Frommer's®

10th Edition

Canada

by
Wayne Curtis
Herbert Bailey Livesey
Bill McRae
Anistatia R. Miller & Jared M. Brown
Marilyn Wood

Macmillan • USA

MACMILLAN TRAVEL

A Simon & Schuster Macmillan Company
1633 Broadway
New York, NY 10019

Find us online at **www.frommers.com**

ISBN 0-02-862051-8
ISSN 1044-2251

Editors: Ron Boudreau, Dan Glover, and Margot Weiss
Special thanks to Marie Morris
Production Editor: Stephanie Mohler
Design by Michele Laseau
Digital Cartography by John Decamillas and Ortelius Design

Front cover photo: Moraine Lake in Banff National Park, Alberta

SPECIAL SALES

Bulk purchases (10+ copies) of Frommer's and selected Macmillan travel guides are available to corporations, organizations, mail-order catalogs, institutions, and charities at special discounts, and can be customized to suit individual needs. For more information, write to Special Sales, Macmillan General Reference, 1633 Broadway, New York, NY 10019.

Manufactured in the United States of America

Contents

7 Newfoundland & Labrador 165

by Wayne Curtis

8 Montréal 199

by Herbert Bailey Livesey

12 Toronto & the Golden Horseshoe 372

by Marilyn Wood

13 Southern & Midwestern Ontario 440

by Marilyn Wood

14 North to Ontario's Lakelands & Beyond 458

by Marilyn Wood

15   Manitoba & Saskatchewan   491

by Marilyn Wood

16   Alberta & the Rockies   528

by Bill McRae

17   Vancouver   614

by Anistatia R. Miller & Jared M. Brown

18   Victoria & the Best of British Columbia   665

by Anistatia R. Miller & Jared M. Brown

19 The Yukon & the Northwest Territories: The Great Northern Wilderness   754

by Bill McRae

Index   800

List of Maps

ABOUT THE AUTHORS

Wayne Curtis is a freelance writer whose articles have appeared in the *New York Times, National Geographic Traveler,* and *Outside* and on the Discovery Channel Online. He's also the author of *Frommer's Northern New England; Frommer's Nova Scotia, New Brunswick & Prince Edward Island;* and *Maine: Off the Beaten Path* (Globe Pequot). For the past decade he's lived in coastal Maine but can be found in the warm months exploring from Vermont to Newfoundland, fingers crossed, in an aging Volkswagen camper.

Herbert Bailey Livesey has written about travel and food for many magazines, including *Travel & Leisure, Food & Wine,* and *Playboy.* He is a coauthor of *Frommer's Europe from $50 a Day* and *Frommer's New England* and the author of *Frommer's Montréal & Québec City* and *Frommer's Walking Tours: Spain's Favorite Cities.*

Bill McRae was born and raised in rural Montana, though he spent the better years of his youth attending university in Great Britain and France. His previous books include *The Montana Handbook,* published by Moon Publications, and *The Pacific Northwest,* published by Lonely Planet. He makes his home in Portland, Oregon.

One month after their first visit to British Columbia, **Jared M. Brown** (a former hotel manager and chef) and **Anistatia R. Miller** sold their Manhattan apartment and moved to Vancouver. Authors of *Shaken Not Stirred: A Celebration of the Martini* (HarperPerennial) and *Frommer's Vancouver & Victoria,* they've written about food and drink for *Icon, Wine Spectator, Wine & Dine,* and *Au Juice.*

Formerly the editorial director of Macmillan Travel, **Marilyn Wood** is an acclaimed travel writer and editor. Once a resident of Toronto, she has covered the city and all of central Canada for years and is author of *Frommer's Toronto.* She has also written *Frommer's London from $60 a Day, Frommer's Wonderful Weekends from New York, Frommer's Wonderful Weekends from San Francisco,* and *Frommer's Wonderful Weekends from Boston.*

AN INVITATION TO THE READER

In researching this book, we discovered many wonderful places—hotels, restaurants, shops, and more. We're sure you'll find others. Please tell us about them, so we can share the information with your fellow travelers in upcoming editions. If you were disappointed with a recommendation, we'd love to know that, too. Please write to:

Frommer's Canada, 10th Edition
Macmillan Travel
1633 Broadway
New York, NY 10019

AN ADDITIONAL NOTE

Please be advised that travel information is subject to change at any time—and this is especially true of prices. We therefore suggest that you write or call ahead for confirmation when making your travel plans. The authors, editors, and publisher cannot be held responsible for the experiences of readers while traveling. Your safety is important to us, however, so we encourage you to stay alert and be aware of your surroundings. Keep a close eye on cameras, purses, and wallets, all favorite targets of thieves and pickpockets.

WHAT THE SYMBOLS MEAN

✪ Frommer's Favorites

Our favorite places and experiences—outstanding for quality, value, or both.

The following abbreviations are used for credit cards:

AE	American Express	EU	Eurocard
CB	Carte Blanche	JCB	Japan Credit Bank
DC	Diners Club	MC	MasterCard
DISC	Discover	V	Visa
ER	enRoute		

FIND FROMMER'S ON-LINE

Arthur Frommer's Outspoken Encyclopedia of Travel (www.frommers.com) offers more than 6,000 pages of up-to-the-minute travel information—including the latest bargains and candid, personal articles updated daily by Arthur Frommer himself. No other Web site offers such comprehensive and timely coverage of the world of travel.

The Best of Canada   1

Planning a trip to such a vast and diverse country can present you with a bewildering array of choices. We've scoured all of Canada in search of the best places and experiences, and in this chapter we share our very personal and opinionated choices. We hope they'll give you some ideas and get you started.

1 The Best Travel Experiences

- **Hiking Gros Morne National Park** (Newfoundland): When the earth's land masses broke apart and shifted 500 million years ago, a piece of the earth's mantle, the very shell of the planet, was thrust upward to form tableland mountains of rock here. Spend a week or more trekking along amazing coastal trails, venturing to scenic waterfalls, and strolling along landlocked fjords. See chapter 7.
- **Watching the World Go By in a Québec City Cafe:** On a sunny Saturday in late June or September, sit outside at Le Marie-Clarisse restaurant in the Quartier Petit-Champlain. From there you can watch the goings-on in one of the oldest European communities in the New World. A folksinger may do a half-hour set, then be followed by a classical guitarist. See chapter 10.
- **Houseboating on the Trent-Severn Waterway** (Ontario): The Trent-Severn Waterway will take you 240 miles via 44 locks from Trenton to Georgian Bay on Lake Huron. Enjoy drawing into the locks or being drawn up or let down by the lock master. You can cruise aboard a fully equipped houseboat that usually sleeps up to six; weekly rentals on the canal system in summer average C$1,000 (US$714). Call **Big Rideau Boats** (☎ 613/828-0138) or **Houseboat Holidays** (☎ 613/382-2842). See chapter 11.
- **Seeing the Polar Bear in Churchill** (Manitoba): In October or November, travel by train or plane to Churchill and the shores of Hudson Bay to view hundreds of magnificent polar bear, who migrate to the bay's icy shores and even lope into Churchill itself. In the evening, you can glimpse the famous aurora borealis (northern lights). Either take **VIA Rail's Hudson Bay** (☎ 800/561-3949) train, a 2-night/1-day trip from Winnipeg, or fly in on **Canadian Airlines International** (☎ 800/426-7000 in the U.S. or 800/665-1177 in Canada). See chapter 15.

- **Horseback Riding in the Rockies:** Rent a cabin on a rural guest ranch and get back in the saddle again. Spend a day fishing, then return to the lodge for a country dance or barbecue. Ride a horse to a backcountry chalet in the rugged mountain wilderness. Forget the crowded park highways and commercialized resort towns and just relax. **Brewster's Kananaskis Guest Ranch** (☎ **800/691-5085** or 403/673-3737) in Kananaskis Village, near Banff, Alberta, offers a variety of guided horseback trips, ranging from C$125 to C$140 (US$91 to US$102) per day, including all food, lodging, and the horse you ride in on. See chapter 16.
- **Taking the Inside Passage Ferry** (Vancouver): Every year, 700,000 people pay thousands of dollars for Vancouver-to-Alaska cruises. But insiders know that C$102 (US$71) is all you need to spend. The 15-hour Inside Passage ferry cruise aboard the MV *Queen of the North* takes you from Vancouver Island's Port Hardy into an otherwise inaccessible coastline stretching north to the town of Prince Rupert and the southern tip of the Alaskan Panhandle. Orcas swim past the ferry, bald eagles soar overhead, and rare white black-bears known as kermodei emerge from old-growth forests to fish for salmon along the rain-forested coast while you lounge on the deck. Contact **BC Ferries** at ☎ **604/386-3431.** See chapter 17.
- **Dogsledding Through Baffin Island:** Spectacular fjords, knife-edged mountains draped with glaciers, and friendly craft-oriented Inuit villages make this rarely visited island—the world's fifth largest—a great off-the-beaten-path destination. Arrange a dogsled tour to the floe edge, where the protected harbor ice meets the open sea and where seals, polar bears, and bowhead whales converge. A week-long dogsledding trip with **NorthWinds,** an Iqaluit-based outfitter (☎ **819/979-0551**), costs C$2,300 (US$1,638). See chapter 19.

2 The Best Family Vacations

- **Fundy National Park and Vicinity** (New Brunswick): You'll find swimming, hiking, and kayaking at this dramatic national park. And don't overlook biking in the hills east of the park or a day spent rappelling or rock climbing at Cape Enrage. See chapter 5.
- **Prince Edward Island's Beaches:** The red-sand beaches will leave your kids' white swim trunks a bit pinkish, but it's hard to beat a day or three splashing around these tepid waters while admiring pastoral island landscapes. See chapter 6.
- **Club Tremblant** (Laurentian Mountains; ☎ **800/567-8341** in the U.S. and Canada, or 819/425-2731): This resort faces Mount Tremblant, eastern Canada's highest peak, with a ski village at the base and gondola and chairlifts to the top, summer and winter. Ten lakes and connecting rivers around the mountain offer boating, swimming, and windsurfing. There are indoor and outdoor pools, plus inviting biking and hiking trails. A day-care program for children 3 to 13 lets parents take a break. Most lodgings are one- to three-bedroom suites. See chapter 9.
- **Ottawa:** In this family-friendly city, you and your kids can watch soldiers strut their stuff and red-coated Mounties polish their equestrian and musical skills. Canoeing or skating on the canal is lots of fun, and Ottawa boasts a host of live museums to explore—like the National Aviation Museum, the National Museum of Civilization, and the National Museum of Science and Technology. See chapter 11.
- **The Muskoka Lakes** (Ontario): This region is filled with resorts that welcome families. Kids can swim, canoe, bike, fish, and more. Since most resorts offer children's programs, parents can enjoy a rest as well. See chapter 14.

- **Whistler/Blackcomb Ski Resorts** (British Columbia): Whistler and Blackcomb's twin ski resorts have family-oriented outdoor activities ranging from downhill and cross-country skiing, snowboarding, snowshoeing, and snowmobiling lessons during winter to horseback riding, mountain biking, golfing, in-line skating, paragliding, heli-skiing, swimming, kayaking, and rafting summer trips custom-designed for families with school-age children. See chapter 18.
- **The Klondike Gold Rush Route** (the Yukon): Follow the Klondike Gold Rush, traveling from Skagway, Alaska, up over White Pass to the Yukon's capital, Whitehorse. Canoe through the once-daunting Miles Canyon on the mighty Yukon River. Drive to Dawson City and visit the gold fields, walk the boardwalks of the old town center, and listen to recitations of Robert Service poetry. Pan for gold and attend an old-fashioned musical revue at the opera house. Inexpensive public campgrounds abound in the Yukon, making this one of the more afford-able family vacations in western Canada. See chapter 19.

3 The Best Nature & Wildlife Viewing

- **Fundy Tides at Hopewell Rocks** (Highway 114, south of Moncton, New Brunswick): The force of Fundy's tremendous tides are nowhere as impressive as at Hopewell Rocks, where great rock "sculptures" created by the winds and tides rise from the ocean floor at high tide. See chapter 5.
- **Birds and Caribou on the Avalon Peninsula** (Newfoundland): In one busy day you can view a sprawling herd of caribou, the largest puffin colony in North America, and an extraordinary gannet roost visible from mainland cliffs. See chapter 7.
- **Whales at Baie Ste-Catherine** (Québec): At Baie Ste-Catherine, about a 2-hour drive northeast of Québec City, and along the northern shore to the resort area of La Malbaie, hundreds of resident beluga and minke whales are joined by several additional species of their migratory cousins, including humpbacks and blues. From mid-June to early October the graceful giants can often be sighted from land, but whale-watching cruises depart from Baie Ste Catherine for closer looks. See chapter 10.
- **Pelicans in Prince Albert National Park** (Saskatchewan): On Lavallee Lake roosts the second-largest pelican colony in North America. Bison, moose, elk, caribou, black bear, and red fox also roam free in this million acres of wilderness. See chapter 15.
- **Wood Buffalo at Elk Island National Park** (east of Edmonton): Before home-steaders put the plow to the northern Canadian prairies, bison, elk, deer, moose, beaver, and dozens of other animals roamed the land. This small and easily acces-sible national-park preserves the original prairie-lake ecosystem and large numbers of wildlife, including two species of bison and a genetically pure herd of prairie elk. See chapter 16.
- **Bald Eagles Near Victoria** (British Columbia): Just a few miles north of Victoria is one of the world's best bald-eagle spotting sites: Goldstream Provincial Park. Counts have been as high as 3,700 eagles during the month of January. See chapter 18.
- **Orcas Off Vancouver Island** (British Columbia): At Tofino and Ucluelet on Vancouver Island's west coast, you can watch pods of feeding gray whales on their annual migration north. But it's on the east coast, at Alert Bay, where you'll find the perfect on-shore spot for watching orcas as they glide through the Johnstone Strait in search of salmon or rub their tummies on the pebbly beaches at Robson Bight. See chapter 18.

- **Musk Oxen on Banks Island** (Northwest Territory): This tundra-covered island is home to the world's largest population of musk oxen. Flights from Inuvik visit Aulavik National Park, established to protect the island's 10,000 musk ox; also watch for caribou, grizzly bear, and whales during the flight. Hike through delicate tundra and marshland, a mass of tiny blossoms in summer. **Arctic Nature Tours** (☎ 867/777-3300) in Inuvik runs a daylong flight and excursion for C$400 (US$286). See chapter 19.

4 The Best Views

- **Cape Enrage** (New Brunswick): Just east of Fundy National Park, you'll find surprisingly harsh coastal terrain of high rocky cliffs pounded by the sea. Route 915 offers a wonderful detour off the beaten path. See chapter 5.
- **Bonavista Peninsula** (Newfoundland): The peninsula's northernmost tip offers a superb vantage point for spotting icebergs, even into midsummer. You'll also see puffins, whales, and one of the most scenic lighthouses in eastern Canada. See chapter 7.
- **Terrasse Dufferin in Québec City:** This classic boardwalk promenade with benches and green-and-white–roofed gazebos runs along the cusp of the bluff rearing up behind the original colonial settlement. At its back is the landmark Château Frontenac, and out front is the long silvery sweep of the mighty St. Lawrence, where ferries glide back and forth and cruise ships and Great Lakes freighters and tankers put in at the port. To the east is the trailing edge of the Adirondacks, and downriver you can see the last of the Laurentian Mountains. See chapter 10.
- **Niagara Falls:** This is still a wonder of nature despite its commercial exploitation. You can experience the falls from the decks of the *Maid of the Mist,* which takes you into the roaring maelstrom, or look down from the cockpit of a helicopter. The least scary view is from the Skylon Tower. See chapter 12.
- **Agawa Canyon** (northern Ontario): To see the northern Ontario wilderness that inspired the Group of Seven, take the Agawa Canyon Train Tour on a 114-mile trip from the Soo to Hearst through the Agawa Canyon, where you can spend a few hours exploring scenic waterfalls and vistas. The train snakes through a vista of deep ravines and lakes, hugging the hillsides and crossing gorges on skeletal trestle bridges. See chapter 14.
- **Takakkawa Falls in Yoho National Park** (British Columbia): One of Canada's highest falls, Takakkawa Falls plunges more than 1,200 feet into a glacier-carved valley. Hike up to the base of the falls, hear the roar of crashing water, and stand in clouds of mist. See chapter 16.
- **Moraine Lake in Banff National Park** (Alberta): Ten snow-clad peaks towering more than 10,000 feet high rear up dramatically behind this tiny, eerily green lake. Rent a canoe and paddle to the mountains' base. See chapter 16.
- **Vancouver as Seen from Mount Seymour** (British Columbia): This small ski area overlooks Vancouver, the Burrard Inlet, the Straight of Georgia, and Vancouver Island. On a clear day, the entire city and the coastal islands spread out below. You can see a similar view from Grouse Mountain, which is easily accessible by a tram. See chapter 17.

5 The Most Dramatic Drives

- **Cape Breton's Cabot Trail** (Nova Scotia): This 280-kilometer (175-mile) loop through the uplands of Cape Breton National Park is one of the world's greatest excursions. You'll visit Acadian fishing ports, pristine valleys, and some of the most picturesque rocky coastline in the world. See chapter 4.

- **Viking Trail** (Newfoundland): This beautiful drive through Gros Morne National Park to Newfoundland's northern tip is wild and solitary. You'll pass vistas filled with quirky geology and wind-raked coasts, then finish up at one of the world's great historic sites—L'Anse aux Meadows. Keep an eye peeled for icebergs. See chapter 7.
- **The Icefields Parkway** (Highway 93 through Banff and Jasper national parks): This is one of the world's grandest and most beautiful mountain drives. Cruising along it is like a trip back to the ice ages. The parkway climbs past glacier-notched peaks to the Columbia Icefields, a sprawling cap of snow, ice, and glacier at the very crest of the Rockies. See chapter 16.
- **Highway 99** (British Columbia): The Sea to Sky Highway from Vancouver to Lillooet takes you from a dramatic seacoast past glaciers, pine forests, and a waterfall that cascades from a mountaintop and through Whistler's majestic glacial mountains. The next leg of the 4-hour drive winds up a series of switch-backs to the thickly forested Cayoosh Creek valley and on to the craggy, arid mountains surrounding the Fraser River gold-rush town of Lillooet. See chapter 18.
- **The Dempster Highway** (from Dawson City to Inuvik): Canada's most northerly highway, the Dempster is a year-round gravel road across the top of the world. From Dawson City, the road winds over the Continental Divide three times, crosses the Arctic Circle, and fords the Peel and Mackenzie rivers by ferry before reaching Inuvik, a native community on the mighty Mackenzie River delta. See chapter 19.

6 The Best Walks & Rambles

- **Cape Breton Highlands National Park** (Nova Scotia): You'll find bog and wood-land walks aplenty at Cape Breton, but the best trails follow rugged cliffs along the open ocean. The Skyline Trail is among the most dramatic pathways in the province. See chapter 4.
- **North Head Trail** (St. John's, Newfoundland): This trail runs from downtown St. John's along the harbor, through the picturesque Battery neighborhood, then climbs the open bluffs overlooking the Narrows and the open ocean beyond. Where else can you hike from downtown shopping to cliff-side whale watching? See chapter 7.
- **Old Montréal:** Wander the streets, where you'll find some remains—both above and below the streets—of what founder Paul de Chomedey, sieur de Maisonneuve, christened Ville-Marie in 1642. Above ground, buildings have been restored into homes, stores, restaurants, and nightclubs. Horse-drawn carriages clop and creak along the cobblestone streets, past the heart of the district, place Jacques-Cartier, which is lined with cafes. Below ground, a tunnel leads from the new Museum of Archaeology to the old Custom House. See chapter 8.
- **Lake Superior Provincial Park** (Ontario): Follow any trail in this park to a rewarding vista. The 16-kilometer (10-mile) Peat Mountain Trail leads to a panoramic view close to 500 feet above the surrounding lakes and forests. The moderate Orphan Lake Trail offers views over the Orphan Lake and Lake Superior, plus a pebble beach and Baldhead River falls. The 26-kilometer (16-mile) Toawab Trail takes you through the Agawa Valley to the 81-foot Agawa Falls. See chapter 14.

- **Johnston Canyon** (Banff National Park): Just 15 miles west of Banff, Johnson Creek cuts a deep, very narrow canyon through limestone cliffs. The trail winds through tunnels, passes waterfalls, edges by shaded rock faces, and crosses the chasm on footbridges before reaching a series of iridescent pools, formed by springs that bubble up through highly colored rock. See chapter 16.
- **Plain of Six Glaciers Trail** (Lake Louise): From Chateau Lake Louise, a lakeside trail rambles along the edge of emerald-green Lake Louise, then climbs up to the base of Victoria Glacier. At a rustic teahouse you can order a cup of tea and a scone—each made over a wood-burning stove—and gaze up at the rumpled face of the glacier. See chapter 16.
- **West Coast Trail** (Vancouver Island): The first 7 kilometers (4 miles) of Vancouver Island's West Coast Trail aren't too difficult. The trail takes you through an incredible rain forest edged by a sandy beach, roaring surf, and awe-inspiring views of migrating gray whales, basking sea lions, and soaring eagles. See chapter 18.

7 The Best Biking Routes

- **Cabot Trail** (Nova Scotia): This long loop around Cape Breton National Park is rough and rugged on the legs, but you'll come away with a headful of indelible memories. See chapter 4.
- **Confederation Trail** (Prince Edward Island): This 350-kilometer (217-mile) end-to-end pathway is still being pieced together. But you can already explore 225 kilometers (140 miles) along the old rail line that once stitched this island province together. See chapter 6.
- **Old Port Route** (Montréal): The city has 148 miles of biking paths, and the Métro permits bicycles in the last car of its trains. One popular route is from the Old Port, west along the side of the Lachine Canal. A little under 7 miles one way, it's tranquil, vehicle-free, and mostly flat. You can rent bicycles at the Old Port. See chapter 8.
- **Ile d'Orléans** (Québec): You can enjoy a day or two of biking around this bucolic island 15 minutes downriver from Québec City. A main road runs around the island, never far from water's edge. You can stop at a pick-your-own orchard or strawberry field or in a tiny village with 18th- and 19th-century houses and churches. Two roads cut across the island at the southern end, and a third does the same a little beyond midpoint. You can rent bikes on the island. See chapter 10.
- **The Niagara Region:** This very flat area is ideal biking terrain. A bike path runs along the Niagara Parkway, which follows the Niagara River. You'll bike past fruit farms, vineyards, and gardens with picnicking spots. See chapter 12.
- **Highways 1 and 93 Through Banff and Jasper National Parks:** This well-maintained wide highway winds through some of the most dramatic mountain scenery in the world. Take the Bow River Parkway, between Banff and Lake Louise, and Highway 93A between Athabasca Falls and Jasper for slightly quieter peddling. Best of all, there are seven hostels (either rustic or fancy) at some of the most beautiful sights along the route, so you don't have to weigh yourself down with camping gear. See chapter 16.
- **Seawall** (Vancouver): Vancouver's Seawall surrounds the Stanley Park shoreline on the Burrard Inlet and English Bay. Built just above the high-tide mark, it offers nonstop breathtaking views, no hills, and no cars. See chapter 17.

8 The Best Culinary Experiences

- **Fresh Atlantic Seafood:** Fresh boiled lobster in New Brunswick, pan-fried cod in Newfoundland, succulent Digby scallops in Nova Scotia, and plump cultivated mussels from the inlets of Prince Edward Island are among the area's most savory treats. Watch also for regional favorites, like cod cheeks and fish-and-brewis. See chapters 4 to 7.
- **Newfoundland Berries:** "The Rock" isn't exactly known for its lush agricultural lands, but the flinty soil and damp bogs produce a riot of berries late in summer. Look for luscious strawberries as well as native bakeapples and partridgeberries. See chapter 7.
- **Dining at the Best in Montréal:** Montréal boasts one of the hottest dining scenes in Canada. The current favorite is **Toqué!** (☎ **514/499-2084**), the kind of restaurant that raises the gastronomic expectations of an entire city. The silky greeting-to-tab performance of the kitchen and wait staff is a pleasure to observe, and the postnouvelle presentations are both visually winning and completely filling. No restaurant in eastern Canada surpasses this contemporary French gem. See chapter 8.
- **Sampling Smoked Meat in Montréal:** Somewhere between pastrami and corned beef, this deli delight appears to have had its origins with the immigrations of eastern Europeans during the late 19th century. Meat eaters are ravenous at the sight and aroma of it, and the place to inhale smoked meat is **Chez Schwartz** on The Main (☎ **514/842-4813**). Elegant it's not; immensely satisfying it is. See chapter 8.
- **Eating Ethnic in Toronto:** If you explore the city's neighborhoods, you'll find ethnic dining spots in Little Italy, Little Portugal, and Greek sections of the Danforth. Order spaghettini with seafood, garlic, capers, white wine, and a touch of anchovies at **Trattoria Giancarlo** (☎ **416/533-9619**); poached fillet of cod at **Chiado** (☎ **416/538-1910**); or imaginatively updated Greek at **Pan on the Danforth** (☎ **416/466-8158**). Each is situated at the heart of its ethnic neighborhood. See chapter 12.
- **Feasting on Danish Specialties:** Enjoy seven superlative dishes, from *frikadeller* (Danish meat patties served with red cabbage and potato salad) to *aeggekage* (a Danish omelet served with home-baked bread) at the warmly inviting **Bistro Dansk,** Saskatoon (☎ **204/775-5662**). See chapter 15.
- **Going Organic in Calgary:** You'll walk through a quiet tree-filled park on an island in the Bow River to reach the bustling **River Cafe** (☎ **403/261-7670**). At the restaurant's center, an immense wood-fired oven and grill produces soft, chewy flat breads and smoky grilled meats and vegetables, all organically grown and freshly harvested. On warm summer evenings, picnickers loll in the grassy shade, nibbling this and that from the cafe's picniclike menu. See chapter 16.
- **Dining at a Hotel in Lake Louise:** At its cozy dining room with a low ceiling in an old log lodge, the **Post Hotel** (☎ **403/522-3989**) serves up the kind of sophisticated yet robust cuisine that perfectly fits the backdrop of glaciered peaks, deep forest, and glassy streams. Both the wine list and the cooking are French and hearty, with the chef focusing on the best of local ingredients—lamb, salmon, and Alberta beef. After spending time out on the trail, a meal here will top off a quintessential day in the Rockies. See chapter 16.
- **Enjoying Dim Sum in Vancouver's Chinatown:** With its burgeoning Chinese population, Vancouver's Chinatown has more than half a dozen dim-sum parlors

where you can try steamed or baked barbecued-pork buns, dumplings filled with fresh prawns and vegetables, or steamed rice-flour crêpes filled with spicy beef. See chapter 17.

- **Attending Salmon Barbecues in British Columbia:** The annual salmon barbecues that take place in cities, towns, and villages throughout coastal British Columbia pay tribute to a tradition that dates back thousands of years. Nothing is quite as good as Pacific sockeye salmon, hot smoked over alder wood. See chapter 18.

9 The Best Festivals & Special Events

- **International Busker Festival** (Halifax, Nova Scotia): In early August, the 10-day International Busker Festival brings together talented street performers from around the world, performing in their natural habitat. Best of all, it's free. See chapter 4.
- **International Jazz Festival** (Montréal): Ten days every summer glorify America's truest art form with the immensely successful International Jazz Festival, in operation since 1979. Big stars always appear, but their concerts cost money. No problem: Hundreds of free concerts are held, most often in the streets and plazas of midtown. See chapter 8.
- **Winter Carnival** (Québec City): Think Mardi Gras in New Orleans, without the nudity (well, maybe a little). Ice sculptures, parades, a canoe race across the frozen St. Lawrence, and an impressive castle of ice are among the principal features. The general jollity is fueled by a nasty drink called Caribou, whiskey sloshed with red wine. See chapter 10.
- **Toronto International Film Festival** (Ontario): Up there right behind Cannes, this film festival, now the second-largest in the world, shows more than 250 films for 10 days in early September. See chapter 12.
- **Stratford Festival** (Ontario): This summer-long festival of superb repertory theater, launched by Tyrone Guthrie in 1953, produces shows that frequently move successfully to Broadway and beyond (for example, Christopher Plummer in *Barrymore*). Productions, which run from May to October or early November on three stages, range from classic to contemporary. You can also participate in informal discussions with company members. See chapter 13.
- **Northern Trapper's Festival** (The Pas, Manitoba): This festival celebrates the traditions of the frontier pioneers each February with world-championship dogsled races, ice fishing, beer fests, bannock baking, moose calling, and more. See chapter 15.
- **Calgary Stampede** (Alberta): In all of North America, there's nothing quite like the Calgary Stampede. Of course it's the world's largest rodeo, but it's also a series of concerts, an art show, an open-air casino, a carnival, a street dance—you name it, it's undoubtedly going on somewhere. In July, all of Calgary is converted into a party and everyone's invited. See chapter 16.
- **Symphony of Fire** (Vancouver): This 4-night fireworks extravaganza takes place over English Bay in Vancouver. Three of the world's leading manufacturers are invited to represent their countries in competition against one another, setting their best displays to music. On the 4th night, all three companies launch their finales. Last year over 500,000 people showed up each night. The best seats are at the "Bard on the Beach" Shakespeare festival across False Creek. See chapter 17.
- **Kamloops Cattle Drive** (southern British Columbia): This rollicking 7-day trail ride draws about 1,000 people annually. A parade of wagons, horses, and cows sets

off from a different location every August, driving the cattle along a predetermined route through the High Country's sagebrush mesas to a triumphant finish (and huge party) in Kamloops. Beginners are welcome, and horses (even space on wagons) can be rented. See chapter 18.

10 The Best Luxury Hotels & Resorts

- **Kingsbrae Arms** (St. Andrews, New Brunswick; ☎ 506/529-1897): This new deluxe inn manages the trick of being opulent and comfortable at the same time. This shingled manse is lavishly appointed, beautifully landscaped, and well situated for exploring charming St. Andrews. See chapter 5.
- **Dalvay-by-the-Sea** (Grand Tracadie, Prince Edward Island; ☎ 902/672-2048). This intimate resort (just 30 rooms and cottages) is situated on a quiet stretch of beach. The Tudor mansion was built by a business partner of John D. Rockefeller, and the woodwork alone is enough to keep you entertained for your stay. Bring your bike. See chapter 6.
- **Hôtel Vogue** (Montréal, Québec; ☎ 800/465-6654 or 514/285-5555): What was just an anonymous mid-rise office building has turned into the king of the hill of Montréal hotels. The Vogue targeted international executives on the go, and little was left to chance. Even the standard rooms come with fax machines, four phones, computer ports, bathroom TVs, and whirlpool baths. Tins of caviar are tucked into the minibars. People with cell phones at the ready fill the lobby espresso bar and adjacent dining room. Even after two changes in management, the Vogue remains steady on its course. See chapter 8.
- **Langdon Hall** (Cambridge, Ontario; ☎ 800/268-1898 or 519/740-2100): This quintessential English country house, built in 1902 for the granddaughter of John Jacob Astor, is now a small country-house hotel where you can enjoy 200 acres of lawns, gardens, and woodlands. Rooms feature the finest amenities, fabrics, and furnishings. Facilities include a full spa, a pool, a tennis court, a croquet lawn, and an exercise room. The airy dining room overlooking the lily pond offers fine continental cuisine. See chapter 13.
- **Manitowaning Lodge Golf & Tennis Resort** (Manitowaning, Ontario; ☎ 705/859-3136): This resort on Manitoulin Island is an idyllic island retreat. A lodge and cottages are set on 11 acres of beautiful gardens. The lodge, with its huge hand-hewn beams, a mask of the Spirit of Manitowaning, and images of the Native-American protective spirit, provides a serene setting to restore the spirit. This unpretentious place delivers on the promise of luxurious peace and quiet. See chapter 14.
- **Chateau Lake Louise** (Banff National Park, Alberta; ☎ 800/441-1414 or 403/522-3511): First of all, there's the view. Across a tiny gem-green lake rise massive cliffs shrouded in glacial ice. And then there's the hotel. Part hunting lodge, part European palace, the Chateau is its own community, with sumptuous boutiques, sports rental facilities, seven dining areas, two bars, magnificent lobby areas, and beautifully furnished guest rooms. See chapter 16.
- **Hotel Macdonald** (Edmonton, Alberta; ☎ 800/441-1414 or 403/424-5181): When the Canadian Pacific bought and refurbished this landmark hotel in the 1980s, all the charming period details were preserved, while all the inner workings were modernized and brought up to snuff. The result is a regally elegant but friendly small hotel. From the kilted bellman to the gargoyles on the walls, this is a real class act. See chapter 16.

- **Canadian Pacific Chateau Whistler Resort** (Whistler, British Columbia; ☎ 800/441-1414 in the U.S., 800/606-8244 in Canada, or 604/938-8000): Canadian-Pacific's Chateau Whistler has sterling service and excellent accommodations right next to the Blackcomb Mountain ski lift. The après-ski lounge has comfortable sitting with a great view of the lifts. Ski and bike valet service, as well as storage, a full-service spa and health club, and Whistler's best buffet-style brunch top off the experience. See chapter 18.

11 The Best Bed & Breakfasts

- **Shipwright Inn** (Charlottetown, Prince Edward Island; ☎ 902/368-1905): This in-town seven-room B&B is within easy walking distance of all the city's attractions yet has a settled and pastoral feel. It's informed by the Victorian sensibility without being over the top. See chapter 6.
- **Tickle Inn** (Cape Onion, Newfoundland; ☎ 709/452-4321 June to September or 709/739-5503 October to May): The Tickle Inn may not be at the end of the world, but you can surely see it from here. Located in a wonderful 1890 home in a remote cove, this cordial B&B is run by the great-grandson of the house's builder. See chapter 7.
- **Les Passants du Sans Soucy** (Montréal, Québec; ☎ 514/842-2634): The only B&B in Old Montréal has a lot more going for it than that enviable distinction. Indeed, it almost qualifies as a boutique hotel, but with much lower prices. Housed in a renovated 1723 building, it makes the most of its stone walls and exposed dark ceiling beams, using them to contain brass or wrought-iron beds and cushy sofas. A fireplace is the focal point of the common room. Breakfast includes café au lait and pain au chocolat. See chapter 8.
- **Clifton Manor Inn** (Bayfield, Ontario; ☎ 519/565-2282): You'll find instant romance at this elegant house, built in 1895 for the reve (bailiff or governor) of Bayfield. All the bathrooms have candles and bubble bath, and one has a deep tub for two. Four comfortable rooms are named after an artist or composer. All rooms have cozy touches like mohair throws, sheepskin rugs, wingback chairs, fresh flowers, and so on. Breakfast consists of egg dishes like omelets or crêpes, plus fresh fruit often plucked from the trees in the garden. See chapter 13.
- **Beild House** (Collingwood, Ontario; ☎ 705/444-1522): On Fridays, you can sit down to a splendid five-course dinner before retiring to the bed that belonged to the duke and duchess of Windsor. A sumptuous breakfast will follow the next morning. This handsome 1909 house contains 17 rooms, seven with private bath. See chapter 14.
- **Nakiska Ranch** (Clearwater, British Columbia; ☎ 604/674-3655): This B&B is set at the edge of the mountains along an alpine creek where moose and deer graze amid towering Douglas firs and lupine-filled alpine meadows. You can choose rooms in the main two-story log chalet or one of two separate, secluded two-story log cabins with full kitchens that look like they're straight from the pages of *Metropolitan Home.* Congenial Swiss service and a hearty breakfast await before you set out on a day hike or a Nordic ski run through nearby Wells Gray Provincial Park. See chapter 18.
- **Pearson's Arctic Home Stay** (Baffin Island, Northwest Territories; ☎ 867/979-6408): Staying at this lovely private home overlooking Frobisher Bay is like staying at a museum of Inuit arts and crafts. The innkeeper is the town's former mayor and currently the island's public coroner, so you also get a real insight into life and death on Baffin Island. See chapter 19.

12 The Best Camping & Wilderness Lodges

- **Green Provincial Park** (Tyne Valley, Prince Edward Island; ☎ 902/831-2370): Can't afford your own well-maintained estate? This provincial campground makes a decent substitute. Set on a quiet inlet, the 219-acre park is built around an extravagant gingerbread mansion that's open to the public. See chapter 6.
- **Gros Morne National Park** (Newfoundland): Backpackers will find wild, spectacular campsites in coastal meadows along the remarkable Green Gardens Trail. Car campers should head to Trout River Pond, at the foot of one of Gros Morne's dramatic landlocked fjords. See chapter 7.
- **Sir Sam's Inn** (Eagle Lake, Ontario; ☎ 705/754-2188): You'll have to search a bit for this remote stone-and-timber lodge, built in 1917 in the woods above Eagle Lake for politician and militarist Sir Sam Hughes. You can stay in the inn or in new chalets or lakefront suites. At this friendly yet sophisticated place you can play tennis, swim, sail, windsurf, water-ski, canoe, or mountain bike. See chapter 14.
- **Arowhon Pines** (Algonquin Park, Ontario; ☎ 705/633-5661 in summer or 416/483-4393 in winter): Located 8 miles off the highway down a dirt road, this is one of the most entrancing places anywhere. You can enjoy peace, seclusion, and natural beauty, plus comfortable accommodations and fresh, good food. There are no TVs or phones—just the call of the loons, the gentle lapping of the water, the croaking of the frogs, and the splash of canoe paddles cutting the smooth surface of the lake. See chapter 14.
- **Tunnel Mountain** (Banff, Alberta; **403/762-1500**): If you find Banff too expensive and too crowded, these campgrounds—three within 5 kilometers (3 miles) of town—are a great antidote. There are showers and real toilets, and most sites have full hookups. And you'll pay just one-tenth of what hotel dwellers are paying for equally good access to the Rockies. See chapter 16.
- **Emerald Lake Lodge** (Yoho National Park, Alberta; ☎ 250/343-6321): This historic log lodge sits on the edge of a glacial lake just below the rim of the Continental Divide. Rent a cabin that sleeps four and come here in winter, when the snowbound lodge is a center for cross-country ski expeditions. See chapter 16.
- **Bowron Lakes Provincial Park** (British Columbia): Every summer canoeists and kayakers set out to navigate the perfect 120-kilometer (72-mile) circle of six alpine lakes, with minimal portages in between. A 1949 Wells Gray map listed the Bowron Area as "uncharted mountains"; there are no roads or other signs of civilization beyond the launch point, except some well-placed cabins, campsites, and shelters set up and maintained by the province for the public. It's a 7-day trip, but the memories will last a lifetime. See chapter 18.
- **Wells Gray Park Backcountry Chalets** (British Columbia; ☎ 888/SKI-TREK or 250/587-6444): Since they aren't accessible by car, you have to hike, ski, or travel by horse to these three fully equipped log chalets built inside one of the province's largest and most spectacular parks. True adventurers can opt for packages that include chalet hopping, hiking deeper into the wilderness each day. See chapter 18.

2 Introducing Canada: A Confederation of Provinces

by Bill McRae

Canada's sheer amount of elbow space can make you dizzy. At 3.8 million square miles (200,000 more than the United States), this colossal expanse contains only 25.5 million people—barely 3 million more than California alone. Most of the population is clustered in a relatively narrow southern belt that boasts all the nation's large cities and nearly all its industries. The silent Yukon and Northwest Territories—where 51,000 people dot 1.5 million square miles—remain a frontier, stretching to the Arctic shores and embracing thousands of lakes that no one has ever charted, counted, or named. It's impossible to easily categorize this land or its people—just when you think you know Canada, you discover another place, another temperament, another hidden side.

1 Canada Today

Canada has always been a loosely linked country, a confederation of provinces, not a union of states. Canadians are quick to tell you that theirs is a "cultural mosaic" of people, not a "melting pot." These factors account in great part for two of Canada's most striking characteristics: its cultural vitality and its habits of mistrust and contention. While the country has weathered many storms in the past, recent events indicate that it will continue to face extremely divisive social and cultural challenges, some with the potential to alter its political cohesion and economic power.

The ongoing debate on the Québec "question" serves to divide the majority of English-speaking and French-speaking Canadians. Twenty-five years after the heyday of the Québec separatist movement, many Canadians cynically evaluated the current independence movement as simply an employment program for regional politicians. But then Québec again faced a referendum in October 1995, asking whether the French-speaking province should separate from the rest of Canada, and suddenly Canada teetered on the brink of splitting apart. The vote went in favor of the prounity camp by a razor-thin margin, but the issue was hardly resolved: In all likelihood, it lives to be reborn as another referendum.

Meanwhile, as public officials debate separatism, Québec's younger generation is voting with its feet. Many of its brightest and best are heading west, particularly to more prosperous British Columbia and Alberta. However, these western provinces—no lovers of Ottawa—themselves dream of loosening the federal laws that bind them to eastern Canada.

In 1999 the huge Northern Territories will be divided into two smaller territories. The eastern half, which takes in Baffin Island, the land around Hudson's Bay, and most of the Arctic islands, will be called Nunavut and essentially function as an Inuit homeland. (As for what becomes of the rest of the Northwest Territories, no one seems to have thought much about that; there's not even a name yet for the new territory.)

Nunavut lacks adequate resource development or industry to become self-sufficient, and billions of Canadian tax dollars will still flow into Nunavut from Ottawa. At the same time, all non–Inuit-owned business will be forced to leave Nunavut or become at least partly owned by Inuits, and federal government agencies will come under Inuit control. While the territory of Nunavut will give its native people more control over their lands and government, it looks like a recipe for short-term socioeconomic destabilization.

The success of the Nunavut negotiations has emboldened other native groups to settle their own land claims with the Canadian government. While many of the claims in northern Canada can be settled by transferring government land and money to native groups, those in southern Canada are more complex. Some tribes assert a prior claim to land currently owned by non-Indians; in other areas, native groups refuse to abide by environmental laws that seek to protect endangered runs of salmon. The situation in a number of communities has moved on beyond protests and threats to armed encounters and road barricades. The path seems set for more and increasingly hostile confrontations between official Canada and its native peoples.

Elements of the Canadian economy are still adapting to the landmark Free Trade Agreement concluded with the United States in 1989. While free trade hasn't done much to revive the smokestack industries that once were the engines of eastern Canada, the agreement, combined with the weak dollar, has actually been good for much of Canada's huge agricultural heartland. However, the globalization of trade is transforming the Canadian economy in ways that produce confusion and hostility in the average citizen. Many Canadians are deeply ambivalent about being so closely linked to their powerful southern neighbor, and the trade agreement (and U.S. culture in general) often gets the blame for everything that's going wrong with Canada.

Public interest in protecting the environment runs high, and this is reflected in public policy. Recycling is commonplace and communities across the country have made great strides in balancing economic interests with environmental goals. On Vancouver Island, for example, environmentalists and timber companies agreed in 1995 on forestry standards that satisfy both parties. When salmon fishing boats blockaded an Alaska ferry in Prince Rupert in 1997, the issue for the Canadians was perceived as overfishing by Americans. Salmon have been reduced to an endangered species in much of the Pacific Northwest, and the Canadians consequently don't think much of U.S. fisheries policies.

Canada is challenged internally on many fronts. Social and economic forces are working to fragment a cohesive sense of national identity. Whether the long-standing cultural and political institutions that have guided the country successfully for so many years will survive is a question that'll be answered in the very near future.

Canada

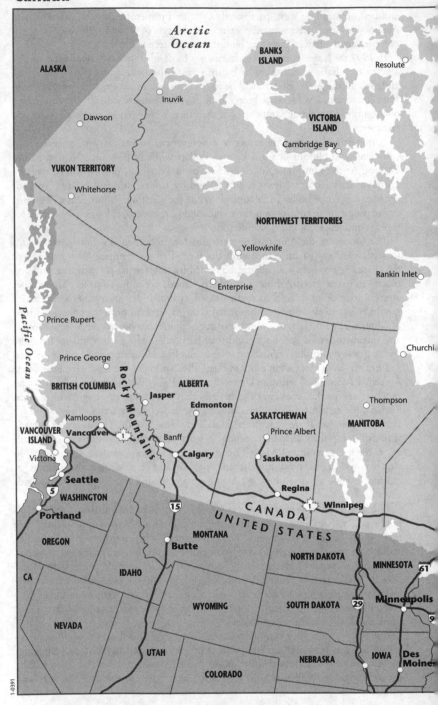

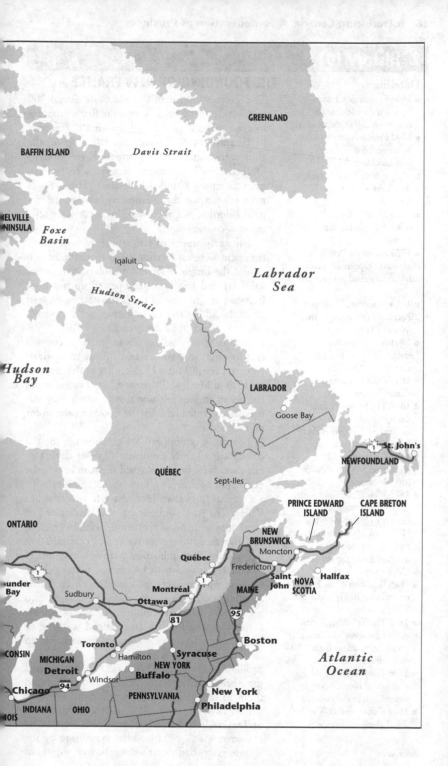

2 History 101

Dateline

- **1608** Samuel de Champlain founds the settlement of Kebec—today's Québec City.
- **1642** French colony of Ville-Marie established, later renamed Montréal.
- **1759** British defeat French at the Plains of Abraham. Fall of Québec City.
- **1763** All of "New France" (Canada) ceded to the British.
- **1775** American Revolutionary forces capture Montréal but are repulsed at Québec City.
- **1813** Americans blow up Fort York (Toronto) in the War of 1812.
- **1841** Act of Union creates the United Provinces of Canada.
- **1855** Ottawa becomes Canada's capital.
- **1869** The Hudson's Bay Company sells Rupert's Land to Canada. It becomes the Province of Alberta.
- **1873** Creation of the Northwest Mounted Police (the Mounties).
- **1875** West Coast community of Gastown incorporated as the city of Vancouver. The Northwest Mounted Police build the log fort that developed into the city of Calgary.
- **1885** Rebellion of the Metis under Louis Riel in western Saskatchewan.
- **1887** The Transcontinental Railroad reaches Vancouver, connecting Canada from ocean to ocean.
- **1896** The Klondike gold rush brings 100,000 people swarming into the Yukon.
- **1914** Canada enters World War I alongside Britain.

continues

THE FOUNDING OF NEW FRANCE

The Vikings landed in Canada more than 1,000 years ago, but the French were the first Europeans to get a toehold in the country. In 1608 Samuel de Champlain established a settlement on the cliffs overlooking the St. Lawrence River—today's Québec City. This was exactly a year after the Virginia Company founded Jamestown. Hundreds of miles of unexplored wilderness lay between the embryo colonies, but they were inexorably set on a collision course.

The early stages of the struggle for the new continent were explorations, and there the French outdid the English. Their fur traders, navigators, soldiers, and missionaries opened up not only Canada but also most of the United States. At least 35 of the 50 United States were either discovered, mapped, or settled by the French.

Gradually, they staked out an immense colonial empire that, in patches and minus recognized borders, stretched from Hudson Bay in the Arctic to the Gulf of Mexico. Christened New France, it was run on an ancient seigniorial system, whereby settlers were granted land by the Crown in return for military service.

The military obligation was essential, for the colony knew hardly a moment of peace during its existence. New France blocked the path of western expansion by England's seaboard colonies with a string of forts that lined the Ohio-Mississippi Valley. The Anglo-Americans were determined to break through, and so the frontier clashes crackled and flared, with the native tribes participating ferociously. These miniature wars were nightmares of savagery, waged with knives and tomahawks as much as with muskets and cannons, characterized by raids and counter-raids, burning villages, and massacred women and children. According to some historians, the English introduced scalping to America by offering a cash bounty for each French scalp the native braves brought in!

The French retaliated in kind. They converted the Abenaki tribe to Christianity and encouraged them to raid deep into New England territory where, in 1704, they totally destroyed the town of Deerfield, Massachusetts. The Americans answered with a punitive blitz expedition by the famous green-clad Roger's Rangers, who wiped out the main Abenaki village and slaughtered half its population.

By far the most dreaded of the tribes was the Iroquois, who played the same role in the Canadian east as the Sioux (another French label) played in the American west. Astute politicians, the Iroquois learned to play the English against the French and vice versa, lending their scalping knives first to one side, then to the other. It took more than a century before they finally succumbed to the whites' smallpox, firewater, and gunpowder—in that order.

THE FALL OF QUEBEC

There were only about 65,000 French settlers in the colony, but they more than held their own against the million Anglo-Americans, first and foremost because they were natural forest fighters—one Canadian trapper could stalemate six redcoats in the woods. Mainly, however, it was because they made friends with the local tribes whenever possible. The majority of tribes sided with the French and made the English pay a terrible price for their blindness.

Even before French and English interests in the New World came to the point of armed struggle in the Seven Years' War, the British had largely taken control of Acadia, though its lush forests and farmlands were dotted with French settlements. The governors knew there would be war, so, suspicious of Acadia's French-speaking inhabitants, they decided on a bold and ruthless plan: All Acadians who would not openly pledge allegiance to the British sovereign would be deported. The order came in 1755, and French-speaking families throughout the province were forcibly moved from their homes, many resettling in the French territory of Louisiana, where their Cajun language and culture are still alive today. To replace the Acadians, shiploads of Scottish and Irish settlers arrived from the British Isles, and the province soon acquired the name Nova Scotia—New Scotland.

When the final round of fighting began in 1754, it opened with a series of shattering English debacles. The French had a brilliant commander, the marquis de Montcalm, exactly the kind of unorthodox tactician needed for the fluid semiguerrilla warfare of the American wilderness.

Britain's proud General Braddock rode into a French-Indian ambush that killed him and scattered his army. Montcalm led an expedition against Fort Oswego that wiped out the stronghold and turned Lake Ontario into a French waterway. The following summer he repeated the feat with Fort William Henry, at the head of Lake George, which fell amid ghastly scenes of massacre, later immortalized by James

Some 60,000 Canadians die in combat.
- **1920** The Northwest Territories separated from the Yukon.
- **1930** Depression and mass unemployment hit Canada.
- **1939** Canada enters World War II with Britain.
- **1947** Huge oil deposits discovered at Leduc, southwest of Edmonton. Start of the Alberta oil boom.
- **1959** Opening of St. Lawrence Seaway turns Toronto into a major seaport.
- **1967** Montréal hosts World Expo.
- **1968** Parti Québécois founded by René Lévesque. Beginning of separatist movement.
- **1970** Kidnap-murder of Cabinet Minister Pierre Laporte. War Measures Act imposed on Québec Province.
- **1976** Montréal becomes site of the Olympic Games.
- **1988** Calgary hosts the Winter Olympics.
- **1989** Canada-U.S. Free Trade Agreement eliminates all tariffs on goods of national origin moving between the two countries.
- **1993** Conservative party is swept out of power in elections.
- **1995** Québec votes narrowly to remain in Canada.
- **1997** Jean Chrétien reelected prime minister.

Fenimore Cooper in *The Last of the Mohicans.* Middle New York now lay wide open to raids, and England's hold on America seemed to be slipping.

Then, like a cornered boxer bouncing from the ropes, the British came back with a devastating right-left-right that not only saved their colonies but also won them the entire continent.

The first punches were against Fort Duquesne, in Pennsylvania, and against the Fortress of Louisbourg, on Cape Breton, both of which they took after bloody sieges. Then, where least expected, came the ultimate haymaker, aimed straight at the enemy's solar plexus—Québec.

In June 1759 a British fleet nosed its way from the Atlantic down the St. Lawrence River. In charge of the troops on board was the youngest general in the army, 32-year-old James Wolfe, whose military record was remarkable and whose behavior was so eccentric that he had the reputation of being "mad as a march hare."

The struggle for Québec dragged on until September, when Wolfe, near desperation, played his final card. He couldn't storm those gallantly defended fortress walls, though the British guns had shelled the town to rubble. Wolfe therefore loaded 5,000 men into boats and rowed upriver to a cove behind the city. Then they silently climbed the towering cliff face in the darkness, and when morning came Wolfe had his army squarely astride Montcalm's supply lines. Now the French had to come out of their stronghold and fight in the open.

The British formed their famous "thin red line" across the bush-studded Plains of Abraham, just west of the city. Montcalm advanced on them with five regiments, all in step, and in the next quarter of an hour the fate of Canada was decided. The redcoats stood like statues as the French drew closer—100 yards, 60 yards, 40 yards. Then a command rang out, and (in such perfect unison that it sounded like a single thunderclap) the English muskets crashed. The redcoats advanced four measured paces, halted, fired, advanced another four paces with robot precision—halted, fired again. Then it was all over.

The plain was covered with the fallen French. Montcalm lay mortally wounded, and the rest of his troops fled helter-skelter. Among the British casualties was Wolfe himself. With two bullets through his body, he lived just long enough to hear that he'd won. Montcalm died a few hours after him.

Today, overlooking the boardwalk of Québec, you'll find a unique memorial to these men—a statue commemorating both victor and vanquished of the same battle.

THE U.S. INVASION

The capture of Québec determined the war and left Britain ruler of all North America down to the Mexican border. Yet, oddly enough, this victory generated Britain's worst defeat. For if the French had held Canada, the British government would certainly have been more careful in its treatment of the American colonists.

As it was, the British felt cocksure and decided to make the colonists themselves pay for the outrageous costs of the French and Indian Wars. The taxes slapped on all imports—especially tea—infuriated the colonists to the point of open rebellion against the Crown.

But if the British misjudged the temper of the colonists, the Americans were equally wrong about the mood of the Canadians. Washington felt sure that the French in the north would join the American Revolution, or at least not resist an invasion of American soldiers. He was terribly mistaken on both counts.

The French had little love for either of the English-speaking antagonists. But they were staunch Royalists and devout Catholics, with no sympathy for the "godless" republicans from the south. Only a handful changed sides, and most French Canadians fought grimly shoulder to shoulder with their erstwhile enemies.

Thirty-eight years later, in the War of 1812, another U.S. army marched up the banks of the Richelieu River where it flows from Lake Champlain to the St. Lawrence. And once again the French Canadians stuck by the British and flung back the invaders. The war ended in a draw, but with surprisingly happy results. Britain and the young United States agreed to demilitarize the Great Lakes and to extend their mutual border along the 49th parallel to the Rockies.

LOYALISTS & IMMIGRANTS

One of the side effects of the American Revolution was an influx of English-speaking newcomers for Canada. About 50,000 Americans who had remained faithful to George III, the United Empire Loyalists, migrated to Canada because they were given rough treatment in the States. They settled mostly in Nova Scotia and began to populate the almost empty shores of what is now New Brunswick.

After the Napoleonic Wars, a regular tide of immigrants came from England, which was going through the early and cruelest stages of the Industrial Revolution. They were fleeing from the new and hideously bleak factory towns, from workhouses, starvation wages, and impoverished Scottish farms. Even the unknown perils of the New World seemed preferable to these blessings of the Dickens era.

By 1850 more than half a million immigrants had arrived, pushing Canada's population above two million. The population centers began to shift westward, away from the old seaboard colonies in the east, opening up the territories eventually called Ontario, Manitoba, and Saskatchewan.

With increased population came the demand for confederation, largely because the various colony borders hampered trade. Britain complied rather promptly. In 1867 Parliament passed an act creating a federal union out of the colonies of Upper and Lower Canada, Nova Scotia, and New Brunswick. British Columbia hesitated over whether to remain separate, join the United States, or merge with Canada, but finally voted itself in. Remote Newfoundland hesitated longest of all. It remained a distinct colony until 1949, when it became Canada's 10th province.

THE METIS REBELLION

Geographically, Canada stretched from the Atlantic to the Pacific, but in reality most of the immense region in between lay beyond the rule of Ottawa, the nation's capital. The endless prairies and forest lands of the West and Northwest were inhabited by about 40,000 people, more than half of them nomadic tribes pushed there by the waves of white settlers from the east. They lived by hunting, fishing, and trapping, depending largely on buffalo for food, clothing, and shelter. As the once enormous herds began to dwindle, life grew increasingly hard for the nomads. Adding to their troubles were whiskey traders peddling poisonous rotgut for furs and packs of outlaws who took what they wanted at gunpoint.

Ordinary law officers were nearly useless. In 1873 the federal government therefore created a quite extraordinary force: the Northwest Mounted Police, now called the Royal Canadian Mounted Police (and now rarely mounted). The scarlet-coated Mounties earned a legendary reputation for toughness, fairness, and the ability to hunt down wrongdoers. And unlike their American counterparts, they usually brought in prisoners alive.

But even the Mounties couldn't handle the desperate uprising that shook western Saskatchewan in 1885. As the railroad relentlessly pushed across the prairies and the buffalo vanished, the people known as Metis felt that they had to fight for their existence. The Metis, offspring of French trappers and native women, were superb hunters and trackers. The westward expansion had driven them from Manitoba to the banks of the Saskatchewan River, where some 6,000 of them now made their last stand against iron rails and wooden farmhouses. They had a charismatic leader in Louis Riel, a man educated enough to teach school and mad enough to think that God wanted him to found a new religion.

With Riel's rebels rose their natural allies, the Plains tribes, under chiefs Poundmaker and Big Bear. Together, they were a formidable force. The Metis attacked the Mounted Police at Duck Lake, cut the telegraph wires, and proclaimed an independent republic. Their allies stormed the town of Battleford, then captured and burned Fort Pitt.

The alarmed administration in Ottawa sent an army marching westward under General Middleton, equipped with artillery and Gatling machine guns. The Metis checked them briefly at Fish Creek but had to fall back on their main village of Batoche. There the last battle of the west took place—long lines of redcoats charging with fixed bayonets, the Metis fighting from house to house, from rifle pits and crude trenches, so short of ammunition that they had to shoot lead buttons instead of bullets.

Batoche fell (you can still see the bullet marks on the houses there), and the rebellion was completely crushed shortly afterward. Louis Riel was tried for treason and murder. Though any court today probably would've found him insane, the Canadian authorities hanged him.

RAILROADS, WHEAT & WAR

The reason that the army was able to crush Riel's rebellion so quickly was also the reason for its outbreak: the Canadian Pacific Railway. The railroad was more than a marvel of engineering—it formed a steel band holding the country together, enabling Canada to live up to its motto, *A Mari Usque ad Mare* ("From Sea to Sea").

Though the free-roaming prairie people hated the iron horse, railroads were vital to Canada's survival as a nation. They had to be pushed through, against all opposition, if the isolated provinces weren't to drift into the orbit of the United States and the Dominion cease to exist. As one journalist of the time put it: "The whistle of a locomotive is the true cradle song and anthem of our country."

As the country's transportation system developed, the central provinces emerged as one of the world's biggest breadbaskets. In 1 decade, wheat production zoomed from 56 million bushels to more than 200 million, putting Canada on a par with the United States and Russia as a granary.

And despite the bitterness engendered by Riel's execution, in the following year Canada elected its first prime minister of French heritage. Sir Wilfrid Laurier had one foot in each ethnic camp and proved to be a superlative leader—according to some, the best his country ever produced. His term of office, from 1896 to 1911, was a period in which Canada flexed its muscles like a young giant and looked forward to unlimited growth and a century of peaceful prosperity—just like an equally optimistic American neighbor to the south.

With the onset of World War I, the Dominion went to war allied with Britain and likewise tried to fight it on a volunteer basis. It didn't work. The tall, healthy Canadians, together with the Australians, formed the shock troops of the British Empire and earned that honor with torrents of blood. The entire western front in France was littered with Canadian bones. The flow of volunteers became a trickle, and in 1917 the Dominion was forced to introduce conscription. The measure ran into violent opposition from the French-speaking minority, who saw conscription as a device to thin out their numbers.

The draft law went through, but it strained the nation's unity almost to the breaking point. The results were ghastly. More than 60,000 Canadians fell in battle, a terrible bloodletting for a country of 250,000. (In World War II, by contrast, Canada lost 40,000 from a population of 11.5 million.)

TOWARD WORLD POWER

Between the world wars, the fortunes of Canada more or less reflected those of the United States, except that Canada was never foolish enough to join the "noble experiment" of Prohibition. Some of its citizens, in fact, waxed rich on the lucrative bootlegging trade across the border.

But the Great Depression, coupled with disastrous droughts in the western provinces, hit all the harder in Canada. There was no equivalent of Roosevelt's New Deal in the Dominion. The country staggered along from one financial crisis to the next until the outbreak of World War II totally transformed the situation. The war provided the boost Canada needed to join the ranks of the major industrial nations. And the surge of postwar immigration provided the numbers required to work the new industries. From 1941 to 1974 Canada doubled in population and increased its gross national product nearly tenfold.

With the discovery of huge uranium deposits in Ontario and Saskatchewan, Canada was in the position to add nuclear energy to its power resources. And the opening of the St. Lawrence Seaway turned Toronto—more than 1,000 miles from the nearest ocean—into a major seaport.

All these achievements propelled Canada into its present position: a powerhouse of manufacturing and trading, with a standard of living to match that of the United States. But, simultaneously, old ghosts were raising their heads again.

TROUBLE IN QUEBEC

As an ethnic enclave, the French Canadians had won their battle for survival with flying colors. From their original 65,000 settlers they had grown to more than six million, without receiving reinforcements from overseas.

The French Canadians had preserved and increased their presence by means of large families, rigid cultural cohesion, and the unifying influence of their Catholic faith. But they had fallen far behind the English-speaking majority economically and politically. Few of them held top positions in industry or finance, and they enjoyed relatively little say in national matters.

What rankled most with them was that Canada never recognized French as a second national language. In other words, the French were expected to be bilingual if they wanted good careers, but the English-speakers got along nicely with just their own tongue. On a general cultural basis, too, the country overwhelmingly reflected Anglo-Saxon attitudes rather than an Anglo-French mixture.

By the early 1960s this discontent led to a dramatic radicalization of Québécois politics. A new separatist movement arose that regarded Québec not as simply 1 of 10 provinces but as *l'état du Québec*, a distinct state that might, if it chose, break away from the country. The most extreme faction of the movement, the Front de Libera-tion du Québec (FLQ), was frankly revolutionary and terrorist. It backed its demands with bombs, arson, and murder, culminating in the kidnap-killing of Cabinet Min-ister Pierre Laporte in October 1970.

The Ottawa government, under Prime Minister Pierre Trudeau, imposed the War Measures Act and moved 10,000 troops into the province. The police used their exceptional powers under the act to break up civil disorders, arrested hundreds of suspects, and caught the murderers of Laporte. And in the 1973 provincial elections, the separatists were badly defeated, winning only 6 seats from a total of 110.

The crisis eventually calmed down. In some ways its effects were beneficial. The federal government redoubled its efforts to remove the worst grievances of the French Canadians. Federal funds flowed to French schools outside Québec (nearly half the schoolchildren of New Brunswick, for example, are French-speaking). French Canadians were appointed to senior positions. Most important, all provinces were asked to make French an official language, which entailed making signs, government forms, transportation schedules, and other printed matter bilingual. Civil servants had to bone up on French to pass their exams and the business world began to stipulate bilingualism for men and women aiming at executive positions. All these measures were already afoot before the turmoil began, but there's no doubt that bloodshed helped to accelerate them.

UNION OR SEPARATION?

Ever since the violent crisis, Canadian politicians of all hues have been trying to patch up some sort of compromise that would enable their country to remain united. They appeared close to success when they formulated the so-called Meech Lake Accord in the 1980s—only to see it destroyed by a series of opposition moves stemming from not only French Canadians but also native-Canadian groups. The separatist Parti Québécois rallied its forces and staged a political comeback. The rift between Québec's French and English speakers is today wider than ever.

Québec's premier set up a commission to study ways to change the province's constitutional relationship with Ottawa's federal government. This aroused the ire of other provinces, which failed to see why Québec should be granted a "special" position in Canada. So the proposals, memorandums, and referendums go on and on; each one vetoed by the other camp and none coming closer to a solution.

By now, most Canadians are heartily tired of the debate, though nobody seems to have a clear idea how to end it. Some say that secession is the only way out; others favor the Swiss formula of biculturalism and bilingualism. For Québec, the breakaway advocated by Francophone hotheads could spell economic disaster. Most of Canada's industrial and financial power is in the English-speaking provinces. An independent Québec would be a poor country. But all of Canada would be poorer by losing the special flavor and rich cultural heritage imparted by the presence of La Belle Province.

3 Canada's Cultural Mosaic

Canada's people are even more diverse than its scenery. In the eastern province of Québec live six million French Canadians, whose motto, *Je me souviens* ("I remember"), has kept them "more French than France" through 2 centuries of Anglo domination. They've transformed Canada into a bilingual country where everything official—including parking tickets and airline passes—comes in two tongues.

The English-speaking majority of the populace is a mosaic rather than a block. Two massive waves of immigration—one before 1914, the other between 1945 and 1972—poured 6.5 million assorted Europeans and Americans into the country, providing muscles and skills as well as a kaleidoscope of cultures. Thus, Nova Scotia is as Scottish as haggis and kilts, Vancouver has a Germanic core alongside a Chinatown, the plains of Manitoba are sprinkled with the onion-shaped domes of

Ukrainian churches, and Ontario offers Italian street markets and a theater festival featuring the works of Shakespeare at, yes, Stratford.

You can attend a native-Canadian tribal assembly, a Chinese New Year dragon parade, an Inuit spring celebration, a German Bierfest, a Highland gathering, or a Slavic folk dance. There are group settlements on the prairies where the working parlance is Danish, Czech, or Hungarian, and entire villages speak Icelandic. For Canada hasn't been a "melting pot" in the American sense, but rather has sought "unity through diversity" as a national ideal.

NATIVE CANADIANS

There are actually more native Canadians living in Canada today than existed at the time of the first white settlements. Anthropologists have estimated that the original population was about 200,000. This population began to decline with the arrival of the Europeans. By the early 20th century it was down to almost half, and common belief labeled the native peoples a dying race. At the last census, however, the total had reached 282,000.

Ethnically, Canada's native peoples are the same as some tribes in the United States. Some tribes, such as the Cree, Sioux, and Blackfoot, are found on both sides of the border. In Canada they belong to 10 distinct linguistic groups, subdivided into widely differing local dialects. Their customs, religion, and methods of hunting and warfare were similar to those of tribes near the border in the United States. The treatment they received, however, was rather different.

In the 1870s—before most white settlers reached the west—the Canadian government began to negotiate a series of treaties with the prairie tribes. By the end of the decade, most of the western tribes had agreed to treaties in which they surrendered their lands in return for guaranteed reservations, small cash payments for each member, supplies of seeds and tools, and assistance in changing over to farming for a livelihood. By and large, with a few inglorious exceptions, those treaties were kept.

The Canadian government wielded much greater control over the white settlers than its counterpart in Washington. It was thus able to prevent the continual incursions by gold prospectors, buffalo hunters, railroad companies, and squatters that sparked most of the Indian wars south of the border. The Mounties, as distinct from the U.S. Cavalry, actually protected native tribes. As Blackfoot chief Crowfoot said: "The police have shielded us from bad men as the feathers of birds protect them from the winter frosts. If the police had not come, very few of us would have been left today."

The decline of the native population was due mainly to sickness brought in by the whites. In addition, tens of thousands of erstwhile nomadic hunters simply couldn't bear a life tied to one patch of soil; they died from sheer discouragement, unwilling to continue an existence that appeared joyless and stale.

Today the country has 574 separate native-Canadian communities, known as "bands." A few—a very few—of them still roam the northern regions. The others share 2,110 reserves, though less than two-thirds actually live on reservations. Today they're successful farmers, nurses, builders, secretaries, doctors, teachers, clergy, salespeople, and industrial workers, both on and off the reserves. In 1973 the government accepted a proposal by the National Indian Brotherhood by which increasing numbers of bands now manage their own schools. Instead of trying to erase their past, the new school curricula include history and native-language courses for children who've almost forgotten their native tongues.

This is only fair, since the very name Canada derives from the Huron word for settlement, *kanata*.

THE INUIT

Inuit means "people," and that's what the Canadian Eskimos call themselves. So remote was their native habitat, so completely isolated from the rest of the world, that they were unaware that any people except themselves existed.

The Eskimos are a unique people, the Canadian branch even more so than the others. There are only around 80,000 Eskimos in the world, forming part of four nations: Russia, the United States, Canada, and Denmark (in Greenland, a Danish possession). This makes the Eskimos the only natives of the same ethnic group to live in both Asia and America.

Some 22,000 Inuit live in Canada today, and we have no idea how many there might've been originally. They inhabited the Far North, the last portion of the country to be explored, much later than the other Arctic lands of the globe. While their cousins elsewhere were trading with the white settlers, the Inuit initially had limited contact with Europeans.

The Inuit were traditionally coastal people who lived by fishing and by hunting seal, whale, and polar bear. These animals supplied their food, clothing, light, and heat (in the form of blubber-fueled lamps and stoves) and were used to their last shred of skin. The Inuit's earliest contact was with whalers, frequently with tragic results. The Inuit were gentle people, intensely hospitable and so averse to violence that their language had no term for war.

When the first British and American whaling ships touched Baffin Bay in the 1820s, they found that the Inuit had no conception of private property and of food and clothing that wasn't shared with whomever needed it. The Inuit marveled at the white sailors' wooden whaleboats, firearms, iron tools, and glass bottles—none of which they'd ever seen. They had no idea of the dangers associated with these wonders.

Murder and rape were the least of them. Liquor was far more destructive, but worst of all were the diseases the whalers introduced. For all its harshness, the Arctic was a healthy region, free of bacteria. The Inuit might have starved and froze to death, but they rarely succumbed to illness. So their bodies had no resistance to the measles, smallpox, and tuberculosis that the whites brought in along with their rum and gadgetry.

The Inuit—particularly their children—died like flies. The only doctors available were a handful of missionaries, usually with limited medical supplies. Today's Inuit are a race of survivors, the strain that somehow battled through a century that killed uncounted numbers of their kind.

It wasn't until the 1950s that the Canadian government took serious steps to assure the Inuit their rightful place in their Arctic homeland. As air transportation and radio communications broke down the isolation of the Far North, the government introduced improved educational, health, and welfare services. The Inuit are now full citizens in every respect (not in name only), electing members of the Territorial Council of the Northwest Territories and running their own communities.

They've ceased to be nomads and have moved into permanent settlements. But unlike the prairie tribes, the Inuit are still basically hunters, though nowadays they use rifles instead of the traditional harpoons. But don't compare their hunting with weekend activity. The Inuit hunt in order to eat, and no one is more ecologically conscious than they are. Everything in their prey is used—a walrus represents a minisupermarket—and they kill nothing for pleasure and not one animal more than is absolutely necessary.

The Inuit Tapirisat (Inuit Brotherhood) is their nonpolitical organization dedicated to preserving the Inuktetut language and culture and to helping them achieve full participation in Canada's society. This would include legal rights to some of the enormous lands the Inuit once roamed and used, but without establishing fixed borders for their domain. Some of these areas have been found to contain valuable deposits of oil, natural gas, and minerals, which makes the question of ownership more than merely academic.

If you want a glimpse of the Inuit soul, look at their art, which you'll find in stores all over Canada. Their artistry shouldn't surprise you: The Inuit are perhaps the greatest needle (fish bone) experts in the world, and their completely waterproof sealskin kayak canoe is possibly the best-designed vehicle in marine history.

But Inuit carvings of people and animals have a quality all their own. They're imbued with a sense of movement, a feeling for anatomy, almost a smell. Their expressions are so hauntingly lifelike, yet so curiously abstract, that they give you an eerie notion of having seen them before in some strange dream.

4 Wilderness & Wonder: Canada's National & Provincial Parks

THE NATIONAL PARKS

Canada is in the process of creating several new national parks in the Far North. Recently accorded agreements with the region's native peoples call for the development of parks on part of the land that was once administered by the government. Additionally, Parks Canada operates hundreds of Historic Parks that feature historic buildings or sites (often with summer programs and activities). But these exceptions aside, we've listed the national parks, offering a quick rundown on the defining characteristics of each.

Kejimkujik National Park (Nova Scotia): There are two parts to this park. The first is a wilderness of rolling hills and lakes in the heart of Nova Scotia. The other part preserves a stretch of wild and undeveloped southern coastline flanked by steep cliffs. This section of the park protects the rare shorebird, the piping plover, and marine animals.

Cape Breton Highlands National Park (Nova Scotia): This far-flung coastal wilderness, similar in terrain and grandeur to the Scottish Highlands, appealed to hearty Scots who founded small settlements among the mountains. The Cabot Trail highway rings the park, with tremendous views down from pink granite coastal cliffs.

Fundy National Park (New Brunswick): Covered bridges, the world's highest tides, and plenty of hiking trails characterize this small coastal park on the southern New Brunswick coast.

Kouchibouguac National Park (New Brunswick): A small, low-key park on the Acadian Coast, Kouchibouguac features beaches, bike paths, and hikes to salt marshes and offshore dunes. Swimmers will enjoy the park's pleasant lagoon waters, known as the warmest north of the Carolinas.

Prince Edward Island National Park (Prince Edward Island): This park combines a popular stretch of sandy beach on the Gulf of St. Lawrence and Green Gables House, a Victorian estate that served as the setting for the popular children's tale *Anne of Green Gables*.

Gros Morne National Park (Newfoundland): A spectacular preserve with glacier-carved mountains and fjords, Gros Morne stretches along the west coast of Newfoundland. Hiking trails lead to Western Brook Pond, which is in fact a fresh-water fjord lined by cliffs towering 2,000 feet high.

Terra Nova National Park (Newfoundland): A scenic spot on the Labrador Sea, Terra Nova is covered with dense coniferous forests that provide backcountry adventure. Sea kayakers come here to probe the multitudes of tiny inlets and coves found along the headlands.

La Mauricie National Park (Québec): A maze of lakes, rivers, and deep forest, La Mauricie is popular with canoe-campers who paddle through the extensive natural water system much as did the early Indians and French trappers. In winter, 50 miles of cross-country ski trails are groomed, with warming huts every 3 miles.

Mingan Archipelago National Park (Québec): A string of 47 limestone islands along the northern shores of the Gulf of St. Lawrence, Mingan is uninhabited except by seabirds and marine mammals.

Forillon National Park (Québec): At the end of the Gaspé Peninsula, this park is famous for its 600-foot-high limestone cliffs that drop into the Gulf of St. Lawrence. Hiking trails lead to dizzying overlooks; watch for whales in summer.

St. Lawrence Islands National Park (Ontario): Canada's smallest national park, these 23 islands in the St. Lawrence River are part of the larger Thousand Islands area. The tiny flower-covered islands are mostly undeveloped and offer free campsites to those with boats.

Pukaskwa National Park (Ontario): Ontario's largest national park, Pukaskwa is in the boreal forests on the north shore of Lake Superior. Preserved as a wilderness, it can be accessed by boat only.

Bruce Peninsula National Park (Ontario): The rugged 50-mile Bruce Peninsula juts into Lake Huron and is popular with long-distance hikers on the Bruce Trail. From a point near the park's headquarters at Tobermory, ferries leave for Manitoulin Island.

Georgian Bay Islands National Park (Ontario): A collection of 50 islands in Lake Huron's Georgian Bay, this park is popular with boaters, who are able to access the more remote islands. Water taxis are available to Beausoleil Island, the park headquarters.

Point Pelee National Park (Ontario): Point Pelee is famous for its bird watching (this peninsula of sand in Lake Erie is at the junction of two migratory flyways) and for the fall gathering of monarch butterflies, which flock here before their annual migration.

Riding Mountain National Park (Manitoba): Manitoba's only national park, Riding Mountain is a habitat crossroads where prairie, boreal forest, and deciduous life zones intersect. Wolf, moose, bison, and elk are found here in great numbers. The park is popular with summertime campers, who fish and boat in the many lakes.

Grasslands National Park (Saskatchewan): The first national park to preserve the native prairie ecosystem, this park in southern Saskatchewan protects the only remaining black-tailed prairie-dog colony in Canada. Other wildlife includes coyotes, deer, pronghorn, and many bird species.

Prince Albert National Park (Saskatchewan): Located where the southern prairies give way to the lake country, this national park is the nesting ground for one of Canada's largest colonies of white pelicans; moose, wolf, caribou, and bison also live here. The early environmentalist/author Grey Owl lived here in the 1930s; his cabin still stands on Ajawaan Lake.

Waterton Lakes National Park (Alberta): Joined with Montana's Glacier National Park, this international peace park is famed for its beautiful lakes glimmering in glacial basins between finlike mountain ranges. The most popular activity is the boat ride from the Canadian to the U.S. side of the park.

Banff National Park (Alberta): The most popular destination in all Canada, Banff Park is extremely beautiful and often crowded. The views onto towering cliff-sided mountains are unforgettable; easy hiking trails to lakes and alpine meadows make this a popular park for families. Banff Townsite and Lake Louise Village provide world-class accommodations and boutiques.

Jasper National Park (Alberta): The largest park in the Canadian Rockies, Jasper sits astride the central crest of the continent. The Columbia Icefields, natural hot springs, shimmering glacial lakes, soaring mountain peaks, and superb long-distance hiking trails make this one of the gems of the Canadian Park system.

Yoho National Park (British Columbia): *Yoho* means "awe" in Cree, and the park's many lakes, towering peaks, and mighty waterfalls (Takakkawa Falls drops 1,200 ft.) certainly provoke it. The Kicking Horse River is one of the best white-water rivers in the Rockies, and glacier-fed Emerald and O'Hara lakes are famed beauty spots.

Glacier National Park (British Columbia): Heavy snowfalls maintain more than 400 glaciers and snowfields in this park located at the crest of the rugged Columbia Mountains; more than 14% of the park's landscape is covered in permanent ice.

Kootenay National Park (British Columbia): A collection of natural marvels on the western slopes of the Rockies' Main Range, Kootenay is noted for its rugged lime-stone canyons, Radium Hot Springs resort, and highly colored mineral springs.

Elk Island National Park (Alberta): A major preserve of the wildlife that once roamed the northern prairies, Elk Island is just east of Edmonton. Moose, two species of bison, a large number of elk, beaver, and other species are all easily viewed from hiking trails.

Wood Buffalo National Park (Alberta/Northwest Territory): The world's largest national park, Wood Buffalo protects many animal species, including the once-feared-extinct wood buffalo and the whooping crane. The park also preserves unique eco-systems, like the Peace-Athabasca river delta and a natural salt plain.

Pacific Rim National Park (British Columbia): The only national park on Vancouver Island, Pacific Rim is comprised of three units: Long Beach; Broken Group Islands, an archipelago of more than 100 islets in Barkley Sound; and the West Coast Trail, a long-distance trail that skirts the rugged coastline.

Gwaii Haanas National Park (British Columbia): On the southern end of the Queen Charlotte Archipelago, Gwaii Haanas is jointly administered by Parks Canada and the Haida Nation. The 138-island park is filled with ancient village and totem sites sacred to the Haida.

Mount Revelstoke National Park (British Columbia): Roads lead to the top of Mount Revelstoke, a peak in the Selkirk Mountains. Hiking trails lead into inland rain forests and alpine meadows.

Kluane National Park (Yukon): Canada's highest peaks and largest nonpolar ice caps are in this rugged park on the Gulf of Alaska. Long-distance trails lead to enormous valley glaciers; the park's mighty rivers are popular with white-water rafters.

Nahanni National Park (Northwest Territories): Known throughout the world for its superlative rafting and canoeing, Nahanni is also famous for massive Virginia Falls, twice as high as Niagara.

Ivvavik National Park (Yukon): Fronting onto the Arctic Ocean and accessible only by small aircraft, Ivvavik was formed to protect the porcupine caribou herd. Approximately 10% of the world's caribou live here.

Vuntut National Park (Yukon): Just south of Ivvavik National Park, Vuntut is a habitat preserve for caribou, grizzly bear, and other Arctic animals. The park was the hunting grounds for the native Gwitchin, who called the area Old Crow Flats.

Aulavik National Park (Northwest Territories): Banks Island is home to the largest musk oxen herds in the world, and this Arctic island park is designed to preserve their fragile tundra habitat.

Ellesmere Island National Park (Northwest Territories): The most northerly and second largest of Canada's national parks, this remote and rugged wilderness of tundra, glacier, and mountains is literally at the top of the world.

Auyuittuq National Park (Northwest Territories): *Auyuittuq* means "the land that never melts," and much of this precipitously rugged fjord-bit park on Baffin Island is covered with a permanent ice cap. A long-distance fjord-to-fjord hiking trail leads across the park, accessing some of the world's longest rock faces, popular with climbers.

THE BEST OF THE PROVINCIAL PARKS

Canada has hundreds of provincial parks (British Columbia alone has 330), many of them simply campgrounds or public beaches in popular recreation areas. Others contain sites of great scenic or historic interest and definitely deserve a detour. Below are some that we consider outstanding.

Mont Orford (Québec): Always popular with family camping groups, this mountainous park is ablaze with autumn color each year. The hiking paths through hardwood forest that are so popular in summer become cross-country ski trails when the snow falls.

Algonquin Provincial Park (Ontario): A wilderness of lakes and deep forest, Algonquin is perfect for extended canoe-camping trips, with nearly 1,000 miles of charted routes.

Dinosaur Provincial Park (Alberta): The Badlands of Alberta are filled with Cretaceous-era dinosaur-bone fossils, and this park protects one of the richest quarry areas. You can tour or join a dig and watch fossils being prepared at the visitor center.

Head-Smashed-In Buffalo Jump (Alberta): The Plains Indians once stampeded bison off cliffs as part of their yearly food-gathering cycle. This interpretive center preserves one of these cliffs and relates the area's natural and human history.

Mount Robson (British Columbia): The highest peak in the Canadian Rockies, Mount Robson towers above glacial lakes and roaring rivers just west of Jasper National Park.

Strathcona (British Columbia): Strathcona is the largest wilderness park on Vancouver Island, with lots of skiing and hiking. The high point, though, is the 2-day hiking trail into Dalla Falls; at more than 1,440 feet, they're the highest in North America.

Planning a Trip to Canada 3

by Bill McRae

This chapter can save you money, time, and headaches. Here's where you'll find travel know-how, such as when to visit, what documents you'll need, and where to get more information. These basics can make the difference between a smooth ride and a bumpy one.

1 Visitor Information & Entry Requirements

VISITOR INFORMATION

The various provincial offices below dispense visitor information. Canadian consulates do not.

- **Alberta Economic Development and Tourism,** Commerce Place, 10155 102nd St., Edmonton, AB, T5J 4L6 (☎ **800/661-8888**).
- **Tourism British Columbia,** Parliament Building, Victoria, BC, V8V 1X4 (☎ **800/663-6000** or 250/387-1642).
- **Travel Manitoba,** 155 Carlton St., Winnipeg, MB, RC3 3H8 (☎ **800/665-0040**).
- **Tourism New Brunswick,** P.O. Box 12345, Fredericton, NB, E3B 5C3 (☎ **800/561-0123**).
- **Newfoundland and Labrador Dept. of Tourism,** Culture and Recreation, P.O. Box 8700, St. John's, NF, A1B 4J6 (☎ **800/563-6353** or 709/729-2806).
- **Nova Scotia Dept. of Tourism,** P.O. Box 130, Halifax, NS, B3J 2M7 (☎ **800/565-0000**).
- **Northwest Territories Economic Development and Tourism,** P.O. Box 1320, Yellowknife, NWT, X1A 2L9 (☎ **800/661-0788**).
- **Ontario Travel,** Queen's Park, Toronto, ON, M7A 2E5 (☎ **800/668-2746**).
- **Tourism Prince Edward Island,** West Royalty Industrial Park, Charlottetown, PEI, C1E 1B0 (☎ **800/463-4734**).
- **Tourisme Québec,** C.P. 979, Montréal, PQ, H3C 2W3 (☎ **800/363-7777**).
- **Tourism Saskatchewan,** 500–1900 Albert St., Regina, SK, S4P 4L9 (☎ **800/667-7191**).

- **Tourism Yukon,** P.O. Box 2703, Whitehorse, YK, Y1A 2C6 (☎ 403/ 667-5340).
- **Nunavut Tourism,** P.O. Box 1450, Iqaluit, NT, X0A 0H0, (☎ 800/491-7910).

For general information about Canada's national parks, contact **Canadian Heritage,** Publications Unit, Room 10H2, Hull, Québec, K1A 0M5 (☎ 819/994-6625; fax 819/953-8770).

ENTRY REQUIREMENTS

U.S. citizens, permanent U.S. residents, or British, Australian, New Zealand, or Irish nationals, require neither passports nor visas. You should, however, carry some identifying papers, such as a passport or birth, baptismal, or voter's certificate to show your citizenship; in most cases, a driver's license is all you're asked to provide. Permanent U.S. residents who aren't U.S. citizens must have their Alien Registration Cards.

Customs regulations are very generous in most respects but get pretty complicated when it comes to firearms, plants, meats, and pets. Fishing tackle poses no problems, but the bearer must possess a nonresident license for the province or territory where he or she plans to use it. You can bring in free of duty up to 50 cigars, 200 cigarettes, and 2 pounds of tobacco, providing that you're over 16 years of age. You're also allowed 40 ounces of liquor or wine.

An important point: Any person under 19 requires a letter from a parent or guardian granting him or her permission to travel to Canada. The letter must state the traveler's name and duration of the trip. It's essential that teenagers carry proof of identity; otherwise, their letter is useless at the border.

For more details concerning customs regulations, write to **Customs and Excise,** Connaught Building, Sussex Drive, Ottawa, ON, K1A 0L5.

2 Money

Canadians use dollars and cents, but with a very pleasing balance: The Canadian dollar is worth around 75¢ in U.S. money, give or take a couple of points' daily variation. So your American money gets you roughly 27% more the moment you exchange it for local currency. And since the price of many goods is roughly on a par with that in the United States, the difference is real, not imaginary. (Before you get too excited, however, remember that sales taxes are astronomical.) You can bring in or take out any amount, but if you're importing or exporting sums of $5,000 or more, you must file a report of the transaction with U.S. Customs. Most tourist places in Canada will take U.S. cash, but for the best rate you should change your funds into Canadian currency.

If you do spend American money at Canadian establishments, you should understand how the conversion is done. Often by the cash register there'll be a sign reading "U.S. Currency 25%." This 25% is the "premium," and it means that for every U.S. greenback you hand over, the cashier will see it as $1.25 in Canadian dollars. Thus, for an $8 tab you need pay only $6 in U.S. bills.

When you cash U.S. traveler's checks at a bank, most banks will charge you a $2 fee per transaction (not per check). Hotels, restaurants, and shops don't charge fees as a rule, but their exchange rate may be somewhat lower than the current figure.

The best rate of exchange is usually through use of an ATM with a bank card. Not only is it convenient not to have to carry cash and checks, but you'll get the best commercial rate. It's always wise to bring in sufficient Canadian cash to pay for an initial cab or bus and a meal.

The Canadian Dollar & the U.S. Dollar

The prices cited in this guide are given first in Canadian dollars, then in U.S. dollars (which have been rounded to the nearest dollar). Note that the Canadian dollar is worth 25% less than the American dollar but buys nearly as much. As we go to press, $1 Canadian is worth about 75¢ U.S.

Here's a quick table of equivalents:

Canadian $	U.S. $
1	0.72
5	3.60
10	7.20
20	14.30
50	35.70
80	57.10
100	71.40

A final word: Canada has no $1 bills. The lowest paper denomination is $2. Single bucks come in brass coins bearing the picture of a loon—hence their nickname "loonies." There's also a new two-toned $2 coin.

3 When to Go

THE WEATHER

In southern and central Canada, the weather is the same as in the northern United States. As you head north, the climate becomes Arctic, meaning long and extremely cold winters, brief and surprisingly warm summers (with lots of flies), and magical springs.

As a general rule, spring runs from mid-March to mid-May, summer from mid-May to mid-September, fall from mid-September to mid-November, and winter from mid-November to mid-March. Pick the season best suited to your tastes and temperament, and remember that your car should be winterized through March and that snow sometimes falls as late as April (in 1995 a foot of snow blanketed Prince Edward Island in May). September and October bring autumn foliage and great opportunities for photographers.

Evenings tend to be cool everywhere, particularly on or near water. In late spring and early summer, you'll need a supply of insect repellent if you're planning bush travel or camping.

With the huge size of some provinces and territories, you naturally get considerable climate variations inside their borders. Québec, for instance, sprawls all the way from the temperate south to the Arctic, and the weather varies accordingly. British Columbia shows the slightest changes: It rarely goes above the 70s in summer or drops below the 30s in winter.

HOLIDAYS

National holidays are celebrated throughout the country, meaning that all government facilities close down, as well as banks, but some department stores and a scattering of smaller shops stay open. If the holiday falls on a weekend, the following Monday is observed.

Canadian holidays include New Year's Day, Good Friday, Easter Monday, Victoria Day (in mid- to late May), Canada Day (July 1), Labour Day, Thanksgiving (in mid-October), Remembrance Day (November 11), Christmas Day, and Boxing Day (December 26). In addition, you may run into provincial holidays.

4 The Outdoor Adventure Planner

SPORTS A TO Z

BIKING   Most of Canada's highways are wide and well maintained, and thus well suited for long-distance bicycle touring. Most resort areas have ample supplies of rentals, so you don't have to worry about transporting your own (it's a good idea to call ahead and reserve a bike). You'll need to be in good shape to embark on a long bike trip and able to deal with minor bike repairs.

While most hiking trails are closed to mountain bikes, other trails are developed specifically for backcountry biking. Ask at national-park and national-forest information centers for a map of mountain-bike trails.

Probably the most rewarding biking anywhere is in Banff and Jasper national parks. The Icefields Parkway, running between the parks, is an eye-popping route past soaring peaks and glaciers and is wide and well graded.

CANOEING & KAYAKING   Much of Canada was first explored by canoe, as low-lying lakes and slow rivers form vast waterway systems across the central and northern parts of the country. Canoes are still excellent for exploring the backcountry. Several-day canoe-camping trips through wilderness waterways make popular summer and early-fall expeditions for small groups; you'll see lots of wildlife (especially mosquitoes) and keep as gentle a pace as you like. Generally speaking, the longer the trip, the more experience you should have with a canoe and with wilderness conditions (weather, wildlife, and chance of injury). Lake-filled Manitoba is a good place to plan a canoe trip.

DOGSLEDDING   Just imagine taking a traditional dogsled out into the Arctic ice floes and snowy tundra. Outfitters in the North run several-day trips to see the aurora borealis in early spring, and in late spring they offer trips out to the floe edge where wildlife viewing is great: This is your best chance to see a polar bear. You'll get a turn at driving the dog team and will sleep in comfort in special room-sized tents heated with small stoves (no igloos!). Outfitters will usually provide all the gear necessary for the weather, though you should be prepared to get a little cold. Outfitters on Baffin Island provide dogsled trips ranging from part-day to a week out on the tundra amid dramatic mountain and fjord scenery; February to May is the best time.

FISHING   Angling is another sport enjoyed across the entire country. The famed salmon fisheries along the Atlantic and Pacific coasts face highly restricted catch limits in most areas, and outright bans on fishing in others. However, not all salmon species on all rivers are threatened, and rules governing fishing change quickly, so check locally with fishing outfitters to find out if a season will open while you're visiting. Other species aren't so heavily restricted and probably make a better focus for a fishing-oriented vacation. Trout are found throughout Canada, some reaching great size in the thousands of lakes in the north country; northern pike and walleye are also wary fish that grow to massive size in the North. The Arctic char, a cousin of the salmon, is an anadromous fish running in the mighty rivers that feed into the Arctic Ocean; char fishing is often combined with other backcountry adventures by Arctic outfitters.

Fishing in Canada is regulated either by local government or by tribes, and appropriate licenses are necessary. Angling for some fish is regulated by season; in some areas, catch-and-release fishing is enforced. Be sure to check with local authorities before casting your line.

Perhaps Canada's most famous fishing hole is Great Slave Lake. This deep and massive lake is home to enormous lake trout and northern pike; the latter can reach lengths over 6 feet. You'll want to plan a trip with an outfitter, as weather conditions change rapidly and maneuvering small craft can be dangerous.

HIKING   Almost every national and provincial park in Canada is webbed with hiking trails, ranging from easy, interpretive nature hikes to long-distance trails into the backcountry. Late summer and early fall is a good time to plan a walking holiday, since spring comes late to much of Canada—trails in the high country may be snowbound until July.

Most parks have developed free hiking and trail information, as well as details on accessible trails for people with mobility concerns. Before setting out, be sure to request this information and buy a good map. If you're taking a long trip, make sure to evaluate your fitness and equipment before you leave; once in the backcountry, there's no way out except on foot, so make sure that your boots fit and you understand the risks you're undertaking.

Though there are great trails and magnificent scenery across Canada, for many people the Canadian Rockies, with their abundance of parks and developed trail systems, provide the country's finest hiking.

HORSEBACK RIDING   Holidays on horseback have a long pedigree in western Canada. Most outfitters and guest ranches offer a variety of options. Easiest are short rides that take a morning or an afternoon; you'll be given an easygoing horse and sufficient instruction to make you feel comfortable no matter what your previous riding ability. Longer pack trips take riders off into the backcountry on a several-day guided expedition, with lodging either in tents or at rustic camps. These trips are best for those who don't mind "roughing it": You'll probably go a day or two without showers or flush toilets, and you'll end up saddle sore and sunburned. While these trips are generally open to riders with varying degrees of experience, it's a good idea to spend some time on horseback before heading out: You get very sore if you haven't been in a saddle for a while. The Canadian Rockies in Alberta are filled with guest ranches offering a wide range of horseback activities.

SEA KAYAKING   Though it may seem like a newer sport, sea kayaking is an ancient activity: The Inuit have used hide-covered kayaks for centuries. New lightweight kayaks make it possible to transport these crafts to remote areas and explore previously inaccessible areas along sheltered coasts; kayaks are especially good for wildlife viewing. Most coastal towns in British Columbia will have both kayak rentals and instruction, as well as guided trips. Handling a kayak isn't as easy as it looks, and you'll want to have plenty of experience in sheltered coves before heading out onto the surf. Be sure to know the tide schedule and weather forecast before setting out, as well as what the coastal rock formations are. You'll need to be comfortable on the water and ready to get wet, as well as be a strong swimmer. One of the best places in the world to practice sea kayaking is in the sheltered bays, islands, and inlets along the coast of British Columbia.

SKIING   It's no wonder that Canada, a mountainous country with heavy snowfall, is one of the world's top ski destinations. If you've never skied before, then you've got a basic choice between the speed and thrills of downhill skiing, or the more

Zen-like pleasure of cross-country skiing. Both sports are open to all ages, though downhill skiing is less forgiving of older bones and joints and carries a higher price tag: A day on the slopes, with rental gear and lift ticket, can easily top $80.

For **downhill skiing,** the Canadian Rockies are the primary destination. The 1988 Winter Olympics were held at Nakiska, just outside of Banff National Park, and the park itself is home to three other ski areas, including Lake Louise, the country's largest. If you're just learning to ski or are skiing with the family, then the easier slopes at Banff Mount Norquay are made to order. At all these ski areas, instruction, rentals, and day care are available, and world-class lodging is available at Banff and Lake Louise. The slopes are usually open from November to May.

The dry, heavy snows of eastern Canada make this the best destination for a **cross-country skiing** vacation. The Laurentians, north of Québec, are a range of low mountains with many ski trails and small resort towns with rural French-Canadian charm. The best skiing is from January to March.

WHITE-WATER RAFTING Charging down a mountain river in a rubber raft is one of the most popular adventures for many people visiting Canada's western mountains. Trips range from daylong excursions that demand little of a participant other than sitting tight, to long-distance trips through remote backcountry where all members of the crew are expected to hoist a paddle through the rapids. Risk doesn't correspond to length of trip: Individual rapids and water conditions can make even a short trip a real adventure. On long trips, you'll be camping in tents and spending evenings by a campfire. Even on short trips, plan on getting wet; it's not unusual to get thrown out of a raft, so you should be comfortable in water and a good swimmer if you're floating an adventurous river (outfitters will always provide life-jackets).

Jasper National Park is a major center for short yet thrilling white-water trips. For a weeklong white-water adventure in a wilderness setting, contact an outfitter about trips through Nahanni National Park.

SHOULD YOU USE AN OUTFITTER OR PLAN YOUR OWN TRIP?

A basic consideration for most people who embark on an adventure vacation is time versus money. If you have time on your hands and have basic skills in dealing with sports and the outdoors, then planning your own trip can be fun and satisfying. On the other hand, making one phone call and writing one check makes a lot more sense if you don't have a lot of time and lack the background to safely get you where you want to go.

TRANSPORTATION & EQUIPMENT In general, the more remote the destination, the more you should consider an outfitter. In many parts of Canada, simply getting to the area where your trip begins requires a great deal of planning. Frequently, outfitters will have their own airplanes or boats or work in conjunction with someone who does. These transportaiion costs are usually included in the price of an excursion and are usually cheaper than the same flight or boat trip on a chartered basis.

The same rule applies to equipment rental. Getting your raft or canoe to an out-of-the-way lake can be an adventure in itself. But hire an outfitter and they'll take care of the hassle.

Another option is to use an outfitter to "package" your trip. Some outfitters offer their services to organize air charters and provide equipment for a fee but leave you to mastermind the trip.

SAFETY Much of Canada is remote and given to weather extremes. What might be considered a casual camping trip or boating excursion in more populated or temperate areas can become life-threatening in the Canadian backcountry—which often starts right at the edge of town. Almost all outfitters are certified as first-aid providers, and most will carry two-way radios in case there's a need to call for help. Local outfitters also know the particular hazards of the areas where they lead trips. In some areas, like the Arctic, where hazards range from freakish weather, ice-floe movements, and polar bears, outfitters are nearly mandatory.

OTHER PEOPLE   Most outfitters will only lead groups out on excursions after signing up a minimum number of participants. This is usually a financial consideration for the outfitter, but for participants, this can be both good and bad news. Traveling with the right people can add to the trip's enjoyment, but the wrong companions can lead to exasperation and disappointment. If you're sensitive to other peoples' idiosyncrasies, ask the potential outfitter specific questions regarding who else is going on the trip.

SELECTING AN OUTFITTER

An outfitter will be responsible for your safety and your enjoyment of the trip, so make certain that you choose one wisely.

All outfitters should be licensed or accredited by the province and be happy to provide you with proof. This means that they're bonded, carry the necessary insurance, and have the money and organizational wherewithal to register with the province. This rules out fly-by-night operations and college students who've decided to set up business for the summer. If you're just starting to plan an excursion, ask the provincial tourist authority for its complete list of licensed outfitters.

Often a number of outfitters offer similar trips. When you've narrowed down your choice, call and talk to the outfitters in question. Ask questions and try to get a sense of who these people are; you'll be spending a lot of time with them, so make sure you feel comfortable. If you have special interests, like bird or wildlife watching, be sure to mention them. A good outfitter will also take your interests into account when planning a trip.

If there's a wide disparity in prices between outfitters for the same trip, find out what makes the difference. Some companies economize on food. If you don't mind having cold cuts for each meal of your weeklong canoe expedition, then perhaps the least expensive outfitter is okay. However, if you prefer a cooked meal, or alcoholic beverages, or choice of entrees, then be prepared to pay more. On a long trip, it might be worth it to you.

Ask how many years an outfitter has been in business and how long your particular escort has guided this trip. While a start-up outfitting service can be perfectly fine, you should know what level of experience you're buying. If you have questions, especially for longer or more dangerous trips, ask for referrals.

OUTFITTERS & ADVENTURE-TRAVEL OPERATORS

All outfitters should be licensed by the province, and local tourist offices can provide listings of outfitters who operate in the areas you intend to visit. Most outfitters offer trips in specific geographic areas only, though some larger outfitters package trips across the country. In the chapters that follow, we'll recommend lots of local operators and tell you about the outings they run. We've found a few, though, that operate in more than one region of Canada.

Whitewolf Adventure Expeditions, 1355 Citadel Dr., no. 41, Port Coquitlam, BC, V3C 5X6 (☎ **800/661-6659**), offers canoe and white-water trips in rivers across northern and western Canada.

Canusa Cycle Tours, P.O. Box 45, Okotoks, AB, T0L 1T0 (☎ **403/560-5859**), offers guided cycle tours along some of Canada's most scenic highways.

Canada North Outfitting, P.O. Box 3100, 87 Mills St., Almonte, ON, K0A 1A0 (☎ **613/256-4057;** fax 613/256-4512), offers fishing and hiking trips in several locations in the Arctic, including Ellesmere National Park.

WHAT TO PACK

Be sure that it's clearly established between you and your outfitter what you're responsible for bringing along. If you need to bring a sleeping bag, find out what weight of bag is suggested for the conditions that you'll encounter. If you have any special dietary requirements, bring them along.

While it's fun and relatively easy to amass the equipment for a backcountry expedition, none of the equipment will do you any good unless you know how to use it. Even though compasses aren't particularly accurate in the North, bring one along and know how to use it. If you're trekking on your own, bring along a first-aid kit.

For all summer trips in Canada, make sure to bring along insect repellent, as mosquitoes are particularly numerous and hungry in the North. If you know you're heading into bad mosquito country, consider buying specialized hats with mosquito netting attached. Sunglasses are a must, even above the Arctic Circle. The farther north you go in summer, the longer the sun stays up; the low angle of the sun can be particularly annoying. In winter, the glare off snow can cause sun blindness. For the same reasons, sunscreen is a surprising necessity.

Summer weather is changeable in Canada. If you're planning outdoor activities, be sure to bring along wet-weather gear, even in high summer. The more exposure you'll have to the elements, the more you should consider bringing high-end Gortex and artificial-fleece outerwear. The proper gear can make the difference between a miserable time and a great adventure.

If you're traveling in Canada in winter, you'll want to have the best winter coat, gloves, and boots that you can afford. A coat with a hood is especially important, as Arctic winds can blow for days at a time.

5 Getting There

BY PLANE

Canada is served by almost all the international air carriers. The major international airports in the east are in Halifax, Toronto, and Montréal; in the west they're in Winnipeg, Edmonton, Calgary, and Vancouver.

Air Canada (☎ 800/776-3000) has by far the most flights between the United States and Canada (including 18 daily from New York to Toronto), but most major U.S. and Canadian carriers fly daily between major cities in Canada and the United States as well, including **America West** (☎ 800/292-9378), **American Airlines** (☎ 800/433-7300), **Canadian Airlines** (☎ 800/426-7000), **Delta** (☎ 800/221-1212), **Northwest** (☎ 800/447-4747), **United** (☎ 800/241-6522), and **US Airways** (☎ 800/428-4322).

If you're looking for the cheapest fare possible, you have a few options, including charter flights. Try calling the **Council on International Educational Exchange (Council Charters),** 205 E. 42nd St., New York, NY 10017 (☎ **800/223-7402**). **Travel Avenue,** 10 S. Riverside Plaza, Suite 1404, Chicago, IL 60606 (☎ **800/ 333-3335** or 312/876-1116), is a reputable rebator that often offers remarkable bargains.

See the box "Cyber Deals for Net Surfers," below, for Internet resources.

BY CAR

Hopping across the border by car is no problem, since the U.S. freeway system leads directly into Canada at 13 points. Once across the border you can link up with the Trans-Canada Highway, which runs from St. John's, Newfoundland, to Victoria, British Columbia—a total of 5,000 miles.

BY TRAIN

Amtrak serves the East Coast with four main routes into Canada. The *Adirondack,* which starts at New York City's Pennsylvania Station, is a day train that travels daily via Albany and upstate New York to Montréal. The *Montrealer* travels nightly from New York City's Penn Station through Vermont to Montréal. Round-trip coach fares range from US$102 to US$300. The *Maple Leaf* links New York City and Toronto via Albany, Buffalo, and Niagara Falls, departing daily from Penn Station. Round-trip coach fares range from US$140 to US$195. From Chicago, the *International* carries passengers to Toronto via Port Huron, Michigan, for a round-trip coach fare ranging from US$110 to US$195. On the West Coast, the *Mt. Baker* runs between Seattle and Vancouver, British Columbia. Round-trip fare is US$38.

From Buffalo's Exchange Street Station you can make the trip to Toronto on the Toronto/Hamilton/Buffalo Railway (THB), which is a two-car Budd train. In Toronto you can make connections to Montréal, Ottawa, and so on.

Connecting services are available from other major cities along the border in addition to these direct routes. Call **Amtrak** at ☎ **800/USA-RAIL** for further information and fares. Remember that the prices don't include meals; you can buy meals on the train or carry your own food.

BY FERRY

Ocean ferries operate from Maine to Nova Scotia and New Brunswick, and from Seattle and Port Angeles, Washington, to Victoria and Vancouver, British Columbia. For details, see the relevant chapters.

6 Package Tours & Escorted Tours

Tour packages divide into two main categories: tours that take care of all the details and tours that simply give you a package price on the big ticket items and leave you free to find your own way. Independent tours give you much more flexibility but require more effort on your part. Those who prefer not to drive and don't relish the notion of getting from train or bus stations to hotels on their own might prefer an escorted tour. But if you're the kind of traveler who doesn't like to be herded around in a group and wants to be able to linger at various sights at your leisure, a bus tour will drive you to distraction. The samples below will give you an idea of your choices.

INDEPENDENT PACKAGES

Air Canada offers an array of package deals specially tailored to trim the costs of your vacation. Collectively, these packages come under the title "Air Canada's Canada." This term covers a whole series of travel bargains ranging from city packages to fly/drive tours, escorted tours, motor-home travel, ski holidays, and Arctic adventures. For details, pick up the brochure from an Air Canada office, have it sent to you by calling ☎ **800/776-3000,** or visit their Web site at **www.aircanada.ca**.

Cyber Deals for Net Surfers

It's possible to get some great deals on airfare, hotels, and car rentals via the Internet. So grab your mouse and start surfing before you head to Canada—you could save a bundle on your trip. The Web sites I've highlighted below are worth checking out, especially since all services are free (but don't forget that time is money when you're on-line).

Air Canada (www.aircanada.ca) and **Canadian Airlines (www.cdnair.ca)**   On Wednesdays, the Web sites of these two airlines offer highly discounted flights to Canada for the following weekend. You need to reserve the flight on Wednesday or Thursday to fly on Friday (after 7pm only) or Saturday (all day) and return on Monday or Tuesday (all day). For Air Canada, you need to register with its Web Specials page; thereafter they'll e-mail you every Wednesday about available discounts. There's no need to register for the Canadian Airlines site, where every Wednesday morning they post their specials.

Microsoft Expedia (www.expedia.com)   The best part of this multipurpose travel site is the Fare Tracker: You fill out a form on the screen indicating that you're interested in cheap flights to Canada from your hometown, and, once a week, they e-mail you the best airfare deals. The site's Travel Agent will steer you to bargains on hotels and car rentals, and you can book everything, including flights, right on-line. This site is even useful once you're booked: Before you go, log on to Expedia for oodles of up-to-date travel info, including weather reports and foreign exchange rates.

Preview Travel (www.reservations.com and **www.vacations.com)**   Another useful site, Reservations.com has a Best Fare Finder that'll search the Apollo computer reservations system for the three lowest fares for any route on any days of the year. Say you want to go from New York to Montréal and back between December 6 and 13: Just fill out the form on the screen with times, dates, and destinations, and within minutes, Preview will show you the best deals. If you find an airfare you like, you can book your ticket on-line—you can even reserve hotels and car rentals on this site. If you're in the preplanning stage, head to Preview's Vacations.com site, where you can check out the latest package deals by clicking on Hot Deals.

Travelocity (www.travelocity.com)   This is one of the best travel sites out there. In addition to its Personal Fare Watcher, which notifies you via e-mail of the lowest airfares for up to five destinations, Travelocity will track in minutes the three

---

Canadian Airlines operates an array of package tours in conjunction with World of Vacations, including a number of fly/rail packages. Contact **World of Vacations, 3507 Frontage Rd., Suite 100, Tampa, FL 33607 (☎ 800/237-0190).**

FULLY ESCORTED TOURS

Collette Tours offers a wide variety of trips by bus, including several in the Rockies and several in the Atlantic Provinces. A 10-day tour of Newfoundland includes the seldom-visited northern peninsula and the Viking site at L'Anse aux Meadows, as well as a visit to Labrador. Shorter trips explore the Toronto/Niagara area and some combine Québec with New England or the Yukon with Alaska. An escorted train tour goes from Vancouver to Banff aboard the *Rocky Mountaineer.* Ask for its *USA and*

lowest fares for any routes on any dates. You can book a flight then and there, and if you need a rental car or hotel, they'll find you the best deal via the SABRE computer reservations system (a huge database used by travel agents worldwide). Click on Last Minute Deals for the latest travel bargains.

Trip.Com (www.thetrip.com) This site is really geared toward the business traveler, but vacationers-to-be can also use Trip.Com's valuable fare-finding engine, which will e-mail you every week with the best city-to-city airfare deals on your selected route or routes.

E-Savers Programs Several major airlines offer a free e-mail service known as **E-Savers,** via which they'll send you their best bargain airfares on a weekly basis. Once a week (usually Wednesday), subscribers receive a list of discounted flights to and from various destinations. Now here's the catch: These fares are available only if you leave the very next Saturday (or sometimes Friday night) and return on the following Monday or Tuesday. It's really a service for the spontaneously inclined and travelers looking for a quick getaway. But the fares are cheap, so it's worth taking a look. If you have a preference for certain airlines (in other words, the ones you fly most frequently), sign up with them first. *Another caveat:* You'll get frequent-flier miles if you purchase one of these fares, but you can't use miles to buy the ticket.

Here's a list of airlines and their Web sites, where you can not only get on the e-mailing lists but also book flights directly:

- **American Airlines:** www.americanair.com
- **America West:** www.americawest.com
- **Continental Airlines:** www.flycontinental.com
- **Delta:** www.delta-air.com
- **Northwest Airlines:** www.nwa.com
- **TWA:** www.twa.com
- **United:** www.ual.com
- **US Airways:** www.usairways.com

Epicurious Travel (travel.epicurious.com), another good travel site, allows you to sign up for all these airline e-mail lists at once.

—Jeanette Foster
Jeanette Foster is coauthor of *Frommer's Hawaii from $60 a Day* and *Frommer's Honolulu, Waikiki & Oahu.*

Canada brochure by contacting **Collette Tours,** 162 Middle St., Pawtucket, RI 02860 (☎ **800/248-8991**).

If your destination is the Canadian Rockies, contact **Brewster Transportation** at ☎ **800/661-1152** for tours in the west. Some packages include stays at guest ranches, hikes across glaciers, and white-water raft trips.

7 Getting Around

Canada is a land of immense distances, so transportation from point A to point B forms a prime item in your travel budget as well as your timetable. Here are some sample distances (in miles) between major cities: Montréal to Vancouver, 3,041;

Vancouver to Halifax, 3,897; Toronto to Victoria, 2,911; Winnipeg to St. John's, 3,159; Calgary to Montréal, 2,299; St. John's to Vancouver, 4,723; Ottawa to Victoria, 2,979.

BY PLANE

Canada has two major transcontinental airlines: **Air Canada** (☎ 800/776-3000) and **Canadian Airlines** (☎ 800/426-7000). Together with their regional partner companies, they handle most of the country's air transport. There are also numerous small local outfits, but these will concern you only when you get into their particular territories.

Within Canada, Air Canada operates daily service between 18 major cities, and its schedules dovetail with a string of allied connector carriers such as Air Nova, Air Ontario, and NWT Air to serve scores of smaller Canadian towns. Fares vary widely with day of the week and the availability of seats.

BY CAR

Canada has scores of rental-car companies, including **Hertz** (☎ 800/654-3131), **Avis** (☎ 800/331-1212), **Dollar** (☎ 800/800-4000), **Thrifty** (☎ 800/367-2277), and **Budget** (☎ 800/527-0700). Nevertheless, rental vehicles tend to get tight during the tourist season, from around mid-May through summer. It's a good idea to reserve a car as soon as you decide on your vacation.

The biggest and most thoroughly Canadian car-rental outfit is **Tilden Interrent,** with 400 locations coast to coast and affiliates in the United States and throughout the world. To book a Tilden car or get additional information while in the United States, contact **National Car Rental** (☎ 800/CAR-RENT). In Canada, contact the local stations listed in this book or **Tilden Interrent headquarters** at 250 Bloor St. E., Suite 1300, Toronto, ON, M4W 1E6 (☎ 800/387-4747).

Tilden rentals offer a Roadside Assistance Program. In case of an accident, a breakdown, a dead battery, a flat tire, a dry gas tank, getting stuck, or locking yourself out of your car, you can call ☎ 800/268-9711, available 24 hours, and get an immediate response for roadside help anywhere in Canada.

Members of the **American Automobile Association (AAA)** should remember to take their membership cards since the Canadian Automobile Association (CAA) extends privileges to them in Canada.

GASOLINE As in the United States, the trend in Canada is toward self-service stations, and in some areas you may have difficulty finding the full-service kind. Though Canada (specifically Alberta) is a major oil producer, gasoline isn't particularly cheap. Gas sells by the liter and pumps at around 55¢ to 60¢ per liter ($2.20 to $2.40 per gallon); prices vary slightly from region to region. Filling the tank of a medium-sized car will cost you roughly $19 (US$14).

DRIVING RULES Wearing seat belts is compulsory (and enforced) in all provinces, for all passengers. Throughout the country, pedestrians have the right-of-way and crosswalks are sacrosanct. The speed limit on the autoroutes (limited-access highways) is 100 kilometers per hour (62 m.p.h.). Right turns cannot be made at red lights unless a sign or green arrow makes an exception.

BY TRAIN

Most of Canada's passenger rail traffic is carried by the government-owned **VIA Rail** (☎ 800/561-3949). You can traverse the continent very comfortably in sleeping cars, parlor coaches, bedrooms, and roomettes. Virtually all of Canada's major cities (save Calgary) are connected by rail, though service is less frequent than it used to be. Some

The *Rocky Mountaineer*: One of the World's Great Train Trips

It's billed as "The Most Spectacular Train Trip in the World," and it may very well be. Operated by the privately owned Great Canadian Railtour Company, this sleek blue-and-white train winds past foaming waterfalls, ancient glaciers, towering snowcapped peaks, and roaring mountain streams. The *Rocky Mountaineer* gives you the option of traveling either east from Vancouver, traveling west from Jasper or Calgary, or taking a round-trip. The journey entails 2 days on the train and 1 night in a hotel and lets you see the Rocky Mountains as you never would behind the wheel of a car.

The train operates from late May into October, entirely in daylight hours. For information and bookings, contact the **Great Canadian Railtour Company,** Suite 104, 340 Brooksbank Ave., North Vancouver, BC, V7J 2C1 (☎ **800/665-7245**).

luxury trains, like *The Canadian,* boast dome cars with panoramic picture windows, hot showers, and elegant dining cars.

You can also purchase a Canrailpass that gives you 12 days of unlimited travel throughout the VIA national network; if you do this, travel within 30 days. A Canrailpass costs C$577 (US$433) in high season and C$395 (US$296) in low season. Seniors 60 and over and students receive a 10% discount on all fares. Fares for children up to 11 are half the adult rate.

FAST FACTS: Canada

American Express See the city chapters that follow for the locations of individual American Express offices. To report lost or stolen traveler's checks, call ☎ **800/221-7282.**

Electricity Canada uses the same electrical current as does the United States, 110 to 115 volts, 60 cycles.

Embassies & Consulates All embassies are in Ottawa, the national capital; the **U.S. embassy** is at 100 Wellington St., Ottawa, ON K1P 5T1 (☎ **613/238-4470**). For the other embassies in Ottawa, see "Fast Facts" in chapter 11.

You'll find **U.S. consulates** in the following locations: Nova Scotia—Cogswell Tower, Suite 910, Scotia Square, Halifax, NS, B3J 3K1 (☎ 902/429-2480); Québec—2 place Terrasse-Dufferin (P.O. Box 939), Québec City, PQ, G1R 4T9 (☎ 418/692-2095) and Complexe Desjardins, South Tower, Ground Floor, Montréal, PQ, H5B 1E5 (☎ 514/398-9695); Ontario—360 University Ave., Toronto, ON, M5G 1S4 (☎ 416/595-1700); Alberta—Room 1050, 615 Macleod Trail SE, Calgary, AB, T2G 4T8 (☎ 403/266-8962); British Columbia—1095 W. Pender St., Vancouver, BC, V6E 2Y4 (☎ 604/685-4311).

There's a **British consulate general** at 777 Bay St., Toronto (☎ 416/593-1267), and an **Australian consulate general** at 175 Bloor St. E., Toronto (☎ 416/323-1155).

Emergencies In life-threatening situations, call ☎ **911.**

Liquor Laws Beer and wine are sold in supermarkets and most grocery stores; spirits are sold only in government liquor stores. The minimum drinking age is 19.

Mail At press time, it costs 42¢ to send a first-class letter or postcard within Canada, and 48¢ to send a first-class letter or postcard from Canada to the United States.

First-class airmail service to other countries is 84¢ for the first 10 grams (about half an ounce). Rates are expected to go up.

Taxes   In January 1991 the Canadian government imposed the goods and service tax (GST), a 7% federal tax on virtually all goods and services. Some hotels and shops include the GST in their prices, others add it on separately. When included, the tax accounts for the odd hotel rates, such as $66.04 per day, that you might find on your final bill. The GST is also the reason you pay 50¢ for a newspaper at a vending machine, but 54¢ over a shop counter: The machines haven't been geared for the new price.

Thanks to a government provision designed to encourage tourism, you can **reclaim the GST** portion of your hotel bills and the price of goods you've purchased in Canada—in due course. The minimum GST rebate is $7 (the tax on $100) and the claim must be filed within a year of purchase. You must submit all your original receipts (which will be returned) with an application form. Receipts from several trips during the same year may be submitted together. Claims of less than $500 can be made at certain designated duty-free shops at international airports and border crossings. Or you can mail the forms to **Revenue Canada,** Customs and Excise, Visitors' Rebate Program, Ottawa, ON, K1A 1J5. You can get the forms in some of the larger hotels, in some duty-free shops, or by phoning ☎ **613/ 991-3346** outside Canada or 800/66-VISIT in Canada.

The rebate doesn't apply to car rentals or restaurant meals. And the GST isn't levied on airline tickets to Canada purchased in the United States.

Time   Six time zones are observed in Canada. In winter, when it's 7:30pm Newfoundland standard time, it's 6pm Atlantic standard time (Labrador, Prince Edward Island, New Brunswick, and Nova Scotia); 5pm eastern standard time (Québec and most of Ontario); 4pm central standard time (western Ontario, Manitoba, and most of Saskatchewan); 3pm mountain standard time (northwestern Saskatchewan, Alberta, eastern British Columbia, and the Northwest Territories); and 2pm Pacific standard time (the Yukon and most of British Columbia).

Each year, on the first Sunday in April, daylight saving time comes into effect in most of Canada and clocks are advanced by 1 hour. On the last Sunday in October, Canada reverts to standard time. During these summer months, all of Saskatchewan observes the same time zone as Alberta.

Nova Scotia 4

by Wayne Curtis

Nova Scotia is one of those rare destinations that's more than the sum of its parts. It's home to an extravagant variety of landscapes and attractions, and the province seems to change kaleidoscopically as you travel along: historic villages, bucolic farmlands, dramatic coasts, melancholy bogs, and dynamic downtowns. (About the only terrain it doesn't offer is towering mountain peaks.) Nova Scotia is compact enough that you needn't spend all your time in a car, yet with fewer than a million residents, it's unpopulated enough to provide empty places when you're seeking solitude.

Culturally, Nova Scotia is also diverse, although the contrast isn't quite as distinct as in New Brunswick or Québec. The name of the province translates as "New Scotland" in Latin, and you'll detect the strong influence of Scottish culture—from the brogue heard in remote parts of Cape Breton to the Highland games staged in various locales. But you'll also find Acadian culture near Yarmouth, and in Halifax, you'll encounter a diversity enriched by recent immigration from Asia, Africa, and elsewhere.

In the end, what impresses me most about Nova Scotia is this: I'll finish up a ramble on a back road somewhere and finally pull up to the main highway. And what I'll see is this: nothing. No cars in either direction. If this were New England, I'd be tapping my fingers to the turn signal while awaiting an opening between RVs and impatient cars. Not here. There's still a sense of remoteness, of being surrounded by big space and a profound history. More than once I had the fleeting sense that I was visiting New England, but 60 or 70 years ago, well before anyone referred to tourism as an industry.

1 Exploring Nova Scotia

Visitors to Nova Scotia would do well to spend some time poring over a map and this travel guide before leaving home. The hardest chore will be to narrow down your options before you set off. There are numerous loops and circuits available, made more complicated by ferry links to the United States, New Brunswick, Prince Edward Island, and Newfoundland. Figuring out where to go and how to get there is the hardest part.

VISITOR INFORMATION

Every traveler to Nova Scotia should have a copy of the massive (350-plus–page) official tourism guide, which is the province's best effort to put travel-guide writers like me out of business. This comprehensive, colorful, and free guide lists all hotels, campgrounds, and attractions within the province, with brief descriptions and current prices. (Unfortunately, restaurants are given only limited coverage.)

The guide, entitled *Nova Scotia: The Doer's and Dreamer's Complete Guide,* is available starting each March by phone (☎ 800/565-0000 in North America or ☎ 902/425-5781 outside North America), mail (P.O. Box 130, Halifax, NS, B3J 2M7), fax (902/453-8401), and e-mail (nsvisit@fox.nstn.ns.ca). If you'd rather wait until you arrive in the province before obtaining a copy, ask for one at the numerous visitor information centers, where you can also request the excellent free map.

The province operates about a dozen official **Visitor Information Centres** throughout Nova Scotia, as well as in Portland, Maine, and Wood Islands, Prince Edward Island. These are mostly seasonal, and are amply stocked with brochures and tended by knowledgeable staffers. In addition, virtually every local tourist information center has racks of brochures covering the entire province. You won't ever come up short for information.

One note about the official tourism names for parts of the province: In the guide and on the maps, you'll see frequent references to various "trails," for example, the Evangeline Trail, the Cabot Trail, the Sunrise Trail. These aren't actually routes, but names for regions. My hunch is that the number-one question at visitor centers is, "Excuse me, but where does this trail go?" Answer: It doesn't.

For general questions about travel in the province, call **Nova Scotia's information hot line** at ☎ 800/565-0000 (North America) or 902/425-5781 (outside North America).

GETTING THERE

BY CAR & FERRY　Most travelers reach Nova Scotia overland by car from New Brunswick. Plan on about 4 hours of driving from the U.S. border at Calais, Maine, to Amherst (at the New Brunswick–Nova Scotia border). Incorporating ferries into your itinerary can significantly reduce driving time. Daily ferries connect both Portland and Bar Harbor, Maine, to Yarmouth, Nova Scotia, at the peninsula's southwest end.

The seasonal **Portland-Yarmouth ferry** takes approximately 11 hours and costs around C$112 (US$80) for each adult passenger, C$56 (US$40) for children, and C$112 (US$80) for each vehicle. Cabins are available for an additional fare, ranging from about C$30 (US$22) (day cabin) to C$231 (US$165) for an overnight suite. Reservations are essential. Call **Prince of Fundy Cruises** at ☎ 800/341-7540 or 207/775-5616.

Bay Ferries (☎ 888/249-7245) operates the seasonal **Bar Harbor–Yarmouth ferry,** which takes 6 hours and costs approximately C$112 (US$80) for car *and* driver. Cabins range from C$50 to C$78 (US$36 to US$56). Reservations are vital during the peak summer season.

To shorten the slog around the Bay of Fundy, a 3-hour ferry links **Saint John, New Brunswick,** and **Digby, Nova Scotia.** The ferry sails year-round, with as many as three crossings daily each way in summer. Summer rates are C$23 (US$16) for adults, C$11.50 (US$8) for children, and C$50 (US$36) per vehicle. Like the Bar Harbor ferry, this crossing is run by **Bay Ferries** (☎ 888/249-7245).

For those traveling further afield, ferries also connect Prince Edward Island to Caribou, Nova Scotia, and Newfoundland to North Sydney, Nova Scotia. See the

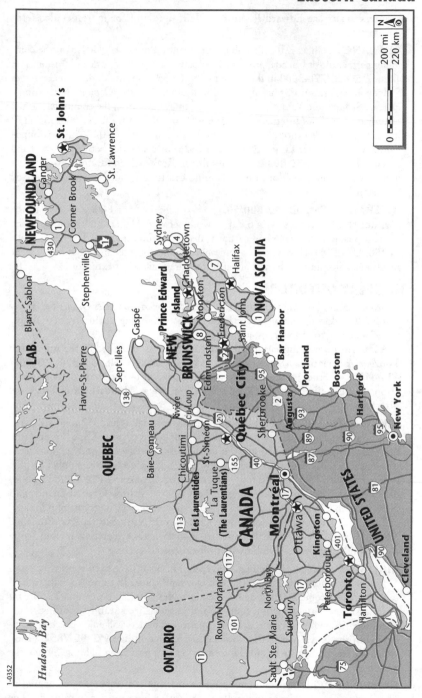

chapters on Prince Edward Island and Newfoundland for more detailed ferry information.

BY PLANE   Halifax is the air hub of the Atlantic Provinces. **Air Nova,** the commuter partner of Air Canada, provides direct service from New York and Boston. The airline (☎ **800/776-3000** in the U.S. or 800/565-3940 in the Maritimes) also serves Sydney and Yarmouth, plus about a dozen other Atlantic Canada destinations. Halifax, Sydney, and Yarmouth are also served by **Air Atlantic,** the commuter partner of Canadian Airlines International (☎ **800/426-7000** in the U.S., 800/665-1177 in the Maritime Provinces, 902/427-5500 locally, or 709/576-0274 in Newfoundland). **Northwest Air Link** (☎ **800/225-2525**) offers service between Boston and Halifax; **Icelandair** (☎ **800/223-5500**) flies to Reykjavik and Europe. Routes that involve connections at Montréal or Toronto can turn a short hop into an all-day excursion.

BY TRAIN   Via Rail (☎ **800/561-3949** in the U.S. or 800/561-3952 in the Maritimes) offers train service 6 days a week between Halifax and Montréal. The entire trip takes between 18 and 21 hours, depending on direction. The fare is about C$180 (US$129) each way, with significant discounts for those buying at least 1 week in advance. Sleeping berths and private cabins are available at extra cost.

THE GREAT OUTDOORS

Nova Scotia's official travel guide (*Doers and Dreamers Complete Guide*) has a very helpful "Outdoors" section in the back that lists camping outfitters, bike shops, whale-watching tour operators, and the like.

A free brochure listing various adventure outfitters is published by the **Adventure Tourism Association,** 1800 Argyle St., Suite 402, Halifax, NS, B3J 3N8 (☎ **902/ 423-4480**). Internet users looking for more detailed information on outdoor recreation may benefit from this handy Web site: **www.whatasite.com/outdoor. directory**.

BIKING   The low hills of Nova Scotia (the highest peak is just 532m, or 1,745 ft.) and the gentle, largely empty roads make for wonderful cycling. Cape Breton is the most challenging of destinations; the south coast and Bay of Fundy regions yield wonderful ocean views while making few demands on cyclists. A number of bike outfitters can aid your trip planning. **Freewheeling Adventures** (☎ **902/857-3600**) offers guided bike tours throughout Nova Scotia, Prince Edward Island, and Newfoundland. Walton Watt's guide, *Nova Scotia by Bicycle,* is very helpful for anyone planning a serious bike expedition; write **Bicycle Nova Scotia,** P.O. Box 3010 South, Halifax, NS, B3J 3G6. For an Internet introduction to cycling in Nova Scotia and beyond, point your Web browser to **fox.nstn.ca/~cycling**.

BIRD WATCHING   More than 400 species of birds have been spotted in Nova Scotia, ranging from odd and exotic birds blown off course in storms to majestic bald eagles, of which some 250 nesting pairs reside in Nova Scotia, mostly on Cape Breton Island. Many whale-watching tours also offer specialized seabird-spotting tours, including trips to puffin colonies. More experienced birders will enjoy checking regularly with the **Nova Scotia Bird Society's** information line (☎ **902/852-2428**), which features up-to-date recorded information about intriguing sightings around the province.

CAMPING   With backcountry options rather limited (especially compared to New Brunswick and Newfoundland), Nova Scotia's forte is drive-in camping. The 20 provincial parks with campgrounds are uniformly clean, friendly, well managed,

Nova Scotia, Cape Breton Island & Prince Edward Island

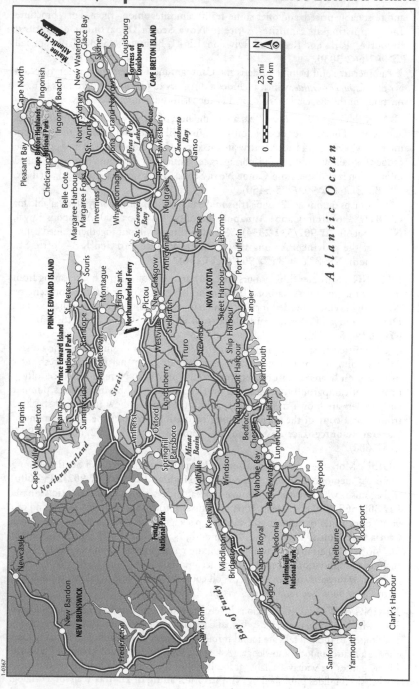

and reasonably priced, and offer some 1,500 campsites among them. For a brochure and map listing all campsites, write to **Nova Scotia Department of Natural Resources,** Parks and Recreation Division, RR #1, Belmont, NS, B0M 1C0, or call ☎ **902/662-3030.**

Another free and helpful guide is the Campground Owners Association of Nova Scotia's *Camper's Guide,* which includes a directory of private campgrounds that are members of the association. Ask for it at the visitor information centers.

CANOEING   Nova Scotia offers an abundance of great canoeing on inland lakes and ponds. The premier destination is **Kejimkujik National Park** in the southern interior, which has 44 backcountry sites accessible by canoe. A number of other fine canoe trails allow paddlers and portagers to venture off for hours or days. General information is available from **Canoe Nova Scotia,** 5516 Spring Garden Rd., Halifax, NS, B3J 3G6 (☎ **902/425-5450).**

Tour maps outlining 22 canoe trips in detail in Annapolis County are available for C$16 (US$36) from **Canoe Annapolis County,** P.O. Box 100, Annapolis Royal, NS, B0S 1A0 (☎ **902/532-2334).** Several outfitters will put together guided canoe tours of the province. Among them: **Scotia Paddle and Scull,** 34 Joffre St., Dartmouth, NS, B2Y 3C8 (☎ **902/463-0136).**

FISHING   Saltwater fishing tours are easily arranged on charter boats leaving from many of the province's harbors. Inquire locally at the visitor information centers. No fishing license is needed for tours on charters. For saltwater regulations, contact **Department of Fisheries and Oceans,** P.O. Box 550, Halifax, NS, B3J 2S7 (☎ **902/426-5952).**

Committed freshwater anglers come to Nova Scotia in pursuit of the elusive Atlantic salmon, which requires a license separate from that for other freshwater fish. **Salmon licenses** must be obtained from a provincial Natural Resources office, provincial campground, or licensed outfitter. Other freshwater species popular with anglers are brown trout, shad, smallmouth bass, rainbow trout, and speckled trout. For a copy of the current fishing regulations, contact the **Department of Natural Resources License Section,** P.O. Box 68, Truro, NS, B2N 5B8 (☎ **902/424-6608).**

GOLF   More than 50 golf courses are located throughout Nova Scotia. Among the most memorable are the **Cape Breton Highland Links** (☎ **902/285-2600)** in Ingonish, which features a dramatic ocean-side setting. **Golf Atlantic Canada** (☎ **800/565-0001)** represents 106 golf courses throughout Atlantic Canada and can arrange tee times or custom golf-vacation packages with a single phone call. **Nova Scotia Golf Tours,** 17 Tulip St., Dartmouth, NS, B3A 2S5 (☎ **800/565-3885** or 902/465-7414) arranges 4- and 9-day golfing packages that begin in Halifax. Tours include transportation, greens fees, and accommodations.

A handy directory of Nova Scotia's golf courses (with phone numbers) is published in the "Outdoor" section of the *Doers and Dreamers Guide.*

HIKING & WALKING   Serious hikers head for Cape Breton Highlands National Park, which is home to the most dramatic terrain in the province. But you're certainly not limited to these. Trails are found throughout Nova Scotia, although in many cases they're a matter of local knowledge. (Ask at the visitor information centers.) Published hiking guides are widely available at local bookstores. Especially helpful are the back-pocket-sized guides published by **Nimbus Publishing of Halifax** (call for a catalog: ☎ **800/646-2879** or 902/455-4286).

SAILING   Any area with so much convoluted coastline is clearly inviting to sailors and gunkholers. Tours and charters are available almost everywhere there's a decent-sized harbor. Those with the inclination and skills to venture out on their own can rent 16-foot Wayfarers by the hour and maneuver among the islands at **Sail Mahone Bay** (☎ **902/624-8864**) on the south shore near Lunenburg. The province's premier sailing experience is an excursion aboard the *Bluenose II,* which is virtually an icon for Atlantic Canada. See "Lunenburg," below.

SEA KAYAKING   Nova Scotia is increasingly attracting the attention of kayakers worldwide. Kayakers traveling on their own should be especially cautious on the Bay of Fundy side, since the massive tides create strong currents that overmatch even the fittest of kayakers. Nearly 40 kayak outfitters do business in Nova Scotia, and offer everything from 1-hour casual paddles to intensive weeklong trips; consult the directory in the *Doers and Dreamers Guide.*

Among the most respected outfitters is **Coastal Adventures,** P.O. Box 77, Tangier, NS, B0J 3H0 (☎ **902/772-2774**). The group is led by kayak guru Scott Cunningham, and features trips throughout the Maritimes and Newfoundland. For kayaking on Cape Breton, check with **Island Seafari,** 20 Paddys Lane, Louisbourg, NS, B0A 1M0 (☎ **902/733-2309**).

WHALE WATCHING   If you're on the coast, you're not far from a whale-watching operation. Around 2 dozen whale-watching outfits offer trips in search of finback, humpback, pilot, and minke whales, among others. Digby Neck offers the highest concentration of whale-watching excursions, but you'll find them in many other coves and harbors. Just ask the staff at visitor information centers to direct you to the whales.

2 Minas Basin & Cobequid Bay

If you're not fully content unless you're off the beaten track, a detour along the Minas Basin and Cobequid Bay will be one of the highlights of your trip. With the exception of Truro, this region is rural and quiet, and full of hidden surprises. You can turn down a dirt road, shut off your car's engine, and hear not much other than the wind and maybe a blackbird or two. You can trek along spectacular hiking trails, or picnic alone on a long stretch of remote and misty coast.

There's also a rich history here, but it tends to be hidden and subtle rather than preening and obvious. And don't look for the quaint seaside villages or the hard-edged, rocky coast for which Nova Scotia is famous; that will have to wait until Yarmouth and the South Shore. The natural drama here is pegged to the region's profound remoteness and the powerful but silent tides, among the highest in the world.

PARRSBORO

Samuel de Champlain stumbled upon amethyst while exploring Partridge Island in 1607. He and his crew brought the gemstones back to France, where they were cut, polished, and are now part of the French crown jewels.

A few miles away and a few centuries later, another discovery was made near Parrsboro. In 1986 two scientists uncovered the one of the world's largest caches of dinosaur fossils—some 100,000 pieces of fossilized dinosaur bones dating back 200 million years, the cusp between the Jurassic and the Triassic periods. The trove included skulls, teeth, and bones that belonged to dinosaurs, lizards, sharks, and crocodiles. These finds have gone a long way in expanding our understanding of prehistoric animals.

Parrsboro's richness in gems and fossils stems from a confluence of two events: It's at the seam where two continents collided back in the days of primeval ooze (evidence: the fossils found here are the same as you'll find in parts of Africa); and the region's shores are exposed to the world's highest tides, which means that constant erosion reveals new geological treasures.

ESSENTIALS

GETTING THERE Parrsboro is reached via Route 2 from either Springhill (46km/27 miles) or Truro (90km/54 miles).

VISITOR INFORMATION The **Parrsboro Tourist Info Centre** (☎ 902/254-3266) faces the bandstand and small park in the village center. It's open daily in summer from 8:30am to 8:30pm.

ROCKHOUNDING

It's somewhat ironic that in an area that boasts outstanding seacoast landscapes, so many people spend their time with eyes glued to the ground. But this is a rockhound and fossil-scavenger's paradise, and you're missing out on the area's unique character if you admire only the landscape.

If you're an experienced rock hound, you know the drill. If you're a novice, you'll want guidance. Start with a trip to the **Fundy Geological Museum** (see below) to get up to speed on the region's unique geology. Then sign up for a guided mineral- or fossil-collecting tour with either the museum or Eldon George.

Another option is to explore with **Dinatours** (☎ 902/254-3700), an outfit that maintains a headquarters and gift shop in a converted lobster boat at the causeway near the museum. Sonja Prell and Randy Corcoran offer various guided collecting tours both on foot and by boat around the Minas Basin. Costs range from C$40 (US$28) per adult, C$20 (US$14) for children under 16, for a 6-hour boat trip to the mineral-rich Five Islands, to C$20 (US$14) for a 2¹/₂-hour interpretive walking tour. (Some minimums apply on boat tours.)

The modern **Fundy Geological Museum,** 6 Two Island Rd. (☎ 902/254-3814; Web site: www.nova-scotia.com/fundgeomuseum), does a fine job putting the region's complex geology into context. Operated by the Cumberland Geological Society, the museum starts off with displays and a video presentation to help you brush up on various epochs and eras (does Jurassic comes before or after Triassic?). Then you can view various minerals and fossils on display, and learn what to look for when you head out on your own. Kids seem especially fascinated by the dioramas featuring dinosaurs. There's more than enough to engage curious adults, but it's displayed in a fashion that makes it accessible to most children. Field trips are regularly scheduled to mineral- and fossil-rich areas; ask at the front desk for a schedule. Admission is C$3.50 (US$2.50) for adults, C$1.75 (US$1.25) for children 6 to 17, C$2.75 (US$2) for seniors, and C$8.50 (US$6) for families. In summer, it's open daily from 9:30am to 5:30pm (closed Mondays in winter).

Eldon George is a celebrity in rock-collecting circles for his extraordinary finds—including the world's smallest dinosaur footprints (they're about the size of a penny, from dinosaurs as big as sparrows). His **Parrsboro Rock and Mineral Shop & Museum,** 39 Whitehall Rd. (☎ 902/254-2981), sells prospecting gear along with raw and polished stones. You can see the famed footprints, huge amethyst geodes, and other wondrous geological displays at the small museum. George himself is often here and is congenial and accessible. He and his son also lead guided tours (1 to 3 hours) to collecting areas, with rates starting at C$10 (US$7) per person for a minimum of three or four people. Donations are requested for the museum. The shop and museum are open Monday to Saturday from 9am to dusk and Sunday by chance (closed Christmas to April). From town, bear right at the war memorial and follow the road toward Ottawa House. Look for the shop on your left, with the brown dinosaur in front.

HIKING

Just 3 kilometers (1.8 miles) southwest of town is **Partridge Island,** connected to the mainland by a pebbly causeway. You can park along the beach, then hike out to the high, tree-studded island, which offers trails for exploring. You'll get great views of Minas Basin and the stupendous tides. Keep your eyes peeled for amethyst and other rare stones.

   Cape Chignecto Provincial Park (about 45km/28 miles west of Parrsboro on Route 209) was being developed as a hiking destination when I last visited and promises to be spectacular. The provincial park is by far the largest (10,600 acres) and is wild and remote, with coastal cliffs as high as 600 feet above tide-raked Advocate Bay and the Bay of Fundy. A hiking trail around the shoreline is currently under construction. When completed, the circuit will be about 30 kilometers (18 miles), with some six backcountry campsites available for overnighting. Day hikes to secluded beaches are also an option; an interior trail is being developed for mountain biking. For more information, contact the **Department of Natural Resources,** 4917 Main St. (P.O. Box 130), Oxford, NS, B0M 1P0 (☎ **902/447-2155**).

ACCOMMODATIONS

If you're equipped for camping, one of the province's true gems is **Glooscap Park and Campground** (☎ 902/254-2529), on the coast about 6 kilometers (3.6 miles) from the village. (Look for directional signs in town.) There are 56 sites spread about a tall bluff of grass and forest. A steel staircase leads to the beach, where you can walk for miles along crumbling cliffs and watch the huge tides slosh in and out. (This is a popular area to scout for fossils.) This is managed by the town and is a well-run, old-fashioned campground, of the sort that's harder to find these days—you actually park and camp on grassy lawns, not on gravel pads. It's C$8 (US$6) for a tent site; C$14 (US$10) for a trailer site with hookups.

Gillespie House Inn. 358 Main St., Parrsboro, NS, B0M 1S0. ☎ **902/254-3196.** 5 rms (all share 2 baths). C$45 (US$32) double. Rates include continental breakfast. V. Closed Nov–Apr.

This handsome 1890s Victorian farmhouse sits on a shady rise—an easy walk from the village center—and was originally home to prominent shipbuilders and merchants. Innkeepers Lori Lynch and David Beattie offer a pleasant, homey atmosphere with five guest rooms, which share two baths (one has a handsome claw-foot tub). The guest rooms have lustrous maple floors, but are a bit Spartan. Room 3 is the largest and brightest of the bunch; Room 5 has wonderful maple wainscoting. Public spaces are limited, although there's a small TV room and a first-floor sauna and hot tub. No smoking.

The Maple Inn. 17 Western Ave. (P.O. Box 457), Parrsboro, NS, B0M 1S0. ☎ **902/254-3735.** 9 rms (6 with bath; 3 share 2 baths). C$53–C$90 double (US$38–US$64). Rates include full breakfast. AE, MC, V.

The Maple Inn, in a peaceful village setting, is actually two century-old homes joined together. The pair of sturdy, yellow-and-brown buildings served as the town's hospital for 30 years, but has been made over in a glossy, country-Victorian style with dried flowers and period furniture. It's likely to be considered a bit overly renovated by those who prize historic authenticity, but it's comfortable and cheerful, and many of the rooms are quite spacious. The third-floor suite is perfect for families, with its king canopied bed and spare room with two twin beds (the suite also has the inn's only in-room TV). The three shared-bath guest rooms offer especially good value; of these, cozy Room 4 has a sitting area in the bay window. No smoking.

TRURO

Truro is the region's commercial hub, with a tidy downtown surrounded by a sprawling mass of strip malls and shopping plazas. The town (pop. 12,000) has served as a traveler's crossroads since 1858, when the rail line between Montréal and Halifax first passed through. (Passenger rail service is still available.) With a convenient location just off the Trans-Canada Highway and a profusion of motels and chain restaurants, Truro still serves the traveler well. It is, however, best regarded as an intermediate stop rather than a destination.

ESSENTIALS

GETTING THERE   Truro is located on Route 102, just south of the junction with Route 104 (the Trans-Canada Highway). Truro is also served by **Via Rail** (☎ **800/ 561-3949** in the U.S. or 800/561-3952 in the Maritimes), which connects Moncton to Halifax. The train station is at 104 Esplanade St., next to the downtown Esplanade Mall.

VISITOR INFORMATION   The **Truro Information Centre and Tourist Bureau** (☎ **902/893-2922**) is located in a glass-walled pavilion downtown at Victoria Square (corner of Prince and Willow streets). It's open daily from mid-May to early November from 8am to 8pm; closed the rest of the year.

EXPLORING TRURO

Aficionados of public spaces—especially of parks that trace their ancestry back to the turn of the century—will enjoy **Victoria Park,** a 1,000-acre retreat flanking a shady gorge not far from the town center. It's well used by Truro residents, and a bit worn and shabby around the edges. But park your car and stroll past the playing fields and playground, following the brook into the dusky glen. Elaborate arrangements of staircases, boardwalks, and bridges work their way up into the narrowing gorge, which is lined with Norway spruce and hemlock. Local kids are at play here, some swimming in the waterfalls, others intent on triggering rock slides on hapless hikers. Younger children often find the upper reaches of the gorge especially magical.

The park is open daily from dawn to dusk; admission is free. It's located at Brunswick Street and Park Road. It's a bit tricky to track down; your best bet is to ask for a map and directions at the visitor center.

EXPERIENCING THE TIDAL BORE

Let it be said: The tidal bore is one of the more overrated attractions in Nova Scotia. The bore is a low wave around a meter in height that rolls upstream ahead of the incoming tide, marking the moment the flow of rivers and brooks change direction. The bore tends to be especially pronounced around Cobequid Bay, where the tides are greatly amplified (up to 50 ft.) thanks to its funnel-like shape. I'm told the tidal bore can be truly impressive at times, but this has not been my experience. The bore is an interesting geographic quirk, nothing more, and offers little to inspire awe or wonder. If you happen to be in the area when the bore is due, by all means swing by and have a look. I just wouldn't rearrange travel plans to view it.

In Truro, visitors are directed to **Tidal Bore Park** along the Salmon River, located on a grassy slope next to a motel and restaurant (take Exit 14 off Route 102). *Be forewarned:* the site is not all that charming. A busy highway runs along one side of the viewing area, and power lines clutter the horizon. But you get a good view of the bore steadfastly chugging up the muddy river. Ask at the visitor center for tide times, check the local paper, or call **Dial-a-Tide** (☎ **902/426-5494**).

A better way to experience the bore is to incorporate some outdoor adventure that would be fun even without the bore. Several outfitters based south of Truro offer motorized Zodiac (raft) trips that follow the bore's progress upstream. **Tidal Bore Rafting** (☎ **902/752-0899**) offers half-day adventures on the Shubenacadie River that includes a riverside lunch. **Shubenacadie Tidal Bore Park Rafting** (☎ **800/565-7238**) has 2- and 4-hour trips; as many as 75 adventurers at a time follow the bore in a herd of noisy Zodiacs. Other options include trips with **Shubenacadie River Adventure Tours** in South Maitland (☎ **902/471-6595**) and **Shubenacadie River Runners Ltd.** in Maitland (☎ **800/856-5061** or 902/261-2770). Plan on paying C$40 to C$65 (US$28 to US$46) per person, depending on the length of the tour. Times, of course, vary according to the tide. Call for information.

A SCENIC DRIVE

If you're headed from Truro southwestward along the Fundy coast toward Digby, Route 215 offers a wonderful coastal detour from Maitland to Windsor. This winding, fast, and rather narrow road (not suggested for bicycling) passes through a number of quiet hamlets, some with handsome early buildings. But the chief appeal comes in the sudden vistas of lush green farmland (often accompanied by the fulsome smells of cows) and broad views of expansive Minas Basin beyond. At the town of Walton, there's a handsome lighthouse on rocky bluff with a nearby picnic area just off the main route (it's well marked). This detour runs 93 kilometers (56 miles) from South Maitland to Brooklyn. Few services for tourists are offered along the route, other than a handful of restaurants, B&Bs, and campgrounds. Look for general stores and farm stands if you need a snack.

ACCOMMODATIONS & DINING

Truro is located where the main highway from the west diverges to Cape Breton (north arm) and Halifax (south arm). As such, the town is home to about a dozen motels and B&Bs. Among the chains are the **Comfort Inn,** 12 Meadow Dr. (☎ **800/228-5150** or 902/893-0330), and **Best Western Glengarry,** 150 Willow St. (☎ **800/567-4276** or 902/893-4311).

The Palliser Motel & Restaurant. Tidal Bore Rd. (Rte. 102/Exit 14), Truro, NS, B2N 5G6. ☎ **902/893-8951.** Fax 902/895-8475. E-mail: palliser@auracom.com. 42 rms. TV. C$47 (US$33) double. Rates include buffet breakfast (discounts in off-season). AE, DC, ER, MC, V.

This vintage 1950s-era motel is arrayed in a horseshoe pattern around a well-tended lawn that slopes down toward the Palliser Restaurant and the viewing area for the tidal bore. Rooms are simple and basic, as are the meals at the restaurant (fried scallops, fried haddock, lobster rolls). The Palliser has the most character of any Truro motel, but it's unlikely anyone will find it necessary to spend more than a night here. The bore is floodlit at night for after-dark viewing.

WOLFVILLE

The trim and tidy Victorian village of Wolfville (pop. 3,500) has a distinctly New England feel to it, both in its handsome architecture and its layout: a small commercial downtown just 6 blocks long is surrounded by shady neighborhoods of elegant homes. And it's not hard to trace that sensibility to its source. The area was largely populated in the wake of the American Revolution by transplanted New Englanders, who forced off the Acadian settlers who had earlier done so much to tame the wilds.

The town's mainstay these days is handsome **Acadia University,** which has nearly as many full-time students as there are residents of Wolfville. The university's presence gives the small village an edgier, more youthful air. Don't miss the university's **Art Gallery at the Beveridge Arts Centre** (☎ 902/585-1373), which showcases both contemporary and historic Nova Scotian art.

EXPLORING WOLFVILLE

Strolling the village is the activity of choice. The towering elms and maples that shade the extravagant Victorian architecture provide the dappled light and rustling sounds for an ideal stroll. A good place to start is the **Wolfville Tourist Bureau** at Willow Park (☎ 902/542-7000 or 902/542-7117), on the north edge of downtown.

One of the more intriguing sights in town occurs each summer day at dusk, in an unprepossessing park surrounded by a parking lot a block off Main Street. At **Robie Swift Park,** a lone chimney (dating from a long-gone dairy plant) rises straight up like a stumpy finger pointed at the heavens. Around sunset, between 25 and 100 chimney swifts flit about and then descend into the chimney for the night. Alas, the swifts have been declining in number in recent years, ever since predatory merlins starting nesting nearby and found in the swifts an easy target.

Long before New Englanders showed up here, hardworking Acadians had vastly altered the local landscape. They did this in large part by constructing a series of dikes outfitted with ingenious log valves, which allowed farmers to convert the saltwater marshes to productive farmland. At the **Grand-Pré National Historic Site,** Route 1, Grand-Pré (☎ 902/542-3631), a short drive east of Wolfville, you can learn about these dikes along with the tragic history of the Acadians, who populated the Minas Basin between 1680 and their expulsion in 1755.

More a memorial park than a living-history exhibit, Grand-Pré ("great meadow") has superbly tended grounds that are excellent for idling, a picnic lunch, or simple contemplation. Among the handful of buildings, you'll find a graceful **stone church,** built in 1922 on the presumed site of the original church. Evangeline Bellefontaine, the revered (albeit fictional) heroine of Longfellow's epic poem, was born here; look for the statue of the tragic heroine in the garden. It was created in 1920 by Canadian sculptor Philippe Hérbert and the image has been reproduced widely since. Admission is C$2.50 (US$1.80) for adults, C$2 (US$1.40) for seniors, C$1.10 (US80¢) for children 6 to 16, and C$7 (US$5) for families. It's open May 15 to October 15, daily from 9am to 6pm.

ACCOMMODATIONS

Gingerbread House Inn. 8 Robie Tufts Dr. (P.O. Box 819), Wolfville, NS, B0P 1X0. ☎ 888/542-1458 or 902/542-1458. Fax 902/542-4718. E-mail: gingerbread@valleyweb.com. 6 rms, including 3 suites (4 with shower only). TV. C$65–C$139 (US$46–US$99) double. C$10 (US$7) discount in off-season. Rates include full breakfast. MC, V.

The ornate Gingerbread House Inn was originally the carriage house for the building now housing Victoria's Historic Inn (see below). A former owner went woodshop–wild, adding all manner of swirly accoutrements and giving the place a convincingly authentic air. The guest rooms are a modern interpretation of the gingerbread style, and are generally quite comfortable, although the two rooms in the back are dark and small. The floral Carriage House Suite is the most spacious, and features luxe touches like a propane fireplace and two-person Jacuzzi. The budget choice is the lovely Terrace Room, which is rather minuscule but has a lovely private deck on the second floor under a gracefully arching tree. Breakfasts tend toward the elaborate, and are served by candlelight. No smoking.

✪ **Tattingstone Inn.** 434 Main St. (P.O. Box 98), Wolfville, NS, B0P 1X0. ☎ **800/565-7696** or 902/542-7696. Fax 902/542-4427. 10 rms. A/C TV TEL. C$85–C$128 (US$60–US$91) double; C$158 (US$112) suite. AE, MC, V.

"We sell romance and relaxation," says innkeeper Betsy Harwood. And that pretty well sums it up. This handsome Italianate-Georgian mansion dates back to 1874 and overlooks the village's main artery. The inn is furnished with a mix of reproductions and antiques, and traditional and modern art blend equally well. The attitude isn't over-the-top Victorian as one might guess by looking at the manse, but decorated with a more deft touch by mixing informal country antiques and regal Empire pieces. The rooms in the Carriage House tend to be a bit smaller, but are still pleasant and showcase fine examples of modern Canadian art. Young children disrupt the romantic atmosphere, so only kids older than 12 are welcome. No smoking.

Dining: The spacious semiformal dining room is rather refined, and diners sup amid white tablecloths and stern Doric columns. Dinner is served nightly in summer from 5:30 to 9:30pm. Ask for a seat on the enclosed porch, which captures the lambent early evening light to good effect. House specialties include the rack of lamb and the chicken served with pear-and-ginger sauce; the latter uses pears grown on the property. Entrees range in price from C$16 to C$26 (US$11 to US$19).

Facilities: Heated outdoor pool, steam room, tennis court.

Victoria's Historic Inn. 416 Main St., Wolfville, NS, B0P 1X0. ☎ **800/556-5744** or 902/542-5744. Fax 902/542-7794. 15 rms. A/C TV TEL. C$79–C$145 (US$56–US$103) double. Breakfast C$3.75 (US$2.70) additional for guests. AE, ER, MC, V.

Victoria's Historic Inn was constructed by apple mogul William Chase in 1893, and is architecturally elaborate. This sturdy Queen Anne–style building features bold pediments and massed pavilions, which have been adorned with balusters and ornate Stick-style trim. Inside, the effect is a bit as if you'd wandered into one of those stereoscopic views of a Victorian parlor. Where the nearby Tattingstone Inn resists theme decor, Victoria's Historic Inn embraces it. There's dense mahogany and cherry woodworking throughout, along with exceptionally intricate ceilings. The deluxe Chase Suite features a large sitting room with a gas fireplace and oak mantle. The less expensive third-floor rooms are smaller and somewhat less historic in flavor.

Dining: Dinner is served Tuesday to Sunday from mid-April to December in the inn's sumptuous dining room. Entrees might include filet mignon, grilled Atlantic salmon with lobster sauce, or Digby scallops with a spinach-and-chardonnay sauce. Main courses are C$25 to C$30 (US$18 to US$21).

DINING

In addition to these restaurants, the dining rooms mentioned in "Accommodations," above, serve some of the most elegant meals in town, but at a price.

Al's Sausages. 314 Main St. ☎ **902/542-5908.** All selections C$5 (US$3.60) or less. V. Mon–Sat 9am–6:30pm, Sun 11am–5pm. DELI.

Al Waddell has attracted a loyal local following since he started vending his home-made sausages from this uninspired storefront in the early 1990s. Among Al's usual offerings: Polish, German, hot Italian, and honey garlic sausages. Most are lower in fat than the usual sausage; some are not. (Especially not is the sausage nugget plate, which features breaded and deep-fried sausage pieces.) You won't find a better cheap lunch: a sausage on a bun with soup is just C$4.50 (US$3.20).

Chez la Vigne. 117 Front St. ☎ **902/542-5077.** Reservations suggested. Lunch C$6–C$11 (US$4.30–US$8); dinner C$13–C$25 (US$9–US$18). AE, ER, MC, V. Daily 11am–10pm (until 9pm in winter). FRENCH.

Chez la Vigne is located on a quiet side street a few steps off Main Street. It's been through changes in the past 2 years—new chef, new artwork on the walls, more houseplants scattered about—but has maintained the philosophy that everyone should be able to afford a good meal. Dishes range from the country-simple (pasta with a light bean-and-olive-oil sauce tossed with ham and fava beans) to the rather more complex (rabbit stuffed with herbs and rice). The quality varies, but more often than not, it's very good.

3 Annapolis Royal

Annapolis Royal is Nova Scotia's most historic town—it even bills itself, with justi-fication, as "Canada's birthplace." The nation's first permanent settlement was estab-lished at Port Royal, just across the river from the present-day Annapolis Royal, in 1605 by a group of doughty settlers that included Samuel de Champlain. (Champlain called the beautiful Annapolis Basin "one of the finest harbours that I have seen on all these coasts.") The strategic importance of this well-protected harbor was proven in the tumultuous later years, when a series of forts was constructed on the low hills overlooking the water.

Annapolis Royal today is truly a treat to visit. Because the region was largely over-looked by later economic growth (trade and fishing moved to the Atlantic side of the peninsula), it requires little in the way of imagination to see Annapolis Royal as it once was. (The current population is just 700.) The original settlement was rebuilt on the presumed site. Fort Anne overlooks the upper reaches of the basin, looking much as it did when abandoned in 1854. And the village itself maintains much of its original historic charm, with narrow streets and historic buildings fronting the now-placid waterfront.

Indeed, Annapolis Royal is also considered by many historians to be the birthplace of historic preservation. Starting early in this century, town residents have been unusually active in preserving the character of the place. As testament to their dedication, note that some 150 buildings and homes in town are officially designated heritage sites.

For anyone curious about Canada's history, Annapolis Royal is one of Nova Scotia's don't-miss destinations.

ESSENTIALS

GETTING THERE Annapolis is located at Exit 22 of Route 101. It is 206 kilo-meters (124 miles) from Halifax, and 133 kilometers (80 miles) from Yarmouth.

VISITOR INFORMATION The **Annapolis District Tourist Bureau** (☎ 902/532-5454) is located 1.2 kilometers (0.7 miles) north of the town center (follow Prince Albert Road and look for the Annapolis Royal Tidal Generating Station). It's open daily in summer from 8am to 8pm.

EXPLORING THE TOWN

Start by seeking out the tourist bureau at the **Annapolis Royal Tidal Generating Station** (☎ 902/532-5454), where the extreme tides have been harnessed to pro-duce electricity. The dam is opened when the tide flows in, then closed before it flows out. Water is then released through turbines to generate electricity. It's the only tidal generator in North America, and the world's largest straight-flow turbine. Learn about the generator at the free exhibit center, or on brief tours of the plant. Tours are offered Monday to Friday from 9am to 3pm, and visitors must be at least 16 years old; a C$2.50 (US$1.80) donation is suggested.

Before leaving the center, be sure to request a copy of the free *Footprints with Footnotes* walking-tour brochure. The annotated map provides architectural and historic context for a stroll around downtown and the waterfront. Take a moment to note that as you walk down lower St. George Street, you're walking down the oldest town street in Canada.

What you'll remember most from a visit to the ✪ **Fort Anne National Historic Park,** entrance on St. George Street (☎ **902/532-2321**), are the impressive grassy earthworks that cover some 35 acres of high ground overlooking the confluence of the Annapolis River and Allains Creek. The first fort on this site was built by the French around 1643. Since then, dozens of buildings and fortifications have occupied this site. You can visit the 1708 gunpowder magazine (the oldest building of any Canadian National Historic Site), then peruse the museum located in the 1797 British field-officer's quarters. The model of the site as it appeared in 1710 is particularly intriguing. If you find all the history a bit tedious, ask a guide to borrow a croquet set and practice your technique on the lush rolling lawns. Admission to the grounds is free and they're open year-round; museum admission is C$2.75 (US$2) for adults, C$2.25 (US$1.60) for seniors, C$1.35 (US95¢) for children, and C$7 (US$5) for families. It's open May 15 to October 15, daily from 9am to 6pm; off-season by appointment only. Closed holidays.

You don't need to be a flower nut to enjoy an hour or two at these exceptional ✪ **Historic Gardens,** 441 St. George St. (☎ **902/532-7018**). Created in 1981, the 10-acre grounds are uncommonly beautiful, with a mix of formal and informal gardens dating from varied epochs. The gardens overlook a beautiful salt marsh (now diked and farmed) and include a geometric Victorian garden, a knot garden, a rock garden, and a colorful perennial border garden. Rose fanciers should allow plenty of time—some 2,000 rose bushes track the history of rose cultivation from the earliest days through the Victorian era to the present day. A garden cafe (see below) offers an enticing spot for lunch. Admission is C$4 (US$2.80) for adults, C$3.50 (US$2.50) for seniors and students, and C$10.75 (US$8) for families. It's open mid-May to mid-October, daily from 8am to dusk.

Canada's first permanent settlement, Port Royal was located on an attractive point with sweeping views of the Annapolis Basin. After the dreadful winter of 1604 spent on an island in the St. Croix River (the current Maine–New Brunswick border), the survivors moved to a better-protected location, now the ✪ **Port Royal National Historic Park,** 10 kilometers (6 miles) south of Route 1, Granville Ferry (turn left shortly after passing the tidal generating station; ☎ **902/532-2321**). Settlers lived here for 8 years in a high style that approached decadent, given the savage surroundings. Many of the handsome, compact French-style farmhouse buildings were designed by Samuel de Champlain to re-create the comfort they might have enjoyed at home.

While the original settlement was abandoned and eventually destroyed, this 1939 re-creation is convincing in all the details. You'll find a handful of costumed interpreters engaged in traditional handicrafts, like woodworking, and they're happy to fill you in on life in the colony during those harsh early years, an "age of innocence" when the French first forged an alliance with local natives. Allow at least an hour to wander and explore. Admission is C$2.75 (US$2) for adults, C$2.25 (US$1.60) for seniors, C$1.35 (US95¢) for children, and C$8 (US$6) for families. It's open May 15 to October 15, daily from 9am to 6pm.

ACCOMMODATIONS

For modern motel-like accommodations near town, try **Wandlyn Inn–Annapolis Royal** (☎ **902/532-2323**) on Highway 101, Exit 22 (south of town). Doubles are C$65 to C$95 (US$46 to $US67).

Garrison House Inn. 350 St. George St., Annapolis Royal, NS, B0S 1A0. ☎ **902/532-5750.** Fax 902/532-5501. 7 rms. C$55–C$82 (US$39–US$58) double. AE, MC, V. Open May–Oct; phone/fax in advance for weekends rest of year. Street parking.

The historic Garrison House sits across from Fort Anne in the town center, and has bedded and fed guests since it first opened as an inn in 1854. Flowers make the inn welcoming, and the guest rooms are comfortable. Room 7 is tucked in the back of the house, away from the hubbub of St. George Street, and has two skylights to let in the wonderfully dappled light. The well-regarded Garrison House restaurant is open daily for dinner (breakfast for guests, also; not included in room rate). The menu is refreshing and eclectic, with selections like Acadian jambalaya. Prices range from C$20 to C$25 (US$14 to $US18).

Hillsdale House. 519 St. George St. (P.O. Box 148), Annapolis Royal, NS, B0S 1A0. ☎ **902/532-2345.** 10 rms. C$65–C$95 (US$46–US$67) double. Rates include full breakfast. MC, V. Closed mid-Oct to mid-May.

This pale-yellow clapboard Italianate home dates to 1849 and sits just across the road from its sister property, the slightly fancier Queen Anne Inn. (Both are owned by the same innkeeper, but managed separately.) The first floor features a Georgian-style sitting room with furniture that's both nice to look at and comfortable to sit on. The carpeted guest rooms are handsome if rather basic, furnished with antiques that aren't overly elaborate. Only the top-floor rooms have air-conditioning. And this may be good news: there's not a single television in the place. No smoking.

Queen Anne Inn. 494 St. George St., Annapolis Royal, NS, B0S 1A0. ☎ **902/532-7850.** 10 rms (2 with shower only). C$50–C$95 (US$36–US$67) double. Rates include full breakfast. MC, V.

This Second Empire mansion, built in 1865, looks like the city hall of a small city. You won't miss it driving into town. Like the Hillsdale House across the street, the Queen Anne (built for the sister of the Hillsdale's owner) has benefited from a preservation-minded owner, who has restored the Victorian detailing to its former luster. This includes the zebra-striped dining room floor (alternating planks of oak and maple), and the grand central staircase. The guest rooms are more elegant than those across the way. With its towering elms, the parklike grounds are shady and inviting. No smoking.

DINING

Fat Pheasant. 200 St. George St. ☎ **902/532-5315.** Reservations suggested on weekends. Main courses C$5–C$15 (US$3.60–US$11). MC, V. Daily 11:30am–9pm. ECLECTIC.

The Fat Pheasant offers creative dining on two levels in what used to be the town post office. The decor is a blend of modern and traditional, with eggplant walls, oak antiques, and an unobtrusive pheasant theme. The menu is likewise creative, and the chef manages to surprise even with run-of-the-mill items, like a grilled cheese sandwich with chutney. Among the selections are steamed mussels, haddock chowder, beef stir-fry in a peppered mango glaze, and blackened tuna with tomato rati.

✪ **Newman's.** 218 St. George St. ☎ **902/532-5502.** Reservations recommended. Main courses C$7–C$25 (US$5–US$18). V. July–Aug daily 11:30am–9pm; June and Sept Tues–Sun 11:30am–9pm; May and Oct Tues–Sun 11:30am–2:30pm and 5:30–8:30pm. SEAFOOD.

Newman's is located in an oddly out-of-place pink Spanish Revival building on Annapolis Royal's historic waterfront. But don't let that confuse you. Inside, you'll find some of the most carefully prepared food in Nova Scotia, ordered from a substantial menu. It's hard to nail down a specialty—the kitchen does so much so very well. The seafood is especially delectable (grilled Atlantic salmon with tarragon sauce, halibut sautéed with sliced almonds), as are the generous, old-fashioned desserts (bananas with chocolate and whipped cream, homemade strawberry shortcake). Unexpected bonus: The wine list is surprisingly creative.

Secret Garden. 471 St. George St. ☎ **902/532-2200.** Lunch C$4–C$8 (US$2.80–US$6). MC, V. Daily in summer 11:30am–4:30pm. LIGHT FARE.

Located at the edge of the Historic Gardens, the Secret Garden is the ideal location for a light lunch on one of those beguilingly warm days touched with a mild breeze. The best seats are on the patio, which occupies a shady spot under a huge American elm and overlooking the knot garden. The selections are tasty and light, with fare like tuna sandwiches and penne in a spicy tomato sauce. There's also a children's menu.

4 Kejimkujik National Park

About 43 kilometers (25 miles) southeast of Annapolis Royal is a popular national park that's a world apart from coastal Nova Scotia. Kejimkujik National Park, founded in 1968, is located in the heart of south-central Nova Scotia, and it is to lakes and bogs what the south coast is to fishing villages and fog. Bear and moose are the full-time residents here; park visitors are the transients. The park, which was largely scooped and shaped during the last glacial epoch, is especially popular with canoeists, although hikers can occupy themselves here as well. Bird watchers are also drawn to the park, especially in pursuit of barred owls, pileated woodpeckers, and loons.

ESSENTIALS

GETTING THERE Kejimkujik National Park is approximately midway on Kejimkujik Scenic Drive (Route 8), which extends 115 kilometers (71 miles) between Annapolis Royal and Liverpool. The village of **Maitland Bridge** (pop. 130) is near the park's entrance. Plan on about a 2-hour drive from Halifax.

VISITOR INFORMATION The park's **visitor center** (☎ 902/682-2772) is open daily and features slide programs and exhibits about the park's natural history.

FEES Entrance fees are charged from mid-May to the end of October. Daily fees are C$3 (US$2.10) for adults, C$2.25 (US$1.60) for seniors, C$1.50 (US$1.10) for children 6 to 16, and C$7 (US$5) for families; 4-day passes are available in all categories for the price of 3 days. Children under 6 are free at all national parks.

EXPLORING THE PARK

The park's 381 square kilometers (147 sq. miles) of forest, lake, and bog are peaceful and remote. Part of what makes it such is the lack of access by car. One short, forked park road from Route 8 gets you partway into the park. Then you need to continue on foot or by canoe.

Canoeing is really the optimal means of voyaging in the park. Bring your own, or rent a canoe at **Jake's Landing,** in the park on the road to Grafton Lane (☎ 902/682-2196), for C$4 (US$2.80) per hour, or C$20 (US$14) per day. (The same rate applies to rentals of bikes, paddleboats, kayaks, and rowboats.) Canoeists can cobble together wilderness excursions from one lake to the other, some involving slight portaging. Multiday trips are easily arranged to backcountry campsites and are the best way to get to know the park. Canoe route maps are provided at the visitor center. Rangers also lead short guided canoe trips for novices.

The park also has 14 **hiking trails,** ranging from easy strolls to more extensive overnight hikes. The 6-kilometer (4-mile) **Hemlocks and Hardwoods Trail** loops through stately groves of 300-year-old hemlocks; the 3-kilometer (1.8-mile) **Merrymakedge Beach Trail** skirts a lakeshore to end at a lovely beach. The free hiking-trail brochure available at the visitor center will help you decide where to go.

CAMPING

Backcountry camping may be the park's chief draw. So nice are the 44 backcountry sites that they actually cost more than the drive-in campsites. The canoe-in and hike-in sites are assigned individually, which means you needn't worry about noisy neighbors playing "La Bamba" over and over on their car stereo. Backcountry rangers keep the sites in top shape, and each is stocked with firewood for the night. Most sites can handle a maximum of six campers. Naturally, there's high demand for the best sites; you're better off here midweek when fewer weekenders are down from Halifax. You can also reserve backcountry sites in advance for an additional fee of C$3.75 (US$2.70); call the **visitor center** (☎ **902/682-2772**). The backcountry camping fee is C$16.50 (US$12) per night.

The park's drive-in campground at Jeremys Bay offers 329 sites, some of which are quite close to the water's edge. Campground rates are C$13.50 (US$10) per night. (During the shoulder seasons in spring and fall, campsites are available for C$50/US$36 for 5 consecutive nights.)

5 Digby to Yarmouth

This 113-kilometer (70-mile) stretch of coast is bracketed by two towns that serve as gateways to Nova Scotia. While the South Shore—the stretch between Yarmouth and Halifax—serves to confirm popular conceptions of Nova Scotia (small fishing villages, shingled homes), the Digby-to-Yarmouth route seems determined to confound them. Look for Acadian enclaves, fishing villages with more corrugated steel than weathered shingle, miles of sandy beaches, and spruce-topped basalt cliffs that seem transplanted from Labrador.

DIGBY

The unassuming port town of Digby (pop. 2,300) is located on the water at Digby Gap—where the Annapolis River finally forces an egress through the North Mountain coastal range. Set at the south end of the broad watery expanse of the Annapolis Basin, Digby is home to the world's largest inshore scallop fleet, which drags the ocean bottom for tasty and succulent Digby scallops. Ferries to Saint John, NB, sail year-round from a dock a few miles north of downtown.

The town is named after Admiral Sir Robert Digby, who arrived here from New England in 1783. He led a group of loyalists who found relations with their neighbors rather strained following the War of Independence. Today, Digby is an active community where life centers around fishing boats, neighborhoods of wood-frame houses, and no-frills seafood restaurants. It's certainly worth a brief stopover when heading to or from the ferry.

ESSENTIALS

GETTING THERE Digby is Nova Scotia's gateway for those arriving from Saint John, NB, via ferry. The ferry terminal is on Route 303 north of Digby. If you're arriving by ferry and want to visit the town before pushing on, watch for signs directing you downtown from the bypass. Otherwise, you'll end up on Route 101 before you know it.

From other parts of Nova Scotia, Digby is accessible via Exit 26 off Route 101.

VISITOR INFORMATION The **Visitor Information Centre** (☎ **902/ 245-5714**) is located on the harbor at 110 Montague Row. It's open daily mid-June to mid-October from 9am to 8:30pm.

EXPLORING DIGBY

Water Street runs along the water (of course), with its views of the scallop fleet from various points. A grassy promenade extends from the visitor information center to the small downtown; parking is usually plentiful.

Learn about the scallop industry at the **Lady Vanessa** fisheries exhibit, 34 Water St. (☎ **902/245-4555**). Set in a 98-foot scallop dragger, it features videos and exhibits about the prized local catch. It's open daily throughout the summer; admission is C$1.75 (US$1.25). The exhibit is not open in winter.

Continue walking northward on Water Street and you'll arrive at **Royal Fundy Fish Market** (☎ **902/245-5411**) at the head of Fisherman's Wharf. You can buy fresh scallops or smoked fish, including locally popular "smoked chicks"—slang for smoked herring. They got their name when early Digby settlers had to settle for these rather than poultry during impoverished Christmas dinners.

ACCOMMODATIONS

Digby is an entryway for those arrive or departing by ferry, and as such it has a number of basic motels. Two within walking distance of the promenade and downtown are the cottage-style efficiency units of **Seawinds Motel,** 90 Montague Row (☎ **902/ 245-2573**), which offers good sea views; and the rather more basic **Siesta Motel** just across the street at 81 Montague Row (☎ **902/245-2568**).

✪ **The Pines.** Shore Rd., P.O. Box 70, Digby, NS, B0V 1A0. ☎ **800/667-4637** or 902/ 245-2511. Fax 902/245-6133. Web site: www.gov.ns.ca/resorts. 83 rms, 30 cottages. TV TEL. C$135–C$270 (US$96–US$192) double; cottages C$270 (US$192) and up. AE, DC, DISC, ER, MC, V.

The Pines, situated on 300 acres with marvelous views of the basin, is redolent of an earlier era when old money headed to fashionable resorts for an entire summer. Built in 1929 in a Norman chateau style, the inn today is owned and operated by the Province of Nova Scotia, and should silence those who believe that government can't do anything right. The imposing building of stucco and stone is surrounded by the eponymous pines, which rustle softly in the wind. Throughout, the emphasis is more on comfort than historical verisimilitude, although the gracious lobby features old-world touches like Corinthian capitals, floral couches, and parquet floors. The guest rooms vary slightly as to size and views (ask for a water-view room; there's no extra charge), and all now have ceiling fans, although air-conditioning is said to be on the way. The cottages have one to three bedrooms and most feature wood fireplaces.

Dining: The Annapolis Dining Room is open for all three meals, and the cuisine might best be described as Nova Scotian with a French flair. Look for entrees like roasted pork tenderloin with apples and a cider sauce, or poached char infused with green Chinese tea. Entrees are priced from C$13 to C$27 (US$9 to $US19). Dinner reservations are advised.

Services: The concierge can arrange for baby-sitting, dry cleaning, laundry or VCR rentals. Also offered: afternoon tea, turndown service, courtesy car to the ferry, and a tour desk.

Facilities: The hotel has a very appealing pool and fitness center complex just down the lawn from the main building; the heated outdoor pool is surrounded by glass walls to block the wind while allowing views. The resort also has hiking trails, shuffleboard, bike rentals, two night-lit tennis courts, an 18-hole golf course, sauna, children's center, shopping arcade, and a range of services for business travelers.

DINING

A meal at The Pines (see above) offers a grand setting. Otherwise, the handful of downtown seafood restaurants are more or less interchangeable, serving up heaps of the local specialty: fried scallops. Of these, the spot with the best harbor view is the **Fundy Restaurant,** 34 Water St. (☎ **902/245-4950**); ask for a seat in the solarium. If you'd like your scallops with a more exotic tang, head to **Kaywin Restaurant,** 51 Water St. (☎ **902/245-5543**), a Chinese-Canadian restaurant that serves scallops stir-fried with vegetables, as well as the more common fried variant.

YARMOUTH

The constant lament of Yarmouth restaurateurs and shopkeepers is this: The steady stream of summer tourists arriving via ferry rarely linger long enough to appreciate their city before they mash the accelerator and speed off to higher-marquee venues along the coast.

There may be a reason for that. Yarmouth is a pleasant burg that offers some note-worthy historic architecture dating from the golden age of seafaring. But the town's not terribly unique, and thus not high on my list of places I'd choose to spend a few days. It's too big (pop. 7,800) to be charming; too small to generate urban buzz and vitality. It has more of the flavor of a handy pit stop than a destination.

By all means plan to dawdle a few hours while awaiting the ferry (Portland-bound passengers could enjoyably spend the night here prior to their early-morning departure), or to while away an afternoon looping around the coast. Take the time to follow the self-guided walking tour, enjoy a meal, or wander around the newly renovated waterfront, where efforts to coax it back from decrepitude have started to take root.

Then: onward.

ESSENTIALS

GETTING THERE   Yarmouth is located where two of the province's principal highways—Route 101 and Route 103—converge. It's approximately 300 kilometers (180 miles) from Halifax. Yarmouth is the gateway for two daily ferries (seasonal) connecting to Maine. **Air Canada** serves Yarmouth with one flight daily from Halifax; call ☎ **800/776-3000** in the United States or 800/565-3940 in the Maritimes. The airport is located a few minutes' drive east of town on Starrs Road. For more information, see "Exploring Nova Scotia," at the beginning of this chapter.

VISITOR INFORMATION   The **Yarmouth Visitor Centre** (☎ **902/742-6639**) is at 228 Main St., just up the hill from the ferry in a modern, shingled building you simply can't miss. It's open May to October daily from 8am to 7pm.

EXPLORING THE TOWN

The tourist bureau and the local historical society publish a very informative **walking-tour brochure** covering downtown Yarmouth. It's well worth requesting at the visitor information center. The guide offers general tips on what to look for in local architectural styles (how *do* you tell the difference between Georgian and classic revival?), as well as brief histories of significant buildings. The whole tour is 4 kilometers (2.5 miles) long.

The most scenic side trip—and an ideal excursion by bike or car—is to
✪ **Cape Forchu** and the Yarmouth Light. Head west on Main Street (Route 1) for
2.2 kilometers (1.3 miles) from the visitor center, then turn left at the horse statue.
The road winds picturesquely out to the cape, past seawalls and working lobster
wharves, meadows and old homes.

When the road finally ends, you'll be at the red-and-white striped concrete lighthouse that marks the harbor's entrance. (This modern lighthouse dates to the early
1960s, when it replaced a much older octagonal light that succumbed to wind and
time.) There's a tiny photographic exhibit on the cape's history in the visitor center
in the keeper's house.

Leave enough time to ramble around the dramatic rock-and-grass bluffs—part of
Leif Ericson Picnic Park—that surround the lighthouse. Don't miss the short trail
out to the point below the light. Bright-red picnic tables and benches are scattered
about; bring lunch or dinner if the weather is right.

The two-story **Firefighters Museum of Nova Scotia,** 451 Main St. (☎ 902/
742-5525), will appeal mostly to confirmed fire buffs, historians, and impression-
able young children. The museum is home to a broadly varied collection of early fire-
fighting equipment, with early hand-drawn pumpers the centerpiece of the collection.
Also showcased here are uniforms, badges, helmets, and pennants. Look for the photos of notable Nova Scotian fires ("Hot Shots"). Admission is C$2 (US$1.40)
for adults and C$4 (US$2.80) for families. It's open July and August, Monday to
Saturday from 9am to 9pm and Sunday from 10am to 5pm (closed Sunday the rest
of the year and limited hours Monday to Saturday).

The **Yarmouth County Museum,** 22 Collins St. (☎ 902/742-5539), consists of
the museum itself (with displays of seafaring artifacts, Victorian furniture, paintings,
costumes, and examples of early decorative arts) and the Pelton-Fuller House, just
next door. The Queen Anne–style Fuller house (ca. 1895) was the summer home of
Primrose and Alfred Fuller. Mr. Fuller, a Nova Scotia native, was best known as the
founder of the famed Fuller Brush Co. The home was donated to the museum in
1996, and is richly furnished with antiques, much as it was left. Admission to the
museum and Pelton-Fuller house is C$4 (US$2.80) for adults (C$2.50/US$1.80
museum or house only), C$2 (US$1.40) for students, C$1 (US70¢) for children, and
C$8 (US$6) for families. It's open June to mid-October, Monday to Saturday from
9am to 5pm and Sunday from 2 to 5pm; mid-October to May, Tuesday to Sunday
from 2 to 5pm. (House open summers only.)

ACCOMMODATIONS

Campers will discover there are no provincial parks within easy striking distance of
Yarmouth. But 9 miles west of town on Route 1 is the **Lake Breeze Campground**

(☎ 902/649-2332), a privately run spot with the appealingly low-key character of a small municipal campground. It has 32 sites, some right on the shores of tiny Lake Darling, and is impeccably well cared for by owners Del and Pearl Kuehner.

Yarmouth is home to a number of chain motels. Among them are the **Best Western Mermaid Motel,** 545 Main St. (☎ **800/772-2774** or 902/742-7821), with rates of C$90 to C$100 (US$64 to US$71) double; **Comfort Inn,** 96 Starrs Rd. (☎ **902/742-1119**), at C$70 to C$95 (US$50 to US$68) double; and the **Rodd Grand Hotel,** 417 Main St. (☎ **902/742-2446**), C$80 to C$115 (US$57 to US$82) double.

Churchill Mansion Inn. Rte. 1 (9 miles west of Yarmouth), Yarmouth, NS, B5A 4A5. ☎ **902/649-2818.** 10 rms. C$40–C$60 (US$28–US$43) double. DISC, MC, V. Closed Nov to mid-May.

Between 1891 and 1920, the Churchill Mansion was occupied just 6 weeks a year, when Aaron Flint Churchill, a Yarmouth native who amassed a shipping fortune in Atlanta, Georgia, returned to Nova Scotia to summer. This extravagant mansion with its garish furnishings, situated on a low bluff overlooking the highway and a lake, was converted to an inn in 1981 by Bob Benson, who is likely to be found on a ladder or with a hammer in hand when you arrive. ("It never ends," he sighs.)

The home is built on three tiers, echoing Churchill's Savannah mansion, and furnished with flea-market antiques and a spooky portrait of Churchill in the hallway. The mansion boasts some original carpeting, lamps, and woodwork, although it can be a little threadbare, flaky, or water-stained in other spots. This is a popular destination among those who like quirky history and don't mind a little mustiness, as well as among kids with lively imaginations. Are there any ghosts? "Oh, yeah," says Benson, adding that they do only good things, never bad.

Harbour's Edge B&B. 12 Vancouver St., Yarmouth, NS, B5A 2N8. ☎ **902/742-5655** or 902/742-2387. 3 rms (1 with private hallway bath). C$75–C$95 (US$53–US$67) double. Rates include full breakfast. MC, V. Head toward Cape Forchu (see above); watch for the inn shortly after turning at the horse statue.

This exceptionally attractive early Victorian home (1864) sits on 2 leafy acres and 250 feet of harbor frontage. You can lounge on the lawn while watching herons and king-fishers below, making it hard to believe you're right in town and only a few minutes from the ferry terminal. Harbour's Edge opened in 1997 after 3 years of intensive restoration (it had previously been abandoned for 5 years). All the rooms are lightly furnished, which serves to nicely highlight the architectural integrity of the design. The three guest rooms all have high ceilings and handsome spruce floors. The Ellen Brown Room is my pick: it has fine oak furniture and a great view of the harbor, although the private bath is down the hall. No smoking.

Lakelawn Motel. 641 Main St., Yarmouth, NS, B5A 1K2. ☎ **902/742-3588.** 31 rms (some with shower only). TV. C$49–C$64 (US$35–US$45) double. AE, DC, DISC, ER, MC, V. Closed Nov–Apr.

The clean, well-kept Lakelawn Motel offers basic motel rooms done up in colors that were fashionable some years ago, like harvest-orange and brown plaid. It's been a downtown Yarmouth mainstay since the 1950s, when the centerpiece Victorian house (where the office is located) was moved back from the road to make room for the motel wings. Looking for something a bit cozier? The house also has four B&B-style guest rooms upstairs, each furnished nicely with antiques.

DINING

Harris Quick and Tasty. Rte. 1, Dayton. ☎ **902/742-3467.** Sandwiches C$2.40–C$12 (US$1.70–US$9); main courses C$6.50–C$18.25 (US$4.60–US$13). AE, MC, V. Daily 11am–9pm (until 8pm in winter). Located just east of Yarmouth on the north side of Rte. 1. SEAFOOD.

The name about says it all. This vintage 1960s restaurant has no pretensions (it's the kind of place that still lists cocktails on the menu), and is hugely popular with locals. The Harrises sold the place a couple of years ago, but new owner Paul Surette is committed to preserving the place as is. The restaurant is adorned with that sort of paneling that was rather *au courant* about 30 years ago, and the meals are likewise old-fashioned and generous. The emphasis is on seafood, and you can order your fish either fried or broiled. The "Scarlet O'Harris" lobster club sandwich is notable, as is the seafood casserole.

Queen Molly's Brewpub. 96 Water St. ☎ **902/742-6008.** Main courses C$8–C$15 (US$6–US$11). AE, MC, V. Daily 11:30am–10pm. BREW PUB.

Yarmouth's first (and Nova Scotia's fourth) brew pub opened in the summer of 1997 on the newly spiffed-up waterfront. It occupies an old warehouse dating to the mid-1800s, and you can see the wear and tear of the decades on the battered floor and the stout beams and rafters. The place has been cleaned up nicely (it still had the gleam and luster of new construction when I visited), and looks poised to age well. The menu features basic pub fare, with more ambitious meals like New York steak with a peppercorn-mushroom-brandy demi-glace. The beers are very good, especially the best bitter. In summer, there's outdoor seating on a deck with a view of the harbor across the parking lot.

6 The South Shore

The Atlantic coast between Yarmouth and Halifax is that quaint, maritime Nova Scotia you see on laminated place mats and calendars. It's all lighthouses and weathered shingled buildings perched at the rocky edge of the sea, as if tenuously trespassing on the good graces of the sea. If your heart is set on exploring this fabled landscape, make sure you leave enough time to poke in all the nooks and crannies along this stretch of the coast.

As rustic and beautiful as it is, you may find it a bit stultifying to visit *every* quaint village along the entire coastline—involving about 350 kilometers (210 miles) of twisting road along the water's edge. A more sane strategy would be to sit down with a map and target two or three villages, then stitch together selected coastal drives near the chosen villages with speedier links on Route 103, which runs straight and fast a short distance inland.

It's sensible to allow more time here for one other good reason: fog. When the cool waters of the Arctic currents mix with the warm summer air over land, the results are predictable and soupy. The fog certainly adds atmosphere. It also can slow driving to a crawl.

SHELBURNE

Shelburne is a historic town with an unimpeachable pedigree. Settled in 1783 by United Empire Loyalists fleeing New England after the unfortunate outcome of the late war, the town swelled with newcomers and by 1784 was believed to have a population of 10,000—larger than Montréal, Halifax, or Québec. With the decline of boatbuilding and fishing in this century, the town edged into that dim economic twilight familiar to other seaside villages (it now has a population of about 3,000), and the waterfront began to deteriorate, despite valiant preservation efforts.

And then Hollywood came calling with hat in hand. In 1992 the film *Mary Silliman's War* was filmed here. The producers found the waterfront to be a fair facsimile of Fairfield, Connecticut, around 1776. The crew spruced the town up a bit and buried power lines along the waterfront.

Two years later director Roland Joffe arrived to film the spectacularly miscast *Scarlet Letter,* starring Demi Moore, Gary Oldman, and Robert Duvall. The film crew buried more power lines, built some 15 "historic" structures near the waterfront (most demolished after filming), dumped tons of rubble to create dirt lanes (since removed), and generally made the place look like 17th-century Boston.

When the crew departed, they left behind three buildings and an impressive shingled steeple you can see from all over town. Among the "new old" buildings is the waterfront cooperage across from the Cooper's Inn. The original structure, clad in asphalt shingles, was considered an eyesore and was torn down, replaced by the faux 17th-century building. Today, barrel makers painstakingly make and sell traditional handcrafted wooden barrels in what amounts to a souvenir of a notable Hollywood flop.

ESSENTIALS

GETTING THERE   Shelburne is 223 kilometers (134 miles) southwest of Halifax on Route 3. It's a short hop from Route 103 via either Exit 25 (southbound) or Exit 26 (northbound).

VISITOR INFORMATION   The **Shelburne Tourist Bureau** (☎ 902/875-4547) is located in a tidy waterfront building at the corner of King and Dock streets. It's open mid-May to October, daily from 9am to 8pm.

EXPLORING HISTORIC SHELBURNE

The central **historic district** runs along the waterfront, where you can see legitimately old buildings, Hollywood fakes (see above), and spectacular views of the harbor from small, grassy parks. (Note that some of the remaining *Scarlet Letter* buildings weren't meant to last, and may have been demolished by the time you arrive.) A block inland from the water is Shelburne's more commercial stretch, where you can find services that include banks, shops, and a wonderful bakery (see "Dining," below).

The **Shelburne Historic Complex,** Dock St. (P.O. Box 39), Shelburne, NS, B0T 1W0 (☎ 902/875-3219), is an association of three local museums located within steps of one another. The most engaging is the **Dory Shop,** right on the waterfront. On the first floor you can admire examples of the simple, elegant craft (said to be invented in Shelburne), and view videos about the late Sidney Mahaney, a master builder who worked in this shop from the time he was 17 until he was 96.

Then head upstairs, where all the banging is going on. There you'll meet Sidney's son and grandson, still building the classic boats using traditional methods. "The dory is a simple boat, but there are a lot of things to think about," says the grandson with considerable understatement. While you're there, ask about the difference between a Shelburne dory and a Lunenburg dory.

The **Shelburne County Museum** features a potpourri of locally significant artifacts from the town's Loyalist past. Most intriguing is the 1740 fire pumper; it was made in London and imported here in 1783. If you keep track of such things, it's said to be the "oldest fire pumper in Canada." Behind the museum is the austerely handsome **Ross-Thomson House,** built from 1784 to 1785. The first floor contains a general store as it might have looked in 1784, with bolts of cloth and cast-iron teakettles. Upstairs is a militia room with displays of antique and reproduction weaponry.

Admission to all three museums is C$4 (US$2.90) for adults; children under 16 are free. Individual museums cost C$2 (US$1.40) for adults. They're open in summer daily from 9:30am to 5:30pm. Closed mid-October to May (Dory Shop closes at the end of September).

ACCOMMODATIONS

Just across the harbor from Shelburne is the **Islands Provincial Park** (☎ 902/ 875-4304), which offers 64 campsites on 484 acres. Some are right on the water and have great views of the historic village across the way. No hookups for RVs.

✪ **Cooper's Inn.** 36 Dock St., Shelburne, NS, B0T 1W0. ☎ **800/688-2011** or 902/875-4656. E-mail: coopers@ns.sympatico.ca. 10 rms (2 with shower only). C$65–C$95 (US$46–US$67) double; C$145 (US$103) suite. Rates include full breakfast. AE, DC, ER, MC, V.

Located facing the harbor in the Dock Street historic area, the impeccably historic Cooper's Inn was originally built by Loyalist merchant George Gracie in 1785. Subsequent additions and updating have been historically sympathetic. The downstairs sitting and dining rooms set the mood nicely, with worn wood floors, muted wall colors (mustard and khaki-green), classical music in the background, and even a book of Leonard Cohen poems on the table. The rooms in the main building mostly feature painted wood floors (they're carpeted in the cooper-shop annex), and are decorated in a comfortably historic-country style.

The new third-floor suite was deftly designed by a talented architect and features wonderful detailing, two sleeping alcoves, and harbor views. It's worth stretching your budget for. The George Gracie Room features a four-poster bed and water view; the small Roderick Mornash room has a wonderful claw-foot tub perfect for a late-evening soak.

Dining: The two small, elegant dining rooms serve the best meals in town, with sophisticated dishes like Atlantic salmon with citrus sauce, and beef tenderloin with a port and salsa sauce. The inn has a growing reputation for its scallops sautéed in pine-nut butter. Lobster is usually available in one incarnation or another. Dinner is served nightly from 6 to 9pm, and reservations are strongly recommended. Entrees range from C$13 to C$21 (US$9 to US$15).

DINING

For a full dinner out, see "Cooper's Inn," above.

Shelburne Pastry. 151 Water St. ☎ **902/875-1168.** Sandwiches C$3.50–C$4.25 (US$2.50– US$3); main courses C$7–C$10 (US$5–US$7). No credit cards. Summer Mon–Sat 9am–6pm; limited days/hours in winter. BAKERY/CAFE.

When a family of German chefs set about to open the Shelburne Pastry shop in 1995, the idea was to sell fancy pastries. But everyone who stopped by during the restoration of the Water Street building asked if they would be selling bread. So they added bread. And today it's among the best you'll taste in the province—especially the delectable Nova Scotian oatmeal brown bread. The simple cafe also offers great pastries (try the pinwheels), as well as sandwiches served on their own bread, and filling meals from a limited menu that includes German bratwurst and chicken cordon bleu. Everything is made from scratch, and everything (except the marked-down day-old goods) is just-baked fresh. You'll find good value for your dollar here.

LUNENBURG

Lunenburg is one of Nova Scotia's most historic and appealing villages, a fact recognized in 1995 when UNESCO declared the old downtown a World Heritage Site. The town was first settled in 1753, primarily by German, Swiss, and French colonists. It was laid out on the "model town" plan then in vogue (Savannah, Georgia, and Philadelphia, Pennsylvania, were also set out along these lines), which meant seven north-south streets intersected by nine east-west streets. Such a plan worked quite well in the coastal plains. Lunenburg, however, is located on a harbor flanked by steep hills, and the model town plan saw no reason to bend around these. As a result, some of the streets can be downright exhausting to walk.

About 70% of the downtown buildings date from the 18th and 19th centuries, and many of these are possessed of a distinctive style and are painted in bright colors. Looming over all is the architecturally unique Lunenburg Academy, with its exaggerated mansard roof, pointy towers, and extravagant use of ornamental brackets. It sets the tone for the town the way the Citadel does for Halifax. The first two floors are still used as a public school (the top floor was deemed a fire hazard some years ago), and the building is open to the public only on special occasions.

What makes Lunenburg so appealing to visitors is its vibrancy and life. Yes, it's historic, but this is not an ossified village. There's life, including a subtle countercultural tang that dates back to the 1960s. Look and you'll see evidence of the tie-dye-and-organic crowd in the scattering of natural-food shops and funky boutiques.

ESSENTIALS

GETTING THERE   Lunenburg is 103 kilometers (62 miles) southwest of Halifax on Route 3.

VISITOR INFORMATION   The **Lunenburg Tourist Bureau** (☎ 902/ 634-8100) is located at the top of Blockhouse Hill Road. It's open daily in summer from 9am to 8pm. It can be tricky to find; look for the "?" signs posted around town and follow those. If you find yourself on Lincoln Street, head uphill and you'll end up nearby. You can also call up local information on the Web at **www.lunco.com**.

EXPLORING LUNENBURG

Leave plenty of time to explore Lunenburg by foot. When exploring, note the architectural influence of later European settlers—especially Germans. Some local folks made their fortunes from the sea; I'd wager that real money was made by carpenters who specialized in ornamental brackets, which elaborately adorn dozens of homes.

Many of the homes also feature a distinctive architectural element that's known as the "Lunenburg bump"—a dormer with a bay window installed directly over the front door. Other homes feature the more common Scottish dormer.

Well worth visiting is **St. John's Anglican Church** at Duke and Cumberland streets. The original structure was rendered in simple New England–meetinghouse style, built in 1754 of oak timbers shipped from Boston. Between 1840 and 1880, the church went through a number of additions and was overlaid with ornamentation and shingles to create a fine example of the "carpenter Gothic" style. It's open to the public.

Guided 1¹/₂-hour **walking tours** that include lore about local architecture and legends are hosted daily by a knowledgeable historian. Tours depart at 10am, 1pm, 4pm, and 7pm from the Atlantic Fisheries Museum; the cost is C$8 (US$6).

For a view from the water, you can enjoy a 1¹/₂-hour sail on the *Eastern Star*, a 48-foot wooden ketch berthed in the harbor. Tours average around C$20 (US$14) per adult, with several sailings daily. Call ☎ **902/634-3535.** Further afield, **Lunenburg Whale Watching Tours** (☎ 902/527-7175) sail from a tiny wharf at Blue Rocks (see below) in pursuit of the massive sea mammals; harbor and bird-watching tours are also offered.

For bike rentals, see Blue Rocks Road B&B, below.

The sprawling ✪ **Fisheries Museum of the Atlantic,** on the waterfront (☎ 902/ 634-4794), is professionally designed and curated and manages to take a topic that some might consider a little, well, dull, and make it fun and exciting. You'll find aquarium exhibits on the first floor, including a touch-tank where kids can play with

The Dauntless *Bluenose*

Take a Canadian dime out of your pocket and have a close look. That graceful schooner on one side? That's the *Bluenose*, Canada's most recognized and storied ship.

The *Bluenose* was built in Lunenburg in 1921 as a fishing schooner. But it wasn't just any schooner. It was meant to be an exceptionally *fast* schooner. U.S. and Canadian fishing fleets had raced informally for years. Starting in 1920 the *Halifax Herald* sponsored the International Fisherman's Trophy, which was captured that first year by Americans sailing out of Massachusetts.

Peeved, the Nova Scotians set about taking it back. And did they ever. The *Bluenose* retained the trophy for 18 years running, despite the best efforts of Americans to recapture it. The race was shelved as World War II loomed; in the years after the war, fishing schooners were displaced by long-haul, steel-hulled fishing ships, and the schooners sailed into the footnotes of history. The *Bluenose* was sold in 1942 to labor as a freighter in the West Indies. Four years later it foundered and sank off Haiti.

What made the *Bluenose* so unbeatable? A number of theories exist. Some said it was because of last-minute hull-design changes. Some said it was frost "setting" the timbers as the ship was being built. Still others claim it was blessed with an unusually talented captain and crew.

The replica *Bluenose II* was built in 1963 from the same plans as the original, in the same shipyard, and even by some of the same workers. It's been owned by the province since 1971, and sails throughout Canada and beyond as Nova Scotia's seafaring ambassador. When it's in port in Lunenburg—which won't be very often in 1998, when it's on national tour—you can sign up for 2-hour harbor sailings, costing C$20 (US$14) for adults and C$10 (US$7) for children 12 and under. To find out where the ship is currently, call the **Bluenose II Preservation Trust** (☎ **800/763-1963** or 902/634-1963).

starfish and hermit crabs. (Look also for the massive 15-lb. lobster, estimated to be 25 to 30 years old.) Detailed dioramas depict the whys and wherefores of fishing from dories, colonial schooners, and other historic vessels. You'll also learn a whole bunch about the *Bluenose*, a replica of which ties up in Lunenburg when it's not touring elsewhere (see the box "The Dauntless *Bluenose*," above). Outside, you can tour two other ships—a trawler and a salt-bank schooner—and visit a working boat shop. Allow at least 2 hours to probe all the corners of this engaging museum. Admission is C$7 (US$5) for adults, C$5.50 (US$3.90) for seniors, C$2 (US$1.40) for children, and C$17 (US$12) for families. It's open June to mid-October, daily from 9:30am to 5:30pm; mid-October to May, Monday to Friday from 8:30am to 4:30pm.

ACCOMMODATIONS

Blue Rocks Road B&B. 579 Blue Rocks Rd., Lunenburg, NS, B0J 2C0. ☎ **800/818-3426** or 902/634-8033. 3 rms (1 private bath; 2 others share 1 bath). C$55–C$65 (US$39–US$46) double. Rates include full breakfast. MC, V. Closed mid-Oct to mid-May.

Outdoorsy folks who like a place where they can put their feet up will be right at home here. Merrill and Al Heubach offer three guest rooms in their cozy 1879 home, a short drive (or pleasant 20-min. walk) to downtown Lunenburg. It's on the way to scenic Blue Rocks, and Al runs **Lunenburg Bicycle Barn** (☎ **902/634-3426**)— a complete bike shop and rental operation—from an outbuilding behind the house.

The handsomely painted floors and pleasant veranda with a view across marsh to the water beyond make the place instantly relaxing. You'll share the first-floor living areas with the owners, who are very tidy and knowledgeable about the area. The morning coffee is organic and strong. No smoking.

✪ **Boscawen Inn.** 150 Cumberland St., Lunenburg, NS, B0J 2C0. ☎ **800/354-5009** or 902/634-3325. Fax 902/634-9293. 20 rms (1 with private hallway bath). C$50–C$120 (US$36–US$85). Rates include full breakfast. AE, ER, MC, V.

This imposing 1888 mansion occupies a prime hillside site just a block from the heart of town. It's almost worth it just to get access to the main-floor deck and its views of the harbor. Most of the rooms are in the main building, which had a newer wing added in 1945. The decor is Victorian, but not aggressively so. Even if you prefer Shaker to Victorian, you'll still do OK here, as everything has been appointed with measured taste. Some of the rooms, including two spacious suites, are located in the 1905 MacLachlan House, just below the main house. A few things to know: Room 6 lacks a shower but has a nice tub. Guests on the third floor will need to navigate steep steps. Two rooms have televisions, and in-room phones are available on request. Breakfast is buffet-style, with both hot and cold dishes. Pets are OK, as long as they get along with the house dog.

Dining: The inn's restaurant serves reliable and sometimes imaginative dinners nightly in season from 5:30 to 9pm. The ground-floor dining room is more banally modern than one might expect in this historic mansion, but the meals are quite good. Entrees emphasize seafood, and might include a mixed seafood platter, Digby scallops, or Cornish game hen with a wine sauce. Main courses are C$13 to C$18 (US$9 to $US13).

Kaulbach House Historic Inn. 75 Pelham St., Lunenburg, NS, B0J 2C0. ☎ **800/568-8818** or 902/634-8818. E-mail: kaulbach@istar.ca. Web site: www.lunco.com/kaulbach. 7 rms. TV. C$58–C$105 (US$42–US$75) double. Rates include full breakfast. AE, MC, V. Closed mid-Dec to mid-Mar.

The in-town Kaulbach House is decorated appropriately for its elaborate architecture: in high Victorian style, although rendered somewhat less oppressive with un-Victorian colors, like pink and green. The house also reflects the era's prevailing class structure: The nicest room (the tower room) is on top, and features two sitting areas and a great view. The least intriguing rooms are the former servants' quarters on street level. No smoking.

DINING

Note also that the Boscawen Inn (see above) serves well-regarded meals in a fine Victorian mansion.

Lion Inn. 33 Cornwallis St. ☎ **902/634-8988.** Reservations suggested. Main courses C$10–C$17 (US$7–US$12). AE, MC, V. Mon–Sat 5:30–9pm. CONTINENTAL.

The tiny Lion Inn seats just 24 diners in two compact dining rooms (one smoking, one non) in an 1835 home on a Lunenburg side street. The interior is simply appointed with Windsor chairs and pale greenish walls. Diners' comments tend to focus on the food, which more often than not is prepared with sophistication and flair. Lamb and lobster specials are usually featured in summer. Other entrees include baked salmon with a white-wine-and-dill sauce, and peppercorn steak served with a Madeira sauce.

✪ **Magnolia's Grill.** 128 Montague St. ☎ **902/634-3287.** Reservations not accepted. Main courses C$5–C$12 (US$3.60–US$9). AE, MC, V. Daily 11:30am–10pm. Closed Nov–Mar. SEAFOOD/ECLECTIC.

This is a bright, cheerful, funky storefront with a checkerboard linoleum floor, lively rock playing in the background, and walls adorned with old Elvis and Beatles iconography. It also serves some of the most delectable food in town. Look for barbecue pork sandwiches, chicken tostadas, and mussels and pasta—or whatever else is fresh and the kitchen feels like scrawling on the blackboard. The restaurant is especially famed for its fish cakes (served with a homemade rhubarb relish) and the Key lime pie, which are usually on the blackboard. Reservations are not accepted, so come at off-peak hours or come expecting a wait.

Old Fish Factory Restaurant. 68 Bluenose Dr. (at the Fisheries Museum). ☎ **902/ 634-3333.** Reservations recommended (ask for a window seat). Lunch C$7–C$11 (US$5–US$8); dinner C$12–C$28 (US$9–US$20). AE, DC, DISC, ER, MC, V. Daily 11am–9:30pm. Closed mid-Oct to early May. SEAFOOD.

The Old Fish Factory Restaurant is—no surprise—located in a huge old fish factory, which it shares with the Fisheries Museum. This large and popular restaurant can swallow whole bus tours at once; come early and angle for a window seat or a spot on the patio. Also no surprise: The specialty is seafood, which tends to involve medleys of varied fish. At lunch you might order a cold seafood sandwich (made with crab, scallops, and lobster). At dinner, there's a phyllo pastry filled with a blend of salmon, haddock, and scallops. Lobster is served four ways, and there's steak for more terrestrial tastes.

MAHONE BAY

Mahone Bay, first settled in 1754 by European Protestants, is postcard-perfect Nova Scotia. It's tidy and trim with an eclectic Main Street that snakes along the bay and is lined with inviting shops. This is a town that's remarkably well cared for by its 1,100 residents; architecture buffs will find a range of styles to keep them ogling.

A **visitor information center** (☎ **902/624-6151**) is located at 165 Edgewater St., near the three church steeples. It's open daily in summer from 9am to 7:30pm.

The **Mahone Bay Settlers Museum,** 578 Main St. (☎ **902/624-6263**), provides historic context for your explorations (closed Mondays). A good selection of historic decorative arts are on display. Before leaving, be sure to request a copy of *Three Walking Tours of Mahone Bay,* a handy brochure that outlines easy historic walks around the compact downtown.

Mahone Bay is the natural habitat of the boutique. The town is populous with carved and painted wooden signs, and shops selling pewter to pottery.

DINING

One of the area's small treasures is the **Tingle Bridge Tea House** (☎ **902/ 624-9770**), about 3 kilometers (1.8 miles) outside of town on the road to Lunenburg. The place sits with some formality atop a grassy slope, with a view down to the bay. It's perfect for a relaxing pot of tea late in the afternoon (there's a selection of about 55 teas), along with a slice of their lauded cheesecake. Open Wednesday to Sunday from noon to 6pm. Luncheon is C$6 to C$8 (US$4.30 to US$6); biscuits and desserts, C$4 to C$7 (US$2.85 to US$5).

Innlet Cafe. Edgewater St. ☎ **902/624-6363.** Reservations suggested for dinner. Main courses C$12–C$21 (US$9–US$15) (mostly C$13–C$15/US$9–US$11). MC, V. Daily 11:30am–8:30pm. SEAFOOD/GRILL.

The best seats are on the stone patio, which has a view of the harbor and the famous three-steepled townscape of Mahone Bay. If you end up inside, nothing lost. The clean lines and lack of clutter make it an inviting spot, and the informal and relaxed attitude will put you at ease. The menu is all over the place (oven-braised lamb shank to scallop stir-fry), but the smart money hones in on the unadorned seafood. Notable are the "smoked and garlicked mackerel," and the mixed seafood grill.

✪ **Mimi's Ocean Grill.** 662 Main St. ☎ **902/624-1342.** Main courses C$10–C$16 (US$7–US$11). AE, MC, V. Summer daily 11:30am–9:30pm; limited hours off-season. Open May–Dec. ECLECTIC.

Set under an overarching tree in a historic colonial-style home painted a rich Cherokee red, Mimi's offers some of the region's most wonderful cooking amid a relaxed and informal atmosphere. The whimsical wall paintings put you immediately at ease (this is no period piece with stiff chairs and stiff service), and the servers are jovial without overdoing it. The menu changes regularly to reflect available ingredients. For lunch you might opt for the shrimp and lobster roll, or mussel linguini with pesto cream. For dinner, how about Asian seafood stew or maple-wood salmon? If the weather's right, angle for a table on the narrow front porch, where you can enjoy a glimpse of the bay and the ongoing parade of Main Street.

CHESTER

Chester is a short drive off Route 103 and has the feel of an old-money summer colony, perhaps somewhere along the New England coast, around 1920. It was first settled in 1759 by immigrants from New England and Great Britain, and today has a population of 1,250. The village is noted for its regal homes and quiet streets. The atmosphere here is uncrowded, untrammeled, lazy, and slow—the way life used to be in summer resorts throughout the world.

The **Chester Visitor Information Centre** (☎ 902/275-4616) is in the old train station on Route 3 on the south side of town. It's open daily from 10am to 5pm in summer.

WHAT TO SEE & DO

Like so many other towns in Nova Scotia, Chester is best seen out of your car. But unlike other towns, where the center of gravity seems to be in the commercial district, here the focus is on the graceful, shady residential areas that radiate out from the Lilliputian village.

In your rambles, plan to head down Queen Street to the waterfront, then veer around on South Street, admiring the views out toward the mouth of the harbor. Continue on South Street past the yacht club, past the statue of the veteran (in a kilt), past the sundial in the small square. Then you'll come to a beautiful view of Back Harbour. At the foot of the small park is a curious municipal saltwater pool, filled at high tide. On warmer days, you'll find what appears to be half the town out splashing and shrieking in the bracing water.

For an even slower pace, plan an excursion out to the **Tancook Islands,** a pair of lost-in-time islands with a couple hundred year-round residents. The islands, accessible via a short ferry ride, are good for walking the lanes and trails. There's a small cafe on Big Tancook, but little else to cater to travelers. Several ferry trips are scheduled daily between 6am and 6pm. The ferry ties up on the island, however, so don't count on a last trip back to the mainland. Tickets are C$5 (US$3.60) round-trip; children under 12 are free.

In the evening, the intimate **Chester Playhouse,** 22 Pleasant St. (☎ 800/363-7529 or 902/275-3933), hosts plays, concerts, and other high-quality performances throughout the summer season. Tickets are usually C$16 (US$11) for adults. Call for a schedule or reservations.

ACCOMMODATIONS

Graves Island Provincial Park (☎ 902/275-4425) is just 3 kilometers (1.8 miles) north of the village on Route 3. The 125-acre estatelike park has 73 sites, many dotting a high grassy bluff with unrivaled views out to the spruce islands of Mahone Bay.

☼ Haddon Hall. 67 Haddon Hill Rd., Chester, NS, B0J 1J0. ☎ **902/275-3577.** Fax 902/275-5159. 9 rms. A/C TV TEL. C$150–C$400 (US$106–US$284) double. Rates include continental breakfast. AE, DC, ER, MC, V.

If there's no fog, Haddon Hall has the best view of any inn in Atlantic Canada, bar none. Perched atop an open hill with panoramic views of island-studded Mahone Bay, this very distinctive inn dates to 1905 and was built in what might be called "heroic Arts & Crafts" style. You'll recognize the bungalow form of the main house, but it's rendered in an outsized manner. Three stylish guest rooms are located in the main house; the remaining six are scattered in cottages around the property. Four rooms have wood fireplaces, three have Jacuzzis, two have kitchenettes. The styling is eclectic—a woodstove and twig furniture mark the rustic Log Cabin, spare continental lines are featured in the main house—but everything is united by understated good taste.

Dining: The delightful dining room is open April to mid-October, serving dinner nightly from 5:30 to 8:30pm. Make reservations early, and ask for a table on the front porch with its sweeping vistas. The creative menu might include grilled lamb and papaya, or vegetable strudel with basil and feta. Prix-fixe dinners are C$34 (US$24).

Facilities: The inn has a tennis court and outdoor pool and can arrange for boat tours. Ask about using the free bikes or visiting the inn-owned island for picnics or tours.

Mecklenburgh Inn. 78 Queen St., Chester, NS, B0J 1J0. ☎ **902/275-4638.** E-mail: frnthrbr@auracom.com. 4 rms (all share 2 baths). C$59–C$69 (US$42–US$49) double. Rates include full breakfast. AE, V. Closed late Oct to May.

The informal Mecklenburgh Inn is located on a low hill in one of Chester's appealing residential neighborhoods. The inn is dominated by porches on the first and second floors, which invariably are populated with guests sitting and rocking and watching the town wander by. Rooms are modern Victorian and generally quite bright. Baths are shared, but the inn provides Tartan robes to guests. Children over 10 are welcome; smoking on the porch only.

7 Halifax

During a recent stop at the sprawling Nova Scotia visitor center near Amherst, I heard an older couple ask an eager young staffer why they should bother to visit Halifax. "It's just a city, isn't it?," they asked.

"Well," the staffer responded brightly, "It's the second largest natural harbor in the world, after Sydney, Australia!" And then she seemed at a loss for words.

Oh, dear. I hope that's not the best the tourism folks can come up with. In fact, Halifax is a fun, vibrant, exciting city that's loaded with history but not staid, modern but not slick, big enough to get lost in but not big enough to be intimidating.

Should you bother to visit? By all means.

This unusually pleasing harborside setting, now home to a city of some 115,000, first attracted Europeans in 1749, when Col. Edward Cornwallis established a military outpost here. (The site was named after George Montagu Dunk, 2nd Earl of Halifax.) Halifax plodded along as a colonial backwater for the better part of a century; one historian wrote that it was generally regarded as "a rather degenerate little seaport town."

But its natural advantages—including the well-protected harbor and its location near major fishing grounds and shipping lanes—eventually allowed Halifax to emerge as a major port and military base. In recent years, the city has grown aggressively (it annexed adjacent suburbs in 1969) and carved out a niche as the vital commercial and financial hub of the Maritimes. The city is also home to a number of colleges and universities, which gives it a youthful air. Skateboards and bicycles sometimes seem to be the vehicles of choice. In addition to the many attractions, downtown Halifax hosts wonderful restaurants and hotels.

ESSENTIALS

GETTING THERE   All roads lead to Halifax, so it's no problem finding the place by car. The fastest route is via Route 102 from Truro; allow a little more than 2 hours from the provincial border at Amherst.

Halifax International Airport is 35 kilometers (21 miles) north of downtown Halifax in Elmsdale. (Take Route 102 to Exit 6.) Nova Scotia's notorious fogs make it advisable to call before heading out to the airport to reconfirm flight times.

More than 100 departures daily serve Atlantic Canada's largest city. Airlines serving Halifax include Air Canada, Air Nova, Canadian Airlines International, Air Atlantic, and Icelandair. (See "Exploring Nova Scotia," earlier in this chapter, for phone numbers.)

Airbus (☎ 902/873-2091) offers frequent shuttles from the airport to major downtown hotels daily from 6:30am to 11:15pm. The rate is C$11 (US$8) one-way, C$18 (US$13) round-trip.

Via Rail (☎ 800/561-3949 in the U.S. or 800/561-3952 in the Maritimes) offers train service 6 days a week between Halifax and Montréal. The entire trip takes between 18 and 21 hours, depending on direction. Stops include Moncton and Campbellton (and bus connections to Québec). Halifax's CN Station is within walking distance of downtown attractions at Barrington and Cornwallis streets.

VISITOR INFORMATION   The **Halifax International Visitor Centre** (☎ 800/565-0000 or 902/490-5946) is located downtown at 1595 Barrington St., at the corner of Barrington and Sackville. It's open daily from 8:30am to 7pm in summer (until 6pm in winter), it's huge, and it's staffed with friendly folks who will point you in the right direction or help you make room reservations.

If you're on the waterfront, stop by the **Red Store Visitor Information Centre** (☎ 902/424-4248) at Historic Properties.

GETTING AROUND   Parking in Halifax is problematic. Long-term metered spaces are in high demand downtown, and many of the parking lots and garages fill up fast. If you're headed downtown for a brief visit, you can usually find a 2-hour meter. But if you're looking to spend a day, I'd suggest venturing out early to ensure a spot at a parking lot. Your best bet is along Lower Water Street, south of the Maritime Museum of the Atlantic, where you can park all day for around C$6 (US$4.30).

Metro Transit operates buses throughout the city. Route and timetable information is available at the information centers or by phone (☎ 902/490-6600). Bus fare is C$1.35 (US$1) for adults and C90¢ (US65¢) for seniors and children.

Between Monday and Saturday **a bright yellow bus named Fred** (☎ 902/423-6658) cruises a loop through downtown, passing each stop about every 20

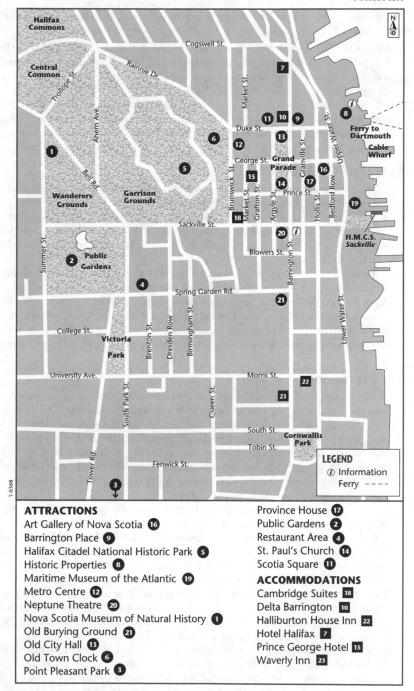

Halifax

LEGEND
ⓘ Information
Ferry ----

ATTRACTIONS
Art Gallery of Nova Scotia ⑯
Barrington Place ⑨
Halifax Citadel National Historic Park ⑤
Historic Properties ⑧
Maritime Museum of the Atlantic ⑲
Metro Centre ⑫
Neptune Theatre ⑳
Nova Scotia Museum of Natural History ①
Old Burying Ground ㉑
Old City Hall ⑬
Old Town Clock ⑥
Point Pleasant Park ③

Province House ⑰
Public Gardens ②
Restaurant Area ④
St. Paul's Church ⑭
Scotia Square ⑪

ACCOMMODATIONS
Cambridge Suites ⑱
Delta Barrington ⑩
Halliburton House Inn ㉒
Hotel Halifax ⑦
Prince George Hotel ⑮
Waverly Inn ㉓

1-0368

minutes. It's free. Stops include the Maritime Museum, the Grand Parade, and Barrington Place Shops. Request a schedule and map at the visitor center.

EVENTS The annual **Nova Scotia International Tattoo** (☎ 902/451-1221) features military and marching bands totaling some 2,000, plus military and civilian performers. This rousing event takes place in early July, and is held indoors at the Halifax Metro Center. Tickets are C$12 to C$24 (US$9 to US$17).

In early August expect to see a profusion of street performers ranging from avant-garde fire-eaters to comic jugglers. They descend on Halifax each summer for the 10-day **International Busker Festival** (☎ 902/429-3910). Performances take place all around city streets, and are often quite remarkable. Donations are requested.

EXPLORING HALIFAX

Halifax is fairly compact and easily reconnoitered on foot or by mass transportation. The major landmark is the Citadel—the stone fortress that looms over downtown from its grassy perch. From the ramparts, you can look into the windows of the 10th floors of downtown skyscrapers. The Citadel is only 9 blocks from the waterfront—albeit 9 sometimes steep blocks—and you can easily roam both areas in 1 day.

A lively neighborhood worth seeking out runs along **Spring Garden Road,** between the Public Gardens and the library (at Grafton Street). You'll find intri-guing boutiques, bars, and restaurants along these 6 blocks, set amid a mildly bohemian street scene. If you have strong legs and a stout constitution, you can start on the waterfront, stroll up and over the Citadel to descend to the Public Gardens, then return via Spring Garden to downtown, perhaps enjoying a meal or two along the way.

THE WATERFRONT

Halifax's lovingly rehabilitated waterfront is at its most inviting and vibrant between Sackville Landing (at the foot of Sackville Street) and the Sheraton Casino, near Purdy Wharf. (You could keep walking, but north of here the waterfront lapses into an agglomeration of stark modern towers with sidewalk-level vents that lash passersby with unusual odors.) On sunny summer afternoons, the waterfront is bustling with tourists enjoying the harbor, business folks playing hooky while sneaking an ice-cream cone, and baggy-panted skateboarders striving to stay out of trouble. Plan on at least 3 or 4 hours to tour and gawk from end to end.

The city's most extensive parking (fee charged) is available near Sackville Landing, and that's a good place to start a walking tour.

Make your first stop the waterfront's crown jewel, the ✪ **Maritime Museum of the Atlantic,** 1675 Lower Water St. (☎ 902/424-7490). Everything from birch-bark canoes to the *Titanic* is the subject of this stand-out museum, which opened at this prime waterfront location in 1982. Visitors are greeted by a 10-foot lighthouse lens from 1906, then proceed through a parade of shipbuilding and seagoing eras. Visit the deckhouse of a coastal steamer (ca. 1940). Learn the colorful history of Samuel Cunard, a Nova Scotia native (born 1787) who founded the Cunard Steam Ship Co. to carry the royal mail and along the way established an ocean dynasty.

Learn about the tragic Halifax Explosion of 1917, when two warships collided in Halifax harbor not far from the museum, detonating tons of TNT. More than 1,700 people died, and windows were shattered 100 kilometers (60 miles) away. You'll also learn that 150 victims of the *Titanic* disaster are buried in Halifax (out of 1,503 dead), where rescue efforts were centered. Perhaps the most poignant exhibit is the lone deck chair from the *Titanic,* a metaphor made real. Also memorable are the Age of Steam exhibit, and Queen Victoria's barge.

Admission is charged June 1 to October 15; it's C$4.50 (US$3.20) for adults, C$1 (US70¢) for children, and C$10 (US$7) for families. Admission is free October 16 to May 31. Hours from June to mid-October are Monday to Saturday from 9:30am to 5:30pm (to 8pm Tuesday) and Sunday from 1 to 5:30pm. From mid-October to May, the museum is closed Mondays, and it shuts down at 5pm from Wednesday to Sunday.

On the water in front of the Maritime Museum is the unusually handsome **CSS** *Acadia,* 1675 Lower Water St. (☎ **902/424-7490**). This 1913 vessel is part of the Maritime Museum ("our largest artifact"), but may be viewed independently for a small fee. The *Acadia* was used by the Canadian government to chart the ocean floor for 56 years, until her retirement in 1969. Much of the ship is open for self-guided tours, including the captain's quarters, upper decks, wheelhouse, and the oak-paneled chart room. If you want to see more of the ship, ask about the guided half-hour tours (four times daily), which offer access to the engine room and more. Admission is free with a museum ticket, or costs C$1 (US70¢), which may be applied to your museum admission. It's open Monday to Saturday from 9:30am to 5:30pm and Sunday from 1 to 5pm. Closed mid-October to June 1.

Close by on Lower Water Street is the **HMCS** *Sackville* (☎ **902/429-5600**). This blue-and-white corvette (a speedy warship smaller than a destroyer) is tied up along a wood-planked wharf behind a small visitor center. There's a short multimedia presentation to provide some background. The ship is outfitted as it was in 1944, and is now maintained as a memorial to the Canadians who served in World War II. Admission is free and hours are Monday to Saturday from 10am to 5pm and Sunday from 1 to 5pm.

In addition to these attractions, the waterfront walkway is studded with small diversions, intriguing shops, take-out food emporia, and minor monuments. Think of it as an alfresco scavenger hunt.

Among other treasures, look for **Summit Plaza,** commemorating the historic gathering of world leaders in 1995, when Halifax hosted the G-7 Economic Summit. There's North America's oldest operating **Naval Clock,** which dates back to 1772. You can visit the **Ferry Terminal,** which is hectic during rush hour with commuters coming and going to Dartmouth across the harbor. It's also a cheap way to enjoy sweeping city and harbor views. The passenger-only ferry runs at least every half hour, and the fare is C$1.50 (US$1.10) each way.

At **Cable Wharf,** several boats offer on-the-water adventures ranging from 1-hour harbor tours for C$12 (US$9) to 5-hour deep-sea fishing trips for C$37 (US$26). Contact **Murphy's on the Water** (☎ **902/420-1015**) for reservations or information.

The waterfront's **shopping** core is located in and around the 3-block **Historic Properties,** near the Sheraton. These stout buildings of wood and stone are Canada's oldest surviving warehouses, and were once the center of the city's booming shipping industry. Today, the historic architecture is stern enough to provide ballast for the somewhat precious boutiques and restaurants they now house. Especially appealing is the granite-and-ironstone **Privateers' Warehouse,** which dates to 1813.

If you're feeling that a pub crawl might be in order, the Historic Properties area is also a good place to wander around after working hours in the early evening. There's a contagious energy that spills out of the handful of public houses, and you'll find a bustling camaraderie and live music.

THE CITADEL & DOWNTOWN

Downtown Halifax cascades 9 blocks down a slope between the imposing stone Citadel and the waterfront. There's no fast and ready tour route; don't hesitate to follow your own desultory course, alternately ducking down quiet streets and striding along busy arteries. A good spot to regain your bearings periodically is the **Grand Parade,** where military recruits once practiced their drilling. It's a lovely urban landscape—a broad terrace carved into the hill, presided over by St. Paul's (see below) and City Hall, a grand bit of Victorian exuberance dating back to 1888. If the weather's nice, this is also a prime spot for a picnic lunch and furtive people-watching.

Also see "Gardens & Open Space," below, for other fair-weather explorations nearby.

Looming over Halifax is ✪ **The Citadel** (☎ 902/426-5080). Even if this stalwart stone fort on Citadel Hill weren't here, it would be worth the uphill trek for the astounding views alone. The panoramic sweep across downtown and the harbor finishes up with vistas out toward the broad Atlantic beyond. At any rate, an ascent makes it obvious why this spot was chosen for the harbor's most formidable defenses: There's simply no sneaking up on the place.

Four forts have occupied the summit since Col. Edward Cornwallis was posted to the colony in 1749. The Citadel has been restored to look much as it did in 1856, when the fourth fort was built out of concern over bellicose Americans. The fort has never been attacked.

The site is impressive to say the least: sturdy granite walls topped by grassy embankments form a rough star; in the sprawling gravel and cobblestone courtyard, you'll find convincingly costumed interpreters in kilts and bearskin hats marching in unison, playing bagpipes, and firing the noon cannon. The former barracks and other chambers are home to exhibits about life at the fort. If you still have questions, stop a soldier, bagpiper, or washerwomen and ask.

The Citadel is the perfect place to launch an exploration of Halifax: It provides a good geographic context for the city, and anchors it historically as well. This National Historic Site is the most heavily visited in Canada, and it's not hard to see why.

From mid-May to mid-October, the admission is C$6 (US$4.30) for adults, C$4.50 (US$3.20) for seniors, C$3 (US$2.10) for youths 6 to 16, and C$14.75 (US$11) for families; children under 6 are free. It's free the rest of the year. Limited parking at the site costs C$2.75 (US$2). From mid-June to August the site is open daily from 9am to 6pm; from September to mid-June it's open daily from 9am to 5pm.

Forming one end of the Grand Parade, **St. Paul's Church,** 1749 Argyle St., near Barrington Street (☎ 902/429-2240), was the first Anglican cathedral established outside of England and is Canada's oldest Protestant place of worship. Part of the building, which dates from 1750, was fabricated in Boston and erected in Halifax with the help of a royal endowment from King George II. A classic white Georgian building, St. Paul's has fine stained-glass windows. A piece of flying debris from the explosion of 1917 (see "Maritime Museum of the Atlantic," above) is lodged in the wall over the doors to the nave. It's open daily from 9am to 4:30pm; Sunday services are at 8, 9:15, and 11am. There are free guided tours from Tuesday to Saturday in summer.

Located in an ornate sandstone building between the waterfront and the Grand Parade, the **Art Gallery of Nova Scotia,** 1741 Hollis St., at Cheapside (☎ 902/424-7542), features 16 galleries that contain the largest and best art collection in the Maritimes. The emphasis is on provincial artists, but you'll also find a good selection of other works by Canadian, British, and European artists. The folk-art collection, located on the mezzanine level, attracts international attention. At press time, plans are underway for an expansion of the gallery into the neighboring Provincial Building. When open in 1998, the new wing will feature, among other attractions, the extravagantly painted house—the *whole* house, that is—of noted Nova Scotian folk artist Maud Lewis. Admission is C$2.90 (US$2.10) for adults, C$1.45 (US$1) for seniors and children, and C$6.35 (US$4.50) for families. Opening hours are Tuesday to Friday from 10am to 5pm and Saturday and Sunday from noon to 5pm (it's open Thursdays in summer to 9pm).

Canada's oldest seat of government, **Province House,** on Hollis Street near Prince Street (☎ **902/424-4661**), has been home to the Nova Scotian legislature since 1819. This exceptional Georgian building is a superb example of the rigorously symmetrical Palladian style. And like a jewel box, its dour stone exterior hides true gems of ornamental detailing and artwork inside; note especially the fine plasterwork, rare for a Canadian building of this era.

Within the building also roost a number of fine stories. My favorite: Look for the headless falcons in several rooms. It's said that they were decapitated by an agitated legislator with a free-swinging cane who mistook them for eagles during a period of feverish anti-American sentiment in the 1840s. Learn more about this and other local intrigue on the free tour. Admission is free. Open July and August, Monday to Friday from 9am to 5pm and Saturday, Sunday, and holidays from 10am to 4pm; the rest of the year the hours are Monday to Friday from 9am to 4pm.

On the far side of the Citadel from downtown, the **Nova Scotia Museum of Natural History,** 1747 Summer St. (☎ 902/424-7353), offers a good introduction to the flora and fauna of Nova Scotia. Galleries include geology, botany, mammals, birds, plus exhibits of archaeology and Mi'kmaq culture. Especially noteworthy are the extensive collection of lifelike ceramic fungus and the colony of honeybees that freely come and go from their indoor acrylic hive through a tube connected to the outdoors. Allow about 1 hour. Admission is C$3.50 (US$2.50) for adults, C$3 (US$2.10) for seniors, C$1 (US70¢) for children, and C$8 (US$6) for families. Open June to mid-October Monday to Saturday from 9:30am to 5:30pm (to 8pm Wednesday) and Sunday from 1 to 5:30pm. From mid-October to May, it's open Tuesday to Saturday from 9:30am to 5pm (to 8pm Wednesday) and Sunday from 1 to 5pm.

GARDENS & OPEN SPACE

The **Old Burying Ground,** at the corner of Spring Garden and Barrington (☎ 902/429-2240), was the first burial ground in Halifax, and between 1749 and 1844 some 12,000 people were interred here. (Only 1 in 10 graves are marked with a headstone, however.) You'll find wonderful examples of 18th- and 19th-century gravestone art—especially winged heads and winged skulls. (No rubbings allowed.) Also exceptional is the Welsford-Parker Monument (1855) near the grounds' entrance, which honors Nova Scotians who fought in the Crimean War. This ornate statue features a lion with an unruly Medusa-like mane. The grounds are imbued with a mystical grace a couple of hours before sunset, when the light slants magically through the trees and the traffic seems far away. The cemetery was fully restored in 1991. Admission is free and hours are daily 9am to 5pm from June to September.

At the south end of Halifax on Point Pleasant Drive, **Point Pleasant Park** is one of Canada's finest urban parks, and there's no better place for a walk along the water on a balmy day. This 186-acre park occupies a wooded peninsular point, and served for years as one of the linchpins in the city's military defense. You'll find the ruins of early forts and a nicely preserved Martello tower. Halifax has a 999-year lease from Great Britain for the park, for which it pays one shilling—about 10¢—per year. You'll also find a lovely gravel carriage road around the point, a small swimming beach, miles of walking trails, and groves of graceful fir trees. The park is about 2 kilometers (1.2 miles) south of the Public Gardens (head south on South Park Street near the Public Gardens and continue on Young). It's open daily during daylight hours. No bikes are allowed on weekends or holidays.

The ✪ **Public Gardens,** Spring Garden and South Park Street, literally took seed in 1753, when it was founded as a private garden. It was acquired by the Nova Scotia Horticultural Society in 1836, and assumed its present look in 1875, during the peak of the Victorian era. As such, it's one of the nation's Victorian masterpieces, more rare and evocative than any mansard-roofed mansion. You'll find wonderful examples of many of last century's dominant trends in outdoor landscaping, from the "natural" winding walks and ornate fountains to the duck ponds and fussy Victorian bandstand. (Stop by on Sundays in summer for free concerts.) Adding to the historic feel, you'll usually find dowagers feeding pigeons, and smartly uniformed guards slowly walking the grounds. Whatever you might think of high Victorian style in furnishings and interiors (and I won't hold it against you if you find it off-putting), the Victorians sure knew how to design gardens that remain inviting more than a century later. Admission is free. The gardens are open from spring to late fall daily from 8am to dusk.

A ROAD TRIP TO PEGGY'S COVE

About 43 kilometers (26 miles) southwest of Halifax is the picturesque fishing village of Peggy's Cove (pop. 120). The village offers a postcard-perfect tableau: octagonal lighthouse (surely one of the most photographed in the world), tiny fishing shacks, and graceful fishing boats bobbing in the postage-stamp-sized harbor. The bonsailike perfection hasn't gone unnoticed by the big tour operators, however, so it's a rare summer day when you're not sharing the experience with a few hundred of your close, personal bus-tour friends. The village is home to a handful of B&Bs and boutiques (Wood n' Wool, The Christmas Shoppe), but scenic values draw the day-trippers with cameras and lots of film.

If you'd like to view the coast from the water side, consider signing up for a boat tour aboard the 42-foot "So Much To Sea," operated by **Peggy's Cove Water Tours** (☎ **902/823-1060** or 902/456-3411). The 3-hour tour includes a pass by the puffin colony on Pearl Island.

ACCOMMODATIONS

At the larger hotels you'll discover this: Virtually all guest rooms and lobbies were fully renovated in 1995, the year of the international G-7 Summit. As such, they're all in quite good condition. Staffers still love to gossip about the conference, when delegations from the seven major economic powers commandeered whole hotels for the duration.

VERY EXPENSIVE

✪ **Prince George Hotel.** 1725 Market St., Halifax, NS, B3J 3N9. ☎ **800/565-1567** or 902/ 425-1986. Fax 902/429-6048. E-mail: pghotel@atcon.com. 206 rms and suites. A/C TV TEL MINIBAR. C$160–C$170 (US$114–US$121) double; from C$200 (US$142) suite. Parking C$9 (US$6). AE, CB, DC, DISC, MC, V.

This contemporary and large downtown hotel features clean and understated styling, with all the underpinnings of elegance, like highly polished wainscoting, plush carpeting, and the discreet use of marble. Expect modern and comfortably appointed hotel rooms; the hotel was built in 1986, but all rooms were fully renovated in 1995, when the Japanese legation to the G-7 Summit meeting took over the hotel. Rooms have a selection of complimentary tea and coffee, along with irons and boards, coffeemakers, and hair dryers. The hotel is popular among business travelers, but the cordial staff makes individual travelers feel very much at home. It's nicely situated near the Citadel and restaurants, and linked to much of the rest of downtown via underground passageways.

Dining: Georgios on the first floor features contemporary bistro styling, with a menu to match. Dinners include burgers and pizza (all under C$10/US$7), along with more ambitious offerings like cilantro-and-lemon fettuccine, pine-nut crusted strip-loin of beef, and grilled halibut (C$12 to C$18/US$9 to $US13).

Services: Concierge, limited room service, valet parking, safe-deposit boxes. Baby-sitting, dry cleaning, and laundry may be arranged.

Facilities: There's a business center on premises, and a health club with an indoor pool, sauna, and whirlpool.

EXPENSIVE

Delta Barrington. 1875 Barrington St., Halifax, NS, B3J 3L6. ☎ **902/429-7410.** Fax 902/420-6524. 202 rms. A/C TV TEL MINIBAR. C$110–C$175 (US$78–US$124) double. Valet parking C$15 ($11); self-parking C$6 (US$4.30) weekends, C$9 (US$6) midweek. AE, DC, DISC, ER, JCB, MC, V.

Convenience and location form the cornerstones of the Delta Barrington, located just 1 block from the waterfront, 1 block from the Grand Parade, and connected to the Metro Centre and much of the rest of downtown by Pedway. It's a modern large hotel, but one that's been designed and furnished with an eye more to comfort than flash. The guest rooms are decorated with a contemporary country decor, with pine headboards and country-style reproduction furniture. The king rooms are spacious, furnished with sofas and easy chairs. Some rooms face the pedestrian plaza and have been soundproofed to block the noise from the evening rabble, but these windows don't open (most other rooms have opening windows). The quietest rooms face the courtyard, but lack a view. Pets allowed.

Dining: McNab's restaurant has a distinguished country-estate atmosphere, and is open for three meals daily. Luncheon entrees are under C$10 (US$7) and feature robust sandwiches and more elaborate fare like stuffed sole and asparagus and ricotta crêpes. For dinner, look for peppered shrimp, lamb loin with wild-mushroom strudel, and seared beef tenderloin with a Madeira jus.

Services: Concierge, 24-hour room service, nightly turndown, valet parking, safe-deposit boxes, and weekend children's programs. *Extra Charge:* Baby-sitting, dry cleaning, and laundry.

Facilities: There's an indoor pool and fitness room, along with health club, sauna, and whirlpool.

✪ Halliburton House Inn. 5184 Morris St., Halifax, NS, B3J 1B3. ☎ **902/420-0658.** Fax 902/423-2324. E-mail: halhouse@newedge.net. 28 rms (2 with shower only). A/C TV TEL. C$110–C$160 (US$78–US$114) double. Rates include continental breakfast and limited parking. AE, ER, MC, V.

The Halliburton House is a rare treasure: a well-appointed, well-run, and elegant country inn located in the heart of downtown. Named after former resident Sir Brenton Halliburton (Nova Scotia's first chief justice), the inn is spread among three town house–style buildings, which are connected via gardens but not internally. The main building was constructed in 1809 and converted to an inn in 1995 when it was modernized without any loss of native charm. All guest rooms are subtly furnished with fine antiques, but few are so rare that you'd fret about damaging them. The rooms are rich and masculine in tone, and light on frilly stuff. Among my favorites:

Room 113, which is relatively small but has a lovely working fireplace and unique skylit bathroom. Halliburton is the inn of choice among businesspeople, but it's also a romantic spot for couples. Smoking allowed in the library only.

Dining: This is home to one of Halifax's finest dining rooms; see "Dining," below.

Services: Room service is available, as are VCRs on request. Afternoon refreshments are set out. *Extra charge:* baby-sitting, dry cleaning, laundry.

Hotel Halifax. 1990 Barrington St., Halifax, NS, B3J 1P2. ☎ **800/441-1414** or 902/425-6700. Fax 902/425-6214. 300 rms. A/C MINIBAR TV TEL. C$115–C$155 (US$82–US$110) double. AE, ER, JCB, MC, V. Parking C$10 (US$7).

The Hotel Halifax is a slick and modern downtown hotel that offers the premium service Canadian Pacific Hotels are known for. It's located just a block off the waterfront and connected via skyway, but navigating involves a confusing labyrinth of parking garages and charmless concrete structures. Inside, the hotel has the muffled, sanctuarylike feel of a businessman's lair. About half the rooms have views of the harbor, and many have private balconies.

Dining: The Crown Dining Room offers informal bistro cuisine. Prices are quite reasonable, with most everything under C$13 (US$9). Entrees might include halibut with mango relish or cedar-plank salmon, along with a selection of pastas. The Sunday brunch is among the best in town.

Services: Children's program (including a special juice-and-cookie turndown service), concierge, limited room service, safe-deposit boxes, complimentary coffee, shopping arcade, and car-rental desk. *Extra charge:* Valet parking, dry cleaning, laundry, and baby-sitting.

Facilities: There's a fitness facility with indoor pool and sundeck.

MODERATE

Cambridge Suites. 1583 Brunswick St., Halifax, NS, B3J 3P5. ☎ **888/417-8483** or 902/420-0555. Fax 902/420-9379. 200 rms. A/C TV TEL MINIBAR. From C$110 (US$78) 1 bedrm suite. Rates include continental breakfast. Children under 18 stay free in parents' rm. AE, DC, ER, MC, V. Parking C$6 (US$4.30).

The popular Cambridge Suites chain hotel is nicely located near the foot of the Citadel and well-positioned for exploring Halifax. It's perfect for families—most units are two-room suites featuring kitchenettes with microwaves, two phones, coffeemakers, and hair dryers. Expect comfortable, inoffensive decor.

The rooftop fitness center has a whirlpool, sauna, weights, and exercise bikes. There's also a sundeck with barbecue grills, room service, safe-deposit boxes, and a concierge. *Extra charge:* self-service laundry, baby-sitting, dry cleaning, valet parking.

Waverly Inn. 1266 Barrington St., Halifax, NS, B3J 1Y5. ☎ **800/565-9346** or 902/423-9346. Fax 902/425-0167. E-mail: waverly@ra.isisnet.com. Web site: www.isisnet.com/waverly. 32 rms (7 with shower only). A/C TV TEL. Summer C$109–C$145 (US$77–US$103); off-season C$79–C$109 (US$56–US$77). Rates include light breakfast and parking. ER, MC, V.

The Waverly Inn has been adorned in high Victorian style as befits its 1866 provenance. Flamboyant playwright Oscar Wilde was a guest in 1882, and one suspects he had a hand in the decorating scheme. There's walnut trim, upholstered red furniture, and portraits of sourpuss Victorians at every turn. The headboards in the guest rooms are especially elaborate—some look like props from Gothic horror movies; guests of delicate constitution might suffer from a fitful slumber. Room 130 has a unique Chinese wedding bed and a Jacuzzi (nine rooms have private Jacuzzis). There's a common deck on which to enjoy sunny afternoons; a first-floor hospitality room stocks complimentary snacks and beverages for guests.

INEXPENSIVE

A short way from downtown but convenient to the bus lines are university dorm rooms open to travelers throughout the summer. **Dalhousie University** (☎ 902/ **494-8840**) has two-bedroom units in a 33-story tower on Fenwick Street. Rates are C$46 (US$33) per day (C$4/US$2.80 additional for parking), which includes access to the athletic facility. **Saint Mary's University** (☎ **888/345-5555** or 902/ 420-5486, or 902/420-5591 after 4:30pm) has 600 dorm rooms and apartments spread about its campus, which is located between Dalhousie University and Point Pleasant. Rates are C$33 (US$23) double, C$61 (US$43) for four guests in a two-bedroom apartment.

Budget motels and hotels are rare downtown, with most located along arterials leading into the city. The **Econo Lodge** (☎ **902/443-0303**) has 33 basic rooms at 560 Bedford Hwy., with rates starting at C$71 (US$50) double in summer. Across the MacKay Bridge in Dartmouth, just off Exit 3 on the Circumferential Highway, is the equally basic **Future Inns** (☎ **800/565-0700** or 902/465-6555), with rooms starting at C$57 (US$40) double.

DINING

If you find yourself wandering aimlessly around the waterfront near dinnertime, you'll do no better than to head to **The Brewery,** a sort of upscale diner's mall and office complex off Lower Water Street near Spring Garden Road. This creative adaptation of a stout old brewery has been deftly done, and hosts a limited selection of fine restaurants, including The Left Bank, City Deli, Cheelin (the city's best Chinese restaurant), and daMaurizio (the city's best restaurant, period; see below).

EXPENSIVE

✪ **daMaurizio.** 1496 Lower Water St. (in The Brewery). ☎ **902/423-0859.** Reservations highly recommended. Main courses C$17–C$23 (US$12–US$16). AE, DISC, ER, MC, V. Mon–Sat 5:30–10pm. ITALIAN.

Halifax's best restaurant does everything right. Located in a cleverly adapted former brewery, the vast space has been divided into a complex of hives with columns and exposed brick that add to the atmosphere and heighten the anticipation of the meal. The decor shuns decorative doodads for clean lines and simple class. Much the same might be said of the menu. You could start with an appetizer of squid quick-cooked with olive oil, tomato, and chilies, or an avocado salad garnished with crab and shrimp. You won't be disappointed if you order pasta appetizers—like the pumpkin-filled ravioli served with citrus duck sauce. The main courses tax even the most decisive of diners: There's veal scaloppini with prosciutto and arugula, marinated Atlantic salmon with fresh herbs, and seafood braised with tomato and cilantro. The kitchen doesn't try to dazzle with creativity, but relies instead on the best ingredients and a close eye on perfect preparation.

Halliburton House Inn. 5184 Morris St. ☎ **902/420-0658.** Reservations recommended. Main courses C$17–C$28 (US$12–US$20). AE, ER, MC, V. Daily 5:30–10pm. EUROPEAN.

The intimate, dusky Halliburton House—home to the city's best small hotel (see above)—also hosts one of its better restaurants. The setting is quiet and wonderful, and the menu small but inventive. Appetizers tend toward familiar favorites like bouillabaisse and a smoked trout plate. But the entrees sail before a more creative wind, with offerings like buffalo rib eye, Creole-curried lamb, and seafood *vol-au-vent* (in puff pastry). The fresh seafood is always reliable.

✪ **Ryan Duffy's Steak and Seafood.** 5640 Spring Garden Rd. ☎ **902/421-1116.** Reservations helpful. Main courses C$14–C$24 (US$10–US$17). AE, DC, DISC, ER, MC, V.

Dining rm Sun–Thurs 5–10pm, Fri–Sat 5–11pm. Grill Mon–Sat 11:30am–midnight (approx.),
Sun 5–11pm. STEAK HOUSE.

Located on the upper level of a moderately chichi shopping mall on Spring Garden,
Ryan Duffy's will at first strike diners as a knockoff of a middle-brow chain, like
TGIFriday's. It's not. It's many notches above. The house specialty is steak, for which
the place is justly famous. The beef comes from corn-fed Hereford, black angus, and
short horn, and is wonderfully tender. Steaks are grilled over a natural wood
charcoal, and can be prepared with garlic on request. The more expensive cuts
are trimmed right at the table. The rest of the menu—including the veggies accompanying the steak—tends to be yawn-inspiring but is easily worth enduring if you're
feeling carnivorous.

MODERATE

Il Mercato. 5475 Spring Garden Rd. ☎ **902/422-2866.** Main courses C$9–C$12
(US$6–US$9). AE, DC, MC, V. Mon–Sat 11am–11pm. NORTHERN ITALIAN.

Light-colored Tuscan sponged walls, big rustic terra-cotta tiles on the floor, and a
fountain amid the hubbub of the room will whisk you promptly to northern Italy.
You'll also find a good selection of meals at prices that approach bargain level.
Pastas run C$9 to C$12 (US$6 to $US9); every entree is less than C$15 (US$11).
The focaccias are superb and come with a decent salad. Non-Italian entrees include
a seafood medley and grilled strip-loin with wild-mushroom sauce.

Mundo Latino. 1813 Granville St. ☎ **902/429-0411.** Reservations recommended. Lunch
C$6–C$10 (US$4.30–US$7); main courses C$10–C$18 (US$7–US$13). AE, ER, MC, V. Mon–Sat
11am–10pm. ECLECTIC/LATINO.

Mundo Latino—one of Halifax's newer entries in the international dining category—
is upscale without being stuffy, eclectic without being zany. Dining is on three
levels—I'd ask for the more spacious and airy second level—with the open kitchen
on the second floor. The colors are richly hued, like burgundy, mustard, and peach,
and the lightly mottled walls lend a festive, tropical air. The menu pulls off the feat
of being at once exotic and familiar. Some examples: rotisserie chicken served with
Brazilian rice; Atlantic squid stuffed with pine nuts, raisins, and shrimp;
and gratinated shark served on a chunky tomato sauce. The Brazilian seafood stew
(prepared with coconut milk and cashews) is especially delectable.

Sweet Basil Bistro. 1866 Upper Water St. (in Historic Properties). ☎ **902/425-2133.**
Reservations recommended. Main courses C$8–C$17 (US$6–US$12). AE, DC, ER, MC, V. Daily
11:30am–11pm. SEAFOOD/CONTEMPORARY.

If hunger overtakes you while snooping around the waterfront's shopping district, this
should be your destination. It has the feel of a trattoria, but the menu far transcends
the limited offerings that implies. Pastas are well represented (especially good is the
squash ravioli with Parmesan and hazelnut sauce), but you'll also fine spicy tanger-
ine chicken, pork tenderloin with caramelized apples, and scallops and shrimp on
lemongrass skewers. The best name? Slash 'n Burn Salmon, a spicy fillet served with
a mango-basil sauce.

INEXPENSIVE

Granite Brewery. 1222 Barrington St. ☎ **902/423-5660.** Reservations usually not necessary. Main courses C$6–C$12 (US$4.30–US$9). AE, DC, MC, V. Mon–Sat 11:30am–12:30am,
Sun noon–11pm. BREW PUB.

Eastern Canada's pioneer brew pub—this was the first—is housed in an austere building far down Barrington Street, near the Westin Hotel. The starkly handsome 1834
stone building has a medium-fancy dining room upstairs with red tablecloths and

captain's chairs. The pubbier downstairs is more boisterous and informal. You can order off the same menu from either spot, and it's what you'd expect at a brew pub. Entrees include steak sandwich, burgers, and Mediterranean meat loaf. Try the "peculiar pork tenderloin," topped with a sauce made with their trademark dark ale. Plans call for a second Granite Brewery restaurant closer to downtown attractions, but no date was set for an opening at press time.

Satisfaction Feast. 1581 Grafton St. ☎ **902/422-3540.** Reservations not accepted. Main courses C$5–C$12 (US$3.60–US$9). AE, MC, V. Mon–Sat 9am–10pm (to 9pm Mon–Thurs in winter), Sun 5–10pm. VEGETARIAN.

Located along the newly cool stretch of Grafton Street, Satisfaction Feast is Halifax's original vegetarian restaurant. The restaurant recently added a canopy and sidewalk tables for summer lounging, and generally spruced the place up. It's still funky and fun, but not so much that it will alarm those who eat meat and vote conservative. Entrees include lasagna, bean burritos, pesto pasta, veggie burgers, and a macrobiotic rice casserole. The vegan fruit crisp is the dessert to hold out for. Satisfaction Feast also does a brisk business in takeout; think about a hummus-and-pita picnic atop nearby Citadel Hill.

HALIFAX AFTER DARK

For organized entertainment, stop by the visitor center and ask for a copy of *Where Halifax,* a comprehensive monthly guide to the city's entertainment. Among the city's premier venues for shows are the downtown **Halifax Metro Centre,** 5248 Duke St. (☎ 902/451-1202 for recorded information), which hosts sporting events and major concerts, such as Garth Brooks, Bob Dylan, a monster-truck rally, and the Elvis Stojko skating tour.

The **Neptune Theatre,** 1593 Argyle St. (☎ 902/429-7070), benefited from a recent 2-year, C$13.5-million renovation and now also includes an intimate 200-seat studio theater. Top-notch dramatic productions are offered throughout the year. (The main season runs October to May, with a summer season filling in the gap.) Main-stage tickets range from C$21 to C$33 (US$15 to US$23).

For a more informal dramatic night out, there's the **Grafton Street Dinner Theater,** 1741 Grafton St. (☎ 902/425-1961), which typically offers light musicals and mysteries with a three-course dinner (choice of prime rib, salmon, or chicken Kiev).

For disorganized entertainment: The young and restless seem to congregate in pubs, nightclubs, and on street corners along two axes that converge at the public library: **Grafton Street** and **Spring Garden Road.** (In fact, the small park fronting the library may be *the* hangout scene in early evening.) If you're thirsty, wander the neighborhoods around here and you're likely to find a spot that could serve as a temporary home for the evening.

A number of popular clubs offer live music around town. Check *The Coast,* Halifax's free weekly newspaper (widely available), for details. Among the clubs offering more consistent fare is the **Palace Cabaret,** 1721 Brunswick St. (☎ 902/429-5959), with a cover charge typically around C$5 (US$3.60).

8 The Eastern Shore

When I was growing up we had two ways to drive to my grandparents' house: the short cut and the long cut. The Eastern Shore is the long cut between Halifax and Cape Breton Island. The twisting roads are longer and slower than Route 102 and Route 104, but you'll be rewarded with glimpses of a fierce and rugged coastline that's much wilder and more remote than the coast south of Halifax. Communities tend to be further apart, and those that you come upon have fewer services and fewer tourists. With its rugged terrain and remote locales, this is the preferred destination for those drawn to the outdoors and looking for solitude.

Be forewarned that this region isn't always breathtakingly scenic if you limit yourself to the main routes. To get the most out of the Eastern Shore, you should be committed to making periodic detours down dead-end roads to coastal peninsulas, where you might come upon wild roses blooming madly in the fog, or inland to the lush forest, home of moose and sudden dusk.

ESSENTIALS

GETTING THERE Route 107 and Route 7 run along or near the coast from Dartmouth to Stillwater (near Sherbrooke). A patchwork of other routes—including 211, 316, 16, and 344—continue onward along the coast to the causeway to Cape Breton. (It's all pretty obvious on a map.) An excursion along the entire coastal route—from Dartmouth to Cape Breton Island with a detour to Canso—is 422 kilometers (253 miles).

VISITOR INFORMATION Several tourist information centers are staffed along the route. You'll find the best stocked and most helpful centers at **Sheet Harbor** (open daily 9am to 7pm), **Sherbrooke Village** (at the museum, open 9:30am to 5:30pm daily), and **Canso,** 1297 Union St. (☎ **902/366-2170**).

EXPLORING THE EASTERN SHORE

This section assumes travel northeastward from Halifax toward Cape Breton. If you're traveling the opposite direction, hold the book upside down.

Between Halifax and Sheet Harbor the route plays hide-and-seek with the coast, touching the water periodically before veering inland. The most scenic areas are around wild and open **Ship Harbor,** and **Spry Harbor,** noted for its attractive older homes and islands looming offshore.

Between Ship and Spry harbors is the town of Tangier, home to **Coastal Adventures** (☎ **902/772-2774**), which specializes in kayak tours. It's run and owned by Scott Cunningham and Gayle Wilson. Cunningham literally wrote the book on Nova Scotia kayaking—he's the author of the definitive guide to paddling the coast. This well-run operation is situated on a beautiful, island-clogged part of the coast, but specializes in multiday trips throughout Atlantic Canada. You're best off writing (P.O. Box 77, Tangier, NS, B0J 3H0) or calling for a brochure in advance.

Northeast of Spry Harbor watch for signs to **Taylor Head Provincial Park** (no phone). A 3-mile corrugated dirt road offers access to several attractive hiking trails, or you can continue to the end. Short trails through a scrubby wood lead to a long and beautiful fine-grained sand beach with views out to evergreen-clad islands. Bathers splash around on weekends, but weekdays it's often empty and wild. Admission is free.

Sheet Harbor (pop. 900) is a pleasant, small town with a campground, a couple of small grocery stores, two motels, and a visitor information booth, behind which is a short nature trail and boardwalk that descends to rocky cascades. Inland from Sheet Harbor on Route 374 is the **Liscomb Game Sanctuary,** which is a popular destination for hearty, self-contained explorers equipped with map, compass, canoe, and fishing rod. There are no services to speak of for casual travelers.

Continuing on Route 211 beyond historic **Sherbrooke Village** (see below), you'll drive through a wonderful landscape of lakes, ocean inlets, and upland bogs and soon come to the scenic **County Harbor Ferry.** The 12-car cable ferry crosses each direction every half hour; it's a picturesque crossing of a broad river encased by rounded and wooded bluffs. The fare is C$1.75 (US$1.25) for car and driver. The ferry isn't always running, so it's wise to check at the Canso or Sherbrooke visitor centers before setting off.

Further along (you'll be on Route 316 after the ferry), you'll come to **Tor Bay Provincial Park.** It's 4 kilometers (2.4 miles) off the main road, but well worth the detour on a sunny day. The park features three sandy crescent beaches backed by grassy dunes and small ponds that are slowly being taken over by bog and spruce forest. The short boardwalk loop is especially picturesque.

Way out on the eastern tip of Nova Scotia's mainland is the end-of-the-world town of **Canso** (pop. 1,200). It's a rough-edged fishing and oil-shipping town, often wind-swept and foggy. The chief attraction here is **Grassy Island National Historic Site** (☎ **902/366-3136**). First stop by the small interpretive center on the waterfront and ask about the boat schedule. A park-run boat will take you out to the island, which once housed a lively community of fishermen and traders from New England. (The interpretive center features artifacts recovered from the island.) A trail links several historic sites on this island, which tends to be a bit melancholy whether foggy or not. The boat serves the island from May to mid-August daily from 10am to 6pm. Fares are C$2.50 (US$1.80) for adults, C$2 (US$1.40) for seniors, and C$1.50 (US$1) for children 6 to 16; children under 6 are free.

Route 16 between the intersection of Route 316 and Guysborough is an uncommonly **scenic drive.** The road runs high and low along brawny hills, affording soaring views of Chedabucto Bay and grassy hills across the way. Also pleasant, although not quite as distinguished, is Route 344 from Guysborough to the Canso causeway. The road twists, turns, and drops through woodlands with some nice views of the strait. It will make you wish you were on a motorcycle.

About half the town of Sherbrooke comprises ✪ **Sherbrooke Village,** Route 7, Sherbrooke (☎ **902/522-2400**), a historic section surrounded by low fences, water, and fields. (It's managed as part of the Nova Scotia Museum.) You'll have to pay admission to get in, but it's well worth it. This is the largest restored village in Nova Scotia, and it's unique in several respects. For one, almost all of the buildings are on their original sites (only two have been moved). Also, many homes are still occupied by local residents, and private homes are interspersed with the buildings open to the public. The church is still used for services on Sundays, and you can order a meal at the old Sherbrooke Hotel. (The fish cakes and oven-baked beans are good.)

Some 25 buildings are open to the public, ranging from a very convincing general store to the operating blacksmith shop and post office. Look also for the temperance hall, courthouse, printery, boatbuilding shop, drugstore, and school house. These are staffed by genial costumed interpreters, who can tell you about life in the 1860s. Be sure to ask about the source of the town's early prosperity, which may surprise you. Admission is C$6 (US$4.30) for adults, C$5 (US$3.60) for seniors, C$3 (US$2.10) for children, and C$18 (US$13) for families. It's open daily from 9:30am to 5:30pm (closed mid-October to June 1).

ACCOMMODATIONS & DINING

Other than a handful of motels and B&Bs, there are few accommodations available on the Eastern Shore. This is one area where it definitely behooves normally spontaneous travelers to plan ahead.

Liscomb Lodge. Rte. 7, Liscomb Mills, NS, B0J 2A0. ☎ **800/665-6343** or 902/779-2307. Fax 902/779-2700. 30 rms, 15 chalets, 5 cottages. TV TEL. C$110 (US$78) double; inquire about packages. AE, DC, ER, MC, V.

This modern complex, owned and operated by the province, consists of a central lodge and a series of smaller cottages and outbuildings. It's situated in a remote part of the coast, adjacent to hiking trails and a popular boating area at the mouth of the Liscomb River. The lodge bills itself as "the nature lover's resort," and indeed it offers good access to both forest and water. But it's not exactly rustic, with well-tended lawns, bland modern architecture, shuffleboard, a marina, and even an oversized outdoor chessboard. (It's a popular stop for bus tours.) The rooms are modern and motel-like, and the cottages and chalets have multiple bedrooms and are well suited to families. Pets are allowed in the chalets only. The dining room is open to the public and serves the usual resort fare. Especially popular is the salmon cooked on a cedar plank. In addition to the shuffleboard and so forth mentioned above, there's an indoor pool and fitness center, tennis court, room service, and a gift shop.

✪ **Seawind Landing Country Inn.** 1 Wharf Rd., Charlos Cove, NS, B0H 1T0. ☎ **800/ 563-4667.** Fax 902/525-2108. E-mail: jcolvin@auracom.com. Web site: www.grassroots.ns.ca/ ~seawind. 12 rms (4 with shower only). C$70–C$95 (US$50–US$68). Rates include deluxe continental breakfast. MC, V.

What to do when your boatbuilding business plummets as the fisheries decline? How about opening an inn. That's what Lorraine and Jim Colvin did, and their 20-acre oceanfront compound is delightful and inviting. Half of the guest rooms are in the 130-year-old main house, which has been tastefully modernized and updated. The others are in a more recent outbuilding—what you lose in historic charm, you make up in brightness, space, ocean views, and double Jacuzzis (all outbuilding rooms have them). The innkeepers are especially knowledgeable about local artists (much of the work on display here was produced nearby) and have compiled an unusually literate and helpful guide to the region for guests to peruse. The property has three private sand beaches, and coastal boat tours and picnic lunches can be easily arranged. The inn serves dinner nightly (inn guests only), featuring local products prepared in a country-French style. No smoking.

9 Pictou

These historic towns are both located on the Northumberland Straits (Nova Scotia's "north shore," which faces Prince Edward Island). Both are convenient to the heavily traveled route between Amherst and Cape Breton. Both have reputations as spots to visit while in transit, although not necessarily as final destinations. Pictou is a bit more settled and scenic than Antigonish, and is well worth an overnight detour.

Pictou was established as part of a development scheme hatched by speculators from Philadelphia in 1760. Under the terms of their land grant, they needed to place some 250 settlers at the harbor. That was a problem. So the company sent a ship called the *Hector* to Scotland in 1773 to drum up some impoverished souls who might be more amenable to starting life over in North America.

This worked out rather better, and the ship returned with some 200 passengers, mostly Gaelic-speaking Highlanders. The voyage was brutal and full of storms, and the passengers were threatened with starvation. But they eventually arrived at Pictou, and disembarked wearing Tartans and playing bagpipes.

The anniversary of their arrival is celebrated in mid-August each year with the **Hector Festival** (☎ **800/353-5338**), when you might spot members of the clans wearing kilts and dining out in high style in memory of their ancestors. Pictou's Scottish enough that you might find yourself a bit wary that the locals might try to slip some beastly haggis into you while you're not paying attention.

ESSENTIALS

GETTING THERE   Pictou is located on Route 106, which is just north of Exit 22 off Route 104 (the south branch of the Trans-Canada Highway). The Prince Edward Island ferry is several kilometers north of town at the coast near Caribou. (See the Prince Edward Island chapter for details on the ferry.)

VISITOR INFORMATION   The **Tourist Information Centre** (☎ 902/485-6213) is located just off the rotary at the junction of routes 106 and 6. It's open daily from 8am to 8pm mid-May to mid-October.

EXPLORING PICTOU

Pictou is a pleasant and historic harborside town with an abundance of interesting architecture. There's a surfeit of dour sandstone buildings adorned with five-sided dormers, and at times you might think you've wandered down an Edinburgh side street. Water Street is especially attractive, and offers an above-average selection of boutiques, casual restaurants, and pubs. Look for the headquarters and factory outlet of **Grohmann Knives,** 116 Water St. (☎ 902/486-4224). Located in a 1950s-mod building with a large knife piercing one corner, you'll find a good selection of quality knives (each with a lifetime guarantee) at marked-down prices. It's open daily; free factory tours are offered between 9am and 3pm.

Pictou's one downside is the huge and unsightly paper mill across the harbor. Even when it's obscured in the fog, you can often tell it's there by the sulfurous smell.

Learn about the hardships endured on the 1773 voyage of the singularly unseaworthy *Hector*—which brought Scottish settlers to the region—at this modern **Hector Heritage Quay,** 29–33 Caladh Ave. (☎ 888/485-4844 or 902/485-8028), on the waterfront in downtown Pictou. You'll pass by intriguing exhibits en route to the museum's centerpiece: a full-sized replica of the 110-foot *Hector* that's currently under construction at the water's edge. Stop by the blacksmith and carpentry shops to get a picture of life in the colonies in the early days. Admission is C$3 (US$2.10) for adults, C$2.25 (US$1.60) for seniors and teens, C$1 (US70¢) for children 6 to 12, and C$8 (US$6) for families; children under 6 are free. It's open May to October, daily from 9am to 9pm.

ACCOMMODATIONS

Braeside Inn. 126 Front St., Pictou NS, B0K 1H0. ☎ 800/617-7701 or 902/485-5046. Fax 902/485-1701. 20 rms. TV TEL. C$55–C$110 (US$39–US$78) double. AE, ER, MC, V. At the end of Water St. make a right on Coleraine St., then left on Front St.

This very pleasant, very friendly inn is situated on 5 leafy acres at the edge of downtown, on a low hill overlooking the harbor. This squarish three-story hotel was built in 1938 as an inn, and it's consistently been one of the town's foremost hostelries. The public rooms are done up in soothing pinks and greens, although it's not very fussy and looks better than it sounds. The TV room has a profusion of wingback chairs and is a good spot to settle in with a book or to catch up on the news before dinner. The guest rooms are all carpeted and comfortable. No smoking in the guest rooms. The well-regarded dining room has hardwood floors and views down a lawn and across the gravel lot to the harbor. Entrees aren't terribly exciting but are well prepared, with selections like rack of lamb, seafood casserole, and roast duckling. Entrees cost from C$18.50 to C$25 (US$13 to US$18). It's also open for lunch (summer only) and breakfast. Dinner reservations are suggested.

Consulate Inn. 157 Water St., Pictou, NS, B0K 1H0. ☎ 800/424-8283 or 902/485-4554. Fax 902/485-1532. 8 rms and suites. TV. C$54–C$115 (US$38–US$82) double. Rates include continental breakfast. AE, MC, V.

No surprise: This doughty 1810 historic home of sandstone and ivy was originally a consulate, in this case used by the Americans. Three guest rooms are upstairs in the main building and share a handsome sitting area; five luxurious suites are in the modern cottage next door. The inn is conveniently located for exploring Pictou; the PEI ferry is just a 10-minute drive away. The room rates offer good value. The Vines is the inn's elegant first-floor restaurant (seasonal), where you'll find white tablecloths and elaborately fanned napkins. It's dim and intimate, and when the kitchen surprises diners, it's invariably for the better. The Study is more informal and centers around a fireplace.

Pictou Lodge Resort. Shore Rd. (P.O. Box 1539), Pictou, NS, B0K 1H0. ☎ **800/495-6343** or 902/485-4322. Fax 902/485-4945. 65 rms. TV TEL. C$79–C$195 (US$56–US$138) double. DISC, MC, V. Follow Shore Rd. from downtown toward PEI ferry; watch for signs. Closed mid-Oct to May.

The original rustic log lodge and a handful of log outbuildings have gone through a number of owners—including Canadian National Railway—since entrepreneurs built the compound on a far-off grassy bluff overlooking a beach early in this century. The current owners acquired it in 1982, and have steadily made improvements. Four new buildings went up in 1995 adding significantly to the number of guest rooms; in 1996 they added a heated outdoor pool and a battery of propane grills for guests. The older log rooms, most of which have kitchenettes, have considerably more character but some regard them as a bit dowdy. The newer rooms have the bland sameness of motel rooms everywhere. The lodge is located about a 10-minute drive from downtown, but has a wonderfully remote feel. Lunch and dinner are served in the Adirondack-style lodge, with its soaring spaces hammered together of time-burnished logs. Entrees range from C$13 to C$25 (US$9 to US$18).

DINING

For an unhurried, relaxed meal in decidedly unstuffy environs, try the **Stone House Cafe,** 13 Water St. (☎ 902/465-6885). There's a decent selection of pizza (including a nasty sounding lobster, scallop, and haddock pizza), and basic meals like smoked pork chops, lasagna, croquettes, and roast chicken. Most entrees are around C$10 to C$15 (US$7 to US$11).

Fougere's. 91 Water St. ☎ **902/485-1575.** Reservations helpful. Main courses C$15–C$20 (US$11–US$14). DC, ER, MC, V. Daily 4–10pm. Closed Jan–Mar. UPSCALE TRADITIONAL.

Fougere's has a new, bright, sparely furnished dining room right downtown that's as appealing as it is tidy. You wouldn't expect much less from Ben Fougere, who long attracted crowds to his old bistro out near the ferry. The fancier digs haven't changed the attitude of his kitchen, which subscribes to the notion that you should be able to get a good roast turkey dinner at a reasonable price. Ben knows how to do the basics better than almost anyone, with a menu that reads like a trip to grandma's house: smoked pork chops, poached salmon, prime rib, and chicken cordon bleu (well, *somebody's* grandmother's house). Save room for the shortcakes topped with this week's berries, or the sinful butterscotch sundae.

Piper's Landing. Rte. 376, Lyons Brook. ☎ **902/485-1200.** Reservations recommended. Lunch main courses C$5–C$10.50 (US$3.50–US$8); dinner main courses C$13–C$22.50 (US$9–US$16). AE, MC, V. Mon–Sat 11:30am–2:30pm and 4–9pm, Sun 11am–9pm. From the Pictou Rotary take Rte. 376 toward Lyons Brook; it's 3km (1.8 miles) on your left. UPSCALE TRADITIONAL.

This contemporary and attractive dining room on a stretch of residential road outside of Pictou began drawing crowds shortly after it opened a few years ago and quickly became a local favorite. Expect some sleight of hand after you settle in. The decor has a spare elegance that's as understated as it is understood. Likewise, the menu looks simple—entrees include grilled beef tenderloin, pork schnitzel, and a seafood platter—but you'll be impressed by the flair in preparation, and the tremendous civility of the service. The wine list, alas, is small and tired.

10 Cape Breton Island

The isolated and craggy island of Cape Breton—Nova Scotia's northernmost landmass—should be high on the list of don't-miss destinations for travelers, especially those with an adventurous bent. The island's chief draw is Cape Breton Highlands National Park, far north on the island's western lobe. But there's also the historic fort at Louisbourg and scenic Bras d'Or Lake, the inland saltwater lake that nearly cleaves the island in two. Above all, there are the picturesque drives. It's hard to find a road that's not a scenic route in Cape Breton. By turns the vistas are wild and dramatic, then settled and pastoral.

When traveling on the island, be alert to the cultural richness. Just as southern Nova Scotia was largely settled by English Loyalists fleeing the United States after they lost the War of Independence, Cape Breton was principally settled by Highland Scots whose families had come out on the wrong side of rebellions against the Crown. You can still see that heritage in the accents of elders in some of the more remote villages, and in the great popularity of British-style folk music.

You'll often hear references to the ✪ **Cabot Trail** when on the island. This is the official designation for the 280-kilometer (175-mile) roadway around the northwest part of the island, which encompasses the national park. It's named after John Cabot, whom many believe first set foot on North American soil near Cape North. (Many don't believe that, however, especially those in Newfoundland.)

If you're in a hurry, you'd do well to base out of Baddeck, which is centrally located, offers the best accommodations and restaurants, and is well positioned for day excursions to the island's two best attractions: the national park and the reconstructed historic settlement of Louisbourg. The southeastern portion of the island—near Isle Madame and Port Hawkesbury—can be picturesque in parts, but isn't nearly as inviting as the rest of the island. I'd encourage travelers to focus more on the west and central sections.

One note: I've divided Cape Breton into two sections: Cape Breton Island and Cape Breton Highlands National Park. Jump ahead to the next section for information on adventures in the park itself.

ESSENTIALS

GETTING THERE   Cape Breton is connected to the mainland via the Canso Causeway, an 80-foot wide, 217-foot deep, 4,300-foot long stone causeway built in 1955 with 10 million tons of rock. The causeway is 271 kilometers (163 miles) from the New Brunswick border at Amherst, 282 kilometers (169 miles) from Halifax.

VISITOR INFORMATION   Nine tourist information centers dot the island. The best stocked (and a strongly recommended first stop) is the bustling **Port Hastings Info Centre** (☎ **902/625-4201**) located just over the Canso Causeway. It's open mid-May to mid-October, daily from 9am to 5pm.

MABOU & VICINITY

Mabou (pop. 400) is situated on a deep and protected inlet along the island's picturesque west shore. Scenic drives and bike rides are a dime a dozen hereabouts; few roads fail to yield up opportunities to break out the camera or just to lean against your vehicle and enjoy the panorama. The residents are strongly oriented toward music in their activities, unusually so, even for musical Cape Breton Island.

Evening entertainment tends to revolve around fiddle playing, square dancing, or a traditional gathering of musicians and storytellers called a *ceilidh* (pronounced *kay*-lee—don't ask). To find out where things are going on, stop by The Mull (see below) and scope out the bulletin board.

In a handsome valley between Mabou and Inverness is the distinctive post-and-beam **Glenora Distillery** (☎ 800/839-0491 or 902/258-2662). This modern distillery began producing single-malt whiskey in 1990 in charred oak barrels. This includes scotch, which can't technically be called such because it isn't made in Scotland. This is currently the only single-malt distillery in North America. Tours are C$4 (US$2.80) and last about half an hour. The bad news? The product is being aged for at least 10 years, and can't be sampled until the year 2000.

The distillery has an adjoining restaurant and nine-room hotel; traditional music is often scheduled for weekends or evenings in the contemporary pub.

ACCOMMODATIONS

✪ **Duncreigan Country Inn.** Rte. 19, Mabou, NS, B0E IX0. ☎ **800/840-2207** or 902/945-2207. 8 rms. TV TEL. C$80–C$130 (US$57–US$92) double. Rates include continental breakfast. AE, MC, V.

The Duncreigan occupies a quiet, wooded bluff just across the bridge from the village. Modern and airy (it was built in 1991), the inn manages to meld contemporary and traditional in a most appealing way. Guest rooms are located in the main lodge and an outbuilding (connected via boardwalk), and the landscaping is beginning to mature quite nicely. The rooms are uniformly wonderful, many decorated in soothing dark-burgundy tones, and all have radios and ceiling fans. Many are furnished with Nova Scotian antiques, with headboards creatively designed by a local artisan to match the furnishings. Room 2 has a superb water view, although my favorite is Room 5 with its wood-burning stove, whirlpool, and deck overlooking the estuary. No smoking. Dinners are served Tuesday to Sunday nights from mid-June to mid-October. Entrees might include grilled salmon, lemon-peppered pork tenderloin, or scallops with pesto. The prix-fixe four-course dinner is C$28.50 (US$20); reservations are suggested.

DINING

The Mull. Rte. 19 (north of village), Mabou. ☎ **902/945-2244.** Reservations accepted for parties of 6 or more. Sandwiches C$4.50–C$7 (US$3.20–US$5); main courses C$12–C$15 (US$9–US$11). AE, DISC, MC, V. Daily 9am–11pm. CAFE.

The Mull is a simple country deli that serves simple, well-prepared food. Lunches tend toward items like seafood chowder, fish-and-chips, and deli-style sandwiches. After 5pm, the dinner menu kicks in, with entrees like grilled halibut, T-bone steak, and scallops in a light wine sauce. Don't expect to be wowed by fancy; do expect a satisfying and filling meal.

CHETICAMP

The Acadian town of Chéticamp (pop. 1,000) is the western gateway to Cape Breton Highlands National Park and the center for French-speaking culture on Cape Breton. It consists of an assortment of restaurants, boutiques, and tourist traps spread along Main Street, which closely parallels the harbor. It's plainly a tourist town—you can tell by the steady stream of RVs lumbering slowly through—but thanks to the short summer season, it seems to have avoided the commercial depredations suffered by other tourist venues, and the views up the coast toward the Highlands remain

outstanding. It's a good place for provisioning, topping off the gas tank, or finding shelter at one of the no-frills motels.

Chéticamp is noted worldwide for its hooked rugs, a craft perfected by early Acadian settlers. In the 1930s artisans formed the **Co-operative Artisanale de Chéticamp,** located at 774 Main St. (☎ **902/224-2170**). There's a small museum downstairs, and you can shop for rugs and local music upstairs. A small restaurant on the premises serves traditional meals.

Flip ahead to the next section for information on national-park activities.

ACCOMMODATIONS

A handful of motels service the thousands of travelers who pass through each summer. **Laurie's Motor Inn,** on Main Street (☎ **800/959-4253** or 902/224-2400), has more than 50 motel rooms in three buildings, with rates of C$85 to C$125 (US$60 to US$89). **Parkview Motel,** Route 19 north of town (☎ **902/224-3232**), is near the park entrance and peacefully away from the hubbub of town. Rooms are around C$80 (US$57) for two.

Pilot Whale Lodge. Rte. 19, Chéticamp, NS, B0E 1H0. ☎ **902/224-2592.** Fax 902/224-1540. 6 cottages. TV. C$100 (US$71) double. Each additional child C$10 (US$7) extra; adults C$20 (US$14) extra. AE, MC, V.

These spanking new cottages (opened summer 1997) all have two bedrooms and full housekeeping facilities, including a microwave. The kitchens are especially a blessing in a town that lacks notable restaurants. These spare, handsome cottages have a bit of an antiseptic, condo air, but are well equipped with TVs and VCRs, gas barbecues, coffeemakers, decks, and woodstoves. The best feature, though, is the grand view toward the coastal mountains. (Cottages 1, 2, 4, and 5 have the best vistas.) Plans call for additional guest rooms in the walk-out basements in 1998, which may poach somewhat on the current privacy of the cottages.

DINING

Chéticamp has a number of family-style restaurants that are adequate for a quick bite to eat. But there's really no place you'd want to linger over a long lunch or dinner. **La Chaloupe,** on Main Street (☎ **902/274-3710**), has a fine harbor view, a good selection of deli sandwiches, and a handful of Acadian specialties. The onion rings are crispy and good; the chowder heavily favors potatoes over fish.

INGONISH

The area includes a number of similarly named towns (Ingonish Centre, Ingonish Ferry, South Ingonish Harbor) which together have a population of about 1,300. Like Chéticamp on the peninsula's east side, Ingonish serves as a gateway to the national park and is home to a park visitor information center and a handful of motels and restaurants. Oddly, there's really no critical mass here—the services are spread along a lengthy stretch of the Cabot Trail, and there's never any sense of arrival. You pass a liquor store, some shops, a post office, and a handful of cottages. Then you're suddenly in the park.

Highlights in the area include a **sandy beach** good for chilly splashing around (near Keltic Lodge), and a number of shorter hiking trails. (See "Cape Breton Highlands National Park," below.) **The Highland Links** golf course (☎ **800/441-1118**) is considered one of the best in Nova Scotia, if not all of Atlantic Canada. South of Ingonish the Cabot Trail climbs and descends the hairy 1,200-foot-high promontory of **Cape Smoky,** which explodes into panoramic views from the top.

ACCOMMODATIONS

A number of serviceable cottage courts and motels are located in this area. These include **Ingonish Chalets** in Ingonish Beach (☎ **902/285-2008**), which has seven cottages for C$129 (US$92) per double and five suites for C$89 (US$63) each. The **Glenghorn Beach Resort** in Ingonish (☎ **902/286-2049**) has 51 units on a spacious property that fronts a sand beach. Some rooms feature painted cinder-block walls and the decorating is a bit dated, with avocado and gold hues that recall a thankfully bygone era. Options include motel rooms and efficiencies, along with cottages. Prices are C$68 to C$110 (US$48 to US$78).

Keltic Lodge. Middle Head Peninsula, Ingonish Beach, NS, B0C 1L0. ☎ **800/565-0444** or 902/285-2880. Fax 902/285-2859. Web site: www.gov.ns.ca/resorts. 72 rms, 26 cottages. TV TEL. C$268–C$283 (US$190–US$201) double. Rates include breakfast and dinner. AE, DC, DISC, ER, MC, V. Open year-round, but main lodge closed in off-season.

The Keltic Lodge is reached after a series of dramatic flourishes: you pass through a grove of white birches, cross an isthmus atop angular cliffs, and then arrive at the stunning, vaguely Tudor resort that dominates the narrow peninsula. The views are extraordinary. Owned and operated by the province, the resort is comfortable without being slick, nicely worn without being threadbare. Some of the guest rooms are painted in that soothing mint green that was popular in the 1940s; most are furnished rather plainly with run-of-the-mill motel furniture. (You expect more for the price.) The cottages are set amid birches and have four bedrooms; you can rent just one bedroom and share a common living room with other guests. Be aware that some of the guest rooms are located at the modern White Birch Inn nearby, which has better views but a more sterile character.

Dining: The management keeps up appearances in the main dining room: No jeans, shorts, or sweat clothes are allowed. The C$40 (US$28) fixed-price dinner menu (included in room rates) offers several selections. Prime rib and lemon-pepper salmon fillet are favorites.

Facilities: The Highland Links—an adjacent 18-hole golf course—is under separate management, but is a major draw (ask about packages). A recent overhaul has boosted the course's reputation among serious duffers, who now come for more than just the ocean views. Also on the grounds: a heated ocean-side pool, game room, laundry service, guest safe, and a great hiking trail that's worth strolling at least once a day. Tennis courts are nearby, as is a sand beach.

BADDECK

Although Baddeck (pronounced "Bah-*deck*") is a good distance from the national park, it's generally considered the de facto "capital" of the Cabot Trail. It offers the best selection of hotels and accommodations along the whole loop, an assortment of restaurants, and a handful of useful services like grocery stores and Laundromats. Baddeck is also famed as having been the summer home of revered inventor Alexander Graham Bell. What's more, it's compact and easy to reconnoiter by foot and is scenically located on the shores of Bras d'Or Lake. This is the best base for those with limited vacation time and those who plan to drive the Cabot Trail in 1 day (figure on 6 to 8 hours). If, however, your intention is to spend a few days exploring the hiking trails and remote coves of the national park, you're better off finding accommodations further north.

The **Baddeck Welcome Centre** (☎ 902/295-1911) is located just south of the village at the intersection of routes 105 and 205. It's open daily in season from 8:30am to 8:30pm.

EXPLORING THE TOWN

Baddeck is much like a New England village, centered around a small commercial boulevard (Chebucto Street) just off the lake. Ask for a free **walking-tour brochure** at the welcome center. A complete tour of the village's architectural highlights won't take much more than 15 or 20 minutes.

Government Wharf (head down Jones Street from the Yellow Cello restaurant) is home to two boat tours, which are by far the best way to experience Bras d'Or Lake. **Amoeba Sailing Tours** (☎ 902/295-2481) offers a mellow cruise on a 50-foot sailboat. **Lock Bhreagh Boat Tours** (☎ 902/295-2016) is more for adrenaline-driven cruisers, with tours on a speedy jet boat. On either trip, you'll pass Alexander Graham Bell's palatial former estate and spend time scanning the skies for bald eagles.

About 200 yards offshore from the downtown wharf is **Kidston Island,** owned by the town. It has a wonderful sand beach with lifeguards, and an old lighthouse to explore. The Lion's Club offers frequent pontoon boat shuttles between 10am and 6pm (noon to 6pm on weekends) across St. Patrick's Channel; it's free and donations are encouraged.

Each summer for much of his life, noted inventor Alexander Graham Bell fled the heat of Washington, D.C., for a hillside retreat high above Bras d'Or Lake. It's now the **Alexander Graham Bell National Historic Site,** Chebucto Street, Baddeck (☎ 902/295-2069). The mansion, still owned and used by the Bell family, is visible across the harbor from various spots around town. But to learn more about Bell's career and restless mind, you should visit this modern exhibit center, perched on a grassy hillside at the north edge of the village. You'll find extensive exhibits about Bell's invention of the telephone at age 29, as well as considerable information about Bell's less-lauded contraptions, like his kites, hydrofoils, and airplanes. There's an extensive discovery area, where kids are encouraged to apply their intuition and creativity in solving problems. Admission is C$3.75 (US$2.70) for adults, C$2.75 (US$2) for seniors, C$2 (US$1.40) for children, and C$9.50 (US$7) for families. It's open daily: July and August from 9am to 8pm, June and September from 9am to 7pm, and October to May from 9am to 5pm.

ACCOMMODATIONS

If the more intimate places below lack vacancies, try **Auberge Gisele,** 387 Shore Rd. (☎ 800/304-0466 or 902/295-2849), a modern 66-room hotel that's popular with bus tours. Rates are C$99 to C$175 (US$70 to US$124) double. Also in town is the **Telegraph House,** Chebucto Street (☎ 902/295-1100), a Victorian-era hotel whose 42 rooms are furnished eclectically with flea-market antiques. (*Historical note:* Bell stayed here when he first visited.) Rates are C$49 to C$92 (US$35 to US$65).

۞ Duffus House Inn. Water St. (P.O. Box 427), Baddeck, NS, B0E 1B0. ☎ 902/295-2172 or 902/928-2678. 7 rms (including 3 suites). C$80–C$105 (US$57–US$75) double; C$115–C$125 (US$82–US$89) suite. Rates include full breakfast. V. Closed mid-Oct to mid-June.

A visit to the Duffus House is like a visit to the grandmother's house everyone wished they had. These two adjacent buildings (constructed in 1820 and 1885) overlook the channel and are cozy and very tastefully furnished with a lovely mix of antiques. It's located far enough from Baddeck's downtown to keep the commotion at arm's length, yet you can still walk everywhere in a few minutes' time. (The inn also has its own dock, where you can swim or just sit peacefully.) The common areas, including the gardens, are comfortably furnished and offer great places to chat with the other guests. The inn is run with considerable good cheer by innkeepers John and Judy Langley. No smoking.

Green Highlander Lodge. Chebucto St., Baddeck, B0E 1B0. ☎ 902/295-2303. E-mail: yellow@atcon.com. 3 rms. TV. C$90–C$120 (US$64–US$85) double. Rates include full breakfast. MC, V.

The Green Highlander is located atop the Yellow Cello, a popular in-town eatery. The three rooms are nicely decorated in a sort of Abercrombie and Fitch gentleman's-fishing-camp motif. (Rooms are named after Atlantic salmon flies.) Blue Charm has a private sitting room. Rosie Dawn and Lady Amherst have private decks that look out to Kidston Island. Ask about the moonlight paddle trips, and the private beach located a mile away. No smoking.

Lynwood Country Inn. 23 Shore Rd., Baddeck, NS B0E 1B0. ☎ 902/295-1995. Fax 902/295-3084. 3 rms. TV. C$90–C$110 (US$64–US$78) double. Rates include continental breakfast. MC, V. Closed mid-Oct to early June.

Located in a deep-red Victorian farmhouse across the street from the welcome center, the Lynwood Country Inn has been furnished with impeccable taste, and has a lean look that will appeal to travelers who abhor clutter. The rooms are simple without seeming empty and feature Persian carpets, hardwood floors, and salmon-tinged walls. Room 2 has rare bird's-eye maple trim. All rooms have private baths; two have Jacuzzis. No smoking. For dining, see below.

DINING

Baddeck Lobster Suppers. Ross St. ☎ **902/295-3307.** Lobster dinner around C$23 (US$16); lunch items C$3–C$7 (US$2.10–US$5). Kids' menu available. MC, V. Daily 11:30am–1:30pm and 4–9pm. Closed Nov 1–June 1. SEAFOOD.

Save your burgeoning appetite for an over-the-top seafood feed at this cavernous, no-frills restaurant. It has all the charm of a Legion Hall, but compensates with mounds of decently prepared seafood. The lobster dinner—which virtually everyone orders—includes one steamed crustacean, plus all you-can-eat mussels, chowder, biscuits, dessert, and drinks. Not in the mood for lobster? There's also a cold salmon or cold ham plate.

☼ **Lynwood Inn.** 23 Shore Rd. ☎ **902/295-1995.** Reservations recommended. Main courses C$12–C$20 (US$9–US$14). MC, V. Daily 5:30pm–9pm. Closed Nov 1–June 1. CONTINENTAL.

Chef Daryl MacDonnell worked as sous-chef at the Ottawa Hilton before heading here to take charge of his own kitchen. He's done a fine job scaling down, and offers a beguilingly simple menu that rarely fails to please. Appetizers might feature local favorite solomon gundy (pickled herring) or steamed mussels. Main courses emphasize sauces, such as a balsamic vinegar sauce on rack of lamb, or a light white-wine sauce with grilled salmon. Fresh flowers adorn the white tablecloths, and the walls are discretely enlivened with a mix of modern art and historic prints.

LOUISBOURG

In the early 18th century, Louisbourg on Cape Breton's easternmost coast was home to an ambitious French fortress and settlement. Despite its brief prosperity and durable construction of rock, it virtually disappeared after the British forced the French out in 1760. Through the miracle of archaeology and historic reconstruction, much of the imposing settlement has been re-created, and today Louisbourg is among Canada's most ambitious national historic parks. It's an attraction everyone coming to Cape Breton Island should make an effort to visit.

And a visit does require some effort. The site, 37 kilometers (22 miles) east of Sydney, isn't on the way to anywhere else, and it's an inconvenient detour from Cape Breton Highlands National Park. As such, it's far too easy to justify *not* going—it's too out of the way, it's a pain to double back, etc. By employing such excuses, you're only cheating yourself. Commit yourself to going, then go. A day spent wandering this wondrous rebuilt town, then walking amid ruins and out along the coastal trail, will be one of the highlights of your trip to Atlantic Canada.

EXPLORING THE VILLAGE OF LOUISBOURG

The peaceable hamlet of Louisbourg—which you'll pass through en route to the historic park—is pleasantly low-key, still scouting for ways to rebound from one devastating economic loss after another, including the cessation of the railway, the decline in boatbuilding, and the loss of the fisheries. Louisbourg is now striving to gear its economy more toward tourism, and you can see the progress year by year.

A short **boardwalk** with interpretive signs fronts the town's tiny waterfront. (You'll get a glimpse of the historic site across the water.) Nearby is a faux-Elizabethan theater, the **Louisbourg Playhouse** (☎ **902/733-2996**). This was originally built near the old town by Disney for filming the movie *Squanto.* After the production wrapped up, Disney donated it to the village, which dismantled it and moved it to a side street near the harbor. Various performances and concerts are staged here throughout summer.

At the ✪ **Fortress of Louisbourg National Historic Park,** Louisbourg (☎ 902/ 733-2280), you'll learn that the historic French village of Louisbourg has had three lives. The first was early in the 18th century, when the French first colonized this area—aggressively—in a bid to stake their claim in the New World. With the help of creative engineers and strong backs, they built an imposing fortress of stone. Imposing, but not impregnable, as the British were to prove when they captured the fort following the siege of 1745.

The fortress had a second, if short-lived, life after it was returned to France following negotiations in Europe. War soon broke out again though, and it was recaptured by the British in 1758. This time they blew it up for good measure.

The final resurrection came in the 1960s, when the Canadian government decided to rebuild one-fourth of the stone-walled town—virtually creating from whole cloth a settlement out of a handful of grass hummocks and some scattered documents about what once was. (The project also served as an economic lifeline for recently unemployed miners.) The historic park was built to re-create life as it looked in 1744, when it was an important French military capital and seaport.

Visitors today arrive at the site after walking through an interpretive center and boarding a bus for the short ride to the site. (Keeping cars at bay does much to enhance the historic flavor.) You'll wander through the impressive gatehouse—perhaps being challenged by a costumed guard—and then begin wandering the narrow lanes and poking around the historic buildings, some of which contain informative exhibits, others of which are restored and furnished with historic reproductions. Chickens, geese, and other barnyard animals peck and cluck. Vendors sell freshly baked bread out of wood-fired ovens.

To make the most of your visit, ask about the free guided tours. And don't hesitate to question the costumed interpreters, who are as knowledgeable as they are friendly. Allow at least a full day to explore. It's an extraordinary destination, as picturesque as it is historic.

Admission from June to September is C$11 (US$8) for adults, C$8.25 (US$6) for seniors, C$5.50 (US$4) for children, and C$27.50 (US$20) for families. Discounts are given in May and October. It's open daily: July and August from 9am to 7pm and May, June, September, and October from 9:30am to 5pm; closed November 1 to April 30. The costumed interpreters are limited in off-season.

ACCOMMODATIONS

Cranberry Cove. 17 Wolfe St., Louisbourg, NS, B0A 1M0. ☎ **902/733-2171.** E-mail: crancove@auracom.com. 7 rms. TEL. C$75–C$130 (US$53–US$91) double. Rates include full breakfast. AE, MC, V. Closed mid-Oct to early May.

You won't miss this attractive, in-town inn when en route to the fortress—it's a three-story Victorian farmhouse painted a boisterous cranberry red. Inside it's decorated in a light Victorian motif. The upstairs rooms are carpeted and typically furnished around themes—Anne's Hideaway is the smallest, but has a nice old tub and butterfly collection; Isle Royale is done up in Cape Breton tartan. My favorite room is also the quirkiest: Field and Stream, with a twig headboard, and mounted deer head and pheasant. Dinner is served nightly from 5 to 8:30pm in the handsome first-floor dining room, which has a polished wood floor and cherry-wood tables and chairs. Entrees range from Cajun shrimp and wild rice to a vegetarian quiche Lorraine and are priced from C$12 to C$19 (US$9 to US$14). No smoking.

Louisbourg Harbor Inn. 9 Warren St. (P.O. Box 110), Louisbourg, NS, B0A 1M0. ☎ **888/ 888-8466** or 902/733-3222. 8 rms (1 with shower only). C$85–C$125 (US$60–US$89) double. Rates include continental breakfast. MC, V.

This golden, century-old clapboard home is conveniently located in the village, a block off the main drag and overlooking the working harbor. The lustrous wood floors were brought back nicely, and the guest rooms are tidy and attractive, with some fussier than others. A nice touch: all rooms facing the harbor have Jacuzzis. Room 1 also has a private balcony and gets wonderful afternoon light. No smoking. Dinner is available by advance reservation in the first-floor dining room. A three-course meal (entree choices often include steak, lobster, or crab) runs C$25 to C$30 (US$18 to US$21).

11 Cape Breton Highlands National Park

✪ **Cape Breton Highlands National Park** is one of the two crown-jewel national parks in Atlantic Canada. (Gros Morne in Newfoundland is the other.) Covering some 950 square kilometers (365 square miles), and stretching across a rugged peninsula from the Atlantic to the Gulf of St. Lawrence, the park is famous for its starkly beautiful terrain. It also features one of the most dramatic coastal drives east of Big Sur, California. One of the great pleasures of the park is that it holds something for everyone, from tourists who prefer to sightsee from the comfort of their car, to those who prefer backcountry adventure in the company of bear and moose.

The mountains of Cape Breton are probably unlike those you're familiar with elsewhere. The heart of the park is fundamentally a huge plateau. In the vast interior, you'll find a flat and melancholy landscape of wind-stunted evergreens, bogs, and barrens. This is called the **taiga,** a name that refers to the zone between tundra and the northernmost forest. In this largely untracked area (which is also Nova Scotia's largest remaining wilderness), you might find 150-year-old trees that are only knee-high.

But it's the park's edges that capture the attention. On the western side of the peninsula, the tableland has eroded into the sea, creating a dramatic landscape of ravines and ragged, rust-colored cliffs pounded by the ocean. The ✪ **Cabot Trail,** a paved road built in 1939, winds dramatically along the flanks of the mountains, offering extraordinary vistas at every turn. On the park's other coastal flank—the eastern, Atlantic side—the terrain is less dramatic, with a coastal plain interposed between mountains and sea. But the lush green hills still offer a backdrop that's exceptionally picturesque.

Note that this section focuses only on the park proper, which offers no lodging or services other than camping. You will find limited lodging and restaurants in the handful of villages that ring the park. See "Cape Breton Island," above.

ESSENTIALS

GETTING THERE   Access to the park is via the Cabot Trail, one of several tourist routes well marked by provincial authorities. The entire loop is 292 kilometers (175 miles). The distance from the park entrance at Chéticamp to the park entrance at Ingonish is 106 kilometers (65 miles).

While the loop can be done in either direction, I would encourage visitors to drive in a clockwise direction solely because the visitor center in Chéticamp offers a far more detailed introduction to the park.

VISITOR INFORMATION   Visitor information centers are located at both Chéticamp and Ingonish and are open daily in summer from 8am to 8pm. The Chéticamp center has more extensive information about the park, including a

20-minute slide presentation, natural-history exhibits, a large-scale relief map, and a very good bookstore specializing in natural and cultural history. The park's main phone number is ☎ **902/224-2306;** in winter, call ☎ 902/285-2691.

FEES   Entrance permits may be purchased at either information center or at tollhouses at the two main park entrances. Permits are required for any activity along the route, even stopping to admire the view. Daily fees are C$3.50 (US$2.50) for adults, C$2.50 (US$1.80) for seniors, C$1.50 (US$1.10) for children 6 to 16, and C$8 (US$6) for families; 4-day passes are C$10.50 (US$45) for adults, C$7.50 (US$5) for seniors, C$4.50 (US$3.20) for children, and C$24 (US$17) for families.

CAMPING

The park has five drive-in campgrounds. The largest are at **Chéticamp** (on the west side) and **Broad Cove** (on the east), both of which have the commendable policy of never turning campers away. Even if all regular sites are full, they'll find a place for you to pitch a tent or park an RV at an overflow area. All the national-park campgrounds are well run and well maintained. Chéticamp and Broad Cove offer three-way hookups for RVs. Rates are C$14 (US$10) for an unserviced site, C$16 (US$11) for electric only, C$20 (US$14) for fully serviced. It costs C$2 (US$1.40) more for a site with a fire pit (otherwise you must build fires at picnic areas within the campground). Remember that you also need to buy a day-use park permit when camping at Cape Breton.

Cape Breton also has two backcountry campsites. ✪ **Fishing Cove** is especially attractive, set on a pristine cove an 8-kilometer (5-mile) hike from the Cabot Trail. Watch for pilot whales at sunset from the cliffs. **Lake of Islands,** the other backcountry site, is 13 kilometers (8 miles) from the trailhead on a remote lake in the interior; it's accessible by mountain bike. Fees are C$14 (US$10) per night; make arrangements at one of the visitor information centers.

SCENIC DRIVES

Cape Breton Highlands National Park offers basically one drive, and with few lapses, it's scenic along the entire route. The most breathtaking stretch is the 44-kilometer (27-mile) jaunt from Chéticamp to Pleasant Bay along the western coast. Double the time you figure you'll need to drive this, as you'll want to spend time at the pull-outs admiring the views and perusing informational signboards. If it's foggy, save yourself the entrance fee and gas money. Without the views, there's little reason to travel and you'd be well advised to wait until it lifts. Until then, you could hike in the foggy forest or across the upland bogs, or explore some of the nearby villages in the atmospheric fog.

You'll want to be very confident in your car's brakes before setting out on the Cabot Trail. The road rises and falls with considerable drama, and when cresting some ridges, you might feel mildly afflicted with vertigo. Especially stressful on the brakes (when traveling clockwise) are the descents to Pleasant Bay, into the Aspy Valley, and off Cape Smoky.

HIKING

The park has 27 hiking trails departing from the Cabot Trail. Many excursions are quite short and have the feel of a casual stroll rather than a vigorous tromp, but those determined to be challenged will find suitable destinations. All trails are listed with brief descriptions on the reverse side of the map you'll receive when you pay your entry fee.

The ✪ **Skyline Trail** offers all the altitude with none of the climbing. You ascend the tableland from Chéticamp by car, then follow a 7-kilometer (4.3-mile) hiking loop out along dramatic bluffs and through wind-stunted spruce and fir. A spur trail descends to a high, exposed point overlooking the surf; it's capped with blueberry bushes. Moose are often spotted along this trail. *Downside:* It's a very popular trek and often crowded.

Further along the Cabot Trail, the half-mile-long **Bog Trail** offers a glimpse of the tableland's unique bogs from a dry boardwalk. **Lone Shieling** is an easy half-mile loop through a verdant hardwood forest in a lush valley that includes 350-year-old sugar maples. A re-creation of a hut of a Scottish crofter (shepherd) is a feature along this trail.

If you're looking to leave the crowds behind, the **Glasgow Lake Lookoff** is a relatively gentle 8-kilometer (4.8-mile) round-trip hike that takes you through barrens and scrub forest to a rocky bald overlooking a series of pristine highland lakes with distant views of the ocean. The trail is alternately swampy and rocky, so rugged footwear is advised.

On the eastern shore, a superb hike is out to **Middle Head,** beyond the Keltic Lodge resort. This dramatic and rocky peninsula thrusts well out into the Atlantic. The trail is wide and relatively flat; you'll cross open meadows with wonderful views north and south. The tip is grassy and open, and offers a fine spot to scan for whales or watch the waves crash in following a storm. Allow an hour or two for a relaxed excursion out and back.

BIKING

The 292-kilometer (175-mile) **Cabot Trail loop** is the iron-man tour for bike trekkers, both arduous and rewarding. The route twists up ravines and plummets back down toward the coast. One breathtaking vista after another unfolds, and the plunging, brake-smoking descent from Mount MacKenzie to Pleasant Bay will be one you're not likely to forget. Campgrounds and motels are well-spaced for 3- or 4-day excursions. As for disadvantages, the road is uniformly narrow, and bikers get the sense that motor-home drivers don't always know where the far side of their rig is located. This can be a bit harrowing.

If you're not inclined to pedal the whole loop, pick and choose. Especially scenic stretches for fit bikers include Chéticamp to Pleasant Bay and back, and the climb and descent from Lone Shieling eastward into the Aspy Valley.

Mountain bikes are allowed on just three trails within the park—check with the visitor center when you arrive for details. The longest backcountry trail is the 13-kilometer (8-mile) route into the Lake of Islands.

5

New Brunswick

by Wayne Curtis

Think of New Brunswick as the Rodney Dangerfield of Atlantic Canada—it just gets no respect. Among Canadians, at any rate, it has a reputation more for pulp mills, industrial forests, cargo ports, and oil refineries (the huge Irving Oil conglomerate is based here) than for quaint villages and charming byways. As such, travelers tend to view New Brunswick as a place you need to drive through—preferably really fast—en route from Québec or Maine to the rest of Atlantic Canada.

There's a grain of truth behind its reputation. But rest assured, New Brunswick has pockets of wilderness and scenic beauty that are unrivaled anywhere in eastern Canada. You'll find sandy beaches on warm ocean waters that will hold their own to anything on Prince Edward Island. Not to mention rocky, surf-pounded headlands that could be in the farthest reaches of Newfoundland. Admittedly, the province's appeal tends to be more hidden than elsewhere. But all that means is that you've got to do more homework to get the most out of it.

Culturally, New Brunswick is Canada in microcosm. It's split between Anglophone and Francophone populations (about one-third of the residents speak French). Its heritage is both proudly Acadian and proudly pro-British—in fact, New Brunswick is sometimes called the "Loyalist Province," since so many Loyalists fleeing the United States settled here after the American Revolution.

But the cultural divide is less contentious than in Québec. Interestingly, French-speaking New Brunswick residents share few cultural roots with French-speaking Québecois. (New Brunswick's French ancestors came mostly from central and western France; Québecois trace their ancestry to Brittany and Normandy.) Acadians celebrate the Feast of the Assumption as their national holiday. In Québec, it's the day of St. Jean Baptiste. With its unusually harmonious detente between two cultures, New Brunswick likes to offer itself as a model for Québec. Québec, in turn, likes to ignore New Brunswick.

1 Exploring New Brunswick

Visitors drawn to rugged beauty should plan to focus on the Fundy Coast, with its stupendous tides, rocky cliffs, and boreal landscape. (The south coast actually feels more remote and northerly than the

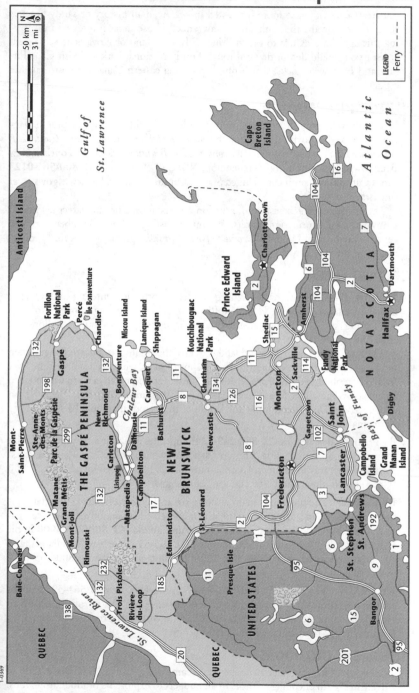

northeast coast.) Those more interested in the Acadian history or sandy beaches should veer toward the Gulf of St. Lawrence. Those most interested in hurrying through the province to get to Prince Edward Island or Nova Scotia . . . well, at least you should detour down through Fundy National Park and visit Cape Enrage and Hopewell Rocks, which number among eastern Canada's most dramatic attractions.

VISITOR INFORMATION

New Brunswick publishes several free directories and guides that are helpful in planning a trip to the province, including the *Accommodation & Campground Guide, Day Adventure Guide,* and the general *Welcome to New Brunswick.* Write to **Tourism New Brunswick,** P.O. Box 12345, Fredericton, NB, E3B 5C3, or call ☎ **800/561-0123** (from Canada and continental United States). On the Web, head to **www.gov.nb.ca/ tourism**.

The province staffs six visitor information centers; most cities and larger towns also have their own information centers. A complete listing of phone numbers for these centers may be found in the *Welcome to New Brunswick* guide, or look for "?" direction signs on the highway.

GETTING THERE

BY CAR The Trans-Canada Highway bisects the province, entering from Québec at St-Jacques. It follows the Saint John River Valley before veering through Moncton and exiting into Nova Scotia at Aulac. The entire distance is about 550 kilometers (330 miles).

The fastest route from New England is to take the Maine turnpike to Bangor, then head east on Route 9 to connect to Route 1 into Calais, which is just across the river from St. Stephen, New Brunswick. A more scenic variation is to drive to Campobello Island across the bridge from Lubec, Maine (see "Passamaquoddy Bay," below), then take a ferry to Deer Island, drive the length of the island, then board a second ferry to the mainland.

BY FERRY Bay Ferries (☎ **888/249-7245**) operates a 3-hour ferry that links Saint John and Digby, Nova Scotia. The ferry sails year-round, with as many as three crossings daily each way in summer. Summer rates are C$23 (US$16) for adults, C$11.50 (US$8) for children, and C$50 (US$36) per vehicle.

BY PLANE The province's main airports are at Fredericton (the provincial capital), Saint John, and Moncton, all of which are served by major rental-car companies. These airports are served by **Air Nova/Air Canada** (☎ **800/776-3000** in the U.S., 800/565-3940 in the Maritimes or 800/563-5151 in Newfoundland), and **Air Atlantic/Canadian Airlines** (☎ **800/426-7000** in the U.S. or 800/665-1177 in Canada).

BY TRAIN Via Rail (☎ **800/561-3949** in the U.S. or 800/561-3952 in the Maritimes) offers train service through the province (en route from Montréal to Halifax) 6 days per week. The train follows a northerly route, with stops in Campbellton, Miramichi, and Moncton.

THE GREAT OUTDOORS

The province has put together a laudable campaign—called **"The New Tide of Adventure"**—to encourage visitors of all budgets to explore its outdoor attractions. A booklet outlines more than 120 miniadventures ranging from a C$10 (US$7) guided hike in the nighttime woods of Fundy National Park to a C$375 (US$266)

3-day bike tour, which includes meals, equipment, and lodging. Ask for the current adventure catalog at any visitor center. Within New Brunswick, make phone reservations by calling ☎ 800/561-1112.

BACKPACKING Among the best destinations for a backcountry tromp are **Mount Carleton Provincial Park** and **Fundy National Park,** both of which maintain backcountry sites. See the appropriate sections below for more information.

BICYCLING The islands and peninsulas of **Passamaquoddy Bay** lend themselves nicely to cruising in the slow lane—especially Campobello, which also has good dirt roads for mountain biking. **Grand Manan** holds appeal for cyclists, although the main road (Route 776) has narrow shoulders and fast cars. Perhaps the best coastal biking is **east of Fundy National Park**—especially the back roads to Cape Enrage. Along the Acadian Coast, **Kouchibouguac National Park** has limited but unusually nice biking trails through mixed terrain (rentals available).

A handy guide is *Biking to Blissville* by Kent Thompson. It costs C$15 (US$11) and is published by **Goose Lane Editions,** 469 King St., Fredericton, NB, E3B 1E5 (☎ 506/450-4251).

BIRD WATCHING **Grand Manan** may be the province's most noted destination for birders, located smack on the Atlantic flyway. (Ur-birder John James Audubon lodged here when studying local bird life more than 150 years ago.) Over the course of a year, as many as 275 species are observed on the island; September is typically the best month for sightings. It's not hard to swap information with other birders. On the ferry, look for excitable folks with binoculars and Tilley hats dashing from port to starboard and back. Talk to them. Boat tours from Grand Manan will bring you to Machias Seal Island, with its colonies of puffins, Arctic terns, and razorbills.

On **Campobello Island,** the mixed terrain also attracts a good mix of birds, including sharp-shinned hawk, common eider, and black guillemot. Ask for a check-list and map at the visitors center. Shorebird enthusiasts flock to **Shepody Bay National Wildlife Area,** which maintains preserves in the mudflats between Alma (near Fundy National Park) and Hopewell Cape.

CANOEING New Brunswick has 3,600 kilometers (2,200 miles) of inland waterways, plus lakes and a protected bay. Canoeists can find everything from glass-smooth waters to daunting rapids. Novices often enjoy the 3-hour **Voyager Canoe Marine Adventure** (☎ 506/876-2443) in Kouchibouguac National Park. More experienced canoeists looking for a longer expedition should head to the **St. Croix River** on the U.S. border, where you can embark on a multiday paddle trip and get lost in the woods, spiritually if not in fact.

FISHING The **Miramichi River** has long attracted famous and not-so-famous anglers, lured by the wily Atlantic salmon. In some considered opinions, this is one of the best salmon rivers in the world. Salmon must be caught on flies, and nonresidents need to hire a guide to go after salmon. For other freshwater species, like bass, and saltwater angling, the restrictions are less onerous. Get up-to-date on the rules and regulations by requesting copies of two brochures: *Sport Fishing Summary* and *Atlantic Salmon Angling.* These are available from **Fish and Wildlife,** P.O. Box 6000, Fredericton, NB, E3B 5H1 (☎ 506/453-2440).

HIKING The province's highest point is in the center of the woodlands region, at **Mount Carleton Provincial Park.** Several demanding hikes in the park yield glorious views. There's also fine hiking at **Fundy National Park,** with a mix of coastal and woodland hikes. **Grand Manan** is a good destination for independent hikers, who enjoy the challenge of finding the trail as much as the hike itself.

An excellent resource is *A Hiking Guide to New Brunswick,* published by **Goose Lane Editions.** It's C$15 (US$11) and available in bookstores around the province, or directly from the publisher at 469 King St., Fredericton, NB, E3B 1E5 (☎ 506/450-4251).

SEA KAYAKING The huge tides that make kayaking so fascinating along the Bay of Fundy also make it exceptionally dangerous—even the strongest kayaker is no match for a fierce ebb tide if they're in the wrong place. Fortunately, the number of skilled sea-kayaking guides has boomed in recent years.

Among the most extraordinary places to explore is **Hopewell Rocks,** which stand like Brancusi statues on the ocean floor at low tide, but offer sea caves and narrow channels to explore at high tide. **Baymount Outdoor Adventures** (☎ 506/734-2660) offers 90-minute sea-kayak tours of Hopewell Rocks for C$30 (US$21). Other kayak outfitters along the Fundy Coast include the **Outdoor Adventure Company** (☎ 800/365-3855 or 506/755-2007) in St. George, and **Fresh Air Adventure** (☎ 800/545-0020 or 506/887-2249) in Alma.

SWIMMING Parts of New Brunswick offer wonderful ocean swimming. The best beaches are along the **Acadian Coast,** especially near Shediac and in Kouchibouguac National Park. The water is much warmer and the terrain more forgiving along the Gulf of St. Lawrence than along the Bay of Fundy.

WHALE WATCHING The **Bay of Fundy** is rich with plankton, and therefore rich with whales. Some 15 kinds of whales can be spotted in the bay, including finback, right, minke, and humpback whales. Whale-watching expeditions sail throughout the summer from Campobello Island, Deer Island, Grand Manan, St. Andrews, and St. George. Any visitor information center can point you in the right direction; the province's *Day Adventure* guide also lists many of the tours, which typically cost around C$40 or C$50 (US$28 or US$36) for 2 to 5 hours of whale watching.

2 Passamaquoddy Bay

The Passamaquoddy Bay region is often the first point of entry for those arriving overland from the United States. The deeply indented bay is wracked with strong tides and currents powerful enough to stymie even doughty fishing boats. It's a place of lasting fogs, spruce-clad islands, bald eagles, and little development. It's also home to a grand old summer colony and a peninsula that can boast of two five-star inns and a rambling turn-of-the-century resort.

If you're arriving through St. Stephen, the best place to stock up on maps and brochures is the **Provincial Visitor Information Centre,** 101 King St. (☎ 506/466-7390), open mid-May to mid-October daily from 10am to 6pm.

CAMPOBELLO ISLAND

Campobello is a compact island (about 16km long and 5km wide—or 10 miles by 3 miles) at the mouth of Passamaquoddy Bay. Among its other distinctions, it's easier to get to from the United States than from Canada. It's connected by a graceful bridge from the Maine town of Lubec. To arrive here from the Canadian mainland without driving through the United States requires two ferries, one of which operates only during summer.

Campobello has been home to both humble fishermen and wealthy families over the years, and both have coexisted quite nicely. (Locals approved when summer folks built golf courses earlier this century, since it gave them a place to graze their sheep.) Today, the island is a mix of elegant summer homes and less-interesting tract homes of a more recent vintage.

ESSENTIALS

GETTING THERE   Campobello Island is accessible year-round from the United States. From Route 1 in Whiting, Maine, take Route 189 to Lubec, where a bridge links Lubec with Campobello. In summer there's another option. From the Canadian mainland, take the free ferry to Deer Island, drive the length of the island, and then board the seasonal ferry to Campobello. The ferry is operated by **East Coast Ferries** (☎ 506/747-2159) and runs from late June to early September. The fare is C$13 (US$9) for car and driver and C$2 (US$1.40) for each extra passenger, with a maximum of C$18 (US$13) per car.

VISITOR INFORMATION   The **Campobello Visitor Information Centre,** P.O. Box 12345, Wilson's Beach, NB, E0G 3L0 (☎ 506/752-2997), is in the town of Campobello, near the ferry landing. It's open mid-May to mid-October daily from 10am to 5pm. Information on local activities is also available at the visitor center of Roosevelt Campobello International Park.

EXPLORING THE ISLAND

The island offers excellent shoreline **walks** at both Roosevelt Campobello International Park (see below) and **Herring Cove Provincial Park** (☎ 506/752-7010). The landscapes are extraordinarily diverse. On some trails you'll enjoy a Currier & Ives tableau of white houses and church spires across the channel in Lubec; 10 minutes later you'll be walking along a wild, rocky coast pummeled by surging waves. Herring Cove has a mile-long beach that's perfect for a slow stroll in the fog. Camping and golf is also offered at the provincial park.

The island's main lure is **Roosevelt Campobello International Park,** Route 774 (☎ 506/752-2922). Like many other affluent Americans, the family of Franklin Delano Roosevelt made an annual trek to the prosperous summer colony at Campobello Island. The island lured folks from the sultry cities with a promise of cool air and salubrious effect on the circulatory system. ("The extensive forests of balsamic firs seem to affect the atmosphere of this region, causing a quiet of the nervous system and inviting sleep," read an 1890 real-estate brochure.) The future U.S. president came to this island every summer between 1883, the year after he was born, and 1921, when he was suddenly stricken with polio. Franklin and his siblings spent those summers exploring the coves and sailing around the bay, and he always recalled his time here fondly. (It was his "beloved island," he said, coining a phrase that gets no rest in local brochures.)

You'll learn much about Roosevelt and his early life at the visitor center, where you can watch a brief film, and during a self-guided tour of the elaborate mansion, covered in cranberry-colored shingles. For a "cottage" this huge, it's surprisingly comfortable and intimate. The park is truly an international park—run by a commission with representatives from both the United States and Canada, making it like none other in the world.

Leave some time to explore farther afield in the 2,800-acre park, which offers scenic coastline and 14 kilometers (8.5 miles) of walking trails. Maps and walk suggestions are available at the visitor center. The park is open daily from 10am to 6pm; admission is free. Closed from mid-October to late May.

ACCOMMODATIONS

Lupine Lodge. Welshpool Rd., Campobello, NB, E0G 3H0. ☎ 506/752-2040. 11 rms (some with shower only). C$50–$C125 (US$36–US$89) double. MC, V. Closed mid-Oct to mid-June.

This handsome compound of log buildings not far from the Roosevelt cottage was built in 1915 by cousins of the Roosevelts. A busy road runs between the lodge and the water, but the buildings are located on a slight rise and have the feel of being removed from civilization. Guest rooms are situated in two long lodges adjacent to the main building and restaurant. The rooms with bay views cost a bit more, but are worth it—they're slightly bigger and better furnished in a log-rustic style. All guests have access to a deck that overlooks the bay. The attractive restaurant exudes rustic summer ease with log walls, a stone fireplace, bay views, and a mounted moose head and swordfish. Three meals are served daily. Dinner entrees include favorites like salmon, T-bone, turkey, and steamed lobster, and are well-priced at C$9 to C$15 (US$6 to US$11).

The Owen House. Rte. 774, Welshpool, Campobello, NB, E0G 3H0. ☎ **506/752-2977.** 9 rms (4 rms share 1 bath). C$78 (US$55) double with shared bath, C$103 (US$73) double with private bath. Rates include full breakfast. V. Closed mid-Oct to Apr.

This three-story clapboard captain's house dates to 1835 and sits on 10 tree-filled acres at the edge of the bay. The first-floor common rooms are nicely decorated in a hectic Victorian manner with Persian and braided carpets and mahogany furniture. The guest rooms are a mixed lot, furnished with an eclectic mélange of antique and modern furniture that sometimes blends nicely, sometimes doesn't. Likewise, some rooms are bright and airy and filled with the smell of salty air; others, like Room 5, are tucked under stairs and rather dark. The four third-floor rooms share a single bath but also have the best views.

ST. ANDREWS

The lovely village of St. Andrews—or St. Andrews By-The-Sea, as the chamber of commerce likes to call it—traces its roots back to the days of the Loyalists. After the American Revolution, New Englanders who supported the British in the struggle were made to feel unwelcome. They decamped first to Castine, Maine, which they presumed was safely on British soil. It wasn't. Uprooted again, the Loyalists dismantled their houses, loaded the pieces aboard ships, and rebuilt them on the welcoming peninsula of St. Andrews.

This historic community later emerged as a fashionable summer resort in the late 19th century, when many of Canada's affluent and well-connected nabobs built homes and gathered annually here for an active social season. Around this time, the Tudor-style **Algonquin Hotel** was built on a low rise overlooking the town, and quickly became the town's social hub and defining landmark.

St. Andrews is beautifully sited at the tip of a long, wedge-shaped peninsula. Thanks to its location off the beaten track, the village hasn't been spoiled much by modern development, and walking the wide, shady streets—especially those around the Algonquin—invokes a more genteel era. Some 250 homes around the village are more than a century old, and a handful date back to the late 18th century.

ESSENTIALS

GETTING THERE   St. Andrews is located at the apex of Route 127, which dips southward from Route 1 between St. Stephen and St. George. The turnoff is well marked from either direction. One **bus** (☎ 506/529-3371) daily connects St. Andrews with Saint John; the one-way fare is approximately C$15 (US$11).

VISITOR INFORMATION   At the western intersection of Route 1 and Route 127 is the seasonal **St. Andrews Tourist Bureau** (☎ 506/466-4858). A better bet is the **Welcome Centre** (☎ 506/529-3000), located at 46 Reed Ave., on your left as you enter the village. It's in a handsome 1914 home overarched by broad-crowned trees. It's open daily from 9am to 6pm in May and September, 9am to 8pm in July and

August. The rest of the year, contact the **Chamber of Commerce** in the same building (☎ **800/563-7397** or 506/529-3555) by writing P.O. Box 89, St. Andrews, NB, E0G 2X0, or e-mailing stachmb@nbnet.nb.ca.

EXPLORING ST. ANDREWS

The chamber of commerce and the town jointly produce a wonderfully informative brochure entitled *Unique Things to See and Do,* which is free at the two visitor information centers. It's well worth tracking down this and the free downtown map before beginning your explorations.

The village's compact and handsome downtown flanks **Water Street,** just off the bay. You'll find low and attractive architecture encompassing a gamut of styles, and an hour or two's worth of browsing at boutiques and art galleries. There's also a mix of restaurants and inns.

Two blocks inland, on King Street, you'll get a dose of local history at the **Ross Memorial Museum,** 188 Montague St. (☎ **506/529-5124**). The historic home was built in 1824; in 1945 the home was left to the town by Rev. Henry Phipps Ross and Sarah Juliette Ross, complete with their eclectic and intriguing collection of period furniture, carpets, and paintings. Open late June to mid-October, Tuesday to Saturday from 10am to 4:30pm; in July and August it's also open Mondays. Admission is by donation.

The 27-acre **Kingsbrae Horticultural Gardens,** 220 King St. (☎ **506/ 529-3335**), was busily under construction when I last visited and was due to open in 1998. The entire project looked very promising, and these elegant hilltop grounds are poised to become a noted stop for garden lovers. The grounds will include 800 varieties of trees and 900 perennials. Among the features in the works: a day-lily collection, an extensive rose garden, and an elaborate maze. Admission is C$6 (US$4.25) for adults, C$4 (US$2.80) for children, students, and seniors; children under 6 are free. The gardens are open mid-May to mid-October daily from 9am to dusk. They're closed from mid-October to mid-May.

Northeast of St. Andrews on Route 127 at Chamcook is ✪ **Ministers Island Historic Site/Covenhoven.** This rugged, 500-plus–acre island is linked to the mainland by sandbar at low tide, and 2-hour tours are scheduled around the tides. (Call ☎ **506/529-5081** for upcoming times.) You'll meet your tour guide on the mainland side, then drive your car out convoy-style across the ocean floor to the magical island estate created in 1890 by Sir William Van Horne.

Van Horne was president of the Canadian Pacific Railway and the person behind the extension of the rail line to St. Andrews. He then built a sandstone mansion— Covenhoven—with some 50 rooms (including 17 bedrooms), a circular bathhouse (where he indulged his passion for landscape painting), and one of Canada's largest and most impressive barns. The estate also features heated greenhouses, which produced grapes and mushrooms, along with peaches that weighed up to 2 pounds each. When Van Horne was home in Montréal, he had fresh dairy products and vegetables shipped daily (by rail, of course) so he could enjoy fresh produce year-round.

One gathers that the discriminating Van Horne may not have been the most accommodating of bosses. He required that the entire dairy barn, including each cow, be washed down after every milking. And he demanded a fresh coat of sawdust be spread over the barn floor each night, with the Van Horne coat of arms meticulously drawn in it by the staff.

Admission is C$5 (US$3.60) for adults and C$2.50 (US$1.80) for youths 13 to 18; children under 12 are free. Call ☎ **506/529-5081** for the recorded tour schedule; the site is closed from mid-October to May.

ACCOMMODATIONS

St. Andrews offers an abundance of B&Bs and inns, including two inns with the very rare five-star classification, as awarded by Canada Select. Those traveling on a tighter budget should head for the **Picket Fence Motel,** 102 Reed Ave. (☎ **506/529-8985**). This trim and tidy motel is near the Algonquin golf course and within walking distance of the village center. Rooms are C$55 to C$65 (US$39 to US$46) in peak season.

The Algonquin. 184 Adolphus St., St. Andrews, NB, E0G 2X0. ☎ **800/441-1414** or 506/529-8823. Fax 506/529-7162. 250 rms and suites. MINIBAR TV TEL. May–Oct C$125–C$215 (US$89–US$153) double. Nov–Apr (limited operations with 51 rms) C$79 (US$56), including continental breakfast. Meal package C$45 (US$32) extra per person per day. Other packages available. AE, CB, DC, DISC, ER, MC, V.

The Algonquin's distinguished pedigree dates back to 1889, when it first opened its doors to wealthy vacationers seeking respite from city heat. The original structure was destroyed by fire in 1914, but the surviving annexes were rebuilt in sumptuous Tudor style; in 1993 an architecturally sympathetic addition was built across the road, linked by a gatehouse-style bridge.

The red-tile-roofed resort commands one's attention through its sheer size and aristocratic bearing. The inn is several long blocks from the water's edge, but perches on the brow of a hill and affords panoramic bay views from the second-floor roof garden and many guest rooms. The guest rooms have recently been redecorated, and are comfortable and tasteful; all have coffeemakers and hair dryers. *One caveat:* The hotel happily markets itself to bus tours and conferences, and if your timing is unfortunate, you may feel a bit overwhelmed and small.

Dining: For fine dining, see below. Informal dining options include The Library (just off the main lobby), and the downstairs lounge.

Services: The resort features a day-adventure desk, bus shuttle to the Saint John airport (C$85/US$60 one-way for one passenger; less if booked as a group), daily children's programs, valet parking, and safe-deposit boxes. *Extra charge:* baby-sitting, laundry, dry cleaning, in-room massage.

Facilities: The Algonquin has two golf courses (one 18-hole, one 9-hole), which are benefiting from an attention-getting redesign and makeover; greens fees begin at C$30 (US$21). Other facilities include two outdoor tennis courts, an outdoor heated pool, bike rentals, beauty salon, gift shop, fitness room, locker room saunas, and an indoor whirlpool.

Hiram Walker Estate Heritage Inn. 109 Reed Ave., St. Andrews, NB, E0G 2X0. ☎ **800/470-4088** or 506/529-4210. E-mail: walkest@nb.sympatico.ca. 9 rms. A/C TV TEL. C$135–C$295 (US$96–US$209) double. Rates include full breakfast. AE, MC, V.

The Walker Estate was built for distillery tycoon Hiram Walker's oldest son in 1912, and the 11-acre grounds and regal, three-story stucco building are imbued with a spare, French-chateaulike elegance. You'll find common rooms ornately furnished with museum-quality antiques, some bordering on the baroque. (Guests who like to put their feet up on the couch won't be comfortable here; see Salty Towers, below.) The bright dining room, where candlelit breakfasts are served, opens onto a lovely patio, which in turn overlooks an octagonal pool and tidy, lush yard (alas, no water views).

Guest rooms are furnished with lovely antiques in upscale chateau style. There's not a bad room in the place—although be forewarned that the third-floor rooms have sloping attic ceilings that make them feel somewhat smaller. Room 6 is the largest, with a comfortable sitting area, nice view of the pool, and a canopy bed. Room 1 is also sizable, with a double Jacuzzi, hardwood floors, and a small chandelier. My top choice: Room 5, with its leopard-print carpet, Empire-style furniture, and a fine corner Jacuzzi. Eight of the nine rooms have electric fireplaces, which generate heat but little charm. Children and pets are welcome with prior approval. No smoking.

Dining: Meals are available nightly to guests only. Three-course meals might include a choice of salmon, pork, or beef tenderloin in a green peppercorn sauce. One seating is offered at 7pm; the fixed-price meal is C$27 (US$19).

Services: A light afternoon tea is served at 3pm daily.

Facilities: There's an outdoor heated pool and hot tub, and the inn is near the Algonquin's golf course.

♦ Kingsbrae Arms. 219 King St., St. Andrews, NB, E0G 2X0. ☎ **506/529-1897.** Fax 506/529-1197. E-mail: kingbrae@nbnet.nb.ca. 8 rms. A/C TV TEL. High season C$225–C$400 (US$160–US$284); low season C$115–C$225 (US$82–US$160). MC, V.

Kingsbrae Arms, like The Walker Estate, is a five-star inn informed by an upscale European elegance. But where the Walker Estate tends to suggest 19th-century France, Kingsbrae brings to mind a more rustic elegance—a bit of Tuscany, perhaps, melded with a genteel London town house. Located atop King Street, this intimate inn occupies an 1897 manor house, where the furnishings—from the gracefully worn leather chesterfield to the Delft-tiled fireplace—all seem to have a story to tell. The grand, shingled home, built by prosperous jade merchants, occupies 1 acre, all of which has been well employed: A heated pool sits amid rose gardens at the foot of a lawn, and immediately next door is the 27-acre Kingsbrae Horticultural Gardens (some guest rooms have wonderful views of the gardens; others a panoramic sweep of the bay). Guest will feel pampered here, with 325-thread count sheets, plush robes, VCRs and hairdryers in all rooms, and a complete guest services suite stocked with complimentary snacks and refreshments. Five rooms have Jacuzzis; all have gas fireplaces. Children 10 and older are welcome, as are pets if you ask in advance. No smoking.

Dining: Registered guests can enjoy a four-course meal in the stately dining room. Advance reservations are required; the fixed-price meal is C$65 (US$46).

Services: The inn can arrange for baby-sitting, dry cleaning, and laundry; an afternoon tea is served.

Facilities: In addition to the heated pool, guests can avail themselves of the Algonquin's facilities (extra charge) a short stroll away.

Salty Towers. 340 Water St., St. Andrews, NB, E0G 2X0. ☎ **506/529-4585.** E-mail: steeljm@nbnet.nb.ca. Web site: www.islands.org/salty.towers. C$38 (US$27) double with shared bath, C$54 (US$38) double with private bath. MC, V.

Behind this somewhat staid Queen Anne home on Water Street lurks the soul of a daft eccentric. Salty Towers is equal parts turn-of-the-century home, 1940s boarding house, and 1960s commune. Overseen with great affability by artist-naturalist Jamie Steel, you enter into a world of wondrous clutter—from the early European landscapes with overly wrought gilt frames, to the washtub bass and a marvelous angel concocted of an old mannequin and tin-can lids. Think "Addams Family meets Timothy Leary."

The guest rooms lack the visual chaos of the public spaces, and are nicely done, furnished with eclectic antiques and old magazines. (Especially nice is Room 2, with hand-sponged walls and a private sitting area surrounded by windows.) The top floor is largely given over to single rooms; these are a bargain at C$28 (US$20) with shared bath. Guests have full run of the large if sometimes confused kitchen. Don't be surprised to find musicians strumming on the porch, artists lounging in the living room, and others of uncertain provenance swapping jokes around the stove. If that sounds pretty good to you, this is your place.

DINING

⊙ **The Algonquin**. 184 Adolphus St. ☎ **800/441-1414** or 506/529-8823. Reservations encouraged during peak season. Dinner C$18–C$24 (US$13–US$17). AE, CB, DC, DISC, ER, MC, V. Daily 7am–10pm. REGIONAL/CONTINENTAL.

The Algonquin's Passamaquoddy Dining Room is elegant without being stuffy, featuring white tablecloths paired with painted farmhouse chairs. Expect expertly prepared resort fare, including prime rib, potato-crusted lamb chops, and cedar-plank salmon with onion marmalade. Never-fail specialties include salmon in its various guises and, for dessert, the maple mousse.

L'Europe. 48 King St. ☎ **506/529-3818**. Reservations recommended. Main courses C$17–C$35 (US$12–US$25). V. Tues–Sat 6–11pm. Closed mid-Oct to Apr. EUROPEAN/CANADIAN.

If the name didn't give it away, the theme at this handsome home a short stroll from Water Street is Europe, from the pewter and dark wood interior to the emphasis on continental fare. The large menu roams the old country from Italy to the Balkans and over to Paris. You'll find cream sauces and flambés, as well as a selection of more straightforward fare, like haddock with butter and almonds, and lamb chops with garlic and parsley. The menu also features Wiener schnitzel, German rolladen (rolled stuffed beef), and beef tenderloin with béarnaise. *Nice touch:* Every meal includes a dab of homemade pâté served with Black Forest farmer bread.

3 Grand Manan Island

Geologically rugged, profoundly peaceable, and indisputably remote, this handsome island of 2,800 year-round residents is a 90-minute ferry ride from Blacks Harbour, southeast of St. George. For adventurous travelers, Grand Manan is a much-prized destination and a highlight of their vacation. Yet it remains a mystifying puzzle for others who fail to be smitten by its rough-edged charm. "Either this is your kind of place, or it isn't," said one island resident. "There's no in-between." The only way to find out is to visit.

Grand Manan is a special favorite among serious birders and enthusiasts of novelist Willa Cather. Hiking the island's noted trails, don't be surprised to come across knots of very quiet people peering intently through binoculars. These are the birders. Nearly 300 different species of birds either nest here or stop by the island during their long migrations, and it's a good place to add to one's life list, with birds ranging from bald eagles to puffins (you'll need to sign up for a boat tour for the latter).

Willa Cather kept a cottage here and wrote many of her most beloved books while living on the island. Her fans are as easy to spot as the birders, say locals. In fact, islanders are still talking about a Willa Cather conference a few summers ago, when 40 participants wrapped themselves in sheets and danced around a bonfire during the summer solstice. "Cather people, they're a wild breed," one innkeeper intoned gravely to me.

ESSENTIALS

GETTING THERE   Grand Manan is connected to Blacks Harbour on the mainland via frequent ferry service in summer. **Coastal Transport** ferries (☎ **506/ 662-3724**), each capable of hauling 60 cars, depart from the mainland and the island every 2 hours between 7:30am and 5:30pm during July and August; three ferries a day serve the island the rest of the year. The round-trip fare is C$8.50 (US$6) per passenger (C$4.25/US$3 ages 5 to 12), C$25.50 (US$18) per car. Boarding the ferry on the mainland is free; tickets are purchased when you leave the island.

No reservations are accepted (although you can buy a ticket for the 7:30am ferry off the island a day in advance); get in line early to secure a spot. A good strategy for departing from Blacks Harbour is to bring a picnic lunch, arrive an hour or two early, put your car in line, and head to the grassy waterfront park adjacent to the wharf. It's an attractive spot; there's even an island to explore at low tide.

VISITOR INFORMATION   The island's **Tourist Information Centre** (☎ 506/662-3442) is open daily in summer in the town of Grand Harbor. It's beneath the museum, across from the elementary school. If the center's closed, ask around at island stores or inns for one of the free island maps published by the **Grand Manan Tourism Association,** which includes a listing of key island phone numbers.

EXPLORING THE ISLAND

Start your explorations before you arrive. As you come abreast of the island aboard the ferry, head to the starboard side. You'll soon see **Seven Day's Work** in the rocky cliffs of Whale's Cove, where seven layers of hardened lava and sill (intrusive igneous rock) have come together in a sort of geological Dagwood sandwich.

You can begin to open the Japanese puzzle box that is local geology at the **Grand Manan Museum** (☎ 506/662-3524) in Grand Harbor, one of three villages on the island's eastern shore. The museum's geology exhibit, located in the basement, offers pointers about what to look for as you roam the island. Birders will enjoy the Allan Moses collection upstairs, which features 230 stuffed and mounted birds in glass cases. The museum also has an impressive lighthouse lens from the Gannet Rock Lighthouse, and a collection of stuff that's washed ashore from the frequent shipwrecks. The museum is open mid-June to October Monday to Saturday from 10:30am to 4:30pm and Sunday from 1 to 5pm. Admission is C$2 (US$1.40) for adults and C$1 (US70¢) for seniors and students; children under 12 are free.

HIKING

Numerous hiking trails lace the island, and offer a popular diversion throughout the summer. Trails may be found just about everywhere, but most are a matter of local knowledge. Don't hesitate to ask at your inn, the tourist information center, or of anyone you might meet on the street. *A Hiking Guide to New Brunswick* (Goose Lane Editions; ☎ 506/450-4251) lists 12 hikes with maps; this handy book is often sold on the ferry.

The most accessible clusters of trails are at the island's northern and southern tips. Head north up Whistle Road to Whistle Beach and you'll find both the Northwestern Coastal Trail and the Seven Day's Work Trail, both of which track along the rocky coast. Near the low lighthouse and towering radio antennae at Southwest Head (follow Route 776 to the end), trails radiate out along cliffs topped with scrappy forest; the views are remarkable when the fog's not in.

BOAT TOURS

A fine way to experience island ecology is to mosey offshore. Several outfitters offer complete nature tours, providing a nice sampling of the world above and beneath the sea. **Island Coast Boat Tours** (☎ 506/662-8181) sets out for 4- to 5-hour expeditions in search of whales and birds. On an excursion you may see minke, finback, or humpback whales, along with exotic birds like puffins and phalaropes. The cost is C$40 (US$28) for adults, C$35 (US$25) for seniors, and C$22 (US$16) for children. **Seaview Adventures** (☎ 800/586-1922 in Canada, or 506/662-3211) offers

3¹/₂-hour educational tours with a unique twist: Divers provide a live underwater video feed to an onboard monitor. Prices are C$41 (US$29) for adults, C$38 (US$27) for seniors, and C$24 (US$17) for children.

ACCOMMODATIONS

Anchorage Provincial Park (☎ 506/662-7022) has 100 campsites scattered about forest and field. There's a small beach and a hiking trail on the property, and it's well situated for exploring the southern part of the island. It's very popular midsummer; call before you board the ferry to ask about campsite availability.

Compass Rose. North Head, Grand Manan, NB, E0G 2M0. ☎ **506/662-8570,** or 514/ 458-2607 Nov–Apr. 9 rms (5 with shared bath). C$59–C$89 (US$42–US$63) double. Rates include full breakfast. MC, V. Closed Nov–Apr.

The shipshape Compass Rose Inn occupies two small but historic homes overlooking the waterfront. All rooms have a water view and are tastefully decorated in a light country style. Among the best rooms: Calico, a corner room with a couch and pine floors, and great windows to watch the ferry come and go. No smoking. Lunch and dinner are served in a remarkably bright and cheerful dining room overlooking the harbor. Seafood is the specialty. Dishes include coquilles St-Jacques, sautéed scallops with rosemary, and pork tenderloin with wild-blueberry chutney. It's open daily for dinner from 5:30 to 8pm, and entree prices are C$13 to C$19 (US$9 to US$14).

✪ **Inn at Whale Cove Cottages.** Whistle Rd. (P.O. Box 233), North Head, Grand Manan, NB, E0G 2M0. ☎ **506/662-3181.** 3 rms, 4 cottages. C$75 (US$53) double including full breakfast; cottages rent by the week only C$400–C$500 (US$284–US$355). MC, V. Closed Nov–Apr.

The Inn at Whale Cove is a delightful, family-run compound set in a grassy meadow overlooking a quiet and picturesque cove. The original building is a cozy farmhouse that dates to 1816. It's been restored rustically with a nice selection of simple country antiques. The guest rooms are comfortable (Sally's Attic has a small deck and a large view); the living room has a couple years' worth of good reading and a welcoming fireplace. The cottages are scattered about the property and vary from one to four bedrooms. (Orchardside is the best.) The 10-acre grounds are wonderful to explore, especially the path down to the quiet cove-side beach. Pets are welcome. Innkeeper Laura Buckley received her culinary training in Toronto and demonstrates a deft touch with local ingredients. The menu might include seafood risotto, salmon in phyllo, or pork tenderloin with a green peppercorn sauce. Dinner is served nightly from 6 to 8:30pm, and entrees are priced from C$11 to C$20 (US$8 to $14).

DINING

In the mood for a dare? Try walking into the **North Head Bakery** (☎ 506/ 662-8862) and walking out without buying anything. *It cannot be done.* This superb bakery has used traditional baking methods and whole grains since it opened in 1990. Breads made daily include a crusty, seven-grain Saint John Valley bread and a delightful egg-and-butter bread. Nor should the chocolate-chip cookies be overlooked. The bakery is on Route 776 on the left when heading south from the ferry.

For a ready-made picnic, detour to **Cove Cuisine** at the Inn at Whale Cove (☎ 506/662-3181). Laura Buckley offers a limited but tasty selection of "new traditional" fixin's, like hummus, tabbouleh, and curried chicken salad to go. The inn is on Whistle Road, which forks off Route 776 near the bakery.

Options for dining out aren't exactly extravagant on Grand Manan. Both inns listed in "Accommodations" offer appetizing meals and decent value.

4 Saint John

Saint John is New Brunswick's largest city, and easily the province's most vibrant metropolis. The streets are bustling with everyone from skateboarders sporting nose rings to impeccably coiffed dowagers shopping at the public market. It's also the only New Brunswick city with an impressive skyline. The peninsular location has forced the downtown to build upwards, and a number of tall buildings—they don't quite qualify as "skyscrapers"—give the place a contemporary aspect when viewed from across the harbor.

Despite the generic modern architecture that dominates from afar, when you actually get downtown you'll find it's laid out on a very human scale. Built on a low hill, the downtown boasts wonderfully elaborate Victorian flourishes along the rows of commercial buildings. (Be sure to look high along the cornices to appreciate the intricate brickwork.) On certain streets at certain drizzly times, you could swear you're in Seattle or Portland, Oregon.

Travelers should be forewarned that making one's way downtown by car from the west can seem like passing through the outer rings of Hell, especially if it's foggy or damp. Belching factories, squalid industrial districts, and charmless subdivisions mark the outlying areas, which are set against bleak and stony hills. It's as if the whole metropolitan area was created by the Ashcan School of American artists. (A 1978 book on New Brunswick put it diplomatically: "Saint John's heavy industries ensure that the city is not famed for beauty, but the setting is magnificent.")

Don't let this put you off—make the effort to find downtown. And it does take some effort. The traffic engineers have been very mischievous here. When you finally arrive, you'll discover a good place to stroll around for an afternoon while awaiting the ferry to Digby, to grab a delicious bite to eat, or to break up village-hopping with an urban overnight.

One final note: Saint John is always spelled out, just like that. It's never abbreviated as St. John. That's to better keep mail aimed for St. John's in Newfoundland from ending up here, and vice versa. Locals will be quick to correct you if you err.

ESSENTIALS

GETTING THERE   Saint John is located on Route 1. It's 107 kilometers (66 miles) from the U.S. border at St. Stephens, and 424 kilometers (265 miles) from Halifax, Nova Scotia.

Year-round **ferry service** connects Saint John to Digby, Nova Scotia. See "Exploring New Brunswick" at the beginning of this chapter for information. Saint John's airport has regular flights to Toronto, Halifax, and other Canadian points; contact **Air Canada/Air Nova** (☎ 800/776-3000 in the U.S., 800/565-3940 in the Maritimes, or 506/632-1500) or **Air Atlantic** (☎ 800/426-7000 in the U.S. or 800/665-1177 in Canada) for more information.

VISITOR INFORMATION   Arriving from the west, look for a contemporary triangular building just off Route 1 (open mid-May to mid-October) where you'll find a trove of information and brochures (☎ 506/658-2940). A smaller seasonal information center is located inside the restaurant overlooking the Reversing Falls on Route 100 (☎ 506/658-2937).

If you've already made your way downtown, your best bet is the **City Centre Tourist Information Centre** (☎ 506/658-2855) inside Market Square, a downtown shopping mall just off the waterfront. Find the center by entering the square at street level at the corner of St. Patrick and Water streets. From mid-June to mid-September the center is open daily from 9am to 8pm. The rest of the year it's open daily from 9:30am to 6pm.

EXPLORING SAINT JOHN

Downtown comes in two flavors: indoor and outdoor. And it's worth exploring both.

If the weather's cooperative, start by wandering around the waterfront. The Visitor and Convention Bureau has published three **walking-tour brochures** that offer plenty of history and architectural trivia. Saint John is noted for the odd and interesting gargoyles and sculpted heads that adorn the brick and stone 19th-century buildings that comprise downtown. If you have time for only one, I'd opt for "Prince William's Walk," an hour-long, self-guided tour of the especially impressive commercial buildings. Request the free tour brochures at the Market Square information center.

If the weather's disagreeable, head indoors. Over the past decade, Saint John has been busy linking up its downtown malls and shops with an elaborate network of underground and overhead pedestrian walkways, dubbed **"The Inside Connection."** It's not just for shopping—two major hotels, the provincial museum, the city library, the city market, the sports arena, and the aquatic center are all part of the network.

The ✪ **New Brunswick Museum,** Market Square (☎ 506/643-2360), opened in modern new quarters downtown in April 1996, and is an excellent stop for anyone in the least curious about the province's natural or cultural history. The collections are displayed on three open floors and offer a nice mix of traditional artifacts and quirky objects. (Among the more memorable items is a dastardly looking "permanent wave" machine from a 1930s beauty parlor.) The exhaustive exhibits include the complete interior of Sullivan's Bar (where longshoremen used to slake their thirst a few blocks away), a massive section of a ship frame, a wonderful geological exhibit, and even a sporty white Bricklin from a failed New Brunswick automobile-manufacturing venture in the mid-1970s. Allow at least 2 hours to enjoy these eclectic and uncommonly well-displayed exhibits. Admission is C$5.50 (US$4) for adults, C$4.50 (US$3.20) for seniors, C$3.50 (US$2.50) for students and youths 4 to 18, and C$12 (US$9) for families; free from 6 to 9pm Wednesday. Open Monday to Friday from 9am to 9pm, Saturday from 10am to 6pm, and Sunday from noon to 5pm.

Hungry travelers venture at their own peril to the ✪ **Old City Market,** 47 Charlotte St. (☎ 506/658-2820). This spacious, bustling, and bright marketplace is crammed with vendors hawking meat, fresh seafood (beautiful fish!), cheeses, flowers, baked goods, and bountiful fresh produce. You can even sample dulse, a snack of dried seaweed from the Bay of Fundy. (One traveler has compared the experience to licking a wharf.) The market was built in 1876 and has been a center of commerce for the city ever since. Note the construction of the roof—some claim it resembles an inverted ship because it was made by boatbuilders. And watch for the small but enduring traces of tradition: The handsome iron gates at either end have been in place since 1880, and the loud bell is rung daily by the Deputy Market Clerk, who signals the opening and closing of the market. A number of vendors offer meals to go, and there's a bright seating area along the market's south side. Open Monday to Thursday from 7:30am to 6pm, Friday from 7:30am to 7pm, and Saturday from 7:30am to 5pm.

Serious antique buffs will find **Loyalist House,** 120 Union St. (☎ 506/652-3590), a mandatory destination. This stately Georgian home of white clapboard was built in 1817 for the Merritt family, who were wealthy Loyalists from Rye, New York. Inside is an extraordinary collection of furniture dating from before 1833, most

Saint John

ACCOMMODATIONS
Earle of Leinster Inn **6**
Parkerhouse Inn & Restaurant **5**
Saint John Hilton **1**

DINING
Billy's Seafood Co. **2**
Il Fornello **3**
Taco Pico **4**

of which were original to the home and have never left. Especially notable are the extensive holdings of Duncan Phyfe Sheraton furniture, and a rare piano-organ combination. Other unusual detailing includes the doors steamed and bent to fit into the curved sweep of the stairway, and the carvings on the wooden chair rails. Tours last 30 to 45 minutes, depending on the number of questions you muster. Admission C$3 (US$2.15) for adults, C$1 (US70¢) for children. Open daily from 10am to 5pm in July and August; Monday to Friday only in May and June. Entrance is by appointment only from mid-September to April.

The gleaming and modern **Canada Games Aquatic Centre,** 50 Union St. (☎ 506/658-4715), was built smack downtown in 1985. It remains a remarkably popular destination for exercise and recreation, and it's open to the public most hours all week long. Facilities include an eight-lane Olympic-size pool, warm-up and leisure pools, water slides, rope swings, whirlpools, and saunas. Also available: weight and exercise rooms (extra charge). Admission is C$5 (US$3.60) for adults; C$4 (US$2.85) for seniors, students, and children; and C$14.50 (US$10) for families. It's open Monday to Thursday from 6am to 10pm, Friday from 6am to 8pm, Saturday from 6:30am to 6pm, and Sunday from 11am to 6pm. Lanes aren't available at all times for nonmembers; call first.

OUTDOOR PURSUITS

Just west of downtown on Route 100 is **Reversing Falls,** an impressive, rocky gorge spanned by a pair of steel bridges. Owing to the massive tides, rapids and low waterfalls in the gorge flow one way during one tide, then reverse during the opposite tide. It's a dramatic sight in a dramatic location, but few tourist photos or descriptions include one important caveat: The gorge is all but overwhelmed by a huge and often stinky paper mill literally yards upriver. If you don't come expecting wild and brutish nature, you're less likely to be disappointed.

There are three ways of enjoying the spectacle. You can scramble down the wooden steps to a park along the river's edge. More sedentary souls can enjoy a meal in **The Falls Restaurant** (☎ 506/635-1999) overlooking the river at the west end of the bridge. The restaurant is peaceful and removed from the urban fray in that chirpy, elevator-music kind of way.

The most dramatic viewing platform is aboard a high-speed boat. **Reversing Falls Jet Boat Rides** (☎ 506/634-8987) runs fun, fast boat trips through the falls at all tides. The always breezy, sometimes damp trip takes 20 minutes and costs C$18 (US$13), which includes use of a raincoat. The specially designed boat departs frequently from Fallsview Park on the east bank of the river, opposite the restaurant and information center. Reservations are helpful during peak season.

Located along the coast across the Saint John River, the **Irving Nature Park,** Sand Cove Road (☎ 506/632-7777), consists of 450 dramatic coastal acres where as many as 240 species of birds have been spotted. Soft wood-chipped trails and marsh boardwalks provide access to a lovely forest and wild, salty seascapes. The observation tower on the "Squirrel Trail" gives a fine vantage of the park and its mudflats, where migrating sandpipers devour shrimp for a week to double their weight before flying 4 days nonstop to Surinam. Seals throng the park in mid-June and mid-October and are so thick on the rocks that they've been described as "a great gray noisy carpet." Irving Nature Park can get very busy—there are some 125,000 visitors a year—and Sundays are the most popular. Call beforehand to ask about the excellent tours. To get there, take Exit 107 off Route 1 and follow Bleury Street to Sand Cove Road. Admission and tours are free. Open daylight hours; the information booth is staffed daily from May to October.

ACCOMMODATIONS

In-town camping is available summers at **Rockwood Park** (☎ 506/652-4050). Some 80 sites are spread across a rocky hill; many overlook downtown, along with the highway and rail yard (expect nighttime noise). RVs requesting full hookups are directed to an area resembling a parking lot, but it's quite serviceable. Other sites vary widely in privacy and scenic attributes. Rates are C$14 (US$10) for a tent site, C$17 (US$12) for hookups. Follow signs to the park from either Exit 111 or Exit 113 off Route 1.

DOWNTOWN

Earle of Leinster Inn. 96 Leinster St., Saint John, NB, E2L 1J3. ☎ **506/652-3275.** 7 rms. TV TEL. C$55–C$60 (US$39–US$43) double. Rates include continental breakfast. MC, V.

Lauree and Stephen Savoie run the Earle of Leinster, a handsome Victorian row house in a working-class neighborhood a 5-minute walk from King's Square. It's an exceptionally welcoming place, with two kitchens for guests to make themselves at home and a pool table and TV in the basement. The Fitzgerald and Lord Edward rooms in the main house are the most historic, with high ceilings and regal furniture. Most of the remaining rooms are in the carriage house, and are a bit more motel-like, although the second-floor loft is quite spacious. The bathrooms are all private, but they're also small. Pets and kids are OK; smoking is not. Ask about the knotty-pine shorefront cottages the Savoies also rent about 25 minutes west.

Parkerhouse Inn & Restaurant. 71 Sydney St., Saint John, NB, E2L 2L5. ☎ **888/457-2520** or 506/652-5054. Fax 506/636-8076. 9 rms. A/C TV TEL. C$79–C$99 (US$56–US$70) double. AE, DC, ER, MC, V.

The Parkerhouse is a grand 1890 in-town mansion designed in high Victorian style. The attention to architectural detail is extraordinary, from the beveled leaded glass in the front doorway to the exquisite carved staircase of regal mahogany. Much of the downstairs is given over to a restaurant, but there's a bright sitting area with a 60-inch television for a slow night at home. (The Imperial Theatre is just next door, so see what's slated before settling in.) Guest rooms are decorated in a light Victorian country motif. Among the best is Room 5, with its sitting room, wood floors, pine armoire, and wonderful morning light. Also notable is Room 4, which features large stained-glass windows in the bathroom. Children over 10 are welcome. No smoking.

Dining: One of Saint John's better restaurants is located on the ground floor. Angle for a seat in the Victorian solarium with its mosaic floor, although the two other dining rooms are cozy and romantic. (An outside dining terrace was under construction when I last visited.) Lunch and dinner are served Monday to Saturday, with lunches of Monte Cristos and burgers; dinners are more ambitious, featuring steaks and fresh seafood, and the menu changes often (main courses C$16 to C$25/US$11 to US$18). Reservations are encouraged.

Saint John Hilton. 1 Market Sq., Saint John, NB, E2L 4Z6. ☎ **800/445-8667** in the U.S., 800/561-8282 in Canada, or 506/693-8484. Fax 509/657-6610. 197 rms. A/C MINIBAR TV TEL. Summer to mid-Oct C$89–C$115 (US$63–US$82) double; off-season C$85–C$99 (US$60–US$70). AE, DC, DISC, MC, V. Free parking weekends; C$9 (US$6) per day weekdays.

This 12-story waterfront hotel was built in 1984 and has all the modern amenities one would expect from an upscale chain hotel. It boasts the best location in Saint John, overlooking the harbor yet just steps from the rest of downtown by street or indoor walkway. Windows in all guest rooms open, which is a nice touch when the breeze is coming from the sea, but not when it's blowing in from the paper mill to the west. The Hilton is connected to the convention center and attracts major events; ask if anything's scheduled before you book if don't want to be overwhelmed by conventioneers.

Dining: The Brigantine Lounge offers light meals from 11:30am to 1am daily. For more refined fare, head to Turn of the Tide, which serves three meals daily in an attractive harborside setting.

Services: Concierge, 24-hour room service, laundry, safe-deposit boxes.

Facilities: Indoor pool, fitness room, Jacuzzi, sauna, indoor parking, game room, on-command video, business center.

ACROSS THE RIVER

Head to **Manawagonish Road** for a selection of budget-priced motels. Unlike many other motel strips, which tend to be notably unlovely, Manawagonish Road is pretty attractive. It winds along a high ridge of residential homes, with views out to the Bay of Fundy. It's about a 10-minute drive into downtown.

Among the motels here are the **Fairport Motel,** 1360 Manawagonish Rd. (☎ **800/251-6158** or 506/672-9700), with its home-cooked-meals restaurant, and the **Seacoast Motel,** 1441 Manawagonish Rd. (☎ **506/635-8700**), where the rooms have stunning views. I can attest to the impeccably clean and brightly lit rooms and cabins run by Dilip and Daxa Patel at **Balmoral Court Motel,** 1284 Manawagonish Rd. (☎ **506/672-3019**). Rates at most Manawagonish motels are under C$60 (US$43) in peak season.

DINING

For lunch, don't overlook the delightful **Old City Market,** mentioned above. With a little snooping, you can turn up excellent light meals and fresh juices in the market, then enjoy your finds in the alley atrium.

✪ **Billy's Seafood Co. Fish Market & Oyster Bar.** 49–51 Charlotte St. (at City Market). ☎ **888/933-3474** or 506/672-3474. Reservations suggested. Lunch specials C$6–C$8 (US$4.20–US$6); dinner entrees C$10–C$20 (US$7–US$14). AE, DC, ER, MC, V. Mon–Thurs 11am–10pm, Fri–Sat 11am–11pm, Sun 4–10pm. SEAFOOD.

When it comes to seafood, Billy Grant's restaurant off King's Square sets the standard. It's got a congenial staff, exceptionally fresh seafood (they sell to City Market customers by day), better prices than the waterfront seafood restaurants, and the chef simply knows how to prepare fish without overcooking. This classy restaurant is cozy and comfortable, painted a soothing deep, deep blue, with Ella Fitzgerald and Dinah Washington usually crooning in the background. Specialties include Atlantic salmon and the pan-fried rainbow trout. Billy's bouillabaisse is also very good. Offerings of beef, veal, and pasta fill out the menu for those not in the mood for fish.

Il Fornello. 33 Canterbury St. ☎ **506/648-2377.** Reservations suggested. Lunch C$7.35–C$15 (US$5–US$11); dinner C$9–C$15 (US$6–US$11); pizza C$6.30–C$14 (US$4.50–US$10). AE, DC, ER, MC, V. Mon–Thurs 11:30am–11pm, Fri–Sat 11:30am–midnight, Sun 4–10pm. ITALIAN.

If you've been to Toronto, you may recognize the name of this place. Canada's biggest city boasts seven Il Fornellos, a successful and classy minichain of Italian eateries. But this is the sole version in the Atlantic Provinces, and owner Paul Grannan has done a nice job converting an old printing office into a dramatic setting for reliable Italian fare. It's housed in a soaring, two-story space, anchored downstairs by a beautiful bar topped with polished red granite. Guests sit in austerely handsome chairs around lustrous wooden tabletops. You can "build your own" pasta by picking shape and sauce, along with add-ins. The same's true for the wood-fired pizza. Or select from a handful of traditional entrees like veal alla panna or chicken asiago. The all-you-can-eat lunch buffet is one of the city's better deals at C$9 (US$6).

Taco Pico. 96 Germain St. ☎ **506/633-8492.** Reservations suggested on weekends. Main courses C$7–C$16 (US$5–US$11) (same menu lunch and dinner). AE, MC, V. Mon–Sat 11am–10pm. GUATEMALAN.

This worker-owned cooperative is owned and run by young Guatemalans, and it's a great spot to expand your repertoire of Latin American cuisine. It's bright, festive, and just a short stroll off King Street. It's also developed a strong local following since it opened in 1994. It boasts a unique menu full of exotic tastes, not the usual dreary Canadian-Mex. Among the most reliably popular dishes are *pepian* (a spicy beef stew with chayote), garlic shrimp, and shrimp taco with potatoes, peppers, and cheese. There's a good selection of fresh juices, including a mildly addictive strawberry-kiwi-banana-milk concoction.

SAINT JOHN AFTER DARK

The best entertainment destination in town is the **Imperial Theatre** (☎ **506/674-4100**) on King's Square. Not always because of the acts that appear here, but because they perform in what the *Toronto Globe and Mail* called the "most beautifully restored theatre in Canada." The theater originally opened in 1913, and hosted performances by luminaries like Edgar Bergen, Al Jolson, and Walter Pidgeon (the latter a Saint John native). After being driven out of business by movie houses, then serving a long interim as home to a Pentecostal church, the theater was threatened with demolition in the early 1980s. That's when concerned citizens stepped in, raising funds to ensure the theater would survive.

The Imperial reopened to much fanfare in 1994, and it's since hosted a wide range of performances from Broadway road shows to local theatrical productions and concerts. Even if nothing is slated during your stay, you can take a short guided tour of the hall to admire the intricate plasterwork and the 9-foot drop chandelier. Tours are offered Monday to Saturday 10am to 5pm; the cost is C$2 (US$1.40) for adults and C$1 (US70¢) for children 12 and under.

5 Fredericton

New Brunswick's provincial capital is a small, historic city of brick and concrete that unfolds lazily along the banks of the wide and sluggish Saint John River. The handsome buildings, broad streets, and wide sidewalks make it feel more like a big, tidy village than a small city. Keep an eye out for the two icons that mark Fredericton: The stately, stubborn elm trees that have resisted Dutch elm disease and still shade the occasional park and byway, and the Union Jack, which you'll see fluttering from various buildings, attesting to long-standing historic ties with the Loyalists who shaped the city.

For travelers, the city can be seen as divided into three zones: the malls and motels near Exit 292 of the Trans-Canada Highway; the impressive, Georgian-style University of New Brunswick on the hillside just south of downtown; and the downtown proper, with its casual blend of modern and historic buildings.

Most visitors focus on downtown. The main artery—where you'll find the majority of the attractions and many restaurants—is Queen Street, which parallels the river between 1 and 2 blocks inland. An odd little limited-access four-lane spur separates much of downtown from the river, but you can still reach the water's edge via The Green.

Fredericton is low-key and appealing in a quiet and understated way. There's really no must-see attraction, but the collective impact of visiting several spots adds up to a very full sense of history and place. Fredericton's subtle charms won't be everyone's cup of tea. My advice: If eastern Canada's allure for you is the shimmering sea, deep woods, and wide open spaces, you won't miss much by bypassing Fredericton. If your passions include history—especially the history of British settlement in North America—then it's well worth the detour.

ESSENTIALS

GETTING THERE Fredericton is easily reached via the Trans-Canada Highway. From the west, follow signs for Woodstock Road, which follows the river to downtown. From Saint John, follow Route 7 to Regent Street, then turn right down the hill. Regent Street ends at the river near museums and attractions.

The **Fredericton Airport** (☎ 506/444-6100) is located 10 minutes southeast of downtown on Route 102, and is served by cab and rental-car companies. For flight information, contact **Air Canada/Air Nova** (☎ 800/776-3000 in the U.S., 800/565-3940 in the Maritimes, or 506/632-1500) or **Air Atlantic** (☎ 800/426-7000 in the U.S. or 800/665-1177 in Canada).

VISITOR INFORMATION Every visit should begin with a stop at the **Fredericton Visitor Centre** at City Hall, 397 Queen St. (☎ 506/460-2129). This is the place to request a **Visitor Parking Pass,** which allows visitors (at least those with out-of-province plates) to park free at city lots and meters around town. While you're here, also request the free *Fredericton Visitor's Guide.* During the peak summer season the office is open daily from 8am to 8pm; in fall it closes at 5pm; the rest of the year it's open weekdays only from 8:15am to 4:30pm.

If you're coming from the west, look for another **information center** just off the Trans-Canada Highway near Exit 289. It's open daily during the peak summer season and closed the rest of the year.

You can request information in advance by visiting the city's Web site at **www.city.fredericton.nb.ca** or e-mailing tourism@city.fredericton.nb.ca.

EXPLORING FREDERICTON

Begin your exploration with a stroll or bike ride along **The Green,** a 3-mile pathway that follows the river from the Sheraton Hotel to the Princess Margaret Bridge. This will allow you to get your bearings, and put you in the right frame of mind for the city's intimate scale.

Fredericton is noted for its distinctive architecture, especially the Victorian and Queen Anne residential architecture. Especially attractive is **Waterloo Row,** a group of privately owned historic homes—some grand, some less so—just downriver of downtown. There's really no single structure that defines the town. It's the sum of the smaller parts that provides the impact.

City Hall, 397 Queen Street, is an elaborate Victorian building with a prominent brick tower and 8-foot clock dial. The second-floor City Council Chamber occupies what was the opera house until the 1940s. Small, rather amateurish tapestries around the visitor's gallery tell the town's history. Learn about these and the rest of the buildings during the free building tours, which are offered daily from mid-May to mid-October on the hour (on the half hour in French). In the off-season, call ☎ 506/452-9616 to schedule a tour.

The surprisingly fine **Beaverbrook Art Gallery,** 703 Queen St. (☎ 506/458-8545), overlooks the waterfront and is home to an impressive collection of

Fredericton

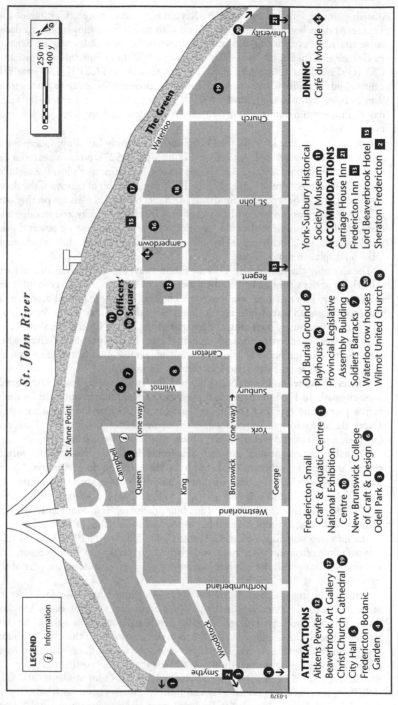

St. John River

The Green

LEGEND
ⓘ Information

250 m
400 y

ATTRACTIONS
Aitkens Pewter ⑫
Beaverbrook Art Gallery ⑰
Christ Church Cathedral ⑲
City Hall ⑤
Fredericton Botanic
 Garden ④
Fredericton Small
 Craft & Aquatic Centre ①
National Exhibition
 Centre ⑩
New Brunswick College
 of Craft & Design ⑥
Odell Park ③
Old Burial Ground ⑨
Playhouse ⑯
Provincial Legislative
 Assembly Building ⑱
Soldiers Barracks ⑦
Waterloo row houses ⑳
Wilmot United Church ⑧
York-Sunbury Historical
 Society Museum ⑪

ACCOMMODATIONS
Carriage House Inn 21
Fredericton Inn 13
Lord Beaverbrook Hotel 15
Sheraton Fredericton 2

DINING
Café du Monde ◆14

1-0370

123

British paintings, including works by Reynolds, Gainsborough, Constable, and Turner. Antique buffs gravitate to the rooms with period furnishings and early decorative arts. Most everyone finds themselves drawn to Salvador Dali's massive *Santiago El Grande* and studies for an ill-fated portrait of Winston Churchill. Admission is C$3 (US$2.15) for adults, C$2 (US$1.40) for seniors, and C$1 (US70¢) for students; children under 6 are free. Open June to September, Monday to Friday from 9am to 6pm, Saturday and Sunday from 10am to 5pm; November to May, Tuesday to Friday from 9am to 5pm, Saturday from 10am to 5pm, and Sunday from noon to 5pm.

Constructed starting in 1880, the ✪ **Legislative Assembly Building,** Queen Street across from the Beaverbrook Art Gallery (☎ **506/453-2527**), boasts an exterior designed in that bulbous, extravagant Second Empire style. But that's just the prelude. Inside it's even more dressed up and fancy. Entering takes a bit of courage if the doors are closed; they're heavy and intimidating, with slits of beveled glass for peering out. (They're a little reminiscent of the gates of Oz.) Inside, it's creaky and wooden and comfortable, in contrast to the cold, unyielding stone of many seats of power. In the small rotunda, look for the razor-sharp prints from John James Audubon's elephant folio, on display in a special case.

The assembly chamber nearly takes the breath away, especially when viewed from the heights of the visitor gallery on the upper floors. (You ascend via a graceful wood spiral stairway housed in its own rotunda.) The chamber is ornate and draperied in that fussy Victorian way, which is quite a feat given the vast scale of the room. Note all the regal trappings, including the portrait of the young Queen Elizabeth. This place just feels like a setting for high drama, whether or not it actually delivers when the chamber is in session. Admission to the assembly is free. It's open in summer daily from 9am to 8pm; off-season, weekdays from 9am to 4pm.

Officer's Square, on Queen Street between Carleton and Regent, is now a handsome city park. In 1785 the park was the center of military activity and used for drills, first as part of the British garrison, and later (until 1914) by the Canadian Army. Today, the only soldiers are local actors who put on a show for the tourists. Look also for music and dramatic events staged at the square in the warmer months.

The handsome colonnaded stone building facing the parade grounds is the former officers' quarters, now the fine **York-Sunbury Historical Society Museum,** Queen Street (☎ **506/455-6041**). This small museum lures visitors with the promise of a stuffed 42-pound frog. It was said to belong to Fred Coleman, who in the late 19th century fed it a nasty concoction of June bugs, cornmeal, buttermilk, and whiskey to give it Rubenesque proportions. After it perished at the hands of some miscreants, the famous frog was displayed at the Burke House Hotel until 1959, when it traveled with little ceremony to the museum. It's displayed on the top floor to ensure that you wander through all the exhibits looking for it—a clever trick on the part of the curator.

Actually, the frog is a disappointment. (Not to mention suspect—it looks like it's made of bad papier-mâché.) But the rest of the museum is nicely done. Displays feature the usual artifacts of life-gone-by, but several exhibits rise well above the clutter, including a fine display on Loyalist settlers. Kids will love the claustrophobic re-creation of a German World War II trench on the second floor—and likely will end up talking more about that on the way home than Fred's portly frog.

Admission is C$2 (US$1.40) for adults, C$1 (US70¢) for students, and C$4 (US$2.85) for families. It's open May and June, Monday to Saturday from 10am to 6pm; July and August, Monday to Saturday from 10am to 9pm and Sunday from noon to 6pm; September to November, Monday to Friday from 9am to 5pm and Saturday from noon to 4pm; December to April, Monday, Wednesday, and Friday from 11am to 3pm or by appointment.

Two blocks upriver of Officers' Square is the **Soldiers' Barracks,** housed in a similarly grand stone building. Check your watch against the sundial high on the end of the barracks, a replica of the original time piece. A small exhibit shows the life of the enlisted man in the 18th century. Along the ground floor, local craftspeople sell their wares from small shops carved out of former barracks.

An entertaining and enlightening way to learn about the city's history is to sign up for a walking tour with the **Calithumpians** of Fredericton's Outdoor Summer Theatre. Costumed guides offer 1-hour tours daily in July and August, pointing out highlights with anecdotes and dramatic tales. Especially recommended is the evening "Haunted Hikes" tour, which runs closer to 2 hours. The tours are free; contact **City Hall Tourist Information** (☎ 506/452-9616) for times.

Outside town, the ✪ **Kings Landing Historical Settlement** (☎ 506/363-4999, or 506/363-4959 for recorded information), is 34 kilometers (21 miles) and about 150 years from Fredericton. This authentic re-creation brings to life the New Brunswick of 1790 to 1910, with 10 historic houses and nine other buildings relocated here and saved from destruction by the flooding during the Mactaquac hydro project. The aroma of freshly baked bread mixes with the smell of horses and livestock, and the sound of the blacksmith's hammer alternates with that of the church bell. More than 160 costumed "early settlers" chat about their lives.

You could easily spend a day exploring the 150 acres, but if you haven't that much time, focus on the **Hagerman House** (with furniture by Victorian cabinetmaker John Warren Moore), the **Ingraham House** with its fine New Brunswick furniture and formal English garden, the **Morehouse House** (where you'll see a clock Benedict Arnold left behind), and the **Victorian Perley House.** The **Ross Sash and Door Factory** will demonstrate the work and times of a turn-of-the-century manufacturing plant.

Afterwards, hitch a ride on the sloven wagon, or relax at the Kings Head Inn, which served up grub and grog to hardy travelers along the Saint John River a century or more ago. Today it serves lemonade, chicken pie, and corn chowder, along with other traditional dishes. Lunch prices are C$8 to C$13 (US$6 to US$9), and dinner is C$13 to C$19 (US$9 to US$13).

Admission to Kings Landing is C$9 (US$6) for adults, C$8 (US$6) for seniors, C$7.25 (US$5) for students over 16, C$5.50 (US$4) for children 6 to 16, and C$24 (US$17) for a family pass. It's open June to mid-October daily from 10am to 5pm. To get there, take exit 259 off the Trans-Canada Highway (Route 2 west).

ACCOMMODATIONS

A handful of motels and chain hotels are located in the mall zone along Regent and Prospect streets (take Exit 292 off the Trans-Canada). Among the classiest of the bunch is the **Fredericton Inn,** 1315 Regent St. (☎ 800/561-8777 or 506/455-1430), situated between two malls. It's a soothing-music-and-floral-carpeting kind of place that does a brisk business in the convention trade. But with its indoor pool and classically appointed rooms, it's a comfortable spot for vacation travelers as well. Peak-season rates are C$73 to C$105 (US$52 to US$75), and up to C$169 (US$120) for suites.

Also accessible via Exit 292 are the **Auberge Wandlyn Inn,** 58 Prospect St. (☎ 506/452-8937), with rates of C$63 to C$95 (US$45 to US$68); the **Comfort**

Inn, 255 Prospect St. (☎ **506/453-0800**), at C$70 to C$95 (US$50 to US$68); and the **Country Inn and Suites,** 455 Prospect St. (☎ **506/459-0035**), C$70 to C$81 (US$50 to US$58).

Carriage House Inn. 230 University Ave., Fredericton, NB, E3B 4H7. ☎ **800/267-6068** or 506/452-9924. Fax 506/458-0799. E-mail: chinn@nbnet.nb.ca. 10 rms (4 rms share 1 bath; 2 with private hall baths). TEL. C$60 (US$43) double with shared bath, C$75–C$85 (US$53–US$60) with private bath. Rates include breakfast. AE, DC, MC, V.

Fredericton's premier bed-and-breakfast is located a short stroll from the riverfront pathway in a quiet residential neighborhood. This imposing three-story Victorian manse was built by a former mayor in 1875. Inside it's a bit somber in that heavy Victorian way, with dark wood trim and deep colors, but the place feels solid enough to resist glaciers. Rooms are eclectically furnished and comfortable but not opulent. Beware the shared bath: Four guest rooms share one small bath, so access could be problematic after morning coffee. Breakfast is served in a sunny room in the rear of the house. Children and pets are welcome (there's a friendly rottweiler named Bailey already on the premises). No smoking.

Lord Beaverbrook Hotel. 659 Queen St., Fredericton, NB, E3B 5A6. ☎ **800/561-7666** in Canada and New England only, or 506/455-3371. Fax 506/455-1441. E-mail: lbh@nbnet.nb.ca. 153 rms. A/C TV TEL. C$95–C$120 (US$67–US$85) double; C$125–C$450 (US$89–US$320) suite. Weekend and off-season discounts. AE, CB, DC, DISC, ER, MC, V.

Don't be put off by first impressions. This stern and hulking 1947 waterfront building is severe and boxy, looking as if it were housing either prisoners or the Ministry of Dourness. But inside the mood lightens considerably, with composite stone floors, Georgian pilasters, and chandeliers. The downstairs indoor pool and recreation area is positively whimsical, a sort of Tiki-room grotto that kids adore. The guest rooms are nicely appointed with traditional reproduction furniture in dark wood. Standard rooms can be somewhat dim, and most of the windows don't open (ask for a room with opening windows when you book). The suites are spacious and many have excellent river views. The hotel, which is part of the Keddy chain, possesses more sentimental charm than polish. If you're looking for a glossier finish, continue down the waterfront to the Sheraton. At press time the hotel's facade was slated for updating, so it might not look quite as grim once you arrive.

Dining: You've got several choices for dining, from the elegant Terrace and Governor's rooms to the informal River Room. The Terrace Room is the main dining area, with an indoor gazebo and seasonal outdoor deck overlooking the river. The menu corrals resort standards, starting with relish trays and puffy white dinner rolls. Main courses, at C$11 to C$17 (US$8 to US$12), range from Oriental shrimp stir-fry to chicken fettuccine Alfredo. The adjacent Governor's Room has higher aspirations, with dinner entrees like duck breast with a raspberry and Grand Marnier coulis, or shrimp Provençale at C$16 to C$25 (US$11 to US$18).

Services: Dry cleaning and laundry, baby-sitting, safe-deposit boxes, airport shuttle (nominal fee).

Facilities: The downstairs recreation area includes a small indoor pool, a Jacuzzi, and limited fitness equipment; conference rooms, business center.

Sheraton Fredericton. 225 Woodstock Rd., Fredericton, NB, E3B 2H8. ☎ **800/325-3535** or 506/457-7000. Fax 506/457-4000. 208 rms, 15 suites. A/C MINIBAR TV TEL. C$140 (US$99) double; C$89 (US$63) weekends. AE, CB, DC, MC, V.

This modern resort hotel, built in 1992, is tall and proud, occupying a prime location along the river about a 10-minute walk from downtown on the riverfront pathway. Much of summer life revolves around the outdoor pool on the deck overlooking

the river, and on Sunday the lobby is surrendered to an over-the-top breakfast buffet. While decidedly up-to-date, the interior is done with classical styling and is comfortable and well appointed. All rooms include irons and hair dryers.

Dining/Entertainment: The lounge is an active and popular spot on many nights,
especially weekends. Across the lobby is Bruno's Seafood Cafe, which offers a surprisingly good alternative to the lackluster restaurants downtown. It's perhaps the only
Sheraton in existence to have boasted emu on the menu; look also for seasonal and
regional specialties, especially those involving fiddleheads. Main courses range from
C$7 to C$23 (US$5 to US$16).

Services/Facilities: The hotel features all the services and amenities you'd expect
from a modern hotel, including a fitness room, indoor and outdoor pools, gift shop,
and complete conference facilities.

DINING

Fredericton is the natural habitat of the family restaurant, and creative cuisine simply isn't on the menu for travelers. Head to Bruno's Seafood Cafe in the Sheraton
or the Terrace Room at the Beaverbrook Hotel for the city's best upscale dining.

Café du Monde. 610 Queen St. ☎ **506/457-5534.** Reservations recommended for dinner.
Lunch main courses C$7.25–C$9 (US$5–US$6); dinner main courses C$9–C$15 (US$6–US$11).
AE, DC, ER, MC, V. Mon–Wed 7:30am–10pm, Thurs–Fri 7:30am–11pm, Sat 9am–11pm, Sun
11am–10pm. CAFE.

This casual cafe offers a relaxed atmosphere that attracts university students studying from thick textbooks, young folks playing cards, and older folks sitting at the bar
smoking and reminiscing. It's part pub, part art gallery, and part inventive restaurant.
While the menu won't get big-city chefs talking, it's as creative as you'll find in
Fredericton, with entrees like Cajun sea bass, spinach and basil lasagna, and bouillabaisse.

6 Fundy National Park

The Fundy Coast east of Saint John is wild, remote, and unpopulated. Plumbed by
few roads, it's also next to impossible to explore unless you have a boat. But there's
one exception: ✪ **Fundy National Park.** This is a gem of a park, a spot that would
make a fine destination for a week's outing, especially for a family. Activities in and
near the park range from hiking to sea kayaking to biking to just splashing around
a seaside pool. Nearby are lovely drives and an innovative adventure center at Cape
Enrage. If a muffling fog moves in to smother the coast, head inland for a hike to a
waterfall. If it's a day of brilliant sunshine, venture along the rocky shores by foot or
boat.

ESSENTIALS

GETTING THERE   Route 114 runs through the center of Fundy National Park.
If you're coming from the west, follow the prominent national-park signs just
east of Sussex. If you're coming from Prince Edward Island or Nova Scotia, head
southward on Route 114 from Moncton.

One word of warning for travel from Moncton: Beware the signs at the Route 15
rotary directing you to Fundy National Park. Moncton's traffic czars send tourists
on a silly, Mr. Toad's Wild Ride around the city's outskirts, apparently to avoid
downtown traffic; after 16 kilometers (10 miles) of driving you'll end up within sight
of the rotary again, just across the river. It's far more sensible to head downtown via
Main Street, cross the river on the first steel bridge (you can see it from about
everywhere), and then turn left on Route 114.

VISITOR INFORMATION   The park's main **Visitor Centre** (☎ 506/887-6000) is located just inside the Alma (eastern) entrance to the park. The stone building is open daily during peak season from 8am to 10pm (with limited hours in the off-season). You can watch a video presentation, peruse a handful of exhibits on wildlife and tides, and shop at the nicely stocked nature bookstore.

The smaller **Wolfe Lake Information Centre** (☎ 506/432-6026) is at the park's western entrance, and is open daily in summer, weekdays-only in spring.

FEES   Park entry fees are charged from mid-May to mid-October. The fee is C$3.50 (US$2.50) for adults, C$2.75 (US$2) for seniors, C$1.75 (US$1.25) for children 6 to 16, and C$7 (US$5) for families; children under 6 are free. Four-day passes are available for the price of 3 days.

EXPLORING FUNDY NATIONAL PARK

Most national-park activities are centered around the Alma (east) side of the park, where the park entrance has a cultivated and manicured air, as if part of a landed estate. Here you'll find stone walls, well-tended lawns, and attractive landscaping, along with a golf course, amphitheater, lawn bowling, and tennis.

Also in this area is a **heated saltwater pool,** set near the bay with a sweeping ocean view. There's a lifeguard on duty and it's a popular destination for families. The pool is open late June to August and is open daily from 11am to 6:45pm. A day pass is C$3.25 (US$2.30) for adults, C$2.25 (US$1.60) for children, and C$8 (US$6) for families; there are discounts for campers and overnight visitors.

Also unique to the park are two **auto trails**—basically overgrown dirt roads that you can explore with the family car. Hastings Auto Trail is one-way so you needn't worry about oncoming vehicles. It's a good way to see some of the great outdoors without suffering the indignities that often result from actual encounters with nature (rain, bugs, blisters, and so on).

HIKING

The park maintains 110 kilometers (66 miles) of trails for hikers and walkers. These range from a 20-minute loop to a 4-hour trek, and pass through varied terrain. The trails are arranged such that several may be linked into a 50-kilometer (30-mile) backpacker's loop, dubbed the **Fundy Circuit,** which typically requires 3 nights in the backcountry. Preregistration is required, so ask at the visitor center.

Among the most accessible hikes is the **Caribou Plain Trail,** a 3.4-kilometer (2-mile) loop that provides a wonderful introduction to the local terrain. You'll hike along a beaver pond, on a boardwalk across a raised peat bog, and through lovely temperate forest. Read the interpretive signs to learn about the deadly "flarks," which lurk in bogs and can kill a moose.

The **Third Vault Falls Trail** is a 7.4-kilometer (4.4-mile) in-and-back hike that takes you to the park's highest waterfall, about 45 feet high. The trail is largely a flat stroll through leafy woodlands until you begin a steady descent into a mossy gorge. You round a corner and there you are, suddenly facing the cataract.

All the park's trails are covered in the pullout trail guide you'll find in *Salt & Fir,* the booklet you'll receive when you pay your entry fee.

CAMPING

The national park maintains four drive-in campgrounds and 15 backcountry sites. The two main campgrounds are near the Alma entrance. **Headquarters Campground** is within walking distance of Alma, the saltwater pool, and numerous other attractions. Since it overlooks the bay, this campground tends to be cool and subject to fogs. **Chignecto Campground** is higher on the hillside, sunnier, and warmer. You can down-hike to Alma on an attractive hiking trail in 1 to 2 hours. Both campgrounds have hookups for RVs, flush toilets, and showers, and sites may be reserved in advance (☎ 800/213-7275 or 506/887-6000).

The **Point Wolfe** and **Wolfe Lake** campgrounds lack RV hookups and are slightly more primitive (Wolfe Lake lacks showers), but are the preferred destinations for campers seeking a quieter camping experience. Rates at all campgrounds are C$11 to C$18 (US$8 to US$13) depending on services required; Wolfe Lake has pit toilets only and is C$9 (US$6) per night.

Backcountry sites are scattered throughout the park, with only one located directly on the coast (at the confluence of the coast and Goose River). Ask at one of the visitor centers for more information or to reserve a site (mandatory). Backcountry camping fees are C$2.50 (US$1.80) per person per night.

A ROAD TRIP TO CAPE ENRAGE

Cape Enrage is a blustery and bold cape that juts impertinently out into Chignecto Bay. It's also home to a wonderful adventure center that could be a model for similar centers worldwide.

✪ **Cape Enrage Adventures** traces its roots back to 1993, when a group of Harrison Trimble High School students in Moncton decided to do something about the decay of the cape's historic lighthouse, which had been abandoned in 1988. They put together a plan to restore the light and keeper's quarters and establish an adventure center. It worked. Today, with the help of experts in kayaking, rock climbing, rappelling, and other rugged sports, a couple dozen high-school students staff and run this program throughout the summer months.

Part of what makes the program so notable is its flexibility. Day adventures are scheduled throughout the summer, from which you can pick and choose, as if from a menu. These include rappelling workshops, rock-climbing lessons, kayak trips, and canoeing expeditions. Prices range from C$40 (US$28) per person for rock workshops to C$50 (US$36) per canoe or kayak for other trips. (*Note to parents:* This is an ideal spot to drop off restless teens for a few hours while you indulge in scenic drives or a trip to Hopewell Rocks.)

Families looking to endure outdoor hardships together should inquire about custom adventures. For about C$170 (US$120) per person, the center will organize a 2-night adventure vacation that includes equipment, instruction, food, and lodging. You pick your own adventures—maybe a sea-kayak trip early one morning, followed by a whole afternoon of rappelling. It's entirely up to you.

As if running the center didn't keep the students busy enough, they also operate a restaurant (open to the public), called **The Keeper's Lunchroom.** Light but tasty meals include a fish chowder, soups, and fresh-from-the-oven biscuits. Prices are very reasonable.

For more information about the program, contact **Cape Enrage Adventures,** Site 5-5, RR #1, Moncton, NB, E1C 8J5 (☎ **506/856-2417,** or 506/887-2273 after May 15; fax 506/856-3480).

A ROAD TRIP TO THE HOPEWELL ROCKS

There's no better place to witness the extraordinary power of the Fundy tides than at ✪ **Hopewell Rocks** (☎ 506/734-3429), located about 40 kilometers (24 miles) northeast of Fundy National Park on Route 114. Think of it as a natural sculpture garden. At low tide (the best time to visit), eroded columns as high as 50 feet tower above the ocean floor. They're sometimes called the "flowerpots," on account of the trees and plants that still flourish on their narrowing summits.

You park at the new visitor center and restaurant and wander down to the shore. Signboards fill you in on the natural history. If it's the bottom half of the tide, you can descend the steel staircase to the sea floor and admire these wondrous freestanding rock sculptures, chiseled by waves and tides.

The site can be crowded, but understandably so. If your schedule allows it, come early in the day when the sun is fresh over Nova Scotia across the bay, the dew is still on the ground, and most travelers are still sacked out in bed. The park charges an entry fee of C$4 (US$2.80) per carload.

If you arrive at the top half of the tide, consider a sea-kayak tour around the islands and caves. **Baymount Outdoor Adventures** (☎ 506/734-2660) runs tours daily for C$30 (US$21) per person.

ACCOMMODATIONS

Fundy Park Chalets. Rte. 114 (P.O. Box 72), Alma, NB, E0A 1B0. ☎ **506/887-2808.** 29 cabins. TV. C$68 (US$48) for 1–4 people; discounts in spring and fall. MC, V. Closed Oct to mid-May.

These storybooklike cabins are set amid birch and pines just inside the park's eastern entrance, and will have immediate appeal to fans of classic motor courts. The steeply gabled white clapboard cabins have interiors that will bring to mind a national-park vacation around 1950—painted wood floors, pine paneling, metal shower stalls, small kitchenettes. Two beds are located in the main rooms, separated by a hospital-like track curtain that pulls around one bed. What the cabins lack in privacy they more than make up for in convenience and a retro charm. The golf course, playground, tennis courts, lawn bowling, and saltwater pool are all within walking distance.

DINING

Seawinds Dining Room. Rte. 114 (near park headquarters), Alma. ☎ **506/887-2098.** Reservations helpful. Sandwiches C$3–C$7 (US$2.15–US$5); main courses C$9–C$16 (US$6–US$11). MC, V. Daily 8am–9:30pm in summer. Closed Oct–May. PUB FARE/CANADIAN.

Seawinds overlooks the park golf course, and it serves as a de facto clubhouse for hungry duffers. The handsome and open dining room is decorated in rich forest green and mahogany hues, and has hardwood floors, a flagstone fireplace, and wrought-iron chandeliers. The menu offers enough variations to please most anyone. Lunches include a variety of hamburgers, fish-and-chips, and bacon-and-cheese dogs. Dinner is somewhat more refined, with main courses like grilled trout, roast beef, and fried clams.

7 Moncton

Moncton, a city of some 60,000 inhabitants, offers a mix of the antique and the modern. Brick buildings with elaborate facades and cornices exist cheek by jowl with boxy office towers of a less ornamental era. Moncton's low and unobtrusive skyline is dominated by an unfortunate concrete tower that houses a cluster of microwave antennae. It looks like a project designed by a former Soviet bureaucrat in a bad mood, but serves as a good landmark to keep yourself oriented.

The residents are also a mix of old and new. Moncton makes the plausible claim that it's at the crossroads of the Maritimes, and hasn't been bashful about using its geographic advantage to promote itself as a business hub. As such, much of the hotel and restaurant trade caters to the gray-flannel set, at least on weekdays. But walk along Main Street in the evening or on weekends, and you're likely to spot spiked hair, grunge flannel, skateboards, and other youthful fashion statements from current and lapsed eras. There's life here.

For families, Moncton offers a good stopover if you're traveling with kids. Magnetic Hill and Crystal Palace both offer entertaining (albeit somewhat pricey) ways to fill an afternoon. The latter is an especially appealing destination on rainy days.

ESSENTIALS

GETTING THERE   Moncton is at the crossroads of several major routes through New Brunswick, including Route 2 (the Trans-Canada Highway) and Route 15.

Moncton's airport is about 10 minutes from downtown on Route 132 (head northeast on Main Street from Moncton and keep driving). The city is served by daily flights on **Air Nova/Air Canada** (☎ **800/776-3000** in the U.S. or 800/565-3940 in the Maritimes) and **Air Atlantic/Canadian Airlines** (☎ **800/426-7000** in the U.S. or 800/665-1177 in Canada).

Via Rail's (☎ **800/561-3949** in the U.S. or 800/561-3952 in the Maritimes) line from Montréal to Halifax stops in Moncton 6 days a week. The rail station is downtown on Main Street, next to Highfield Square. (Look for the prominent train trestle.)

VISITOR INFORMATION   Moncton's primary **visitor center** (☎ **506/ 853-3590**) is downtown at 655 Main St., in the lobby of modern **City Hall.** It's open daily from 8am to 8pm during peak summer season. During the warmer months, "ambassadors" also staff a **Tourist Information Centre** (☎ **506/853-3540**) at Lutes Mountain on the Trans-Canada Highway.

EXPLORING MONCTON

Moncton's downtown can be easily reconnoitered on foot—once you find parking, which can be vexing. (Look for the paid lots a block or so north and south of Main Street.) The most active stretch of Main Street is the few blocks between City Hall (home to the visitor center) and the train underpass. Here you'll find cafes, newsstands, hotels, and restaurants, along with a handful of intriguing shops.

Moncton's **Tidal Bore** is a low wave that rolls up the Petitcodiac River at the leading edge of the turning tide. Sadly, the bore has been living up to its name since a dam and causeway were constructed upstream in 1968. Silt has built up in the chocolatey-brown river below the causeway, which some say has reduced the height and drama of the bore. The wave, when it comes up around the bend of the river, is rather tiny. (Think of the Stonehenge scene in *Spïnal Tap.*) It's more dramatic in winter and fall, I'm told, but in the summer it's not all that impressive.

The bore rolls in twice daily on the tides (at Bore Park it's illuminated at night with banks of floodlights). Check the arrival time in the brochure produced by the tourism authority, or swing by Bore Park on Main Street (across from the Hollins Lincoln Mercury dealership) and note the time of the next bore on the digital clock. The park has bleachers to sit on and railings to lean against while awaiting the ripple.

A simple way to get a good sense of Moncton's past is to spend 45 minutes or so roaming through the **Moncton Museum,** 20 Mountain Rd., at King Street (☎ **506/ 853-3003**). This handsome, modern museum opened in 1973 (note the clever reuse of the old City Hall facade) and displays various artifacts of city life on two floors, including early hotel dishware, fashions, and intriguing, grainy photos of downtown in the early days. Admission is by donation. Open daily in July and August from 10am to 8pm; 9am to 5pm the rest of the year.

Architecture buffs should inquire at the museum's front desk about visiting the **Free Meeting House** next door. Constructed in 1821 and restored in 1990, the meetinghouse has historically served as a gathering point for a wide range of denominations. Inside, it's simplicity itself, with neatly enclosed pews and sunlight streaming in through the windows.

Located on Moncton's northwest outskirts, **Magnetic Hill,** Trans-Canada Highway Exit 488 (☎ 800/217-8111), began as a simple quirk of geography. Cars that stopped at the bottom of a short stretch of downhill started to roll back uphill! Or at least what appeared to be uphill. It's a nifty illusion—not to pull back the curtain, but it works because the slope is on the side of a far larger hill, which tilts the whole countryside and effectively skews one's perspective. Starting in the 1930s, locals capitalized on the phenomenon by opening canteens and gift shops nearby. By the 1950s, the hill boasted the largest souvenir shop in the Maritimes.

This mysterious stretch of country road was preserved for posterity when a bypass was built around it, and today you can still experience the mystery. The atmosphere is a bit more glossy than a half-century ago, however. You enter a well-marked drive with magnet-themed road signs and streetlights, pay a C$2 (US$1.40) toll at a gatehouse, and wind around a comically twisting road to wait your turn before being directed to the hill.

Young kids often find the "uphill roll" entertaining—for about 3 yards. Then their attention is riveted by the two amusement complexes that have sprouted in the fields on either side of the road. Attractions within a few hundred yards of the hill include **Wharf Village** (a quaint collection of boutiques and snack bars designed to look like a seaside village), a minigolf course, a sizable zoo, video arcades, go-cart racing, batting cages, a driving range, a kiddie train, and bumper boats. But the chief attraction is the **Magic Mountain Water Park,** which features wave pools and numerous slides, including the towering Kamikaze Slide where daredevils can reach speeds of 64 kilometers per hour (40 m.p.h.).

Despite—or perhaps because of—the unrepentant cheesiness, Magnetic Hill is actually a great destination for families weary of beaches, hikes, and the dreary natural world. Just be aware that nothing's cheap after you fork over C$2 (US$1.40) to roll up the hill; an afternoon here can put a serious hurt on your wallet.

The water park is open daily from 10am to 8pm during peak season; until 6pm in shoulder season. Other attractions open at varied hours; call for information. Admission for Magnetic Hill is C$2 (US$1.40) per car. Magic Mountain Water Park costs C$19.50 (US$14) for a full day (age 12 or older), and C$14 (US$10) for children ages 4 to 11; a family pass costs C$59 (US$42). Half-day and evening rates are available. Additional charges apply for the Pier Mini Golf: C$4.95 (US$4) for ages 12 and older, and C$3.75 (US$2.70) for children 4 to 11; the Magnetic Hill Zoo: C$6 (US$4.30) for adults, C$5 (US$3.60) for youths 12 to 18 and seniors, C$3.75 (US$2.65) for children 4 to 11, and C$15 (US$11) per family (4 persons). The park accepts American Express, MasterCard, and Visa.

The indoor amusement park at **Crystal Palace,** Champlain Place Mall (Trans-Canada Highway Exit 504-A West), Dieppe (☎ 506/859-4386), will make an otherwise endless rainy day seem short. The spacious enclosed park includes a four-screen cinema, shooting arcades, numerous games (ranging from old-fashioned SkeeBall to cutting-edge video games), medium-sized roller coaster, carousel, swing ride, laser tag, bumper cars, mini-airplane and mini-semitruck rides, minigolf, batting cages, and a virtual-reality ride. In summer, outdoor activities include go-carts and bumper boats. The park will particularly appeal to kids under the age of 12, although teens will likely find video games to occupy them. To really wear the kids down, you can stay virtually inside the park by booking a room at the adjoining Best Western (see below).

Crystal Palace is open daily. Admission is free; rides are one to three tickets each (C$1/US70¢ per ticket or 10 for C$7.50/US$5). Unlimited ride passes are also available for C$21 (US$15), which doesn't include the go-carts.

ACCOMMODATIONS

Several chain hotels have set up shop near Magnetic Hill (Trans-Canada Highway Exit 488). These include **Comfort Inn** at 2495 Mountain Rd. (☎ **800/228-5150** or 506/384-3175); **Country Inn & Suites** at 2475 Mountain Rd. (☎ **800/ 456-4000** or 506/852-7000); and **Holiday Inn Express,** also just off the exit on Mountain Road (☎ **800/595-4656** or 506/384-1050.) At these hotels, you'll find rooms that range from a low of C$80 (US$57) to a high of C$100 (US$71).

Best Western Crystal Palace. 499 Paul St., Moncton, NB, E1A 6S5. ☎ **800/561-7108** or 506/858-8584. Fax 506/858-5486. 115 rms. A/C MINIBAR TV TEL. C$103–C$165 (US$73–US$117) double. Ask about value packages, which include amusement-park passes. AE, DC, DISC, ER, MC, V.

This modern, three-story chain hotel (built in 1990) adjoins the Crystal Palace amusement park and is a short walk from the region's largest mall. As such, it's surrounded by acres of asphalt and has little in the way of innate charm. Most rooms are modern but unexceptional—not counting the 12 fantasy suites that go over-the-top with themes like "Deserted Island" (sleep in a thatched hut) or "Rock 'n' Roll" (sleep in a 1959 replica pink Cadillac bed). Some rooms face the indoor pool, others the vast parking lot.

Dining/Entertainment: For entertainment there's the amusement park, obviously. Also within the amusement complex is the hotel's restaurant, McGinnis Landing, which offers basic pub fare. Prices are relatively high at C$12 to C$20 (US$9 to US$14) for main dinner courses, but specials are always available and the restaurant caters well to younger appetites.

Services/Facilities: Indoor pool, hot tub, sauna, safe, baby-sitting, limited room service, dry cleaning (Monday to Friday), conference rooms.

Hotel Beauséjour. 750 Main St., Moncton, NB, E1C 1E6. ☎ **800/441-1414** or 506/ 854-4344. Fax 506/858-0957. 310 rms. A/C MINIBAR TV TEL. C$87–C$107 (US$62–US$76) double summer and weekends; C$116–C$153 (US$82–US$109) double remainder of year. AE, DC, ER, MC, V.

The downtown Hotel Beauséjour is one of the Canadian Pacific properties, and with that lineage comes certain expectations of elegance. These expectations are handily met, with nice touches throughout like down comforters, hair dryers, and irons and ironing boards in all rooms. The imposing building, constructed in 1972, is boxy, bland, and concrete, and the entrance courtyard is sterile and off-putting in a cold-war Berlin sort of way. Inside the decor is inviting in a spare, international modern manner. The property is superbly maintained, with rooms and public areas recently renovated. Nothing is threadbare. The third-floor pool was recently enclosed, and now offers year-round swimming. (There's also a pleasant outdoor deck overlooking the distant marshes of the Petitcodiac River.) The hotel is a favorite among business travelers, but in summer and on weekends leisure travelers largely have it to themselves—hence the lower rates.

Dining: In addition to the very elegant ✪ **Windjammer** (see below), the hotel has a basic cafe/snack bar, a piano bar and lounge, and a rustic, informal restaurant called L'Auberge, which serves three meals a day. The lunches at L'Auberge offer good value, with most dishes under C$10 (US$7).

Services: 24-hour room service, dry cleaning, laundry service, turndown service, safe-deposit boxes, baby-sitting, valet parking.

Facilities: Indoor pool, health club, conference rooms, business center, washer/dryer, beauty salon, shopping arcade.

DINING

Boomerang's Steakhouse. 130 Westmoreland St. ☎ **506/857-8325.** Call-ahead seating in lieu of reservations. Hamburgers and grilled sandwiches C$7–C$9 (US$5–US$6); dinners C$12–C$18 (US$9–US$13). AE, DISC, ER, MC, V. Daily 4–10pm. STEAK HOUSE.

Boomerang's is a unabashed knockoff of the Aussie-themed Outback Steakhouse chain, right down to the oversized knives. But since this is the only Boomerang's (it's not a chain), the service is rather more personal, and the Aussie-whimsical decor is done with a lighter hand. It's a handsome spot with three dining rooms, all quite dim with slatted dividers, drawn shades, and ceiling fans, which creates the impression that it's blazingly hot outside. (That's a real trick in February in New Brunswick.) The menu features the usual stuff from the barbie, including grilled chicken breast and ribs. The steak selection is grand and ranges from an 8-ounce bacon-wrapped tenderloin to a 14-ounce porterhouse. The burgers are also excellent.

✪ **The Windjammer.** 750 Main St. (in the Hotel Beauséjour). ☎ **506/854-4344.** Reservations recommended. Main courses C$19.25–C$31.25 (US$14–US$22). AE, DC, ER, MC, V. Daily 6–9pm. CONTINENTAL.

Tucked off the lobby of Moncton's best hotel is The Windjammer, an intimate dining room that serves the city's best meals. With its heavy wood and nautical theme, it resembles the private officers' mess of a very exclusive ship. The menu is ambitious, with creative dishes like pan-fried shrimp and scallops with black pepper and spicy dried banana, and Atlantic salmon baked with Moroccan spices. Despite the seafaring decor, the chef also serves up treats for carnivores, including tournedos of caribou with jus and blueberries, and sautéed duck confit with Asian pesto. Intrigued by the fan of ostrich breast marinated in ginger and garlic and served with a black pepper sauce? Plan ahead, since it requires 24 hours notice.

8 Kouchibouguac National Park

Much is made of the fact that this sprawling park has all sorts of ecosystems worth studying, from sandy barrier islands to ancient peat bogs. But that's a little bit like saying Disney World has nice lakes. It causes one's eyes to glaze over, and it entirely misses the point. In fact, this artfully designed national park is a wonderful destination for relaxing biking, hiking, and beach-going. If you can, plan to spend a couple of days here doing a whole lot of nothing. The varied ecosystems (which, incidentally, are spectacular) are just an added attraction.

Kouchibouguac is, above all, a place for bikers and families. The park is laced with well-groomed bike trails made of finely crushed cinders that traverse forest and field, and along rivers and lagoons. Where bikes aren't permitted (such as on boardwalks and beaches), there are usually clusters of bike racks for locking them up while you continue on foot. If you camp here, bring a bike; there's no need to ever use your car.

Families can easily divide their days to keep kids entertained. Mornings might be spent at the broad and sandy beach, and afternoons biking along the lagoon, crossing a springy bog on a boardwalk, or poking around in a paddleboat.

While the park is ideal for campers, day-trippers also find it a worthwhile destination. *One tip:* Plan to remain here until sunset. The trails tend to empty out, and the dunes, bogs, and boreal forest take on a rich, almost iridescent hue as the sun sinks over the spruce.

Be aware that this is a fair-weather destination. If it's blustery and rainy, there's little to do here except take damp and melancholy strolls on the beach. It's best to save a visit here for more cooperative days.

By the way, the ungainly name is a Mi'kmaq Indian word meaning "River of the Long Tides." It's pronounced "*Koosh*-uh-*boog*-oo-*whack*." If you don't get it right, don't worry. Few do.

ESSENTIALS

GETTING THERE   Kouchibouguac National Park is between Moncton and Miramichi. The exit for the park off Route 11 is well marked.

VISITOR INFORMATION   The park is open from mid-May to mid-October. The **Visitors Centre** (☎ 506/876-2445) is just off Route 134, a short drive past the park entrance. It's open from 8am to 8pm during peak season, with shorter hours in the off-season. There's a slide show to introduce you to the park's attractions, and a small collection of field guides to peruse.

FEES   A daily pass is C$3.50 (US$2.50) for adults, C$1.75 (US$1.25) for children 6 to 16, C$2.75 (US$2) for seniors, and C$7 (US$5) for families; children under 6 are free. Four-day passes are also available. A map of the park (helpful) costs C$1 (US70¢) at the information center. You should have permits for everyone in your car when you enter the park. There are no formal checkpoints, only occasional roadblocks during summer to ensure compliance.

CAMPING

Kouchibouguac is at heart a camper's park, best enjoyed by those who plan to spend at least a night here. **South Kouchibouguac,** the main campground, is centrally located and very nicely laid out with 311 sites, most quite large and private. The 46 sites with electricity are nearer the river and somewhat more open. The newest sites (1 to 35) lack grassy areas for pitching tent, and campers have to pitch tents on gravel pads. It's best to bring a good sleeping pad, or ask for another site. Sites are C$16.75 (US$12) per night. Reservations are accepted for about half the campsites; call ☎ 800/213-7275. The remaining sites are doled out on a first-come, first-served basis.

The park also maintains three backcountry sites. **Sipu** is on the Kouchibouguac River and is accessible by canoe or foot, **Petit Large** by foot or bike, and **Pointe-à-Maxime** by canoe only. Backcountry sites cost C$10 (US$7) per night for two, including firewood.

BEACHES

The park features some 15 kilometers (9 miles) of sandy beaches, mostly along barrier islands of sandy dunes, delicate grasses and flowers, and nesting plovers and sandpipers. ✪ **Kellys** is the principal beach, and it's one of the best-designed and best-executed recreation areas I've come across in eastern Canada. At the forest's edge, a short walk from the main parking area, you'll find showers, changing rooms, a snack bar, and some interpretive exhibits. From here, you walk some 600 yards across a winding boardwalk that's plenty fascinating on its own. It crosses salt marsh, lagoons, and some of the best-preserved dunes in the province.

The long, sandy beach features water that's comfortably warm, with waves that are usually quite mellow—they lap rather than roar, unless a storm's offshore. A roped-off section of about 100 yards is overseen by lifeguards; elsewhere you're on your own. For very young children who still equate waves with certain death, there's supervised swimming on a sandy stretch of the quiet lagoon.

EQUIPMENT RENTALS

Ryans—a cluster of buildings between the campground and Kellys Beach—is the place for renting bikes, canoes, kayaks, paddleboats, and canoes. Bikes rent for C$4.60 (US$3.30) per hour (C$23.30/US$17 daily, C$29/US$21 for 2 days). Most of the water-sports equipment rents for about C$6 to C$7 (US$4.30 to US$5) per hour, with double kayaks around C$10 (US$7) per hour. It's located on the lagoon, so you can explore up toward the dunes or upstream on the winding river.

HIKING

The hiking and biking trails are as short and undemanding as they are attractive. The one hiking trail that requires slightly more fortitude is the Kouchibouguac River Trail, which runs for some 13 kilometers (8 miles) along the banks of the river.

The ✪ **Bog Trail** is just 1.8 kilometers (1.2 miles) each way, but it opens the door to a wonderfully alien world. The 4,500-year-old bog is a classic domed bog, made of peat from decaying shrubs and other plants. At the bog's edge you'll find a wooden tower ascended by a spiral staircase that affords a panoramic view of this eerie habitat.

Callanders Beach and **Cedar Trail** are at the end of a short dirt road. There's an open field with picnic tables, a small protected beach on the lagoon (there are fine views of dunes across the way), and a 1-kilometer (0.6-mile) hiking trail on a boardwalk that passes through a cedar forest, past a salt marsh, and through a mixed forest. This is a good alternative for those who'd prefer to avoid the larger crowds at Kellys Beach.

OUTSIDE THE PARK

There's little development just outside the park gates—a couple of take-out restaurants, some small, poorly stocked grocery stores, and that's about it. Head south toward Richibucto and Bouctouche for a slightly wider selection of accommodations and restaurants.

Kayakouch (☎ 506/876-1199) offers guided kayak tours along the Saint-Louis River and an open lagoon a few kilometers south of the park. You may see gray seals and terns, and you'll get a loon's-eye view of the terrain hereabouts. A half-day tour runs C$50 (US$36) per person (tax not included); an evening paddle takes 3 hours and costs C$25 (US$18) per person. The base camp is on Route 134 north of the bridge, in Saint-Louis-de-Kent.

ACCOMMODATIONS & DINING

Habitant Motel and Restaurant. Rte. 134 (RR #1, Box 2, Site 30), Richibucto, NB, E0A 2M0. ☎ **506/523-4421.** Fax 506/523-9155. 29 rms. A/C TV TEL. C$60–C$90 (US$43–US$64) double. AE, CB, DC, DISC, ER, MC, V.

At about 15 kilometers (9 miles) from the park entrance, Habitant is the best choice for overnighting if you're exploring Kouchibouguac by day. It's a modern, mansard-roofed, Tudor-style complex—well, let's just say "architecturally mystifying"—with a restaurant and small campground on the premises. The rooms are decorated in a contemporary motel style and are very clean. The motel features a distinctive indoor pool.

Dining: The restaurant next door serves three meals a day, and is informal, comfortable, and reasonably priced. Seafood dinners are the specialty, including a heaping "fisherman's feast" for C$23 (US$16). Most main courses are C$8 to C$15 (US$6 to US$11). *One nice touch:* there's a self-serve wine cellar, where wines are sold at liquor-store prices. There's a decent selection of bottles under C$20 (US$14), and even a handful under C$10 (US$7).

9 The Acadian Peninsula

The Acadian Peninsula is that bulge on the northeast corner of New Brunswick, forming one of the arms of the Baie des Chaleurs (Québec's Gaspé Peninsula forms the other.) It's a land of low and generally nondescript houses, miles of shoreline (much of it beaches), modern concrete harbors filled with commercial fishing boats, and residents proud of their Acadian heritage. (You'll see the *stella maris* flag everywhere—the French tricolor with a single gold star in the field of blue.)

On a map it looks like much of the coastline would be wild and remote out here. Unfortunately, it's not. While a number of picturesque farmhouses dot the route, and you'll come upon brilliant meadows of hawkweed and lupine, the coast is more defined by manufactured housing that's been erected on squarish lots between the sea and fast two-lane highways.

Other than the superb Acadian Village historical museum near Caraquet, there are few organized attractions in the region. It's more a place to unwind while walking on a beach, or just idle harborside while watching fishing boats come and go.

ESSENTIALS

VISITOR INFORMATION Each of the areas mentioned below maintains a visitor information center. **Caraquet Tourism Information** is located at 51 bd. St-Pierre est (☎ 506/726-2676). This office offers convenient access to other activities in the harbor (see below), and there's plenty of parking. Shippagan dispenses information from a wooden lighthouse near the Marine Centre.

GETTING THERE Route 11 is the main highway serving the Acadian Peninsula.

CARAQUET

The historic beach town of Caraquet—widely regarded as the spiritual capital of Acadian New Brunswick—just keeps on going and going, geographically speaking. It's spread thinly along a commercial boulevard parallel to the beach. Caraquet once claimed the honorific "longest village in the world" when it ran to some 22 kilometers (13 miles) long. As a result of its length, Caraquet lacks a well-defined downtown or any sort if urban center of gravity; there's one stoplight, and that's where Boulevard St-Pierre est changes to Boulevard St-Pierre ouest. (Most establishments mentioned below are somewhere along this boulevard.)

A good place to start a tour is the **Callefour de la Mer** (51 boulevard St-Pierre est), a modern complex overlooking the man-made harbor. It has a spare, Scandinavian feel to it, and here you'll find the tourist information office (see above), a seafood restaurant, snack bar, children's playground, and two short strolls that lead to picnic tables on jetties with fine harbor views.

While you're here you can sign up for a whale watch or rent a bicycle in the shingled buildings next to the information center. But the best way to view the harbor and bay is by sea kayak. You can rent a kayak from **Tours Kayaket** (☎ 800/704-3966 or 506/727-6309) for C$12 (US$9) an hour (C$24/US$17 for a double kayak) and putter around inside the seawall, or venture out into the bay if conditions are agreeable. For C$45 (US$32) per person, guides will take you on a 3- to 4-hour excursion to an island or sandbar; if the wind's ripping, you'll be trailered to a protected river about 10 minutes from downtown.

New Brunswick sometimes seems awash in Acadian museums and historic villages. If you're interested in visiting just one, ✪ **Village Historique Acadien,** Route 11, 6 miles west of Caraquet (☎ 506/726-2600), is the place to hold out for. Some 45 buildings—most of which were dismantled and transported here from other villages on the peninsula—depict life as it was lived in an Acadian settlement between the years 1770 and 1890. The historic buildings are set throughout 458 acres of woodland, marsh, and field. You'll learn all about the exodus and settlement of the Acadians from costumed guides, who are also adept at skills ranging from letterpress printing to blacksmithing. Plan on spending at least 2 to 3 hours exploring the village.

In 1997 construction began on a second phase that will nearly double the size of the village. Some 25 new buildings (all but one are replicas) will be devoted to continuing the saga, showing Acadian life from 1890 to 1939, with a special focus on industry. Plans also call for an old-style hotel within the new village, which will house students enrolled in multiday workshops in traditional Acadian arts and crafts. Construction of phase two is expected to take 2 to 3 years.

Admission is C$8.75 (US$6) for adults, C$5 (US$3.60) for children 6 to 16, C$7.25 (US$5) for seniors, C$22 (US$16) per family; children under 6 are free. Prices are discounted in September. Open daily in summer from 10am to 6pm (to 5pm in September). Closed October to May.

ACCOMMODATIONS

Camping is at **Caraquet Provincial Park** (☎ 506/727-1706), a few minutes' drive west of downtown. It's a rather cozy sliver of coastal land for the 109 sites, but pleasant enough with its own beach and snack bar. Rates are C$17.50 (US$12) with electricity and C$15 (US$11) without.

Hotel Paulin. 143 bd. St-Pierre ouest. ☎ **506/727-9981.** Fax 506/727-3300. 10 rms (5 share 2 baths). C$45–C$85 (US$32–US$60) double. MC, V.

This attractive Victorian hotel, built in 1891, has been operated by the Paulin family for the past three generations, and it's only acquired more charm with each passing year. It's a three-story red clapboard building with a green-shingled mansard roof, located just off the main boulevard and overlooking the bay. (Some of the charm has been compromised by encroaching buildings nearby.) The lobby puts one immediately in mind of summer relaxation, with royal-blue wainscoting, canary-yellow walls, and stuffed furniture upholstered in white with blue piping. The rooms, which are all on the second floor, are varied, but only the suite (good for families) has an unobstructed ocean view. Expect rooms sparely furnished with antiques, but quite cozy. Because few guests want to share baths, the current generation of Paulin is considering making suites of the shared bath rooms, each with private bath. Ask before you book. Hotel Paulin's first floor houses a handsome well-regarded restaurant. Specialties include a delectable crab mousse and a cure for the sweet tooth: brown sugar pie.

DINING

Caraquet is a good place for seafood, naturally. There are no standout restaurants, but several inexpensive to moderate spots along the main drag serve fresh seafood that's nicely prepared.

For a delicious and sophisticated snack, head to **Les Blancs d'Arcadia,** a handsome compound of yellow farm buildings hard against the forest just east of town. The specialties here are cheese and yogurt from the milk of a Swiss breed of goats called Saanen. The goats are raised indoors year-round; you can learn about the goats and the cheese- and yogurt-making processes on a tour of the operation, which includes tastings. The tour is C$6 (US$4.30).

Not in the mood for a tour? There's a small shop to buy fresh cheeses and milk. I heartily recommend both the peppercorn and garlic soft cheeses. **Les Blancs d'Arcadia,** 340-A bd. St-Pierre est (☎ 506/727-5952) is en route to Bas Caraquet on Route 145 (watch for the goat sign on the right shortly after you pass the road to St-Simon). Reservations for tours are appreciated.

Café Phare. 186 bd. St-Pierre ouest. ☎ **506/727-9469.** Breakfast C$1.50–C$6 (US$1.10–US$4.30); lunch and dinner C$3–C$7 (US$2.15–US$5). MC, V. Sun–Mon 9am–5pm, Tues–Thurs 9am–10pm, Fri–Sat 9am–midnight. CAFE.

Café Phare, located in a wood-frame house on Caraquet's main drag, has a relaxed, hip, and inviting atmosphere that's a perfect stop for the road-weary traveler. Order up a cappuccino while browsing the well-thumbed selection of French and English magazines. The menu includes tasty salads and generous sandwiches (the pastrami's especially good). The soups are made fresh daily and are usually delicious.

GRANDE-ANSE

Grande-Anse is a wide-spot-in-the-road village of low, modern homes near bluffs overlooking the bay. The town is lorded over by the stern, stone Saint Jude Church. The best view of the village, and a good spot for a picnic, is along the bluffs just below the church. (Look for the QUAI sign 50 yd. west of the church). Here you'll find a small man-made harbor with a fleet of fishing boats, a tiny sand beach, and some grassy bluffs where you can park overlooking the bay.

If you'd prefer picnic tables, head a few miles westward to **Pokeshaw Park.** Just offshore is a large kettle-shaped island ringed with ragged cliffs that rises from the waves, long ago separated from the cliffs you're now standing on. An active cormorant rookery thrives among the eerie skeletons of trees, lending the whole affair a somewhat haunted and melancholy air. There's a small picnic shelter for inclement weather. It's open daily from 9am to 9pm; admission is C$1 (US70¢) per car, C$2 (US$1.40) for a motor home.

For the full-blown ocean-swimming experience, head to **Plage Grande-Anse,** located 2 kilometers (1.2 miles) east of town. This handsome beach has a snack bar near the parking area and is open from 10am to 9pm daily. The cost is C$3 (US$2.15) for adults.

Deep vermilion hues and liturgical strains piped in all the rooms mark the modern **Pope Museum,** Route 184, Grande-Anse (☎ 506/732-3003), founded in 1985—the year after the Pope visited Moncton. The devout will enjoy the portrait gallery featuring portraits of all 264 popes. But all will be fascinated by the intricate model of the Vatican, which occupies much of the central hall (the top of the dome stands about 6 ft. high). Other models of houses of worship include smaller versions of the Florence cathedral, Bourges cathedral, Cheops pyramid, and the Great El Hakim mosque. Head upstairs for displays of various Roman Catholic artifacts and contemporary religious accoutrements, including vestments and chalices. Most descriptions are bilingual, but a handful are in French only. Admission is C$5 (US$3.60) for adults, C$2.50 (US$1.80) for children, C$3.50 (US$2.50) for seniors, and C$10 (US$7) for families. Open daily from 10am to 6pm. Closed September to May.

10 Mount Carleton Provincial Park

New Brunswick isn't all sandy beaches and rushing tides. There's the whole, vast interior, a sprawling land marred by few roads and filled with rolling hills, dense forest, and tenacious blackflies (at least in early summer). This isn't wilderness—most of the land is employed as a vast timber plantation to feed the province's voracious paper and lumber mills. But in 1969 New Brunswick carved out some of the choicest land and set it aside as wilderness park. Mount Carleton Provincial Park contains 7,052 acres of azure lakes, pure streams, thick boreal forest, and gently rounded mountains, the largest of which are ledgy and afford excellent views. When visiting, look for moose, black bear, coyote, bobcat, and more than 100 species of birds. And, of course, blackflies.

ESSENTIALS

GETTING THERE Mount Carleton Provincial Park is 43 kilometers (26 miles) east of Saint-Quentin on Route 180. Be aware that Saint-Quentin is the nearest community for supplies; there are no convenient general stores just outside the park gates. The park is also accessible from Bathhurst to the east, but it's a 115-kilometer (69-mile) drive on a road that's mostly paved but gravel in spots. There are no services along the road and frequent logging trucks.

VISITOR INFORMATION The park's gates are open daily from 7am to 10pm. A **small interpretive center** (☎ 506/235-2025) is located at the entrance gate, and offers background on the park's natural and cultural history.

FEES The day-use fee is C$4 (US$2.85) per car.

CAMPING

Armstrong Brook is the principal destination for visiting campers. It has 88 sites split between the forest near Lake Nictau's shore (no lakeside sites) and an open and grassy field. Campers can avail themselves of hot showers and a bathhouse for washing up. The toilets are either pit or composting toilets. A path leads to the lake's edge; there's a spit of small, flat pebbles that's wonderful for swimming and sunbathing.

Four backcountry sites are located high on the slopes of Mount Carleton (preregistration required). The sites, which require a 4-kilometer (2.4-mile) hike, offer views into a rugged valley and a great sense of remoteness. Water is available, but should be treated (beavers are nearby). No fires are permitted, so bring a stove. The fee is C$5 (US$3.60) per night.

Two other remote campsites on the shores of Lake Nictau are accessible either by canoe or a moderate walk. Register in advance; the fee is C$9 (US$6) per night.

HIKING & BIKING

The park has 10 hiking trails that total 62 kilometers (37 miles). The helpful park staff at the gatehouse will be happy to direct you to a hike that suits your experience and mood.

The park's premier hike is to the summit of **Mount Carleton,** the province's highest point at 2,697 feet. While that's not going to impress those who've hiked in the

Canadian Rockies, height is relative here, and the views seem endless. The summit is marked by a craggy comb of rocks that afford a 360° view of the lower mountains and the sprawling lakes. The trailhead is about a 25-minute drive from the gatehouse; allow about 4 hours for a round-trip hike of about 10 kilometers (6 miles).

Overlooking Nictau Lake is **Mount Sagamook,** at an altitude of 2,555 feet. It's a steep and demanding hike of about 3 kilometers (1.8 miles) to the summit, where you're rewarded with spectacular views of the northern park.

For the truly gung-ho, there's the ridge walk that connects Sagamook and Carleton via **Mount Head.** The views from high above are unforgettable; you'll need to set up a shuttle with two cars to do the whole ridge in 1 day.

If you've got a mountain bike, bring it. The gravel roads are perfect for exploring. Motor vehicles have been banned from two of the roads, which take you deep into the woods past clear lakes and rushing streams.

6 Prince Edward Island

by Wayne Curtis

Prince Edward Island may not be the world's leading manufacturer of relaxation and repose, but it's certainly a major distribution center. Visitors soon suspect there's something about the richly colored landscape of azure seas and henna-tinged cliffs capped with lush farm fields that triggers an obscure relaxation hormone, resulting in a pleasant ennui. It's hard to conceive that verdant Prince Edward Island and boggy, blustery Newfoundland share a planet, never mind the same gulf.

The north coast is lined with red-sand **beaches,** washed with the warmish waters of the Gulf of St. Lawrence. Swimming here isn't quite like a tepid dip in North Carolina, but it's quite a bit warmer than in Maine or New Hampshire further down the Eastern seaboard. Away from the beaches you'll find low, rolling hills, blanketed in trees and crops, especially potatoes, for which the island is justly famous. Small **farms** make up the island's backbone—one-quarter of the island is dedicated to agriculture, with that land cultivated by more than 2,300 individual farms.

The island was first explored in 1534 by Jacques Cartier, who discovered the Mi'kmaq living here. Over the next 2 centuries, dominion over the island bounced between Great Britain and France (who called it Isle St-Jean). Great Britain was awarded the island in 1763 as part of the Treaty of Paris; just over a century later, the first Canadian Confederation was held at Charlottetown and bore fruit with the creation of Canada in 1867. (Prince Edward Island didn't join the confederation until 1873.) The island is named for Edward Augustus (1767–1820), the son of George III of England.

Today, the island retains much of its bucolic flavor of a century ago, and pockets of kitsch and sprawl are happily few, mostly concentrated around Cavendish, Charlottetown, and Summerside. Here you'll find campy tourist attractions and all-too-familiar strip malls. Elsewhere, though, you're certain to find yourself on winding back roads through farmlands that make you wish for a bicycle.

Indeed, Prince Edward Island is steeped in the slower pace of an earlier era; milkmen still make their quiet rounds, and you return soda-pop bottles for refilling, not just recycling. Indeed, the population has grown only from 109,000 in 1891 to about 125,000 today. You should take your cue from this comforting cadence and do yourself this favor: schedule 1 or 2 extra days into your vacation, and make absolutely no plans. You won't regret this.

Prince Edward Island

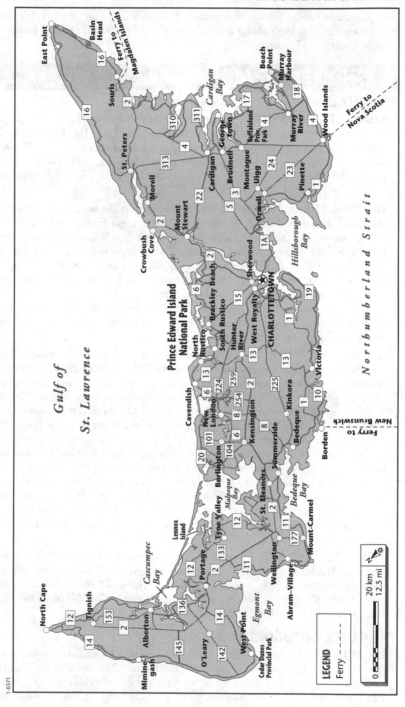

This chapter is divided into the counties that neatly trisect the province. It's easy to remember: They rise in order of royal hierarchy—**Prince** to **Queens** to **Kings**—in the direction of England.

1 Exploring Prince Edward Island

ESSENTIALS

VISITOR INFORMATION   Tourism PEI publishes a comprehensive free guide to island attractions and lodgings that's well worth picking up. The *Visitors Guide* is available at all information centers on the island or in advance by calling ☎ 800/ 463-4734 or 902/368-4444. You can also request it by e-mail (tourpei@gov.pe.ca) or mail (P.O. Box 940, Charlottetown, PEI, C1A 7M5). The official **PEI Web site** is **www.gov.pe.ca**.

GETTING THERE   By Car   If you're coming from the west, you'll arrive via the **Confederation Bridge,** which opened with great fanfare in June 1997. Sometimes you'll hear it referred to as the "fixed link," a reference to the guarantee Canada made in 1873 to provide a permanent link from the mainland. The dramatic 12.9-kilometer (7.7-mile) bridge is open 24 hours a day and takes about 10 or 12 minutes to cross. Unless you're high up in a van, a truck, or an RV, the views are mostly obstructed by the concrete Jersey barriers.

The bridge toll is C$35 (US$25) round-trip. No fare is paid when you travel to the island; the entire toll is collected when you leave. Credit cards are accepted. Call ☎ **888/437-6565** for more information.

By Ferry   For those arriving from Cape Breton Island or other points east, **Northumberland Ferries Limited** (☎ **888/249-7245** or 902/566-3838) provides seasonal service between Caribou, Nova Scotia (just north of Pictou), and Woods Island, Prince Edward Island. Ferries with a 250-car capacity run from May to mid-December. During peak season (June to mid-October), ferries depart each port every 90 minutes between 6am and 6pm, with an additional ferry at 8pm. The crossing takes about 75 minutes.

No reservations are accepted; it's best to arrive at least an hour before departure to improve your odds of getting on the next boat. Early morning ferries tend to be less crowded. Fares are C$40 (US$28) for car and driver, C$9.50 (US$7) per additional adult, and C$5 (US$3.60) per child. Major credit cards are honored. As with the bridge, fares are paid upon exiting the island; the ferry to the island is free. (Discussions were underway in 1997 to possibly change the pay-when-leaving system; call first to confirm.)

By Air   The island's main airport is a few miles north of Charlottetown. Commuter flights to Halifax are just half an hour; direct flights from Toronto are offered summers only. For more information, contact **Air Nova** (☎ **800/776-3000** in the U.S. or 800/565-3940 in Eastern Canada) or **Air Atlantic** (☎ **800/426-7000** in the U.S., 800/665-1177 in Eastern Canada, or 902/427-5500).

THE GREAT OUTDOORS

BICYCLING   The main off-road bike trail is the ✪ **Confederation Trail.** Eventually, the trail will cover some 350 kilometers (210 miles) from Tignish to Souris along the old path of the ill-fated provincial railway. At present, some 225 kilometers (135 miles) have been completed, mostly in Prince and Kings counties; Queens County is still largely under development. The pathway is covered mostly in rolled stone dust, and makes for good travel with a mountain bike or hybrid. Services are steadily being developed by groups along the route, with bike rentals and inns cropping up; ask at the local tourist bureaus for updated information on completed segments.

MacQueen's (☎ 902/962-3397) at 430 Queen St. in Charlottetown organizes custom bike tours, with prices including bike rentals, accommodations, maps, luggage transfer, and emergency road service. Five- and 7-night tours are C$649 and C$839 (US$461 and US$596), respectively. Rentals are also available at C$22 (US$16) per day or C$88 (US$63) per week. MacQueen's can be reached via e-mail at **biketour@peinet.pe.ca**. For rentals and repairs, you might also try **Smooth Cycle** (☎ 800/310-6550 or 902/566-5530) at 172 Prince St. in Charlottetown.

FISHING   For a taste of deep-sea fishing, head to the north coast where you'll find plenty of outfitters happy to take you out on the big swells. The greatest concentration of services are at North Rustico and Covehead Bay; see the "Queens County" section, below. Rates are quite reasonable, generally about C$15 to C$20 (US$11 to US$14) for 3 hours or so.

Numerous trout fishing holes attract inland anglers, although, as always, the best spots are a matter of local knowledge. A good place to start your inquiries is at **Island Rods and Flies,** 18 Birch Hill Dr., Charlottetown (☎ 902/566-4157), which specializes in fly-fishing equipment. Information on obtaining the required fishing license may be had from any visitor information center, or by contacting the **Department of Environmental Resources,** P.O. Box 2000, Charlottetown, PEI, C1A 7N8 (☎ 902/368-4683).

GOLF   A dozen golf courses on the island lure duffers from the mainland to try their hand on gracefully rolling courses, many of which are along the sea. Among the best are the **Links at Crowbush Cove** (☎ 902/652-2356), which opened in 1993. Sand dunes and persistent winds add to the challenge. Another perennial favorite is the pastoral **Brudenell River Provincial Golf Course** (☎ 902/652-2342) near Montague.

SWIMMING   Among Prince Edward Island's chief attractions are its sand beaches. You'll find them all around the island, tucked in among dunes and crumbling cliffs. Thanks to the moderating influence of the Gulf of St. Lawrence, the water temperature is more humane than elsewhere in Atlantic Canada, and usually doesn't result in unbridled shrieking and hand-wringing among bathers. The most popular beaches are at **Prince Edward Island National Park** along the north coast, but you can easily find beaches where crowds are few. Among the best: **Cedar Dunes Provincial Park** on the southwest coast, and **Poverty Beach** on the southeast coast.

2 Queens County

This county occupies the center of the province, is home to the island's largest city, and hosts the greatest concentration of traveler services. It's neatly cleaved by the Hillsborough River, which is spanned by a bridge at Charlottetown. Cavendish on the north shore is the most tourist-oriented part of the province; if the phrase "Ripley's Believe It or Not Museum" makes you feel a bit queasy, you might consider avoiding this area, which has built a vigorous tourist industry around a fictional character, Anne of Green Gables. On the other hand, much of the rest of the county—not including Charlottetown—is quite pastoral and untrammeled.

ESSENTIALS

GETTING THERE   Route 2 is the fastest way to travel east-west through the county, although it lacks charm. Route 6 is the main route along the county's north coast; following the highway involves a number of turns at intersections, so keep a sharp eye on the directional signs.

VISITOR INFORMATION   The **Cavendish Visitors Centre** (☎ **902/963-2391** in summer or 902/566-7050 off-season) is open June to mid-September, daily from 8am to 10pm, and is just north of the intersection of Route 13 and Route 6.

CAVENDISH

Cavendish is the home of the fictional character Anne of Green Gables. If you mentally screen out the tourist traps constructed over the last couple of decades, you'll find in the area a bucolic mix of woodlands and fields, rolling hills and sandy dunes— a fine setting for a series of pastoral novels.

However, the tremendous and enduring popularity of the novels has attracted droves of curious tourists, who in turn have attracted droves of entrepreneurs who've constructed plenty of new buildings. The bucolic character of the area has thus become somewhat compromised.

ANNE-O-RAMA

All visitors to Prince Edward Island owe it to themselves to read *Anne of Green Gables* at some point. Not that you won't enjoy your stay here without doing this. But if you don't, you may feel a bit out of touch, unable to understand the inside references that seep into many aspects of Prince Edward Island culture, much the way sand gets into everything at the beach. (Even gas stations in Cavendish sell Anne dolls.) In fact, Anne has become so omnipresent and popular on the island that in 1994 a licensing authority was created to control the crushing glacier of Anne-related products.

Some background: *Anne of Green Gables* was written by Lucy Maud Montgomery in 1908. It's a fictional account of Anne Shirley, a precocious and bright 11-year-old who's mistakenly sent from Nova Scotia to the farm of the taciturn and dour Matthew and Marilla Cuthbert. (They'd requested a boy orphan to help with farm chores.) Anne's vivid imagination and outsized vocabulary get her into a series of pickles, from which she generally emerges beloved by everyone who encounters her. It's a bright, bittersweet story and went on to huge popular success, spawning a number of sequels as well as a long-running cable TV series.

The best place to start an Anne tour is at **Green Gables** (☎ **902/672-6350**) itself, located on Route 6, just west of the intersection with Route 13. The house is operated by Parks Canada, which opened a new visitor center on the site in 1997. Watch a 7-minute video presentation about Montgomery, view a handful of exhibits, then head out to explore the farm and trails. The farmhouse dates to the mid-19th century and belonged to cousins of Montgomery's grandfather. It was the inspiration for the Cuthbert farm and has been furnished according to descriptions in the books.

If you're a diehard Anne fan, you'll delight in the settings where characters ventured, such as the Haunted Woods and Lover's Lane. But you may need as active an imagination as Anne's to edit out the golf carts puttering through the landscape at the adjacent Green Gables Golf Course, or the busloads of tourists crowding through the house and moving herdlike down the paths. Come very early or very late in the day to avoid the largest crowds.

Green Gables is open daily from mid-May to October. During the peak summer season (late June to August), the house and grounds are open from 9am to 8pm. Admission is C$2.50 (US$1.80) for adults, C$2 (US$1.40) for seniors, C$1.25 (US90¢) for children, and C$6 (US$4.30) for families.

A walking trail leads from Green Gables to **L. M. Montgomery's home** (☎ 902/ 963-2231). (If headed there by car, watch for signs on Route 6 just east of the Route 13 intersection.) Montgomery was raised by her grandparents at this house, where she lived from 1876 to 1911. This is where she wrote *Anne of Green Gables*. It's open daily June to September; during peak season the hours are daily from 9am to 7pm. Admission is C$2 (US$1.40) for adults and C$1 (US70¢) for children.

About 20 kilometers (12 miles) west of Cavendish near the intersection of routes 6 and 20 is the **Anne of Green Gables Museum at Silver Bush** (☎ 902/436-7329). It's in the home of Montgomery's aunt and uncle; the author was married here in 1911. For the best view of the "Lake of Shining Waters," take the wagon ride. Open daily June to October; peak-season hours are 9am to 7:30pm. Admission is C$2.50 (US$1.80) for adults and C75¢ (US50¢) for children under 16.

Very near the museum is the **Lucy Maud Montgomery Birthplace** (☎ 902/ 886-2099), where the author was born in 1874. The house is decorated in the Victorian style of the era, and includes Montgomery mementos, like her wedding dress. Open mid-May to mid-October daily from 9am to 5pm (to 7pm in July and August). Admission is C$2 (US$1.40) for adults and C50¢ (US35¢) for children 6 to 12; children under 6 are free.

Finally, watch for performances. The musical *Anne of Green Gables* plays summers at the **Confederation Arts Centre** (☎ 800/565-0278 or 902/566-1267) in Charlottetown, as it has since dinosaurs roamed the earth. Tickets are C$20 to C$36 (US$14 to US$26).

ACCOMMODATIONS

Nondescript motels and cottages dot the Cavendish area, but be aware that many are focused on volume and rapid turnover rather than providing a quality experience. If you arrive without reservations, check the board at the visitor information center, which lists up-to-the-minute vacancies.

Green Gables Bungalow Court. Rte. 6 (Hunter River RR #2), Cavendish, PEI, C0A 1N0. ☎ 800/965-3334 or 902/892-3542. 40 cottages. TV. C$75–C$105 (US$53–US$75) for up to 4 people. MC, V. Closed mid-Sept to June.

Located next to the Green Gables house, this pleasant cluster of one- and two-bedroom cottages began as a government make-work project promoting tourism in the 1940s. As a result, they're quite sturdily built, and nicely arrayed among lawn and pines. All have kitchens and refrigerators, and many have outdoor gas grills for evening barbecues. The linoleum floors and Spartan furnishings take on a certain retro charm after a few hours of settling in. Some cabins were trimmed out with cheap sheet paneling, others have the original pine paneling; ask for one with the latter. The beach is about 1 kilometer (0.6 miles) away, accessible via walking path, and there's a small heated outdoor pool on the premises.

Shining Waters Country Inn. Rte. 13, Cavendish, PEI, C0A 1N0. ☎ 902/963-2251. 10 rms, 20 housekeeping cottages. TV. Inn rms C$65–C$78 (US$46–US$55) double, including continental breakfast; cottages C$86–C$112 (US$61–US$80). AE, ER, MC, V. Closed mid-Oct to mid-May.

The Shining Waters Inn is across from the visitor information center and a 5-minute walk from the Cavendish Beach. For Anne fans, there's also this connection: The farmhouse was the home of the fictional Rachel Lynde (the real Mrs. Pierce Macneill), when the building was located on a farm (now the golf course) next to Green Gables. In 1942 the building was hauled here by horses. Despite the colorful history and distinguished pedigree, the place is somewhat charmless, offering basic accommodations with industrial carpeting and linoleum that don't create much of a farmhouse feel, despite the straw hats adorning guest-room doors. Many guest rooms in the inn are small; the cottages are packed together gracelessly out back. On the plus side, there's an outdoor pool and Jacuzzi.

DINING

Cavendish itself offers limited opportunities for creative dining. Both places mentioned below require a 10- to 15-minute drive, but they're worth it. See also the box "Lobster Suppers," below.

Herb Garden. Rte. 244, Hunter River. ☎ **902/621-0765.** Reservations encouraged. Main courses C$14–C$19 (US$10–US$14). MC, V. Daily 11am–9pm most of the year; closed Mon–Wed in winter. Located on Rte. 244 between Rte. 13 and Stanley Bridge. BAKERY/EUROPEAN.

Watch for the restaurant's understated sign on Route 224 outside of Hunter River. Many harried travelers find the Herb Garden by sailing past, then making an abrupt U-turn. Set off the road, it's modern and bright inside, and noted for its innovative cooking.

Prince Edward Island Preserve Co. Rte. 13 and Rte. 224, New Glasgow. ☎ **902/964-2524.** Breakfast and lunch main courses C$2–C$8 (US$1.40–US$6); dinner C$9–C$16 (US$6–US$11). AE, ER, MC, V. July–Aug daily 8am–9:30pm; limited hours June and Sept; closed Oct–May. LIGHT FARE.

The Prince Edward Island Preserve Co. is a worthwhile stop for the delicious home-made preserves (free samples are offered, and you can watch the canning process). And while you're here, why not enjoy a light meal in the modern annex off the showroom? In this popular and often crowded spot, you can order from a menu with a small but appealing selection; the smoked fish platter and lobster chowder are just the ticket on a drizzly afternoon.

NORTH & SOUTH RUSTICO

Just east of Cavendish are a pair of attractive villages that have fewer tourist traps and are more amenable to exploring by foot or bike than Cavendish. While out of the hubbub, they still provide easy access to the national park and Anne-land, with beaches virtually at your doorstep.

North Rustico clusters around a scenic harbor, with views out toward Rustico Bay. Plan to park and walk around, perusing the deep-sea fishing opportunities (see below) and peeking in the shops. In South Rustico, head off Route 6 and up the low hill overlooking the bay. Here you'll find a handsome cluster of buildings, including the sandstone **Farmer's Bank of Rustico,** established with the help of a visionary local cleric in 1864 to help farmers get ahead of the hand-to-mouth cycle. The stern building was being restored in 1997; look for exhibits to explain the history in upcoming summers. Next door is handsome **St. Augustine's Parish Church** (1838) and a cemetery beyond. If the door's open, head in for a look at this graceful structure.

DEEP-SEA FISHING

Prince Edward Island's north shore is home to the greatest concentration of deep-sea fishing boats. For about C$15 (US$11) per person, you'll get 3 hours out on the seas, searching for mackerel, cod, and flounder. Don't worry about lack of prior experience; equipment is supplied, crew members are very helpful, and most will even clean and filet your catch for you.

In North Rustico, about half a dozen captains offer fishing trips. Among them: **Aiden Doiron's Deep-Sea Fishing** (☎ 902/963-2442), **Bob's Deep-Sea Fishing**

Lobster Suppers

The north shore of Prince Edward Island is the home to the famous lobster suppers, which are your best bet if your appetite demands one of the succulent local crustaceans. These suppers took root some years ago as events held in church basements, in which parishioners would bring a covered hot dish to share and the church would provide a lobster. Everyone would contribute some money, and the church netted a few dollars. Outsiders discovered these good deals, the fame of the dinners spread, and today several establishments offer the bountiful lobster dinners, although few are raising money for charity these days.

Expect a large and fairly impersonal dining experience (Fisherman's Wharf can accommodate 500 diners at a time), especially if you have the misfortune to pull up after a couple of bus tours have unloaded. Lobster is naturally the main feature, although there's usually roast beef, ham, or other alternatives. This is typically accompanied by an all-you-can-eat buffet with a button-bursting selection of rolls, salads, chowder, mussels, desserts, and more. The cost? Figure on C$20 to C$30 (US$14 to US$21) per person, depending on the options.

St. Ann's Church Lobster Suppers (☎ 902/621-0635) remains a charitable organization, as it was 3 decades ago when it was the first and only lobster supper on Prince Edward Island. Located in a modern church hall in the small town of St. Ann, just off Route 224 between routes 6 and 13, St. Ann's has a full liquor license and the home-cooked food is served to your table (no buffet lines). Lobster dinners are served Monday to Saturday from 4 to 9pm. As befits a church, it's closed on Sundays.

Fisherman's Wharf Lobster Suppers (☎ 902/963-2669) in North Rustico boasts a 60-foot salad bar to go with its lobster; it's open daily from noon to 9pm. And near the Prince Edward Island Preserve Co. in New Glasgow is **New Glasgow Lobster Suppers** (☎ 902/964-2870). Meals include unlimited mussels and chowder; it's on Route 258 (just off Route 13) and is open daily from 4:30 to 8:30pm.

(☎ 902/963-2666), and **Bearded Skipper's Deep-Sea Fishing** (☎ 902/963-2334). East of North Rustico, at Covehead Harbor (within the national park), try **Richard's Deep-Sea Fishing** (☎ 902/672-2376) or **Salty Seas Deep-Sea Fishing** (☎ 902/672-3246).

ACCOMMODATIONS

Barachois Inn. Church Rd., S. Rustico (mailing address: P.O. Box 1022, Charlottetown, PEI, C1A 7M4). ☎ **902/963-2194.** 4 rms. C$115–C$135 (US$82–US$96) double. Rates include full breakfast. MC, V. Closed Nov–Mar.

The proudly Victorian Barachois Inn was built in 1870 and is a soothing retreat for road-weary travelers. It's topped with a lovely mansard roof adorned with pedimented dormers, and boasts a fine garden and historic furnishings throughout. Two of the rooms are suites and offer a bit more room for unwinding. No smoking.

Shaw's Hotel. Rte. 15, Brackley Beach, PEI, C1E 1Z3. ☎ **902/672-2022.** Fax 902/672-3000. 16 rms, 20 cottages. TV in cottages only. Inn: C$165–C$210 (US$117–US$149) double, including breakfast and dinner; cottages: C$195–C$260 (US$138–US$185) double. AE, MC, V. Closed Oct–May.

Shaw's is a delightful compound located down a peaceful, tree-lined dirt road at the edge of a marsh-edged inlet. It's been in the same family for generations, and even with the addition of some cottages over the years and a regimen of modernization, the place still has the feel of a farm-stay vacation in the 19th century. The hotel's centerpiece is the Victorian farmhouse with the lipstick-red mansard roof. Sixteen guest rooms are located upstairs here; on the first floor is the lobby and spacious dining room with views toward the water. The cottages, with one to four bedrooms, are spread around the grounds in an unobtrusive manner that doesn't impinge on the peaceable air.

Dining: The spare but handsome main dining room serves breakfast and dinner daily. The dinner menu changes frequently, but typical entrees might include filet mignon au poivre, poached halibut with béarnaise, or penne with smoked salmon in a vodka cream sauce. Prices range from C$16.50 to C$22.50 (US$12 to US$16). The Lobster Trap Lounge, located in a nearby outbuilding, is open until 1am daily, and offers more casual fare like chicken pot pie, nachos, and steamed island mussels.

Services: You can rent sailboards from an outfitter based on the grounds, and the beach is just 601 yards away.

DINING

See also Shaw's Hotel, above, and Dalvay-by-the-Sea, listed under "Prince Edward Island National Park," below.

Cafe St. Jean. Rte. 6, Oyster Bed Bridge. ☎ **902/963-3133.** Reservations helpful. Lunch C$7–C$9 (US$5–US$6); dinner C$12–C$25 (US$9–US$18) (mostly C$15–C$18/US$11–US$13). Daily 11:30am–9pm. Closed Oct–May. Located where Rte. 6 crosses the Wheatley River, at the southern tip of Rustico Bay. ECLECTIC.

There's a strong emphasis on local and Celtic music at Cafe St. Jean, with original tunes in the background, live music on the deck some evenings, and even CDs and tapes for sale at the cash register. Don't worry—this isn't a ploy to compensate for the quality of the food. The kitchen often scales culinary heights and produces zesty originals (including a killer potato-fennel soup), but meals can be inconsistent at times, especially at lunch. The menu should appeal to most taste buds: There's Cajun salmon with a Creole sauce, shrimp with peppercorns, and chateaubriand.

3 Prince Edward Island National Park

Prince Edward Island National Park encompasses a 40-kilometer (24-mile) swath of red-sand beaches, wind-sculpted dunes topped with marram grass, vast salt marshes, and placid inlets. The park is located along the island's sandy north-central coast, which is broached in several spots by broad inlets that connect to harbors. As a result, you can't drive along the entire park's length in one shot. The coastal road is disrupted by inlets, requiring backtracking to drive the entire length. And, actually, there's little point in doing so. It's a better use of your time to pick one spot, then settle in and enjoy your surroundings.

The national park also oversees the Green Gables house and grounds; see "Cavendish," above.

ESSENTIALS

GETTING THERE   From Charlottetown, Route 15 offers the most direct route to the eastern segments of the park. To head to the Cavendish area, take Route 2 to Hunter River, then head north on Route 13.

VISITOR INFORMATION   Two visitor centers provide information on park destinations and activities between June and October. The **Cavendish Visitors Centre** (☎ **902/963-2391** or 902/963-7830) is near the intersection of routes 6 and 13;

it's open daily from 9am to 10pm in the peak summer season (it closes earlier the rest of the summer).

The **Brackley Visitors Centre** (☎ **902/672-7474**) is at the intersection of routes 6 and 15; it's open in July and August, daily from 9am to 9pm; June, September, and October, daily from 9:30am to 5pm. In the off-season, contact the **park administration office** (☎ **902/672-6350**) near the Dalvay Hotel.

FEES   Between June and September, visitors to the national park must stop at one of the tollhouses to pay entry fees. Daily rates in 1997 were C$3 (US$2.15) for adults, C$2 (US$1.40) for seniors, C$1.50 (US$1.10) for children 6 to 16, and C$6.50 (US$4.65) for families. Ask about multiday passes if you plan to visit for more than 3 days.

BEACHES

Prince Edward Island National Park is nearly synonymous with its beaches. The park is home to two kinds of sandy strands: popular and crowded beaches with changing rooms, lifeguards, snack bars, and other amenities; and all the other beaches. Where you go depends on your temperament. If it's not a day at the beach without the wafting aroma of other people's coconut tanning oil, head to Brackley Beach or Cavendish Beach. The latter is within walking distance of the Green Gables House and many other amusements (see "Cavendish," above), and makes a good destination for families.

If you'd just as soon be left alone with the waves, sun, and sand, you'll need to head a bit further afield, or just keep walking down the beaches until you leave the crowds behind. I won't reveal the best spots here for fear of crowding. But suffice it to say, they're out there.

HIKING & BIKING

Hiking is limited compared to Atlantic Canada's other national parks, but you will find a handful of pleasant strolls. And, of course, there's the beach, which is perfect for long walks.

The park maintains eight trails for a total of 20 kilometers (12 miles). Among the most appealing is the **Homestead Trail,** which departs from the Cavendish campground. The trail offers a 5.5-kilometer (3.3-mile) loop, and an 8-kilometer (4.8-mile) loop. The trail skirts wheat fields, woodlands, and estuaries, with frequent views of the distinctively lumpy dunes at the west end of the park. Mountain bikes are allowed on this trail, and it's a busy destination on sunny days. The two short trails at the Green Gables House—**Balsam Hollow** and **Haunted Wood**—are rather lovely but invariably crowded. Avoid them if you're looking for a *relaxing* walk in the woods.

CAMPING

Prince Edward Island National Park has three campgrounds. Reservations are not accepted, so plan to arrive early in the day for the best selection of sites. Campground fees start at C$17 (US$12) per night (slightly less at Rustico Island).

The most popular (and first to fill) is **Cavendish.** It has more than 300 sites spread among piney forest and open, sandy bluffs; the sites at the edge of the dunes overlooking the beach are naturally the most popular. The sites aren't especially private or scenic. A limited number of 2-way hookups are available for RVs, and the campground has free showers, kitchen shelters, and evening programs.

The **Stanhope** campground lies just across the park road from lovely Stanhope Beach. The road isn't heavily traveled, so you don't feel much removed from the water's edge. Most sites are forested, and you're afforded more privacy than at Cavendish. Two-way hookups, free showers, and kitchen shelters are offered.

To my mind, the best campground is **Rustico Island.** It's down a dead-end sand spit, with a number of sites overlooking a placid cove and the rolling countryside beyond. It lacks hookups for RVs, which may explain why sites are usually available here after other campgrounds fill up. The sites are mostly wooded, very large and quite private, and there's a hushed and settled air that hovers over the place. Supervised swimming is 4 kilometers (2.5 miles) away at Brackley Beach. If you'd rather have quiet than a lifeguard, turn left out the campground gate and walk or bike down the gated dirt road to the pleasant (and often deserted) beach at the mouth of Rustico Bay.

ACCOMMODATIONS & DINING

Also see listings for "Cavendish" and "North & South Rustico," above.

✪ **Dalvay-by-the-Sea.** Off Rte. 6, Grand Tracadie (mailing address: P.O. Box 8, Little York, PEI, C0A 1P0). ☎ **902/672-2048.** Fax 902/672-2741. E-mail: dalvay@isn.net. 26 rms, 4 cottages. C$180–C$300 (US$128–US$213) double. Rates include breakfast and dinner. National-park entrance fees also charged. 2-night minimum in summer. AE, ER, MC, V.

This imposing Tudor mansion was built in 1895 by Alexander MacDonald, a partner of John D. Rockefeller. The place is unusually large for a private home, but it's quite intimate for a luxury resort. There are glimpses of the ocean across the road from the upper floors, but the landscaping largely focuses on a beautiful pond out front. Inside, you'll be taken aback by the extraordinary cedar woodwork in the main entryway, and the grand stone fireplace. The guest rooms are elegantly appointed and wonderfully solid and quiet; in the evening you'll hear mostly the roar of the sea. No smoking in guest rooms.

Dining: The well-regarded dining room sends fireworks out of the kitchen, with exuberant dishes like salmon with roasted seaweed and a tomato-coriander salsa. For dessert, try the espresso parfait with poached figs. For those not on the meal plan, entrees run C$17 to C$25 (US$12 to US$18). Make reservations for a better shot at a window seat.

Services/Facilities: The inn is just across the road from one of the park's better beaches; there's also tennis, croquet, lawn bowling, horseshoes, canoeing, bike rentals, a two-hole fairway, and nearby nature trails. An afternoon tea is served from 2 to 4pm.

4 Charlottetown

It's not hard to figure out why early settlers put the province's political and cultural capital where they did: It's on a point of land between two rivers and within a large protected harbor. For ship captains plying the seas, this quiet harbor with ample anchorage and wharf space must have been a welcome sight. Of course, travelers rarely arrive by water these days (unless a cruise ship is in port), but the city's harborside location does translate into a lovely setting today for one of Atlantic Canada's most graceful and relaxed cities.

Named after Queen Charlotte, consort of King George III, Charlottetown is home to some 40,000 people—nearly one of every three Prince Edward Islanders. Within Canada, the city is famous for hosting the 1864 conference that 3 years later led to the creation of the independent Dominion of Canada. For this reason, you're never far from the word "confederation," which graces buildings, malls, and bridges. (In a historic twist, Prince Edward Island itself declined to join the new confederation until 1873.)

Charlottetown

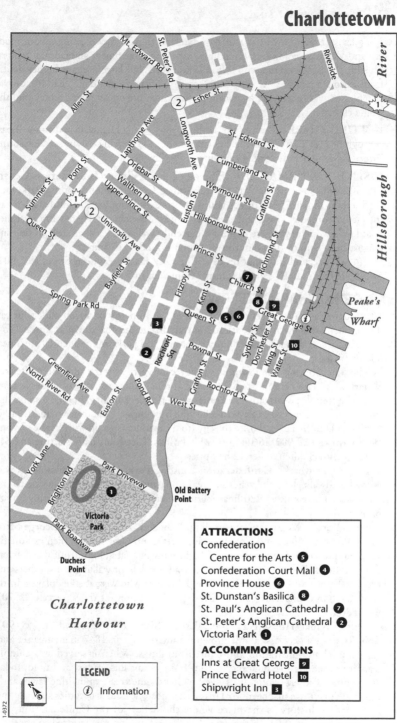

River

Hillsborough

Peake's
Wharf

Charlottetown
Harbour

Duchess
Point

Old Battery
Point

Victoria
Park

ATTRACTIONS
Confederation
  Centre for the Arts **5**
Confederation Court Mall **4**
Province House **6**
St. Dunstan's Basilica **8**
St. Paul's Anglican Cathedral **7**
St. Peter's Anglican Cathedral **2**
Victoria Park **1**

ACCOMMMODATIONS
Inns at Great George **9**
Prince Edward Hotel **10**
Shipwright Inn **3**

LEGEND
i Information

1-0372

Today, the downtown has a brisk, urban feel to it, with a pleasing mix of modern and Victorian commercial buildings, as well as government and cultural centers. Outside the business core, you'll find leafy streets and large, elegant homes dating from various eras from the early 19th century to the present day. Charlottetown is also blessed with a number of pocket parks, which provide a quiet respite amid the gentle clamor.

GETTING THERE   Both Route 1 (the Trans-Canada Highway) and Route 2 pass through or near Charlottetown. For information on arriving by air, see "Exploring Prince Edward Island" at the beginning of this chapter.

VISITOR INFORMATION   The city's main **Visitor Information Centre** (☎ 902/368-4444) is on Water Street next to Confederation Landing Park; look for the big, brown "?" to direct you to a brick building with helpful staffers, an interactive computer kiosk, and an ample supply of brochures. There's also a vacancy board to let you know where rooms are currently available. It's open daily in July and August from 8am to 10pm; in the off-season from 8am to 5pm.

There's a second information center at **City Hall** on Queen Street (☎ 902/566-5548) that's open daily in summer from 8am to 5pm.

EXPLORING CHARLOTTETOWN

Charlottetown is a compact city that's easy to reconnoiter once you park your car. Three main areas merit exploration: the waterfront, the downtown area near Province House and the Confederation Court Mall, and parks and residential areas near Victoria Park.

The waterfront has been spruced up in recent years with the addition of **Peake's Wharf,** a collection of touristy boutiques and restaurants that attracts hordes in summer. The complex is attractive and offers good people-watching, but has a somewhat formulaic feel to it (you can't even tell if the buildings are old or new) and is rather lacking in local character. To see the city from the water, sign up with **Peake's Wharf Boat Cruises** (☎ 902/566-4458), which offers three tours daily starting at C$12 (US$9), with children under 12 half price.

Next to the wharf is **Confederation Landing Park,** an open, modern park with a lazy boardwalk along the water's edge, lush lawns, and benches nicely situated for indolence. There's also a 220-boat marina where you can scope out freshly arrived pleasure craft.

From Peake's Wharf, you can stroll up leafy and attractive **Great George Street** to the Province House and Confederation Arts Centre (see below), then explore the shops and restaurants of downtown Charlottetown. Watch for historical characters: Some students dressed in period costume lead free 1-hour walking tours; others portray the Fathers of Confederation—the politicians who were the key players in the confederation conference. Check with the visitor center for times, or call ☎ 902/629-1864.

The **Province House National Historic Site,** 165 Richmond St. (☎ 902/566-7626), is a neoclassical downtown landmark built in 1847 in an area set aside for colonial administration and church buildings. When it served as a colonial legislature, the massive building rose up from vacant lots of dust and mud; today, as the provincial legislature, it's ringed by handsome trees, an inviting lawn, and a bustling downtown just beyond. This stern sandstone edifice occupies a special spot in Canadian history as the place where the details of the Confederation were hammered out in 1864. In the early 1980s the building was restored to appear as it would have in 1864. Especially impressive is the second-floor Confederation Chamber, where a staffer is on hand to explain what took place and why Prince

Edward Island itself waited 9 years to join. Some modest exhibits fill in the details. Be sure also to view the Legislative Assembly, where legislators have been meeting since 1847. It's surprisingly small, but perhaps appropriate given that PEI's legislature has just 27 members, making it the smallest in Canada. Admission is free but donations are requested. It's open July and August daily from 9am to 6pm and September to June Monday to Friday from 9am to 5pm.

Part of the Confederation Centre of the Arts (which includes three theaters, see "Charlottetown After Dark," below), the **Confederation Centre Art Galley and Museum,** at Queen and Grafton streets (☎ 902/628-6111), is the largest art gallery in Atlantic Canada. The center is housed in a bland and boxy modern complex of glass and rough concrete; about the best that can be said of it is that it doesn't detract too much from the stylishly classical Province House next door. Inside, the gallery is spacious and nicely arranged on two levels, and features displays from the permanent collection as well as imaginatively curated changing exhibits. Admission is C$3 (US$2.15) for adults, C$2 (US$1.40) for seniors and children, and C$5 (US$3.60) for families; free admission on Sunday. It's open in summer daily from 10am to 8pm and off-season Tuesday to Saturday from 11am to 5pm and Sunday from 1 to 5pm.

ACCOMMODATIONS

A number of moderately priced motels are situated along the city's main access roads and across from the airport a few miles from downtown. Scout here if you're on a tight budget.

Two motels are situated within easy walking distance of downtown attractions. The **Islander Motor Lodge,** 146–148 Pownal St. (☎ 902/892-1217), has 49 rooms a few minutes' walk from Province House. Rooms are under C$100 (US$71) for two. **Best Western MacLauchlans,** 238 Grafton St. (☎ 800/528-1234 or 902/566-2979) has 148 rooms and 25 suites in two buildings a couple blocks east of the Confederation Court Mall. Rooms and suites range from about C$100 to C$125 (US$71 to US$89).

Inns at Great George. 589 Great George St., Charlottetown, PEI, C1A 4K3. ☎ 800/361-1118 or 902/892-0606. Fax 902/628-2079. 39 rms (5 rms share 2 baths). A/C TV TEL. C$135–C$205 (US$96–US$146) double. Rates include continental breakfast. AE, DC, ER, MC, V. Free parking.

The Inns at Great George opened in 1997 and quickly established itself as one of the classiest Charlottetown hostelries. The inn encompasses six striking buildings on and around historic Great George Street. Twenty-four rooms are located in the old (1846) Pavilion Hotel; others are in smaller town houses and homes nearby. All rooms have been thoroughly updated and refurbished with antiques, down duvets, hair dryers, and early black-and-white prints; all but two rooms are carpeted. The more expensive rooms have fireplaces and Jacuzzis, but many of the others have claw-foot tubs, perfect for soaking in after a day of roaming the city. The inn features a small fitness room. It also has safe-deposit boxes and limited room service from an affiliated restaurant and can arrange for baby-sitting, dry cleaning, and laundry.

Prince Edward Hotel. 18 Queen St., Charlottetown, PEI, C1A 8B9. ☎ 902/566-2222. Fax 902/566-2282. 211 rms. A/C MINIBAR TV TEL. Peak season C$159–C$319 (US$113–US$227) double; off-season C$145–C$219 (US$103–US$156) double. AE, DC, DISC, ER, MC, V. Parking C$8/US$6 per day.

A modern, boxy, 10-story hotel overlooking the harbor, The Prince Edward Hotel is part of the Canadian Pacific chain and has all the amenities expected by business travelers, including coffeemakers, hair dryers, irons and ironing boards, free exercise bikes delivered to your room, and even cordless phones (about half the rooms are cordless). You enter the hotel to a two-story atrium (home to a well-regarded restaurant), then head up to the guest rooms. The better rooms are furnished with reproduction Georgian-style furniture; others have those oak and beige-laminate furnishings that are virtually invisible. The higher rooms have the better views; there's a C$20 (US$14) premium for water views, but the city views are actually nicer (and you can usually glimpse the water, anyway). Pets allowed.

Dining: The Selkirk (see below) may be the city's best restaurant, with upscale service and presentation to complement a fine menu. Summers only, the Anchor and Oar serves tasty lunches for C$6 to C$12 (US$4.30 to US$9) on a patio near the harbor.

Services: Concierge, room service (to 2am), dry cleaning, laundry, nightly turn-down, afternoon tea, baby-sitting, safe-deposit boxes, valet parking.

Facilities: Indoor pool and fitness room, sauna, outdoor hot tub, business center, conference rooms, shopping arcade, beauty salon.

✪ Shipwright Inn. 51 Fitzroy St., Charlottetown, PEI, C1A 1R4. ☎ **902/368-1905.** Fax 902/ 628-1905. E-mail: shipwright@isn.net. Web site: www.isn.net/shipwrightinn. 7 rms. A/C TV TEL. C$95–C$150 (US$67–US$107) double. Rates include continental breakfast. AE, DC, ER, MC, V. Free parking.

Judy and Jordan Hill made their mark with Charlottetown's Edwardian Inn, but they wanted something more central. The Shipwright Inn was the answer. This under-stated Victorian home was built by a shipbuilder, and expertly renovated and refurbished. It's decorated with period furniture and with a deft touch—don't expect over-the-top Victoriana here. All rooms have lovely wood floors (some with original ship-planking floors), and three are in a recent addition, which was built with many nice touches. Amenities include hair dryers and down duvets in all rooms, and about half the rooms have Jacuzzis, gas fireplaces, or both. Among the best: the Ward Room, a suite with a private deck, and the Purser's State Room, which shares a lovely deck with another room. The inn is located right in the city, but has a settled, pastoral farmhouse feel to it. No smoking; pets allowed with prior permission from Piper, the resident black lab.

DINING

A locally popular spot for cheap eats is **Cedar's Eatery** at 81 University between Fitzroy and Kent (☎ 902/892-7377). The specialty here is Lebanese dishes like *yabrak* (stuffed vine leaves) and *kibbee* (ground beef with crushed wheat and spices). There are also sandwiches and burgers. Lunch specials are C$5 (US$4), dinner specials C$8 (US$6).

Piazza Joe's Italian Eatery and Bistro. 189 Kent St. ☎ **902/894-4291.** Reservations not accepted. Main courses C$8–C$16 (US$6–US$11); individual pizzas C$8 (US$6) and up. AE, ER, MC, V. Daily 11am–midnight. PIZZA/ITALIAN.

Piazza Joe's, located in a handsome, historic building, 1 long block from the Confederation mall, has gone a bit overboard with the Tuscan-style washed tones and fake ivy climbing fake trellises. But it works in a comic-book kind of way. The place is pleasantly casual and can be loud on weekends, but there's friendly service, a long menu, and lots of comic-book mixed drinks. The wood-fired pizza is consistently quite good; take your chances on the rest of the selections, like linguini primavera or spaghetti alla Bolognese.

Piece a Cake. 119 Grafton St. (at Confederation Court Mall). ☎ **902/894-4585.** Reservations recommended. Lunch main courses C$7–C$14 (US$5–US$10); dinner main courses C$12–C$18 (US$9–US$13). AE, DC, ER, MC, V. Daily 11am–11pm. ECLECTIC.

This very modern, very handsome restaurant occupies the second floor of a building connected to the Confederation Court Mall. With hardwood floors, high ceilings, rich custard-colored walls, and window frames suspended whimsically from the ceiling, there's a welcoming, airy grace to the spot. The menu is broad enough to snare most any taste—lunches range from chicken crèpes to Thai scallop salad to blackened chicken in a cilantro cream sauce. Dinners are similarly eclectic, and include a range of striking pastas. Among the most creative: "penne on fire," with charred onions, grilled zucchini, toasted nuts, and a tangerine-serrano relish. If you're cursed with an adventurous palate and can't afford the Selkirk (see below), this is your next best choice.

⚫ **The Selkirk.** In the Prince Edward Hotel, 18 Queen St. ☎ **902/566-2222.** Reservations encouraged. Breakfast main courses C$6–C$9 (US$4.30–US$6); lunch main courses C$6–C$13 (US$4.30–US$9); dinner main courses C$20–C$28 (US$14–US$20). AE, DC, DISC, ER, MC, V. Daily 6:30am–2pm and 5–11pm. NEW CANADIAN.

Charlottetown's most stylish restaurant is smack in the middle of the lobby of the high-end Prince Edward Hotel. Yet it has a more informal character than many upscale hotel restaurants, with an eclectic mix of chairs and a piano player providing the live soundtrack. The menu is also more ambitious and creative than you'll find elsewhere in the city. The signature appetizer is lobster and prawns served with a three-melon salsa, or you might opt for pheasant confit. Main courses could include sashimi of salmon, oysters, and scallops with a sauce of lime, ginger, and garlic; or a Maritime jambalaya with lobster, mussels, shrimp, scallops, and salmon. Carnivores aren't ignored, with a selection that includes duck breast with a raspberry-and-green-peppercorn vinaigrette, or beef tenderloin with a shiitake ragout. The only downside: The lobby location can get clamorous at times, especially when conferees are milling about. Ask for one of the tables under the mezzanine, near the piano.

Sirenella. 83 Water St. ☎ **902/628-2271.** Reservations recommended. Lunch main courses C$6–C$12 (US$4.30–US$9); dinner main courses C$8–C$18 (US$6–US$13). AE, ER, MC, V. Mon–Fri 11am–2pm; daily 5–10pm. Closed Sun in winter. ITALIAN.

Sirenella has traditionally been one of Charlottetown's better kept secrets—one of those legendary hidden trattorias that delivered far more than diners might expect for the money. Unfortunately, it's been slipping with sketchy service and indifferent preparation. The place still has diehard fans, and the menu remains quite good with selections like grilled calamari, lasagna made with Atlantic salmon, and rigatoni with sun-dried tomatoes and black olives. Sirenella is also noted for its ravioli, but it usually sells out early, so arrive soon after opening if you have your heart set on it. Desserts? Eh. Our tiramisu was frozen in the middle, smacked of freezer burn, and cost C$6 (US$4.30) a slice.

CHARLOTTETOWN AFTER DARK

A good resource for evening adventure is *Buzz,* a free monthly newspaper that details ongoing and special events around the island with an emphasis on Charlottetown. It's widely available; look in visitor centers or area bars and restaurants.

For culture with a capital "C," check out the **Confederation Centre of the Arts** (☎ **800/565-0278** or 902/566-1267), where three stages bustle with activity in the warm weather months. The musical *Anne of Green Gables,* a perennial favorite, is performed here throughout the summer, as are revivals and new shows.

The art-house **City Cinema,** 64 King St. (☎ **902/368-3669**), has an excellent lineup of domestic and foreign films throughout the year; there's typically a choice of two films each evening.

Outdoor libations are on tap at **Victoria Row,** on Richmond Street behind the Confederation Centre. Several restaurants and pubs cluster here and serve meals and drinks on street-side patios; some offer live music. **Kelly's,** 136 Richmond (☎ 902/ 628-6569), has the best selection of microbrews. The row is a popular destination for university students and younger locals.

Myron's, 151 Kent St. (☎ 902/892-4375), features a dance club and cabaret on two floors with a robust 22,000 square feet of entertainment space. Performers range from country to rock. For live Celtic-flavored music, head for **The Olde Dublin Pub,** 113 Sydney St. (☎ 902/892-6992).

5 Kings County

After a visit to Charlottetown and the island's central towns, Kings County comes as a bit of surprise. It's far more tranquil and uncluttered than Queens County (Anne's reach is much diminished here), and the landscapes are woodlots alternating with corn, grain, and potato fields. While much is made of the county's two great commercial centers on the coast—Souris and Montague—it's good to keep in mind that these each have a population of around 1,500. In some parts of North America, that wouldn't even rate a dot on the map.

ESSENTIALS

GETTING THERE   Several main roads—including highways 1, 2, 3, and 4— connect eastern Prince Edward Island with Charlottetown and points west. The ferry to Nova Scotia sails from Woods Island on the south coast. See "Exploring Prince Edward Island," above, for more information.

VISITOR INFORMATION   A helpful visitor center is located at the old railway depot in Montague near the river. It's open daily in summer.

MONTAGUE

Montague is the region's main commercial hub, but it's decidedly a hub in low gear. It's compact and attractive, with a handsome business district on a pair of flanking hills sloping down to a bridge across the Montague River. (A century and a half ago, the town was called Montague Bridge.) Shipbuilding was the economic mainstay in the 19th century; today, it's dairy and tobacco.

EXPLORING THE OUTDOORS

Cruise Mananda (☎ 800/986-3444 or 902/838-3444) offers seal- and bird-watching tours daily during peak season aboard restored fishing boats; the cost is C$15 (US$11) for adults and C$7.50 (US$5) for children under 12. Trips depart from the marina on the Montague River, just below the visitor center in the old railway depot.

Southeast of Montague (en route to Murray River) is the **Buffaloland Provincial Park** (☎ 902/652-2356), where you'll spot a small herd of buffalo. These were a gift to Prince Edward Island from the province of Alberta, and they now number about 25. Walk down the 100-yard fenced-in corridor into the paddock and ascend the wooden platform for the best view of the shaggy beasts. Often they're hunkered down at the far end of the meadow, but they sometimes wander near. It's right off Route 4; watch for signs. Open year-round.

Brudenell River Provincial Park (☎ 902/652-8966) is one of the province's more active and better-bred parks, and a great spot to work up an athletic glow on a sunny afternoon. On its 1,500 riverfront acres you'll find a superb 18-hole golf course, a full-blown resort (see below), tennis, lawn bowling, wildflower garden, playground, campground, and nature trails. Kids' programs like Frisbee golf, shore-line scavenger hunts, and crafts workshops are scheduled daily in summer. You can also rent canoes, kayaks, and jet skis from private operators located within the park. The park is open daily from 9am to 9pm. Admission is free. Head north of Montague on Route 4, then east on Route 3 to the park signs.

ACCOMMODATIONS

Brudenell River Resort. Rte. 3 (P.O. Box 67), Cardigan, PEI, C0A 1G0. ☎ **800/565-7633** or 902/652-2332. Fax 902/652-2886. Web site: www.Rodd-Hotels.ca/. 101 rms. TV TEL. Peak season C$130–C$180 (US$92–US$128) hotel, C$99–C$107 (US$70–US$76) chalets; off-season C$90–C$130 (US$64–US$92) hotel, C$69–C$79 (US$49–US$56) chalets. AE, DC, ER, MC, V. Closed mid-Oct to mid-May.

The attractive Brudenell River Resort was built in 1991, and its sleek, open, and vaguely Frank Lloyd Wright–esque design reflects its recent vintage. Guests choose between the luxurious hotel rooms or the curious clusters of chalets, which look a bit like pavilions left over from some forgotten world exposition. The chalets are perfectly fine and offer good value (especially if your goal is to spend most of your time on the links), but the construction feels a bit shoddy; at the least, spend a few extra few dollars on a chalet with a kitchenette for a more open and homey feeling. The main hotel is more stately, and the architects and designers clearly knew when to pull back and let a graceful simplicity stand on its own. All hotel rooms but three have balconies or terraces. Pets are permitted for a C$10 (US$7) additional fee.

Dining: The Gordon Dining Room on the first level overlooks the golf course. It's a bit cavernous (it seats 100), but the high-backed chairs carve out a sense of intimacy. Breakfast and dinner are served; you'll enjoy what might be described as creative country-club cuisine, with entrees like charbroiled steak, sole in a puff pastry, and pasta primavera. Entrees range from C$14 to C$19 (US$10 to US$14).

Services: Dry cleaning and baby-sitting are available by request and at extra cost.

Facilities: In addition to the superb golf course, the resort has two pools (indoor and out), river swimming, a Jacuzzi, sauna, two night-lit tennis courts, health club, jogging and hiking trails, and a children's center.

DINING

Windows on the Water. 106 Sackville St. (corner of Main St.), Montague. ☎ **902/838-2080.** Reservations encouraged. Lunch main courses C$7–C$10 (US$5–US$7); dinner main courses C$10–C$19 (US$7–US$14). MC, V. Daily 11:30am–9pm. SEAFOOD.

If you haven't yet dined on PEI mussels, this is the place to let loose. The blue mussels are steamed in a root mirepoix, with sesame, ginger, and garlic. It's a winner. Main courses include sole stuffed with crab and scallop and topped with hollandaise, and grilled scallop and tenderloin brochettes. The appealing and open dining room features press-back chairs and a lively buzz, but if the weather's agreeable, angle for a seat on the deck. This is one of a handful of memorable restaurants in eastern Prince Edward Island. One last word: chowder.

SOURIS & NORTHEAST PRINCE EDWARD ISLAND

Some 44 kilometers (26 miles) northeast of Montague is the town of **Souris,** an active fishing town attractively set on a gentle hill overlooking the harbor. Souris ("*Soo*-ree") is French for "mouse"—so named because early settlers were beset by voracious field mice, which destroyed their crops. The town is the launching point for an excursion to the Magdalen Islands and makes a good base for exploring northeastern Prince Edward Island, considered by most urban residents to be the island's outback—remote and sparsely populated.

EXPLORING THE AREA

Several good beaches may be found ringing this wedge-shaped peninsula that points like an accusing finger toward Nova Scotia's Cape Breton Island. **Red Point Provincial Park** (☎ 902/357-2463) is 13 kilometers (8 miles) northeast of Souris and offers a handsome beach and supervised swimming, along with a campground that's popular with families. Another inviting and often empty beach is a short distance northeast at **Basin Head,** which features a "singing sands" beach that allegedly sings (actually, it's more like a squeak) when you walk on it.

At the island's far eastern tip is the aptly named **East Point Lighthouse** (☎ 902/357-2106). You can simply enjoy the dramatic setting, or take a tour of the building. Ask for your East Point ribbon while you're here. If you make it to the North Cape Lighthouse on the western shore, you'll receive a Traveller's Award documenting that you've traveled Prince Edward Island tip-to-tip. Admission to the lighthouse is C$2.50 (US$1.80) for adults and C$1 (US70¢) for children.

ACCOMMODATIONS

✪ **Inn at Bay Fortune.** Rte. 310 (off Rte. 2), Bay Fortune, PEI, C0A 2B0. ☎ **902/687-3745,** or 860/296-1348 off-season. Fax 902/687-3540. E-mail: innbayft@peinet.ca. 11 rms (2 with shower only). TEL. Summer C$120–C$180 (US$85–US$128) double; fall C$95–C$150 (US$67–US$106) double. Rates include full breakfast. AE, MC, V. Closed mid-Oct to late May.

This exceptionally attractive shingled compound on 46 acres was built by playwright Elmer Harris in 1910 as a summer home, and soon a became a nucleus for a colony of artists, actors, and writers. (Most recently, the home was owned by Canadian actress Colleen Dewhurst, who sold it to current innkeeper David Wilmer in 1988.) Wilmer pulled out the stops in renovating, adding to the quirky tower and expertly refurbishing the guest rooms around a grassy, courtyardlike enclosure. The rooms are cozy with a mix of antiques and custom-made furniture; the tower rooms are small but romantic. Eight of the rooms have wood-burning fireplaces, and an additional six rooms with Jacuzzis were slated for completion by summer 1998. Be sure to visit the television room atop the tower with its panoramic views. The inn is home to Prince Edward Island's best restaurant; see below.

DINING

✪ **Inn at Bay Fortune.** Rte. 310 (off Rte. 2), Bay Fortune. ☎ **902/687-3745.** Reservations strongly recommended. Main courses C$21–C$26 (US$15–US$19). AE, MC, V. Daily 5–9pm. Closed mid-Oct to late May. CREATIVE CONTEMPORARY.

Chef and co-owner Michael Smith has put tiny Bay Fortune on Canada's culinary map. This is without a doubt the province's best restaurant, and may well be the best in Atlantic Canada. Smith—a New York native who trained at the Culinary Institute of America and apprenticed at New York's Bouley—uses no cream or butter sauces, and instead draws on his network of local farmers and fishermen, as well as his kitchen garden, to ensure products that burst with flavor. "We're trying to take fine dining off its pedestal and make it accessible to the average person," Smith says. Among his repertoire of creations: roast venison and emu stew in cheddar sage broth with cabernet prunes and a walnut cake; and Arctic char with parsnip pancakes, arugula, cranberry chutney, and merlot sauce. Serious gourmands should inquire about the tasting menu (C$50/US$36), and the 1-day tasting class (C$150/US$107), in which Smith and his team share their secrets and serve you lunch and dinner.

6 Prince County

Prince County encompasses the western end of Prince Edward Island and offers a varied mix of lush agricultural land, rugged coastline, and unpopulated sandy beaches. This is Prince Edward Island with calluses. With a few exceptions, the region is a bit more ragged around the edges in a working-farm, working-waterfront kind of way. It typically lacks the pristine-village charm of Kings County or much of Queens County.

Within this unrefined landscape, however, you'll find pockets of considerable charm, such as the village of Victoria on the south coast at the county line, and in Tyne Valley near the north coast, which is reminiscent of a Cotswold hamlet.

ESSENTIALS

GETTING THERE   Route 2 is the main highway connecting Prince County with the rest of the island. Feeder roads typically lead from or to Route 2. The **Confederation Bridge** from the mainland connects to Prince County at Borden Point, southeast of Summerside.

VISITOR INFORMATION   The best source of travel information for the county is **Gateway Village** (☎ 902/368-5465) at the end of the Confederation Bridge. It's open in the summer, daily from 8am to 10pm.

VICTORIA

The town of Victoria—located a short detour off Route 1 between the Confederation Bridge and Charlottetown—is a tiny and unusually scenic village that's attracted a number of artists, boutique owners, and craftspeople. The village is perfect for strolling—parking is near the wharf and off the streets, keeping the narrow lanes free for foot traffic. Wander the short, shady lanes while admiring the architecture, much of which is in that elemental farmhouse style, clad in clapboard or shingle and constructed with sharply creased gables. (Some elaborate Victorians break the mold.) What makes the place so singular is that the village, which was first settled in 1767, has utterly escaped the creeping sprawl that has plagued so many otherwise attractive places. The entire village consists of 4 square blocks, which are surrounded by potato fields and the Northumberland Strait. It's not hard to imagine how the village looked a century ago.

EXPLORING VICTORIA

The **Victoria Seaport Museum** is in a shingled square lighthouse near the town parking lot. (You can't miss it.) You'll find a rustic local-history museum with the usual assortment of artifacts from the last century or so. In summer it's open Tuesday to Sunday from noon to 5pm; admission is by donation.

In the middle of town is the well-regarded **Victoria Playhouse** (☎ 800/925-2025 or 902/658-2025). Built in 1913 as a community hall, the building has a unique raked stage (it drops 7 in. over 21 ft.) to create the illusion of space, four beautiful stained-glass lamps, and a proscenium arch (also unusual for a community hall). Plays staged here in summer attract folks out from Charlottetown for the night. It's hard to say what is more enjoyable: the high quality of the acting, or the wonderful big-night-out air of a professional play in a small town where nothing else is going on. There's also a Monday-night concert series, with performers offering up everything from traditional folk to Latin jazz. Tickets are C$15.50 (US$11) for adults, C$13.50 (US$10) for seniors and students, and C$8 (US$6) for children 12 and under.

ACCOMMODATIONS

Orient Hotel. Main St. (mailing address: P.O. Box 162, Charlottetown, PEI, C1A 7K4). ☎ **800/ 565-6743** or 902/658-2503. Fax 902/658-2078. E-mail: orient@pei.sympatico.ca. 6 rms (3 with shower only). C$80–C$120 (US$57–US$85) double. Rates include full breakfast. AE, DC, MC, V. Closed mid-Oct to mid-May.

The Orient has been a Victoria mainstay for years—a 1926 guide notes that the inn had 20 rooms at C$2.50 (US$1.80) per night (of course, then a trip to the bathroom required a walk to the carriage house). The Orient has been modernized in recent years (all rooms now have private baths), but retains much of its antique charm. The rooms are painted in warm pastel tones and furnished eclectically with flea-market antiques. While some of the updating has diminished the charm—such as the velour furniture in the lobby and the industrial carpeting—the place has a friendly low-key demeanor, much like the village itself. Mrs. Proffit's Tea Shop on the first floor serves three meals daily (dinner by reservation). The light lunches are appropriate to a tearoom, and include tea sandwiches, fish cakes, and soups and salads. Prices are C$4 to $9 (US$2.80 to US$6).

DINING

Landmark Cafe. Main St. ☎ **902/658-2286.** Reservations helpful. Sandwiches around C$5 (US$3.60); main courses C$11–C$15 (US$8–US$11). MC, V. Daily 11am–9:30pm. Closed mid-Sept to mid-June. CAFE.

Located across from the Victoria Playhouse, the Landmark Cafe occupies a small and cozy storefront teeming with shelves filled with crockery, pots, jars, and more, some of which is for sale. But the effect is more funky than Ye Olde Quainte, and the limited menu very inviting. The steamed mussels and vine leaves with feta cheese are a favorite of regulars. Other offerings include salads, lasagna, meat pie, and tarragon-steamed salmon.

TYNE VALLEY

The village of Tyne Valley is just off Malpeque Bay and is one of the more attractive and pastoral areas of western Prince Edward Island. The village of gingerbread homes is surrounded by verdant barley and potato fields. Azure inlets encroach here and there; these are the arms of the bay, which is famous for its succulent Malpeque oysters. A former 19th-century shipbuilding center, the village now attracts artisans and others in search of a quiet lifestyle. A few very good restaurants, inns, and shops cater to visitors.

EXPLORING TYNE VALLEY

Lesley Dubey oversees the knitting of the island's most striking wool sweaters at **Shoreline Sweaters and Tyne Valley Studio Art Gallery,** Route 12 (☎ 902/ 831-2950). She's most famous for her sweater design featuring a subtle lobster pattern, but other garments—made from island-spun wool—are just as well done. Noted island artisans are featured in the gallery. Open May to October.

Just north of the village on Route 12 is the lovely ✪ **Green Provincial Park** (☎ 902/831-2370). Once the site of an active shipyard, the 219-acre park is now a lush riverside destination with emerald lawns and verdant trees, and has the feel of a turn-of-the-century estate—which, in fact, it was. In the heart of the park is the extravagant gingerbread mansion (1865) once owned by James Yeo, a merchant, shipbuilder, and landowner, who in his time was the island's wealthiest and most powerful man.

The **Historic Yeo House** and **Green Park Shipbuilding Museum** (☎ 902/ 831-2206) are now the park's centerpieces. Managed by the Prince Edward Island

Museum and Heritage Foundation, exhibits in two buildings provide a good view of the prosperous life of a shipbuilder and the golden age of Prince Edward Island shipbuilding. The museum and house are open daily in summer from 10am to 5pm. Admission is C$3 (US$2.15) for adults; children under 12 are free.

When leaving the area, consider taking the very scenic drive along the bay on Route 12 from Tyne Valley to MacDougall.

ACCOMMODATIONS

Green Provincial Park (☎ 902/831-2370) offers camping on grassy sites over-looking an arm of Malpeque Bay.

✪ **Doctor's Inn.** Rte. 167 (P.O. Box 92) Tyne Valley, PEI, C0B 2C0. ☎ **902/831-3057.** 2 rms (both share 1 bath). C$55 (US$39) double. Rates include breakfast. MC, V.

A stay at the Doctor's Inn is a bit like visiting relatives you didn't know you had. Upstairs in this handsome in-town farmhouse are just two guest rooms, which share a bath. (Note that you could rent them both for less than the cost of many fancy inns.) There's an upstairs sitting area, and the extensive organic gardens out back to peruse. It's a pleasant retreat, and innkeepers Jean and Paul Offer do a fine job making guests feel relaxed and at home.

Dining: The Offers serve up one of Atlantic Canada's most memorable dining experiences. They cater to a maximum of six people on any night at a single sitting. You first gather for appetizers and wine in the sitting room, then move to the large dining-room table. The extraordinary salads feature produce from the Offer's garden (they grow more than 2 dozen kinds of lettuce), and you'll have a choice of entrees, which are cooked on the woodstove in an old-fashioned kitchen. Look for scallops, Arctic char, salmon, veal, or whatever else the Offers can get fresh. Desserts are fresh-baked and wonderful. Reservations are requested at least 24 hours in advance; dinner is served at 7pm. A four-course meal with wine is C$40 (US$28) per person.

DINING

Also see the Doctor's Inn, above.

✪ **Seasons in Thyme.** Rte. 178, Tyne Valley. ☎ **902/831-2124.** Reservations encouraged. Main courses C$17–C$20 (US$12–US$14). AE, ER, MC, V. Summer daily 11am–2pm and 4–10pm; dinner-only in spring and fall. ECLECTIC.

The Doctor's Inn provides the organic produce for Seasons in Thyme, where meals are creatively prepared by chef Stefan Czapalay, who trained in Europe and Canada's largest cities. The restaurant, which is adjacent to historic Britannia Hall (a 120-seat theater), gets consistently high marks for its creative cuisine. You can typically chose between unadulterated meals (steamed mussels straight from the sea), or those that have benefited from Czapalay's deft touch with homegrown herbs (peppered salmon layered with basic-scented potato purée, or star-anise–scented lobster). Wonderful desserts include a French, Belgian, and Swiss chocolate pâté, and gingerbread pudding with rhubarb turnovers.

WESTERN PRINCE COUNTY

Prince Edward Island's far western coast—from West Point to North Cape—is well suited to a driving tour or exploring more leisurely by bike. You'll find vast agricultural lands and open ocean views, and a more rugged beauty than elsewhere on the island. What you won't find are many tourist services—or even many of the usual services. Even general stores are infrequent, and it's surprisingly hard to find fresh fish or produce, especially given the number of fishmongers and vegetable stands elsewhere in the province.

EXPLORING WESTERN PRINCE COUNTY

At the southwest tip of the island is the **Cedar Dunes Provincial Park** (☎ 902/859-8785). Set on 100 ocean-side acres, the park features extensive beaches (with lifeguards) and views across the strait to New Brunswick and down to the Confederation Bridge. You'll get a good illustration of the shifting sand here: The changing room has been all but engulfed in sand over the past few years.

Edging the beach is the distinctive black-and-white **West Point Lighthouse Museum** (☎ 902/859-3605). It's open in summer and features displays about lighthouse history and local lore, including rooms with some of the original furnishings. This is also the headquarters of the PEI Lighthouse Society, so it's a good stop for information about other island lights. If you're not afraid of heights, scramble up the narrow stairs to the beacon at the top, where you'll be rewarded with sweeping ocean views. Admission is C$2.50 (US$1.80) for adults and C$7 (US$5) for families. The lighthouse also houses an inn and restaurant (see below).

Closer to the northern tip of the island, photogenic **Elephant Rock** is a huge and striking stone formation grazing at the edge of the sea. Unlike many "famous animal" stone formations, this has the distinction of actually looking like the animal, complete with prominent trunk. You don't even need to use your imagination. It was created by the sea's action on eroding sandstone, and has been attracting attention since 1982. In recent years it's been discreetly reinforced to prevent further erosion, but one assumes the sea will eventually win out. The formation is accessible via an ill-maintained dirt road off Route 182 south of North Cape; watch for signs. It's on a privately owned piece of land, so you may have to pay C$2 (US$1.40) to park, depending on the season and time of day.

North Cape is a blustery, dramatic point where the seas swirl around from north and west, mixing off the point. You can take pictures of the lighthouse (1866), walk along the low, crumbling cliffs, then visit the small **Interpretive Centre and Aquarium** (☎ 902/882-2991) for a bit more information about local marine life and history. (Above the center is the Wind & Reef Restaurant, which offers seafood with a view of the sea.) Admission to the center is C$2 (US$1.40) for adults and C$1 (US70¢) for seniors and children. It's open from late May to mid-October.

And all those strange towering devices next to the center? That's the **Atlantic Wind Test Site,** where an array of traditional and state-of-the-art windmills are being refined to better harness the winds. You can admire the eerie sound they make in the cape's persistent breeze, but the site itself is closed to the public. Guides at the center can answer any questions you might have.

ACCOMMODATIONS & DINING

West Point Lighthouse. RR #2, West Point, PEI, C0B 1V0. ☎ 800/764-6854 or 902/859-3605. Fax 902/859-3117. 9 rms. C$85–C$130 (US$60–US$92) double. Off-season discounts (May–June 15 and after Sept 9). AE, MC, V. Closed Oct–May.

Two of the nine guest rooms at the West Point Lighthouse are actually in the lighthouse itself—something quite unique. One room, Keepers Quarters, faces landward and has a low ceiling; hold out for the Tower Room, with a 13-foot ceiling, extravagant canopy bed, and unrivaled views. (Book well in advance.) The other guest rooms are in a newer addition and are the size of cozy motel rooms, but are nicely decorated with quilts and full baths. The best of these is #9, a corner room with a wonderful breeze and great views. The first-floor restaurant is a popular destination for daytrippers who venture here for the beach and seafood. Breakfast (not included in room rates) is under C$5 (US$3.60), lunch is mostly under C$10 (US$7), and dinners range widely from C$10 to C$26 (US$7 to $19). Expect traditional dinner entrees like fisherman's platter, seafood fettuccine, chicken breast, and steak and scallops.

Newfoundland & Labrador

by Wayne Curtis

If you have but one atom of adventure in you, you'll know it after a few minutes poring over a map of Newfoundland and Labrador. Your electrons begin to pulse madly. Your heart races. All those isolated harbors! All those miles of remote lakes! And those extraordinary names that freckle the map: Jerry's Nose, Snook's Arm, Leading Tickles, Heart's Delight, Happy Adventure, Chapel Island, St. Bride's, Mistaken Point, Misery Hill, Breakheart Point, Cape Pine, Shuffle Board.

Newfoundland and Labrador may be the Eastern seaboard's last best place. (These two distinct geographic areas are administered as one province, so sometimes the phrase "Newfoundland and Labrador" refers to a single place, sometimes to two places.) Wild, windswept, and isolated, the province often reveals a powerful paradox. While the landscape is rocky and raw—at times it looks as if the glaciers had receded only a year or two ago—the residents display a genuine warmth that makes visitors feel right at home.

1 Exploring Newfoundland & Labrador

Two or three weeks is enough for a bare-bones tour of the whole island, though you'll be frustrated by all that you leave out. You're better off selecting a few regions and focusing on those.

Note that Newfoundland keeps its own clock, and "Newfoundland time" is a *half*-hour ahead of Atlantic time.

VISITOR INFORMATION

Visitor information centers aren't as numerous or well-organized in Newfoundland as they are in Nova Scotia or Prince Edward Island, where almost every small community has a place to harvest brochures and ask questions. You're better off stocking up on maps and information either in St. John's or just after you disembark from the ferries, where excellent centers are maintained.

The *Newfoundland and Labrador Travel Guide,* published by the province's department of tourism, is hefty and helpful, with listings of all attractions and accommodations. Request a free copy before arriving by calling ☎ **800/563-6353** or 709/729-2830. You may also request it by fax (709/729-1965), e-mail (info@ tourism.gov.nf.ca), or mail (P.O. Box 8730, St. John's, NF, A1B 4K2). The guide is available on the ferries and at the province's information centers.

GETTING THERE

Air transportation to Newfoundland is typically through Gander or St. John's. Flights originate in Montréal, Toronto, Halifax, and London, England. Airlines serving the island include **Air Canada/Air Nova** (☎ **800/776-3000** in the U.S. or 800/422-6232 in Canada), **Air Atlantic** (☎ **800/426-7000**), **Air Labrador** (☎ **800/563-3042** within Newfoundland, or 709/896-3387), and **Interprovincial Airlines** (☎ **800/563-2800** within Newfoundland or 709/576-1666 elsewhere). Flight time from Toronto to St. John's is about 3 hours.

Ferry service connects the island to North Sydney, Nova Scotia. Year-round ferries run to Port aux Basques with as many as three sailings each way daily in summer.

The crossing takes about 5 hours; one-way fares are C$19 (US$14) for adults, plus C$59 (US$42) per automobile. A seasonal ferry connects North Sydney with Argentia on the southwest tip of the Avalon Peninsula. This crossing is offered three times weekly in summer and takes 14 hours. The one-way fare is C$52.50 (US$37) for adults and C$118 (US$84) per automobile. On both ferries, children 5 to 12 years old are half-price; children under 5 are free. Reserved reclining seats and private cabins are available.

Seasonal ferries also connect Lewisport, Newfoundland, with Goose Bay, Labrador. The trip takes about 38 hours. Call ☎ **800/563-6353** for information on schedules and fares.

For all ferries, advance reservations are strongly advised during the peak travel season. As many as 100 cars have been backed up at Port aux Basques awaiting the next berth off the island. The reservation policy is quite fair: When you reserve over the phone with a credit card, you pay a C$25 (US$18) deposit. You can cancel or change your reservations up to 48 hours before departure for a full refund of your deposit. The balance is due at the terminal; you're required to check in at least 1 hour before sailing to hold your reservation. Many passengers check in a few hours early and nap in their cars. The terminals have recently been modernized, and all have snack bars, rest rooms with free showers, and up-to-date facilities.

Call **Marine Atlantic** for reservations or more information (☎ **800/341-7981**). Details are also available on their Web site at **www.marine-atlantic.com**.

GETTING AROUND

Newfoundland has no rail service, but several bus lines connect the major ports and cities. **DRL Coachlines** (☎ **709/738-8090**) has one bus daily from Port aux Basques to St. John's. The one-way fare is C$90 (US$64).

Airports served by scheduled interisland flights include Deer Lake, St. Anthony, and Stephenville on Newfoundland, and Wabush and Happy Valley-Goose Bay in Labrador. Call **Interprovincial Airlines** (☎ **800/563-2800** within Newfoundland or 709/576-1666 elsewhere) or **Air Labrador** (☎ **800/563-3042** within Newfoundland or 709/896-3387 elsewhere) for route and schedule information.

THE GREAT OUTDOORS

BIKING Bike touring in Newfoundland is for the hearty. It's not that the hills are necessarily brutal (although many are), but the weather can be downright demoralizing. The happiest bike tourists seem to be those who allow themselves frequent stays in motels or inns, where they can find hot showers and places to dry their gear.

Newfoundland & Labrador

Among the outfitters arranging bike tours are **Aspenwood Hike and Bike Tours,** P.O. Box 622, Springdale, NF, A1C 5K8 (☎ **709/673-4255**), and **Freewheeling Adventures,** RR #1, Hubbards, NS, B0J 1T0 (☎ **902/857-3600**).

BIRD WATCHING If you're from a temperate or tropical climate, bird watching won't get much more interesting or exotic than in Newfoundland and Labrador. Seabirds typically attract the most attention, and eastern Newfoundland and the Avalon Peninsula is especially rich in bird life. **Baccalieu Island,** reached by tour boat, is home to an astounding 3.3 million Leach's storm petrels. Just south of St. John's is the **Witless Bay Ecological Reserve,** where three islands host the largest colony of breeding puffins and kittiwakes in the western Atlantic. On the southern Avalon, **Cape St. Mary's** features a remarkable sea stack, just yards from easily accessible cliffs, that's home to a cacophonous colony of gannets.

CAMPING In addition to the two national parks, Newfoundland maintains a number of provincial parks open for car camping. (About a dozen of these were "privatized" in 1997, and are now run as commercial enterprises.) These are listed in the provincial travel guide, as are most privately run campgrounds.

CANOEING A glance at a map shows that rivers and lakes abound in Newfoundland and Labrador. Canoe trips can range from placid puttering around a pond near St. John's, to world-class descents of Labrador rivers hundreds of miles long. The Department of Tourism produces a free brochure outlining several canoe trips; call ☎ **800/563-6353.** A popular guide—*Canyons, Coves and Coastal Waters*—is sold in bookstores around the province, or it can be ordered by mail from **Newfoundland Canoeing Association,** P.O. Box 5961, St. John's, NF, A1C 5X4.

FISHING Newfoundland and Labrador is legendary among serious anglers, especially those stalking the cagey Atlantic salmon, which can weigh up to 40 pounds. Other prized species include landlocked salmon, lake trout, brook trout, and northern pike. One fishing license is needed for Atlantic salmon, one for other fish, so be sure to closely read the current *Newfoundland & Labrador Hunting and Fishing Guide* for current regulations. It's available at most visitor centers, or by calling ☎ **800/ 563-6353** or 709/576-2830. To request it by mail, write the **Department of Tourism, Culture & Recreation,** P.O. Box 8730, St. John's, NF, A1B 4K2.

HIKING & WALKING Newfoundland has an abundance of trails, but you'll have to work a bit harder to find them than in the provinces to the south. Casual hiking trails tend to be centered around national parks and historic sites, where they are often fairly short—good for a half-day hike, rarely more. Many communities also have short hiking trails, especially on the Avalon. Ask around.

The best clusters are at **Gros Morne National Park,** which maintains around 100 kilometers (60 miles) of trails. In addition to these, there's also off-track hiking on the dramatic Long Range for backpackers equipped to set out for a couple of days. Ask at the park visitor center for more information.

SEA KAYAKING Novices should stick to guided tours. **Eastern Edge Outfitters** (☎ **709/782-7465**) offers a variety of tours, mostly on the Avalon Peninsula. Rates range from C$100 (US$71) for a 1-day tour, to C$1,200 (US$852) for an 11-day tour, which includes all equipment and meals.

At **Terra Nova National Park,** 2-hour sea-kayak tours leave from the Marine Interpretation Centre and explore protected Newman's Cove. (See "Terra Nova National Park," below.)

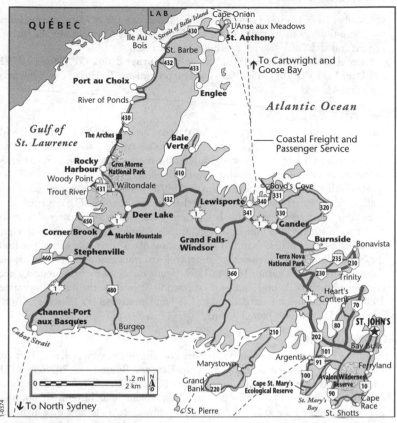

2 Southwestern Newfoundland

For most travelers arriving by ferry, this region is the first introduction to The Rock. And it's like starting the symphony without a prelude, jumping right to the crescendo. There's instant drama in the brawny, verdant mountains along the Trans-Canada Highway and in the intriguing coastal villages that await exploration. And you may be surprised that winds can blow with such intensity yet not attract any comment from the locals.

ESSENTIALS

GETTING THERE   Southwestern Newfoundland is commonly reached via ferry from Nova Scotia to Port aux Basques. See "Exploring Newfoundland & Labrador," above for ferry information. The Trans-Canada Highway (Route 1) links the major communities of southwestern Canada. Port aux Basques is 905 kilometers (543 miles) from St. John's via the Trans-Canada Highway.

VISITOR INFORMATION   In Port aux Basques, the **Provincial Interpretation and Information Centre** (☎ 709/695-2262) is located on the Trans-Canada Highway about 2 miles from the ferry terminal. It's open daily mid-May to the end of October from 6am to 11pm. You can't miss it. It's the modern, ecclesiastical-looking building on the right. Inside are displays to orient you about the island's regions and racks with enough brochures to sink a ship.

Helpful information centers are also found in **Corner Brook** (☎ 709/639-9792) and **Deer Lake** (☎ 709/635-2202). Look for prominent "?" signs to direct you from the Trans-Canada.

PORT AUX BASQUES

Port aux Basques is a major gateway for travelers arriving in Newfoundland, with ferries connecting to Nova Scotia year-round. It's an excellent way station for those arriving late on a ferry, or departing early in the morning. Otherwise, it can easily be viewed in a couple of hours when coming or going.

The **Gulf Museum,** 118 Main St. (☎ 709/695-3408), across from the Town Hall, has a quirky assortment of artifacts related to local history. The museum's centerpiece is a Portuguese astrolabe dating from 1628, which was recovered from local waters in 1981. Other intriguing items include a display about the *Caribou,* a ferry torpedoed by a German U-boat in 1942 with a loss of 137 lives, and bric-a-brac from the Newfie Bullet, the much-maligned, much-loved train that ran between Port aux Basques and St. John's from 1898 to 1969. (Some railcars were being restored near the Hotel Port aux Basques and were expected to be open to the public in summer 1998.) The museum is open daily from 1 to 8pm; admission is C$2 (US$1.40) for adults and C$1 (US70¢) for children.

ACCOMMODATIONS

About half a dozen hotels and B&Bs offer no-frills shelter to travelers at Port aux Basques. The two largest are **Hotel Port aux Basques,** Route 1 (☎ 709/695-2171) and **St. Christopher's Hotel,** Caribou Road (☎ 800/563-4779). Both might be described as "budget modern," with clean, basic rooms in architecturally undistinguished buildings. I'd give St. Christopher's the edge since it's located on a high bluff with attractive views of the town and the harbor. Both have around 50 rooms, and both charge about C$60 (US$43) for a double.

CORNER BROOK

With a population of 25,000, Corner Brook is Newfoundland's second largest city. On the map it looks promising—it's located on the hill-flanked Humber Arm, a well-protected ocean inlet and famed salmon fishing area. With the residential areas stacked neatly on the hills around the commercial center in the valley, it's got great topographical interest.

Alas, the downtown is disappointing for sightseeing. Simplifying somewhat (quite a bit, actually), the city center consists of one huge paper mill and two small malls. The enclosed malls offer a basic selection of goods but little charm. If you do venture downtown, search out attractive, tree-lined **West Street,** where you'll find coffee shops, restaurants, and pharmacies.

ACCOMMODATIONS

Corner Brook is home to several basic chain motels. Among others, you'll find the **Best Western Mamateek Inn,** 64 Maple Valley Rd., (☎ 800/563-8600 or 709/639-8901) out near the highway, and the **Holiday Inn,** 48 West St. (☎ 709/634-5381), which is within easy walking distance of the city's best restaurant. Plan on C$80 (US$57) and up for a room for two.

Glynmill Inn. 1 Cobb Lane (near West St.), Corner Brook, NF, A2H 6E6. ☎ **800/563-4400** in Canada only, or 709/634-5181. Fax 709/634-5106. 57 rms, 24 suites. A/C TV TEL. C$77–C$135 (US$55–US$96) double. AE, DC, ER, MC, V.

This in-town Tudor inn is set in a quiet parklike setting an easy stroll to the services and attractions of West Street. Built in 1924 (and extensively renovated in 1994), the four-story hotel has a surfeit of charm and appealing detailing. The rooms are tastefully decorated with colonial reproductions; the popular Tudor Suite has a private Jacuzzi. You'll get far more character here than at the chain motels in town, and for about the same price. The inn's two dining rooms are quite popular among local diners, with steaks especially popular. The setting feels a bit institutional (they do a rousing business with conventions and banquets), but the food is quite good. Dinner entrees run from C$12 to C$21 (US$9 to US$15).

DINING

✪ Thirteen West. 13 West St. ☎ **709/634-1300.** Reservations recommended on weekends. Lunch main courses C$8–C$14 (US$6–US$10); dinner main courses C$12–C$26 (US$9–US$19). AE, DC, ER, MC, V. Mon–Fri 11:30am–2:30pm; Sun–Thurs 5:30–9:30pm, Fri 5:30–10:30pm, Sat 5:30–10:30pm. ECLECTIC.

Corner Brook's best restaurant could easily compete with the better restaurants of St. John's or Halifax in both quality of the food and the pleasantly casual attitude. Tucked along shady West Street in an unobtrusive building (there's a patio fronting the street for the rare balmy night), the kitchen does an outstanding job preparing top-notch meals, and the staff knows how to make good service seem easy. The menu is creative, with entrees like a terrifically tender strip-loin in a four-peppercorn crust, and a Cajun-style pan-roasted chicken breast with tiger shrimp.

DEER LAKE

Deer Lake is an unassuming crossroads town where travelers coming from the south either continue on the Trans-Canada Highway toward St. John's or veer northwest to Gros Morne National Park, some 71 kilometers (43 miles) distant. There's little reason to linger here other than to stop briefly at the visitors center, gas up, and then push on.

Well, that's not exactly true. There are the **strawberries.** If you arrive here when the berries are in season (mid- to late July some years; early August in others), do yourself a favor and stop at one of the several seasonal roadside stands for a pint or two. They're plump, they're cheap, and they're sinfully sweet and flavorful— nothing at all like the tasteless commercial berries that have lately taken over grocery stores in the United States and elsewhere.

3 Gros Morne National Park

"Gros Morne" translates roughly from the French as "big gloomy," and if you arrive on a day when ghostly bits of fog blow across the road and scud clouds hover in the glacial valleys, you'll get a pretty good idea how this area got its name. Even on brilliantly sunny days there's something about the stark mountains, lonely fjords cut off from the ocean, and miles of tangled spruce forest that can trigger a mild melancholy.

✪ **Gros Morne National Park** is one of Canada's true treasures, and few who visit here fail to come away awed. The park is divided into two sections, north and south, riven by the multiarmed Bonne Bay (locally pronounced "Bombay"). Alas, a ferry connecting the two has not operated for years, so exploring both sections by car requires backtracking. The park's visitor center and most tourist services are found in the village of Rocky Harbour in the north section. But you'd be shortchanging your-self to miss a detour through the dramatic southern section, a place that looks like it had a rough birth, geologically speaking.

If you'd prefer to let someone else do the planning for you, contact **Gros Morne Adventure Guides** (☎ 709/458-2722), which organizes guided sea-kayaking and hiking excursions around the park. Prices range from C$35 to C$90 (US$25 to US$64) per person per trip.

ESSENTIALS

GETTING THERE   From the Trans-Canada Highway in Deer Lake, turn west on Route 430 (the Viking Trail). This runs through the northern section of the park. For the southern section, turn left (south) on Route 431 in Wiltondale.

VISITOR INFORMATION   The main national-park **visitor information center** (☎ 709/458-2066) is just south of Rocky Harbour on Route 430. It's open daily from 9am to 10pm. The center features exhibits on park geology and wildlife; there's also a short film about the park

FEES   All visitors must obtain a permit for any activity within the park. Daily fees are C$3 (US$2.10) for adults, C$2.25 (US$1.60) for seniors, C$1.50 (US$1.10) for children 6 to 16, and C$6 (US$4.30) for families; children under 6 are free. Four-day passes are available for the price of 3 days.

GROS MORNE'S SOUTHERN SECTION

The road through the southern section dead-ends at Trout River, and accordingly it seems to discourage unadventurous visitors who like loops and through-routes. That's too bad, because the south contains some of the park's most dramatic terrain. Granted, you can glimpse the rust-colored Tablelands from north of Bonne Bay near Rocky Harbour, thereby saving the 50-kilometer (30-mile) detour. But without ac-tually walking through the desolate landscape you miss much of the impact. The south also contains several lost-in-time fishing villages that predate the park's creation in 1973.

The region's scenic centerpiece is **Trout River Pond,** a landlocked fjord some 15 kilometers (9 miles) long. You can hike along the north shore to get a great view of the Narrows, where cliffs nearly pinch the pond in two. For a more relaxed view, sign up for a boat tour, which surrounds you with breathtaking panoramic views. ✪ **Tableland Boat Tours** (☎ 709/451-2101) offers excursions aboard the *Lady Catherine,* a 40-passenger tour boat. Two-and-a-half hour trips are offered daily at 10am, 1pm, and 4pm in July and August (1pm only in June and September). The cost is C$25 (US$18) for adults and C$9.25 (US$7) for children 6 to 16; children under 6 are free. Tickets are sold at a gift shop between the village of Trout River and the pond; watch for signs.

HIKES & WALKS

The **Tablelands Trail** departs from barren Trout River gulch and follows an old gravel road up to Winterhouse Brook Canyon. You can bushwhack along the rocky river a bit further upstream, or turn back. It's about 2 kilometers (1.2 miles) each way, depending on how adventurous you feel. This is a good trail to get a feel for the unique ecology of the Tablelands. Look for the signboards that explain the geology at the trailhead and at the roadside pull-off on your left prior to reaching the trailhead.

Experienced hikers looking for a challenge should seek out the ✪ **Green Gardens Trail.** There are two trailheads to this loop; I'd recommend the second one (closer

Journey to the Center of the Earth

If you see folks walking around the Tablelands looking twitchy and excited, they're probably amateur geologists. The Tablelands are one of the world's great geological celebrities and a popular destination among pilgrims who love the study of rock.

To the uninitiated, the Tablelands area—south of Woody Point and the south arm of Bonne Bay—will seem rather bleak and barren. From a distance, the muscular hills rise up all rounded and rust-colored, devoid of trees or even that pale-green furze that seems to blanket all other hills. Up close, you discover just how barren they are—little plant life seems to have established a toehold.

There's a reason for that. Some 570 million years ago, this rock was part of the earth's mantle, that part of the earth just under the crust. Riding on continental plates, two land masses collided forcefully hereabouts, and a piece of the mantle was driven up and over the crust, rather than being forced under, as is usually the case. Years of erosion followed, and what's left is a rare glimpse of the earth's skeleton. The rock is so laced with magnesium that few plants can live here, giving it a barrenness that seems more appropriate for a desert landscape in the American Southwest than the rainy mountains of Newfoundland.

to Trout River). You'll start by trekking through a rolling, infertile landscape, and then the plunge begins as you descend down, down, down wooden steps and a steep trail toward the sea. The landscape grows more lush by the moment, and soon you'll be walking through extraordinary coastal meadows on crumbling bluffs high above the surf.

The trail follows the shore northward for about 4 or 5 kilometers (2.5 or 3 miles), and it's one of the most picturesque coastal trails I've hiked anywhere in the world. In July the irises and a whole symphony of other wildflowers are blooming wildly. The entire loop is about 16 kilometers (9.6 miles) and is rugged and very hilly; allow about 5 or 6 hours. An abbreviated version involves walking clockwise on the loop to the shore's edge, then retracing one's steps back uphill. That's about 9 kilometers (5.4 miles).

CAMPING

The two **drive-in campsites** in the southern section—**Trout River Pond** and **Lomond**—both offer showers and nearby hiking trails. Of the two, Trout River Pond is more dramatic, located on a plateau overlooking the pond; a short stroll brings you to the pond's edge with wonderful views up the fjord. Lomond is near the site of an old lumber town and is popular with anglers. Camping is C$15.25 (US$11) per site.

ACCOMMODATIONS

Victorian Manor. Main St. (P.O. Box 165), Woody Point, NF, A0K 1P0. ☎ **709/453-2485.** 3 rms (2 with shared bath), 3 efficiency units, 1 guest house. C$50–C$70 (US$36–US$50) double; C$125 (US$89) guest house. Rates include continental breakfast. AE, MC, V.

This 1920 home is one of the most impressive in the village, but that doesn't mean it's extravagant. It's more solid than flamboyant, set in a residential neighborhood near the town center and a few minute's walk to the harbor. The attractive guest house has its own whirlpool. If that's booked, ask for one of the efficiencies, which cost about the same as the rooms but afford much greater convenience, especially considering the slim dining choices in town.

DINING

Seaside Restaurant. Main St., Trout River. ☎ **709/451-3461.** Main courses C$9–C$19 (US$6–US$14). MC, V. Daily noon–10pm. Closed Oct–June. SEAFOOD.

The Seaside has been a Trout River institution for years, and it's clearly a notch above the tired fare you often find in tiny coastal villages. The restaurant is nicely polished without being swank, and features magnificent harbor views. The pan-fried cod is superb, as are a number of other seafood dishes, like shrimp and lobster. (Sandwiches and burgers are at hand for those who don't care for seafood.) I've heard the desserts are quite good, such as the partridgeberry parfait, but the service was so numbingly slow that I didn't dare order dessert after lunch for fear of missing an entire day of hiking. Other diners report no problems with service.

GROS MORNE'S NORTHERN SECTION

Gros Morne's northern section flanks Route 430 for some 75 kilometers (45 miles) between Wiltondale and St. Paul's. The road winds through the abrupt, forested hills south of Rocky Harbour; beyond these, the road levels out, following a broad coastal plain covered mostly with bog and tuckamore. East of the plain rises the extraordinarily dramatic monoliths of the Long Range. This section contains the park's visitor center as well as the park's one must-see attraction: Western Brook Pond.

The hardscrabble fishing village of **Rocky Harbour** is home to the greatest concentration of tourist services, including motels, B&Bs, Laundromats, and small grocery stores. One caveat, however: Rocky Harbour and the surrounding area lack a well-lit, well-stocked grocery store of the sort one might expect near a national park of international importance. What you'll find are small fishing villages with small grocery stores—the sorts of places where you'll want to check the dates on bread and milk real carefully.

If you have time for only one activity in Gros Morne—and heaven forbid that's the case—make it the boat trip up ✪ **Western Brook Pond.** The trip begins a 20-minute drive north of Rocky Harbour. Park at the Western Brook Pond trailhead, then set off on an easy 45-minute hike across the northern coastal plain, with interpretive signs explaining the wildlife and bog ecology you'll see along the way. (I watched a moose and her calf munching their way down a stream.) Always ahead, the mighty monoliths of the Long Range rise high above, inviting and mystical, more like a 19th-century scene from the Rockies than the Atlantic seaboard.

You'll soon arrive at the pond's edge, where there's a small collection of outbuildings near a wharf. Once aboard one of the vessels (there are two), you'll set off into the maw of the mountains, winding between the sheer rock faces that define this landlocked fjord. The spiel on the boat is recorded, but even that unfortunate bit of cheese fails to detract from the grandeur of the scene. You'll learn about the glacial geology and the remarkable quality of the water, which is considered among the purest in the world. Bring lots of film and a wide-angle lens. The trip lasts about 2^1/$_2$ hours. The cost is C$27 (US$19) for adults and C$6 (US$4.30) for students 6 to 16 (must be accompanied by an adult); children under 6 free when with parents. For reservations, contact the **Ocean View Motel** (☎ 709/458-2730) in Rocky Harbour.

HIKES & WALKS

Even if you're not planning on signing up for the **Western Brook Pond** boat tour (reconsider!), you owe yourself a walk up to the pond's wharf and possibly beyond. The 45-minute one-way trek from the parking lot north of Sally's Cove follows well-trod trail and boardwalk through bog and boreal forest. When you arrive at the wharf, the view to the mouth of the fjord will take your breath away. An outdoor exhibit explains how glaciers shaped the landscape in front of you, and it's one of the best such exhibits you'll ever see.

Two spur trails continue on either side of the pond for a short distance. The **Snug Harbour Trail,** which follows the northern shore to a primitive campsite (registration required), is especially appealing. After crossing a seasonal bridge at the pond outlet, you'll pass through scrubby woods before emerging on a long and wonderful sand and pebble beach; this is a great destination for a relaxed afternoon picnic and requisite nap. The hike all the way to Snug Harbour is about 8 kilometers (4.8 miles) one-way.

CAMPING

The northern section has three campgrounds open to car campers. The main campground is **Berry Hill,** which is just north of Rocky Harbour. There are 146 drive-in sites, plus six walk-in sites on the shores of the pond itself. It's just a 10-minute drive from the visitor center, where evening activities and presentations are held.

Shallow Bay has 50 campsites, mostly open, and is near the park's northern border and an appealing 4-kilometer (2.5-mile) sand beach. Both these campgrounds have showers and flush toilets.

ACCOMMODATIONS

Rocky Harbour has more tourist services than any other village in or around the park, but it still can't handle the influx of travelers in July and August. Two or three bus tours can pretty much fill up the town. One B&B owner told me she turned away 20 people seeking a room one night in July. It's an unwise traveler who arrives without a reservation.

The largest motel in town is the **Ocean View Motel** (☎ 709/458-2730), located on the harbor. It has 44 basic rooms (some have small balconies with bay views), but everything feels a bit thin here, from the carpeting to the walls to the furnishings. It's popular with bus tours, and often fills up fast. Rooms are C$65 to C$70 (US$46 to US$50) double in season.

Gros Morne Cabins. P.O. Box 151, Rocky Harbour, NF, A0K 4N0. ☎ **709/458-2020** or 709/458-2369. 22 cabins. TV. C$60 (U$43) 1 bedrm; C$75 (US$53) 2 bedrms. Prices are for 2; add C$5 (US$3.60) per extra person. Open year-round; off-season rates available. AE, MC, V.

My favorite thing about the Gros Morne Cabins? Pulling up and seeing the long lines of freshly washed sheets billowing in the sea breeze, like a Christo installation. The trim and tidy log cabins are clustered tightly along a grassy rise overlooking Rocky Harbour, and all have outstanding views toward the Lobster Cove Head Lighthouse. Inside they're new and clean, more antiseptic than worn. You can base yourself here for a week easily; each is equipped with a kitchenette, gas barbecues are scattered about, and the complex includes Endicott's Store and a Laundromat. There's also a pizza place just across the street for relaxed sunset dining at your own picnic table. Pets are welcome.

Wildflower Inn. Main St. N., Rocky Harbour, NF, A0K 4N0. ☎ **709/458-3000.** 6 rms (2 with private bath; 4 share 2 bathrms). C$50–C$60 (US$36–US$43) double. Rates include continental breakfast. MC, V.

This 60-year-old home near the village center was modernized and updated prior to its opening as a B&B in 1997, giving it a casual country look inside. The guest rooms are tastefully appointed if a bit small (I didn't get a chance to see the two rooms with private bath, which were under construction), and the neighborhood isn't especially scenic (there's an auto-repair shop across the way). But the house is very peaceful, the innkeepers exceptionally friendly (as is their black Lab), and this is a great choice for those seeking lodging with a comfortable, homey feel.

DINING

Fisherman's Landing. Main St., Rocky Harbour. ☎ **709/458-2060.** Sandwiches C$3.50–C$7 (US$2.50–US$5); main courses C$7–C$15 (US$5–US$11). MC, V. Summer 6am–11pm; limited hours off-season. SEAFOOD.

Fisherman's Landing is still the newcomer in town, and with its industrial carpeting and generic chain-restaurant chairs and tables, it will take some more time before it starts to develop its own personality. But it does offer efficient service and dependable meals, with specialties like fish-and-chips, cod tongues, and squid rings. For breakfast, there's the traditional Newfie fisherman's breakfast of a mug of tea served with homemade bread and molasses.

4 The Great Northern Peninsula

The Great Northern Peninsula is that stout cudgel that threatens the shores of Labrador. If Newfoundland can even be said to have a beaten track, rest assured that the peninsula is well off it. It's not as mountainous or starkly dramatic as Gros Morne, but the road unspools for kilometer after kilometer through tuckamore and evergreen forest, along restless coast and the base of geologically striking hills. There are few services and even fewer organized diversions. But it has early history in spades, a handful of fishing villages clustering along the rocky coast, and some of the most unspoiled terrain anywhere. The road is in very good condition, with the chief hazard being the stray moose or caribou. In the spring, the infrequent polar bear may wander through a village, often hungry after a long trip south on ice floes.

ESSENTIALS

GETTING THERE   Route 430, which is also called the Viking Trail, runs from Deer Lake (at the Trans-Canada Highway) to St. Anthony, a 433-kilometer (260-mile) jaunt. Scheduled flights on **Air Labrador** (☎ **800/563-3042** within Newfoundland or 709/896-3387 elsewhere), and **Interprovincial Airlines** (☎ **800/563-2800** within Newfoundland or 709/576-1666 elsewhere) stop at St. Anthony, where rental cars are available. The airport is located on Route 430 approximately 30 kilometers (18 miles) west of St. Anthony.

VISITOR INFORMATION   For information about the Great Northern Peninsula and the Viking Trail, contact the **Viking Trail Tourism Association,** P.O. Box 430, St. Anthony, NF, A0K 4S0 (☎ **709/454-8888;** e-mail: viking@thezone.net). Visitor centers are located at St. Anthony and Hawkes Bay.

PORT AU CHOIX

A visit to Port au Choix (pronounced "Port-a-*Shwaw*") requires a 13-kilometer (8-mile) detour off the Viking Trail, out to a knobby peninsula that's home to a sizable fishing fleet. The windswept lands overlooking the sea are low, predominantly flat, and lush with grasses. Simple homes speckle the landscape; most are of recent vintage, many are mobile.

The story of **Port au Choix National Historic Site,** Point Riche Road, Port au Choix (☎ **709/861-3522**), began back in 1967 when a local businessman began digging the foundation for a new movie theater in town. He came upon some bones. A lot of bones. In fact, what he stumbled upon turned out to be a remarkable burial ground for what are now called the Maritime Archaic Indians.

This group of hunters populated parts of Atlantic Canada starting 7,500 years ago, far predating the Inuit, who arrived only around 4,000 years ago. These early natives relied chiefly on the sea, and among artifacts recovered here are slate spears and antler harpoon tips, which featured an ingenious toggle that extended after being thrust into flesh. One of the enduring historical mysteries is the disappearance of the Maritime Archaic Indians from the province about 3,500 years ago; to this day no one can explain their sudden departure.

You'll learn about this fascinating historic episode at the new visitor center, which opened in 1997. From here, staffers will be able to direct you to various sites, including the original burial ground, now surrounded by village homes. You can also visit the nearby lighthouse, scenically located on a blustery point thrusting into the Gulf of St. Lawrence. Admission is C$2.75 (US$2) for adults, C$2.25 (US$1.60) for seniors, and C$1.50 (US$1.10) for children. Open daily mid-June to mid-September from 9am to 7pm.

L'ANSE AUX MEADOWS

Newfoundland's northernmost tip is not only exceptionally remote and dramatic, it's one of the most historically significant spots in the world. At ○ **L'Anse aux Meadows National Historic Site,** Route 436, L'Anse aux Meadows (☎ **709/623-2608**), a Viking encampment dating from about 1,000 years ago, was discovered in 1960 and has been thoroughly documented by archaeologists in the 4 decades since. This unusually well-conceived and well-managed site probes this historic chapter in European expansion, and an afternoon spent here goads the imagination.

In the late 1950s a pair of determined archaeologists named Helge Ingstad and Anne Stine Ingstad pored over 13th-century Norse sagas searching for clues about where the Vikings might have landed on the shores of North America. With just a few scraps of description, the Ingstads began cruising the coastlines of Newfoundland and Labrador, asking locals about unusual hummocks or odd findings.

At L'Anse aux Meadows, they struck gold. In a remote cove noted for its low, grassy hills, they found the remains of an ancient Norse encampment that included three large halls, along with a forge where nails were made from locally obtained pig iron. As many as 100 people lived here for a time, including some women. (Spindle whorls and bone knitting needles attest to that.) The Vikings abandoned the settlement after a few years to return to Greenland and Denmark. It's telling that no graves have ever been discovered here.

Start your visit by viewing the recovered artifacts in the visitor center and watching the half-hour video about the site's discovery. Then I would suggest signing up for one of the free guided tours of the site. The guides offer considerably more information than the simple markers around the grounds. Near the original encampment are several re-created sod-and-timber buildings, depicting how life was lived 1,000 years ago. These are tended by costumed interpreters, who have a wonderful knack of staying in character without making their questioners feel like dorks. If you time it right, you might be rewarded with a bit of flat bread cooked old-style over an open fire.

Admission is C$5 (US$3.60) for adults, C$4.25 (US$3) for seniors, C$2.75 (US$2) for children, and C$10 (US$7) for families. Open daily from 9am to 8pm. Closed mid-September to mid-June.

ACCOMMODATIONS

✪ **Tickle Inn at Cape Onion.** RR #1, Cape Onion, NF, A0K 4J0. ☎ **709/452-4321** (June–Sept) or 709/739-5503 (Oct–May). Web site: home.thezone.net/~tickle. 4 rms (all share 2 baths). C$50–C$60 (US$36–US$43) double. Rates include deluxe continental breakfast. MC, V. Closed Oct–May.

If you're seeking that end-of-the-world flavor, you'll be more than a little content here. Set on a remote cove at the end of a road near Newfoundland's northernmost point (you can see Labrador across the straits), the Tickle Inn occupies a solid fisherman's home built around 1890 by the great-grandfather of the current inn-keeper, David Adams. (He's a school counselor in St. John's the rest of the year.) After lapsing into decrepitude, the home was expertly restored in 1990 and has recaptured much of the charm of a Victorian outport home. The guest rooms are small but comfortable, and they share two washrooms. Before dinner, guests often gather in the parlor and enjoy snacks and complimentary cocktails. One of the highlights of a stay here is exploring the small network of hiking trails maintained by Adams, which ascend open bluffs to painfully beautiful views of the Labrador Straits. The inn is about a 40-minute drive from L'Anse aux Meadows. No smoking.

Dining: Meals are served family-style at 7:30 each evening. (Your only other option for a meal is to drive a considerable distance to the nearest restaurant.) The food here is excellent, featuring very local cuisine. You might have a Newfoundland minestrone with homegrown vegetables and herbs, or crispy baked cod garnished with squid rings. Time your visit for berry season and you can expect such delights as the northern berry flan for dessert.

5 Terra Nova National Park

You've probably heard travelers rave about Gros Morne National Park as you discussed your impending trip to Newfoundland. At the same time, you may have heard a deafening silence that fell on the island's other national park, Terra Nova, on the island's eastern shore.

As it turns out, there's a reason for that. Words like *dramatic* and *grandeur* don't really apply. This is an exceedingly pleasant park with lots of boreal forest and coastal landscape, along with a surfeit of low, rolling hills. Within its boundaries, forest and shoreline are preserved for wildlife and recreation and make for good exploration. But the terra, however nova, just won't take your breath away. (With one possible exception: the cliffy hills at the mouth of Newman Sound.) More than likely, a visit here will leave you soothed and relaxed, like a good walk in the woods.

ESSENTIALS

GETTING THERE Terra Nova is located on the Trans-Canada Highway. It's about 240 kilometers (144 miles) from St. John's, and 630 kilometers (378 miles) from Port aux Basques.

VISITOR INFORMATION In 1997 visitor information was consolidated at the new **Marine Interpretation Centre** (☎ **709/533-2801**) at the Saltons Day-Use Area, about 5 kilometers (3 miles) north of the Newman Sound Campground. It's open daily from June to mid-October from 9am to 9pm (restricted hours after Labour Day).

EXPLORING THE PARK

A trip to the park should begin with a visit to the **Marine Interpretation Centre** (see above), which was newly built in 1997. It's located on a scenic part of the sound, with high hills across the way. Encased in verdant hills, the sound looks suspiciously like a lake, but oceangoing sailboats tied up at the wharf suggest that it's otherwise.

HIKING & BOATING

The park has 60 kilometers (37 miles) of maintained **hiking trails.** Many of these are fairly easy treks of an hour or so through undemanding woodlands. The main exception is the **Outport Trail,** a 17.5-kilometer (10.5-mile) pathway that winds in and around the south shore of Newman Sound near abandoned fishing settlements. Another popular trek, and justly so, is the 4.5-kilometer (2.7-mile) **Coastal Trail,** which runs between Newman Sound Campground and the Marine Interpretation Centre. You'll get great views of the sound, and en route you'll pass the wonderfully named Pissing Mare Falls.

Trail maps and advice on other hikes are available at the Marine Interpretation Centre.

The park lends itself quite nicely to **sea kayaking.** If you've brought your own boat, ask for route suggestions at the information center. (Overnight trips to Minchin and South Broad coves are good options, as is a day exploration of Swale Island.) If you're a paddling novice, sign up with **Terra Nova Adventure Tours** (☎ 709/256-8687), located at the Marine Interpretation Centre. The crew leads guided tours of the sound four times daily. The tours last between 2 and 3 hours and cost C$33 (US$23) for adults. Reservations aren't required.

For a more passive view from the water, consider a tour with **Ocean Watch Tours** (☎ 709/533-6024), which sails in a converted fishing boat four times daily from the wharf at the Marine Interpretation Centre. You'll see bald-eagle nests, old outport villages, and, with some luck, whales and icebergs.

CAMPING

Terra Nova's main campground is at **Newman Sound.** It has 417 campsites (mostly of the gravel-pad variety) set in and around spruce forest and sheep-laurel clearings. The lengthy amenities list includes free showers, limited electrical hookups, grocery store and snack bar, evening programs, Laundromat, and hiking trails. Camping fees are C$14 to C$16 (US$10 to US$11).

ACCOMMODATIONS & DINING

Campgrounds are the only option within the park itself. At the edge of the park, try the following.

Terra Nova Park Lodge. Rte. 1, Port Blandford, NF, A0C 2G0. ☎ **709/543-2525.** Fax 709/543-2201. 79 rms, including 5 suites. A/C TV TEL. C$80–C$200 (US$57–US$142) double. AE, DISC, MC, V.

This modern three-story resort is a short drive off Route 1 about 2 kilometers (1.2 miles) south of the park's southern entrance. Most notably, it's adjacent to the well-regarded, 6,500-yard Twin River Golf Course, one of Atlantic Canada's more scenic links. The hotel isn't lavish and lacks a certain personality. It feels rather inexpensively built (pray that you don't have heavy-footed children staying overhead), and features bland, cookie-cutter rooms. On the other hand, it's clean, comfortable, and well located for a golfing holiday or exploring the park.

Dining: The Clode Sound Dining Room is open daily for all three meals. It offers standard resort fare, with dinners such as fried cod, filet mignon, pork chops and applesauce, and surf and turf. Entrees are priced from C$12 to C$20 (US$9 to US$14).

Facilities: There's a heated outdoor pool, fitness room, sauna, Jacuzzi, two tennis courts, and game room. And, of course, the golf course.

6 The Bonavista Peninsula

The Bonavista Peninsula juts northeast into the sea from just south of Terra Nova National Park. It's a worthy side trip for travelers fascinated by the island's past. You'll find a historic village, a wonderful new historic site, and one of the province's most intriguing lighthouses. It's also a good spot for scouting for whales, puffins, and icebergs.

About halfway out the peninsula you'll come to **Trinity,** an impeccably maintained old village. Some longtime visitors grouse that it's becoming overly popular and a bit prettified with too many B&Bs and traffic restrictions. That may be. But there's still a palpable sense of history to this profoundly historic spot. And anyway, it's the region's only destination to find good shelter and a decent meal.

From Trinity it's about 40 kilometers (24 miles) out to the tip of the peninsula. Somewhere along the route, which isn't especially picturesque, you'll wonder if it's worth it. Yes, it is. Keep going. Plan to spend at least a couple of hours exploring the dramatic, ocean-carved point and the fine fishing village of Bonavista with its two excellent historic properties.

ESSENTIALS

GETTING THERE The Bonavista Peninsula can be reached from the Trans-Canada Highway via—depending on the direction you're coming from—Route 233, Route 230, or Route 230A. Route 230 runs all the way to the tip of the cape; Route 235 forms a partial loop back, and offers some splendid water views along the way. The round-trip from Clarenville to the tip is approximately 240 kilometers (144 miles).

VISITOR INFORMATION The **Southern Bonavista Bay Tourist Chalet** (☎ 709/462-3306) is located on Route 230 just west of the intersection with Route 235. It's open daily in summer.

TRINITY

The tiny coastal hamlet of Trinity was once more populous than St. John's. For more than 3 centuries, from its first visit by Portuguese fishermen in the 1500s until well into the 19th century, Trinity benefited from a long and steady tenure as a hub for traders, primarily from England, who supplied the booming fishing economy of Trinity Bay and eastern Newfoundland.

Technological advances (including the railroad) doomed Trinity's merchant class, and the town lapsed into an extended economic slumber. But even today, you can see lingering traces of the town's former affluence, from the attractive flourishes in much of the architecture, to the rows of white picket fences all around the village (no rustic quiggly fences for Trinity).

In recent years the provincial government and concerned individuals have taken a keen interest in preserving Trinity, and it's clearly benefiting from a small revival in which many homes have been made over as bed-and-breakfasts. Several buildings are open to the public as provincial historic sites, and two others as local historical museums. Plan on 2 or 3 hours to wander about and explore.

Start your adventure into history at the **Trinity Interpretation Centre** (☎ 709/464-2042) at the Tibbs House. (It's a bit tricky to find, since signs don't seem to be a priority. Follow the one-way road around the village and continue straight past the parish hall. Look on the left for the pale-green home with the prominent gable.) Here you can pick up a walking-tour map and get oriented with a handful of historical exhibits.

A minute's walk away is the brick **Lester-Garland Premises,** where you can learn about the traders and their times. This handsome Georgian-style building is a convincing replica (built in 1997) of one of the earlier structures, built in 1819. The original was occupied until 1847, when it was abandoned and began to deteriorate. It was torn down (much to the horror of local historians) in the 1960s, but much of the building hardware, including some doors and windows, were salvaged and warehoused until the rebuilding.

Next door is the **Ryan Building,** where a succession of the town's most prominent merchants kept shop. The grassy lots between these buildings and the water were once filled with warehouses, none of which have survived. A good imagination is helpful in envisioning the former prosperity.

A short walk away is the **Hiscock House,** a handsome home where Emma Hiscock raised her children and kept a shop after the untimely death of her husband in a boating accident at age 39. The home has been restored to appear as it might have in 1910, and helpful guides can fill in the details. All the buildings mentioned so far are provincial sites open mid-June to mid-October daily from 10am to 5:30pm; admission is free.

The most entertaining way to learn about the village's history is through the **Trinity Pageant** (☎ 888/464-1100 or 709/464-3232). On Wednesday, Saturday, and Sunday, at 2pm, actors lead a peripatetic audience through the streets, acting out episodes from Trinity's past. Tickets are C$6 (US$4.30); children under 12 are free.

ACCOMMODATIONS

All three properties mentioned below are in the heart of Trinity's historic area.

✪ **Campbell House.** High St., Trinity, Trinity Bay, NF, A0C 2S0. ☎ **709/464-3377.** Web site: www.newcomm.net/campbell. 4 rms, all with private bath (3 rms with detached hall bath). TEL. C$89 (US$63) double. Rates include full breakfast. AE, DC, ER, MC, V. Closed mid-Oct to late May.

This handsome 1840 home and its nearby cottage—both clad in traditional white clapboard with green trim—are set amid lovely gardens on a twisting lane overlooking Fisher's Cove. All four rooms have water views. Two rooms are on the second floor of the main house and have a nice historic flair, even to the point that they'll require some stooping under joists if you're over 5-foot-10-inches tall. The two other rooms are in a lovely and simple pine-paneled cottage just below the gardens, and feature an adjacent waterfront deck and a full kitchen on the first floor. Reserve well in advance for July and August, when the inn rarely has a free room. There's no smoking, and no children under age 8.

Hangashore Bed & Breakfast. 1 Ash's Lane, Trinity, Trinity Bay, NF, A0C 2S0. ☎ **709/ 464-3807,** or 709/754-7324 off-season. 3 rms (all share 2 baths). C$75 (US$53) double. Rates include full breakfast. AE, MC, V. Closed Nov–May.

The Hangashore opened in June 1997, and is owned by the same folks who run the always-cordial Monkstown Manor in St. John's. This is a place for travelers who don't require much space. The rooms in this historic 1850 home are cozy (read: tiny), just as they would have been in, well, 1850. But they're utterly uncluttered in a modern Scandinavian sort of way, and painted with bold, welcoming colors. There's a parlor with television and telephone downstairs, and the relaxed breakfasts are served around a pine picnic-style table in a room of eye-searing yellow. Pets are allowed.

Village Inn. Barbour's Lane (P.O. Box 10), Trinity, Trinity Bay, NF, A0C 2S0. ☎ **709/ 464-3269.** Fax 709/464-3700. E-mail: beamish@nf.sympatico.ca. Web site: www3.nf.sympatico. ca/beamish. 12 rms (6 with shared bath). C$52–C$72 (US$37–US$51) double. MC, V. Closed Nov–Apr.

With eight rooms in the main inn and four in the guest house, the Village Inn is Trinity's largest hostelry. It has a pleasantly lived-in feel, with eclectic but leaning-toward-Victorian furniture, and the small dining room feels as if it hasn't changed a whit in 75 years. Innkeepers Christine and Peter Beamish do a fine job making guests feel at home; they also run **Ocean Contact,** a well-respected whale-watch operation that deploys a 26-foot rigid-hull inflatable. Ask about tour availability when you book your room. No smoking is allowed, but "small, well-behaved pets" are. The dining room serves meals from 8am until well into the evening. Lunch includes sand-wiches and burgers, and the evening selection is equally basic (meat loaf, fried cod, liver and onions) but well prepared. Meals are reasonably priced at C$7 to C$17 (US$5 to US$12).

DINING

Hungry travelers have a few choices in addition to the dependable Village Inn (see above). The tiny **Old Trinity Cookery** (☎ **709/464-3615**), next to the museum, serves up traditional Newfoundland meals, including eggs Benedictine (*not* eggs Benedict, and don't get them started on the difference) beginning at 8am. On the wharf is the **Dock Marina Restaurant,** which, despite its name and oceanfront lo-cation, specializes in meaty steaks.

BONAVISTA

The ✪ **Ryan Premises National Historic Site** (☎ 709/772-5364) opened in June 1997 with Queen Elizabeth herself presiding over the grand opening. Located in downtown Bonavista, the new site is an exceedingly photogenic compound of white clapboard buildings at the harbor's edge. For more than a century, this was the town's most prominent salt-fish complex, where fishermen sold their catch and bought all the sundry goods needed to keep an outport functioning. Michael Ryan opened for business here in 1857; his heirs kept the business going until 1978. The spiffy com-plex today features an art gallery, local history museum, gift shop, handcrafted furniture store, theater, and the best interpretive exhibit I've seen on the role of the codfish industry in Newfoundland's history.

The property is open daily in summer from 10am to 6pm. Admission is C$2. 50 (US$1.80) for adults, C$2 (US$1.40) for seniors, and C$1.50 (US$1.10) for children.

On the far side of the harbor, and across from a field of magnificent irises, is the beautiful **Mockbeggar Property** (☎ 709/729-2460). Named after an English seaport that shared characteristics with Bonavista, the home was occupied by promi-nent Newfoundland politician F. Gordon Bradley. It's been restored to how it ap-peared when Bradley moved here in 1940, and features much of the original furniture. With a few telltale exceptions (note the wonderful 1940s-era carpet in the formal dining room), it shows a strong Victorian influence. The house is managed as a provincial historic site, and admission is free. It's open daily in summer from 10am to 5:30pm.

JUST NORTH OF TOWN

The extraordinary ✪ **Cape Bonavista Lighthouse** is located 6 kilometers (3.6 miles) north of town on a rugged point. Built in 1843, the lighthouse is fundamentally a stone tower around which a red-and-white wood-frame house has been constructed.

The keepers' quarters (the light-keeper and his assistant both lived here) has been restored to the year 1870. You can clamber up the narrow stairs to the light itself, and inspect the ingenious clockwork mechanism that kept six lanterns revolving all-night long between 1895 and 1962. (With some help—it took 15 minutes to wind the counterweight by hand, a job that had to be performed every 2 hours.) This light served mariners until 3 decades ago, when its role was usurped by an inelegant steel tower and beacon. Open daily in summer from 10:30am to 6pm; admission is free.

Below the lighthouse on a rocky promontory cleft from the mainland is a robust **puffin colony.** Hundreds of these stumpy, colorful birds hop around the grassy knob and take flight into the sea winds. They're easily seen from just below the lighthouse; bring binoculars for a clearer view. Red-footed common murres dive for fish below, and whales are often sighted just offshore. This is the only place I've ever had whales and puffins in sight through my binoculars at the same time. (And there was a beautiful iceberg just off to my left.)

7 The Baccalieu Trail

The Baccalieu Trail forms a loop around the long, narrow, and unnamed peninsula that separates Conception Bay from Trinity Bay. It doesn't have the distinguished 18th-century pedigree of neighboring Bonavista Peninsula, which was the region's mercantile center in the early days. But I think the history here is actually more intriguing in a quirky kind of way. Episodes here feature the mysterious Amelia Earhart, the cranky Rockwell Kent, and the pioneers of both the Arctic exploration and transatlantic communication. There's also excellent bird watching, if you're willing to brave a choppy boat ride. As at Bonavista, be aware that the drive isn't uninterruptedly scenic. But you'll come upon vistas that will absolutely leave you speechless.

ESSENTIALS

GETTING THERE   The Baccalieu Trail is comprised of routes 80, 70, and 60. The entire detour to Bay de Verde and back from the Trans-Canada is about 260 kilometers (156 miles).

VISITOR INFORMATION   The **Provincial Interpretive and Information Centre** is on the Trans-Canada Highway just west of Route 80 in Whitbourne. It's open daily in season from 8:30am to 8:30pm. The **Kearny Tourist Chalet** (☎ 709/596-3042) in Harbour Grace is on Route 70 at the south end of town; it's open from 10am to 7pm in season. The **Bay Roberts Tourist Information Centre** is in the red caboose behind the McDonald's on Route 70 and is open Monday to Saturday from 10am to 7pm.

BACCALIEU ISLAND

This is a don't-miss destination for serious birders. Cliff-girded **Baccalieu Island,** about 3.5 kilometers (2 miles) off the peninsula's tip, is 5 kilometers (3 miles) long and has a rich history as a fishing center and location of an important lighthouse. Today it's better known for the vast colonies of seabirds, 11 species of which breed here. These include puffins, northern fulmar, common murre, and northern gannet. The island is also home to thick-billed murre and razorbills, and a staggering three-million-plus Leach's storm petrels. Access to the island is by boat only. For information about tours, contact **Baccalieu Bird Island Tours** (☎ 709/587-2860).

Boat tours leave from the village of **Bay de Verde,** which itself is worth the excursion even if you're not intending to visit the island. A road now reaches this remote fishing village, but it still very much has the feel of a outport untouched by modern trends. It's dominated by trim, old-fashioned houses on rocky terraces overlooking the harbor.

HARBOUR GRACE

Harbour Grace is a lovely historical town that sprawls along a waterfront with views out to Conception Bay. It's not a picture-perfect town—there's plenty of charmless modern architecture mixed among the historic—but you'll get a good sense of the region's rich history with an hour's poking around.

Near the Harbour Grace Visitor Centre at the south end of town are two modest memorials to transportation before the roads came through. *The Spirit of Harbour Grace,* a DC-3 airplane from Labrador Air, is mounted in a graceful banked turn, like a trout rising to take a fly. Just offshore and slightly off-kilter is the **SS** *Kyle,* an exceptionally handsome coastal steamer, which is aground and listing to port. The *Kyle* was one of the last of the wood- and coal-burning coastal steamers. Launched in 1913, it actively plied Newfoundland's waters until 1967, when a northeaster blew it from its moorings and it came to rest on a mussel bed. A paint job in 1997 made the steamer rather more festive once again.

Harbour Grace occupies a prominent niche in the history of early-20th-century aviation. A cluster of pioneer pilots used the town airfield as a jumping off point for crossings of the Atlantic. Indeed, Newfoundland was abuzz with daring pilots during aviation's pioneer days. The first nonstop crossing of the Atlantic was by J. Alcock and A. W. Brown, who flew from Newfoundland to Ireland in 1919, 8 years before Charles Lindbergh left New York to become the first solo pilot to cross the Atlantic. In 1928 Amelia Earhart flew to Wales from Newfoundland, and 4 years later became the first woman to solo the transatlantic trip, taking off from Harbour Grace.

You can revisit this rich history at the **Harbour Grace Airfield,** the first aerodrome in Newfoundland. It's a stunningly beautiful and pristine spot on a hillside overlooking the harbor and the town—it appears not to have changed a bit since Earhart took off for Europe more than a half-century ago. You can scramble atop the monolith at the top of the airfield to get a sweeping view out into Conception Bay, with the lush, grassy airstrip stretching out below.

Find the airfield by driving 1 mile north of the information center on Route 70, then turning left (away from the water). The paved road soon stops; you don't. Continue 1.5 kilometers (0.9 miles) from Route 70, and turn right on another dirt road. Continue 1.6 kilometers (1 mile), passing the end of the airstrip, then turn right and drive to the top of the low hill. There's a small plaque commemorating the early fliers.

ACCOMMODATIONS

There are several motels and a number of family-style restaurants along the Baccalieu Trail, especially on the southern stretches of Route 70. Carbonear has two basic, serviceable motels: **Fong's Motel** (☎ 709/596-5114) and **Carbonear Motel** (☎ 709/596-5662), where rooms range from C$45 to C$65 (US$32 to US$46).

✪ **Garrison Inn.** Water St., Harbour Grace, NF, A0A 2M0. ☎ **709/596-3658.** 4 rms (2 rms share 1 bath). C$54 (US$38) double with shared bath, C$64 (US$45) private bath. Rates include full breakfast. MC, V.

Innkeeper Jerry Dick came here from Ontario with an academic background in historic preservation. And it shows in every room of this splendidly restored 1811 home—wide pine floors, warm and welcoming colors, well-chosen antiques that seem to have never left the room. This intimate inn is a wonderful surprise—historic without being shabby, refined without too much gloss. It's located across the road from the local-history museum and offers glimpses of the harbor from some rooms and the gardens. This is one of the more inviting inns on the island, and quite a bargain given the high quality of the experience. No smoking.

Dining: Jerry Dick not only knows historic preservation, he knows his way around a kitchen and prepares a fine meal, often using local salmon. (A couple of examples: marinated salmon steaks with a kiwi salsa, poached salmon with a partridgeberry hollandaise.) Herbs are from the kitchen garden just outside the back door. There's one seating nightly Wednesday to Sunday, and dinners are by reservation only (the public is welcome). The cost is C$20 (US$14) for a three-course meal.

BRIGUS

The trim and tidy harbor-front village of Brigus is clustered with wood-frame homes and narrow lanes that extend out from the picturesque harbor. Brigus is remembered by some art historians as the town that gave the boot to iconoclastic American artist Rockwell Kent, who lived here—briefly—around 1914 to 1915. World War I was on, and Kent was suspected of "pro-German activities." His crime? Singing songs in Pennsylvania Dutch. Kent eventually returned to Newfoundland in 1968 as a guest of the premier, and forgave the province and the people. "It was wartime," he said.

The **Brigus Museum,** 4 Magistrates Hill (☎ 709/528-3298), is one of the finest small museums in the province. Local history is the focus on the two compact floors of this 1820 stone barn, which has been nicely curated with a limited but well-chosen selection of intriguing artifacts. These include a beautiful plate hand-painted by Rockwell Kent during his brief but controversial residency here. Admission is C$1 (US70¢) for adults and C50¢ (US35¢) for children. Open daily mid-June to early September.

The **Hawthorne Cottage National Historic Site,** Village Center, Brigus (☎ 709/528-4302), an elaborate gingerbread cottage on a lovely landscaped yard in the town center, was home to Captain Bob Bartlett. Bartlett was with the support crew accompanying Robert E. Peary on his successful trip to the North Pole in 1909, and has been lauded as the "greatest ice navigator of the century." The cottage was originally built in 1830, moved here from 10 kilometers (6 miles) away in 1833, and is now furnished much as it might have been by the local gentry at the turn of the century. Admission is C$2.25 (US$1.60) for adults, C$1.75 (US$1.25) for seniors, and C$1.25 (US90¢) for children 6 to 16; children under 6 are free. Open daily from 10am to 6pm in summer.

8 St. John's

St. John's is a world apart from the rest of Newfoundland. The island's small outports and long roads through spruce and bog are imbued with a deep melancholy. St. John's, on the other hand, is vibrant and bustling. Coming into the city after traveling the hinterlands is like stepping from Kansas into Oz—the landscape seems to suddenly burst with color and life.

This attractive port city of just over 100,000 residents crowds the steep hills around a deep harbor. Like Halifax, Nova Scotia, and Saint John, New Brunswick, St. John's also serves as a magnet for youth culture in the province, and the clubs and restaurants tend to have a more cosmopolitan feel and sharper edge.

The geographical centerpiece of St. John's harbor is impressive geographically—it's well protected from the open sea by stony hills. Ships sail through the Narrows, a rocky defile of the sort you'd expect to see Hercules astraddle, hidden from view at the north end of the harbor.

This is very much a working harbor, the hub of much of the province's commerce. As such, it's not terribly quaint. Across the way is a charmless oil-tank farm, along with off-loading facilities for tankers. A major container-ship wharf occupies the head of the harbor. Along the water's edge on Harbour Street downtown you'll usually find hulking ships tied up; pedestrians are welcome to stroll and gawk, but wholesale commerce is the focus here, not boutiques.

ESSENTIALS

GETTING THERE St. John's is located 131 kilometers (79 miles) from the ferry at Argentia, 905 kilometers (543 miles) from Port aux Basques. The **St. John's International Airport** offers flights to Halifax, Montréal, Ottawa, Toronto, and London, England. See "Getting There," above, for ferry and airline information.

The airport is 6 kilometers (4 miles) from downtown; taxis from the airport to downtown hotels are approximately C$12 (US$9) for one traveler, C$2 (US$1.40) for each additional traveler.

VISITOR INFORMATION In summer, visitor information can be obtained from the **Tourist Information Rail Car** (☎ 709/576-8514) on Harbour Drive, along the waterfront. Off-season, look for information at **City Hall** (☎ 709/576-8106) on New Gower Street. The e-mail address is cityedev@nfld.com.

GETTING AROUND **Metrobus** serves much of the city. Fares in 1997 were C$1.50 (US$1.10) for a single trip. Route information is available at the visitor information center or by calling ☎ 709/722-9400. Taxis are plentiful around St. John's, and charge an initial fee of C$2 (US$1.40) plus 10¢ per sixteenth of a mile. One of the larger and more dependable outfits in the city is **Bugden Taxi** (☎ 709/726-4400).

EXPLORING ST. JOHN'S

Parking is rarely a problem in downtown St. John's. Bring loonies and quarters to feed the meters. Once you park you can continue easily by foot; the downtown area is compact enough.

DOWNTOWN

You'll come to ✪ **Signal Hill** (☎ 709/772-5367) for the history, but stay for the views. Signal Hill is St. John's most visible and most visit-worthy attraction. The rugged, barren hill is the city's preeminent landmark, rising up over the entrance to the harbor and topped by a craggy castle with a flag fluttering high overhead (that's the signal of the name). The layers of history here are rich and complex—flags have flown atop this hill since 1704, and over the centuries a succession of military fortifications occupied these strategic slopes, as did three different hospitals. The "castle" (called Cabot Tower) dates to 1897, built in honor of Queen Victoria's Diamond Jubilee and the 400th anniversary of John Cabot's arrival in the New World. The hill also secured a spot in history in 1901, when Nobel laureate Guglielmo Marconi received the first wireless transatlantic broadcast—three short dots indicating the letter S in Morse code, sent from Cornwall, England—on an antennae raised on a kite 400 feet in the air in powerful winds.

A good place to start a tour is at the interpretive center, where you'll get a good briefing about the hill's history. Four days a week, military drills and cannon firings

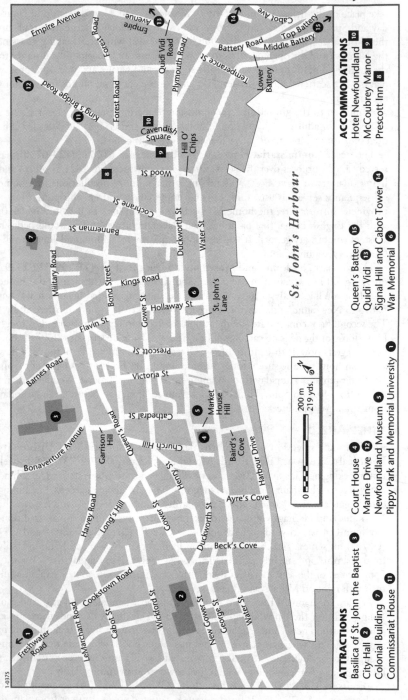

St. John's

St. John's Harbour

200 m
219 yds.
0

1-0375

take place in the field next to the center (Wednesday and Thursday at 7pm; Saturday and Sunday at 3 and 7pm). From here, you can following serpentine trails up the hill to the Cabot Tower, where you'll be rewarded with breathtaking views of the Narrows and the open ocean beyond. (Cape Spear can be seen in the distance to the south.) Look for icebergs in the early summer, and whales anytime. Interpretive placards are scattered about the summit, and feature engaging photos from various epochs.

Admission to the grounds is free; admission to the interpretive center is C$2.25 (US$1.60) for adults, C$1.75 (US$1.25) for seniors, and C$1.25 (US90¢) for children 6 to 16; children under 6 are free. Open daylight hours.

The stellar **Commissariat House,** King's Bridge Road (☎ 709/729-6730), has served varied purposes over the years. Originally constructed in 1821 as offices and living quarters to serve Fort William and other military installations, the home subsequently served as a rectory, nursing home, and children's hospital. Now a provincial historic site, the home has been restored to look as it would in 1830, with the English china, fine paintings, and elaborate furnishings as would befit an assistant commissary general. It's open daily from 10am to 5:30pm mid-June to mid-October. Free admission.

The compact **Newfoundland Museum,** 285 Duckworth St. (☎ 709/729-2329), offers a good introduction to the natural and cultural history of the island. On the first floor you'll learn about the flora and fauna, and find out that the moose was not native to Newfoundland, but introduced. (Twice, actually—once unsuccessfully.) The second floor concentrates on the various native cultures, from Beothuk through Inuit (look for the delicate carvings of bear heads). The more sparsely exhibited third floor suggests how 19th-century life was lived in Newfoundland's outports. Allow about an hour for a leisurely tour. Summer hours are Friday to Wednesday from 10am to 6pm and Thursday from 10am to 9pm; winter, Tuesday, Wednesday, and Friday from 9am to 5pm, Thursday from 9am to 9pm, and Saturday and Sunday from 10am to 6pm. Free admission.

FARTHER AFIELD

An abundant selection of northern plants make the **Memorial University Botanical Garden at Oxen Pond,** Mount Scio Road (☎ 709/737-8590), well worth seeking out (it's tucked over a wooded ridge on the city's western edge, behind Pippy Park). The main plots are arranged in gracious "theme gardens," including cottage garden, rock garden, and a peat garden. Among the most interesting: the Newfoundland Heritage Garden, with examples of 70 types of perennials traditionally found in island gardens. Admission is C$2 (US$1.40) for adults and C$1 (US70¢) for seniors and children 5 to 17. Open May to November; hours are daily from 10am to 5pm in July and August, and Wednesday to Sunday from 10am to 5pm the rest of the season. To get there, drive on Thorburn Road past Avalon Mall, then turn right on Mount Scio Road.

The low, octagonal **Fluvarium,** in Pippy Park off Allandale Road at the edge of Long Pond near the University (☎ 709/754-3474), actually descends three stories into the earth. The second level features exhibits on river ecology, including life in the riffles (that's where trout spawn) and in shallow pools, which are rich with nutrients. On the lowest level you'll find yourself looking up into a deep pool that's located alongside the building. Watch for brown trout swimming lazily by.

Admission is C$4 (US$2.80) for adults, C$3.25 (US$2.30) for seniors and students, and C$2.75 (US$2) for children. It's open daily in summer from 9am to 5pm. Guided tours leave on the hour; feeding time is 4pm.

OUTDOOR PURSUITS

The region's most dramatic hiking trail happens to be within city limits. ○ **North Head Trail** runs from atop Signal Hill to the inviting cluster of cliff-side buildings called the Battery at the water's edge below. It twists along bluffs with peerless views of the Narrows, Cape Spear, and the high, ragged cliffs to the north. For a half-day adventure, walk from downtown to the Battery, ascend the trail, spend some time at Signal Hill, then return to town via Signal Hill Road. If you're pressed for time and plan to drive to the trail, park atop Signal Hill rather than at the Battery, where space is tight and the road harrowingly narrow.

Pippy Park (☎ 709/737-3655) is on the city's hilly western side and contains 3,350 acres of developed recreation land and quiet trails. The popular park is home to the city campground and Fluvarium (see above), as well as golf, picnic sites, and playgrounds.

QUICK EXCURSIONS

Quidi Vidi (pronounced "kitty vitty") is a tiny harbor village that sets new standards for the definition of "quaint." The village is tucked in narrow, rocky defile behind Signal Hill, where a narrow ocean inlet provides access to the sea. It's photogenic in the extreme, and a wonderful spot to investigate by foot or bike (it's rather more difficult by car). The village consists mostly of compact homes, including the oldest home in St. John's, with very few shops open to the public. To get to Quidi Vidi, follow Signal Hill Road to Quidi Vidi Road; turn right onto Forest Road.

Some 11 kilometers (7 miles) southeast of downtown is North America's most easterly point, and home to dramatic **Cape Spear National Historic Site** (☎ 709/772-5367). Here you'll find a picturesque lighthouse dating back to 1836 and underground passages from abandoned World War II gun batteries. A visitor center will orient you nicely; leave plenty of time to walk the hiking trails and scout for whales surfacing out to sea. Admission to the lighthouse, which has been restored to the appearance it had in 1839, is C$2.25 (US$1.60) for adults, C$1.75 (US$1.25) for seniors, and C$1.25 (US90¢) for children 6 to 16; children under 6 are free. Open year-round.

ACCOMMODATIONS

Campers should head to municipal **Pippy Park Campground** (☎ 709/737-3669), just a few miles from downtown off Allandale Road. The campground has 184 sites, most with full hookups, and a sociable tenting area. Rates range from about C$9 (US$6) for a tent site, to C$20 (US$14) for a fully serviced site. It often books up in summer, so it's wise to call ahead for reservations.

Budget options (rooms around C$60/US$43) include the serviceable **Centre City Motel,** 389 Elizabeth Ave. (☎ 709/726-0092), and the adequate **1st City Motel,** 479 Kenmount Rd. (☎ 709/722-5400).

EXPENSIVE

○ **Hotel Newfoundland.** Cavendish Sq. (P.O. Box 5637), St. John's, NF, A1C 5W8. ☎ **800/828-7447** in the U.S., 800/268-9411 in Canada, or 709/726-4980. Fax 709/726-2025. Web site: www.cphotels.ca. 301 rms. A/C MINIBAR TV TEL. C$109–C$234 (US$77–US$166) double. AE, CB, DC, DISC, ER, MC, V.

The Hotel Newfoundland was built in 1982 in a starkly modern style, but it boasts a refined sensibility and attention to detail that's reminiscent of a lost era. What I like most about the hotel is how the designers and architects hide their best surprises. The lobby has one of the best views of the Narrows in the city, but you have to wander around to find it. It's a wonderful effect, and one that's used nicely throughout. (This helps compensate for the somewhat generic, conference-hotel feel of the decor.) About half the guest rooms have stupendous harbor views; all have ironing boards, coffeemakers, and bathrobes.

Dining: The very elegant Cabot Club is among the best restaurants in town, and features a mix of traditional favorites and continental dining (try the medaillons of caribou with partridgeberry confit). Jackets are requested for men; it's open weekdays for lunch and daily for dinner. Dinner entrees are C$21 to C$32 (US$15 to US$23). The more casual Outport Cafe is open for three meals daily; you can get fish and brewis and tasty cod served up a variety of ways.

Services: Concierge, 24-hour room service, dry cleaning, laundry service, safe-deposit boxes, baby-sitting.

Facilities: Indoor pool, Jacuzzi, sauna, health club (with computerized golf course simulator), business center, beauty salon, shopping arcade.

MODERATE

McCoubrey Manor. 8 Ordnance St., St. John's, NF, A1C 3K7. ☎ 888/753-7577 or 709/722-7577. Fax 709/579-7577. E-mail: mccmanor@nfld.com. 4 rms. TV TEL. C$89–C$129 (US$63–US$91) double. Rates include continental breakfast. AE, MC, V.

McCoubrey Manor offers the convenient location of the Hotel Newfoundland (it's just across the street), but with Victorian charm and a more casual B&B atmosphere. The pair of adjoining 1904 town houses are decorated in what might be called a "contemporary Victorian" style and are quite inviting. The two upstairs rooms have private double Jacuzzis; three rooms have fireplaces. Room 3 has an attractive 1940s-era bathroom and corner fireplace; Room 2 has a sunken Jacuzzi, oak mantled fireplace, and lustrous trim of British Columbia fir. There's a washer and dryer on premises for guests; one of the rooms even has a full kitchen (C$10/US$7 extra to use it). No smoking; kids older than toddler age are welcome.

Monkstown Manor. 51 Monkstown Rd., St. John's, NF, A1C 3T4. ☎ 888/754-7377 or 709/754-7324. Fax 709/722-8557. E-mail: krussel@pigeoninlet.nfnet.com. 4 rms, 3 house-keeping units (all share baths). C$55 (US$39) double. Rates include continental breakfast. AE, MC, V.

A stay here is like a visit with old college friends. This narrow Victorian home, a short drive or moderate walk from downtown, is run with an infectious congeniality, more like a dormitory than an inn. More likely than not there's someone playing music on the ground floor or guests chatting at length about bands they saw the night before. (The owners are very musical, and run a production company that specializes in Newfoundland folk music.) The guest rooms in the main house have buttery wooden floors and funky decorating; the units with small kitchens are a couple doors away. The two shared baths in the main house have Jacuzzis, so at times you might have to wait your turn. Pets are welcome. No smoking.

Prescott Inn. 19 Military Rd. (P.O. Box 204), St. John's, NF, A1C 2C3. ☎ 709/753-7733. Fax 709/579-7774. 16 rms (7 rms share 3 baths), 7 units at the Battery with kitchen and private baths. TV TEL. C$50–C$105 (US$35–US$75) double. Rates include full breakfast. MC, V.

The Prescott Inn is comprised of an unusually attractive grouping of wood-frame town homes painted a vibrant lavender-blue. Some of the historical detailing has been restored inside, but mostly the homes have been modernized. Some rooms have carpeting, others have hardwood floors. All are furnished with eclectic antiques that rise above flea-market quality but aren't quite collectible. The lower priced rooms share washrooms, and are among the city's better bargains. All guests are welcome to relax on the shared balcony that runs along the back of the building. Room 3 may be the best of the bunch, and is the only guest room with a private Jacuzzi. If you want a room with one of the best views in the city, ask about their new guest rooms at the Battery, a scenic villagelike neighborhood perched precariously over the harbor a short drive away. The Battery units all have private baths and kitchens. No smoking.

◐ Winterholme. 79 Rennies Mill Rd., St. John's, NF, A1C 3R1. **☎ 800/599-7829** or 709/739-7979. Fax 709/753-9411. E-mail: winterholme@nf.sympatico.ca. 7 rms, 5 apts. TV TEL. C$89–C$119 (US$63–US$85) double; C$129–C$179 (US$92–US$127) suite. AE, ER, MC, V.

This handsome and stout Victorian mansion was built in 1904 for C$120,000 (US$85,200), when C$120,000 was more than chump change. The place is an architectural marvel, with prominent turrets, bowfront windows, bold pediments, elaborate molded-plaster ceilings, and woodwork extravagant enough to stop you in your tracks. (The oak woodwork was actually carved in England and shipped here for installation.) Room 7 is one of the most lavish I've seen; the former billiards room features a fireplace and two-person Jacuzzi, along with a plasterwork ceiling and a supple leather wing chair. Room 1 is oval-shaped and occupies one of the turrets; it also has a Jacuzzi. The attic rooms are a little less extraordinary, but still appealing with their odd angles and nice touches. It's located a 10- to 15-minute walk from downtown. No smoking in guest rooms.

DINING

Budget travelers should migrate toward the pubs along George Street, where you can find good deals on basic fare. Better yet, head up the hill to the intersection of LaMarchant and Freshwater streets. Within a 2-block radius, you'll find cheap Chinese, Italian, Mexican, and fish-and-chips, among others, at both eat-in and takeout establishments.

EXPENSIVE

The Cellar. Baird's Cove (near waterfront, just downhill from Supreme Court building). **☎ 709/579-8900.** Reservations encouraged. Lunch main courses C$8–C$15 (US$6–US$11); dinner main courses C$15–C$26 (US$11–US$19). AE, DC, DISC, ER, MC, V. Mon–Fri 11:30am–2:30pm; Sun–Thurs 5:30–9:30pm, Fri 5:30–10pm, Sat 5:30–10:30pm. ECLECTIC.

The classy interior is a surprise here—the restaurant is located on a nondescript street and through a nondescript entrance. Inside, it's intimate and warm, not unlike an upper-crust gentleman's club. The kitchen has been turning out fine meals for some time now, developing a reputation for creativity and consistency. The menu is constantly in play, but look for reliable standbys like the delicious gravlax and the homemade bread and pastas. Fish is prepared especially well here, with some cuts paired with innovative flavors like ginger and pear butter.

◐ Stone House. 8 Kenna's Hill. **☎ 709/753-2380.** Reservations suggested. Lunch main courses C$9–C$14 (US$6–US$10); dinner main courses C$18–C$29 (US$13–US$21). AE, ER, MC, V. Mon–Fri 11:30am–2:30pm; Sun–Thurs 6–10pm, Fri–Sat 5–11pm. Drive north on King's Bridge Rd. to Kenna's Hill. HAUTE NEWFOUNDLAND.

Here's a menu you won't soon forget: Slow-roasted seal-flipper with pork scruncions. Roast caribou with juniper-berry sauce. Labrador partridge stuffed with partridgeberry dressing and wrapped in bacon. No surprise, Stone House is noted for its wild-game dishes. But it also caters to less adventurous palates with dishes like chicken breast stuffed with Camembert and currants, and poached salmon served on spinach and finished with hollandaise. Meals served in this 1834 home are gourmet with a capital "G," served by formally attired and entirely capable waiters.

MODERATE

Casa Grande. 108 Duckworth. ☎ **709/753-6108.** Reservations appreciated. Lunch main courses C$7–C$8 (US$5–US$6); dinner main courses C$10–C$16 (US$7–US$11). AE, DC, ER, MC, V. Mon–Fri 11:30am–2:30pm; Mon–Thurs 5–10pm, Fri–Sat 5–11pm, Sun 5–10pm. MEXICAN.

If you've developed Mexican-food withdrawal after all those outport meals of fried fish, plan to satisfy your cravings here—you won't find better Mexican food in Newfoundland, and you'd be hard-pressed to find it better anywhere in Atlantic Canada. Seating is on two floors of a narrow storefront just down the hill from the Hotel Newfoundland. Angle for the front room of the upper level, where you'll get views of the harbor. It's often crowded and the service can be irksome, but come prepared for a wait and you'll get excellent value for your money.

Classic Cafe. 364 Duckworth. ☎ **709/722-4083.** Breakfast and lunch main courses C$4–C$11 (US$2.85–US$8); dinner main courses C$8–C$17 (US$6–US$12). DC, ER, MC, V. Daily 24 hr. NEWFOUNDLAND.

This come-as-you-are spot is appropriately named—it's truly classic St. John's, and everyone seems to drop in here at one time or another. There's an intimate dining room with good deals on lobster dinners upstairs in this 1894 hillside home. But the real action is in the crowded street-level bistro. Breakfast is served 24 hours a day—but don't expect a limp croissant and tea. Macho breakfasts (for example, 8-oz. sirloin with eggs, toast, home fries, and baked beans) appeal to a mixed group, from burly longshoremen to hungover pale musicians. Nonbreakfast entrees in the evening are surprisingly good, and include mushroom caps stuffed with shrimp, rack of lamb, and a very fresh seafood medley.

✪ **Stella's.** 106 Water St. ☎ **709/753-9625.** Reservations suggested. Lunch C$4–C$9 (US$2.85–US$6); main courses C$11–C$14 (US$8–US$10). MC, V. Tues–Fri noon–3pm; Wed 6–9pm, Thurs–Fri 6–10pm, Sat noon–10pm. NATURAL/WHOLE FOODS.

This is *the* destination for those pining away for an oversized plate of fresh greens after too much time in the canned-vegetable hinterlands. The cozy two-level dining room on Water Street is often hectic and the service strained, but the food is consistently outstanding. Among your choices: pan-fried cod, chicken burrito, curried scallops, Thai veggie stir-fry, and Oriental almond tofu. There's no soda, but a good selection of wonderful homemade concoctions, including "bogwater"—a mix of carrot, ginger, and celery juices. The partridgeberry milkshake is also a winner.

ST. JOHN'S AFTER DARK

The nightlife in St. John's is extraordinarily vibrant, and you'd be doing yourself an injustice if you didn't spend at least one evening on a pub crawl.

The first stop for a little local music and cordial imbibing should be **George Street,** which runs for several blocks near New Gower and Water streets, close to City Hall. Every St. John's resident confidently asserts that George Street contains more bars per square foot than anywhere else on the planet. I have been unable to track down a global authority that verifies pubs-per-square-foot, but a walk down the street did little to buck their claims.

George Street is packed with energetic pubs and lounges, some fueled by beer, others by testosterone, still more by righteous Gaelic fiddling. The best strategy for selecting a pub is a slow ramble around 10pm, vectoring into spots with appealing music wafting from the door. At places with live music, cover charges are universally very nominal and rarely top C$5 (US$3.60).

To get started: If you're looking for good local folk music, arrive early to get seats at the **Blarney Stone,** George Street (☎ 709/754-1798), which puts on few airs and features wonderful Newfoundland and Irish folk music. **Trapper John's,** 2 George St. (☎ 709/579-9630), is also known for outstanding provincial folk music, but tries a bit harder for that "Ye Olde Newfoundeland" character. This is a traditional "screeching-in" spot for visitors (You have to ask what this is when you get there).

For blues, there's the lively **Fat Cat,** 5 George St. (☎ 709/722-6409). For a more upscale spot with lower decibel levels, try **Christian's Bar,** 23 George St. (☎ 709/753-9100), which offers the nonalcoholic option of specialty coffees.

If George Street's beery atmosphere reminds you of those nights in college you'd just as soon forget, a few blocks away are two pubs tucked down tiny alleys known for their genial public-house atmospheres. The **Duke of Duckworth,** 325 Duckworth St. (☎ 709/739-6344), specializes in draft beers and pub lunches. **The Ship Inn,** 265 Duckworth St. (☎ 709/753-3870), is a St. John's mainstay and features a variety of local musical acts that seem to complement rather than overwhelm the pub's cozy atmosphere.

9 The Southern Avalon Peninsula

The Avalon Peninsula—or just "the Avalon," as it's commonly called—is home to some of Newfoundland's most memorable and dramatic scenery, including high coastal cliffs and endless bogs. More good news: It's also relatively compact and manageable, and can be viewed on long day trips from St. John's, or in a couple of days of scenic poking around. It's a good destination for anyone short on time yet wanting to get a taste of the wild. The area is especially notable for its bird colonies, as well as its herd of wild caribou. The bad news? It's thrust out in the sea where cold and warm currents collide, resulting in legendary fogs and blustery, moist weather. Bring a rain suit and come prepared for bone-numbing dampness.

While snooping about, also listen for the distinctive Irish-influenced brogue of the residents. You'll find no more vivid testimony to the settlement of the region by Irish pioneers.

ESSENTIALS

GETTING THERE   Several well-marked, well-maintained highways follow the coast of the southern Avalon Peninsula; few roads cross the damp and spongy interior. A map is essential.

VISITOR INFORMATION   Your best bet is to stop in the St. John's tourist bureaus (see above) or at the well-marked tourist bureau just up the hill from the Argentia ferry before you begin your travels. Witless Bay has a tourist information booth at the edge of the cobblestone beach and is stocked with a handful of brochures. It's open irregularly.

WITLESS BAY

Witless Bay is about 35 kilometers (21 miles) south of St. John's and makes an easy day trip. The main attraction here is the Witless Bay Ecological Reserve, a cluster of islands located a couple of miles offshore. Here you'll find the ✪ **largest puffin colony in North America,** along with the second largest murre colony. Access is by tour boat, several of which you'll find headquartered along Route 10 between Bay Bulls and Bauline East. **Captain Murphy's Bird Island & Whale Tours** (☎ 709/

334-2002) is based in Witless Bay and offers several trips daily; tours last 2 to 2¹/₂ hours and cost C$25 (US$18) for adults. In Bauline East, south of Witless Bay, the 30-foot **Molly Bawn** (☎ **709/334-2621**) offers 1-hour tours in search of puffins, whales, and icebergs. Tours depart every 1¹/₂ hours during peak season; the cost is C$15 (US$11) for adults and C$10 (US$7) for children under 12.

FERRYLAND

Historic Ferryland is among the most picturesque of the Avalon villages, set at the foot of rocky hills on a harbor protected by a series of abrupt islands at its mouth.

Ferryland was among the first permanent settlements in Newfoundland. In 1621, the **Colony of Avalon** was established here by Sir George Calvert, First Baron of Baltimore (he was also behind the settlement of Baltimore, Maryland). Calvert sunk the equivalent of C$4 million (US$2.8 million) into the colony, which featured luxe touches like cobblestone roads, slate roofs, and fine ceramics and glassware from Europe. So up-to-date was the colony that privies featured drains leading to the shore just below the high-tide mark, making these the first flush toilets in North America. The colony was later sacked by the Dutch and then the French during ongoing squabbles over territory, and eventually it was abandoned.

Recent excavations have revealed much about life here nearly 4 centuries ago. Visit the modern **archaeological museum** (☎ **709/432-3200**) with its numerous glass-topped drawers filled with engrossing artifacts, then ask for a tour of the archaeological site, which is included in the cost of admission. The site is open daily mid-June to mid-October; admission is C$2 (US$1.40) for adults.

After your visit, take a walk to the lighthouse at the point (about 1 hr. round-trip), where you can scan for whales and icebergs. Ask for directions at the museum.

ACCOMMODATIONS

The Downs Inn. Rte. 10, Ferryland, NF, A0A 2H0. ☎ **709/432-2808** or 709/432-2659. 4 rms (all share 1 bath). C$55 (US$40) double. No credit cards.

This attractive building overlooking the harbor served as a convent between 1914 and 1986, when it was converted to an inn. The furnishings reflect its heritage as an institution rather than a historic building—there's dated carpeting and old linoleum, and the furniture is uninspired. (Much of the religious statuary was left in place—a nice touch.) Ask for one of the two front rooms, where you can watch for whales from your windows. No smoking.

Dining: The front parlor has been converted to a tearoom, where you can order a nice pot of tea and a light snack, like carrot cake or a rhubarb tart. Some sandwiches are available. Everything is under C$3 (US$2.10). Innkeeper Aidan Costello also operates Southern Shore Eco Adventures and can create custom tour packages for kayaking, hiking, or whale watching.

AVALON WILDERNESS RESERVE

Where there's bog, there's caribou. Or at least that's true in the southern part of the peninsula, which is home to the island's largest caribou herd, numbering some 13,000. You'll see signs warning you to watch for caribou along the roadway; the landscape hereabout is so misty and primeval, though, that you may feel you should also watch for druids in robes with tall walking staffs.

The caribou roam freely throughout the 1,700-square-kilometer (656-sq.-mile) reserve, so it's largely a matter of happenstance to find them. Your best bet is to scan the high upland barrens along Route 10 between Trepassey and Peter's River (an area that's actually out of the reserve). You'll commonly see caribou here. As of 1997, plans were in the works to build a government-run visitor center to inform travelers about the herd and its habits. Check with the **Provincial Parks Division** (☎ 709/729-2421) in St. John's for more information.

CAPE ST. MARY'S

The ✪ **Cape St. Mary's Ecological Reserve** (☎ 709/729-2431) is off the beaten track—some 100 kilometers (60 miles) from the Trans-Canada Highway—but worth every kilometer of it. Start your visit at the visitor center, which offers a good introduction to the indigenous bird life. Then walk for 15 minutes along a grassy cliff-top pathway—through harebell, iris, and dandelion—to arrive at a remarkable sea stack that's teeming with bird life. As you approach, the domed top of this dramatic cliff looks snowcapped. Then you realize it's covered with gannets, a member of the booby family. These handsome seabirds have cappuccino-colored heads and black-tipped wings, with wingspans up to 6 feet. Some 5,400 pair of gannets noisily nest here, along with 10,000 pair of murre, 10,000 kittiwake, and 100 razorbill.

Visitors observe the colony from the top of a 300-foot cliff, peering across a perilous abyss. (Looking down at the surging surf and hundreds of birds on the wing *below* is not recommended for acrophobes.) You're close enough to get a good view even in a heavy fog. This is a remarkable site, extraordinary enough to make birders out of those normally disinterested in the natural world.

The reserve is open daily May to October. There's a small charge to view the excellent exhibits in the visitor center.

ACCOMMODATIONS

Bird Island Resort. Rte. 100, St. Bride's, NF, A0B 2Z0. ☎ **709/337-2450.** Fax 709/337-2903. 20 rms. TV. C$59–C$69 (US$42–US$49) double. MC, V.

This modern, nothing-special motel is located behind Manning's Foodex, where you'll stop to ask for a room. The basic rate will get you a motel room, but given the dearth of interesting dining opportunities in town, you're better off spending the few extra dollars for a kitchenette. The vinyl-sided units are located on grounds with lovely views, but the room views are somewhat limited. If you do plan to eat out, head to **Atlantica Inn and Restaurant,** just down the road, for basic diner fare.

10 The Labrador Coast

Labrador may be sparsely settled, but it has been inhabited for thousands of years. The Innu (Indian) culture in Labrador goes back 8,000 years, and the Inuit (Eskimo) culture, 4,000 years.

The Vikings sighted Labrador in 986, but didn't come ashore until 1010. Traces of the Vikings remain in the shape of "fairy holes"—deep, cylindrical holes in the rocks, angled away from the sea, where they were thought to have moored their boats.

The 16th century brought Basque whalers, as many as 2,000 of them in galleons, and they returned to Europe with 20,000 barrels of whale oil in what might be one of the globe's first oil booms. It has been said that the whale oil of Newfoundland and Labrador was as valuable to the Europeans as the gold of South America. Vestiges of a whaling station remain on Saddle Island, off the coast of Red Bay on the Labrador Straits.

Next came the British and French fishermen, fur traders, and merchants, who first came here in summers to fish, hunt, and trade, and established permanent settlements in the 1700s. Many of the Europeans married Innu and Inuit women, but conflicts between Inuit whalers and the European settlers along the south coast prompted the Inuit communities to move to the Far North, where they remain today.

Only about 30,000 people live in Labrador: 13,000 in western Labrador, 8,000 in Happy Valley-Goose Bay, with the remaining residents spread along the coast. Approximately four-fifths of those born here will remain here, with strong ties to family and neighbors. These close-knit communities welcome visitors warmly.

For most visitors to the "Big Land," there are three destinations: **Labrador West,** including Labrador City and Wabush, reached by train from Sept-Iles, Québec (pronounced "Set-*teel*"), and via Route 389, also from Québec; the **Labrador Straits,** with tiny fishing villages and the rushing Pinware River, reached by ferry from Newfoundland; and **Central Labrador,** the commercial and industrial hub centered around Happy Valley-Goose Bay.

THE LABRADOR STRAITS

The Labrador Straits are the easiest part of Labrador to explore from Newfoundland. The southeast corner of Labrador is served by ferries shuttling between St. Barbe, Newfoundland, and Blanc Sablon, Québec. (Blanc Sablon is on the Québec-Labrador border.) From Blanc Sablon, you can travel on the one and only road, which runs 80 kilometers (48 miles) northward, dead-ending at Red Bay.

Ferries are timed such that you can cross over, drive to Red Bay, and be back for the later ferry to Newfoundland. Such a hasty trip isn't recommended, however. Better to spend a night, when you'll have a chance to meet the people, who are the most compelling reason to visit.

The **M/S *Northern Princess*** (☎ 709/931-2309 or 418/461-2056) runs from May 1 until ice season, usually sometime in early January. The crossing takes about 90 minutes and reservations are encouraged in summer (half the ferry can be reserved; the other half is first-come, first-served). One-way fares are C$9 (US$6) for adults, C$4.75 (US$3.40) for children, and C$18.50 (US$13) for automobiles.

The **Visitor Information Centre** (☎ 709/931-2013) in the small, restored **St. Andrews Church** in L'Anse au Clair, the first town after the ferry, is open from June to August. The tourist association has developed several footpaths and trails in the area, so be sure to ask about them; also ask about the "fairy holes."

EXPLORING THE LABRADOR STRAITS

Drive the "slow road" that connects the villages of the Labrador Straits. Traveling southwest to northeast, here is some of what you'll find along the way.

In L'Anse au Clair, **Moore's Handicrafts,** 8 Country Rd., just off Route 510 (☎ 709/931-2022), sells handmade summer and winter coats, traditional cassocks, moccasins, knitted items, handmade jewelry, and other crafts, as well as homemade jams. They also do traditional embroidery on Labrador cassocks and coats, and if you stop on the way north and choose your design, they'll finish it by the time you return to the ferry—even the same day. Prices are very reasonable. It's open daily, often until late.

The **Point Amour Lighthouse** (1858), at the western entrance to the Strait of Belle Isle, is the tallest lighthouse in the Atlantic Provinces and the second tallest in all of Canada. The walls of the slightly tapered, circular tower are 6.5 feet thick at the base. You'll have to climb 122 steps for the view. The dioptric lens was imported from Europe at a cost of C$10,000 (US$7,100), quite a sum for its day. The lighthouse, which kept watch for submarines during World War II, is still in use and has a light-keeper. It's open to the public June to mid-October from 8am to 5pm

(☎ 709/927-5826). The lighthouse is a 3.3-kilometer (2-mile) drive away from the main road.

After you pass the fishing settlements of **L'Anse au Loup** ("Wolf's Cove") and **West St. Modeste,** the road follows the scenic Pinware River, where the trees become noticeably taller. Along this stretch of road, you'll see glacial erratics—those odd boulders deposited by the melting ice cap. **Pinware Provincial Park,** 43 kilometers (26 miles) from L'Anse au Clair, has a picnic area, hiking trails, and 15 campsites. The 50-mile-long Pinware River is known for salmon fishing.

The highway ends in **Red Bay.** The **Visitor Centre** (☎ 709/920-2197) showcases artifacts from the late 1500s, when Basque whalers came in numbers to hunt the right and bowhead whales. Starting in 1977, excavations turned up whaling implements, pottery, glassware, and even partially preserved seaman's clothing. From here you can also arrange tours of **Saddle Island,** the home of Basque whaling stations in the 16th century. Free transportation to archaeological sites on the island is available in summer Monday to Saturday from 9am to 4pm. You can also opt to view Saddle Island from the observation level on the third floor.

ACCOMMODATIONS

Beachside Hospitality Home. 9 Lodge Rd., L'Anse au Clair, Labrador, A0K 3K0. ☎ 800/ 563-8999 or 709/931-2662. 6 rms (all with shared bath). C$38–C$45 (US$27–US$32) double. MC, V.

A stay here offers an excellent opportunity to meet a local family and learn firsthand about life in this region of Labrador. Three bedrooms have a separate entrance and share two full baths. There is a whirlpool bath and guests have access to a telephone. Delicious home-cooked meals are available by arrangement, or you can cook for yourself in the kitchen or outdoors on the grill.

Grenfell Louie A. Hall. 3 Willow Ave. (P.O. Box 137), Forteau, Labrador, A0K 2P0. ☎ 709/ 931-2916. 5 rms (all share 2 baths). C$40 (US$28) double. V.

History buffs love the Grenfell Hall—it was built in 1946 by the International Grenfell Association as a nursing station, and there's plenty of reading material about the coast's early days. The rooms are furnished with basic, contemporary-country furniture, and there's a common room with a TV, VCR, and fireplace. Meals are available on request, and the innkeepers can arrange to transport you to and from the ferry. (If you're just curious about the place, you're invited to stop in for a C$2/ US$1.40 per person tour.) No smoking.

LABRADOR WEST

The most affluent and industrialized part of Labrador, Labrador West lies on the Québec border and is home to the twin towns of **Wabush** and **Labrador City,** 7 kilometers (4 miles) apart. The two towns share many attractions, activities, and services. This region offers top-notch cross-country skiing and has hosted two World Cup events. Labrador West is also home to the largest open-pit iron-ore mine in North America, which produces almost half of Canada's iron ore. For indoor activities, go to the **Labrador West Arts and Culture Centre,** which draws performers from throughout North America.

For more information about activities in the area, contact **Labrador West Tourism Development Corporation** (☎ 709/282-3337).

CENTRAL LABRADOR

From the North West River and Mud Lake to the Mealy Mountains, a visit to the interior of Labrador will bring you deep into a land of lakes, rivers, and spruce forests, where the horizon looks the same in every direction. Many believe that the Lake Melville area is "Markland, the land of forests" in the Viking sagas.

Three displays of local history are exhibited in the local mall, the **Northern Lights Building** (☎ 709/896-5939) at 170 Hamilton River Rd. Look for the **Military Museum** (uniforms, weapons, and other items from the Royal Newfoundland Regiment), **Trapper's Brook Animal Displays** (Labrador animals), and the **Newfie Bullet Model Railway** ("one of the largest collections of O Gauge Lionel toy trains on the east coast of Canada"). Admission to all three is free; the building is open Monday to Saturday from 10am to 5:30pm.

ACCOMMODATIONS

Convenient to the airport, TransLab Highway, and marine dock, the full-service **Labrador Inn** (☎ 800/563-2763 or 709/896-3351) provides comfort and hospitality. The well-kept modern building has 74 rooms; doubles are C$75 to C$94 (US$53 to US$67) and a suite is C$150 (US$107). The restaurant serves traditional Canadian cuisine with some local dishes, including game meats and seafood.

Montréal 8

by Herbert Bailey Livesey

The distinct cultures that inhabit Canada have been called the Twin Solitudes. One, English and Calvinist in origin, is portrayed as staid, smug, and work obsessed. The other, French and Catholic, is more creative and lighthearted—inclined to see pleasure as the purpose of labor. Or so goes the stereotype. These two peoples live side by side throughout Québec and in the nine provinces of English Canada, but the blending occurs in a particularly intense fashion in Québec Province's largest city, Montréal. French speakers, known as Francophones, constitute 66% of the city's population, while most of the rest of its residents speak English.

There's an impression, buttressed by rashes of *Vente* ("For Sale") signs, that Montréal is in a steep decline. A bleak mood prevails in many quarters, brought about by a lingering recession and uncertainty over the future. There's a large measure of truth in this. After all, it's possible that Québec may choose to fling itself into independence, an event that could lead to increased Anglo flight and a loss of federal subsidies—even outright civil war.

But to many American city dwellers, Montréal might seem an urban paradise. A study by Population Action International pronounced that it tied with what it deemed the two other most livable cities in the world, Seattle and Melbourne. There are many reasons. The subway system, the Métro, is modern and swift. The streets are clean and safe. There are rarely more than 60 homicides a year in Montréal, compared to the hundreds of murders that occur annually in U.S. cities of comparable size. Montréal's best restaurants are the equal of their south-of-the-border compatriots in almost every way, yet they're as much as 30% or 40% cheaper. And the government gives visitors back most of the taxes it collects.

Yet the defining dialectic of Canadian life is language, the thorny issue that might yet tear the country apart. It manifests itself in the assumption of many Québécois that a separate state is the only way to maintain their culture. The role of Québec in the Canadian federation is the most volatile issue in Canadian politics. People talk about separation in Québec as often as those elsewhere discuss the weather. Would a politically independent Québec continue to share a common currency, a common central bank, and an open-borders relationship with the rest of Canada? Would the North American Free Trade Agreement (NAFTA) be extended to an independent

Québec? Would the Atlantic Provinces, cut off from the rest of Canada, apply to the United States for statehood?

The reasons for the intransigence of the Québécois go back 2 centuries. After the "Conquest" (as French Québecers call it) in 1759, the English made a few concessions to French-Canadian pride, including allowing them a Gallic version of jurisprudence. But a kind of linguistic racism prevailed, with wealthy Scottish and English bankers and merchants ensuring that French Canadians were repeatedly denied access to the upper echelons of business and government. Intentionally or thoughtlessly, Anglophones lowered an opaque ceiling on Francophone advancement.

Resentment over this treatment festered for years, and in the 1960s the Québécois began to assert pride in their French roots. This fueled a burgeoning nationalism, punctuated by a series of violent extremist acts. By 1976, mainstream sentiments of the French-speaking majority in the province resulted in the election of the separatist Parti Québécois. Its leader, René Lévesque, promoted a referendum on sovereignty in 1980, but the measure was defeated.

Federalists later attempted to assuage the Québécois sensitivities with formal recognition of the province as a "distinct society." Those efforts failed, leading with glacial certainty to the sovereignty referendum of October 30, 1995. That vote went in favor of the pro-unity camp, but only by a margin of barely 1%. While recent polls suggest that the pro-sovereignty position is losing support, heated debate, threats, ideological posturing, and off-and-on negotiations will continue for years to come.

None of this fractious history should deter you, however. The Québécois are gracious hosts. While Montréal may be the largest French-speaking city outside Paris, most Montréalers grow up speaking both French and English and switch effortlessly from one to the other as the situation dictates. Telephone operators go from French to English the instant they hear an English word from the other party, as do most store clerks, waiters, and hotel staff. This is less true in country villages and in Québec City, but there's virtually no problem that can't be solved with a few French words, some expressive gestures, and a little goodwill.

1 Orientation

ARRIVING

BY PLANE Montréal's two international airports, **Dorval** and **Mirabel,** are served by most of the world's major airlines. All the major car-rental agencies have desks at the airports.

By far the greatest number of visitors fly into Dorval from other parts of North America on **Air Canada** (☎ 800/776-3000), **American Airlines** (☎ 800/397-9635), **Canadian Airlines** (☎ 800/665-1177), **Delta** (☎ 800/337-5520), or **Northwest** (☎ 800/225-2525). **Continental** (☎ 800/231-0856) uses Mirabel. In the United States, Air Canada flies out of New York (Newark and La Guardia), Miami, Tampa, Chicago, Los Angeles, and San Francisco. Other carriers that serve Montréal are **USAirways** (☎ 800/432-9768), **Air France** (☎ 800/847-1106), **British Airways** (☎ 800/247-9297), **SAS** (☎ 800/221-2350), and **Swissair** (☎ 800/879-9154). From Dorval it takes about 30 minutes to get downtown.

Travelers arriving from Europe and other countries outside North America arrive at Mirabel. The ride downtown from Mirabel takes about 45 minutes.

BY CAR Interstate 87 runs due north from New York City to link up with Canada's Autoroute 15, and the entire 400-mile journey is on expressways.

From Boston, I-93 north joins I-89 just south of Concord, New Hampshire. At White River Junction you can continue north on I-89 to Lake Champlain, crossing the lake by roads and bridges to join I-87 and Canada Autoroute 15, or you can pick up I-91 at White River Junction to go due north toward Sherbrooke, Québec. At the border I-91 becomes Canada Route 55 and joins Route 10 through Estrie to Montréal.

The Trans-Canada Highway runs right through the city, connecting both ends of the country.

The distance from Boston to Montréal is approximately 510 kilometers (320 miles), from Toronto, 540 kilometers (335 miles), and from Ottawa, 190 kilometers (120 miles). Once you're in Montréal, Québec City is an easy 3-hour drive away.

See also "Driving Rules" under "Getting Around," later in this chapter.

BY TRAIN   For **VIA Rail information** from the United States, call ☎ 800/989-2626. Montréal is a major terminus on Canada's VIA Rail network, with its station at 935 rue de la Gauchetière ouest (☎ 514/871-1331). The city is served by comfortable VIA Rail trains—some with dining cars, sleeping cars, and cellular phones—from other cities in Canada. There's scheduled service to and from Québec City via Trois-Rivières, and to and from Ottawa, Toronto, Winnipeg, and points west.

Amtrak (☎ 800/872-7245) runs one train daily to Montréal from Washington, New York, and intermediate stops. The *Adirondack* takes about 10-plus hours, if all goes well, but delays aren't unusual. Passengers from Chicago can get to Montréal most directly by taking Amtrak to Toronto, then switching to VIA Rail.

Seniors 62 and older are eligible for a 15% discount on some Amtrak trains on the U.S. segment of the trip. VIA Rail also has senior discounts.

Don't forget to bring along proof of citizenship (a passport or birth certificate) for passing through Customs.

BY BUS   Montréal's main bus terminal is the **Terminus Voyageur,** 505 bd. de Maisonneuve est (☎ 514/842-2281). The **Voyageur** company operates buses between here and all parts of Québec, with frequent runs through Estrie (the Eastern Townships) to Sherbrooke, to the various villages in the Laurentides, and to Québec City. Morning, noon, early-afternoon, and midnight buses cover the distance between Toronto and Montréal in about 7 hours.

From Boston or New York there's daily bus service to Montréal on **Greyhound/Trailways** (☎ 800/231-2222). The trip from Boston takes about 8 hours; from New York City, with five buses daily, it takes 9 hours.

VISITOR INFORMATION

Québec tourism authorities produce volumes of detailed and useful publications, and they're easy to obtain by mail, phone, or in person. To contact **Tourisme Québec,** write C.P. 979, Montréal, PQ, H3C 2W3 or call ☎ 800/363-7777, operator 806 (in the Montréal area, call ☎ 514/873-2015).

The main information center for visitors is the large and efficiently organized **Infotouriste,** at 1001 rue du Square-Dorchester, between rues Peel and Metcalfe in the downtown hotel and business district. From June to early September the office is open daily from 8:30am to 7:30pm; from early September to May the hours are daily from 9am to 6pm. Its bilingual staff can help with questions about the entire province, as well as Montréal.

The city has its own **information bureau** at 174 rue Notre-Dame (☎ 514/871-1595), at the corner of rue place Jacques-Cartier. The hours from Easter to mid-October are daily from 9am to 7pm; from mid-October to Easter it's open Thursday to Sunday from 9am to 5pm.

CITY LAYOUT

The city borders the St. Lawrence River. As far as its citizens are concerned, that's south, looking toward the United States, though the river runs more nearly north and south at this point, not east and west. For that reason, it has been observed that Montréal is the only city in the world where the sun rises in the north. Don't fight it: Face the river. That's south. Turn around. That's north.

When examining a map of the city, note that such prominent streets as Ste-Catherine and René-Lévesque are said to run "east" and "west"; the dividing line is boulevard St-Laurent, which runs "north" and "south." To ease confusion, the directions given in this chapter conform to local tradition, since they're the ones that will be given by natives.

MAIN ARTERIES & STREETS In downtown Montréal, the principal streets running east-west are **boulevard René-Lévesque, rue Ste-Catherine, boulevard de Maisonneuve,** and **rue Sherbrooke.** Prominent north-south arteries are **rue Crescent, rue McGill, rue St-Denis,** and **boulevard St-Laurent,** the line of demarcation between east and west Montréal (most of the downtown area of interest to visitors and businesspeople lies to the west). Near Mont-Royal Park, north of the downtown area, major streets are **avenue du Mont-Royal** and **avenue Laurier.** In Old Montréal, **rue St-Jacques, rue Notre-Dame,** and **rue St-Paul** are the major streets, along with **rue de la Commune,** which hugs the St. Lawrence River.

FINDING AN ADDRESS Boulevard St-Laurent is the dividing line between east and west (*est* and *ouest*) in Montréal. There's no equivalent division for north and south. Numbers start at the river and climb from there, as the topography does. For instance, if you're driving north on boulevard St-Laurent and pass no. 500, that's Old Montréal, near rue Notre-Dame; no. 1100 is near boulevard René-Lévesque, no. 1500 near boulevard de Maisonneuve, and no. 3400 near rue Sherbrooke. Even numbers are on the west side of north-south streets and the south side of east-west streets; odd numbers are on the east and north sides, respectively. For more help, check the handy Address Locator map in the free *Montréal Tourist Guide,* available everywhere.

In earlier days, Montréal was split ethnically between those who spoke English, centered in the city's western regions, and those who spoke French, concentrated to the east. Things still sound more French when you walk from west to east. Though boulevard St-Laurent is the east-west divider for the street numbering system, the spiritual split comes farther west, at about avenue de Bleury/avenue de Parc.

MAPS You'll find good street plans inside the free tourist guide supplied by the Greater Montréal Convention and Tourism Bureau and distributed widely throughout the city. The bureau also provides a large foldout city map for free.

NEIGHBORHOODS IN BRIEF

Downtown This area contributes the most striking elements of Montréal's dynamic skyline and contains the main rail station, as well as most of its first-class hotels, principal museums, corporate headquarters, and largest department stores. Loosely bounded by rue Sherbrooke to the north, boulevard René-Lévesque to the south, boulevard St-Laurent to the east, and rue Drummond to the west, it incorporates the neighborhood once known as the "Golden Square Mile," an Anglophone district characterized by dozens of mansions erected by wealthy Scottish and English merchants and industrialists. Many of these homes were torn down after World War II to make room for skyscrapers, but some remain, often converted to institutional use. At the northern edge of the downtown area is the handsome urban campus of McGill University.

The Underground City   In the long Montréal winter, people escape down escalators and stairways into *la ville souterraine,* which amounts to a parallel subterranean universe. Down there, in a controlled climate that's forever spring, it's possible to arrive at the rail station, check into a hotel, go out for lunch at any of hundreds of fast-food counters and full-service restaurants, see a movie, attend a concert, conduct business, go shopping, and even take a swim—all without unfurling an umbrella or donning an overcoat. This "city" evolved when major building developments in the downtown area—such as Place Ville-Marie, Place Bonaventure, Complexe Desjardins, Palais des Congrès, and Place des Arts—put their below-street levels to profitable use, leasing space for shops and other purposes. Over time, in fits and starts and with no master plan in place, these spaces connected with Métro stations and with one another. It became possible to ride long distances and walk the shorter ones, through mazes of corridors, tunnels, and plazas. Without the convenience of a logical street grid, the area can be confusing to navigate. There are plenty of signs, but make careful note of landmarks at key corners as you make your way . . . and expect to get lost anyway.

Rue Crescent   One of Montréal's major dining-and-nightlife districts lies in the western shadow of the massed phalanxes of downtown skyscrapers. It holds hundreds of restaurants, bars, and clubs of all styles between Sherbrooke and René-Lévesque, centering on rue Crescent and spilling over onto neighboring streets. The raucous party atmosphere never quite fades, building to crescendos as weekends approach, especially in warm weather, when its largely 20- and 30-something denizens spill out into sidewalk cafes and onto balconies.

Vieux-Montréal   The city was born here in 1642, down by the river at Pointe-à-Callière, and today activity centers around place Jacques-Cartier, especially in summer, where cafe tables line narrow terraces and sun worshipers, flower sellers, itinerant artists, and strolling visitors congregate. The area is larger than it might seem at first, bounded on the north by rue St-Antoine, once the "Wall Street" of Montréal and still home to many banks, and on the south by the recently developed Old Port, a linear park bordering rue de la Commune that gives access to the river and provides welcome breathing room for cyclists, in-line skaters, and picnickers. To the east, Old Montréal is contained by rue Berri, and to the west by rue McGill. Several small but intriguing museums are housed in historic buildings, and the district's architectural heritage has been substantially preserved, its restored 18th- and 19th-century structures adapted for use as shops, studios, cafes, bars, offices, and apartments.

Latin Quarter   Boulevard St-Denis, from rue Ste-Catherine to rue de Bullion, running from downtown to the Plateau Mont-Royal section, is the thumping central artery of Montréal's Latin Quarter, thick with cafes, bistros, offbeat shops, and lively nightspots. It's to Montréal what boulevard St-Germain is to Paris, and it isn't difficult to imagine that you've landed on the Left Bank when you're strolling around here. At the southern end of St-Denis, near the concrete campus of the Université du Québec à Montréal, the avenue is decidedly student-oriented, with alternative rock issuing from the inexpensive bars and boîtes. Farther north, above Sherbrooke, a raffish quality persists along the facing rows of three- and four-story row houses and the average age of residents and visitors rises past 30. The prices are higher, too, and some of the city's better restaurants are located here.

Plateau Mont-Royal Due north of the downtown area, this may be the part of the city where Montréalers feel most at home—away from the chattering pace of downtown and the crowds of heavily touristed Vieux-Montréal. Bounded by boulevard St-Joseph to the north, rue Sherbrooke to the south, avenue Papineau to the east, and rue St-Dominique to the west, it has a throbbing ethnicity that fluctuates in tone and direction with each new surge in immigration. St-Denis (see above) runs the length of the district, but parallel St-Laurent owns the more polyglot flavor. Known to all as "The Main," it was once the boulevard first encountered by foreigners tumbling off ships at the waterfront. They simply shouldered their belongings and walked north on St-Laurent, peeling off into adjoining streets when they heard familiar tongues, saw people who looked like them, and smelled the aromas of food they once cooked in the old country. New arrivals still come here to start their lives again, creating a patchwork of colors and cultures. Without its people and their diverse interests, St-Laurent would be just another paper-strewn urban eyesore. But these ground-floor windows are filled with glistening golden chickens, collages of shoes and pastries and aluminum cookware, curtains of sausages, and the daringly far-fetched garments of Montréal's active fashion industry. Many warehouses and former tenements have been converted to house this panoply of shops, bars, and low-cost eateries, with their often garish signs drawing the eye from the still-dilapidated upper stories.

Prince Arthur & Duluth These two essentially pedestrian streets connect boulevard St-Laurent with St-Denis, 8 blocks east. The livelier rue Prince-Arthur is lined with ethnic restaurants, primarily Greek and Portuguese, but with Asian places starting to join them. Mimes, jugglers, and street musicians try to cajole passersby into parting with their spare change. Four blocks north of rue Prince-Arthur, Duluth is fairly quiet in the blocks near St-Laurent but more engaging near St-Denis. The mix of cuisines is much like that on Prince Arthur. Visitors are evident in greater numbers on Prince Arthur, many of them attracted by menus promising bargain lobster dinners for less than $10 at some times of the year.

Parc du Mont-Royal Not many cities have a mountain at their core. In actuality, it's not a mountain but a high hill. Still, Montréal is named for it—the "Royal Mountain"—and one of the unique urban pleasures you'll find here is driving, walking, or taking a horse-drawn calèche to the top for an unparalleled view of the city, the island, and the St. Lawrence, especially at dusk. The park, which encompasses the mountain, was designed by the famous American landscape architect Frederick Law Olmsted, whose other credits include New York's Central Park. On its far slope are two cemeteries—one Anglophone, one Francophone—silent reminders of the linguistic and cultural division that persists in the city. With its skating ponds, hiking and running trails, and even a short ski run, the park is well used by Montréalers, who refer to it simply as "the mountain."

Chinatown Just north of Vieux-Montréal, south of boulevard René-Lévesque, and centered on the intersection of rue Clark and rue de la Gauchetière (pedestrianized at this point), Montréal's pocket Chinatown appears to be mostly restaurants and a tiny park, with the occasional grocery, laundry, church, and small business. Most signs are in French or English, as well as Chinese. Community spirit is strong—it's had to be to resist the bulldozers of redevelopment—and Chinatown's inhabitants remain faithful to their traditions despite the encroaching modernism all around them. In recent years, concerned investors from Hong Kong, wary of their uncertain future with mainland China, have poured money into the neighborhood, producing signs that its shrinkage has been halted, even reversed. The area is colorful and deserves a look, though the best Chinese restaurants are actually in other parts of the city.

The Gay Village   The city's gay enclave runs east along rue Ste-Catherine from rue St-Hubert to rue Papineau. A small but vibrant district, it's filled with clothing stores, small eateries, a bar/disco complex in a former post office building, and the Gay and Lesbian Community Centre, at 1355 rue Ste-Catherine est.

Ile Ste-Hélène   Ile Ste-Hélène (St. Helen's Island) in the St. Lawrence River was altered extensively to become the site of Expo '67, Montréal's very successful world's fair. In the 4 years before Expo opened, construction crews reshaped the island and doubled its surface area with landfill, then went on to create beside it an island that hadn't existed before, Ile Notre-Dame. Much of the earth needed to do this was dredged up from the bottom of the St. Lawrence, and 15 million tons of rock from the excavation of the Métro and the Décarie Expressway were carried in by truck. Bridges were built and 83 pavilions constructed. When Expo closed, the city government preserved the site and a few of the exhibition buildings. Parts were used for Olympic Games events in 1976, and today the island is home to Montréal's popular new casino and an amusement park, La Ronde.

2   Getting Around

For a city of more than a million inhabitants, Montréal is remarkably easy to get to know and negotiate. The two airports that serve it are nearby (one is only 14 miles away), and, once you're in town, the Métro is fast and efficient. Of course, walking is the best way to get to know this vigorous, multidimensional city.

BY PUBLIC TRANSPORTATION

Dial ☎ 514/AUTOBUS (288-6287) for information about the Métro and city buses.

BY METRO   For speed and economy, nothing beats Montréal's Métro system. Clean, relatively quiet trains whisk you through an ever-expanding network of underground tunnels, with 65 stations at present and more scheduled to open. A single ride is C$1.85 (US$1.30), and a strip of six tickets is C$8 (US$6). You might save money by buying the 1-day tourist pass for C$5 (US$3.55) or the 3-day pass for C$12 (US$9). See p. 206 for a map of the system.

Buy tickets at the booth in any station, then slip one into the slot in the turnstile to enter the system. Take a transfer (*correspondence*) from the machine just inside the turnstiles of every station to be able to transfer free from a train to a bus at any other Métro station. Remember to take the transfer ticket at the station where you first enter the system. (When starting a trip by bus and intending to continue on the Métro, ask the bus driver for a transfer.) Most connections from one Métro line to another can be made at the Berri-UQAM (Université de Québec à Montréal), Jean-Talon, and Snowdon stations. Métro trains run daily from 5:30am to 12:38am.

BY BUS   Buses cost the same as Métro trains, and Métro tickets are good on buses, too. Exact change is required to pay bus fares in cash. While routes extend across the entire city, buses don't run as frequently or as swiftly as the Métro.

BY TAXI   There are plenty of taxis in Montréal, run by several private companies. Cabs come in a variety of colors and styles, so their principal distinguishing feature is the plastic sign on the roof. At night, it's illuminated when the cab is available. Fares

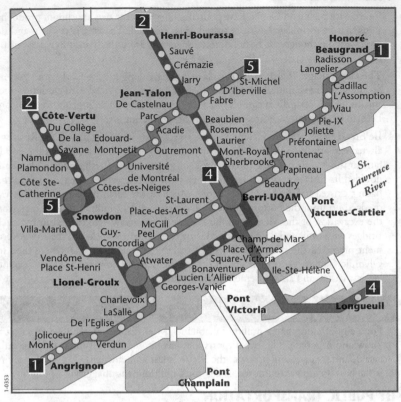

aren't cheap. Most short rides from one point to another downtown cost about C$5 (US$3.55). Members of hotel and restaurant staffs can call cabs, many of which are dispatched by radio. They line up outside most large hotels or can be hailed on the street.

BY CAR

The 24-hour hot line for emergency service provided by the **Canadian Automobile Association (CAA),** which is affiliated with AAA, is ☎ **514/861-7575** in Montréal.

For information on **road conditions** in and around Montréal, call ☎ **514/636-3026;** outside Montréal, call ☎ **514/636-3248.**

RENTALS Major agencies include **Avis,** 1225 rue Metcalfe (☎ 800/321-3652 or 514/866-7906); **Budget,** Gare Centrale, 895 rue de la Gauchetière (☎ 800/268-8970 or 514/938-1000); **Hertz,** 1475 rue Aylmer (☎ 800/263-0678 or 514/842-8537); **Thrifty,** 1600 rue Berri (☎ 800/367-2277 or 514/845-5954); and **Tilden,** 1200 rue Stanley (☎ 800/387-4747 or 514/878-2771).

Gas in Québec is somewhat more expensive than across the border. It costs about C$25 (US$18) to fill a tank with unleaded.

PARKING Parking can be difficult on the heavily trafficked streets of downtown Montréal. There are plenty of parking meters, with varying hourly rates. (Look around before walking off without paying. Meters are set well back from the curb so that they won't be buried by plowed snow in winter.) Most downtown shopping complexes have underground parking lots, as do the big hotels. Some of the hotels don't charge extra to take cars in and out of their garages during the day, which can save money for those who plan to do a lot of sightseeing by car.

DRIVING RULES The limited-access expressways in Québec are called *autoroutes*, and speed limits and distances are given in kilometers. Most highway signs are in French only, though Montréal's autoroutes and bridges often bear dual-language signs. Seat-belt use is required by law while driving or riding in a car in Québec. Turning right on a red light is prohibited in Montréal and throughout the Province of Québec, except where specifically allowed by an additional green arrow.

FAST FACTS: Montréal

American Express Offices of the **American Express Travel Service** are at 1141 rue de Maisonneuve ouest (☎ **514/284-3300**), and La Baie (The Bay), 585 rue Ste-Catherine ouest (☎ **514/281-4777**). For lost or stolen cards, call ☎ **800/268-9824.**

Currency Exchange There are currency-exchange offices at the airports, in the train station, in and near Infotouriste at Dorchester Square, and near Notre-Dame cathedral at 86 rue Notre-Dame. The **Bank of America Canada,** 1230 Peel, offers foreign-exchange services Monday to Friday from 8:30am to 5:30pm and Saturday from 9am to 5pm.

Doctors & Dentists The front desk at hotels can contact a doctor quickly. If it's not an emergency, call your consulate and ask for a recommendation. Even if the consulate is closed, a duty officer should be available to help. For **dental information,** call the 24-hour hot line at ☎ **514/342-4444.** In an **emergency** requiring an ambulance, dial ☎ **911.**

Drugstores The branch of **Pharmaprix** at 5122 Côte-des-Neiges at rue Queen Mary (☎ **514/738-8464**) is open 24 hours; the one at 901 rue Ste-Catherine est at rue St-André (☎ **514/842-4915**) is open daily from 8am to midnight.

Embassies & Consulates The consulate general for the **United States** is at 1155 rue St-Alexandre (☎ **514/398-9695**). **Great Britain** has a consulate at 1155 rue University, Suite 901 (☎ **514/866-5863**). Other English-speaking countries have their embassies in Ottawa.

Emergencies Dial ☎ **911** for the police, firefighters, or an ambulance.

Hospitals Hotel staffs and consulates can offer advice and information. Hospitals with emergency rooms are **Hôpital Général de Montréal** (☎ **514/937-6011**) and **Hôpital Royal Victoria** (☎ **514/842-1231**). **Hôpital de Montréal pour Enfants** (☎ **514/934-4400**) is a children's hospital with a poison center.

Liquor Laws All hard liquor in Québec is sold through official government stores operated by the Québec Société des Alcools. Wine and beer can be bought in grocery stores and supermarkets. The legal drinking age in the province is 18.

Newspapers & Magazines Montréal's prime English-language newspaper is the *Montréal Gazette.* Most large newsstands and those in the larger hotels also carry the *Wall Street Journal,* the *New York Times, USA Today,* and the *International Herald Tribune.* So do the several branches of the **Maison de la Presse Internationale,** one of which is at 550 rue Ste-Catherine ouest, and the large bookstore, **Champigny,** at 4380 rue St-Denis. For information about current happenings in Montréal, pick up the Friday or Saturday editions of the *Gazette.* The free monthly booklet *Montréal Scope* and the free pocket-sized quarterly *Montréal Le Guide* are available in some shops and many hotel lobbies.

Pets   Dogs and cats can be taken into Québec, but the Canadian Customs authorities at the frontier will want to see a rabies vaccination certificate less than 3 years old signed by a licensed veterinarian. If a pet is less than 3 months old and obviously healthy, the certificate isn't likely to be required. Check with U.S. Customs about bringing the pet back into the States. Most hotels in Montréal don't accept pets.

Police   Dial ☎ **911** for the police.

Post Office   The main post office is at 1250 rue University, near Ste-Catherine (☎ **514/395-4909**), and is open Monday to Friday from 8am to 5:45pm. A convenient post office in Vieux-Montréal is at 155 rue St-Jacques.

Taxes   Most goods and services in Canada are taxed 7% by the federal government. The Province of Québec tacks on an extra 6.5% tax on goods and services, including those provided by hotels. In Québec, the federal tax appears on the bill as the TPS (elsewhere in Canada, it's called the goods-and-services tax [GST]), and the provincial tax is known as the TVQ. You may receive a rebate on both the federal and provincial tax on items you've purchased but not used in Québec, as well as on lodging. To take advantage of this, request the necessary forms at duty-free shops and hotels and submit them, with the original receipts, within a year of the purchase. Contact the Canadian consulate or Québec tourism office for up-to-the-minute information about taxes and rebates.

Telephones   The telephone system, operated by **Bell Canada,** closely resembles the American system. All operators (dial "0" to get one) speak French and English and respond in the appropriate language as soon as callers speak to them. Pay phones in Québec require 25¢ for a 3-minute local call. **Directory information** calls (dial **411**) are free. When calling a Canadian number from the States, dial as you would at home, with "1," the area code, and the number. No international prefix is required.

Time   Montréal, Québec City, and the Laurentians are all in the eastern time zone. Daylight saving time is observed as in the United States, moving clocks ahead 1 hour in the spring and back 1 hour in the fall.

Transit Information   Dial ☎ **514/AUTOBUS** (**288-6287**) for details about the Métro and city buses. For airport transportation, call **Autocar Connaisseur/Gray Line** (☎ **514/934-1222**).

Useful Telephone Numbers   For **Alcoholics Anonymous,** call ☎ 514/376-9230; **24-hour pharmacy,** ☎ 514/842-4915 or 514/738-8464; **Gay and Lesbian Association of UQAM,** ☎ 514/987-3039; **Sexual Assault Center** (a 24-hour crisis line), ☎ 514/934-4504; the **suicide action line,** ☎ 514/723-4000; **lost or stolen Visa cards,** ☎ 800/361-0152 (for American Express, see above); **Canada Customs,** ☎ 514/283-2953; **U.S. Customs,** ☎ 514/636-3875; and **road conditions** in and around Montréal, ☎ 514/636-3026.

3 Accommodations

Montréal hoteliers make everyone welcome, partly because there are more rooms in the city than can be filled with certainty throughout the year. With that competition and with the robustness of the U.S. dollar in relation to its Canadian counterpart, this is a place to splurge or at least step up in class.

Except in bed-and-breakfasts, you can almost always count on special discounts and package deals, especially on weekends, when the hotels' business clients have gone home.

Choose the familial embrace of a B&B and expect to get to know a Montréaler or two and to pay relatively little for that privilege. By the nature of the trade, they're among the most outgoing and knowledgeable guides. For information about downtown B&Bs, contact **Relais Montréal Hospitalité,** 3977 av. Laval, Montréal, PQ, H2W 2H9 (☎ **800/363-9635** or 514/287-9635; fax 514/287-1007), or **Bed and Breakfast Downtown Network,** 3977 av. Laval (at rue Sherbrooke), Montréal, PQ, H2X 3C8 (☎ **800/267-5180** or 514/289-9749). For B&Bs in Plateau Mont-Royal, try the new **Hébergement Touristique du Plateau Mont-Royal,** 1301 rue Rachel est, Montréal, PQ, H2J 2K1 (☎ **800/597-0597** or 514/597-0166; fax 514/ 597-0496), operated by the people who manage the popular Auberge de La Fontaine. All three are referral agencies for homeowners who have one or more rooms available for guests. Accommodations and individual rules vary significantly, so ask all pertinent questions up front, such as if children are welcome, smoking is allowed, or all guests share bathrooms. Deposits are usually required, with the balance payable on arrival.

Nearly all hotel staff members, from front-desk personnel to porters, are reassuringly bilingual. The busiest times are July and August, especially during the several summer festivals, and during annual holidays (Canadian or American). At those times, book well in advance, especially if you're looking for special rates or packages. At most other times, expect to find plenty of available rooms.

Note: The rates below don't include federal or provincial taxes. All rooms have a private bath unless otherwise noted. In the top two price categories, hair dryers, cable color TVs, and in-room movies are to be expected, as are restaurants, bars, meeting rooms, and parking garages.

DOWNTOWN

See the "Downtown Montréal" map (p. 226) to locate hotels in this section.

VERY EXPENSIVE

✪ **Hôtel Vogue.** 1425 rue de la Montagne (between Maisonneuve and Ste-Catherine), Montréal, PQ, H3G 1G3. ☎ **800/465-6654** or 514/285-5555. Fax 514/849-8903. 134 rms, 20 suites. A/C MINIBAR TV TEL. C$159–C$275 (US$114–US$196) double; from C$375 (US$268) suite. Children under 16 stay free in parents' rm. Lower weekend rates. AE, DC, ER, MC, V. Valet parking C$15 (US$11). Métro: Peel.

The Vogue has been creating a stir since it opened in 1990 after completing a stunning conversion of an undistinguished office building. Not a few observers feel that it has displaced the Ritz-Carlton at the apex of the local luxury hotel pantheon. Confidence resonates from every staff member, and luxury breathes from its lobby to its well-appointed guest rooms. Feather pillows and duvets dress the oversize beds, and rooms are decked with fresh flowers, cherry-wood furniture, and an enormous marble bath with Jacuzzi. Other amenities are fax/modem outlets, safes, in-room movies, bathroom TVs, and plush robes. All of this suits the international clientele to a tee.

Dining/Entertainment: The Société Café serves three meals a day, with outside tables in summer. The lobby bar, L'Opéra, has piano music Thursday to Saturday.

Services: Concierge, 24-hour room service, dry cleaning, baby-sitting.

Facilities: Small exercise room, coin-operated laundry, parking garage.

✪ **Le Westin Mont-Royal.** 1050 rue Sherbrooke ouest, Montréal, PQ, H3A 2R6. ☎ **800/ 228-3000** or 514/284-1110. Fax 514/845-3025. 300 rms, 27 suites. A/C MINIBAR TV TEL. C$105–C$250 (US$107–US$179) double; from C$370 (US$264) suite. Rates include breakfast. Children under 18 stay free with parents or in adjoining rm for C$75 (US$54). Weekend rates and special packages available. AE, CB, DC, ER, MC, V. Valet parking C$19 (US$13); self-parking C$11 (US$8). Métro: Peel.

This used to be Le Quatre Saisons, a member of the esteemed Four Seasons chain and a worthy competitor of the nearby Ritz-Carlton. A rather chilly lobby is softened by banks of plants and flowers. The rooms are large, with comfortable, if slightly dated, furnishings. Robes are ready for your use, and security is enhanced by in-room safes. On-demand movies can be chosen from a library of over 60 titles. There are 12 no-smoking floors.

Dining/Entertainment: Zen, an upscale Chinese restaurant, offers lunch and dinner daily. Buffet breakfasts and lunches are served in the lobby bar, L'Apèro, which features piano music in the evenings.

Services: Concierge, 24-hour room service, in-room massage, car and limo rentals, secretarial services.

Facilities: Impressive health club with heated outdoor pool, aerobics classes, weight machines, whirlpool, sauna, workout gear or swimsuits on request; car-rental desk; boutiques.

Montréal Bonaventure Hilton. 1 place Bonaventure (at Mansfield), Montréal, PQ, H5A 1E4. ☎ **800/445-8667** in the U.S., 800/267-2575 in Canada, or 514/878-2332. Fax 514/878-3881. 377 rms, 18 suites. A/C MINIBAR TV TEL. C$179–C$234 (US$128–US$167) double; C$345–C$980 (US$246–US$700) suite. Children of any age stay free in parents' rm. Weekend packages available. AE, CB, DC, ER, MC, V. Valet parking C$18.75 (US$13); self-parking C$13.75 (US$10). Métro: Bonaventure.

The Hilton's main entrance is at de la Gauchetière and Mansfield, but the lobby is on the 17th floor. It has elevator access to Central Station and the Underground City. From aloft, the place Bonaventure exhibition center looks like it has a hole in the top. That's the 2¹/₂-acre rooftop garden, with strolling pheasants, paddling ducks, and a heated pool. All guest rooms have color TVs in the bedrooms and smaller black-and-white sets in the baths, as well as views of the city or the garden. There's an executive floor. All rooms, public and private, have recently undergone renovation.

Dining: Le Castillon is the hotel's French restaurant. La Bourgade is less expensive. Both have summer dining terraces.

Services: Concierge, 24-hour room service, baby-sitting.

Facilities: Year-round heated outdoor pool, fitness center with sauna, business center.

✪ Ritz-Carlton Kempinski Montréal. 1228 rue Sherbrooke ouest (at Drummond), Montréal, PQ, H3G 1H6. ☎ **800/426-3135** in the U.S., 800/363-0366 in Canada, or 514/842-4212. Fax 514/842-2268. 185 rms, 45 suites. A/C MINIBAR TV TEL. C$145–C$240 (US$104–US$171) double; from C$350 (US$250) suite. Children under 14 stay free in parents' rm. Packages available. AE, CB, DC, ER, MC, V. Self-parking or valet C$15 (US$11), with in/out privileges. Métro: Peel.

In 1912, the Ritz-Carlton opened its doors to the carriage trade, and that clientele has remained faithful. However, the carriages have since given way to Rolls-Royces and Lamborghinis. You'll always see a few of these (or at least a Cadillac limo or custom-built Lincoln) parked in readiness near the front door. Male patrons used to be required to wear jackets in the public rooms after 5pm, but the management has eased up on that requirement. Baths are equipped with robes, makeup mirrors, and speakers carrying TV sound. Recent visits have revealed signs of slippage in service and maintenance, but not enough to damage its still-glowing reputation, and needed renovations are underway.

Dining/Entertainment: The Café de Paris is favored for its afternoon tea and weekday power breakfasts. Meals are served on the terrace in summer. There's piano music in the Ritz Bar and Le Grand Prix, with dancing nightly in the latter.

👥 Family-Friendly Hotels

Delta Montréal *(see p. 213)* The Activity Centre for supervised play and crafts-making is a big draw for small kids, along with the pool and (for bigger kids) the electronic-games room. Besides, children under 18 stay free with their parents and kids under 6 eat for free.

Holiday Inn Montréal Midtown *(see p. 213)* Two kids under 19 stay free with their parents, kids 12 and under eat for free, and everyone gets to enjoy free in-room movies and the big pool; special packages for families are offered.

Complexe Desjardins *(see below)* The glass-enclosed elevators scooting up and down through the heart of the complex are fun for kids, as is the indoor pool and the subterranean levels of the Underground City. Children stay free with their parents.

Services: Concierge, 24-hour room service, same-day dry cleaning and laundry, twice-daily maid service, baby-sitting, secretarial services.

Facilities: In-room movies, modest fitness room, barbershop, newsstand, gift shop.

EXPENSIVE

Complexe Desjardins. 4 Complexe Desjardins, Montréal, PQ, H5B 1E5. ☎ **800/361-8234** or 514/285-1450. Fax 514/285-1243. 572 rms, 28 suites. A/C MINIBAR TV TEL. C$99–C$170 (US$71–US$121) double; from C$380 (US$271) suite. Children under 18 stay free in parents' rm. Packages available. AE, DC, ER, MC, V. Valet parking C$15 (US$11); self-parking C$9 (US$6). Métro: Place-des-Arts.

This used to be Le Meridien, but nothing much besides the name has changed. It's still an integral part of the striking Complexe Desjardins, across from the Place des Arts and the Montréal Museum of Contemporary Art. The rooms, decorated in rest-ful tones, are comfortable enough, with extras like in-room movies; however, the baths are on the skimpy side. Glass-enclosed elevators glide up to rooms and down to the lower levels of the complex, with a shopping plaza and an indoor pool. Chinatown is a block away, and Vieux-Montréal, the downtown district, and the eth-nic neighborhoods along The Main are within easy walking distance. The hotel is usually the official headquarters of Montréal's annual jazz festival. No-smoking floors are available.

Dining/Entertainment: Café Fleuri provides all meals, while Le Club, with a French menu, serves only lunch and dinner. Le Bar overlooks Complexe Desjardins and has piano music nightly.

Services: Concierge, 24-hour room service, dry-cleaning and laundry service, express checkout, valet parking.

Facilities: Indoor pool, exercise room with whirlpool and sauna, business center.

La Reine Elisabeth (Queen Elizabeth). 900 bd. René-Lévesque ouest (at Mansfield), Montréal, PQ, H3B 4A5. ☎ **800/441-1414** or 514/861-3511. Fax 514/954-2256. 1,020 rms, 60 suites. A/C MINIBAR TV TEL. C$99–C$205 (US$71–US$146) double; Entree Gold Floor rates about C$50 (US$36) higher; from C$310 (US$221) suite. Various discounts, weekend, and ex-cursion packages available. Children 18 and under stay free in parents' rm. AE, CB, DC, DISC, ER, MC, V. Parking C$12 (US$9). Métro: Bonaventure.

Montréal's largest hotel has lent its august presence to the city since 1958. Its 21 floors sit atop VIA Rail's Gare Centrale, with place Ville-Marie, place Bonaventure, and the Métro all accessible by underground arcades. That desirable location makes it a choice for heads of state and celebrities, even though other hotels in town offer higher standards of personalized pampering. They close the gap by staying on the Entree Gold floor, which has a lounge serving complimentary breakfast and cocktail-hour canapés. The less-exalted rooms are entirely satisfactory, with most of the expected comforts and gadgets (including in-room movies), in price ranges to satisfy most budgets. No-smoking floors are available.

Dining/Entertainment: The Beaver Club (see "Dining," below) has a combo for dancing on Saturday nights. Several more casual bistro/bars serve meals in a variety of settings.

Services: Concierge, 24-hour room service, dry-cleaning and laundry service, baby-sitting, valet parking.

Facilities: Small health club with instructors, business center, beauty salon, shopping arcade, parking garage.

Le Centre Sheraton. 1201 bd. René-Lévesque ouest (between Drummond and Stanley), Montréal, PQ, H3B 2L7. ☎ **800/325-3535** or 514/878-2000. Fax 514/878-3958. 824 rms, 40 suites. A/C TV TEL. C$160–C$230 (US$114–US$164) double; from C$280 (US$200) suite. Children under 17 stay free in parents' rm. Weekend rates available. AE, DC, DISC, ER, MC, V. Valet parking C$10 (US$7); self-parking C$9 (US$6) with in/out privileges. Métro: Bonaventure or Peel.

Le Centre Sheraton rises near Gare Centrale, a few steps off Dorchester Square, and within a short walk of the rue Crescent dining and nightlife district. A high glass wall transforms the lobby atrium into an immense greenhouse, big enough to shelter two royal palms and a luxuriance of tropical plants. The staff is efficient and the rooms are comfortable, if anonymous. Earnest people in suits make up most of the clientele. They gravitate to the executive Towers section, which bestows complimentary breakfast and a private lounge. Half the rooms have minibars; all have coffeemakers and in-room movies. Some floors are reserved for nonsmokers.

Dining/Entertainment: The Boulevard serves three meals a day; the Musette, breakfast and lunch only. Jazz is performed Tuesday to Saturday evenings in the Impromptu Bar.

Services: Concierge in Towers, 24-hour room service, dry cleaning, baby-sitting, secretarial services, express checkout, valet parking, airport transport.

Facilities: Indoor pool, fitness center with whirlpool and sauna.

MODERATE

Château Versailles. 1659 rue Sherbrooke ouest (at Guy), Montréal, PQ, H3H 1E3. ☎ **800/ 361-3664** in the U.S., 800/361-7199 in Canada, or 514/933-3611. Fax 514/933-6867. 70 rms in the town houses, 107 rms in the tower. A/C TV TEL. C$119–C$139 (US$85–US$99) double. Children 16 and under stay free in parents' rm. Special weekend rates Nov–May, summer packages available. AE, CB, DC, ER, MC, V. Valet parking C$8.50 (US$6). Métro: Guy.

Long a local favorite, this place has been somewhat overpraised. Though it began as a European-style pension in 1958, the owners have since expanded into four adjacent pre–World War I town houses and added a modern tower across the street. I'd choose the former over the motelish tower, even though it has no elevator and the furnishings verge on dowdy. The rooms are of good size and comfortable enough, some with minibars. A few antiques are spotted around the public rooms. Service remains more personal than in the big downtown hotels, and breakfast and afternoon tea are served in a small dining room with a fireplace (the orange juice is freshly squeezed, the croissants are warm and flaky). There are two no-smoking floors, plus a French restaurant in the tower. Price and location keep both popular, so reserve well in advance.

Delta Montréal. 450 rue Sherbrooke ouest, Montréal, PQ, H3A 2T4. ☎ **800/877-1133** or 514/286-1986. Fax 514/284-4342. 453 rms, 6 suites. A/C MINIBAR TV TEL. C$109–C$149 (US$78–US$106) double; from C$250 (US$179) suite. Children under 18 stay free in parents' rm; children under 6 eat for free. Weekend rates available. AE, DC, ER, MC, V. Parking C$12 (US$9). Métro: Place-des-Arts.

A well-maintained property, this unit of the Canadian chain is targeted to business travelers with its expansive business center and large health club. However, its supervised children's crafts and games center makes it clear that families are welcome, too. The rooms have angular dimensions, escaping the boxiness of many contemporary hotels. Most have small balconies; all have coffee machines. Room service is available around the clock. The better-than-average health club has an aerobics instructor, a whirlpool, a sauna, massage, an indoor lap pool, an outdoor pool, and two squash courts. Enter the 23-story tower from avenue du Président-Kennedy. Courtesy airport transportation is available on request.

Holiday Inn Montréal Midtown. 420 rue Sherbrooke ouest (at av. du Parc), Montréal, PQ, H3A 1B4. ☎ **800/465-4329** in the U.S., 800/387-3042 in Canada, or 514/842-6111. Fax 514/842-9381. 485 rms. A/C TEL TV. C$104–C$150 (US$74–US$107) double. Two children 19 and under stay free in parents' rm; children 12 and under eat for free. Summer and family packages available. AE, DC, ER, MC, V. Parking C$11.50 (US$8). Métro: Place-des-Arts.

Not to be confused with the Holiday Inn Select Centre Ville, this upper-middle entry stands out among the hotels clustered around the intersection of rue Sherbrooke and rue City Councillors. It's one of the city's best values in its class, especially for economizing families. The bathrooms are compact. No-smoking and executive floors are available, and coin-operated washers and dryers are provided for guests' use. A large heated indoor pool is attended by a lifeguard. The adjoining fitness center has weights, exercise bikes, a whirlpool, and a sauna.

✪ Montagne. 1430 rue de la Montagne (north of Ste-Catherine), Montréal, PQ, H3G 1Z5. ☎ **800/361-6262** or 514/288-5656. Fax 514/288-9658. 138 rms. A/C TV TEL. C$129–C$139 (US$92–US$99) double. AE, CB, DC, DISC, ER, MC, V. Parking C$10 (US$7). Métro: Peel.

Two white lions stand sentinel at the front door, with a doorman in a pith helmet. Noah extends his influence inside, in a crowded lobby that incorporates a pair of 6-foot carved elephants, two gold-colored crocodiles, and a nude female figure with stained-glass butterfly wings sitting atop a splashing fountain. On the mezzanine is the main dining room, Le Lutétia. Light meals are available beside the pool on the roof, 20 stories up, and there's dancing under the stars. Off the lobby, a lounge featuring a piano player and jazz duos leads to a spangly disco that empties into a pub with a terrace on rue Crescent. After all that, the relatively serene guest rooms seem downright bland. Stop in for a drink, anyway.

INEXPENSIVE

Castel St-Denis. 2099 rue St-Denis, Montréal, PQ, H2X 3K8. ☎ **514/842-9719.** Fax 514/843-8492. 18 rms. A/C TV. C$55 (US$39) double. Extra person C$10 (US$7). MC, V. No parking. Métro: Berri-UQAM or Sherbrooke.

Among the budget choices in the Latin Quarter, the St-Denis is one of the most desirable. It's a little south of rue Sherbrooke, among the cafes of the lower reaches of the street, and 2 long blocks from the Terminus Voyageur. Most of the rooms are fairly quiet, and all are tidy and simply decorated, if hardly chic. The friendly bilingual owner is a good source for nearby restaurants and attractions.

Lord Berri. 1199 rue Berri (between René-Lévesque and Ste-Catherine), Montréal, PQ, H2L 4C6. ☎ **888/363-0363** or 514/845-9236. Fax 514/849-9855. 148 rms, 6 junior suites. A/C TV TEL. High season, C$82 (US$59) double, C$130 (US$93) suite; low season, C$75

(US$54) double, C$109 (US$78) suite. Extra person C$7 (US$5). AE, CB, DC, ER, MC, V. Outdoor parking C$10 (US$7). Métro: Berri-UQAM.

After a stint as a Days Inn, this economy hotel has returned to its old name, along with some needed upgrading. It's near St-Denis and a 5-minute walk from Old Montréal. Its Italian restaurant has a sidewalk terrace. The room decor is as interesting as a bus schedule, but the Latin Quarter location and fair tariffs make up for it. Several floors are set aside for nonsmokers.

VIEUX-MONTREAL
VERY EXPENSIVE

✪ **Inter-Continental Montréal.** 360 rue St-Antoine ouest (at Bleury), Montréal, PQ, H2Y 3X4. ☎ **800/361-3600** or 514/987-9900. Fax 514/847-8550. 335 rms, 22 suites. A/C MINIBAR TV TEL. C$180–C$305 (US$129–US$218) double; from C$350 (US$250) suite. Packages available. AE, CB, DC, DISC, ER, MC, V. Valet parking C$16 ($11). Métro: Square-Victoria.

A few minutes' walk from Notre-Dame and the restaurants and nightspots of Vieux-Montréal, this striking luxury hotel opened in 1991 and became an instant candidate for inclusion among the top three properties in town. Its new tower houses the sleek reception area and guest rooms, while the restored annex, the Nordheimer building (1888), contains some of the hotel's restaurants and bars. (Take a look at the early-19th-century vaults down below.) The guest rooms are quiet and well lit, with photographs and lithographs by local artists on the walls and with in-room movies. The turret suites are fun, with their round rooms and wraparound windows. All rooms have two or three phones and coffee machines. Robes are supplied. Four floors are reserved for nonsmokers, and there are executive floors with a lounge.

Dining/Entertainment: Les Continents serves all three meals and Sunday brunch. Le Cristallin, the lobby piano bar, has music nightly. In the Nordheimer building is congenial Chez Plume, popular for lunch and after work.

Services: Concierge, 24-hour room service, same-day laundry/valet Monday to Friday, complimentary newspaper, nightly turndown, express checkout, valet parking.

Facilities: Health club with small enclosed rooftop pool, sauna and steam rooms, massage, weight room, business center.

MODERATE

✪ **Les Passants du Sans Soucy.** 171 rue St-Paul ouest, Montréal, PQ, H2Y 1Z5. ☎ **514/842-2634.** Fax 514/842-2912. 9 rms. A/C TV TEL. C$110–C$120 (US$79–US$86) double; C$160 (US$114) suite. Extra person C$10 (US$7). Rates include full breakfast. AE, DC, ER, MC, V. Parking C$7.50 (US$5). Métro: Place d'Armes.

This delightful B&B in Vieux-Montréal is a 1723 house on even older foundations craftily converted by the bilingual owners. (Its seemingly misspelled appellation is a play on the name of one of them, Daniel Soucy.) Exposed brick, beams, and a marble floor form the entry, which leads to a sitting area and a breakfast nook with a skylight. Nine guest rooms are upstairs, and each has mortared stone walls, a buffed wood floor, a clock radio, fresh flowers, lace curtains, and a wrought-iron or brass bed. The inn is 8 blocks from place Jacques-Cartier.

✪ **Vieux-Port.** 97 rue de la Commune est (near St-Gabriel), Montréal, PQ, H2Y 1J1. ☎ **514/876-0081.** Fax 514/876-8923. 27 rms. A/C TV TEL. C$110–C$165 (US$79–US$118) double. Extra person C$10 (US$7). Rates include full breakfast. AE, DC, ER, MC, V. Parking C$7.50 (US$5). Métro: Place d'Armes.

Expanding on their own fine example, the owners of Sans Soucy (above) have produced this larger, more luxurious inn in an 1882 building, adding a romantic cellar restaurant. Polished hardwood floors, massive beams, and original windows shape the hideaway rooms, 15 of which face the waterfront. Many have whirlpool baths. There's no smoking in the rooms. Drinks and sandwiches are served on the rooftop terrace, which has unobstructed views of the Old Port, a particular treat when fireworks are scheduled at La Ronde. The restaurant, Les Ramparts, sticks to traditional fare, carefully prepared and adroitly served. At one end of the dining room is a fragment of the colonial fortification.

PLATEAU MONT-ROYAL
MODERATE

La Fontaine. 1301 rue Rachel est (at Chambord), Montréal, PQ, H2J 2K1. ☎ **800/597-0597** or 514/597-0166. Fax 514/597-0496. 18 rms, 3 suites. A/C TV TEL. C$120–C$140 (US$86–US$100) double; C$175–C$185 (US$125–US$132) suite. Extra person $10. Children under 12 stay free in parents' rm. Rates include buffet breakfast. AE, DISC, ER, MC, V. Free parking behind the inn or on the street. Métro: Mont-Royal or Sherbrooke.

At the northern edge of Lafontaine Park, this urban inn (no elevator) is a bit far from the action (except in summer, when free concerts are given in the park and the tennis courts and jogging and cycling paths are well used). It has clean, sprightly rooms in bright colors; the baths are equipped with hair dryers. The suites have whirlpools, and many of the other rooms have terraces or balconies. Those in the new section are roomier; units in back are quieter. You may use the terrace on the third floor and have access to a small kitchen that's kept stocked with complimentary cookies, tea, and juice. The lobby gets crowded for breakfast.

4 Dining

Montréal boasts over 4,000 restaurants. Until only a few years ago, they were overwhelmingly French. There were a few *temples de cuisine* that delivered (or pretended to) haute standards, scores of accomplished bistros employing humbler ingredients and less grand settings, and some places serving the hearty fare of the colonial era (game, maple syrup, and root vegetables). There were places that presented the cooking of Asia and the Mediterranean, but they didn't enjoy the same favor they did in other North American cities. Québec was French, and that was that.

In the 1980s, when waves of food crazes washed over Los Angeles, Chicago, Toronto, and New York (introducing Cajun, Tex-Mex, Southwestern, and the fusion cuisines known as Franco-Asian, Pacific Rim, and Cal-Ital), the diners of Montréal were resolute, sticking to their traditions. Now that's changing, for a number of reasons. The recession of the early 1990s, from which Canada has been slow to recover, put many restaurateurs out of business and forced others to streamline their operations. Immigration continued to grow, and with it came the introduction of still more foreign cooking styles. Montréalers began sampling the exotic edibles emerging in new storefront eateries—Thai, Moroccan, Vietnamese, Portuguese, Turkish, Mexican, Indian, Szechuan, and Japanese. Innovation and intermingling of styles, ingredients, and techniques was inevitable. The city, long among the elite gastronomic centers, is now as cosmopolitan in its tastes and offerings as any on the continent.

Picking through this forest of tempting choices can be both gratifying and bewildering. Besides the places below, there are many worthy possibilities, especially along rues Crescent, St-Denis, and St-Laurent. Nearly all have menus posted outside, prompting the local pastime of stopping every few yards for a little mouthwatering reading and comparison shopping before deciding on a place for dinner.

It's a good idea to make a reservation to dine at one of the city's top restaurants. Unlike in larger American and European cities, however, a few hours or a day in advance is usually sufficient. Dress codes are all but nonexistent, except in a handful of the luxury restaurants, but adults who show up in the equivalent of T-shirts and jeans are likely to feel uncomfortably out of place at the better establishments.

This city's moderately priced bistros, cafes, and ethnic eateries offer outstanding food, congenial surroundings, and amiable service. And, speaking of value for money, the table d'hôte (fixed-price) meals are eye-openers. Entire two- to four-course meals, often with a beverage, can be had for little more than an à la carte main course alone. Even the best restaurants offer them, so table d'hôte represents a considerable savings as well as the chance to sample some excellent restaurants at reasonable prices. (Prices don't include the 7% federal tax and 6.5% provincial tax that are added to the restaurant bill. Food purchased in a market or grocery store isn't taxed.)

Since parking space is at a premium in most restaurant districts, take the Métro or a taxi to the restaurant (most are within a block or two of a Métro station) or ask if valet parking is available when making a reservation.

DOWNTOWN

See the "Downtown Montréal" map (p. 226) to locate restaurants in this section.

VERY EXPENSIVE

✪ **The Beaver Club.** In Le Reine Elisabeth Hotel, 900 bd. René-Lévesque ouest. ☎ **514/861-3511.** Reservations recommended. Jacket advised for men. Main courses C$23–C$35 (US$16–US$25); table d'hôte lunch C$17–C$29 (US$12–US$21); table d'hôte dinner C$32–C$38 (US$23–US$27). AE, CB, DC, DISC, ER, MC, V. Mon–Fri noon–3pm and 6–11pm; Tues–Sat 6–11pm. Métro: Bonaventure. FRENCH.

Dine here under the glassy gazes of a polar bear, musk ox, and bison, for the restaurant takes its name from an organization of socially prominent explorers and trappers begun in 1785. Stained glass and carved wood panels depict their early adventures in the wilderness and undergird the clubby tone of the dining room, a magnet for the city's power brokers for decades (though, with 225 seats, it's hardly exclusive). Lunch is the time for the gentlest prices. The menu changes twice a year, but if you can eat only one meal here, lean toward the roast beef. The determined dieter will appreciate the nutritional information provided for each lunch dish. On Saturday a trio begins playing at 7:30pm for dancing. Men are expected to wear jackets.

Les Halles. 1450 rue Crescent (between Ste-Catherine and Maisonneuve). ☎ **514/844-2328.** Reservations recommended. Lunch main courses C$10.25–C$23 (US$7–US$16); dinner main courses C$25–C$31 (US$18–US$22); table d'hôte lunch C$23 (US$16); table d'hôte dinner C$32 (US$23) or C$45 (US$32). AE, DC, ER, MC, V. Tues–Fri 11:45am–2:30pm; Mon–Sat 6–11pm. Métro: Guy-Concordia or Peel. FRENCH.

Les Halles thrives as one of the town's most accomplished French restaurants. It's more expensive than it should be, however, so consider coming here for lunch. Despite the prices, this isn't an "event" place, draped with brocade and glinting with Baccarat. The tables are close, the service is correct but chummy, and animated conversations often start up between strangers—all of which promote the idea of a bistro, not a gastronomic temple. Beef, lamb, and game dishes are the stars on the menu, but seafood, simply prepared, is also good. The ingredients are rarely exotic, yet the kitchen dresses them in unexpected ways. Main courses and desserts come in such hefty portions that you don't need appetizers.

EXPENSIVE

Chez Pauzé. 1657 rue Ste-Catherine ouest (near rue Bishop). ☎ **514/932-6118.** Reservations suggested on weekends. Main courses C$15.75–C$40.75 (US$11–US$29); table d'hôte C$21.50–C$46.50 (US$15–US$33). AE, DC, ER, MC, V. Daily 11:30am–4pm; Sun–Wed 5–10:30pm, Thurs–Sat 5–11:30pm. Métro: Guy-Concordia. SEAFOOD.

Go in summer, when a terrace covered by a green awning pushes from the building out into a poplar-shaded lot. Opened in 1862, the V. Pauzé store sold fruit and oysters, evolving into Montréal's oldest fish house and moving to this site in 1947. About the only meat offered is that in the surf 'n' turf; everything else is fresh from the briny, including Arctic char, grouper, and Dover sole. A new French chef has dramatically upgraded the kitchen's performance. There are 225 seats in the gloomy interior, while up to 200 people can catch the breezes outside. A piano player tinkles away on Friday and Saturday.

MODERATE

Katsura. 2170 rue de la Montagne (between Maisonneuve and Sherbrooke). ☎ **514/849-1172.** Reservations recommended. Main courses C$13–C$25 (US$9–US$18); table d'hôte lunch C$8–C$19 (US$6–US$14); table d'hôte dinner C$27–C$43 (US$19–US$31). AE, DC, ER, MC, V. Mon–Fri 11:30am–2:30pm; Mon–Thurs 5:30–10:30pm, Fri–Sat 5:30–11:30pm, Sun 5:30–9:30pm. Métro: Peel or Guy-Concordia. JAPANESE.

A tuxedoed maître d' welcomes you at the door and leads you into a conventional Western dining room with plush chairs or into rooms enclosed by opaque paper screens that allow you to sit on tatami mats at low Japanese tables. Whichever venue you choose, waitresses in kimonos move quickly but almost silently under the soothing tinkle of music on the stereo. Katsura has been around long enough to be accorded credit for introducing sushi to Montréal, and it's prepared to near-perfection here. Sample a lot of it, though, and the bill shoots into a far pricier category. The sushi bar in back is a refuge for those who arrive without a reservation when the place is full.

✪ **Le Taj.** 2077 rue Stanley (near Sherbrooke). ☎ **514/845-9015.** Lunch buffet C$9 (US$6); main courses C$9–C$17 (US$6–US$12). AE, DC, ER, MC, V. Sun–Fri 11:30am–2:30pm; daily 5–10:30pm. Métro: Peel. NORTHERN INDIAN.

A large relief temple sculpture occupies pride of place in this dramatic setting of cream and apricot. Back in the corner, a chef works diligently over an open tandoor oven. His specialty is the mughlai repertoire of the north of the Indian subcontinent. The seasonings on the scores of dishes he sends forth are more tangy than incendiary (but watch out for the coriander sauce). Spicy or mild, all are perfumed with turmeric, saffron, ginger, cumin, mango powder, and garam masala. For a rare treat, order the marinated lamb chops roasted in the tandoor; they arrive at the table still sizzling and nested on braised vegetables. Vegetarians have a choice of eight dishes, the chickpea-based *channa masala* among the most complex. The main courses are huge, arriving in a boggling array of bowls, saucers, cups, and dishes, all with *nan* (flat bread) and basmati rice. Evenings are quiet, and lunches are busy but not hectic.

INEXPENSIVE

La Maison Kam Fung. 1008 rue Clark (near Gauchetièrie est). ☎ **514/878-2888.** Main courses C$7–C$12 (US$5–US$9). AE, DC, ER, MC, V. Daily 10am–2pm and 5–10:30pm. Métro: Place d'Armes. SZECHUAN/CANTONESE.

Weekends are the event days, when Chinese dispersed throughout the suburbs return home for the comfort food. While regular meals are served in the evening, midday is reserved for dim sum. Here's the drill: Go to the second floor, obtain a ticket from

---

😀 Family-Friendly Restaurants

Le 9e *(see below)* What looks like a ship's dining room is found on the ninth (9e) floor of Eaton department store. Kids can pretend they're on a fantasy voyage, and since "Le Neuvième" is a noisy place, they can be as enthusiastic as they like.

Pizzédélic *(see p. 223)* Pizza never fails to please the younger set, and this place caters to any taste, with toppings that stretch the imagination.

McDonald's For something familiar, but with a twist, this McDonald's, only a block from Notre-Dame at the corner of rue Notre-Dame and St-Laurent, deserves a mention. Located in the former home of Antoine Lamet de la Mothe Cadillac, the founder of Detroit and a governor of Louisiana, it offers the usual menu, along with pizzas and the Québec favorite, *poutine* (french fries covered with a cheese gravy).

---

the young woman at the podium, and wait. Once summoned to a table, be alert to the carts being trundled out of the kitchen. They're stacked with covered baskets and pails, most of which contain dumplings of one kind or another, such as balls of curried shrimp or glistening envelopes of pork nubbins or scallops, supplemented by such items as fish purée slathered on wedges of sweet pepper and, for the venturesome, steamed chicken feet and squid. Simply order until sated. Resist the desire to gather up the first five items that appear. Much more is on the way. If you opt for the relative peacefulness of dinner, they're proud of their live seafood, cooked to order.

Le Commensal. 1204 av. McGill College (at Ste-Catherine). ☎ **514/871-1480.** Reservations not accepted. Dishes priced by weight: C$1.75 (US$1.25) per 100 g (about 3.5 oz.). AE, MC, V. Daily 7am–midnight. Métro: McGill. VEGETARIAN.

Le Commensal serves vegetarian fare buffet-style. Most of the dishes are so artfully conceived, with close attention to aroma, color, and texture, that even avowed meat eaters won't feel deprived. The only likely complaint is that those dishes that are supposed to be hot are too often lukewarm. Patrons circle the table helping themselves, then pay the cashier by weight. The second-floor location affords a view, which compensates for the utilitarian decor. There's no tipping.

Le Commensal has eight other locations at recent count, one of the most convenient at 2115 St-Denis, at rue Sherbrooke (☎ **514/845-2627**).

Le 9e. 677 rue Ste-Catherine (in Eaton department store). ☎ **514/284-8421.** Table d'hôte C$7.95 (US$6). AE, MC, V. Mon–Sat 11:30am–3pm; Thurs–Fri 4:30–7pm. Métro: McGill. LIGHT FARE.

Opened in 1931, "Le Neuvième," on the ninth floor of the old-line department store, is a replica of an art-deco dining room aboard the ocean liner *Ile de France,* complete with murals, marble columns, and giant alabaster vases. Menu items include soups, sandwiches, salads, and daily specials that come with soup, dessert, and coffee. A new feature is a pasta table, where plates are prepared to order, with choice of sauce. It comes with salad. Some of the waiters and waitresses, in their starched black-and-white uniforms, look as if they might've been around at the inauguration. Expect noise and children.

VIEUX-MONTREAL
EXPENSIVE

✪ **Claude Postel.** 443 rue St-Vincent (near Notre-Dame). ☎ **514/875-5067.** Reservations recommended. Table d'hôte lunch C$20–C$26 (US$15–US$19); main courses C$27–C$34

(US$19–US$24); table d' hote dinner C$44 (US$31). AE, CB, DC, ER, MC, V. Daily noon–2:30pm and 5–11pm. Métro: Place d'Armes or Champ-de-Mars. FRENCH.

One of the most upbeat places in Vieux-Montréal is named for its chef-owner, who once shook the skillets at Bonaparte. He has surpassed his former employer on every count and continues to widen the gap, as with the recent addition of a summer dining terrace. The 1862 building has been both a morgue and a hotel that once had Sarah Bernhardt as a guest. The animated Mr. Postel almost dances through his dining room, greeting regulars and newcomers with equal warmth, suggesting off-menu items and possible wines. The crowd is largely composed of businesspeople and government employees, but the restaurant attracts visiting celebrities as well. They come for such dishes as seafood ravioli on a bed of vegetables steamed in lobster bouillon. Items change daily, but caribou, venison, scallops, and salmon frequently appear in creative guises. A luncheon express menu of two courses with coffee lets you sample his wares for only C$11.95 (US$9). There's valet parking from 6pm.

Postel has a **takeout shop** nearby, at 75 rue Notre-Dame, with most of the makings of a satisfying picnic, including baguettes, cheeses, sandwiches, and quiches.

✪ La Marée. 404 place Jacques-Cartier (near Notre-Dame). ☎ 514/861-8126. Reservations required. Table d'hôte lunch C$14–C$17 (US$10–US$12); main courses C$24–C$30 (US$17–US$21). AE, DC, DISC, ER, MC, V. Mon–Fri noon–3pm; daily 5:30–11:30pm. Métro: Champ-de-Mars. FRENCH.

Despite the T-shirted masses who fill the terrace of this 1807 house on the west side of the plaza, dining of high order takes place behind these stone walls. Begin with the setting: fireplaces, paintings of fish and game, delicately figured wallpaper, and furnishings recalling Louis XIII and the Sun King. Candlelight enhances the romantic mood in the evening, while power lunches prevail at midday. Known for its refined and precise treatment of seafood, the kitchen is lauded for such fabrications as trout stuffed with salmon-and-lobster mousse and lobster with tomato, fresh basil, and white-wine sauce. Natural flavors are allowed to prevail, and presentations aren't flashy. In cooler weather, chateaubriand tops the list. Service is disciplined, of that level of professionalism characterized by a smoothly avuncular solicitude. There's no dress code, but you'll want to look at least casually stylish.

MODERATE

✪ Casa de Matéo. 440 rue St-François-Xavier (near St-Paul). ☎ 514/844-4154. Reservations suggested for Fri–Sat nights. Daily lunch specials C$10 (US$7); main courses C$13–C$18 (US$9–US$13). AE, CB, DC, ER, MC, V. Mon–Fri 11:30am–10pm, Sat–Sun 4–11pm. Métro: Place d'Armes. MEXICAN.

Stepping into Casa de Matéo feels like wandering into a party already in progress. Expect a gleeful greeting any night, and on Fridays and Saturdays between 7 and 10pm, mariachis come to carry the fiesta to a higher register. Birdbath-sized margaritas arrive with chips and salsa at the center horseshoe bar, which is encased with rough terra-cotta tiles. Lending authenticity is a cheerful staff from Mexico, Guatemala, and other Latin American countries, most of whom are delighted to be addressed in even a few words of Spanish. With these generous servings, you can skip the appetizers. But that would mean missing the *plato Mexicano,* a sampler of all the starters. Since that's a meal in itself, others may want to stop there. But *that* would mean missing the *pescado Veracruzano,* whole red snapper quickly marinated and fried and served with a nest of crisp vegetables. The usual burritos and enchiladas are easy to forget.

The owner has opened a new trattoria, **Pavarotti** (☎ 514/844-9656), down the street, and a sushi restaurant, **Tokyo** (☎ 514/844-6695), around the corner on rue St-Paul.

La Gargote. 351 place d'Youville (at St-Pierre). ☎ **514/844-1428.** Main courses and lunch table d'hôte C$10–C$13 (US$7–US$9). MC, V. Daily noon–2pm and 5:30–10pm. Métro: Square-Victoria. FRENCH.

Though it's across from Montréal's history museum, visitors haven't yet discovered this spirited little bistro. That's just as well, since it's already packed with locals and businesspeople, especially at lunch. When they pay attention to their plates and not their companions, they derive considerable satisfaction from such classics as duck sausage l'orange and veal kidney in sauce Diable. The surroundings are the Vieux-Montréal norm, relying for decor on stone and brick walls and rough-cut beams overhead. Meals are also put up for takeout, meant for offices, but as useful for a picnic in the waterfront park.

✪ **Le Bourlingueur.** 363 St-François-Xavier (near St-Paul). ☎ **514/845-3646.** Reservations suggested on weekends. Table d'hôte lunch or dinner C$9.45–C$15.65 (US$7–US$11). AE, DC, ER, MC, V. Mon 11:30am–3pm, Tues–Fri 11:30am–9pm, Sat–Sun 5–9pm. Métro: Place d'Armes. FRENCH.

While it doesn't look especially promising on first approach, this registers as a real find in Vieux-Montréal. That star up there is for the almost unbelievably low prices they charge for 8 to 10 four-course meals daily. The chalkboard menu changes with market availability, making it possible to dine here twice a day for a week without repeating anything except the indifferent salad. The specialty is seafood—watch for the cold lobster with herb mayonnaise. Well short of chic, this restaurant doesn't make the most of its stone walls and old beams, choosing instead to put paper place mats on the pink tablecloths. No matter—not at these prices and relative quality. The crowd is diverse—you'll be dining with the widest possible range of ages, genders, and occupations. Lunch is busiest.

✪ **Sawatdee.** 457 rue St-Pierre (near rue Notre-Dame). ☎ **514/849-8854.** Main courses C$8–C$20 (US$6–US$12). AE, MC. Tues–Fri noon–2:30pm and 5–10pm, Sat–Sun 5–11pm. Métro: Square-Victoria or Place d'Armes. THAI.

While it may be a stretch to describe this as one of the hundred best restaurants in Canada, as it has been proclaimed, Sawatdee is certainly a welcome addition. It recently moved here from a remote location west of downtown, and along with it came an impressive collection of museum-quality statuary and tapestries, which deserves close examination. The lunch buffet is cheap and filling, but not wonderful. For something memorable, show up for dinner, and make it clear that you want genuine Thai seasonings, not the wan versions usually served to non-Asians.

INEXPENSIVE

Chez Better. 160 rue Notre-Dame (near place Jacques-Cartier). ☎ **514/861-2617.** Main courses $7.50–$8.50; table d'hôte C$12.75–C$14.75 (US$9–US$11). AE, DC, ER, MC, V. Daily 11am–11pm. Métro: Champ-de-Mars. GERMAN.

They aren't making a half-hearted boast with the name. This and the other five outposts of this growing local chain are named for the founder, a Canadian born in Germany. Presumably he grew homesick for a taste of his native land and opened his first restaurant to assuage that hunger. Think variations of knackwurst, sauerkraut, fries, and 100 brands of beer and that gives the general outline of the menu. Forget grease and oozing fat globules, though, for these are remarkably lighthearted sausages, brightly seasoned with herbs, curry, hot pepper, and even truffle shavings. A trivet of three mustards sits on each table. While sausage plates are the stars, there are also mixed grills, chicken schnitzels, grilled smoked pork chops, salads, and 10 preparations of mussels. In this 1811 building in Vieux-Montréal, the ground floor is for nonsmokers, the upstairs for puffers. Service can be disjointed, but rarely to the point of irritation.

Two other branches you're likely to encounter are 4382 bd. St-Laurent (☎ 514/845-4554) and 1430 rue Stanley (☎ 514/848-9859).

Le Jardin Nelson. 407 place Jacques-Cartier (at rue de la Commune). ☎ 514/861-5731. Reservations accepted only by phone. Main courses C$5.75–C$9.85 (US$4.10–US$7). AE, MC, V. May to Labour Day daily 11:30am–3am; Labour Day to Nov daily 11:30am–midnight (later on weekends); Nov–Apr Sat–Sun 11:30am–5pm. Métro: Place d'Armes. FRENCH/LIGHT FARE.

Near the foot of the hill, a passage leads into the paved garden court in back of a handsome 1812 stone building. The kitchen specializes in crêpes, their fillings determining their destinies as main courses or desserts. Mild invention keeps the results intriguing, as with the mélange of semicrisp veggies rolled in a thin buckwheat pancake laced with threads of spinach. Soups, omelets, salads, and sandwiches are also available. A crabapple tree shades the garden, a horticultural counterpoint to midday and evening concerts by jazz combos (Friday to Sunday) and classical chamber groups (Monday to Thursday).

PLATEAU MONT-ROYAL
EXPENSIVE

✪ **Toqué!** 3842 rue St-Denis (at Roy). ☎ 514/499-2084. Reservations recommended. Main courses C$22–C$26 (US$16–US$19); *menu dégustation* C$60 (US$43). AE, DC, ER, MC, V. Daily 6–11pm. Métro: Sherbrooke. CONTEMPORARY FRENCH.

This is the sort of restaurant that can single-handedly raise a city's gastronomic expectations. A meal here is virtually obligatory for anyone who admires superb food dazzlingly presented. Normand Laprise teamed up with Christine Lamarche to create a place as postmodernist in its cuisine as in its decor, which is largely bright colors and minimalist fixtures, with a wall down the middle to separate smokers from nonsmokers. Success has forced the owners to forego the open kitchen that used to be in front—they needed the space for tables. Postnouvelle might be an apt description, for though presentations are eye-openers, the portions are sufficient and the singular combinations of ingredients intensely flavorful. This food bears comparison to the Wolfgang Puck school (French and Asian techniques applied to top-of-the-bin Californian ingredients), but experimentation is kept on a tether by the chefs' professionalism, and missteps are few. The menu is never set in stone. If fiddleheads are good at market in the morning, they might replace the listed asparagus that night. Consider just one recent dish: sautéed scallops nestled with flageolet bean salsa laced with cumin, coriander, and jalapenos, the light heat countered with salsify and cinnamon-touched plantain chips. Duck, venison, and foie gras are memorable, while salmon is often the most desirable fish entree. An exciting cheese selection can precede dessert. The restaurant fills up later than most, with prosperous-looking suits and women with sparkles at throat and wrist. Allow 2 hours for dinner and call at least a day ahead for reservations.

Witloof. 3619 rue St-Denis (at Sherbrooke). ☎ 514/281-0100. Reservations recommended. Table d'hôte C$12–C$16 (US$9–US$11); main courses C$13.50–C$16 (US$10–US$11). AE, DC, ER, MC, V. Mon–Wed 11:30am–11pm, Thurs–Fri 11:30am–midnight, Sat 5pm–midnight, Sun 5–11pm. Métro: Sherbrooke. BELGIAN.

Its name is Flemish for "endive," and when Witloof sticks to the Belgian dishes in which it specializes, it's one of the most gratifying restaurants in town. It contrives to be both a casual and an elegant place, manifest in the snowy linen tablecloths covered with butcher paper. Steaming casseroles of mussels with tents of frites on the side are deservedly the most popular on the menu, but the classic Belgian stew, waterzooi, is a close second. The pastas are adequate. Because it's always busy, the kitchen can fall behind on orders, but the convivial atmosphere dissuades grousing. Several Belgian beers, including Blanche de Bruges, are available and go well with most of this food. The restaurant has a large selection of desserts, from crème caramel to praline crêpes.

MODERATE

Buona Notte. 3518 bd. St-Laurent (near Sherbrooke). ☎ **514/848-0644.** Reservations recommended. Main courses C$8.50–C$13 (US$6–US$9); table d'hôte C$19–C$33 (US$14–US$24). AE, DC, MC, V. Mon–Fri 11:30am–midnight, Sat 5pm–midnight, Sun 10am–3pm and 5pm–midnight. Métro: St-Laurent. CONTEMPORARY ITALIAN.

With its high ceiling masked by electric fans, wrapped pipes, and heating ducts, Buona Notte could easily be in New York's SoHo. A principal component of the decor are plates painted by celebrity diners, among them Michael Bolton, Ben Kingsley, Danny DeVito, and Winona Ryder. They're boxed (the plates, that is) and arrayed along one wall. Funk and hip-hop thump over the stereo, people in black cruise the tables, the wait staff looks ready to leap at the next casting call. The front opens up in warm weather. Yet while the food inevitably takes second place to preening, it's surprisingly good. Pastas prevail, tumbled with crunchy vegetables or silky walnut sauce or any of 10 or more combinations. The kitchen exhibits less reliance on meat than the norm and makes an imaginative risotto with two cheeses and two sauces. Rims of plates are usually dusted with minced parsley and paprika, an overdone device that tends to look messy rather than decorative. The breads are dense and chewy.

✪ **L'Express.** 3927 rue St-Denis (at Roy). ☎ **514/845-5333.** Reservations recommended. Main courses C$10–C$16 (US$7–US$11). AE, CB, DC, ER, MC, V. Mon–Fri 8am–3am, Sat 10am–3am, Sun 10am–2am. Métro: Sherbrooke. FRENCH.

No obvious sign announces this place, only its name discreetly spelled in white tiles embedded in the sidewalk. Apart from that bit of implicit snobbery, there's no need for it to call attention to itself, since *tout* Montréal knows exactly where it is. The food, fairly priced for such an "in" place, is prepared with a sensitivity to lightness in saucing but in substantial helpings. Seasonal adjustments veer from vinegary octopus-and-lentil salad in summer to full-flavored duck breast with chewy chanterelles in a sauce with the scent of deep woods. Or simply stop by for a *croque monsieur* (like a grilled cheese sandwich) or a bagel with smoked salmon and cream cheese. Reservations are usually necessary for tables, but single diners can often find a seat at the bar, where meals are also served.

INEXPENSIVE

Au Coin Berbère. 73 rue Duluth (east of St-Laurent). ☎ **514/844-7405.** Main courses C$9–C$17 (US$6–US$12). MC, V. Tues–Sun noon–2:30pm and 7–10:30pm. Métro: Mont-Royal. ALGERIAN.

This earnest little retreat may be all but empty, but don't let that deter you. Couscous is the specialty, the name of the North African dish and of the grain pasta that's its one essential ingredient. Here it's both tasty and a bargain and may be appealing to vegetarians eager for something other than salads. The staff pushes the most expensive versions as shamelessly as in a Moroccan medina, but accepts your decision to take the cheaper one with falling-off-the-bone duck, scented with cilantro and mint and zinged with optional harisa sauce. Dates stuffed with almond paste are dessert, and mint tea a perfect topper. It's fully licensed.

The Bagel Factory. 74 rue Fairmount ouest. ☎ **514/272-0667.** Most items C$3–C$9 (US$2.15–US$6). No credit cards. Daily 24 hours. Métro: Laurier. BAGELS.

Québec bagels are a must-try treat when in Montréal. Natives insist that they're superior to the more famous New York version, and they have a case. Thinner and lighter, they have an agreeably chewy texture that doesn't remind eaters of teething rings. This tiny place is as good a place as any to sample them. It offers a substantial variety, including an extra-large one called Bozo, available for takeout only. Potato latkes, cheese blintzes, and bagel spreads are also sold.

✪ Chez Schwartz Charcuterie Hébraïque de Montréal. 3895 bd. St-Laurent (north of Prince Arthur). ☎ **514/842-4813.** Most items C$4–C$12 (US$2.85–US$9). No credit cards. Sun–Thurs 9am–1am, Fri 9am–2am, Sat 9am–3am. Métro: St-Laurent. DELI.

Before the imposition of French-first language laws, this was called Schwartz's Montréal Hebrew Delicatessen. To many ardent fans, including this writer, it's the only place on the continent to indulge in the guilty treat of smoked meat. Housed in a long, narrow space, it has a lunch counter and a collection of simple tables and chairs crammed almost impossibly close to one another. Any empty seat is up for grabs. Few mind the inconvenience or proximity to strangers, for they're soon delivered plates described either as small (meaning large) or large (meaning humongous) heaped with slices of the trademark delicacy, along with piles of rye bread. Most people also order sides of french fries and one or two mammoth garlicky pickles. There are a handful of alternative edibles, but tofu and leafy green vegetables aren't among them. Schwartz's has no liquor license.

Pizzédélic. 3500 bd. St-Laurent (near Sherbrooke). ☎ **514/282-6784.** Main courses C$6.50–C$14.50 (US$4.65–US$10). MC, V. Sun and Wed–Thurs 11:30am–1am, Tues 11:30am–2am, Fri–Sat 11:30am–3am. Métro: St-Laurent. ITALIAN.

Pizza here runs the gamut from traditional to as imaginative as anyone might conceive, with toppings from feta cheese to escargots to artichokes to pesto. All arrive on thin, not quite crispy crusts. The difference over ordinary pizzerias is the use of fresh, not canned ingredients, as in the antipasto plate of grilled vegetables and calamari strips. Pastas and meat dishes are also available. The front opens in warm weather, and there's a terrace in back. Another conveniently located Pizzédélic is downtown at 1329 rue Ste-Catherine (☎ **514/526-6011**).

ILE STE-HELENE
VERY EXPENSIVE

✪ Nuances. 1 av. du Casino (in the Casino de Montréal). ☎ **514/392-2708.** Reservations recommended. Main courses C$28–C$38.50 (US$20–US$28); table d'hôte C$32–C$39.75 (US$23–US$28). AE, DC, ER, MC, V. Daily 5:30–11pm. Métro: Ile Ste-Hélène. FRENCH.

The last place you might expect to find haute cuisine is a gambling casino, atop five floors of bleeping buzzers and blinking lights. But that's where the latest entry in Montréal's gastronomic sweepstakes is. Even with just a year on the scene, it shouldered its elegant way into the top trio. The designers didn't stint on what they deemed the appropriate trappings, not with this mahogany paneling, soaring ceiling, Villeroy & Boch china, and lavish deployment of leather and linen and gleaming brass. A maître d' seats you, a captain explains the evening's possibilities, a waitress takes your order and serves. She brings some remarkable creations. There is, for one, the thick slab of ostrich (tastes like beef, not chicken) sandwiched en crôute with exotic mushrooms and a delicate meaty sauce. The *plateau de fromage* boasts several admirable Québec-produced cheeses, not available in the States because they're made of nonpasteurized cow's milk. Get to dessert and the waitress might suggest a dish of praline mousse and chocolate sherbet, which is surmounted by latticed towers of spun sugar. Should an event need to be celebrated, this has to be the place.

PICNICKING

When planning a picnic or a meal to eat back in your hotel room, consider a stop at **La Vieille Europe,** 3855 bd. St-Laurent, near St-Cuthbert (☎ **514/842-5773**), a compact storehouse of culinary sights and smells. Choose from wheels of pungent cheeses, garlands of sausages, pâtés, cashews, honey, fresh peanut butter, or dried fruits. Coffee beans are roasted in the back. A stroll to the north along boulevard St-Laurent reveals other possibilities for mobile edibles.

Better still, make the short excursion by Métro (the Lionel-Groulx stop) to **Marché Atwater,** the public market at 3025 rue St-Ambroise. The long shed is bordered by stalls of gleaming produce and flowers, the two-story center section given to wine purveyors, food counters, bakeries, and cheese stores. The best representatives of the last two are **La Fromagerie** (☎ **514/932-4653**), whose highly knowledgeable attendants know every detail of production of the 450 to 550 North American and European cheeses on offer, and the **Boulangerie Première Moison** (☎ **514/932-0328**), which fills its space with the tantalizing aromas of baskets of breads and cases of pastries. (There's another branch of the bakery in the Gare Centrale.) From either location, it isn't far by taxi to Parc du Mont-Royal, a wonderful place to enjoy a picnic.

In Old Montréal, pick up supplies at the **dépanneur** (convenience store) at 8 rue St-Paul (at rue St-Jean-Baptiste), which keeps late hours, and then take them to place Jacques-Cartier or the Old Port, both only steps away. Dépanneurs also sell wine, but there's a bigger selection at the **SAQ Selection,** 440 bd. de Maisonneuve ouest, and a shop selling cheeses and crackers is conveniently across the hall. A more upscale possibility is the **takeout shop** at 75 rue Notre-Dame operated by the owner of Claude Postel restaurant, stocked with appetizing cheeses, pâtés, quiches, and baguettes.

5 Seeing the Sights

A superb Métro system, a fairly logical street grid, wide boulevards, and the vehicle-free Underground City all aid in the swift, uncomplicated movement of people from one destination to another. The difficulty, as in every great city, lies in making choices that fit your interests and the time available. After all, the possibilities include a hike up imposing Mont Royal in the middle of the city, biking along the redeveloped waterfront or out beside the Lachine Canal, visits to museums or historic homes, and taking in a hockey or baseball game. With riverboat rides, the fascinating Biodôme, a sprawling amusement park, and the unique Cirque du Soleil, Montréal also assures kids of a good time.

A number of the following sights opened or expanded in 1992. That's no coincidence. They were planned to coincide with that year's celebration of Montréal's 350th birthday. Efforts to enhance the city's cultural attractions have continued since then, as the opening of the Biosphère on Ile Ste-Hélène demonstrates.

A **Montréal Museums Pass** allows you entry to 19 of the city's museums. It costs C$15 (US$11) for adults for 1 day or C$28 (US$20) for 3 days; for families, the price is C$30 (US$21) for 1 day or C$60 (US$43) for 3 days. For information, call ☎ **514/845-6873.**

DOWNTOWN

✪ **Musée des Beaux-Arts (Museum of Fine Arts).** 1379–1380 rue Sherbrooke ouest (at Crescent). ☎ **514/285-2000.** Permanent collection free; temporary exhibits C$10 (US$7) adults, C$5 (US$3.55) seniors and students, C$2 (US$1.40) children 12 and under. Half-price Wed 5:30–9pm. Tues and Thurs–Sun 11am–6pm, Wed 11am–9pm. Métro: Peel or Guy-Concordia.

Montréal's most prominent museum was opened in 1912, in Canada's first building designed specifically for the visual arts. The original neoclassical pavilion is on the north side of Sherbrooke. Years ago, museum administrators recognized that the collection had outstripped its building, and curators were forced to make painful decisions about what few items could be placed on view at any one time. That problem was solved with the late-1991 completion of the stunning new annex, the Jean-Noël Desmarais Pavilion, across the street. It was designed by Montréal architect Moshe Safdie, who first gained international notice with his Habitat housing complex at the 1967 Expo. Along with two substreet floors and underground galleries connecting the new building with the old, it tripled the exhibition space.

For the best look at the results, enter the new annex, take the elevator to the top, and work your way down. The permanent collection is largely devoted to international contemporary art and Canadian art after 1960, as well as to European paintings, sculpture, and decorative arts from the Middle Ages to the 19th century. On the upper floors, for example, are many of the gems of the collection—paintings by El Greco, Reynolds, Renoir, Monet, Picasso, and Cézanne and sculptures by Rodin and Lipshitz. On the subterranean levels are works by 20th-century modernists, including abstract expressionists of the post–World War II New York School.

From the lowest level of the new pavilion, follow the understreet corridor past primitive artworks from Oceana and Africa, then up the elevator into the old building, with its display of pre-Columbian ceramics, Inuit carvings, and Amerindian crafts. The rest of that building is used primarily for temporary exhibits.

Across the street, the street-level store has an impressive selection of books, games, and folk art, and there's a cafe. If you have time for only a short visit, make it to the fourth floor. For an extra bonus, be sure to walk to the sculpture court on that level for a splendid panoramic city view.

Musée Juste Poure Rire (Just for Laughs Museum). 2111 bd. St-Laurent (north of Sherbrooke). ☎ **514/845-4000.** Admission C$7.95 (US$6). Tues–Sun 1–8pm. Closed 2 months in winter when the new exhibition is being installed. Métro: St-Laurent. Bus: 55.

This engagingly off-center museum opened on April Fool's Day 1993, a byproduct of the annual "Just for Laughs" festival. It may seem a quixotic endeavor, given the differences in tastes between the French and English (witness Jerry Lewis). But it must be remembered that Francophone Québecers share a North American culture and sensibility. Somehow this place works, as delicate a commodity as humor is, and in both languages. Mammoth shows with lavish exhibits are mounted for several months at a time. They've included clips of famous clowns, cartoons, TV sitcoms, comic shorts, and Québécois folk music. Puns, one-liners, and double entendres abound, not a few of them risqué, others as black as humor gets. Preteens are likely to be baffled. Videos and historic film clips hold museum-goers, many of them students, enthralled for hours. It also houses a 250-seat cabaret-theater, a humor hall of fame, a shop, and a cafe.

Musée McCord (McCord Museum of Canadian History). 690 rue Sherbrooke ouest (at Victoria). ☎ **514/398-7100.** Admission C$7 (US$5) adults, C$5 (US$3.55) seniors, C$4 (US$2.85) students, C$1.50 (US$1.05) children 7–11, C$14 (US$10) families; children under

Downtown Montréal

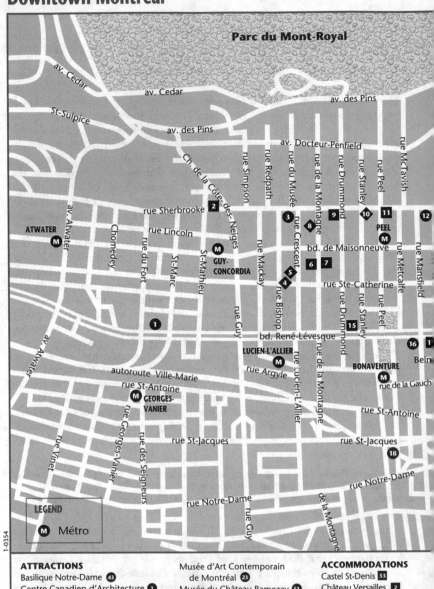

Parc du Mont-Royal

ATWATER

GUY-CONCORDIA

PEEL

LUCIEN-L'ALLIER

BONAVENTURE

GEORGES-VANIER

LEGEND

Ⓜ Métro

1-0354

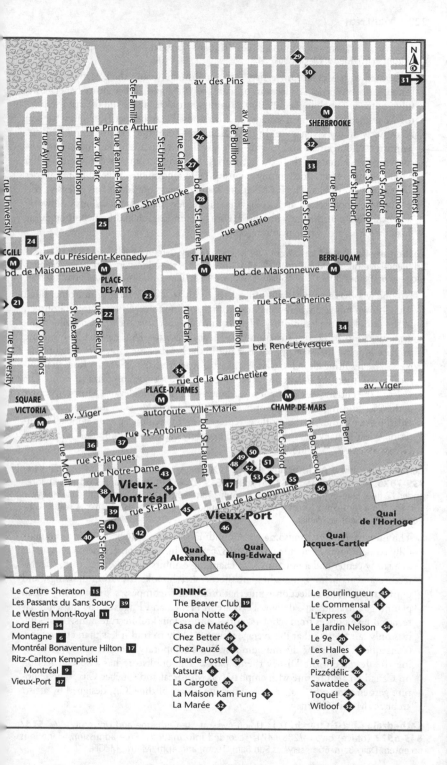

Le Centre Sheraton ▮15
Les Passants du Sans Soucy ◆39
Le Westin Mont-Royal ▮11
Lord Berri ▮34
Montagne ▮6
Montréal Bonaventure Hilton ▮17
Ritz-Carlton Kempinski
   Montréal ▮9
Vieux-Port ◆47

DINING
The Beaver Club ▮19
Buona Notte ◆27
Casa de Matéo ◆44
Chez Better ◆49
Chez Pauzé ◆4
Claude Postel ◆48
Katsura ◆8
La Gargote ◆40
La Maison Kam Fung ◆35
La Marée ◆52

Le Bourlingueur ◆45
Le Commensal ◆14
L'Express ◆30
Le Jardin Nelson ◆54
Le 9e ◆20
Les Halles ◆5
Le Taj ◆10
Pizzédélic ◆26
Sawatdee ◆38
Toqué! ◆29
Witloof ◆32

227

11 free; free to all 10am–noon Sat–Sun. Tues–Fri 10am–6pm, Sat–Sun 10am–5pm (in summer, daily from 9am). Métro: McGill. Bus: 24.

Associated with McGill University, this museum showcases the eclectic—and not infrequently eccentric—collections of scores of 19th- and 20th-century benefactors. Objects from its holdings of 29,000 costumes, artifacts, and 750,000 historic photos are rotated in and out of storage, so it isn't possible to be specific about what will be on view at any given time. In general, expect furniture, clothing, china, silver, paintings, photographs, and folk art that reveal the rural and urban life of English-speaking immigrants of the past 3 centuries. An atrium connects the original 1905 building with a wing added during extensive 1992 renovations. Beyond it are galleries for temporary exhibits. The First Nations room displays portions of an extensive collection of ethnology and archaeology, including jewelry and meticulous beadwork. The exhibits are intelligently mounted, with texts in English and French, though the upstairs rooms are of narrower interest.

Cathédrale-Basilique Marie-Reine-du-Monde (Mary Queen of the World Cathedral). Bd. René-Lévesque (at Mansfield). ☎ 514/866-1661. Free admission; donations accepted. Mon–Fri 6:30am–7:30pm, Sat 7:30am–8:30pm, Sun 8:30am–7:30pm. Métro: Bonaventure.

No one who has seen both will confuse this with St. Peter's Basilica in Rome, but a scaled-down homage was the intention of its guiding force, Bishop Ignace Bourget, in the middle of the last century. He was moved to act after the first Catholic cathedral burned in 1852. Construction lasted from 1875 to 1894, delayed by his desire to place it not in the Francophone east but in the heart of the Protestant Anglophone west. The resulting church covers less than a quarter of the area of its Roman inspiration, and there are no curving arcades to embrace a sweeping plaza in front. The stairs to the entrance are only a few yards away from the boulevard. Most impressive is the 252-foot-high dome, about half the size of the original. A local touch is provided by the statues on the roofline, representing the region's patron saints. The interior is less visually rewarding than the exterior. A planned restoration is expected to cost at least $7.5 million.

Centre Canadien d'Architecture (CCA). 1920 rue Baile (at the corner of Fort). ☎ 514/939-7026. Admission C$5 (US$3.55) adults, C$3 (US$2.15) seniors and students, children under 12 free. June–Sept Tues–Wed and Fri–Sun 11am–6pm, Thurs 11am–9pm; Oct–May Wed and Fri–Sun 11am–5pm, Thurs 11am–9pm. Guided tours on request. Métro: Atwater, Guy-Concordia, or Georges-Vanier.

The understated but handsome CCA building fills a city block, joining a thoughtfully contemporary structure with the 1875 Shaughnessy House. The CCA doubles as a study center and a museum with changing exhibits devoted to the art of architecture and its history, including architects' sketchbooks, elevation drawings, and photography. The collection is international and encompasses architecture, urban planning, and landscape design. Texts are in French and English. The museum has received rave notices from scholars, critics, and serious architecture buffs. That said, it is only fair to note that the average visitor is likely to find it less than enthralling. Consequently, in 1997 the museum installed a temporary summer exhibit examining the designs of the Disney theme parks. The bookstore has a special section on Canadian architecture with emphasis on Montréal and Québec City. The sculpture garden across the Ville-Marie autoroute is part of the CCA, designed by artist/architect Melvin Charney.

Cathédrale Christ Church. 1444 Union Ave. (at Ste-Catherine and University). ☎ 514/843-6577 (office) or 514/288-6421 (recorded information). Free admission; donations accepted. Daily 8am–6pm; services Sun 8am, 10am, and 4pm. Métro: McGill.

This Anglican cathedral stands in glorious Gothic contrast to the city's glassy downtown skyscrapers, reflected in the postmodernist Maison des Coopérants office tower. Sometimes called the "floating cathedral" because of the many tiers of malls and corridors of the Underground City beneath it, the building was erected in 1859. The original steeple, too heavy for the structure, was replaced by a lighter aluminum version in 1940. Christ Church Cathedral hosts concerts throughout the year, notably from June to August on Wednesday at 12:30pm.

Musée d'Art Contemporain de Montréal (Museum of Contemporary Art). 185 rue Ste-Catherine ouest. ☎ **514/847-6226.** Admission C$6 (US$4.30) adults, C$4 (US$2.85) seniors, C$3 (US$2.15) students, C$12 (US$9) families; children under 12 free; free to all Wed 6–9pm. Tues and Thurs–Sun 11am–6pm, Wed 11am–9pm. Métro: Place-des-Arts.

The only museum in Canada devoted exclusively to contemporary art moved into this new facility at the Place-des-Arts in 1992 after years in an isolated riverfront building. "Contemporary" is defined here as art produced since 1939. It showcases the work of Québec and other Canadian artists but is supplemented by a collection of 3,400 works by such notables as Jean Dubuffet, Max Ernst, Jean Arp, Ansel Adams, Larry Poons, Antoni Tàpies, Max Ernst, Robert Mapplethorpe, and Montréal photographer Michel Campeau. A few larger pieces are on the ground floor, but most are one flight up, with space for temporary exhibits to the right and selections from the permanent collection on the left. No single style prevails, so expect to see minimalist installations small and large; video displays; evocations of Pop, Op, and abstract expressionism; and accumulations of objects simply piled on the floor. That the works often arouse strong opinions signifies a museum that's doing something right.

VIEUX-MONTREAL

Across the street from the Hôtel de Ville (see below) is the focus of summer activity in Vieux-Montréal: **place Jacques-Cartier,** between rues Notre-Dame and Commune. The most enchanting of the old city's squares has cobblestoned streets sloping down toward the port past ancient stone buildings that survive from the 1700s. Its outdoor cafes, street musicians, flower sellers, and horse-drawn carriages recall the Montréal of a century ago. Montréalers insist that they never go to a place so thronged by visitors, which begs the question of why so many of them congregate here. They take the sun and sip sangria on the bordering terraces on warm days, enjoying the unfolding pageant just as much as you will.

✪ Basilique Notre-Dame. 110 rue Notre-Dame ouest (on place d'Armes). ☎ **514/842-2925.** Basilica free; museum C$1 (US70¢) adults, C50¢ (US35¢) students. Basilica June 24–Labour Day daily 7am–8pm; rest of year daily 7am–6pm; tours mid-May to June 24 and Labour Day to mid-Oct Mon–Fri 9am–4pm (4:30pm in summer). Museum Sat–Sun 9:30am–4pm. Métro: Place d'Armes.

Big enough to hold 4,000 worshipers and breathtaking in the richness of its interior, this magnificent church was designed in 1829 by an Irish-American Protestant architect, James O'Donnell. He was so inspired by his work that he converted to Catholicism after it was done. He had good reason. None of the hundreds of churches on the island of Montréal approaches this interior in its wealth of exquisite detail, most of it carved from rare woods delicately gilded and painted. O'Donnell, one of the proponents the Gothic Revival style in the early middle decades of the 19th century, is the only person honored by burial in the crypt.

The main altar was carved from linden wood, the work of Victor Bourgeau. Behind it is the Chapel of the Sacred Heart, much of it destroyed by a deranged arsonist in 1978 but rebuilt and rededicated in 1982. It's such a popular place for weddings that couples have to book it a year and a half in advance. The chapel altar was cast in bronze by Charles Daudelin of Montréal, with 32 panels representing birth, life, and death. Next to the chapel is a bell, nicknamed Le Gros Bourdon, weighing more than 12 tons; it has a low, resonant rumble that vibrates right up through the feet and is tolled only on special occasions.

Vieux-Port (Old Port). Stretching along the waterfront from rue McGill to rue Berri. Interpretation center at 333 rue de la Commune ouest (at McGill). ☎ **514/496-7678.** Port and interpretation center free. Tram rides C$3.50 (US$2.50) adults, C$2.50 (US$1.80) seniors and students, C$1.50 (US$1.05) children under 13. Charges vary for other attractions. Interpretation center mid-May to early Sept daily 10am–9pm; hours for specific attractions vary. Métro: Champ-de-Mars, Place d'Armes, or Square-Victoria.

Since 1992, Montréal's once-dreary commercial wharf area has been transformed into an appealing 1.2-mile, 133-acre promenade and park with public spaces, exhibition halls, family activities, bike paths, and a permanent flea market. Cyclists, in-line skaters, joggers, strollers, lovers, and sunbathers all make use of the park in good weather. A variety of harbor cruises leaves from here. To get an idea of all there is to see and do, hop aboard the small Balade tram that travels throughout the port. During even-numbered years in spring, the acclaimed Cirque du Soleil sets up here under its bright yellow-and-blue big top. There's also a large-scale wraparound IMAX theater. At the far eastern end of the port is a clock tower built in 1922, with 192 steps leading past the exposed clockworks to observation decks at three levels (admission free). Most cruises, entertainment, and special events take place from mid-May to October, and information booths with bilingual attendants assist visitors during that period. Quadricycles, bicycles, and in-line skates are available for rent.

✪ Pointe-à-Callière (Montréal Museum of Archaeology and History). 350 place Royale (at the corner of Commune). ☎ **514/872-9150.** Admission C$8 (US$6) adults, C$5.50 (US$3.90) seniors, C$4 (US$2.85) students, C$2.50 (US$1.80) children 6–12, C$14 (US$10) families; children under 6 free. July–Aug Tues–Fri 10am–6pm, Sat–Sun 11am–6pm; Sept–June Tues–Fri 10am–5pm, Sat–Sun 11am–5pm. Métro: Place d'Armes.

A first visit to Montréal might best begin here. Built on the site where the original colony was established in 1642 (Pointe-à-Callière), the modern Museum of Archaeology and History engages you in rare and beguiling ways. Go first to the 16-minute multimedia show in an auditorium that actually stands above exposed ruins of the earlier city. Images pop up, drop down, and slide out on rolling screens accompanied by music and a playful bilingual narration that keeps the history slick and painless, with enough quick cuts and changes to keep even the youngest viewers from fidgeting.

Pointe-à-Callière was the point where the St-Pierre River merged with the St. Lawrence. Evidence of the many layers of occupation at this spot—from Amerindians to French trappers to Scottish merchants—were unearthed during archaeological digs that lasted for more than a decade. They're in display cases set among ancient building foundations and burial grounds below street level. The bottom shelves of the cabinets are for items dating from before 1600, and there are other shelves for consecutive centuries.

Wind your way through the complex until you find yourself in the dynamic new building you first entered, which echoes the triangular Royal Insurance building (1861) that stood there for many years. Its tower contains L'Arrivage cafe and provides a fine view of Old Montréal and the Old Port. At the end of the self-guided subterranean tour, in the Custom House, are more exhibits and a well-stocked gift shop. Allow at least an hour for a visit.

Hôtel de Ville (City Hall). 275 rue Notre-Dame (at the corner of Gosford). ☎ **514/ 872-3355.** Free admission. Daily 8:30am–4:30pm. Métro: Champ-de-Mars.

This is a relatively recent building by Old Montréal standards, finished in 1878. The French Second Empire design makes it look as though it had been imported from Paris. Balconies, turrets, and mansard roofs detail the exterior, seen at its best when illuminated at night. It was from the balcony above the awning that a bad-mannered Charles de Gaulle proclaimed, "Vive le Québec Libre!" in 1967, thereby straining relations with the federal Canadian government for years. Fifteen-minute guided tours are given throughout the day on weekdays May to October. The Hall of Honour is made of green marble from Campagna, Italy, with art-deco lamps from Paris and a bronze-and-glass chandelier from France that weighs a metric ton. In the display cabinet to the left by the elevator are gifts from mayors of other cities around the world. Council Chamber meetings, on the first floor, are open to the public. The chamber boasts a hand-carved ceiling and five stained-glass windows representing religion, the port, industry and commerce, finance, and transportation. The mayor's office is on the fourth floor.

Centre d'Histoire de Montréal. 335 place d'Youville (at St-Pierre). ☎ **514/872-3207.** Admission C$4.50 (US$3.20) adults, C$3 (US$2.15) students, children 6–17, and seniors; children under 6 free. Late Jan to early May and early Sept to mid-Dec Tues–Sun 10am–5pm; early May to mid-June daily 9am–5pm; mid-June to early Sept daily 10am–5pm. Closed mid-Dec to end of Dec. Métro: Square-Victoria.

Built in 1903 as Montréal's Central Fire Station, the redbrick-and-sandstone building is now the Montréal History Centre, tracing the city's history from the first Amerindians, to the European settlers who arrived in 1642, to the present day. Throughout its 14 rooms, carefully conceived presentations chart the contributions of the city fathers and mothers and subsequent generations. The development of the railroad, Métro, and related infrastructure are recalled, as is that of domestic and public architecture in imaginative exhibits, videos, and slide shows. On the second floor, reached by a spiral staircase, are memorabilia from the early 20th century. Labels are in French, so ask at the front desk for a visitor's guide in English. One or two rooms are given to temporary exhibits.

Eglise Notre-Dame-de-Bonsecours (Notre Dame de Bonsecours Chapel). 400 rue St-Paul (at the foot of Bonsecours). ☎ **514/282-8670.** Chapel free; museum C$5 (US$3.55) adults; fees for seniors, students, and children not set at press time. Chapel May–Oct daily 9am–5pm; Nov–Apr daily 10am–3pm. Museum May–Oct Tues–Sun 9am–4:30pm; Nov–Apr Tues–Sun 10:30am–2:30pm. Métro: Champ-de-Mars.

Just east of Marché Bonsecours (see below), this is called the Sailors' Church because of the wooden ship models hanging inside, given as votive offerings by fishers and other mariners. The first church, the project of an energetic teacher, Marguerite Bourgeoys, was built in 1678. She arrived with Maisonneuve to undertake the education of the children of Montréal in the latter half of the 17th century. Eventually, she and several sister teachers founded a nuns' order called the Congregation of Notre-Dame, Canada's first. The present church, dating from 1771 to 1773, has a small museum downstairs with 58 stage sets dedicated to her life and work. A carving of the Madonna has been displayed in both churches. Due to a theft, the carving now on view is a replica (the recovered original is locked up). The pioneering Bourgeoys was recognized as a saint in 1982. There's an excellent view of the harbor and the old quarter from the church's tower.

Marché Bonsecours. 350 rue St-Paul (at the foot of St-Claude). ☎ **514/872-4560.** Free admission. Daily 9am–5pm. Métro: Champ-de-Mars.

This imposing neoclassical building with a long facade, a colonnaded portico, and a silvery dome was built in the mid-1800s and first used as Montréal's City Hall, then for many years after 1878 as the central market. Restored in 1964, it housed city government offices; in 1992 it became the information and exhibition center for the celebration of the city's 350th birthday. It continues to be used as an exhibition space, and room has been made for shopping stalls. The architecture alone makes a visit worthwhile.

Musée du Château Ramezay. 280 rue Notre-Dame (east of place Jacques-Cartier). ☎ **514/861-3708.** Admission C$5 (US$3.55) adults, C$3 (US$2.15) seniors and students, C$10 (US$7) families; children under 6 free. June–Sept daily 10am–6pm; Oct–May Tues–Sun 10am–4:30pm. Métro: Champ-de-Mars.

Built by Gov. Claude de Ramezay in 1705, the château was the home of the city's royal French governors for 4 decades, before being taken over and used for the same purpose by the British conquerors. In 1775 an army of American revolutionaries invaded and held Montréal, using this as their headquarters. Benjamin Franklin, sent to persuade Québecers to rise with the colonists against British rule, stayed here for a time but failed to persuade the city's people to join his cause. After the American interlude, the château was used as a courthouse, a government office building, a teachers' college, and headquarters for Laval University before being converted into a museum in 1895. Old coins and prints, portraits, furnishings, tools, a loom, Amerindian artifacts, and other memorabilia related to the economic and social activities of the 18th century and first half of the 19th century fill the main floor. In the cellar are the original vaults of the house. Descriptive placards are in both French and English.

Musée Marc-Aurèle Fortin. 118 rue St-Pierre (at Youville). ☎ **514/845-6108.** Admission C$4 (US$2.85) adults, C$2 (US$1.40) seniors and students; children under 12 free. Tues–Sun 11am–5pm. Métro: Square-Victoria.

This is Montréal's only museum dedicated to the work of a single French-Canadian artist. Landscape watercolorist Marc-Aurèle Fortin (1888–1970) interpreted the beauty of the Québec countryside, such as the Laurentians and Charlevoix. His work is on the ground floor, while temporary exhibits usually feature the work of other Québec painters.

ELSEWHERE IN THE CITY

✪ **Biodôme de Montréal.** 4777 av. Pierre-de-Coubertin (next to Olympic Stadium). ☎ **514/868-3000.** Admission C$9.50 (US$7) adults, C$6.50 (US$4.65) seniors and students, C$4.75 (US$3.50) children 6–17; children under 6 free. Daily 9am–6pm (to 8pm in summer). Métro: Viau.

Near the Botanical Garden and next to the Olympic Stadium (see below) is the engrossing Biodôme, possibly the only environmental museum of its kind. Built as the velodrome for the 1976 Olympics, it has been refitted to house replications of four ecosystems: a Laurentian forest, the St. Lawrence ecosystem, a tropical rain forest, and a polar environment. They feature appropriate temperatures, flora, fauna, and changing seasons. With 4,000 creatures and 5,000 trees and plants, the Biodôme incorporates exhibits gathered from the old aquarium and the modest zoos at the Angrignon and Lafontaine parks. It also has a game room for kids called Naturalia, a shop, and a cafe.

Stade Olympique (Olympic Stadium). 4141 av. Pierre-de-Coubertin (at bd. Pie IX). ☎ **514/252-8687.** Funicular ride C$7.25 (US$5) adults, C$5.25 (US$3.75) students and children. Guided tours, recorded train tours, and a multimedia presentation are available. Public swim periods are scheduled daily, with low admission rates. Cable car mid-June to early Sept

Mon noon–9pm, Tues–Thurs 10am–9pm, Fri–Sat 10am–11pm; early Sept to mid-Jan and mid-Feb to mid-June Tues–Sun noon–6pm. Closed Tues off-season and closed mid-Jan to mid-Feb. Métro: Pie-IX or Viau (choose the Viau station for the guided tour).

Centerpiece of the 1976 Olympics, Montréal's controversial stadium and its associated facilities provide considerable opportunities for both active and passive diversion. It incorporates a natatorium with six pools, including one of competition dimensions with an adjustable bottom and a 50-foot-deep version for scuba diving. The stadium seats 60,000 to 80,000 spectators, who come here to see the Expos, the CFL Montréal Alouettes, rock concerts, and trade shows.

It has a 65-ton retractable Kevlar roof winched into place by 125 tons of steel cables attached to a 626-foot inclined tower that looms over the arena like an egret bobbing for fish in a bowl. When everything functions as was intended, it takes about 45 minutes to raise or lower the roof. In reality, the roof malfunctions frequently and high winds have torn large rents in the fabric. That's only one reason why what was first known as "The Big O" was scorned as "The Big Owe," after cost overruns led to heavy increases in taxes. A decision has been made to spend $37 million to construct a fixed Teflon roof.

The tower, which leans at a 45° angle, also does duty as an observation deck, with a funicular that whisks 90 passengers to the top in 95 seconds. On a clear day, the deck bestows a 35-mile view over Montréal and into the neighboring Laurentides. A free shuttle bus links the Olympic Park and the Botanical Garden.

La Biosphère. 160 chemin Tour-de-l'Isle (Ile Ste-Hélène). ☎ **514/283-5000.** Admission C$6.50 (US$4.65) adults, C$5 (US$3.55) seniors and students, C$4 (US$2.85) children 7–17, C$16 (US$11) families; children under 7 free. June–Sept daily 10am–8pm; Oct–May Tues–Sun 9am–6pm. Métro: Ile Ste-Hélène, then the shuttle bus.

Not to be confused with the Biodôme at Olympic Park, this new project is in the geodesic dome designed by Buckminster Fuller to serve as the American Pavilion for Expo '67. A fire destroyed the sphere's acrylic skin in 1976, and it served no purpose other than as a harbor landmark until 1995. The motivation behind the Biosphère is unabashedly environmental, with four exhibit areas, a water theater, and an amphitheater all devoted to promoting awareness of the St. Lawrence/Great Lakes ecosystem. Multimedia shows and hands-on displays invite active participation. In the highest point of the so-called Visions Hall is an observation level with an unobstructed river view. The Connections Hall offers a "Call to Action" presentation with six giant screens and three stages. There's a preaching-to-the-choir quality to all this that slips over the edge into zealous philosophizing. But the various displays and exhibits are put together thoughtfully and will divert and enlighten you, at least for a while.

Musée David M. Stewart. Vieux Fort, Ile Ste-Hélène. ☎ **514/861-6701.** Admission C$5 (US$3.55) adults, C$3 (US$2.15) seniors and students, C$10 (US$7) families; children under 7 free. Mid-May to Labour Day daily 10am–6pm; rest of year Wed–Mon 10am–5pm. Métro: Ile Ste-Hélène, then a 15-min walk.

After the War of 1812, the British prepared for a possible future American invasion by building this moated fortress. The duke of Wellington ordered its construction as another link in the chain of defenses along the St. Lawrence. Completed in 1824, it was never involved in armed conflict. The British garrison left in 1870, after confederation of the former Canadian colonies. Today the low stone barracks and blockhouses contain the museum, which displays maps and scientific instruments that helped Europeans explore the New World, as well as military and naval artifacts, uniforms, and related paraphernalia from the time of Jacques Cartier (1535) through the end of the colonial period.

From late June to late August, the fort comes to life with reenactments of military parades by La Compagnie Franche de la Marine and the 78th Fraser Highlanders, daily at 11am, 2:30pm, and 5pm. The presence of the French unit is an unhistorical sop to Francophone sensibilities, since New France had become English Canada almost 65 years before the fort was erected.

PLATEAU MONT-ROYAL

Musée de Hospitalières de l'Hôtel-Dieu de Montréal. 201 av. des Pins ouest. ☎ **514/849-2919.** Admission C$5 (US$3.55) adults, C$3 (US$2.15) seniors and students 12 and over. Mid-June to mid-Oct Tues–Fri 10am–5pm, Sat–Sun 1–5pm. Mid-Oct to mid-June Wed–Sun 1–5pm. Métro: Sherbrooke. Bus: 144.

Opened in 1992 to coincide with the city's 350th birthday, this unusual museum, in the former chaplain's residence of Hôtel-Dieu Hospital, traces the history of Montréal from 1659 to the present and focuses on the evolution of health care spanning 3 centuries in the history of the hospital, including an exhibit of medical instruments. It bows to missionary nurse Jeanne Mance, who arrived in 1642 and founded the first hospital, the only woman among the first settlers who left France with Maisonneuve. The museum's three floors are filled with memorabilia, including paintings, books, reliquaries, furnishings, and a reconstruction of a nun's cell. Its architectural high point is a marvelous "floating" oak staircase brought to the New World in 1634 from the Maison-Dieu hospital in La Flèche, France. The original Hôtel-Dieu was built in 1645 near the site of the present Notre-Dame, in Vieux-Montréal. This building was erected in 1861.

Oratoire St-Joseph (St. Joseph's Oratory). 3800 chemin Queen Mary (on the north slope of Mont Royal). ☎ **514/733-8211.** Free admission; donations requested at the museum. Daily 7am–9pm; museum daily 10am–5pm. The 56-bell carillon plays Wed–Fri noon–3pm, Sat–Sun noon–2:30pm. Métro: Côtes-des-Neiges.

This huge basilica, with its giant copper dome, was built by Québec's Catholics to honor St. Joseph, patron saint of Canada. Dominating the north slope of Mont Royal, its imposing dimensions are seen by some as inspiring, by others as forbidding. It came into being through the efforts of Brother André, a lay brother in the Holy Cross order who enjoyed a reputation as a healer. By the time he'd built a small wooden chapel in 1904 near the site of the basilica, he was said to have effected hundreds of cures. Those celebrated powers attracted supplicants from great distances, and Brother André performed his work until his death in 1937. His dream of building this shrine to his patron saint became a reality in 1967. He's buried in the basilica and was beatified by the pope in 1982, a status one step below sainthood.

The basilica is largely Italian Renaissance in style, its dome recalling the shape of Florence's Duomo, but of much greater size and less grace. Inside is a museum where a central exhibit is the heart of Brother André. Outside, a Way of the Cross lined with sculptures was the setting of scenes for the film *Jesus of Montréal.* Brother André's wooden chapel, with his tiny bedroom, are on the grounds and open to the public. Pilgrims, some ill, come to seek intercession from St. Joseph and Brother André, and often climb the middle set of steps on their knees. At 862 feet, the shrine is the highest point in Montréal. A cafeteria and snack bar are on the premises. Guided tours are offered at 10am and 2pm daily in summer and on weekends in September and October (donation only).

PARKS & GARDENS

✪ **Jardin Botanique (Botanical Garden).** 4101 rue Sherbrooke est (opposite Olympic Stadium). ☎ **514/872-1400.** Outside gardens, greenhouses, and Insectarium, May–Oct C$8.75

(US$6) adults, C$6.50 (US$4.65) seniors and students, C$4.50 (US$3.20) children 6–17; Nov–Apr C$6.50 (US$4.65) adults, C$5 (US$3.55) seniors and students, C$3.25 (US$2.30) children. A ticket for the Botanical Garden, Insectarium, and Biodôme, good for 2 consecutive days, C$14.75 (US$11) adults, C$11 (US$8) seniors, and C$7.50 (US$5) children. Daily 9am–5pm (to 8pm in summer). Métro: Pie-IX; walk up the hill to the gardens, or from mid-May to mid-Sept take the shuttle bus from Olympic Park (Métro: Viau).

This garden spreads across 180 acres. Begun in 1931, it has grown to include 26,000 types of plants in 31 specialized segments, ensuring something beautiful and fragrant year-round. Ten large conservatory greenhouses shelter tropical and desert plants, and bonsai and penjings, from the Canadian winter. One greenhouse, the Wizard of Oz, is especially fun for kids. Roses bloom here from mid-June to the first frost, May is for lilacs, and June is for flowering hawthorn trees. Inaugurated in 1991, the 6-acre **Chinese Garden,** a joint project of Montréal and Shanghai, is the largest of its kind ever built outside Asia, with pavilions, inner courtyards, ponds, and myriad plants indigenous to China. The serene **Japanese Garden** fills 15 acres and contains a cultural pavilion with an art gallery, a tearoom where the ancient tea ceremony is observed, and a Zen garden. The grounds are also home to the **Insectarium,** displaying some of the world's most beautiful insects, not to mention some of its sinister ones (see "Especially for Kids," below). Birders should bring along binoculars on summer visits to spot some of the more than 130 species that spend at least part of the year in the Botanical Garden. In summer, an outdoor aviary is filled with Québec's most beautiful butterflies. Year-round, a free shuttle bus links the Botanical Garden and nearby Olympic Park; a small train runs regularly through the gardens and is worth the small fee charged.

Parc du Mont-Royal. ☎ 514/844-4928 (general information) or 514/872-6559 (special events). Daily 6am–midnight. Métro: Mont-Royal. Bus: No. 11; hop off at Lac des Castors.

Montréal is named for the 761-foot hill that rises at its heart—the "Royal Mountain." Joggers, cyclists, dog walkers, and others use it religiously. On Sundays hundreds of folks congregate around the statue of George-Etienne Cartier to listen and sometimes dance to improvised music, and Lac des Castors (Beaver Lake) is surrounded by sunbathers and picnickers in summer (no swimming allowed). In winter, cross-country skiers follow the miles of paths, snowshoers tramp along trails laid out for them, and there's a tow for the short downhill run above the lake. In the cold months, the lake fills with whirling ice-skaters. The large refurbished Chalet Lookout near the crest of the hill provides a sweeping view of the city and an opportunity for a snack. Up the hill behind the chalet is the spot where, tradition has it, Maisonneuve erected his wooden cross in 1642. Today the cross is a 100-foot-high steel structure rigged for illumination at night and visible from all over the city. Park security is provided by mounted police. On the northern slope of the mountain are three cemeteries—Catholic, Protestant, and Jewish.

Parc Lafontaine. Rue Sherbrooke and av. Parc Lafontaine. ☎ 514/872-2644. Free admission; small fee for use of tennis courts. Daily 24 hours. Tennis courts, daily 9am–10pm in summer. Métro: Sherbrooke.

The European-style park near downtown is one of the city's oldest. In testament to the dual identities of the populace, half the park is landscaped in the formal French manner, the other in the more casual English style. Among its several bodies of water is a lake used for paddle-boating in summer and ice-skating in winter. Snowshoeing and cross-country trails curl through the trees. The amphitheater is the setting for free outdoor theater and movies in summer. Joggers, bikers, picnickers, and tennis buffs (there are 14 outdoor courts) share the space.

ESPECIALLY FOR KIDS

IMAX Theatre. Old Port, quai King Edward (end of bd. St-Laurent). ☎ **514/349-4629** (shows and times). Admission C$11.95 (US$9) adults, C$9.75 (US$7) seniors and students, C$7.50 (US$5) children 4–11, C$33.95 (US$24) families (4 people); double feature plus laser show C$13 (US$9) all ages. Year-round. Call for current schedule of shows in English. Métro: Place d'Armes.

The images and special effects are larger-than-life, sometimes in 3-D and always visually dazzling, thrown on a seven-story screen. Recent films made the most of the Andrettis racing Indy cars and cameras swooping low over Alaskan wildlife and glaciers. Running time is usually under an hour. Arrive for shows at least 10 minutes before starting time, earlier on weekends and evenings.

Insectarium. In the Botanical Garden, 4101 rue Sherbrooke (at bd. Pie IX). ☎ **514/872-1400.** May–Oct C$7 (US$5) adults, C$6.50 (US$4.65) seniors, C$4.50 (US$3.20) children 6–17; Nov–Apr C$6.50 (US$4.65) adults, C$5 (US$3.55) seniors, C$3.25 (US$2.30) children. Summer daily 9am–7pm; rest of year daily 9am–5pm. Métro: Pie-IX; walk up the hill to the gardens or in summer take the shuttle bus from Olympic Park (Métro: Viau).

A recent addition to the Botanical Garden, this bilevel structure near the Sherbrooke gate exhibits the collections of two avid entomologists: Georges Brossard (whose brainchild this place is) and Father Firmia Liberté. More than 3,000 mounted butterflies, scarabs, maggots, locusts, beetles, tarantulas, and giraffe weevils are displayed, and live exhibits feature scorpions, tarantulas, crickets, cockroaches, and praying mantises. Of course, kids are delighted by the creepy critters. Their guardians are apt to be less enthusiastic, except in summer in the Butterfly House, when beautiful live specimens flutter among the nectar-bearing plants.

La Ronde Amusement Park. Parc des Iles, Ile Ste-Hélène. ☎ **800/361-8020** or 514/872-6222. Unlimited all-day pass C$23.04 (US$16) 12 and over, C$11.41 (US$8) under 12, C$50.90 (US$36) family. Reserved seating for fireworks, from C$24.57 (US$18) including all rides. Ground admission only C$11.85 (US$8); parking C$7.02 (US$5). Mid-May to late June daily 10am–9pm; late June to Labour Day Sun–Thurs 11am–11pm, Fri–Sat 11am–midnight. Métro: Papineau and bus no. 169, or Ile Ste-Hélène and bus no. 167.

Montréal's ambitious amusement park fills the northern reaches of Ile Ste-Hélène with more than 30 rides, an international circus, a medieval village, roller coasters, and places to eat and drink. Thrill-seekers will love Le Boomerang, Le Monstre, and Le Cobra (a stand-up roller coaster that incorporates a 360° loop and reaches speeds in excess of 97 kmph/60 m.p.h.). A big attraction every year is the International Fireworks Competition, held on Saturdays in June and Sundays in July (postponed in bad weather). The pyromusical displays are launched at 10pm and last at least 30 minutes. (Some Montréalers choose to watch them from the Jacques Cartier Bridge, which is closed to traffic then. Take along a Walkman to listen to the accompanying music.)

Planetarium de Montréal. 1000 rue St-Jacques (at Peel). ☎ **514/872-4530.** Admission C$5.50 (US$3.90) adults, C$4 (US$2.85) seniors and students, C$2.75 (US$1.95) children 6–17. Jan 29 to mid-June and Labour Day to Dec 18 Tues–Sun 2:30–7:15pm; mid-June to Labour Day, Dec 24, and Jan 2–8 daily 2:30–7:15pm. Métro: Bonaventure (Cathédrale exit).

A window on the night sky with its mythical monsters and magical heroes, Montréal's planetarium is downtown, 2 blocks south of Windsor Station. Changing shows under the 65-foot dome dazzle and inform kids at the same time. Shows change with the seasons, exploring time and space travel and collisions of celestial bodies. The Christmas show in December and early January, "Star of the Magi," is based on recent investigations by historians and astronomers into the mysterious light that guided the Magi. Shows in English alternate with those in French.

6 Special Events & Festivals

Montréal's answer to Québec City's Winter Carnival is February's **La Fête des Neiges** (Snow Festival), with events like harness racing, barrel jumping, racing beds on ice, canoe racing, snowshoeing, skating, and cross-country skiing. The less athletically inclined can cheer from the sidelines, then inspect the snow and ice sculptures. It's held mostly on Ile Notre-Dame, in the Port and Vieux-Montréal, and in Parc Maisonneuve. Call ☎ **514/872-6093** for details.

Early in June, some 45,000 biking enthusiasts converge on Montréal to participate in a grueling daylong race before more than 120,000 spectators. **La Tour de l'Ile de Montréal,** which began in 1984, attracts almost as many women as men. Call ☎ **514/847-8356** for details.

Screenings of new and experimental films stimulate controversy and forums on the latest trends in film and video at halls and cinemas throughout the city in June at the **International Festival of Cinema and New Media** (☎ **514/843-4711**).

International Formula I drivers burn rubber around the Gilles-Villeneuve racetrack on Ile Notre-Dame for the running of the **Molson Grand Prix of Canada,** held the second weekend in June. Call ☎ **514/350-0000** for details.

St-Jean Baptiste Day (June 24) honors St. John the Baptist, the patron saint of French Canadians. It's marked by more festivities and far more enthusiasm throughout Québec Province than national Dominion Day on July 1. It's their "national" holiday.

Montréal boasts a long jazz tradition, and its enormously successful **Festival International de Jazz** has been celebrating it since 1979. Major stars have headlined over the years, but it costs money to hear the big names. Fortunately, hundreds of other concerts are free, often given on the streets and plazas. The festival runs from late June to early July; for information and tickets, call ☎ **888/515-0515,** operator 11. You can reserve seats through Ticketron.

The **Just for Laughs Festival** almost equals the more famous jazz festival in magnitude. It even gave rise to the opening of a humor museum. More than 650 comics perform in many venues, some for free, some not. Among them have been such stars as Tim Allen, Jerry Seinfeld, Lily Tomlin, and Jim Carrey. Francophone and Anglophone comics from 14 countries participate. It's held along rue St-Denis and rue de Maisonneuve in the last 2 weeks of July. Call ☎ **514/845-3155** for details.

The open-air theater in La Ronde amusement park on Ile Ste-Hélène is the best place to view the pyrotechnics of the **Benson & Hedges International Fireworks Competition,** though they can be enjoyed from almost any point overlooking the river. Tickets to the show also provide entrance to the amusement park. Kids love the whole explosive business. The 90-minute shows are staged by companies from several countries. Since parking is limited, it's best to use the Métro. It's held Saturdays in June, but different days in July. Bad weather postpones performances. Call ☎ **514/935-5161** for details.

Late August brings the **World Film Festival,** with some 500 screenings over 12 days, drawing the usual throngs of directors, stars, and wanna-bes. It isn't as gaudy as Cannes, but it's taken almost as seriously. Various movie theaters play host. Call ☎ **514/933-9699** for details.

The **International Festival of New Dance** is a 12-day showcase that invites troupes and choreographers from Canada, the United States, and Europe to various performance spaces in mid-October. Call ☎ **514/287-1423** for details.

7 Outdoor Activities & Spectator Sports

OUTDOOR ACTIVITIES

BICYCLING   Cycling is hugely popular, and Montréal enjoys a network of 240 kilometers (149 miles) of paths. Heavily used routes are the 11-kilometer (6.8-mile) path along the Lachine Canal leading to Lac St-Louis, the 16-kilometer (10-mile) path west from the St-Lambert Lock to the city of Côte Ste-Catherine, and Angrignon Park with its 6.5-kilometer (4-mile) path and inviting picnic areas (take the Métro, which accepts bikes in the last two doors of the last car, to Angrignon station). You can rent bikes at the Vieux-Port (at the end of boulevard St-Laurent) for C$6.50 to C$7 (US$4.65 to US$5) per hour or C$20 to C$22 (US$14 to US$16) per day. **Velo Aventure** on quai King Edward is a principal source (see also "In-Line Skating," below). You can rent bikes, along with the popular four-wheel Q Cycles, at the place Jacques-Cartier entrance to the Old Port. The Q Cycles, for use in the Old Port only, are C$4.25 (US$3) per half an hour for adults and C$3.50 (US$2.50) per half an hour for children.

CROSS-COUNTRY SKIING   Parc Mont-Royal has a 2.1-kilometer (1.3-mile) cross-country course called the *parcours de la croix*. The Botanical Garden has an ecology trail used by cross-country skiers. The problem for either is that you have to supply your own equipment. Just an hour from the city, in the Laurentides, are almost 20 ski centers, all offering cross-country as well as downhill skiing. See chapter 9.

HIKING   The most popular—and obvious—hike is up to the top of Mont Royal. Start downtown on rue Peel, which leads north to a stairway, which in turn leads to a half-mile path of switchbacks called Le Serpent. Or opt for the 200 steps that lead up to the Chalet Lookout, with the reward of a panoramic view of the city. Figure about 1¼ miles one-way.

IN-LINE SKATING   Over 230 pairs of in-line skates and all the relevant protective gear can be rented from **Velo Aventure** (☎ 514/847-0666) on quai King Edward in the Vieux-Port. The cost is C$8.50 (US$6) weekdays or C$9 (US$6) weekends for the first hour and C$4 (US$2.85) for each additional hour. A deposit is required. Lessons on skates are available for C$25 (US$18) for 2 hours.

JOGGING   There are many possibilities. One is to follow rue Peel north to Le Serpent switchback path on Mont Royal, continuing uphill on it for 800 meters (half a mile) until it peters out. Turn right and continue 2 kilometers (1 mile) to the monument of George-Etienne Cartier. From here, either take a bus back downtown or run back down the same route or along avenue du Parc and avenue des Pins (turn right when you get to it). It's also fun to jog along the Lachine Canal.

SWIMMING   Alas, the St. Lawrence is too polluted for swimming. Bordering the river, though, is the artificial **Plage de l'Ile Notre-Dame** (☎ 514/872-6093), the former Regatta Lake from Expo '67. The water is drawn from the Lachine Rapids and treated by a mostly natural filtration system of sand, aquatic plants, and ultraviolet light (and a bit of chlorine) to make it safe for swimming. The cost is C$7 (US$5) for adults, seniors, and students and C$2.50 (US$1.80) for children 6 to 17. To get there, take the Métro to the Ile Ste-Hélène station.

   If you prefer a pool but are staying in a hotel that doesn't have one, you can take the Métro to Viau station and **Olympic Park,** 4141 Pierre-de-Coubertin (☎ 514/252-4622), which has six pools, open Monday to Friday from about 9:30am to 9pm and Saturday and Sunday from 1 to 4pm. Call ahead to confirm swim schedules, which are affected by competitions and holidays.

The Great American Pastime Goes North

U.S. broadcast networks and the team owners of Major League Baseball suffer night sweats over worse things than labor strife and laws banning the sale of beer in their stadiums. It's the terror of a World Series featuring the Toronto Blue Jays or the Montréal Expos (or—quelle calamité!—*both*) that truly keeps them up at night.

Ratings plummet whenever a playoff game takes place in either of those cities, as happened with Toronto in the early 1990s. When colorless teams from undesirably small TV markets in the Midwest match up, network executives shrug their shoulders and comfort themselves with a resigned, "At least they ain't Canadians."

This is unfortunate, for Canadians are as enthusiastic about the American game as anyone else—at least after their national religion, hockey, is taken into account. Even though there's the ever-present possibility of games being called off on account of snow, professional baseball has been a fixture in Montréal (off and on, admittedly) since the last century. The Expos were preceded by the Royals, who played their first game in 1828 in the Eastern League. There was a gap from 1916 to 1928. Then the Royals were reincarnated in the International League as a triple-A farm club associated with the Brooklyn Dodgers. They signed Jackie Robinson in 1945, 2 years before Branch Rickey brought him up to The Show. Robinson paid off handsomely: In his first game for the Royals, he hit a three-run homer, scored four times, and stole two bases.

Many of the game's greats have passed through Montréal—usually on their climb up, sometimes on their way down. Walter Alston managed them in the 1950s, and his and other Royals teams of the postwar era had batting orders that included, however briefly, Don Newcombe, Bobby Morgan, Junior Gilliam, Gil Hodges, Roy Campanella, Chuck Connors (yes, the actor), and a pitcher named Tommy Lasorda.

The Royals expired for good in the early 1960s but were followed by the Expos in 1969, named for the 1967 World's Fair held in Montréal and now housed in a stadium built for the 1976 Olympics (though it's a notoriously bad place to see a game and has terrible turf). Persistent success hasn't been their lot, but they, too, have had their favorite stars. When red-headed Rusty Staub was playing, Montréalers gave him the nickname "Le Grand Orange."

The **City of Montréal Department of Sports and Leisure** (☎ 514/872-6211) can provide information about other city pools, indoor or out. Admission to the pools varies from free to about C$4 (US$2.85) for adults or C$2 (US$1.40) for children, with the exception of the Plage de l'Ile Notre-Dame (see above).

SPECTATOR SPORTS

Montréalers are as devoted to ice hockey as other Canadians, with plenty of enthusiasm left over for baseball and soccer. There are several prominent annual sporting events of other kinds, such as the Molson Grand Prix in June, the Player's Ltd. International men's tennis championship in late July, and the Montréal Marathon in September.

BASEBALL The **Montréal Expos,** part of the National League, continue to play at Stade olympique (Olympic Stadium), 4549 Pierre-de-Coubertin (Métro: Pie-IX), from April to September. You can make ticket reservations by phone, with a credit card, by calling ☎ 514/790-1245. Tickets start at C$5 (US$3.55) for general admission.

FOOTBALL   Canadian professional football returned to Montréal after a 3-year experiment with U.S. teams. What was briefly the Baltimore Colts is now the **Montréal Alouettes.** The CFL team plays at the Stade olympique (Olympic Stadium) on a schedule that runs from June to September. Call for information at ☎ 514/254-2400.

HOCKEY   The NHL's **Montréal Canadiens** play at the new Centre Molson at 1260 rue de la Gauchetière (Métro: Bonaventure), replacing the beloved old Forum. They've won 24 Stanley Cup championships since 1929. The season runs from October to April, with playoffs continuing to mid-June. Tickets are about C$15 to C$94 (US$11 to US$67). You can get ticket and schedule information by calling ☎ 514/932-2582.

HORSE RACING   Popularly known as Blue Bonnets Racetrack, the **Hippodrome de Montréal** at 7440 bd. Décarie, in Jean-Talon (☎ 514/739-2741; Métro: Namur, then take the shuttle bus), is the host facility for international harness-racing events, including the Coupe des Elevers (Breeders Cup). Restaurants, bars, a snack bar, and pari-mutuel betting can make for a satisfying evening or Sunday-afternoon outing. There are no races on Tuesday and Thursday. General admission is free, but the VIP section costs C$5 (US$3.55). Races begin at 7:30pm on Monday, Wednesday, Friday, and Saturday and at 1:30pm on Sunday.

8 Shopping

THE SHOPPING SCENE

You'll find much to delight you in Montréal. Its bubbling fashion industry, from couture to ready-to-wear, enjoys a history that reaches back to the earliest trade in furs and leather. Beyond that, it's unlikely that any reasonable need can't be met here. After all, there are some 1,500 shops in the Underground City alone, plus many more than that at street level and above.

MAJOR SHOPPING STREETS   Try **rue Sherbrooke** for fashion, art, and luxury items, including furs and jewelry. **Rue Crescent** has a number of scattered upscale boutiques, while funkier **boulevard St-Laurent** covers everything from budget practicalities to off-the-wall designer clothing. Look along **rue Laurier** between St-Laurent and de l'Epée for home-furnishings stores and young Québécois designers. **Rue St-Paul** in Vieux-Montréal has a growing number of art galleries. At least 35 antique stores line **rue Notre-Dame** between Guy and Atwater. **Rue Ste-Catherine** near Christ Church Cathedral has most of the major department stores and myriad satellite shops, while **rue Peel** is known for men's fashions and some crafts. As in many cities, some of the best shops in Montréal are in its museums, tops among them being Pointe-à-Callière in Vieux-Montréal as well as the Museum of Fine Arts and the McCord Museum, both on rue Sherbrooke in the city center.

EXCHANGE RATES   Some stores put out signs offering better exchange rates to attract customers carrying U.S. funds. If you pay with a credit card, however, you're likely to get the best deal (provided that the exchange rate doesn't drop precipitously after your visit). Your credit-card company will convert the charges from Canadian into U.S. dollars based on the actual exchange rate posted on the day they process your transaction. Visa and MasterCard are the most popular bank cards in this part of Canada; Discover is rarely accepted by shops, and American Express reluctantly.

TAXES & REFUNDS   Save your sales receipts from any store in Montréal or the rest of Québec and ask shopkeepers for tax-refund forms. After returning home, mail the originals (not copies) to the specified address with the completed form. Refunds usually take a few months but are in the currency of your home country. A small service fee is charged. For faster refunds, follow the same procedure but hand in the receipts and form at a duty-free shop designated in the government pamphlet *Goods and Services Tax Refund for Visitors,* available at tourist offices and in many stores and hotels.

SHOPPING A TO Z

ANTIQUES   The best places to shop for antiques and collectibles are in the over 2 score storefronts clustered along **rue Notre-Dame** between rues Guy and Atwater. Or visit **Antiques Puces Libres,** 4240 rue St-Denis, near Rachel (☎ **514/842-5931;** Métro: Mont-Royal), where three fascinatingly cluttered floors are packed with pine and oak furniture, lamps, clocks, vases, and more, most of it late-19th- and early-20th-century French-Canadian art nouveau.

ARTS & CRAFTS   Founded more than 50 years ago, the **Dominion Gallery,** 1438 rue Sherbrooke ouest, at Bishop (☎ **514/845-7471;** Métro: Guy), features both international and Canadian painting and sculpture in 14 rooms spread over four floors. A choice collection of craft items is displayed in a gallery setting at the **Guilde Canadienne des Métiers d'Art Québec,** 2025 rue Peel, at Maisonneuve (☎ **514/ 849-6091;** Métro: Peel). Among the objects are blown glass, paintings on silk, pewter, tapestries, and ceramics. The stock is particularly strong in jewelry and Inuit sculpture. **L'Empreinte,** 272 rue St-Paul est, Vieux-Montréal (☎ **514/861-4427;** Métro: Champ de Mars), is a craftpersons' collective, a block off place Jacques-Cartier. The ceramics, textiles, glassware, and other items often occupy that vaguely defined borderland between art and craft. The quality is uneven.

BOOKS   The superchain of which this flagship store, **Chapters,** 1171 rue Ste-Catherine ouest (☎ **514/849-8825;** Métro: Guy), is a unit was a result of a merger between the Smithbooks and Coles booksellers. Thousands of titles are available in both French and English. At the large **Museum of Fine Arts Bookstore,** 1380 rue Sherbrooke ouest, near Bishop (☎ **514/285-1600,** ext. 350; Métro: Guy), next to the new museum annex, you'll find books on art, gardens, fashion, interior design, cooking, and biographies, as well as folk art and reproductions. The needs of travelers are served by the good stock of guidebooks and maps (many in English) at **Ulysse,** 4176 rue St-Denis (☎ **514/843-9447**) and 560 av. du Président-Kennedy (☎ **514/ 843-7222**). It also sells accessories like maps, day packs, money pouches, electrical adapters, and coffeemakers.

CLOTHING   For Men   One of the many links in a popular Canadian chain, **America,** 1101 Ste-Catherine ouest, at Stanley (☎ **514/289-9609;** Métro: Guy or Peel), carries both casual and dressy clothes. There's a women's section upstairs. At **Brisson & Brisson,** 1472 rue Sherbrooke ouest, near MacKay (☎ **514/937-7456;** Métro: Guy), apparel of the nipped and trim British and European schools fill three floors, from makers as diverse as Burberry, Brioni, and Valentino. Armani and Hugo Boss styles prevail at **Club Monsieur,** 1407 rue Crescent, near Maisonneuve (☎ **514/843-5476;** Métro: Guy), for those with the fit bodies to carry them, as well as the required discretionary income.

For Women   Sonia Kozma designs the fashions at **Ambre,** 201 rue St-Paul ouest, at place Jacques-Cartier (☎ **514/982-0325;** Métro: Champ de Mars), including suits, cocktail dresses, and dinner and casual wear made of linen, rayon, and cotton. Browse at **Artefact,** 4117 rue St-Denis, near Rachel (☎ **514/842-2780;** Métro:

Mont-Royal), among articles of clothing and paintings by up-and-coming Québécois designers and artists, as well as garments imported from Nepal and Indonesia. **Kyoze,** Centre Mondial du Commerce, 393 rue St-Jacques ouest, 2nd floor (☎ 514/ 847-7572; Métro: Champ de Mars), features the eye-catching creations of Québécois and other Canadian designers, including jewelry and accessories.

For Men & Women The British origins of the updated **Marks & Spencer,** place Montréal Trust, 1500 av. McGill College, at Ste-Catherine (☎ 514/499-8558; Métro: Peel or McGill), grow less obvious as it spreads over several continents, but the clothing still represents a favorable price-to-value ratio. It also sells quality foods and confections. At **Polo Ralph Lauren,** 1290 rue Sherbrooke, near Montagne (☎ 514/288-3988; Métro: Guy), the international designer has set up shop in a town house in the poshest part of town, near the Ritz-Carlton. Apparel for the well-heeled family is what you'll find.

DEPARTMENT STORES Most department stores are located along a 12-block strip of **rue Ste-Catherine** (except for Holt Renfrew), from rue Guy eastward to Carré Phillips at Aylmer. Most of the stores below have branches elsewhere.

Since 1925, **Eaton,** 677 rue Ste-Catherine ouest, at Alymer (☎ 514/284-8411; Métro: McGill), has offered a conventional range of middle-of-the-road goods at reasonable prices. It's also Montréal's largest store and is connected to the 225-shop Eaton Centre, a shopping mall that's part of the Underground City. The beautiful **Henry Birks et Fils,** 1240 Carré Phillips, at Union (☎ 514/397-2511; Métro: McGill), with its dark-wood display cases, stone pillars, and marble floors, is a living part of Montréal's Victorian heritage. The merchandise encompasses jewelry, pens and desk accessories, watches, leather goods, glassware, and china. **Holt Renfrew,** 1300 rue Sherbrooke ouest, at Montagne (☎ 514/842-5111; Métro: Guy or Peel), is a showcase of international style for men and women, offering prestigious names like Armani, Gucci, and Lagerfeld. The firm began as a furrier in 1837. No retailer has a more celebrated name than the 300-year-old Hudson's Bay Company, shortened in Québec to **La Baie** (The Bay), 585 rue Ste-Catherine ouest, near Aylmer (☎ 514/281-4422; Métro: McGill). The main store emphasizes clothing but also offers crystal, china, and Inuit carvings. Its Canadiana Boutique features famous Hudson's Bay blankets.

A FLEA MARKET In the Vieux-Port, a few steps from place Jacques-Cartier, the **Marché aux Puces,** at bd. St-Laurent (☎ 514/843-5949; Métro: Champ de Mars), is an old dockside warehouse that has been divided into stalls where vendors sell collectibles; knickknacks; jewelry; odd lots; new, used, and antique furniture; new and vintage clothing; souvenirs; tools; and junk. Hours change frequently, but from spring to fall it's usually open Monday to Friday from 11am to 7pm and Saturday and Sunday from 11am to 10pm. Call before making a special trip.

9 Montréal After Dark

Montréal's reputation for effervescent nightlife stretches back to the 13-year experiment with Prohibition south of the border. A fortune was made by Canadian distillers and brewers, not much of it legal, and Americans streamed here for temporary relief from alcohol deprivation. That the city enjoyed a sophisticated and slightly naughty reputation as the Paris of North America added to the allure.

Nightclubbing and barhopping remain popular, with much later hours than those of archrival Toronto, still in thrall to Calvinist notions of propriety and early bedtimes.

Montréalers' nocturnal pursuits are often as cultural as they are social. The city boasts its own outstanding symphony, French- and English-speaking theater companies, and the incomparable Cirque du Soleil (Circus of the Sun). It's also on the standard concert circuit that includes Chicago, Boston, and New York, so internationally known entertainers, rock bands, orchestra conductors and virtuosos, and ballet and modern dance companies pass through frequently.

In summer, the city becomes livelier than usual with several enticing events: the **Festival de Théâtre des Amériques** (late May), the **Benson & Hedges International Fireworks Competition** (mid-June), the ✪ **International Jazz Festival** (early July), and the ✪ **Just for Laughs Festival** (late July). And every year, in late September or early October, a **Festival International de Nouvelle Danse** is held, attracting modern-dance troupes and choreographers from around the world.

For details concerning current performances or special events, pick up a free copy of *Montréal Scope,* a weekly ads-and-events booklet, at any large hotel reception desk, or the free weekly newspapers *Mirror* (in English) or *Voir* (in French). Place des Arts puts out a monthly calendar of events, *Calendrier des Spectacles,* describing concerts and performances to be held in the various halls of the performing-arts complex. You can find these publications in most large hotels or near the box offices in Place des Arts. Montréal's newspapers, the French-language *La Presse* and the English *Gazette,* carry listings of films, clubs, and performances in their Friday and Saturday editions.

Concentrations of pubs and nightclubs underscore the city's linguistic dichotomy, too. While there's a great deal of mingling between the two cultures, the parallel blocks of rue Crescent, rue Bishop, and rue de la Montagne north of rue Ste-Catherine have a pronounced Anglophone character, while Francophones dominate the Latin Quarter, with college-age patrons most evident along the lower reaches of rue St-Denis and their yuppie elders gravitating to the nightspots of more uptown blocks of the same street. Vieux-Montréal, especially along rue St-Paul, has a more universal quality, where many of the bars and clubs feature live jazz, blues, and folk music. In the Plateau Mont-Royal area, boulevard St-Laurent, parallel to St-Denis, known locally as "The Main," has become a miles-long haven of chic restaurants and clubs, roughly from avenue Viger to St-Viatur. St-Laurent is a good place to end up in the wee hours, as there's always some place with the welcome mat still out.

THE PERFORMING ARTS
THEATER

The annual **Festival de Théâtre des Amériques** is an opportunity to see dramatic and musical stage productions that are international in scope, not simply North American. There have been works from Vietnam and China as well as from Canada, the United States, and Mexico. The plays are performed in the original languages, as a rule, with simultaneous translations in French and/or English, when appropriate. For information, call ☎ 514/842-0704.

Centaur Theatre. 453 rue St-François-Xavier (near rue Notre-Dame). ☎ **514/288-3161.** Tickets C$20–C$30 (US$14–US$21) adults, C$16 (US$11) students, C$12 (US$9) seniors. Métro: Place d'Armes.

The former Stock Exchange (1903) is now home to Montréal's principal English-language theater. A mix of classics, foreign adaptations, and works by Canadian playwrights is presented. Off-season, the theater is rented out to other groups, both French- and English-speaking. Performances are held October to June, Tuesday to Saturday at 8pm, Sunday at 7pm, and Saturday (and most Sundays) at 2pm.

Saidye Bronfman Centre for the Arts. 5170 Côte-Ste-Catherine (near Décarie). ☎ **514/ 739-2301** (information), 514/739-7944 or 514/739-4816 (tickets). Tickets C$25–C$45 (US$18– US$32) adults, C$15–C$20 (US$11–US$14) seniors and students. Métro: Côte-Ste-Catherine. Bus: 129 ouest.

Montréal's Yiddish Theater was founded in 1937 and is housed in the Saidye Bronfman Centre, not far from St. Joseph's Oratory. It stages two plays a year in Yiddish, and they run for 3 to 4 weeks, usually in June and October. At other times, the 300-seat theater hosts dance and music recitals, a bilingual puppet festival, occasional lectures, and three English-language plays. Across the street, in the Edifice Cummings House, is a small Holocaust museum and the Jewish Public Library. The center takes its name from philanthropist Saidye Bronfman, widow of Samuel Bronfman, who was a founder of the Seagram Company. She died in 1995 at age 98.

The box office is usually open Monday to Thursday from 11am to 8pm and Sunday from noon to 7pm—call ahead. Performances are held Tuesday to Thursday at 8pm and Sunday at 1:30 and 7pm.

DANCE

Frequent appearances by notable dancers and troupes from other parts of Canada and the world augment the accomplished local company, among them Paul Taylor, the Feld Ballet, and Le Ballet National du Canada. During summer, the native company often performs at the outdoor Théâtre de Verdure in Parc Lafontaine. In winter, they're scheduled at venues around the city, but especially in the several halls at the Place des Arts. The fall season is kicked off by the inevitably provocative **Festival International de Nouvelle Danse,** in early October.

✪ **Les Grands Ballets Canadiens.** Salle Wilfrid-Pelletier in Place des Arts, 200 bd. de Maisonneuve ouest. ☎ **514/849-8681.** Tickets C$12–C$40 (US$9–US$29). Métro: Place-des-Arts.

This prestigious company has developed a following far beyond national borders over more than 35 years, performing both classical and modern repertory. In the process, it has brought prominence to many gifted Canadian choreographers and composers. The troupe's production of *The Nutcracker Suite* is always a big event in Montréal the last couple of weeks in December. The box office is open Monday to Saturday from noon to 8pm. Performances are held from late October to early May at 8pm.

CLASSICAL MUSIC & OPERA

L'Opéra de Montréal. Salle Wilfrid-Pelletier in Place des Arts, 260 bd. de Maisonneuve ouest. ☎ **514/985-2222** (information) or 514/985-2258 (tickets). Tickets usually C$30–C$94 (US$21–US$67). Métro: Place-des-Arts.

Founded in 1980, this outstanding opera company mounts seven productions a year in Montréal, with artists from Québec and abroad participating in such productions as *Madame Butterfly, Il Trovatore, Faust,* and *La Nozze di Figaro.* Video translations are provided from the original languages into French and English. The box office is open Monday to Friday from 9am to 5pm. Performances are held from September to June, usually at 8pm, in three theaters at Place des Arts and occasionally other venues.

✪ **Orchestre Métropolitan de Montréal.** Maisonneuve Theatre in Place des Arts, 260 bd. de Maisonneuve ouest. ☎ **514/598-0870.** Tickets C$15–C$30 (US$11–US$21). Métro: Place-des-Arts.

This orchestra has a regular season at Place des Arts but also performs in St-Jean-Baptiste church and tours regionally. Most of the musicians are in their mid-30s or younger. The box office is open Monday to Saturday from noon to 8pm.

Performances are held from mid-October to early April, usually at 8pm. Outdoor concerts are given in Parc Lafontaine in August.

○ **Orchestre Symphonique de Montréal.** Salle Wilfrid-Pelletier in Place des Arts, 260 bd. de Maisonneuve ouest. ☎ **514/842-9951.** Tickets C$10–C$50 (US$7–US$36). Métro: Place-des-Arts.

The world-famous orchestra, under the baton of Swiss conductor Charles Dutoit (and Zubin Mehta before him), performs at Place des Arts and at Notre-Dame, as well as around the world, and may be heard on numerous recordings. In the well-balanced repertoire are works from Elgar, Rabaud, and Saint-Saëns, in addition to Beethoven and Mozart. The box office is open Monday to Saturday from noon to 8pm. Performances are usually at 8pm, during a full season that runs from September to May, supplemented by Mozart concerts in Notre-Dame in June and July and interspersed with free performances at three parks in the metropolitan region.

LANDMARK CONCERT HALLS & VENUES

There are many venues around the city, so check the papers upon arrival to see who's playing where. Big-name rock bands and pop stars usually play **Centre Molson,** 1260 rue de la Gauchetière ouest (☎ 514/932-2582), also the new home of the Montréal Canadiens hockey team. If a concert is scheduled, printed flyers, posters, and radio and TV ads make certain that everyone knows. The box office is open Monday to Friday from 10am to 6pm (to 9pm on days of events).

A broad range of Canadian and international performers, usually of a modest celebrity unlikely to fill the larger Centre Molson, use the **Spectrum de Montréal,** 318 rue Ste-Catherine ouest (☎ 514/861-5851; Métro: Place-des-Arts), a converted movie theater. Rock acts like Marilyn Manson and Phish are the usual fare, but comedians are sometimes booked and the space also hosts segments of the annual jazz festival. Seats are available on a first-come, first-served basis. The box office is at 318 Ste-Catherine ouest (at Bleury) and is open Monday to Saturday from 10am to 9pm and Sunday from noon to 5pm. Call ☎ 514/285-4200 for information, 514/842-2112 for tickets, or 514/285-4275 for guided-tour reservations.

Founded in 1963 and in its striking new home in the heart of Montréal since 1992, ○ **Place des Arts** mounts musical concerts, opera, dance, and theater in five halls: Salle Wilfrid-Pelletier (2,982 seats), where the Montréal Symphony Orchestra often performs; the Maisonneuve Theatre (1,460 seats), where the Métropolitan Orchestra of Montréal and the McGill Chamber Orchestra perform; the Jean-Duceppe Theatre (755 seats); the new Cinquième Salle (350 seats); and the small Studio-Théâtre du Maurier Ltée (138 seats). Noon performances are often scheduled. The Museum of Contemporary Art moved into the complex in 1992. The box office is open Monday to Saturday from noon to 8pm, and performances are usually at 8pm.

Pollack Concert Hall. McGill University, 555 rue Sherbrooke ouest. ☎ **514/398-4547.** Métro: McGill.

In a landmark building dating from 1899 and fronted by a statue of Queen Victoria, this hall is in nearly constant use, especially during the university year. Among the attractions are concerts and recitals by professionals, students, or soloists from McGill's music faculty. Recordings of some of the more memorable concerts are available on the university's own label, McGill Records. Concerts are also given in the campus's smaller **Redpath Hall,** 3461 rue McTavish (☎ 514/398-4547). Performances are at 8pm and are usually free.

Théâtre de Verdure. Lafontaine Park. ☎ **514/872-2644.** Métro: Sherbrooke.

In a popular park in Plateau Mont-Royal, this open-air venue presents free music and dance concerts and theater, often with well-known artists and performers. Sometimes it shows outdoor movies. Many in the audience pack picnics. Performances are held from June to August; call for days and times. Performances are free.

Théâtre St-Denis. 1594 rue St-Denis (at Emery). ☎ **514/849-4211.** Métro: Berri-UQAM.

Recently refurbished, this theater in the heart of the Latin Quarter hosts a variety of shows, including pop singers and comedians, as well as segments of the Just for Laughs Festival in July. It's actually two theaters, one seating more than 2,000, the other almost 1,000. The box office is open daily from noon to 9pm. Performances are usually at 8pm.

A CIRCUS EXTRAORDINAIRE

✪ **Cirque du Soleil.** Old Port, quai Jacques-Cartier. ☎ **800/361-4595** or 514/522-2324. Tickets C$12–C$39 (US$9–US$28) adults, C$6–C$27 (US$4.30–US$19) children. Métro: Champ-de-Mars.

Through the exposure generated by its frequent tours across North America, this circus enjoys an ever-multiplying following. One reason, curiously, is the absence of animals in the troupe, which means that no one need be troubled by the possibility of mistreated lions and elephants. What is experienced during a Cirque du Soleil performance is nothing less than magical, a celebration of pure skill and theater, with plenty of clowns, trapeze artists, tightrope walkers, and contortionists. The show is offered from late April to early June in odd-numbered years only, as it goes on the road during even-numbered years. Look for the yellow-and-blue tent at the Vieux-Port, which means that it's in residence. The box office is open Tuesday to Sunday from 9am to 9pm. Performances are Tuesday to Friday at 8pm, Saturday at 4 and 8pm, and Sunday at 1 and 5pm.

COMEDY & MUSIC CLUBS
COMEDY

The 1980s explosion in comedy venues has cooled, but Montréal still has a couple of places to sample the fading phenomenon, mostly because it's the home to the **Just for Laughs Festival** every July. For information, call ☎ **514/845-2322.**

Comedy Nest. 1740 bd. René-Lévesque (at Guy). ☎ **514/932-6378.** Cover C$10 (US$7). Métro: Guy-Concordia.

This club, in the Hôtel Nouvel, features mostly local talent, with occasional appearances by better-known visiting comics. Shows are Wednesday to Sunday at 8:30pm, plus Friday and Saturday at 11:30pm. Drinks are C$4 to C$7 (US$2.85 to US$5). The dinner-and-show package is C$20 (US$14) Wednesday to Sunday and C$26 (US$19) Friday and Saturday; dinner starts at 6:30pm.

Comedyworks. 1238 rue Bishop (near Ste-Catherine). Cover up to C$12 (US$9). ☎ **514/398-9661.** Métro: Guy-Concordia.

There's a full card of comedy at this long-running club, up the stairs from Jimbo's Pub on a jumping block of Bishop south of Ste-Catherine. Monday is open-mike night, while on Tuesday and Wednesday improvisation groups usually work off the audience. Headliners of greater or lesser magnitude—usually from Montréal, Toronto, New York, or Boston—take the stage Thursday to Sunday. No food is served, just drinks. Reservations are recommended, especially on Friday, when early arrival may be necessary to secure a seat. Shows are daily at 9pm, with extra 11:15pm performances on Friday and Saturday. Most drinks are C$4 to C$8 (US$2.85 to US$6), and there's a one-drink minimum.

FOLK, ROCK & POP

Scores of bars, cafes, theaters, clubs, and even churches present live music on at least an occasional basis, if only at Sunday brunch. The performers, local or touring, traffic in every idiom, from metal to reggae to folk to unvarnished Vegas. In most cases, they stay in one place for only a night or two. Here are a select few that focus their energies on the music.

Café Campus. 57 rue Prince-Arthur est (near St-Laurent). ☎ **514/844-1010.** Cover C$3 (US$2.15) and up. Métro: Sherbrooke.

When anyone over 25 shows up inside this bleak club on touristy Prince-Arthur, it's probably a parent of one of the musicians. Alternative rock prevails, but metal and retro-rock bands also make appearances. Followers of the scene may be familiar with such groups as Bootsauce, Come, and Elastica, all of whom have appeared.

Club Soda. 5240 av. du Parc (near Bernard). ☎ **800/361-4595** or 514/270-7848. Cover C$10 (US$7) and up. Métro: Place-des-Arts, then no. 80 bus north.

At one of the city's larger venues for attractions below the megastar level, performers are given a stage before a hall seating up to 450. Three bars lubricate audience enthusiasm. Musical choices hop all over the charts—folk, rock, blues, country, Afro-Cuban, heavy metal, you name it. Acts for the annual jazz and comedy festivals are booked here, too. The box office is open Monday to Saturday from 10am to 6pm and Sunday and evenings when shows are scheduled.

Déjà Vu. 1224 rue Bishop (near Ste-Catherine). ☎ **514/866-0512.** No cover. Métro: Guy-Concordia.

Over a club called Bowser and Blue, this casual room puts on live music every night. The management has eclectic tastes, hiring bands that specialize in old-time rock, country, blues, and whatever else takes their fancy. They run a loose, fun place with three floors and two small dance floors, and they keep it relatively inexpensive.

Hurley's Irish Pub. 1225 rue Crescent (south of Ste-Catherine). ☎ **514/861-4111.** No cover. Métro: Peel or Guy-Concordia.

The Irish have been one of the largest immigrant groups in Montréal since the famine of the 1840s, and their musical tradition thrives here. Celtic instrumentalists and dancers perform every night of the week. Guinness and other drinks go for C$3 to C$5.50 (US$2.15 to US$3.90).

✪ Le Pierrot/Aux Deux Pierrots. 114 and 104 rue St-Paul est (west of place Jacques-Cartier). ☎ **514/861-1686.** Cover, Le Pierrot, C$2 (US$1.40) Fri–Sat, free other nights; Aux Deux Pierrots, C$3 (US$2.15) Thurs, C$5 (US$3.55) Fri–Sat. Métro: Place d'Armes.

Perhaps the best known of Montréal's *boîtes-à-chansons,* Le Pierrot is an intimate French-style club. The singer interacts animatedly with the crowd, often bilingually, and encourages them to join in the lyrics. Le Pierrot is open year-round, daily from early June to late September and Thursday to Sunday the other months, with music into the wee hours. Its sister club next door, the larger Aux Deux Pierrots, features live bands playing rock on Friday and Saturday nights, half in French and half in English. The terrace joining the two clubs is open on Friday and Saturday nights in summer. Le Pierrot is open only May to September. Drinks are C$3 to C$4.50 (US$2.15 to US$3.20).

JAZZ & BLUES

The respected and heavily attended **Festival International de Jazz,** held for 10 days every summer, sustains interest in the most original American art form. For information, call ☎ **514/871-1881.** Scores of events are scheduled, indoors and out, many of them free. "Jazz" is broadly interpreted to include everything from Dixieland to world beat to the unclassifiable experimental. Artists represented in the past have included Thelonious Monk, Pat Metheny, John Mayall, and B. B. King. Piano legend Oscar Peterson grew up here and often returns to perform in his hometown.

There are many more clubs than the sampling that follows. Pick up a copy of *Mirror* or *Hour,* distributed free everywhere, or buy the Saturday edition of the *Gazette* for the entertainment section. These publications have full listings of the bands and stars appearing during the week.

Biddle's. 2060 rue Aylmer (north of Sherbrooke). ☎ **514/842-8656.** No cover. Métro: McGill.

Downtown, in an area where there isn't much other after-dark action, this longtime stalwart is a club/restaurant with hanging plants and faux art-nouveau glass. It fills up early with lovers of barbecued ribs and jazz. The live music starts around 5:30pm (at 7pm Sunday and Monday) and continues until closing time. Charlie Biddle plays bass Tuesday to Friday when he doesn't have a gig elsewhere. He and his stand-ins favor jazz of the swinging mainstream variety, with occasional digressions into more esoteric forms. It's open Sunday from 4pm to 12:30am, Monday to Thursday from 11:30am to 1:30am, and Friday and Saturday from 11:30am to 2:30am. Drinks are $5 to $6.50 (US$3.55 to US$4.65), and there's a per-person minimum Friday and Saturday. There's a mandatory paid coat check.

✪ L'Air du Temps. 191 rue St-Paul ouest (at St-Francois-Xavier). ☎ **514/842-2003.** Cover C$5–C$25 (US$3.55–US$18). Métro: Place d'Armes.

A Montréal tradition since 1976, L'Air du Temps is a jazz emporium of the old school—a little seedy and beat-up with no gimmicks to distract from the music. The main room and an upper floor in back can hold more than 135, and the bar stools and tables fill up quickly. Get there by 9:30pm or so to secure a seat. The bands go on at 10:30pm or thereabouts. L'Air du Temps doesn't serve food, just a wide variety of drinks, but there are several good midpriced restaurants nearby. The club doesn't take reservations and is open Thursday to Monday from 9pm to 3am. Drinks are C$3.50 to C$7.75 (US$2.50 to US$6).

Le Grand Café. 1720 rue St-Denis (near Ontario). ☎ **514/289-9945.** Cover up to C$10 (US$7). Métro: Berri-UQAM.

The French of Canada are as enthusiastic about jazz as their European brethren, as is evident in this funky joint deep in the Latin Quarter. The stage is upstairs, large enough to hold large combos and small bands. Sometimes the management brings on blues or rock as a change of pace. When it's chilly out, they stoke up the fireplace. The big windows in front give a preview of what's going on inside, and they open up in summer. It's open daily from 11am to 3am. Drinks are C$3.50 to C$5.50 (US$2.50 to US$3.90).

Le Quai des Brumes. 4481 rue St-Denis (at Mont-Royal). ☎ **514/499-0467.** No cover. Métro: Mont-Royal.

Loosely translated, the name means "foggy dock," a reference of elusive significance. But it's an atmospheric place in which to attend to jazz, blues, and rock. Jazz gets lots of play upstairs in the Central Bar. The crowd has been described as "a fairly uniform group of post-1960s Francophone smokers." It's open daily from 2pm to 3am. Drinks are C$3 to C$5 (US$2.15 to US$3.55).

Les Beaux Esprits. 2073 rue St-Denis (at Sherbrooke). ☎ **515/844-0882.** No cover. Métro: Sherbrooke.

Blues gets a wide hearing in this musical city, as demonstrated here in the thumping heart of the youthful Latin Quarter. Simple and unpretentious, the place attracts avid fans of the music, mostly of university age. Local musicians perform nightly from 8pm to 3am. Drinks are C$3 to C$5 (US$2.15 to US$2.55).

DANCE CLUBS

Montréal's dance clubs change in tenor and popularity in mere eye blinks, and new ones sprout like toadstools after a heavy rain and wither as quickly. For the latest fever spots, quiz concierges, guides, waiters—anyone who looks as if they might follow the scene. Here are a few that appear likely to survive the whims of night-birds and landlords. Expect to encounter steroid abusers with funny haircuts guarding the doors.

Batalou. 4372 bd. St-Laurent (at Marie-Anne). ☎ **514/845-5447.** No cover. Métro: Mont-Royal.

A sensual tropical beat issues from this club-with-a-difference on The Main, a hot, happy variation from the prevailing grunge and murk of what might be described as mainstream clubs. Though most of the patrons revel in their ancestral origins in the Caribbean and Africa, the sources of the live and recorded music, an ecumenical welcome is extended to all. Admittedly, the hip-waggling expertise of the dancers might be intimidating to the uninitiated. Things get going about 10pm every night but Monday, and there are live shows Tuesday and Wednesday. Drinks are C$3.50 to C$7 (US$2.50 to US$5).

Hard Rock Cafe. 1458 rue Crescent (near Maisonneuve). ☎ **514/987-1420.** No cover. Métro: Guy-Concordia.

No surprises here, not with clones all around the world. The hamburgers are good enough and not too expensive, guitars and costumes and other rock memorabilia decorate the walls, and the usual Hard Rock souvenirs are available. The formula continues to work, and it gets crowded at lunch and weekend evenings. It's open daily from 11:30am to 3am, and the disco starts at 10pm. Drinks are C$3.45 to C$6 (US$2.45 to US$4.30).

Métropolis. 59 rue Ste-Catherine est (near St-Laurent). ☎ **514/288-5559.** Cover Thurs–Fri C$5 (US$3.55), Sat C$8 (US$6). Métro: Berri-UQAM.

Housed in a handsome old opera house dating from the 1890s is a monster club that can accommodate 2,200 gyrating bodies. The sound system for mostly rock and some jazz acts is state-of-the-art, and there are six bars on three levels. The neighborhood is scruffy, but not especially worrisome, not far from the campus of the Université du Québec. It's open Thursday to Saturday from 10pm to 3am. Drinks are C$3 to C$5.50 (US$2.15 to US$3.90).

Salsathèque. 1220 rue Peel (at Ste-Catherine). ☎ **514/875-0016.** Métro: Peel.

It's been on the scene for years, so they're obviously doing something right. The big upstairs room is all glittery, bouncing, mirrored light, the better to get the dancers moving to the mambo, merengue, and other infectious tropical beats. Open every night but Tuesday from 9pm to 3am, it rarely kicks into high before midnight. The house band comes on at 11 or thereabouts, and they bring in other acts. The major source of entertainment, though, is the patrons themselves, a highly proficient lot on the dance floor. Drinks run about C$3.50 to C$7 (US$2.50 to US$5).

BARS & CAFES

There's an abundance of restaurants, bars, and cafes along the streets near the downtown commercial district, from Stanley to Guy between Ste-Catherine and

Maisonneuve. **Rue Crescent,** in particular, hums with activity from late afternoon until far into the evening, especially after 10pm on a cool summer weekend, when the street swarms with young people moving from club to bar to restaurant. **Boulevard St-Laurent,** another nightlife hub, abounds in bars and clubs, most with a distinctive European (particularly French) personality, as opposed to the Anglo flavor of the rue Crescent area. Increasingly active **rue St-Paul,** west of place Jacques-Cartier in Vieux-Montréal, falls somewhere in the middle on the Anglophone-Francophone spectrum. It's also a little more likely to get rowdy on late weekend nights. In all cases, bars tend to open around 11:30am and go late. Last call for drinks is 3am, but patrons are often allowed to dawdle over them until 4am.

Le Continental Bistro Americain. 4169 rue St-Denis (at Rachel). ☎ **514/845-6842.** No cover. Métro: Mont-Royal.

The after-curtain crowd from the Théâtre St-Denis gathers here for drinks or late meals, which range far enough afield to be called "international." A guy with a cigarette clenched in his lips sits at the upright piano when the mood strikes, sometimes spelled by a guitarist or two. Their music is often submerged beneath the high buzz of conversation. The designer, Jacques Sabourin, fashioned the revivalist deco decor, including the bar, which doubles as a display counter. The bar is open Tuesday to Saturday from 6am to 12:30am and Saturday and Monday from 6am to midnight. Drinks are C$4 to C$7 (US$2.85 to US$5).

Le Swimming. 3643 bd. St-Laurent (north of Sherbrooke). ☎ **514/282-7665.** Métro: Sherbrooke.

A nondescript entry and a stairway that smells of stale beer leads to a trendy pool hall that attracts as many men and women who come to drink and socialize as to play pool. Many Montréal bars have pool tables, but this one has 13, along with nine TVs and a terrace. Some nights they have comedy (in French) or bands. Two people can play pool for an hour for C$8 (US$6), three play for C$9 (US$6), and four for C$10 (US$7).

Le Tour de Ville. In the Radisson Hôtel des Gouverneaurs, 777 rue University. ☎ **514/879-1370.** Métro: Square-Victoria.

Memorable. Breathtaking. The view, that is, from Montréal's only revolving bar/restaurant. The best time to go is when the sun is setting and the city lights are beginning to wink on. In the bar, one floor down from the restaurant, the same wonderful vistas are augmented by a dance floor, a band is featured Thursday and Friday from 9pm to 1am and Saturday from 9pm to 2am. There's no cover, but drinks are from C$5.50 to C$9 (US$3.90 to US$6). The bar opens at 6pm. The food in the restaurant is okay and not too expensive.

Lutetia Bar. In L'Hôtel de la Montagne, 1430 rue de la Montagne (north of Ste-Catherine). ☎ **514/288-5656.** Métro: Guy-Concordia.

Within sight of the trademark lobby fountain with its nude bronze sprite sporting stained-glass wings, this appealing bar draws a standing-room-only crowd of youngish to middle-aged professionals after 5:30pm. Monday to Friday a piano player performs; Friday and Saturday evenings, there's a jazz duo. In summer, the hotel opens the terrace bar on the roof by the pool.

Ritz Bar. In the Ritz-Carlton Kempinski Montréal, 1228 Sherbrooke ouest (at Drummond). ☎ **514/842-4212.** Métro: Peel.

A mature, prosperous crowd seeks out the quiet Ritz Bar in the Ritz-Carlton, adjacent to its semilegendary Café de Paris. Anyone can take advantage of the tranquil room and the professionalism of its staff. The dress code of jackets and ties for men has been eased, but most men will be more at ease with at least a jacket. Piano music tinkles just above the level of consciousness during cocktail hour Monday to Friday from 5 to 8pm from mid-May to August and from 5 to 11pm from September to mid-May. The bar is off the hotel lobby, to the right.

Sir Winston Churchill Pub. 1455 rue Crescent (near Ste-Catherine). ☎ **514/288-0623.**

The twin upstairs/downstairs bar/cafes are rue Crescent landmarks. One reason is the sidewalk terrace (open in summer, enclosed in winter), a vantage for checking out the pedestrian traffic. Inside and down the stairs, it attempts to imitate a British pub with marginal success. The mixed crowd is dominated by questing young professionals. They mill around a total of 17 bars and 2 dance floors. Winnie's, on the second floor, is a restaurant with a terrace of its own and a new cigar lounge. During the 5-to-8pm happy hour, drinks are two for one.

Thursday's. 1449 rue Crescent (near Ste-Catherine). ☎ **514/288-5656.** Métro: Guy-Concordia.

This is a prime watering hole of the young professional set, who are ever alert to the possibilities of companionship. The pubby bar spills onto the terrace that hangs over the street. There's a glittery dance club in back connected to a restaurant called Les Beaux Jeudis, in the same building. Thursday's presumably takes its name from the Montréal custom of prowling nightspots on Thursday evening in search of the perfect date for Friday. The disco opens at 9pm.

Whisky Café. 5800 bd. St-Laurent (at Bernard). ☎ **514/278-2646.** Métro: Outremont.

Those who enjoy Scotch, particularly single-malt imports like Cragamore and Glenfiddich, will find 30 labels to sample here. The trouble is that the Québec government applies stiff taxes for the privilege, so 70 ☎ of the patrons stick to beer. The decor is sophisticated, with exposed beams and vents, handmade tiled tables, and large wood-enclosed columns, but the real decorative triumph is the men's urinal, with a waterfall for a pissoir. Women are welcome to tour it. A new cigar lounge has been added.

GAY & LESBIAN CLUBS

K.O.X. 1450 rue Ste-Catherine (near Amherst). ☎ **514/523-0064.** Cover C$2–C$4 (US$1.40–US$2.90). Métro: Beaudry.

Despite the arch name, this dance space has survived and prospered, drawing an enthusiastic mixed crowd of men and women. House music is the beat of choice, blended by DJs who take their jobs seriously. Drinks and admission prices are reasonable, and there's no cover for the Sunday tea dance. The disco is closed Monday, Wednesday, and Thursday. Drinks are C$2.25 to C$4 (US$1.60 to US$2.85).

O'Side. 4075A rue St-Denis (near Rachel). ☎ **514/849-7126.** Métro: Mont-Royal.

This lesbian bar, welcoming women of all ages, has pool tables. The talkative staff and customers are good sources for information about gay activities and events in the city. Occasionally there's live music. Men are turned away at the door.

Sky Pub. 1474 rue Ste-Catherine est (near Amherst). ☎ **514/529-6969.** Métro: Beaudry.

Adjudged the city's best gay club by many, it has thrived for years. The spiffy decor and thumping music in the upstairs disco contribute to the popularity. Women are welcome Thursday nights, and there are usually appearances by drag performers earlier in the week. It has an outdoor terrace in summer.

GAMBLING

In 1993, the **Montréal Casino** (☎ **800/665-2274** or 514/392-2746), Québec's first, opened on Ile Notre-Dame in the former French Pavilion, which was left over from Expo '67. The casino has 113 gaming tables, including roulette, blackjack, midi-baccarat, and 2,738 slot machines. (No craps tables, though.) It can accommodate 8,000 people, most of whom come to try their luck, of course, but the five restaurants, especially Nuances (see "Dining," earlier in this chapter), have been getting good notices, and there are several bars, live shows, and two shops selling gifts and souvenirs. Gambling hours are daily from 9am to 5am, and patrons must be 18 or over. No alcoholic beverages are served in the gambling areas. The originally strict dress code has been relaxed, the only absolutely verboten item being sweatpants. To avoid rejection, keep your attire neat and reasonably tasteful. To get to the casino, take the Métro to the Ile Ste-Hélène stop, which is adjacent to Ile Notre-Dame, and walk or take the shuttle bus from there.

Resorts Near Montréal: The Laurentides & the Estrie Region

9

by Herbert Bailey Livesey

For respite from urban stresses, Montréalers need drive only 30 minutes or so to the north or east to find themselves in the heart of either the Laurentides or Estrie. Lakes and mountains have invited development of year-round vacation retreats and ski centers in both areas. The pearl of the Laurentides is Mont Tremblant (at 3,175 feet the highest peak in eastern Canada), but the region boasts 18 other ski centers with scores of trails at every level of difficulty.

Bucolic Estrie, known as the Eastern Townships when it was a haven for English Loyalists and their descendants, is blessed with a trio of memorable country inns on Lake Massawippi and promotes four seasons of outdoor diversions. It has fewer ski centers, and the hotels serving them are generally smaller and less extensive in their facilities, but the area's many lakes and gentler pastimes give it an edge for warm-weather vacations. Since the people of these regions rely heavily on tourism, you'll find that knowledge of at least rudimentary English is widespread, even outside the hotels and ski resorts.

1 Exploring the Laurentides & the Estrie Region

Most of the major resorts and ski centers of the Laurentides ("Laurentians" in English) are within sight of the limited-access Autoroute 15 and the roughly parallel but slightly slower Route 117. Both roads follow scenic routes through tidy hamlets and villages, with humpbacked hills giving way to higher and higher mountains.

In Estrie, the same observations hold for Autoroute 10, which runs east from Montréal to Sherbrooke, except that the terrain rises and falls less dramatically. In this chapter, the suggestions for enjoying both regions are laid out as driving tours, beginning with the towns or other sites of interest closest to Montréal and ending with those most distant.

VISITOR INFORMATION

Québec tourism authorities produce volumes of detailed and highly useful publications, and they're easy to obtain by mail, by phone, or in person. To contact **Tourisme Québec,** write C.P. 979, Montréal,

PQ, H3C 2W3 or call ☎ **800/363-7777,** operator 806 (in the Montréal area, call ☎ 514/873-2015).

GETTING AROUND

The limited-access expressways in Québec are called autoroutes, and speed limits and distances are given in kilometers. Most highway signs are in French only, though Montréal's autoroutes and bridges often bear dual-language signs. Seat-belt use is required by law while driving or riding in a car in Québec. Turning right on a red light is prohibited throughout the Province of Québec, except where specifically allowed by an additional green arrow.

For information on **road conditions** in and around Montréal, call ☎ **514/636-3026;** outside Montréal, call ☎ **514/636-3248.** To get from downtown Montréal to the Laurentian Autoroute 15, take ring Route 40 around the city.

THE GREAT OUTDOORS

There doesn't seem to be an outdoor sport or game yet conceived that doesn't enjoy at least one or two venues somewhere in the Laurentides or Estrie.

BIKING   Both strenuous mountain biking and gentler forms of cycling are possible throughout the region, especially in Mont Tremblant Park and on roads around the hotels. **Rentals** are available at a concession stand in the park (☎ **818/688-2281**), which has 100 kilometers (62 miles) of trails. Magog, in Estrie, has an 18$\frac{1}{2}$-kilometer (11-mile) bike path linking its Lake Mephremagog with Mont Orford.

BIRD WATCHING   The lakes of Québec's mountain regions are home to an estimated 16,000 loons, a native waterfowl that gives its name to the dollar coin. Excellent divers and swimmers, the birds are unable to walk on land, which makes nesting a trial, and they're identified by a distinctive call that might be described as an extended mournful giggle.

CANOEING   From June to September, **Escapade Nature** in Ste-Agathe-des-Monts (☎ **514/226-6521**) conducts canoe trips along the rivers Diable and Rouge from a few hours in duration to made-to-measure expeditions of up to a week. Canoes, equipment, and guides are part of the package.

CROSS-COUNTRY SKIING   Among the best cross-country trails in the Laurentides are at the **Hôtel l'Estérel** (☎ **514/228-2571**) and on the grounds of the monastery **Domaine du St-Bernard,** near Mont Tremblant.

In Estrie, 35 kilometers (22 miles) of courses run across **Lake Massawippi** and over the low surrounding hills. The bike path between **Lake Mephremagog** and **Mont Orford** becomes a cross-country trail in winter.

DOGSLEDDING   In St-Jovite, **Chinook Aventure** (☎ **819/425-6518**) introduces novices to the sport with 1-hour to whole-day guided outings. Guests at the **Hôtel l'Estérel** (☎ **514/228-2571**) have that opportunity, too. For longer, more venturesome expeditions of up to 4 days, meals and lodging provided, contact **Les Expéditions Tapini** (☎ **819/586-2064**). The outfitter is based in Ste-Anne-du-Lac, 47 kilometers (29 miles) north of Mont Laurier, an excursion in itself. In Waterloo, near Exit 90 off Autoroute 10, **Safari Tour** (☎ **514/539-0501**) schedules daily excursions by reservation.

DOWNHILL SKIING   Half a century ago the first ski schools, rope tows, and trails began to appear, and today there are over 20 ski centers within a 40-mile radius of Montréal. These sprawling resorts and modest lodges and inns are packed each winter with skiers, some of them through April. Trails for advanced skiers typically have short pitches and challenging moguls, with broad, hard-packed avenues for beginners and the less experienced. In addition to the 19 ski centers scattered along Autoroute 15, there are four prominent centers in Estrie, near Autoroute 10; they're smaller and tend to be more family-oriented. Bromont, Orford, Owl's Head, and Sutton cooperate through their **Ski East Network** to offer a lift ticket acceptable at all four centers (☎ 819/820-2020). For information on **ski packages** in Estrie, call ☎ 800/355-5755.

GARDEN & VINEYARD TOURS   **Les Jardins de Rocailles,** 1319 rue Lavoie in Val-David (☎ 819/322-6193), is a small but delightful floral retreat with more than 250 varieties of flowers and shrubs. There's a cafe with a terrace from which to observe. All four of the vineyards in and around Dunham in Estrie conduct tours. Three are along Route 202, west of the town: **L'Orpailleur** (☎ 514/295-2763), **Les Trois Clochers** (☎ 514/295-2034), and **Domaine** (☎ 514/295-2020). Outside of Magog, **Le Vignoble Le Cep d'Argent** (☎ 819/864-4441) offers tastings and a simple cafe.

GOLF   Courses in the Laurentides now number almost 30, most of them 18 holes and open to the public. Reservations are required and daily fees are C$25 to C$40 (US$18 to US$29). Most of the resort hotels covered in this chapter can make arrangements, but three have courses on their premises—**Gray Rocks** (☎ 819/425-2771) and the **Hôtel l'Estérel** (☎ 514/228-2571) both feature 18-hole courses, and **Le Chantecler** (☎ 514/229-3555) makes do with a 9-hole course. In Estrie there are 25 more courses, also open to the public, with greens fees at C$24 to C$34 (US$17 to US$24) for 18 holes.

SAILING & WINDSURFING   You can rent small sailboats and sailboards at the lakefront in Ste-Agathe-des-Monts, where there's also a **sailing school** (☎ 819/326-2282). The larger lake resorts in both the Laurentides and Estrie rent or make available canoes, pedal boats, and sailing dinghies. Yamaska Park in Granby, for example, rents sailboards, kayaks, sailboats, and rowboats, as does the recreational park at Mont Orford.

SCUBA DIVING   The many clear lakes of the Laurentides have visibility of up to 50 feet. Notable are Lac Tremblant, at the base of the mountain of the same name, and the several lakes in or near the Papineu-Labelle wildlife preserve, west of Tremblant and St-Jovite. Information, dive classes, and rental equipment are available through the **Centre de Plongée Lac-des-Ecorces** (☎ 819/585-3472), in the village of that name near the town of Mont Laurier, 110 kilometers (68 miles) north of St-Jovite.

TENNIS   All the large resorts and many of the smaller auberges have courts, including **Manoir St-Sauveur** (☎ 514/227-1811), **Mont Gabriel** (☎ 514/229-3547), **Hôtel l'Estérel** (☎ 514/228-2571), **Club Tremblant** (☎ 819/425-2731), and **Manoir Hovey** (☎ 819/842-2421).

WHITE-WATER RAFTING   Several companies offer rafting trips of 4 to 5 hours on the Rivière Rouge (Red River), which flows down to the Ottawa River. Access is via Route 158 west of Autoroute 15 (Exit 39) toward Lachute and on Route 148 past Calumet, turning north on chemin de la Rivière Rouge. Launching points are clearly marked. Passengers must weigh at least 40 kilograms (88 lb.). Guides, rafts, safety helmets, and jackets are provided, as is an end-of-trip meal.

Inquire ahead to determine details and make reservations. Two of the more prominent companies are **Aventure en Eau Vive** (☎ 819/242-6084) and **Nouveau Monde** (☎ 818/242-7238).

2 The Laurentides

St-Sauveur-des-Monts: 60 kilometers (37 miles) N of Montréal

Expect no spiked peaks or high ragged ridges. The rolling hills and rounded mountains of the Laurentian Shield are among the oldest in the world, worn down by wind and water over eons. They average 300 to 520 meters (1,000 to 1,700 ft.), with the highest being Mont Tremblant, at 968 meters (3,000 ft.). In the lower precincts, nearest Montréal, the terrain resembles a rumpled quilt, its folds and hollows cupping a multitude of ponds and lakes. Farther north, the summits are higher and craggier, with patches of snow persisting into spring, but these are still not like the Alps or Rockies. They're welcoming and embracing rather than awe-inspiring.

The busiest times are July and August, the Christmas–New Year's period, and February and March. At other times, reservations are easier to get, prices lower, and crowds less dense. May and September are often characterized by warm days, cool nights, and just enough people so that the streets don't seem deserted. In May and June, the indigenous blackflies can seem as big and as ill-tempered as buzzards, so take along an effective insect repellent. Some of the resorts, inns, and lodges close down for a couple of weeks in spring and fall. A handful are open only for a few winter months.

March and April are when the maple trees are tapped and **cabanes à sucre** (sugar shacks) open, some selling only maple candies and syrup, others serving full meals featuring the principal product and even staging entertainments. In mid-July, the region's annual **Fête de Vins** (Wine Festival) is held for 2 days in St-Jérôme, and the emphasis is on gastronomy and wine tasting; a dozen restaurants in the area participate.

July and August usher in glorious days in the Laurentians. An attractive event in late July/early August is the 4-day **Festival International du Blues Tremblant,** and during the last 2 weeks in September the leaves put on an unsurpassed color show. Skiers can usually expect reliable snow from early December to mid-April.

Prices can be difficult to pin down. The large resorts have so many types of rooms, cottages, meal plans, discounts, and packages that a travel agent may be needed to pick through the thicket of options. Remember that Montréalers fill the highways when they "go up north" on weekends, particularly during February and March, so plan ahead when making reservations.

Pet owners, take note: Few Laurentian resorts accept animals.

ESSENTIALS

VISITOR INFORMATION For an orientation to the entire region, stop at **La Maison du Tourisme des Laurentides,** 14142 rue de la Chapelle (RR #1), St-Jérôme, PQ, J7Z 5T4 (☎ 800/561-6673, 514/436-8532, or 514/476-1840 in Montréal; fax 514/436-5309), at Exit 39 off the Laurentian Autoroute 15. Perhaps most important to the traveler, the staff can make reservations for lodging throughout the Laurentides, either by phone or in person. The service is free. The red-roofed stone cottage is off the highway to the east; take Route 158 and follow the signs. It's open daily: late June to the end of August from 9am to 8:30pm and the rest of the year from 9am to 5pm.

GETTING THERE **By Car** The fast and scenic **Autoroute des Laurentides,** also known as Autoroute 15, goes straight from Montréal to the Laurentian Mountains. Just follow the signs to St-Jérôme. The exit numbers are actually the distance in

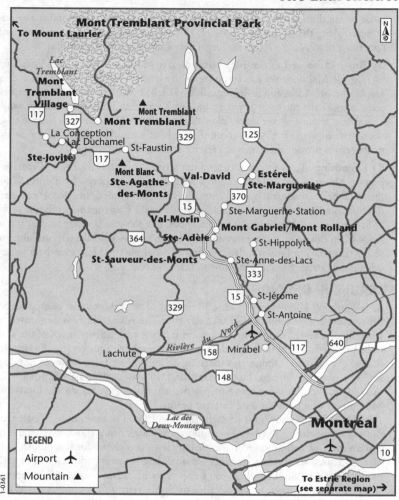

kilometers the village is from Montréal. One likely stop, for instance, is the Laurentian Tourism House at Exit 39 in St-Jérôme, and St-Jérôme is 39 kilometers (24 miles) from Montréal. This is a pretty drive, once you get out of the clutches of the tangle of expressways surrounding Montréal. The Autoroute des Laurentides gives a sweeping, panoramic introduction to the area, from the rolling hills and forests of the lower Laurentians to the mountain drama of the upper Laurentians.

Those with the time to meander can exit at St-Jérôme and pick up the older, parallel Route 117, which plays tag with the autoroute all the way to Ste-Agathe-des-Monts, where the highway ends. Most of the region's more appealing towns are strung along or near Route 117. As you approach each town, you'll see signs directing you to the local tourism information office, where attendants provide helpful tips on lodging, restaurants, and things to do. North of Ste-Agathe, Route 117 becomes the major artery, continuing deep into Québec's north country and finally ending at the Ontario border hundreds of miles from Montréal.

Be aware that Québec's equivalent of the Highway Patrol maintains a strong presence along the stretch of Autoroute 15 between St-Faustin and Ste-Adèle, and remember that radar detectors are illegal here and subject to confiscation.

By Bus   Limocar Laurentides buses depart Montréal's Terminus Voyageur, 505 bd. de Maisonneuve est, stopping in the larger Laurentian towns, including Ste-Agathe, Ste-Adèle, and St-Jovite; call ☎ **514/842-2281** for schedules. An express bus can make the run to St-Jovite and Mont Tremblant in less than 2 hours, while a local bus, making all the stops, takes almost 3. From Montréal to Ste-Adèle takes about 1½ hours, 15 minutes more to Val-Morin and Val-David. Some of the major resorts provide their own bus service at an additional charge.

By Limousine   Taxis and limousines await arrivals at both Dorval and Mirabel airports in Montréal and will take you to any Laurentian hideaway—for a price. While the fare for the 1-hour trip by limo from Dorval is steep, four or five people can share the cost and dilute the pain. Mirabel is actually in the Laurentians, 5 minutes south of St-Antoine and 35 minutes from the slopes. Ask the standard fare to your inn or lodge when calling to make reservations. The inn usually will take responsibility for seeing that a taxi or limo is indeed waiting at the airport and may even help to find other guests arriving at the same time to share the cost.

ST-SAUVEUR-DES-MONTS

As it's only 60 kilometers (37 miles) north of Montréal, you can easily visit St-Sauveur-des-Monts (pop. 5,864) on a day trip. The village square is dominated by a handsome church, and the streets around it bustle with activity much of the year, so be prepared to have difficulty finding a parking place in season (try the large lot behind the church). Dining and snacking on everything from crêpes to hot dogs are big activities, evidenced by the many cafes. In season, there's a tourist kiosk on the square. Pick up some bread or pastries at nearby Page, as do the locals and Montréalers who have weekend cottages nearby.

The area is well known for its night skiing—23 well-lit trails, only 3 fewer than those available during the day. The mountain is wide, with a 700-foot vertical drop and a variety of well-groomed trails, making it a good choice for families. In summer, St-Sauveur-des-Monts becomes Canada's largest water park, featuring a wave pool and a mountain slide where you go up in chairlifts and come down in tubes.

The **Bureau Touristique de la Vallée de St-Sauveur,** in Les Galeries des Monts, 75 av. de la Gare (☎ **514/227-2564**), is open year-round, daily from 9am to 5pm.

ACCOMMODATIONS

Manoir St-Sauveur. 246 chemin du Lac-Millette, St-Sauveur-des-Monts, PQ, J0R 1R3. ☎ **800/ 361-0505** or 514/227-1811. Fax 514/227-8512. 163 rms, 37 suites. A/C MINIBAR TV TEL. Mid-June to mid-Oct C$99–C$118 (US$71–US$84) single or double; from C$180 (C$129) suite. Mid-Oct to mid-June C$89–C$108 (US$64–US$77) single or double; from C$160 (US$114) suite. Extra person C$10 (US$7). Children 17 and under stay free in parents' rm. Packages available. AE, DC, ER, MC, V. Take Exit 60 off Autoroute 15.

This is one of the region's several large resort hotels, with a monster outdoor pool and a comprehensive roster of four-season activities: Its facilities include a fitness center with weight machines and a sauna, an indoor pool, racquetball, squash, tennis, in-house movies, and a shop. A warm personality isn't included. It isn't really necessary, considering that the rooms are commodious and comfortable, blandly modern with light-wood furnishings. The main building is easily spotted from the road, with its green roof and many dormers. The front desk is reluctant to quotes rates, which they adjust according to season, demand, and occupancy rate, so keep asking if they have anything cheaper.

Relais St-Denis. 61 rue St-Denis, St-Sauveur-des-Monts, PQ, J0R 1R4. ☎ **800/997-4766** or 514/227-4766. Fax 514/227-8504. 18 rms, 24 suites. A/C MINIBAR TV TEL. C$98–C$108 (US$71–US$77) double; C$118 (US$84) suite. Meal plans with breakfast and/or dinner available. AE, DC, ER, MC, V.

Set back from the road, the cream-colored U-shaped building is surrounded by birches and evergreens and extensive gardens. The Relais resembles a country club, complete with a heated outdoor pool and nearby golf. The rooms are of good size, with fireplaces and large baths. Those in the new wing are larger and more polished, with whirlpool baths. Note that the suites are only C$10 (US$7) more than the regular rooms. Ski and golf packages are available, as are therapeutic massages. Reception is in the building with the green awning.

DINING

Les Prés. 231 rue Principale. ☎ **514/227-8580.** Main courses C$5.50–C$13 (US$3.90–US$9). AE, MC, V. Mon–Thurs 11am–9pm, Fri 11am–2am, Sat 9am–11pm, Sun 9am–10pm. LIGHT FARE.

Utilizing a well-preserved Victorian house, Les Prés is only one of a number of fetching casual eateries clustered near the village square. Several of them are units of Montréal chains, as is this one, whose name means "the meadows." Daily lunch specials offer soup, a main course, and coffee, and there's a brunch menu every day. Fondues, salads, pastas, and vegetarian dishes are other possibilities. In summer, the front porch and a large side deck have vantages for watching the street activity.

MONT GABRIEL

Mont Gabriel is only 4 kilometers (2¹/₂ miles) from St-Sauveur-des-Monts. To get there, follow Autoroute 15 to Exit 64 and turn right at the stop sign. Though popular in summer, Mont Gabriel comes into its own each winter, when skiers schuss down its 21 trails and slopes and then slide back up on the seven T-bar lifts, the triple-chair lift, or the quadruple-chair lift. Eight trails are lit for night skiing. Cross-country trails girdle the mountain and range through the surrounding countryside.

ACCOMMODATIONS & DINING

Mont Gabriel. 1699 chemin Montée Gabriel, PQ, J0R 1G0. ☎ **800/668-5253** in Canada, 514/229-3547, or 514/861-2852 in Montréal. Fax 514/229-7034. 126 rms. TV TEL. C$98 (US$70) double. Rates include breakfast. MAP and other packages available. Discounts for stays of 2–5 nights. AE, ER, MC, V. Take Exit 64 from Autoroute 15.

Perched high above highways and the valley and looking like the rambling log "cottages" of the turn-of-the-century wealthy, this desirable hotel is only 20 miles from Montréal's Dorval Airport. Set on a 1,200-acre forest estate, the resort complex features golf and tennis programs in summer and ski packages in winter. The spacious rooms in the Tyrol section are the most desirable, many with views of the hills, while those in the Old Lodge are more rustic. Some rooms have air-conditioning and minibars, but you must request these. With the Club Package comes three meals a day and unlimited access to all sports facilities, and prices include tax and service charge.

Dining/Entertainment: Meals are served in the resort's dining rooms and at poolside. In the evening there's dancing in the main lodge.

Services: Summer activity programs for children.

Facilities: Indoor pool, sauna, whirlpool, and exercise room; heated outdoor pool (summer only); par-71 golf course; six tennis courts.

STE-ADELE

You can take Route 117, which swings directly into Ste-Adèle to become its main street, boulevard Ste-Adèle, or take Exit 67 off Autoroute 15 North. The village (pop. 7,800), 67 kilometers (42 miles) north of Montréal, is a near-metropolis compared to the other Laurentian villages lining the upper reaches of Route 117. What makes it seem big are its services: police, doctors, ambulances, a shopping center, art galleries, and a larger collection of places to stay and dine than elsewhere in the Laurentians. As rue Morin mounts the hill to Lac Rond, Ste-Adèle's resort lake, you can easily see why the town is divided into a lower part (*en bas*) and an upper part (*en haut*).

The **Bureau Touristique de Ste-Adèle,** 333 bd. Ste-Adèle (☎ **514/229-2921,** ext. 207), is open daily: July and August from 9am to 7pm and September to June from 9am to 5pm. One of the main streets, **rue Valiquette,** is lined with cafes, galleries, and bakeries, but **Lac Rond** is the center of summer activity. Canoes, sailboats, and *pédalos* (pedal-powered watercraft), rented from several docks, glide over the surface, while swimmers splash and play at shoreside beaches.

In winter, ski trails descend to the shores of the frozen lake. Rent downhill ski equipment or book lessons at **Le Chantecler** resort, which has 22 trails served by 6 chairlifts and two T-bars. Some of the trails end right by the main hotel. At the town's **Centre Municipal,** Côtes 40/80, 1400 rue Rolland (☎ **514/229-2921**), the trails are good for beginners. Three T-bar lifts carry you up the slopes for the run down five trails.

ACCOMMODATIONS

Champêtre. 1435 bd. Ste-Adèle (Rte. 117), Ste-Adèle, PQ, J0R 1L0. ☎ **800/363-2466** or 514/229-3533. Fax 514/229-3534. 48 rms. A/C TV TEL. C$57–C$129 (US$41–US$92) double. Rates include continental breakfast. Extra person C$10 (US$7). Children 12 and under stay free in parents' rm. Lower rates for stays longer than 1 night and in spring/fall. Packages available. Discounts and full breakfast available for stays longer than 2 nights. AE, DC, ER, MC, V.

You can stretch your budget by choosing lodging places that offer accommodations alone, without the sports and meal packages promoted by the region's comprehensive resorts. A case in point is this unpretentious auberge, somewhere between a motel and a condominium block. Of the several kinds of accommodations, the most appealing are the midpriced rooms called Chalet Nest and Whirlpool Nest. The least expensive for two people are the Champêtre rooms, with a queen-size or two twin beds, cable color TV, and AM/FM radio. There's a Franklin fireplace (with firewood) in each room. The auberge has a breakfast room with a small pool surrounded by a hedge.

Excelsior. 3655 bd. Ste-Adèle (Hwy. 117), Ste-Adèle, PQ, J0R 1L0. ☎ **800/363-2483** or 514/229-7676. Fax 514/229-8310. 105 rms. A/C TV TEL. Old section, from C$60 (US$43) double. New section, C$80 (US$57) double including breakfast, C$135 (US$96) double including breakfast and dinner. AE, MC, V. Coming from Montréal, take Exit 67 off the autoroute.

A number of motel units are scattered along a slope beside Route 117 south of the central structure, about a mile north of town. They used to constitute a Days Inn, which explains the no-frills aspect of that section and the aesthetic differences from its more desirable main building farther down the road. Architectural distinctions aside, the management maintains high standards of housekeeping, and all rooms have cable color TVs and share no fewer than four indoor and outdoor pools, a tennis court, squash courts, an exercise room, a sauna, a whirlpool, and the Amadéus restaurant/bar. Many rooms have balconies and some are reserved for nonsmokers. Elaborate spa treatments are available, including hydrotherapy, mineral and algae wraps, massages, and salt baths. A full 1-day package is C$139 (US$99).

L'Eau à la Bouche. 3003 bd. Ste-Adèle (Hwy. 117), Ste-Adèle, PQ, J0R 1L0. ☎ **800/ 363-2582** from Montréal, or 514/229-2991. Fax 514/229-7573. 23 rms, 2 suites. A/C TV TEL. From C$125 (US$89) double; from C$205 (US$146) suite. Rates include breakfast. Packages available. AE, DC, ER, MC, V.

L'Eau à la Bouche started as a roadside restaurant and the chef-owners later added the hotel. It's a Relais & Châteaux, an organization that places its emphasis on gastronomy rather than physical exertion. That it does here, and admirably, as the separate recommendation of its restaurant suggests (see "Dining," below). However, the hotel faces the Mont Chantecler ski trails, is across the road from a golf course, and has a heated outdoor pool. Inside is a large living room with a brick fireplace and bar and sofas set about in conversation groups. Substantial breakfasts are served there, at tables with bentwood chairs and green-and-white–checkered cloths. The guest rooms boast queen- or king-size beds, ceiling fans, and reproductions of Québec country furniture. The large baths have hair dryers and robes. All rooms contain sitting areas, six with fireplaces and balconies or patios. There is no elevator and no porters, but you can obtain help with your luggage if necessary.

Le Chantecler. 1474 rue de Chantecler (C.P. 1048), Ste-Adèle, PQ, J0R 1L0. ☎ **800/ 363-2420** or 514/229-3555. Fax 514/229-5593. 280 rms, 20 suites. MINIBAR TV TEL. C$89 (US$64) double including breakfast, C$170–C$250 (US$121–US$179) double including breakfast and dinner; from C$292 (US$209) suite. Children 6 and under stay free in parents' rm. Many packages available. AE, DC, ER, MC, V. Take Exit 67 off Autoroute 15, turn left at the 4th traffic light onto rue Morin, then turn right at the top of the hill.

Sprawled across steep slopes cupping Lac à la Truite, this resort is composed of several stone buildings of varying heights, its roofs bristling with steeples and dormers. It has 22 slopes for all levels of skiers, including a 622 foot vertical drop, and a ski school. The rooms are decorated with pine furniture made locally; most have air-conditioning. Many of the suites have fireplaces, and most have whirlpool baths. A bountiful buffet breakfast is served in the glass-enclosed dining room, which overlooks the active slopes and the lake with its small beach. Apart from the dings and dents that typically afflict heavily used family resorts, it's all maintained reasonably well.

Dining/Entertainment: There's a dining room with a terrace, a piano bar, a disco (winter only), movies in the projection room, and a summer-stock theater.

Services: Baby-sitting, day camp, dry cleaning, ski lockers.

Facilities: Ski school, 22 runs on 4 mountains (including 13 night-lit runs), ski chalet (with cafeteria and bar), cross-country trails, ice-skating, indoor sports complex (with pool, sauna, Jacuzzi, squash, racquetball, badminton, some fitness equipment), 18-hole and lit 9-hole golf courses, six lit tennis courts, windsurfing, canoeing, paddleboats, rowboats, mountain bikes.

DINING

✪ **L'Eau à la Bouche.** 3003 bd. Ste-Adèle (Hwy. 117). ☎ **800/363-2582** from Montréal or 514/229-2991. Reservations recommended. Main courses C$31–C$38 (US$22–US$27); fixed-price lunch from C$15 (US$11); fixed-price 5-course dinner C$45–C$65 (US$32–US$46). AE, MC, V. Daily 6–9pm. CONTEMPORARY FRENCH.

Owners Anne Desjardins and Pierre Audette leave no doubt where their priorities lie. Their nearby hotel (see above) is entirely satisfactory, but this, the restaurant, is their love child, with the glow-in-the-dark reviews to prove it. False modesty isn't a factor—*l'eau à la bouche* means "mouth-watering," and the kitchen delivers. The faux Provençal interior employs heavy ceiling beams, white plaster walls, and pine paneling to set the mood. On one occasion, the preappetizer was a dollop of salmon tartare laced with flecks of ginger and sweet red pepper. It provided an interlude to appreciate the generous martinis that exceed the skimpy Québec norm and study the carefully assembled wine list. A good deal is the three glasses of vintage clarets for C$30 (US$21), which can accompany a choice of three fixed-price meals. Native ingredients and hefty portions are meshed with nouvelle presentations, as with the fanned leaves of rosy duck breast garnished with slivered broccoli and a timbale of puréed sweet potato. Fiddleheads appear in their short spring season paired with baby asparagus heads; game dishes arrive in fall. The desserts are impressive, but the cheese plate (pungent nubbins of French and Québec varieties delivered with warm baguette slices) is special. The young staff contrives to be both efficient and unintrusive. A meal here might be the most memorable—and pricey—dining experience of a Laurentian visit.

STE-MARGUERITE & ESTEREL

To get to Ste-Marguerite (pop. 2,000) or the even less populous Estérel, only 2 miles apart, follow Autoroute 15 north to Exit 69. Or if driving from Ste-Adèle, look for a street heading northeast named chemin Ste-Marguerite. It becomes a narrow road that crosses the Laurentian Autoroute (at Exit 69), bridges the Rivière du Nord, and leads into an area of many lakes bordered by upscale vacation properties.

Ste-Marguerite and Estérel are 85 kilometers (53 miles) and 88 kilometers (55 miles) north of Montréal, respectively. In summer, information about the area is available from **Pavillon du Parc,** 74 chemin Masson, in Ste-Marguerite-du-Lac-Masson (☎ 514/228-3525); year-round, go to the nearby tourist bureau of Ste-Adèle (see above).

ACCOMMODATIONS & DINING IN ESTÉREL

L'Estérel. Bd. Fridolin-Simard (C.P. 38), Ville d'Estérel, PQ, J0T 1E0. ☎ **888/378-3735** from Montréal, or 514/228-2571. Fax 514/228-4977. 135 rms. A/C TV TEL. C$252–C$309 (US$180–US$221) double, including breakfast and dinner and use of most facilities. Lower rates Dec–May. Discounts for stays of 3 or more nights. Packages available. AE, CB, DC, DISC, ER, MC, V. Take the Limocar bus from Montréal into Ste-Adèle; the hotel picks up guests there.

One of the more prominent Laurentian resorts lies a few miles past Ste-Marguerite in the town of Estérel. This year-round complex is capable of accommodating 300 guests on its 5,000-acre estate with three linked lakes. Occupying an expanse of otherwise vacant lakeshore, L'Estérel offers conventionally conventional guest rooms. Those with a view of the lake are more expensive.

Rates include use of all indoor facilities and the tennis courts. For a special winter experience, inquire about the dogsled trips through the woods and over the frozen lake. There are 85 kilometers (53 miles) of cross-country ski trails, nearby downhill skiing, ice-skating on a rink, and in summer an 18-hole golf course and school, tennis, nature trails, horseback riding, sailing, parasailing, and waterskiing.

DINING IN STE-MARGUERITE

✪ **Le Bistro à Champlain.** 75 chemin Masson. ☎ **514/228-4988.** Reservations recommended. Main courses C$15–C$25 (US$11–US$18); fixed-price 3-course dinners C$23 and C$30 (US$16 and US$21); *menu dégustation* C$70 (US$50). AE, MC, V. Summer Tues–Sat 6–10pm, Sun noon–10pm; rest of the year Thurs–Sat 6–10pm, Sun noon–10pm. FRENCH.

On the shore of Lac Masson is one of the most honored restaurants in the Laurentians. Its 1864 building used to be a general store, and it retains the rough-hewn board walls, exposed beams, wood ceiling, and cash register. Gastronomy, not hardware, is now the motivation for customers who routinely motor up from Montréal for dinner. The 35,000-bottle cellar is a big reason, and 20 of the stocked wines can be sampled by the glass. (You can actually get a 3-oz. taste of fabled Sauterne Château d'Yquem.) Tours of the cellar are often conducted by the waiter/sommelier or his equally enthusiastic boss, a practicing radiologist. The food matches the wines, arriving flavorful and attractively presented. For those caught up in the current fad, there's a comfortably appointed cigar lounge with dozens of single-malt scotches available.

VAL-DAVID

Follow Route 117 north to Exit 76 to reach Val-David. To those who know it, the faintly bohemian enclave of **Val-David** (pop. 3,225), 80 kilometers (50 miles) north of Montréal, conjures up images of cabin hideaways set among hills rearing above ponds and lakes and laced with creeks tumbling through fragrant forests. The village celebrated its 76th anniversary in 1997.

The **tourist office** is on the main street at 2501 rue de l'Eglise (☎ 888/322-7030 or 819/322-2900). It's open daily: June 20 to Labour Day from 9am to 7pm and Labour Day to June 19 from 10am to 4pm. Another possibility for assistance is **La Maison du Village,** a cultural center that mounts art exhibits in a two-story wooden building at 2495 rue de l'Eglise (☎ 819/322-2900, ext. 237). Note that this far north into the Laurentians, the telephone area code changes to 819.

A favorite activity in Val-David is visiting the studios of local artists, including the **pottery workshop** of Kinya Ishikawa, at 2435 rue de l'Eglise (☎ 819/322-6868), where you can view the artist's work and discuss it with him.

Or you can enjoy a picnic beside the North River in the **Parc des Amoureax,** 4 kilometers (2½ miles) from the main road through town. Watch for the sign SITE PITTORESQUE and turn at chemin de la Rivière.

Val-David sits astride a 200-kilometer (124-mile) parkway that's a trail for cycling in summer and for cross-country skiing in winter.

The village sponsors an annual **art festival,** when painters, sculptors, ceramicists, jewelers, pewtersmiths, and other craftspeople display their work. It features concerts and other outdoor activities.

ACCOMMODATIONS & DINING

La Sapinière. 1244 chemin de la Sapinière, Val-David, PQ, J0T 2N0. ☎ 800/567-6635 or 819/322-2020. Fax 819/322-6510. 66 rms, 4 suites. A/C TV TEL. C$99–C$109 (US$71–US$78) double; C$145–C$155 (US$104–US$111) suite. Rates include breakfast and dinner. Extra person C$75 (US$54). AE, MC, V. Drive through downtown and find the sign to the inn on the right.

This sedate lakeside inn celebrated its 61st anniversary in 1997. It's a tranquil lakeside retreat, upper-middle-class in tone, with a largely 40-plus clientele. They return faithfully year after year, in large part to escape childish shrieks and orchestrated hyperactivity. Demanding diners, they're treated to a menu of five-course meals that's changed daily and embellished with wines from a 10,000-bottle cellar. The lake is private, with motorized boats banned. Shuffleboard and croquet are popular, but there are two tennis courts and a pool, with golf and hiking and cross-country trails available nearby.

Vieux Foyer. 3167 chemin Doncaster, Val-David, PQ, J0T 2N0. ☎ 800/567-8327 in Canada, or 819/322-2686. Fax 819/322-2687. 22 rms, 3 chalets. A/C. C$140–C$190 double (US$100–US$136); C$230 (US$164) chalet for 2. Rates include breakfast and dinner. Extra person C$65

(US$46). Weekly rates, off-season rates, and packages available. MC, V. Follow the signs through the town about 3km (1¹/₂ miles) to the inn.

This Swiss-style inn stands beside its own private pond. Armchairs are drawn up to the big fireplace in the main sitting room. The guest rooms are smallish and plain vanilla, with views of the surrounding forested hills. Some have whirlpools. There are also three chalets that hold up to eight people. With the auberge's popularity and limited number of rooms, advance reservations are a necessity most of the year. Facilities include a heated outdoor pool and a skating rink, bicycles and pedal boats are available, and cross-country skiing is nearby.

DINING

Le Grand Pa. 2481 rue de l'Eglise. ☎ **818/322-3104.** Pizzas and sandwiches C$4–C$14 (US$2.85–US$10). MC, V. Sun and Tues–Thurs noon–11pm, Fri–Sat noon–midnight. ITALIAN/ CANADIAN.

Near the tourist office, an open deck reaches out to the sidewalk, crowded with resin chairs and tables. Patrons tuck into a dozen versions of pizzas, baked in the brick oven inside. With their puffy crusts and fresh ingredients, they're the star attractions, often taken with pitchers of beer or sangria. Full meals are also available, and in summer a barbecue pit is fired up. Friday and Saturday nights they lay on live music by small combos.

STE-AGATHE-DES-MONTS

With a population approaching 10,000, Ste-Agathe-des-Monts, 85 kilometers (53 miles) north of Montréal, is the largest town in the Laurentians. Follow Autoroute 15 north to Exit 83 or 86. Ste-Agathe marks the end of the autoroute.

Early settlers and vacationers flocked here in search of land fronting on Lac des Sables, and entrepreneurs followed the crowds. Ste-Agathe's main street, rue Principale, is the closest to citification in these mountains, but it's only a touch of urbanity. Follow rue Principale from the highway through town and end up at the town dock on the lake. Watch out for four-way stops along the way.

The dock and surrounding **waterfront park** make Ste-Agathe a good place to pause for a few hours. One possibility is renting a bicycle from **Jacques Champoux Sports,** 74 rue St-Vincent (☎ **819/326-3480**), for the 3-mile ride around the lake. Lake cruises, beaches, and watercraft rentals seduce many people into lingering for days. For a night or two, the motels near town on Route 117 are sufficient, but for longer stays, consider a lakeside lodge.

The **Bureau Touristique de Ste-Agathe-des-Monts,** 190 rue Principale est (☎ **819/326-0457**), is open daily: from 9am to 8:30pm in summer and from 9am to 5pm the rest of the year.

Alouette cruises (☎ **819/326-3656**) depart the dock at the foot of rue Principale from mid-May to late October. It's a 50-minute, 19-kilometer (12-mile) voyage on a boat equipped with a bar and running commentary of the sights that observes, among other things, that Ste-Agathe and the Lac des Sables are famous for water-ski competitions and windsurfing. The cost for the cruise is C$11 (US$8) for adults, C$10 (US$7) for seniors, C$6 (US$4.30) for children 5 to 15; children under 5 are free. There are half a dozen departures a day; call for exact times.

ACCOMMODATIONS

Lac des Sables. 230 rue St-Venant, Ste-Agathe-des-Monts, PQ, J8C 2Z7. ☎ **800/567-8329** or 819/326-3994. Fax 819/326-9159. 19 rms. A/C TV. C$78–C$110 (US$56–US$79) double. Rates include breakfast. Extra person C$20 (US$14). AE, MC, V.

All the rooms in this small lakefront auberge have whirlpool baths, their chief distinguishing feature. Those with double Jacuzzis and a view of the lake are slightly more expensive. The small terrace overlooking the lake is a good vantage for watching the sunset. Downstairs is a games room with a pool table and pinball machine. The inn is about 2¹/₂ kilometers (1¹/₂ miles) from the village center and within walking distance of the beach and boating. English is spoken by the hosts, who also own the nearby Auberge du Comte de Watel.

ACCOMMODATIONS & DINING

Note that **Chez Girard** (see "Dining," below) also offers rooms.

La Sauvagine. 1592 Rte. 329 nord, Ste-Agathe, PQ, J8C 2Z8. ☎ **819/326-7673.** 9 rms, 7 with bath. C$75–C$130 (US$54–US$93) double with or without bath. Rates include breakfast. MC, V.

For something a little different, check this out—an 1890s auberge housed in a deconsecrated chapel. (An order of nuns added the chapel when they ran the property as a retirement home.) Antiques and semiantiques are scattered throughout, with an impressive armoire in the surprisingly elegant dining room. New owner René Kissler gathered many culinary awards in his native Belgium and has already started accumulating them here. Only two rooms share a bath; five have TVs. The restaurant is open nightly for dinner. The inn is 2 kilometers (1¹/₄ miles) north of Ste-Agathe, on the road to St-Donat.

DINING

Chez Girard. 18 rue Principale ouest, St-Agathe-des-Monts, PQ, J8C 1A3. ☎ **819/326-0922.** Reservations recommended. Main courses C$14.50–C$23.50 (US$10–US$17); 3-course table d'hôte lunch C$12.75–C$16.75 (US$9–US$12); 4-course table d'hôte dinner C$20–C$32 (US$14–US$23). AE, ER, MC, V. Tues–Wed and Sat–Sun 5–10pm, Thurs–Fri 11am–10pm. FRENCH.

Head toward the town dock and near the end of rue Principale, on the left, is a Québec-style house with a crimson roof: Chez Girard. In good weather diners can sit on the terrace overlooking the lake. Game is a central interest of the kitchen in autumn, while the summer menu emphasizes lighter pasta and seafood dishes. Among the respective possibilities are tournedos of caribou with mushrooms and wild grain rice and tortellini with razor clams, langostinos, and scallops in goat-cheese sauce. The kitchen prides itself on using the freshest ingredients and on the absence of a deep fryer. Lunch is served only in summer.

The auberge also has lodgings, five rooms and three suites, in two village houses. Most units have fireplaces, whirlpool baths, and TV. They go for C$100 to C$120 (US$71 to US$86) double with breakfast or C$125 to C$170 (US$89 to US$121) double with breakfast and dinner; suites are C$110 (US$79) with breakfast. All have access to a private beach.

ST-JOVITE & MONT TREMBLANT

Follow Route 117 about 37 kilometers (23 miles) north from Ste-Agathe to the St-Jovite exit; it's 122 kilometers (76 miles) north of Montréal. To get to Mont Tremblant, turn right on Route 327, just before the church in St-Jovite. Most vacationers make their base at one of the resorts or lodges scattered along Route 327. Mont Tremblant is 45 kilometers (28 miles) north of Ste-Agathe and 130 kilometers (80 miles) north of Montréal.

St-Jovite (pop. 4,118) is the commercial center for the most famous and popular of all Laurentian districts, the area surrounding Mont Tremblant, at 650 meters

(2,135 ft.), the highest peak in the Laurentians. In 1894 the provincial government set aside 1,492 square kilometers (almost 1,000 square miles) of wilderness as **Mont Tremblant Provincial Park,** and the foresight of this early conservation effort has yielded outdoor enjoyment to skiers and four-season vacationers ever since.

The mountain's name comes from a legend of the area's first inhabitants. When the first Amerindians arrived here early in the 17th century, they named the peak after their god, Manitou. When humans disturbed nature in any way, Manitou became enraged and made the great mountain tremble—*montagne tremblante.*

St-Jovite, a pleasant community, provides all the expected services, and its main street, rue Ouimet, is lined with cafes and shops, including Le Coq Rouge, which sells folk art and country antiques. The village of Mont Tremblant, though several miles nearer the large resorts and the mountain itself, has only the most basic services, including a market and post office but no pharmacy.

Tourist information, including maps of local ski trails, is available at the **Bureau Touristique de Mont Tremblant,** rue du Couvent at Mont Tremblant (☎ 819/425-2434), open daily from 9am to 9pm in summer and from 9am to 5pm the rest of the year; and at the **Tourist Bureau of St-Jovite/Mont Tremblant,** 305 chemin Brébeuf in St-Jovite (☎ 819/425-3300), open daily in summer from 9am to 7pm and the rest of the year from 9am to 5pm.

SKIING, SUMMER WATER SPORTS & MORE

Water sports in summer are as popular as the ski slopes and trails in winter, because the base of Mont Tremblant is surrounded by no fewer than 10 lakes: Lac Tremblant, a gorgeous stretch of water 10 miles long, and also Lac Ouimet, Lac Mercier, Lac Gelinas, Lac Desmarais, and five smaller bodies of water, not to mention rivers and streams. From June to mid-October, **Grand Manitou Cruises,** chemin Principale in Mont Tremblant (☎ 819/425-8681), offers a 75-minute narrated tour of Lac Tremblant, focusing on its history, nature, and legends.

Mont Tremblant, which has the same vertical drop—3,175 feet—as Mont Ste-Anne near Québec City, draws the biggest downhill ski crowds in the Laurentians. Founded in 1939 by Philadelphia millionaire Joe Ryan, **Station Mont Tremblant** is one of the oldest ski areas in North America, and the first to create trails on both sides of a mountain. It was the second in the world to install a chairlift. There are higher mountains with longer runs and steeper pitches, but something about Mont Tremblant compels people to return time and again.

Today Mont Tremblant has the snowmaking capability to cover 328 acres, making skiing possible from early November to late May and keeping at least 30 trails open at Christmastime (as opposed to nine in 1992). There are now 43 downhill runs and trails, including the recently opened Dynamite and Verige trails, with 810-foot and 745-foot drops, respectively, and the Edge, a peak with two gladed trails. The several lifts are for gondolas and chairs, no T-bars. There's plenty of cross-country action on 90 kilometers (56 miles) of maintained trails. And in summer, choose from golf, tennis, horseback riding, boating, swimming, biking, hiking, and more.

ACCOMMODATIONS

Château Beauvallon. 616 Montée Ryan (Box 138), Mont Tremblant, PQ, J0T 1Z0. ☎ and fax **819/425-7275.** 12 rms, 6 with bath. Summer C$64 (US$46) double with or without bath, including full breakfast, taxes, and services; winter C$110 (US$79) double with or without bath, including breakfast and dinner. Children 12 and under stay for half price in parent's rm. Packages available. No credit cards. Free parking.

An antidote to the impersonal bustle of Mont Tremblant's big resorts is this modest inn, a white gambrel-roofed and gabled structure with yellow shutters set back from the road and bordered by a log fence. The château's beach is a short stroll away on Lac Beauvallon, and its boats are moored nearby. Built in 1942, it was once part of the Mont Tremblant Lodge resort. Today this seclusion is much of its appeal, along with the low tariffs, and little happens to disturb the tranquillity. The rustic rooms have knotty-pine paneling. Up to 30 guests can be seated in the dining room, and meals are preceded by drinks beside the lounge's fireplace.

✪ **Club Tremblant.** Av. Cuttle, Mont Tremblant, PQ, J0T 1Z0. ☎ **800/567-8341** in the U.S. and Canada, or 819/425-2731. Fax 819/425-5617. 100 suites. TV TEL. From C$111 (US$79) per person. Rates include breakfast and dinner. Children 6–12 are charged C$40 (US$29). Rates are lower for stays of 2 days or more. Packages available. AE, DC, ER, MC, V. Turn left off Montée Ryan, then right on Lac Tremblant N. and follow signs for less than a mile.

Terraced into a hillside sloping steeply to the shore of Lac Tremblant, this handsome property consists of several lodges in blessedly muted alpine style. Essentially a concentration of privately owned condominiums operated by a single management, the accommodations represent excellent value and that greatest of luxuries—space. For the price of a single room at many other resorts in the region, you get a suite of one to three bedrooms. A typical suite has a fireplace, a balcony, a sitting room with cable TV and dining table, a full kitchen with cookware and dishwasher, and one or two bathrooms with Jacuzzi, and clothes washer and dryer. Nearly all have views of the lake and Mont Tremblant, which rises from the opposite shore. This is a family resort, so expect childish yips and squeals in the dining rooms in peak months—July, August, February, and March. A drawback on the hottest days of summer is the lack of air-conditioning, but they'll deliver a portable fan on request.

Dining/Entertainment: The dining room employs a largely French menu, with a five-course table d'hôte. A bar with a stone fireplace and picture windows is an inviting spot any evening, and there's usually piano music Thursday to Saturday nights.

Services: Day-care program for children 3 to 13, lifeguarded swimming areas. During ski season, a 22-passenger bus shuttles between the lodge and the slopes.

Facilities: Indoor and outdoor pools, Jacuzzi, workout room (with weight machine, Exercycles, rowing machines), four tennis courts, six nearby golf courses. A new spa with therapeutic baths and massages opened in late 1997.

Gray Rocks. 525 chemin Principale, Mont Tremblant, PQ, J0T 1Z0. ☎ **800/567-6767** or 819/425-2771. Fax 819/425-3474. 122 rms, 56 condos. A/C TEL. C$198–C$360 (US$141–US$257) double or condo. Rates include breakfast and dinner. Discounts for children sharing parents' rm. Meals optional in condos. Ski-school packages available. AE, DISC, ER, MC, V.

The area's dowager resort has been under new management since 1993, and its ministrations are evident, not least in the new 18-hole golf course. The accommodations are in a huge rambling main lodge, in the cozier Le Château lodge, or in one of the resort's four-person cottages. Only the condos have TVs. That minor lack aside, the resort covers most other recreational bases, including golf, tennis, a spa, horseback riding, and boating. And there's not only a private airport for guests who fly in but also a seaplane base for joyrides over Lac Ouimet. There's a complete playground with attendants to provide child care, as well as a program of free swimming lessons.

Dining/Entertainment: The dining room serves three meals daily, and there's a bar with piano and other music for dancing.

Services: Room service, child-care program, same-day dry cleaning/laundry, bicycle rental, junior and adult tennis school.

Facilities: Par-72 golf course, indoor pool and fitness center, 22 tennis courts, horseback riding, sailboat rentals, shuffleboard, croquet, skiing, lifts, ski school, and access to 90 kilometers (56 miles) of cross-country skiing.

Tremblant: A Resort Village

Not merely a hotel with a pool, Tremblant is a complete and growing resort village stretching from the mountain's skirts to the shores of 10-mile-long Lac Tremblant. At recent count, there were several hotels and condo complexes, 14 shops (including a liquor store), and nine eating places and bars. When the snow is deep, skiers here like to follow the sun around the mountain, making the run down slopes with an eastern exposure in the morning and down the western-facing ones in the afternoon.

To get to the village, drive 5 kilometers (3 miles) north of St-Jovite on Route 117; then take Montée Ryan and follow the blue signs for about 9.5 kilometers (6 miles). The Limocar bus from Montréal stops at the entrance, and there's door-to-door transport from Dorval and Mirabel airports Friday to Sunday.

Lodging at Tremblant: You can make reservations for hotels, B&Bs, chalets, and condos at the resort and in the surrounding area through the central numbers (☎ 800/461-8711 or 819/681-2000) or by contacting the establishments directly. The general reception area is in a building labeled LES CÈDRES; take the right turn just before the old church. Here are the more prominent hotels, all of which incorporate privately owned condos:

Château Mont Tremblant. Mont Tremblant, PQ, J0T 1Z0. ☎ **819/441-1414.** 316 rms and suites. A/C TV TEL. C$135–C$185 (US$96–US$132) double; C$199 (US$142) suite. AE, DC, ER, MC, V.

This very new luxury entry of the Canadian Pacific chain commands a crest above the village, as befits its stature among the Tremblant hostelries. It has a health club and indoor and outdoor pools.

Les Suites Tremblant. Mont Tremblant, PQ, J0T 1Z0. ☎ **800/461-8711.** 569 condos. TEL TV. C$62–C$114 (US$44–US$81) 1-bedrm condo; C$130–C$234 (US$93–US$167) 2-bedrm condo. AE, DC, ER, MC, V.

A collection of several buildings, each with slightly different profiles of decor and amenities, this is the choice for families, couples traveling together, or those who require economical accommodation. The most expensive two-bedroom unit, at C$234 (US$167), can accommodate up to six, bringing the cost down to less than C$39 (US$28) per person. All have kitchenettes, for greater savings, and many have fireplaces and/or washing machines.

Dining/Entertainment: In addition to the hotel bars and restaurants, there are many freestanding places at which to get a meal, a snack, or a cocktail and hear some music. Serving a variety of kinds of food implicit in their names are Pizzateria, Coco Pazzo, Crêperie Catherine, Aux Truffes, Le Savoie (fondues), Mexicali Rosa's, and Le Gascon. The Microbrasserie la Diable pours craft beers to accompany live jazz on weekends and P'tit Caribou brings in pop performers weekly. On the summit of the mountain is Le Rendezvous, a cafe with a circular fireplace, and the 1,000-seat Le Grand Manitou restaurant complex, with a dining room called La Légende, plus a bistro and cafeteria.

Services: Supervision for children 2 to 6 at Kids' Kamp, ski rentals and repair, a gondola to take visitors and residents from the parking lot to the village.

Facilities: In winter, 61 slopes and trails in all, served by 10 ski lifts, including two base-to-summit high-speed quads, triple-chair lifts, double-chair lifts; ski school; ski shop; access to cross-country ski trails. In summer, lake swimming, boat cruise (extra fee), chairlift rides to the top of Mont Tremblant (extra fee), 11 lighted Har-Tru tennis courts, 18-hole St. Andrews Golf Club, and a dozen other indoor and outdoor amusements.

Marriott Residence Inn. Mont Tremblant, PQ, J0T 1Z0. ☎ **888/272-4000.** 127 rms and condos. A/C TV TEL. C$109 (US$78) double; C$139–C$229 (US$99–US$164) condo. Rates include breakfast. AE, DC, ER, MC, V.

Near the terminus of the lower chairlift running through the central part of the village, this midlevel hotel has its own restaurant, a heated outdoor pool, and indoor parking. The higher-priced condos have two bedrooms.

DINING

Though most Laurentian inns and resorts have their own dining facilities and often require that guests use them, especially in winter, Mont Tremblant and vicinity have several decent independent dining places.

Antipasto. 855 rue Ouimet, St-Jovite. ☎ **819/425-7580.** Main courses C$12–C$20 (US$9–US$14). MC, V. Daily 4–11pm. ITALIAN.

Antipasto is housed in an old train station moved to this site, so there's the expected railroad memorabilia on the walls, but the owners have resisted the temptation to play up the theme to excess. Captain's chairs are drawn up to big tables with green Formica tops and paper place mats. Almost everyone orders the César salad (their spelling), which is dense and flavorful, perhaps a little too strong for some tastes—the half portion is more than enough as a first course. Individual pizzas emerge from the brick ovens in 30 versions, costing C$9.50 to C$18 (US$7 to US$13), on a choice of regular or whole-wheat crust. Pastas, for C$8.50 to C$20 (US$6 to US$14), are available in even greater variety, those with shellfish among the winners. The sauces are savory, if a bit thin. There are outdoor tables in summer.

Brunch Café. 816 rue Ouimet, St-Jovite. ☎ **819/425-8233.** Main courses C$8–C$16 (US$6–US$11); table d'hôte C$9–C$15 (US$6–US$11). MC, V. Apr–Oct daily 8am–10pm; Nov–Mar daily 8am–4pm. INTERNATIONAL.

While the menu lists many sandwiches, salads, pastas, and pizzas, one of the most satisfying choices are the sausages picked from a roster of six designer varieties, served with sauerkraut, mustard, and pan fries. They have complementary *bières en fût* (beer on tap), plus an interesting selection of refreshing regional microbrews and imports. Food takes a while to arrive. The cafe is downtown, not far from Antipasto, which is under the same management. There are umbrellas over the tables facing the main street, close tables inside. Live music is on offer most summer weekends.

La Table Enchantée. 600 Rte. 117 nord, Lac Duhamel. ☎ **819/425-7113.** Reservations usually required. Main courses C$14.50–C$24.25 (US$10–US$17); table d'hôte C$16.50–C$24.25 (US$12–US$17). AE, MC, V. Tues–Sun 5–10pm. Closed mid-Oct to mid-Nov and 2 weeks in May. QUEBECOIS.

Tables in this tidy little restaurant support some of the region's most carefully prepared dishes. The kitchen adheres to the traditional Québec repertoire with an occasional detour—their Frenchified medaillons of red deer, for instance. A favored starter is the clam chowder or, in the short spring, fiddleheads. Then perhaps try the pâté called *cretons*, followed by Québécois *cipaille*, a pot pie layered with pheasant, guinea hen, rabbit, veal, and pork. Dessert might be *grand-pères au sirop d'érable* (dumplings in maple syrup).

3 The Estrie Region

80 kilometers (48 miles) SE of Montréal

The Estrie region serves, in part, as Québec's breadbasket, a largely pastoral area marked by billowing hills and the 2,600-foot peak of Mont Orford, centerpiece of a provincial park and the region's premier downhill ski area. Only a short distance from Mont Orford is Sherbrooke, the industrial and commercial capital of Estrie (also known as the Eastern Townships and Les Cantons de l'Est), and throughout the Mont Orford–Sherbrooke area are serene glacial lakes that attract summer fishers, sailors, and swimmers. Estrie is Québec's best-kept secret, so it's mostly Montréalers and Québécois who occupy rental houses to ski, fish, cycle, or launch their boats.

Once out of Montréal, drive east along the arrow-straight Autoroute 10 past silos and fields, herds of cows, and meadows strewn with wildflowers. Cresting the hill at kilometer 100 is an especially beguiling view of mountains and countryside stretching toward New England, not far over the horizon.

At the earliest signs of spring thaw, the Estrie region leaps into gear as crews penetrate every "sugar bush" (stand of sugar maples) to tap the sap and "sugar off." Maple-sugar festivals result, and numerous farms host "sugaring parties" at which guests partake of considerable country repasts topped by traditional maple-syrup desserts.

Autumn has its attractions, for in addition to the glorious fall foliage (usually best in the weeks fore and aft the third weekend in September), Estrie orchards sag under the weight of apples of every variety, and cider mills hum day and night to produce what has been described as the "wine" of Québec. It's not unusual for visitors to help with the apple harvest, paying a low price for the baskets they gather themselves. The cider mills throw open their doors for tours and tastings.

Although town names such as Granby, Waterloo, and Sherbrooke are obviously English, Estrie is now about 90% French-speaking. A few words of French and a little sign language are sometimes necessary, since the area draws fewer Anglophone visitors than do the Laurentides.

On the drive from Montréal, one of the first Estrie towns of interest is **Rougemont,** at Exit 37 off Autoroute 10 and 22 kilometers (13½ miles) along Route 112, known for its orchards and cider mills. The main street is dotted all year with little stands selling various sorts of apples, apple products, vegetables, and homemade bread. At **St-Césaire,** a few miles farther along 112, small stands and shops specialize in locally made handcrafts. The next town, **St-Paul-d'Abbotsford,** was founded in the late 1700s by Scottish settlers. Abbotsford became the name of the town in 1829, the "St-Paul" added later by the French inhabitants.

Another possible detour is 27 kilometers (17 miles) south of Autoroute 10. Take Exit 55 onto Route 233 sud to Route 104 est (briefly) to Route 235 sud. This soon becomes the main street of **Mystic.** Sixty-four people live there, a wide spot in a side road that enjoyed a short-lived prosperity from 1868 to 1880, when an ironworks was here and the railroad passed through. Among its landmarks are an 1882 brick church in the center and an unusual 12-sided barn on the south side. Mystic is home to a fetching enterprise called **L'Oeuf** (☎ 514/248-7529), a combination B&B, restaurant, chocolatier, and food shop. It's open Wednesday to Sunday for lunch and dinner.

From Mystic, it's a short drive south to **Stanbridge East.** The Missiquoi Museum, open in summer only, stands beside the Aux Brochets River, housed in a photogenic 1860 mill with a waterwheel. There's a picnic area beside it. To return to the Autoroute, continue east to Dunham, pick up Route 213 north, make a short jog west on Route 104, and then north again on Route 139.

For extended stays in the region, consider basing yourself in one of the several inns along the shores of Lac Massawippi, especially in and around **North Hatley,** and take day trips from there.

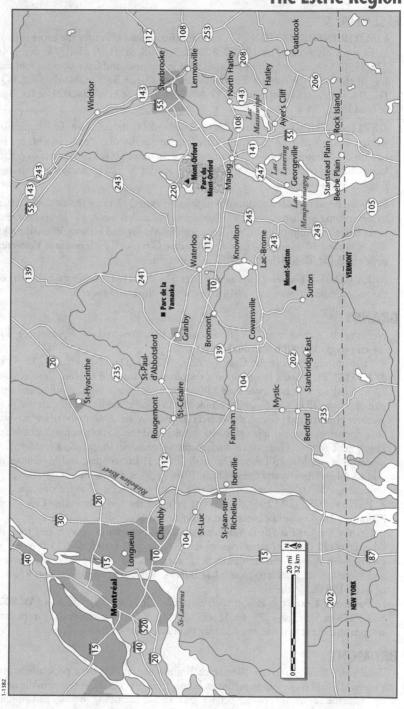

1-1382

ESSENTIALS

VISITOR INFORMATION The **tourist information office** for the Estrie region, at Exit 68 off Autoroute 10 (☎ **800/263-1068** or 514/375-8774; fax 514/375-3530), is open daily from 10am to 6pm in summer and from 9am to 5pm the rest of the year. Or contact **Tourisme Estrie,** 25 rue Bocage, Sherbrooke, PQ, J1L 2J4. For more information, call ☎ **800/355-5755** or 819/820-2020, or fax 819/566-4445.

GETTING THERE **By Car** Leave the island of Montréal by the Champlain Bridge, which leads to Autoroute 10, heading for Sherbrooke. People in a hurry can remain on Autoroute 10—and plenty of express buses do this, too—but to get to know the countryside, turn off the Autoroute at Exit 37 and go north the short distance to join Route 112.

By Bus Local buses leave Montréal to follow Route 112 more than a dozen times a day, arriving in Sherbrooke, 160 kilometers (100 miles) away, 3¹/₂ hours later. Express buses use Autoroute 10, making a stop in Magog and arriving in Sherbrooke in 2 hours and 10 minutes (2¹/₂ hr. from Québec City). Call the **Terminus Voyageur** in Montréal at ☎ **514/842-2281** for information.

AREA CODE The telephone area code is **514** or **819,** depending on the part of the region called (towns with a 514 area code are closer to Montréal).

GRANBY

North of the autoroute at Exit 68, this largely industrial and not especially beguiling city (pop. 41,500) has a couple of surprises.

First among them is the **Granby Zoo,** 347 bd. David-Bouchard (☎ **514/372-9113**), the second most important zoological garden in Québec Province. Its 70 wooded acres harbor more than 1,000 mammals, exotic birds, reptiles, and amphibians from all over the world. Founded in 1953, the zoo has an educational program for children and presents shows every day in summer. Among the newer exhibits are a nocturnal cave, a display of robotic whales, and the Afrika pavilion, notable for its group of gorillas. There are restaurants, picnic areas, gift shops, and free rides. The zoo is open late May to Labour Day, daily from 10am to 5pm, and September to mid-October Saturday and Sunday from 10am to 5pm. Admission is C$16 (US$11) for adults, C$9 (US$6) for students 5 to 17, and C$5 (US$3.55) for children 2 to 4. Parking is C$3 (US$2.15). You'll spot signs for the zoo after taking Exit 68 off Autoroute 10. The visitor entrance is on boulevard David-Bouchard nord.

Granby also has **Parc de la Yamaska,** with a 3-kilometer (2-mile) hiking trail, 40 kilometers (25 miles) of cross-country ski trails, and 22 kilometers (13¹/₂ miles) of cycling trails along an old railroad track between Granby and the towns of Bromont and Waterloo. Another attraction is **Lac Boivin,** with a fountain that shoots a plume of water 150 feet in the air.

Tourisme Granby is at 650 rue Principale, Granby, PQ, J2G 8L4 (☎ **800/567-7273** or 514/372-7273; fax 514/372-7782). It's open summer daily from 8am to 7pm and the rest of the year Monday to Friday from 8:30am to 5pm.

BROMONT

Take Exit 78 off Autoroute 10 to reach Bromont (pop. 5,000), a popular destination for day and night skiing, mountain biking (rent bikes at the entrance to the town opposite the tourist office—see below), golf, horseback riding, hiking, and zipping down alpine and water slides. Shoppers have two of the largest **factory outlets** in

Canada—Versants de Bromont and Les Manufacturiers de Bromont—and the area's largest **flea market,** with 350 stalls set up in the local drive-in from 9am to 5pm the first Sunday in May to the second Sunday in November.

The **tourist office** is at 150 rue Champlain (☎ 514/534-2200).

ACCOMMODATIONS & DINING

Château Bromont. 90 rue Stanstead, Bromont, PQ, J2L 1K6. ☎ **800/304-3433** or 514/534-3433. Fax 514/534-0514. 154 rms. A/C MINIBAR TV TEL. C$158 (US$113) double. Rate includes breakfast. Spa, ski, and other packages available. AE, DC, DISC, ER, MC, V.

All the rooms at the château have rocking chairs and loft beds, and half have fireplaces. Some no-smoking rooms are available. A landscaped terrace and two hot tubs look up at the mountain. The staff is young and bilingual. Les Quatre Canards restaurant serves lunch and dinner, and there's a bistro bar, L'Equestre, and the Château Terrasse Bar-BBQ. In addition to indoor and outdoor pools and Jacuzzis, a sauna, a small gym, and squash and racquetball courts, there's a European spa featuring mud and algae baths (use of the spa facilities costs extra).

KNOWLTON

Those who shop for amusement, not mere necessity, will want to make this a destination. Knowlton is compact, but its two main shopping streets have a number of stores that reveal a creeping chic personified by Liz Claiborne, Ralph Lauren, and their peers.

Knowlton is on the southeast corner of **Lac Brome** and is part of the five-village municipality known as Lac Brome (pop. 4,824). It's one of the last towns in the region where a majority of the residents have English as their mother tongue. The first settler here was Paul Holland Knowlton, a Loyalist from Vermont. He arrived in 1815 and established a farm where the golf course is now located. By 1834 he had added a sawmill, a blacksmith shop, a gristmill, and a store. He also founded the first high school.

Another Knowlton resident, Reginald Aubrey Fessenden, invented a wireless radio in 1906, a year ahead of Marconi, and relayed a message from Brant Rock, Massachusetts, to ships in the Caribbean. Large mansions overhang the lake on either side of town. The town hosts a **Blue Grass Festival** in June, and the **Brome Fair** is held over Labour Day weekend.

The **tourist information office** is in the local museum, the **Musée Historique du Comté de Brome** (Brome County Historical Museum), 130 Lakeside St. (Route 243; ☎ 514/243-6782). This museum fills five historic buildings, including the town's first school, established by Paul Holland Knowlton. Exhibits focus on town life, with re-creations of a schoolroom, bedroom, parlor, and kitchen. The Martin Annex (1921) is dominated by a 1917 Fokker single-seat biplane, the foremost German aircraft in World War I. Also on the premises are collections of old radios and 18th- to early-20th-century weapons. The museum sells books about the area. Admission is C$3.50 (US$2.50) for adults, C$2 (US$1.40) for seniors and students, and C$1.50 (US$1.05) for children. The museum is open only mid-May to mid-September, Monday to Saturday from 10am to 4:30pm and Sunday from 11am to 4:30pm.

SUTTON

A pleasant outing from Knowlton or anywhere in the vicinity, Sutton (pop. 1,587) is a town with a number of promising cafes and the region's best bookstore, the **Book Nook,** 14 rue Principale sud (☎ 514/538-2207), which is open daily. Nearby **Mont**

Sutton is known in summer for its 54 kilometers (33 miles) of hiking trails linking with the Appalachian Trail and for its glade skiing in winter. The surrounding country roads are popular with bikers. For more information, drop by the **Sutton Tourist Association** (☎ 514/538-2646), opposite the bookstore.

MONT ORFORD

Exit 115 north off the Autoroute leads into one of Québec's most popular provincial parks. The **Bureau d'Information Touristique Magog-Orford** is at 55 rue Cabana (via Route 112), Magog, PQ, J1X 2C4 (☎ 800/267-2744 or 819/843-2744; fax 819/847-4036). It's open daily: in summer from 8:30am to 7:30pm and in winter from 9am to 5pm.

From mid-September to mid-October, the **Mont Orford Provincial Park** blazes with autumn color, and in winter visitors come for the more than 20 miles of ski trails and slopes, with a vertical drop of 1,500 feet, or for the extensive network of cross-country ski and snowshoe trails.

Mont Orford is a veteran ski area compared to Bromont (see above) and has long provided slopes of choice for the moneyed families of Estrie and Montréal. The other two mountains in the area, Owl's Head and Mont Sutton, are more family-oriented and less glitzy. These four ski centers have banded together to form **Ski East,** enabling skiers to purchase an all-inclusive 5-day ticket good at all four areas anytime. Similarly economical lesson plans are available.

Orford has another claim to fame in the **Centre d'Arts Orford** (☎ 819/843-3981), set on a 222-acre estate in the park and providing music classes for talented young musicians in summer. From early July to mid-August, a series of classical and chamber-music concerts is given in connection with **Festival Orford.** Prices are C$12 to C$22 (US$9 to US$16) for professional organizations, free for student performances. Concerts are held Thursday to Sunday. A complete luncheon is served outside following the Saturday concert. Visual-arts exhibitions at the center are open to the public, and walking trails connect it to a nearby campground.

ACCOMMODATIONS

Cheribourg. 2603 Rte. 141 nord (C.P. 337), Magog, PQ, J1X 3W9. ☎ **800/567-6132** in Québec, or 819/843-3308. Fax 819/843-2639. 97 rms, 65 chalets. A/C TV TEL. C$90 (US$64) per day double, from C$435 (US$310) per week chalet. Extra adult C$12 (US$9). Children under 12 stay free in parents' rm. Discounts and packages available. AE, DC, DISC, ER, MC, V. Take Exit 118 from Autoroute 10.

These clusters of attached structures with sharply angled orange roofs are easy to spot on the way to Mont Orford and Lac Memphrémagog. Opened only in 1971, it's nevertheless one of the area's oldest resorts, set on 200 acres in Mont Orford Park. You have access to clay tennis courts, two outdoor pools, an exercise room, a sauna, a Jacuzzi, mountain bikes, a kids' playground, and a disco in summer. The rooms, most of which have two queen-size beds, are decorated with bleached pine furniture. Two- or three-room chalets are a frugal choice for families or groups of up to six, all equipped with a fireplace and kitchenette with utensils. Reasonable prices and the good location offset the heavily used look of the interiors and the harried demeanor of the staff. The Cheribourg is open year-round.

MAGOG & LAC MEMPHREMAGOG

Magog (pop. 14,500) came by its handle through the corruption of an Amerindian word. The Abenaki name *Memrobagak* ("Great Expanse of Water") somehow became *Memphrémagog,* which was eventually shortened to *Magog.* The town is at the northernmost end of Lac Memphrémagog (pronounced "Mem-*free*-ma-gog"), *not* on Lac

Magog, which is about 8 miles north of Magog. Lac Memphrémagog straddles the U.S.-Canadian border. It has its own legendary marine creature, nicknamed Memphre, which supposedly surfaced for the first time in 1798. Other sightings have been claimed since then.

For the Magog-Orford tourist information office, see "Mont Orford," above.

Magog has a fully utilized waterfront, and in July each year the **International Crossing of Lac Memphrémagog** creates a big splash. Participants start out in Newport, Vermont, at 6am and swim 38.5 kilometers (24 miles) to Magog, arriving around 3:30 or 4pm. For a less taxing experience, take a 1¹/₂-hour **cruise** aboard the *Aventure I* or *Aventure II* (☎ 819/843-8068). The cost is C$11 (US$8) for adults and C$6 (US$4.30) for children 11 and under; a daylong cruise is C$40 (US$29). The boats leave from Point Merry Park, the focal point for many of the town's outdoor activities.

An 18-kilometer (11-mile) bike path links the lake with Mont Orford. In winter it's transformed into a **cross-country ski trail,** and a 2¹/₂-kilometer-long (1¹/₂-mile) **skating rink** is created on the lakeshores. Snowmobiling trails crisscross the region. Other popular activities are golf, tennis, and horseback riding.

Drive west from Magog on Route 112 and watch for the first road on the left on the far side of the lake; take chemin Bolton 19 kilometers (12 miles) south to the turnoff for the **Benedictine Abbey of St-Benoît-du-Lac,** Chemin Fisher (☎ 819/843-4080). There's no mistaking the abbey, with its granite steeple that thrusts into the sky above the lake, against the backdrop of Owl's Head Mountain. Though St-Benoît-du-Lac dates only from 1912, the serenity of the site is timeless. Some 40 monks help keep the art of Gregorian chant alive in their liturgy, which you can attend. For the 45-minute service (times below), walk to the rear of the abbey and down the stairs; follow the signs for the oratoire and sit in back to avoid a lot of otherwise obligatory standing and sitting.

Admission to the abbey is free but donations are accepted. It's open daily from 6am to 8pm; mass with Gregorian chant is given at 11am, and vespers with Gregorian chant are given at 5pm (at 7pm on Thursday). There are no vespers on Tuesday in July and August.

The abbey receives 7,000 pilgrims a year, 60% of them between 16 and 25. It maintains separate **hostels** for men (☎ 819/843-4080) and women (☎ 819/843-2340). Make reservations in advance, figuring about C$35 (US$25) per person. A bleu cheese known as L'Ermite, among Québec's most famous, is produced at the monastery, along with a creamy version and Swiss and cheddar types. They're on sale in the little shop, open Monday to Saturday from 9 to 10:45am and 2 to 4:30pm. It also sells chocolate from Oka, honey, a nonalcoholic cider, and tapes of religious chants. You may wish to peek into the tiny stone chapel to the left at the entrance to the property, opposite the small cemetery. Visitors during the last 2 weeks of September or the first 2 weeks of October may want to help pick apples in the orchard.

LAKE MASSAWIPPI & NORTH HATLEY

Southeast of Magog, reachable by Route 141 or 108, east of Autoroute 55, is **Lake Massawippi,** easily the most alluring resort area in Estrie. Set among rolling hills and fertile farm country, the 12-mile-long lake with its scalloped shoreline was discovered in the early years of this century by people of wealth and power, many of whom were American Southerners trying to escape the sultry summers of Virginia and Georgia. They built grand "cottages" on slopes in prime locations along the lakeshore, with enough bedrooms to house their extended families and friends for months at a time. Several of these have been converted into inns.

Three local hostelries offer an inn-to-inn cross-country ski package called **Skiwippi,** offering you a fine dinner and accommodation each night. In winter, the lands around the lake have 56 kilometers (35 miles) of cross-country ski trails, and the special 3- or 6-night packages allow takers to spend brisk days skiing between the exemplary Auberge Ripplecove, Manoir Hovey, and Auberge Hatley (see "North Hatley," below). In summer, there's a comparable golf version. For the less athletically inclined, a similar package (*sans* skis), called **A Moveable Feast,** is available. Book these packages through any of the three inns.

The jewel of Lake Massawippi, **North Hatley** (pop. 704), only half an hour from the U.S. border and 138 kilometers (85½ miles) from Montréal, has a river meandering through it. Old photographs show flocks of people coursing along the main village street. It has a variety of lodgings and places to dine, a few shops, golf, horseback riding, a marina, a post office, a laundry, and a general store. An English-language theater, the **Piggery,** on a country road outside town (☎ 819/842-2431), presents plays of an often-experimental nature during summer; a restaurant serves light meals from 5 to 7:30pm.

ACCOMMODATIONS & DINING

✪ **Auberge Hatley.** 325 rue Virgin (P.O. Box 330), N. Hatley, PQ, J0B 2C0. ☎ 819/842-2451. Fax 819/842-2907. 25 rms. A/C TEL. C$220–C$370 (US$157–US$264) double. Rates include breakfast, dinner, and gratuities. AE, MC, V. Take Exit 29 from Autoroute 55 and follow Rte. 108 east, watching for signs.

This acclaimed gastronomic resort occupies a hillside above the lake, not far from the town center. All rooms have bath with tub or shower, and over half have Jacuzzis and/or fireplaces. They're thinking about adding TVs, for those who care. An abundance of antiques, many of them sizable Québécois country pieces, are joined by complementary reproductions. There's a pool, and the staff advises on nearby activities. But there's no uncertainty where owners Liliane and Robert Gagnon place their priorities: the pleasures of the table.

The dining room has a bank of windows looking over the lake. Tables are set with Rosenthal china, fresh flowers, and candles. It's a necessarily soothing environment, since dinner can easily extend over 3 hours. Updated but essentially classical French techniques are applied to such ingredients as salmon, bison, and wild boar. Most herbs and some vegetables come from the Gagnons' hydroponic farm, and the ducks and pheasants come from their 100-acre game island. A particular treat is the meal-ending selection of cheeses, served with the waiter's careful description.

La Raveaudière. 11 Hatley Centre (P.O. Box 8), N. Hatley, Québec J0B 2C0. ☎ 819/842-2554. 7 rms. C$115–C$145 (US$82–US$104) double. Rates include breakfast. MC, V. Drive south along the lakeshore road from the center of town, bearing left up the hill. The inn is on the left.

The owners do little to promote their property, and from the outside the inn looks like the ordinary 1890s farmhouse it once was. But this must be one of the most exquisitely decorated lodgings on the lake, a sophisticated urbanite's notion of a proper country place. It sits next to a golf course, to which guests have access, but most visitors settle into the plush seating to read and chat with their ebullient hosts. There are no TVs and no room phones, and only four units are air-conditioned. They served dinner for a while, but success was too draining. There are no facilities for children under 12.

✪ **Manoir Hovey.** Chemin Hovey (P.O. Box 60), N. Hatley, PQ, J0B 2C0. ☎ 800/661-2421 or 819/842-2421. Fax 819/842-2248. 35 rms. A/C TEL. C$190–C$416 (US$136–US$297) double. Rates include full breakfast, dinner, tax, gratuities, and use of most recreational facilities. AE, MC, V. Take Exit 29 off Autoroute 55 and follow Rte. 108 east, watching for signs.

Named for Capt. Ebenezer Hovey, a Connecticut Yankee who came on the lake in 1793 and was the first white settler, the columned manor was built in 1899. Encompassing 20 acres and 1,600 feet of lakefront property, it's one of Québec's most complete resort inns, a member of the international Romantik Hotels group. Many of the rooms have fireplaces, balconies, and whirlpool baths; most have TVs; several are for nonsmokers. The library adjoining the reception area has floor-to-ceiling bookshelves and a stone fireplace. A lighted tennis court, touring bikes, a modestly equipped exercise room, a heated outdoor pool, and two beaches add to its appeal. In winter, they push a heated cabin out onto the lake for ice fishing. The dining room serves contemporary French cuisine, with a menu that changes with the seasons and features fresh herbs, vegetables, and edible flowers from the kitchen garden. Hearthealthy dishes are featured, all fragrant and full-bodied, in attractive presentations. Steve and Kathy Stafford are the gracious hosts.

Manoir Le Tricorne. 50 chemin Gosselin, N. Hatley, PQ, J0B 2C0. ☎ **819/842-4522.** Fax 819/842-2692. 12 rms. C$115–C$225 (US$82–US$161) double. Rates include full breakfast. AE, MC, V. Take Rte. 108 west out of N. Hatley and follow the signs.

While the core of this house is 125 years old, it looks as if it were erected 5 years ago. The exterior is shocking-pink and white, the interior decked out in best middle-brow *Good Housekeeping* manner, with lots of duck decoys, birdcages, and tartans. The decorative scheme won't be to everyone's taste, but all is immaculate and there's ample room to move about. Three rooms have fireplaces; five have Jacuzzis. There are no phones or TVs, but they are available in the common room. Arriving guests are welcomed with glasses of port. Breakfast menus are changed regularly, with fruit omelets one day and eggs Benedict the next. Up the hill is a pool, and one of the two ponds is stocked for fishing. Spectacular views of Lake Massawippi are provided from all over the hilltop property. Children over 8 are welcome.

DINING

Le Moulin. 225 rue Mill. ☎ **819/842-2380.** Main courses C$8–C$17 (US$6–US$12); table d'hôte lunch C$13 (US$9); table d'hôte dinner C$23 (US$16). MC, V. May–Nov daily noon–2:30pm and 5:30–10pm (closed Mon–Tues rest of year). BELGIAN.

With its big beams, wavy floors, and plywood bar, this former grist mill has a casual air, the better to dig into the house specialty, *moules et frites*—a pot of mussels with a choice of six sauces, a plate of fries on the side. They come in large or small servings, priced accordingly, and an agreeable variation on the standard burger lunch. Steak is another possibility, and the table d'hôte meals are more elaborate. There's also a terrace.

Pilsen. 55 rue Principale. ☎ **819/842-2971.** Reservations recommended on weekends. Main courses C$7–C$20 (US$5–US$14). MC, V. Wed–Sun 11:30am–9pm (bar to 3am Fri–Sat). INTERNATIONAL.

All drives through North Hatley pass the Pilsen, a pub/restaurant in the center of town. There's a covered terrace in front and a narrow deck overhanging the river that feeds the lake. The place fills up quickly on warm days, the better to watch boats setting out or returning. Patrons enjoy the renditions of nachos, burgers, pastas, and lobster bisque. Vegetarian plates are available. There's an extensive choice of beers, including local microbrews Massawippi Blonde and Townships Pale Ale. Park behind the restaurant.

ACCOMMODATIONS & DINING IN AYER'S CLIFF

✪ **Auberge Ripplecove.** 700 rue Ripplecove (P.O. Box 26), Ayer's Cliff, PQ, J0B 1C0. ☎ **800/668-4296** or 819/838-4296. Fax 819/838-5541. 21 rms and cottages, 5 suites. TEL. C$184–C$330 (US$131–US$236) double or cottage for 2; C$310–C$400 (US$221–US$286) suite. Rates include breakfast and dinner, most recreational facilities, and gratuities. AE, MC, V. Take Rte. 55 to Exit 21; follow Rte. 141 east, watching for signs.

A warm welcome is extended by the staff of this handsome inn, and impeccable housekeeping standards are observed throughout. The core structure dates from 1945, but subsequent expansions have added rooms, suites, and cottages. About half have gas fireplaces, balconies, whirlpool tubs, and cable TVs, and the suites add stocked minibars. The 12-acre property beside Lake Massawippi has a private beach, tennis courts, and a heated outdoor pool. Instruction and equipment are available for sailing, sailboarding, waterskiing, canoeing, kayaking, and cross-country skiing. Golf courses and riding stables are a short drive away.

The inn's award-winning lakeside restaurant fills up most nights in season with diners drawn to the kitchen's contemporary French creations, prettily garnished and interpreted by the young new chef. Such exotica as wapiti and caribou appear on the card. Recent renovations included installation in the lobby of an ornate 14-foot-high breakfront built in 1880 and the hull of a fishing dory recycled as a buffet table in the dining room. Innkeeper Jeffrey Stafford is the brother of the owner of the Auberge Hovey in North Hatley.

Québec City & the Gaspé Peninsula

10

by Herbert Bailey Livesey

Québec City is the soul of New France. It was Canada's first settlement and today is the capital of politically prickly Québec, a province larger than Alaska. With its splendid location above the St. Lawrence River and its virtually unblemished old town—a tumble of slate-roofed granite houses clustered around the august Château Frontenac—it is a haunting evocation of the motherland, as romantic as any on the continent. Because of its history, beauty, and unique stature as the only walled city north of Mexico, the historic district of Québec was named a UNESCO World Heritage site in 1985.

Québec City is almost solidly French in feeling, spirit, and language. About 95% of its population speaks the mother tongue. Perhaps because of that homogeneity and its status as the putative capital of a future independent nation, its citizens seem to suffer less over what might happen down the road. They're also aware that a critical part of their economy is based on tourism and are far less likely to vent the open hostility that Americans can encounter in English Canada. There are far fewer bilingual residents here than in Montréal, but many of Québec City's 648,000 citizens speak some English, especially those who work in hotels, restaurants, and shops. This is also a college town, and thousands of young people study English as a second language. Note that the average Québécois will go out of his or her way to communicate—in halting English, sign language, simplified French, or a combination of all three.

You can spend almost all your visit in Vieux-Québec, the old walled city, since many hotels, restaurants, and visitor-oriented services are there. The original colony was built right down by the St. Lawrence at the foot of Cap Diamant (Cape Diamond). It was there that merchants, traders, and boatmen earned their livelihoods, but due to unfriendly fire in the 1700s, this Basse-Ville (Lower Town) became primarily a wharf and warehouse area, and residents moved to safer houses atop the steep cliffs forming the rim of Cap Diamant. That trend is being reversed today, with several new auberges and many attractive bistros and shops bringing new life to the area.

Haute-Ville (the Upper Town), the Québécois later discovered, was not immune from cannon fire either, as British general James Wolfe was to prove. Nevertheless, the division into Upper and Lower Towns persisted for obvious topographical reasons. The Upper

Town remains enclosed by fortification walls, and several ramplike streets and a cliff-side funicular (*funiculaire*) connect it to the Lower Town. (A fatal 1996 accident closed the funicular indefinitely, but it should be running again by the time you read this.)

Strolling through old Québec is comparable to exploring similar quarters in northern Europe. Carriage wheels creak behind muscular horses, sunlight filters through leafy canopies to fall on drinkers and diners in sidewalk cafes, stone houses huddle close, and childish shrieks of laughter echo down cobblestoned streets. In addition, Québec has a bewitching vista of river and mountains that the Dufferin promenade bestows. In winter the city takes on a Dickensian quality, with lamp-glow behind curtains of falling snow.

Once you've had a chance to explore the city, you may want to consider a trip to Ile d'Orléans, an agricultural and resort island within sight of the Château Frontenac; a drive along the northern coast to the provincial park and ski center at Mont Ste-Anne; on to the resort villages of Charlevoix and the possibility of a whale-watching cruise; or a drive through the picturesque riverside villages on the southern bank of the St. Lawrence.

1 Orientation

ARRIVING

BY PLANE   Twelve miles from the city, **Jean-Lesage International Airport** is small, despite the grand name. Buses from there to several large hotels in town are operated by **Autobus La Québécoise** (☎ 418/872-5525). The trip costs C$9 (US$6) one-way or C$17 (US$12) round-trip. Buses leave at variable times, depending on the season, but roughly every $1^1/_2$ hours from 8:45am to 8:45pm from Monday to Friday and every 2 hours from 9am to 8:30pm on Saturday and Sunday. A taxi into town costs about C$28 (US$20).

BY CAR   From New York City and points south, follow I-87 to Autoroute 15 to Montréal, picking up Autoroute 20 to Québec City. Take 73 Nord across Pont Pierre-Laporte and exit onto boulevard Champlain immediately after crossing the bridge. This skirts the city at river level. Turn left at Parc des Champs-de-Bataille (Battlefields Park) and right onto the Grande Allée. Alternatively, take Autoroute 40 from Montréal, which follows the north shore of the St. Lawrence. The trip takes about $2^1/_2$ hours.

From Boston, take I-89 to I-93 to I-91 in Montpelier, Vermont, which connects with Autoroute 55 in Québec to link up with Autoroute 20. Or follow I-90 up the Atlantic coast, through Portland, Maine, to Route 201 west of Bangor, then Autoroute 173 to Lévis, where there's a car-ferry to Québec City, a 10-minute ride across the St. Lawrence. The ferry between Lévis and Québec City runs daily, every 30 minutes between 6am and 3:45pm and every 60 minutes from 3:45pm to 3:45am. It costs C$4.50 (US$3.20) for the car, C$1.50 (US$1.05) for passengers 12 and up, and C$1.10 (US80¢) for passengers 5 to 11; children under 5 are free.

BY TRAIN   The train station in Québec City, **Gare du Palais,** 450 rue de la Gare-du-Palais (☎ 418/692-3940), is a handsome building, but the Lower Town location isn't central. Plan on a moderately strenuous uphill hike or a C$6 (US$4.30) cab ride to the Upper Town. That's C$6 per ride, incidentally, not per passenger, as an occasional cabby may pretend.

BY BUS   The bus station, **Gare d'Autobus de la Vieille Capitale,** at 320 rue Abraham-Martin (☎ 418/525-3000), is near the train station. It's an uphill climb or quick cab ride to Château Frontenac and the Upper Town. A taxi should cost about C$6 (US$4.30), the same as from the train station.

VISITOR INFORMATION

The **Greater Québec Area Tourism and Convention Bureau** operates two useful information centers in and near the city. One is in the Upper Town of Québec City at 60 rue d'Auteuil (☎ 418/692-2471), another in suburban Ste-Foy, at 3300 av. des Hôtels, near the Québec and Pierre-Laporte bridges (☎ 418/651-2882). The Upper Town center is open early June to Labour Day, daily from 8:30am to 7:45pm; Labour Day to mid-October, daily from 8:30am to 5:15pm; and the rest of the year, Monday to Friday from 9am to 4:45pm.

The provincial government's tourism department operates an **information office** on place d'Armes, down the hill from Château Frontenac, at 12 rue Ste-Anne (☎ 800/363-7777 from other parts of Québec, Canada, and the U.S., or 514/873-2015). It's open daily: mid-June to September 1 from 8:30am to 7:30pm and September 2 to mid-June from 9am to 5pm. The office has many brochures, including details about cruise and bus tour operators; a souvenir shop; a 24-hour ATM (*guichet automatique*); a currency-exchange office; and a free accommodations reservation service.

Parks Canada operates an information kiosk in front of Château Frontenac; open daily from 9am to noon and 1 to 5pm. From June to August, bilingual university students on motorbikes station themselves near the visitor sites in the Upper and Lower Towns to answer questions. Spot them by the flags on the backs of their bikes.

CITY LAYOUT

Within the walls of the Upper Town the principal streets are **rues St-Louis** (which becomes the **Grande-Allée** outside the city walls), **Ste-Anne,** and **St-Jean,** and the pedestrians-only **terrasse Dufferin,** essentially a boardwalk overlooking the river. In the Lower Town, major streets are **rues St-Pierre, Dalhousie, St-Paul,** and, parallel to it, **St-André.**

If it were larger, the historic district, with its winding and plunging streets, might be confusing to negotiate. As compact as it is, though, few visitors have difficulty finding their way around. Most streets are only a few blocks long, so when you know the name of the street, it's fairly easy to find a specific address.

There are good maps of the Upper and Lower Towns and the metropolitan region in the *Greater Québec Area Tourist Guide,* provided by any tourist office.

NEIGHBORHOODS IN BRIEF

Haute-Ville   The Upper Town is surrounded by ramparts and stands on a bluff above the Fleuve St-Laurent (St. Lawrence River). It includes most of the sites for which the city is famous, among them Château Frontenac, the terrasse Dufferin, and the Citadelle, begun by the French in the 18th century. Most of the buildings of the Haute-Ville are at least 100 years old, made of granite in similar styles, with few jarring modern intrusions. The Dufferin pedestrian promenade attracts crowds in all seasons for its magnificent views of the river and the land to the south.

Basse-Ville   At river level, the Lower Town is connected to Haute-Ville by several streets and stairways. Basse-Ville encompasses place Royale, the restored quartier du Petit-Champlain, the small Notre-Dame-des-Victoires church, and the Musée de la Civilisation, a highlight of any visit.

Grande-Allée This major artery runs from the St-Louis Gate in the fortified walls to avenue Taché. It passes the stately Parliament building and numerous terraced bars and restaurants, and later skirts the Musée du Québec and the Plains of Abraham. The city's large contemporary hotels are on or near the Grande-Allée.

2 Getting Around

Once you're within or near the walls of the Haute-Ville, virtually no place of interest, hotel, or restaurant is out of walking distance. In bad weather or when traversing between opposite ends of Lower and Upper Towns, a taxi might be necessary, but in general, walking is the best way to explore.

BY PUBLIC TRANSPORTATION

BY BUS Local buses run quite often and charge C$1.85 (US$1.30) in exact change; tickets purchased in a *dépanneur* (convenience store) cost C$1.50 (US$1.05). No. 7 travels up and down rue St-Jean. No. 11 shuttles along Grande-Allée/rue St-Louis, and, along with nos. 7 and 8, also travels well into suburban Ste-Foy, for those who want to visit the shopping centers there. One-day bus passes are available for C$3.75 (US$2.65).

BY FUNICULAR Although there are streets and stairs between the Upper Town and the Lower Town, there has been a funicular as well, operating along an inclined 210-foot track between the terrasse Dufferin and the quartier du Petit-Champlain. At this writing, it's closed indefinitely, due to a fatal accident in 1996. It's likely to have been repaired by the time you get here, but if not, there's a shuttle van (*navette*) that runs from place d'Armes in the Upper Town to the corner of rue du Porche and Notre-Dame in the Lower Town. It leaves every 10 minutes during the day and evening and costs C$1 (US70¢) per passenger; children 10 and under ride free.

BY TAXI

They're everywhere, but they cluster in the largest packs near the big hotels and some of the larger squares of the Upper Town. In theory, they can be hailed, but your best bet is to find one of their ranks, such as the one in place d'Armes or in front of the Hôtel-de-Ville (City Hall). Restaurant managers and hotel bell captains can also summon one for you. Fares are expensive, in part to compensate for the short distances of most rides. To call a cab, try **Taxi Coop** (☎ **418/525-5191**) or **Taxi Québec** (☎ **418/525-8123**).

BY HORSE-DRAWN CARRIAGE

A romantic—and expensive—way to see the city is in a horse-drawn carriage, called a calèche. You can hire one at place d'Armes or on rue d'Auteuil, just within the city walls near the tourist information office. A 30-minute tour with an English-speaking driver/guide is about C$50 (US$36). Carriages operate all summer, rain or shine.

BY CAR

RENTALS Car-rental companies include **Avis,** at the airport (☎ **800/879-2847** or 418/872-2861) and in the city (☎ 418/523-1075); **Budget,** at the airport (☎ **800/268-8900** or 418/872-9885) and in the city (☎ 418/692-3660); **Hertz Canada,** at the airport (☎ **800/654-3131** or 418/871-1571) and in the city (☎ 418/694-1224); **Thrifty,** at the airport (☎ **800/367-2277** or 418/877-2870) and in the city (☎ 418/683-1542); and **Tilden,** at the airport (☎ **418/871-1224**) and in the city (☎ 418/694-1727). A firm emphasizing economy is **Discount** (☎ **418/692-1244**), at 12 rue Ste-Anne, in Vieux-Québec.

PARKING   On-street parking is very difficult in the cramped quarters of old Québec. When a rare space on the street is found, be sure to check the signs for hours that parking is permissible. Where meters are in place, the charge is C25¢ per 15 minutes up to 120 minutes. Metered spots are free on Sundays, before 9am and after 6pm Monday to Wednesday and Saturday, and before 9am and after 9pm on Thursday and Friday.

Many of the smaller hotels have special arrangements with local garages, so their guests receive a C$3 or C$4 (US$2.15 or US$2.85) discount on the cost of a day's parking, usually C$10 (US$7) per day or more. Check with your hotel before parking in a lot or garage.

If your hotel or auberge doesn't have access to a lot, there are plenty available, clearly marked on the foldout city map available at tourist offices.

FAST FACTS: Québec City

American Express   There's no office right in town, but for lost traveler's checks, call ☎ **800/221-7282.** American Express keeps a customer service desk in two shopping centers in Ste-Foy, a bus or taxi ride away: **Les Galeries de la Capitale,** 5401 bd. des Galeries (☎ **418/627-2580**); and **Place Laurier,** 2740 bd. Laurier (☎ **418/658-8820**).

Consulate   The **U.S. Consulate** is near Château Frontenac, facing Jardin des Gouverneurs at 2 place Terrasse-Dufferin (☎ **418/692-2095**).

Currency Exchange   Conveniently located near Château Frontenac, the bureau de change at 19 rue Ste-Anne and rue des Jardins is open Monday, Tuesday, and Friday from 10am to 3pm and Wednesday and Thursday from 10am to 6pm. On weekends, it's possible to change money in hotels and shops, but you'll get an equal or better rate at an ATM, such as the one at the corner of rues Ste-Anne and des Jardins.

Dentists   Call ☎ **418/653-5412** Monday between 9am and 8pm; Tuesday and Wednesday between 8am and 8pm; Thursday between 8am and 6pm; and Friday between 8am and 4pm. For weekend emergencies, call ☎ **418/656-6060.**

Doctors   For emergency treatment, call **Info-Santé** at ☎ **418/648-2626** 24 hours a day, or the **Hôtel-Dieu de Québec Hospital** emergency room at ☎ **418/ 691-5042.**

Drugstores   **Caron and Bernier,** in the Upper Town at 38 côte du Palais (☎ **418/692-4252**), is open Monday to Friday from 8:15am to 8pm and Saturday from 9am to 3pm. In an emergency, it's necessary to travel to the suburbs to **Pharmacie Brunet,** in Les Galeries Charlesbourg, 4266 Première Avenue (1er or First Avenue), in Charlesbourg (☎ **418/623-1571**), open 24 hours.

Emergencies   For the **police,** call ☎ **911.** For **Marine Search and Rescue** (the Canadian Coast Guard) call ☎ **800/463-4393** (St. Lawrence River) or 418/ 648-3599 (Greater Québec area) 24 hours a day. For the **Poison Control Center,** call ☎ **800/463-5060** or 418/656-8090. For pet injuries or illnesses, call **Vet-Medic** at ☎ **418/647-2000,** 24 hours a day. (Incidentally, pet owners must pick up after their animals.)

Liquor Laws   All hard liquor in Québec is sold through official government stores operated by the Québec Société des Alcools. Wine and beer can be bought in grocery stores and supermarkets. The legal drinking age in the province is 18.

Newspapers & Magazines   Québec City's English-language newspaper, the *Chronicle-Telegraph,* is the equivalent of a small-town paper, published weekly on Wednesday. Major Canadian and American English-language newspapers and magazines are available in the newsstands of the large hotels and at vending machines around tourist corners in the old town. The leading French-language newspapers are *Le Soleil* and *Le Journal de Québec.*

Police   For the **Québec City police,** call ☎ **911.** For the **Sûreté du Québec,** comparable to state police, call ☎ **418/623-6262.**

Post Office   The main post office (bureau de poste) is in the Lower Town, at 300 rue St-Paul near rue Abraham-Martin, not far from carré Parent (Parent Square) by the port (☎ **418/694-6176**). Hours are Monday to Friday from 8am to 5:45pm. A convenient branch in the Upper Town, half a block down the hill from Château Frontenac, is at 3 rue Buade (☎ **418/694-6102**), with the same hours.

Rest Rooms   Find them in the tourist offices and on the ground floor of the commercial complex at 41 rue Couillard, just off rue St-Jean (it's wheelchair accessible).

Taxes   Most goods and services in Canada are taxed 7% by the federal government. The province of Québec adds an extra 6.5% tax on goods and services, including hotel stays. In Québec, the federal tax appears on the bill as the TPS (elsewhere in Canada, it's called the GST), and the provincial tax is known as the TVQ. You may receive a rebate on both the federal and provincial tax on items you've purchased but not used in Québec, as well as on lodging. To take advantage of this, request the necessary forms at duty-free shops and hotels and submit them, with the original receipts, within a year of the purchase. Contact the Canadian consulate or Québec tourism office for up-to-the-minute details about taxes and rebates.

Time   Québec City is on the same time as New York, Boston, Montréal, and Toronto. It's an hour behind Halifax.

Transit Information   Call ☎ **418/627-2511.**

Useful Telephone Numbers   For **Alcoholics Anonymous,** call ☎ **418/529-0015,** daily 8am to midnight. **Health Info,** a 24-hour line answered by nurses, ☎ **418/648-2626. Tel-Aide,** for emotional distress including anxiety and depression, ☎ **418/686-2433.**

Weather   For the **forecast,** call ☎ **418/640-2736,** 24 hours a day. For **tides,** ☎ **418/648-7293,** 24 hours daily.

3 Accommodations

Staying in one of the small hotels or auberges within the Upper Town's walls can be one of Québec City's memorable experiences. That isn't to imply that it'll be enjoyable, though. Standards of comfort, amenities, and prices fluctuate so wildly from one small hotel to another—even within a single place—that you should shop around and examine your room before registering. From rooms with private baths, minibars, and cable TVs to walk-up budget accommodations with linoleum floors and toilets down the hall, Québec has something to suit most tastes and wallets.

If cost is a prime consideration, note that prices drop significantly from November to April, except around Christmas and Winter Carnival. On the other hand, if you want conventional luxuries and Château Frontenac is fully booked, you'll need to go outside the walls to the newer part of town. Most of the high-rise chain hotels out there are in walking distance of the Old City or are only a quick bus or taxi ride away. Though Québec City has many fewer luxury and first-class hotels than Montréal, there are still enough of them to provide for the businesspeople and well-heeled visitors who flock here year-round. And in recent years, a clutch of new small hotels and inns have greatly enhanced the lodging stock.

Québec City's inexpensive auberges are generally smaller places, often converted residences or hostelries carved out of several row houses. They offer fewer of the usual electronic gadgets (air-conditioning and TVs are far from standard) and may be several floors high, without elevators. Even with an advance reservation, always ask to see two or three rooms before making a choice. Unless otherwise noted, all rooms in the lodgings below have private baths.

Many owners of private homes make one or more rooms available for guests and provide breakfast. This kind of bed-and-breakfast doesn't have a sign out front. The only way to locate and reserve one is through one of organizations that maintains listings. One is **Bonjour Québec,** 3765 bd. de Monaco, Québec, PQ, G1R 1N4 (☎ **418/527-1465**). These B&B rooms are generally C$35 to C$70 (US$25 to US$50) for a double. When making arrangements, be clear about your needs. Some hosts don't permit smoking, or children, or pets. They might have only one or two baths in the entire place, to be shared by four or five rooms, or all their rooms might be fourth-floor walkups, or they might be far from the center of things. As with the inexpensive lodgings below, TVs and air-conditioning are exceptions. A deposit is usually required, and minimum stays of 2 nights are common. Credit cards may not be accepted.

Note: See the "Québec City" map (p. 298) to locate most of the hotels in this section.

UPPER TOWN
VERY EXPENSIVE

Château Frontenac. 1 rue des Carrières (at St-Louis), Québec, PQ, G1R 4P5. ☎ **800/828-7447** or 418/692-3861. Fax 418/692-1751. 613 rms, 24 suites. A/C MINIBAR TV TEL. Mid-May to mid-Oct C$190–C$309 (US$136–US$221) double; C$385–C$800 (US$275–US$571) suite. Mid-Oct to mid-May C$125–C$214 (US$89–US$153) double; C$300–C$600 (US$214–US$429) suite. AE, CB, DC, DISC, ER, MC, V. Parking C$14.25 (US$10).

Québec's magical "castle" turned 100 years old in 1993. To celebrate, the management added a new 66-room wing, and since the hotel serves as the symbol of the city, care was taken to replicate the original architectural style. In the past, the hotel has hosted Queen Elizabeth and Prince Philip, and during World War II, Churchill and Roosevelt had the entire place to themselves for a conference. Château Frontenac was built in phases, following the landline, so the wide halls take crooked paths. The price of a room depends on its size, its location, its view or lack of one, and how recently it was renovated. In-room movies are available, and some rooms are no-smoking.

Dining/Entertainment: The fare in the dining rooms has yet to measure up to the grandeur of the physical spaces, though the kitchen of Le Champlain strives to improve. The casual Café de la Terrasse offers a buffet breakfast and dinner and dancing on Saturday. Two bars overlook the terrasse Dufferin. Le Bistro is the lower-level snack bar.

Services: Concierge, room service (6:30am to 11:30pm), dry cleaning, laundry service, baby-sitting, limo service, massage, secretarial services, express checkout, valet parking.

Facilities: Indoor pool, kiddie pool, large gym overlooking Governor's Park, Jacuzzi, and business center.

MODERATE

Many of the hotels and auberges below are on or near the Jardin des Gouverneurs, immediately south of Château Frontenac.

Au Jardin du Gouverneur. 16 Mont-Carmel (at Haldimand), Québec, PQ, G1R 4A3. ☎ 418/692-1704. Fax 418/692-1713. 16 rms, 1 suite. A/C TV. C$60–C$125 (US$43–US$89) double. Rates include breakfast. Extra person over 12 C$15 (US$11), under 12 C$5 (US$3.55). AE, MC, V. Parking C$6 (US$4.30) in nearby garage.

Graced with a distinctive white stucco front and blue-gray trim, this hotel is housed in a 150-year-old building at the upper corner of the park for which it's named, a former home of prominent Québec politicians. The rooms are serviceable rather than memorable, but good enough to represent value. About half have views of the park. Château Frontenac and terrasse Dufferin are at the downhill end of the park.

Château Bellevue. 16 rue Laporte, Québec, PQ, G1R 4M9. ☎ 800/463-2617 or 418/692-2573. Fax 418/692-4876. 57 rms. A/C TV TEL. Late Oct to Apr 30 C$59–C$109 (US$42–US$78) double. Winter Carnival and May to late Oct C$79–C$119 (US$56–US$85) double. Extra person C$10 (US$7). Packages available Oct–May. AE, CB, DC, ER, MC, V. Free valet parking.

Occupying several row houses at the top of Parc des Gouverneurs, this minihotel has a pleasant lobby with leather couches and chairs and a helpful staff as well as some of the creature comforts that smaller auberges in the neighborhood lack. While some rooms suffer from unfortunate decorating choices, they're quiet for the most part. A few higher-priced units overlook the park. The hotel's private parking is directly behind the building, a notable convenience in this congested part of town.

Vieux Québec. 1190 rue St-Jean (near Collins), Québec, PQ, G1R 4J2. ☎ 800/361-7787 or 418/692-1850. Fax 418/692-5637. 28 rms and suites. TV TEL. May to mid-Oct, Christmas week, and Winter Carnival C$99–C$129 (US$71–US$92) single or double. Last 2 weeks in Oct C$69–C$99 (US$49–US$71) single or double. Nov 1–Dec 26 C$59–C$89 (US$42–US$64) single or double. Jan–Apr C$69–C$99 (US$49–US$71) single or double. Extra person C$10 (US$7). AE, DC, ER, MC, V. Parking C$6 (US$4.30).

This century-old brick hotel has been renovated with care. The rooms are equipped with sofas, two double beds, cable color TVs, and modern baths. Most have kitchenettes. With these homey layouts, it's understandably popular with families, skiers, and the groups of visiting high-schoolers who descend on the city in late spring. Some rooms have air-conditioning, but you can save a little money in summer by taking one without it. Many moderately priced restaurants and nightspots are nearby.

INEXPENSIVE

Auberge de Jeunesse. 19 Ste-Ursule (at rue Dauphine), Québec, PQ, G1R 4E1. ☎ 800/461-8585 from elsewhere in the province except Montréal, 418/694-0755, or 514/252-3117 from Montréal or outside the province. Fax 418/694-2278 or 514/251-3119 from Montréal or outside the province. 281 beds. C$14–C$15.40 (US$10–US$11) members; C$18.25–C$19.75 (US$13–US$14) nonmembers. Private rms C$40 (US$29). Half price for children 9–13; children under 9 free. AE, MC, V.

An ugly two-story brick building up a steep hill from rue St-Jean, this youth hostel has some rooms with two beds and a few with double beds, but most units have four. There are also dorms with 10 to 12 beds. The renovated cafeteria is open most of the year, and breakfast is about C$4 (US$2.85). Lockers are available for luggage, skis, and bicycles. There's a laundry, a lounge with a pool table, and a backyard with picnic tables. Guests can use the common kitchen. There's no curfew.

La Chouette. 71 rue d'Auteuil (near St-Louis), Québec, PQ, G1R 4C3. ☎ **418/694-0232.** 10 rms. A/C TV TEL. Summer C$70 (US$50) double; winter C$55 (US$39) double. AE, MC, V. Parking C$6 (US$4.30).

Across from Esplanade Park and near Porte St-Louis, this auberge has an accomplished Asian restaurant, Apsara (see "Dining," later in this chapter), on the main floor. A spiral stairway leads up to the rooms, all of which have full baths. The tourist office, the Citadelle, and Winter Carnival or Québec Summer Festival activities are only minutes away.

Manoir de l'Esplanade. 83 rue d'Auteuil (at St-Louis), Québec, PQ, G1R 4C3. ☎ **418/ 694-0834.** Fax 418/692-0456. 36 rms. A/C TV TEL. Summer C$65–C$90 (US$46–US$64) double. Winter rates 45% less. Extra person C$10 (US$7). AE, MC, V. Parking nearby C$6 (US$4.30).

Though not as well appointed as some of the similar places along the nearby Grande-Allée, it's clean and all rooms have air-conditioning and private bath—neither of which can be assumed to be present at this price. Some have double beds. Students like this place, which used to be a nunnery. It faces the St-Louis Gate, and the tourist office is 50 yards down the street.

St-Louis. 48 rue St-Louis (near Ste-Ursule), Québec, PQ, G1R 3Z3. ☎ **418/692-2424.** Fax 418/692-3797. 27 rms (13 with bath). May 1–Oct 15 C$49 (US$35) double without bath, C$79 (US$56) double with bath; Oct 16–Apr 30 C$49 (US$35) double without bath, C$65 (US$46) double with bath. Rates include breakfast. Extra person C$10 (US$7). MC, V. Nearby parking C$6 (US$4.30).

The rooms come in a variety of configurations, with occasional features that add some visual interest, like a carved fireplace mantel or a stained-glass window. But the reasons to stay here are the low prices and good location near city hall. Some rooms have a sink and shower but no toilet, and some have a color or black-and-white TV. Only two units have air-conditioning; the rest have fans.

ON OR NEAR THE GRANDE-ALLEE
EXPENSIVE

Hilton International Québec. 3 place Québec, PQ, G1K 7889. ☎ **800/445-8667** or 418/ 647-2411. Fax 418/847-6488. 565 rms, 39 suites. A/C MINIBAR TV TEL. C$129–C$235 (US$92–US$168) double; from C$335 (US$239) suite. Extra person C$20 (US$14). Children stay free in parents' rm. Packages available. AE, CB, DC, DISC, ER, MC, V. Parking C$16 (US$11). Head east along Grande-Allée and just before the St-Louis Gate in the city wall, turn left on rue Dufferin, then left again as you pass the Parliament building; the hotel is 1 block ahead.

Superior on virtually every count to the other midrise contemporary hotels outside the old town, this Hilton is true to the breed, the clear choice for executives and those leisure travelers who can't bear to live without their gadgets. The location, across from the city walls and near Parliament, is excellent. It's also connected to Place Québec shopping complex, which has 75 shops and 2 cinemas, and the Convention Centre.

The public rooms are big and brassy, Hilton-style, while the uninspired guest rooms are in need of freshening. Most have one or two large beds plus in-room movies. Upper floor views of the St. Lawrence River, old Québec, and the Laurentian Mountains are grand. The staff is generally efficient and congenial. No-smoking rooms are available.

Dining/Entertainment: Le Caucus restaurant serves buffet-style as well as à la carte meals. Fridays and Saturdays are theme nights, with live entertainment.

Services: Airport shuttle, room service, dry cleaning, laundry service, baby-sitting, car rental.

Facilities: Heated outdoor pool (summer only), health club with sauna and whirlpool, jogging track, business center.

✪ **Le Capitole.** 972 rue St-Jean (1 block west of Porte St-Jean), PQ, G1R 1R5. ☎ **800/363-4040** or 418/694-4040. Fax 418/694-1916. 40 rms. A/C MINIBAR TV TEL. July to mid-Oct C$135–C$185 (US$96–US$132) double. Mid-Oct to June C$99–C$175 (US$71–US$125) double. Packages available. AE, MC, V.

As happily eccentric as the three business hotels below are conventional, the entrance to this hotel is squeezed almost to anonymity between a restaurant, a theater, and the Cinema de Paris on place d'Youville. The rooms borrow from art deco and throw in stars in the carpets and clouds on the ceiling. Most tubs have whirlpools and beds have down comforters. All rooms have VCRs, CD players, coffeemakers, and hair dryers.

Dining/Entertainment: Ristorante Il Teatro is half continental and half showbiz, with platinum records on the walls, plates autographed by celebrities, and a busy terrace. Down the central hall is the Théâtre Capitole, which presents live shows when it isn't hosting weddings and banquets.

Services: Concierge, room service, dry-cleaning and laundry service, library of free videos.

Loews Le Concorde. 1225 place Montcalm (at Grande-Allée), Québec, PQ, G1R 4W6. ☎ **800/235-6397** from the U.S., 800/463-5256 from Canada, or 418/647-2222. Fax 418/647-4710. 400 rms, 22 suites. A/C MINIBAR TV TEL. C$129–C$215 (US$92–US$154) double; from C$215 (US$154) suite. Extra person over 17, C$20 (US$14). Special off-season rates available, along with weekend and ski packages. AE, DC, ER, MC, V. Parking garage C$14 (US$10).

From outside, the building is an insult to the skyline, blighting a neighborhood of late-Victorian town houses. But once you enter you might forget the affront (at least if you have business to do and can't be bothered with aesthetics). The standard rooms have marble baths with hair dryers, prints of Québec City street scenes, in-room movies, and three phones. They bestow spectacular views of the river and the old city, even from the lower floors. There are seven no-smoking floors and seven business-class floors. Of all the hotels listed, this is the farthest from the old town, about a 10-minute walk to the walls and then another 10 minutes to the center of the Haute-Ville.

Dining/Entertainment: L'Astral is a revolving rooftop restaurant, with a bar and live piano music Tuesday to Sunday. Le Café serves light lunch or dinner. La Place Montcalm offers buffet or à la carte breakfasts.

Services: Concierge, room service (6am to midnight), dry-cleaning and laundry service.

Facilities: Small fitness facility with sauna and some exercise equipment, outdoor heated pool (April to November; access to pool in a private club during other months).

Radisson Gouverneurs. 690 bd. René-Lévesque est, Québec, PQ, G1R 5A8. ☎ **800/333-3333**, 800/463-2820 from eastern Canada and Ontario, or 418/647-1717. Fax 418/647-2146. 377 rms, 14 suites. A/C TV TEL. C$140–C$160 (US$100–US$114) double; from C$195 (US$139) suite. Extra person C$15 (US$11). Children under 16 stay free in parents' rm. AE, DC, DISC, ER, MC, V. Parking C$11 (US$8). Turn left off Grande-Allée onto Dufferin, just before the St-Louis Gate in the city wall. Once past Parliament, take the 1st left. The hotel is 2 blocks ahead.

Part of Place Québec, a multiuse complex, the hotel is connected to the city's convention center. It's 1 block from the Hilton, 2 blocks from Porte (Gate) Kent

🙂 Family-Friendly Hotels

Château Frontenac *(see p. 285)* This is a fairy-tale castle posing as a hotel. Little princes and princesses have an indoor pool just for them and a kids' activity center during summer.

Vieux Québec *(see p. 286)* Popular with families and school groups, it's in a good location for exploring Upper or Lower Town.

Radisson Gouverneurs *(see p. 288)* The rooftop pool is a treat, with its water route from indoors to the outside. Winter Carnival activities are an easy walk away.

in the city wall, and not far from Parliament, a location likely to fit almost any businessperson's needs. It is, however, an uphill climb from the old city (like all the hotels and inns along or near the Grande-Allée). Some rooms have minibars; all have in-room movies. There are three no-smoking floors and two executive floors. Reception is two levels up.

Dining: Le Café serves buffet and à la carte meals.

Services: Room service, dry-cleaning and laundry service, baby-sitting.

Facilities: Outdoor pool (open only in summer); fully equipped and staffed health club with Exercycles, sauna, and whirlpool.

INEXPENSIVE

✪ **Relais Charles-Alexander.** 91 Grande-Allée est (at Galipeault), Québec, PQ, G1R 2H5. ☎ **418/523-1220.** Fax 418/523-9556. 19 rms (14 with bath). A/C TV. C$69–C$89 (US$49–US$64) double. Rates include breakfast. MC, V. Parking nearby C$6 (US$4.30).

On the ground floor of this charming brick-faced B&B is an art gallery that also serves as the breakfast room. This stylish use of space extends to the guest rooms, which are crisply maintained and decorated with eclectic antique and wicker pieces and reproductions. The rooms in front are larger; most have showers, not tubs. They're quiet, for the most part, since the inn is just outside the orbit of the sometimes raucous Grande-Allée terrace bars. Yet the St-Louis Gate is less than a 10-minute walk away from the hubbub.

LOWER TOWN

VERY EXPENSIVE

✪ **St-Antoine.** 10 rue St-Antoine (at Dalhousie), Québec, PQ, G1K 4C9. ☎ **888/692-2211** or 418/692-2211. Fax 418/692-1177. 22 rms, 9 suites. A/C TV TEL. C$179–C$299 (US$128–US$214) double; C$299–C$439 (US$213–US$313) suite. Rates include breakfast. Extra person C$20 (US$14). Children under 12 stay free in parents' rm. AE, DC, MC, V. Free parking. Follow rue Dalhousie around the Lower Town to rue St-Antoine. The hotel is next to the Musée de la Civilisation.

The centerpiece of this uncommonly attractive boutique hotel is the 1830 maritime warehouse that contains the lobby and meeting rooms, with the dark beams and stone floor still intact. Buffet breakfasts and afternoon wine and cheese are set out in the lobby, where you can relax in wing chairs next to the hooded fireplace. Canny mixes of antique and reproduction furniture are in both public and private areas. The guest rooms, in an adjoining modern wing and a separate, newly remodeled 1727 house, are spacious, with extra touches like custom-made iron bedsteads and tables. The big baths have robes and hair dryers. Several rooms have private terraces. Prices are highest for the 13 rooms with river views, but as a large parking lot intervenes, those without the view are a better deal. The eight new suites have kitchenettes, fax machines, and computer jacks.

MODERATE

✪ **Dominion 1912.** 126 rue St-Pierre (at St-Paul), Québec, PQ, G1K 4A8. ☎ **888/ 833-5253** or 418/692-2224. Fax 418/692-4403. 40 rms. A/C MINIBAR TV TEL. Nov–Apr C$89–C$129 (US$63–US$92) double. May–Oct C$99–C$159 (US$71–US$114) double. Rates include breakfast. AE, DC, ER, MC, V. Parking C$5–C$10 (US$3.55–US$7).

If there was only enough space to recommend one hotel in the city, this would be it. The owners stripped the inside of the 1912 Dominion Fish & Fruit building down to the studs and pipes and started over. Even the least expensive rooms are large, the beds heaped with linen-covered pillows and covered with feather duvets. Neutral colors extend to the spacious baths and the robes hanging there. A fruit basket awaits. Modem outlets are at desktop level. Chairs embrace sitters for work or leisure. A continental breakfast is set out in the handsome lobby and can be taken out to the terrace in back. For lodgings this good, the prices are remarkably low, but as soon as a few lingering kinks are worked out, it can be fairly assumed that the rates will rise significantly. Go now.

Le Priori. 15 rue Sault-au-Matelot (at rue St-Antoine), Québec, PQ, G1K 3Y7. ☎ **800/ 351-3992** or 418/692-3992. Fax 418/692-0883. 21 rms, 5 suites. TV TEL. C$125–C$145 (US$89–US$104) double; C$155–C$290 (US$111–US$207) suite. AE, DC, ER, MC, V. Parking C$8 (US$6).

A forerunner of the blossoming Lower Town hotel scene, 2 blocks behind the Auberge St-Antoine, Le Priori provides a playful postmodern ambiance behind the somber facade of a 1766 house. Hot French designer Philippe Starck inspired the owners, who deployed versions of his conical stainless-steel sinks in the rooms and sensual multinozzle showers in the small baths. Queen-size beds have black tubular frames and soft duvets. The dim lighting doesn't help readers, however, and in some rooms, a claw-foot tub sits beside the bed. Suites have sitting rooms with wood-burning fireplaces, kitchens, and baths with Jacuzzis. The hotel houses the new Zenith restaurant, replacing the admirable Laurie Raphaël, which moved to larger quarters.

St-Pierre. 79 St-Pierre (behind the Musée de la Civilisation), Québec, PQ, G1K 4A3. ☎ **888/ 268-1017** or 418/694-7981. 24 rms, 8 suites. A/C TV TEL. C$119–C$169 (US$85–US$120) single or double; C$189–C$199 (US$135–US$142) suite. Rates include breakfast. AE, MC, V. Parking nearby C$6 (US$4.30).

The paint was still drying and a few startup bugs were evident when I saw it soon after its 1997 opening, but this is another welcome entry in the lengthening roster of Basse-Ville auberges. The full breakfasts are special, cooked to order by the chef in the open kitchen. The commodious suites cost little more than a double, a possible extra luxury for a longer visit, especially since they have modest kitchen facilities. The window air-conditioners are somewhat underpowered for the extra space, if that's a consideration. Robes and hair dryers are provided. The 19th-century building started out as headquarters for a fire insurance company.

4 Dining

Once you're within the ancient walls, walking along streets that look to have been transplanted intact from Brittany or Provence, you might imagine that one superb dining experience after another is in store.

Alas, that isn't true. If that French tire company decided to cast its hotly contested stars on Québec restaurants, they might grudgingly part with three or four. The truth is that this gloriously scenic city has only one or two restaurants that even approach comparison with the best of Paris, Manhattan, or Montréal. While it's easy to eat well in the capital (even, in a few isolated cases, quite well), the dining highlight of your stay will lie elsewhere.

But that's not to imply that you're in for barely edible meals served by sullen waiters. By sticking to any of the many competent bistros, the handful of Asian eateries, and one or two of the emerging nuovo Italiano trattorias, you'll do fine. Another step up, two or three ambitious enterprises tease the palate with hints of higher achievement. Even the blatantly touristy restaurants along rue St-Louis and around place d'Armes can produce decent meals.

As throughout the province, the best dining deals are the table d'hôte (fixed-price) meals. Most full-service restaurants offer them, if only at lunch. As a rule, they include at least soup or salad, a main course, and dessert. Some places add in an extra appetizer and/or a beverage, for the approximate à la carte price of the main course alone.

Curiously, for a city standing beside a great waterway and a day's sail from some of the world's best fishing grounds, seafood isn't given much attention. Mussels and salmon are on most menus, but cherish any place that goes beyond those staples. Game is popular, however, and everything from venison, rabbit, and duck to more exotic quail, goose, caribou, and wapiti is available.

At the better places, and even some of those that might seem inexplicably popular, reservations are all but essential during traditional holidays and the festivals that pepper the social calendar. Other times, it's usually necessary to book ahead only for weekend evenings. Dress codes are only required in a few restaurants, but Québecers are a stylish lot. "Dressy casual" works almost everywhere. Remember that for the Québécois, *dîner* (dinner) is lunch, and *souper* (supper) is dinner, though for the sake of consistency, I've used the word *dinner* in the common American sense. They tend to have that evening meal earlier than Montréalers, at 6 or 7pm rather than at 8pm. When figuring costs, add the $13^1/_2$% in federal and provincial taxes.

Note: See the "Québec City" map (p. 298) to locate most of the restaurants in this section.

UPPER TOWN
EXPENSIVE

✪ **Le St-Amour.** 48 rue Ste-Ursule (near St-Louis). ☎ **418/694-0667.** Reservations recommended for dinner. Main courses C$18.50–C$24.50 (US$13–US$18); table d'hôte lunch C$9.50 (US$7); table d'hôte dinner C$26.50–C$29.50 (US$19–US$21); gastronomic dinner C$48 (US$34). AE, DC, ER, MC, V. Mon–Fri noon–2:30pm; daily 6–11pm. CONTEMPORARY FRENCH.

Here you'll find a gratifying dining experience that touches all the senses, and the energetic chef/owner tirelessly scours away any imperfections. This is a restaurant for the coolly attractive and romantically inclined. You pass through the front room with lace curtains and potted greenery into a covered terrace lit by candles and flickering Victorian gas fixtures. Up above, the roof is retracted on warm nights, revealing a splash of stars. The house, built in the 1820s, is a little off the tourist track. A hint of the imagination the kitchen brings to bear is seen in the halibut with snow crab bound with an orange-shellfish cream sauce. The award-winning chefs have a sure hand with game, with the seasonally adjusted menu often suggesting caribou and wapiti steak, as well as quail, duck, and rabbit. The long wine list has some not-too-expensive choices, and the chocolate desserts are especially tempting.

Serge Bruyère. 1200 rue St-Jean (at côte de la Fabrique). ☎ **418/694-0618.** Reservations recommended for dinner. Main courses C$9.50–C$26.50 (US$7–US$19); table d'hôte lunch

C$8–C$14 (US$6–US$10); table d'hôte dinner C$14–C$26 (US$10–US$19); gastronomic dinners C$55 and C$99 (US$39 and US$71). AE, DC, MC, V. Daily 11:30–2pm and 5:30–10:30pm. ECLECTIC.

The eponymous owner bought the wedge-shaped building in 1979 and set about creating a multilevel dining emporium with something for everyone. Serge Bruyère died young and tragically. His executive chef carries on, along a similar path. At ground level is a casual **cafe** with a cold case displaying salads and pastries. Up a long staircase at the back is his **Chez Livernois,** with three semicircular windows looking down on the street. This bistro is best for lunches, concentrating on grills and pastas that come with rounds of crusty, chewy bread. Foods are adroitly seasoned.

Another flight up is the formal **La Grand Table,** offering a pricey menu that's both imaginative and immaculately presented. Gaps between the eight courses of the gastronomic extravaganza stretch on—and on—for an entire evening. Whether the unquestionably showy creations justify the raves and sedate pace of the meal is up to you. Dress well and arrive with a healthy credit card.

Finally, around back in a vaulted rathskeller is a new addition, **Falstaff.** Aspiring to a Bavarian ambiance, but with a largely Alsatian menu, it sends out choucroute, schnitzel, spätzle, and such, washed down with German beers and occasional helpings of oompah music.

MODERATE

Apsara. 71 rue d'Auteuil (near St-Louis Gate). ☎ **418/694-0232.** Main courses C$10–C$13 (US$7–US$9). AE, MC, V. Mon–Fri 11:30am–2pm; daily 5:30–11pm. SOUTH ASIAN.

Near the tourist office and the city walls, this 1845 Victorian row house is home to one of the city's best Asian restaurants. The interior looks like the British consulate in Shanghai might, welcoming diners who come for a gastronomic tour that arches from Vietnam to Cambodia to Thailand. Head straight for the last stop, since the Thai dishes are clearly masters over the mostly wan alternatives. This cuisine Asiatique includes satays, *mou sati* (brochettes), breaded shrimp in a zingy sauce, and spicy roast beef. An enticing possibility is the seven-course sampler meal for two at C$36 (US$26). The house wines aren't expensive but aren't very good, either. Have a beer.

Les Frères de la Côte. 1190 rue St-Jean (near côte de la Fabrique). ☎ **418/692-5445.** Reservations recommended. Main courses C$9–C$13 (US$6–US$9); table d'hôte C$12–C$15 (US$9–US$11). AE, DC, ER, MC, V. Daily 11:30am–11pm. MEDITERRANEAN.

At the east end of the old town's liveliest nightlife strip, this casual cafe/pizzeria is as loud as a dance club, all hard surfaces with patrons shouting over the music. None of this discourages a single soul—even on a Monday night. Chefs in straw hats in the open kitchen out back crank out a dozen kinds of pizza (thin-crusted, with unusual toppings that work) and about as many pasta versions, which are less interesting. Bountiful platters of fish and meats, often in the form of brochettes, make appetizers unnecessary. Keep this spot in mind when kids are in tow. There's no way they could make enough noise to bother other customers. Outside tables are available in warm weather, and breakfast is served there June 24 to September 5 from 8am to 10am.

INEXPENSIVE

Chez Temporel. 25 rue Couillard (near côte de la Fabrique). ☎ **418/694-1813.** Most items C$2–C$6.25 (US$1.40–US$4.45). No credit cards. Sun–Thurs 7:30am–1:30am, Fri–Sat 7:30am–2:30am. LIGHT FARE.

This Latin Quarter cafe with a tile floor and wooden tables attracts denizens of nearby Université Laval. They read *Le Monde,* play chess, swap philosophical insights, and clack away at their laptops from breakfast until well past midnight. It could be a Left

Bank hangout for Sorbonne students and their profs. Capture a table and you can hold it forever for just a cappuccino or two. Croissants, jam, butter, and a bowl of café au lait cost half as much as a hotel breakfast. Later, drop by for a croquemonsieur, quiche, or plate of cheese with a beer or glass of wine. Only 20 people can be seated downstairs, another 26 upstairs, where the light is filtered through stained-glass windows.

Le Casse-Crêpe Breton. 1136 rue St-Jean (near St-Stanislas). ☎ **418/692-0438.** Most items C$3.25–C$6 (US$2.30–US$4.30). No credit cards. Mon–Wed 7:30am–midnight, Thurs–Sun 7:30am–1am. CREPES/LIGHT FARE.

Eat at the bar and watch the crêpes being made or attempt to snag one of the five tables. Main-course crêpes come with two to five ingredients of your choice. Dessert versions are stuffed with jams or fruit and cream. Soups, salads, and sandwiches are as inexpensive as the crêpes. The name of the cafe is a play on the word *casse-croûte*, which means "break crust." It's open more than 16 hours a day, which is useful, but when it gets busy, the service is glacial. Beer is served in bottles or on tap.

ON OR NEAR THE GRANDE-ALLEE

EXPENSIVE

Le Paris-Brest. 590 Grande-Allée est (at Chevrotière). ☎ **418/529-2243.** Reservations recommended. Main courses C$17.50–C$28 (US$13–US$20); table d'hôte lunch C$9–C$14 (US$6–US$10); table d'hôte dinner C$18–C$23 (US$13–US$16). AE, DC, ER, MC, V. Mon–Fri 11:30am–2:30pm; Mon–Sat 6–11:30pm, Sun 5:30–11:30pm. CONTEMPORARY FRENCH.

Named for a French dessert, this fashionable hideaway is the best along the Grande-Allée. By itself, that's well short of a rave, given the competition. But this place is a whole league ahead, not just a notch. It gives a polished performance from greeting to reckoning. The vaguely art-moderne interior employs mahogany paneling, soft lighting, lush flower arrangements, and a temperature-controlled walk-in wine repository.

Game is featured, including caribou steaks, venison, and pheasant. Escargots Provençales or au Pernod is a savory starter to be followed by such standards as lamb noisettes and seafood cassoulette. The staff is so alert and attentive that even single diners are made welcome. Find the entrance on rue de la Chevrotière, under 200 Grande-Allée. There's a small patio for outdoor dining, and free valet parking is available from 5:30pm.

MODERATE

Le Graffiti. 1191 av. Cartier (near Grande-Allée). ☎ **418/529-4949.** Reservations recommended. Main courses C$12.75–C$19 (US$9–US$14); table d'hôte C$18–C$27.50 (US$13–US$20). AE, MC, V. Mon–Sat 5–11pm, Sun noon–10pm. CONTEMPORARY FRENCH/ITALIAN.

These 2 or 3 blocks of rue Cartier off Grande-Allée are just outside the perimeter of tourist Québec, far enough removed to avoid flashy banality, close enough to remain convenient. This ebullient place blends bistro with trattoria, often on the same plate. Emblematic are the pike with leeks and grilled almonds and the sautéed rabbit with puréed carrot, broccoli florets, and angel-hair pasta powerfully scented with tarragon. Choice seats are in the glassed-in terrace, the better to scope the street scene.

Momento. 1144 av. Cartier (near Grande-Allée). ☎ **418/647-1313.** Reservations suggested at dinner. Main courses C$12.50–C$17 (US$9–US$12); table d'hôte lunch C$9–C$11 (US$6–US$8); table d'hôte dinner C$13–C$20 (US$9–US$14). AE, MC, V. Mon–Fri 11:15am–11pm, Sat–Sun 5pm–midnight. CONTEMPORARY ITALIAN.

Considering its manic popularity elsewhere on the continent, updated Italian cooking was late arriving in Québec. The city had the usual parlors shoveling overcooked

---

👪 Family-Friendly Restaurants

Les Frères de la Côte *(see p. 292)* Here you'll find a dozen varieties of pizza, served up in a casual and boisterous atmosphere.

Au Petit Coin Breton *(see p. 294)* The waitresses' costumes are fun—and so's the food, especially when it's served outside.

Le Cochon Dingue *(see p. 295)* It's big and loud so kids can let themselves go here (to a point). And eating in a place called "The Crazy Pig" is something to write home to Grandma about.

---

spaghetti with thin tomato sauce, but not the kind of spiffy neo-trattoria that trafficks in light-but-lusty dishes. This racy spot is helping to take up the slack, and though it lags somewhat in execution compared to its rival, Le Graffiti, it's a welcome antidote to the city's prevailing Franco-Italian clichés. The pizza crusts are almost as thin as crêpes, and the all-veggie version is a winner, as are the not-too-sweet desserts.

INEXPENSIVE

Au Petit Coin Breton. 655 Grande-Allée est. ☎ **418/525-6904.** Most menu items C$6.75–C$14.75 (US$4.80–US$11). AE, DC, ER, MC, V. Summer daily 10am–midnight; winter daily 10am–11pm. CREPES.

At this "Little Corner of Brittany," the crêpe's the thing, be it for breakfast, brunch, a light lunch, a snack, or dessert. Stone, brick, and wood set the mood, as do waiters and waitresses in Breton costume—the women in tall caps and collars of lace, long dresses, and aprons. After onion soup or salad, choose one (or several) of the more than 80 varieties of the savory dinner crêpes and sweet dessert crêpes. Brunch might be the best choice, when four of you can order the ham-and-asparagus crêpe with béchamel sauce. Often every last seat is taken, especially on the terrace on a sunny day, making a wait inevitable and service slow. A second location, 1029 rue St-Jean, at the corner of rue Ste-Ursule, has a similar menu and hours (☎ 418/694-0758).

LOWER TOWN
EXPENSIVE

✪ **Laurie Raphaël.** 117 rue Dalhousie (at St-André). ☎ **418/692-4555.** Reservations recommended. Main courses C$20–C$27 (US$14–US$19); table d'hôte lunch C$9.50–C$12.50 (US$7–US$9); table d'hôte dinner C$26–C$44 (US$19–US$31). AE, DC, ER, MC, V. Mon–Fri noon–2pm and 6am–10pm, Sat 6–10pm, Sun 10:30am–2pm and 6–10pm. CONTEMPORARY FRENCH.

In 1996, the owners moved from a cramped space in the Auberge Le Priori to these larger, more glamorous quarters suitable for the city's most accomplished kitchen. An amuse-gueule arrives with the cocktail, which might be the special Kir Royale, a sparkling wine laced with blackberry liqueur. After a suitable interlude, the waiter turns up and happily explains every dish on the menu in as much detail as you care to absorb. Appetizers aren't really necessary, since the main course comes with soup or salad, but they're so good that a couple might wish to share one—perhaps the lightly fried calamari rings with a garnish of edible nasturtium blossoms. Main courses run to caribou and salmon in unconventional guises, often with Asian touches. Coupled with a concern for "healthy" saucing and exotic combinations, the food closely resembles that of elevated California restaurants. In no time, the place ascends to the level of contented babble that's music to a restaurateur's ears. The service may at times be forgetful, but that's quibbling, for this is a restaurant that's all but alone at the pinnacle of the local dining pantheon.

MODERATE

L'Ardoise. 71 rue St-Paul (near Navigateurs). ☎ **418/694-0213.** Reservations suggested at dinner. Main courses C$8–C$16 (US$6–US$11); table d'hôte C$18 or C$24 (US$13 or US$17). AE, MC, V. Daily 7am–midnight. BISTRO FRENCH.

This is one of several bistros wrapping around the corner of rues St-Paul and Sault-au-Matelot. Most are inexpensive and cater more to locals than to tourists . . . so far. Mussels are staples at Québec restaurants, prepared in the Belgian manner, with bowls of frites on the side. Here they come with eight sauces. Despite their popularity, the chef is reluctant to serve them in warmer months, explaining that the farmed variety available then tends to be mealy.

That he cares about what he sends out of his kitchen is evident. His food is vibrant and flavorful, served at banquettes along the walls and at tables both inside and on the sidewalk. Piaf and Azvanour clones warble laments on the stereo. This is a place to leaf through a book, sip a double espresso, and meet neighbors.

☼ Le Café du Monde. 57 rue Dalhousie (at Montagne). ☎ **418/692-4455.** Reservations recommended on weekends. Main courses C$9–C$17 (US$6–US$12); table d'hôte lunch C$8–C$12 (US$6–US$9); table d'hôte dinner C$18–C$23 (US$13–US$16). AE, DC, ER, MC, V. Mon–Fri 11:30am–11pm, Sat–Sun brunch 9:30am–11pm. FRENCH/INTERNATIONAL.

This convivial spot near the Musée de la Civilisation enjoys ever-increasing popularity. While it promotes the world dishes promised in its name, the atmosphere is definitely Lyonnaise brasserie. That's seen in the culinary origins of its most-ordered items—pâtés, quiches, confit de canard, and several versions of mussels with frites—prepared in a kitchen overseen by a chef from Brittany. One of his extravaganzas is a five-course evening meal, Le Ciel, La Terre, La Mer (Sky, Earth, Sea—a kind of upscale surf 'n' turf). Pastas and couscous are some of the non-French preparations. Imported beers are favored beverages, along with wines by the glass. Service is friendly but easily distracted. Waiters and customers sit down at the upright piano for impromptu performances.

☼ L'Echaudé. 73 rue Sault-au-Matelot (near St-Paul). ☎ **418/692-1299.** Main courses C$12–C$26.50 (US$9–US$19); table d'hôte lunch C$9–C$13 (US$6–US$9); table d'hôte dinner C$23 (US$16). AE, DC, ER, MC, V. Mon–Wed 11:30am–2:30pm and 5:30–10pm, Thurs–Fri 11:30am–2:30pm and 5:30–11pm, Sat 5:30–11pm, Sun 10am–2:30pm and 5:30–10pm. TRADITIONAL/NOUVELLE BISTRO.

The latest addition to the necklace of restos rounding this Basse-Ville corner, and by most measures, the most polished, it has sidewalk tables with butcher paper on top and a zinc-topped bar inside the door. The grilled meats and fish and seafood stews blaze no new trails, but they're very satisfying and prove an excellent price-value ratio. They keep 24 brands of beer on ice and cellar 125 varieties of wine, a generous 10 of which are available by the glass. Azvanour on the stereo and wisps of Gitanes complete the Left Bank ambiance.

Le Cochon Dingue. 46 bd. Champlain (at Marché-Champlain). ☎ **418/692-2013.** Main courses $9.75–$15 (US$7–US$11); table d'hôte lunch C$7.50–C$13 (US$5–US$9); table d'hôte dinner C$17–C$20 (US$12–US$14). AE, ER, MC, V. Mon–Fri 7am–midnight, Sat–Sun 8am–midnight. BISTRO/INTERNATIONAL.

This "Crazy Pig" faces the ferry dock and lighthouse in the Lower Town and has some sidewalk tables and several indoor dining rooms with rough fieldstone walls and black-and-white floor tiles. It makes stout efforts to be a one-stop eating center, with long hours to cover every possibility. Choose from mussels, steak frites, hefty plates of chicken-liver pâté with pistachios, spring rolls, smoked salmon, half a dozen salads, onion soup, pastas, quiches, sandwiches, grilled meats, and more than 20 desserts. Wine is sold by the glass, quarter liter, half liter, or bottle, at reasonable prices, and there's a menu for kids 10 and under. The same people also own the nearby, smaller **Le Lapin Sauté,** 52 rue Petit-Champlain (☎ 418/692-5325).

Le Marie-Clarisse. 12 rue du Petit-Champlain (at Sous-le-Fort). ☎ **418/692-0857.** Main courses C$8–C$11.75 (US$6–US$8); table d'hôte lunch C$9.75–C$14.75 (US$7–US$11); table d'hôte dinner C$16.70–C$19.70 (US$12–US$14). DC, ER, MC, V. Mon–Fri 11:30am–2:30pm, Mon–Sat 6–10pm; terrace open 11:30am–10pm. BISTRO/SEAFOOD.

Nothing much beyond sustenance is expected of restaurants at the flooded intersections of galloping tourism. That's why this modest little cafe is such a happy surprise. There it sits, at the bottom of Breakneck Stairs, a few yards from the funicular terminal, the streets around it teeming with crowds. And yet it serves what many consider to be the best seafood in town, chosen by a finicky owner who makes his selections personally at market. A more pleasant hour can't be passed anywhere in Québec City, over shrimp scented with anise or a selection of terrines and pâtés, out on the terrace on an August afternoon or cocooned by the stone fireplace in January. Just skip the vegetables, unless the chef has learned to remove them from the pot while they still have some fiber.

Le Zénith. 17 du Sault-au-Matelot (in the Auberge Le Priori). ☎ **418/692-2962.** Table d'hôte lunch C$9.50–C$12.50 (US$7–US$9); table d'hôte dinner C$26–C$44 (US$19–US$31). AE, DC, ER, MC, V. Daily 7am–11pm. CONTEMPORARY FRENCH.

While this replacement for the departed Laurie Raphaël doesn't come within hailing distance of the champ, it's a thoroughly pleasant spot in which to take nourishment and pass an hour or so. There's a dining patio in back of the old stone house and the interior is made more intimate when the windows are closed and logs are set to flame in the fireplace. Service is none too vigilant, but what arrives on the plate compensates, with creative takes on French recipes. Keep it in mind for breakfast, too.

5 Seeing the Sights

Wandering at random through the streets of Vieux-Québec is a singular pleasure. On the way, you can happen on an ancient convent, blocks of gabled houses with steep tin roofs, a battery of 18th-century cannons in a leafy park, or a bistro with a blazing fireplace on a chilly day. This is such a compact city that it's hardly necessary to plan precise itineraries. Start at the terrasse Dufferin and go off on a whim, down Breakneck Stairs to the Quartier Petit-Champlain and place Royale, or up to the Citadelle and onto the Plains of Abraham, where Wolfe and Montcalm fought to the death in a 20-minute battle that changed the destiny of the continent.

Most of what there is to see is within the city walls, in the Lower Town. It's fairly easy walking. While the Upper Town is hilly, with sloping streets, it's nothing like San Francisco, and only people with physical limitations will experience difficulty. If rain or ice discourages exploration on foot, tour buses and horse-drawn calèches are options.

LOWER TOWN

The **Escalier Casse-Cou** (Breakneck Stairs) connects the terrasse Dufferin at the top of the cliff with rue Sous-le-Fort at the base. The name will be self-explanatory as soon as you see the stairs. They lead from Haute-Ville to the Quartier Petit-Champlain in Basse-Ville. A stairway has existed here since the settlement began, but human beings weren't the only ones to use it. In 1698, the town council forbade citizens to take their animals up or down the stairway or face a fine.

A short walk from the bottom of Breakneck Stairs, via rue Sous-le-Fort, is picturesque ✪ **place Royale,** Lower Town's literal and spiritual heart. In the 17th and 18th centuries, it was the town marketplace and the center of business and industry. Dominating the square is the **Eglise Notre-Dame-des-Victoires,** the oldest stone church in Québec, built in 1688 and restored in 1763 and 1969. The paintings, altar, and large model boat suspended from the ceiling were votive offerings brought by early settlers to ensure safe voyages. The church usually is open during the day, unless a wedding is underway.

An empty storefront on the square was refurbished in 1997 to become a **welcome center,** 215 rue du Marché-Finlay (☎ **418/643-6631**), open June 5 to October 1, daily from 10am to 6pm. Across the square from the church stands the **Maison des Vins** (House of Wines). In addition to the wines on sale, the store invites the public to examine the cool subterranean vaults of the old stone house.

All the rest of the buildings on the square have been restored, save one. The stone facade at the northeast corner, with metal and painted plywood covering its doors and windows, isn't simply abandoned—there's nothing behind that wall but an empty lot. Note the ladders on some of the other roofs, a common Québec device for removing snow and fighting fires. Folk dances, impromptu concerts, and other festive gatherings are often held near the bust of Louis XIV in the square.

✪ **Musée de la Civilisation.** 85 rue Dalhousie (at St-Antoine). ☎ **418/643-2158.** Admission C$7 (US$5) adults, C$6 (US$4.30) seniors, C$4 (US$2.85) students over 17, C$2 (US$1.40) ages 12–16; children under 12 free. Free to all Tues (except summer). June 24–Sept 4 daily 10am–7pm; Sept 5–June 23 Tues and Thurs–Sun 10am–5pm, Wed 10am–9pm.

Try to set aside at least 2 hours for a visit to this special museum, one of the most engrossing in all Canada. Designed by Boston-based, McGill University–trained Moshe Safdie and opened in 1988, it's an innovative presence in the historic Basse-Ville, near place Royale. A dramatic atrium lobby sets the tone with a massive sculpture rising like jagged icebergs from the watery floor, a representation of the mighty St. Lawrence at spring breakup. Through the glass wall in back you can see the 1752 Maison Estèbe, now restored to contain the museum shop. It stands above vaulted cellars that you can view.

In the galleries upstairs are four permanent exhibits, supplemented by up to six temporary shows on a variety of themes. The museum's mission has never been entirely clear, leading to some opaque metaphysical meanderings in its early years. Never mind. Through highly imaginative display techniques, hands-on devices, computers, holograms, videos, and even an ant farm, the curators have assured that you'll be so enthralled that you won't pause to question the intent. Notice, as an example of their thoroughness, how a squeaky floorboard has been installed at the entrance to a display of dollhouse-size old Québec houses. If time is short, definitely use it to take in Memoires (Memories), the permanent exhibit that's a sprawling examination of Québec history, moving from the province's roots as a fur-trading colony to the present. Furnishings from frontier homes, tools of the trappers' trade, old farm implements, 19th-century religious garments, old campaign posters, and a re-created classroom from the past envelop you with a rich sense of Québec's daily life from generation to generation. Exhibit texts are in French and English. There's a cafe on the ground floor.

Explore Sound & Light Show. 63 rue Dalhousie (at St-Antoine). ☎ **418/692-1759.** Admission C$5.50 (US$3.90) adults, C$4.50 (US$3.20) seniors, C$3.50 (US$2.50) ages 7–25. Apr 15–Oct 15 daily 11am–5pm.

Québec City

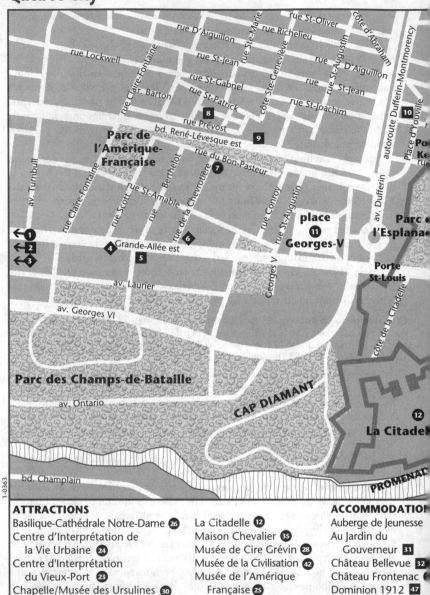

1-0363

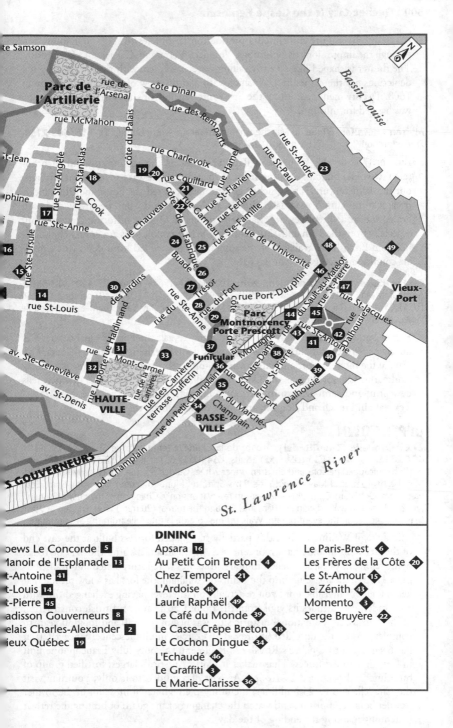

Parc de l'Artillerie

te Samson

rue de l'Arsenal

côte Dinan

rue des Remparts

rue McMahon

côte du Palais

rue Charlevoix

rue St-André

Bassin Louise

rue St-Paul

t-Jean

phine

rue Ste-Angèle

rue St-Stanislas

18

rue Couillard

rue Hamel

rue St-Flavien

23

17

rue Ste-Anne

Cook

19 20

21

côte de la Fabrique

22

rue Chauveau

rue Carneau

rue St-Flavien

rue Ferland

rue Ste-Famille

16

rue Ste-Ursule

24

25

rue de l'Université

48

49

Vieux-Port

15

Buade

26

46

rue St-Pierre

14

rue St-Louis

30

des Jardins

27

Trésor

rue Port-Dauphin

côte de la Montagne

rue du Sault-au-Matelot

47

rue St-Jacques

Dalhousie

28

rue du Fort

44

45

42

rue St-Antoine

40

av. Ste-Geneviève

rue Laporte

rue Haldimand

31

Mont-Carmel

33

29

Parc Montmorency Porte Prescott

rue Notre-Dame

43

41

37

32

av. St-Denis

rue de la Carrière

rue des Carrières

terrasse Dufferin

Funicular

36

38

39

HAUTE-VILLE

35

rue Sous-le-Fort

rue St-Pierre

rue Dalhousie

34

r. du Marché

Champlain

BASSE-VILLE

S GOUVERNEURS

rue du Petit-Champlain

bd. Champlain

St. Lawrence River

DINING

bews Le Concorde **5**

Apsara **16**

Le Paris-Brest **6**

Manoir de l'Esplanade **13**

Au Petit Coin Breton **4**

Les Frères de la Côte **20**

t-Antoine **41**

Chez Temporel **21**

Le St-Amour **15**

t-Louis **14**

L'Ardoise **48**

Le Zénith **43**

t-Pierre **45**

Laurie Raphaël **49**

Momento **3**

adisson Gouverneurs **8**

Le Café du Monde **39**

Serge Bruyère **22**

elais Charles-Alexander **2**

Le Casse-Crêpe Breton **18**

ieux Québec **19**

Le Cochon Dingue **34**

L'Echaudé **46**

Le Graffiti **3**

Le Marie-Clarisse **36**

299

A splashy 30-minute multimedia production chronicles the Age of Exploration through the impressions of Columbus, Vespucci, Verrazano, Cartier, and Champlain. The theater is shaped like an early sailing vessel, complete with rigging. Among the depictions are the difficulties of Champlain and his crew of 28 who came here in 1608. Twenty men died during the first winter, mainly of scurvy and dysentery (one was hanged for mutiny).

Maison Chevalier. 60 rue du Marché-Champlain (at rue Notre-Dame). ☎ **418/643-2158.** Free admission. June 1–Oct 1 daily 10am–5pm.

Built in 1752 for ship-owner Jean-Baptiste Chevalier, the existing structure incorporated two older buildings, dating from 1675 and 1695. It was run as an inn throughout the 19th century. The Québec government restored the house in 1960, and it became a museum 5 years later. Inside, with its exposed wood beams, wide-board floors, and stone fireplaces, are changing exhibits on Québec history and civilization, especially from the 17th and 18th centuries. While exhibit texts are in French, guidebooks in English are available at the sometimes unattended front desk. (It's also an air-conditioned refuge on hot days.)

Centre d'Interprétation du Vieux-Port. 100 rue St-André (at Rioux). ☎ **418/648-3300.** Admission May to Labour Day C$2.75 (US$1.95) adults, C$2 (US$1.40) seniors, C$1.50 (US$1.05) ages 6–16, C$6 (US$4.30) family. May to Labour Day daily 10am–5pm; schedule varies rest of year (call for hours).

Part of Parks Canada, this interpretation center reveals the Port of Québec as it was during its 19th-century maritime zenith. Four floors of exhibits illustrate that era. You can see the modern port and city from the top level, where reference maps identify landmarks. One of these is the Daishowa Pulp and Paper Mill (1927), which sells newsprint and cardboard to international markets, including the *New York Times*. Texts are in French and English, and most exhibits invite touching.

UPPER TOWN

✪ **La Citadelle (The Citadel).** 1 côte de la Citadelle (enter off rue St-Louis). ☎ **418/ 694-2815.** Admission C$5 (US$3.55) adults, C$4 (US$2.85) seniors, C$2.50 (US$1.80) ages 7–17; handicapped persons and children under 7 free. Guided 55-min. tours, daily Apr to mid-May 10am–4pm; mid-May to mid-June 9am–5pm; mid-June to Labour Day 9am–6pm; Sept 9am–4pm; Oct 10am–3pm. Nov–Mar, group reservations only. Changing of the guard (30 min.) July 2 to Labour Day Wed–Sun at 10am and beating the retreat (20 min.) Wed, Fri, Sun at 7pm. May be canceled in the event of rain. Walk up the côte de la Citadelle from the St-Louis gate.

The duke of Wellington had this partially star-shaped fortress built at the east end of the city walls in anticipation of renewed American attacks after the War of 1812. Some remnants of earlier French military structures were incorporated into it, including a 1750 magazine. Dug into the Plains of Abraham, the fort has a low profile that keeps it all but invisible until you're actually on it. Never having exchanged fire with an invader, it continues its vigil from the tip of Cap Diamant. British construction of the fortress, now a national historic site, was begun in 1820 and took 30 years to complete. As events unfolded, it proved an exercise in obsolescence. Since 1920, it has been home to Québec's Royal 22e Régiment, the only fully Francophone unit in Canada's armed forces. That makes it North America's largest fortified group of buildings still occupied by troops. As part of a guided tour only, you may visit the Citadelle and its 25 buildings, including the regimental museum in the former powder house and prison, and watch the changing of the guard or beating the retreat (ceremony marking the ending of the day).

Basilique-Cathédrale Notre-Dame. 20 rue Buade (at côte de la Fabrique). ☎ **418/ 694-0665.** Free admission to basilica and guided tours. "Act of Faith" sound-and-light show,

C$7 (US$5) adults, C$5 (US$3.55) seniors, C$3 (US$2.15) students 12 and over with ID; children 11 and under free. Basilica daily 8am–2:30pm. Guided tours May–Oct daily 9am–2:30pm. "Act of Faith" multimedia sound-and-light show, May–Thanksgiving (mid-Oct) daily 3:30, 5, 6:30, 8pm (and at 9pm July–Aug).

The oldest Christian parish north of Mexico has seen a tumultuous history of bombardment, reconstruction, and restoration. Parts of the basilica date to the original 1647 structure, like the bell tower and portions of the walls. The interior is flamboyantly baroque, shadows wavering by the fluttering light of votive candles. Paintings and ecclesiastical treasures still remain from the time of the French regime, including a chancel lamp given by Louis XIV. In summer, the basilica is the backdrop for a multimedia sound-and-light show called "Act of Faith," which dramatically recalls 5 centuries of Québec's history and that of this building itself.

The basilica is connected to the group of old buildings that makes up Québec Seminary. To enter that complex, go to 7 rue de l'Université.

Chapelle/Musée des Ursulines. 12 rue Donnacona (at rue des Jardins). ☎ **418/694-0694.** Museum C$3 (US$2.15) adults, C$2 (US$1.40) seniors, C$1.50 (US$1.05) students; chapel free. Museum Sept–Apr Tues–Sun 1–4:30pm; May–Aug Tues–Sat 10am–noon and 1–5pm. Chapel May–Oct same days and hours as museum.

The chapel is notable for the sculptures on its pulpit and two retables. They were created by Pierre-Noel Levasseur between 1726 and 1736. Though the present building dates only to 1902, much of the interior decoration is nearly 2 centuries older. The tomb of the founder of this teaching order, Marie de l'Incarnation, is to the right of the entry. She arrived here in 1639 at the age of 40 and was declared blessed by Pope John Paul II in 1980. The museum displays accoutrements of the daily and spiritual life of the Ursulines. On the third floor are exhibits of vestments woven with gold thread by the Ursulines. A cape made of drapes from the bedroom of Anne of Austria and given to Marie de l'Incarnation when she left for New France in 1639 is on display. There are also musical instruments and Amerindian crafts, including the flèche, or arrow sash, still worn during Winter Carnival. Some of the docents are nuns of the still-active order. The Ursuline convent, built as a girls' school in 1642, is the oldest one in North America.

Château Frontenac. 1 rue des Carrières, place d'Armes. ☎ **418/692-3861.** Guided tours: May 1–Oct 15, daily 10am–6pm; Oct 16–Apr 30 Sat–Sun 12:30–5pm. Tours, C$5.50 (US$3.90) adults, C$4.50 (US$3.20) seniors, C$3.50 (US$2.50) children 6–16.

Opened in 1893 to house railroad passengers and encourage tourism, the monster version of a Loire Valley palace is the city's emblem, its Eiffel Tower. You can see the hotel from almost every quarter, commanding its majestic position atop Cap Diamant. Those curious about the interior may wish to take one of the 50-minute guided tours; to make reservations, call ☎ **418/691-2166.**

Musée de Cire Grévin (Wax Museum). 22 rue Ste-Anne (at Trésor). ☎ **418/692-2289.** Admission C$6 (US$4.30) adults, C$3 (US$2.15) seniors and students; children under 6 free. Summer daily 9am–10pm; winter daily 10am–5pm.

Occupying a 17th-century house, this briefly diverting wax museum, renovated in 1994, provides a superficial skim of Québec's history and heroes. Generals Wolfe and Montcalm are portrayed, of course, along with effigies of politicians, singers, Olympic gold medalists, and other newsmakers. Texts are in French and English.

Musée de L'Amérique Française. Québec Seminary, 2 côte de la Fabrique. ☎ **418/643-2159.** Admission C$3 (US$2.15) adults, C$2 (US$1.40) seniors and students over 17, C$1 (US70¢) children 12–16; children under 12 free. June 24–Sept 1 daily 10am–5:30pm; Sept 2–June 23 Tues–Sun 10am–5pm. Guided tours of exhibits and some buildings, daily in summer, rest of the year Sat–Sun.

Housed in the historic Québec Seminary, with a history dating from 1659, the Museum of French America focuses on the beginnings and the evolution of French culture and civilization in North America. Its extensive collections include paintings by European and Canadian artists, engravings and parchments from the early French regime, old and rare books, coins, early scientific instruments, and even mounted animals and an Egyptian mummy. The mix makes for an engrossing visit.

The museum is in three parts of the large seminary complex. In the Guillaume Couillard wing, adjacent to the Basilique-Cathédrale Notre-Dame, is the entrance hall and information desk. In the Jérôme Demers wing, bordering rue de l'Université, down the hill, are the exhibition galleries. Third is the beautiful François Ranvoyze wing, with its trompe-l'oeil ornamentation, which served as a chapel for the seminary priests and students. It's now open only during summer for guided tours. Concerts are held in the chapel.

Musée du Fort. 10 rue Ste-Anne (at place d'Armes). ☎ **418/692-1759.** Admission C$6 (US$4.30) adults, C$5 (US$3.55) seniors, C$3.50 (US$2.50) students and children under 18. Apr–Nov and Dec 26–Jan 6 daily 10am–5pm.

Bordering place d'Armes, not far from the UNESCO World Heritage monument, this commercial enterprise presents a sound-and-light show using a 400-square-foot model of the city and surrounding region. The 30-minute production concerns itself primarily with the six sieges of Québec, including the famous battle on the Plains of Abraham. Commentary is in French or English. Military and history buffs are the ones most likely to enjoy it.

NEAR THE GRANDE-ALLEE

For an amazing view, enter the government office tower called **Edifice Marie-Guyant,** 1033 rue de la Chevrotière, at boulevard René-Lévesque (☎ **418/644-9841**), and look for signs and special elevators labeled "Anima G, 31e Etage." On the 31st floor are unobstructed panoramic vistas of the city and river. Anima G is open Monday to Friday from 10am to 4pm and Saturday and Sunday from 1 to 5pm; it's closed mid-December to January 5.

Musée du Québec. 1 av. Wolfe-Montcalm (at av. George VI). ☎ **418/643-2150.** Admission (excluding special exhibits) C$5.75 (US$4.10) adults, C$4.75 (US$3.40) seniors, C$2.75 (US$1.95) students; children under 16 free; free for everyone Wed. June 1–Sept 7 daily 10am–5:45pm (Wed to 9:45pm); Sept 8–May 31 Tues–Sun 11am–5:45pm (Wed to 8:45pm). Bus: 11.

In the southern reaches of Battlefields Park, just off the Grande-Allée and a half-hour walk or a short bus ride from the Upper Town, this art museum now occupies two buildings, one a former prison. They're linked by a soaring glass-roofed "Grand Hall" housing the reception area, a stylish cafeteria, and a shop.

The 1933 building houses the permanent collection, North America's largest aggregation of Québec art, filling eight galleries with works from the beginning of the colony to the present. Traveling exhibits and musical events are often arranged. The new addition is the 1867 Baillairgé Prison, which in the 1970s became a youth hostel nicknamed the "Petite Bastille." One cell block has been left intact as an exhibit. In this building, four galleries house temporary shows, and the tower contains a provocative sculpture called *Le Plongeur* (The Diver) by David Moore. Also incorporated in the building is the Battlefields Interpretation Centre (see below).

A children's playroom is stocked with toys and books. A very capable cafe/restaurant serves lunch Monday to Saturday, Sunday brunch, and dinner Wednesday and Saturday.

Parc des Champs de Bataille (Battlefields Park). Interpretation Centre in the Musée du Québec, av. Wolfe-Montcalm. ☎ **418/648-5641.** Free admission to park. Interpretation center, martello tower no. 1, astronomy tower, and bus tour in summer, C$2 (US$1.40) ages 18–64, C$1.50 (US$1.05) ages 13–17 and 65 and over; children under 13 free. Late May to Labour Day daily 10am–5:30pm; early Sept to late May Tues–Sun 11am–5:45pm.

Covering more than 250 acres of grassy knolls, sunken gardens, monuments, fountains, and trees, Battlefields Park stretches over the Plains of Abraham, where Wolfe and Montcalm engaged in their swift but crucial battle in 1759. It's a favorite place for all Québécois when they want some sun, a jog, or a bike ride.

Be sure to see the **Jardin Jeanne d'Arc** (Joan of Arc Garden), just off avenue Laurier between the Loews Le Concorde and the Ministry of Justice. The statue was a gift from some anonymous Americans, and it was here that "O Canada," the country's national anthem, was sung for the first time. Within the park are two **martello towers,** cylindrical stone defensive structures built between 1808 and 1812, when Québec feared an invasion from the United States.

Battlefields Park contains almost 5,000 trees representing more than 80 species. Prominent among these are sugar maple, silver maple, Norway maple, American elm, and American ash. There are frequent special activities, including theatrical and musical events, planned in the park during summer.

Year-round, the park interpretation center provides an in-depth look at the historic significance of the Plains of Abraham to Québec over the years. A new **Discovery Pavilion** at 835 av. Wilfrid-Laurier serves as a reception and information center and starting point for bus and walking tours of the park. In summer, a shuttle bus tours the park in 45 minutes with narration in French and English.

The **obelisk** at the lower end of the Parc des Gouverneurs is dedicated to both Wolfe and Montcalm, the winning and losing generals in the momentous battle of September 13, 1759. Wolfe, wounded in the fighting, lived only long enough to hear of his victory. Montcalm died after Wolfe, knowing that the city was lost.

Hôtel du Parlement. Grande-Allée est (at av. Dufferin). ☎ **418/643-7239.** Free admission. Guided tours, early Sept to May Mon–Fri 9am–4:30pm; June 24 to Labour Day Mon–Fri 9am–4:30pm, Sat, Sun 10am–4:30pm. No visitors June 1–23.

Since 1968, what the Québécois choose to call their National Assembly has occupied this imposing Second Empire château built in 1886. Twenty-two bronze statues of some of the most prominent figures in Québec's tumultuous history gaze out from the facade. You can tour the sumptuous chambers of the building with a guide for no charge, but tour times change without warning. Highlights are the Assembly Chamber and the Room of the Old Legislative Council, where parliamentary committees meet. Throughout the building, representations of the fleur-de-lys and the initials "VR" (Victoria Regina) remind you of Québec's dual heritage.

ESPECIALLY FOR KIDS

Québec is such a storybook town that children often delight in simply walking around in it.

As soon as possible, head for **terrasse Dufferin,** which has those coin-operated telescopes kids like. In decent weather, there are always street entertainers—a Peruvian musical group or men who play saws or wineglasses. A few steps away at place d'Armes are **horse-drawn carriages,** and not far in the same direction is the **Musée de Cire** (Wax Museum), on place d'Armes at 22 rue Ste-Anne.

Also at place d'Armes is the top of Breakneck Stairs. Halfway down, across the road, are the monstrous **cannons** ranged along the battlements on rue des Remparts.

The gun carriages are impervious to the assaults of small humans, so kids can scramble over them at will.

At the bottom of Breakneck, on the left, is a **glassblowing workshop,** the Verrerie la Mailloche. In the front room craftspeople give glassblowing demonstrations, always intriguing and informative, especially for children who haven't seen it before. The glass is melted at 2,545°F and worked at 2,000°F. Also in the Lower Town, at 86 rue Dalhousie, the playful **Musée de la Civilization** keeps kids occupied for hours in its exhibits, shop, and cafe.

Military sites are usually a hit, at least with boys. The **Citadelle** has tours of the grounds and buildings and colorful **Changing of the Guard** and **Beating Retreat** ceremonies.

The **ferry** to Lévis across the St. Lawrence is inexpensive, convenient from the Lower Town, and exciting for kids. The crossing, over and back, takes less than an hour.

To run off the kids' excess energy, head for the **Plains of Abraham,** which is also Battlefields Park. Get there by rue St-Louis, just inside the St-Louis Gate, or, more vigorously, by the walkway along terrasse Dufferin and the promenade des Gouverneurs, with a long set of stairs. Acres of grassy lawn give children room to roam and provide the perfect spot for a family picnic.

Or even better, consider the **Village des Sports** (☎ **418/844-2551**) in St-Gabriel-de-Valcartier, about a 20-minute drive north of downtown. In summer, it's a water park, with slides, a huge wave pool, and diving shows. In winter, those same facilities are put to use for snow-rafting on inner tubes, ice slides, and skating.

6 Special Events & Festivals

Usually, Québec is courtly and dignified, but all that's cast aside when the symbolic snowman called Bonhomme (Good Fellow) presides over 10 days of merriment in early February during the annual **Carnaval d'Hiver** (Winter Carnival). More than a million revelers descend, eddying around the monumental ice palace and ice sculptures and attending a full schedule of concerts, dances, and parades. The mood is heightened by the availability of plastic trumpets and canes filled with a concoction called Caribou, the principal ingredients of which are cheap whisky and sweet red wine. Perhaps its presence explains the eagerness with which certain Québecers participate in the canoe race across the treacherous ice floes of the St. Lawrence. You must make hotel reservations far in advance. Scheduled events are free.

On June 24, **St-Jean Baptiste Day** honors St. John the Baptist, the patron saint of French Canadians. It's marked by more festivities and far more enthusiasm throughout Québec Province than national Dominion Day on July 1. It's their "national" holiday.

The largest cultural event in the French-speaking world, the **Festival d'Eté International** (International Summer Festival) has attracted artists from Africa, Asia, Europe, and throughout North America since it began in 1967. The more than 250 events showcase theater, music, and dance, with 600 performers from 20 countries. One million people come to watch and listen. Jazz and folk combos perform free in an open-air theater next to City Hall, visiting dance and folklore troupes put on shows, and concerts, theatrical productions, and related events fill the days and evenings. It's held for about 10 days in mid-July. Call ☎ **418/651-2882** for details.

During the 5-day **Medievales de Québec** (Québec Medieval Festival), hundreds of actors, artists, entertainers, and other participants from Europe, Canada, and the United States converge on Québec City in period dress to re-create scenes from 5 centuries ago, playing knights, troubadours, and ladies-in-waiting. Parades, jousting tournaments, recitals of ancient music, and La Grande Chevauchée (Grand Cavalcade) featuring hundreds of costumed horseback riders are the highlights. Fireworks are the one modern touch. It's held only in odd-numbered years for about a week in early to mid-August. Call ☎ **418/692-1993** for more information.

7 Shopping

SHOPPING AREAS   The compact size of the old town, upper and lower, makes it especially convenient for shopping. There are several **art galleries** in the Upper Town featuring Inuit and folk art that deserve attention. **Antique shops** proliferate along rue St-Paul in the Lower Town, the heaviest concentration running east from the parking lot opposite the Vieux-Port Interpretation Centre. Other **streets to browse** are rue St-Jean, both within and outside the city walls, and rue Garneau and côte de la Fabrique, which branch off the east end of St-Jean. There's a shopping concourse on the lower level of Château Frontenac.

The **Quartier du Petit-Champlain,** especially along rue du Petit-Champlain and rue Sous-le-Fort, offers many possibilities (clothing, souvenirs, gifts, household items, collectibles) and so far avoids the trashiness that often afflicts heavily touristed areas.

ARTS & CRAFTS   Crafts, handmade sweaters, and Inuit art are among the desirable items that aren't seen everywhere else. An official igloo trademark identifies authentic Inuit (Eskimo) art, though the differences between the real thing and the manufactured variety become apparent with a little careful study. Inuit artworks, usually carvings in stone or bone, are best buys not because of low prices but because of their high quality. Expect to pay hundreds of dollars for even a relatively small piece.

For Inuit art in stone, bone, and tusk, check out **Aux Multiples,** 69 rue Ste-Anne (☎ **418/692-1230**). Prices are high, from C$100 to C$10,000 (US$71 to US$7,142) and more, but competitive with goods of similar quality. **Galerie d'Art du Petit-Champlain,** 88¹/₂ rue du Petit-Champlain (☎ **418/692-5647**), features the wood carvings of Roger Desjardins, who applies his skills to meticulous renderings of waterfowl. Artists hang their prints and paintings of Québec scenes along **rue du Trésor** between rue Ste-Anne and rue Baude, a pedestrian lane mostly covered by awnings. Some of the artists, positioned near adjacent sidewalk cafes, draw portraits or caricatures. **Boutique Alsacia,** at 141 rue St-Paul (☎ **418/692-4064**), carries works by Québécois artisans as well as Alsatian ceramics. Nearby, the larger **Renaud & Cie,** 82 rue St-Paul (☎ **418/692-0144**), has a large stock of porcelain dinnerware, especially Royal Doulton and Noritake, while the other half of the store is given to kitchenware.

BOOKS & RECORDS   Most of Québec City's bookstores cater to the solidly French-speaking citizenry and students at the university, but a few shops carry some English books for visitors. One is **Librairie du Nouveau Monde,** 103 rue St-Pierre in Old Québec (☎ **418/694-9475**), which features titles dealing with Québec history and culture, including books in English. For travel books and accessories, visit **Librairie Ulysses,** 4 bd. René-Lévesque, near avenue Cartier (☎ **418/529-5349**). **Maison de la Presse Internationale,** 1050 rue St-Jean (☎ **418/694-1511**), stocks magazines, newspapers, and paperbacks from around the world.

Two floors of recorded music, mostly CDs with some cassettes, constitute the stock of **Archambault,** at 1095 rue St-Jean (☎ **418/694-2088**). The helpful staff goes to some lengths to find what you want.

A FARMERS MARKET   Not far from the 1916 train station is the **Marché du Vieux-Port,** a colorful farmers market with rows of booths heaped with fresh fruits and vegetables, relishes, jams, handicrafts, flowers, and honey from local hives. Above each booth hangs a sign with the name and phone number of the seller. A lot of them bear the initials I.O., meaning that they come from Ile d'Orléans, 10 miles outside the city. The market is enclosed, and the central part of it is heated.

WINE   A supermarket-size **Société des Alcools** (☎ 418/643-4334) store is at 1059 av. Cartier (near rue Fraser), with thousands of bottles in stock. Another attractive possibility is the **Maison des Vins,** on place Royale in the Lower Town. The ground floor of this old Québec house is a liquor store, with a good choice of wines. But down in the cellar (*les caves*) is their collection of rare and special wines and champagnes.

8 Outdoor Activities & Spectator Sports

OUTDOOR ACTIVITIES

The waters and hills around Québec City provide ample opportunities for recreation. There are two centers in particular to keep in mind for most winter and summer activities, both within easy drives from old Québec. Thirty minutes from Québec City, off Route 175 north, is the provincial **Parc de la Jacques-Cartier** (☎ 418/848-3169). Closer by 10 minutes or so is **Parc Mont-Ste-Anne** (☎ 418/827-4561), 40 kilometers (24 miles) northeast of the city. Both are mentioned repeatedly below.

BIKING   Given the Upper Town's hilly topography, biking isn't a particularly attractive option. But bicycles are available at a shop in the flatter Lower Town, near the lighthouse. They rent for about C$6 (US$4.30) per hour or C$30 (US$21) per day from **Location Petit-Champlain,** 94 rue du Petit-Champlain (☎ 418/692-2817), which also rents strollers; it's open daily from 9am to 11pm. You can also rent bikes on relatively level **Ile d'Orléans,** across the bridge from the north shore at the gas station (☎ 418/828-9215). For more vigorous mountain biking, the **Mont-Ste-Anne recreational center** (☎ 418/827-4561) has 200 kilometers (124 miles) of trails.

CAMPING   There are almost 30 campgrounds in the greater Québec area, with as few as 20 campsites and as many as 368. All make showers and toilets available. One of the largest is in the **Parc de Mont-Ste-Anne,** and it accepts credit cards. One of the smallest, but with a convenience store and snack bar, is **Camping La Loutre** (☎ 418/846-2201) on Lac Jacques-Cartier in the park of the same name. It's north of the city, off Route 175. The booklet available at the tourist offices provides details about all the sites.

CANOEING   The several lakes and rivers of **Parc de la Jacques-Cartier** are fairly easy to reach, yet in the midst of virtual wilderness.

CROSS-COUNTRY SKIING   Greater Québec has 22 cross-country ski centers with 278 trails. In town, the **Parc des Champs-de-Bataille** has 11 kilometers (6 miles) of groomed cross-country trails, a convenience for those who don't have cars or the time to get out of town. Those who do have transportation should consider Station Mont-Ste-Anne, which has more than 225 kilometers (140 miles) of cross-country trails at all levels of difficulty; equipment is available for rent.

DOGSLEDDING   **Aventures Nord-Bec** (☎ 418/889-8001), 665 rue Ste-Aimé in St-Lambert-de-Lévis, about 20 minutes south of the city, offers dogsledding expeditions. While they aren't the equivalent of a 2-week mush across Alaska, there are choices of half-day to 5-day expeditions, and you do get a sense of what that experience is like. You get a four-dog sled meant for two and take turns standing on the runners and sitting on the sled. (Shout "Yo" to go left, "Gee" to go right.) Part of the route passes beneath high-tension wires, but it's still a hushed world of snow and evergreens. With the half-day trip costing C$69 (US$49) per adult, C$59 (US$42) for students, and C$20 (US$14) for children, it's undeniably expensive, especially for families, but the memory will stay with you. Providing similar experiences are **Aventure Québec** (☎ 418/827-2227) and **Norac Expédition** (☎ 418/848-2551).

DOWNHILL SKIING Foremost among the five area downhill centers is the one at **Parc Mont-Ste-Anne,** the largest ski area in eastern Canada, with 51 trails (many of them lit for night skiing) and 11 lifts. From November 15 to March 30, a daily shuttle operates between downtown hotels and alpine and cross-country ski centers. The cars or minivans are equipped to carry ski gear and cost about C$18 (US$13) round-trip per person. For information, call ☎ 418/525-4953 or 418/525-5191.

FISHING From May to early September, anglers can wet their lines in the river that flows through the **Parc de la Jacques-Cartier** and at the national wildlife reserve at **Cap-Tourmente** (☎ 418/827-3776), on the St. Lawrence, not far from Mont-Ste-Anne. Permits are available at many sporting-goods stores.

GOLF Parc Mont-Ste-Anne has two 18-hole courses, plus practice ranges and putting greens. Reservations are required, and fees are C$28 to C$33 (US$20 to US$24). The only night-lit facility in Québec City is the 9-hole course at the **Club de Golf** in Val-Bélair, 1250 rue Gabin (☎ 418/845-2222), about 15 minutes west of the city. Reservations are required; a round costs C$14 (US$10) on weekends. There are 2 dozen courses in the area, most of them in the suburbs of Ste-Foy, Beauport, and Charlesbourg. All but three in the nearby suburbs are open to the public.

ICE-SKATING Outdoor rinks are located at place d'Youville and Parc de l'Esplanade inside the walls, and at Parc de Champs-de-Bataille (Battlefields Park), where rock climbing, camping, canoeing, and mountain biking are also possible.

SWIMMING Those who want to swim should plan to stay at one of the handful of hotels with pools. Château Frontenac has a new one, and the Radisson Gouverneurs has a heated outdoor pool you can enter from inside. Other possibilities are the Hilton and Loews Le Concorde.

Village des Sports, a two-season recreational center at 1860 bd. Valcartier in St-Gabriel-de-Valcartier (☎ 418/844-2200), has an immense wave pool and water slides as well as 38 trails for snow-rafting. It's about 20 minutes west of the city.

SPECTATOR SPORTS

The Nordiques, Québec's representatives in the misnamed National Hockey League, departed in 1995 for Denver, leaving the city without a team in any of the professional major leagues. For diehard hockey fans, however, there's the new Rafales, the Québec team in the International Hockey League. They play at the **Colisée de Québec,** 250 bd. Wilfred-Hamel, ExpoCité (☎ 418/691-7211).

Harness races take place at the **Hippodrome de Québec,** 2205 av. du Colisée, parc de l'Exposition (☎ 418/524-5283). Admission to the clubhouse is C$5 (US$3.55) general admission. Races take place year-round Wednesday to Monday at 1:30pm or 7:30pm (times vary from season to season, call ahead). Le Cavallo clubhouse is open year-round.

9 Québec City After Dark

While Québec City can't pretend to match the volume of nighttime diversions in exuberant Montréal, there's more than enough to do. And apart from theatrical productions, almost always in French, a knowledge of the language is rarely necessary. Drop in at the tourism information office for a list of events.

Check the "Night Life" section of the **Greater Québec Area Tourist Guide** for suggestions. A weekly information leaflet called *L'Info-Spectacles,* listing headline attractions and the venues in which they're appearing, is found at concierge desks and in many bars and restaurants, as is the free tabloid-size *Voir,* which provides greater detail. Both are in French, but salient points aren't difficult to decipher.

THE PERFORMING ARTS

The **Québec Symphony Orchestra,** Canada's oldest, performs at the Grand Théâtre de Québec from September to May; the **Québec Opéra** mounts performances there in the spring and fall, as does, more occasionally, the **Danse-Partout** dance company.

Many of the city's churches host sacred and secular music concerts, as well as special Christmas festivities. Among them are the Cathedral of the Holy Trinity, the Eglise St-Jean-Baptiste, and the Chapelle Bon-Pasteur. Outdoor performances in summer are staged beside the City Hall in the Jardins de l'Hotel-de-Ville, in the Pigeonnier at Parliament Hill, on the Grande-Allée, and at place d'Youville.

Agora. 120 rue Dalhousie (Vieux-Port). ☎ **418/648-4370.**

This 6,000-seat amphitheater at the Old Port is the scene of classical and contemporary music concerts and a variety of other shows in summer. The city makes a dramatic backdrop. The box office, in the adjacent Naturalium, is open daily from 10am to 6pm.

Colisée de Québec. 250 bd. Wilfrid-Hamel (ExpoCité). ☎ **418/691-7211.**

Rock concerts by name attractions on the order of Phil Collins and Supertramp are generally held in this arena, located in a park on the north side of the St-Charles River. The box office is open Monday to Friday: in summer from 9am to 4pm and in winter from 10am to 5pm.

Grand Théâtre de Québec. 269 bd. René-Lévesque est (at av. Turnbull). ☎ **418/643-8131.**

Classical music concerts, opera, dance, and theatrical productions are performed in two halls, one of them housing the largest stage in Canada. Visiting conductors, orchestras, and dance companies often perform here when resident organizations are away. Québec's Conservatory of Music is underneath the theater. The box office is open Monday to Friday from 10am to 6pm.

Kiosque Edwin-Bélanger. 390 av. de Bernières (near the Musée du Québec). ☎ **418/648-4050.**

The bandstand at the edge of the Battlefields Park is the site of a 10-week music season from mid-June to late August. Performances are Wednesday to Sunday and range from operas, chorales, and classical recitals to jazz, pop, and blues. All are free.

Théâtre Capitole. 972 rue St-Jean (near Porte St-Jean). ☎ **800/261-9903** (ticket office).

A mixture of live shows and attractions are offered on an irregular schedule in the historic 1,312-seat theater. Dramatic productions and comedic performances are in French, but they also host rock groups and occasional classical recitals.

LIVE-MUSIC CLUBS

Most bars and clubs stay open until 2 or 3am, closing earlier if business doesn't warrant the extra hour or two. Cover charges and drink minimums are all but unknown in the bars and clubs that provide live entertainment. There are three principal streets among which to choose for nightlife: the **Grande-Allée, rue St-Jean,** and the emerging **avenue Cartier.**

Café des Arts. 1000 rue St-Jean (at the corner of Auteuil). ☎ **418/694-1499.** Cover charge usually C$5–C$10 (US$3.55–US$7), depending on the attraction.

New in 1997, this unusual enterprise above the Eldorado boutique puts on theatrical pieces, poetry readings, dance, and jazz. On Friday nights, traditional Québécois music is showcased, and on Saturday they serve dinner. They're licensed to sell wine and beer.

Chez Son Père. 24 rue St-Stanislas (near St-Jean). ☎ **418/692-5308.** No cover.

A musical institution in Québec since 1960, this is the place where French-Canadian folksingers often get their start. The stage is on the second floor, with the usual brick walls and sparse decor. A young, friendly crowd is in attendance. The club is a few steps uphill from bustling rue St-Jean.

D'Orsay. 65 rue Baude (opposite the Hôtel de Ville). ☎ **418/694-1582.** No cover.

Visitors whose complexions have cleared up and are well into their mortgages will want to keep this chummy pub/bistro in mind. Most of the crowd is on the far side of 35, and they start up conversations easily. There's a small dance floor with a DJ, and in summer a folk singer perches on a stool on the terrace.

Kashmir. 1018 rue St-Jean (near St-Stanislas). ☎ **418/694-1648.** No cover (usually).

Upstairs, according to an erratic schedule, the show bar that has replaced Café Blues puts on an eclectic variety of musical and artistic presentations, including rock, blues, and art exhibits, with the added attraction of dancing 3 or 4 nights a week. Pass the time before the evening's performances at the pool tables or poker machines.

Le d'Auteuil. 35 rue d'Auteuil (near Porte Kent). ☎ **418/692-2263.** No cover.

University students and hip 20- and 30-somethings play pool in the bar until the bands start thumping upstairs. Live performers are booked almost every night of the year. Sometimes, they're semifamiliar names like April Wine and The Tea Party; more often they're local alternative bands or "homage" rock groups. Recent renovations have given the 1822 hall a splashy new look.

L'Emprise. 57 rue Ste-Anne (at rue des Jardins). ☎ **418/692-2480.** No cover.

Listening to jazz, usually of the mainstream or fusion variety, is a long-standing tradition in this agreeable room. The bar, off the lobby of the once-elegant Hôtel Clarendon, has large windows and art-deco touches. Seating is at tables and around the bar. It has a mellow atmosphere, with serious jazz fans who come to listen. Music is nightly from about 10:15pm.

Les Yeux Bleus. 1117^1/2 rue St-Jean. ☎ **418/694-9118.** No cover.

At the end of an alleyway off rue St-Jean, it looks tumbledown from the outside, but isn't intimidating inside. The music is mostly Québécois *chanson,* partly international pop.

Palais Montcalm. 995 place d'Youville (near Porte St-Jean). ☎ **418/670-9011** (ticket office). No cover.

The main performance space is the 1,100-seat Raoul-Jobin theater, with a mix of dance programs, classical music concerts, and plays. More intimate recitals and jazz groups are seen in the much smaller Café-Spectacle.

Théâtre du Petit-Champlain. 78 rue du Petit-Champlain (near the funiculaire). ☎ 418/692-2631. No cover.

Québécois and French singers fill this roomy cafe/theater with cabarets and revues. Have a drink on the patio before the show. The box office is open Monday to Friday from 1 to 5pm; to 7pm the night of a show. Performances are usually Tuesday to Saturday.

DANCE CLUBS

Chez Dagobert. 600 Grande-Allée (near Turnbull). ☎ 418/522-0393. No cover.

The top disco in Québec City, this three-story club has an arena arrangement on the ground floor for live bands, with raised seating around the sides. Upper floors have a large dance floor, more bars, TV screens to keep track of sports events, and video games. Sound, whether live or recorded, is a hair short of bedlam, and more than a few habitués are seen to use earplugs. Things don't start jamming until well after 11pm. The crowd divides into students and their more fashionably attired older brothers and sisters. A whole lot of eyeballing and approaching goes on.

Le Bistro Plus. 1063 rue St-Jean (near St-Stanislas). ☎ 418/694-9252. No cover.

A dance floor in back, with a light show, is full of writhing young bodies—very young, in many cases. During the week, the music is recorded, with live groups on some weekends. It gets raucous and messy, especially after the 4-to-7pm happy hour, but it's happy, too, with a pool table and TVs tuned to sports to keep people entertained.

Maurice. 575 Grande-Allée est. ☎ 418/640-0711. No cover.

Bidding to challenge Chez Dagobert at the top rung of the nightlife ladder, this triple-tiered enterprise occupies a converted mansion at the thumping heart of the Grande-Allée scene. The dance room rotates live Latin and blues bands, filling the gaps with house music. Theme nights are frequent, and the balconies, cigar lounge, and Le Charlotte bar can accommodate over 1,000 post-Boomers.

Vogue/Sherlock Holmes. 1170 d'Artgny (off Grande-Allée). ☎ 418/529-9973. No cover.

This pair of double-decked bars is far less frenetic than Chez Dagobert, with a small disco upstairs in Vogue, and the pubby eatery Sherlock below, with a pool table and dart board. Grad students and Gen-Xers in their first jobs make up most of the clientele.

BARS & CAFES

The strip of **Grande-Allée** between place Montcalm and place George-V, near the St-Louis Gate, has been compared to the boulevard St-Germain in Paris. That's a real stretch, but it's lined on both sides with cafes, giving it a passing resemblance. Many have terraces abutting the sidewalks, so cafe hopping is an active pursuit. Eating is definitely not the main event. Meeting and greeting and partying are, aided in some cases by glasses of beer so tall that they require stands to hold them up. This leads to a beery frat-house atmosphere that can get sloppy and dumb as the evening wears on. But early on, it's fun to sit and sip and watch. The following bars are away from the Grande-Allée melee.

Aviatic Club. Gare-du-Palais (near rue St-Paul, Lower Town.) ☎ **418/522-3555.**

A local favorite with the after-work crowd since 1945, it's in the front of the city's train station. The theme is aviation (which may seem odd given the venue) signaled by two miniature planes hanging from the ceiling. Food is served, along with local and imported beers. Behind the bar, the **Pavillon** (☎ **418/522-0133**), a casual Italian restaurant with pizza, pasta, and pool tables, is under the same ownership.

L'Astral. 1225 place Montcalm (at the Grande-Allée). ☎ **418/647-2222.**

Spinning slowly above a city that twinkles below like tangled necklaces, this restaurant and bar in the Loews Le Concorde unveils a breathtaking 360° panorama. Many people come for dinner. Make it for drinks and the view.

Le Pape-Georges. 8 rue Cul-de-Sac (at bd. Champlain, Lower Town). ☎ **418/692-1320.**

This cozy wine bar features jazz or a French singer from Thursday to Sunday at 10pm. Light fare is served during the day.

St-Alexandre Pub. 1087 rue St-Jean (near St-Stanislas). ☎ **418/694-0015.**

Roomy and sophisticated, this is the best-looking bar in town. It's done in a noncliché British-pub mode, with polished mahogany, exposed brick, and a working fireplace that's a particular comfort 8 months of the year. It claims to serve 40 single-malt scotches and more than 200 beers, 20 on tap, along with hearty food that complements the brews. Sometimes they present jazz duos, usually on Mondays. Large front windows provide easy observation of the busy St-Jean street life.

GAY & LESBIAN CLUBS

The gay scene in Québec City is a small one, centered in the Upper Town just outside the city walls, on **rue St-Jean** between avenue Dufferin and rue St-Augustin, and also along **rue St-Augustin** and nearby **rue d'Aiguillon,** which runs parallel to rue St-Jean. One popular bar/disco, frequented by both men and women (and by men who look like women), is **Le Ballon Rouge,** at 811 rue St-Jean (☎ **418/647-9227**).

EVENING CRUISES

Dancing and cruising are the pursuits of passengers on the MV *Louis Jolliet* (☎ **418/692-1159**), which offers a 4-hour evening cruise from 7 to 11pm. Snack food and a complete bar lubricate the evening. The fare is C$48.75 (US$49). Cruises depart from quai Chouinard at the port.

The sleek **Bateau-Mouche** (☎ **800/361-0130** or 418/692-4949) has arrived in Québec, following in the footsteps of its sister vessel in Montréal. Dinner cruises cost C$58.75 (US$42) and last from 7 to 10pm. You board at 6:15pm at Bassin Louise at the port.

10 Day Trips from Québec City

You can combine these four trips and complete them in a day. It'll be a breakfast-to-dark undertaking, especially if you spend much time exploring each destination, but the farthest of the destinations is only 25 miles from Québec City.

Bucolic Ile d'Orléans, with its maple groves, orchards, farms, and 18th- and 19th-century houses, is a mere 15 minutes away. The famous shrine of Ste-Anne-de-Beaupré and the Mont Ste-Anne ski area are only about half an hour from the city by car. With two or more days available, continue along the northern shore to Charlevoix, where inns and a new casino invite an overnight stay. Then take the ferry across the river—in summer and early fall you might even sight a whale. At Rivière-du-Loup on the opposite shore, drive back toward Québec City.

While it's preferable to drive through this area, tour buses go to Montmorency Falls, the shrine of Ste-Anne-de-Beaupré, and circle the Ile d'Orléans. If you wish to join a tour, contact **Visite Touristique de Québec** (☎ 418/563-9722), which offers English-only tours; **Old Québec Tours** (☎ 418/624-0460); **Maple Leaf Sightseeing Tours** (☎ 418/687-9226); or **Gray Line** (☎ 418/622-7420).

ILE D'ORLEANS

The island is only a short drive from Québec City. Follow rue Dufferin (in front of Parliament) to connect with Autoroute 440 north, heading toward Ste-Anne-de-Beaupré. In about 15 minutes, the Ile d'Orléans bridge will be on the right. At the island end, you can rent bikes at the convenience store, **Dépanneur Godbout** (☎ 418/828-9215).

After arriving on the island, turn right on Route 368 east toward Ste-Pétronille. In the house on the right is the **tourist information office** (☎ 418/828-9411), selling a useful guidebook (C$1) for the island. In summer it's open daily from 9am to 7pm; off-season hours are Monday to Friday from 9am to 5pm. A good substitute for the Ile d'Orléans guide is the Greater Québec guide, which includes a short tour of the island. You can rent a driving-tour cassette at the tourist office, and cycling maps are also available there.

Until 1935, the only way to get to Ile d'Orléans was by boat in summer or over the ice in winter. The building of the bridge permitted the fertile fields of Ile d'Orléans to become Québec City's primary market garden. During harvest periods, fruits and vegetables are picked fresh on the farms and trucked daily into the city. In mid-July hand-painted signs posted by the main road announce FRAISES: CUEILLIR VOUS-MÊME ("Strawberries: Pick 'em Yourself"). The same invitation is made during apple season in September and October. Farmers hand out baskets and quote the price, paid when the basket's full. Bring along a bag or box to carry away the bounty.

Three stone churches on the island date back to the days of the French regime, due in part to the island's long isolation from the mainland. There are only seven such churches left in all of Québec. And firm resistance to development has kept many of its old houses intact. This could easily have become just another sprawling bedroom community, but it has remained a rural farming area. Island residents work to keep it that way. They have plans to bury their telephone lines and to put in a bike lane to cut down on car traffic.

A coast-hugging road circles the island, which is 34 kilometers (21 miles) long and 8 kilometers (5 miles) wide, and another couple of roads bisect it. On the east side of the island are many farms and picturesque houses; on the west side, an abundance of apple orchards.

There are six tiny villages on Ile d'Orléans, each with a church as its focal point. Take it slow and spend a full day and a night—eat in a couple of restaurants, visit a sugar shack, skip stones at the beach, and spend the night at one of the waterside inns. But if you're strapped for time, you can do a quick circuit of the island in half a day. Drive as far as St-Jean, then take Route du Mitan across the island, and return to the bridge, and Québec City, via Route 368 west.

STE-PÉTRONILLE

The first village you reach on the recommended counterclockwise tour is Ste-Pétronille, 3 kilometers (2 miles) from the bridge. With 1,050 inhabitants, it's best

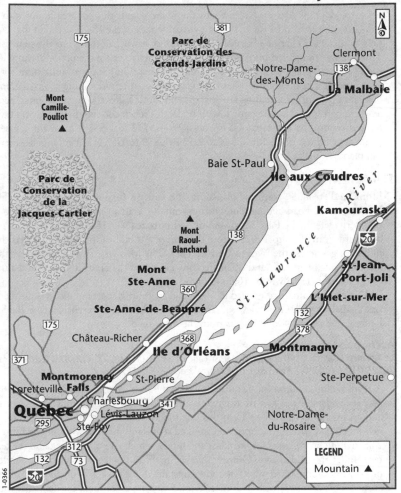

LEGEND
Mountain ▲

1-0366

known for its Victorian inn, La Goéliche (see below), and claims the northernmost stand of red oaks in North America, dazzling in autumn. The church dates from 1871, and its houses were once the summer homes of wealthy English in the 1800s. Even if you don't stay at the inn, drive down to the water's edge to a small public area with benches. Strolling down the picturesque rue Laflamme is another pleasant way to while away an hour or two.

All the lodgings recommended below for the Ile d'Orléans are of the auberge type, meaning that they have five or more rooms and have full-service dining rooms open to guests and nonguests. But there are also many B&B inns and *gîtes* (homes with a room or two available). Cheaper and less elaborate than auberges, many of them provide leaflets and photos to the tourist office.

Accommodations & Dining

La Goéliche. 22 av. du Quai, Ste-Pétronille, PQ, G0A 4CO. ☎ **888/511-2248** or 418/828-2248. Fax 418/828-2745. 18 rms, 2 suites. TEL. C$54.50–C$74.50 (US$39–US$53) double; C$110 (US$79) suite. Rates include breakfast. AE, MC, V. Free parking.

On a rocky point at the western tip of the island stands this country house with a wraparound porch and a pool. This is a virtual replica of the 1880 Victorian that was here until 1996. That one burned to the ground, leaving nothing but the staircase. This one was completed in record time and managed to retain the period flavor with tufted chairs, Tiffany-style lamps, and a few antiques. Only the two suites have TVs. The river slaps at the foundation of the glass-enclosed terrace dining room, a grand observation point for watching cruise ships and Great Lakes freighters steaming past. The dining room is well regarded, with updated French cooking that's easy on butter and cream. Expect to pay C$17 to C$27 (US$12 to US$19) for main courses, while table d'hôte meals run C$13 to C$33 (US$9 to US$24). A modified American plan is available.

ST-LAURENT

From Ste-Pétronille, continue on Route 368 east. In 6 kilometers (4 miles) is St-Laurent, once a boatbuilding center turning out 400 craft a year. To learn more about that heritage, visit **Le Parc Maritime de St-Laurent** (☎ **418/828-2322**), an active boat yard from 1908 to 1967. Before the bridge was built, it provided islanders the means to get across the river to Québec City. The Maritime Park incorporates the old Godbout Boatworks and offers demonstrations of the craft. It's open mid-June to early October, daily from 10am to 5pm.

The town's church was erected in 1860, and there are a couple of picturesque roadside chapels as well. Good views of farmlands and the river are available from the St-Laurent golf course—follow signs from the main road.

Accommodations & Dining

Le Canard Huppé. 2198 chemin Royal, St-Laurent, PQ, G0A 3Z0. ☎ **418/828-2292.** 8 rms. C$125 (US$89) double. Rates include full breakfast. AE, DC, ER, MC, V.

A roadside inn reminiscent of those found in the motherland, this tidy young place takes considerable pride in its kitchen. Local products and a light touch with butter and cream are its hallmarks. Turn this one menu item over in your mind: crimson raviolis stuffed with duck confit and smoked snails and drizzled with lobster butter. The inviting bistro/bar is for breakfast and lunch, which you can also take on the terrace under the linden tree. Dinner is in the main dining room, where the service meets professional standards. The rooms upstairs don't have TVs or phones but are attractively decorated, with firm mattresses. Smoking is confined to the baths, with the fan on.

Dining

Le Moulin de St-Laurent. 754 chemin Royal. ☎ **418/829-3888.** Reservations recommended at dinner. Main courses C$11–C$23 (US$8–US$16); table d'hôte lunch C$10–C$16 (US$7–US$11); table d'hôte dinner C$23–C$45 (US$16–US$32). AE, DC, ER, MC, V. Daily 10:30am–2pm and 6–10pm. Closed mid-Oct to May 1. COUNTRY FRENCH.

This former flour mill, in operation from 1720 to 1928, has been transformed into one of the island's most romantic restaurants. Rubble-stone walls and hand-wrought beams form the interior, and candlelight glints off hanging copper and brass pots. On a warm day, sit on the terrace beside the waterfall; be sure to wander upstairs to see the Québécois antiques. Lunch can be light—an omelet or a plate of assorted pâtés or cheeses, perhaps. There are at least half a dozen main courses to choose from, only one of them fish, despite all that water out there. On weekends, a small combo plays in the evenings. The owners also have a cottage for rent at the shore.

ST-JEAN

St-Jean, 6 kilometers (4 miles) from St-Laurent, was home to sea captains, and the homes in the village appear more prosperous than others on the island. The yellow bricks that comprise the facades of several of the houses were ballast in boats that came over from Europe. The village church was built in 1732, and the walled cemetery is the final resting place of many fishers and seafarers.

On the left as you enter the village is one of the island's largest and best-preserved houses: **Mauvide-Genest Manor,** 1451 av. Royale (☎ **418/829-2630**). Dating from 1752, it's filled with period furnishings. A beggar's bench on view was so named because a homeless person who appeared at the door late in the day would be offered a bed for the evening (otherwise, he might cast a spell on the house). A small chapel was added in 1930; the altar was made by Huron Indians. Admission is C$4 (US$2.85) for adults, C$2.50 (US$1.80) for seniors and students, C$2 (US$1.40) for children under 14, and C$10 (US$7) for families. It's open June to August daily from 10:30am to 5:30pm; other times by appointment. The dining room here is open in summer, daily from 11am to 9pm. The table d'hôte lunch is C$8 (US$6) and the table d'hôte dinner is C$18 (US$13). Next to the manor house is an active summer theater.

If you're pressed for time, pick up Route du Mitan, which crosses Ile d'Orléans from here to St-Famille on the west side of the island. Route du Mitan, not easy to spot, is on the left just past the church in St-Jean. A detour down that road is a diverting drive through farmland and forest. Return to St-Jean and proceed on Route 368 east to St-François.

ST-FRANÇOIS

The 9-kilometer (5½-mile) drive from St-Jean to St-François exposes vistas of the Laurentian Mountains off to the left on the western shore of the river. Just past the village center of St-Jean, you can see Mont Ste-Anne, its slopes scored by ski trails. At St-François, home to about 500 people, the St. Lawrence, a constant and mighty presence, is 10 times wider than when it flows past Québec City. Regrettably, the town's original church (1734) burned in 1988. At St-François, 24 kilometers (15 miles) from the bridge, the road becomes Route 368 west.

Dining

Chaumonot. 425 av. Royale, St-François. ☎ **418/829-2735.** Reservations recommended. Main courses C$18–C$27 (US$13–US$19); table d'hôte C$30 (US$21). AE, MC, V. Daily 11am–3pm and 5–9pm (to 10pm July–Aug). Closed mid-Oct to Apr 30. QUEBECOIS.

At this riverside inn, the food reflects what farmers have eaten on this island for generations—pork chops, lamb, salmon, *tourtière* (meat pie), pheasant pâté, tomato-and-onion relish, and plenty of warm bread. The kitchen mixes in a few relatively modern touches, such as quiche Lorraine and shrimp and duck pâté. Picture windows look out on the river.

The inn has eight tidy guest rooms. They're quite ordinary, but if you wish to stay the night, doubles with breakfast go for C$98 to C$138 (US$70 to US$99). The place is named for Jesuit priest Pierre Chaumonot, who led the Hurons to the island in 1651 to protect them from the attacking Algonquins.

STE-FAMILLE

Founded in 1661 at the northern tip of Ile d'Orléans, Ste-Famille is the oldest parish on the island. With 1,660 inhabitants, it's 8 kilometers (5 miles) from St-François and 19 kilometers (12 miles) from the bridge. Across the road from the triple-spired church (1743) is the convent of Notre-Dame Congregation, founded in 1685 by Marguerite Bourgeoys, one of Montréal's prominent early citizens. This area supports dairy and cattle farms and apple orchards.

Anglers might wish to swing by **Etang de Pêche Richard-Boily,** 4739 chemin Royal (☎ 418/829-2874), where they can wet their lines for speckled or rainbow trout in a stocked pond, daily from 9am to sunset. It isn't *quite* like fishing in a rain barrel. Poles and bait are supplied—no permit is required—and you pay only for what you catch, about C30¢; the fish run 9 to 12 inches. They'll clean, cut, and pack what you catch. Some island restaurants can even be persuaded to cook the fish for you. For more passive activity, buy a handful of fish pellets for C25¢, toss them on the water, and watch the ravenous trout jump.

On the same property is a *cabane à sucre,* the traditional "sugar shack" where maple syrup is made. They demonstrate the equipment and explain the process that turns the sap of a tree into syrup. Free tastes are offered and several types of products are for sale.

Farther along, near the village church, you might wish to visit the **Boulangerie G. H. Blouin** (☎ 418/829-2590), run by a family of bakers that has lived on the island for 300 years, and a little shop called **Le Mitan** (☎ 418/829-3206), which stocks local crafts and books about the island.

Dining

L'Atre. 4403 chemin Royal, Ste-Famille. ☎ **418/829-2474.** Reservations required. Main courses C$17.50–C$23.80 (US$13–US$17); table d'hôte C$29.50–C$39.50 (US$21–US$28); 9-course La Grande Fête C$58 (US$41). AE, MC, V. May to mid-Oct daily 6–9:30pm. QUEBECOIS.

For what will be a lasting memory of an island visit, park in the lot marked by the restaurant's sign and wait for the 1954 sedan to arrive from the restaurant. (It used to be a horse-drawn carriage, but that was given up for safety reasons.) The driver deposits diners at a 1680 Québécois house with wide floorboards and whitewashed walls at least 2 feet thick. The rooms are furnished with rough country antiques and reproductions and illuminated by oil lamps. "L'Atre" means the fireplace, and that's where most of the food is cooked. The menu is short and to the point, and traditional through and through, including such burly standards as *soupe aux légumes et fines herbes* (vegetable soup flavored with herbs), *boeuf au vin rouge* (beef stewed in red wine), and *tourtière* (meat pie). Dessert can be either maple-sugar pie or island-grown berries. All this is delivered by servers clothed according to the era they're re-creating.

ST-PIERRE

By Ile d'Orléans standards, St-Pierre is a big town, with a population of about 2,000. Its central attraction is the island's oldest church (1717). Services are no longer held there; it now contains a large handcraft shop in the back, behind the altar, which is even older than the church (1695). The pottery, beeswax candles, dolls, scarves, woven rugs, and blankets aren't to every taste but are worth a look.

Thousands of migrating snow geese, Canada geese, and ducks stop by in spring, a spectacular sight when they launch themselves into the air in flapping hordes so thick that they almost blot out the sun.

Accommodations & Dining

Le Vieux Presbytère. 1247 av. Mgr. d'Esgly, St-Pierre, PQ, G0A 4E0. ☎ **888/828-9723** or 418/828-9723. Fax 418/828-2189. 6 rms (4 with bath), 2 cottages. C$55–C$85 (US$39–US$61) double; C$60–C$70 (US$43–US$50) cottage. Rates include breakfast. Half board available. MC, V.

Down the street running past the front of the church, the former 1790 rectory has been converted to a homey auberge. Filled with antiques and simply old pieces, its sitting and dining rooms and glassed sunporch coax strangers into conversation. For privacy, choose one of the cottages, 100 feet from the main house; for more space and enough beds for a family of five, ask for room no. 1.

A fireplace warms the dining room much of the year. The kitchen is fond of exotic game, including ostrich, bison, and wapiti. Main courses run C$8.50 to C$26 (US$6 to US$19), with a table d'hôte of C$49 (US$35), which includes a bottle of wine.

Heading back across the bridge toward Québec City, you'll get a fine view of the next destination.

MONTMORENCY FALLS & STE-ANNE-DE-BEAUPRE

Take Autoroute 40, north of Québec City, going east. At the end of the autoroute, where it intersects with Route 138, the falls come into view. A **tourist information booth** (☎ **418/663-2877**) is beside the parking area at the falls, just after the turn-off from the highway. It's open daily: early June to early September from 9am to 7pm and mid-September to mid-October from 11am to 5pm. Admission to the falls is free.

The **waterfall** is surrounded by a provincial park where you can stop for the view or a picnic from early May to late October. At 274 feet, the falls, named by Samuel de Champlain for his patron, the duc de Montmorency, are 100 feet higher than Niagara, a boast that no visitor is spared. They are, however, far narrower. In winter, the plunging waters contribute to a particularly impressive sight, when the freezing spray sent up by the falls builds a mountain of white ice at the base, called the "Sugarloaf," which sometimes grows as high as 100 feet. On summer nights, the falls are illuminated and in the last 2 weeks of July there's a fireworks festival overhead. The water's yellow cast comes from the high iron content of the river bed. Manoir Montmorency, above the falls, was opened in 1994, replacing an earlier structure that burned down. Lunch and dinner are served there daily, except Monday and Tuesday dinner from January to March.

From Montmorency Falls, it's a 20-minute drive along Route 138 east to the little town of Ste-Anne-de-Beaupré. The highway goes right past the basilica, with an easy entrance into the large parking lot on the left. A **reception booth** at the southeastern side of the basilica, 10018 av. Royale (☎ **418/827-3781**), is open from early May to mid-September daily from 8:30am to 5pm. The basilica itself is open year-round. Masses are held daily but hours vary.

Legend has it that French mariners were sailing up the St. Lawrence in the 1650s when they ran into a terrifying storm. They prayed to their patroness, Ste. Anne, to save them, and when they survived they dedicated a wooden chapel to her on the north shore of the river, near the site of their perils. Not long afterward, a laborer on the chapel was said to have been cured of lumbago, the first of many documented miracles. Since that time pilgrims have come here—more than a million a year—to pay their respects to Ste. Anne, the mother of the Virgin Mary and grandmother of Jesus.

Reactions to the religious complex that has resulted inevitably vary. To the faithful, this is a place of wonder, perhaps the most important pilgrimage site in North America. Others see it as a building that lacks the grandeur its great size is intended to impart, a raw and ponderous structure without the ennobling patina of age. The former group will want to schedule at least a couple of hours to absorb it all; the latter won't need more than 15 minutes to satisfy their curiosity.

The towering basilica is the most recent building raised on this spot in Ste. Anne's honor. After the sailors' first modest wooden chapel was swept away by a flood in the 1600s, another chapel was built on higher ground. Floods, fires, and the ravages of time dispatched later buildings, until a larger, presumably sturdier structure was erected in 1887. In 1926, it, too, was gutted by fire.

As a result of a lesson finally learned, the present basilica is constructed of stone, following an essentially neo-Romanesque scheme. Marble, granite, mosaics, stained glass, and hand-carved wood are employed with a generous hand. The pews are of wood with hand-carved medallions at the ends, each portraying a different animal. Behind the main altar are eight side chapels and altars. The conviction that miracles routinely occur here is attested by the hundreds of crutches, canes, braces, and artificial limbs strapped to columns and stacked on the floor of the vestibule, left behind by the devout who no longer needed them.

Other attractions in Ste-Anne-de-Beaupré are the **Way of the Cross,** with life-size cast-iron figures, the Scala Santa Chapel (1891), and the Memorial Chapel (1878), with a bell tower and altar from the late 17th and early 18th centuries, respectively. More commercial than devotional are the **Historial,** a wax museum, and the **Cyclorama,** a 360° painting of Jerusalem.

Driving north on Route 360 toward Mont Ste-Anne, about 2 miles from Ste-Anne-de-Beaupré, on the left, is a factory outlet strip mall called **Promenades Ste-Anne** (☎ 418/827-3555). It has shops selling discounted merchandise from Dansk, Liz Claiborne, Mondi, Marikita (crafts), and Benetton, as well as a bistro serving California-style food. The mall is open daily.

ACCOMMODATIONS & DINING

La Camarine. 10947 bd. Ste-Anne, Beaupré, PQ, G0A 1E0. ☎ **800/567-3939** or 418/ 827-5703. Fax 418/827-5430. 31 rms. TV TEL. C$99–C$129 (US$71–US$92) double. AE, DC, MC, V. Go just past the Promenades Ste-Anne outlet center, turning left off Rte. 138.

Why they named it after a bitter berry is uncertain, but this inn has a kitchen equaled by only a bare handful of restaurants in the entire province—and that includes Montréal. (Reservations essential for dinner, the only meal served.) It bears a resemblance to that variety of fusion cookery that joins French, Italian, and Asian techniques and ingredients. The menu changes frequently, and they're justly proud of their wine cellar. The table d'hôte dinner is C$40 to C$50 (US$29 to US$35).

The guest rooms gracefully blend antique and contemporary notions, some with fireplaces, air-conditioning, and/or Exercycles. Two have Jacuzzis. The ski slopes of Mont Ste-Anne are a short drive away.

MONT STE-ANNE: SKIING & SUMMER SPORTS

Continue along Route 360 from Ste-Anne-de-Beaupré to the large ski and recreational area of Mont Ste-Anne. The park entrance is easy to spot from the highway.

Like Montréal, Québec City has its Laurentian hideaways. But there are differences: The Laurentians sweep down close to the St. Lawrence at this point, so Québécois need drive only about 30 minutes to be in the woods. And since Québec City is much smaller than Montréal, the resorts here are more modest in size and fewer in number, but their facilities and amenities are equal to those elsewhere in the Laurentian range.

The park's 78 square kilometers (30 sq. miles) surround a 2,625-foot-high peak. In summer, there's camping, golfing, in-line skating, biking, hiking, rock climbing, jogging, paragliding, and a 150-mile network of mountain-biking trails (you can rent bikes at the park). An eight-passenger gondola to the top of the mountain operates daily between late June and early September, weather permitting.

In winter, the park is Québec's largest and busiest ski area. Twelve lifts, including the gondola and three quad-chair lifts, transport downhill skiers to the starting points of 50 trails and slopes.

Condos are available for rent, and there are seven restaurants on the park grounds or in the vicinity. Golf, camping, and cycling packages are offered. For information and reservations, call ☎ **418/827-2002** or fax 418/827-6666.

CHARLEVOIX

Take Route 138 as far as Baie St-Paul, 87 kilometers (61 miles) from Québec City. Baie St-Paul has a year-round **tourist office** at 4 rue Ambroise-Fafard (☎ **514/665-4454**); it's open daily: mid-June to Labour Day from 9am to 9pm and the rest of the year from 9am to 5pm.

The Laurentians move closer to the shore of the St. Lawrence as they approach what used to be called Murray Bay, at the confluence of the Malbaie River and the St. Lawrence. While there's no pretending that the entire length of Route 138 from Beaupré is fascinating, moose sightings aren't uncommon, and the Route 362 detour from Baie St-Paul is scenic, with wooded hills slashed by narrow stream beds and billowing meadows ending in harsh cliffs plunging down to the river. The air is scented by sea salt and rent by the shrieks of gulls.

From Baie St-Paul to Cap à l'Aigle, a few miles beyond La Malbaie, there are several good-to-memorable inns. Nearby Pointe-au-Pic has a new casino, a smaller offshoot of the one in Montréal. The northern end of the region is marked by the confluence of the Saguenay River and the St. Lawrence. From mid-June to late October, these waters attract six species of whales—so many that you can see them from shore, though whale-watching cruises are increasingly popular. See the section on Baie St-Catherine below for information about whale-watching cruises.

In 1988, Charlevoix was named a UNESCO World Biosphere Reserve. While only 1 of 325 such regions throughout the world, it was the first so designated to include human settlement.

BAIE ST-PAUL

The first town of any size reached in Charlevoix via Route 138, this attractive community of 6,000 holds on to a reputation as an artists' retreat that began developing at the turn of the 20th century. Over a dozen boutiques and galleries and a couple of small museums show the work of local painters and artisans. Given the setting, it isn't surprising that many of the artists are landscapists, but other styles and subjects are represented.

One undertaking, opened in 1992, is **Le Centre d'Exposition,** 23 rue Amroise-Fafard (☎ **418/435-3681**), a brick-and-glass museum with three floors of work by mostly regional artists, both past and present. Inuit sculptures are included, and temporary one-person and group shows are mounted often. Admission is C$3 (US$2.15) for adults and C$2 (US$1.40) for seniors and students; children under 12 are free. It's open daily: September to May from 9am to 5pm and June to August from 9am to 7pm.

Accommodations

La Maison Otis. 23 rue St-Jean-Baptiste, Baie St-Paul, PQ, G0A 1B0. ☎ **800/267-2254** or 418/435-2255. Fax 418/435-2464. 30 rms. A/C TV TEL. C$160–C$258 (US$114–US$184) double. Rates include breakfast and dinner. AE, DC, ER, MC, V.

The prices may look steep, but remember that with big breakfasts and dinners included, lunch is almost redundant. A wide range of facilities and amenities allows guests who reserve far enough in advance to customize their lodgings. Combinations of fireplaces, whirlpools, stereo systems, VCRs, four-poster beds, and suites sleeping four are available, distributed through three buildings. A long porch fronts the colorful main street, and on the premises are a kidney-shaped indoor pool, a sauna, and a jovial piano bar. Housekeeping is meticulous.

ST-IRÉNÉE

From Baie St-Paul, take Route 362 toward La Malbaie. It roller-coasters over bluffs above the river, and in about 33 kilometers (20 miles) is this cliff-top hamlet of fewer than 800 year-round residents. Apart from the setting, the best reason for dawdling here is the lengthy music and dance festival held every summer. **Domaine Forget,** 398 chemin les Bains (☎ **418/452-8111**), offers concerts from mid-June to late August on Wednesdays, Saturdays, some Friday evenings, and Sundays at 2pm. This performing-arts festival was initiated in 1977, with the purchase of a large property overlooking the river. Existing buildings and the surrounding lawns were used to stage the concerts and recitals. Their success prompted the construction of a new 600-seat hall, completed in 1996. While the program emphasizes classical music with solo instrumentalists and chamber groups, it's peppered with appearances by jazz combos. Tickets are C$20 to C$26 (US$14 to US$19), with children under 12 free.

POINTE-AU-PIC

From St-Irénée, the road starts to bend west after 10 kilometers (6 miles) as the mouth of the Malbaie River starts to form. Pointe-au-Pic is one of the trio of villages collectively known as La Malbaie, or Murray Bay, as it was known to the wealthy Anglophones who made this their resort of choice from the Gilded Age on through the 1950s. Though inhabitants of the region wax poetic about their hills and trees and wildlife "where the sea meets the sky," they have something quite different to preen about now.

The **Casino de Charlevoix,** 183 av. Richelieu, Route 362 (☎ **800/665-2274** or 418/665-5300), is the second of Québec's recently approved gambling casinos (the first is in Montréal and the third opened in the Ottawa/Hull area in 1996). It's about as tasteful as such places get this side of Monte Carlo. Cherry-wood paneling and granite floors enclose the 303 slot machines and 15 tables, including blackjack, roulette, stud poker, and minibaccarat (no craps). Only soft drinks are allowed at the machines and tables, so players have to go to an adjacent bar to mourn their losses. And there's a dress code, forbidding, among other items, bustiers and "clothing associated with organizations known to be violent." Admission is free to persons 18 and over. The casino is open June to September, daily from 10am to 4am; October to May, Monday to Friday from 11am to 1am and Saturday and Sunday from 11am to 3am. Signs are frequent on Route 362 coming from the south, and on Route 138 from the north.

Opened in 1975, the **Musée de Charlevoix,** 1 chemin du Havre, at the intersection with Route 362/boulevard Bellevue (☎ **418/665-4411**), moved to its present quarters in 1990. Folk art, sculptures, and paintings by regional artists figure prominently in the permanent collection, supplemented by frequent temporary exhibits with diverse themes. Admission is C$4 (US$2.85) for adults and C$3 (US$2.15) for seniors and students; children under 12 are free. The museum is open June 26 to September 4, daily from 10am to 6pm; September 5 to June 25, Tuesday to Friday from 10am to 5pm and Saturday and Sunday from 1 to 5pm.

Accommodations & Dining

✪ Falaises. 18 chemin des Falaises, Pointe-au-Pic, PQ, G0T 1M0. ☎ **800/386-3731** or 418/665-3731. Fax 418/665-6194. 48 rms. TV TEL. C$99–C$249 (US$71–US$178) double. MAP available. AE, DC, ER, MC, V.

Falaises means "bluffs," and most rooms enjoy engrossing views of the Charlevoix coast. They're of good size, with furniture that serves its purpose. Most have whirlpool baths and some have balconies. The owners might want to rethink the dining room's pink-and-white color scheme, but just about everything else ranks it among the province's best, starting with the graceful service. The food is memorable, starting one recent evening with silky chilled cucumber soup with flecks of crabmeat and a plate of zucchini blossoms that the chef, by some legerdemain, had stuffed with lobster mousse. Finish with the plate of four cheeses and the frozen lime sorbet.

The auberge is half a mile from the casino—watch carefully on the left for the sign, difficult to read until you're on top of it.

Manoir Richelieu. 181 rue Richelieu, Pointe-au-Pic, PQ, G0T 1M0. ☎ **888/294-0111** or 418/665-3703. Fax 418/665-3093. 372 rms. A/C TV TEL. C$115–C$125 (US$82–US$89) and up. Rates include breakfast. MAP, golf, and other packages available. AE, DC, ER, MC, V.

As this town has long been the haven of swells summering in Murray Bay, there has been a resort hotel here since 1899 (the present one dates from 1929). The opening of the casino across the drive-up circle has changed that. To the mix of elderly people who've been coming here since they were young and families who've discovered that they can be together and still have time for themselves have been added those people who'll go anywhere for the opportunity to lose money. With the large numbers coursing through the halls, there's no denying that individuals get lost and services sometimes fall short, like the dysfunctional voice-mail system.

Buffet-lovers are bound to be pleased with the dozens of platters and trays set out for all three meals in the main dining room. There are sit-down menus, too. The informal Winston Pub is an able alternative. Golf on the hillside course provides the bonus of river views. A fitness center has weight machines and a sauna. The house band plays on past midnight for dancing.

CAP À L'AIGLE

Route 362 rejoins Route 138 in La Malbaie, the area's largest town, with almost 4,000 inhabitants. It serves as a provisioning center, with supermarkets, hardware stores, and gas stations. The **tourist information office** at 630 bd. de Comporté is open daily: mid-June to Labour Day from 9am to 9pm and the rest of the year from 9am to 5pm. Continue through the town center and across the bridge, making a sharp right on the other side. This is Route 138, with signs pointing to Cap à l'Aigle.

William Howard Taft spent many summers in Murray Bay, starting in 1892 and extending well past his one-term presidency. For much of that time, the only way to get here was by boat, for the railroad didn't arrive until 1919. Given his legendary girth, it can be assumed that Taft knew something about the good life. Some of the other folks who made this their summer home, namely the Cabots of Boston, the duke of Windsor, and Charlie Chaplin, could confirm that Taft loved the region. And if any of them could return today, they might choose what's arguably the premier auberge in Murray Bay.

Accommodations & Dining

✪ La Pinsonnière. Cap à l'Aigle, PQ, G0T 1B0. ☎ **418/665-4431.** Fax 418/665-7156. 26 rms, 1 suite. May 1–Oct 7 and Christmas C$130–C$295 (US$93–US$211) double. Nov–Apr C$100–C$275 (US$71–US$196) double. MAP available but not required. AE, MC, V.

In all Canada, this is one of only eight member hostelries in the prestigious Relais & Châteaux. As aficionados know, properties included in this organization offer limited size, comfort bordering on luxury in the guest rooms, and an emphasis on food and wine. The rooms come in five categories, the priciest of which have Jacuzzis and gas fireplaces.

Dining: You'll know where the owners focus their laserlike attention when you're seated in the serene dining room beside the picture window, anticipating dinner. With drinks and menus comes the customary *amuse-guele*—say, quail's legs on a bed of slivered asparagus and fettuccine tossed with plump mussels, spiked with a spray of pungent tarragon and brightened with an edible pansy—immediately followed by soup. The main event, often a succulent veal chop with a nest of shaved carrots, fiddleheads, and purple potatoes, is superb. Wines are a particular point of pride here, and the owner needs no urging to conduct tours of his impressive cellar.

Facilities: Indoor pool, sauna, tennis, massages.

ST-SIMÉON

Rejoin Route 138 and continue 33 kilometers (20 miles) to the ferry at St-Siméon to cross to Rivière-du-Loup on the other side of the St. Lawrence, returning to Québec City along the south shore. If there's no time, it's only 150 kilometers (93 miles) back to the city the way you came on the north shore.

Once in St-Siméon, signs direct cars and trucks down to the ferry terminal. Boarding is on a first-come, first-served basis, and ferries leave on a carefully observed schedule, weather permitting, from late March to early January. Departure times of the five daily sailings vary substantially from month to month, however, so get in touch with the company **Clarke Transport Canada** (☎ **418/862-9545**) to obtain a copy of the schedule. One-way fares are C$9.80 (US$7) for adults, C$6.50 (US$4.65) for seniors and children 5 to 11, and C$24.85 (US$18) for cars. MasterCard and Visa are accepted. Arrive at least 30 minutes before departure, 1 hour ahead in summer. The boat is equipped with a luncheonette, lounges, and a newsstand. Voyages take 65 to 75 minutes.

From late June to September, you may enjoy a bonus. That's when the **whales** are most active, and when pelagic (migratory) species join the resident minke and beluga whales, they're estimated at more than 500 in number. They prefer the northern side of the Estuary, roughly from La Malbaie to Baie Ste-Catherine, at the mouth of the Saguenay River. Since that's the area the ferry steams through, sightings are always possible, especially in summer.

BAIE STE-CATHERINE

To enhance your chances of seeing whales, continue northeast from St-Siméon on Route 138, arriving in 33 kilometers (20 miles) at Baie Ste-Catherine, near the mouth of the Saguenay. Half a dozen companies offer cruises to see the whales or the majestic Saguenay Fjord from here or from Tadoussac, on the opposite shore. They use different sizes and types of watercraft, from powered inflatables called zodiacs that carry 10 to 25 passengers to stately catamarans and cruisers that carry up to 500. The zodiacs don't provide food, drink, or narration, while the larger boats have snack bars and naturalists on board to describe the action. The small boats, though, are more maneuverable, darting about at each sighting to get closer to the rolling and breeching behemoths.

Most cruises are 2 to 3 hours. One of the most active companies offering trips is **Croisières AML,** with offices in Québec City (☎ **418/692-1159**), Pointe-au-Pic

(☎ **418/665-3666**), and Baie Ste-Catherine (☎ **418/237-4274**). From June to mid-October, they have up to four departures daily, with fares at C$30 (US$21) for adults and C$20 (US$14) for children 6 to 12. You're issued lifejackets and waterproof overalls, but expect to get wet anyway. It's cold out there, too, so layers and even gloves are a good idea. People on the large boats sit at tables inside or ride the observation bowsprit, high above the waves. Big boats are the wimp's choice in whale watching. And next time, mine, too.

From Baie Ste-Catherine, it's less than a half-hour drive back to St-Siméon and the ferry across to the opposite shore.

11   The Gaspé Peninsula: A Great Escape

The southern bank of the St. Lawrence sweeps north and then eastward toward the Atlantic. At the river's mouth the thumb of land called the Gaspé Peninsula—Gaspésie in French—pokes into the Gulf of St. Lawrence. The Gaspé is a primordial region heaped with aged, blunt hills covered with hundreds of square miles of woodlands. Over much of its northern perimeter, their slopes fall directly into the sea, then back away to define the edges of a coastal plain. Winter is long and harsh, the crystal days of summer made all the more precious.

The fishing villages huddled around the coves cut from the coast are as sparsely populated as they've always been, with many of the young residents moving inland toward brighter lights. That leaves the crash of the surf, eagles and elk in the high grounds, and timber to be harvested gingerly by lumber companies, the principal industry.

All that makes it the perfect place for camping, hiking, biking, hunting, and fishing in near-legendary salmon streams. Almost every little town has a modest but clean motel and a restaurant to match. The purpose of a trip is a complete escape from the cities, and your destination is the tip of the thumb, the village of Percé and the famous rock for which it's named. From Québec City, driving around the peninsula and back to the city takes about 5 days, assuming only an overnight stay when you get to Percé. The first half of the trip is the most scenic, while the underside of the peninsula is largely a flat coastal plain beside a regular shoreline. That southern shore is the route of the Via Rail trains, a thrice-weekly service recently restored between Montréal, Québec, and intermediate stops on the way to the town of Gaspé. The train, called the *Chaleur,* makes a stop at Lévis, opposite Québec City, and the ferry ride is complimentary for VIA Rail passengers. It leaves Lévis at 10:35pm on Monday, Thursday, and Saturday and arrives at Percé at 10:34am the next morning. Passengers in sleeping cars have the use of showers and a domed lounge car.

FROM RIVIERE-DU-LOUP TO RIMOUSKI

Past Rivière-du-Loup along Route 132, the country slowly grows more typically Gaspésien. Bogs on the river side of the road yield bales of peat moss, shipped to gardeners throughout the continent. Past the town of Trois-Pistoles (the name comes from a French coin, the pistole, not from firearms) are miles of low rolling hills and fenced fields for dairy cattle. Along the roadside, hand-painted signs advertise *pain de ménage* (homemade bread) and other baked goods for sale.

Rimouski (pop. 40,000) is the region's largest city. It has the look of a boomtown, with many new buildings, but those not there on business are likely to pass on through. The highway skirts the center of town along the riverbank. Rimouski marks the start of the true Gaspé, free of the gravitational pull of Greater Québec. The number of the two-lane highway is 132, which runs all the way around the peninsula to join itself again at Mont-Joli. Thus the confusing signs: 132 est (east) and 132 ouest (west).

JARDINS DE METIS

Near Grand Métis is the former Reford estate, now a ✪ **public garden** (☎ 418/ 775-2221) that's easily the north shore's stellar attraction. It was last owned by a woman with such a passion for gardening that even in Gaspé's relatively severe climate she was able to cultivate a horticultural wonderland of some 100,000 plants in 2,500 varieties. Full of fragrances and birdsong and tumbling water, the six sections are laid out in the informal English manner. Butterflies float and hummingbirds zip among the blossoms, all but oblivious to humans. The provincial government took the gardens over in 1962, and you can visit them June 1 to mid-October, daily from 8:30am to 6:30pm. Admission is C$7 (US$5) for adults, C$6 (US$4.30) for seniors and students, C$3 (US$2.15) for ages 6 to 14, and C$20 (US$14) for families; children under 6 are free. Elsie Reford's mansion now houses a museum of limited interest and a busy restaurant, open from 9am to 6:30pm. Nine concerts of classical music are given in the evenings of 3 weekends in July and August.

As you drive on to Matane, you'll note that the foothills off to the right of the highway get larger and move closer to the coast, and the roadside communities are farther apart.

MATANE

The highway enters town and passes gas stations and a new shopping center whose traffic rivals the bustle in Rimouski. But the focal point is the Matane River, a thoroughfare for the annual migration of up to 3,000 spawning salmon. They begin their swim up the Matane in June through a specially designed dam that facilitates their passage, continuing to September. Near the lighthouse the town maintains an **information bureau,** open daily from 9am to 8pm.

ACCOMMODATIONS

Riôtel. 250 av. du Phare est, Matane, PQ, G4W 3N4. ☎ **800/463-7468** or 418/566-2651. Fax 418/562-7365. 96 rms, 1 suite. A/C TV TEL. C$119–C$135 (US$85–US$96) double; C$170 (US$121) suite. Packages and Sept–May discounts available. AE, CB, DC, DISC, ER, MC, V. Free parking.

On the water near the harbor, the former Hôtel des Gouverneurs is now part of a small Gaspé chain. It hasn't changed much. Half its rooms have ocean views, some have minibars. The licensed dining room serves all meals, with dinner main courses running C$14 to C$23 (US$10 to US$16). A piano bar helps pass an evening, and on premises are a heated pool, a sauna, an exercise room, and a lighted tennis court. You may be encouraged to eat at the beach restaurant next door. Don't.

It takes 5 nonstop driving hours to get to Percé from Matane, so plan to spend a full day getting there. There are frequent picnic grounds, a couple of large nature preserves, and ample opportunities to sit by the water and collect driftwood. While towns along the way are smaller and more spread out, you'll find many modest motels, gîtes, and tourist cabins. Simple sustenance isn't a problem, either, for there are many casse-croûtes, the roadside snack stands also known as cantines.

STE-ANNE-DES-MONTS & PARC DE LA GASPESIE

Ste-Anne (pop. 6,000), another fishing town, has a **tourist information booth** on Route 132, half a mile past the bridge, and also stores, garages, gas stations, and other necessary services.

Rising higher inland are the Chic-Choc mountains, the northernmost end of the Appalachian range. Most of them are contained by the Parc de la Gaspésie and adjoining preserves. Turn onto Route 299 in Ste-Anne-des-Monts and head for the Gîte du Mont-Albert, about 40 kilometers (25 miles) south. The road climbs into the mountains, some of which are naked rock at the summits. Back there, the rivers brim with baby salmon and speckled trout, and the forests and meadows sustain herds of moose, caribou, and deer.

ACCOMMODATIONS & DINING

Gîte du Mont-Albert. Parc de la Gaspésie, C.P. 1150, Ste-Anne-des-Monts, PQ, G0E 2G0. ☎ **418/763-2288.** 48 rms. C$80–C$170 (US$57–US$121) double. AE, MC, V.

Reservations are essential for a meal or lodging at this remote lodge, operated as a training ground for people planning to enter the hospitality profession. Rooms in the main lodge or outlying cottages are summer-camp rustic, but food served in the dining room is considerably more sophisticated than you might expect.

MONT ST-PIERRE: PERFECT FOR HANG-GLIDING

Back on Route 132, turning right from Ste-Anne, the highway becomes a narrow band crowded up to water's edge by sheer rock walls. Offshore, seabirds perch on rocks, pecking at tidbits. High above the shore are many waterfalls that spill from the cliffs beside the highway.

Around a rocky point and down a slope, Mont St-Pierre is much like other Gaspésian villages except for the eye-catching striations in the rock of the mountain east of town. Such geological phenomena are quickly forgotten at the startling sight of hang gliders suddenly appearing overhead. The site is regarded as nearly perfect for the sport due to its favorable updrafts. In late July and early August the town holds a 2-week **Fête du Vol-Libre** (Hang-Gliding Festival), when the sky is filled with birdmen and birdwomen in flight hundreds of feet above the town, looping and curving on the air currents until landing in the sports grounds behind city hall. For more information about the event, contact the **Corporation Vol Libre,** C.P. 82, Mont St-Pierre, Gaspésie (☎ **418/797-2222;** fax 418/797-2558).

PARC NATIONAL FORILLON

Soon the road winds up into the mountains, over a rise, down into the valley, and again up to the next. The settlements get smaller, but still there are roadside stands advertising fresh-baked homemade bread and fresh fish. At Petite-Rivière-au-Renard, Route 197 heads southwest toward Gaspé while Route 132 continues east to the tip of the peninsula. Shortly after that intersection is the **reception center** for Parc National Forillon (☎ **418/368-5505**). Bilingual attendants on duty there can advise on park facilities, regulations, and activities. Route 132 continues along the edge of the park until it turns south at a lighthouse into the grounds.

Chosen because of its representative terrain, the park's 238 square kilometers (92 sq. miles) of headlands capture a surprising number of the features characteristic of eastern Canada. A rugged coastline, dense forests, and an abundance of wildlife attract hikers and campers from all North America. On the northern shore are sheer rock cliffs carved by the sea from the mountains, and on the south is the broad Bay of Gaspé. The park has a full program of nature walks, trails for hiking and cycling, beaches, sea kayaking, picnic spots, and campgrounds. A daily pass to enter the park is C$3.50 (US$2.50) for adults, C$2.75 (US$1.95) for seniors, C$1.75 (US$1.25) for students and children 6 to 16, and C$8.25 (US$6) for families. Camping fees are C$15.50 to C$19 (US$11 to US$14) per night. Of the 371 campsites at four designated campgrounds, 77 have electricity. Only four are open all year; most of the others are closed from October 16 to May 29.

   Croisière Forillon (☎ **418/892-5629** in summer or 418/368-2448 in winter) operates "discovery" cruises from Cap-des-Rosiers harbor daily in the warm months. Their 95-passenger *Félix-Leclerc* steams around the rim of the headlands past colonies of seals and seabirds. Fares are C$16 (US$11) for adults and C$10 (US$7) per child. Whales are sometimes encountered, but cruises specifically intended to get close to those magnificent creatures are provided by **Croisières Baie de Gaspé** (☎ **418/892-5500**). The *Narval,* a powered inflatable, is the means of transport, with a capacity of 48 passengers. It leaves from Grande-Grave Harbor, on the south shore of the park. Fares are C$32 (US$23) for adults, C$27 (US$19) for seniors and students, and C$10 (US$7) for children. Reserve in advance, if possible.

GASPE

Jacques Cartier stepped ashore here in 1534 to claim the land for the king of France. He erected a wooden cross to mark the spot. Today Gaspé is important economically because of its deep-water port and the three salmon rivers that empty into it. Otherwise unprepossessing, it doesn't offer much to detain travelers. The principal attraction is the **Gaspésie Museum,** at Jacques Cartier Point on Route 132 (☎ **418/368-5710**), which endeavors to tell the story of Cartier's landing, and the granite dolmens out front are reminiscent of the explorer's native Brittany.

PERCE

As you wind through the hills and along the water toward Percé, the Pic de l'Aurore (Peak of the Dawn), dominating the town's northern reaches, comes into view. Over the hill from the Pic, Percé Rock and the bird sanctuary of Ile Bonaventure appear. The rock is Percé's most famous landmark, a narrow butte rising straight out of the water and pierced by a sea-level hole at its far end. In the sunlight of late afternoon it's especially striking.

   The town of Percé (*"Pair-*see") isn't large, and except for a few quiet, well-groomed inland residential streets, it's confined to the main road that winds along the shore. Little private museums, cafes, snack bars, gift shops, restaurants, and motels line the highway, and people in bathing suits or shorts and T-shirts give it all a beach-party ambiance. But perhaps because the only way to get here is by this fairly long drive, it has thus far avoided the honky-tonk aspect that afflicts many beach communities closer to big cities.

   An **information center** is in town at 142 Rte. 132, open daily from 8am to 8pm in summer (shorter hours off-season).

EXPLORING THE AREA

After checking into a motel, most people take a boat trip out to the Rock and to the humpbacked bird sanctuary, Ile Bonaventure. A provincial park, the island's lure is the quantity, rather than the diversity, of its tens of thousands of nesting birds. Among them are gannets, cormorants, puffins, black guillemots, kittiwakes, and razorbills. For a photographic exhibit of the island's history, visit the **Information Centre** (☎ **418/782-2721**) at the foot of the Percé wharf. Naturalists are on the island to answer questions. Transportation is provided to and from Percé wharf. Birders and hikers can get off at the dock, later picking up one of the ferries that arrive two or three times an hour from 8am to 5pm. Fares are C$13 (US$9) for adults and C$5 (US$3.55) for children under 12.

   A glass-bottomed **catamaran,** *Capitaine Duval* (☎ **418/782-5401** or 418/782-5355), sails from the same wharf on whale-watching cruises. The cat has a lounge, large windows, bar service, rest rooms, and a bilingual crew. Tours go to Percé Rock, Bonaventure Island, and even Forillon National Park. For underwater explorations of the area, contact the **Club Nautique de Percé** (☎ 418/782-5403 in summer or 418/782-5222 in winter; fax 418/782-5624), which can lead you to a dozen or more dive sites. The water is about 50°F to 64°F (10°C to 18°C) from June to August and about 57°F (14°C) until mid-October.

The **Parc de l'Ile-Bonaventure-et-du-Rocher-Percé Interpretation Centre,** on l'Irlande Road (☎ 418/782-2240), focuses on the ecology of the Gulf of St. Lawrence and the natural features of Ile Bonaventure. A 10-minute film of the bird colonies is shown here, and there are saltwater aquariums. June to mid-October it's open daily from 9am to 5pm, with shorter hours the rest of the year.

More? Take a picnic up to the roadside rest just north of the Pic de l'Aurore, then take in different views of Percé Rock. At low tide walk out to the fossil-filled rock on a sandbar, a temptation few visitors resist.

ACCOMMODATIONS & DINING

La Normandie. 221 route 132 ouest, C.P. 129, Percé, PQ, G0C 2L0. ☎ 800/463-0820 or 418/782-2112. Fax 418/782-2337. 45 rms. A/C TV TEL. C$99–C$135 (US$71–US$96) double. Packages available. AE, CB, DC, ER, MC, V. Closed Nov–Apr.

Slightly south of the center, this small hotel occupies a building more stylish than others in town, sheathed in weathered wood. All rooms have small sitting areas, and those facing the water have decks. There's an exercise room and sauna for guests' use. The Normandie's handsome dining room is respected as one of the peninsula's most ambitious. Unobstructed views of the Rock are provided to every bentwood-and-wicker chair in the place, and the five-course table d'hôte dinners (at C$23 to C$37/US$16 to US$26) are admirable exercises in the culinary arts. Almost always offered are lobster, salmon, scallops, and an especially good halibut steak poached with orange and white wine sauce.

Les Trois Soeurs. Percé, PQ, G0C 2I0. ☎ 800/463-9700 or 418/782-2183. Fax 418/782-2610. 57 rms, 2 suites, 1 bungalow. A/C MINIBAR TV TEL. C$55–C$99 (US$39–US$71) double; C$95–C$125 (US$68–US$89) suite; C$155 (US$111) bungalow. AE, DC, ER, MC, V. Open May 15–Oct 20.

This unpretentious motel is one of the first you encounter when entering town, but it's only a short walk from the center. Several conveniences are available here, including an inexpensive Laundromat and provisions for baby-sitting. Coffee, juice, and croissants are served in the lobby. From one of the picnic tables on the lawn above the beach you get an up-close view of the high end of the Rock, looming like a beached supertanker. The owners, blessed with seven gorgeous daughters who often stop by in summer to help out, recently opened a restaurant, **Maison Mathilde,** in an adjacent 125-year-old building. Specializing in seafood, but with pizzas, chicken, and beef dishes also available, its table d'hôte meals are only C$12 to C$25 (US$9 to US$18).

DINING

Gargantua. Chemin des Falls. ☎418/782-2852. Reservations recommended. Table d'hôte C$27–C$37 (US$19–US$26). V. Mid-May to mid-Oct daily 4–10pm. Drive south on Rte. 132 from town, watching for the sign L'AUBERGE DU GARGANTUA on the right. CANADIAN.

The owner doesn't sit at your table to take your order anymore. All those ups and downs are a chore when you're 80. But he's still pretty spry around his log cabin mountaintop restaurant, and dining here is as much fun as ever. Check this procession of courses: A plate of hors d'oeuvres that includes a bowl of periwinkles (sea snails) extracted from their shells with pins. A big tureen of soup from which you serve yourself, repeatedly, if you wish. A choice of several fish and game main courses with copious portions of veggies from the garden out back. Sweets from the dessert buffet. All are served by the busy but infectiously cheerful staff, most of whom speak English. For country cooking at its best, don't miss this experience.

La Maison du Pêcheur. Place du Quai. ☎ **418/782-5331.** Reservations recommended at dinner. Main courses C$9–C$20 (US$6–US$14); table d'hôte C$20 or C$39 (US$14 or US$28). AE, DC, DISC, ER, MC, V. Early May to mid-Oct daily 11:30am–3pm and 5:30–10pm. SEAFOOD.

Everybody's favorite Percé eating place is at the end of the wharf, its windows offering views of harbor activity and the Rock. The decor is subdued nautical framed by a open-beam ceiling and rough-pine walls. Lunch is a complete meal with a choice of meat or fish for about C$12 (US$9), and that can include lobster. It's brought to the table by a congenial staff. The boardwalk-level bar/cafe, open from 8am to 3am, is a convenient stop for a drink or an espresso at the end of a long day, but it also serves very tasty sandwiches and pizzas.

HEADING EAST & SOUTH

Leaving Percé, Route 132 quickly bends back to the west. The southern shore of the Gaspé, on the Baie de Chaleur, is distinct from the north, with much more farming and commercial activity, fields of wildflowers, and small houses flanked by the day's wash flapping in the breeze. The mountains disappear over the horizon. Here the air is warmer and more humid.

FROM BONAVENTURE TO NEW RICHMOND

Continue west along Route 132 to Bonaventure (pop. 3,000) and, on the right, you'll see the **Musée Acadien du Québec à Bonaventure** (Acadian Museum of Québec at Bonaventure), 95 av. Port-Royal (☎ **418/534-4000**), devoted to Québec's Acadian forebears and to outstanding Acadians of the present day. Its exhibits are sophisticated and well worth a brief look. Ask for the text in English. It's open late June to Labour Day, daily 9am to 8pm; the rest of the year, Monday to Friday from 9am to noon and 1 to 5pm and Saturday and Sunday from 1 to 5pm. Admission is C$4 (US$2.85) for adults and C$3 (US$2.15) for students and seniors; children under 6 are free.

Farther east, just outside New Richmond (pop. 4,100), is a contrasting museum that examines Québec's British heritage: the **British Heritage Centre,** 351 bd. Perron ouest (☎ **418/392-4487**). Union Jacks flutter out front in this otherwise resolutely French region. But as this coast was settled in large part by United Empire Loyalists fleeing the American Revolution, it's a historically accurate touch. Twenty buildings from the late 1700s to the early 1900s comprise the museum. Guided tours are available in summer, and the 80 acres and many trails are conducive to strolling. Admission is C$4 (US$2.85) for adults, C$3 (US$2.15) for seniors and students, and C$8 (US$6) for families. It's open mid-June to Labour Day, daily from 9am to 6pm.

CARLETON

After passing through New Richmond, Route 299 heads north in Gaspésie Provincial Park to the Gîte du Mont-Albert (see above) and then to Ste-Anne-des-Monts on the St. Lawrence shore. Route 132, though, continues southwestward as far as Matapédia, where it turns north to return to the St. Lawrence at Mont-Joli. Long before Matapédia, but after passing through New Richmond, is Carleton (pop. 2,650), a port and resort town and a convenient overnight stop.

Accommodations

Baie Bleue. Rte. 132 (C.P. 150), Carleton, PQ, G0C 1J0. ☎ **800/463-9099** or 418/364-3355. Fax 418/364-6165. 93 rms, 2 suites. A/C TV TEL. C$68–C$96 (US$49–US$69) double; from C$115 (US$82) suite. AE, DC, ER, MC, V.

The guest rooms are comfortable, if unremarkable, and limited room service is available, hardly standard on the Gaspé. The upstairs restaurant with an ocean view changes its menu daily, and on the premises are an outdoor pool and a tennis court.

DRIVING ON TO NEW BRUNSWICK

If you're heading south to New Brunswick, you have two options. From Miguasha, not far west of Carleton, there's regular ferry service to Dalhousie, New Brunswick. It costs C$12 (US$9) one-way and can shave perhaps 30 minutes off the trip in summer traffic. At the least, the 15-minute crossing is a break from driving. Or you can continue along Route 132 to cross the western end of the Baie de Chaleur at Pointe-à-la-Croix, where a bridge spans the bay to Campbellton, New Brunswick.

11 Ottawa & Eastern Ontario

by Marilyn Wood

Ottawa's physical beauty is striking. It sits high atop a bluff above the confluence of the Ottawa, Gatineau, and Rideau rivers, with the gently rolling contours of the Gatineau Hills as a northern backdrop. The Gothic Parliament buildings brood romantically above the city, reminiscent of a Turner painting; the Rideau Canal cuts a vibrant swath through the city, worthy of any Dutch palette in summer or winter; and the daffodils in Rockcliffe Park would have inspired Wordsworth to sing had he seen them.

Ottawa has not yet really been visited by choked downtown streets and that imprisoned feeling that afflicts most cities. It has, in fact, a haunting romance to it, especially if you take the time to walk down to Victoria Island. Here, at the tip of the island, as the river rushes by the bluffs where the Gothic Parliament buildings and a statue of Champlain stand, you can still capture in your imagination the spirit of those early days when the river drew fur traders and explorers westward and great logs rolled down the river in this rough-and-ready town. Today, Ottawans boast that you can still see the hills and rivers from downtown and indeed in a short time you can be among them. And where else in North America can you see sentries in scarlet and busby changing guard just as they do at Buckingham Palace, and skate and boat on a canal reminiscent of Amsterdam, and wonder at the three million tulips that blaze and sway throughout the city in early May?

But Ottawa seemed an unlikely candidate to serve as Canada's capital when it was chosen back in the mid-19th century. The two provinces of **Upper Canada** (Ontario) and **Lower Canada** (Québec) were fused into the United Provinces of Canada, but their rivalry was so bitter that the legislature had to meet alternately in Toronto and Montréal. Casting around for an acceptable site for the new capital, Queen Victoria selected the brawling village of Ottawa in 1858, probably hoping that its location, right on the Ontario-Québec border, would resolve French-speaking and English-speaking differences. Her choice was not met with much praise: Essayist Goldwin Smith called it "a sub-Arctic lumber village, converted by royal mandate into a political cockpit," while the American press remarked that it was an excellent choice because any soldiers who tried to capture it would get lost in the woods trying to find it.

Certainly, for nearly a century the city languished in a provincialism as dull as its gray-flanneled denizens, and developed a reputation for sobriety and propriety. Still, even during its early days, it managed to throw up some colorful characters, not the least of whom was Canada's longest-lasting prime minister, William Lyon Mackenzie King, who conducted World War II with the guidance of his dog, his deceased mother, and frequent spiritual consultations with former prime minister Sir Wilfrid Laurier, who was by then 2 decades dead.

In the 1960s, perhaps because of Canada's newly expressed nationalism, or perhaps because the government wished to create a real capital, Ottawa changed. The **National Arts Centre** was built (Hull also underwent, and is still undergoing, a massive transformation), ethnic restaurants multiplied, the **Byward Market** area and other historic buildings were renovated, and public parks and recreation areas were created. And the process has continued into the present with the building of the **National Gallery of Canada,** the equally fabulous **Museum of Civilization,** and most recently, the **Casino de Hull.** It's a city full of unexpected pleasures—you can ski, fish, and hike through wilderness only 12 minutes away from downtown; watch the dramatic debates and pomp of parliamentary proceedings; and then visit a rustic French inn across the river in Québec.

After visiting Ottawa, you may wish to linger for a few days in eastern Ontario. I've covered all the highlights: **Kingston,** a very appealing lakefront town with its own weekly market, is the gateway to the mighty **St. Lawrence River, the Thousand Islands,** and **St. Lawrence National Park.** East from **Port Hope**—a worthy stop for antique hounds—stretches the **Bay of Quinte** and **Quinte's Isle,** a tranquil region of farms and orchards largely settled by Loyalists. It's still off the beaten track—except to those in the know, who come to explore the pretty small towns, to go antiquing, or to enjoy the beaches, dunes, and waterfront activities.

1 Orientation

GETTING THERE   The airport is located about 20 minutes south of the city. **Air Canada** (☎ 800/776-3000) and **Canadian Airlines** (☎ 800/426-7000) are the main airlines serving Ottawa. A **shuttle** (☎ 613/736-9993) operates between the airport and downtown for C\$9 (US\$6) one-way or C\$14 (US\$10) round-trip for adults, and C\$4 (US\$2.85) one-way and round-trip for seniors and students. The trip takes about 20 minutes.

Driving from New York, take Highway 81 to Canada's 401 east to 16 north. From the west, come via Toronto taking Highway 401 east to Route 16 north. From Montréal, take Highway 17 to Highway 417.

VIA Rail trains arrive at the station at 200 Tremblay Rd., at boulevard St-Laurent in the southeastern area of the city. From here buses connect to downtown. For VIA Rail information, contact **VIA Rail Canada** (☎ 613/244-8289 for reservations) or call your local Amtrak office.

Buses arrive at the Central Bus Station at 265 Catherine St., between Kent and Lyon. **Voyageur Colonial** (☎ 613/238-5900) provides service from other Canadian cities and the United States.

VISITOR INFORMATION   The **Ottawa Tourism and Convention Authority** at 130 Albert St., on the 18th floor (☎ 613/237-5158), is open Monday to Friday from 9am to 5pm, but the best place to pick up information is at the **National Capital Commission's Information Centre** at 90 Wellington St., right across from Parliament Hill (☎ 613/239-5000). It's open daily from 8:30am to 9pm in summer and from 9am to 5pm in winter. The commission also runs the "Infotent" on the Parliament Hill lawn, where visitors book free tours of Parliament. It's open mid-May to Labour Day. From mid-May to about the third week in June, hours are daily from 9am to 5pm; at other times, weekdays from 9am to 8pm and weekends and holidays from 9am to 5pm.

For information about Hull, contact **Outaouais Tourist Association,** Maison du Tourisme, 103 rue Laurier, Hull, PQ, J8X 3V8 (☎ **819/778-2222**), which is open from 8:30am to 5pm weekdays and 9am to 4pm weekends in winter, and from 8:30am to 8pm Monday to Friday and 9am to 5pm Saturday and Sunday in summer.

CITY LAYOUT   The Ottawa River arches around the city; the compact downtown area, where most major attractions are clustered within walking distance, is located south of the river.

The Rideau Canal, which sweeps past the National Arts Centre, divides the downtown area into two—Centre Town and Lower Town. In **Centre Town,** you'll find Parliament Hill, the Supreme Court, and the National Museum of Natural Sciences. In **Lower Town** are the National Gallery of Canada, the Byward Market (a vibrant center for restaurants and nightlife), and along Sussex Drive (which follows the Ottawa River's course), the Canadian War Museum, the Royal Canadian Mint, and farther out, the prime minister's residence, diplomat's row, and finally Rockcliffe Park. The area south of the Queensway, west to Bronson and east to the canal, is known as the **Glebe,** containing some restaurants and clubs, on Bank Street from First to Fifth avenues. North across the river, in Québec, lies **Hull,** reached by the Macdonald-Cartier and Alexandra bridges from the east end of town, and the Portage and Chaudière bridges from the west end. At the end of the Alexandra Bridge stands the curvaceous Museum of Civilization, and nearby are some of the city's very best French restaurants and the most lively nightlife action (which continues until 3am). North of Hull stretch the Gatineau Hills and ski country.

Finding your way around can be a little mystifying, since streets have a habit of disappearing and reappearing a few blocks farther on, and some streets change their names several times. For example, the main street starts in the west as Scott Street, changes to Wellington Street as it passes through downtown west in front of the Parliament buildings, changes again to Rideau Street in downtown east, and finally to Montréal Road on the eastern fringes of town. So carry a map. The information office will provide you with a perfectly serviceable one.

Just a few pointers: The main east-west streets going south from the river are **Wellington, Laurier,** and **Somerset;** the Rideau Canal demarcates the east from the west; the main north-south streets starting in the west are **Bronson, Bank,** and **Elgin.**

GETTING AROUND   The best way to get around is to walk. The only public transportation available is the 130-route bus network operated by the Ottawa-Carleton **Regional Transit Commission (OC Transpo).** Pick up a system map at their office at 294 Albert St. (at Kent), between 8:30am and 6pm weekdays. For daily information about schedules, where to buy tickets, and more, call ☎ **613/741-4390** between 7am and 9pm weekdays, 8am and 9pm Saturday, or 9am and 6pm Sunday. Fares change by type of route and are displayed in the front window of each bus. As of 1997, the fare on green express routes is C$2.70 (US$1.95) and on regular black and red routes, C$1.85 (US$1.35). Children 6 to 11 pay C$1 (US70¢) on all routes. Tickets can be bought at outlets such as newsstands, Shopper's Drug Marts, and PharmaPlus; otherwise you need the exact fare. All routes converge downtown at the Rideau Centre. Bus stops are color-coded to indicate the type of route. Routes begin to close down at midnight and there's no service after 1am.

In Hull, buses are operated by the **Société de Transport l'Outaouais** (STO; ☎ **819/770-7900**). Transfers between the two systems are obtainable when you pay your fare on the bus.

Ottawa

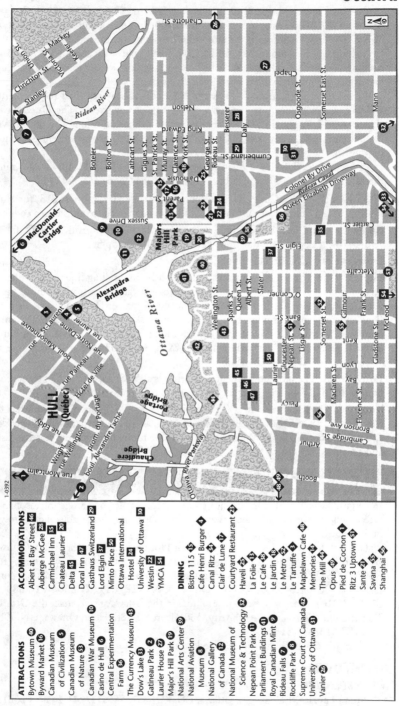

333

Car-rental agencies based in Ottawa include **Tilden** (☎ 613/737-7023), **Budget** (☎ 800/527-0700 in the U.S. or 800/268-8900 in Canada), and **Thrifty** (☎ 800/367-2277), all with offices at the airport and various downtown locations.

Parking will cost about C$3 (US$2.15) per half hour, with about a C$9 (US$6) maximum at most local garages. Your best parking bets are the municipal parking lots, which are marked with a large green *P* in a circle.

When driving, remember that Ontario has a **compulsory seat-belt requirement,** and pay careful attention to the city's system of one-way streets. The **Queensway** (Highway 417) cuts right across the city, adding to the confusion. The downtown entrance to the highway is at O'Connor Street. Exit the highway at Kent Street for downtown.

Taxis cost C$2 (US$1.45) when you step in and C$1.95 (US$1.40) for each mile thereafter plus C10¢ (US7¢) per bag. Call **Blue Line** (☎ 613/238-1111).

FAST FACTS   Area Code   The telephone area code for Ottawa is **613,** for Hull it's 819. When calling from Ottawa to Hull, you don't need to use the area code.

Embassy   The U.S. embassy is located at 100 Wellington St. (☎ 613/238-4470). It's open Monday to Friday from 8:30am to 5pm.

Emergencies   Call ☎ **911** for police, fire, or ambulance.

Liquor   The government controls liquor distribution, selling liquor and wine at certain stores and beer at others. Liquor stores generally open from 10am to 6pm Monday to Wednesday and Saturday, and until 9pm on Thursday and Friday. Beer outlets open from noon to 8pm Monday to Wednesday and Saturday, until 9pm on Thursday and Friday. The legal drinking age is 19 in Ottawa, 18 in Hull. There is a liquor outlet at 181 Bank St. (☎ **613/233-0394**) and a beer store at 1546 Scott St. (☎ **613/729-4828**).

Post Office   The most convenient post office is at 59 Sparks St., at Confederation Square (☎ **613/844-1545**); open Monday to Friday from 8am to 6pm.

Taxes   In Ontario there's an 8% provincial sales tax (PST) plus a restaurant tax of 8%, a room tax of 5%, and a liquor tax of 16%, as well as the national 7% goods-and-services tax (GST). In Québec there's a 6¹/2% tax on food, liquor, merchandise, and accommodations.

2 Accommodations

In Ottawa, accommodations do not come cheap. While you can get a reasonably priced double at bed-and-breakfasts and at the universities, there's no real downtown budget hotel.

The best deal (and most interesting option) for the budget traveler is the **Ottawa Bed and Breakfast,** an organization that represents about 10 homes, which rent for C$63 to C$75 (US$45 to US$54) per double with breakfast. For information, contact Robert Rivoire, 488 Cooper St., Ottawa, ON, K1R 5H9 (☎ **800/461-7889** or 613/563-0161). For more B&B possibilities in the Ottawa area, contact the **Ottawa Tourism and Convention Authority,** 130 Albert St., 18th Floor, Ottawa, ON, K1P 5G4 (☎ **613/237-5150**).

Note: Add 5% hotel tax and 7% GST to the rates quoted here.

DOWNTOWN
VERY EXPENSIVE

✪ **Château Laurier.** 1 Rideau St., Ottawa, ON, K1N 8S7. ☎ **613/241-1414.** Fax 613/562-7030. 425 rms. A/C MINIBAR TV TEL. C$180–C$200 (US$129–US$143) double. Special packages available. AE, CB, DC, DISC, ER, MC, V. Parking C$15 (US$11).

A granite and sandstone replica of a Loire château, the Château Laurier has attracted royalty and celebrities since its 1912 opening. It's ideally situated at the bottom of Parliament Hill, with many rooms offering views over the Ottawa River to the Gatineau Hills. The spacious rooms, with high ceilings and original moldings, are decorated with Louis XV–style reproductions. The executive Entree Gold Floor has its own concierge and such extras as complimentary continental breakfast, honor bar, and overnight shoe-shine.

Dining/Entertainment: At Wilfrid's, guests enjoy a wonderful view of the Parliament buildings and rub shoulders with government mandarins. The chef uses Canadian ingredients in classic continental-style dishes priced from C$15 to C$30 (US$11 to US$21). Zoe's Lounge, an atrium-lit room with soaring columns, stucco, chandeliers, and potted palms, is a lovely place for afternoon tea or cocktails.

Services: Concierge, 24-hour room service, valet, twice-daily maid service.

Facilities: Large indoor swimming pool, sauna, steam room, massage salon, and exercise room. Kids' playroom next to pool, plus welcome kit and children's menus in all restaurants.

Delta Ottawa. 361 Queen St., Ottawa, ON, K1R 7S9. ☎ **800/268-1133** or 613/238-6000. Fax 613/238-2290. 266 rms, 62 suites. A/C MINIBAR TV TEL. C$230–C$310 (US$164–US$221) double. Weekend packages available. AE, CB, DC, ER, MC, V. Parking C$11.50 (US$8).

The Delta has a brilliant skylit marble lobby complete with a welcoming fire in winter and island-style front desks for a more personal welcome. Rooms are spacious and modern and very attractively decorated in a refreshingly different way (colorful floral duvet covers on the beds, for example); a substantial number are one- or two-bedroom suites with kitchenettes and more than half have balconies.

Dining/Entertainment: Facilities include the casual Gallery-Cafe, The Capital Club for more formal intimate dining, and Jester's lounge for cocktails and snacks.

Services: Concierge, room service (6:30am to 11pm), valet, twice-daily maid service.

Facilities: Indoor swimming pool, saunas, exercise room, water slide, children's creative center, Nintendo and video room, two self-service Laundromats.

The Westin Hotel. 11 Colonel By Dr., Ottawa, ON, K1N 9H4. ☎ **800/228-3000** or 613/560-7000. Fax 613/560-7359. 478 rms. A/C MINIBAR TV TEL. C$195–C$235 (US$139–US$168) double. AE, CB, DC, ER, MC, V. Parking C$19 (US$14) per day.

Located right in downtown Ottawa, the Westin has views over the canal from its atrium lobby. The hotel also connects directly to both the Rideau Centre and the Ottawa Congress Centre. The elegantly furnished rooms have oak furniture, brass lamps, and half-poster beds; 10 are specially equipped for travelers with disabilities.

Dining/Entertainment: The popular dining spot Daly's commands a close-up view onto the canal and serves three meals a day. Hartwells, a bar just off the lobby, is a popular dance spot Tuesday to Saturday.

Services: Concierge, 24-hour room service, shoe-shine, and valet.

Facilities: Health club with indoor pool, squash courts, whirlpool, and saunas.

EXPENSIVE

✪ **The Albert at Bay Suite Hotel.** 435 Albert St. (at Bay), Ottawa, ON, K1R 7X4. ☎ **613/238-8858.** Fax 613/238-1433. 195 suites. A/C TV TEL. C$109–C$205 (US$78–US$146) 1-bedrm unit for 2; C$159–C$255 (US$114–US$182) 2-bedrm unit. Weekend rates C$89 (US$64) double. AE, CB, DC, DISC, ER, MC, V. Parking C$8 (US$6) per day.

This conveniently located hostelry, originally built as apartments, is one of Ottawa's best buys, especially for triples or quads. All units are suites, the smallest being a one-bedroom (with a den off the living room) with a sofa bed; a fully furnished living room that opens onto a terrace; two bathrooms; and a kitchen that's fully equipped for four, with appliances and dishes, plus iron and ironing board.

Services: Daily valet service, laundry service.

Facilities: Exercise room with a whirlpool and a spacious terrace, 24-hour convenience store.

✪ **Carmichael Inn and Spa.** 46 Cartier St. (at Somerset), Ottawa, ON, K2P 1J3. ☎ **613/ 236-4667.** Fax 613/563-7529. 10 rms. TV TEL. C$129–C$169 (US$92–US$121) double. Rates include breakfast. AE, ER, MC, V. Free parking.

Steps away from the canal and a few blocks from the Parliament buildings, the Carmichael Inn and Spa was a Supreme Court judge's residence, a convent, and a senior-citizens' home before being converted to an inn. It's named after the Group of Seven artist Frank Carmichael, and the decor throughout recalls the Group of Seven's art as well as their life and times. All the rooms have modern conveniences, and each is furnished differently with a mixture of authentic antiques and reproductions. Room 204 is particularly attractive, with its bay window, large armoire, and marble-top coffee table. Some rooms are air-conditioned. A good continental breakfast is served. Guests can relax on the couches in front of the marble fireplace in the comfortable lounge or laze in an Adirondack chair on the veranda.

Services: Valet service, newspaper delivery, in-room massage and other spa treatments (hydrotherapy, aromatherapy, and reflexology), secretarial services.

✪ **Lord Elgin.** 100 Elgin St., Ottawa, ON, K1P 5K8. ☎ **800/267-4298** or 613/235-3333. Fax 613/235-3223. 312 rms. A/C TV TEL. C$145 (US$104) double. Children under 19 stay free in parents' rm. AE, CB, DC, ER, MC. Parking C$11.50 (US$8) per day.

Only 3 blocks south of Parliament Hill and across from the National Arts Centre, the Lord Elgin offers good value. Built in 1941, this dignified stone edifice with its green copper roof was named after the eighth earl of Elgin, once Canada's governor-general. In recent years, rooms have been enlarged and the decor made light throughout with pastels. Many of the tile and faux-granite bathrooms have windows that open—a benefit bestowed by the building's age. About half the rooms have fridges.

Dining: The lobby bar is comfortably furnished with wingbacks and club chairs; the Connaught dining room is an airy galleria famous among Ottawans for its liver (but don't worry—there are other choices).

Minto Place Suite Hotel. 433 Laurier Ave. W. (at Lyon St.), Ottawa, ON, K1R 7Y1. ☎ **613/ 232-2200.** Fax 613/232-6962. 417 suites. A/C TV TEL. C$141–C$156 (US$101–US$111) studio suite; C$174–C$210 (US$124–US$150) 1-rm suite; C$216–C$226 (US$154–US$161) 2-rm suite. Children under 18 stay free in parents' rm. Weekend rates available. AE, DC, ER, MC, V. Parking C$12 (US$9).

The Minto Place has more than 400 studio and one- and two-bedroom suites, each very well equipped and attractively furnished. The upper floor units have magnificent views. Each suite's kitchen contains a fridge, microwave, coffeemaker, toaster, and kettle, plus pots, pans, and silverware. Some also have an electric stove and dishwasher. The spacious, comfortable living rooms are fully furnished and have desks, computer-compatible multiline telephones, and dining tables. Bedrooms contain large closets and chests of drawers. Your bathroom will also have a phone and hair dryer, and there's an additional half bath in some suites.

Dining: Two restaurants are conveniently located at the base of the tower.

Services: Room service is available from 7:30am to 1am.

Facilities: 20-meter lap pool, whirlpool, sauna, well-equipped fitness center.

MODERATE

Auberge McGee's Inn. 185 Daly Ave., Sandy Hill, Ottawa, ON, K1N 6E8. ☎ **613/237-6089.** Fax 613/237-6201. 14 rms (12 with private bath). A/C TV TEL. C$60–C$70 (US$43–US$50) double with shared bath, C$90–C$102 (US$64–US$73) double with private bath; C$130–C$160 (US$93–US$114) deluxe rm with Jacuzzi. AE, MC, V. Free parking. From downtown, take Laurier Ave. E. and turn left at Nelson St.

On a quiet street only blocks from the University of Ottawa, this inn occupies a handsome Victorian home with a steep dormer roof. Proprietor Anne Schutte has decorated each room distinctively, often with touches reflective of her Anglo-Peruvian upbringing. All the queen-size rooms have minibars; some have Jacuzzis. Breakfast is served in an elegant room with a carved cherry-wood fireplace and Oriental-style rugs. No smoking.

Doral Inn. 486–488 Albert St., Ottawa, ON, K1R 5B5. ☎ **800/263-6725** or 613/230-8055. Fax 613/237-9660. 37 rms. A/C TV TEL. C$80–C$135 (US$57–US$96) double. Extra person C$10 (US$7). Children under 12 stay free in parents' rm. AE, DC, DISC, ER, MC, V. Parking C$7 (US$5).

A great choice for the price, the Doral Inn occupies a conveniently located and handsome Victorian brick town house. The comfortably furnished rooms have modern brass beds, desk/drawers, and armchairs. On the ground floor, two handsome bay-windowed rooms serve as a comfortable lounge/sitting room and a breakfast room. Guests also have use of a nearby pool and health club and laundry facilities. There's a cafe on the premises where you can purchase a full breakfast.

✪ **Gasthaus Switzerland.** 89 Daly Ave., Ottawa, ON, K1N 6F6. ☎ **613/237-0335.** Fax 613/594-3327. 19 rms, 3 suites. A/C TV TEL. C$88–C$118 (US$63–US$84) double; from C$168 (US$120) suite. Rates include breakfast. AE, CB, DC, ER, MC, V. Free parking.

Located in an old stone building in downtown Ottawa, this bed-and-breakfast has the familiar hallmarks of red gingham and country pine associated with typical rustic Swiss hospitality. There's a comfortable sitting room with cable TV, and guests can use the garden and its barbecue in summer. A Swiss-style breakfast buffet of breads, eggs, cheese, and cereal is served. The Gasthaus is at the corner of Cumberland and Daly, across the canal and near the market area just south of Rideau.

INEXPENSIVE

Carleton University, Tour and Conference Centre. 1125 Colonel By Dr., Ottawa, ON, K1S 5B6. ☎ **613/520-5611.** Fax 613/520-3952. 1,400 rms. C$45.50 (US$32) double. Rates include all-you-can-eat breakfast. MC, V. Parking C$5 (US$3.55) weekdays, free on weekends.

In summer this university, 6¹/₂ kilometers (4 miles) southwest of the city, has single and double accommodations in several residences. Only two buildings are air-conditioned. A snack bar, cafeteria, lounge, and some sports facilities are available.

Ottawa International Hostel. 75 Nicholas St., Ottawa, ON, K1N 7B9. ☎ **613/235-2595.** Fax 613/569-2131. 130 beds. C$15 (US$11) members, C$19 (US$14) nonmembers. MC, V. Parking C$5.35 (US$3.80) 1st night, C$3.20 (US$2.30) subsequent nights.

Formerly the Carleton County Jail (1862–1972), this hostel, conveniently located near the Byward Market and Parliament Hill, is certainly unique. The old chapel is now used as a dining room, and the walls between cells have been removed to create small dorms housing anywhere from two to eight beds per room. Attractive lounges, a kitchen, laundry, and bike/skate rentals are available. Reservations are recommended.

University of Ottawa Residences. 85 University St., Room 339, Ottawa, ON, K1N 6N5.
☎ **613/562-5771.** Fax 613/562-5157. 900 rms. C$45 (US$32) a night. MC, V. Parking C$9
(US$6).

Between May and the end of August, the University of Ottawa Residences in Stanton
Hall offer singles and twins with shared bathroom down the hall. Rooms are not air-
conditioned but fans can be rented. Bonuses include an indoor pool, health club,
squash/racquetball courts, game room, and Laundromat, all located nearby.

YMCA/YWCA. 180 Argyle St. (at O'Connor), Ottawa, ON, K2P 1B7. ☎ **613/237-1320.** Fax
613/788-5095. 264 rms (26 with bath). A/C TEL. C$44 (US$31) single without bath, C$50.50
(US$36) single with bath; C$54 (US$39) double without bath. Children under 12 stay free in
parents' rm. MC, V. Parking C$2.75 (US$2).

This exceptional 15-story Y has mainly single rooms with shared washroom facilities,
although a few have private bath; some doubles are available. There are TV lounges
and laundry facilities, plus the added attractions of an indoor pool, gym, exercise
rooms, handball and squash courts, cafeteria, and free local phone calls. And, of
course, the price is right.

AN EXPENSIVE RESORT IN THE GATINEAU HILLS

✪ **The Château Cartier Sheraton.** 1170 Aylmer Rd., Aylmer, PQ, J9H 5E1. ☎ **819/
777-1088.** Fax 819/777-7161. 129 rms and suites. A/C TV TEL. C$150–C$170 (US$107–
US$121) double. AE, DC, DISC, ER, MC, V. Free parking.

Across the river, 15 minutes from Ottawa in the Gatineau Hills, the Château Cartier
Sheraton provides a resort experience on 152 acres. It's well designed and comfortable throughout, from the welcoming pink-marble lobby to the large Nautilus room
overlooking the golf course. The spacious rooms have couches and well-lit desks, plus
tile and marble bathrooms equipped with hair dryers. Most rooms are king- or queen-
size suites with parlor and bedroom separated by French doors, and have two TVs
and two telephones. In addition, four suites have fireplaces; two have Jacuzzis.

Dining/Entertainment: The stylish dining room, with French windows that open
onto the patio, overlooks the golf course. A lounge with a circular bar, club chairs,
and a small dance floor features a pianist on weekends.

Services: Valet, room service until 10pm.

Facilities: 18-hole golf course that doubles as a cross-country skiing area in winter; one racquetball and one squash court; two tennis courts. The indoor pool with
a wraparound terrace is perfect for catching rays. Health club with Nautilus.

3 Dining

For a real Ottawa tradition, stop at **Hooker's** stand in the center of the Byward Market and purchase a **beaver tail,** a local specialty. Don't worry, we're not talking about
rodent parts—a beaver tail is actually a very tasty deep-fried whole-wheat pastry served
either with cinnamon, sugar, and lemon, or with garlic butter and cheese, or with
raspberry jam. And not only are beaver tails delicious, they're dirt cheap, too!

For delicious homemade ice cream, Ottawans flock to **Lois 'n' Frimas,** 361 Elgin
St. (☎ **613/235-8060**). It's open daily from 11am to 11pm (until midnight on Friday and Saturday in summer).

CENTRE TOWN
MODERATE

Le Café. In the National Arts Centre. ☎ **613/594-5127.** Reservations recommended.
Main courses C$14–C$23 (US$10–US$16). AE, DC, ER, MC, V. May–Sept Mon–Sat

11:30am–midnight, Sun 11:30am–8pm; Oct–Apr Mon–Fri noon–midnight, Sat 5pm–midnight. CANADIAN.

The National Arts Centre's Le Café commands a marvelous canal view from its summertime terrace and offers fine food year-round in a relaxing setting. The menu features imaginatively prepared dishes that use prime Canadian ingredients like New Brunswick salmon, Petrie Island mussels, Nova Scotia scallops, venison, and lamb. You might start with the Cape Breton seafood chowder made with scallops, clams, and salmon, and follow with Mariposa farm-raised breast of Muscovy duck served with blueberries deglazed in blackberry vinegar. Among the desserts, the Canadian specialties are Newfoundland screech cake (a rum-flavored cake) and golden maple creme caramel.

The Mill. 555 Ottawa River Pkwy. ☎ **613/237-1311.** Reservations required (even at lunch). Main courses C$11–C$17 (US$8–US$12). AE, ER, MC, V. Mon–Fri 11:30am–2:30pm, Sun 10:30am–2pm; Mon–Sat 4:30–11pm, Sun 4:30–10pm. CANADIAN.

The Mill occupies a delightful setting on the Ottawa River, where it does a solid job with traditional dishes such as prime rib, lemon pepper chicken, and surf and turf. Erected in the 1840s, when Ottawa was a lusty, hell-raising lumber town, it now has an atrium dining room and several other dining areas upstairs and down with a magnificent river view.

Ritz 3 Uptown. 226 Nepean St. ☎ **613/238-8752.** Reservations recommended. Pasta courses C$9–C$12 (US$6–US$9); main courses C$13–C$17 (US$9–US$12). AE, DC, ER, MC, V. Mon–Fri 11:30am–11pm, Sat 5–11pm, Sun 5–10pm. ITALIAN.

Located in a town house, the Ritz 3 Uptown has a casual bistro ambiance, with tables covered in white tablecloths and walls adorned with contemporary Canadian art. There's a wine bar in the back. You can order a variety of pastas, including gnocchi and linguini as well as such specials as chicken puttanesca or beef tenderloin with red pesto butter. Great desserts, all under C$6 (US$4.30), include Italian trifle, sbaglione, and apricot and apple crêpe cake.

There's also a popular branch at 89 Clarence St. (☎ **613/789-9797**).

INEXPENSIVE

Shanghai. 651 Somerset St. W. (near Bronson). ☎ **613/233-4001.** Reservations recommended on weekends. Main courses C$8–C$15 (US$6–US$11). AE, MC, V. Tues–Fri 11am–2pm; Tues–Thurs and Sun 4:30–11pm, Fri–Sat 4:30pm–1am. SHANGHAI/SZECHUAN.

Shanghai offers comfort, attractive decor, and some very fine food of Szechuan, Cantonese, Shanghai, and other Asian origins. Soups include Chinese melon and Chinese greens, and a hot and sour soup which might be followed by such tempting specialties as coconut curry chicken in a spicy peanut sauce, seafood supreme in spicy garlic sauce, or beef with Shanghai bok choy and roasted garlic. Regular dishes like honey garlic spareribs round out the menu. Instead of the usual uninspired Chinese desserts, there's a smooth mandarin mousse cake and also litchi cheesecake.

THE BYWARD MARKET AREA
EXPENSIVE

Le Jardin. 127 York St. ☎ **613/241-1424.** Reservations recommended. Main courses C$18–C$30 (US$13–US$21). AE, DC, ER, MC, V. Daily 5:30–11pm. FRENCH.

In a handsome Victorian gingerbread house with three intimate dining rooms, Le Jardin impresses with fabric-covered walls, rich drapery, antique furnishings, and fresh flowers; there's a Gaspé quilt in one room and a fireplace in another. The restaurant selects the freshest ingredients possible. At dinner hors d'oeuvres might include quail and pheasant pâté served with coriander and pineapple chutney, shrimps flambéed with vodka and papaya coulis, or caviar from the Caspian Sea. I like the beef fillet with snails and red-wine sauce and the lobster blanquette with morels and vegetables. Among the desserts, there's cheesecake with fresh strawberries and apricot glaze, and—most tempting of all—chocolate terrine with raspberry delight.

MODERATE

Bistro 115. 110 Murray St. ☎ **613/562-7244.** Reservations recommended. Main courses C$14–C$18 (US$10–US$13); 3-course prix-fixe C$26 (US$19). AE, ER, MC, V. Daily 11:30am–10:30pm. FRENCH.

This place affects a very French atmosphere with lace tablecloths, floral banquettes, and a trellis-covered dining terrace in the back. The fixed price is a great deal—you'll get something like chicken liver and brandy pâté or shrimp-and-mango salad with yogurt to start, followed by pan-fried caribou with wild-mushroom sauce or grilled tuna with a beurre blanc of red pepper. A la carte choices might include cioppino or filet mignon with Roquefort butter. For dessert there's often a fine white-chocolate raspberry tart.

✪ **Clair de Lune.** 81B Clarence St. ☎ **613/241-2200.** Reservations recommended. Main courses C$9–C$18 (US$6–US$13). AE, ER, MC, V. Daily 11:30am–2:30pm; Sun–Wed 6–11pm, Thurs–Sat 6pm–midnight. FRENCH.

The market area has an astounding number of restaurants and cafes. One of my special favorites is Clair de Lune, a little gem of a French bistro that serves a reasonable two-course lunch, featuring dishes such as mussels steamed with Indonesian spices and rabbit chasseur (prepared hunter style, with tomatoes and onions). At dinner the menu has several appealing appetizers like the asparagus tart with goat cheese and leeks or fresh and smoked salmon rillettes with capers, scallions, and mustard-seed mayonnaise. Among the main courses there might be beef tenderloin with a Jack Daniel's portobello-mushroom jus or salmon fillet baked in a five-herb pink peppercorn crust splashed with balsamic vinaigrette. Cap it all off with the chocolate tulip with yogurt and brandy. Moreover, Clair de Lune is a snappily decorated spot with a handsome glass-block bar, and rich dark mahogany tables that make for a pleasant meal. In summer the rooftop terrace is the place to sample tapas ranging in price from C$3 to C$6 (US$2.15 to US$4.30) plus such items as grilled fish and brochettes.

The Courtyard Restaurant. 21 George St. ☎ **613/241-1516.** Reservations recommended. Main courses C$15–C$22 (US$11–US$16). AE, DC, ER, MC, V. Mon–Sat 11:30am–2pm, Sun 11am–2pm; Mon–Sat 5:30–9:30pm, Sun 5–9pm. CONTINENTAL.

With a distinct air of old Montréal, the Courtyard Restaurant is set in a gray stone building with a high-ceilinged, stone-walled dining room and an outdoor cafe with colorful parasols. The menu, though, is rather predictable—old standbys such as filet mignon with béarnaise, salmon teriyaki, and veal Oscar. Lunch dishes such as chicken breast with mango are priced from C$8 to C$10 (US$6 to US$7). The Outdoor Café is a popular meeting spot, and Sunday brunch is accompanied by live classical music.

Haveli. 87 George St. ☎ **613/241-1700.** Reservations recommended. Main courses C$10–C$16 (US$7–US$11). AE, MC, V. Mon–Fri 11:45am–2:15pm, Sun noon–2:30pm; Mon–Wed 5:30–10pm, Thurs–Sat 5:30–10:30pm, Sun 5–9pm. INDIAN.

Popular Indian stars like Jagjit and Chitra, Anup Jalota, and Chanchal have all gone upstairs in the Market Mall to dine in this comfortable restaurant. The extensive menu offers a wide selection of vegetarian dishes—*aloo gobi, senza jalfraize, dal*—and meat and fish preparations. Special dishes include Bhuna shrimp and chicken *makhni,* and of course, items from the tandoor oven (including the most expensive dish on the menu, lobster tails marinated in Indian spices and broiled in the tandoor oven). The best deals are the lunch and Sunday buffets; on Sunday, south Indian specialties like *dhosa* are served.

✪ Sante. 45 Rideau St. ☎ **613/241-7113.** Reservations recommended. Main courses C$14–C$20 (US$10–US$14). AE, DC, ER, MC, V. Mon–Sat 11:30am–3pm and 5–10pm. In July and Aug Sante may close for Sat lunch, so call ahead. INTERNATIONAL.

Sante specializes in dishes that use healthy fresh ingredients and reflect a multicultural approach to cuisine. The tables are graced with fresh flowers, the walls with works by local artists, and if you're lucky, you'll be seated at a table with armchairs. Start with the delicious callaloo soup, chicken satay, or Bali spring rolls. Follow with a sizzling hot plate like the seafood with basil-coconut-cream sauce, or with the Thai spicy shrimp stir-fried in tamarind, garlic, lemongrass, and chilies. It's an interesting and innovative menu, with other specialties like almond citrus chicken with snow peas, mushrooms, lime, and sake; Java scallops spiced and sautéed with coconut, tamarind, and cinnamon; or kingfish with basil, pine nut, and garlic.

INEXPENSIVE

La Folie. 15 Clarence St. ☎ **613/562-0705.** Reservations not accepted. Pizzas and other dishes C$8–C$11 (US$6–US$8). AE, ER, MC, V. Sun–Thurs 11:30am–11pm, Fri–Sat 11:30am–midnight. Shorter hours in winter. PIZZA/MEDITERRANEAN.

La Folie gets rave reviews and draws a large crowd to its two patios and its small dining room. The front outdoor patio sports super scarlet-and-gray fringed umbrellas, while the back patio has an awning. The kitchen turns out innovative food—a characteristic entry from their roster of a dozen different wood-burning oven pizzas had toppings of smoked salmon, red onion, capers, and dill. Even the calzones are creative, such as the curried lamb with fontina cheese. Salads and daily specials are also available, and so, too, are some divine desserts—apricot and apple crêpe cake or chocolate sabayon cake.

Memories. 7 Clarence St. ☎ **613/232-1882.** Reservations not accepted. Sandwiches and light fare C$6–C$9 (US$4.30–US$6). AE, MC, V. Mon 11:30am–11pm, Tues–Fri 11:30am–midnight, Sat 10:30am–midnight, Sun 10am–11pm. BISTRO.

Next door to La Folie, Memories is another very attractive and well-frequented cafe that offers a light menu and notable desserts. You can get sandwiches such as ham-and-cheese with marinated mushrooms and Dijon mustard on a croissant, plus salads, soups, pâtés, and pastas. For Saturday and Sunday brunch you'll find the usual croissants, quiches, and eggs as well as luscious waffles served with your choice of fruit toppings. The tables out front fill up quickly.

IN VANIER

✪ Il Vagabondo. 186 Barrette St. ☎ **613/749-4877.** Reservations recommended. Pasta courses around C$10 (US$7); main courses C$10–C$18 (US$7–US$13). AE, DC, ER, MC, V. Tues–Fri 11:30am–2:30pm; Mon–Sat 5–11pm, Sun 5–10pm. ITALIAN.

A little off the beaten track across the bridge in Vanier, this Italian bistro in a corner house has a lot going for it. The cozy bilevel dining room has an oak bar, colorful tablecloths, and a tiled floor. A blackboard lists specials—like *pollo a basilico* (basil chicken) or *fettuccine con erbe* (fettuccine with an herb sauce)—but you'll need to come early because they quickly disappear. The à la carte menu includes veal *al limone* (veal splashed with lemon), marsala, or *alla Maltese* (in butter, white wine, cream, and fresh orange juice), and cannelloni fiorentina with tomato sauce. The veal is of superb quality and comes in large portions with vegetables added as a garnish.

OTTAWA SOUTH

This arbitrary designation refers to an area that stretches from Wellington Street to the Queensway, along Bank and Elgin streets in particular. Here you find cafes that carry free literature, such as the *Peace Information News,* and a medley of food stores and other neighborhood services and vendors. It's heaven if you're on a budget.

MODERATE

✪ **Le Metro.** 315 Somerset St. W. (between Bank and O'Connor). ☎ **613/230-8123.** Reservations strongly recommended. Main courses C$13–C$20 (US$9–US$14). AE, ER, MC, V. Mon–Fri 11:30am–2:30pm; daily 6–10:30pm. FRENCH.

At this romantic bistro in a town-house setting, gilded statuary and lavish flower arrangements accent the rooms, silver candelabra set off the tables, and French songs add to the atmosphere. The menu changes daily, reflecting what's really fresh and outstanding at the local markets. You might begin with a shrimp bisque, smoked duck carpaccio, or a pheasant terrine with blueberry Cumberland sauce, and then choose from 10 or so entrees, which might include breast of duck with olive sauce, salmon with fine herbs, pepper steak, or rack of lamb with a mint sauce.

✪ **Savana Cafe.** 431 Gilmour (between Bank and Kent). ☎ **613/233-9159.** Reservations recommended. Main courses C$10.50–C$15 (US$8–US$11). AE, ER, MC, V. Tues–Fri 11:30am–3pm; Mon–Sat 5–10pm. CARIBBEAN.

The Savana Cafe has caught Ottawans' imaginations with its tropical flavor, brilliantly colored Caribbean art, and spicy cuisine. Start with the fabulous kalaloo (or callaloo) soup made Caribbean-style—it's the real thing, with okra, spinach, thyme, Congo peppers, and lime. Among my main course favorites are spicy Thai noodles; fresh grilled marlin with wasabi mousseline; cubana chicken stuffed with bananas and cream cheese and served with jalapeno salsa; and lamb glazed with guava and served with two chutneys. Most dishes can be ordered mild, medium, or hot (go on, ask for hot!). In winter, the fire adds a welcome touch; in summer, so does the patio.

THE GLEBE

The Glebe refers to the southern part of Ottawa, an area that stretches from just south of the Queensway to the Rideau Canal and from Bronson Avenue to Rideau.

✪ **Canal Ritz.** 375 Queen Elizabeth Dr. ☎ **613/238-8998.** Reservations recommended. Pizza and pasta C$8–C$13 (US$6–US$9); fish courses about C$12 (US$9). AE, ER, MC, V. Mon–Sat 11:30am–11pm, Sun 11:30am–10pm. Summer hours extended. INTERNATIONAL.

Located right on the canal, the Canal Ritz occupies a fabulous old boathouse with outdoor dining and an airy two-story interior. The real specialty here is pizza fresh from the wood-burning oven. There's a delightful choice: pears and Brie on braised onions; shrimp, cappicola ham, figs, and mozzarella; or pesto, mozzarella, and plum tomato, to name a few. A variety of fettuccine dishes, charcoal-grilled fish, and brochettes are other options. Canal Ritz is also known for desserts—among them the caramel pecan cheesecake and the *zuccotto* (consisting of sponge cake, hazelnut cream, and chocolate mousse iced in white chocolate and glazed in dark). In fact, this is a chocoholic's paradise.

OTTAWA WEST

MODERATE

Maplelawn Cafe. 529 Richmond Rd. ☎ **613/722-5118.** Reservations recommended. Main courses C$17–C$20 (US$12–US$14); prix-fixe C$23 (US$16) and C$25 (US$18). AE, DC, MC, V. Mon–Fri 11:30am–2pm, Sun 11am–2:30pm; Sun–Thurs 5:30–8:30pm, Fri–Sat 6–9pm. CONTEMPORARY.

Cafe seems a misnomer for this splendid restaurant located in a restored 1831 Georgian stone mansion with an adjoining 1-acre walled garden. It's particularly lovely in summer when the gardens are in bloom and patrons can relax in the courtyard dining area. There are four elegant dining rooms, each with deep casement windows and art for sale hanging on the walls. Service is gracious and the food is well prepared. Expect to savor such dishes as grilled marinated breast of chicken with a rich Bourbon gravy and just the right accompaniments—corn bread, charred peppers, and roasted okra—or grilled pork loin with a fruit salsa. There's always a fish of the day as well as other daily specials. The oak-paneled fireside lounge is an inviting place for an aperitif.

✪ **Opus Bistro.** 1331 Wellington St. ☎ **613/722-9549.** Reservations required. Main courses C$10–C$20 (US$7–US$14). MC, V. Tues–Sat 11:30am–11pm. CONTEMPORARY.

A small West End restaurant, the Opus Bistro is worth visiting to savor the finely prepared, continentally inspired food. The one-room restaurant has a clean and simple decor and a small bar up front. Their reasonably priced main dishes reflect diverse international flavors. One day's menu might feature jumbo shrimp and bay scallops flambéed with tequila, sun-dried tomatoes, fresh herbs, garlic, and white wine; or grilled filet mignon with a red-wine reduction; or grilled chicken tossed with chilies, tomatoes, green onions, and red peppers, flambéed with vodka cream sauce on a pepper linguini. The selection changes daily—but if the crab cakes *en filo* are among the appetizers, try them. They're delicious when served with a cilantro-lime dipping sauce.

HULL
EXPENSIVE

✪ **Café Henri Burger.** 69 rue Laurier. ☎ **819/777-5646.** Reservations recommended. Main courses C$15–C$25 (US$11–US$18); 4-course prix-fixe dinner C$40 (US$29). AE, ER, MC, V. Mon–Fri noon–2:30pm; Mon–Sat 6–10pm. The Terrace is open daily in summer noon–11pm. FRENCH.

"Let's go to Burger's" used to be a byword in Ottawa in the early 1920s when Henri Burger, chef at the Château Laurier, founded his restaurant, Café Henri Burger. Although he died in 1936, the name still attracted people to this landmark brick building overlooking the Museum of Civilization and across the river to Parliament Hill.

The cafe continues to excel. The lunch menu still offers a fine array of dishes from bouillabaisse to grilled leg of lamb with roast garlic and rosemary and half-lobster salad. At night, the fixed-price of appetizer, soup, entree, dessert, and coffee might include such appetizers as a Napoleon of roasted peppers and goat cheese or warm salad of chicken livers and fennel with a pastis vinaigrette. Follow these with pan-roasted salmon served with a curried-beet-and-carrot broth or pepper-crusted roast sirloin with pinot reduction sauce. For dessert, the classic *tarte au citron* (lemon tart) is a must.

Le Tartuffe. 133 rue Notre-Dame, Hull. ☎ **819/776-6424.** Reservations recommended. Main courses C$22.75–C$26.50 (US$16–US$19). AE, ER, MC, V. Mon–Fri 11:30am–2pm; Mon–Tues 5–9:30pm, Wed–Sat 5–10pm. Closed Mon from Oct–May. FRENCH

This is a small, relaxed, town-house restaurant with inspired cuisine. The price of your three-course meal (soup, appetizer, and main course) will be determined by the main course you select. You might start with a plate of mussels flavored with curry and accompanied by vegetable julienne or with snails parmentier with leeks and pastis. Main courses include grilled salmon with tarragon, and veal medaillons with morelles, cognac, and cream.

MODERATE

✪ **Le Pied de Cochon.** 248 rue Montcalm. ☎ **819/777-5808.** Reservations recommended. Main courses C$14–C$18 (US$10–US$13); 3-course prix-fixe C$23 (US$16). AE, DC, ER, MC, V. Tues–Fri noon–2pm and 6–10pm, Sat 6–11pm. FRENCH.

When people need a reliable spot offering classically good cuisine, they head for this unpretentious spot, which you'd pass by if you didn't know it was there. The food is fresh and good and the atmosphere casual. When local Québecois fill this place at lunchtime, it positively radiates happiness. The decor is simple, but what really counts is what's served on the small menu. At lunch there might be such choices as salmon in puff pastry or crusty veal kidneys with shiitake mushrooms on the C$12.50 (US$9) prix-fixe menu. At dinner, a similar table d'hôte, priced at C$23 (US$16), includes such additional entrees as grilled duck breast with a raspberry-vinegar sauce or pheasant in champagne sauce. A la carte choices range from rib of veal with Armagnac sauce Nearby to a delicious rack of lamb persille. The last, consisting of an eight-chop rack, is a bargain at a mere C$16 (US$11).

DINING IN QUEBEC

✪ **L'Oree du Bois.** Chemin Kingsmere, Old Chelsea. ☎ **819/827-0332.** Reservations required. Main courses C$14–C$19 (US$10–US$14); 4-course prix-fixe C$22.50 (US$16). AE, ER, MC, V. May–Oct Tues–Sun 5:30–10pm; Nov–Apr Tues–Sat 5:30–10pm. From Hull, take Autoroute 5 north to Old Chelsea, Exit 12. FRENCH.

In the heart of the Gatineau region, this traditional restaurant offers traditional Québec regional cuisine. The management grows its own herbs, produces smoked fish on the premises, and also makes their own chocolates and flavored oils and vinegars. For a good start to your meal, try the duckling pâté with orange and pistachio, or snails with mushrooms, smoked bacon, and parsley sauce. Among the main courses, the braised duckling is spiced up with a green and black peppercorn sauce and scallops and shrimps are enhanced with basil and sun-dried tomatoes. The plate of local cheeses makes a fine finish.

TWO REAL PUBS OUTSIDE OTTAWA

For both of these pubs, take Highway 417 west to Highway 5, then go north to Carp.

✪ **The Cheshire Cat.** 2193 Richardson Side Rd., Carp. ☎ **613/831-2183.** Main courses C$9–C$11 (US$6–US$8). MC, V. The kitchen is open Mon–Sat 11:30am–9pm and Sun noon–9pm. The bar stays open until 11pm Sun–Wed and until 1am Thurs–Sat. ENGLISH.

Located in a stone cottage that formerly housed a school, this English-style pub with wood-burning stove and good pub food is as authentic as you're likely to find outside England. A variety of sandwiches are available, plus such main courses as liver and bacon; mixed grill; sausage, eggs, and chips; and shepherd's pie. On summer days the garden is a lovely spot to relax and imagine yourself back in England's green and pleasant land.

✪ **The Swan at Carp.** Falldown Lane, Carp. ☎ **613/839-7926.** Most items C$6–C$9 (US$4.30–US$6). AE, ER, MC, V. Mon–Sat 11am–1am, Sun 11am–11pm. ENGLISH.

Another corner of England waits here at the Swan, a more Victorian-style English pub, located in a brick house complete with separate public bar as well as lounge bar. It was originally a Presbyterian manse built in 1902. The Dugdale/Nadeau families opened it as a pub in 1987, naming it after a pub they ran in Stoke, England. Since there are no videos or TV, you'll find good conversation, real ale at cellar temperature, Brit-inspired events like the Dambusters Anniversary celebration, and honest pub fare like bangers and mash, Guinness stew, fish-and-chips, and "afters" like sherry trifle.

4 Seeing the Sights

Most of Ottawa's major sights are clustered together downtown, so you can easily walk from one to another—from Parliament Hill to the Byward Market, from the National Gallery to the Museum of Civilization.

Paul's Boat Lines Ltd., 219 Colonnade Rd., in Nepean (☎ **613/225-6781,** or 613/235-8409 in summer), operates two cruises: the **Ottawa River cruise,** which takes you along Embassy Row to Rockcliffe Park and departs from the dock in Hull, east of Alexandra Bridge in Jacques Cartier Park; and the **Rideau Canal cruise,** which leaves from the docks opposite the Arts Centre and goes down the canal to the Experimental Farm and Carleton University. River cruises, which last 1 1/2 hours, leave at 11am, and 2, 4, and 7:30pm. The canal trip leaves at 10 and 11:30am, and 1:30, 3, 4:30, 7, and 8:30pm, and takes 1 1/4 hours. Each trip costs C$12 (US$9) for adults, C$10 (US$7) for seniors, and C$6 (US$4.30) for children.

The *Sea Prince II* also cruises daily along the Ottawa River from both Ottawa and Hull docks. The adult fare is C$13 (US$9), students and seniors pay C$11 (US$8), and children ages 6 to 12 C$6 (US$4.30). The boat also hosts dinner-dance cruises, theme events, and day cruises to Château Montebello. For more information, contact the **Ottawa Riverboat Company,** 30 Murray St., Suite 100 (☎ **613/ 562-4888**).

PARLIAMENT HILL

Standing on a bluff jutting into the Ottawa River, the ✪ **Parliament buildings,** with their high, pitched copper roofs, are truly spectacular. In 1860 Prince Edward, later Edward VII, laid the cornerstone of the Parliament buildings, which were finished in time to host the inaugural session of the first Parliament of the new Dominion of Canada in 1867. If you enter through the south gate, you will pass the **Centennial Flame,** lit by Lester Pearson on New Year's Eve 1966 into 1967 to mark the passing of 100 years since this historic event.

The Parliament buildings (especially the Centre Block) represent the heart of Canadian political life, housing the House of Commons and the Senate. You may attend the **House of Commons** sessions and observe the 295 elected members debating in the handsome green chamber with its tall stained-glass windows. Parliament is usually in recess from the end of June to early September and occasionally between September and June, including the Easter and Christmas holidays. Otherwise, the House usually sits from 11am to 6:30pm on Monday, from 10am to 6:30pm on Tuesday and Thursday, from 2pm to 8pm on Wednesday, and from 10am to 4pm on Friday. The 104 appointed members of the Senate sit in an opulent red chamber with murals depicting Canadians fighting in World War I.

The great 302-foot tower rising from the Centre Block—the **Peace Tower**—houses a 53-bell carillon, a huge clock, an observation deck, and the **Memorial Chamber,** which commemorates Canada's war dead, most notably the 66,650 who lost their lives in World War I. Stones from the battlefields are lodged in the chamber's walls and floors. Atop the tower rises a bronze mast, 35 feet high, flying a Canadian flag. When Parliament is in session the tower is lit.

When you go up to the tower, see if you notice anything strange about the elevator. Does it travel vertically as practically every other elevator does? Not quite. For the first 98 feet of your journey it travels on a 10° angle. This special elevator replaced the two elevators that you used to have to take to reach the observatory.

A fire in 1916 destroyed the original Centre Block; only the **Library** at the rear was saved. A glorious 16-sided dome, supported outside by huge flying buttresses and beautifully paneled inside with Canadian white pine, features a marble statue of the young Queen Victoria and magnificent carvings—Gorgons, crests, masks, and hundreds of rosettes. The original floor was an intricate pattern of oak, cherry, walnut, and ash.

The Centre Block is flanked by the **East and West blocks.** The West Block, containing parliamentary offices, is closed to the public. But you can go into the East Block, which used to house offices of prime ministers, governors-general, and the Privy Council, to see four historic rooms: the original governor-general's office, restored to the period of Lord Dufferin (1872–78); the offices of Sir John A. Macdonald and Sir Georges-Etienne Cartier (the principal Fathers of Confederation); and the Privy Council Chamber with anteroom.

Stroll the grounds, dotted with statues honoring such political figures as William Lyon Mackenzie King and Sir Wilfrid Laurier. Behind the Centre Block stretches a promenade with great views of the river. Here, too, you will find the old Centre Block's bell, which crashed to the ground shortly after tolling midnight on the night of the 1916 fire. At the bottom of the cliff behind the Parliament buildings (accessible from the entrance locks on the Rideau Canal), a pleasant path leads along the Ottawa River.

TOURS Free tours of the **Centre Block and library** are given daily year-round, except on Christmas, New Year's Day, and Canada Day (July 1). Although the precise times for tours in English in 1998 were not available at press time, they should be very similar to the 1997 tour times, which were as follows: Labour Day to late May, every 20 and 50 minutes after the hour from 9am to 3:50pm; June to Labour Day, from 9am to 7:50pm weekdays and from 9am to 4:50pm weekends. The last tour excludes a visit to the Peace Tower. From Victoria Day to Labour Day you need to make same-day reservations for tours at the Infotent (east of Centre Block). For more information on tour hours, call ☎ 613/992-4793.

Tours of the **East Block** historic offices are usually given daily from July to Labour Day. For more information, call ☎ 613/992-4793.

Discover the Hill Walking Tours, exploring the events and personalities that shaped the Hill and the nation, are also given daily from the end of June to September 1. Make reservations at the Infotent.

✪ **CHANGING OF THE GUARD** From late June to late August, a colorful half-hour ceremony is held daily on the Parliament Hill lawn (weather permitting). Two historic regiments—the Governor-General's Foot Guards (red plumes) and the Canadian Grenadier Guards (white plumes)—comprise the Ceremonial Guard. The parade of 125 soldiers in busbies and scarlet jackets (guard, colour party, and band) assembles at Cartier Square Drill Hall (by the canal at Laurier Avenue) at 9:30am and marches up Elgin Street to reach the hill at 10am. Upon arrival on the hill, the Ceremonial Guard splits into two groups, one division of the old guard positioned on the west side of the Parliament Hill lawn and two divisions of the new guard, or "duties," on the east side. The ceremony includes the inspection of dress and weapons of both groups to ensure that the new guard is appropriately turned out and to determine if the old guard is still properly regaled and has no deficiencies in the equipment after their tour of duty. The colours are then marched before the troops and are saluted. The guards also compliment each other by presenting arms. Finally, the outgoing guard commander gives the key to the guard room to the incoming guard commander, signifying that the guard has been changed. If you can understand what some of those sergeant-majors yell, you're a natural-born soldier.

✪ **SOUND & LIGHT SHOW**   From May to August, Canada's history unfolds in a dazzling half-hour display of sound and light against the dramatic backdrop of the Parliament buildings. Weather permitting, two performances are given per night, one in English, the other in French. There's bleacher seating for the free show. For more information, contact the **National Capital Commission** at ☎ 613/239-5000.

OTHER TOP ATTRACTIONS

The Byward Market. At the junction of Sussex, Rideau, St. Patrick, and Kind Edward sts. May 1–Nov 1 Mon–Sat 9am–6pm, Sun 10am–6pm; winter daily 10am–6pm.

A colorful traditional farmers market still sells all kinds of local food and vegetable products. The market building also houses two floors of boutiques displaying a wide variety of wares and crafts. During market season you can enjoy the outdoor cafes and watch life drift by over a cold beer or glass of wine.

Take some time to wander past the stalls, piled high with fresh, shining locally grown produce. Pick up some fruit and cheese from the **International Cheese shop** (☎ 613/241-5411), some desserts from **Aux Délices** (☎ 613/241-9292), and take your picnic back down to the canal.

Explore, too, the Sussex courtyards, which extend from George to St. Patrick streets along Sussex Drive.

Canadian Museum of Civilization. 100 Laurier St. in Hull. ☎ **819/776-7000.** Admission C$5 (US$3.55) adults, C$4 (US$2.85) seniors and ages 13–17, C$3 (US$2.15) children 2–12. Free to all Sun 9am–noon. Tickets to CINEPLUS range from C$5.50 to C$11 (US$4 to US$8). May–June and Labour Day to Oct 9 Fri–Wed 9am–6pm, Thurs 9am–9pm; July to Labour Day Sat–Wed 9am–6pm, Thurs–Fri 9am–9pm; Oct 10–Apr 30 Tues–Wed and Fri–Sun 9am–5pm, Thurs 9am–9pm.

Alberta architect Douglas Cardinal designed this spectacular museum, which rises from the banks of the Ottawa River as though its curvilinear forms had been sculpted by wind, water, and glacier. The exhibits within tell the history of Canada and its various ethnic peoples, but somehow the exhibits don't live up to the promise of the building itself. The **Grand Hall** is devoted to six native-Canadian tribes of the west coast, featuring an impressive collection of huge totem poles. Recently installed permanent exhibits include **From Time Immemorial,** which re-creates a west-coast archaeological dig, and the Canadian **Children's Museum** invites kids to explore and understand other cultures.

The **CINEPLUS** theater contains an IMAX and an OMNIMAX (dome-shaped) screen that propel the viewer giddily into any film's action.

✪ **National Aviation Museum.** Rockcliffe Airport. ☎ **613/993-2010.** Admission C$5 (US$3.55) adults, C$4 (US$2.85) seniors and students, C$1.75 (US$1.25) children 6–15; children 6 and under free. Free to all Thurs 5–9pm. May 1 to Labour Day Fri–Wed 9am–5pm, Thurs 9am–9pm; rest of year Tues–Wed and Fri–Sun 10am–5pm, Thurs 10am–9pm. From Sussex Dr., take Rockcliffe Pkwy. and exit at the National Aviation Museum.

This collection of more than 115 aircraft is one of the best of its kind in the world. In the main exhibit hall, a "Walkway of Time" traces aviation history from the turn of the century through two world wars to the present. There's a replica of the Silver Dart, which rose from the ice of Baddeck Bay, Nova Scotia, in February 1909, performing the first powered flight in Canada. It flew for 9 minutes—not bad, considering it looks as though it were built out of bicycle parts and kites.

✪ **National Gallery of Canada.** 380 Sussex Dr. (at St. Patrick St.). ☎ **613/990-1985.** Free admission; fees charged for special exhibits. April 1–Sept 9 Fri–Wed 10am–6pm, Thurs 10am–8pm; Sept 10–Mar 31 Wed and Fri–Sun 10am–5pm, Thurs 10am–8pm. Guided tours given daily at 11am and 2pm. Register at the information desk. Closed major holidays.

Moshe Safdie's National Gallery, a rose-granite crystal palace, shines like a candelabra on a promontory overlooking the Ottawa River and Parliament Hill. A dramatic long glass concourse leads to the Grand Hall commanding glorious views of Parliament Hill. Natural light also fills the galleries, thanks to ingeniously designed shafts with reflective panels.

The museum displays about 800 works from its great collection of Canadian art. Among the highlights are the fabulous Rideau Convent Chapel (1888), a rhapsody of wooden fan vaulting, cast-iron columns, and intricate carving created by architect priest Georges Bouillon; the works of early Québecois artists such as Antoine Plamondon, Joseph Legare, Abbé Jean Guyon, and Frère Luc; turn-of-the-century talents Homer Watson and Ozias Leduc; Tom Thomson and the Group of Seven; Emily Carr and David Milne; and the Montréal Automatistes Paul-Emile Borduas and Jean-Paul Riopelle. The European masters are also represented, and contemporary galleries feature pop art and minimalism, plus later abstract works, both Canadian and American. Facilities include two restaurants, a gift shop/bookstore, and an auditorium.

MORE ATTRACTIONS

The Canadian Museum of Nature. At the corner of Metcalfe and McLeod sts. ☎ **613/ 566-4700.** Admission C$4 (US$2.85) adults, C$3 (US$2.15) students, C$2 (US$1.45) ages 6–16 and seniors, C$9 (US$6) for families; children under 6 free. Half price on Thurs 9:30am–5pm, free 5–8pm. May 1 to Labour Day Fri–Wed 9:30am–5pm, Thurs 9:30am–8pm; rest of year Fri–Wed 10am–5pm, Thurs 10am–8pm.

Seven permanent exhibit halls trace the history of life on earth from its earliest beginnings 4,200 million years ago. The dinosaur hall and mineral galleries are the museum's most popular highlights. A huge tree of life traces the evolutionary threads of life from 500 million years ago to the present. Kids will enjoy the Discovery Den activity area, and on the third floor they can trade their "natural" treasures.

National Museum of Science & Technology. 1867 bd. St-Laurent (at Lancaster Rd.). ☎ **613/991-3044.** Admission C$6 (US$4.30) adults, C$5 (US$3.55) seniors and students, C$2 (US$1.45) ages 6–15; C$12 (US$9) family maximum (2 adults, 2 children). May 1 to Labour Day Sat–Thurs 9am–6pm, Fri 9am–9pm; rest of year Tues–Sun 9am–5pm. Closed Dec 25. Appointments needed to enter the observatory (call ☎ 613/991-3053 8am–4pm).

In this interactive museum, you can pull levers to demonstrate physical principles such as viscosity, climb aboard a steam locomotive, launch a Black Brant rocket from a mini–control room, observe the heavens in the evening through Canada's largest refracting telescope (appointments necessary), see chicks hatching, and try to walk through the Crazy Kitchen, where everything looks normal but the floor is tilted at a sharp angle. The permanent exhibits deal with Canada in space, land and marine transportation, communications, and all kinds of modern industrial and household technology. The outdoor technology park adjacent to the museum features machines and devices that have been developed, from the windmill and lighthouse to radar and rocket.

✪ **Royal Canadian Mounted Police Musical Ride.** 8900 St. Laurent Blvd. N. ☎ **613/ 993-3751.** At St. Laurent Blvd. N., take Sussex Dr. east past Rideau Hall and pick up Rockville Driveway; turn left at Sandridge Rd. and continue to the corner of St. Laurent.

The famous Musical Ride mounted drill team was first produced in Regina in 1878. Horses and riders practice at the Canadian Police College and the public is welcome to attend. Check before you go, though, because the ride is often on tour and schedules are extremely tentative.

The Supreme Court. Wellington St. (at Kent). ☎ **613/995-4330,** or 613/995-5361 for tour information.

The lofty art-deco building houses three courtrooms—one for the Supreme Court, two for the Federal Court. Three sessions are held during the year; the court does not normally sit during July, August, and September. While in session, the court usually hears appeals Monday to Thursday from 10:30am to 1pm and 2:30 to 4pm. The first and third Mondays of each month are usually reserved for the hearing of motions for leave to appeal. Thirty-minute tours are given daily every half hour from 9am to 4:30pm May to Labour Day (closed Saturday and Sunday from noon to 1pm). From Labour Day to April, tours are given Monday to Friday by reservation only.

Billings Estate Museum. 2100 Cabot St. ☎ **613/247-4830.** Admission C$2.50 (US$1.80) adults, C$2 (US$1.45) seniors, C$1 (US70¢) ages 5–17; children under 5 free. May 1–Oct 31 Sun–Thurs noon–5pm. Go south on Bank St., cross the Rideau River at Billings Bridge and take Riverside East; turn right on Pleasant Park and right on Cabot.

At this imposing house, set on 8 acres, you can look into the social life of a period spanning from 1828, when pioneer Braddish Billings built the house, to the 1970s, when the home was turned into a museum. Visitors may use the picnic area and stroll the grounds; tea is served on the lawn on Sunday, Wednesday, and Thursday from June 1 to September 1 from 1 to 4pm.

Bytown Museum. 540 Wellington St. (at Commissioner). ☎ **613/234-4570.** Admission C$2.50 (US$1.80) adults, C$1.25 (US90¢) seniors and students, C50¢ (US35¢) children. Apr to mid-May and mid-Oct to Nov Mon–Fri 10am–4pm. Mid-May to mid-Oct Mon–Sat 10am–5pm, Sun 1–5pm. Closed Dec–Mar.

Housed in Ottawa's oldest stone building (1827), which served originally as the Commissariat for food and material during building of the Rideau Canal, the museum displays possessions of Lieutenant-Colonel By, the canal's builder, as well as artifacts that reflect the social history of early Bytown/Ottawa. There are three period rooms and a number of changing exhibits. The museum is located beside the Ottawa Locks, between Parliament Hill and the Château Laurier Hotel.

Canadian War Museum. 330 Sussex Dr. ☎ **819/776-8627.** Admission C$3.50 (US$2.50) adults, C$2 (US$1.45) seniors and youths 13–17, C$1 (US70¢) children 2–12; free for everyone Sun 9:30am–noon. Fri–Wed 9:30am–5pm, Thurs 9:30am–8pm. Closed Christmas Day. *Note:* The museum will close from Sept 1998 to June 1999 for renovations.

Kids love to clamber over the tanks that are stationed outside the War Museum, and they seem to love almost as much imagining themselves in battle in the life-size replica of a World War I trench. The collection, which traces Canadian military history, contains airplanes, cars (including a Mercedes used by Adolf Hitler), guns, mines, uniforms (including that of Canadian air ace Billy Bishop, who's credited with shooting down the Red Baron), and military equipment, plus several large displays complete with sound effects showing famous battles such as the Normandy D-day landings.

The Currency Museum. 245 Sparks St. ☎ **613/782-8914.** Admission C$2 (US$1.45) adults; children under 8 free. May to Labour Day Mon–Sat 10:30am–5pm, Sun 1–5pm; Labour Day–Apr Tues–Sat 10:30am–5pm, Sun 1–5pm.

At the Bank of Canada, this museum will set you thinking creatively about money. It houses the world's most complete collection of Canadian notes and coins and traces the history of money—beads, wampum, and whale teeth—from early China to the modern era.

Laurier House. 335 Laurier Ave. E. ☎ **613/992-8142.** Admission C$2.25 (US$1.60) adults, C$1.75 (US$1.25) seniors, C$1.25 (US90¢) ages 6–16. Oct–Mar Tues–Sat 10am–5pm, Sun 2–5pm; Apr–Sept Tues–Sat 9am–5pm, Sun 2–5pm.

This comfortable Victorian home built in 1878 is filled with mementos of the two Canadian prime ministers who lived here: from 1897 to 1919, Sir Wilfrid Laurier, Canada's seventh prime minister (and first French-Canadian PM); from 1923 to 1950, William Lyon Mackenzie King, prime minister for 21 years. In the library where King held seances is the crystal ball that King supposedly had seen and coveted in London but said he couldn't afford (an American bought it for him when he overheard King's remarks). You'll also see the portrait of his mother, in front of which he used to place a red rose daily, and also a copy of the program Abraham Lincoln held the night of his assassination, plus copies of Lincoln's death mask (completed 4 years before his death) and hands. Lester B. Pearson's library has also been re-created and contains the Nobel Peace Prize medal he won for his role in the 1956 Arab-Israeli dispute.

Royal Canadian Mint. 320 Sussex Dr. ☎ **613/993-8990.** Admission C$2 (US$1.40); children under 6 free. Tours daily May–Aug 9am–5pm, Sept–Apr 9am–4pm.

From an elevated walkway you can watch gold and silver being transformed into special commemorative coins, medals, and investment tokens. Built as a branch of the Royal Mint in London, this mint struck its first coin in 1908. In 1931 it became an independent operation, but since 1976, circulating coinage has been made in Winnipeg.

PARKS & GARDENS

Ottawa has numerous parks, but the biggest and most attractive isn't a park at all—it's the **Central Experimental Farm,** at the Driveway and Prince of Wales Drive (☎ **613/991-3044**)—1,200 acres of green open space, now completely surrounded by Ottawa suburbia. Its famous greenhouses hold a spectacular chrysanthemum show every November. The farm itself has livestock barns housing cows, pigs, sheep and horses, which the kids'll love. There's also an ornamental flower garden and an arboretum with 2,000 different varieties of trees and shrubs. From May to early October, visitors can ride in wagons drawn by Clydesdales, weather permitting, from 10 to 11:30am and 2 to 3:30pm Monday to Friday. In winter there are sleigh rides. Admission is C$3 (US$2.15) for adults and C$2 (US$1.45) for students, seniors, and children ages 3 to 15. The agricultural museum, barns, and tropical greenhouse are open daily March to November from 9am to 5pm. From December to February, except Christmas and New Year's days, the barns and tropical greenhouse are open daily 10am to 4pm.

Another star attraction in the Ottawa area is ✪ **Gatineau Park.** Only 3 kilometers (2 miles) from the Houses of Parliament lie 88,000 acres of woodland and lakes named after notary-turned-explorer Nicolas Gatineau of Trois-Rivières. The park was inaugurated in 1938, when the federal government purchased land in the Gatineau Hills to stop forest destruction. Black bear, timber wolf, otter, marten, and raccoon are regular residents; they're joined by white-tailed deer, beaver, and more than 100 species of birds. If you're lucky, you might spy a lynx or a wolverine.

Park facilities include 90 miles of **hiking trails** and supervised **swimming beaches** at Meech Lake, Lac Philippe, and Lac la Pêche. Vehicle access fees to beach areas are C$6 (US$4.30). Boats (canoes, kayaks, and rowboats) can be rented at Lac Philippe and Lac la Pêche for C$25 (US$18) a day. Call ☎ **819/456-3555** to make reservations. Motorboats are not permitted on park lakes except on Lac la Pêche, where motors up to 10 horsepower may be used for **fishing.** Most lakes can be fished (if it's not allowed, it's posted). A Québec license is required and can be obtained at many convenience stores around the park.

Camping facilities are at or near Lac Philippe, accessible by highways 5, 105, and 366; there are also 35 canoe camping sites at Lac la Pêche. For information on this and other camping facilities, call the **Gatineau Park Visitor Centre,** 318 Meech Lake Rd., Old Chelsea, PQ, J0X 1N0 (☎ **819/827-2020**), or write the **National Capital Commission,** 40 Elgin St., Suite 202, Ottawa, ON, K1P 1C7. Reservations are vital (add C$3/US$2.15). Call ☎ **819/456-3016** from mid-May to September between 9am and 4pm. Fees are C$15 to C$18 (US$11 to US$13) per site per day; C$9 (US$6) for seniors.

In winter, hiking trails become cross-country ski trails, marked by numbers on blue plaques, with chalets along the way. Winter camping is available at Lac Philippe.

While you're in the park, visit the summer retreat of Mackenzie King at **Kingsmere.** You can have tea in a summer cottage there and inspect the architectural fragments he dragged here from the parliamentary building after the 1916 fire and from London's House of Commons after the 1941 blitz. The Moorside tearoom is open only from May 1 to Oct 31 from 11am to 6pm. For reservations, call ☎ **819/827-3405.**

To get to the park, you can take several routes: cross over to Hull and take boulevard Taché (Route 148) to the Gatineau Parkway, which leads to Kingsmere, Ski Fortune, and eventually to Meech Lake. Or come up Highway 5 north, take Exit 12 for Old Chelsea, turn left and proceed 1.2 kilometers (³⁄₄ mile) on Meech Lake Road to the Gatineau Park Visitor Centre. To reach Lac Philippe, take Highway 5 north out of Hull and then Highway 105 to the intersection of Highway 366 west. Just before you reach Ste-Cecile-de-Masham, you can turn off to Lac Philippe; to reach Lac la Pêche, keep going along the Masham road to St-Louis-de-Masham and enter the park just beyond.

ESPECIALLY FOR KIDS

Kids love the bands, rifles, and uniforms they see on Parliament Hill at the **Changing of the Guard.** The **National Aviation Museum** is a fantasyland for budding pilots. The perennial favorites at the **Canadian Museum of Nature** are the dinosaurs, the animals, and the Discovery Den, which was specially created for children. Extraspecial attractions at the **Canadian Museum of Civilization** are the Children's Museum and CINEPLUS for action movies. Kids enjoy petting the animals at the agriculture museum as well as picnicking or taking a hayride at the **Central Experimental Farm.** At the **National Museum of Science and Technology,** the hands-on exhibits will keep them entertained while they learn. And they'll love watching horses and riders in the Musical Ride practice their moves at the **Canadian Police College.** All of these attractions are described in detail elsewhere in this chapter.

When it's time to let off some steam, there's **canoeing** or **boating** at Dow's Lake; **biking** along the canal or **ice-skating** on it; plus activities outside the city in Gatineau Park.

Outside Ottawa, you'll find a few more fun places for kids. **Storyland,** RR #5, off Highway 17 about 6 miles northwest of Renfrew (☎ **613/432-2222**), has a puppet theater, paddleboats, minigolf, a petting zoo, and more. Admission is C$7.50 (US$5) for adults and children 5 and over, and C$6 (US$4.30) for children 2 to 4 and seniors 60 and over. It's open daily from the second week in June to Labour Day from 9:30am to 6pm. Another nearby family amusement park, **Logos Land Resort,** RR #1, Cobden (☎ **613/646-2313**), has five water slides, minigolf, paddleboats, and sleigh rides and cross-country skiing in winter. Admission is C$12 (US$9), and it's open from 10am to 7pm daily from the first weekend in June to Labour Day.

A SCENIC DRIVE

A very picturesque and interesting drive, the **Ottawa River Parkway** starts in the west end at Carling Avenue and runs along the river into Wellington Street, all the way offering glorious views over the islands in the river.

From Confederation Square, proceed along Sussex Drive to St. Patrick Street, where you can turn left into **Nepean Point Park.** Here, you and the statue of Samuel de Champlain can share a beautiful river view.

Across the road is **Major's Hill Park,** between the Château Laurier and the National Gallery, where the noonday gun is fired (at 10am on Sunday to avoid disturbing church services). You can watch the lighting of the cannon.

Just beyond the Macdonald-Cartier Bridge stands **Earnscliffe,** originally the home of Sir John A. Macdonald and now the impressive residence of the British high commissioner.

Farther along Sussex Drive you cross the Rideau River, whence you can look down upon the modern Ottawa City Hall pat in the middle of Green Island overlooking Rideau Falls, before proceeding past the prime minister's house, well-sheltered by trees at 24 Sussex Dr., and on to **Government House,** at no. 1, still often referred to as Rideau Hall, the governor-general's residence. On the 88-acre grounds is a red oak planted by President Kennedy and a sapling planted by President Nixon (which local wags note has grown rather crooked). For tours of the grounds and the interior public rooms, call ☎ **613/998-7113.**

The drive then becomes the **National Capital Commission Driveway,** a beautiful route along the Ottawa River and through **Rockcliffe** Park. Where the road forks in the park, follow the right fork to Acacia Avenue to reach the Rockeries, where carpets of daffodils and narcissus in April herald spring.

5 Special Events & Festivals

Ottawa's biggest event is the **Canadian Tulip Festival** in May, when the city is ablaze with 200 varieties of tulips stretching around public buildings, monuments, embassies, private homes, and along driveways. (Probably the best viewing is at Dow's Lake.) The festival began in 1945, when the people of the Netherlands sent 100,000 tulip bulbs to Canada in appreciation of the role Canadian troops played in liberating Holland. Queen Juliana of the Netherlands, who had spent the war years in Canada during the occupation, arranged for an annual presentation of bulbs to celebrate the birth of her daughter, Princess Margriet, in Ottawa in 1943 (to ensure that the princess was born a citizen of the Netherlands, the Canadian government proclaimed her room in the Ottawa Civic Hospital part of Holland).

Now the festival has a flurry of spectacular events, including fireworks, concerts, parades, and flotilla on the canal, which accompany the medley of floral sculptures, floral tapestries, and garden displays. For festival information, contact the Canadian Tulip Festival (☎ **613/567-5757**).

In early June the National Museum of Natural Science holds a **Children's Festival,** an extravaganza of dance, mime, puppetry, and music, all for the kids.

Late June brings **Le Franco,** a 5-day celebration of French-speaking Canada, featuring classical and other musical concerts, fashion shows, street performers, games and competitions, crafts, and, of course, French cuisine. For information, call ☎ **613/741-1225.**

On July 1, Canadians flock to the city to celebrate **Canada Day,** a huge birthday party complete with all kinds of entertainment, including fireworks. For 10 days in mid-July the city is filled with the sound of jazz at the **Ottawa International Jazz Festival.** Local, national, and international artists give more than 125 performances at more than 20 venues. For information, call ☎ **613/594-3580.**

On Labour Day weekend, 150 brilliantly colored balloons fill the skies over Ottawa, while below on the ground, people flock to musical events and midway rides during the **Gatineau Hot Air Balloon Festival.** For information, call ☎ **819/ 243-2330.**

When the ice hog breaks through the ice of the Rideau Canal, it's time for **Winterlude,** a snow and ice extravaganza that features parades, bands, floats, fireworks, speed skating, snowshoe races, ice boating, curling, and more. One quite colorful event is the bed race on the canal, while the most exciting event may be the harness racing on ice. The carnival usually takes place the first or second week in February. For information, call ☎ **613/239-5000.**

Other major events include the National Capital Air Show in June; the National Capital Dragon Boat Race Festival in July; and the 10-day **Super-Ex (Central Canada Exhibition)** (☎ **613/237-7222**), in mid- to late August.

For additional information on any event listed here, contact the **Convention and Tourist Bureau,** 130 Albert St. (☎ **613/237-3959**).

6 Outdoor Activities & Spectator Sports

OUTDOOR ACTIVITIES

BIKING   More than 160 kilometers (100 miles) of bike paths run along the Ottawa and Rideau rivers, the Rideau Canal, and in Gatineau Park, and more miles are being added. A blue, black, and white cyclist logo marks all bikeways.

From April to Canadian Thanksgiving, you can rent bikes from **Rent a Bike,** 1 Rideau St., in the parking lot behind the Château Laurier Hotel (☎ **613/ 241-4140**). Town bikes, sport bikes, mountain bikes, and in-line skates are all available, with standard bikes from C$7 (US$5) an hour to C$25 (US$18) for 24 hours or C$80 (US$57) per month, and performance bikes from C$30 (US$21) per day to C$95 (US$68) per month. The company will also provide maps of the best day trips around the city for you to follow on your own as well as through guided tours.

Bikes can also be rented at **Dow's Lake Marina** (☎ **613/232-5278**).

BOATING/CANOEING   At **Dow's Lake Pavilion,** 1001 Queen Elizabeth Dr., you can rent bikes, in-line skates, paddleboats, and canoes (C$11/US$8 an hour, C$40/US$29 a day) at the **marina** (☎ **613/232-5278**), and also relax and dine at several restaurants. The $3-million glass-and-steel complex, which looks like a cluster of sails from a distance, makes a great haven after a winter skate or a summer running or biking jaunt.

Boats can also be rented in **Gatineau Park** at Lac la Pêche and Lac Philippe (☎ **819/827-2020**) for C$7 (US$5) per hour or C$25 (US$18) per day.

GOLF   The **Château Cartier Sheraton** (☎ 819/777-1088; greens fee C$20/ US$14) in Québec has a golf course on the premises. Other fine courses in Ottawa include the **Edelweiss Golf and Country Club** (☎ 819/459-2980); **Canadian Golf and Country Club** (☎ 613/780-3565; greens fee C$34.50/US$25); **Le Club de Golf Mont Cascades** (☎ 819/459-2980); and **Manderley on the Green** (☎ 613/ 489-2092; greens fee C$24/US$17).

Ottawa's Pride & Joy: The Rideau Canal

Built to avoid using the St. Lawrence River (once so vulnerable to American attack) for transporting troops and supplies to Canada's interior, the Rideau Canal is one of Ottawa's greatest assets. In summer you can walk or cycle along the canal paths, or else canoe or boat your way along before stopping in at the canal-side beer garden at the National Arts Centre. In winter, it's turned into a glorious skating rink worthy of any Dutch artist's palette, as people come and go to work, skating with their briefcases, and families take to the ice with children perched atop their backs or drawn upon sleighs.

Construction of the canal began in 1826, and the 123-mile engineering feat was completed in 1832. Starting in Ottawa, the canal follows the course of the Rideau River to its summit on Upper Rideau Lake, which is connected to Newboro Lake, where the canal descends the Cataraqui River (through a series of lakes controlled by dams) to Kingston. In Ottawa, a flight of eight locks allows boats to negotiate the 80-foot difference between the artificially constructed portion of the canal and the Ottawa River—a sight not to be missed. (You can observe this astounding maneuver between Parliament Hill and the Château Laurier Hotel.)

HIKING & NATURE WALKS   A band of protected wetlands and woodlands surround the capital on the Ontario side of the Ottawa River and here visitors can find ideal hiking areas. At **Stony Swamp Conservation Area** in the region's west end, there are 39 kilometers (24 miles) of trails, including the Old Quarry Trail, the Jack Pine Nature Trail, and the Sasparilla Trail. Call ☎ 613/239-5000 for information. It's also good for cross-country skiing and snowshoeing. Regional maps are available from Canada's Capital Information Centre at 14 Metcalfe St.

Gatineau Park has a network of hiking trails, some long enough for a genuine day hike. Call the visitor center for information (☎ 819/827-2020). West of the city in Kanata, **Riverfront Park** has nature trails along the Ottawa River. Call ☎ 613/592-4281. On the Québec side in Luskville, a trail leads to Luskville Falls from the Chemin de Hotel de Ville. **The Rideau Trail,** which runs from Ottawa to Kingston, is the area's major serious hiking trail.

HORSEBACK RIDING   Near Edelweiss Valley, **Captiva Farm,** RR #2, Wakefield (☎ 819/459-2769), offers trail rides year-round on 20 kilometers (12.8 miles) of trails through the Gatineau Hills. Hourly charges are C$22 (US$16) for adults, C$10 (US$7) for children (each additional hour is C$11/US$8) and riders can go with or without a guide. Reservations are required.

About 40 kilometers (25 miles) west of the city, **Pinto Valley Ranch,** Fitzroy Harbour (☎ 613/623-3439), offers trail rides for C$20 (US$14) an hour, as well as pony riding and a petting zoo for the kids.

ICE-SKATING/IN-LINE SKATING   During the winter, the **Rideau Canal** is flooded to a 3-foot depth, becoming the world's longest and most romantic skating rink—it stretches 9$\frac{1}{2}$ kilometers (6 miles) from the National Arts Centre to Dow's Lake and Carleton University. (Every morning the radio news reports ice conditions.) Skates can be rented at three places: at Dow's Lake, opposite the NAC, and at Fifth Avenue, all for about C$15 (US$11) for 2 hours. The canal is fully serviced with heated huts, sleigh rentals, boot check and skate-sharpening services, food concessions, and rest rooms. The season usually runs from late December to late February.

In-line skates are available at the Rent a Bike facility behind the Château Laurier and also from Dow's Lake marina at a cost of C$15 (US$11) for 2 hours.

SKIING   Few out-of-town visitors ski the areas around Ottawa, heading instead for Québec's more sophisticated resorts. In many ways, the following ski resorts are more compelling summer tourist attractions with their water parks and other fun facilities. (See "St-Jovite & Mont Tremblant" in chapter 9 and "Mont Ste-Anne: Skiing & Summer Sports" in chapter 10 for two of Québec's best-loved ski resorts.)

Mont Cascades, just 30 minutes north of Ottawa across the Gatineau River, outside of Cantley on Highway 307 (☎ 819/827-0301), has 13 trails, one triple- and three double-chair lifts, and two T-bars. The longest run is 2,200 feet. There are two day lodges with cafeteria and restaurant-bar at the hill. Night skiing is available. During the summer you can enjoy coming down six thrilling water slides and spend the whole day cooling off in the state-of-the-art water park.

Twenty-nine kilometers (18 miles) from the city, **Edelweiss Valley,** Route 366, Wakefield (☎ 819/459-2328), has 24 runs, four lifts (including three double-chairs and one quad), ski school, night skiing, and a warm cozy lodge, plus overnight accommodations. Lift rates for adults are C$30 (US$21) per day. Tennis and golf are summer attractions.

Mont Ste-Marie, 89 kilometers (55 miles) north of Ottawa at Lac Ste-Marie (☎ 819/467-5200), offers skiing on twin peaks, with a 1,250-foot drop, and a 3-kilometer (2-mile) ski run. There are two quads and a Poma. Mont Ste-Marie also offers cross-country skiing. Lift rates are C$29 (US$21) a day.

Gatineau Park, with 185 kilometers (115 miles) of groomed trails, offers the best **cross-country skiing.** In town you can also ski along the bike paths that parallel the Eastern or Western parkways.

SWIMMING   Pools that are open to the public include those at the universities and the YMCA (see "Accommodations," above). You can also swim in the Gatineau Park lakes: Meech, Lac la Pêche, and Lac Philippe.

WHITE-WATER RAFTING   While you're in Ottawa, you can enjoy the thrills and spills of white-water rafting from May to September, depending on the river. **Equinox Adventures,** 5334 Yonge St., no. 609, Toronto (☎ 800/785-8855 or 416/222-2223), has a base camp on the Ottawa River and offers 1- and 2-day white-water rafting trips on the Ottawa, Magnetawan, and Madawaska rivers, plus instruction in canoeing and kayaking. They also operate sea-kayaking trips along the Bruce Peninsula and canoeing trips in Algonquin Provincial Park (see chapter 14). Prices start at C$70 (US$50) per person per day during the week.

Other companies operating similar trips and facilities include: **River Run,** P.O. Box 179, Beachburg, ON, K0J 1C0 (☎ 800/267-8504 or 613/646-2501); **Esprit Rafting Adventures,** Box 463, Pembroke, ON, K8A 6X7 (☎ 819/683-3241); **OWL Rafting,** Box 29, Forester's Falls, ON, K0J 1V0 (☎ 613/646-2263 in summer or 613/238-7238 in winter); and **Wilderness Tours,** Box 89, Beachburg, ON, K0J 1C0 (☎ 613/646-2291).

SPECTATOR SPORTS

The **Ottawa Senators** (☎ 613/599-0300) are in their fifth season in the National Hockey League (their former incarnation won a string of Stanley Cups earlier in this century) and currently play at the Corel Centre in Kanata. Tickets cost C$28 to C$80 (US$20 to US$57); call **Ticketmaster** (☎ 613/755-1166). **The Ottawa Lynx** (☎ 613/747-5969), the Triple A affiliate of the Montréal Expos, play baseball at Jetform Park, 300 Coventry Rd. Tickets, which are generally available, cost C$4.25 to C$8.25 (US$3 to US$6); call ☎ 613/749-9947.

7 Ottawa After Dark

Ottawa's culture and nightlife pickings are somewhat meager, really only extending to the National Arts Centre, several bars, the Byward Market area, and one or two dance clubs, the raciest of which are concentrated across the river in Hull. The biggest news in this area is the opening of the **Casino de Hull,** 1 bd. du Casino (☎ **800/665-2274** or 819/772-2100), which is open daily from 11am to 3am. It's not just your typical run-of-the-mill casino: A strict dress code is upheld (no blue jeans, jogging outfits, cutoffs, shorts or beachwear allowed) and both the exterior and interior are dramatically landscaped with tropical plants, pools, and waterfalls. There are 45 gaming tables and 1,250 slot machines. The complex also has two restaurants—fine dining in Baccara and excellent buffet in Banco—and two bars. Shuttles operate from hotels to the casino for C$9 (US$5) per round-trip.

For Ottawa entertainment information, call **Chez Nightlife** (☎ **613/562-1111**) for a taped message, and secure any of the following: *Where,* a free guide usually provided in your hotel; *Ottawa* magazine; or the Friday edition of the *Ottawa Citizen.*

THE PERFORMING ARTS

Besides the ensemble at the National Arts Centre, the **Ottawa Little Theatre,** 400 King Edward Ave. (☎ **613/233-8948**), offers good productions of such popular shows as *Lettice and Lovage* by Peter Shaffer and *The Sisters Rosensweig* by Wendy Wasserstein. The company started in 1913 in an old church that burned down in 1970, but it now has a fully equipped, modern theater. Tickets are C$10 (US$7). The **Great Canadian Theatre Company,** 910 Gladstone Ave. (☎ **613/236-5196**), specializes in Canadian contemporary drama and comedy and performs from September to May. Tickets are C$20 (US$14).

The National Arts Centre. 53 Elgin St. (at Confederation Sq.). ☎ **613/996-5051.** For reservations, call Ticketmaster (☎ 613/755-1166) or visit the NAC box office, Mon–Sat noon–9pm; Sun and holidays when performances are scheduled noon to curtain time. Guided tours available.

Canadian and international musical, dance, and theater artists—including the resident National Arts Centre (NAC) Orchestra—perform at this marvelous center. The building, created by architect Fred Lebensold, is made of three interlocking hexagons with terraces and spectacular views of the Rideau Canal and Ottawa River. There are three auditoriums: the European-style **Opera,** seating 2,300; the 950-seat **Theatre,** with its innovative apron stage; and the 350-seat **Studio,** suitable for experimental works. The **National Arts Centre Orchestra** (☎ **613/996-5051**) performs in seven or eight main concert series. The center also offers classic and modern drama in English and French.

A free monthly *Calendar of NAC Events* is available from the **NAC Marketing and Communications Department,** Box 1534, Station B, Ottawa, ON, K1P 5W1. For information, call ☎ **613/996-5051.** See "Dining," above, for the center's canal-side Le Café.

FOLK, ROCK & JAZZ CLUBS

As the guy who runs the place puts it, "everyone from politicians to truck drivers" crams into **Patty's Place Pub,** 1186 Bank St. (☎ **613/730-2434**), to raise a jug or two, tuck into some real fish-and-chips or Irish stew, and listen to the stirring Irish ballads rendered by a folk singer (resident Thursday to Saturday). It's the kind of place where you're tossed into the fray and wind up having a good old time playing darts, chatting, singing, and wassailing.

For a more rollicking scene, try **Molly McGuire's,** 130 George St. (☎ 613/241-1972), a cavernous pub where rock-and-roll and jazz bands belt out their sounds Wednesday to Monday. For local and national acoustic folk talent in a relaxed atmosphere, go to **Rasputin's,** 696 Bronson Ave. (☎ 613/230-5102). The **Bravo Bar-Ristorante,** 292 Elgin St. (☎ 613/233-0057), is a fun place to drop in for a drink and some pool and has good Italian cuisine and Sunday brunch, too. **Vineyards,** 54 York St., in the market (☎ 613/241 4270), features jazz on Wednesday and Sunday nights.

Mainly blues action can be found upstairs at the **Rainbow Bistro,** 76 Murray St. (☎ 613/241-5123), which features live music nightly and has hosted such artists as KD Lang, Colin James, and Buckwheat Zydeco. There's always someone worth hearing, and on Thursday, Friday, and Saturday there are free matinees between 3 and 7pm.

DANCE CLUBS

Nightlife closes down at 1am (11pm on Sunday) in Ottawa, but across the river in Hull, it continues until 3am every night of the week. The hottest discos/dance bars are found there, but note that the strip where most clubs are located has developed a reputation for late-night fights and muggings.

IN HULL   Tucked away off Promenade du Portage is the dance bar **Le Bop** (☎ 819/777-3700), and farther along the street you'll find **Au Zone,** 117 Promenade du Portage (☎ 819/771-6677), where the decor will transport you to a surreal Camelot. It attracts a young crowd with rock and R&B sounds, and is open nightly until 3am. **Shalimar,** 84 Promenade du Portage (☎ 819/770-7486), is a disco-pub.

IN OTTAWA   **Hartwells,** in the Westin, 11 Colonel By Dr. (☎ 613/560-7000), attracts an over-25 crowd for dancing to DJ tunes Tuesday to Saturday (cover charged). On Saturday nights there's dancing to live entertainment at **Zoe's** in the Château Laurier, 1 Rideau St. (☎ 613/241-1414).

BARS

In the Byward Market area, **Vineyards,** 54 York St. (☎ 613/241-4270), is one of the city's coziest hangouts, with its downstairs cellarlike atmosphere, stone floors, and red-and-white-checked tablecloths. Five different house wines are featured (from C$6/US$4.30 a glass), plus more than 60 different varieties. There's live jazz on Sunday and Wednesday nights. Snacks are available, too. It's open Monday to Saturday from 4pm to 1am. Also popular is **Tramps,** on William Street (☎ 613/241-5523).

For quiet drinking with a piano background, **Friday's Victorian Music Parlour,** 150 Elgin St. (☎ 613/237-5353), with its clubby atmosphere, old London engravings, and comfortable wingbacks, plus an inviting fire in winter, is a good choice, especially for single women who just want to have a quiet, dignified drink. The pianist entertains nightly. A similar parlor upstairs at the **Full House Restaurant,** 337 Somerset St. W. (☎ 613/238-6734), provides piano entertainment and a jolly atmosphere Wednesday to Saturday nights.

For a truly relaxing ambiance where you sink into plush upholstery and enjoy the lilting piano strains, go to the **Delta Ottawa Hotel's lobby bar,** 361 Queen St. (☎ 613/238-6000); for jazz, go to **Zoe's,** at the Château Laurier, 1 Rideau St. (☎ 613/232-6411) or **The Lounge,** at the Westin Hotel, 11 Colonel By Dr. (☎ 613/650-7000).

For pub-style conviviality, check out the **Brig,** in the Byward Market area at 23 York St. (☎ 613/562-6666), and the **Elephant and Castle,** at 50 Rideau St.

(☎ 613/234-5544). At **Maxwell's,** at 340 Elgin St. (☎ 613/232-5771), an attractive contemporary-style bar, you can stop in and meet people.

For some real down-home Québecois fun and atmosphere, visit **Les Raftsmen,** 60 rue St-Raymond, Hull (☎ 819/777-0924), a large tavern (brasserie) decked out in log-cabin style with cart wheels for decoration. At lunch or dinner you'll find plenty of joie de vivre and reasonably priced traditional French Canadian cuisine—tourtière and pigs' feet as well as spaghetti, sandwiches, burgers, chicken, steak, and fish—all under C$13 (US$9), and most under C$6 or C$7 (US$4.30 or US$5). Dinner is served until 9pm, but the place is open Monday to Saturday from 7am to 3am. There's entertainment every night.

MORE ENTERTAINMENT

FILM The **ByTowne Cinema,** 325 Rideau St., shows alternative foreign and independent films. For a complete bimonthly calendar, call ☎ 613/789-4600. The **Canadian Film Institute,** 2 Daly St. (☎ 613/232-6727), offers regular programs of Canadian and international art films. Screenings take place every Saturday and Sunday at the **National Archives Auditorium** at 395 Wellington St., with general admission costing C$8 (US$6).

SON ET LUMIERE In summer, don't miss the evening spectacular on Parliament Hill—a sound-and-light show relating Canadian history and culture. There are two shows nightly (one in French and one in English), and admission is free. English performances are given first on Thursday and Saturday at 9:30pm in May; on Monday, Tuesday, Thursday, and Saturday at 9:30pm in June; on Wednesday, Friday, and Saturday at 10:30pm in July; and Monday, Tuesday, Thursday, and Saturday at 9pm and Wednesday, Friday, and Sunday at 10pm in August and September.

8 Exploring Eastern Ontario

East from Port Hope, which is a worthy stop for antique hounds, stretches the Bay of Quinte and Quinte's Isle, a tranquil region of farms and orchards largely settled by Loyalists. It's still off the beaten track—except to those in the know, who come to explore the pretty, small towns, to go antiquing, or to enjoy the beaches, dunes, and waterfront activities. Kingston, a very appealing lakefront town with its own weekly market, is interesting both architecturally and historically. It's also the gateway to the mighty St. Lawrence River, the Thousand Islands, and the St. Lawrence National Park.

To get from Ottawa to the region covered in the following sections, take Highway 16 south to Highway 401 west, which strings together the towns, parks, and townships from Brockville to Port Hope. From Toronto, take Highway 401 east. A particularly beautiful detour is the Thousand Islands Parkway, which runs parallel to the 401 between Brockville and Kingston.

9 Along the St. Lawrence: The Thousand Islands & More

The mighty St. Lawrence River was the main route into the heart of Upper Canada from the 17th century to the mid-19th century, traveled first by explorers, fur traders, and missionaries and later by settlers en route to Ontario and the plains west. The river is a magnificent and humbling sight—in some places it is 12 miles wide.

If you're driving, Highway 401 is the fastest route connecting the townships, or you can take the more scenic Highway 2.

THE THOUSAND ISLANDS

Today the St. Lawrence continues as a major shipping route into Canada and the Great Lakes. But visitors know it for the Thousand Islands. According to a native-Canadian legend, petals of heavenly flowers fell to earth and were scattered on the river, creating Manitouana, the Garden of the Great Spirit, and as we know it, the Thousand Islands.

St. Lawrence Islands National Park (The Thousand Islands) is headquartered at 2 County Rd. 5, Mallorytown, ON, K0E 1R0 (☎ 613/923-5261). Canada's smallest national park, it encompasses the St. Lawrence and its islands, stretching about 80 kilometers (49.6 miles) from Kingston to Brockville. The visitor center and headquarters is on the mainland in Mallorytown, where there is a picnic area, beach, and nature trail. Access to the park island facilities is via boat only; mooring costs C$14 to C$24 (US$10 to US$17) overnight, depending on the size of the boat. Most of the islands have docking and picnicking facilities, available on a first-come, first-served basis. The largest campground has 18 sites, the smallest two. Three consecutive nights is the docking limit at each island. Parking is C$5 (US$3.55) per car at the Mallorytown Landing.

Each island has a pretty self-contained microclimate. In summer the park staff give interpretive programs (ask at the park's headquarters at Mallorytown Landing, located between Gananoque and Brockville).

You can also savor the island-river landscape aboard one of the many cruise boats that operate from Kingston (see below) and Gananoque. From May to mid-October, boats leave from Gananoque on 1- and 3-hour trips. Adult prices are C$11 (US$8) and C$16 (US$11), respectively, and C$6 (US$4.30) for children 7 to 12.

The **Thousand Islands Gananoque Boat Line** (☎ 613/382-2144, or 613/382-2146 for 24-hour information) operates cruises from May to October. Three-hour and 1-hour cruises are available for C$16 and C$11 (US$11 and US$8), respectively. The charge for children 7 to 12 on both is C$6 (US$4). The longer cruise stops at the fantastical Boldt Castle (admission C$5/US$4). Note, though, that you'll need a passport, and a valid U.S. visa if you're not an American citizen, to visit the castle. Call ahead for the schedule. Boats leave from the waterfront in Gananoque.

The same company also operates 1-hour trips from Ivy Lea, leaving from west of the International Bridge on the Thousand Islands Parkway. The cost is C$11 (US$8) for adults and C$6 (US$4) for children 7 to 12.

For a dramatic view from above, climb the **Skydeck** on Hill Island near Ivy Lea, which soars 400 feet above the river. You'll be rewarded with a 40-mile panorama.

EXPLORING THE THOUSAND ISLANDS FROM KINGSTON

Kingston is a great leaping-off point for the Thousand Islands, especially for visitors from Toronto. In summer, cruise boats meander through the more than 1,800 islands, past such extraordinary sights as **Boldt Castle,** built on Heart Island by millionaire George Boldt at the turn of the century as a gift for his wife. (When she died suddenly, the work was abandoned, and so it stands a relic to lost love.)

The best way to see the park is to charter your own houseboat (see below). Alternatively, several cruise boats leave from various points along the St. Lawrence. From Kingston Harbour at City Hall, you can take a 3-hour cruise on the *Island Queen,* a whistle-blowing triple-deck paddle wheeler. It costs C$17 (US$12) for adults and C$8.50 (US$6) for children 4 to 12. Or there's a 90-minute cruise aboard the *Island Bell* that takes in the Kingston Harbour and waterfront. It costs C$12 (US$9) for adults and C$6 (US$4.30) for children 4 to 12; children under 4 are free. For cruise information, call the *Island Queen Showboat* (☎ 613/549-5544 or 613/549-5545).

Southern Ontario

144

Sudbury

17

11

North Bay

17

17

6

ALGONQUIN
PROVINCIAL PAR

Manitoulin
Island

6

60

South
Baymouth

Georgian

McKellar

Oxtongue
Lake

Fathom Five
Prov. Park

Tobermory

Bay

Parry
Sound

*Lake
Rosseau*

*Lake
Joseph*

Huntsville

Bruce Peninsula
Nat. Park

11

6

Port Carling

*Lake
Muskoka*

Bracebridge

Georgian Bay Islands
Nat. Park

69

Gravenhurst

Haliburto

*Lake
Huron*

Penetanguishene

Midland

12

Orillia

Wasaga
Beach

400

11

12

Lindsay

21

Collingwood

26

*Lake
Simcoe*

Barrie
Lindsay

Peterborough

Keene

see Muskoka Lake Region map

400

28

6

Newcastle

Oshawa

401

Po
Ho

Goderich

Elora

Fergus

★ Toronto

Lake

Bayfield

8

Elmira

St. Jacobs

21

6

Mississauga

401

Stratford

Waterloo

Kitchener

QEW

Burlington

21

7

8

Cambridge

Hamilton

Niagara-on-
the-Lake

St. Marys

401

8

104

7

Woodstock

2

Brantford

St. Catharines

Niagara Falls

London

2

*Welland
Canal*

QEW

402

3

Nanticoke

QEW

Fort
Erie

90

"to Windsor &
Leamington/
Point Pelee
Nat. Park"

401

St. Thomas

Port
Colborne

Buffalo

Lake Erie

90

1-0393

360

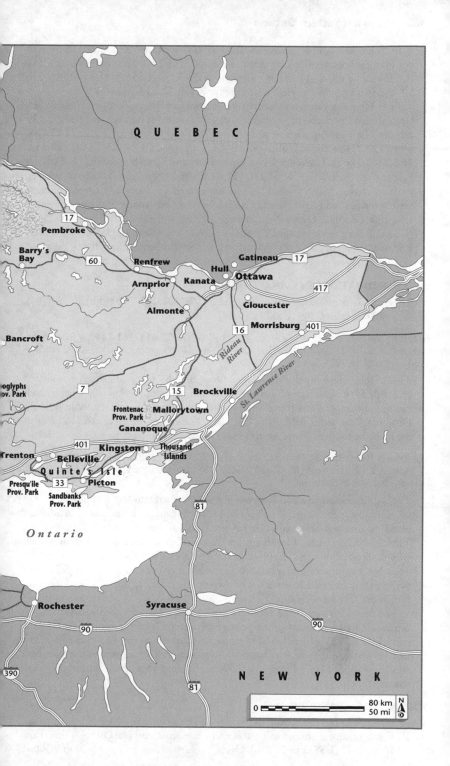

QUEBEC

Pembroke 17

Barry's
Bay

60 Renfrew

Gatineau 17

Hull

Arnprior Kanata Ottawa

417

Almonte Gloucester

Bancroft 16 Morrisburg 401

Rideau River

oglyphs
ov. Park 7

15 Brockville

St. Lawrence River

Frontenac Mallorytown
Prov. Park

Gananoque

Trenton 401 Kingston Thousand
Islands

Belleville

Quinte's Isle

Presqu'ile 33 Picton
Prov. Park

Sandbanks
Prov. Park

Ontario

Rochester Syracuse

90 90

390

NEW YORK

81

0   80 km
0   50 mi

N

In season, the nimble catamaran *Sea Fox II* also cruises the islands and the harbor from the bottom of Brock Street in Kingston. The 2-hour islands tour costs C$13 (US$9) for adults, C$11 (US$8) for seniors, and C$6 (US$4.30) for children 6 to 12; children under 6 are free. For information, call ☎ 613/542-4271.

From Kingston you can also cruise the Rideau Canal or explore the Thousand Islands aboard a **houseboat.** For information on houseboat holidays and rentals, contact the following: **Aquaventures,** P.O. Box 70, Brockville, ON, K6V 5T7 (☎ 888/498-2727); **Houseboat Holidays,** RR #3, Gananoque, ON, K7G 2V5 (☎ 613/382-2842); or **St. Lawrence River Houseboat and Cruiser Rentals,** c/o Halliday Point, Wolfe Island, ON, K0H 2Y0 (☎ 613/385-2290). Most houseboats sleep up to six and have a fully equipped kitchen, hot and cold running water, and a propane system for heat and light. Weekly rentals on the canal system in summer average C$1,100 (US$786). On the St. Lawrence, in August the cost starts at about C$600 (US$429) for a weekend, and C$900 to C$1,215 (US$643 to US$893) per week. Prices are higher in July, less in May, June, and September, and also during the week. Boats are fully equipped—you need only bring sleeping bags and towels.

ACCOMMODATIONS IN GANANOQUE

There's a 67-room **Travelodge** on King Street (☎ 800/267-7820 or 613/382-4781), with doubles from C$99 (US$71).

Athlone Inn. 250 King St. W., Gananoque, ON, K7G 2G6. ☎ **613/382-2440.** 4 suites, 6 motel units. A/C TV. C$85–C$185 (US$61–US$132) suite in the main inn; C$65–C$90 (US$46–US$64) motel rm. AE, MC, V.

The Athlone Inn, located in a Victorian home built by a local industrialist, is known primarily for its food, served in a handsome dining room (see below). The inn itself has four attractive suites (three with gas fireplaces and one with a double Jacuzzi). Furnishings are traditional Ethan Allen–style. The gilt-framed pictures and a love seat are welcome touches. There are also some nicely kept motel units.

✪ **Trinity House Inn.** 90 Stone St., Gananoque, ON, K7G 1Z8. ☎ **613/382-8383.** 6 rms, 2 suites. A/C TV. Summer C$80–C$160 (US$57–US$114) double; C$200 (US$143) suite. Off-season discounts available. MC, V.

The Trinity House Inn is an impressive redbrick Victorian home built in 1859. In addition to the six rooms, there's a one-bedroom suite with kitchen in an adjacent building that was originally Gananoque's jail, and there's also a Jacuzzi suite. Throughout, the period furnishings are fine—Oriental rugs and screens, brass beds with flouncy pillows and skirts—and at night guests will find a rose at turndown. There's a comfortable sitting room with marble fireplace and also an art gallery displaying local art in the basement. The owners also offer day sailing aboard their 30-foot yacht, *The Lady Trinity.*

The Bistro has two dining rooms, a bar-lounge, a glass-enclosed veranda, and an outdoor terrace overlooking the ponds and waterfalls of the garden. Among the specialties are chilled-peach-and-champagne soup which can be followed by such items as orange roughy with a mango salsa, chicken with asparagus over a tomato basil coulis, or rack of lamb Provençale. Open Thursday to Tuesday from 5:30pm in summer.

DINING IN GANANOQUE

At the Athlone Inn (see above), the food is classic continental—rack of lamb, chicken Kiev, sole meunière, shrimp with garlic and white wine, and veal Oscar—priced from C$16 to C$22 (US$11 to US$16). Open Tuesday to Sunday from 5:30 to 9:30pm.

Cook Not Mad. 110 Clarence St. ☎ **613/382-4361.** C$35 (US$25) 3-course prix-fixe menu. AE, MC, V. Wed–Thurs and Sun 5:30–7:30pm, Fri–Sat 5:30–8pm. CANADIAN.

Located in a historic home, this restaurant specializes in regional Canadian cuisine, offering a daily changing fixed-price menu. A sample menu might begin with cauliflower, fennel, and asparagus soup, or Québec smoked trout with carrot slaw. Next you might have a choice of swordfish grilled with coconut, ginger, noodles, and basil, or lamb loin with rosemary jus. To finish there might be a dark-chocolate tart with chocolate sauce. The wine list features Niagara wines as well as international selections.

The Golden Apple. 45 King St. W. ☎ **613/382-3300.** Reservations recommended. Main courses C$17–C$30 (US$12–US$21). MC, V. May 1–Oct 31 daily 11am–3pm and 5–9pm. Nov 1–Dec 31 Sat–Sun 11am–3pm; Thurs–Sun 5–9pm. Closed Jan–Apr. CONTINENTAL.

Situated in an early-19th-century limestone farmhouse, The Golden Apple has an authentic country ambiance with its pine accents. The cuisine ranges from chicken parmigiana to prime rib, veal Normande, and stuffed sole. In summer, the flagstone terrace is very pleasant.

A SIDE-TRIP TO UPPER CANADA VILLAGE

About 50 kilometers (31 miles) east of Brockville along Route 2, **Upper Canada Village,** just east of Morrisburg (☎ **613/543-3704**), is Ontario's answer to Williamsburg, a riverfront community representing Canadian frontier life in the 1860s. Some 40 structures and interiors, restored with painstaking accuracy using hand-forged nails and wooden dowel pegs, appear as if still inhabited. In the woolen mill the waterwheel spins, the old machinery turns, and the wool is woven into soft blankets; the clang of hammer on anvil rings out from the blacksmith's shop, while a heady smell of fresh bread wafts from the bake shop near Willard's Hotel. Stop at the hotel for lunch or dinner. The village artisans, dressed in period costume, operate the 19th-century machinery and will answer any questions you may have. Admission is C$12.50 (US$9) for adults, C$11.50 (US$8) for seniors, C$9 (US$6) for students, C$6 (US$4.30) for children 5 to 12, and C$29 (US$21) for families; children under 6 are free. Open May to Canadian Thanksgiving daily from 9:30am to 5pm.

10 Kingston

About a 2-hour drive from Ottawa and about a 3-hour drive from Toronto (172km/103 miles southwest of Ottawa, 255km/153 miles northeast of Toronto), Kingston stands at the confluence of Lake Ontario, the Rideau Canal, and the St. Lawrence Seaway. This makes for splendid scenery, best viewed by taking a **free ferry trip to Wolfe Island,** the largest of the nearby Thousand Islands. Ferries leave at frequent intervals for this sparsely populated island that doubles as a marvelous, quiet rural retreat. (See "Exploring the Thousand Islands from Kingston," above, for more information.) A stroll along Kingston's waterfront, site of many hotels and restaurants as well as the maritime museum and attractive gardens, is also a must.

Then there's Kingston's history, more than 300 years of it. It lingers on in the fine old limestone public buildings and private residences that line the downtown streets and give the city a gracious air; the martello towers that once formed a string of defense works guarding the waterways along the U.S.-Canadian border; and the Wren-style St. Georges Church, which contains a Tiffany window.

During the summer, **Confederation Park** is the site for band concerts and other performances; during the winter you might catch a local ice-hockey contest. In

Market Square on Tuesday, Thursday, and Saturday, a colorful market is held, and on Sunday it's the place to rummage for antiques.

ESSENTIALS

VISITOR INFORMATION Contact the **Kingston Tourist Information Office,** 209 Ontario St., Kingston, ON, K7L 2Z1 (☎ 613/548-4415).

GETTING THERE If you're driving from Ottawa, take Highway 16S to the 401W and drive to the Kingston exits. Or you can take the more scenic Highway 2 instead of the 401. From Toronto, take the 401E to the Kingston exits.

Several daily **trains** come from Ottawa (☎ 613/244-8289), Toronto (☎ 416/366-8411), and Montréal (☎ 514/989-2626) to Kingston.

EXPLORING THE TOWN

The best way to explore Kingston is aboard the **tour trolley** that leaves from in front of the Kingston Tourist Information Office, on the waterfront across from the City Hall, every hour on the hour from May to September between 10am and 5pm (until 7pm in July and August). The tour lasts 50 minutes and costs C$8 (US$6) for adults and C$6 (US$4.30) for seniors and youths.

Fort Henry. On Hwy. 2, just east of Kingston. ☎ 613/542-7388. Admission C$8.75 (US$6) adults, C$4.65 (US$3.30) children 5–16. Mid-May to Sept daily 10am–5pm.

Fort Henry broods above the town on a high promontory, eerily unchanged since it was rebuilt in the 1830s (it was originally built in 1812). Here, all summer long the Fort Henry Guard, complete with their goat mascot named David, perform 19th-century drills, musters, and parades. Regular programming includes a music and marching display by the fife-and-drum band, an exhibition of infantry drill, and a mock battle with artillery support, all brought to a close with the firing of the garrison artillery and the lowering of the Union Jack. Part of the fort—officers' quarters, men's barracks, kitchens, and artisans' shops—has been restored to show the military way of life circa 1867.

Royal Military College. On Point Frederick. ☎ 613/541-6000, ext. 6652. Free admission. July to Labour Day daily 10am–5pm.

The Royal Military College, Canada's West Point, is also close to the fort. The campus occupies the site of a Royal Navy Dockyard, which played a key role in the War of 1812. Although you can tour the grounds, only the museum, located in a large martello tower, is open to the public. It houses displays about the college's history and Kingston's Royal Dockyard, plus the Douglas collection of small arms and weapons.

Bellevue House. 35 Centre St. ☎ 613/545-8666. Admission C$2.75 (US$1.95) adults, C$2.20 (US$1.55) seniors, C$1.40 (US$1) students and children 6 and over. June 1 to Labour Day daily 9am–6pm; Apr 1–30 and Labour Day to Oct 31 daily 10am–5pm. Closed at other times.

On July 1, 1867, the Canadian Confederation was proclaimed in Kingston's Market Square. The Confederation's chief architect, and Canada's first prime minister, Sir John A. Macdonald, is closely identified with the city of Kingston, his home for most of his life, and he is commemorated in several places. The most notable is Bellevue House, an Italianate villa, jokingly referred to as "Pekoe Pagoda" and "Tea Caddy Castle" by the local citizenry. It has been restored to the period of 1848 to 1849, when Macdonald lived there as a young lawyer and rising member of Parliament.

Agnes Etherington Art Centre. University Ave. at Queen's Crescent. ☎ **613/545-2190.** Free admission. Tues–Fri 10am–5pm, Sat–Sun 1–5pm.

Located on the campus of Queen's University, the Agnes Etherington Art Centre displays a comparatively extensive collection in seven galleries. The collection's emphasis is Canadian, although it also contains European old masters and African sculpture. The center's heart is the original 19th-century home of benefactor Agnes Richardson Etherington (1880–1954) and features three rooms furnished in period style. *Note:* The gallery will be closed for most of 1998 and 1999 for major expansion. It will reopen in 2000.

ON THE WATERFRONT

A great free 30-minute trip can be taken aboard the ferry to **Wolfe Island.**

For serious hiking, the Rideau Trail runs 388 kilometers (241 miles) along the canal from Kingston to Ottawa. For more information, contact the **Rideau Trail Association** (☎ **613/545-0823**).

Kingston is very much a waterfront defense town. Along the waterfront, **Confederation Park** stretches from the front of the old 19th-century town hall down to the magnificent yacht basin, which is worth a look. Within walking distance of the marina is one of the finest martello towers, built during the Oregon Crisis of 1846 to withstand the severest of naval bombardments. The **Murney Tower** (☎ **613/544-9925**) is now a museum where you can see the basement storage rooms, the barrack room, and the gun platform. Open daily from 10am to 5pm from mid-May to Labour Day. Admission is C$2 (US$1.45) for adults; children under 6 are free.

While you're exploring downtown and along the waterfront, visit the **City Hall,** 2162 Ontario St. (☎ **613/546-4291**), where you can take a self-guided tour. If you can't afford the time, at least view the stained-glass windows in Memorial Hall, each one commemorating a World War I battle. Open weekdays only from 8:30am to 4:30pm.

For an understanding of the great shipping days on the Great Lakes, visit the **Marine Museum of the Great Lakes,** 55 Ontario St. (☎ **613/542-2261**), which documents the change from sail in the 17th century to steam in the early 19th century and from the great schooners in the 1870s to today's bulk carriers that still ply the Great Lakes. Other exhibits recapture the area's boat- and shipbuilding industry. Open daily mid-April to mid-December from 10am to 5pm; January to March Monday to Friday from 10am to 4pm. Adults pay C$5.45 (US$3.90) to see the ship and the museum, and students and seniors pay C$4.95 (US$3.55); children under 6 are free.

A SIDE TRIP TO FRONTENAC PROVINCIAL PARK

Frontenac Provincial Park, near Sydenham (☎ **613/376-3489**), is a wilderness park with more than 182 kilometers (113 miles) of hiking trails that explore such intriguing areas as Moulton Gorge, the Arkon Lake bogs, and the Connor-Daly mine.

There's also terrific canoe-camping here. You could combine this adventure with sea kayaking through the Thousand Islands by contacting a local outfitter. All equipment—canoes, kayaks, paddles, life jacket, car-top carrier, tent, sleeping bags, stove, and utensils—is provided for a modest fee, ranging from C$22 to C$26 (US$16 to US$19) per person per day. The trips run from April to November. For information, contact **Frontenac Outfitters** (☎ **613/376-6220** in season or 613/382-1039 off-season).

ACCOMMODATIONS

For B&B accommodations, contact **Kingston Area Bed and Breakfast** (☎ 613/ 542-0214), a reservation service, for a fine selection of homes throughout the area. Rates are C$60 to C$65 (US$43 to US$46) double; children 1 to 10 are charged C$10 (US$7), children 11 and over, C$15 (US$11).

Two chains have commandeered the spectacular position overlooking the harbor— the **Holiday Inn,** 1 Princess St. (☎ 800/549-8400 or 613/549-8400), charging C$155 (US$111) for a double in summer; and the **Howard Johnson's,** 237 Ontario St. (☎ 888/825-4656 or 613/549-6300), charging C$140 to C$160 (US$100 to US$114). Other possibilities are the **Ramada Inn,** 1 Johnson St. (☎ 888/ 548-6726 or 613/549-8100), also on the lakefront, with doubles from C$150 (US$107); or the **Best Western Fireside,** 1217 Princess St. (☎ 800/528-1234 or 613/549-2211), with doubles for C$125 (US$89), and some very popular, fun fantasy suites.

MODERATE

✪ **Hochelaga Inn.** 24 Sydenham St. S., Kingston, ON, K7L 3G9. ☎ and fax **613/549-5534.** 23 rms. A/C TV TEL. C$130–C$175 (US$93–US$125) double. Extra person C$10 (US$7). Rates include breakfast. AE, DC, ER, MC, V.

All rooms are furnished differently in this elegant Victorian home with a charming garden. My favorite is no. 301, an oddly shaped space, with a carved bed set on a diagonal, a large armoire, and a love seat. Three steps lead to a delightful 11-sided tower with windows, and a stepladder goes into a tiny sitting area. Atop the ladder you'll find a futon—you can sleep here under the Gothic windows. Many other rooms are furnished in oak pieces along with wing chairs and brass table lamps. Guests can enjoy the large sitting room, complete with a carved ebony fireplace, or sit on the outdoor veranda, overlooking the gardens.

✪ **Hotel Belvedere.** 141 King St. E., Kingston, ON, K7L 2Z9. ☎ **800/559-0584** or 613/ 548-1565. Fax 613/546-4692. 20 rms. TV TEL. C$109–C$209 (US$78–US$149) double. Rates include continental breakfast. AE, DC, ER, MC, V.

The place to stay in Kingston is the Hotel Belvedere, a carefully restored mansardroofed brick residence. The individually decorated rooms have pleasant sitting areas; most are air-conditioned. Room no. 207 has an art-deco flavor featuring a scalloped-style bed, Madame Récamier sofa, and sideboard, all set on marble floors. In room no. 204 there's a brilliant marine-blue tile fireplace, tasseled curtains, kneehole dresser, and a bed sporting a lace-embroidered coverlet. Guests can relax in the elegant sitting room, with a turquoise marble coal-burning fireplace and tall French windows that open onto a porch prettily decorated with flowers and plants in classical urns.

Queen's Inn. 125 Brock St., Kingston, ON, K7L 1S1. ☎ **613/546-0429.** 17 rms. A/C TV TEL. C$89–C$109 (US$64–US$78) double. Lower rates in winter. Rates include continental breakfast. AE, DC, ER, MC, V.

Downtown the Queen's Inn, in an old three-story stone building, offers nicely decorated rooms that sport light-oak furnishings. For me, the rooms with the most character are on the third floor tucked under the eaves. The Coppers dining room has an outdoor patio; there's also a sports bar with large-screen TV.

INEXPENSIVE

There's also a **Comfort Inn** at 1454 Princess St. (☎ 800/228-5150 or 613/ 549-5550), charging C$105 (US$75) double.

Alexander Henry. 55 Ontario St., Kingston, ON, K7L 2Y2. ☎ **613/542-2261.** Fax 613/542-0043. 19 cabins. C$45–C$65 (US$32–US$46) double; C$70 (US$50) Captain's Cabin. Rates include continental buffet breakfast. AE, MC, V. Closed Oct to mid-May.

You'll find a unique B&B at the Marine Museum aboard the 3,000-ton icebreaker *Alexander Henry.* The accommodations are not exactly roomy, and you may think twice about drinking the water, but it's certainly different. The Captain's Cabin comes with double bed, a desk large enough to spread out navigational charts, a sitting area with a table, and a bathroom with a shower. There are also two twin-bedded rooms aboard.

Donald Gordon Centre. 421 Union St., Kingston, ON, K7L 3N6. ☎ **613/545-2221.** 80 rms. A/C TV TEL. C$85 (US$61) double. AE, MC, V.

Good reasonably priced accommodations can be found at the university's Donald Gordon Centre. All rooms have private bath. The spaces are furnished in typical study-bedroom fashion. Other building facilities include a dining room, a lounge, and a basement bar and game room.

A NEARBY RETREAT ON WOLFE ISLAND

General Wolfe Hotel. Wolfe Island, ON, K0H 2Y0. ☎ **613/385-2611.** Fax 613/385-1038. 6 rms. A/C TV TEL. C$35–C$105 (US$25–US$75) double. AE, MC, V.

This has to be one of the most spectacular values in the region. Located on Wolfe Island, near the ferry docks, it's mainly known for its dining room but also rents rooms. A small room furnished with a double bed, side table, chair, and TV rents for C$35 (US$25)! A suite containing a double and single bed and a sitting room equipped with refrigerator goes for C$75 (US$61), while a two-room suite accommodating six tops out at C$105 (US$75).

The dining rooms afford views of the ferry landing and waterfront—great for sunset viewing. The food is continental—say, pheasant bourguignonne or salmon Wellington—and very reasonably priced. Open mid-May to Labour Day daily for lunch and dinner; at other times the restaurant closes Monday. In winter when the river is frozen (from January to early April), the owners operate a shuttle to Dawson's Point connecting to the mainland. There's also a cocktail lounge with dancing on weekends.

DINING

Another top choice for dining is the General Wolfe Hotel (see above).

✪ **Chez Piggy.** 68R Princess St. ☎ **613/549-7673.** Reservations recommended on weekends. Main courses C$10–C$22 (US$7–US$16). AE, DC, MC, V. Mon–Fri 11:30am–2pm, Sat 11:30am–2:30pm, Sun 11am–2:30pm; Mon–Sat 5:30–10pm. CONTINENTAL/ECLECTIC.

Just off Princess Street, in a complex of renovated buildings, you'll find Chez Piggy occupying an 1820s building that probably once was a stable. In front there's a paved courtyard where you can sit outdoors. Inside, there's a long bar with brown high director's chairs, and a dining room enhanced by two glorious Tunisian rugs. The small menu might feature seven or so dinner entrees plus daily specials. Try the saffron chicken breast with pine nuts served with couscous and harissa, or the rack leg of lamb with coulis of carrot and beet, or any one of the pastas (linguini with smoked salmon, for example). To begin, there are several salads and such dishes as mussels piri piri (steamed with Portuguese lemon-chili oil) or Stilton pâté. Brunch dishes, most under C$10 (US$7), are interesting and different—teriyaki chicken breast or liver with bacon, onion confit, and home fries.

Gencarelli. 629 Princess St. ☎ **613/542-7976.** Reservations recommended. Pasta courses under $13 (US$9); main courses C$11–C$36 (US$8–$26). AE, MC, V. Mon–Sat 11am–2pm and 4–10:30pm, Sun 4–9pm. ITALIAN.

A local favorite for years, Gencarelli continues to serve good Italian food in an intimate series of dining rooms. Pastas like fettuccine, tortellini, and rigatoni can be married to a sauce of your choice, or you can select such dishes as cannelloni parmigiana or lasagna al forno, including a salad. The C$36 (US$26) dish is two lobster tails. The dessert specialty is the chocolate-amaretto cheesecake.

Kingston Brewing Company. 34 Clarence St. ☎ **613/542-4978.** Burgers, sandwiches, and main courses under C$10 (US$7). AE, DC, ER, MC, V. Mon–Sat 11am–1am, Sun 11:30am–1am. LIGHT FARE.

At the Kingston Brewing Company, you can peer behind the bar and view the huge brewing tanks. Beer, several ales, and a pleasant lager are brewed without chemicals and other substances that adulterate modern mass-produced beers. The most famous of the brews is Dragon's Breath ale, a dark rich ale. Locals come here for the charbroiled ghetto chicken wings served with a spicy barbecue sauce and the smoked beef and ribs plus typical bar fare. It's either served inside at polished wood tables or in the back courtyard garden or sidewalk patio.

11 Quinte's Isle

Prince Edward County, an island surrounded by Lake Ontario and the Bay of Quinte, has retained much of its early character and its relaxed pace. It's 265 kilometers (157 miles) southwest of Ottawa and was settled by United Empire Loyalists in the 1780s, and many of their descendants still live, work, and farm here. Their solid attachment to the past shows in the quiet streets of such historic towns and villages as Picton, Bloomfield, and Wellington.

ESSENTIALS

VISITOR INFORMATION Contact the **Prince Edward County Chamber of Tourism & Commerce,** 116 Main St. (P.O. Box 50), Picton, ON, K0K 2T0 (☎ 613/476-2421).

GETTING THERE If you're driving from Trenton, take Highway 33S; from Belleville, Highway 62S off the 401; and from Kingston, Highway 49S off the 401.

WELLINGTON & BLOOMFIELD

Drive through **Wellington** and you can't help but notice how well kept the houses and their gardens are. You'll feel like you're in an English village.

Bloomfield, settled in the early 1800s, has been strongly influenced by the Methodists and the Quakers. The latter were harassed in their native New York for their pacifism during the American Revolution, and fled to Canada with the Loyalists. Two Quaker cemeteries in town are part of that legacy. Today this pretty town has become a haven for retirees, artists, and craftspeople. You'll find several potteries, craft shops, and antique stores, including **Bloomfield Pottery,** at 274 Main St. (☎ 613/ 393-3258), and the **Village Art Gallery,** at 313 Main St. (☎ 613/393-2943).

ACCOMMODATIONS

In Wellington

Tara Hall. 146 Main St., Wellington, ON, K0K 3L0. ☎ **613/399-2801.** Fax 613/399-1104. 4 rms. A/C TV. C$75 (US$54) double. Extra person C$24 (US$17). Rates include breakfast. V. Free parking.

Tara Hall is a landmark 1839 home built by a wealthy local merchant. Originally the whole upper front floor served as a ballroom; today it has been divided into three guest rooms. Each room is furnished pleasantly with some antiques. A full and formal breakfast is served, the table set with linen. No smoking.

In Bloomfield

Cornelius White House. 8 Wellington St., Bloomfield, ON, K0K 1G0. ☎ **613/393-2282.** 3 rms (1 with bath), 2 suites (both with bath). A/C. C$55–C$85 (US$39–US$61) double. Extra person in suite C$15 (US$11). Rates include breakfast. V.

This 19th-century redbrick house offers a lovely view over meadows dotted with Holsteins. There are two doubles, a twin, and two suites, each furnished differently. One has an iron-and-brass bed; another is furnished in pine (rocker, dresser, bed, and chest). A full breakfast (or continental, if you prefer) is served in the 1867 dining room, which has wide pine floors and a brick fireplace. Guests also have use of a comfortable sitting room. A cottage is also available with a small kitchen.

✪ **Mallory House.** RR #1, Bloomfield, ON, K0K 1G0. ☎ **613/393-3458.** 3 rms (none with bath). C$60 (US$43) double. Rates include full breakfast. No credit cards.

Mallory House offers three really appealing accommodations sharing 1 1/2 baths in an old 1810/1850 farmhouse. One is furnished with a brass bed and marble-top dresser, another has twin brass beds, and the third has a mahogany four-poster and marble-top dresser among the furnishings. The bathroom features an old-fashioned tub. Two sitting rooms are available to guests, both very comfortably furnished with antiques, Oriental rugs, good books, and a marble fireplace. The house is surrounded by lawns, shrubs, trees, and flower gardens. It's a really fine accommodation and a great value, watched over by Hobbes, the black mutt, and two old cats.

DINING

In Bloomfield

✪ **Angelines.** In the Bloomfield Inn, 29 Stanley St. W. ☎ **613/393-3301.** Reservations recommended. Main courses C$12–C$25 (US$9–US$18). MC, V. June–Sept daily 5:30–9pm; Sun only 11:30am–2pm. Oct–May Thurs–Sun 5:30–9pm. CONTINENTAL.

The Bloomfield Inn is mainly known for its restaurant, Angelines, which is operated by a young Austrian chef and located in an 1869 house. Umbrellaed tables are on the lawn out front. The cuisine is seasonal and the chef grows his own herbs. Dinner entrees might include beef tenderloin with a red-pepper coulis sauce, roasted rabbit in a creamy olive sauce, and trout served with a bouillabaisse-style broth; there are always several vegetarian dishes offered along with prix-fixe menus. Afternoon teas are also served; it's then that the chef, who specializes in pastries, really comes into his own, offering Sacher torte and other fine Austrian pastries and tortes.

FROM BLOOMFIELD TO PICTON-GLENORA

Picton is the hub and county town of Prince Edward County. East of the town lies the mysterious **Lake on the Mountain,** a small clear lake 200 feet above Lake Ontario. From one side of the escarpment there's a fabulous view of the ferry crossing Picton Bay, water, and islands stretching into infinity. It's a great place for a picnic. The Lake on the Mountain was called Lake of the Gods by the Mohawks. Nobody has as yet discovered the source of this lake set atop a mountain. Is it an ancient volcanic crater, a meteorite hole, a sinkhole caused by rain, or what?

The other major attraction, 11 miles west of Picton, is **Sandbanks and North Beach Provincial Parks.** Sandbanks Park has some of the highest (more than 80 ft.) freshwater dunes anywhere—a spectacular sight. Consisting of two dune systems linked by fields and woods, it also fosters diverse plant and animal life. Some of the more unusual plants are bluets, hoary puccoon, butterfly weed, sea rocket, and spurge. Among the bird species that have been recorded here are the long-billed marsh wren, pileated woodpecker, northern oriole ruby, and golden crowned kinglets; the best time to spot birds is spring and fall.

The park has prime sandy beaches and facilities for swimming, windsurfing, sailing, canoeing, and boating (rentals available). There are several self-guided nature trails in the park. Camping (549 sites) is available in four areas for C$18.15 to C$21 (US$13 to US$15) per day. Entry to the park is C$8 (US$6) per vehicle. Park officials begin taking reservations April 1. Open from May to October. For information, call headquarters at ☎ 613/393-3319.

The **Black River Cheese Company** is 13 kilometers (8 miles) southeast of Picton outside Milford on County Road 13 (☎ **613/476-2575**). Stop for the cheese—and the rich ice cream. Open daily from 9am to 5pm.

The best way off Quinte's Isle is to take the rewarding 15-minute ferry trip from Glenora across to Adolphustown. The ferry operates every 15 minutes in summer, less frequently in winter, and has been operating since settlement began.

ACCOMMODATIONS

Isaiah Tubbs Resort. RR #1, Picton, ON, K0K 2T0. ☎ **800/724-2393** or 613/393-2090. Fax 613/393-1291. 630 rms. A/C TV TEL. C$110–C$145 (US$79–US$104) double; C$175–C$195 (US$125–US$139) kitchenette suite; C$195–C$210 (US$139–US$150) Jacuzzi suite. Lakeside cabin C$900–C$1,000 (US$643–US$714) per week. AE, ER, MC, V.

This miniresort spread over 30 acres on West Lake offers very attractive accommodations. The Carriage House rooms, located in the original building's oldest part, have kitchenettes, comfy pine furnishings (including rockers and tables), original beamed ceilings, brick fireplaces, and microwaves. Upstairs there's a sleeping loft furnished with bunk beds, TV, and shower. Standard rooms, with sloping ceilings, are furnished in Ethan Allen country style. Two lodges each feature a living room with fieldstone fireplace and two bedrooms, one upstairs with skylights and a Jacuzzi tub. Some have sunporches. Facilities include outdoor and indoor pools, two tennis courts, a beach, windsurfing equipment and lessons, canoes and paddleboats, bike rentals, and nature trails.

Merrill Inn. 343 Main St. E., Picton, ON, K0K 2T0. ☎ **613/476-7451.** 14 rms. A/C TV TEL. C$95–C$135 (US$68–US$96) double. Extra person C$10 (US$7). Rates include continental breakfast. AE, ER, MC, V.

The rooms at the Merrill Inn are individually decorated with antiques. Room no. 101, for example, features a high-back Victorian bed, wing chairs, and bay windows. One room has a Jacuzzi, another a fireplace. There's a comfortable sitting room, a pub serving eight beers on tap plus pub fare (shepherd's pie, bangers and mash) and more elaborate dishes like poached salmon with dill cream or mussels Provençale. Facilities include a barbecue area and a sunporch.

DINING

Waring House Restaurant. Hwy. 33, just west of Picton. ☎ **613/476-7492.** Reservations recommended. Main courses C$11–C$29 (US$8–US$21). MC, V. Summer daily 11am–2pm and 5–9:30pm; winter usually Tues–Sun 11:30am–2pm and 5–9pm. CONTINENTAL.

The Waring House Restaurant is located in an old stone house surrounded by pretty shrubbery. Pine floors, archival photographs, and other regional memorabilia set the country tone. The menu features local produce as much as possible—rosemary garlic lamb, Cajun chicken with a tangy Dijon Apricot sauce, and a pasta of the day. The inviting pub has a big brick-and-beam fireplace.

12 Port Hope, Presqu'île Provincial Park & Trenton

If you're driving from Ottawa, take Highway 16 south to 401 west, which will bring you to the attractive old lakefront town of Port Hope, where antique stores line the main street. It's situated at the mouth of the Ganaraska River, 72 miles east of Toronto. From Toronto, take 401 east.

If you'd like to stay in Port Hope, **The Carlyle,** 86 John St. (☎ 905/885-8686), occupies the old 1857 Bank of Upper Canada building. Rates are C$95 (US$68) for doubles and C$135 (US$96) for suites. Some rooms are also located in a building behind the bank; these have fireplaces and rent for C$125 (US$89). The dining room, open daily for lunch and dinner, offers casual, moderately priced food—lasagna, burgers, chicken Kiev, and seafood dishes.

Sixty-five kilometers (40 miles) east of Port Hope lies Trenton, the starting point for the **Trent-Severn Canal,** a 386-kilometer-long (240-mile-long) waterway that travels northeast via 44 locks to Georgian Bay on Lake Huron. It is also the western entrance to the Loyalist Parkway (Highway 33), leading to Quinte's Isle.

Halfway between Port Hope and Trenton on Highway 401 is Brighton, the gateway town to **Presqu'île Provincial Park.** This 2,000-acre area of marsh and woodland offers superb **bird watching** (attracting birds from both the Atlantic and Mississippi flyways), camping, and a mile-long beach. Major bird-watching weekends are organized in spring and fall. The visitor center is open from Victoria Day to Labour Day. For information, call the headquarters at ☎ 613/475-2204. Admission is C$7 (US$5) per car.

Serpent Mounds Park, RR #3 (☎ 705/295-6879), is in Keene, which can be reached by driving north from Port Hope on Highway 28. The park has 120 campsites and offers swimming and self-guided nature trails. The name comes from the Indian burial mounds it contains—one is shaped like a serpent. Admission is C$6 (US$4.30) per car.

Farther north on Route 28 is **Peterborough,** which is at the center of the Kawartha lakes—the series of lakes connected by the Trent-Severn Waterway from Trent to Georgian Bay. Here you can watch the boats traveling through the locks and being lifted 62 feet from one water level to another at the **visitor center** (☎ 705/750-4900) on the waterway on Hunter Street East.

Continuing northeast on Highway 28 from Peterborough, you'll come to Stony Lake, where you'll discover, at its eastern end (on Northey's Bay Road) near the town of Stonyridge, **Petroglyphs Provincial Park** (☎ 705/877-2552). Although the hiking trails, two lakes, and forests are appealing, the petroglyphs themselves—hundreds of symbolic shapes and figures—attract visitors. To this day, some members of the Ojibwa Anishinabe Nation revere this as a sacred site. It's believed that these petroglyphs were carved by an Algonquin-speaking people between 6,500 and 1,100 years ago. About 300 distinct carvings have been identified alongside 600 indecipherable figures. The park also has several short hiking trails and picnic areas. Open from 10am to 5pm from the second Friday in May to Canadian Thanksgiving. Admission is C$7 (US$5) per car.

12 Toronto & the Golden Horseshoe

by Marilyn Wood

Once lampooned as a dull and ugly city, Toronto, now with a metropolitan population of 4.6 million, has burst forth from its stodgy past and grabbed attention as one of North America's most exciting cities.

How did it happen? Unlike most cities, Toronto got a second chance to change its image with a substantial blood transfusion from other cultures. A post–World War II influx of large numbers of Italians, Chinese, and Portuguese, plus Germans, Jews, Hungarians, Greeks, Indians, West Indians, Vietnamese, Thais, and French Canadians, infused this once-conservative community with new energy. Now Toronto vibrates with street cafes, restaurants, cabarets, boutiques, theater, music, noise, and life.

The city continues to grow rapidly and has blossomed with major developments— from theaters and concert halls to sports stadiums and major downtown projects like the BCE building, the Canadian Broadcasting complex, and the planned basketball facility for the Raptors. With the victory of a conservative provincial government in the last election, however, this explosive growth has slowed and health and other social services have been severely curtailed by cost-cutting and downsizing. Already there are signs of how this parsimony is affecting urban life. The streets are looking shabbier than they ever used to and panhandling is common.

Until now, Toronto has always managed to preserve its past while building a new future, as illustrated by Holy Trinity Church and Scadding House, one of the city's oldest residences, standing proudly against the futuristic Eaton Centre.

In Toronto, people walk to work from their restored Victorian town houses, no developer can erect downtown commercial space without including living space, the subway gleams, and the streets are safe. Here old buildings are saved and converted to other uses, and architects design around the contours of nature instead of just bulldozing the trees. It is a city created not only with flair and imagination, but also a sense of traditional values. It's not surprising that *Fortune Magazine* recently voted it the best place in the world to work and raise a family.

At the end of this chapter, we cover our favorite parts of the stretch of the Ontario lakefront that is often called the Golden Horseshoe. *Golden* because the communities along the lake are wealthy, *horseshoe* because of its shape, this stretch of the Ontario lakefront from Niagara-on-the-Lake to Toronto offers the visitor some golden opportunities: **Niagara Falls** itself; **Niagara-on-the-Lake,** home of the famous Shaw Festival; the **Welland Canal,** an engineering wonder; Niagara **wineries;** and Dundurn Castle and Royal Botanical Gardens in Canada's steel town of **Hamilton.** Niagara Falls, Niagara-on-the-Lake, St. Catharines to Port Colborne, and Hamilton can be visited together. The best way to see them is to take the Niagara Parkway from Niagara-on-the-Lake to Niagara Falls and then drive to Port Colborne on Lake Erie and follow the Welland Canal north to Port Dalhousie on Lake Ontario. Although this is, for the most part, a densely populated area with a tangled network of roads, there are several scenic routes: the parkway and the Wine Route, which takes you from Stoney Creek to Niagara Falls.

1 Orientation

ARRIVING

BY PLANE   More than 20 major airlines serve Toronto, with regularly scheduled flights departing and arriving at **Pearson International Airport,** in the northwest corner of metropolitan Toronto, about 30 minutes from downtown.

The most spectacular of the three terminals is the Trillium Terminal 3 (☎ 905/612-5100), used by American, Canadian Airlines, British Airways, Air France, Alitalia, KLM, and most of United's flights. This supermodern facility has moving walkways, a huge food court, and hundreds of stores. Airport facilities include the exceptionally useful Transport Canada Information centers in all terminals, where a staff fluent in 10 languages will answer questions about the airport, airline information, transportation services, and tourist attractions (☎ **905/676-3506**).

Here are a few useful airline reservation numbers: **Air Canada** (☎ 800/776-3000); **US Airways** (☎ 800/428-4322); **American Airlines** (☎ 800/433-7300); **Canadian Airlines** (☎ 800/426-7000); **Delta Airlines** (☎ 800/221-1212); **United Airlines** (☎ 800/241-6522); and **Northwest Airlines** (☎ 800/225-2525, or 800/444-4747 for international).

To get from the airport to downtown, take Highway 427 south to the Gardiner Expressway East. A taxi along this route will cost about C\$40 (US\$29). A slightly sleeker way to go is by flat-rate limousine, which will cost C\$36.50 to C\$38 (US\$26 to US\$27). Two limo services are **Aaroport** (☎ 416/745-1555) and **AirLine** (☎ 905/676-3210). Also very convenient is the **Airport Express** bus (☎ 905/564-6333), which travels between the airport, the bus terminal, and all major downtown hotels—Harbour Castle Westin, the Royal York, Crown Plaza Toronto Centre, the Sheraton Centre, and the Delta Chelsea Inn—every 20 minutes all day. The adult fare is C\$12.50 (US\$9) one-way, C\$21.50 (US\$15) round-trip; the service is free for children under 11 accompanied by an adult. In addition, most first-class hotels run their own hotel limousine services, so check when you make your reservation.

The cheapest way to go is by subway and bus, which will take about an hour. The **TTC** has an airport bus (#58A) traveling between the Lawrence West subway station and Terminal Two at Pearson airport for a total fare of C\$4 (US\$2.85), C\$2 of which is a supplement due at the airport. For more information, call ☎ **416/393-4636.**

BY CAR   From the United States you are most likely to enter Toronto via Highway 401, or via Highway 2 and the Queen Elizabeth Way if you come from the west. If you come from the east via Montréal, you'll also use highways 401 and 2.

Here are a few approximate driving distances to Toronto: from Boston, 566km (340 miles); from Buffalo, 96km (58 miles); from Chicago, 534km (320 miles); from

Metropolitan Toronto

Cincinnati, 501km (301 miles); from Detroit, 236km (142 miles); from Minneapolis, 972km (583 miles); and from New York, 495km (297 miles).

BY TRAIN   Both **VIA Rail's** and Amtrak's passenger trains pull into the massive, classically proportioned Union Station on Front Street, 1 block west of Yonge opposite the Royal York Hotel. The station has direct access to the subway so you can easily reach any Toronto destination from here. For **VIA Rail** information, call ☎ **416/366-8411;** in the United States, call your travel agent or **Amtrak** at ☎ **800/ 872-7245.**

BY BUS   Out-of-town buses arrive and depart from the Metro Toronto Coach Terminal, 610 Bay St., at Dundas Street, and provide frequent and efficient service from Canadian and American destinations. **Greyhound** (☎ **800/231-2222**) services Buffalo, Niagara Falls, Windsor, Detroit, Ottawa, and Western Canada; Trentway-Wagar (☎ **416/393-7911**) travels west from Montréal and Québec, and **Ontario Northland** (☎ **416/393-7911**) has service from towns such as North Bay and Timmins.

VISITOR INFORMATION

Contact **Tourism Toronto,** 207 Queen's Quay W., Suite 509, in the Queen's Quay Terminal at Harbourfront (P.O. Box 126), Toronto, ON, M5J 1A7 (☎ **800/ 363-1990** or 416/203-2600); open Monday to Friday from 9am to 5pm. Take the Harbourfront LRT down to the terminal building. There's also an information center in the Metro Toronto Convention Centre at 255 Front St. W. You can also check out Tourism Toronto's Web site at **www.tourism-toronto.com**; their e-mail address is mtcvaadm@pathcom.com.

More conveniently located is the drop-in Travel Ontario Visitor Information Centre, in the Eaton Centre on Yonge Street at Dundas. It's located on Level 1 and is open year-round Monday to Friday from 10am to 9pm, Saturday from 9am to 6pm, and Sunday from noon to 5pm. It has city and Ontario travel information.

You can also contact **Ontario Travel,** Queen's Park, Toronto, ON, M7A 2R9 (☎ **800/ONTARIO** or 416/314-0944).

CITY LAYOUT

MAIN STREETS & ARTERIES   Toronto is laid out in a grid system. Yonge Street (pronounced "Young") is the main south-north street, stretching from Lake Ontario in the south to well beyond Highway 401 in the north (it's the longest street in the world); the main east-west artery is Bloor Street, which cuts right through the heart of downtown. Yonge Street divides western cross streets from eastern cross streets.

Downtown usually refers to the area stretching south from Eglinton Avenue to the lake between Spadina Avenue in the west and Jarvis Street in the east. I have divided this large area into downtown (from the lake to College/Carlton streets), midtown (College/Carlton streets to Davenport Road), and uptown (north from Davenport Road). In the first you will find all the lakeshore attractions—Harbourfront, Ontario Place, Fort York, Exhibition Place, the Toronto Islands—plus the CN Tower, City Hall, SkyDome, Chinatown, the Art Gallery, and Eaton Centre. Midtown includes the Royal Ontario Museum, the University of Toronto, Markham Village, and chic Yorkville, a prime place to browse and dine alfresco. Uptown is a fast-growing residential and entertainment area for the young, hip, and well-heeled.

Because metropolitan Toronto is spread over 634 square kilometers (255 sq. miles) and includes East York and the cities of (from west to east) Etobicoke, York, North York, and Scarborough, some primary attractions exist outside the central core, such as the Ontario Science Centre, the Metropolitan Zoo, and Canada's Wonderland—so be prepared to journey somewhat.

UNDERGROUND TORONTO   It is not enough to know Toronto's streets; you also need to know the warren of subterranean walkways that enable you to go from Union Station to Atrium on Bay at Dundas. Currently, you can walk from Yonge and Queen Street Station west to the Sheraton Centre, then south through the Richmond-Adelaide Centre, First Canadian Place, and Toronto Dominion Centre all the way (through the dramatic Royal Bank Plaza) to Union Station. En route, branches lead off to the Stock Exchange, Sun Life Centre, and Metro Hall. Additional passageways link Simcoe Plaza to 200 Wellington West and to the CBC Broadcast Centre. Other walkways exist around Bloor and Yonge, and elsewhere in the city (ask for a map of these at the tourist information office). So if the weather's bad, you can eat, sleep, dance, and go to the theater without even donning a raincoat.

2 Getting Around

BY PUBLIC TRANSPORTATION

The **Toronto Transit Commission** (TTC) operates public transit, an overall interconnecting subway, bus, and streetcar system (☎ **416/393-4636** from 7am to 10pm for information). For adults, fares (including transfers to buses or streetcars) are C$2 (US$1.45) for one token and C$8 (US$6) for five; for students and seniors, fares are C$1.35 (US95¢) for one token and C$10.70 (US$8) for 10; for children 2 to 12, fares are C50¢ (US35¢) for one token and C$4 (US$2.85) for 10. You can purchase from any subway collector a special C$6.50 (US$4.65) pass good for unlimited travel for one person after 9:30am weekdays, and good for up to six persons anytime Saturday, Sunday, and holidays (maximum of two adults). To use surface transportation, you need a ticket, a token, or exact change. Tickets and tokens may be obtained at subway entrances or stores that display the sign TTC TICKETS MAY BE PURCHASED HERE.

BY SUBWAY   It's a joy to ride—fast, quiet, and sparkling clean. It's a very simple system to use, designed basically in the form of a cross: The Bloor Street east-west line runs from Kipling Avenue in the west to Kennedy Road in the east, where it connects with Scarborough Rapid Transit traveling from Scarborough Centre to McCowan. The Yonge Street north-south line runs from Finch Avenue in the north to Union Station (Front Street) in the south. From here, it loops north along University Avenue and connects with the Bloor line at the St. George Station. A Spadina extension runs north from St. George to Wilson. The subway operates from 6am to 1:30am Monday to Saturday and on Sunday from 9am to 1:30am. For route information, pick up a *Ride Guide* at subway entrances or call ☎ **416/393-4636.**

A Light Rapid Transit connects downtown to Harbourfront. It operates from Union Station along Queen's Quay to Spadina, stopping at Queen's Quay ferry docks, York Street, Simcoe Street, and Rees Street, and then continuing up Spadina to the Spadina/Bloor subway station. A transfer is not required, as the LRT links up underground with the Yonge-University subway line.

Smart commuters (and visitors!) park their cars for a low all-day parking fee at subway terminal stations—Kipling, Islington, Finch, Wilson, Warden, Kennedy, and McCowan; or at smaller lots at Sheppard, York Mills, Eglinton, Victoria Park, and Keele. You'll have to get there early, though.

BY BUS & STREETCAR   Where the subway leaves off, buses and streetcars take over to carry you east-west or north-south along the city's arteries. When you pay your fare (on streetcar, bus, or subway) always pick up a transfer—if you want to transfer to another mode of transportation, you won't have to pay another fare.

BY TAXI

As usual, taxis are an expensive mode of transportation: C$2.50 (US$1.80) the minute you step in and then C25¢ (US18¢) for each additional 0.275 kilometers. These fares mount up, especially in rush hours. Nevertheless, here are the major companies: **Diamond** (☎ 416/366-6868), **Yellow** (☎ 416/504-4141), and **Metro** (☎ 416/504-8294).

BY CAR

The Canadian Automobile Association (CAA), 60 Commerce Valley Dr. E., Thornhill (☎ 905/771-3111), provides aid to any driver who is a member of AAA.

RENTALS   You can rent cars from any of the major companies at the airport. In addition, **Budget** has a convenient location at 141 Bay St. (☎ 416/364-7104), and **Tilden** is at 930 Yonge St. (☎ 416/925-4551).

PARKING   Parking costs are extremely high, and metered street parking is only allowed for short periods. Parking downtown runs about C$4 (US$2.85) per half hour, with C$15 to C$18 (US$11 to US$13) maximum. After 6pm and on Sunday, rates go down to C$6 (US$4.30) or thereabouts. Generally, the city-owned lots, marked with a big green *P,* are slightly cheaper. Observe the parking restrictions— the city will tow your car away.

DRIVING RULES   You can turn right on a red light after coming to a full stop and checking the intersection, but watch out for signs forbidding such turns at specific intersections. Watch carefully also for one-way streets and no-left- and no-right-turn signs. The driver and front-seat passenger must wear their seat belts or, if caught, pay a substantial fine. The speed limit within the city is 50 kilometers per hour (30 m.p.h.). You must stop at pedestrian crosswalks. If you are following a streetcar and it stops, you must stop well back from the rear doors so that passengers can exit easily and safely. (Where there are concrete safety islands in the middle of the street for streetcar stops, this rule does not apply, but still, exercise care.)

FAST FACTS: Toronto

Area Code   Toronto's area code is **416;** outside the new city limits (including Mississauga), the area code is **905.**

Dentist   For emergency dental services, call ☎ 416/485-7121 or call the **Royal College of Dental Surgeons** ☎ 416/961-6555 for a referral.

Doctor   The College of Physicians and Surgeons, 80 College St. (☎ 416/ 961-1711), operates a referral service from 9am to 5pm.

Drugstores (Late-Night Pharmacies)   **Shoppers Drug Mart,** 360 Bloor St. W., at Spadina Avenue (☎ 416/961-2121), stays open daily until midnight. They operate many other branches downtown. The other big chain is **PharmaPlus,** with a store at 68 Wellesley St., at Church Street (☎ 416/924-7760), that's open daily from 8am to midnight.

Embassies & Consulates   While all embassies are in Ottawa, many nations maintain consulates in Toronto, including the following: **Australian Consulate-General,** 175 Bloor St. E., Suite 314, at Church Street. (☎ 416/323-1155);

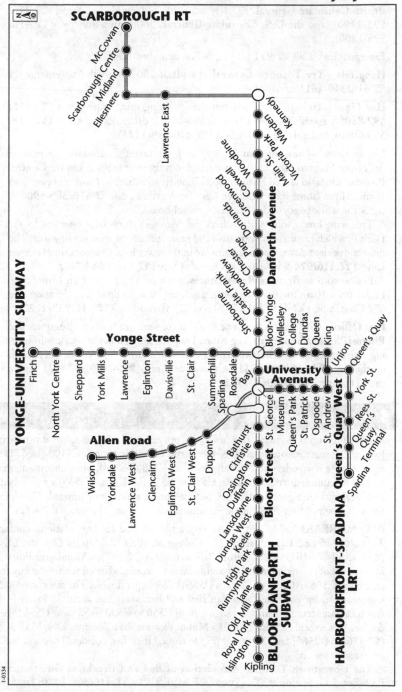

SCARBOROUGH RT

McCowan
Scarborough Centre
Midland
Ellesmere
Lawrence East
Kennedy

Warden
Victoria Park
Main St.
Woodbine
Coxwell
Greenwood
Donlands
Pape
Chester
Broadview
Castle Frank
Sherbourne

Danforth Avenue

YONGE-UNIVERSITY SUBWAY

Yonge Street

Finch
North York Centre
Sheppard
York Mills
Lawrence
Eglinton
Davisville
St. Clair
Summerhill
Rosedale
Bay
Spadina

Bloor-Yonge
Wellesley
College
Dundas
Queen
King
Union
Queen's Quay

University Avenue

St. George
Museum
Queen's Park
St. Patrick
Osgoode
St. Andrew

Queen's Quay
King St.
Queen's St.
Queen's Quay
Spadina Terminal

Allen Road

Wilson
Yorkdale
Lawrence West
Glencairn
Eglinton West
St. Clair West
Dupont
Bathurst
Christie
Ossington
Dufferin
Lansdowne
Dundas West
Keele
High Park
Runnymede
Jane
Old Mill
Royal York
Islington
Kipling

Bloor Street

BLOOR-DANFORTH SUBWAY

HARBOURFRONT-SPADINA LRT

Queen's Quay West

T-0334

British Consulate-General, 777 Bay St., Suite 2800, at College Street (☎ 416/593-1290); and the **U.S. Consulate-General,** 360 University Ave. (☎ 416/595-1700).

Emergencies Call ☎ **911** for fire, police, or ambulance.

Hospitals Try **Toronto General Hospital,** 200 Elizabeth St. (emergency ☎ **416/340-4611** or 416/340-4800).

Hot Lines Help is available from the following lines: **rape crisis** (☎ **416/597-8808**), **assault victims** (☎ **416/863-0511**), **drug/alcohol crisis** (☎ **416/595-6000**), and **suicide prevention** (☎ **416/598-1121**).

Liquor Laws The minimum drinking age is 19 and public drinking is permitted daily from 11am to 2am. Liquor, wine, and some beers are sold at **Liquor Control Board of Ontario** (LCBO) stores, open Monday to Saturday. Most are open from 10am to 6pm (some stay open evenings). For locations, call ☎ **416/365-5900** or check the white pages under "Liquor Control Board."

True wine lovers will want to check out **Vintages** stores (also operated by the LCBO), which carry a more extensive and more specialized selection of wines. The most convenient downtown locations are in the lower level concourse of Hazelton Lanes (☎ **416/924-9463**) and at Queen's Quay (☎ **416/864-6777**).

Beer is sold at **Brewers Retail Stores,** most of which are open Monday to Friday from 10am to 10pm and Saturday from 10am to 8pm. Two locations are 572 Church St. (☎ **416/921-6036**) and 227 Gerrard St. (☎ **416/923-2122**).

Post Office Postal services can be found at convenience stores or drugstores like **PharmaPlus** or **Shopper's Drug Mart.** Look for the sign in the window indicating such services. Post office windows are also open throughout the city in Atrium on the Bay (☎ **416/506-0911**), Commerce Court (☎ **416/956-7452**), and at the TD center (☎ **416/360-7105**).

3 Accommodations

Although Toronto has many fine hotels, it's not easy to find good values downtown. Even at the more moderate establishments you can expect to pay C$100 (US$71) a night. Only a few budget hotels charge less than C$90 (US$64), while unconventional options like university dorms start at C$45 to C$50 (US$32 to US$35) a night. Bed-and-breakfasts are a good budget bet, but their prices are creeping upward. The situation is not helped by a 5% Ontario accommodations tax and the national 7% GST.

BED & BREAKFASTS For interesting, truly personal accommodations, contact **Toronto Bed and Breakfast,** at 253 College St. (P.O. Box 269), Toronto, ON, M5T 1R5 (☎ **416/588-8800** from 9am to noon and 2 to 7pm Monday to Friday), for their list of homes offering bed-and-breakfast accommodations within the city for an average C$65 to C$90 (US$46 to US$64) a night per double. The association will reserve rooms for you. **Metropolitan Bed and Breakfast** lists about 25 lovely bed-and-breakfast accommodations, ranging from C$50 to C$90 (US$36 to US$64) per double. Write them at Suite 269, 615 Mount Pleasant Rd., Toronto, ON, M4S 3C5 (☎ **416/964-2566;** fax 416/960-9529) to request their free booklet. They will make reservations for you.

The Downtown Toronto Association of Bed and Breakfast Guesthouses, P.O. Box 190, Station B, Toronto, ON, M5T 2W1 (☎ **416/368-1420;** fax 416/368-1653) represents about 30 no-smoking B&Bs, with room prices ranging from C$60 to C$85 (US$43 to US$61) per double. The best time to call is between 8:30am and 7pm.

Bed and Breakfast Homes of Toronto, Box 46093, College Park Post Office, 444 Yonge St., Toronto, ON, M5B 2L8 (☎ **416/363-6362**), is a cooperative of about 18 independent B&B operators offering rooms from C$60 to C$135 (US$43 to US$96) per double.

DOWNTOWN

The downtown area runs from the lakefront to College/Carlton streets between Spadina and Jarvis.

Note: See the "Downtown Toronto" map (p. 396) to locate hotels in this section.

VERY EXPENSIVE

King Edward Hotel. 37 King St. E., Toronto, ON, M5C 2E9. ☎ **416/863-9700.** Fax 416/367-5515. 315 rms and suites. A/C MINIBAR TV TEL. C$195–C$330 (US$139–US$236) double; from C$385 (US$275) suite. Weekend packages available. AE, CB, DC, ER, MC, V. Parking C$24 (US$17). Subway: King.

In its heyday, The King Eddy, as this hotel is affectionately known, welcomed the Prince of Wales (later Edward VIII), hosted a dinner for Cecil B. DeMille that transformed the Crystal Ballroom into a 15th-century castle complete with moat, and attracted anybody who was anybody. Today, this vintage 1903 hotel is once again one of the city's top hostelries. The hotel's original elements, such as imported marble Corinthian columns and sculpted ceilings, have been restored to their former elegance. The lobby soars 40 feet to a glass dome that lets the sun stream in.

The modest number of rooms guarantees personal service. All units are extremely spacious, beautifully decorated with mahogany antique reproductions and floral prints, and come fully equipped with telephones in the bedroom and bathroom, and such niceties as bathrobes, makeup mirrors, hair dryers, and marble bathtubs.

Dining: The Lobby Lounge offers afternoon tea and cocktails. The famous old Victorian Room has been turned into the Café Victoria, where baroque plasterwork is matched with extravagant potted shrubs. Eight-foot-high windows in the main-floor Consort Bar look out onto King Street. For formal dining, Chiaro's specializes in fine continental cuisine, with dinner entrees priced from C$25 to C$30 (US$18 to US$21).

Services: 24-hour room and concierge service, complimentary shoe-shine and newspaper.

Facilities: Health club.

Radisson Plaza Hotel Admiral. 249 Queen's Quay W., Toronto, ON, M5J 2N5. ☎ **800/333-3333** or 416/203-3333. Fax 416/203-3100. 157 rms. A/C MINIBAR TV TEL. C$175–C$220 (US$125–US$157) double. Extra person C$20 (US$14). Weekend packages available. AE, DC, ER, MC, V. Parking C$15 (US$11). Subway: Union, then take the LRT.

As the name and the harbor-front location suggest, the Radisson Plaza Hotel Admiral has a strong nautical flavor. Rooms are elegantly furnished with campaign-style chests of drawers with brass trimmings, marble-top side tables, and desks. Extra amenities include two phones, real hangers, and, in the bathroom, a hair dryer and clothesline.

Dining: The Commodores Dining Room, which looks out onto the harbor and Lake Ontario, offers classic continental cuisine, with main courses ranging from C$20 to C$28 (US$14 to US$20). The Galley serves a more modest menu, while the adjacent Bosun's Bar offers light snacks.

Services: Concierge, 24-hour room service, complimentary newspaper.

Facilities: On the horseshoe-shaped roof deck overlooking the lake is a resortlike pool and cabana-style bar-terrace. There's also a squash court.

The Royal York. 100 Front St. W., Toronto, ON, M5J 1E3. ☎ **800/441-1414** or 416/863-6333. 1,365 rms and suites. A/C MINIBAR TV TEL. C$175–C$230 double (US$125–US$164); from C$300 (US$214) suite. Extra person C$20 (US$14). Add C$50 (US$36) for Entree Gold service. Many special packages available. AE, DC, DISC, MC, V. Parking C$18 (US$13). Subway: Union.

To many citizens and regular visitors, the Royal York is Toronto, because in its 35 banquet and meeting rooms many of the city's historical and social events have taken place. Conveniently located for the business and theater districts, it is a huge enterprise, and as such, not to everyone's taste. Still, there is a magnificence to this hotel, which opened in 1929. The vast lobby is crowned by an incredible inlay-coffered ceiling, lit by large cast-bronze chandeliers.

Units vary in size, but a standard room will have a king-size bed and antique reproduction furnishings, including an armchair and a well-lit desk. Nice features include solid wood doors, windows that open, and wall moldings. Rooms for travelers with disabilities are exceptionally well equipped for wheelchair guests and for those guests who have hearing or visual impairments. Entree Gold provides a superior room on a private floor with private lounge, complimentary breakfast and newspaper, and nightly turndown.

Dining/Entertainment: Of the 10 restaurants and lounges, the Acadian Room offers Canadian cuisine in an elegant atmosphere; the Royal Tea Room serves afternoon tea; Benihana offers a show of Japanese finesse; the York Station has bar lunches. The Lobby Bar features a sports screen, while the Library Bar is more intimate. Four more dining venues are downstairs.

Services: Concierge, 24-hour room service.

Facilities: Skylit indoor lap pool with hand-painted trompe-l'oeil murals and potted palms, exercise room, saunas, steam rooms and whirlpool, business center, barbershop and beauty salon, shopping arcade.

Sheraton Centre. 123 Queen St. W., Toronto, ON, M5H 2M9. ☎ **800/325-3535** or 416/361-1000. Fax 416/947-4854. 1,382 rms and suites. A/C TV TEL. C$265 (US$189) double. Extra person C$20 (US$14). 2 children under 18 can stay free in parents' rm. Special packages available. AE, DC, ER, MC, V. Parking available in underground City Hall parkade, which connects to the hotel, for C$22 (US$16) per day. Additional charge for valet parking. Subway: Osgoode.

A city in itself, the Sheraton Centre contains dozens of shops in the Plaza, eight restaurants and bars, and two movie theaters. It's conveniently located at the heart of the city's underground passageways, right across from City Hall and near the Convention Centre. At the back of the lobby, you'll even find 2 acres of landscaped gardens with a waterfall and summer terrace. In this 43-story complex, rooms are spacious, attractively furnished, and well equipped with coffeemakers, hair dryers, irons/ironing boards, and voice mail. The Club level in the Queen Tower provides such extra amenities as a private lounge with complimentary continental breakfast and hors d'oeuvres, and rooms with combo fax/printer/copier, ergonomic chair, and two-line speaker phone.

Dining/Entertainment: In the shopping concourse, Good Queen Bess, an authentic English pub (shipped from England in sections), is one of the few places around where you can enjoy a mug of Newcastle Brown. Off the lobby, Reunion is a lively bar, with several videos, a pool table, and upbeat music, while the second-floor Long Bar and Lounge provides a spectacular view of City Hall. The premier restaurant is Postcards Cafe & Grill, which at dinner features cuisine from the Americas. Here the "Fast Break Breakfast" is served in 5 minutes or it's free.

Services: Concierge, 24-hour room service, valet.

Facilities: Indoor/outdoor pool (20 ft. inside, 60 ft. outside), sundeck, exercise room with LifeFitness and Cybex equipment, sauna, game room, hot tub, business center.

○ **Westin Harbour Castle.** 1 Harbour Sq., Toronto, ON, M5J 1A6. ☎ **800/228-3000** or 416/869-1600. Fax 416/361-7448. 980 rms. A/C MINIBAR TV TEL. C$160–C$300 (US$114–US$214) double. Extra person C$20 (US$14). Children under 17 stay free in parents' rm. Special weekend packages (double occupancy) available. AE, DC, ER, MC, V. Parking C$21 (US$15). Subway: Union, then take the LRT.

Located right on the lakefront, the Westin is ideally situated for visiting Harbourfront and is linked to downtown by a Light Rapid Transit system. Guest rooms, all with a lake view, are located in two towers joined at the base by a five-story podium. All rooms are furnished with marble-top desks and night tables, table and floor lamps, and an extra phone in the bathroom. There are 442 no-smoking rooms.

Dining/Entertainment: On the 38th floor of the south tower, the Lighthouse is a revolving restaurant with fabulous views that is open for breakfast, lunch, and dinner, with entrees from C$17 to C$38 (US$12 to US$27). Chinese cuisine is offered in the ground-floor Grand Yatt. Tea is served in the Lobby Lounge, along with cocktails and a continental breakfast. Off the main lobby, the Chartroom offers a quiet haven for a drink, with piano entertainment in the evenings.

Services: Concierge, 24-hour room service, laundry/valet.

Facilities: Fitness center with indoor pool, whirlpool, sauna, steam room, two outdoor tennis courts, two squash courts, and massage clinic.

EXPENSIVE

Delta Chelsea Inn. 33 Gerrard St. W. (between Yonge and Bay), Toronto, ON, M5G 1Z4. ☎ **800/268-1133** or 416/595-1975. Fax 416/585-4302. 1,594 rms and suites. A/C TV TEL. C$235–C$250 (US$168–US$179) double; from C$250 (US$179) suite. Extra person C$20 (US$14). Children under 18 stay free in parents' rm. Weekend and other packages available. AE, DC, ER, MC, V. Parking C$18 (US$13) per day. Subway: College.

The Delta Chelsea Inn is still one of Toronto's best buys—particularly for families and on weekends, when special packages are offered—although prices have shot up and the lobby can be mobbed with people at checkout. All rooms have bright, modern furnishings, and 400 rooms have minibars, some kitchenettes. Rooms in the south tower feature dual phones with data jacks, call-waiting, and conference-call features.

Dining/Entertainment: Wittles offers casual but elegant dining, while the Market Garden is an attractive self-service cafeteria with an outdoor courtyard selling everything from salads to grilled items at reasonable prices. The children's menu offers good value, and children 6 and under eat free. The Chelsea Bun offers live entertainment daily and Dixieland jazz on Saturday afternoons (lunch buffets and Sunday brunch are also served here); for a relaxing drink, there's the Elm Street Lounge or Deck 27 on the 27th floor, which offers writing desks and telephones for the final wrap-up at the end of the day.

Services: 24-hour room service, baby-sitting (for a fee), valet pickup.

Facilities: Two swimming pools, whirlpool, sauna, fitness room, lounge, and game room (with three pool tables), and—a blessing for parents—a children's creative center where 3- to 8-year-olds can play under close and expert supervision. It's open until 10pm on Friday and Saturday. Business center in the new tower.

MODERATE

Bond Place Hotel. 65 Dundas St. E., Toronto, ON, M5B 2G8. ☎ **416/362-6061.** Fax 416/360-6406. 286 rms. A/C TV TEL. C$130 (US$93) single or double. Extra person C$15 (US$11). Children 14 and under stay free in parents' rm. AE, DC, DISC, ER, MC, V. Parking C$12 (US$9). Subway: Dundas.

Ideally located just 1 block from Yonge Street and the Eaton Centre, the Bond Place Hotel offers all the appurtenances of a first-class hotel at reasonable prices. The rooms are pleasantly decorated in somewhat old-fashioned Scandinavian-style. Off the lobby, the casual Garden Café is open all day, while downstairs, Freddy's serves lunch and dinner and complimentary hors d'oeuvres from 5 to 7pm.

Hotel Victoria. 56 Yonge St. (at Wellington), Toronto, ON, M5E 1G5. ☎ **416/363-1666.** Fax 416/363-7327. 48 rms. A/C TV TEL. C$90–C$107 (US$64–US$76) double. Extra person C$15 (US$11). Children under 12 stay free in parents' rm. Special weekend rates available. AE, DC, DISC, MC, V. Subway: King.

In search of a small, personal hotel? Try the six-floor Hotel Victoria, only 2 blocks from the Hummingbird Centre. The rooms are either standard or select (the latter are larger). Rooms have modern furnishings, a gray-and-burgundy decor, and private baths. The small and elegant lobby retains the marble columns, staircase, and decorative moldings of an earlier era. A complimentary *Globe and Mail* is included in the room price. There's an attractive restaurant and lounge, as well as a lobby bar.

The Strathcona. 60 York St., Toronto, ON, M5J 1S8. ☎ **416/363-3321.** Fax 416/363-4679. 193 rms. A/C TV TEL. May–Oct C$90–C$100 (US$64–US$71) double; Nov–Apr C$70 (US$50) double. AE, CB, DC, MC, V. Nearby parking C$12 (US$9). Subway: Union.

Currently one of the city's best buys, the Strathcona is located right across from Union Station and the Royal York Hotel, within easy reach of all downtown attractions. Although the rooms are small, they are decently furnished with modern blond-wood furniture, gray carpeting, brass floor lamps, and private baths. Guests receive a complimentary newspaper and have fitness-club access.

INEXPENSIVE

Neill Wycik College Hotel. 96 Gerrard St. E. (between Church and Jarvis), Toronto, ON, M5B 1G7. ☎ **800/268-4358** or 416/977-2320. Fax 416/977-2809. 304 rms (none with bath). C$46–C$55 (US$33–US$39) double; C$50–C$62 (US$36–US$44) family rm (2 adults plus children). MC, V. Closed Sept to early May. Nearby parking C$9 (US$6). Subway: College.

Right downtown, the Neil Wycik College Hotel offers basic accommodations at extremely reasonable rates, from early May to late August. Since these are primarily student accommodations, rooms contain only the most essential furniture—beds, chairs, and desks. Family rooms have two single beds and room for three rollaways. Four to five bedrooms share two bathrooms and one kitchen. If you wish to cook, you have to furnish your own utensils. Other building facilities include a TV lounge, rooftop sundeck, sauna, a laundry room on the 22nd floor, and a breakfast cafeteria.

Toronto International Hostel. 160 Mutual St. (at Gerrard), Toronto, ON, M5B 2M2. ☎ **416/971-4440.** Fax 416/971-4088. 225 beds. A/C. For members C$26 (US$19) per person in a double rm, C$22.50 (US$16) per person in a 4-person rm; C$30.30 (US$22) and C$26.80 (US$19), respectively, for nonmembers. Membership C$25 (US$18) per year. MC, V. Parking C$7 (US$5) in nearby lot. Subway: Dundas.

The hostel accommodations are arranged in suites of four rooms sharing two bathrooms. Furnishings are simple: bed, closet, and sink with a kitchen in each suite. Each floor has a common room with TV, and there are laundry facilities and an exercise room on the premises. Guests have access to a complete health facility with squash courts, track, and pool in an adjacent building for only C$1 (US70¢).

MIDTOWN

The midtown area runs north from College/Carlton streets, between Spadina and Jarvis, to where Dupont crosses Yonge.

Note: See the "Midtown Toronto" map (p. 402) to locate hotels in this section.

🏛 Family-Friendly Hotels

Sheraton Centre *(see p. 382)* This hotel operates a Very Important Kids program, which includes a free welcome gift for each child upon check-in, free dining from the kid's menu for children under 12 accompanied by an adult in Postcards Cafe, plus two complimentary hours at Kids & Quackers, which is a supervised play area for kids ages 18 months to 12 years, and, of course, in-room Super Nintendo. Plus, don't forget that the hotel has two movie theaters on the premises.

Four Seasons *(see below)* Free bicycles, video games, and the pool should keep kids occupied. Meals are served in Animal World wicker baskets or on Sesame Street plates, and complimentary room-service cookies and milk on arrival make them feel special.

VERY EXPENSIVE

✪ **Four Seasons Hotel.** 21 Avenue Rd., Toronto, ON, M5R 2G1. ☎ **800/332-3442** in the U.S., 800/268-6282 in Canada, or 416/964-0411 locally. Fax 416/964-2301. 380 rms and suites. A/C MINIBAR TV TEL. C$290–C$365 (US$207–US$261) double; from C$415 (US$296) suite. Extra person C$30 (US$21). Children under 18 stay free in parents' rm. Weekend rates available. AE, CB, DC, ER, MC, V. Parking C$20 (US$14). Subway: Bay.

In the heart of Bloor-Yorkville, the Four Seasons has a well-deserved reputation for personal service, quiet but unimpeachable style, and total comfort. The lobby, with its marble-and-granite floors, Savonnerie carpets, and stunning fresh-flower arrangements, epitomizes the style. The extra-large rooms, with dressing rooms and marble bathrooms, are elegant and well furnished. Extra amenities include hair dryers, makeup and full-length mirrors, tie bars, and closet safes. Corner rooms have balconies.

Four Seasons Executive Suites have additional seating areas, two televisions, and deluxe telephone with two lines and conference-call capability. No-smoking rooms are available.

Dining/Entertainment: Truffles, on the second floor, provides a lavish setting of fine woods, fabric, and furnishings for extraordinary modern French cuisine. Main courses, priced from C$28 to C$37 (US$20 to US$26), might include oven-baked halibut in tomato caper sauce or pan-seared five-spice duck breast with lemongrass jus. The Studio Café serves meals all day. Light lunches, evening hors d'oeuvres, and Sunday brunch are served in La Serre, where a pianist entertains in the evening. The lobby bar is a pleasant area for afternoon tea and cocktails. Special kids' menus are available.

Services: 24-hour concierge, 24-hour room service and valet pickup, 1-hour pressing, complimentary newspaper, complimentary shoe-shine, twice-daily maid service, baby-sitting, doctor on call, courtesy limo to downtown.

Facilities: Business center, health club with an indoor/outdoor pool, whirlpool, Universal equipment, and massage. Bicycles and video games are also available for kids.

✪ **Intercontinental.** 220 Bloor St. W. (at St. George), Toronto, ON, M5S 1T8. ☎ **416/960-5200.** Fax 416/960-8269. 209 rms. A/C MINIBAR TV TEL. C$265–C$345 (US$189–US$246) double. Parking C$22 (US$16). Subway: St. George.

The Intercontinental is small enough to provide personal service. The spacious rooms are well furnished with comfortable French-style armchairs and love seats. The marble bathrooms, with separate showers, are large and equipped with every amenity—at elephone, a clothesline, large fluffy towels, a bathrobe, and scales. All rooms also feature closet lights, a large desk-table, full-length mirror, and a two-line telephone with data port.

Dining/Entertainment: Signatures offers fine dining, with dinner entrees from C$16 to C$28 (US$11 to US$20) and one of the best brunches in town. The Harmony Lounge, with its marble bar, fireplace, and cherry paneling, plus an outdoor patio, is a pleasant retreat for cocktails or afternoon tea.

Services: Concierge, 24-hour room service, laundry/valet, nightly turndown, twice-daily maid service, complimentary shoe-shine and newspaper, video check-out in four languages (English, French, Spanish, and Japanese).

Facilities: Lap pool with adjacent patio; fitness room with treadmill, bikes, Stairmaster, and Paramount equipment.

✪ **Park Plaza.** 4 Avenue Rd. (at Bloor), Toronto, ON, M5R 2E8. ☎ **800/268-4927** or 416/924-5471. Fax 416/924-4933. 348 rms and suites. A/C MINIBAR TV TEL. C$260–C$395 (US$186–US$282) double. Children under 18 stay free in parents' rm. AE, DISC, MC, V. Parking C$18 (US$12). Subway: Museum.

The Park Plaza is conveniently located in Yorkville. Purchased in 1997 by Grand Bay Hotels and Resorts, the Park Plaza is currently undergoing extensive renovations. All the 64 rooms and 20 suites in the original South Tower, built in 1935, were recently renovated and redecorated to exceptionally high standards and will remain open during the makeover. The amenities in these rooms already include two telephones with voice mail, louvered closets, and full length mirror, plus hair dryer, bathrobes, and makeup mirror in the bathroom. Suites have additional features: scales, umbrellas, and two-line phones with fax/computer hookups.

Dining/Entertainment: The Roof Restaurant, on the 18th floor, will be open for breakfast, lunch, and dinner. The adjacent lounge, with inviting couches, wood-burning fireplace, and spectacular skyline view—famous as a gathering place for Toronto literati—will be retained. Additional restaurants are also planned.

Services: Concierge, room service, laundry/valet, complimentary newspaper and shoe-shine, nightly turndown, twice-daily maid service.

Facilities: Fitness room, spa, business center.

Sutton Place Hotel. 955 Bay St., Toronto, ON, M5S 2A2. ☎ **800/268-3790** or 416/924-9221. Fax 416/924-1778. 230 rms, 62 suites. A/C MINIBAR TV TEL. C$235–C$300 (US$168–US$214) double; from C$400 (US$286) suite. Extra person C$20 (US$14). Children under 18 stay free in parents' rm. Weekend rates available. AE, DC, ER, MC. Parking C$21 (US$15). Subway: Museum or Wellesley.

This small luxury hotel caters to both a business and leisure clientele attracted by its European flair, elegant decor, and exceptional service. Throughout the public areas you will find authentic antiques, old-master paintings, 18th-century Gobelins, Oriental carpets, and crystal chandeliers. The very spacious rooms are luxuriously furnished in a French style. Each room has a couch, desk, two telephones (allowing hookup to a fax or PC via a modem), bathrobes, and hair dryers.

Dining: Accents Restaurant and Bar, open daily for breakfast, lunch, and dinner, offers a continental bistro-style menu at night.

Services: Concierge, 24-hour room service, laundry/valet, complimentary shoe-shine, twice-daily maid service.

Facilities: Indoor pool with sundeck, sauna, massage, fully equipped fitness center, and business center.

MODERATE

Venture Inn. 89 Avenue Rd., Toronto, ON, M5R 2G3. ☎ **800/387-3933** or 416/964-1220. Fax 416/964-8692. 71 rms. A/C TV TEL. C$100–C$150 (US$71–US$107) double. Rates include continental breakfast. Children under 19 stay free in parents' rm. AE, CB, DC, DISC, ER, MC,V. Parking C$6.50 (US$4.65). Subway: Bay or Museum.

Though the Venture Inn is located on a high-priced site in Yorkville, it charges moderate prices for its modern rooms, decorated with pine accents.

INEXPENSIVE

Victoria University. 140 Charles St. W., Toronto, ON, M5S 1K9. ☎ **416/585-4524.** Fax 416/585-4530. 425 rms (none with bath). C$64 (US$46) double. Rates include breakfast. Discounts for seniors and students. MC, V. Closed Sept to early May. Nearby parking C$12 (US$9). Subway: Museum.

For a great summer bargain downtown, stay at Victoria University, across from the Royal Ontario Museum. Rooms in the university residence are available from mid-May to late August. Each is furnished as a study/bedroom and supplied with fresh linen, towels, and soap. Bathrooms are down the hall. Guests enjoy free local calls and use of laundry facilities, as well as access to the dining and athletic facilities (including tennis courts).

METRO EAST

INEXPENSIVE

University of Toronto at Scarborough. Student Village, 1265 Military Trail, Scarborough, ON, M1C 1A4. ☎ **416/287-7369.** Fax 416/287-7323. C$160 (US$114) for 2 nights; each additional night C$80 (US$57) to a maximum of C$470 (US$336) per week. 2-night minimum. MC, V. Closed end of Aug to early May. Free parking. Take the subway to Kennedy, then the Scarborough Rapid Transit to Ellesmere, then bus 95 or 95B to the college entrance. Or take Exit 387 off the 401.

From mid-May to the third week in August, the University of Toronto in Scarborough has accommodations available in town houses for families (two adults and children under 17) that sleep four to six people and contain equipped kitchens. There's a cafeteria, pub, and recreation center.

4 Dining

The multicultural makeup of the city makes dining a delightful round-the-world experience. Supposedly, there are more than 5,000 restaurants in Toronto, but there's room below only for a very short list. I suggest seeking out ethnic dining spots in Little Italy, Little Portugal, Chinatown, and along the Danforth, where you'll find great food at reasonable prices.

SOME DINING NOTES   Dining in Toronto can appear expensive because of the additional 8% provincial sales tax and 7% GST. In addition, expect higher wine prices than those in the United States, again because of higher liquor taxes.

Several dining clusters throughout Toronto also offer good budget meals. In the basement of **Dragon City,** the Asian shopping complex on Spadina Avenue at Dundas Street, you'll find counters selling Indonesian, Japanese, Chinese, and Taiwanese food, plus noodles and seafood. At the **Harbourfront,** Queen's Quay and Pier 4 are dotted with a great variety of restaurants. And you'll find everything from Chinese, Middle Eastern, Japanese, and Mexican fast food to Coney Island hot dogs and a booth specializing in schnitzels at **Village by the Grange,** at 71 McCaul St., conveniently located south of the Art Gallery of Ontario.

In addition to the listings below, don't overlook **Truffles** in the Four Seasons Hotel, where some of the finest dining in the city can be experienced.

DOWNTOWN WEST

Note: See the "Downtown Toronto" map (p. 396) to locate restaurants in this section.

EXPENSIVE

✪ **Acqua.** 10 Front St. W. ☎ **416/368-7171.** Reservations recommended. Main courses C$20–C$29 (US$11–US$21). AE, DC, ER, MC, V. Mon–Fri noon–2:30pm; Mon–Sat 5–11pm. Subway: Union. CALIFORNIA/ITALIAN.

One of Toronto's trendiest and most dramatic restaurants, Acqua evokes the drama and color of Venice at carnival. A brilliant blue door leads into the bar where curvaceous tables stand under sail-like flags. The courtyard dining area in the BCE building is defined by striped poles like those found along Venetian canals.

The cuisine is less easily defined. Roasted black grouper with a pecan crust and apricot yam jus, or herb roasted chicken with sautéed sweetbreads, crimini mushroom, sunchokes, oven-dried tomatoes, and black peppercorn sauce blend Italian and other traditional cuisines. In addition, there are pastas like the pappardelle with braised rabbit, roasted tomatoes, pearl onions, and truffle-scented natural juices. Start with warm herbed goat cheese with pan-seared polenta, roasted portobello mushrooms, and chiffonade of basil. Winning desserts include the Belgian chocolate and raspberry crème brûlée and the Frangelico bread pudding and sugar pear in Muscat de Beaunes de Venise.

✪ **Canoe.** 54th Floor, Toronto Dominion Bank Tower, 66 Wellington St. W. ☎ **416/ 364-0054.** Main courses C$25–C$32 (US$18–US$23). AE, DC, ER, MC, V. Mon–Fri 11:30am–2:30pm and 5–10:30pm. CANADIAN.

The foyer, with its framed autumn leaves, sets a natural tone for this restaurant, where the floors are fashioned from mushroom-stained walnut and the tables from cherry. On a clear day, the view is magnificent; when the clouds are low and mist envelops the tower, the setting is dramatic. The cuisine spotlights the very best Canadian ingredients (Digby scallops, Alberta beef, Yukon caribou), and includes spa-inspired dishes like the skin-roasted Arctic char on a warm salad of spinach. Other dishes are more heart-warming, like the spice-rubbed strip-loin of beef with French-onion gravy and mash. Canoe keeps an extensive wine list and has great desserts, too. Try the sampling of chocolate desserts for a start.

MODERATE

Jump Cafe & Bar. Commerce Court E., Court Level, Bay and Wellington. ☎ **416/363-3400.** Reservations recommended. Main courses C$17–C$21 (US$12–US$15). AE, DC, ER, MC, V. Mon–Fri 11:30am–5pm; Mon–Sat 5–11:30pm. FUSION.

Tucked away in Commerce Court, this hard-to-find restaurant for power-lunchers vibrates with energy. The streamlined atrium–dining room is broken up by palms and other strategically placed trees and shrubs. A small bar area to the left of the entrance features a good selection of single malts and grappas. In summer, it's pleasant to sit out in Commerce Court.

The menu features fresh daily specials, plus dishes like five-herb marinated halibut with charred corn, pineapple, mango, and spinach salad in a wild-ginger and yellow-tomato vinaigrette, or New York steak in a smoky bourbon peppercorn sauce served with truffle whipped potatoes and grilled portobello mushrooms. At least six pasta dishes are also available. To start, try the richly flavored wild and tame mushroom soup made with six different kinds of fungi, or the terrific Black Tiger shrimp with a Cajun Creole spiced sweet pepper sauce and wild-mushroom ragout. Among the desserts I lust after is the banana coconut cream pie with fresh grated coconut and Jamaican rum butterscotch, but you may be seduced by the dense chocolate cake spiked with rum-soaked raisins and layered with sweet mascarpone filling.

La Fenice. 319 King St. W. ☎ **416/585-2377.** Reservations required. Main courses C$16–C$26 (US$11–US$27). AE, CB, DC, ER, MC, V. Mon–Fri noon–2:30pm; Mon–Sat 5:30–11pm. ITALIAN.

This Italian outpost draws a conservative business crowd at lunchtime and a theater crowd at dinner. The cuisine's hallmarks are fresh ingredients and authentic fine olive oil. A plate of assorted appetizers will include pungent roasted peppers, crisp-grilled zucchini, squid, and a roast veal in tuna sauce (vitello tonnato). Choose from 18 or more pasta dishes—say, *agnolotti al gorgonzola e salvia* made with Gorgonzola, sage, and tomato, or *fettuccine salmonate* made with fresh salmon, dill, leeks, and cream—along with a fine selection of Provimi veal and grilled fresh fish. Desserts include cakes and tortes, plus zabaglione and fresh strawberries and other fruits in season. Downstairs, an attractive pasta bar is open all day for light fare.

Le Select. 328 Queen St. W. ☎ **416/596-6405.** Reservations recommended. Main courses C$14–C$20 (US$10–US$14); fixed price C$20 (US$14). AE, DC, MC, V. Daily 11:30am–5pm; Mon–Thurs 5:30pm–midnight, Fri–Sat 5:30pm–1am, Sun 5:30–11pm. FRENCH.

A mixed crowd of young and middle-aged sophisticates flock to this bistro, one of the longest-lived on Queen Street. It's very French with an authentic zinc bar, breakfronts, fringed fabric lampshades over the tables, French posters, and a jazz background. The crowds come for the moderately priced, good French food—examples include *moules marinières* (mussels cooked in white wine), steak with sautéed shallots and frites, and cassoulet made with duck confit, goose, and pork sausage served on white beans simmered with tomatoes and fresh rosemary. A C$20 (US$14) fixed-price dinner lets you select from five choices per course for appetizer, entree, and dessert.

Mildred Pierce. 99 Sudbury St. ☎ **416/588-5695.** Reservations not accepted. Main courses C$14–C$19 (US$10–US$14). AE, DC, ER, MC, V. Mon–Fri noon–2pm, Sun 11am–3pm; Sun–Thurs 6–10pm, Fri–Sat 6–11pm. Take Queen St. W. to Dovercourt, turn left, then right on Sudbury. The restaurant is located on the left at the back of a parking lot attached to Studio 99. FRENCH/FUSION.

Resembling a movie set, this spot is worth seeking out. Outside, there's a great view of the CN Tower and the downtown skyline. Inside, the room has a theatrical flair: Organza drapes sweep down from the ceiling and a vast mural at the back of the room depicts a Bacchanalian feast painted by artist Rebecca Last.

The open kitchen issues a variety of fine dishes like the beef fillet with a red-wine thyme jus or grilled tiger shrimp with Asian greens, crispy noodles, and a pickled ginger vinaigrette. My favorite dish is baked fillet of salmon with a ragout of roasted Yukon gold potatoes, braised fennel, and sugar snap peas. Start with the chilled shellfish salad of scallops, shrimp, mussels, and clams marinated in tequila and kaffir lime with avocado, mango, and cilantro. For dessert, I recommend the pear tarte tatin served with brandied caramel sauce and vanilla ice cream.

INEXPENSIVE

Rivoli. 332 Queen St. W. ☎ **416/597-0794.** Reservations not accepted. Main courses C$9–C$15 (US$6–US$11). MC, V. Mon–Sat 11:30am–1am. CONTINENTAL.

Rivoli attracts a mixed avant-garde artsy and boomer crowd. Its dinner menu features nine or so eclectic specialties such as *yuhukai,* which is a breast of chicken stuffed with macadamia-nut Thai basil pesto and served with red-plum lime ginger sauce, or liberation lamb—lamb chops marinated in garlic, balsamic vinegar, oil, and herbs and finished with a teriyaki cabernet glaze. In summer the sidewalk patio is jammed. There's pool upstairs and good nightly entertainment in the back room. The dining-room decor is appropriately surreal and basic black.

Vanipha. 193 Augusta Ave. ☎ **416/340-0491.** Reservations accepted only for parties of 6 or more. Main courses C$8–C$12 (US$6–US$9). V. Mon–Sat noon–11pm. THAI/LAO.

Serving some really fine cuisine, Vanipha is housed in a plain but comfortable step-down storefront. Try the pad Thai, mango salad, grilled fish with tamarind sauce, chicken red curry, and, of course, the special treat—sticky rice.

DOWNTOWN EAST

Note: See the "Downtown Toronto" map (p. 396) to locate restaurants in this section.

MODERATE

The Senator. 249 and 253 Victoria St. ☎ **416/364-7517.** Reservations recommended for dinner in the dining rm. Lunch main courses C$8–C$14 (US$6–US$10); dinner main courses C$18–C$24 (US$13–US$17). MC, V. Mon–Fri 7:30am–3:30pm; Tues–Sat 5–11:30pm (5–10pm in the diner), Sun 5–10pm; brunch Sat–Sun 8am–3pm. Subway: Dundas. NORTH AMERICAN.

In the diner, green leatherette booths, tiled floors, and down-home cuisine take you back to the 1940s at this local favorite, conveniently located for the Pantages Theatre. You can still order a full breakfast of bacon and eggs, beans, home fries, and toast for C$5 (US$3.55). At lunch, such comfort foods as meat loaf, macaroni and cheese, burgers with fried onions and corn relish, and creamy rice pudding are served. And, best of all, you can perch on a stool and order up a rich and real old-fashioned milkshake.

In the adjacent dining room, which is decked out in mahogany, mirrors, and stained glass, you can eat dinner, seated in a velvet enclosed booth, and relish any one of the steaks or try dishes like chicken breast with rosemary lemon sauce, prime rib, and grilled swordfish steak with a roasted red-pepper coulis. Desserts are good and the wine list is excellent.

INEXPENSIVE

Movenpick Marche. In the Galleria of the BCE Building, Front St. E. ☎ **416/366-8986.** Reservations not accepted. Most items C$7–C$9 (US$5–US$6). AE, DC, MC, V. Daily 7:30am–2am. Subway: Union. CONTINENTAL.

This is the city's latest innovation in food merchandising. Pick up a tab at the entrance and stroll through the bustling market, where various stands and carts of-fer fresh salads, fish, meats, pizzas, and more. Select and purchase what you want as you go through. At the rotisserie, select a meat for the chef to cook, or at the seafood and raw bar, choose a fish for the grill. Then wander over to the bistro de vin and check out the cases of wine or enjoy a boccalino of an open wine. The chefs and staff are easily identifiable by their boaters. This is a fun place for breakfast, lunch, or dinner.

MIDTOWN WEST

This section of Toronto includes Yorkville, where dining can be pricey but not nec-essarily good. In this section, I've included one or two selections that can be relied upon to deliver quality at a decent price.

Note: See the "Midtown Toronto" map (p. 402) to locate restaurants in this section.

EXPENSIVE

✪ **Boba.** 90 Avenue Rd. ☎ **416/961-2622.** Main courses C$20–C$27 (US$14–US$19). AE, DC, ER, MC, V. Tues–Sat noon–2pm; Mon–Thurs 5:30–10pm, Fri–Sat 5:30–10:30pm. Subway: Bay. FUSION.

Barbara Gordon and Bob Bermann were among the early Toronto restaurateurs to experiment with spicy ethnic flavors at restaurants like the Avocado Club. They continue to provide food lovers with a sophisticated ethnic-inspired modern American cuisine that uses fresh local products. Start, for example, with the grilled eggplant and smoked pepper salad with Woolwich chèvre, or the Thai-flavored steak tartare served with shiitake-mushroom salad and wonton crisps. Asian spices imbue the main dishes with delectable character—rice-paper–wrapped chicken breast on Thai black rice, with a spiced rice-wine-vinegar sauce is a good example. Desserts are also extraordinary, especially the Valrhona chocolate triangle with crème fraîche ice cream, fresh raspberries, and raspberry sauce, or the citrus trio: a divine blood-orange tart in a cookie crust, with lime buttermilk pudding and lemon ice cream.

This finely prepared cuisine is served in a sunny garden area with large, spectacular floral arrangements. Boba attracts a moneyed crowd—some in fine designer wear, others in jeans.

Splendido Bar and Grill. 88 Harbord St. ☎ **416/929-7788.** Reservations recommended well in advance. Main courses C$20–C$29 (US$14–US$21). AE, DC, ER, MC, V. Mon–Sat 5–11pm. Subway: Spadina, then take the LRT south. ITALIAN.

The Splendido Bar and Grill is a scene-stealer, with an absolutely stunning dining room that stretches behind a black-gray granite bar in a riot of brilliant yellow lit by a host of tiny, almost fairylike track lights. It's a loud, lively place, not the spot for a romantic dinner. The menu—Italian with international inspirations—changes monthly. Start with the filling antipasto of grilled chili-marinated prawns, smoked bocconcini, pickled octopus, cranberry bean salad, sweet pepper, and sweet garlic prosciutto with melon, mission fig, octopus salad, scallop sausage, rosemary peppers, roasted garlic, and marinated bocconcini; or the pizzeta with jerk chicken, tomatoes, leeks, fresh cilantro, and pecorino. Special treats among the main courses are the clay-oven–roasted curry-rubbed salmon with lentils, watercress, pickled apples, and papadum, or the boneless rabbit stuffed with mushrooms and served with a wild-morel-mushroom sauce. The dessert list will certainly command your attention, offering such enticements as warm banana cake with a soft chocolate center and banana ice cream, and the lemon meringue tart with vodka blueberry compote.

MODERATE

Boulevard Cafe. 161 Harbord St. (between Spadina and Bathurst). ☎ **416/961-7676.** Reservations recommended for upstairs dining. Main courses C$12–C$16 (US$9–US$11). AE, MC, V. Daily 11:30am–3:30pm and 5:30–11pm. Subway: Spadina, then take the LRT south. PERUVIAN.

A favorite gathering spot of young creative types, the Boulevard Cafe is somehow reminiscent of Kathmandu in the 1960s, although the inspiration is Peru. Peruvian cushions and South American wall hangings soften the upstairs dining room. The outside summer cafe, strung with colored lights, attracts an evening and late-night crowd. The menu features *empanadas* (spicy chicken or beef pastry); tangy shrimp in a spiced garlic, pimiento, and wine sauce; and *tamal verde* (spicy corn, coriander, and chicken pâté) to start. For the main course, the major choice is *anticuchos,* marinated and charbroiled brochettes of your own choosing: sea bass, shrimp, pork tenderloin, beef, or chicken.

✪ **Chiado.** 864 College St. (at Concord Ave.). ☎ **416/538-1910.** Reservations recommended. Main courses C$17–C$28 (US$12–US$20). AE, DC, MC, V. Mon–Sat noon–3pm; Mon–Thurs 5–10pm, Fri–Sat 5pm–midnight. Subway: College, then take the streetcar west. PORTUGUESE.

Chiado refers to the district in Lisbon that is filled with small bistrettos like this one. Beyond the appetizing display at the front of the room, you'll discover a long, narrow dining room decorated with elegant French-style pink chairs and colorful art on the walls. In summer, the storefront opens entirely onto the street, adding to the atmosphere. Among the appetizers, the pinheta of salted cod or the marinated sardines with lemon and parsley will appeal to the true Portuguese; others might prefer the tiger shrimp served with piri-piri sauce. On the main menu, a Portuguese might pine for the poached fillet of cod or the bistretto-style steak with fried egg and fries, while a friend might go for the roast rack of lamb with a red Douro-wine sauce or the braised rabbit in a Madeira wine sauce. To top it all off, choose from the tempting desserts, including *molotov* (egg-white flan), chocolate mousse, and pecan pie.

Il Posto. 148 Yorkville Ave. ☎ **416/968-0469.** Reservations recommended. Pasta C$9.50–C$21 (US$7–US$15); main courses C$19–C$26 (US$14–US$19). AE, MC, V. Mon–Sat noon–2:30pm and 6–10:30pm. Subway: Bay. ITALIAN.

This Yorkville survivor offers an attractive courtyard setting complete with brick terrace under a spreading maple tree. The dessert spread at the entrance is tempting enough—fresh raspberry tarts with kiwi, fresh strawberry tarts, and other delights. The menu features such Italian specialties as *involtino di pollo* (chicken stuffed with eggplant and cheese), *scaloppini champagne* (veal sautéed in champagne), or linguini with seafood. For dessert, you might discover oranges marinated in Grand Marnier, or, of course, the smooth, creamy zabaglione. The restaurant's Italian prints and classical music create a serene dining atmosphere enhanced by handsome bouquets of fresh flowers.

✪ **Trattoria Giancarlo.** 41–43 Clinton St. (at College). ☎ **416/533-9619.** Reservations highly recommended. Pasta and rice C$12–C$14 (US$9–US$10); main courses C$17–C$24 (US$12–US$17). AE, MC, V. Mon–Sat 6–10:30pm. Subway: College, then take the streetcar west. ITALIAN.

This is one of my all-time favorite spots in Little Italy, if not in the whole city. It's small and cozy and thoroughly Italian, with an outside dining area in summer. For a real treat, start with the fresh wild mushrooms brushed with herbs, garlic, and oil, or *crostini chiantigiana* (mattone toasts topped with fresh ricotta, prosciutto, and Chianti-caramelized figs). Follow with any one of six pasta dishes—linguini with oven-roasted tomatoes, sweet onions, and shrimp in a white-wine broth, or the risotto of the day. The grilled fish and meats are superb, like the tender lamb marinated in grappa, lemon, and olive oil or the swordfish grilled with mint, garlic, and olive oil. For dessert try the tiramisu, the crème caramel, or the delicious chocolate-raspberry tartufo. The experience is always memorable and the welcome real.

INEXPENSIVE

Kensington Kitchen. 124 Harbord St. ☎ **416/961-3404.** Reservations not accepted. Main courses C$8–C$13 (US$6–US$9). DC, ER, MC, V. Mon–Sat 11:30am–11pm, Sun 11:30am–10pm. Subway: Spadina, then take the LRT south. MIDDLE EASTERN.

A mixed hip and academic crowd enjoys the food and prices at this comfortable, casual Mediterranean bistro. The menu changes weekly, although it will usually feature such basics as couscous, eggplant Provençale, and *meshwi* (brochettes of marinated chicken, lamb, or kofta). The fresh fish changes daily and varies from salmon to Arctic char, mahimahi, or monkfish spiced with a fresh-mango salsa. The appetizers are

> ### 👪 Family-Friendly Restaurants
>
> **The Senator** *(see p. 390)*   The burgers and shakes at this traditional diner are real hits with the kids.
>
> **Movenpick Marche** *(see p. 390)*   Kids will love strolling through the bustling market and choosing their own pizza or burger from the stands and carts.
>
> **Kensington Kitchen** *(see p. 392)*   There are pita sandwiches, brownies, and other kid-friendly fare. The airplanes and other toys decorating the walls only add to its attraction.

always appealing, like the steamed Prince Edward Island mussels with diced celery, carrots, and onions in a spicy tomato coriander sauce. In summer my favorite spot is on the back deck under the spreading trees.

MIDTOWN EAST/THE EAST END

In the East End along Danforth Avenue, you'll encounter a veritable Little Greece, a late-night mecca, where the streets are lined with tavernas, bouzouki music spills out onto the sidewalk, and restaurant after restaurant bears a Greek name.

Pan on the Danforth. 516 Danforth Ave. ☎ **416/466-8158.** Reservations accepted for parties of 6 or more only. Main courses C$13–C$19 (US$9–US$14). AE, MC, V. Sun–Thurs 5pm–midnight, Fri–Sat 5pm–1am. Subway: Pape. GREEK.

Pan is different from the other kebab houses on the street, thanks to its owner-chef, who produces imaginatively updated Greek cuisine. It's served in a room painted with the brilliant palette of the Mediterranean—gold and azure. You can make a meal from the assortment of 20-odd dips, salads, and appetizers that are offered at this exciting, energetically charged hot spot. Among the more substantial dishes, try the grilled loin of lamb with a fig-and-orange glaze, and served with black-olive mash and marinated artichokes, or the grilled sea bass with tomato, onion, capers, and roasted garlic salsa served with delicious and authentic lemon potatoes.

UPTOWN
EXPENSIVE

✪ **Centro.** 2472 Yonge St. (north of Eglinton). ☎ **416/483-2211.** Reservations recommended. Main courses C$24–C$34 (US$17–US$24). AE, DC, MC, V. Mon–Sat 5–11:30pm. Subway: Eglinton. NORTHERN ITALIAN.

Occupying a huge space with a mezzanine and a downstairs wine and pasta bar, Centro has grand Italian style—dramatic classical columns, brilliant murals, and ultra-moderne Milan-style furnishings. A chic, animated crowd gathers here for the northern Italian cuisine with a California accent. The menu changes monthly, but among the specialties might be grilled Delft blue veal chop with chanterelles and chive cream, rack of Ontario lamb with honey mustard crust and rosemary essence, or sautéed red snapper in a corn and jalapeno sauce. There are three or so pasta dishes, all with flavorsome sauces. Desserts are worth waiting for—lemon mascarpone tart with blackberry sauce and chocolate pecan napoleon with a Southern Comfort sauce being only two examples. Afterwards, you can retire to the downstairs piano bar for a nightcap.

✪ **N 44.** 2537 Yonge St. (just south of Sherwood Ave.). ☎ **416/487-4897.** Reservations recommended. Main courses C$25–C$37 (US$18–US$26). AE, DC, ER, MC, V. Mon–Fri noon–3pm; Mon–Sat 5–10:30pm. Subway: Eglinton. CONTINENTAL.

The name, which refers to the city's latitude, is etched into the glass that encloses the kitchen at the back of this dramatic dining room. Food lovers come here for the inspired cuisine prepared by executive chef Mark McEwan and the 500-plus selections offered from the great cellar. Among the dozen main dishes, you might find a fragrant seafood stew filled with shrimp, scallops, mussels, and sea bass in a tomato curry broth with scented oils; grilled veal tenderloin with herb peppercorn crust, enhanced by an aged balsamic sauce and woodland mushroom risotto; or a deliciously simple 12-ounce aged sirloin with roasted garlic and mashed potatoes. Pizzas and pastas are also featured. Any one of the desserts will bring your meal to a rapturous finish, whether it's crème brûlée with Tahitian vanilla beans and glazed with lemon sugar, or the chocolate torte with a luscious liquid center accompanied by macadamia-nut brittle and cognac pear ice cream. Besides the extraordinary wine list, there are 70 wines by the glass (including 30 dessert wines), a dozen different martinis, and 20-plus single malts, including a 25 year-old Macallan. The upstairs wine bar is open Wednesday to Saturday.

✪ **Scaramouche.** 1 Benvenuto Place. ☎ **416/961-8011.** Reservations recommended. Main courses C$25–C$30 (US$18–US$21). AE, DC, ER, MC, V. Mon–Fri 6–10pm (till 11pm in pasta bar), Sat 6–10:30pm (till midnight in pasta bar). Subway: St. Clair. CONTEMPORARY FRENCH.

A little difficult to find (it's located in the first floor of an apartment building about 4 blocks south of St. Clair Avenue and Yonge Street, off Edmund Street), Scaramouche is certainly worth seeking out. Try to secure a window seat with a city-skyline view. The decor, the large flower arrangements, and the careful presentation of the food make it special.

Although the menu changes every 2 months, to start, there might be fresh lobster and scallop sausage in a lobster nage with roasted pepper aioli, or a terrine of duck foie gras served with grilled apple and mango in a port-wine reduction with toasted brioche. Among the 10 or so main courses, the signature dishes are hickory-smoked and grilled Bay of Fundy salmon on steamed leeks, shallots, and potatoes, with a horseradish white-wine sauce; grilled Rowe Farm filet mignon with roasted shallots and red-wine glaze; or the Arctic char cooked in court-bouillon and served with chervil and chive hollandaise. There's also a pasta-bar menu, which offers similar appetizers and a selection of gnocchi, fusilli, and linguini, all done in excitingly different ways, plus a few meat and fish dishes. The desserts, too, always have an original spin, like the crème brûlée flavored with Tahitian vanilla beans served with fresh berries and berry coulis.

MODERATE

✪ **Pronto.** 692 Mount Pleasant Rd. (just south of Eglinton). ☎ **416/486-1111.** Reservations recommended well in advance. Main courses C$18–C$26 (US$13–US$19). AE, ER, MC, V. Daily 5–10:30pm. Subway: Eglinton. ITALIAN.

Behind the austere black-tile facade, diners will discover a vibrant yet intimate dining room where the chefs can be seen in an open kitchen in the back. The cuisine has a reputation to match the room. Among the long list of appetizers and pastas (which can be ordered as a main course), there might be warm portobello mushrooms with Asiago cheese on grilled radicchio, arugula with balsamic vinaigrette, or Prince Edward Island mussels steamed in a lemongrass ginger broth with leeks and fresh tomato. For your main course, select from the 10 or so carefully prepared entrees, like rack of lamb crusted with grain mustard on a wild-mushroom ragout and home-made dumplings, or the grilled Bay of Fundy salmon on lobster potato and steamed sea asparagus with salsa verde. To finish, even the simple shortbread and lemon curd with blueberry sorbetto is sublime.

5   Seeing the Sights

Although some major sights are centrally located, several favorites lie outside the downtown core—the Ontario Science Centre, Canada's Wonderland, and the zoo—and take extra time and effort to reach. Ideally, you should spend 1 day each at Ontario Place, the Ontario Science Centre, Canada's Wonderland, and Harbourfront. In fact, that's what the kids will definitely want to do.

THE TOP ATTRACTIONS
ON THE LAKEFRONT

Ontario Place. 955 Lakeshore Blvd. W. ☎ **416/314-9811,** or 416/314-9900 for a recording. Gate admission is C$10 (US$7); play-all-day pass C$20 (US$14) adults, C$10 (US$7) children 3–5. IMAX movies after Labour Day C$9 (US$6) adults, C$4.50 (US$3.20) seniors and children under 13 (included in pass in summer). Mid-May to mid-September daily from 10am with most attractions closing at dusk, except for evening events. Open weekends only after Labour Day until mid-September; the Cinesphere is open year-round. Parking C$9 (US$6). Take the subway to Bathurst or Dufferin and buses south from there to Exhibition. Call TTC Information (☎ 416/393-4636) for special bus-service details.

When this 96-acre recreation complex on Lake Ontario opened in 1971, it seemed futuristic, and 27 years later, it still does (although it was revamped in 1989). From a distance, you'll see five steel-and-glass pods suspended 105 feet up on columns above the lake, three artificial islands, and alongside, a huge geodesic dome that looks like a golf ball magnified several thousand times. The five pods contain a multimedia theater, a live children's theater, a high-technology exhibit, and other displays that tell the story of Ontario in vivid kaleidoscopic detail. The dome houses Cinesphere, where a 60- by 80-foot screen shows specially made IMAX movies.

Located under an enormous orange canopy, the Children's Village is the most creative playground you'll find anywhere in the world. In a well-supervised area, children 12 and under can scramble over rope bridges, bounce on an enormous trampoline, explore the foam forest, slide down a twisting chute, or most popular of all, squirt water pistols and garden hoses, swim, and generally drench one another in the water-play section. There are also three specialty children's theaters.

A stroll around the complex reveals two marinas full of yachts and other craft, the HMCS *Haida* (a destroyer, open for touring, that served in both World War II and the Korean War), a miniature 18-hole golf course, plenty of grassland for picnicking and general cavorting, and a wide variety of restaurants and snack bars serving everything from Chinese, Irish, German, and Canadian food to hot dogs and hamburgers. And don't miss the wildest rides in town—the Hydrofuge, the rush river raft ride, the pink twister and purple pipeline (water slides), the bumper boats, and the go-carts. For something more peaceful, you can navigate paddleboats or remote-control boats between the artificial islands.

At night the outdoor **Molson Amphitheatre** accommodates 16,000 under a copper canopy and outside on its grassy slopes, and features top-line entertainers—Kenny G, James Taylor, The Who, Hank Williams, and Lord of the Dance are some recent performers. For information, call ☎ **416/260-5600.**

✪ **Harbourfront Centre.** Queen's Quay W. ☎ **416/973-3000** for information on special events or 416/973-4000 for box office. Take the LRT from Union or Spadina stations.

In 1972, the federal government took over a 96-acre strip of prime waterfront land to preserve the waterfront vista—and since then Torontonians have rediscovered their lakeshore. Abandoned warehouses, shabby depots, and crumbling factories have been refurbished, and a tremendous urban park now stretches on and around the old piers.

Downtown Toronto

ATTRACTIONS
Allan Gardens ⑫
Art Gallery of Ontario ❷
BCE Place ㉟
Bus Station ⑭
CBC Building ㊴
Campbell House ⑲
City Hall ⑳
CN Tower ㊶
Convention Centre ㊵
Eaton Centre ⑮
The Grange ❸
Harbourfront Antiques Market ❽
Hockey Hall of Fame ㉟
Hummingbird Centre ㉞
Kensington Market ❶
Maple Leaf Gardens ⑩
Old City Hall ㉑
Princess of Wales Theatre ㉔
Royal Alexandra Theatre ㉕
Royal Bank Plaza ㊱
Roy Thomson Hall ㉖
St. Lawrence Market ㉝
SkyDome ❼
Toronto Dominion Centre ㉗
Toronto Stock Exchange ㉓
Union Station ㊷

ACCOMMODATIONS
Bond Place Hotel ⑰
Delta Chelsea Inn ⑬
Hotel Victoria ㉛
King Edward Hotel ㉜
Neil Wycik College Hotel ⑪
Radisson Plaza Hotel Admiral ㊸
Royal York ㊲
Sheraton Centre ㉒
Strathcona ㊳
Toronto International Hostel ⑱
Westin Harbour Castle ㊹

DINING
Acqua ㉙
Canoe ㉘
Jump Cafe & Bar ㊷
La Fenice ❻
Le Select ❺
Movenpick Marche ㉚
Rivoli ❹
Senator ⑯

1-0339

396

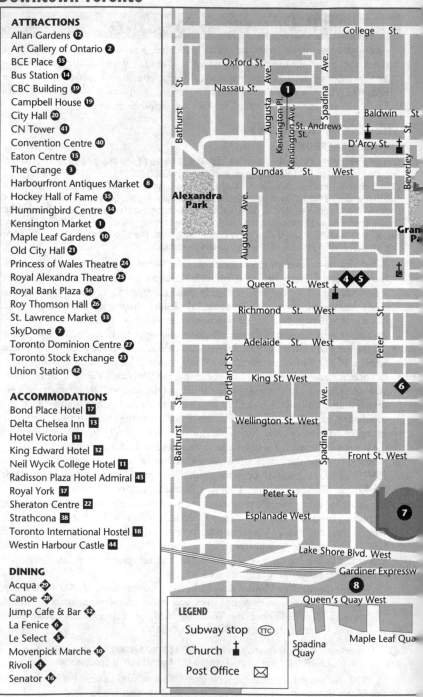

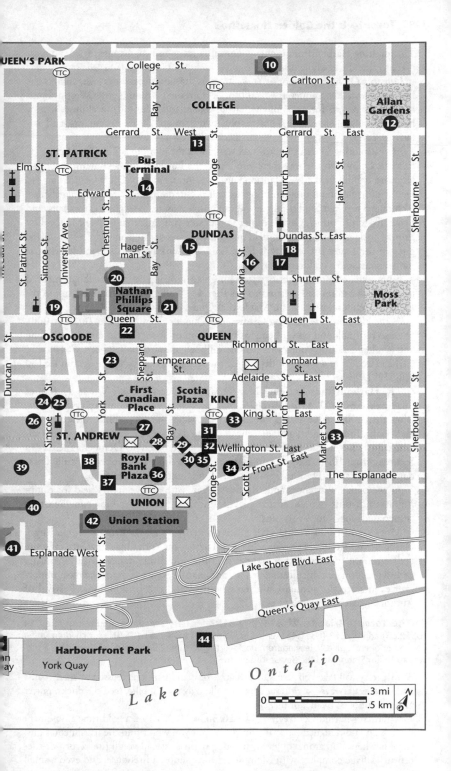

The resulting Harbourfront is one of Toronto's most exciting happenings. It's a great place to spend the whole day.

Queen's Quay, at the foot of York Street, is the closest quay to town, and it's the first point you'll encounter as you approach from the Harbour Castle Westin. From here, boats depart for tours of the harbor and islands. An old warehouse, it now houses the Premiere Dance Theatre, plus two floors of shops, restaurants, and waterfront cafes.

After exploring Queen's Quay, walk west along the glorious waterfront promenade to **York Quay.** On the way there you'll pass the Power Plant, a contemporary gallery, and behind it, the Du Maurier Theatre Centre. At York Quay Centre you can secure information on programming, as well as entertain yourself in several galleries, including The Craft Studio, where you can watch artisans blow glass, throw pots, and make silk-screen prints. On the center's other side you can attend a free Molson Dry Front Music outdoor concert, held all summer long at Molson Place. Also on the quay in the center is the Water's Edge Café, overlooking a small pond for electric model boats and a children's play area.

From here, take the footbridge to John Quay, crossing over the sailboats moored below, to the stores and restaurants on **Pier 4**—Wallymagoo's marine bar and the Pier 4 Storehouse. Beyond, on Maple Leaf Quay, lies the Nautical Centre.

At the **Harbourside Boating Centre,** 283 Queen's Quay W. (☎ 416/203-3000), you can rent sail- and power boats, as well as sign on for sailing lessons or weeklong and weekend sailing courses. A 3-hour sailboat rental costs between C$100 and C$125 (US$71 and US$89), depending on the boat's size; power boats run C$180 (US$129).

The **Harbourfront Antiques Market,** at 390 Queen's Quay W., at the foot of Spadina Avenue (☎ 416/260-2626), will keep antique-lovers browsing for hours. More than 100 antique dealers spread out their wares—jewelry, china, furniture, toys, and books. Indoor parking is adjacent to the market, and a cafeteria serves fresh salads, sandwiches, and desserts for rest stops. It's open May to October, Tuesday to Saturday from 10am to 6pm, Sunday from 8am to 6pm; November to April, Tuesday to Friday from 11am to 5pm, Saturday and Sunday 10am to 6pm.

At the park's west end stands **Bathurst Pier,** with a large sports field for romping around, plus two adventure playgrounds, one for older kids and the other (supervised) for 3- to 7-year-olds.

More than 4,000 events take place annually at Harbourfront, including a Harbourfront Reading Festival, held every Tuesday on York Quay, that attracts some very eminent writers. Other happenings include films, dance, theater, music, children's events, multicultural festivals, and marine events. Two of the most important events are the annual Children's Festival and the International Festival of Authors. Most activities are free.

✪ **The Toronto Islands.** ☎ 416/392-8193 for ferry schedules. Round-trip fare C$4 (US$2.85) adults, C$2 (US$1.45) seniors and youths 15–19, C$1 (US70¢) for children under 15. Ferries operate all day, leaving from docks at the bottom of Bay St. To get there, take a subway to Union Station and the Bay St. bus south.

A little ferry will take you across to 612 acres of island park crisscrossed by shady paths and quiet waterways—a glorious spot to walk, play tennis, bike, feed the ducks, putter around in boats, picnic, or just sit.

Children will find **Centreville** (☎ 416/363-0405), a 19-acre old-time amusement park, built and designed especially for them. But you won't find the usual neon signs, shrill hawkers, and aroma of greasy hot-dog stands. Instead you'll find a turn-of-the-century village complete with Main Street, tiny shops, a firehouse, and even a small working farm where the kids can pet lambs and chicks and enjoy pony rides. They'll also love trying out the miniature antique cars, fire engines, old-fashioned train, the authentic 1890s carousel, the flume ride, and the aerial cars. An all-day ride pass costs C$10 (US$7) for those 4 feet tall and under and C$15 (US$11) for those over 4 feet. Individual ride tickets are C84¢ (US60¢). Open daily from mid-May to Labour Day from 10:30am to 6pm.

DOWNTOWN

CN Tower. 301 Front St. W. ☎ **416/360-8500.** Admission C$13 (US$9) adults, C$11 (US$8) seniors, C$9 (US$6) children 5–12; children under 5 free. Cosmic Pinball, Q-Zar, and Virtual World C$6 (US$4.30) adults, C$5 (US$3.55) children 5–12; children under 5 free. Mid-May to Labour Day daily 9am–11pm; rest of the year daily 10am–10pm. Cosmic Pinball and Q-Zar early June to Labour Day daily 10am–10pm; otherwise Sun–Thurs 11am–5pm, Fri–Sat 11am–9pm. Subway: Union Station, then walk west along Front St.

As you approach the city, the first thing you'll notice is this slender needlelike structure. Tiny colored elevators that look like jumping beans glide to the top of this 1,815-foot-high tower—the tallest freestanding structure in the world.

They whisk you to the 1,136-foot-high seven-level sky pod in just under 1 minute. From here, on a clear day you can't quite see forever, but you can see, I'm told, all the way to Niagara Falls, or even Buffalo, if you wish.

Besides the view, the tower offers several futuristic attractions—Cosmic Pinball, a simulator ride that duplicates the experience of a pinball, catapulting riders at high velocity past flashing lights, flippers, bumpers, and other hazards; Q-Zar, an exhilarating laser tag game; and Virtual World, featuring the computer games Battletech and Red Planet. The latest thrill experience is the Climbing Wall, which is open during summer at a cost of C$6 (US$4.30) per climb. The pod also contains broadcasting facilities, a revolving restaurant, and a nightclub. For lunch, dinner, or Sunday-brunch reservations at the **360 Revolving Restaurant,** call ☎ **416/362-5411.**

Atop the tower sits a 335-foot antenna mast that took 3¹/₂ weeks to erect with the aid of a giant Sikorsky helicopter. It took 55 lifts to complete the operation. Above the sky pod is the world's highest public observation gallery, the Space Deck, at 1,465 feet above the ground. The Outdoor Observation deck one floor below has a glass floor, which makes for a scary experience and a real bird's-eye view of the SkyDome. While you're up there, don't worry about the elements sweeping the tower into the lake: It's built of contoured reinforced concrete covered with thick glass-reinforced plastic, which is designed to keep ice accumulation to a minimum. The structure can withstand the highest winds and the effects of snow, ice, lightning, and earth tremors.

✪ Art Gallery of Ontario. 317 Dundas St. W. (between McCaul and Beverly sts.). ☎ **416/977-0414.** Admission by donation with suggestion of C$5 (US$3.55) adults. A fee (which could be as much as C$11/US$8) is charged for special exhibits. Tues–Fri noon–9pm, Sat–Sun 10am–5:30pm; Grange, Tues–Sun noon–4pm, Wed noon–9pm. Closed Christmas Day and New Year's Day. Subway: St. Patrick on the University line; or take the subway to Dundas and the streetcar west.

The concrete exterior gives no hint of the light and openness inside this beautifully designed gallery. The recently refurbished and expanded gallery and atrium space is dramatic and the paintings are imaginatively displayed. Throughout are audiovisual presentations and interactive computer presentations that provide information on particular paintings or schools of painters.

Although the European collections are fine, I would concentrate on the Canadian galleries. The galleries displaying the Group of Seven—among them Tom Thomson,

F. H. Varley, and Lawren Harris—are extraordinary. In addition, other galleries show the genesis of Canadian art from earlier to more modern artists. Also don't miss the galleries featuring Inuit art.

The Henry Moore Sculpture Centre, possessing more than 800 pieces (original plasters, bronzes, maquettes, woodcuts, lithographs, etchings, and drawings), is the largest public collection of the works of the modern British sculptor. In one room, under a glass ceiling, 20 or so of his large works stand like silent prehistoric rock formations. Along the walls flanking a ramp are color photographs showing Moore's major sculptures in their natural locations, which fully reveal their magnificent dimensions.

The collection of European old masters ranges from the 14th century to the French impressionists and beyond. Among the sculpture you'll find Picasso's *Poupée* and Brancusi's *First Cry,* two beauties.

Behind the gallery and connected by an arcade stands The Grange (1817), Toronto's oldest surviving brick house, which was the gallery's first permanent space. Originally the home of the Boulton family, it was a gathering place for many of the city's social and political leaders as well as such eminent guests as Matthew Arnold, Prince Kropotkin, and Winston Churchill. Today it's a living museum of mid-19th-century Toronto life, meticulously restored and furnished to reflect the 1830s. Entrance is free with admission to the art gallery.

MIDTOWN

✪ **Royal Ontario Museum.** 100 Queen's Park (at Avenue Rd. and Bloor St.). ☎ **416/586-5549.** Admission C$10 (US$7) adults, C$5 (US$3.55) seniors and students; children under 5 free; by donation Tues 4:30–8pm. Mon and Wed–Sat 10am–6pm, Tues 10am–8pm, Sun 11am–6pm. Closed Christmas Day and New Year's Day. Subway: Museum or St. George.

The ROM, as it's affectionately called, is Canada's largest museum, with more than six million objects in its collections.

Among the many highlights is the Chinese collection, one of the world's best, which includes displays of Chinese wall paintings, 14 monumental Buddhist sculptures dating from the 12th through the 16th centuries, Chinese stone sculptures that were part of an original Ming tomb, and a gallery filled with rare jades, glazed tomb figures of warriors, weapons, and horse and chariot fittings, which span 5,000 years.

The Sigmund Samuel Canadiana galleries display a premier collection of early Canadian decorative arts and historical paintings showcased in elaborate period room settings. This collection also contains the famous McCrea models of buildings, farm implements, and tools, which are a representation in miniature of early rural life in Ontario. Other highlights include the Ancient Egypt Gallery with its mummies, the Roman gallery (Canada's most extensive collection), the world-class textile collection, and nine life-science galleries (devoted to evolution, mammals, reptiles, and botany).

A favorite with kids is the Bat Cave Gallery, a miniature replica of the St. Clair bat cave in Jamaica, complete with more than 3,000 very lifelike bats roosting and flying through the air amid realistic spiders, crabs, a wild cat, and snakes. Kids also enjoy the Dinosaur Gallery, featuring 13 dinosaur skeletons, and the Discovery Gallery, a minimuseum where kids and adults can touch authentic artifacts from Egyptian scarabs to English military helmets.

✪ **George R. Gardiner Museum of Ceramic Art.** 111 Queen's Park. ☎ **416/586-8080.** Admission by donation (C$5/US$3.55 suggested). Mon and Wed–Sat 10am–5pm, Tues 10am–8pm, Sun 11am–5pm. Subway: Museum or St. George.

Across the street from the ROM, the George R. Gardiner Museum, North America's only specialized ceramics museum, houses a great collection of 15th- to 18th-century

European ceramics in four galleries. The pre-Columbian gallery contains fantastic Olmec and Maya figures, as well as objects from cultures in Mexico, Ecuador, Colombia, and Peru. The majolica gallery displays spectacular 16th- and 17th-century pieces from Florence, Faenza, and Venice and a Delftware collection of fine 17th-century chargers and other examples.

Upstairs the galleries are given over to porcelain—Meissen, Sèvres, Worcester, Chelsea, Derby, and other great names. All are spectacular. Among the highlights are the pieces from the Swan Service—a 2,200-piece set that took 4 years (1737–41) to make—and an extraordinary collection of Commedia dell'Arte figures.

ON THE OUTSKIRTS

✪ Ontario Science Centre. 770 Don Mills Rd. (at Eglinton Ave. E.). ☎ **416/696-3127,** or 416/696-1000 for OMNIMAX tickets. Admission C$8 (US$6) adults, C$5 (US$3.55) seniors and children 5–16, C$21 (US$15) families; children under 4 free. Same prices, respectively, for OMNIMAX. Special discounts apply if you attend both the Science Centre and OMNIMAX. July–Aug daily 10am–8pm; otherwise Sun–Tues, Thurs, and Sat 10am–5pm, Wed 10am–8pm, Fri 10am–9pm. Closed Christmas Day. Parking C$5 (US$3.55). Take the Yonge St. subway to Eglinton, then the Eglinton bus going east, and get off at Don Mills Rd. If you're driving from downtown, take the Don Valley Pkwy. and follow the signs from Don Mills Rd. north.

Described as everything from the world's most technical fun fair to a hands-on museum of the 21st century, the Science Centre really does hold a series of wonders for adult and child—650 hands-on experiments, no less, in 10 themed exhibit halls. When one million people visit every year, you know that the best time to get to the museum is promptly at 10am—that way you'll be able to play without too much interference and negotiation.

The building itself is another one of architect Raymond Moriyama's miracles. Instead of flattening the ravine and bulldozing the trees on the site, Moriyama designed to the ravine's contours so that a series of glass-enclosed escalators providing views of the natural surroundings take you down an escarpment to the main exhibition halls. Supposedly, Moriyama built penalty clauses into the subcontractors' contracts for each and every tree destroyed!

Wherever you look, there are things to touch, push, pull, or crank. Test your reflexes, balance, heart rate, and grip strength; play with computers and binary-system games and puzzles; and shunt slides of butterfly wings, bedbugs, fish scales, or feathers under the microscope. Tease your brain with optical illusions; land a spaceship on the moon. Watch bees making honey; try to lift sponge building blocks with a mechanical grip; or see how high you can elevate a balloon with your own pedal power. The fun goes on and on.

Throughout, there are small theaters showing films and slide shows on various topics, while at regular times demonstrators present 20-minute expositions on such subjects as lasers, metal casting, and high-voltage electricity (watch your friend's hair stand on end). Another draw is the OMNIMAX Theatre, featuring a 79-foot domed screen which creates spectacular effects. Facilities include a licensed restaurant and lounge, cafeteria, and science shop.

✪ The Metropolitan Zoo. Meadowvale Rd. (north of Hwy. 401 and Sheppard Ave.), Scarborough. ☎ **416/392-5900.** Admission C$12 (US$9) adults, C$9 (US$6) seniors and children 12–17, C$7 (US$5) children 4–11; children under 4 free. Summer daily 9am–7:30pm; winter daily 9:30am–4:30pm. Closed Christmas Day. Take the subway all the way to Kennedy on the Bloor-Danforth line. Then take bus no. 86A north from there. Check with the TTC for schedules (☎ 416/393-4636). Driving from downtown, take the Don Valley Pkwy. to Hwy. 401 east and exit on Meadowvale Rd.

Covering 710 acres of parkland in Scarborough is a unique zoological garden containing some 4,000 animals, plus an extensive botanical collection. The plants and

Midtown Toronto

TORONTO

Midtown

ATTRACTIONS
Allan Gardens **24**
Bata Shoe Museum **6**
Gardiner Museum of
Ceramic Art **16**
Maple Leaf Gardens **23**
Metro Library **21**
Ontario Parliament
Building **19**
Queen's Park **18**
Royal Ontario
Museum (ROM) **15**
University of Toronto **9**
Varsity Stadium **8**

ACCOMMODATIONS
Four Seasons Hotel **13**
Intercontinental **7**
Neil Wycik College
Hotel **25**
Park Plaza **14**
Sutton Place Hotel **20**
Venture Inn **11**
Victoria University **17**

DINING
Boba **10**
Boulevard Cafe **3**
Chiado **1**
Il Posto **12**
Kensington Kitchen **4**
Pan on the Danforth **22**
Splendido **5**
Trattoria Giancarlo **2**

LEGEND
TTC Subway stop

1-0340

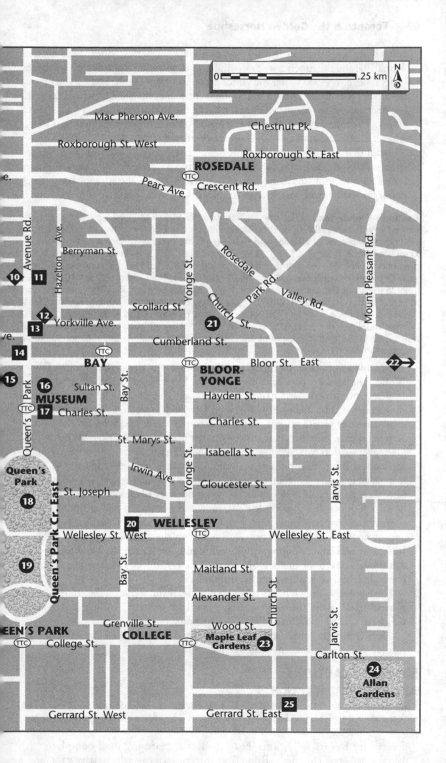

animals are housed either in the eight pavilions—including Africa, Indo-Malaya, Australasia, and the Americas—or in outdoor paddocks. It's a photographer's dream.

Six miles of walkways offer the visitor access to any area of the zoo, or you can use the Zoomobile or monorail. During the warmer months the Zoomobile takes the zoo-goer around the major walkways, viewing the animals contained in outdoor facilities. The monorail, which runs year-round, travels through the beautiful Rouge River Valley where animals native to Canada are displayed.

Facilities include restaurants, picnic tables, gift shop, first aid, and family center; strollers and wheelchairs are also available. The zoo is equipped with ramps and washrooms for travelers with disabilities. The Africa pavilion is also equipped with an elevator for strollers and wheelchairs. Ample parking is available.

Canada's Wonderland. 9580 Jane St., Vaughan. ☎ **905/832-7000,** or 905/832-8131 for concert information at the Kingswood Music Theatre. Pay One Price Passport, for the day, including unlimited use of all rides and shows (excludes parking, special attractions, and the Kingswood Music Theatre), C$36 (US$26) adults, C$18 (US$13) seniors and children 3–6; children under 2 free. Grounds admission only (no rides) C$20 (US$14). May and Labour Day to early Oct weekends only 10am–8pm; June 1–25 Mon–Fri 10am–8pm, Sat–Sun 10am–10pm; June 26 to Labour Day daily 10am–10pm. Hanna Barbera Land and Kids Kingdom close daily at 8pm. "Splashworks" open 11am–7pm, depending on weather and lighting. Parking C$6.50 (US$5). To get there, take the GO Express Bus from Yorkdale or York Mills subway directly to Wonderland. If you're driving, take Yonge St. north to Hwy. 401 and travel west to Hwy. 400 north. Take the Rutherford Rd. exit off Hwy. 400 and follow the signs. Exit at Major Mackenzie if heading south on Hwy. 400.

Thirty minutes (31km / 19 miles) north of Toronto is Canada's answer to Disney World. The 300-acre park features more than 140 attractions, including 50 rides, a 10-acre water park, a participatory play area, and live shows. The newest stomach churner is the Drop Zone, in which riders free-fall 230 feet in an open cockpit. Another terrifying experience can be had aboard the Xtreme Skyflyer, which is a cross between skydiving and hang gliding. Among the most popular rides though are the nine roller coasters, which range from a nostalgic, relatively tame wooden version to the looping inverted Top Gun, the standup looping Sky Rider, and the Vortex, a suspended type of roller coaster. Splash Works is a 20-acre water park, which has a huge wave pool and 16 water rides, including the scary Black Hole, which drops you down a 400-foot slide in complete darkness, and a fun water-play area for kids that contains rotating water guns, pipe water falls, and much more. Top-name entertainers appear at the Kingswood Theatre. To add to the thrills, Klingons, Vulcans, Romulans, and Bajorans along with Hanna-Barbera characters stroll around the park. Additional attractions include Speedcity Raceway, featuring two-seated go-carts, minigolf, batting cages, restaurants, and shops.

You'll probably need 8 hours to see everything. If you picnic on the grounds, forgo souvenirs, and avoid the video games, a family of four can do the park for about C$110 to C$150 (US$79 to US$107), depending on the age of the kids.

Note: Watch out for the extra added attractions that are not included in the admission pass, particularly the many "games of skill."

MORE ATTRACTIONS
ARCHITECTURAL HIGHLIGHTS

Casa Loma. 1 Austin Terrace. ☎ **416/923-1171.** Admission C$8 (US$6) adults, C$5 (US$3.55) seniors and youths 14–17, C$4.50 (US$3.20) children 4–13; children under 4 free. Daily 9:30am–4pm. Gardens are open in summer only. Subway: Dupont, then walk 2 blocks north.

Every city has its folly, and Toronto has a charming one, complete with Elizabethan-style chimneys, Rhineland turrets, secret panels, passageways, and a

An Idyllic Setting for Art: The McMichael Collection at Kleinburg

The McMichael Canadian Art Collection, featuring Canadian, Inuit, First Nations, and contemporary art, is worth the trip 40 kilometers (25 miles) north of downtown—for the setting as well as the art. The log-and-stone gallery sits amidst quiet stands of pine trees on 100 acres of conservation land. Specially designed to house the Canadian landscapes within, the gallery ambiance is established in the lobby—itself a work of art with a pitched roof that soars to a height of 27 feet on massive rafters of Douglas fir. Throughout the gallery panoramic windows look south over white pine, cedar, ash, and birch.

The gallery houses works by Canada's famous group of landscape painters, the "Group of Seven," as well as David Milne, Emily Carr, and their contemporaries. These painters, inspired by the Canadian wilderness early in this century, particularly that of Algonquin Park and northern Ontario, recorded its rugged landscape in highly individualistic styles. An impressive collection of Inuit and contemporary native-Canadian art and sculpture is also on display.

Founded by Robert and Signe McMichael, the gallery began in 1965 when they donated their property, home, and collection of 177 works to the Province of Ontario. Since 1965 the collection has expanded to include more than 5,000 works. Still, its unique atmosphere has been preserved—with log and barn-wood walls, fieldstone fireplaces, and rustic decor, like the hooked rugs and earthenware urns from the original McMichael home.

The gallery is located at 10365 Islington Ave. in Kleinburg (☎ **905/893-1121**). From downtown, take the Gardiner Expressway to Highway 427 north, following it to Highway 7. Go east at Highway 7 and turn left (north) at the first light onto Highway 27. Turn right (east) at Major Mackenzie Drive and left (north) at the first set of traffic lights to Islington Avenue and the village of Kleinburg. Or take the 401 to Highway 400 north. At Major Mackenzie Drive, go west to Islington Avenue and take a right to get to the gallery. Admission is C$7 (US$5) for adults, C$5 (US$3.55) for seniors, C$4 (US$2.85) for students, C$15 (US$11) for families; children under 5 are free. Parking is C$3 (US$2.15). From Victoria Day to Canadian Thanksgiving, hours are daily from 10am to 5pm; from late October to Victoria Day, it's open Tuesday to Sunday from 10am to 4pm. In summer, buses to the gallery operate from the Islington subway station. Trolley service (C$19/US$14 adults, C$17/US$12 children; children under 4 are free) is also available from key downtown hotels.

mellifluous-sounding name: Casa Loma. Sir Henry Pellatt had a lifelong and incurably romantic fascination with medieval castles—so he decided to build his own, from 1911 to 1914, at a cost of C$3.5 million (US$2.5 million). He studied European medieval castles, and gathered materials and furnishings from far-flung sources, bringing marble, glass, and paneling from Europe, teak from Asia, and oak and walnut from prime areas of North America. He imported Scottish stonemasons to build the massive walls that surround the 6-acre site.

It's a fascinating place to explore: Rooms include the majestic Great Hall with its 60-foot ceiling; the Oak Room, where three artisans worked for 3 years to fashion the paneling; the Conservatory, with its elegant bronze doors and stained-glass dome; the battlements and towers; Sir Henry's suite, containing a shower with an 18-inch-diameter shower head; the 1,700-bottle wine cellar; and the 800-foot tunnel to the stables, where horses were quartered amid the luxury of Spanish tile and mahogany.

City Hall. Queen St. W. (at Bay St.) ☎ **416/392-7341.** Self-guided tours Mon–Fri 8:30am–4pm. Subway: Queen St. or Osgoode.

This architectural spectacle houses the mayor's office and the new megacity's administrative offices. Daringly designed in the early 1960s by the Finnish architect Viljo Revell, it consists of a low podium topped by the flying-saucer–shaped Council Chamber, which is enfolded between two curved towers. In front stretches Nathan Phillips Square (named after the mayor who initiated the project), where in summer you can sit and contemplate the flower gardens, fountains, and reflecting pool (which doubles as a skating rink in winter), as well as listen to concerts. Here also stands Henry Moore's *Three-Way Piece No. 2,* locally referred to as *The Archer,* which the city purchased through a public subscription fund. To the east, in contrast, stands Old City Hall, a green-copper-roofed Victorian Romanesque-style building.

Ontario Legislature. Queen's Park. ☎ **416/325-7500.** Tours given daily Victoria Day to Labour Day. Call ahead to check times and also for tours in winter. Subway: Queen's Park.

East of the university, at the top of University Avenue, lies Queen's Park, surrounding the rose-tinted sandstone-and-granite Ontario Parliament buildings, which are profusely carved, with stately domes, arches, and porte cocheres. Drop in between 2 and 3pm when the legislature is in session (in fall, winter, and spring) for some pithy comments during the Question Period.

Royal Bank Plaza. At the corner of Front and Bay sts. Subway: Union.

Shimmering in the sun, the Royal Bank Plaza looks like a pillar of gold, and with good reason. During its construction, 2,500 ounces of gold were used as a coloring agent in the building's 14,000 windows. More importantly, it is a masterpiece of design and architectural drama. Two triangular towers of bronze mirrored glass flank a 130-foot-high glass-walled banking hall. The external tower walls are built in a serrated configuration so they reflect a phenomenal mosaic of color from the skies and surrounding buildings. In the banking hall, check out the work of Venezuelan sculptor Jesus Raphael Soto.

SkyDome. 1 Blue Jays Way. ☎ **416/341-2770.** 1-hr. tours begin most days at 10am (call ahead because schedules change); cost is C$9.50 (US$7) adults, C$7 (US$5) seniors and children. Subway: Union, then follow the SkyWalk signs west.

In 1989 the opening of the downtown 53,000-seat SkyDome, new home to the Toronto Blue Jays baseball team and the Toronto Argonauts football team, was a gala event. The stadium itself represents an engineering feat, featuring the world's first fully retractable roof, which spans more than 8 acres, and a gigantic video scoreboard. So large is it that you could fit a 31-story building inside the complex when the roof is closed. Indeed, there's already an 11-story hotel with 70 rooms facing directly onto the field.

HISTORIC BUILDINGS

Campbell House. 160 Queen St. W. ☎ **416/597-0227.** Admission C$3.50 (US$2.50) adults, C$2.50 (US$1.80) seniors and students, C$2 (US$1.45) children. Mon–Fri 9:30am–4:30pm. Also Sat–Sun noon–4:30pm late May to early October. Subway: Osgoode.

Just across the street from Osgoode Hall, on the opposite corner of University and Queen, sits Sir William Campbell's mansion, built in 1822 by this Loyalist and subsequent chief justice of upper Canada. He retired to his mansion in 1829 where he resided until he died in 1834.

Fort York. Fleet St. (between Bathurst St. and Strachan Ave.). ☎ **416/392-6907.** Admission C$5 (US$3.55) adults, C$3.25 (US$2.30) seniors and youths 13–17, C$3 (US$2.15) children

6–12; children under 6 free. Summer Mon–Fri 10am–5pm, Sat–Sun noon–5pm; winter Tues–Sun noon–4pm. Streetcar: Bathurst streetcar south to the gate.

Established by Lieutenant-Governor Simcoe in 1793 to defend "little muddy York," as Toronto was then known, Fort York was sacked by Americans in 1813. At the fort you can see the soldiers' and officers' quarters, clamber over the ramparts, and view demonstrations and exhibits.

Osgoode Hall. 130 Queen St. W. ☎ **416/947-3300.** Free tours by appointment, except July–Aug, when daily tours are given Mon–Fri at 1:15pm. Subway: Osgoode.

To the west of City Hall extends an impressive, elegant wrought-iron fence in front of an equally gracious public building, Osgoode Hall, currently the home of the Law Society of Upper Canada and the Court of Appeal for Ontario. Folklore has it that the fence was originally built to prevent the cows from getting in and trampling the flower beds. On a conducted tour you can see the splendor of the grand staircase, the rotunda, the Great Library, and the fine portrait and sculpture collection. Building began in 1829 on this structure, troops were billeted here during the Rebellion of 1837, and the buildings now house the headquarters of Ontario's legal profession and several magnificent courtrooms—including one using materials from London's Old Bailey. The courts are open to the public.

MARKETS

Toronto has a colorful and lively tapestry that should not be missed—it's the **Kensington Market,** between Spadina Avenue and Bathurst Street, just south of College Street. If you can struggle out of bed to get there around 5am, you'll see the squawking chickens being carried from their trucks to the stalls. You'll hear the accents of Caribbean Islanders, Portuguese, Italians, and merchants of other nationalities, who spread their wares before them—squid and crabs in pails, chickens, pigeons, bread, cheese, apples, pears, peppers, ginger, and mangoes from the West Indies, salted fish from Portuguese dories, lace, fabrics, and other colorful remnants. There's no market on Sunday.

The other market, the **St. Lawrence,** on Front Street East between Church and Jarvis streets, has a more staid atmosphere, but it's a terrific food market held in a magnificent historic hall. It's open Tuesday to Saturday from 7am to 5pm (Saturday is *the* day).

MUSEUMS

The Bata Shoe Museum. 327 Bloor St. W. (at the corner of St. George). ☎ **416/979-7799.** Admission C$6 (US$4.30) adults, C$4 (US$2.85) students, C$2 (US$1.45) children 5–14; children under 5 free; 1st Tues of month free. Tues–Wed and Fri–Sat 10am–5pm, Thurs 10am–8pm, Sun noon–5pm. Subway: St. George.

Imelda Marcos—or anyone else obsessed by shoes—will love this museum housing the 9,000-item personal collection of the Bata family. Now located in a brand-new building, the three-floor galleries display shoes from all over the world and from every time period. The main gallery, All About Shoes, is home to the plaster cast of the first human footprints that date from 4 million B.C., discovered in Africa by anthropologist Mary Leakey, and then traces the development of shoes, from early sandals to space-age moon boots. It's a truly remarkable display and refreshingly different.

Black Creek Pioneer Village. Steeles Ave. and Jane St. ☎ **416/736-1733.** Admission C$8 (US$6) adults, C$6 (US$4.30) seniors, C$4 (US$2.85) children 5–14; children under 5 free. May–June Mon–Fri 9:30am–4:30pm, Sat–Sun 10am–5pm; July–Sept daily 10am–5pm; Oct–Dec Mon–Fri 9:30am–4pm, Sat–Sun 10am–4:30pm. Closed Jan–Apr. Take the Yonge St. subway north to Finch and transfer to the no. 60 bus that runs along Steeles Ave. W. to Jane St.

Life at this reconstructed village moves at the gentle pace of rural Ontario as it was 100 years ago. You can watch the authentically garbed villagers as they go about their chores—harrowing, seeding, rail splitting, sheep shearing, and threshing. Enjoy the fruits of their cooking, wander through the cozily furnished homesteads, visit the working mill, shop at the general store, and rumble past the farm animals in a horse-drawn wagon. There are over 30 restored buildings to explore.

Hockey Hall of Fame. 30 Yonge St. (at Front St. in BCE Place). ☎ **416/360-7765.** Admission C$10 (US$7) adults, C$5.50 (US$4) seniors and children 2–13; children under 2 free. Mon–Fri 10am–5pm, Sat 9:30am–6pm, Sun 10:30am–5pm. Subway: Union.

Ice-hockey fans will thrill to see the original Stanley Cup (donated in 1893 by Lord Stanley of Preston), a replica of the Montréal Canadiens' dressing room, Terry Sawchuck's goalie gear, Newsy Lalonde's skates, and the stick that Max Bentley used, along with photographs of the personalities and great moments in ice-hockey history. But a fan's greatest thrill should take place at the goal-scoring and goal-keeping arenas, where you have the chance to don goalie gear and face down some of the greats on video.

Marine Museum. Exhibition Place. ☎ **416/392-1765.** Admission C$3.50 (US$2.50) adults, C$2.75 (US$2) children 13–18 and seniors, C$2.50 (US$1.80) children 6–12, children under 6 free. Tues–Fri 10am–5pm, Sat–Sun and holidays noon–5pm. Take the 511 streetcar southbound from Bathurst.

This museum interprets the history of Toronto Harbour and its relation to the Great Lakes. From May to October, visitors can board the fully restored 1932 Ned Hanlan, the last steam tugboat to sail on Lake Ontario. The museum will be closed until July 1998 while it is being remodeled into a more interpretive waterfront-history facility.

NEIGHBORHOODS

CHINATOWN   Stretching along Dundas Street from Bay Street to Spadina Avenue, and north and south along Spadina, Chinatown, home to many of Toronto's 350,000 Chinese residents, is a great area for eating and browsing in fascinating shops. Even the street signs are in Chinese.

If you're interested in things Asian, then go into **Dragon City,** a large shopping mall on Spadina that's staffed and shopped by Chinese. Here you'll find all kinds of stores, some selling exotic Chinese preserves like cuttlefish, lemon ginger, whole mango, ginseng, and antler, and others specializing in Asian books, tapes, and records, as well as fashions and foods. Downstairs, a whole court is given over to Korean, Indonesian, Chinese, and Japanese fast-food restaurants.

As you stroll through Chinatown, stop at the **Kim Moon Bakery** on Dundas Street West (☎ **416/977-1933**), and pick up some Chinese pastries and/or a pork bun. Or go to a tea store. A walk through Chinatown at night is especially exciting— the sidewalks are filled with people, families, and youths, and neon lights shimmer everywhere. Another stopping place might be the **New Asia Supermarket** (☎ **416/591-9314**) around the corner from Dundas at 293–299 Spadina Ave.

QUEEN STREET WEST   Over the years this street, lined with an eclectic mix of stores and clubs, has been known as the heart of the city's funky avant-garde scene. Although recent trends have brought mainstream stores like The Gap, there's still a broad selection of good-value bistros, several secondhand and antiquarian bookstores, and funky fashion stores. East of Spadina, the street is being slowly gentrified, but beyond Spadina it still retains its rough and ready energy.

YORKVILLE   This is the name given to the area that stretches north of Bloor Street, between Avenue Road and Bay Street. In 1853 Yorkville became a village, surrounded then by trees and meadows; in the 1960s it became Toronto's Haight-Ashbury, the mecca for young suburban runaways; and in the 1980s it became the focus of the chic, who shopped at the famous-name boutiques (Hermès, Courrèges, Fabiani, Cartier, Turnbull and Asser) and occupied the restored town houses, as well as the art galleries, cafes, and restaurants.

It's a good place to stroll and browse; you can sit outside and enjoy an iced coffee at one of the many cafes on the south side of Yorkville Avenue and watch the parade go by. Most cafes have happy hours from 4pm to 7 or 8pm. Make sure you wander through the labyrinths of **Hazelton Lanes** between Avenue Road and Hazelton Avenue, where you'll find a maze of shops and offices clustered around an outdoor court in the center of a building that's topped with apartments—the most sought-after in the city. And while you're in the neighborhood (especially if you're an architecture buff), take a look at **Metro Library,** at Bloor Street and Yorkville Avenue, which was designed by Raymond Moriyama.

PARKS & GARDENS

Toronto is blessed with a sizable amount of green space when you include the Toronto Islands, such downtown green spaces as Queen's Park, and the series of parks that extend along the steep ravines of the Humber and Don valleys.

Downtown, the **Allan Gardens,** between Jarvis, Sherbourne, Dundas, and Gerrard streets (☎ **416/392-7259**), still contain the Victorian glass-domed Palm House.

In the northeast section of the city, **Edwards Garden** at Lawrence Avenue and Leslie Street (☎ **416/397-1340**), is a formal garden with a creek cutting through it. Part of a series of parks, it's famous for its rhododendrons but also features gracious bridges, rock gardens, and rose and other seasonal displays. Walking tours are given on Tuesday and Thursday at 11am and 2pm.

In the West End, the 400-acre **High Park** extends from Bloor Street to the Gardiner Expressway and shelters many delights: Grenadier Pond, a small zoo, swimming pool, tennis courts, sports fields, bowling greens, and vast expanses for jogging, picnicking, and bicycling.

ESPECIALLY FOR KIDS

The city puts on a fabulous array of special events for children at **Harbourfront.** In March the **Children's Film Festival** screens 40 films from 15 countries. In April **Spring Fever** celebrates the season with egg decorating, puppet shows, and more; on Saturday mornings in April, **cushion concerts** are given for the 5-to-12 set. In May the **Milk International Children's Festival** brings 100 international children's performers to the city for a week of great entertainment. For additional information, call ☎ **416/973-3000.**

For the last 30 years, the **Young Peoples Theatre,** at 165 Front St. E., at Sherbourne Street (☎ **416/862-2222** for the box office or 416/363-5131 for administration) has been entertaining young people. Its season runs from August to May.

All the attractions that have major appeal to kids of all ages are listed above, but here I've summarized them in what I think is the most logical order, at least from a kid's point of view (the first five, though, really belong in a dead heat).

- **Ontario Science Centre** Kids race to be the first at this paradise of fun hands-on games, experiments, and push-button demonstrations—700 of 'em.
- **Canada's Wonderland** The kids love the rides in the theme park. But watch out for video games and carnival games, which they also love—an unanticipated extra cost.

- **Harbourfront** Kaleidoscope is an ongoing program of creative crafts, active games, and special events on weekends and holidays. There is also a summer pond, winter ice-skating, and a crafts studio.
- **Ontario Place Waterslides** A huge Cinesphere, a futuristic pod, and other entertainment are the big hits at this recreational/cultural park on three artificial islands on the edge of Lake Ontario. In Children's Village, kids 12 and under can scramble over rope bridges, bounce on an enormous trampoline, or drench one another in the water-play section.
- **Metro Zoo** At one of the world's best zoos, modeled after San Diego's, the animals in this 710-acre park really do live in a natural environment.
- **Toronto Islands–Centreville** Riding a ferry to this turn-of-the-century amusement park is part of the fun.
- **CN Tower** Kids especially like the simulator and other cyber games at the base of the tower.
- **Royal Ontario Museum** The top hit is always the dinosaurs.
- **Fort York** The reenactments of battle drills, musket and cannon firing, and musical marches with fife and drum capture kids' attention.
- **Hockey Hall of Fame** Young hockey fans especially like the interactive video displays.
- **Black Creek Pioneer Village** Here kids can watch the way things used to be done.
- **Casa Loma** It's fun to tour the stables and the fantasy rooms.
- **Art Gallery of Ontario** Kids like its hands-on exhibit.

African Lion Safari. Off Hwy. 8 between Hamilton and Cambridge. ☎ **519/623-2620.** Admission C$15 (US$11) adults, C$13 (US$9) seniors and youths 13–17, C$11 (US$8) children 3–12. July to Labour Day daily 10am–5:30pm; Apr–June and Sept–Oct Mon–Fri 10am–4pm, Sat–Sun 10am–5pm. Closed Nov–Mar.

Just a half-hour northwest of Hamilton, you can drive yourself or take the guided safari tram through this 750-acre wildlife park containing rhino, cheetah, lion, white Bengal tiger, giraffes, zebra, vultures, and many other species. Shows and demonstrations are held throughout the day. There are also scenic railroad and boat rides, plus special kids' jungle and water (bring bathing suits) play areas. Admission includes a tour of the six large game reserves plus the rides and shows.

Chudleigh's. On Hwy. 25 north of Hwy. 401 (P.O. Box 76), Milton, ON. ☎ **905/826-1252.** Admission C$3 (US$2.15) adults; children under 4 free. Discounts with purchase available. July–Oct daily 9am–6pm; Nov–June daily 10am–5pm.

A day here will introduce the kids to life on a farm. They'll enjoy the hayrides, pony rides, and, in season, the apple picking, as well as the entertainment area featuring slides, a swinging bridge, a straw maze, and some farm animals. The store also sells pies, cider, and other gourmet foods.

Cullen Gardens & Miniature Village. Taunton Rd., Whitby, ON. ☎ **905/668-6606.** Admission C$8.75 (US$6) adults, C$7 (US$5) seniors and children 3–12. July–Aug daily 9am–9pm; Mid-Apr to June and Sept–Oct daily 10am–6pm; Nov–Dec 10am–10pm. Closed early Jan to mid-Apr.

The miniature village (made to one-twelfth scale) has great appeal. The 27 acres of gardens, including a wildflower garden and bird sanctuary, and the shopping and live entertainment add to the fun. Kids enjoy the splash ponds and playground.

Wild Water Kingdom. 7855 Finch Ave. W. (1 mile west of Hwy. 427), Brampton, ON. ☎ **416/369-WILD** or 905/794-0565. Admission C$17 (US$12) adults, C$13 (US$9) children

4–9 and seniors. Mid-June to late June daily 10am–6pm; July 1 to Labour Day daily 10am–8pm; May 31 to mid-June Sat–Sun only, 10am–6pm. Closed at other times.

Kids love this huge water theme park, complete with a half-acre wave pool, 18 water rides, and giant hot tubs. In between they can use the batting cages, practice on the minigolf circuit, and enjoy the bumper boats.

6 Special Events & Festivals

The big event in May is the 9-day **Milk International Children's Festival,** featuring more than 30 international entertainment troupes—acrobats, mimes, comedians, storytellers, theater companies, and puppeteers. For details, call Harbourfront at ☎ 416/973-3000.

In June, the **Metro International Caravan** (☎ 416/977-0466) is a 9-day feast of arts, food, and entertainment celebrating the cultural life of the city's many ethnic communities, from Armenian to Vietnamese. A Passport admitting you to the 40 pavilions around town is C$14 (US$10) for the whole 9 days (or C$7/US$5 for 1 day).

In late June or early July, the **Queen's Plate** is run at Woodbine Racetrack. Begun in 1859, it is the oldest stakes race in North America. Another big June event is the 10-day **du Maurier Jazz Festival.** Also in late June/early July the 10-day **Fringe Theatre Festival** showcases experimental and new drama featuring more than 80 performing artists/groups. For information, write or call the **Fringe of Toronto Festival,** 720 Bathurst St., Suite 303, Toronto, ON, M5S 2R4 (☎ 416/534-5919).

In July, usually on the third weekend, the **Molson Indy,** a grand-prix race on the IndyCar circuit, is run at the Exhibition Place circuit. Call ☎ 416/872-4639. At the end of July or the beginning of August, a West Indian calypso beat takes over the city when three-quarters of a million people dance, sway, and watch the colorful **Caribana** celebration, Toronto's version of carnival, complete with traditional Caribbean and Latin American foods, moonlight cruises, island picnics, concerts, and arts and crafts exhibits. The high point is the Saturday grand parade, when the city dances to the beat of steel drums as the colorful befeathered and sequined retinue snakes its way downtown, singing and dancing in best Mardi Gras fashion.

In August, the big 18-day event is the **Canadian National Exhibition,** at Exhibition Place, featuring 70-plus midway rides, display buildings, free shows, and grandstand performers. It was first staged in 1878. For information, contact Canadian National Exhibition, Exhibition Place, Toronto, ON, M6K 3C3 (☎ 416/393-6399). On Labour Day, the Canadian Air Show is an added bonus; the Snowbirds, the Canadian Air Force Performance Team, performs. Good vantage points are from the islands or Ontario Place.

In September the ✪**Toronto International Film Festival** (☎ 416/967-7371) is the world's second largest, showing more than 250 films over 10 days.

In October the prestigious 9-day **International Festival of Authors** at Harbourfront (☎ 416/973-3000) draws some of the world's finest authors to readings and other events.

In November the **Royal Agricultural Winter Fair,** a sort of state fair held since 1929, displays the largest fruits and vegetables, along with crafts, farm machinery, and livestock. The royal event is the accompanying horse show traditionally attended by a British royal-family member.

Call **Tourism Toronto** at ☎ 800/363-1990 or 416/203-2600 for additional information on festivals and events.

7 Outdoor Activities & Spectator Sports

For general information on city sports facilities, call the **Department of Parks and Recreation** at ☎ 416/392-1111 Monday to Friday from 8:30am to 4:30pm.

OUTDOOR ACTIVITIES

BIKING   The Martin Goodman Trail, which runs from the Beaches to the Humber River along the waterfront, is ideal for biking. The Lower Don Valley bike trail starts in the city's east end at Front Street East and runs north to Riverdale Park. High Park is another good venue along with the parks along the ravines. Official bike lanes are marked on College/Carlton streets, the Bloor Street Viaduct leading to the Danforth, Beverly/St. George, and Davenport Road. The Convention and Visitors Association has more detailed information on these bike lanes.

Bikes can be rented from **Wheel Excitement,** 5 Rees St. (☎ 416/260-9000), for C$14 (US$10) for the first 2 hours plus C$2 (US$1.45) for each additional hour or C$26 (US$19) a day.

BOATING/CANOEING   Harbourside Boating Centre, 283 Queen's Quay W. (☎ 416/203-3000), rents sail- and power boats and also provides sailing instruction. For 3 hours, sailboats cost from C$100 to C$125 (US$71 to US$89) and power boats C$180 (US$129). Weekend and weeklong sailing courses are offered.

Harbourfront Canoe and Kayak School, 283A Queen's Quay W. (☎ 416/203-2277), rents kayaks for C$30 (US$21) a day or C$15 (US$11) an hour and canoes for C$25 (US$18) and C$10 (US$7), respectively.

Canoes, rowboats, and paddleboats can also be rented on the Toronto Islands just south of Centreville.

CROSS-COUNTRY SKIING   You can ski in Toronto's parks when snow is on the ground. Best bets are Sunnybrook Park and Ross Lord Park, both in North York. For more information, call **Metro Parks** (☎ 416/392-8186).

GOLF   Among the city's half-dozen metro public golf courses, the following stand out:

Don Valley, at Yonge Street south of Highway 401 (☎ 416/392-2465), designed by Howard Watson, is a scenic course with some challenging elevated tees and a par-5 12th hole. It's a good place to start your kids. Greens fees are C$26 to C$33 (US$19 to US$24).

Humber Valley (☎ 416/392-2488) is a par-70 links and valley-land course that has three final holes requiring major concentration. Greens fees are C$25 to C$28 (US$18 to US$20).

The moderately difficult **Tam O'Shanter** course, Birchmount Avenue, north of Sheppard (☎ 416/392-2547), features links holes and water hazards among its challenges. Greens fees are C$25 to C$28 (US$18 to US$20).

There are several outstanding championship courses in the Toronto area. The most famous is the Jack Nicklaus–designed **Glen Abbey Golf Club** in Oakville (☎ 905/844-1800), the course where the Canadian Open is most often played. Green fees at Glen Abbey cost C$145 (US$104). **The Lionhead Golf Club** in Brampton (☎ 905/455-4900) has two 18-hole par-72 courses, charging C$145 (US$104) for the tougher course and C$130 (US$93) for the other course. In Markham, the **Angus Glen Golf Club** (☎ 905/887-5157) has a Doug Carrick–designed par-72 course and charges a C$120 (US$86) greens fee.

HIKING/JOGGING   If you want to jog downtown, places to run include Harbourfront and along the lakefront or through Queen's Park and the University.

The **Martin Goodman Trail,** which runs 20 kilometers (12.4 miles) along the waterfront from the Beaches in the east to the Humber River in the West, is ideal for jogging, walking, or cycling. It links to the **Tommy Thompson Trail,** which travels the parks stretching from the lakefront along the Humber River.

Near the Ontario Science Centre in the Central Don Valley, **Ernest Thompson Seton Park** is also good for jogging and hiking. Parking is available at the Thorncliffe Drive and Wilket Creek entrances.

ICE-SKATING/IN-LINE SKATING   **Nathan Philips Square** in front of City Hall becomes a free ice rink in winter, as does an area at **Harbourfront Centre.** Rentals are available. Artificial rinks are also found in more than 25 parks, including **Grenadier Pond** in High Park—a romantic spot with a bonfire and vendors selling roasted chestnuts. They're open from November to March. In-line skates can be rented from Wheel Excitement (see "Biking," above).

SWIMMING   There are a dozen or so outdoor pools (open June to September) in the municipal parks, including High and Rosedale parks, plus indoor pools at several community recreation centers. For pool information, call ☎ **416/392-1111.**

The **University of Toronto Athletic Centre,** 55 Harbord St. at Spadina Avenue (☎ **416/978-4680**), opens its swimming pool free to the public on Sunday from noon to 4pm. The pool at the **YMCA,** 20 Grosvenor St., can be used on a day pass, which costs C$12.85 (US$9).

There are public beaches on the Toronto Islands (off Hanlan's Point) and Woodbine Beach in the Beaches neighborhood, but quite frankly, the waters of Lake Ontario are polluted, and although people do swim in them, they do so at their own risk. Beaches are signed when they are deemed unsafe, usually after a heavy rainfall.

TENNIS   There are tennis facilities in more than **30 municipal parks.** The most convenient locations are the courts in High Park, Rosedale, and Jonathan Ashridge parks, which are open in summer only. For more information, call the city at ☎ **416/392-1111,** or Metro Parks at ☎ **416/392-8186.**

SPECTATOR SPORTS

Some wag once said that there's only one really religious place in Toronto and that's **Maple Leaf Gardens,** 60 Carlton St. (☎ **416/977-1641**), where the city's ice-hockey team, the NHL's **Maple Leafs,** wield their sticks to the screaming enthusiasm of fans. Tickets are nigh impossible to attain because many are sold by subscription and as soon as the remainder go on sale, lines wind around the block. The only way to secure tickets is to harass your concierge, or haggle with a scalper by the arena. If by boon of God you do find legitimate tickets, they should cost C$24.50 to C$95 (US$18 to US$68). Try calling **Ticketmaster** at ☎ **416/872-5000.**

SkyDome, on Front Street beside the CN Tower, is the home of the American League **Blue Jays,** who were World Series champs in 1992 and 1993, though their fortunes have declined lately. Blue Jays tickets range in price from C$4 to C$30 (US$2.85 to US$21). The **Toronto Argonauts** football team plays in SkyDome from June to November. Argos tickets cost C$10 to C$35 (US$7 to US$25). For Blue Jays or Argonauts tickets, call ☎ **888/654-6529** or 416/341-1234.

In 1995, Toronto acquired an exciting new addition to its sports scene—a brand-new NBA franchise—the **Toronto Raptors,** who immediately charmed the whole city. The team continues to play in SkyDome while negotiations continue about the construction of a new stadium, likely at the foot of Bay Street. For tickets, which cost C$13 to C$108 (US$9 to US$77), call **Ticketmaster** at ☎ **416/872-5000.**

Racing takes place at **Woodbine Racetrack,** Rexdale Boulevard at Highway 427, Etobicoke (☎ 416/675-RACE or 416/675-6110), famous for the Queen's Plate (contested in July), and the North America Cup. About 161 kilometers (100 miles) outside Toronto, **Fort Erie Race Track** (☎ 905/871-3200) is another beautiful racing venue. Harness racing takes place at **Mohawk Raceway,** 30 miles west of the city at Highway 410 and Guelph Line (☎ 416/675-7223).

8 Shopping

Toronto's major shopping areas are the Bloor/Yorkville area for designer boutiques and top-name galleries; Queen Street West for a more funky mixture of fashion, antiques, and bookstores; and a number of shopping malls/centers, like Queen's Quay down on the waterfront, and the 2-block-long Eaton Centre.

ANTIQUES The finest antiques can be found in the Bloor/Yorkville area and in the Mount Pleasant/St. Clair area along the 500 to 700 blocks of Mount Pleasant Road. The more eclectic and often more recent collectibles can be found at various stores along Queen Street West. Markham Village also has several antique stores.

ART Most galleries are open Tuesday to Saturday from 10:30am to 5:30pm, so don't come around on Sunday or Monday. The **Isaacs/Inuit Gallery of Eskimo Art,** 9 Prince Arthur Ave. (☎ 416/921-9985; Subway: Bay/St. George), sells museum-quality Inuit sculpture, prints, drawings, wall hangings, and antiquities from across the Arctic. The gallery also specializes in early native-Canadian art and artifacts. The bilevel **Kinsman Robinson,** 14 Hazelton Ave. (☎ 416/964-2374; Subway: Bay), exhibits such contemporary Canadian artists as Norval Morrisseau, Henri Masson, Robert Katz, and Stanley Cosgrove, plus sculptors Esther Wertheimer, Maryon Kantaroff, Joseph Jacobs, and many others.

BOOKS **Abelard Books,** 519 Queen St. W. (☎ 416/504-2665; Subway: Osgoode, then streetcar west), is one of my favorite rare-book stores in the city. It has a fabulous collection of early editions, with every subject clearly cataloged. Armchairs invite leisurely browsing. A real book-lover's haven. The **Albert Britnell Book Shop,** 765 Yonge St., north of Bloor Street (☎ 416/924-3321; Subway: Bay or Bloor-Yonge), has been a Toronto tradition since 1893. This wonderful store has a great selection of hard- and softcover books displayed handsomely on wooden shelves. The staff is very knowledgeable and helpful. The **Glad Day Bookshop,** 598A Yonge St., 2nd floor (☎416/961-4161; Subway: Wellesley), offers gay fiction, biography, and other nonfiction of interest to the gay community. It also stocks calendars, journals and magazines, and other items.

DEPARTMENT STORES There are numerous Eatons in Toronto. But the flagship store, **Eatons,** 290 Yonge St. (☎ 416/349-7111; Subway: Dundas), is in the four-level Eaton Centre, which stretches 2 blocks from Dundas Street to Queen Street. Arch rival to Eatons, **The Bay,** Queen and Yonge streets (☎ 416/861-9111; Subway: Queen), still has a venerable feel. **Marks & Spencer,** Manulife Centre, 55 Bloor St. W. (☎ 416/967-6674; Subway: Bloor-Yonge), is a branch of the famous British store that's known for good-quality goods and clothes at reasonable prices.

FOOD The specialty bakery **Dufflet Pastries,** 787 Queen St. W., near Bathurst Street (☎ 416/504-2870; Subway: Osgoode, then streetcar west), supplies many restaurants with its pastries and desserts. The special Dufflet cakes include a white-and dark-chocolate mousse, almond meringue, and many other singular creations. Fine coffees and teas are served, too. In Chinatown is the fascinating **Ten Ren Tea,**

454 Dundas St. W., at Huron Street (☎ **416/598-7872;** Subway: St. Patrick, then streetcar west), where you can pick up some fine Chinese tea. The tiny ceramic teapots also make nice gifts in the C$20 to C$30 (US$14 to US$21) price range.

9 Toronto After Dark

The companies to see in Toronto are the National Ballet of Canada, the Canadian Opera Company, the Toronto Symphony, the Toronto Dance Theatre, and Tafelmusik. You can catch major Broadway shows or a performance by one of the many small theater companies that make Toronto one of the leading theater centers in North America. For additional entertainment, there are enough bars, clubs, cabarets, and other entertainment to keep anyone spinning.

For local happenings, check *Where Toronto* and *Toronto Life,* as well as the *Globe and Mail,* the *Toronto Star,* the *Toronto Sun,* and the two free weekly papers, *Now* and *Eye.*

Half-price day-of-performance tickets are available at **T. O. Tix booth** outside the Eaton Centre at Yonge and Dundas streets (open Tuesday to Saturday from noon to 7:30pm and Sunday 11am to 3pm). Call the hot line at ☎ **416/596-8211** for information. For **Ticketmaster's** telecharge service, call ☎ **416/872-1111.**

THE PERFORMING ARTS

The major performing-arts venues include **Massey Hall,** 178 Victoria St. (☎ **416/ 593-4828**), which is a Canadian musical landmark, hosting a variety of musical programming from classical to rock. The **Hummingbird Centre,** 1 Front St. E. (☎ **416/872-2262**), is home to the Canadian Opera Company and the National Ballet; it also presents Broadway musicals, headline entertainers, and other national and international theater, music, and dance companies. **Roy Thomson Hall,** 60 Simcoe St. (☎ **416/593-4828**), is the premier concert hall and home to the Toronto Symphony Orchestra, which performs here September to June. The **St. Lawrence Centre,** 27 Front St. E. (☎ **416/366-7723**), hosts musical and theatrical events and is home to the Canadian Stage Theatre Company in the Bluma Appel Theatre and to Music Toronto and public debates in the Jane Mallett Theatre. And then there's the **Premiere Dance Theatre,** 207 Queen's Quay W. (☎ **416/973-4000**), home to a leading contemporary dance season featuring local companies—the Toronto Dance Theatre, the Danny Grossman Dance Company, and other Canadian and international companies including the Desrosiers Dance Theatre.

OPERA

The **Canadian Opera Company** began life in 1950 with 10 performances of three operas. It now stages eight different operas a season at the Hummingbird Centre and the Elgin Theatre from September to April. Call ☎ **416/363-6671** for administration or 416/872-2262 for tickets.

CLASSICAL MUSIC

The **Toronto Symphony Orchestra** performs at Roy Thomson Hall, 60 Simcoe St. (☎ **416/593-4828** for tickets or 416/593-7769 for administrative offices), from September to June. In June and July, concerts are also given at outdoor venues throughout the city. The world-renowned **Toronto Mendelssohn Choir** also performs at Roy Thomson Hall (☎ **416/598-0422**). This choir, which was founded in 1895, performs the great choral works not only of Mendelssohn, but also of Bach, Handel, Elgar, and others. Its most famous recording, though, is undoubtedly the soundtrack from Spielberg's film *Schindler's List.*

Tafelmusik Baroque Orchestra. 427 Bloor St. W. ☎ **416/964-6337** for tickets or 416/964-9562 for administration.

For 19 seasons this group, celebrated in England as "the world's finest period band," has been playing baroque music on authentic period instruments. Concerts featuring Bach, Handel, Telemann, Mozart, and Vivaldi are given at **Trinity-St. Paul's United Church,** 427 Bloor St. W., and also at **Massey Hall,** 178 Victoria St.

DANCE

Toronto Dance Theatre (☎ 416/967-1365), the city's leading contemporary dance company, burst onto the scene 27 years ago, bringing an inventive spirit and original Canadian dance to the stage. Today, Christopher House directs the company; he joined in 1979 and has contributed 30 new works to the repertoire. Exhilarating, powerful, and energetic—don't miss their Handel Variations, Artemis Madrigals, Sacra Conversazione, and the Cactus Rosary. For tickets, call ☎ **416/973-4000.**

✪ **National Ballet of Canada.** 157 King St. E., Toronto, ON, M5C 1G9. ☎ **416/366-4846,** or 416/872-2262 for tickets. Tickets C$14–C$90 (US$10–US$64).

One of the most beloved and famous of all Toronto's cultural icons is the National Ballet of Canada. It was launched at Eaton Auditorium in Toronto on November 12, 1951, by English ballerina Celia Franca, who served initially as director, dancer, choreographer, and teacher. Among the highlights of its history have been its 1973 New York debut (which featured Nureyev's full-length *Sleeping Beauty*), Baryshnikov's appearance with the company soon after his defection in 1974, and the emergence of such stars as Karen Kain and Kimberly Glasco.

The company performs its regular seasons in Toronto at the Hummingbird Centre in the fall, winter, and spring, as well as giving summer appearances before enormous crowds at the open-air theater at Ontario Place. The repertory includes works by Glen Tetley, Sir Frederick Ashton, William Forsythe, and Jerome Robbins. James Kudelka was appointed artist in residence in 1991 and has created *The Miraculous Mandarin, The Actress,* and *Spring Awakening.*

THEATER

With theaters and theater companies galore, Toronto has a very active theater scene, with a reputation second only to that of Broadway's in all of North America. Many small theater groups are producing exciting offbeat drama—a burgeoning Toronto equivalent of Off Broadway. I have picked out only the few whose reputations have been established rather than bombarding you with a complete list of all the offerings. Your choice will no doubt be made by what's scheduled while you're in town, so to do your own talent-scouting, check the local newspaper or magazine for listings of the myriad productions offered.

Landmark Theaters

The Elgin & Winter Garden Theatres. 189-91 Yonge St. ☎ 416/872-5555 for tickets or 416/314-2871 for tour info. Tickets C$15–C$85 (US$11–US$61). Subway: Dundas.

These two national historic landmarks vie with the Royal Alex for major shows and attention. Both theaters, which opened their doors in 1913, have been restored to their original gilded glory at a cost of C$29 million (US$20.7 million) and are the only double-decker theaters operating today. The downstairs Elgin is larger, seating 1,500 and featuring a lavish domed ceiling and gilded decoration on the boxes and proscenium. The smaller Winter Garden possesses a striking interior, with "tree trunk–like" columns, hand-painted scenic frescoes, and a ceiling of beech boughs and twinkling lanterns. Guided tours are given twice weekly for C$4 (US$2.85).

Ford Centre for the Performing Arts. 5040 Yonge St. ☎ **416/872-2222.** Tickets C$52.50–C$93 (US$38–US$66). Subway: North York Centre.

Located in North York, the center includes the Apotex theater, seating 1,815, the 250-seat Studio theater, and the George Watson recital hall seating 1,000. This is where *Ragtime* premiered before it opened on Broadway.

Pantages Theatre. 244 Victoria St. ☎ **416/872-2222.** Tickets C$60–C$100 (US$43–US$71). Subway: Dundas.

This magnificent old theater, which opened in 1920, has also been restored to the tune of C$18 million. Tours are given Saturday and Sunday for C$4 (US$2.85).

The Princess of Wales Theatre. 300 King St. W. ☎ **416/872-1212.** Tickets C$40–C$95 (US$29–US$68). Subway: St. Andrew/King.

Opened by the late Princess herself, this is a state-of-the-art theater. The interior has been decorated spectacularly by Frank Stella, who painted hundreds of feet of brilliantly colored murals and designed the lighting fixtures.

Royal Alexandra Theatre. 260 King St. W., Toronto, ON, M5V 1H9. ☎ **416/872-1212.** Tickets C$40–C$95 (US$29–US$68). Subway: St. Andrew/King.

Shows from Broadway migrate north to the Royal Alex. Tickets are often snapped up by subscription buyers, so your best bet is to write ahead to the theater at the above address. The theater itself is quite a spectacle. Constructed in 1907, it owes its current lease on life to owner Ed Mirvish, who refurbished it (as well as the surrounding area) in the 1960s. Inside it's a riot of plush reds, gold brocade, and baroque ornamentation, with a seating capacity of 1,493. It's wise to avoid sitting in the second balcony or under the circle.

Theater Companies & Other Notable Venues

The **Canadian Stage Company** performs comedy, drama, and musicals in the St. Lawrence Centre, and also presents free summer Shakespeare performances in High Park. Call ☎ **416/368-3110** for tickets.

Since 1970, the experimental **Factory Theatre,** 125 Bathurst St. (☎ **416/504-9971**), has been a home to Canadian playwriting, showcasing the best new authors, as well as established playwrights.

The **Tarragon Theatre,** located near Dupont and Bathurst at 30 Bridgman Ave. (☎ **416/536-5018**), opened in 1971 and continues to produce original works by such famous Canadian literary figures as Michael Ondaatje, Michel Tremblay, and Judith Thompson. It's a small, intimate theater.

Theatre Passe Muraille, 16 Ryerson Ave. (☎ **416/504-7529**), started in the late 1960s when a pool of actors began experimenting and improvising original Canadian material. Set in another warehouse, there's a main space seating 220, and a back space for 70. Take the Queen Street streetcar to Bathurst.

Buddies in Bad Times, 12 Alexander St. (☎ **416/975-8555**), is Canada's premier gay theater. Its cutting-edge reputation has been built by American Sky Gilbert. In addition to plays that push out social boundaries, the theater also operates a popular bar and cabaret called Tallulah's (see below).

DINNER THEATER, CABARET & COMEDY

For the art of campy impersonation, there's **La Cage Dinner Theatre,** 278 Yonge St. (☎ **416/364-5200**), which hosts a concert given by the shades of Buddy Holly, Roy Orbison, and Elvis among others. For a unique show that can only be likened to Disney's Fantasia performed live on stage, go to **Famous Players Dinner Theatre,** 110 Sudbury St. (☎ **416/532-1137**).

Top comedy clubs include **Yuk-Yuk's,** 2335 Yonge St. (☎ **416/967-6425**), with a cover of C$5 (US$3.55) on Monday, C$8 (US$6) from Tuesday to Thursday, C$10 (US$7) on Friday, and C$15 (US$11) on Saturday. Dinner and show Sunday and weeknights C$22 (US$16), Friday C$27 (US$19), Saturday C$30 (US$21). Also, there's the option of pizza and a show for C$15.25 (US$11), C$20 (US$14), and C$22 (US$16), respectively. Yuk-Yuk's has nurtured comedians like Jim Carrey, Harland Williams, Howie Mandel, and Norm MacDonald, and has also hosted such major American stars as Jerry Seinfeld and Robin Williams.

Another standby is ✪ **Second City,** which has been and still is the cauldron of Canadian comedy. It recently moved from its famous Firehouse to 56 Blue Jays Way (☎ **416/343-0011**). If you enjoy "Saturday Night Live" or "SCTV," you'll love the improvisational comedy of Second City. Dan Aykroyd, John Candy, Bill Murray, Martin Short, Mike Myers, Andrea Martin, and Catherine O'Hara all got their start here. Dinner and show from C$33 (US$24); show-only from C$11 (US$8).

The **Laugh Resort,** 26 Lombard St. (☎ **416/364-5233**), is another venue featuring local and international comedians. Dinner and show packages available.

JAZZ CLUBS

Toronto is a big jazz town—especially on Saturday afternoons when many a hotel lounge or restaurant lays on an afternoon of rip-roaring rhythm. At **Ben Wicks,** at 424 Parliament (☎ **416/961-9425**), there's free jazz, folk, and blues on Saturday from 8:30pm to midnight. The **Chelsea Bun,** at the Delta Chelsea Inn, 33 Gerrard St. W. (☎ **416/595-1975**), is a good spot for Saturday-afternoon jazz, starting usually at 3pm.

✪ **Montréal Bistro/Jazz Club.** 65 Sherbourne St. ☎ **416/363-0179.** Cover depends on band. Subway: Queen/King, then take streetcar east.

One of the city's hottest jazz clubs has a cool atmosphere for an array of local and international jazz artists—George Shearing, Oscar Peterson, Marian McPartland, and Velvet Glove have all appeared here. Entertainment begins at 9pm. It's great, too, because you can order from the menu of the bistro next door.

✪ **Top o' the Senator.** 249 Victoria. ☎ **416/364-7517.** Cover C$12–C$16 (US$9–US$11) weekends, C$8–C$10 (US$6–US$7) weekdays. Subway: Dundas.

Toronto's swankiest jazz club is a long, narrow room with a bar down one side and a distinct 1930s look. It's a great place to hear fine international jazz. Leatherette banquettes, couches alongside the performance area, and portraits of band leaders and artists on the walls add to the atmosphere. Plush couches, Oriental rugs, and a humidor fully stocked with premium Cuban cigars are the attractions of the third-floor lounge.

COUNTRY, FOLK, ROCK & REGGAE

✪ **Bamboo.** 312 Queen St. W. ☎ **416/593-5771.** Cover C$5 (US$3.55) Mon–Wed, C$7 (US$5) Thurs, C$10 (US$7) Fri–Sat. Subway: Osgoode, then a streetcar west.

The Bamboo, which is decked out in Caribbean style and colors, is the club that introduced reggae, calypso, salsa, and world beat to the city. It's also a popular restaurant, mixing Caribbean, Indonesian, and Thai specialties. Thai spicy noodles are really popular, blending shrimp, chicken, tofu, and egg. Lamb and potato rôti and Caribbean curry chicken are other offerings. Music starts at 10pm. The dance floor is very small.

Birchmount Tavern. 462 Birchmount. ☎ **416/698-4115.** Cover C$5 (US$3.55) Sat. Subway: Kennedy Rd.

The city's longtime country venue attracts a broad range of Canadian and American artists. The music goes on Thursday to Sunday from 9pm to 1am.

Chick 'n' Deli. 744 Mt. Pleasant Rd. (south of Eglinton Ave.). ☎ 416/489-3363. No cover. Subway: Eglinton.

At Chick 'n' Deli, Tiffany-style lamps and oak set the background for Top 40 or rhythm and blues every night from 9pm to 1am. The dance floor is always packed. Chicken wings and barbecue are the specialties, along with nachos, salads, and sandwiches. On Saturday afternoons Dixieland sounds start at 4pm.

El Mocambo. 464 Spadina Ave. ☎ 416/968-2001. Cover varies, depending on the band. Subway: College, then streetcar west; or Spadina, then LRT south.

Still a rock-and-roll landmark, El Mocambo is the famous bar where the Stones chose to do their gig back in the 1970s. Today it hosts the likes of Liz Phair upstairs. Monday is the night to see new local bands.

Free Times Cafe. 320 College St. ☎ 416/967-1078. Cover C$4–C$6 (US$2.85–US$4.30). Subway: College, then streetcar west.

This is the club for folk and acoustic music every evening starting at 9pm. Monday night is open house. Up front the small restaurant offers a health-oriented menu.

DANCE CLUBS

Berlin. 2335 Yonge St. ☎ 416/489-7777. Cover C$8 (US$6) Tues, C$5 (US$3.55) Wed and Fri, C$3 (US$2.15) Thurs, C$10 (US$7) Sat–Sun. Subway: Eglinton.

This is one of the city's more sophisticated clubs, attracting a well-heeled crowd ranging from 25 to 50 years old. It plays everything from salsa to retro and even sponsors an Arabian night on Wednesday. Things get started at 9pm and spin until 3:30am Tuesday to Saturday.

Loose Moose. 220 Adelaide St. W. (between Simcoe and Duncan sts.). ☎ 416/971-5252. No cover. Subway: Osgoode.

This is a crowd-pleaser for a younger set who like the multilevel dance floors, the DJ, the billiard tables, and the booze and schmooze, which starts every night at 9pm. There are more than 60 brews available here.

BARS & PUBS

First, here are some favorite hotel bars. The fairly formal **Chartroom,** at the Harbour Castle Westin, 1 Harbour Sq. (☎ 416/869-1600), offers a good view of the lake and the islands ferry. For cozy fireside conversation in winter, or a summer cocktail with a view, I like the **Roof Lounge at the Park Plaza,** 4 Avenue Rd. (☎ 416/924-5471). The **Consort Bar** at the King Edward Hotel, 37 King St. E. (☎ 416/863-9700), is also comfortable. **La Serre,** at the Four Seasons, 21 Avenue Rd. (☎ 416/964-0411), was named by *Forbes* magazine as one of the best bars in the world. Certainly its selection of single malts and martinis is extraordinary; it also welcomes cigar aficionados. The **Chelsea Bun,** at the Delta Chelsea Inn, 33 Gerrard St. W. (☎ 416/595-1975), has a fine selection of single-malts and good musical entertainment. If you prefer a pubby atmosphere, there's the **Good Queen Bess,** in the Sheraton Centre, 123 Queen St. W. (☎ 416/361-1000).

And now for the independents.

Al Frisco's. 133 John St. ☎ 416/595-8201. Subway: Osgoode.

In summer, the extra-large outdoor patio is jammed with a mix of tourists, suits, and other professionals. Mediterranean fare—pizzas, pastas, and modern dishes like grilled sea bass in a sweet-pepper sauce—is also served in the downstairs space that is warmed in winter by several fireplaces. Upstairs the billiard and retro dance crowd gather.

Alice Fazooli's. 294 Adelaide St. W. ☎ **416/979-1910.** Subway: Osgoode.

Baseball art and memorabilia, including a full-scale model of an outfielder making a wall catch, fills this large bar and dining room. It's always jam-packed with an older business crowd either quaffing in the bar or feasting in the back on crabs cooked in many different styles, pizza, pasta, and raw-bar specialties.

Bar Italia & Billiards. 582 College St. ☎ **416/535-3621.** Subway: College, then streetcar west.

The hippest, hottest scene in Little Italy. Young and beautiful gather downstairs while the pool players head upstairs to the six tables in the comfortable lounge.

Brunswick House. 481 Bloor St. W. ☎ **416/964-2242.** Subway: Spadina/Bathurst.

For an experience that's unique and inexpensive, try the Brunswick House, a cross between a German beer hall and an English north-country workingmen's club. Waitresses move through the Formica tables in this cavernous room carrying high trays of frothy suds to a largely student crowd. And while everyone's drinking suds or playing bar shuffleboard, they're entertained by two large-screen TVs. There's music, too, from jazz and live bands to DJ sounds.

Centro. 2472 Yonge St. ☎ **416/483-2211.** Subway: Eglinton.

Centro has a well-patronized bar downstairs from the restaurant. It's a comfortable, relaxing place to listen to the pianist and get to know the sophisticated mid-30s-and-up crowd.

✪ **C'est What?** 67 Front St. E. ☎ **416/867-9499.** Subway: Union.

Downstairs in a historic warehouse building, C'est What? sports rough-hewn walls and a cellarlike atmosphere reminiscent of a Paris cave. Casual and comfortable, it attracts a young, politically conscious crowd drawn by the ethnically diverse cuisine and the broad selection of single-malts and beers. There's live folk-acoustic music 7 nights a week.

Milano. 325 King St. W. ☎ **416/599-9909.** Subway: St. Andrew.

Up front there's a bar and beyond several billiard tables, with a dining area off to the side. In summer, French doors open to the street, making for a pleasant Parisian atmosphere. The bistro-style food consists of pizza, pasta, sandwiches, and such items as tiger shrimp.

✪ **The Rotterdam.** 600 King St. W. (at Portland). ☎ **416/504-6882.** Subway: St. Andrew, then streetcar west.

This beer-drinker's heaven serves 200 different labels as well as 30 different types on draft. It's not so much an after-work crowd that gathers here, but by 8pm the tables in the back are filled and the long bar is jammed. In summer the patio is fun.

Sassafraz/The Catwalk. 100 Cumberland St. ☎ **416/964-2222.** Subway: Bay.

In Yorkville, this is the classy gathering spot at the Bar/Bistro during the day and early evening, and later on at the Catwalk, which has two bars, a double-sided gas fireplace, and a dance floor.

Wayne Gretzky's. 99 Blue Jays Way. ☎ **416/979-7825.** Subway: Union.

Forget the food. Instead, head upstairs to the rooftop patio or to a stool at the long bar which is in essence a shrine to the golden boy of ice hockey.

WINE BARS

In addition to the bar listed here, there's also **Enoteca** at 150 Bloor St. W. in Yorkville (☎ **416/920-9900**) and the very comfortable wine bar upstairs at **N 44,** 2537 Yonge St. (see "Dining," above).

Vines. Downstairs at 38 Wellington St. E. ☎ **416/869-0744.** Subway: King.

Vines provides a pleasant atmosphere to sample a glass of champagne or any of 30 wines, priced between C$4 and C$10 (US$2.85 to US$7) for a 4-ounce glass. Salads, cheeses, and light meals from C$7 to C$10 (US$5 to US$7) are also available.

GAY & LESBIAN BARS

Toronto's large, active gay and lesbian community has created a great, varied nightlife scene.

The Barn/The Stables. 418 Church St. ☎ **416/977-4702.** Subway: Wellesley.

This is one of the city's oldest gay bars. The second-floor dance floor is jammed; the third floor is for "back room" liaisons. There are afternoon underwear parties on Sundays, with sex videos, too. Don't expect to talk.

The Rose Cafe. 547 Parliament St., at Winchester. ☎ **416/928-1495.** Subway: Wellesley or College, then a streetcar east.

This is the city's most popular lesbian bar, with a pool table and game room downstairs that's furnished with old, cozy couches, and a restaurant and dance area upstairs. In summer, the fenced-in patio is the place to cool off.

Tallulah's Cabaret. 12 Alexander St. ☎ **416/975-8555.** Subway: Wellesley.

A place to let it all hang out. Alternative music, flamboyant dancing, and reasonably priced drinks make certain everyone has a good time. Friday is ostensibly women's night, but don't count on it.

Woody's. 467 Church St. (south of Wellesley). ☎ **416/972-0887.** Subway: Wellesley.

A friendly and very popular local bar, Woody's is frequented mainly by men, but welcomes women. It's considered a good meeting place. Next door is **Sailor,** 465 Church St. (☎ **416/972-0887**), a bar/restaurant noted for its weekend brunch from 11am to 4pm.

10 Niagara Falls

130 kilometers (81 miles) S of Toronto, 30 kilometers (18 miles) N of Buffalo, NY

Niagara Falls, with its gimmicks, amusement parks, wax museums, daredevil feats, and a million motels sporting heart-shaped beds, may seem tacky. Certainly the heart of the falls area is overcommercialized. Still, somehow, the falls steal the show, and on the Canadian side, with its parkway and gardens, nature manages to survive with grace.

ESSENTIALS

VISITOR INFORMATION   For information in and around the falls, contact the **Niagara Falls Canada Visitor and Convention Bureau,** 5433 Victoria Ave., Niagara Falls, ON, L2G 3L1 (☎ **905/356-6061**); or the **Niagara Parks Commission,** 7400 Portage Rd. S., Niagara Falls, ON, L2E 6T2 (☎ **905/356-2241** or 905/354-6266). Summer information centers are open at Table Rock House, Maid of the Mist Plaza, Rapids View Parking Lot, and Niagara-on-the-Lake.

GETTING THERE   If you're driving from Toronto, take the QEW Niagara. From the United States, take the Rainbow Bridge directly into Niagara Falls (ON).

   Amtrak and VIA Rail operate trains between Toronto (☎ 416/366-8411) and New York, stopping in St. Catharines and Niagara Falls. Call ☎ 800/USA RAIL in the United States or 800/361-1235 in Canada.

GETTING AROUND   The best way to get around is aboard the **People Movers** (☎ 905/357-9340). Park your car at Rapid View several miles away from the falls, or else at the so-called Preferred Parking (overlooking the falls—it costs more), and then take the People Mover, an attraction in itself. People Movers travel a loop, making nine stops from Rapid View to Spanish Aero Car. Shuttles to the falls also operate from downtown and Lundy's Lane. An all-day pass costs C$4.25 (US$3.05) for adults and $2.25 (US$1.60) for children 6 to 12.

A MONEY-SAVING PASS   Buying an **Explorer's Passport** secures admission to Journey Behind the Falls, Great Gorge Adventure, and the Niagara Spanish Aero Car, plus all-day transportation aboard the People Movers. It costs C$17.75 (US$13) for adults and $9 (US$6) for children 6 to 12. The pass may be purchased at any of the attractions or at the Table Rock information booth.

SEEING THE FALLS

Obviously, the first thing to do is to see the falls, the seventh natural wonder of the world. Ever since the falls were first seen by Fr. Louis Hennepin, a Jesuit priest, in December 1678, people have flocked to see them; today more than 12 million visit annually. Many are honeymooners, although how the trend got started no one quite knows—legend has it that Napoléon's brother started it when he came on his honeymoon, traveling all the way from New Orleans by stagecoach.

   The most exciting way to see the falls is still from the decks of the ✪ *Maid of the Mist,* 5920 River Rd. (☎ 905/358-5781). This sturdy boat takes you practically into the maelstrom—through the turbulent waters around the American Falls, past the Rock of Ages, and to the foot of the Horseshoe Falls where 34.5 million Imperial gallons fall per minute over the 176-foot-high cataract. You'll get wet and your sunglasses will mist, but that will not detract from the thrill.

   Boats leave from the dock on the parkway just down from the Rainbow Bridge. Trips begin in mid-May and operate daily to mid-October (until 8pm from mid-June to early August). Fares are C$10 (US$7) for adults and C$6.25 (US$4.45) for children 6 to 12; children under 6 are free.

   Go down under the falls via the elevator at Table Rock House, which drops you 150 feet down through solid rock to the **Journey Behind the Falls** (☎ 905/ 354-1551). You'll appreciate the yellow biodegradable mackintosh that you're given. The tunnels and viewing portals are open all year, and the admission charge is C$5.75 (US$4.10) for adults and $2.90 (US$2.05) for children 6 to 12; children under 5 are free.

   To view the falls from above most spectacularly, take a 9-minute spin (C$160/ US$114 for two!) in a chopper over the whole Niagara area. Helicopters leave from the Heliport, adjacent to the Whirlpool at the junction of Victoria Avenue and Niagara Parkway, daily from 9am to dusk, weather permitting. Contact **Niagara Helicopters,** 3731 Victoria Ave. (☎ 905/357-5672).

   Or else you can ride up in the external glass-fronted elevators 520 feet to the top of the **Skylon Tower** observation deck at 5200 Robinson St. (☎ 905/356-2651). The observation deck is open from 8am to midnight from June to Labour Day (call for other seasons). Admission is C$6.95 (US$4.95) for adults, C$5.95 (US$4.25) for seniors, and C$3.90 (US$2.80) for children 6 to 12; children under 6 are free.

Niagara Falls

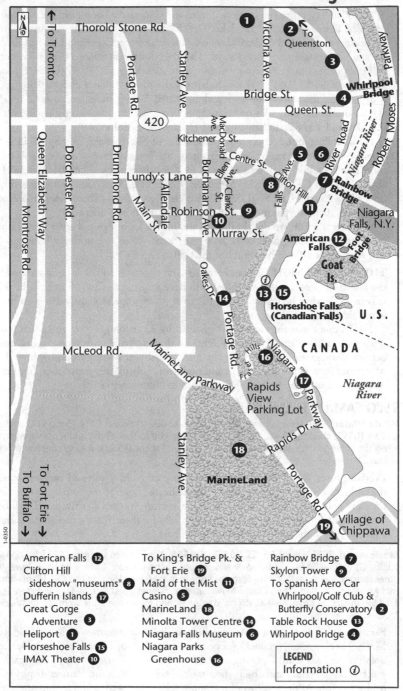

American Falls 12
Clifton Hill
  sideshow "museums" 8
Dufferin Islands 17
Great Gorge
  Adventure 3
Heliport 1
Horseshoe Falls 15
IMAX Theater 10

To King's Bridge Pk. &
  Fort Erie 19
Maid of the Mist 11
Casino 5
MarineLand 18
Minolta Tower Centre 14
Niagara Falls Museum 6
Niagara Parks
  Greenhouse 16

Rainbow Bridge 7
Skylon Tower 9
To Spanish Aero Car
  Whirlpool/Golf Club &
  Butterfly Conservatory 2
Table Rock House 13
Whirlpool Bridge 4

LEGEND
Information ⓘ

A similar perspective can be gained from the observation floors atop the 325-foot **Minolta Tower Centre**, 6732 Oakes Dr. (☎ **905/356-1501**). On-site attractions include a Volcano Mine Ride, Galaxian Space Adventure, Cybermind Virtual Reality, and the free Waltzing Waters show. The tower is open in summer daily from 9am to 11:30pm, and in winter from 9am to 9pm. Admission is C$5.95 (US$4.25) for adults and C$4.95 (US$3.55) for students and seniors; children under 10 are free. A day pass for the observation deck and unlimited entry to the games costs C$18.95 (US$14)—adults only. An unlimited play pass for the games-only is C$13.95 (US$10) and may be purchased by both children and adults.

For a thrilling introduction to the experience of Niagara Falls, stop by the **IMAX Theatre** and view the raging, swirling waters in *Niagara: Miracles, Myths and Magic*, shown on a six-story-high screen. It's at 6170 Buchanan Ave. (☎ **905/358-3611**) and tickets cost C$7.50 (US$5) for adults, C$6.75 (US$4.80) for seniors and children 12 to 18, and C$5.50 (US$3.95) for children 5 to 11. Shows operate on the hour from 10am to 9pm in July and August (shorter hours otherwise).

In winter, the falls are also thrilling to see, for the ice bridge and other formations are quite remarkable (you'll know how remarkable if you've ever seen a building in winter after the firemen have put out the fire).

THE FALLS BY NIGHT   Jean François Gravelet (or Blondin, as he was known), the famed tightrope walker, is believed to have inspired the first effort to light the falls in 1859 when he walked across the river on his rope at night, setting off fireworks that illuminated the gorge.

Today, don't miss the vision of the falls lit by 22 xenon gas spotlights (each producing 250 million candlepower of light), in shades of rose pink, red magenta, amber, blue, and green. You can see it any night of the year starting around 5pm in the winter and 9pm in the summer. In addition, from July to early September, free fireworks are set off every Friday night at 11pm to illuminate the falls.

TWO FAMILY THEME PARKS

White Water. 7430 Lundy's Lane. ☎ **905/357-3380.** Admission C$14.95 (US$11) adults, C$9.95 (US$7) children 12 and under, which allows you to stay all day and return evenings, when the lights go on. Daily 10am–6pm. Closed after Labour Day and through the winter until May.

Everyone loves White Water, where you don your bathing suit and swoop around the corkscrew turns of the five slides into the heated pools at the bottom or frolic in the wave pool. If you prefer to wallow in the hot tub, you can do that, too. The little 'uns can ride three small slides designed specially for them. Take a picnic and spend a greater part of the day (there's also a snack bar).

MarineLand. 7657 Portage Rd. ☎ **905/356-9565.** Admission in summer C$22.95 (US$16) adults, C$19.95 (US$14) children 5–9 and seniors; children under 4 free. Admission lower in other seasons. July–Aug daily 9am–6pm; mid-Apr to mid-May and Sept to mid-Oct 10am–4pm; mid-May to June 10am–5pm. Closed Nov to mid-Apr. Rides open Victoria Day and close the 1st Mon in Oct. In town, drive south on Stanley St. and follow the signs; from the QEW take McCleod Rd. Exit.

Families won't want to miss MarineLand. At the aquarium-theater, King Waldorf, MarineLand's mascot, presides over performances given by killer whales and talented dolphins and sea lions. Opening in 1998 is Friendship Cove, a 4¹/₂-million-gallon killer-whale breeding and observation tank. Another aquarium features displays of freshwater fish. At the small wildlife display, kids enjoy petting and feeding the deer and also seeing bear and Canadian elk.

MarineLand also has theme-park rides, including a roller coaster, Tivoli wheel, Dragon Boat rides, and a fully equipped children's playground. The big thriller is

Dragon Mountain, a roller coaster that loops, double-loops, and spirals its way through 1,000 feet of tunnels.

EXPLORING ALONG THE NIAGARA PARKWAY

The Niagara Parkway makes the Canadian side of the falls much more appealing than the American side. This 35-mile parkway was conceived in 1867 by a group of Americans that included Frederick Law Olmsted, designer of New York City's Central Park, who had become outraged at the peddlers, hawkers, and freak shows who preyed upon Niagara's tourists. Today it provides an unspoiled stretch of parkland and gardens that are exquisitely maintained. A great bike trail parallels the drive.

From Niagara Falls you can drive all the way to Niagara-on-the-Lake, taking in the attractions en route. The first you'll come to is the **Great Gorge Adventure,** 4330 River Rd. (☎ 905/374-1221). Stroll along the scenic boardwalk beside the raging white waters of the Great Gorge Rapids and wonder how it must have felt to challenge this mighty torrent, where the river rushes through the narrow channel at an average speed of 35 kilometers per hour (22 m.p.h.). Admission is C$4.75 (US$3.40) for adults and C$2.40 (US$1.70) for children 6 to 12; children under 6 are free.

Half a mile farther north and you'll arrive at the **Niagara Spanish Aero Car** (☎ 905/354-5711), a cable-car contraption that will whisk you on a 3,600-foot jaunt between two points in Canada, high above the whirlpool, providing excellent views of the surrounding landscape. Admission is C$5 (US$3.55) for adults and C$2.50 (US$1.80) for children 6 to 12; children under 6 are free. It operates daily from May 1 to the third Sunday in October: from 9am to 6pm in May, until 8pm in June, until 9pm in July and August, from 10am to 7:30pm in September, and from 9am to 5pm in October.

At **Ride Niagara,** 5755 River Rd. (☎ 905/374-7433), a simulated plunge over the falls in a hydro-shuttle is the main feature of the 25-minute experience that includes a theater presentation. Admission is C$7.95 (US$6) for adults and C$4.25 (US$3.05) for children 5 to 12; children under 5 are free. Open daily year-round, from 9:15am to 10:30pm in summer, and Monday to Friday from noon to 5pm and Saturday and Sunday from 10:30am to 5pm in winter.

Also on the parkway is the **Whirlpool Golf Club** (☎ 905/356-1140), which offers a scenic course. Greens fees are C$36 (US$26) for 18 holes, C$23 (US$16) for 9 holes.

The next stop is the **School of Horticulture,** for a free view of the vast gardens there, plus a look at the Floral Clock, which contains 25,000 plants in its 40-foot-diameter face. The new **Butterfly Conservatory** is also in the gardens (☎ 905/356-8119). Here, free-flying in a lush tropical setting, more than 2,000 butterflies (50 different international species) float and flutter among such nectar-producing flowers as lantanas and pentas. The large bright-blue luminescent Morpho butterflies from Central and South America are particularly gorgeous. There's also a native butterfly garden outside attracting the more familiar swallowtails, fritillaries, and painted ladies. Open daily from 9am to 5pm with extended summer hours; closed December 25. Admission is C$6 (US$4.30) for adults and C$3 (US$2.15) for children 6 to 12; children under 6 are free.

From here you can drive to **Queenston Heights Park,** site of the battle of that name during the War of 1812. You can take a walking tour of the battlefield. Picnic or play tennis (C$6/US$4.30 an hour) in this shaded arbor before moving to the **Laura Secord Homestead,** Partition Street in Queenston (☎ 905/262-4851). The home of this redoubtable woman contains a fine collection of upper-Canada furniture from the 1812 period, plus artifacts recovered from an archaeological dig. Stop at the candy shop and ice-cream parlor. Tours are given every half hour. Admission is C$1.07 (US75¢). Open from Victoria Day weekend (late May) to Labour Day daily from 10am to 6pm.

Also worth viewing just off the parkway in Queenston is the **Samuel Weir Collection and Library of Art,** RR #1, Niagara-on-the Lake (☎ 905/262-4510), a small personal collection displayed as it was originally when Samuel Weir occupied the house. Mr. Weir (1898–1981), a lawyer from London, Ontario, was an enthusiastic collector of Canadian, American, and European art as well as rare books. Open from Victoria Day to Canadian Thanksgiving, Wednesday to Saturday from 11am to 5pm and Sunday from 1 to 5pm. Admission is free.

From here the parkway continues into Niagara-on-the-Lake, lined with fruit farms like **Kurtz Orchards** (☎ 905/468-2937), and wineries, notably the **Inniskillin Winery,** Line 3, Service Road 56 (☎ 905/468-3554 or 905/468-2187), and **Reif Winery** (☎ 905/468-7738). Inniskillin is open Monday to Saturday from 10am to 6pm June to October and Monday to Saturday from 10am to 5pm November to May. The self-guided free tour has 20 stops explaining the process of wine making. A guided tour is also given daily at 2:30pm in summer and Saturdays-only in winter. At Reif Winery, tours costing C$2 (US$1.45) are given daily from June to Thanksgiving. Both tours are well-worth stopping for, but if you have time only for one, make it the Inniskillin.

Farther along, visit **Dufferin Islands,** where the children can swim, rent a paddleboat, and explore the surrounding woodland areas. Or else you can play a round of golf on the illuminated 9-hole par-3 course. Open the second Sunday in April to the last Sunday in October.

A little farther on, stop for a picnic in **King's Bridge Park** and relax on the beaches before driving on to **Fort Erie** (☎ 905/871-0540), a reconstruction of the fort that was seized by the Americans in July 1814, besieged later by the British, and finally blown up as the Americans retreated across the river to Buffalo. Guards in 1812-to-1814 period uniforms of the British Eighth Regiment will lead you through the museum and display rooms. These guards also stand sentry duty, fire the cannons, and demonstrate drill and musket practice. Admission is C$5 (US$3.55) for adults and C$3 (US$2.15) for children 6 to 16; children under 6 are free. Open daily the first Saturday in May to mid-September and weekends-only to Canadian Thanksgiving from 10am to 6pm.

Also in Fort Erie, the **Mildred M. Mahoney Dolls House Gallery,** on the Niagara Parkway (☎ 905/871-5833), displays more than 120 fully furnished dollhouses representing a variety of styles of architecture from colonial to contemporary. Admission is C$3 (US$2.15) for adults, C$2.50 (US$1.80) for seniors, and C$2 (US$1.45) for children ages 6 to 17; children under 6 are free. Open daily May to December from 10am to 4pm.

Another Fort Erie attraction is the scenic historic **racetrack** (☎ 905/871-3200) that's open in summer.

MORE ATTRACTIONS IN TOWN

The newest attraction is **Casino Niagara,** 5705 Falls Ave. (☎ 905/374-3598), featuring 123 tables that offer blackjack, roulette, baccarat, several different pokers, plus 3,000 slot and video poker machines. The casino contains five restaurants including the Hard Rock Cafe. It's open 24 hours a day 365 days a year.

Founded in 1827, the **Niagara Falls Museum,** 5651 River Rd. (☎ 905/356-2151), has exhibits ranging from Egyptian mummies to an odd mixture of Indian and Asian artifacts, shells, fossils, and minerals, plus the Freaks of Nature display. Open in summer daily from 8:30am to 11pm; in winter from 10am to 5pm. Admission is C$6.75 (US$4.80) for adults, C$6.25 (US$4.45) for seniors, C$4.95 (US$3.55) for students 11 to 18, and C$3.95 (US$2.80) for children 5 to 10; children under 5 are free.

ACCOMMODATIONS

Every other sign in Niagara Falls advertises a motel. In summer, rates go up and down according to the traffic, and some proprietors will not even quote rates ahead of time. So be warned. You can secure a reasonably priced room if you're lucky enough to arrive on a "down night," but with the casino in town, that's becoming a rare occurrence. Still, always request a lower rate and see what happens.

EXPENSIVE

The Americana. 8444 Lundy's Lane, Niagara Falls, ON, L2H 1H4. ☎ **905/356-8444.** Fax 905/356-8576. 120 rms. A/C TV TEL. Late June to late Aug C$130–C$170 (US$93–US$121) double; Sept–June C$80–C$120 (US$57–US$86) double. AE, DISC, ER, MC, V. Free parking.

The Americana, set in 25 acres of grounds, is one of the nicer choices on this motel strip. There's a pleasant tree-shaded area for picnicking right across from the office. The rooms are very large, and some suites have whirlpool tubs and fireplaces.

   Dining: A dining room, lounge, and coffee shop are on the premises.

   Facilities: Tennis and squash courts, two pools, a sauna, a fitness room, and an outdoor swimming pool.

Renaissance Fallsview Hotel. 6455 Buchanan Ave., Niagara Falls, ON, L2G 3V9. ☎ **800/363-3255** or 905/357-5200. Fax 905/357-3422. 262 rms. A/C MINIBAR TV TEL. Summer C$195–C$309 (US$139–US$221) double, from C$220 (US$157) whirlpool rm; winter C$109–C$195 (US$78–US$139) double, from C$175 (US$125) whirlpool rm; spring and fall C$165–C$229 (US$118–US$164) double, from C$189 (US$135) whirlpool rm. AE, DC, DISC, ER, MC, V. Free parking.

The Renaissance offers rooms that are tastefully furnished with oak furniture. Bathrooms have double sinks, hair dryers, and all modern accoutrements. Each Renaissance Club room has three telephones and a whirlpool tub. A rooftop cafe on the 18th floor overlooks the falls. Mulberry's is a more casual restaurant that is open for all three meals.

   Facilities: Indoor pool, a whirlpool, and a health club featuring saunas, squash and racquetball courts, and a fitness and weight room.

Skyline Brock. 5685 Falls Ave., Niagara Falls, ON, L2E 6W7. ☎ **800/263-7135** or 905/374-4444. Fax 905/357-4804. 233 rms. A/C TV TEL. Mid-June to Sept C$129–C$219 (US$92–US$156) double; Oct–Dec and Apr to mid-June C$99–C$145 (US$71–US$104) double; Jan–Mar C$80–C$115 (US$57–US$82) double. Prices based on rm and view. Extra person C$10 (US$7). Children under 18 stay free in parents' rm. Special packages available. AE, DC, DISC, ER, MC, V. Parking C$7 (US$5).

With about 150 rooms facing the falls, the Skyline Brock has been hosting honeymooners and falls visitors since 1929. It still has a certain air of splendor conveyed by the huge chandelier and marble walls in the lobby. City-view rooms are slightly smaller and less expensive. Rooms from the 11th floor up have minibars.

   Dining/Entertainment: The 10th-floor Rainbow Room offers a lovely view over the falls and serves a popular menu that includes half a roast chicken with cranberry sauce, salmon hollandaise, or prime rib, priced from C$16 to C$25 (US$11 to US$18). Isaac's bar is available for drinks and there's also the Lobby Cafe.

Skyline Foxhead. 5875 Falls Ave., Niagara Falls, ON, L2E 6W7. ☎ **800/263-7135,** 905/374-4444, or 905/357-3090. 399 rms. A/C TV TEL. June–Sept C$169–C$279 (US$121–US$199) double; Oct–Dec and Apr–May C$125–C$175 (US$89–US$125) double; Jan–Mar C$90–C$125

(US$64–US$89) double. Prices depend on view. Extra person C$10. Children under 18 stay free in parents' rm. AE, DC, DISC, ER, MC, V. Parking C$7 (US$5).

Also offering rooms with views of the falls, the Foxhead, which has recently undergone an extensive renovation, offers rooms spread over 14 floors, all with either private bath or shower. You may want to request your preference when booking. Rooms have views of the falls, gardens, village, or city. Half the units have balconies.

Dining/Entertainment: The 14th-floor Penthouse Dining Room takes advantage of the view with its large glass windows and serves a daily buffet for breakfast, lunch, and dinner with nightly dancing to a live band (in season). Or there's the Steak and Burger for reasonably priced fare.

Facilities: Outdoor rooftop pool.

MODERATE

Michael's Inn. 5599 River Rd., Niagara Falls, ON, L2E 3H3. ☎ 800/263-9390 or 905/354-2727. Fax 905/374-7706. 130 rms. A/C TV TEL. June 16–Sept 15 C$98–C$208 (US$70–US$149) double, C$235–C$550 (US$168–US$393) bridal suite; Sept 16–Oct 31 and Mar 16–June 15 C$68–C$178 (US$49–US$127) double, C$185–C$335 (US$132–US$239) bridal suite; Nov 1–Mar 15 C$59–C$138 (US$42–US$99) double, C$108–C$235 (US$77–US$168) bridal suite. Rollaway bed C$10 (US$7) extra; crib C$5 (US$3.55). AE, CB, DC, ER, MC, V. Free parking.

Rooms in this four-story white building overlooking the Niagara River gorge are large, have all the modern conveniences, and are nicely decorated. Many have heart-shaped tubs and Jacuzzis; some have themes, like the Garden of Paradise or Scarlett O'Hara rooms. There's a solarium pool out back. The Embers Open Hearth Dining Room is just that—the charcoal pit is enclosed behind glass so you can see all the cooking action. There's a lounge, too.

Village Inn. 5705 Falls Ave., Niagara Falls, ON, L2E 6W7. ☎ 800/263-7135, 905/374-4444, or 905/357-3090. 205 rms. A/C TV TEL. Mid-June to Oct 1 from C$90 (US$64) double (though weekend rates may be as high as C$179/US$128); Oct and Apr to mid-June C$70 (US$50) double. Special packages available. AE, DC, DISC, MC, V. Parking C$4 (US$3).

Located right by Casino Niagara behind the two Skyline hotels, the Village Inn is ideal for families—all rooms are large. Some family suites measure 700 square feet and include a bedroom with two double beds and a living room.

INEXPENSIVE

Nelson Motel. 10655 Niagara River Pkwy., Niagara Falls, ON, L2E 6S6. ☎ 905/295-4754. 25 rms, some with shower only. A/C TV. June 16–Sept 12 C$55–C$90 (US$39–US$64) double; Sept 13 to mid-Nov and mid-Mar to June 15 C$40–C$55 (US$29–US$39) double. Rollaways and cribs extra. MC, V. Closed mid-Nov to mid-Mar. Free parking.

For budget accommodations, try the Nelson Motel, run by John and Dawn Pavlakovich, who live in the large house adjacent to the motel units. The rooms have character, especially the family units, which have a double bedroom adjoined by a twin-bedded room for the kids. Regular units have modern furniture; singles have shower only. All units face the fenced-in pool and neatly trimmed lawn with umbrellaed tables and shrubs (none has a telephone). It's located a short drive from the falls overlooking the Niagara River, away from the hustle and bustle of Niagara itself.

NEARBY ACCOMMODATIONS IN QUEENSTON

✪ **South Landing Inn.** At the corner of Kent and Front sts. (P.O. Box 269), Queenston, ON, L0S 1L0. ☎ 905/262-4634. 23 rms. A/C TV. Mid-Apr to end of Oct C$90–C$110 (US$64–US$79) double; Nov to mid-Apr C$60–C$70 (US$43–US$50) double. AE, MC, V. Free parking.

In the nearby village of Queenston, you'll find the South Landing Inn. The old original inn built in the 1800s has five units with early Canadian furnishings, including poster beds. The rest are in the modern annex. There's a distant view of the river from the inn's balcony. In the original inn you'll also find a cozy dining room with red gingham–covered tables, where breakfast is served for C$4 (US$3).

DINING

Betty's Restaurant & Tavern. 8921 Sodom Rd. ☎ **905/295-4436.** Reservations accepted only for parties of 8 or more. Main courses C$8–C$16 (US$6–US$11). AE, MC, V. Mon–Sat 7am–10pm, Sun 9am–9pm. CANADIAN.

Betty's is a local favorite for honest food at fair prices. It's a family dining room where the art and generosity surface in the food—massive platters of fish-and-chips, breaded pork chops, chicken cutlet, all including soup or juice, vegetable, and potato. There are burgers and sandwiches, too. If you can, save room for the enormous slabs of home-baked pie. Breakfast and lunch also offer good, affordable choices.

Casa d'Oro. 5875 Victoria Ave. ☎ **905/356-5646.** Reservations recommended. Main courses C$15–C$24 (US$11–US$17). AE, DC, DISC, ER, MC, V. Mon–Fri noon–3pm and 4–11pm, Sat 4pm–1am, Sun 4–10pm. ITALIAN.

For fine dining amid an overwhelming array of gilt busts of Caesar, Venetian-style lamps, and classical Roman columns, go to Casa d'Oro. Start with the clams casino or the *brodetto Antonio* (a giant crouton topped with poached eggs and floated on savory broth garnished with parsley and accompanied by grated cheese). Follow with specialties like saltimbocca alla romano or sole basilica (flavored with lime juice, paprika, and basil). Finish with a selection from the dessert wagon or really spoil yourself with cherries jubilee or bananas flambé.

Happy Wanderer. 6405 Stanley Ave. ☎ **905/354-9825.** Reservations not accepted. Main courses C$10–C$26 (US$7–US$19). AE, MC, V. Daily 9am–11pm. GERMAN.

Real Gemütlichkeit greets you at the chalet-style Happy Wanderer, which comes complete with beer steins and game trophies on the walls, and offers a variety of schnitzels, wursts, and other German specialties. Dinner might start with goulash soup and continue with bratwurst, knackwurst, rauchwurst (served with sauerkraut and potato salad), or a schnitzel—wiener, Holstein, or jaeger. All entrees include potatoes, salad, and rye bread. Desserts include, naturally, Black Forest cake and apple strudel.

NIAGARA PARKWAY COMMISSION RESTAURANTS

The Niagara Parkway Commission has commandeered the most spectacular scenic spots, where it operates some reasonably priced restaurants. The **Table Rock Restaurant** (☎ 905/354-3631) and the **Victoria Park Restaurant** (☎ 905/356-2217) are both on the Parkway right by the falls. **Diner on the Green** (☎ 905/356-7221) is also on the Parkway, located at the Whirlpool Golf Course near Queenston. The restaurant listed below offers the best dining experience.

Queenston Heights. 14276 Niagara Pkwy. ☎ **905/262-4274.** Reservations recommended. Main courses C$19–C$26 (US$14–US$19). AE, MC, V. Daily 11:30am–3pm; Sun–Fri 5–9pm, Sat 5–10pm. Closed Jan to mid-Mar. CANADIAN.

The star of the Niagara Parkway Commission's restaurants stands dramatically atop Queenston Heights. Set in the park among fir, cypress, silver birch, and maple, the open-air balcony affords a magnificent view of the lower Niagara River and the rich fruit-growing land through which it flows. (If nothing else, go for a drink on the deck and the terrific view.) Or you can sit under the cathedral ceiling with its heavy crossbeams where the flue of the stone fireplace reaches to the roof. At dinner, selections might include fillet of Atlantic salmon with Riesling chive hollandaise, prime rib, or grilled pork with apples and cider Dijon-mustard sauce. Afternoon tea is served from 3 to 5pm in summer.

11 Niagara-on-the-Lake & the Shaw Festival

128 kilometers (80 miles) S of Toronto, 56 kilometers (35 miles) N of Buffalo, NY

Only 1½ hours from Toronto, Niagara-on-the-Lake is one of North America's best-preserved and prettiest 19th-century villages, with its lakeside location and tree-lined streets bordered by handsome clapboard and brick period houses. In fact, in 1996 it was named the "Prettiest Town in Canada" in the Communities in Bloom competition. Some may find it too cute and too commercialized, but such is the setting for one of Canada's most famous events, the Shaw Festival.

ESSENTIALS

VISITOR INFORMATION   The **Niagara-on-the-Lake Chamber of Commerce and Visitor and Convention Bureau,** 153 King St. (P.O. Box 1043), Niagara-on-the-Lake, ON, L02 1J0 (☎ **905/468-4263**), will help you find accommodations at one of the 120 B&Bs or 15 inns and hotels in town. Its hours are Monday to Friday from 9am to 5pm, Saturday and Sunday from 10am to 5pm.

GETTING THERE   Driving from Toronto, take the QEW Niagara via Hamilton and St. Catharines and exit at Highway 55. From the United States, cross from Buffalo to Fort Erie via the Peace Bridge or from Niagara Falls, New York, via the Rainbow Bridge and then take the QEW to Highway 55. Or cross at the Queenston-Lewiston bridge and follow the signs along the Niagara Parkway into Niagara-on-the-Lake. Allow plenty of time for crossing the border.

Amtrak and VIA operate trains between Toronto (☎ 416/366-8411) and New York that stop in St. Catharines and Niagara Falls. Call ☎ 800/USA-RAIL in the United States or **800/361-1235** in Canada. From St. Catharines or Niagara Falls you can rent a car and drive the rest of the way to Niagara-on-the-Lake.

THE SHAW FESTIVAL

Devoted to the works of George Bernard Shaw and his contemporaries, the festival, which opens in April and runs to November, is housed in three theaters: the historic Court House, the Edwardian Royal George, and the exquisite Festival Theatre, where intermissions can be spent near the reflecting pools and gardens.

The season includes drama, musicals, comedy, and lunchtime performances at the Royal George Theatre. The year's festival program is announced in mid-January, and it is best to book early, as it is difficult to get tickets on short notice unless a particular show bombs. Ticket prices for all three theaters range from C$15 (US$11) for lunchtime performances to C$65 (US$46). For more information, write or phone the **Shaw Festival,** P.O. Box 774, Niagara-on-the-Lake, ON, L0S 1J0 (☎ **800/511-7429** or 905/468-2172).

EXPLORING THE TOWN

Strolling along Queen Street will take you to some entertaining shopping stops: the **Niagara Apothecary Shop,** 5 Queen St. (☎ **905/468-3845**), with its original black-walnut counters and displays of original glass and ceramic apothecary ware; **Greaves Jam,** 35 Queen St. (☎ **905/468-7831**); and **Loyalist Village,** at 12 Queen St. (☎ **905/468-7331**), selling distinctively Canadian clothes and crafts, including Inuit art, native-Canadian decoys, and sheepskins.

The **Niagara-on-the-Lake Golf Club** on Front Street (☎ 905/468-3424) is right on Lake Ontario and has a beautiful 9-hole, par-72 course that can be played for C$30 (US$21) for 18 holes.

Niagara Historical Society Museum. 43 Castlereagh St. (at Davy). ☎ **905/468-3912.** Admission C$3 (US$2.15) adults, C$1 (US70¢) students, C$1.50 (US$1.05) seniors, 50¢ (US35¢) children under 12. May 1–Oct 31 daily 10am–5pm; Nov 1–Dec 31 and Mar–Apr daily 1–5pm; Jan–Feb Sat–Sun 1–5pm.

One of the oldest and largest of its kind in Canada, this museum houses more than 20,000 artifacts pertaining to local history, including collections dating from the 18th and 19th centuries, with many possessions of the United Empire Loyalists who first settled the area at the end of the American Revolution.

✪ **Fort George National Historic Site.** Niagara Pkwy. ☎ **905/468-4257.** Admission C$6 (US$4.30) adults, C$5 (US$3.55) seniors, C$4 (US$2.85) children 6–16, C$20 (US$14) families; children under 6 free. Apr 1–Oct 31 daily 10am–5pm (until 8pm on Sat in July–Aug).

South along the Niagara Parkway is the impressive Fort George National Historic Site. It's easy to imagine taking shelter behind the stockade fence and watching for the enemy from across the river, even though today only condominiums stare back from the opposite riverbank. The fort played a key role in the War of 1812 when the Americans invaded, and was reconstructed in the 1930s. View the guard room with its hard plank beds, the officers' quarters, the enlisted men's quarters, and the sentry posts. In the gunpowder-storage area, no metal fitments are used, for a stray spark could ignite the lot. The self-guided tour includes interpretive films and occasional performances by the Fort George Fife and Drum Corps.

REGIONAL WINERY TOURS

Niagara is set in a fruit- and wine-growing region that has been producing better and better quality wines in the last decade. There are now 30 or so vineyards in the Niagara region. The wines are becoming increasingly sophisticated and so are the vineyard facilities. At Hillebrand, for example, visitors are invited to treat the winery itself as a destination. It features bicycle tours, craft exhibits, concerts, and jazz. Other vineyards offer restaurant and cafe facilities and even accommodations. Pick up a brochure outlining the wine route and follow it from Niagara-on-the-Lake to St. Catharines and through Jordan, Vineland, Beamsville, and Grimsby. Here are just a few recommended vineyard stops along the way: **Inniskillin,** Niagara Parkway at Line 3, RR #1, Niagara-on-the-Lake (☎ 905/468-3554); **Konzelmann Estate Winery,** RR #3, Lakeshore Rd., Niagara-on-the-Lake (☎ 905/935-2866); **Strewn,** 1339 Lakeshore Rd., Niagara-on-the-Lake (☎ 905/468-1229); **Hillebrand,** Hwy. 55, Niagara-on-the-Lake (☎ 905/468-7123), which I particularly recommend, as it hosts special events and offers cafe dining and even bicycle tours; **Henry of Pelham,** 1469 Pelham Rd., St. Catharines (☎ 905/684-8423); **Cave Spring Cellars,** 3836 Main St., Jordan (☎ 905/562-3581); and **Vineland Estates,** 3620 Moyer Rd., RR #1, Vineland (☎ 905/562-7088). Most of these vineyards offer daily tours from May to October (some operate year-round) in which you can see the wine-making process and taste the end results. Call ahead for tour times. Note that some charge a small fee.

ACCOMMODATIONS

During the summer season it can be hard to find lodging, but the **visitors bureau** (☎ 905/468-4263) should be able to find you a room at one of the zillions of bed-and-breakfasts in the region.

EXPENSIVE

Gate House Hotel. 142 Queen St., Niagara-on-the-Lake, ON, L0S 1J0. ☎ **905/468-3263.** Fax 905/468-7400. 10 rms. A/C TV TEL. June–Sept C$160–C$180 (US$114–US$129) double; Oct–Dec and Mar–May C$125–C$150 (US$89–US$107) double; Jan–Feb C$110–C$130 (US$79–US$93) double. Children under 12 stay free in parents' rm. AE, ER, MC, V.

Rooms at the Gate House Hotel are strikingly different from other accommodations in town. They are not country-Canadian, but are decorated in cool, up-to-the-minute Milan style. The turquoise marbleized look is accented with ultramodern basic black lamps, block marble tables, leatherette couches, and bathrooms with sleek Italian accessories and hair dryers. Ristorante Giardino, one of the best places to dine in town, is located in the hotel.

✪ **Oban Inn.** 160 Front St. (at Gate St.), Niagara-on-the-Lake, ON, L0S 1J0. ☎ **905/468-2165.** 22 rms, some with shower only. A/C TV TEL. C$160 (US$94) standard double, C$220 (US$129) double with lake view. Winter midweek and weekend packages available. AE, DC, MC, V.

With a prime location overlooking the lake, the Oban Inn is *the* place to stay. It's a charming white Victorian house with a large veranda. The gardens are a joy to behold and are the source of the bouquets on each table in the dining room and throughout the house. Each comfortable room, though decorated differently, has antique chests and early Canadian–style beds. Each is likely to have a candlewick spread on the bed, a small sofa, dressing table, and old prints on the walls—it's all very homey and comfortably old-fashioned. One or two rooms have showers only, so if you want a bath, be sure to request it.

Dining/Entertainment: Bar snacks and light lunches and dinners are available in the English-style pub, which is furnished with Windsor-style chairs and hunting prints hung above the blazing hearth (piano entertainment, too, on weekends). For fine dining there are more formal dining rooms overlooking Lake Ontario and the gardens.

Pillar & Post Inn. 48 John St. (at King St.), Niagara-on-the-Lake, ON, L02 1J0. ☎ **800/361-6788** or 905/468-2123. Fax 905/468-3551. 123 rms and suites. A/C MINIBAR TV TEL. C$170 (US$121) double; C$185 (US$132) fireplace rm; C$205–C$240 (US$146–US$171) deluxe rms; from C$275 (US$196) suite. AE, DC, ER, MC, V.

The quietly elegant Pillar & Post Inn is located a couple of blocks from the throngs on main street. In recent years it has been transformed into one of the most sophisticated accommodations in town, complete with a spa featuring themed treatment rooms. From the minute you set foot in the light and airy lobby, which has a fireplace, lush planting, and comfortable seating, guests recognize that the emphasis here is on comfort. Although all of the spacious rooms are slightly different, each room contains early Canadian-style furniture, Windsor-style chairs, and historical engravings, plus the usual modern conveniences. The suites all feature cathedral ceilings, redbrick wood-burning fireplaces, pine settles with cushions, four-poster beds, and Jacuzzis. Some rooms facing the pool on the ground level have bay windows and window boxes.

Dining/Entertainment: The two dining rooms, Carriages and the Cannery, are warmed by fires on cool evenings. The menu is eclectic and moderately priced, featuring everything from prime rib with Yorkshire pudding to Szechuan roast duck and bourbon-marinated beef tenderloin with a smoky bacon jus. There's also a comfortable lounge. The adjoining wine bar features a curvaceous bar and a large selection of local Niagara and international wines.

Services: Room service is available from 7am to 10pm Sunday to Thursday (until midnight Friday and Saturday); laundry/valet.

Facilities: The spa offers a full range of body treatments and massage therapies (from C$30 to C$95/US$21 to US$68), plus a Japanese-style warm mineral spring pool, complete with cascading waterfall. There's also an indoor pool, and an attractively landscaped outdoor sauna, and whirlpool. Bikes are available.

Prince of Wales Hotel. 6 Picton St., Niagara-on-the-Lake, ON, L0S 1J0. ☎ **800/263-2452** or 905/468-3246. Fax 905/468-5521. 101 rms. A/C TV TEL. May–Oct C$140–C$245 (US$100–US$175) double; from C$295 (US$211) suite. Extra person C$20 (US$14). Rates slightly less at other times. AE, MC, V.

For a lively atmosphere that retains the elegance of a Victorian inn, the Prince of Wales Hotel has it all: a location right on the main street across from the lovely gardens of Simcoe Park; full recreational facilities; lounges, bars, and restaurants; and attractive rooms, all beautifully decorated with antiques or reproductions. Bathrooms are equipped with bidets, and most rooms have minibars. The hotel's original section was built in 1864 and rooms here are slightly smaller than those in the several additions.

Dining/Entertainment: An impressive old oak bar dominates the quiet bar off the lobby. Royals, the elegant main dining room, is decorated in French style. The dinner menu offers a dozen classics like mustard crusted rack of lamb or salmon with thyme beurre blanc priced from C$18 to C$28 (US$13 to US$20). Three Feathers is a luxuriant greenhouse cafe that is light and airy for breakfast, lunch, or tea. The Queen's Royal lounge, furnished with wingbacks and armchairs, is pleasant for cocktails, afternoon tea, or light evening fare.

Services: Room service is available from 7:30am to midnight; there's also laundry and valet.

Facilities: Indoor pool, sauna, whirlpool, and fitness center.

Queen's Landing. Byron St., Niagara-on-the-Lake, ON, L0S 1J0. ☎800/361-6645 or 905/468-2195. Fax 905/468-2227. 138 rms. A/C MINIBAR TV TEL. C$180 (US$129) double; C$195–C$205 (US$139–US$146) fireplace rm; C$230–C$265 (US$164–US$189) deluxe rm with fireplace and Jacuzzi. Extra person C$20 (US$14). Children under 18 stay free in parents' rm. Special packages available. AE, DC, ER, MC, V.

Overlooking the river, but within walking distance of the theater, the Queen's Landing is a modern Georgian-style mansion offering 71 rooms with fireplaces and 32 with Jacuzzis. The spacious rooms are comfortably furnished with half-canopy or brass beds, wingback chairs, and large desks.

Dining/Entertainment: The Bacchus lounge is cozy, with its fieldstone fireplace, copper-foil bar, and velvet cushioned seating. The circular Tiara dining room looks out over the yacht-filled dock. It's elegantly styled with a grand stained-glass ceiling— a suitable foil for the fine cuisine. At dinner about a dozen dishes are offered, priced from C$20 to C$29 (US$14 to US$21) for such dishes as parsley-crusted sea bass slow-roasted with Estate chardonnay or roasted rack of lamb with tomato bread pudding, leaf spinach, and warm arugula oil. Breakfast, lunch, and Sunday brunch are served here, too.

Services: Room service (from 7am to 11pm), laundry/valet.

Facilities: Indoor pool, whirlpool and sauna, exercise room, lap pool, bicycle rentals.

White Oaks Inn & Racquet Club. Taylor Rd., Niagara-on-the-Lake, ON, L0S 1J0. ☎ **905/688-2550.** Fax 905/688-2220. 75 rms, 15 suites. A/C TV TEL. July–Aug C$145–C$155 (US$104–US$111) double; C$165–C$230 (US$118–US$164) suite. Off-season rates drop slightly. AE, DC, ER, MC, V.

Not far from Niagara-on-the-Lake, the White Oaks Inn and Racquet Club is a fantastic choice for an active vacation. You could spend the whole weekend and not stir outside the resort. The rooms are as good as the facilities, featuring oak beds and furniture, vanity sinks, and additional niceties like a phone in the bathroom. The Executive Suites also have brick fireplaces, marble-top desks, Jacuzzis (some heart-shaped), and bidets. Deluxe suites also have sitting rooms. Additional amenities like hair dryers are found in the rooms.

Dining: There's an outdoor terrace cafe, a restaurant-wine bar, and a pleasantly furnished cafe/coffee shop.

Services: Room service (7am to midnight), valet service.

Facilities: Four outdoor and eight indoor tennis courts, six squash courts, two racquetball courts, Nautilus room, jogging trails, bike rentals, massage therapist, sauna, suntan beds, and a day-care center staffed with fully qualified staff.

MODERATE

Moffat Inn. 60 Picton St., Niagara-on-the-Lake, ON, L02 1J0. ☎ **905/468-4116.** Fax 905/468-4747. 22 rms. A/C TV TEL. Apr 15–Oct 31 and Christmas/New Year holiday period C$85–C$135 (US$61–US$96) double; late Oct to late Apr C$65–C$119 (US$46–US$85) double. Extra person C$10 (US$7). AE, MC, V.

This is a fine choice, with comfortable units. Most are furnished with either brass or cannonball beds, traditional modern furnishings or wicker and bamboo pieces, and feature built-in closets. Additional room amenities include a tea kettle and supplies, and a hair dryer; some rooms have gas fireplaces. Free coffee is available in the lobby and there's also a restaurant and bar for meals. No smoking.

✪ **Old Bank House.** 10 Front St., Niagara-on-the-Lake, ON, L0S 1J0. ☎ **905/468-7136.** 6 rms (4 with private bath), 2 suites (with bath). A/C. C$90 (US$64) rm without bath, C$115–C$125 (US$82–US$89) rm with private bath; C$145 (US$104) suite; C$230 (US$164) 2-bedrm suite for up to 4 people. Rates include full English breakfast. Lower rates in winter. AE, MC, V.

Beautifully situated down by the river, the Old Bank House, a two-story Georgian, was built in 1817 and was in fact the Bank of Canada's first branch. Four rooms have private baths, while two share a bathroom with Jacuzzi. The Rose, the most expensive suite, has two bedrooms, a sitting room, and a bathroom. Several rooms have private entrances, like the charming Garden Room, which also has a trellised deck. All rooms are tastefully decorated. The sitting room, with its fireplace, is extraordinarily comfortable and furnished with eclectic antique pieces.

A NEARBY CHOICE ALONG THE WINE ROAD

The Vintners Inn. 3845 Main St., Jordan, ON, L0R 1S0. ☎ **905/562-5336.** 9 suites. A/C TEL. C$199–C$239 (US$142–US$171) double. AE, ER, MC, V.

Right in the village of Jordan, this modern accommodation has handsome suites, each with an elegantly furnished living room with a fireplace and a bathroom with a whirlpool tub. Seven of the suites are duplexes—one of them, the deluxe loft, has two double beds on its second level—and three are single-level suites with high ceilings. The inn's restaurant, On the Twenty, is across the street.

DINING

In addition to the listings below, consider the dining rooms at the Pillar & Post, Queen's Landing, and the Prince of Wales.

Light meals and lunches can also be enjoyed at the **Shaw Cafe and Wine Bar,** a stylish place with an outside patio at 92 Queen St. (☎ 905/468-4772). Also on Queen at no. 84, the **Epicurean** (☎ 905/468-3408) offers hearty soups, quiches, sandwiches, and other fine dishes in a sunny Provençal-style dining room. Service is cafeteria-style. Half a block off Queen, the **Angel Inn,** 224 Regent St. (☎ 905/468-3411), is a delightfully authentic English pub.

The Buttery. 19 Queen St. ☎ 905/468-2564. Reservations required for Henry VIII feast. Main courses C$15–C$20 (US$11–US$14). AE, MC, V. June–Sept daily 10am–11:30pm; Oct–May daily noon–8pm, except on Fri–Sat when the Henry VIII feast takes place. Afternoon tea served 2–5pm. CANADIAN/ENGLISH/CONTINENTAL.

With its terrace brightened by hanging geraniums, the Buttery has been a main-street dining landmark for years, known for its weekend Henry VIII feasts, in which "serving wenches" ply guests with food and wine, while "jongleurs" and "musickers" entertain. You'll be served "four removes"—broth, chicken, roast lamb, roast pig, sherry trifle, syllabub, and cheese, all washed down with a goodly amount of wine, ale, and mead. This feast takes 2¹/₂ hours and costs C$47.50 (US$34), including tax and a gratuity for Henry VIII.

A full tavern menu is served from 11am to 5:30pm and all day Monday, featuring spareribs, an 8-ounce New York strip, shrimp in garlic sauce, and such English-pub fare as steak, kidney, and mushroom pie and lamb curry. The dinner menu lists eight or so choices; I highly recommend the rack of lamb served with pan juices, or the shrimp curry. Finish with Grand Marnier chocolate cheesecake or mud pie, or take home some of the fresh-baked pies, strudels, dumplings, cream puffs, or scones.

Fans Court. 135 Queen St. ☎ 905/468-4511. Reservations recommended. Main courses C$10–C$20 (US$7–US$14). AE, DC, MC, V. Daily noon–10pm. CHINESE.

Some of the best food in town can be found in this comfortable Chinese spot, decorated with fans, cushioned bamboo chairs, and round tables spread with golden tablecloths. In summer, the courtyard has tables for outdoor dining. The cuisine is primarily Cantonese and Szechuan, with choices such as Singapore beef, moo shu pork, Szechuan scallops, and lemon chicken. If you wish, you can order Peking duck 24 hours in advance.

✪ Ristorante Giardino. In the Gate House Hotel, 142 Queen St. ☎ 905/468-3263. Reservations recommended. Main courses C$22–C$27 (US$16–US$19). AE, ER, MC, V. June–Sept daily noon–2:30pm and 5–10pm; Oct–May daily 5:30–9pm. NORTHERN ITALIAN.

On the ground floor of the Gate House Hotel is this sleek, ultramodern restaurant with gleaming marble-top bar and glass and brass accents throughout. The food is northern Italian with fresh American accents. Main courses include baked salmon seasoned with olive paste and tomato concasse, veal tenderloin marinated with garlic and rosemary, and braised pheasant in a juniper-berry-and-vegetable sauce. There are several pasta dishes, too, plus such appealing appetizers as medaillons of langostine garnished with orange and fennel salad. Desserts include a delicious warm gratin of wild berries and orange zabaglione.

Along the Wine Road
On the Twenty Restaurant & Wine Bar. 3836 Main St., Jordan. ☎ 905/562-7313. Main courses C$20–C$30 (US$14–US$21). AE, DC, MC, V. Daily 11:30am–3pm and 5–10pm. Closed Mon in winter. CANADIAN.

Foodies head for this gardenlike haven overlooking Twenty Mile Creek. It's the domain of chef Michael Olson, who has finally brought some truly fine cuisine to the Niagara Falls area. The appealing dining rooms are in fact located in an old winery. The cuisine features many local ingredients—for example, sauté of Beamsville chicken and forest mushrooms in Mennonite cream with basil buttermilk biscuit; Fundy salmon grilled over herbs with potato pancakes and sweet pepper sauces; or smoked Ontario pork tenderloin with crisp fried shallots and quince-oxtail jus on sweet-potato celery-root gratin. To start, select the Prince Edward Island mussels steamed in lager with caramelized garlic, bacon, and scallions. Naturally, there's an extensive selection of Ontario wines, including some wonderful ice wines to accompany such desserts as lemon tart and fruit cobbler.

Vineland Estates. 3620 Moyer Rd., Vineland. ☎ **905/562-7088.** Reservations recommended. Main courses C$19–C$28 (US$14–US$20). AE, DC, MC, V. Daily 11am–3pm and 5–8:45pm. CONTEMPORARY CANADIAN.

The Vineland Estates dining room is reminiscent of many a California vineyard restaurant, overlooking the vines. On warm days you can dine on a deck under a spreading tree, or in the airy dining room. The chef uses local ingredients wherever possible. Among the appetizers you might find local smoked eel or house-smoked splake (a hybrid fish that's a cross between a lake trout and salmon) and more familiar dishes like the roasted sweet bell-pepper bisque with tomato-chive crème fraîche and Pelee Island treasures. These can be followed by a pasta dish or one of the fresh main courses like the Wellington County lamb with roasted garlic thyme jus or chickpea-crusted halibut with a French lentil ragout. Cheese lovers will appreciate the tasting plate of Canadian farm cheeses including the wonderful Abbey St. Benoit blue ermite. Patrons usually gasp at the delectable desserts—blueberry-and-cherry trifle, for example.

Between Hamilton & Brantford

Ancaster Old Mill Inn. Off Rte. 2, Ancaster. ☎ **905/648-1827.** Reservations recommended. Main courses C$13–C$25 (US$9–US$18). AE, DC, MC, V. Mon–Sat 11:30am–2pm, Sun 9am–2pm; daily 5–8pm. CANADIAN.

To reach the restaurant, you cross the mill race. You'll find pleasant country dining rooms with pine furnishings. One end overlooks the falls, the other the old mill built in 1792. The menu combines traditional favorites (French onion soup) with more innovative cuisine (say, Alaskan-king-crab salad in a lime ginger vinaigrette). Main courses include charcoal-grilled salmon with yellow-pepper beurre blanc, breast of chicken with salsa verde, and prime rib with Yorkshire pudding.

12 St. Catharines to Port Colborne & Hamilton

ST. CATHARINES & THE WELLAND CANAL

In the heart of wine country and the Niagara fruit belt, the historic city of **St. Catharines** is home to two major events: the **Royal Canadian Henley Regatta** in early August and the 10-day **Niagara Grape and Wine Festival,** held in late September.

Year-round you can also observe the operations of the **Welland Canal,** which runs through the town of Port Colborne, south of St. Catharines. Built to circumvent Niagara Falls, the Welland Canal connects Lake Ontario to Lake Erie, which is 327 feet higher than Lake Ontario. Some 27 feet deep, the canal enables large ocean vessels to navigate the Great Lakes. The 26-mile-long canal has seven locks, each with an average lift of 46$^{1}/_{2}$ feet. The average transit time for any vessel is 12 hours. More than a thousand oceangoing vessels travel through in a year, the most common cargoes being wheat and iron ore.

The best places to observe the canal are at the **Welland Canal Viewing and Information Centres,** at Lock 3 in St. Catharines (on Government Road, north of Glendale Avenue off the QEW) and at Lock 8 in Port Colborne. At the first, from a raised platform you can watch ships from over 50 countries passing between Lake Ontario and Lake Erie. The Canal Parkway allows visitors to walk beside the canal and follow the vessels. From the road below the canal you can observe the funnels only moving along above the top of the bank. It's also fun to bike along the canal between Locks 1 and 3.

Also at Lock 3, the **St. Catharines Museum** (☎ 905/984-8880) houses displays illustrating the construction and working of the Welland Canal, as well as pioneer and War of 1812 memorabilia. Kids enjoy the Discovery Room where they can operate a telephone switchboard or dress up in pioneer clothing and enjoy other hands-on fun. Admission is C$3 (US$2.15) adults, C$2 (US$1.45) students and seniors, C$1 (US70¢) children 5 to 13, and C$7 (US$5) for families. Open Labour Day to Victoria Day daily from 9am to 5pm; Victoria Day to Labour Day daily from 9am to 9pm. It's closed December 25 and 26, and New Year's Day.

If you drive to St. Catharines from Niagara-on-the-Lake, on the right just before you enter St. Catharines, you'll find **Happy Rolph Bird Sanctuary and Children's Petting Farm** (☎ 905/935-1484), which the kids will love. It's free and open daily from late May to mid-October from 10am to dusk.

At Port Colborne, the southern end of the canal opens into Lake Erie. A good sense of the area's history and development can be gained at the **Port Colborne Historical and Marine Museum,** 280 King St. (☎ 905/834-7604). The six-building complex downtown has a fully operational blacksmith shop and a tearoom. It's free and open daily May to December from noon to 5pm.

In Vineland, **Prudhomme's Landing-Wet 'n' Wild,** off Victoria Avenue (☎ 905/562-7304), features water slides, a wave pool, go-carts, kids' rides, and miniature golf. An all-day pass costs C$10.65 (US$8) for adults and children 5 or over. Open mid-June to Labour Day daily from 10am to 8pm (water park closes at 7pm).

ATTRACTIONS NEAR HAMILTON

Situated on a landlocked harbor spanned at its entrance by the Burlington Skyway's dramatic sweep, Hamilton has long been known as "Steeltown." Although it has steel mills and smoke-belching chimneys, the town has received an extensive face-lift in the last decade, but, more important, it is home to a couple of worthwhile attractions.

On the northern approaches to the city, the ✪ **Royal Botanical Gardens,** Highway 6 (☎ 905/527-1158), spreads over 3,000 acres. The Rock Garden features spring bulbs in May, summer flowers from June to September, and chrysanthemums in October. The Laking Garden blazes during June and July with iris, peonies, and lilies. The arboretum fills with the heady scent of lilac from the end of May to early June, and the exquisite color bursts of rhododendrons and azaleas thereafter. The Centennial Rose Garden is at its best from late June to mid-September. Admission is C$6 (US$4.30) for adults, C$4 (US$2.85) for seniors, C$3.50 (US$2.50) for students, and C$2 (US$1.45) for children ages 5 to 12; children under 5 are free. The outdoor garden areas are open daily from 9:30am to 6pm; the Mediterranean Garden is open daily from 9am to 5pm.

Forty kilometers (25 miles) of nature trails crisscross the area, while nearby, and still part of the gardens, is **Cootes Paradise,** a natural wildlife sanctuary with trails leading through some 18,000 acres of water, marsh, and wooded ravines. For a trail-guide map, stop in at either the Nature Centre (open daily from 10am to 4pm) or at headquarters at 680 Plains Rd. W. (Highway 2), Burlington. Two tea houses—one overlooking the Rock Garden, the other the Rose Garden—serve refreshments.

Dundurn Castle, Dundurn Park, York Boulevard (☎ 905/546-2872), affords a glimpse of the opulent life as it was lived in this part of southern Ontario in the mid-19th century. It was built between 1832 and 1835 by Sir Allan Napier MacNab, prime minister of the United Provinces of Canada in the mid-1850s and a founder of the Great Western Railway, who was knighted by Queen Victoria for the part he played in the Rebellion of 1837. The 35-plus–room mansion has been restored and furnished in the style of 1855. The gray stucco exterior, with its classical Greek portico, is impressive enough, but inside from the grand and formal dining rooms to Lady MacNab's boudoir, the furnishings are equally rich. The museum contains a fascinating collection of Victoriana. In December the castle is decorated quite splendidly for a Victorian Christmas. From downtown Hamilton, take King Street West to Dundurn Street, turn right, and Dundurn will run into York Boulevard. Admission is C$6 (US$4.30) for adults, C$5.50 (US$3.95) for seniors and students, and C$2.50 (US$1.80) for children ages 6 to 14; children under 6 are free. It's open daily June to Labour Day from 10am to 4pm; the rest of the year, it's open Tuesday to Sunday noon to 4pm. Closed Christmas and New Year's days.

Just a half-hour drive northwest of Hamilton, off Highway 8 between Hamilton and Cambridge, is the **African Lion Safari** (☎ 519/623-2620). You can drive your own car or take the guided safari bus through this 750-acre wildlife park containing rhino, cheetah, lion, tiger, giraffe, zebra, vultures, and many other species. There are scenic railroad and boat rides, plus special kids' jungle and water (bring bathing suits) play areas. Admission, including a tour of the large game reserves plus the rides and shows, costs C$14.95 (US$11) for adults, C$12.95 (US$9) for seniors and youths 13 to 17, and C$10.95 (US$8) for children 3 to 12. Open daily April to October; hours July to Labour Day are from 10am to 5:30pm; at other times it closes earlier.

DINING

Hennepin's. 1486 Niagara Stone Rd. (Hwy. 55 at Creek Rd.), Virgil. ☎ **905/468-1555.** Tapas C$4–C$8 (US$2.85–US$6); main courses C$13–C$24 (US$9–US$17). AE, ER, MC, V. Sun–Wed 11:30–9pm, Fri–Sat 11:30–11pm. CONTEMPORARY.

The region's first tapas bar, Hennepin's offers excitingly different cuisine. The dining rooms are fresh and light and display the works of local artists. Tapas—coconut shrimp, olive-stuffed meatballs, chicken satay, samosas—are served all day in a round-the-world medley. At dinner, in addition to the tapas, there are always such temptations as escargots in Pernod, or pan-seared game pâté with blueberry kirsch sauce to start. At dinner, game and serious meats dominate the main courses—venison bordelaise, liver in a chausseur sauce, steak, and pork tenderloin with a portobello calvados sauce. Even the desserts are seriously rich, like the death-by-chocolate cake. The wine list is extensive; 28 wines are also available by the glass.

Iseya. 22 James St. (between St. Paul and King sts.), St. Catharines. ☎ **905/688-1141.** Reservations recommended for dinner. Main courses C$10–C$27 (US$7–US$19). AE, MC, V. Mon–Fri 11:30am–2:30pm; Mon–Sat 5–10:30pm. JAPANESE.

Iseya is one of the region's few traditional Japanese restaurants, serving sushi/sashimi, as well as teriyaki, tempura, and sukiyaki dishes. This is standard Japanese fare and the sushi is quite fresh.

Rinderlin's. 24 Burgar St., Welland. ☎ **905/735-4411.** Reservations recommended. Main courses C$17–C$30 (US$12–US$21). AE, DC, ER, MC, V. Tues–Fri 11:30am–2pm; Tues–Sat 6–9pm. FRENCH.

An intimate town-house dining spot, Rinderlin's has a very good local reputation for traditional French cuisine. On the dinner menu you might find house-smoked trout with horseradish sauce, rack of lamb with a minted onion-garlic sauce, and local venison with wild mushrooms and game sauce. Desserts are seasonal—my favorite is the white-chocolate torte flavored with brandy and served with a raspberry sauce.

Wellington Court Restaurant. 11 Wellington St., St. Catharines. ☎ **905/682-5518.** Reservations recommended. Main courses C$12–C$23 (US$9–US$16). ER, MC, V. Mon–Sat 11:30am–2:30pm; Tues–Sat 5:30–9:30pm. CONTINENTAL.

In downtown St. Catharines, the Wellington Court is well-worth visiting. Located in an Edwardian town house with a flower trellis, the dining rooms feature contemporary decor with modern lithographs and photographs. The menu features daily specials—the fish and pasta of the day, for example—along with such items as a beef tenderloin in a shallot-and-red-wine reduction, roasted breast of chicken served on gingered plum preserves, and grilled sea bass with cranberry vinaigrette.

13 Southern & Midwestern Ontario

by Marilyn Wood

Part of the long sweep of the Niagara Escarpment, where the land is flat and eminently farmable, this is the pioneer country to which Canada's early settlers came. A landscape dotted with silos, barns, and dairy herds, and broken up by hedgerows, it attracted the Scots to such towns as Elora, Fergus, and St. Mary's; the Germans to Kitchener-Waterloo; the Mennonites to Elmira and St. Jacobs; and the English Loyalists to Stratford and London. This ethnic heritage and the festivals that it nourishes—Oktoberfest, the Highland Games, the Mennonite quilt sale—are part of the area's attraction, but the biggest draw is the world-famous theater festival at Stratford.

1 Exploring Southern & Midwestern Ontario

Windsor sits across from Detroit on the Canadian side of the border. From here visitors can travel along either Highway 401 east or the more scenic Highway 3 (called the Talbot Trail, which runs from Windsor to Fort Erie), stopping along the way to visit some major attractions on the Lake Erie shore.

East of Windsor lies London, and from London it's an easy drive to Stratford. From Stratford visitors can turn west to Goderich and Bayfield on the shores of Lake Huron or east to Kitchener-Waterloo and then north to Elmira, Elora, and Fergus.

VISITOR INFORMATION

Contact **Ontario Travel/Travelinx Ontario,** Queen's Park, Toronto, ON, M7A 2E5 (☎ **800/ONTARIO** from 9am to 8pm, or 416/314-0944). The offices are open Monday to Friday from 8:30am to 5pm (daily from mid-May to mid-September). You can also contact them at their Web site: **www.travelinx.com**.

FARM STAYS

Staying on a farm is a unique way to experience Ontario. You'll enjoy home-cooked meals, the peace of the countryside, and the working rhythms of a dairy or mixed farm. You can choose to stay at all kinds of farms in many different locations. Rates average C$45 to C$70 (US$32 to US$50) double per night, or C$240 (US$171) per week, all meals included. For information, write the **Ontario Vacation Farm Association,** RR #2, Alma, ON, N0B 1A0; or contact Ontario Travel for its free *Farm Vacation Guide.*

THE GREAT OUTDOORS

Some 260 provincial parks in Ontario offer ample opportunities for outdoor recreation. The daily in-season entry fee for a vehicle is C$6 or C$7 (US$4.30 or US$5) depending on the park; campsites cost anywhere from C$13 to C$18 (US$9 to US$13). For more information, contact the **Ontario Ministry of Natural Resources** (☎ 416/314-2000).

Point Pelee National Park offers year-round hiking and bicycle and canoe rentals from April to October. For more information, contact the Superintendent, Point Pelee National Park, RR #1, Leamington, ON, N8H 3V4 (☎ 519/322-2365). If you're driving from Windsor, take Highway 3 east to reach Pelee Island. At Ruthven get on Highway 18 and follow the signs to the park.

BIKING The South Point and Marsh trails in **Rondeau Provincial Park,** near Blenheim (☎ 519/674-1750), are great for cycling.

BIRD WATCHING **Point Pelee National Park,** southeast of Windsor (☎ 519/ 322-2371), is one of the continent's premier bird-watching centers. The spring and fall migrations are spectacular; as many as 100 different species have been spotted in a single day. In fall, it's also the gathering place for flocks of monarch butterflies, which cover the trees before taking off for their migratory flight. Located at the southernmost tip of Canada, which juts down into Lake Erie at the same latitude as northern California, it features some of the same flora—white sassafras, sumac, black walnut, and cedar.

Another good bet is **Jack Miner's Bird Sanctuary,** Road 3 West, 2 miles north of Kingsville off Division Road (☎ 519/733-4034). The famed naturalist established the sanctuary to protect migrating Canadian geese; and the best time to visit is late October and November when thousands of migrating waterfowl stop over. At other times visitors can see the 50 or so Canadian geese and the few hundred ducks, as well as wild turkeys, pheasant, and peacocks. The museum displays artifacts and photographs relating to Jack Miner. Admission is free, it's open Monday to Saturday from 8am to 5:30pm.

BOATING & CANOEING Companies offering trips on the Grand River include the **Grand River Canoe Company,** 132 Rawdon St., Brantford (☎ 519/759-0040), **Canoeing the Grand,** 3734 King St. E., and **Kitchener** (☎ 519/896-0290, or 519/ 893-0022 off-season). Rentals average C$40 to C$50 (US$29 to US$36) a day, C$150 to C$170 (US$107 to US$121) a week.

There are also canoe rentals in **Point Pelee National Park** (☎ 519/322-2371).

GOLF There are a few good courses in Windsor, and in Leamington you'll find **Erie Shores Golf and Country Club,** (☎ 519/329-4231). London offers half a dozen good courses; and Bayfield and Goderich have a couple of 9-hole courses. In Stratford check out the 18-hole course at the **Stratford Country Club** (☎ 519/ 271-3891), and in St. Mary's, the **Science Hill Country Club** (☎ 519/284-3621).

HIKING The 60-kilometer (37-mile) **Thames Valley Trail** follows the Thames River through London, past the University of Western Ontario and into farmlands all the way to St. Mary's. For information, contact **Thames Valley Trail Association,** Box 821, Terminal B, London, ON, N6A 4Z3 (no phone).

The 100-kilometer (62-mile) **Avon Trail** follows the Avon River through Stratford, cuts through the Wildwood Conservation Area, and spans farmlands around Kitchener. It links up with the Thames Valley Trail at St. Mary's and the Grand Valley Trail at Conestoga. For information, contact Avon Trail, Box 20018, Stratford, ON, N5A 7V3 (no phone).

The 124-kilometer (77-mile) **Grand Valley Trail** follows the Grand River from Dunnville, north through Brantford, Paris, and farmlands around Kitchener-Waterloo to the Elora Gorge (see below), connecting with the Bruce Trail at Alton. For information, contact Grand Valley Trails Association, Box 1233, Kitchener, ON, N2G 4G8.

HORSEBACK RIDING   The **Cinch Stables,** 43 Capulet Lane, London (☎ 519/471-3492), offers hour-long trail rides for C$17 (US$12) per person. West of London, in Delaware, the **Circle R Ranch,** RR #1 (☎ 519/471-3799), leads 1-hour trail rides in the Dingman Creek Valley for C$17 (US$12) per person. Reservations are necessary.

SWIMMING   The Elora Gorge is a great place to swim. So is **Rondeau Provincial Park** (☎ 519/674-1750), which is located on Lake Erie (off Highway 21 near Blenheim); lots of other water sports are available here as well.

2 London

If you're driving into Canada from the U.S. Midwest, you certainly should plan on stopping in this pretty university town that sits on the Thames River (pronounced as it's spelled)—particularly if you have kids in tow.

ESSENTIALS

VISITOR INFORMATION   Contact **Tourism London,** 300 Dufferin Ave. (P.O. Box 5035), London, ON, N6A 4L9 (☎ 519/661-5000).

GETTING THERE   If you're driving, London is about 192 kilometers (120 miles) from Detroit via Highway 401, 110 kilometers (68 miles) from Kitchener via Highway 401, 195 kilometers (121 miles) from Niagara Falls via QEW, highways 403 and 401, and 65 kilometers (40 miles) from Stratford via 7 and 4.

You can also fly to London on **Canadian Airlines** (☎ 519/455-8385). A taxi from the airport into town will cost about C$17 (US$12).

VIA operates a Toronto-Brantford-London-Windsor route and also, in conjunction with **Amtrak,** a Toronto-Kitchener-Stratford-London-Sarnia-Chicago route. Both offer several trains a day. The VIA Rail station in London is at 197 York St. (☎ 519/434-2149).

GETTING AROUND   For bus schedules, contact the **London Transit Commission** (☎ 519/451-1347). Exact fare of C$2 (US$1.45) is required, C$1 (US70¢) for children 6 to 12. Or you can purchase five tickets for C$7 (US$5) adults, C$4 (US$2.85) children 6 to 18.

Taxis charge an initial C$2.40 (US$1.72) plus C10¢ (US7¢) each nine-tenths of a kilometer (half a mile) thereafter. There's an additional charge from 11pm to 6am. Taxi companies include **Abouttown Taxi** (☎ 519/432-2244) and **U-Need-A-Cab** (☎ 519/438-2121).

SPECIAL EVENTS   The **London International Air Show,** Canada's largest military air show, ushers in the summer season each June. It's followed by the **Royal Canadian Big Band Festival,** held over the July 1 weekend.

The **Great London Rib-Fest and Hot Air Balloon Fiesta** is usually August 1 or thereabouts. In September, the 10-day **Fair** at the Western Fairgrounds is the seventh largest in Canada.

EXPLORING THE TOWN

Downtown there's a cluster of historic sights. At 401 Ridout North is **Eldon House,** the city's oldest remaining house, built in 1834, which now houses a historic museum (☎ **519/661-5169**). It's open Tuesday to Sunday from noon to 5pm. Admission is C$3 (US$2.15) for adults, C$2 (US$1.45) for seniors, C$1 (US70¢) for children 5 to 16, and free on Tuesday afternoons. The fee includes admission to London Regional Art and Historical Museums. Nearby at nos. 435, 441, and 443 Ridout North are the original Labatt Brewery buildings.

At the **London Regional Art and Historical Museums,** 421 Ridout North (☎ **519/672-4580**), you'll view historical and contemporary works of local, national, and international artists. The building itself—six barrel vaults slotted together to accommodate domed skylights—is striking. Admission is C$3 (US$2.15) for adults, C$2 (US$1.40) for seniors, free for children 1 to 12, or C$5 (US$3.55) for families. Tuesday afternoons are free. It's open Tuesday to Sunday from noon to 5pm. The fee includes admission to Eldon House.

✪ **Children's Museum.** 21 Wharncliffe Rd. S. ☎ **519/434-5726.** Admission C$4 (US$2.85) adults, C$3.25 (US$2.30) children 2 to 12; children under 2 free. Tues–Sat 10am–5pm, Sun noon–5pm. Open Mon June–Aug, holidays, and Mar break.

The incredible Children's Museum occupies several floors of an old school building. A family can easily spend a whole day here—there's more than enough to do. In every room children can explore, experiment, and engage their imaginations. For example, on "The Street Where You Live," kids can dress up in firefighters' uniforms, don the overalls of those who work under the streets, and assume the role of a dentist, doctor, or construction worker. Some rooms contrast how people lived long ago with how they live today. A child can stand in a train station, send a Morse-code message, shop in a general store, and sit in a schoolhouse—all experiences that they can share with their grandparents. More up-to-the-minute experiences can be enjoyed at the photosensitive wall, the zoetrobe, or in the kitchen where children can see exactly how the appliances work. In the garden out back, there's also a fun tree house with a spiral slide. It's fun for children and for adults. I loved it.

✪ **Museum of Indian Archaeology and Lawson Prehistoric Indian Village.** 1600 Attawandaron Rd. (off Wonderland Rd. N., just south of Hwy. 22). ☎ **519/473-1360.** Admission C$3.50 (US$2.50) adults, C$2.75 (US$1.95) seniors and students, C$1.50 (US$1.05) children under 12, C$8 (US$6) families; children under 5 free. Daily May 1 to Labour Day 10am–5pm; Sept–Dec Tues–Sun 10am–5pm; Jan–Apr Wed–Sun only 1–4pm.

This is another sight I wouldn't miss. The museum contains artifacts from various periods of native-Canadian history—projectiles, pottery shards, effigies, turtle rattles, and more. The most evocative exhibit is the on-site reconstruction of a 500-year-old Attawandaron village. Behind the elm palisades, longhouses built according to original specifications and techniques have been erected on the 5 acres where archaeological excavations are taking place. About 1,600 to 1,800 people once lived in the community, about 70 sharing one longhouse. The houses have been constructed of elm, sealed with the pitch from pine trees, and bound together with the sinew of deer hide.

Guy Lombardo Music Centre. 205 Wonderland Rd. S. ☎ **519/473-9003.** Admission C$2 (US$1.45) adults, C$1.75 (US$1.25) seniors; children under 12 free. Mid-May to Labour Day Thurs–Mon 11am–5pm. Limited winter hours; call ahead.

Nostalgia. That's what's captured on Wonderland Road at the outdoor band shell where bandleader Guy Lombardo began playing in the 1930s before he hit the big time and became famous for ringing in the new year at the Waldorf-Astoria in New York. There's also a Guy Lombardo Music Centre filled with memorabilia. Adjacent to the band shell is a restaurant that will help take you on a trip down memory lane (see "Dining," below).

Springbank Park Storybook Gardens. Off Commissioners Rd. W. ☎ **519/661-5770.** Admission C$5.25 (US$3.75) adults, C$4 (US$2.85) seniors, C$3.25 (US$2.30) children 3–14; children under 3 free. May to Labour Day daily 10am–8pm; Labour Day to early Oct Mon–Fri 10am–5pm, Sat–Sun 10am–6pm. Closed Oct–Apr.

The Springbank Park Storybook Gardens is a children's zoo with a storybook theme. Special daily events include the seal feeding at 3:30pm, and a variety of live entertainment. There's also a maze and Playworld, with many activities for children.

Fanshawe Pioneer Village. In Fanshawe Park (entrance off Fanshawe Park Rd., east of Clarke Rd.). ☎ **519/457-1296.** Admission to park C$5.50 per vehicle; Pioneer Village C$5 (US$3.55) adults, C$4 (US$2.85) seniors and students, C$3 (US$2.15) children 3–12; children under 3 free. Village May 1–Nov 30 Wed–Sun 10am–4:30pm. Dec 1 to Dec 20 daily 10am–4:30pm.

The Pioneer Village is a complex comprised of 25-plus buildings where you can see craft demonstrations (broom making, candle dipping, for example), enjoy wagon rides, and imagine what life was like during the 18th century. In **Fanshawe Park** (☎ 519/451-2800) there's a large pool and beach at the 6-kilometer-long (4-mile-long) lake.

ACCOMMODATIONS

For B&B accommodations priced from C$45 to C$70 (US$32 to US$50) per night, contact the **London and Area Bed and Breakfast Association,** 2 Normandy Gardens, London, ON, N6H 4A9 (☎ 519/673-6797).

London also has several modest hotel chains: **Best Western Lamplighter Inn,** 591 Wellington Rd. S. (☎ 519/681-7151), charging C$70 (US$50) double; **Ramada Inn,** 817 Exeter Rd. (☎ 519/681-4900), charging C$75 to C$105 (US$54 to US$75) double; **Holiday Inn Express,** 800 Exeter Rd. (☎ 519/681-1200), with rates of C$85 (US$61) double; and **Comfort Inn,** 1156 Wellington Rd. S. (☎ 519/ 685-9300), charging C$85 (US$61) double.

Delta London Armouries Hotel. 325 Dundas St., London, ON, N6B 1T9. ☎ **519/ 679-6111.** Fax 519/679-3957. 250 rms. A/C MINIBAR TV TEL. C$175 (US$125) double; from C$285 (US$204) suite. Extra person C$10 (US$7). Children under 18 stay free in parents' rm. Special weekend rates available. AE, CB, DC, DISC, ER, MC, V. Parking C$7 (US$5).

This hotel, occupying the old armory, is a worthy example of architectural conservation and conversion. The armory's 12-foot-thick walls form the building's main floor and base, and above the crenellated turrets and ramparts soars a modern glass tower. Inside, the well-equipped rooms are furnished with Federal reproductions. Some rooms (for an additional C$15/US$11) have been specially outfitted for the business traveler with fax, laser printer, cordless speaker phone, halogen-lit desk, and ergonomically designed chair, plus a computer on request. Dining facilities include a restaurant and lounge. A pool and an exercise area now occupy the former drill parade area. There's also a squash court and children's activity center. Services include 24-hour room service.

✪ **Idlewyld Inn.** 36 Grand Ave., London, ON, N6C 1K8. ☎ and fax **519/433-2891.** 17 rms; 10 suites and Jacuzzi rms. A/C TV TEL. C$120 (US$86) double; from $145 (US$104) suite; from $179 (US$128) Jacuzzi rms. Rates include continental breakfast. AE, DC, MC, V. Free parking.

This is the top choice. Located in a house that a wealthy leather industrialist built in 1878, the inn is filled with fine details—8-foot-tall windows, oak and cherry carved fireplaces, casement windows, oak-beamed ceilings, and wallpaper crafted to look like tooled leather in the dining room.

All the rooms are furnished differently. Room 302 has a tiny Romeo and Juliet balcony, while room 202 has a marvelous fireplace of green cabbage-leaf tiles and a scallop-shell marble sink stand. Room 101 is the largest—huge carved cherry columns separate the sitting area from the bedroom, which has a comfortable chaise lounge and a glazed tile fireplace. At breakfast guests help themselves in the large, comfortable kitchen equipped with toasters, coffeemakers, and refrigerators, and can sit on the porch to eat.

DINING

✪ **Anthony's.** 434 Richmond St. ☎ **519/679-0960.** Reservations recommended. Main courses C$17–C$24 (US$12–US$17). AE, DC, ER, MC, V. Mon–Fri 11:30am–2:30pm; Mon–Sat 5–10pm. SEAFOOD.

This seafood-specialty house uses fresh and superb ingredients and presents dishes so well that it stimulates the appetite. For example, the salmon with dill sauce often comes with lime wedges cut into tiny petals placed around a center of caviar. The dinner menu might include a warm salad of smoked tiger shrimp, followed by perch with pine nuts, provincial seafood stew, or beef tenderloin with tarragon sauce. People who really enjoy surprises will want to order the four-course Trust Me dinner, for C$38 (US$27) per person, always a culinary adventure. The open kitchen, with its gleaming copper pots and a mural in the dining room depicting tropical fish, enhances the ambiance. Desserts change daily and are made on the premises, as are the handmade chocolates that conclude the meal. You might be tempted by a lemon tart, a chocolate nocturne gâteau, or sorbet.

✪ **The Horse & Hound.** 939 Hyde Park. ☎ **519/472-6801.** Reservations recommended. Main courses C$15–C$27 (US$11–US$19). AE, DC, ER, MC, V. Tues–Sun 11:30am–2:30pm and 5:30–10pm. Limited menu served between meals and 10pm–1am. CONTINENTAL.

This local favorite, located in a handsome Victorian, has six intimate, elegant dining rooms. Start with warmed Camembert cheese wrapped in phyllo pastry on a black-currant coulis, or leek, corn, and Stilton chowder. Follow with 1 of 10 or so entrees that might include a classic chateaubriand, a flavorsome venison Stroganoff, or poached Atlantic salmon served with a gazpacho and sour-cream sauce. On weekends, jazz or classical duos perform in the downstairs lounge.

Michaels on Thames. 1 York St. ☎ **519/672-0111.** Reservations recommended. Main courses C$12–C$22 (US$9–US$16). AE, DC, ER, MC, V. Mon–Fri 11:30am–2:30pm; daily 5–11pm. CONTINENTAL.

Michaels on Thames has a fine location overlooking the river. In winter a blazing fire makes the dining room cozy. Among the well-prepared and nicely served dishes you might find pan-seared chicken breast with sun-dried tomato, basil and cashew pesto and cream sauce, rack of lamb roasted with mint finished with demiglace and port wine, or salmon with hollandaise. Desserts include a flamboyant cherries jubilee.

Miestro's. 352 Dundas St. ☎ **519/439-8983.** Reservations recommended. Main courses C$16–C$20 (US$11–US$14). AE, ER, MC, V. Tues–Fri 11:30am–2:30pm; Tues–Sat 5:30–10pm. ECLECTIC.

You'll find an unusual selection of dishes at this popular downtown place with an intimate atmosphere. At dinner the choices might include veal sautéed with sun-dried tomato and light basil cream sauce, or Pacific snapper steamed in a ginger, spring-onion, rice-wine, and teriyaki marinade along with a couple of pastas and Indonesian stir-fry or similar dishes.

Wonderland Riverview Dining Room. 284 Wonderland Rd. S. ☎ **519/471-4662.** Reservations recommended. Main courses C$13–C$28 (US$11–US$20). AE, MC, V. Daily 11:30am–2:30pm and 5–9pm. Closed Mon–Tues Jan–Mar. CONTINENTAL.

Still a favorite venue for special family occasions, the Wonderland Riverview Dining Room offers such dishes as rack of lamb with a Dijon mustard sauce, charbroiled beef tenderloin, prime rib, and surf and turf. Around the walls are framed clips of events that took place here in the thirties and forties—dancing to Ozzie Williams, Shep Fields, and Mart Kenney. There's a lovely outdoor dining terrace under the trees and an outdoor dancing area overlooking the river.

LONDON AFTER DARK

The **Grand Theatre,** 471 Richmond St. (☎ 519/672-9030), features drama, comedy, and musicals from September to May. The theater itself, built in 1901, is worth viewing.

Harness racing takes place from October to June at the Western Fairgrounds (☎ 519/438-7203) track Wednesday, Friday, and Saturday. Races usually start at 7:45pm.

London also has a few bars and clubs: **Barneys,** 671 Richmond St. (☎ 519/432-1232), attracts a young professional crowd and has a very popular summer patio; **Jo Kool's,** 595 Richmond at Central (☎ 519/663-5665) is a student hangout.

3 Goderich & Bayfield

Goderich is a good place to stroll. The town's most striking feature is the central octagonal space with the Huron County Courthouse at the center. Another highlight is the **Historic Huron Gaol,** with walls 18 feet high and 2 feet thick. This also houses the **Huron County Museum,** 110 North St. (☎ 519/524-2686). Admission is C$4 (US$2.85) for adults, C$3 (US$2.15) for seniors, C$2.25 (US$1.60) for children 6 to 13, and it's open daily from 10am to 4:30pm.

For **Goderich information,** call ☎ 519/524-6600 or go by the visitor center on Hamilton Street, which is open daily in summer.

Bayfield is a pretty, well-preserved 19th-century town about 13 miles from Goderich and 40 miles from Stratford. Once a major grain-shipping port, it became a quiet backwater when the railroad passed it by. Today the main square, High Street, and Elgin Place are part of a Heritage Conservation District. Walk around and browse in the appealing stores—the **information center** (☎ 519/565-2021) has a helpful walking-tour pamphlet.

ACCOMMODATIONS

Benmiller Inn. RR #4, Goderich, ON, N7A 3Y1. ☎ **519/524-2191.** 47 rms. A/C TV TEL. C$105–C$182 (US$75–US$129) double; C$300 (US$214) deluxe suite. Rates include breakfast buffet. AE, DC, ER, MC, V.

The heart of the inn is the original wool mill (1877), which now contains dining room, bar, reception, and 12 guest rooms. When it was turned into an inn in 1974, many mechanical parts were refashioned into decorative objects—mirrors made from pulley wheels, lamps from gears. The rooms feature barn-board siding, desks, floor lamps, heated ceramic tile in the bathrooms, and handmade quilts. The 17 rooms in Gledhill House, the original mill-owner's home, are extra-large by hotel standards, while the four suites have fireplaces, bidets, and Jacuzzi bathtubs. Ground-floor rooms have pressed-tin ceilings. There are more rooms in the River Mill, which is attached to a silo-style building containing the swimming pool, whirlpool, and running track.

The dining room serves fine continental cuisine. The brick patio overlooking the gardens is a pleasant place to sit and look at the totem pole, brought from British Columbia. Facilities include two tennis courts, billiards, table tennis, and cross-country ski trails.

✪ **Clifton Manor Inn.** 19 The Square, P.O. Box 454, Bayfield, ON, N0M 1G0. ☎ **519/565-2282.** 4 rms. C$110–C$150 (US$79–US$107). No credit cards.

This elegant house was built in 1895 for the reve (bailiff or governor) of Bayfield. The interior features ash wood, etched glass panels in the doors, and other attractive period details. Today owner Elizabeth Marquis has added many touches—Oriental rugs and comfortable sofas and love seats in the living room, and elegant silver and sideboards in the dining room. There are four rooms, each named after an artist or composer. The bathroom in the charming Renoir room has a deep, 6-foot-long tub. Elizabeth provides candles and bubble bath—a lovely romantic touch. The Mozart room offers a canopy bed and tub for two while the entire third floor has been converted into the Mona Lisa. All rooms have cozy touches like mohair throws, sheepskin rugs, wingback chairs, fresh flowers, and so on. Lilac bushes and fruit trees fill the yard. Breakfast consists of egg dishes like omelets or crêpes, plus fresh fruit often plucked from the trees in the garden.

The Little Inn at Bayfield. Main St., P.O. Box 100, Bayfield, ON, N0M 1G0. ☎ **519/565-2611.** Fax 519/565-5474. 20 rms, 10 suites across the street. A/C TV. C$115–C$145 (US$82–US$104) double; from C$225 (US$161) suite. Special packages available. AE, DC, MC, V.

The inn, originally built in 1832, has been thoroughly modernized. The older rooms in the main building are small and have only showers, but they are comfortably furnished with oak or sleigh beds. Rooms in the newer section are larger and feature platform beds and modern furnishings. The suites across the street in the carriage house have platform beds, pine hutches, and feature whirlpool bathrooms, propane-gas fireplaces, and verandas. The popular restaurant is open for lunch and dinner 7 days a week.

DINING

The **Benmiller Inn** (see "Accommodations" above) has a good dining room. For casual dining, Bayfield offers several choices. The **Albion Hotel** on Main Street (☎ 519/565-2641) features a fun, wall-length bar decorated with hundreds of baseball hats and other sports paraphernalia. The fare consists of English specialties plus ribs, pizza, and sandwiches. It also has seven rooms available starting at C$55 (US$39) double, sharing a bath. **Admiral Belfield's,** 5 Main St. is fun, too. A converted general store, it serves diner, deli, and pub fare, and occasionally there's jazz and other entertainment.

✪ **Red Pump.** Main St., Bayfield. ☎ **519/565-2576.** Reservations recommended. Main courses C$15–C$25 (US$11–US$18). AE, MC, V. Daily noon–3pm and 5–9pm. Closed Jan–Mar and Mon–Tues in late fall and winter. INTERNATIONAL.

This very appealing restaurant with an inviting patio serves some of the area's most exciting and eclectic food. Typical main dishes might include steamed chicken breast and scallops with pine-nut, red-pepper, tomato, and balsamic vinegar sauce; barbecued fish; and tiger shrimp stuffed with crab and served with risotto cakes. The decor is lavish and comfortable.

4 Stratford & the Stratford Festival

Home of the world-famous Stratford Festival, this city manages to capture the prime elements of the Bard's birthplace, from the swans on the Avon River to the grass banks that sweep down to it, where you can picnic under a weeping willow before attending a Shakespeare play. It's a very pleasant town with some superb dining and, of course, the famous festival.

ESSENTIALS

VISITOR INFORMATION   Go to the office by the river on York Street at Erie (☎ **519/273-3352**), open from May to mid-October, Sunday to Wednesday from 9am to 5pm and Thursday to Saturday from 9am to 8pm. At other times, contact **Tourism Stratford,** P.O. Box 818, 88 Wellington St., Stratford, ON, N5A 6W1 (☎ **800/561-SWAN** or 519/271-5140).

GETTING THERE   Driving from Toronto, take Highway 401 west to Interchange 278 at Kitchener. Follow Highway 8 west onto Highway 7/8 west to Stratford. From Detroit/Windsor follow Highway 401 east to Exit 218 at Ingersoll, to Highway 19 north and then to Highway 7 east. From Buffalo cross to Fort Erie and take QEW to Exit 100 west onto Highway 403. Take 403 west to Highway 6 north to Highway 401. Take 401 west and then pick up the directions given above from Toronto.

   Amtrak and VIA Rail operate several daily trains along the Toronto-Kitchener-Stratford-London-Sarnia-Chicago route.

SPECIAL EVENTS   Other than the theater festival, there's a **Festival City Days,** in the last week of May. The festival's opening is celebrated with marching bands, floats, and clowns.

EXPLORING THE TOWN

Summer pleasures in Stratford besides theater? Within sight of the Festival Theatre, **Queen's Park** has picnic spots beneath tall shade trees or down by the Avon River where the swans and ducks gather.

   If you turn right onto Romeo Street North from highways 7 and 8, as you come into Stratford, you'll find the **Gallery/Stratford,** 54 Romeo St. (☎ 519/271-5271), located in a lovely old building on the fringes of Confederation Park. Since its 1967 opening, it has mounted Canadian-focused shows. If you're an art lover, do stop in, for you're sure to find an unusual, personally satisfying show in one of the four galleries. It's open daily in summer from 9am to 6pm (Tuesday to Sunday off-season). Admission is C$4 (US$2.85) for adults and C$3 (US$2.15) for seniors and students.

   Stratford is a historic town, and 1-hour **guided tours** of early Stratford are given from July to Labour Day, Monday to Saturday, leaving at 9:30am from the visitor booth by the river. There are also many fine shops worth browsing along Ontario and Downie streets and tucked down along York Street. Antiques lovers will want to visit the nearby town of Shakespeare (7 miles out of town on Highway 7/8). Architecture buffs will want to visit nearby St. Mary's, filled with late-19th-century stone buildings. It's the town where Timothy Eaton of Eatons fame got his start.

A COUPLE OF DAY TRIPS

Only half an hour or so away, **Kitchener-Waterloo** has two drawing cards, the Farmer's Market and its famous 9-day Oktoberfest. For information, write **K-W Oktoberfest,** P.O. Box 1053, 17 Benton St., Kitchener, ON, N2G 4G1, or call ☎ **519/570-4267.** The population of these twin cities is 60% German, many of them Mennonites. At the Saturday market which starts at 6am in the Market Square complex at Duke and Frederick streets, you can sample shoofly pie, apple butter, kochcase, and other Mennonite specialties. For additional information, contact the **Kitchener-Waterloo Area Visitors and Convention Bureau,** 2848 King St. E., Kitchener, ON, N2A 1A5 (☎ **519/748-0800**), open Monday to Friday from 9am to 5pm in winter and daily in summer.

   Five miles north of Kitchener, people enjoy visiting the town of **St. Jacobs,** drawn there by the close to 100 shops that are located in a converted mill, silo, and other

Stratford

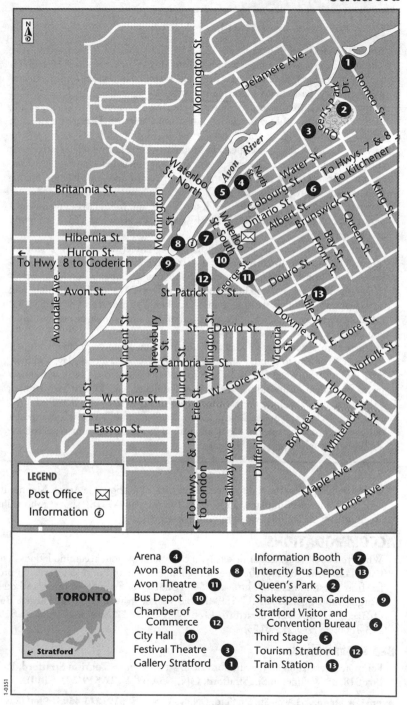

TORONTO

← Stratford

Arena **4**
Avon Boat Rentals **8**
Avon Theatre **11**
Bus Depot **10**
Chamber of Commerce **12**
City Hall **10**
Festival Theatre **3**
Gallery Stratford **1**

Information Booth **7**
Intercity Bus Depot **13**
Queen's Park **2**
Shakespearean Gardens **9**
Stratford Visitor and Convention Bureau **6**
Third Stage **5**
Tourism Stratford **12**
Train Station **13**

1-0351

The Play's the Thing

Since its modest beginnings on July 13, 1953, when *Richard III,* starring Sir Alec Guinness, was staged in a huge tent, Stratford's artistic directors have all built on the radical but faithfully classic base originally provided by Tyrone Guthrie to create a repertory theater with a glowing international reputation.

Stratford has three theaters: the **Festival Theatre,** 55 Queen St. in Queen's Park; the **Avon Theatre,** 99 Downie St.; and the **Tom Patterson Theatre** on Lakeside Drive.

World-famous for its Shakespearean productions, the festival offers both classic and modern masterpieces. Recent productions have included *Camelot, The Taming of the Shrew, Oedipus Rex, Death of a Salesman, Equus,* and *Little Women.* Among the company's famous alumnae are Dame Maggie Smith, Sir Alec Guinness, Sir Peter Ustinov, Christopher Plummer, Irene Worth, and Julie Harris. Present company members include Brian Bedford, Al Waxman, Cynthia Dole, Martha Henry, and Barbara Byrne.

In addition to attending plays, you may enjoy "Meet the Festival," a series of informal discussions with members of the acting company, production, or administrative staff; postperformance discussions following Thursday-evening performances; and backstage or warehouse tours, offered every Wednesday, Saturday, and Sunday morning from early June to mid-October. The tours cost C$5 (US$3.55) for adults and C$3 (US$2.15) for seniors and students and should be reserved when you purchase tickets.

The season begins early in May and continues until mid-November with performances Tuesday to Sunday and matinees on Wednesday, Saturday, and Sunday. Ticket prices range from C$47.75 to C$64 (US$34 to US$46), with lower prices for student, rush, and preview tickets. For tickets, call ☎ 800/567-1600 or 519/273-1600; or write to the **Stratford Festival,** P.O. Box 520, Stratford, ON, N5A 6V2. Tickets are also available in the United States and Canada at Ticketmaster outlets. The box office opens for mail and fax orders only in late January; telephone and in-person sales begin late February.

factory buildings. For those interested in learning more about the Amish-Mennonite way of life, the **Meetingplace,** 33 King St. (☎ 519/664-3518), shows a short film about it (daily in summer, weekends only in winter).

ACCOMMODATIONS

When you book your theater tickets, you can also book your accommodations. The festival can book you into the type of accommodation and price category you prefer, from guest homes for as little as C$40 (US$29) for a double to first-class hotels charging more than C$125 (US$89) double. Call or write the **Festival Theatre Box Office,** P.O. Box 520, Stratford, ON, N5A 6V2 (☎ 800/567-1600 or 519/273-1600; fax 519/273-6173).

BED & BREAKFASTS

For more information on the Stratford B&B scene, write to **Tourism Stratford,** P.O. Box 818, 88 Wellington St., Stratford, ON, N5A 6W1 (☎ 519/271-5140).

Avonview Manor. 63 Avon St., Stratford, ON, N5A 5N5. ☎ **519/273-4603.** 4 rms (2 with bath). C$80–C$90 (US$57–US$64) double. Rates include full breakfast. No credit cards.

Located on a quiet street in an Edwardian house, Avonview Manor has attractive and individually furnished rooms. There are three rooms with queen-size beds (one with private bath); the suite contains four single beds and has a sitting room and private bath. A kitchen equipped with an ironing board is available on the first floor. The living room is very comfortable, particularly in winter in front of the stone fireplace. No smoking, except on the porch. Facilities include an outdoor pool and hot tub.

Brunswick House. 109 Brunswick St., Stratford, ON, N5A 3L9. ☎ **519/271-4546.** 6 rms (none with bath). From C$65 (US$46) double. Rates include full breakfast. No credit cards.

Brunswick House is owned and operated by two writers, Geoff Hancock and Gay Allison. If you stay here, you will enjoy very literary surroundings—portraits of Canadian authors and poetry on the walls, books everywhere, and the chance to run into a literary personality. The nicely decorated rooms with ceiling fans share two baths. One is a family room with a double and two single beds. Each has a personal decorative touch—a Mennonite quilt, posters by an artist friend, a parasol atop a wardrobe. Smoking is restricted to the veranda.

Deacon House. 101 Brunswick St., Stratford, ON, N5A 3L9. ☎ **519/273-2052.** 6 rms. A/C. C$95–C$120 (US$68–US$85) double. Rates include breakfast. V.

A shingle-style house, built in 1907 and home to a prominent surgeon, has been restored by Diane Hrysko and Mary Allen. The guest rooms, all with private baths, are decorated in a country style with iron and brass beds, quilts, pine hutches, oak rockers, and rope-style rugs. My favorites are the quirkily shaped units on the top floor. The living room with fireplace, TV, wingbacks, and sofa is comfortable.

Woods Villa. 62 John St. N., Stratford, ON, N5A 6K7. ☎ **519/271-4576.** Fax 519/271-7173. 6 rms. A/C TV TEL. C$120–C$175 (US$68–US$125) double. Rates include breakfast. DISC, MC, V.

This handsome 1870 house, set on 1 acre, is home to Ken Vinen, who enjoys collecting and restoring Wurlitzers, Victrolas, and player pianos, which are found throughout the house. Ken will happily demonstrate, drawing upon his vast library of early paper rolls and records. The six rooms, all with private bath (five with fireplaces), include a handsome suite with canopy bed. Rooms are large and an excellent value. In the morning coffee is delivered to your room followed by a full breakfast prepared to order and served in the dining room. The extra-large outdoor heated pool and terrace are added bonuses.

HOTELS & MOTELS

Bentley's Inn. 99 Ontario St., Stratford, ON, N5A 3H1. ☎ **519/271-1121.** Fax 519/272-1853. 13 suites. A/C TV TEL. May–Oct C$145 (US$104) double; Nov–Apr C$90 (US$64) double. Extra person C$20 (US$14). AE, DC, ER, MC, V.

Bentley's has soundproofed luxurious duplex suites with two telephones and fully equipped kitchenettes. Period English furnishings and attractive drawings, paintings, and costume designs on the walls make for a pleasant ambiance. Five suites have skylights.

Festival Motor Inn. 1144 Ontario St., Stratford, ON, N5A 6W1. ☎ **519/273-1150.** Fax 519/273-2111. 183 rms. A/C TV TEL. C$84–C$130 (US$60–US$92) double. Extra person C$10 (US$7). Winter rates about 30% lower. AE, DC, MC, V.

With its black-and-white motel-style units, the Festival Motor Inn is set back off highways 7 and 8 in 10 acres of nicely kept landscaped grounds. The place has an Old-English air with its stucco walls, Tudor-style beams, and high-back red settees in the lobby. The Tudor style is maintained throughout the large modern rooms.

Some bedrooms have charming bay windows with sheer curtains, and all rooms in the main building, north wing, and annex have refrigerators. Other facilities include shuffleboard, a dining room, a lounge, and an indoor pool with outdoor patio, whirlpool, and sauna.

Queen's Inn. 161 Ontario St., Stratford, ON, N5A 3H3. ☎ **519/271-1400.** Fax 519/271-7373. 31 rms. A/C TV TEL. May 1–Nov 15 C$105 (US$75) small double; C$130 (US$93) rm with queen-size bed; C$165–C$190 (US$117–US$135) suite. Lower rates off-season. AE, MC, V.

Conveniently located in the town center, the Queen's Inn has recently been restored by the owner of the Elora Mill Inn. The rooms, all with private bath, have been pleasantly decorated in pastels and pine. Facilities include the Boar's Head Pub, and a Southwestern-cuisine restaurant.

Twenty Three Albert Place. 23 Albert St., Stratford, ON, N5A 3K2. ☎ **519/273-5800.** Fax 519/273-5008. 34 rms. A/C TV TEL. C$81–C$100 (US$58–US$71) double; C$110 (US$79) minisuite; C$130–C$140 (US$93–US$105) luxury suite. MC, V.

The Albert Place is right across from the Avon Theatre. Rooms have high ceilings; some have separate sitting rooms, and most units are quite large. Furnishings are simple and modern. Coffee, tea, muffins, and doughnuts are served in the lobby in the morning.

DINING

Stratford is really a picnicking place. Take a hamper down to the banks of the river or into the parks. Plenty of places cater to this. **Rundles,** 9 Cobourg St. (☎ 519/271-6442) will make you a super-sophisticated hamper; **Café Mediterranean,** 10 Downie St., in the Festival Square building (☎ 519/271-9590), has salads, quiches, crêpes, and flaky meat pies and pastries. For takeout, **Picnics Gourmet Food Shop,** 40 Wellington St. (☎ 519/273-6000), offers pasta, grain, and vegetable salads; fish, chicken, and meat entrees; and pâtés, soups, breads and pastries.

EXPENSIVE

✪ **The Church.** At the corner of Brunswick and Waterloo sts. ☎ **519/273-3424.** Reservations required. Main courses C$21.50–C$32 (US$15–US$23); summer fixed-price dinner C$49.25–C$53.25 (US$35–US$38). AE, DC, MC, V. Tues–Sat 11:30am–1am, Sun 11:30am–10pm. May be open Mon if there's a musical performance or some other special event at the theaters. CONTINENTAL.

The decor at The Church is just stunning. The organ pipes and the altar are still intact, along with the vaulted roof, carved woodwork, and stained-glass windows, and you can sit in the nave or the side aisles and dine to the appropriate sounds of, usually, Bach. Fresh flowers, elegant table settings, and a huge table in the center graced with two silver samovars further enhance the experience.

In summer there's a special four-course fixed-price and an à la carte dinner menu, a luncheon on matinee days, and an after-theater menu. Appetizers might include asparagus served hot with black morels in their juices, white wine and cream, or sauté of duck foie gras with leeks citron and mango-and-ginger sauce. Among the selection of eight or so entrees, you might find Canadian caribou with port-and-blackberry sauce, cabbage braised in cream red-wine shallots and glazed chestnuts, or lobster salad with green beans, new potatoes, and truffles scented with caraway. Desserts are equally exciting, like the charlotte of white-chocolate mousse with summer fruit and dark-chocolate sauce or the nougat glace with kiwi sauce.

If you want to dine here during the festival, make reservations in March or April when you buy your tickets; otherwise you'll be disappointed. The upstairs Belfry Bar is a popular pre- and post-theater gathering place.

✪ **The Old Prune.** 151 Albert St. ☎ **519/271-5052.** Reservations required. 3-course fixed-price dinner C$51.50 (US$37). AE, MC, V. Wed–Sun 11:30am–1:30pm; Tues–Sat 5–9pm, Sun 5–7pm. After-theater menu also available Fri–Sat from 9pm. Call ahead for winter hours. CONTINENTAL.

Another of my Stratford favorites is run by two charming, whimsical women— Marion Isherwood and Eleanor Kane. Set in a lovely Edwardian home, The Old Prune has three dining rooms and an enclosed garden patio. The proprietors, former Montréalers, have brought with them some of that Québec flair, which is reflected in both decor and menu. Artist Marion created the subdued, dreamy palette of the walls which are graced with her own inspired paintings.

Chef Bryan Steele selects the freshest local ingredients, many from the dedicated community of organic farmers in the region, and prepares them simply to reveal their abundant flavor. Among the main courses you might find Perth County pork loin grilled with a tamari-and-honey glaze and served with shiitake mushrooms, pickled cucumbers, and sunflower sprouts; steamed bass in Napa cabbage with curry broth and lime leaves; or rack of Ontario lamb with a smoky tomatillo-chipotle pepper sauce. Among the appetizers there might be an outstanding house smoked salmon with lobster potato salad topped with Sevruga caviar or a refreshing tomato consommé with saffron and sea scallops. Desserts, too, are always inspired, like rhubarb strawberry Napoleon with vanilla mousse. The Old Prune is also lovely for lunch or a late supper when such light specialties—priced from C$7 to C$14 (US$5 to US$10)—as sautéed quail and grilled polenta with Italian greens, mushrooms, roasted tomatoes, and balsamic jus and smoked trout terrine are offered.

✪ **Rundles.** 9 Cobourg St. ☎ **519/271-6442.** Reservations required. 3-course fixed-price dinner C$52.50 (US$38). Gastronomic menus C$56.50–C$62.50 (US$40–US$45). AE, ER, MC, V. Wed and Sat–Sun 11:30am–1:30pm; Tues 5–7pm, Wed–Sat 5–8:30pm, Sun 5–7pm. Closed during the winter; it functions occasionally as a cooking school until theater season resumes. INTERNATIONAL.

Rundles provides a premier dining experience in a serene dining room overlooking the river. Proprietor Jim Morris eats, sleeps, thinks, and dreams food, and chef Neil Baxter delivers the exciting, exquisite cuisine to the table. The three-course fixed-price dinner will always offer a full selection of palate-pleasing flavor combinations. Among the five main dishes there might be poached Atlantic salmon garnished with a mixture of Jerusalem artichokes, wilted arugula, and yellow peppers in a light carrot sauce, or fatless pink roast rib eye of lamb with ratatouille and rosemary aioli. All of the appetizers are appealing, from the shaved fennel, arugula, artichoke, and Parmesan salad, to the warm seared Québec foie gras with caramelized endive, garlic-flavored fried potatoes, and tomato-and-basil oil. My dessert choice would be the glazed lemon tart and an orange sorbet, but the hot mango tart with pineapple sorbet is also a dream. Tables are covered with fine white cloths; chairs are swathed in gray fabric and the room features some whimsical contemporary art by Victor Tinkl.

MODERATE

Keystone Alley Cafe. 34 Brunswick St. ☎ **519/271-5645.** Reservations recommended. Main courses C$14–C$19 (US$10–US$14). AE, DC, MC, V. Mon 11am–3pm, Tues–Sat 11am–4pm and 5–9pm. CONTINENTAL.

Theater actors often stop in for lunch—perhaps soup, sandwiches (muffelata with Creole mayonnaise), salads (Jamaican chicken salad with mango and pineapple salsa), or an entree like fish-and-chips or crab-and-jicama ceviche. At night a full dinner menu features eight or so main courses, such as roast sea bass with a potato crust accompanied by jalapeno tartare sauce, roast rack of lamb with a mango sweet-pepper barbecue sauce, or the vegetarian dish and pasta of the day.

York Street Kitchen. 41 York St. ☎ **519/273-7041.** Main courses C$8–C$10 (US$6–US$7). AE, V. Daily 8am–8pm. CANADIAN.

This small narrow restaurant is a fun, funky dining spot loved for its reasonably priced but high-quality fare. You can come here for breakfast burritos and other breakfast fare and for luncheon sandwiches which you can build yourself by choosing from a list of fillings. In the evenings expect to find comfort foods like meat loaf and mashed potatoes or barbecued chicken and ribs.

INEXPENSIVE

Bentley's. 107 Ontario St. ☎ **519/271-1121.** Reservations not accepted. Main courses C$5–C$13 (US$3.55–US$9). AE, DC, ER, MC, V. Daily 11:30am–1am. CANADIAN/ENGLISH.

For budget dining and fun to boot, go to Bentley's, the local watering hole and favorite theater-company gathering spot where you can shoot a game of darts, watch the big game on TV, or relax in one of the wingbacks. In summer you can sit on the garden terrace and enjoy light fare—grilled shrimp, burgers, gourmet pizzas, fish-and-chips, shepherd's pie, or pasta dishes. More substantial dishes like lamb curry, sirloin steak, and salmon baked in white wine with peppercorn dill butter are offered at dinner. Beer drinkers will appreciate the 16 different drafts on tap.

NEARBY ACCOMMODATIONS & DINING

✪ **Jakobstettel Guest House.** 16 Isabella St., St. Jacobs, ON, N0B 2N0. ☎ **519/664-2208.** Fax 519/664-1326. 12 rms. A/C TEL. C$125–C$165 (US$89–US$118) double. Extra person C$15 (US$11). Rates include breakfast. AE, MC, V.

The Jakobstettel Guest House was built in 1898 by mill-owner William Snider as a wedding gift for his wife and five daughters. The house stands on 5 acres of lovely grounds dotted with spruce and maple made even prettier by well-manicured lawns and a trellised rose garden. There's also an outdoor pool, one tennis court, and 2 kilometers (1¼ miles) of trails. Bicycles are available. All rooms have been beautifully furnished with fine antique reproductions, wingback chairs, desks, wicker, and occasionally a brass or four-poster bed. A library, common room, and country kitchen are available for an even more comfortable stay.

✪ **Langdon Hall.** RR #3, Cambridge, ON, N3H 4R8. ☎ **800/268-1898** or 519/740-2100. Fax 519/740-8161. 41 rms, 2 suites. A/C TV TEL. C$209–C$379 (US$150–US$273) double. Rates include continental breakfast. AE, DC, ER, MC, V.

The elegant house that stands at the head of the curving, tree-lined drive was completed in 1902 by Eugene Langdon Wilks, youngest son of Matthew and Eliza Astor Langdon, a granddaughter of John Jacob Astor. It remained in the family until 1987, when its transformation into a small country-house hotel was begun. Today its 200 acres of lawns, gardens, and woodlands make for an ideal retreat. The main house, of red brick with classical pediment and Palladian-style windows, has a beautiful symmetry. Inside, a similar harmony is achieved. Throughout, the emphasis is on comfort rather than grandiosity, whether in the conservatory, the veranda where tea is served, or Wilks's Bar with its comfortable club chairs.

The majority of the rooms are set around the cloister garden. Each room is individually decorated; most have fireplaces. The furnishings consist of handsome antique reproductions, mahogany wardrobes, ginger-jar porcelain lamps, and armchairs upholstered with luxurious fabrics, fine Oriental rugs, pictures, and such nice touches as live plants and terry bathrobes. The light and airy dining room overlooking the lily pond offers fine regional cuisine with main courses priced from C$23 to C$30 (US$16 to US$21). Beyond the cloister, down a trellis arcade, and through a latch gate lies the herb-and-vegetable garden and beyond that the swimming pool (with an attractive pool house), tennis court, and croquet lawn. Other facilities include a whirlpool, sauna, exercise room, billiard room, spa, and cross-country ski trails.

Westover Inn. 300 Thomas St., St. Mary's, ON, N4X 1B1. ☎ **519/284-2977.** Fax 519/284-4043. 22 rms and suites. A/C TV TEL. C$115–C$175 (US$82–US$125) double; C$160–C$225 (US$114–US$162) suite. AE, ER, MC, V.

Graceful accommodations are provided in this Victorian manor house, built in 1867 and featuring carved gingerbread decoration and leaded-glass windows. The house is set on 19 acres, making for a secluded retreat, and there's an outdoor pool. Inside the limestone house, rooms have been furnished in modern antique style with reproductions. Some rooms have balconies. Six rooms are located in the manor itself, including a luxury suite with a whirlpool bathroom. The least expensive and smallest rooms (12 of them) are found in the Terrace, built in the 1930s as a dorm for the priests who attended what was then a seminary. The Thames Cottage, a modern building, also contains two two-bedroom suites. Downstairs in the manor, guests may use the comfortable lounge.

    Dining/Entertainment: The elegant restaurant is known for fine cuisine. Dinner choices might include a Provençale fish stew with fresh fennel, garlic, and lemon, or rack of lamb with a rich Gorgonzola red-wine sauce, or roasted capon with smoked tomato, cumin, and cilantro, priced from C$17 to C$24 (US$12 to US$17). Desserts are enticing: profiteroles filled with chocolate and Kahlúa mousse, lemon tartlets in a shortbread crust, and more. It's open daily from 7:30 to 11am for breakfast, 11:30am to 2pm for lunch (brunch on Sunday), and 5 to 8:30pm for dinner. There's a bar/lounge and delightful patio.

5 Elora & Fergus

If you're driving from Toronto, take Highway 401 west to Highway 6 north to 7 east, then back to 6 north into Fergus. From Fergus take Highway 18 west to Elora.

    Elora has always been a special place. To the natives, the gorge was a sacred site, home of spirits who dwelt within the great cliffs. Early explorers and Jesuit missionaries also wondered at the natural spectacle, but it was Scotsman William Gilkinson who put the town on the map in 1832 when he purchased 14,000 acres on both sides of the Grand River and built a mill and a general store, and named it Elora, after the Ellora Caves in India.

    Most of the houses that the settlers built in the 1850s stand today. You'll want to browse the stores along picturesque Mill Street. For real insight into the town's history, pick up a walking-tour brochure from the tourist booth on Mill Street.

    The **Elora Gorge** is a 350-acre park on both sides of the 70-foot limestone gorge. Nature trails wind through it. Overhanging rock ledges, small caves, a waterfall, and the evergreen forest on its rim are some of the gorge's scenic delights. The park (☎ 519/846-9742) has camping and swimming facilities, plus picnic areas and playing fields. Located just west of Elora at the junction of the Grand and Irvine rivers, it is open from May 1 to October 15 from 10am to sunset. Admission is C$4 (US$2.85) for adults and C$1.75 (US$1.25) for children 6 to 14; children under 6 are free. To camp, for unserviced campsites, it's C$10(US$7) per day, C$13 (US$8) with water and electricity, plus the admission fee. For information, write or call the **Grand River Conservation Authority**, 400 Clyde Rd. (P.O. Box 729), Cambridge, ON, N1R 5W6 (☎ 519/621-2761).

    An additional summer attraction is the **Elora Festival,** a 3-week music celebration held from mid-July to early August. For more information, contact **The Elora Festival,** P.O. Box 990, Elora, ON, N0B 1S0 (☎ 519/846-0331).

Fergus (pop. 7,500) was founded by Scottish immigrant Adam Ferguson. There are more than 250 fine old 1850s buildings to see—examples of Scottish limestone architecture—including the Foundry, which now houses the Fergus market.

The most noteworthy Fergus event is the **Fergus Scottish Festival,** which includes Highland Games, featuring pipe-band competitions, caber tossing, tug-of-war contests, and Highland dancing, and the North American Scottish Heavy Events, held usually on the second weekend in August. For more information on the games, contact **Fergus Scottish Festival and Highland Games,** P.O. Box 25, Fergus, ON, N1M 2W7 (☎ 519/787-0099).

ACCOMMODATIONS & DINING

✪ **Breadalbane Inn.** 487 St. Andrew St. W., Fergus, ON, N1M 1P2. ☎ **519/843-4770.** 6 rms. Doubles C$75–C$185 (US$54–US$132) weekends, C$65–C$145 (US$46–US$104) weekdays. Rates include continental breakfast. AE, MC, V.

This is a favorite dining and lodging choice with the warmth, style, and fare of a British bed-and-breakfast inn. The handsome gray stone structure with ornate grillwork around the front porch was built by the Honorable Admiral Ferguson in 1860 and served as a residence, nursing home, and rooming house before it was converted 23 years ago.

The guest rooms are all extremely comfortable and elegantly furnished with early Canadian-style furniture. In the back, the Coach House contains a suite with fireplace, Jacuzzi tub, and private patio.

Dining: Reservations are recommended for the two dining areas, which have French doors leading into the garden. Here you can dine to the strains of classical music, at darkly polished tables set with Royal Doulton china. Chef/owner Peter Egger bakes his own bread and takes pains with everything. At dinner, start with the smooth chicken-liver pâté with brandy and peppercorns or the baked escargots with garlic and herb butter and follow with such dishes as oven-roasted salmon with a ginger-cucumber sauce or grilled venison medaillons in a black-currant-and-juniper sauce. Prices range from C$18 to C$25 (US$13 to US$18). It's open Tuesday to Sunday from 11:30am to 10pm. The pub, serving typical pub fare, is open daily.

Elora Mill Inn. 77 Mill St. W., Elora, ON, N0B 1S0. ☎ **519/846-5356.** Fax 519/846-9180. 32 rms. A/C TV TEL. C$160 (US$115) double; from C$190 (US$136) suite. Extra person C$25 (US$18). Rates include breakfast. AE, DC, MC, V.

This inn is located in a five-story gristmill built in 1870 and operated until 1974. Downstairs, a lounge with the original exposed beams and a huge stone fireplace overlooks the falls. Upstairs are similarly rustic dining areas. Each guest room is furnished individually, some with four-posters, others with cannonball pine beds. Most beds are covered with quilts, and each room has a comfy rocker or hoop-back chair. Some rooms in adjacent buildings are duplexes and have decks and river views. Many inn rooms have gorge views, and some units have fireplaces.

Dining: The dining room's eight or so appetizers might include Bermuda chowder, a spicy broth of fish, vegetables, spiced sausage, dark rum, and sherry pepper. The main dishes are priced from C$18 to C$32 (US$13 to US$23); the most popular option is the prime-rib cart, followed by a dessert—chocolate decadence or shoofly pie are popular choices. It's open daily for lunch and dinner.

Gingerbread House. 22 Metcalfe St. S., Elora, ON, N0B 1S5. ☎ **519/846-0521.** 5 rms (sharing 4 baths), 2 suites. C$75–C$80 (US$54–US$57) double; C$130–C$200 (US$93–US$143) suite. Rates include breakfast. MC, V.

The Gingerbread House (ca. 1840s) is operated by Petra Veveris, a very gracious, talented, and well-traveled woman who has an eye for decoration and design. The house is filled with antiques and decorative objects acquired on her many overseas expeditions, and each room is comfortably and attractively furnished. The Marco Polo is filled with travel souvenirs from Ecuador, Peru, and Australia. Petra coddles her guests, providing such extras as bathrobes, slippers, and books. A lavish breakfast, for example, crêpes with fresh strawberries and sour cream, is served at a table set with German crystal and silver candlesticks, or privately in the suites. Wine is served on the back veranda every evening. Two suites are available—one with a fireplace, cathedral-ceilinged bedroom, bathroom, dining room, and small kitchen. This suite also has an additional bedroom down the hall. The other suite has a large bedroom, sitting area, porch, and Jacuzzi bathroom.

14

North to Ontario's Lakelands & Beyond

by Marilyn Wood

And where do Torontonians go whenever they feel the urge to flee their high-rises? Usually they head north—toward Georgian Bay, the wilderness of Algonquin Provincial Park, or the cottage-and-resort country of Huronia and the Muskoka Lakes, located about 130 miles north of the city.

1 Exploring Northern Ontario

On weekends most Torontonians head for a particular resort and stay put to unwind. But if you want to explore the whole region, head out from Toronto via Highway 400 north to Barrie. Here you can either turn west to explore Georgian Bay, the Bruce Peninsula, and Manitoulin Island or continue due north to the Muskoka Lakes, Algonquin Provincial Park, and points farther north.

VISITOR INFORMATION

Contact **Ontario Travel/Travelinx Ontario,** Queen's Park, Toronto, ON, M7A 2E5 (☎ **800/ONTARIO** from 9am to 8pm, or 416/314-0944). The offices are open Monday to Friday from 8:30am to 5pm (daily from mid-May to mid-September). You can also contact them at their Web site: **www.travelinx.com.**

THE GREAT OUTDOORS

In the parts of northern Ontario covered by this chapter, you'll find plenty of terrific places to canoe, hike, bicycle, or go freshwater fishing. Some 260 provincial parks in Ontario offer ample opportunities for outdoor recreation. The daily in-season entry fee for a vehicle is anywhere from C$5 to C$10 (US$3.55 to US$7); campsites cost anywhere from C$13 to C$21 (US$9 to US$15). For more information, contact the **Ontario Ministry of Natural Resources** (☎ 416/314-2000).

Topographic maps are vital on extended canoeing/hiking trips and can be secured from the **Canada Map Office,** 130 Bentley Ave., Nepean, ON, K1A 0E9 (☎ 613/952-7000).

BIKING   You'll find networks of biking and hiking trails in the national and provincial parks. Contact the individual parks directly for more information.

Another good route is the **Georgian Cycle and Ski Trail,** which runs 32 kilometers (20 miles) along the southern shore of Georgian Bay from Collingwood via Thornbury to Meaford. The Bruce

Peninsula and Manitoulin Island also offer good cycling opportunities. In the Burk's Falls–Magnetawan area, **The Forgotten Trail** has been organized along old logging roads and railroad tracks. For information, contact the **Huronia Travel Association** in Midhurst at (☎ **705/726-9300**).

CANOEING & KAYAKING   Northern Ontario is a canoeist's paradise. Exceptional canoeing can be enjoyed in Algonquin, Killarney, and Quetico Provincial Parks; along the rivers in the Temagami (Lady Evelyn Smoothwater Provincial Park) and Wabakimi regions; along the Route of the Voyageurs in Algoma Country (Lake Superior Provincial Park); and along the rivers leading into James Bay, like the Missinaibi. Killbear Provincial Park, Georgian Bay, and Pukaskwa National Park also are good places to paddle.

Unfortunately, many areas are getting overcrowded. One of the quietest, least-trafficked areas is the **Missinaibi River** in the Chapleau Game Reserve. Another truly remote canoeing area accessible by plane only is in **Winisk River Provincial Park,** where you're likely to see polar bears who establish their dens in the park. These areas are for advanced canoeists who can handle white water and orient themselves in the wilderness.

For information on all these areas and detailed maps, contact the **Ministry of Natural Resources** (☎ **416/314-2000**) or the provincial parks themselves. For more details, see the individual park entries in this chapter.

Around Parry Sound/Georgian Bay, canoeing and kayaking trips are arranged by **White Squall,** RR #1, Nobel, ON, P0G 1G0 (☎ **705/342-5324**). Day trips are C$100 (US$71); 4-day trips start at C$510 (US$364) and prices include instruction, meals, and equipment.

In Algonquin Provincial Park, several outfitters serve park visitors, including **Algonquin Outfitters,** Oxtongue Lake (RR #1), Dwight, ON, P0A 1H0 (☎ **705/635-2243**), and **Opeongo Outfitters,** Box 123, Whitney, ON, K0J 2M0 (☎ **613/637-5470**). Complete canoe outfitting costs from C$45 to C$55 (US$32 to US$39) a day, depending on the length of trip and extent of equipment. Canoe rentals cost from C$15 to C$30 (US$11 to US$21) a day depending on the type; and from C$90 to C$210 (US$64 to US$150) per week.

Killarney Outfitters, on Highway 637, 3 miles east of Killarney (☎ **705/287-2828,** or 705/287-2242 off-season), offers complete outfitting for C$60 (US$43) a day or C$360 (US$257) per week. Canoe and kayak rentals range from C$18 to C$25 (US$13 to US$18), and C$25 to C$35 (US$18 to US$25), respectively. There's a 10% discount on rentals of 5 or more days.

In the Quetico area, contact **Canoe Canada Outfitters,** Box 1810, 300 O'Brien St., Atikokan, ON, P0T 1C0 (☎ **807/597-6418**); or **Quetico Discovery Tours,** Box 593, 18 Birch Rd., Atikokan, ON, P0T 1C0 (☎ **807/597-2621**).

North of Thunder Bay, there's excellent wilderness camping, fishing, hunting, and canoeing in the Wabakimi (accessed from Armstrong), with plenty of scope for beginners, intermediates, and advanced paddlers. For information, contact **Mattice Lake Outfitters/Wabakimi Air** (☎ **807/583-2483**) which offers 3- to 7-day trips priced from C$910 (US$650) and C$1,106 (US$790) per person, respectively. They will also rent canoes for around C$1,000 (US$710) a week.

In the Cochrane area, contact **Polar Bear Marina** (☎ **705/272-5890**) for information about trips along the Missinaibi, Mattagami, and Abitibi rivers. For additional outfitters, call **Northern Ontario Tourist Outfitters Association** (☎ **705/472-5552**).

Note: In most provincial parks you must register with park authorities and provide them with your route.

FISHING   Ontario is one of the world's largest freshwater fishing grounds, with more than 250,000 lakes and thousands of miles of streams and rivers supporting more than 140 species of fish. The northern area covered in this chapter is the province's best fishing region.

In summer, on Manitoulin Island, fishing for Chinook, coho, rainbow, lake trout, perch, and bass is excellent in Georgian Bay or any of the island lakes—Mindenmoya, Manitou, Kagawong, and Tobacco, to name a few. Trips can be arranged through **Manitou Fishing Charters** (☎ 705/859-2787). The charge is C$130 (US$91) per person per day including overnight accommodations and meals.

Around Nipissing and North Bay there's great fishing for walleye, northern pike, smallmouth bass, muskie, whitefish, and perch. In addition to these, the Temagami region offers brook, lake, and rainbow trout. More remote fishing can be found in the Chapleau and Algoma regions, the James Bay Frontier, and north of Lake Superior.

Many outfitters will rent lakeside log cabins equipped with a propane stove and refrigerator and motorboat to go along with it. The cost varies from about C$910 to C$1,120 (US$650 to US$800) per person for anywhere from 3 to 7 days. Three outfitters to contact are **Smooth Rock Camps** (☎ 807/583-2617), **Thunder Hook Camps** (☎ 807/583-2106), or **Mattice Lake Outfitters** (☎ 807/583-2483) (see above). **Konopelky,** Box 1870, Cochrane, ON, P0L 1C0 (☎ 705/272-4672), rents cabins fully equipped with propane stove, fridge, Coleman lights, and woodstove (some on lakes that are only accessible by aircraft and some in drive-in locations). They offer fishing, moose and bear hunting, and canoe packages on the Missinaibi, Mattagami, and Abitibi rivers. **Polar Bear Camp and Fly-In Outfitters,** P.O. Box 2436, Cochrane, ON, P0L 1C0 (☎ 705/272-5680), offers similar packages. For additional suggestions, contact Ontario Tourism or the Northern Ontario Tourist Outfitters Association.

Note: Fishing limits and regulations must be followed. Licenses are required and will cost about C$15 (US$9). These licenses are usually available at boat shops and sporting goods stores; or contact the **Ministry of Natural Resources** at (☎ 416/314-2000).

GOLF   Barrie has two exceptional courses—**National Pines Golf and Country Club** (☎ 705/431-7000) and the **Horseshoe Resort** golf course. Collingwood offers the scenic Cranberry Resort course. In Bracebridge, you'll find **Muskoka Highlands Golf Course** (☎ 705/646-1060) and farther north near North Bay, **Mattawa Golf Resort.** Thunder Bay has five par-71 or -72 courses, while Timmins and Kenora have one each.

HIKING & BACKPACKING   The region is super for hiking. The **Bruce Trail,** which starts at Queenston, crosses the Niagara escarpment and Bruce Peninsula and ends in Tobermory. The Bruce Trail Association publishes a map that can be obtained from sporting-goods stores specializing in outdoor activities. In the Bruce Peninsula National Park, there are four trails, three of which are linked to the Bruce Trail. There's also a hiking trail around Flowerpot Island in Fathom Five National Park.

Manitoulin Island is another prime hiking area; two of my favorite routes are **The Cup and Saucer Trail** and the trail to **Bridal Veil Falls.**

South of Parry Sound hikers can follow the 66-kilometer (41-mile) **Seguin Trail,** which meanders around several lakes.

In the Muskoka region, trails abound in Arrowhead Provincial Park at Huntsville and the Resource Management Area on Highway 11, north of Bracebridge, and, of course, in Algonquin Park. Algonquin is a great choice for a serious multiday backpacking trip, along the Highland Trail or the Western Uplands Hiking Trail, which combines three loops for a total of 105 miles.

You can do a memorable 7- to 10-day backpacking trip in **Killarney Provincial Park** on the 97-kilometer (60-mile) La Cloche Silhouette Trail, which takes in some stunning scenery.

Sleeping Giant Provincial Park has more than 81 kilometers (50 miles) of trails. The Kabeyun Trail provides great views of Lake Superior and the 800-foot-high cliffs of the Sleeping Giant.

Pukaskwa National Park offers a coastal hiking trail between Pic and Pukaskwa rivers along the northern shore of Lake Superior.

When it's completed, the province's most challenging and longest trail will be **The Voyageur Trail,** starting from South Baymouth on Manitoulin Island through Sault Ste. Marie along the shoreline of Lake Superior to Thunder Bay. Currently the trail is 499 kilometers (310 miles) long, but the plan is for it to extend 1,095 kilometers (680 miles). For information, contact the **Voyageur Trail Association,** Box 20040, 150 Churchill Blvd., Sault Ste. Marie, ON, P6A 6W3 (☎ 705/253-4470).

For additional hiking information, see the park entries later in this chapter.

HORSEBACK RIDING   Harmony Acres, RR #1, Tobermory (☎ 519/596-2735), offers overnight trail rides to the shores of Georgian Bay, as well as 1-hour and day rides.

On Manitoulin Island, **Honora Bay Riding Stables,** RR #1, Little Current, ON, P0P 1K0 (☎ 705/368-2669), operates an overnight trail ride from May to October.

Near Soo and Elliot lakes, **Cedar Rail Ranch,** RR #3, Thessalon (☎ 705/842-2021), offers both hourly and overnight trail rides with stops for swimming breaks along the route.

SKIING & SNOWMOBILING   **Ontario's largest downhill area is the **Blue Mountain Resorts in Collingwood. In the Muskoka region there's downhill skiing at **Hidden Valley Highlands** (☎ 705/789-1773 or 705/789-5942). Up north around Thunder Bay try **Loch Lomond** (☎ 807/475-5250), **Big Thunder** (☎ 807/475-4402), and **Mount Baldy** (☎ 807/683-8441).

You can cross-country ski at Big Thunder and in several provincial parks, such as Sleeping Giant and Kakabeka Falls.

One of the top destinations is the **Parry Sound** area, which has an extensive network of cross-country ski trails and more than 1,047 kilometers (650 miles) of well-groomed snowmobiling trails. There are nine snowmobiling clubs in the area, and the **Chamber of Commerce** (☎ 705/746-4213) can put you in touch with them. For additional information on cross-country skiing, contact the **Georgian Nordic Ski and Canoe Club,** Box 42, Parry Sound, ON, P2A 2X2 (☎ 705/746-5067) which permits day use of its ski trails.

You'll also find groomed cross-country trails at Sauble Beach on the Bruce Peninsula and in many of the provincial parks farther north. Along the mining frontier contact the **Porcupine Ski Runners** (☎ 705/360-1444) in Timmins.

2 From Collingwood/Blue Mountain to Tobermory/Bruce Peninsula National Park

If you head west from Barrie, northwest from Toronto, you'll go along the west Georgian Bay coast from Collingwood up to the Bruce Peninsula. Driving from Toronto, take Highway 400 to Highway 26 west.

Nestled at the base of Blue Mountain, Collingwood is the town closest to Ontario's largest skiing area. Collingwood first achieved prosperity as a Great Lakes port and shipbuilding town that turned out large lake carriers. Many mansions and the Victorian main street are reminders of those days. And just east of Blue Mountain sweep 9 miles of golden sands at Wasaga Beach.

North beyond Collingwood stretches the **Bruce Peninsula National Park,** known for its limestone cliffs, wetlands, and forest. From Tobermory, you can visit an underwater national park.

For visitor information, contact **Georgian Triangle Tourism,** 601 First St., Collingwood, ON, L9Y 4L2 (☎ 705/445-7722).

BLUE MOUNTAIN SKI TRAILS, SLIDES, RIDES & MORE

In winter, people flock to **Blue Mountain Resort,** at RR #3, Collingwood (☎ 705/445-0231), to ski. Ontario's largest resort has 16 lifts, 98% snowmaking coverage on 35 trails, and three base lodges. In addition, there are three repair, rental, and ski shops, a ski school, and day care. Lift rates are C$37 (US$27) daily.

In summer, you can zoom down the **Great Slide Ride,** 3,000 feet of asbestos-cement track, aboard a minibobsled, weaving in and out of trees and careening around high-banked hairpin curves. Naturally, you don't have to go at breakneck speed. The 10-minute ride to the top aboard the triple-chair lift treats you to a glorious panoramic view over Georgian Bay. The slide is open Victoria Day (late May) to Canadian Thanksgiving (U.S. Columbus Day) from 9:30am to dusk. Adults pay C$3.50 (US$2.50); children, C$2.50 (US$1.80); kids under 7 are free; a book of four tickets costs C$11 (US$8) and C$8 (US$6), respectively.

On the **Tube Ride** you ride an inner tube down a series of waterfalls, ponds, and rapids that stretch over 400 feet. Kids must be at least 8 years old to ride. Even more thrilling is the **Slipper Dipper water slide,** consisting of three flumes that loop and tunnel down 400 feet into a splash-down pool. For either of these exhilarating pleasures, adults pay C$4.75 (US$3.40) for five rides; children 8 to 12 C$4 (US$2.85), children under 8 C$2.75 (US$1.95). Open mid-June to Labour Day. Children must be at least 8 years old and 42 inches tall. An all-day pass for unlimited rides on everything costs C$17 (US$12) for adults, C$14 (US$10) for kids 8 to 12, and C$8 (US$6) for children under 8.

Blue Mountain is also famous for its **pottery,** and you can take a free factory tour and perhaps buy a few seconds. A pottery outlet is located at 2 Mountain Rd., on Highway 26 in Collingwood (☎ 705/445-3000).

Three miles east of Collingwood on Highway 26, at Fairgrounds Road, the kids can enjoy testing their mettle and skills at **Blue Mountain Go-Karts** (☎ 705/445-2419). For the really small fry there are minicarts, costing C$4.50 (US$3.20) for 5 minutes, plus bumper boats, a batting cage, a pitching machine, minigolf, a small touch-and-pet animal park, and a game arcade. Open daily from 10am to midnight.

BRUCE PENINSULA NATIONAL PARK

Bruce Peninsula National Park features limestone cliffs, abundant wetlands, quiet beaches, and forest that shelters more than 40 species of orchids, 20 species of ferns, and several insectivorous plants. About 100 species of bird also inhabit the park. Three campgrounds (one trailer, two tent) offer 242 campsites (no electricity).

The **Bruce Trail** winds along the Georgian Bay Coastline, while Route 6 cuts across the peninsula; both end in Tobermory. It's one of Ontario's best-known trails, stretching 700 kilometers (434 miles) from Queenston in Niagara Falls to Tobermory. The most rugged part of the trail passes through the park along the

Georgian Bay shoreline. **Cypress Lake Trails,** from the north end of the Cyprus Lake campground, provide access to the Bruce Trail and also lead to cliffs overlooking the bay. Canoes and nonpowered craft can be used on Cyprus Lake. The best swimming is at Singing Sands Beach and Dorcas Bay, both on Lake Huron on the west side of the peninsula. Winter activities include cross-country skiing, snowshoeing, and snowmobiling. For more information, contact the Superintendent, Bruce Peninsula National Park, Box 189, Tobermory, ON, N0H 2R0 (☎ **519/596-2233**).

AN UNDERWATER NATIONAL PARK

From Tobermory you can visit the underwater national park, **Fathom Five National Marine Park,** P.O. Box 189, Tobermory, ON, N0H 2R0 (☎ **519/596-2233**), where at least 21 known shipwrecks lie waiting for diving exploration around the 19 or so islands in the park. The most accessible is **Flowerpot Island,** which can be visited by tour boat to view its weird and wonderful rock pillar formations. Go for a few hours to hike and picnic. Six campsites are available on the island on a first-come, first-served basis. Boats leave from Tobermory harbor. For more information, contact the Superintendent, Fathom Five National Marine Park, Box 189, Tobermory, ON, N0H 2R0 (☎ **519/596-2233**).

ACCOMMODATIONS

Beaconglow Motel. RR #3, Collingwood, ON, L9Y 3Z2. ☎ **705/445-1674.** Fax 705/445-7176. 33 rms. A/C TV TEL. Motel and efficiency units from C$60 (US$43) double in summer and fall; C$45 (US$32) per person per night for a 2-bedrm standard suite on weekends; C$75 (US$54) per person for luxury 2-bedrm (with VCR, dishwasher, and Jacuzzi) suite. Midweek and other packages available. Special weekly rates available. AE, MC, V.

Beaconglow Motel has nicely furnished efficiency units that range in size from a compact one-bedroom with kitchenette to a two-bedroom/two-bathroom suite with fully equipped kitchen (including coffeemaker, microwave, and dishwasher) and living room with wood-burning fireplace. For fun, there's an indoor pool, whirlpool, sauna, shuffleboard, a game room with pool table, and a library of 375 movies. Reserve at least 3 months ahead for weekend or holiday stays.

✪ Beild House. 64 Third St., Collingwood, ON, L9Y 1K5. ☎ **705/444-1522.** Fax 705/444-2394. A/C. 12 rms. C$360–C$400 (US$256–US$284) for 2 on weekends including meals; C$309–C$365 (US$219–US$259) midweek for same 2-night package for 2. Rates include breakfast. AE, MC, V.

Bill Barclay and his wife Stephanie are the proud, enthusiastic owners of this handsome 1909 house. Bill prepares the breakfasts and gourmet dinners, while his wife is responsible for the inviting decor. The comfortable downstairs public areas are personalized by their collections of folk art, quill boxes from Manitoulin, and sculptures by Stephanie's mother. Two fireplaces make the place cozy in winter. The rooms are individually furnished with elegant pieces. Room 4 contains a bed that was owned by the duke and duchess of Windsor, royal portraits, and a souvenir program of Prince Edward's trip to Canada in 1860. The five rooms on the third floor all have canopied beds and fireplaces. The hotel offers a sumptuous breakfast and a five-course dinner that's even more so, with such dishes as beef fillet with bordelaise sauce, or salmon in phyllo with tarragon mayonnaise.

Blue Mountain Inn. RR #3, Collingwood, ON, L9Y 3Z2. ☎ **705/445-0231.** 98 rms. A/C TV TEL. Ski season from C$109 (US$78) per person per night midweek, C$139 (US$99) per person per night weekends. Off-season from C$99 (US$71) per rm. Condos from C$179 (US$128). Special packages available. AE, MC, V.

Stay here right at the mountain base, and you can beat the winter lift lines. Rooms are simply furnished, with little balconies facing the mountain and overlooking the tennis courts. Guests can also rent one- to three-bedroom condos, either slope-side or overlooking the fairway.

The inn's entertainment facilities include three lounges, a dining room, an outdoor and an indoor pool, squash courts, 12 tennis courts, an 18-hole golf course, mountain-bike and kayak rentals, and a fitness center. Children's programs are also offered.

DINING

✪ **Chez Michel.** Hwy. 26 W., Craigleith. ☎ **705/445-9441.** Reservations recommended. Main courses C$13–C$21 (US$9–US$15). AE, MC, V. Wed–Mon 11:30am–2pm; daily 5–9pm. FRENCH.

Small and charming, Chez Michel has a very French air created by chef-proprietor Michel Masselin, who hails from Normandy. The food is excellent and carefully prepared. Among the specials you might find Cornish hen with a cassis sauce, or rack of lamb with a Dijon crust, along with more traditional favorites like coquilles St-Jacques. There's a good wine list, too, and desserts that are worth waiting for, like the strawberries romanoff.

Christopher's. 167 Pine St. ☎ **705/445-7117.** Reservations recommended. Main courses C$13–C$19 (US$9–US$14). AE, MC, V. Daily 11am–2:30pm and 5–10pm. FRENCH/CONTINENTAL.

Dinner in this handsome Victorian town house might find you sampling such dishes as grilled lamb tenderloin with cider mint sauce, or spinach fettuccine with shrimp, sun-dried tomato, and tomato cream sauce. In summer, afternoon tea is also served.

Spike & Spoon. 637 Hurontario St. ☎ **705/446-1629.** Reservations recommended. Main courses C$13–C$23 (US$9–US$16). MC, V. Tues–Fri noon–2pm; Tues–Sun 5:30–9pm. CONTINENTAL.

Set in an elegant mid-19th-century redbrick house that once belonged to a Chicago millionaire, this restaurant offers food prepared with fresh ingredients and herbs that are grown in the yard out back. There are three dining rooms, each with a different atmosphere, plus a closed-in porch for pleasant summer dining. The bread and the desserts are all freshly made on the premises. Main courses might be poached salmon with roasted-red-pepper cream or rack of lamb with a fresh mint glaze au jus; and there's always a vegetarian dish.

✪ **Swiss Alphorn.** Hwy. 26 W., Craig Leaf. ☎ **705/445-8882.** Reservations not accepted. Main courses C$14–C$20 (US$10–US$14). AE, MC, V. Mon–Fri 4–10pm, Sat–Sun 3–11pm; summer only, daily 11:30–3pm. SWISS.

Bratwurst, Wiener schnitzel, chicken Ticino, and cheese fondue are just some of the favorites served at this chalet-style restaurant, which is loaded with Swiss atmosphere. It's a very popular place; always crowded winter and summer. Save room for the Swiss crêpes with chocolate and almonds.

3 Manitoulin Island

The island, named after the Great Indian Spirit Gitchi Manitou, is for those who seek a quiet, remote, and spiritual place, where life is slow.

ESSENTIALS

VISITOR INFORMATION   Contact the **Manitoulin Tourism Association,** P.O. Box 119, Little Current, ON, P0P 1K0 (☎ 705/368-3021), or stop by the information center at the Swing Bridge in Little Current.

GETTING THERE The island can be reached via **ferry** from Tobermory to South Baymouth, or by road across a swing bridge connecting Little Current to Great Cloche Island and via Highway 6 to Espanola. Ferries operate only from early May to mid-October with four a day in the summer months. The trip takes from 1 3/4 to 2 hours and reservations are necessary. One-way fare is C$11 (US$8) for adults and C$5.50 (US$3.95) for children 5 to 11; an average-size car costs C$24 (US$17) one-way. For information, call the **Owen Sound Transportation Company** at ☎ 519/376-6601 or contact the **Tobermory terminal** at ☎ 519/596-2510.

EXPLORING THE ISLAND

The Indians have lived here for centuries, and today you can visit the **Ojibwa Indian Reserve,** occupying the large peninsula on the island's eastern end—though there really isn't that much to see unless you are genuinely interested in modern life on the reservation. It's home to about 2,500 people of Odawa, Ojibwa, and Potawotami descent; the area was never ceded to the government. Try to time your visit for the big **Wikwemikong Powwow,** held in August. Other powwows are held during the year around the island. It is worth seeking out the few native art galleries like the **Kasheese Studios,** just outside West Bay at highways 540 and 551 (☎ 705/377-4141), which is operated by artists in residence Blake Debassige and Shirley Cheechoo, and the **Ojibwa Cultural Foundation,** also just outside West Bay (☎ 705/377-4902), which opens erratically and then only until 4pm. You can also visit individual artists' studios.

Although there are several communities on the island, the highlights are scenic and mostly outside their perimeters, like the **Mississagi Lighthouse,** located at the western end of the island outside Meldrun Bay. Follow the signs that will take you about 4 miles down a dirt road past the limestone/dolomite quarry entrance (from which materials are still shipped across the Great Lakes) to the lighthouse. There you can see how the light-keeper lived in this isolated area before the advent of electricity. There's a dining room open in summer. From the lighthouse several short trails lead along the shoreline.

Several galleries are well worth visiting. **Perivale Gallery,** RR #2, Spring Bay (☎ 705/377-4847), is the love of Sheila and Bob McMullan, who scour the country searching for the wonderful artists and craftspeople whose work they display in their log cabin/gallery overlooking Lake Kagawong. Glass, sculpture, paintings, engravings, fabrics, and ceramics fill the gallery. From Spring Bay follow Perivale Road east for about 2 miles; turn right at the lake and keep following the road until you see the gallery on the right. Open daily from 10am to 6pm from the May holiday to mid-September.

The island is great for hiking, biking, bird watching, boating, cross-country skiing, and just plain relaxing. Charters also operate from Meldrun Bay. Golf courses can be found in Mindemoya and Gore Bay. Fishing is excellent either in Georgian Bay or in the island's lakes and streams. If you'd like to book an organized fishing expedition, try **Manitou Fishing Charters** (☎ 705/983-2038 or 705/859-2787) in South Baymouth. A 5-hour trip for four is C$250 (US$178).

Honora Bay Riding Stables, RR #1, Little Current, ON, P0P 1K0 (☎ 705/368-2669), offers trail rides, including an overnight program, from May to October. A 3-hour ride is C$25 (US$18). It's 27 kilometers (17 miles) west of Little Current on Highway 540.

There are several nature trails on the island. Among the more spectacular is **The Cup and Saucer Trail,** which starts 18 kilometers (11 miles) west of Little Current at the junction of Highway 540 and Bidwell Road. Also off Highway 540 lies the trail to **Bridal Veil Falls** as you enter the village of Kagawong.

Halfway between Little Current and Manitowaning, stop at **Ten Mile Point** for the view over the North Channel, dotted with 20,000 islands. The best beach with facilities is at **Providence Bay** on the island's south side.

ACCOMMODATIONS

Your best bet is to seek out one of several B&Bs, which will most likely be plain and simple, but clean. Contact **Manitowaning Tourism Association,** Box 119 Little Current, ON, P0P 1K0 (☎ 705/368-3021). Otherwise, try the following:

✪ **Manitowaning Lodge Golf & Tennis Resort.** Box 160, Manitowaning, ON, P0P 1N0. ☎ **705/859-3136.** Fax 705/859-3270. 9 rms, 13 cottages. C$125–C$170 (US$89–US$121) per person. Lower rate is for standard rm; the higher for a 1-bedrm cabin with fireplace. Rates include breakfast and dinner. Special tennis packages available. AE, MC, V. Closed Canadian Thanksgiving (U.S. Columbus Day) to 2nd Fri in May.

This idyllic place lacks the pretension of so many ooh-la-la resorts. It consists of a lodge and cottages set on 11 acres of spectacularly landscaped gardens. Artists were employed to create a whimsical, engaging decor with trompe-l'oeil painting and furniture that sports hand-painted scenes and designs. The buildings themselves have a delightful rustic air created by their beamed ceilings; in the lodge there's a large fieldstone fireplace with a huge carved mask of the Indian Spirit of Manitowaning looming above. The cottages are comfortably furnished with wicker or painted log furniture, beds with duvets and pillows, dhurries, log tables, and hand-painted furnishings. All have fireplaces. None has a TV or phone—it's a real retreat.

The dining room is airy and light. The food features fine local meats like lamb and, of course, fish. You might find Manitowaning poached trout, smoked loin of pork with plum sauce, or tiger shrimp with coconut couscous. Lunch is served alfresco on the terrace overlooking the water.

Facilities include an 18-hole golf course, four tennis courts with pro, a swimming pool surrounded by a deck and gardens set with chaise lounges, a gym, mountain bikes, water sports (canoes, motorboats, and sailboats), and great fishing.

Rock Garden Terrace Resort. RR #1, Spring Bay, ON, P0P 2B0. ☎ **705/377-4652.** 18 motel units, 4 chalet suites. TV. Summer and winter C$86–C$98 (US$61–US$70) per person, including breakfast and dinner. Spring and fall rates slightly lower. Weekend and weekly packages available. MC, V.

This typical family resort, located on the rocks above Lake Mindemoya, has a Bavarian flair. Most accommodations are in motel-style units furnished in contemporary style. There are also four log-cabin–style suites. The dining room seems like an Austrian hunting lodge, with trophies displayed on the oak-paneled walls and a cuisine featuring German-Austrian specialties like Wiener schnitzel, sauerbraten, goulash, and beef rolladen.

Facilities include a kidney-shaped pool, whirlpool, sauna, fitness facilities, a fishing dock, and games like outdoor shuffleboard and chess, as well as bicycle, boat, and canoe rentals.

DINING

The island isn't exactly the place for fine dining. For more sophisticated food, go to the **Manitowaning Lodge Golf & Tennis Resort** (☎ 705/859-3136) or the **Rock Garden Terrace Resort** (☎ 705/377-4642), both near Spring Bay. In Little Current, one of the nicest casual spots on the island for breakfast, lunch, or dinner is **The Old English Pantry,** Water Street (☎ 705/368-3341). At dinner you'll find a pasta and fish dish of the day as well as English specialties like roast beef and Yorkshire, and baked pot pies, priced from C$10.50 to C$17 (US$7 to US$12). Afternoon cream teas and takeout are also available. Only a smaller selection of dishes like quiche, stuffed baked potato, and steak pie is offered after Labour Day. In summer it's open Sunday to Thursday from 9am to 9pm and Friday and Saturday to 11pm; winter hours are Monday to Wednesday from 9am to 5pm and Thursday to Saturday from 9am to 8pm.

4 Along Georgian Bay: Midland & Parry Sound

MIDLAND

Midland is the center for cruising through the thousands of beautifully scenic Georgian Islands, and **30,000 Island Cruises** (☎ 705/526-0161) offers 2¹/₂-hour cruises that follow the route of Brûlé, Champlain, and La Salle up through the inside passage to Georgian Bay. From May to Canadian Thanksgiving (U.S. Columbus Day), boats usually leave the town dock twice a day. Fares are C$14 (US$10) for adults, C$13 (US$9) for seniors, and C$7.50 (US$5) for children 2 to 12.

Midland lies 33 miles east of Barrie and 90 miles north of Toronto. If you're driving from Barrie, take Highway 400 to Highway 12W to Midland.

EXPLORING THE AREA

See the box later in this chapter for details on **Sainte Marie Among the Hurons.** Across from the Martyrs' Shrine, the **Wye Marsh Wildlife Centre** (☎ 705/ 526-7809) is a 150-acre wetland and woodland site offering wildlife viewing, guided and self-guided walks, and canoe excursions in the marsh. A floating boardwalk cuts through the marsh, fields, and woods, where trumpeter swans have been successfully reintroduced into the environment and now number 40 strong. Reservations are needed for the canoe trips (☎ 705/526-7809), offered in July and August and occasionally in September. In winter, cross-country skiing and snowshoeing are available. For information, write Highway 12 (P.O. Box 100), Midland, ON, L4R 4K6. Admission is C$6 (US$4.30) for adults and C$4 (US$2.85) for students and seniors; children under 3 are free. Open Victoria Day (late May) to Labour Day (first Monday in September) daily from 10am to 6pm; other months, daily from 10am to 4pm.

In town, **Freda's,** in an elegant home at 342 King St. (☎ 705/526-4851), serves continental cuisine, with main courses priced from C$9 to C$28 (US$6 to US$20). You can choose from a variety of meat and seafood dishes—steaks, beef Stroganoff, chicken Kiev, coquilles St-Jacques, and more.

EN ROUTE TO THE MUSKOKA LAKES ORILLIA

Traveling to the Muskoka lakeland region, you'll probably pass through Orillia, where you can visit Canadian author/humorist **Stephen Leacock**'s summer home (☎ 705/ 329-1908), a green-and-white mansard-roofed and turreted structure with a central balcony overlooking the beautiful lawns and garden that sweep down to the lake. The interior is filled with heavy Victorian furniture and mementos of this Canadian Mark Twain, author of 35 volumes of humor including *Sunshine Sketches of a Little Town,* which caricatured many of the residents of Mariposa (a.k.a. Orillia). Admission is C$7 (US$5) for adults, C$6.50 (US$4.65) for seniors, C$2 (US$1.45) for students, and C$1 (US70¢) for children 5 to 13. It's open from the end of June to Labour Day, daily from 10am to 7pm; by appointment only in other months.

From Barrie, take Highway 11 to Orillia; and if you're hungry, head north on Highway 11, keeping a lookout for **Paul Weber**'s hamburger place (☎ 705/ 325-3696) at the side of the road. I heartily recommend their burgers and fries, which start at C$3.50 (US$2.50). Take a breather and sit out under the trees at the picnic tables provided.

The Tragic Tale of Sainte Marie Among the Hurons

Midland's history dates from 1639, when the Jesuits established a fortified mission, Sainte Marie Among the Hurons, to bring the word of God to the Huron tribe. However, the mission retreat flourished only for a decade, for the Iroquois, jealous of the Huron-French trading relationship, increased their attacks. By the late 1640s, the Iroquois had killed thousands of Hurons, several priests, and destroyed two villages within 6 miles of Sainte Marie. Eventually, the Jesuits burned down their own mission and fled with the Hurons to Christian Island, about 20 miles away. But the winter of 1649 was harsh: Thousands of Hurons died, leaving only a few Jesuits and 300 Hurons to straggle back to Québec from whence they had come. Their mission had ended in martyrdom. It was 100 years before the native Canadians saw whites again, and by then they spoke a different language.

Today local history is recaptured at the **mission** (☎ **705/526-7838**), 5 miles east of Midland on Highway 12 (follow the HURONIA HERITAGE signs). The blacksmith stokes his forge, the carpenter squares a beam with a broadax, and the ringing church bell calls the missionaries to prayer, while a canoe enters the fortified water gate. A film also depicts the life of the missionaries. Special programs given in July and August include candlelight tours and also a 1¹/₂-hour canoeing trip (at extra cost). Admission is C$7.25 (US$5) for adults, C$4.50 (US$3.20) for students; children under 6 are free. It's open mid-May to mid-October daily from 10am to 5pm; closed mid-October to May 16.

Just east of Midland on Highway 12 rise the twin spires of the **Martyrs' Shrine** (☎ **705/526-3788**), a memorial to the eight North American martyr saints. As six were missionaries at Sainte Marie, this imposing church was built on the hill overlooking the mission, and thousands make pilgrimages here each year. The bronzed outdoor stations of the cross were imported from France. Admission is C$2 (US$1.45) for adults; children under 16 are free. It's open mid-May to mid-October daily from 8:30am to 9pm.

GEORGIAN BAY ISLAND NATIONAL PARK

The park consists of 59 islands in Georgian Bay and can be reached via water taxi from Honey Harbour, a town north of Midland right on the shore. (As you're taking Highway 400 north, branch off to the west at Port Severn to reach Honey Harbour.) Hiking, swimming, fishing, and boating are the name of the game in the park. In summer and on weekends and holidays, the boaters really do take over—but it's a quiet retreat weekdays, late August, and off-season. The park's center is on the largest island, Beausoleil, which also has camping and other facilities. For more information, call or write the Superintendent, **Georgian Bay Islands National Park,** Box 28, Honey Harbour, ON, P0E 1E0 (☎ **705/756-2415**).

ACCOMMODATIONS

Chez Vous Chez Nous Couette et Cafe. RR #3 (in Lafontaine), Penetang, ON, L9M 1R3. ☎ **705/533-2237.** 7 rms. C$50–C$90 (US$36–US$64) double. Rates include breakfast. No credit cards.

Georgette Robitaille takes care of the accommodations at this 55-acre working farm where she decorated all seven rooms in different color schemes, often featuring her own art. Singles, doubles, and twins are available. There's a separate entrance to the guest rooms, which are incredibly clean and well kept. Georgette's breakfasts are excellent and pleasantly presented. Dinners are available on request.

THE PARRY SOUND AREA

Only 225 kilometers (140 miles) north of Toronto and 161 kilometers (100 miles) south of Sudbury, the Parry Sound area is the place for active vacations. For information, contact the **Parry Sound Area Chamber of Commerce** (☎ 705/746-4213) or the **information center** at (☎ 705/378-5105).

There's excellent canoeing and kayaking; if you need an outfitter, contact **White Squall,** RR #1, Nobel, ON, P0G 1G0 (☎ 705/342-5324), which offers both day trips and multiday excursions.

The *Island Queen* cruises through the 30,000 islands for 3 hours. It leaves the town dock once or twice a day and charges C$16 (US$11) for adults and C$8 (US$6) for children. For information, contact **30,000 Island Cruise Lines,** 9 Bay St., Parry Sound, ON, P2A 1S4 (☎ 705/746-2311).

And there are many winter diversions as well—loads of cross-country ski trails and more than 1,000 kilometers (650 miles) of well-groomed snowmobiling trails. For additional information on cross-country skiing, contact the **Georgian Nordic Ski and Canoe Club,** Box 42, Parry Sound, ON, P2A 2X2 (☎ 705/746-5067), which permits day use of their ski trails.

KILLBEAR PROVINCIAL PARK

Nature lovers will head for **Killbear Provincial Park,** P.O. Box 71, Nobel, ON, P0G 1G0 (☎ 705/342-5492, or 705/342-5227 for reservations), farther north up Highway 69; it offers 4,000 glorious acres set in the middle of 30,000 islands. There are plenty of water sports—swimming at a 3-kilometer (1.9-mile) beach on Georgian Bay, snorkeling or diving off Harold Point, and fishing for lake trout, walleye, perch, pike, and bass. The climate is moderated by the bay, which explains why trillium, wild leek, and hepatica bloom. Among the more unusual fauna are the Blandings and Map turtles that inhabit the bogs, swamps, and marshes.

There are three **hiking trails,** including 3.5-kilometer (2.2-mile) Lookout Point, which leads to a commanding view over Blind Bay to Parry Sound; and the Lighthouse Point Trail, which crosses rocks and pebble beaches to the lighthouse at the peninsula's southern tip. There's also **camping** at 883 sites in seven campgrounds, costing from C$16.25 to C$19.75 (US$12 to US$14). The daily vehicle entry fee is C$7 (US$5).

ACCOMMODATIONS

The inn below is exquisite and expensive, but there are other places to stay in the area. Contact the **Parry Sound and District Bed and Breakfast Association,** P.O. Box 71, Parry Sound, ON, P2A 2X2 (☎ 705/746-5399), for its accommodations listings, priced from C$50 (US$36) and up, double. There's also a **Comfort Inn,** 112 Bowes St. (☎ 705/746-6221) and the modest, family-oriented **Resort Tapatoo,** Box 384, Parry Sound, ON, P2A 2X5 (☎ 705/378-2208), located at the edge of Otter Lake, which rents cottages, rooms, and suites, and offers boating, windsurfing, waterskiing, canoeing, fishing, and swimming in an indoor pool. Rates range from C$98 to C$150 (US$70 to US$107), (C$21.75/US$15 per person additional for meals).

✪ **Inn at Manitou.** McKellar, ON, P0G 1C0. ☎ **705/389-2171.** Fax 705/389-3818. 32 rms, one 3-bedrm country house. A/C TEL. July–Aug C$219–C$359 (US$155–US$255) midweek, C$229–C$369 (US$212–US$262) weekends; June and Sept C$199–C$284 (US$141–US$202) midweek, C$221–C$306 (US$157–US$217) weekends; May and Oct C$179–C$239 (US$127–US$170) midweek, C$199–C$262 (US$141–US$186) weekends. All rates are per person per day based on double occupancy and include breakfast, lunch, afternoon tea, and dinner. A variety of special packages are available. Special musical, cooking, and other events scheduled. AE, ER, MC, V. Closed late Oct to early May.

The Inn at Manitou is simply spectacular. Everything about the foyer glows; the space is luxuriously furnished in Franco-Oriental style. Beyond the foyer and a sitting area, a veranda stretches around the building's rear with wicker and bamboo chairs overlooking the tennis courts. To the foyer's left is the very inviting Tea Room with a view of the lake. A steep staircase leads down to the swimming and boating dock.

The accommodations are up the hill in several cedar lodges overlooking the lake. Standard rooms are small and simple; deluxe units contain fireplaces, small sitting areas, and private sundecks, while the luxury rooms each feature a sizable living room with a fireplace, whirlpool bath, sauna, and private deck.

Dining/Entertainment: Downstairs in the main building you'll find the Club Lounge nightclub, a billiard room, and the open-to-view wine cellar, filled with fine vintages, where twice-weekly wine tastings are held. The resort's cuisine is also renowned and is part of the reason the Relais and Châteaux organization awarded the property the distinguished Gold Shield. At dinner a casual three-course bistro menu and a more elaborate four-course gourmet menu are offered along with a special spa menu. Afterwards, guests can retire to the Tea Room for coffee, petit fours, and truffles.

Facilities: The spa facilities, in a separate building, offer a full range of body treatments. Other amenities include an outdoor heated pool, 20 tennis courts (including one indoor), bikes, sailboats, canoes, Windsurfers, and exercise equipment, plus pitch-and-putt facilities and an instructional golfing range.

5 The Muskoka Lakes

To settlers coming north in the 1850s, this region, with its 1,600-plus lakes north of the Severn River, was impossible to farm and difficult to traverse. But even then the wilderness attracted sports-people and adventurers like John Campbell and James Bain, who explored the three major lakes—Rosseau, Joseph, and Muskoka. They later started the Muskoka Club, purchased an island in Lake Joseph, and began annual excursions to the district. Roads were difficult to cut and waterways became the main transportation routes. It wasn't until the late 1800s that a fleet of steamers was running on the lakes and the railway arrived. Muskoka was then finally effectively linked by water and rail to the urban centers in the south.

The area was wired for tourism. Some folks gambled that people would pay to travel to the wilderness if they were wined and dined once they got there. The idea caught on and grand hotels like Clevelands House, Windermere House, and Deerhurst were opened. The lakes became the enclave of the well-to-do from Ontario and the United States. By 1903 there were eight big lake steamers, countless steam launches, and supply boats (floating grocery stores) serving a flourishing resort area.

And though the advent of the car ended the era of the steamboats and grand hotels, the area still flourishes. The rich have been joined by families in their summer cottages and sophisticated young professionals from Toronto. While many resorts don't look so impressive from the road, just take a look at the other side and remember that they were built for steamship approach.

ESSENTIALS

VISITOR INFORMATION　For information on the region, contact **Muskoka Tourism,** on Highway 11 at Severn Bridge, RR #2, Kilworthy, ON, P0E 1G0 (☎ 705/689-0660).

GETTING THERE　You can drive from the south via Highway 400 to Highway 11, from the east via highways 12 and 169 to Highway 11, and from the north via

The Muskoka Lakes Region

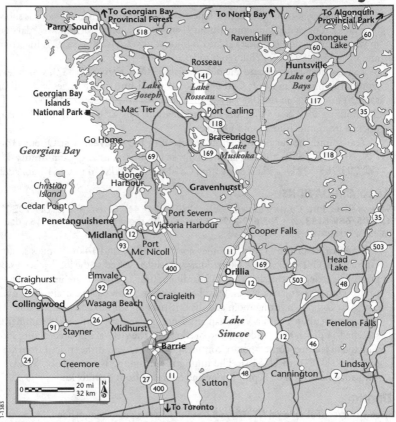

Highway 11. It's about 160 kilometers (100 miles) from Toronto to Gravenhurst, 15 kilometers (9 miles) from Gravenhurst to Bracebridge, 25 kilometers (15½ miles) from Bracebridge to Port Carling, and 34 kilometers (21 miles) from Bracebridge to Huntsville.

VIA Rail (☎ **416/366-8411**) services Gravenhurst, Bracebridge, and Huntsville from Toronto's Union Station.

MUSKOKA B&Bs   If you don't want to pay resort rates or restrict yourself to staying at an American Plan resort, contact the **Muskoka Bed and Breakfast Association,** 175 Clairmont Rd., Gravenhurst, ON, P1P 1H9 (☎ **705/687-4511**), which represents 28 or so bed-and-breakfasts throughout the area. Prices range from C$45 to C$100 (US$32 to US$71) double.

GRAVENHURST

Gravenhurst is Muskoka's first town—the first you reach if you're driving from Toronto and the first to achieve town status (in 1887 at the height of the logging boom).

The **Norman Bethune Memorial House** is the restored 1890 birthplace of Dr. Norman Bethune, at 235 John St. N. (☎ **705/687-4261**). In 1939 this surgeon, inventor, and humanitarian died tending the sick in China during the Chinese Revolution. Tours of the historic house include a modern exhibit on Bethune's life.

A visitor center displays gifts from Chinese visitors and an orientation video is shown. The house is open daily in summer from 10am to noon and 1 to 5pm; weekdays only in winter. Admission is C$2.25 (US$1.60) for adults, C$1.75 (US$1.25) for seniors, and C$1.25 (US90¢) for children 6 to 16.

You can also cruise aboard the old steamship **RMS** *Segwun* (1887), which leaves from Gravenhurst and Port Carling. Aboard you'll find two lounges and a dining salon. The cruises on the lake vary from 1 hour at a cost of C$9.75 (US$7) to a full day's outing for C$50 (US$36). For information, call ☎ **705/687-6667.** Cruises operate from mid-June to mid-October.

Year-round theater performances are given in the **Gravenhurst Opera House** (☎ 705/687-5550) and in summer only at the **Port Carling Community Hall** (☎ 705/765-5221). Tickets range from C$20 to C$25 (US$14 to US$18) for adults.

ACCOMMODATIONS

Severn River Inn. Cowbell Lane off Hwy. 11 (P.O. Box 44), Severn Bridge, ON, P0E 1N0. ☎ **705/689-6333.** Fax 705/689-2691. 8 rms (all with shower), 2 suites. A/C. $85 double. Rates include breakfast. V.

The Severn River Inn (19km/12 miles north of Orillia and 14km/9 miles south of Gravenhurst) is located in a 1906 building, which has served as the local general store, post office, telephone exchange, and boardinghouse. The rooms are individually furnished with pine and oak pieces, brass beds, flounce pillows, lace curtains, and quilts. The suite contains a sitting room and the original old bathtub and pedestal sink. The intimate restaurant, with a Victorian ambiance, is candlelit at night. In summer the screened-in porch and outdoor patio overlooking the river are favored dining spots. The menu features contemporary continental cuisine, with dishes priced from C$14 to C$19 (US$10 to US$14). The dining room/lounge is open daily: Sunday to Thursday from 8am to 10pm, Friday and Saturday from 8am to 1am.

DINING

Ascona Place. Bethune Dr. ☎ **705/687-5906.** Reservations recommended. Main courses C$17–C$23 (US$12–US$16). AE, ER, MC, V. Summer daily 11:30am–2pm and 5–9pm. Closed Mon–Tues Labour Day to Victoria Day. FRENCH/CONTINENTAL.

Named after a small picturesque village in southern Switzerland, Ascona Place offers a pretty courtyard for outside dining in July and August. The menu features classic continental cuisine plus one or two Swiss specialties, such as an *émincé* of veal Swiss-style in white wine and cream sauce with mushrooms. You may either dine in the wine cellar, a cozy nook hung with wine bottles, or in the larger Ascona Room, hung with Swiss banners, wicker lampshades, and a set of Swiss cow bells. Desserts are exquisite—double-chocolate mousse cake, apple strudel, homemade meringues and sorbets, or an iced soufflé with French Marc de Bourgogne.

BRACEBRIDGE: SANTA'S WORKSHOP

Halfway between the equator and the North Pole, Bracebridge bills itself as Santa's summer home, and Santa's Village (☎ 705/645-2512) is an imaginatively designed fantasyland full of delights—pedal boats and bumper boats on the lagoon, a roller-coaster sleigh ride, a Candy Cane Express, carousel, and Ferris wheel. At Elves' Island kids can crawl on a suspended net and over or through various modules—the Lunch Bag Forest, Cave Crawl, and Snake Tube Crawl. Rides, water attractions, and roving entertainers are all part of the fun. Santa's Village is open mid-June to Labour Day only, daily from 10am to 6pm. Admission is C$14.95 (US$11) for adults, C$9.95 (US$7) for seniors and children 2 to 4; children under 2 are free.

The Bracebridge area has a few outstanding resorts.

ACCOMMODATIONS & DINING

✪ Inn at the Falls. 1 Dominion St., P.O. Box 1139, Bracebridge, ON, P1L 1V3. ☎ **705/ 645-2245.** Fax 705/645-5093. 37 rms and suites. A/C TV TEL. C$82–C$195 (US$58–US$138) double. Rates include breakfast. AE, DC, MC, V.

This attractive inn occupies a Victorian house on a quiet street overlooking Bracebridge Falls. The inviting gardens are filled with delphiniums, peonies, roses, and spring flowers, plus there's an outdoor heated pool. Each room is individually decorated, with antiques and English chintz. Some units have fireplaces, Jacuzzis, and balconies; others have views of the falls.

The Fox and Hounds is a popular local gathering place at lunch or dinner. In winter the fire crackles and snaps, but in summer the terrace is filled with flowers and umbrellaed tables. There's also the more elegant Victoria's, for upscale continental fare.

Patterson Kaye Lodge. Golden Beach Rd. (off Hwy. 118), RR #1, Bracebridge, ON, P1L 1W8. ☎ **705/645-4169.** Fax 705/645-5720. 30 rms. TV. High season C$687–C$825 (US$491– US$589) per person per week, depending on the type of accommodation. Rates include breakfast and dinner. Special weekend packages available; also special reductions during certain weeks. European plan, only winter and spring, C$70–C$80 (US$50–US$57). AE, MC, V.

For a secluded, casual lodge, ideal for families, Patterson Kaye Lodge fits the bill. Located on Lake Muskoka 3 miles west of town, the main lodge has a variety of rooms, while cottages of various sizes accommodating a total of 100 people are scattered around the property.

Facilities: Outdoor heated pool; free waterskiing with instruction is run from the dock; hot tub; two tennis courts; a number of organized activities. Of course, there's plenty of fishing, golf, and riding nearby, and use of canoes, sailboats, kayaks, and paddleboats is free. You can rent motorboats as well.

Tamwood Resort. Hwy. 118, RR #1, Bracebridge, ON, P1L 1W8. ☎ **800/465-9166** or 705/ 645-5172. 35 rms. A/C MINIBAR TV TEL. MAP 3-night package C$305–C$362 (US$218– US$259) per person; weekly rates C$671–$800 (US$479–US$571) per person. Special discount weeks available. MC, V.

A great choice for families, Tamwood Lodge is a moderate-size log lodge on Lake Muskoka, 6 miles west of town. The air-conditioned main lodge has 35 units, all simply but nicely decorated, and there are a few cottages. The four deluxe loft accommodations are stunningly appointed in pine and feature two bedrooms with skylights, plus a loft area, two bathrooms, an efficiency kitchen, and a living room with Franklin stove and balcony from which you can dive into Lake Muskoka. Three new waterfront units come complete with fireplaces. Knotty-pine furnishings and large granite fireplaces imbue the lounge and main dining room with character.

Facilities: Indoor and outdoor swimming, fishing, tennis, volleyball, badminton, and shuffleboard, plus free waterskiing and boating, and all the winter sports imaginable. There's also lots of organized family fun—such as baseball games, marshmallow roasts, and bingo. Kids are also supervised and there's a game room.

PORT CARLING

As waterways became the main means of transportation in the region, Port Carling became, and still is, the hub of the lakes. It became a boatbuilding center when a lock was installed connecting Lakes Muskoka and Rosseau, and a canal between Lakes Rosseau and Joseph opened all three to navigation. The **Muskoka Lakes Museum** (☎ 705/765-5367) captures the flavor of this era. July and August it's open Monday to Saturday from 10am to 5pm and Sunday from noon to 4pm; June, September, and October it's open Tuesday to Saturday from 10am to 4pm and Sunday from noon to 4pm. Admission is C$2.25 (US$1.60) for adults and C$1.25 (US90¢) for seniors and students.

ACCOMMODATIONS

Clevelands House. Minett P.O., near Port Carling, ON, P0B 1G0. ☎ **705/765-3171.** Fax 705/765-6296. Accommodates up to 450 people in 86 rms, 21 suites, 30 bungalows, and several cottages. A/C TV TEL. Doubles C$150–C$200 (US$107–US$142) per person per night, C$850–$1,100 (US$604–US$781) per person per week; suites from $200 (US$142) daily per person and from C$1,100 (US$781) per week. Cottages and bungalows rent for a C$4,000 (US$2,840) minimum weekly rate. Rates depend on the number of people in the rm and the type of accommodation. Rates include all meals. Special family week, off-season discounts, and packages available. AE, DC, MC, V.

The very name has a gracious ring, and indeed this resort has been providing the ultimate in luxury since 1869. Much larger than the hostelries I recommended in nearby Bracebridge, it is very much a full-facility resort. The lodge is a magnificent clapboard structure with a veranda that runs around the lakeside giving views over the well-kept flower gardens. There's a dance floor set out on the dock with a sundeck on top. Accommodations vary in size and location, and have solid old-fashioned furniture; the luxury suites, though, are supermodern, with private sundecks.

Facilities: Sixteen tennis (two lighted), two racquetball courts, a 9-hole golf course, bike rentals, a huge children's playground and full children's program, outdoor swimming pool plus several kids' pools, fitness center, and good fishing, swimming, boating, and waterskiing on Lake Rosseau.

Sherwood Inn. P.O. Box 400, Lake Joseph, Port Carling, ON, P0B 1J0. ☎ **705/765-3131.** Fax 705/765-6668. 40 rms. C$120–C$176 (US$86–US$126) per person in the inn; C$159–C$242 (US$114–US$173) per person double in cottages; rates include breakfast and dinner. B&B rates and special packages available. AE, ER, MC, V. From Hwy. 400, take Hwy. 69 north to Foot's Bay. Turn right and take 169 south to Sherwood Rd. Turn left just before the junction of Hwy. 118. Or you can arrive via Gravenhurst and Bala or Bracebridge and Port Carling.

Accommodations here are either in the lodge or in beachside cottages. The latter are very appealing, with fieldstone fireplaces, comfortable armchairs, TVs, telephones, and screened porches overlooking the lake. Some are more luxurious than others and have additional features like VCRs or private docks. The older rooms in the lodge feature painted wood paneling while the newer wing has air-conditioning and the rooms are furnished with wicker.

✪ Windermere House. Off Muskoka Rte. 4 (P.O. Box 68), Windermere, ON, P0B 1P0. ☎ **800/461-4283** or 705/769-3611. Fax 705/769-2168. 78 rms. TEL. C$105–C$180 (US$75–US$129) per person per night. Rates include breakfast and dinner. Weekly rates and European Plan also available. AE, ER, MC, V.

This striking stone-and-clapboard turreted building overlooks lawns that sweep down to Lake Rosseau. Originally built in 1864, it was renovated in 1986. Out front stretches a long, broad veranda furnished with Adirondack chairs and geranium-filled window boxes. Rooms are variously furnished, with some in the main house and others in cottages and buildings scattered around the property. Some rooms have air-conditioning, some only overhead fans. All have private baths and are furnished in modern style, some with a bamboo/rattan look. The dining room, which is open to the public, offers fine modern continental cuisine. There's nightly entertainment in the lounge.

Services include room service from 7am to 10pm, and laundry/dry cleaning. A full children's program is offered during July and August. Among the facilities are an outdoor swimming pool, tennis courts, golf, and all kinds of water sports (fishing, windsurfing, sailing).

HUNTSVILLE

Since the late 1800s lumber has been the name of the game in Huntsville, and today it's Muskoka's biggest town, with major manufacturing companies.

You can see some of the region's early history at the **Muskoka Pioneer Village and Museum,** 88 Brunel Rd., Huntsville (☎ 705/789-7576), open June to Canadian Thanksgiving (U.S. Columbus Day), daily from 11am to 4pm until September 30, weekends only in October from 11am to 4pm, or by a visit to Brunel Locks in nearby Brunel. Admission is C$6 (US$4.30) for adults and C$4 (US$2.85) for children 6 to 12; children under 6 are free.

Robinson's General Store on Main Street (☎ 705/766-2415) in Dorset is so popular it was voted Canada's best country store. Woodstoves, dry goods, hardware, pine goods, and moccasins—you name it, it's here.

ACCOMMODATIONS

Cedar Grove Lodge. P.O. Box 996, Huntsville, ON, P0A 1K0. ☎ **705/789-4036.** Fax 705/789-6860. 8 rms (none with bath), 19 cabins. C$80–C$240 (US$57–US$171) per person. Rates include all meals. Weekly rates and special packages available. AE, MC, V. Take Grassmere Resort Rd., off Hwy. 60.

On Peninsula Lake, 12 kilometers (7¹/₂ miles) from Huntsville, Cedar Grove Lodge is a very attractive and well-maintained resort. The main lodge contains eight rooms sharing three bathrooms; the rest of the accommodations are one-, two-, or three-bedroom log cabins like the Hermit Thrush, which contains pine furnishings, a field-stone fireplace, a porch overlooking the lake, bar/sink and refrigerator, and conveniently stored firewood; or the Chickadee, a smaller version of the same, for two only. The main lodge contains a comfortable large sitting room with stone fireplace, TV, and piano, along with the pretty lakeside dining room.

Facilities include two tennis courts, a hot tub, kid's beach, and game room. There's free waterskiing, plus sailboarding, canoeing, and windsurfing for an extra charge; cross-country skiing and skating on the lake are offered in winter.

✪ Deerhurst Resort. 1235 Deerhurst Dr., Huntsville, ON, P1H 2E8. ☎ **800/441-1414** or 705/789-6411. Fax 705/789-2431. 350 rms and suites. A/C TV TEL. C$109–C$279 (US$78–US$199) double; $209–C$750 (US$149–US$536) suite. AE, CB, DC, DISC, ER, MC, V. Take Canal Rd. off Hwy. 60 to Deerhurst Rd.

Catering to well-heeled families and now a slick, mainly Toronto crowd, the Deerhurst Inn originally opened in 1896, but has expanded throughout the last 2 decades, scattering building units all over the property. It's located on 900 acres of rolling landscape fronting on Peninsula Lake. The guest rooms range from hotel rooms in the Terrace and Bayshore buildings to fully appointed one-, two-, or three-bedroom suites, many with fireplaces and/or whirlpool. These suites come fully equipped with all the comforts of home, including stereos, TVs, and VCRs; some have fully functioning kitchens complete with microwaves, dishwashers, and washer/dryers. The most expensive suites are the three-bedroom units on the lake.

Dining/Entertainment: The lodge features a lounge with a massive stone fireplace and comfortable furnishings. The adjacent dining room offers romantic dining overlooking the lake (prix-fixe dinner for C$33/US$24, à la carte C$19 to C$27/US$13 to US$19), while the Cypress Lounge provides a chic cocktail environment. Other dining options include Steamers Restaurant and Pub at the golf course. Live entertainment includes a musical show in the theater as well as in the lounge.

Facilities: The indoor sports complex has three tennis courts, three squash courts, one racquetball court, an indoor pool, a whirlpool and sauna, and a full-service spa. Outdoor facilities include a pool, eight tennis courts, a beach, canoes, kayaks, sailboats, paddleboats, waterskiing, windsurfing, horseback riding, and two 18-hole golf courses. The full winter program includes on-site cross-country skiing, snowmobiling, dog-sledding, and downhill skiing at nearby Hidden Valley Highlands. A children's activity program operates during the summer and on weekends year-round.

✪ **Grandview Inn.** RR #4, Huntsville, ON, P0A 1K0. ☎ **705/789-4417.** Fax 705/789-6882. 200 rms. A/C TV TEL. C$164–C$258 (US$117–US$184) in high season (late July and Aug). Outdoors and other packages, plus meal plans available. Children under 19 stay free in parents' rm. AE, ER, MC, V.

If Deerhurst is for the folks on the fast track, the Grandview Inn has a more measured pace. This smaller resort retains the natural beauty and contours of the original farmstead even while providing the latest in resort facilities. Eighty accommodations are traditional hotel-style rooms, but most units are suites located in a series of buildings, some right down beside the lake, others up on the hill with a lake view. All are spectacularly furnished. Each executive suite contains a kitchen, a dining area, a living room with a fireplace and access to an outside deck, a large bedroom, and a large bathroom with a whirlpool bath.

Dining/Entertainment: The Mews contains a reception area, a comfortable lounge/entertainment room furnished with sofas and wingbacks, and conference facilities. The main dining room, located in the original old farmhouse, is decorated in paisleys and English chintz, and has an inviting patio with an awning overlooking the gardens. Snacks are also served in summer at the Dockside Restaurant right on the lake, and at the golf clubhouse year-round.

Facilities: Outdoor and indoor pools, a 9-hole golf course, two outdoor tennis courts and one indoor, exercise room, waterskiing, windsurfing, sailing, canoeing, and cross-country skiing. Mountain bikes are also available, and boat cruises are offered aboard a yacht. Nature trails cross the property and a resident naturalist leads guided walks.

6 Algonquin Provincial Park

Immediately east of Muskoka lie Algonquin Park's 7,770 square kilometers (3,000 sq. miles) of wilderness—a haven for the naturalist, camper, and fishing and sports enthusiast. It's an especially memorable destination for the canoeist, with more than 1,610 kilometers (1,000 miles) of canoe routes available for paddling. One of Canada's largest provincial parks, it served as one source of inspiration for the famous Group of Seven artists. A sanctuary for moose, beaver, bear, and deer, Algonquin Park offers camping, canoeing, backpacking trails, and plenty of fishing for speckled, rainbow, and lake trout; and small-mouth black bass (more than 230 lakes have native brook trout and 149 have lake trout).

There are eight **campgrounds** along Highway 60. The most secluded sites are found at **Canisbay** (248 sites) and **Pog Lake** (281 sites). **Two Rivers** and **Rock Lake** have the least secluded sites; the rest are average. In addition, four remote wilderness campgrounds are set back in the interior: **Rain Lake** with only 10 sites; **Kiosk** (17 sites) on Lake Kioshkokwi; **Brent** (28 sites) on Cedar Lake, which is great for pickerel fishing; and **Achray** (39 sites), the most remote site on Grand Lake where Tom Thomson painted many of his great landscapes. The scene that inspired his Jack Pine is a short walk south of the campground. Call the **Visitor Centre** (☎ **613/637-2828**), for more information.

Among the **hiking trails** is the 2.4-kilometer (1½ mile) self-guided trail to the 325-foot-deep Barron Canyon on the park's east side. In addition, there are 16 day trails. The shortest is the **Hardwood Lookout Trail,** which goes through the forest to a fine view of Smoke Lake and the surrounding hills. Other short walks are the **Spruce Bog Boardwalk** and the **Beaver Pond Trail,** a 2-kilometer (1.2-mile) walk with good views of two beaver ponds.

For longer backpacking trips, the **Highland Trail** extends from Pewee Lake to Head, Harness, and Mosquito lakes for a round trip of 35 kilometers (22 miles). The **Western Uplands Hiking Trail** combines three loops for a total of 169 kilometers (105 miles) beginning at the Oxtongue River Picnic Grounds on Highway 60. The first 32-kilometer (20-mile) loop will take 3 days; the second and third loops take longer. There's also a **mountain bike** trail. Call the visitors center below for more information on all trails.

Fall is a great time to visit—the maples usually peak in the last week of September. Winter is wonderful too; visitors can **cross-country ski** on 80 kilometers (50 miles) of trails. Three trails lie along the Highway 60 corridor with loops ranging from 5 kilometers (3 miles) to 24 kilometers (15 miles). Mew Lake Campground is open in winter, and skis can be rented at the west gate. Spring offers the best **trout fishing** and great **moose viewing** in May and June. During summer, the park is most crowded, but it's also when park staff lead expeditions to hear the timber wolves howling in response to naturalists' imitations.

More than 250 **bird species** have been recorded in the park including the rare gray jay, spruce grouse, and many varieties of warbler. The most famous bird is the common loon, which is found nesting on nearly every lake.

Information centers are located at both the west and east gates of the park, plus there's a super **Visitor Centre** (☎ **613/637-2828**), about 43 kilometers (27 miles) from the west gate and 10 kilometers (6 miles) from the east gate, which houses exhibits on the park's flora and fauna and history. It also has a restaurant, bookstore and theater. Visitors can sign up here for conducted walks and canoe outings.

For additional **information,** contact the park at P.O. Box 219, Whitney, ON, K0J 2M0 (☎ **705/633-5572**).

ACCOMMODATIONS

✪ **Arowhon Pines.** Algonquin Park, ON, P0A 1B0. ☎ **705/633-5661** in summer or 416/483-4393 in winter. Fax 705/633-5795 in summer or 416/483-4429 in winter. 50 rms. From C$170 (US$121) daily, C$980 (US$700) weekly, per person, double occupancy in standard accommodations. 20% discount in spring and 5% in fall except on weekends. Rates include all meals. V. Closed mid-Oct to mid-May.

Arowhon Pines has to be one of the most enchanting places I have ever visited. Operated by a delightful couple, Eugene and Helen Kates, it's located 8 kilometers (5 miles) off Highway 60 down a dirt road, so you're guaranteed total seclusion, quiet, and serenity. Cabins are dotted throughout the pine forests that surround the lake. Each is furnished differently with assorted Canadian pine antiques, and each varies in layout, although they all have bedrooms with private baths, and sitting rooms with fireplaces. You can opt either for a private cottage, or for one that contains anywhere from 2 to 12 bedrooms and shares a communal sitting room with a stone fireplace. Sliding doors lead onto a deck. There are no TVs and no telephones—just the sound of the loons, the gentle lap of the water, the croaking of the frogs, and the sound of oar paddles cutting the smooth surface of the lake.

Dining: At the heart of the resort is a hexagonal dining room set down beside the lake with a spacious veranda. A huge fireplace is at the room's center. Helen and Eugene are extremely gracious hosts and pay close attention to the details so that everything is artfully done, right down to the bark menus at mealtimes. The food is good, with fresh ingredients, and there's plenty of it. No alcohol is sold in the park, so if you wish to have wine with dinner you'll need to bring your own. Dinner begins with soup and a buffet spread of appetizers—pâtés, salads, garlic chicken wings, moules mariniere, etc.—and follows with such dishes as salmon with sorrel sauce or pork stuffed with apples and prunes. Desserts are arranged on a harvest table—a wonderful spread of trifle, chocolate layer cake, almond tarts, fresh-fruit salad, and more. Breakfast brings a full selection, all cooked to order.

Facilities: You can swim in the lake, or canoe, sail, row, or windsurf. There are also two tennis courts, a sauna, a game room where a film is shown in the evening, plus miles of hiking trails.

Killarney Lodge. Algonquin Park, ON, P1H 2G9. ☎ **705/633-5551.** Fax 705/633-5667 (summer only). 26 cabins. High season C$160–C$220 (US$114–US$157) per person double. Off-season rates about 30% less. Rates include all meals. MC, V. Closed mid-Oct to mid-May. Enter the park on Hwy. 60 from either Dwight or Whitney.

The Killarney Lodge is not as secluded as Arowhon Pines (the highway is still visible and audible), but it, too, has charm. The cabins all stand on a peninsula that juts out into the Lake of Two Rivers. Each is made of pine logs and has a deck. Furnishings include old rockers, Ethan Allen–style beds, desks, chests, and braided rugs. A canoe comes with every cabin. Home-style meals are served in an attractive rustic log dining room. Guests can relax in the log cabin lounge warmed by a woodstove.

DINING

Spectacle Lake Lodge. Barry's Bay. ☎ **613/756-2324.** Reservations recommended in summer. Main courses C$12–C$17 (US$9–US$12). MC, V. Daily 8am–8pm. Closed last 2 weeks of Nov. Head 17 km (10^1/2 miles) west of Barry's Bay, 35 km (22 miles) east of Algonquin Park, south off Hwy. 60. CANADIAN.

The lodge's rustic dining room looks out over the lake. Traditional fare includes salmon trout and orange roughy, as well as Italian favorites like spaghetti with meatballs and veal parmigiana. Breakfast and lunch are served, too.

There are also nine nicely kept cottages available for rent, some with full housekeeping facilities including fridge and stove. The rates are C$45 to C$60 (US$32 to US$43) per person, depending on the cabin's size. Canoe and pedal boats are available, as are snowmobiles. Facilities include a comfortable sitting room with a hearth and games available, as well as a dining room and a decent wine cellar. Additional amenities include a health club, bikes, and a tennis court; all kinds of water sports are available, as is cross-country skiing in winter.

7 The Haliburton Region

East of Bracebridge along Highway 118 is the Haliburton Highlands, a region of lakes, mountains, and forests.

For information on the region, contact the **Haliburton Highlands Chamber of Commerce,** in Minden (☎ 705/286-1760).

HALIBURTON VILLAGE

The **Haliburton Highlands Museum,** on Bayshore Acres Road, 1 kilometer (half a mile) north of the village off Highway 118 (☎ 705/457-2760), provides some insight into how the pioneers who settled the region in the late 1800s lived. It's open from 10am to 5pm, daily from Victoria Day (late May) to Canadian Thanksgiving (U.S. Columbus Day); in winter, Tuesday to Saturday only. Admission is C$2 (US$1.50) for adults, C$1 (US70¢) for children.

Many artists and craftspeople have settled in the area and some of their works can be seen at the **Rail's End Gallery,** on York Street (☎ 705/457-2330), open Labour Day to July 1, Tuesday to Saturday from 10am to 5pm; July 1 to Labour Day, Monday to Saturday from 10am to 5pm and Sunday from noon to 4pm.

AN EAGLE LAKE HIDEAWAY

✪ **Sir Sam's Inn.** Eagle Lake P.O., ON, K0M 1M0. ☎ **705/754-2188.** Fax 705/754-4262. 25 rms. Summer C$125–C$145 (US$89–US$104) per person weekdays, C$265–C$295 (US$189–US$211) per person for a 2-night weekend. Rates include breakfast and dinner. Weekly rates and rm-only rates available. Off-season rates drop about 10%. AE, ER, MC, V. Follow the signs to Sir Sam's ski area. From Hwy. 118, take Rte. 6 to Sir Sam's Rd.

Sir Sam's takes some finding. That's the way politician/militarist Sir Sam Hughes probably wanted it when he built his 14-bedroom stone-and-timber mansion in 1917 in the woods above Eagle Lake. The atmosphere is friendly yet sophisticated. A comfy sitting room with a large stone fireplace serves as its focal point.

Accommodations are either in the inn or in a series of new chalets or in two lakefront suites. The chalets have fetching bed-sitting rooms with light-pine furnishings, wood-burning fireplaces, small private decks, and such amenities as minirefrigerators and kettles. Some have whirlpool baths. Inn rooms are a little more old-fashioned, except in the Hughes Wing, where they're similar to the chalets with whirlpool bath and fireplace. The suites come equipped with full kitchens and also contain whirlpools.

Dining/Entertainment: The pretty dining room serves upscale continental cuisine and offers a fixed-price dinner for C$33 (US$24). Among the decor of the Gunner's Bar is Sir Sam's gun rack; the bar has a small dance floor.

Facilities: Exercise room with rowing machine and stationary bicycle, two tennis courts, outdoor pool overlooking the lake, beach, and sailing, windsurfing, waterskiing, canoeing, paddleboats, and mountain bikes. Massage available by appointment. Sir Sam's ski area and cross-country skiing is close by.

8 Some Northern Ontario Highlights: Driving Along Highways 11 & 17

From the Muskoka region, Highway 11 winds upward toward the province's northernmost frontier via North Bay, Kirkland Lake, Timmins (using Route 101), and Cochrane before sweeping west to Nipigon. There it links up briefly with Highway 17, the route that travels the northern perimeters of the Great Lakes from North Bay via Sudbury, Sault Ste. Marie, and Wawa, to Nipigon. At Nipigon, highways 11 and 17 combine and lead into Thunder Bay. They split again west of Thunder Bay, with Highway 17 taking a more northerly route to Dryden and Kenora and Highway 11 proceeding via Atikokan to Fort Frances and Rainy River.

TRAVELING HIGHWAY 11 FROM HUNTSVILLE TO NORTH BAY, COBALT & TIMMINS

From Huntsville, Highway 11 travels north past **Arrowhead Provincial Park** (☎ 705/789-5105), which has close to 400 campsites. The road heads through the town of Burk's Falls, at the head of the Magnetawan River, and the town of South River, the access point for **Mikisew Provincial Park** (☎ 705/386-7762), with its sand beaches on the shore of Eagle Lake.

From South River the road continues to **Powassan,** famous for its excellent quality cedar strip boats. Stop in at B. Giesler and Sons to check out these very reliable specimens.

Next stop is **North Bay,** situated on the northeast shore of Lake Nipissing. The town originated on the northern Voyageurs route traveled by fur traders, explorers, and missionaries. Noted for its nearby hunting and fishing, North Bay became world-famous in 1934 when the Dionne quintuplets were born in nearby Corbeil. The quintuplets' original home is now a local museum.

From North Bay, Highway 11 continues north to New Liskeard. Along the route you'll pass **Temagami,** at the center of a superb canoeing region. Its name is Ojibwa, meaning "deep waters by the shore." The region is also associated with the legendary figure Grey Owl, who first came to the area in 1906 as a 17-year-old boy named Archie Belaney. Archie had always dreamed of living in the wilderness among the Indians; eventually he learned to speak Ojibwa and became an expert in forest and wilderness living. He abandoned his original identity and name, renamed himself Grey Owl, married an Indian woman, and became accepted as a native trapper. He subsequently published a series of books that quickly made him a celebrity.

Finlayson Point Provincial Park (☎ 705/569-3205) is located on Lake Temagami. The small park—only 232 acres—is a great base for exploring the lake and its connecting waterways. Steep rugged cliffs, deep clear waters dotted with 1,300 islands, and magnificent stands of tall pines along its shoreline make for an awesome natural display. The park offers 113 secluded campsites (many on the lakeshore), plus canoeing, boating, swimming, fishing, hiking, and biking.

Lady Evelyn Smoothwater Provincial Park is 45 kilometers (28 miles) northwest of Temagami and encompasses the highest point of land in Ontario Maple Mountain and Ishpatina Ridge. Waterfalls are common along the Lady Evelyn River, with Helen Falls cascading more than 80 feet. White-water skills are required for river travel. There are no facilities. For more information, contact District Manager, **Temagami District,** Ministry of Natural Resources, P.O. Box 38, Temagami, ON, P0H 2H0 (☎705/569-3205).

Next stop is **Cobalt,** which owes its existence to the discovery of silver here in 1903. Legend has it that blacksmith Fred LaRose threw his hammer at what he thought were fox's eyes, but he hit one of the world's richest silver veins. Cobalt was also in the ore; hence the name of the town. By 1905 a mining stampede extended to Gowganda, Kirkland Lake, and Porcupine.

A little farther north, **New Liskeard** is situated at the northern end of Lake Timikaming at the mouth of the Wabi River. Strangely enough, this is a dairy center, thanks to the "Little Clay Belt," a glacial lake bed that explains the acres of farmland amongst the rock and forest.

Even farther north, **Kap-kig-iwan Provincial Park (☎ 705/544-2050)** lies just outside of **Englehart,** also the name of the river that rushes through the park, and is famous for its "high falls," which give the park its name. Park recreational facilities are limited to 64 campsites and self-guided trails.

Farther along Highway 11, **Kirkland Lake** produces more than 20% of Canada's gold. One original mine is still in production after 50 years, and others have opened more recently.

At **Iroquois Falls,** a town on the Abitibi River, it's said that some Iroquois once raided the Ojibwa community near the falls. After defeating the Ojibwa, the Iroquois curled up to sleep in their canoes that were tied along the riverbank. But when the Ojibwa cut the canoes loose, the Iroquois were swept over the falls to their deaths.

From Iroquois Falls, you can take Route 101 southwest to **Timmins.** Along the way you'll pass the access road to **Kettle Lakes Provincial Park,** 896 Riverside Dr.,

Timmins (☎ 705/363-3511). The park's name refers to the depressions that are formed as a glacier retreats. It has 137 camping sites, five trails, three small beaches, and 22 lakes to fish and enjoy.

In Timmins visitors can tour the **Hollinger Gold Mine,** James Reid Road (☎ 705/267-6222). Discovered by Benny Hollinger in 1909, the mine produced more than $400-million worth of gold in its day. Today visitors don helmets, overalls and boots, and grab a torch before walking down into the mine to observe a scaling bar, slusher, mucking machine, and furnace at work and to view the safety room to which the miners rushed in the event of a rockfall. At the surface there's a panoramic view from the Jupiter Headframe and ore samples to be inspected along the Prospector's Trail. Admission is C$17 (US$12) for adults, C$15 (US$11) for students, and C$6 (US$4.30) for surface tours only; it's open daily July to August and Wednesday to Sunday May to June and September to October; call ahead in winter.

For additional city information, contact **Timmins Convention and Visitors Bureau,** 54 Spruce St. S. (**705/264-0811**).

COCHRANE: STARTING POINT OF THE *POLAR BEAR EXPRESS*

Back on Highway 11, the next stop is Cochrane, at the junction of the Canadian National Railway and the Ontario Northland Railway. From here, the famous ✪ *Polar Bear Express* departs to Moosonee and Moose Factory, making one of the world's great railroad/nature excursions. The train travels 4¹/₂ hours, 299 kilometers (186 miles) from Cochrane along the Abitibi and Moose rivers (the latter, by the way, rises and falls 6 feet twice a day with the tides) to Moosonee on James Bay, gateway to the Arctic.

Your destination, **Moosonee** and **Moose Factory,** on an island in the river, will introduce you to frontier life—still challenging, although it's easier today than when native Cree and fur traders traveled the rivers and wrenched a living from the land 300 years ago. You can take the cruiser *Polar Princess* or a freighter-canoe across to Moose Factory (site of the Hudson's Bay Company, founded in 1673) and see the 17th-century Anglican church and other sights. If you stay over, you can also visit **Fossil Island** and the **Shipsands Waterfowl Sanctuary.**

Trains operate from the end of June to Labour Day. Tickets are limited because priority is given to the excursion passengers. Fares are C$48 (US$34) round-trip for adults and C$24 (US$17) for children ages 5 to 12. Various 3-day/2-night and 4-day/3-night packages are also offered from North Bay and Toronto. For information, contact **Ontario Northland** at 555 Oak St. E., North Bay, ON, P1B 8L3 (☎ 705/472-4500), or at Union Station, 65 Front St. W., Toronto, ON, M5J 1E6 (☎ 416/314-3750). Note that from June to Labour Day you'll need to make your lodging reservations well in advance.

For additional information on Cochrane, contact the **Cochrane Board of Trade,** P.O. Box 1468, Cochrane, ON, P0L 1C0 (☎ **705/272-4926**).

ACCOMMODATIONS IN COCHRANE

The **Chimo Motel** on Highway 11 (☎ 705/272-6555) offers one- or two-bedroom efficiencies as well as Jacuzzi rooms. Rates are C$65 to C$75 (US$46 to US$54) double. Another option is the **Westway Motel,** 21 First St. (☎ 705/272-4285), at only C$65 (US$46) double.

EN ROUTE FROM COCHRANE TO NIPIGON

From Cochrane, Highway 11 loops farther north past the turnoff to **Greenwater Provincial Park** (☎ 705/272-6335). This 13,215-acre park has good camping (90 sites in three campgrounds), swimming, boating (rentals available), hiking, and fishing on 26 lakes. One of the park's more challenging trails goes along Commando Lake. Spectacular views of the northern lights are an added attraction.

Highway 11 continues west past **Rene Brunelle Provincial Park** (☎ 705/367-2692) and **Kapuskasing,** where General Motors has its cold-weather testing facility, to **Hearst,** known as the "moose capital" of Canada, at the northern terminus of the Algoma Central railway.

It continues all the way to **Lake Nipigon Provincial Park** (☎ 807/887-5000) on the shores of Lake Nipigon. The lake is famous for its black sandy beaches. Park facilities include 60 camping sites, boat rentals, and self-guided trails.

The nearby town of **Nipigon** stands on Lake Superior at the mouth of the Nipigon River. It's where the world-record brook trout, weighing 14½ pounds, was caught. At this point highways 17 and 11 join and run all the way into Thunder Bay.

TRAVELING HIGHWAY 17 ALONG THE PERIMETER OF THE GREAT LAKES

Instead of traveling north from North Bay up Highway 11 to explore the northern mining frontier, you could choose to take Highway 17 along the perimeter of the Great Lakes. I consider this the more scenic and interesting route.

SUDBURY

The road travels past Lake Nipissing through Sturgeon Falls to Sudbury, a nickel-mining center. With a population of 160,000, this is northern Ontario's largest metro area. This rough-and-ready mining town has a landscape so barren that U.S. astronauts were trained here for lunar landings.

Sudbury's two major attractions are **Science North,** 100 Ramsey Lake Rd. (☎ 705/522-3701, or 705/522-3700 for recorded information) and **Big Nickel Mine** (see below). The first occupies two giant stainless-steel snowflake-shaped buildings dramatically cut into a rock outcrop overlooking Lake Ramsey. Inside you can conduct experiments, such as simulating a hurricane, monitoring earthquakes on a seismograph, or observing the sun through a solar telescope. In addition to the exhibits, a 3-D film and laser experience, *Shooting Star,* takes the audience on a journey five billion years into the past, charting the formation of the Sudbury Basin. A theatrical performance in another theater tells the story of the naturalist Grey Owl. There's also a water playground (where kids can play and adults can build a sailboat), space-exploration and weather command centers, and a fossil-identification workshop. Open year-round, daily in May and June from 9am to 5pm, July to Canadian Thanksgiving (U.S. Columbus Day) from 9am to 6pm; call ahead for winter hours (usually 10am to 4pm). Admission is C$8.95 (US$6) for adults and C$6.50 (US$4.65) for students and seniors; children under 5 are free. A combined admission with the mine will save money.

At the **Big Nickel Mine,** 100 Ramsey Lake Rd., Sudbury, (☎ 705/522-3701), visitors are taken underground for a 30-minute tour. On the surface visitors can view a mineral-processing station, measure their weight in gold, and enjoy some other video programs. Open May to Canadian Thanksgiving, same hours as Science North. Admission is C$8.95 (US$6) for adults and C$6.50 (US$4.65) for students and seniors; free for children under 5. A combined admission with Science North will save money.

The **Path of Discovery** is a 2-hour bus tour that provides the only public access to INCO Ltd., the biggest nickel producer in the Western world. On the tour visitors observe the surface processing facilities and one of the world's tallest smokestacks.

The tour is operated from July to Labour Day daily at 10am and 2pm. Contact **Science North** at ☎ **705/522-3701.**

For further information on Sudbury, contact either the **Sudbury and District Chamber of Commerce** (☎ **705/673-7133**) or the **Community Information Service and Convention and Visitors Service** (☎ **705/674-3141**).

Accommodations

Your best bets for lodgings are the chains—**Comfort Inn,** 2171 Regent St. S. (☎ **705/522-1101**), and 440 2nd Ave. N. (☎ **705/560-4502**); **Ramada Inn,** 85 St. Anne Rd. (☎ **705/675-1123**); or **Venture Inn,** 1956 Regent St. S. (☎ **705/ 522-7600**). There's also the **Sheraton Four Points,** 1696 Regent St. S. (☎ **705/ 522-3000**).

A CROWN JEWEL: KILLARNEY PROVINCIAL PARK

Less than an hour's drive southwest of Sudbury is **Killarney Provincial Park** (☎ **705/287-2900**), sometimes called the "crown jewel" of the province's park system. This 119,795-acre park on the north shore of Georgian Bay features numerous lakes and a spectacular range of quartzite ridges. It's only accessible on foot or by canoe. More than 100 species of birds breed in the park, including kingfishers and loons on the lakes in the summer. Four members of the Group of Seven painted in the region: Frank Carmichael, Arthur Lismer, A. Y. Jackson, and A. J. Casson.

The park has 122 **campsites** at the George Lake campground near the entrance to the park.

The park is a paradise for the canoeist (rentals are available in the park). Compared to Algonquin Park, it's much quieter—you only have to cross one lake to find total privacy at Killarney, while at Algonquin you may have to canoe across three lakes.

Three **hiking trails** loop from the campground and can be completed in 3 hours.

For a more ambitious backpacking tour, the park's **La Cloche Silhouette Trail** winds for more than 97 kilometers (60 miles) through forest and beaver meadows past crystal-clear lakes. The trail's main attraction is Silver Peak, which towers 1,214 feet above Georgian Bay offering views of 81 kilometers (50 miles) on a clear day. This is a serious undertaking; it will take 7 to 10 days to complete the whole trail.

The best **fishing** is in Georgian Bay; sadly, acid rain has killed off most of the fish in the lakes.

DRIVING WEST FROM SUDBURY

From Sudbury it's 305 kilometers (189 miles) west along Highway 17 to Sault Ste. Marie, or the Soo, as it's affectionately called.

At Serpent River you can turn off north to the town of Elliot Lake and **Mississagi Provincial Park** (☎ **705/848-2806**), and the river of the same name. The park has 90 campsites, swimming, and also offers some fine canoeing. Hikers will find short self-guided trails as well as trails from 6 to 16 kilometers (3.7 to 10 miles) long.

Continuing along Highway 17, which borders the North Channel, will bring you past the access point to **Fort St. Joseph National Park** (☎ **705/941-6203**) on St. Joseph Island (between Michigan and Ontario) and into the Soo, 305 kilometers (189 miles) west of Sudbury.

SAULT STE. MARIE

The highlights of any visit are the **Soo locks,** the **Agawa Canyon Train,** and the **Bon Soo,** one of North America's biggest winter carnivals, celebrated in late January and early February.

The Soo, at the junction of Lakes Superior and Huron, actually straddles the border. The twin cities, one in Ontario and the other in Michigan, are separated by the St. Marys River rapids, and now are joined by an international bridge. Originally the Northwest Fur Trading Company founded a post here in 1783, building a canal to bypass the rapids from 1797 to 1799. That canal was replaced later by the famous **Soo locks**—four on the American side and one on the Canadian. The locks are part of the St. Lawrence Seaway system, which enables large international cargo ships to navigate from the Atlantic along the St. Lawrence to the Great Lakes. Lake Superior is about 23 feet higher than Lake Huron and the locks raise and lower the ships. There's a viewing station at both sets of locks or you can take a 2-hour cruise for C$17 (US$12) adults, C$13 ($9) youths, and C$8.50 (US$6) children, through the lock system daily from June to about October 10. For information, contact **Lock Tours Canada,** Roberta Bondar Park Dock off Foster Drive, Box 325, Sault Ste. Marie, ON, P6A 5L8 (☎ **705/253-9850**).

The Algoma Central Railway, which operates the ✪ **Agawa Canyon Train Tours,** was established in 1899. The Canadian artists known as the Group of Seven used to shunt up and down the track in a converted boxcar that they used as a base camp for canoe excursions into the wilderness. Today the tour train takes you on a 184-kilometer (114-mile) wilderness trip from the Soo to the Agawa Canyon, where you can enjoy a 2-hour stopover and view the waterfalls, walk the nature trails, or enjoy a picnic. The train snakes through a vista of deep ravines and lakes, hugging the hillsides and crossing gorges on skeletal trestle bridges. The most spectacular time to take the trip is in the fall from mid-September to mid-October. The train operates daily from early June to mid-October; on weekends only January to March. Fares are C$50 to C$60 (US$36 to US$43) for adults, C$15 (US$11) for children and students (June to August); or C$59 (US$24) for adults, C$34 (US$24) for children 5 to 18, and C$10 (US$7) for children under 5 (September to October); C$53 (US$38), C$27 (US$19), and C$11 (US$8), respectively, from January to March. You can, of course, ride the passenger train from the Soo to Hearst, although there are no stops en route. Round-trip costs C$125 (US$89). For information, contact the **Algoma Central Railway,** Passenger Sales, P.O. Box 130, 129 Bay St., Sault Ste. Marie, ON, P6A 6Y2 (☎ **705/946-7300**).

The surrounding area offers great fishing, snowmobiling, cross-country skiing, and other sports opportunities. For cross-country skiing information, call the **Stokely Creek Ski Touring Centre,** at **Stokely Creek Lodge,** Karalash Corners, Goulais River (☎ **705/649-3421**). Contact the **Sault Ste. Marie Chamber of Commerce,** 360 Great Northern Rd. (☎ **705/949-7152**) for more sports information.

Accommodations

Whatever you do, make your reservations in advance. If you're taking the Algoma Train, the most conveniently located hotel is the **Quality Inn Bayfront,** right across from the train station, which has 110 rooms including 18 suites (six with Jacuzzi tubs). Facilities include indoor pool, exercise room, and Italian restaurant. Rates are C$98 to C$180 (US$70 to US$129) double.

You can also try the other chains: the **Holiday Inn,** 208 St. Marys River Dr., on the downtown waterfront (☎ **705/949-0611**), or **Comfort Inn,** 333 Great Northern Rd. (☎ **705/759-8000**). The **Ramada,** 229 Great Northern Rd. (☎ **705/ 942-2500**), has great facilities for families—water slide, bowling, indoor golf, and more.

LAKE SUPERIOR PROVINCIAL PARK

Alona and Agawa bays are in ✪ **Lake Superior Provincial Park** (☎ **705/ 856-2284**). The 1,540-square-kilometer (955-sq.-mile) park, one of Ontario's largest, offers the haunting shoreline and open waters of Longfellow's "Shining Big-Sea Water," cobble beaches, rugged rocks, and limitless forests. Dramatic highlights include Lac Mijinemungsing, the Devil's Chair, and Old Woman Bay. At the park's east end the Algoma Central Railway provides access to the park along the Agawa River.

The magnificent scenery has attracted artists for years, including the Group of Seven. Among the most famous paintings of the park are Frank Johnston's *Canyon and Agawa,* Lawren Harris's *Montreal River,* A. Y. Jackson's *First Snows,* and J. E. H. MacDonald's *Algoma Waterfall and Agawa Canyon.* As for wildlife, you may see moose as well as caribou, which once were common here and have been reintroduced along the coast areas and offshore islands. More than 250 species of birds have been identified here; about 120 different types nest in the area.

Some 269 camping sites are available at three **campgrounds.** The largest, at Agawa Bay, has a 3-kilometer (1.9-mile) beach. Crescent Lake, at the southern boundary, is the most basic, while Rabbit Blanket Lake is well located for exploring the park's interior.

The park has eight canoe routes, ranging in length from 3 to 56 kilometers (1.9 to 35 miles), and in difficulty from easy to challenging, with steep portages and white water. Rentals are available at the campgrounds, but outfitter services are limited. Contact the **Wawa Chamber of Commerce,** P. O. Box 858, Wawa, ON, P0S 1K0 (☎ 705/856-4538).

The 11 **hiking trails** range from short interpretive trails to rugged overnight trails up to 55 kilometers (34 miles) long. The most accessible is the **Trapper's Trail,** which features a wetlands boardwalk from which you can watch beaver, moose, and great blue heron. The 16-kilometer (10-mile) **Peat Mountain Trail** leads to a panoramic view close to 500 feet above the surrounding lakes and forests. The 26-kilometer (16-mile) **Toawab Trail** takes you through the Agawa Valley to the 81-foot Agawa Falls. The **Orphan Lake Trail** is popular due to its moderate length and difficulty, plus its panoramic views over Orphan and Superior lakes, a pebble beach, and Baldhead Falls. **The Coastal Trail,** along the shoreline, is the longest at 55 kilometers (34 miles), stretching from Sinclair Cove to Chalfant Cove, and will take 5 to 7 days to complete. The fall is the best time to hike, when the colors are spectacular and the insects are few.

In winter, although there are no formal facilities or services provided, visitors can cross-country ski, snowshoe, and ice-fish at their own risk.

Wawa, the White River & Winnie-the-Pooh, Too

From the park, it's a short trip into **Wawa,** 230 kilometers (142 miles) north of the Soo, the site of the famous salmon derby. Wawa serves as a supply center for canoeists, fishermen, and other sports folks.

East of Wawa lies the **Chapleau Game Reserve,** where there's some of Ontario's best canoeing and wildlife viewing in **Chapleau Nemegosenda River Provincial Park**—200 kilometers (124 miles) northeast of the Soo and 100 kilometers (62 miles) west of Timmins. It's accessible from Chapleau or by Emerald Lake on Highway 101 to Nemegosenda Lake. There are no facilities. Nonresidents need a permit to camp, costing C$10 (US$8) per person per night. For additional information contact **Ontario Parks,** Ministry of Natural Resources, 190 Cherry St., Chapleau, ON, P0M 1K0 (☎ 705/864-1710, ext. 237).

Ninety-eight kilometers (61 miles) farther on along Highway 17 from Wawa is **White River,** birthplace of Winnie-the-Pooh. In 1916, Winnipeg soldier Harry Colebourne, on his way to Europe from his hometown Winnipeg, bought a mascot for his regiment here and named it Winnie. When he shipped out from London he couldn't take the bear cub, so it went to the London Zoo, where it became the inspiration for A. A. Milne's classic character.

Just outside White River are the spectacular **Magpie High Falls.**

PUKASKWA NATIONAL PARK

Southwest of White River on the shores of Lake Superior is Ontario's only national park in the wilderness, **Pukaskwa National Park,** Hattie Cove, Heron Bay, ON, P0T 1R0 (☎ **807/229-0801**). It's reached via Highway 627 from Highway 17. The interior is only accessible on foot or by boat.

In this 1,878-square-kilometer (388-sq.-mile) park survives the most southerly herd of **woodland caribou**—only 40 of them. Lake Superior is extremely cold, and for this reason rare Arctic plants are also found here.

Hattie Cove is the center of most park activities and services including a 67-site campground, a series of short walking trails, access to three sand beaches, and parking facilities and a visitor center.

The 60-kilometer (37-mile) **Coastal Hiking Trail** winds from Hattie Cove south to the North Swallow River and requires proper planning and equipment (camping areas are located every half- to full-day's hike apart). A 15-kilometer (9-mile) day hike along this trail can be taken to the White River Suspension Bridge. There are also backcountry trails.

In winter cross-country skiers can use 6 kilometers (3.7 miles) of groomed trails or hazard the fast slopes and sharp turns created by the topography. Snowshoers are welcome, too.

CANOEING THE WHITE & PUKASKWA RIVERS

The White and Pukaskwa rivers offer white-water adventure. The easily-accessed White River can be paddled any time during the open-water season. Many wilderness adventurers start from nearby **White Lake Provincial Park** and travel 4 to 6 days to the mouth of the White River and then paddle about an hour north on Lake Superior to Hattie Cove.

The Pukaskwa River is more remote, more difficult (with rugged and long portages and an 850-foot drop between the headwaters at Gibson Lake and the river mouth at Lake Superior), and navigable only during the spring runoff. The best place to start is where the river crosses Highway 17 near Sagina Lake and paddle to Gibson Lake via Pokei Lake, Pokei Creek, and Soulier Lake. Otherwise you'll have to fly in from White River or Wawa.

Outfitters include **Pukaskwa Country Outfitters,** P.O. Box 603, Marathon, ON, P0T 2E0 (☎ **807/229-0265**), **Naturally Superior Adventures,** RR #1 Lake Superior, Wawa ON, P0S 1K0 (☎ **705/856-2939** or 705/856-7107), and **U-Paddle-It,** P.O. Box 374, Pinewood Drive, Wawa, ON, P0S 1K0 (☎ **705/856-1493**).

MORE PROVINCIAL PARKS

From White River it's 270 kilometers (167 miles) to **Nipigon** and **Nipigon Bay,** which offer fine rock, pine, and lake vistas. From here it's another 12 kilometers (7¹/₂ miles) to **Ouimet Canyon Provincial Park** (☎ **807/977-2526**), at the location of a spectacular canyon 330 feet deep, 500 feet wide, and a mile long. When you stand on the edge of the canyon and gaze out over the expanse of rock and forest below, you can sense the power of the forces that shaped, built, and split the earth's crust and then gouged and chiseled this crevasse—one of Eastern Canada's most striking canyons. The park is for day use only.

About 25 kilometers (15¹/₂ miles) on, the next stop is **Sleeping Giant Provincial Park** (☎ 807/977-2526), named after the rock formation that the Ojibwa Indians say is Nanabosho (the Giant), who was turned to stone after disobeying the Great Spirit. The story goes that Nanabosho, who had led the Ojibwa to the north shore of Lake Superior to save them from the Sioux, discovered silver one day, but fearing for his people, he told them to bury it on an islet at the tip of the peninsula and keep it a secret. Vanity got the better of one of the chieftains, who made silver weapons for himself. Subsequently, he was killed in battle against the Sioux. Shortly afterwards Nanabosho spied a Sioux warrior leading two white men in a canoe across Lake Superior to the source of the silver. To keep the secret, he disobeyed the Great Spirit and raised a storm that sank and drowned the white men. For this, he was turned into stone.

Take Route 587 south along the Sibley Peninsula, which juts into the lake. Among the park's natural splendors are bald eagles, wild orchids, moose, and more than 190 species of birds. Facilities include 168 campsites at Marie Louise Campground plus about 40 interior sites. There's a beach at the campground.

The trail system consists of three self-guided nature trails, three walking trails, and a network of about 70 kilometers (43.4 miles) of hiking trails including the 2-day Kabeyun Trail, which originates at the spectacular Thunder Bay lookout and follows the shoreline south to Sawyer Bay. The park has great cross-country skiing with 30 kilometers (19 miles) of trails.

THUNDER BAY

Just before you enter Thunder Bay, stop and honor Terry Fox at the **Monument and Scenic Lookout.** Not far from this spot he was forced to abandon his heroic cross-Canada journey to raise money for cancer research.

To access the remote **Wabakimi region,** take Route 527 north just east of Thunder Bay. It will take you to Armstrong, the supply center for this wilderness region.

From the port city of **Thunder Bay**—an amalgam of Fort William and Port Arthur—wheat and other commodities are shipped out via the Great Lakes all over the world. Fifteen grain elevators still dominate the skyline. You can't really grasp the city's role and its geography unless you take the **Harbor Cruise.** Other highlights include **Old Fort William** (☎ 807/473-2344), about 10 miles outside the city on the Kaministiquia River. From 1803 to 1821 this reconstructed fort was the headquarters of the North West Fur-Trading Company, which was later absorbed by the Hudson's Bay Company.

Thunder Bay is also the center for ice climbing and dogsled excursions. For information on the latter, call **Norwest Dog Sled Adventures** in Thunder Bay (☎ 807/964-2070).

Accommodations

For B&B accommodations, contact the **North of Superior B&B Association** at ☎ 807/475-4200.

Your best bets are the chains: **The Best Western NorWester,** 2080 Hwy. 61, RR #4, ON, P7C 4Z2 (☎ 807/473-9123), which has rooms for C$85 (US$61) double, plus an indoor pool and lounge-restaurant; **Comfort Inn by Journey's End,** 660 W. Arthur St. (☎ 807/475-3155), where rooms are C$100 (US$71) double; and the **Venture Inn,** 450 Memorial Ave. (☎ 807/345-2343), which also has a lounge-restaurant and indoor pool and rents rooms for C$90 (US$64) double.

Airlane Motor Hotel. 698 W. Arthur St., Thunder Bay, ON, P7E 5R8. ☎ **807/473-1600.** 154 rms. A/C MINIBAR TV TEL. C$102.95 (US$74) double. AE, MC, V.

The recently renovated Airlane Motor Hotel has modern rooms that are well equipped, plus free in-room coffee. Facilities include an indoor pool and fitness center, as well as a lounge-restaurant and dance club. Suites with whirlpools are available, too.

The White Fox Inn. RR #4, 1345 Mountain Rd., Thunder Bay, ON, P7C 4Z2. ☎ **807/ 577-3699.** 9 rms. A/C TV TEL. C$110–C$220 (US$79–US$157) double. AE, DC, MC, V.

Set on 15 acres, with a view of the Norwester Mountain range, this inn was originally a lumber magnate's home. The individually decorated rooms have fireplaces and VCRs, while the three largest rooms have in-room Jacuzzis. There's also a fine dining room serving Mediterranean cuisine. Nearby you'll find a variety of outdoor activities.

FROM THUNDER BAY TO FORT FRANCES/RAINY RIVER VIA HIGHWAY 11

From Thunder Bay it's 480 kilometers (298 miles) along the Trans-Canada Highway to **Kenora.** Several provincial parks line the route.

Kakabeka Falls Provincial Park, 435 James St. S., Suite 221, Thunder Bay (☎ 807/473-9231), with its spectacular 130-foot-high waterfall, lies 29 kilometers (18 miles) out along the Trans-Canada Highway. The gorge was carved out of the Precambrian Shield when the last glaciers melted. Fossils dating back 1.6 billion years have been found in the park. The park has several nature trails, plus safe swimming at a roped-off area above the falls. Two campgrounds provide 166 sites (from C$10 to C$17/US$7 to US$12, depending on season and site). In winter, there are 13 kilometers (8 miles) of groomed cross-country ski trails.

Atikokan is the gateway to ✪ **Quetico Provincial Park** (☎ 807/597-2737), primarily a wilderness canoeing park. The 4,662-square-kilometer (1,800-sq.-mile) park has absolutely no roads and only two out of the six entrance stations are accessible by car (those at French Lake and Nym Lake, both west of Thunder Bay). Instead, there are miles of interconnecting lakes, streams, and rivers with roaring white water dashing against granite cliffs. It's one of North America's finest canoeing areas. Dawson Trail Campgrounds, with 133 sites at French Lake, is the only accessible site for car camping. Extended hikes are limited to the 13-kilometer (8-mile) trip to Pickerel Lake; there are also six short trails in the French Lake area (three interpretive). The park can be skied, but there are no groomed trails. Also in the park on some rocks near Lac la Croix you can see 30 ancient pictographs representing moose, caribou, and other animals, as well as hunters in canoes.

Fort Frances is an important border crossing to the United States and the site of a paper mill. Another 90 kilometers (56 miles) will bring you to **Rainy River** at the extreme western point of Ontario across from Minnesota. The district abounds in lakeland scenery, much of it in **Lake of the Woods Provincial Park,** RR #1, Sleeman (☎ 807/488-5531), which is 43 kilometers (26 miles) north of Rainy River. This shallow lake has a 185-yard-long beach and is good for swimming and waterskiing. In spring you can fish for walleye, northern pike, and large- and smallmouth bass. Canoes and boats can be rented in nearby Morson. The park has 100 campsites as well as a couple of easy nature trails to hike.

Almost due north of Thunder Bay via Route 527 lies **Wabakimi Provincial Park,** which has some fine canoeing and fishing. It's accessible from Armstrong.

FROM THUNDER BAY TO KENORA VIA HIGHWAY 17

Instead of taking Highway 11 west from Thunder Bay as described above, you can take Highway 17, which follows a more northerly route. Just follow 17 where it branches off at Shabaqua Corners, about 56 kilometers (34 miles) from Thunder Bay. Continue northwest to Ignace, the access point for two provincial parks.

At Ignace, turn off onto Highway 599 to **Sandbar Lake** (☎ **807/934-2995,** or 807/934-2233 for local Natural Resources office), which offers more than 12,350 acres of forest with nine smaller lakes plus the large one from which it takes its name. The park's most notable inhabitants are the painted turtle, whose tracks can often be seen in the sand; the spotted sandpiper; the loon; the common merganser; as well as several species of woodpecker. The campground has 75 sites; the beach has safe swimming; there are several short and long canoe routes plus several hiking trails, including the 2-kilometer (1.2-mile) **Lookout Trail,** which begins on the beach.

Turtle River Provincial Park is a 120-kilometer-long (74-mile-long) waterway from Ignace to Mine Centre. The canoe route begins on Agimak Lake at Ignace and follows a series of lakes into the Turtle River ending on Turtle Lake just north of Mine Centre. The park also includes the famous log castle built by Jimmy McQuat in the early 1900s on White Otter Lake. Follow Highway 599 farther north and it will lead to the remote Albany and Apawapiskat rivers, which drain into James Bay.

Back on Highway 17 from Ignace it's another 40 kilometers (24 miles) to the turn-off on Highway 72 to **Ojibway Provincial Park** (☎ 807/737-2033), which has only 45 campsites but offers swimming, boating, and self-guided trails.

Back on Highway 17, it's only a short way beyond Highway 72 to **Aaron Provincial Park** (☎ 807/938-6534, or 807/223-3341 for Natural Resources office), where you'll find close to 100 campsites, facilities for boating and swimming, plus some short nature trails. Nearby Dryden is the supply center for Aaron.

From Dryden it's about 43 kilometers (26 miles) to Vermilion Bay where Route 105 branches off north to Red Lake, the closest point to one of the province's most remote provincial parks, **Woodland Caribou** (☎ 807/727-2253). Offering superb fishing, the 1,111,500-acre park has no facilities except picnic tables and boat rentals nearby. It's home to one of the largest herds of woodland caribou south of the Hudson Bay lowlands. It's also inhabited by black bear, great blue heron, osprey, and bald eagles. There are 1,600 kilometers (992 miles) of canoe routes. Contact the **Northern Ontario Tourist Outfitters Association** (☎ 705/472-5552) for information on fly-in camps. Back on Highway 17 from Vermilion Bay, it's only 72 kilometers (43 miles) until the road links up with Highway 71 just outside Kenora, just shy of the Manitoba border.

Accommodations & Dining Near Kenora

Totem Lodge. Box 180, Sioux Narrows, ON, P0X 1N0. ☎ **807/226-5275.** Fax 807/226-5187. 27 cabins, 3 rms. A/C TV. C$160 (US$114) per person per night. Cabins without meals from C$1,600 (US$1,143) per week. Weekly and special packages available. MC, V. Access is off Hwy. 71, 1 mile north of Sioux Narrows.

At the end of Long Bay on Lake of the Woods, this lodge caters to outdoor enthusiasts and families who come for the superb fishing and hunting. The main lodge is an A-frame featuring a dining room, lounge, and decks with umbrellaed tables overlooking the water. The timber-and-stone decor is appropriately rustic. The cabins have full modern baths, beds with Hudson's Bay blankets, fireplaces, and screened-in porches or outdoor decks, plus cooking facilities. The rooms above the boathouse lack cooking facilities but do have fridges.

Facilities: Sixteen-foot fishing boats, canoes, Windsurfers, and wet jets can be rented, and the management will arrange fly-out fishing trips. Fish-cleaning facilities and freezer service are available.

Wiley Point Lodge. Box 180, Sioux Narrows, ON, P0X 1N0. ☎ **807/543-4090.** 3 rms, 7 cabins. Fishing packages C$160 (US$114) per person per night based on 2 per boat (this includes boat, gas, and bait). Hunting packages also available. MC, V.

This lodge is more remote, only accessible by boat, and therefore offers more of a wilderness experience. The main lodge has three suites, plus there are seven cabins (two- or three-bedroom), all with full bath, fridge and screened-in porch. The lodge contains a dining room, lounge, and deck overlooking the lake. Facilities include a beach with diving raft, paddleboats, Windsurfers, and wet skis for rent; hot tub; sauna; and exercise room. Spring and fall bear hunts are offered, as well as more traditional hunting.

Manitoba & Saskatchewan

by Marilyn Wood

Visitors don't exactly flock to these two provinces at Canada's center, but that can be a plus if you like wide open spaces. Part of the great prairies, Manitoba and Saskatchewan boast some beautiful wilderness and parkland and an almost infinite chain of lakes, making them terrific choices for fishing, canoeing, wildlife watching, and more.

Manitoba is famous for its friendly people, who not only brave long harsh winters, but till the southern prairie lands in summer, making the region a breadbasket for the nation and the world. Outside of Winnipeg, along the southern border and under the dome of a huge prairie sky, wheat, barley, oats, and flax wave at the roadside, the horizon is limitless, and grain elevators pierce the skyline. Beyond the province's southern section, which is punctuated by Lake Winnipeg and Lake Manitoba, stretches one of the last wilderness frontiers, a paradise for anglers and outdoors enthusiasts of all sorts. Here you'll find many of the province's 100,000 lakes, which cover about 20% of Manitoba. You'll also see polar bears and beluga whales and hear the timber wolves cry on the lonesome tundra surrounding the Hudson Bay port of Churchill.

Five times the size of New York State, with a population of about one million, Saskatchewan, another of Canada's prairie provinces, produces 60% of Canada's wheat. Here you'll find a hunting and fishing paradise in the northern lakes and forests; several summer playgrounds (including Prince Albert National Park and 31 provincial parks); and the cities of Regina, the capital, and Saskatoon.

1 Exploring Manitoba & Saskatchewan

The Trans-Canada Highway (Highway 1) cuts across the southern part of both provinces. In Manitoba, you can stop along Highway 1 at Whiteshell Provincial Park in the east. You can return to the highway or visit the shores of Lake Winnipeg at Grand Beach Provincial Park and then head south via Selkirk and Lower Fort Garry to Winnipeg, the provincial capital. From Winnipeg, you can take the train north to Churchill to explore the Northern tundra around Hudson Bay. On your return trip to Winnipeg, you can pick up Highway 1 again and drive west across the province, stopping for a detour either to Riding Mountain National Park or Spruce Woods Provincial Park before exiting into Saskatchewan.

Highway 1 leads from Manitoba to Regina, with a stop perhaps at Moose Mountain Provincial Park along the way. From Regina it's a 2¹/₂-hour or so drive to Saskatoon, and about another 2¹/₂-hour drive to Prince Albert National Park (you can stop at Batoche en route). From Prince Albert you can return via Fort Battleford National Historic Park either to Saskatoon and then to Highway 1 at Swift Current, or you can take Route 4 directly from Battleford to Swift Current. From here the Trans-Canada Highway heads west to the Alberta border.

VISITOR INFORMATION

Contact **Travel Manitoba,** Department SV6, 7–155 Carlton St., Winnipeg, MB, R3C 3H8 (☎ 800/665-0040). Or you can visit the information center at 31 Forks Market Rd., open in summer Sunday to Thursday from 10am to 6pm and Friday and Saturday from 10am to 6pm; the rest of the year, daily from 10am to 6pm. For taped info on the latest happenings, call ☎ 204/942-2535. For information on Manitoba's provincial parks, call ☎ 800/214-6497 or 204/945-6784.

In Saskatchewan, contact **Tourism Saskatchewan,** 500–1900 Albert St., Regina, SK, S4P 4L9 (☎ 800/667-7191 or 306/787-2300); open Monday to Friday from 8am to 7pm and Saturday and Sunday from 10am to 4pm.

THE GREAT OUTDOORS

The major playgrounds in Manitoba are **Riding Mountain National Park,** plus these provincial parks: **Whiteshell, Atikaki, Spruce Woods, Duck Mountain,** and **Grass River.** Call ☎ 800/214-6497 or 204/945-6784 for information.

Saskatchewan has 80,290 square kilometers (31,000 sq. miles) of water and 3 million acres are given over to parks—one million alone constitute Prince Albert National Park. In addition, there are 31 provincial parks. The major ones are **Cypress Hills** (☎ 306/662-4411), **Moose Mountain** (☎ 306/577-2131), **Lac La Ronge** (☎ 306/425-4234), and **Meadow Lake** (☎ 306/236-7680). At the parks you can camp for anywhere from C$11 to C$17 (US$8 to US$12) in addition to a C$6 (US$4.30) entry fee. Some parks, such as Cypress Hills and Moose Mountain, also have cabins for an average of C$40 to C$65 (US$29 to US$46) for a one-bedroom cabin, and C$65 to C$100 (US$46 to US$71) for a two-bedroom.

Summers can be simply magnificent, with warm sunny days and cool refreshing evenings and nights. Average winter temperatures are pretty harsh—−18°C to −12°C (0°F to 9°F)—but that doesn't stop winter-sports enthusiasts.

BIRD WATCHING   In Manitoba, there's a goose sanctuary at **Whiteshell Provincial Park.** Gull Harbour's **Hecla Provincial Park,** on Lake Winnipeg, has a wildlife-viewing tower; the Grassy Narrow Marsh located there is home to a wide variety of waterfowl. **Riding Mountain National Park** boasts more than 200 species of birds. And many varieties stop near **Churchill** on their annual migrations.

In Saskatchewan, **Moose Mountain Provincial Park** is home to many waterfowl and songbirds, including the magnificent blue heron and the red-tailed hawk. As you might expect, **Prince Albert National Park** has a wide variety of bird life, with the highlight being an enormous colony of white pelicans at Lavallee Lake. And there's even a waterfowl park right in the middle of downtown **Regina,** where more than 60 species can be seen. A naturalist is on duty weekdays.

CANOEING   In Manitoba the best places to canoe are in **Riding Mountain National Park, Whiteshell Provincial Park,** and the chain of lakes around Flin Flon, which is right on the border between the two provinces.

In Saskatchewan, **Prince Albert National Park** has some fine canoeing, and plenty of other northern water routes offer a challenge to both novice and expert. Some 55

Manitoba

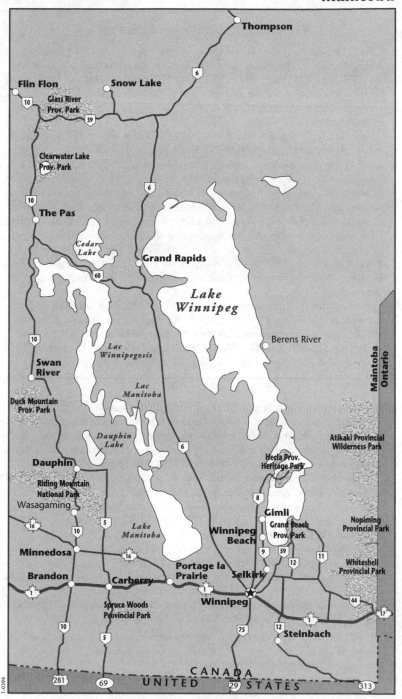

Farm & Ranch Vacations on the Prairies

There's no better way to really get the feel of the prairies than to stay on a farm or ranch. Contact the **Manitoba Country Vacations Association,** c/o Susan Sure, Box 27B, RR #2, Winnipeg, MB, R3C 2E6 (☎ **204/633-3326**), for details about farm accommodations. Rates average C$45 to C$70 (US$32 to US$50) per day for adults and C$30 (US$21) for children—a very reasonable price for such an exciting, authentic experience.

Just outside Riding Mountain National Park, **Riding Mountain Guest Ranch,** Box 11, Lake Audy, MB, R0J 0Z0 (☎ **204/848-2265;** fax 204/848-4658), offers much more than a simple farm vacation. Guests at the 720-acre ranch enjoy horseback riding, hiking, and loon watching at the lake. Accommodations consist of four rooms, plus a dorm room with 12 beds and a bunkhouse accommodating another 12. The ranch also features a lounge with stone fireplace, a sunroom veranda, a billiard room, a sauna, and a hot tub. In summer, guests can take trail rides. Evenings are given over to campfire sing-alongs. In winter, the ranch has 20 kilometers (12.4 miles) of cross-country ski trails. There's a minimum stay of 1 week. Prices range from C$1,317 to C$1,944 (US$935 to US$1,380) per person per week, including all meals and programs, plus transfers between the Winnipeg airport and the ranch.

In Saskatchewan farm vacations average C$45 to C$55 (US$32 to US$39) double for a bed and a real farm breakfast (additional meals can be arranged). For information, contact **Saskatchewan Country Vacations Association,** RR #5, Box 43, Saskatoon, SK, S7K 3J8 (☎ **306/931-3353**); or **Tourism Saskatchewan,** 1919 Saskatchewan Dr., Regina, SK, S4P 3V7 (☎ **306/787-2300**).

canoe routes have been mapped, traversing terrain that has not changed since the era of explorers and fur traders. You can get to all but three of the routes by road. Various outfitters will supply tents, camping equipment, and canoes; look after your car; and transport you to your trip's starting point. Most outfitters are located in either Flin Flon or Lac La Ronge, 400 kilometers (250 miles) north of Saskatoon.

Churchill River Canoe Outfitters in La Ronge, Saskatchewan (☎ **306/635-4420**), offers a selection of packages. Canoes and kayaks can be rented for about C$25 (US$18) a day or they can outfit you for a real wilderness expedition. You can also rent cabins from C$70 to C$190 (US$50 to US$136) per night.

Canoe Ski Discovery Company, 1618 9th Ave. N., Saskatoon, SK, S7K 3A1 (☎ **306/653-5693**), offers several canoeing and cross-country skiing wilderness ecotours in Prince Albert National Park, Lac La Ronge Provincial Park, and along the Churchill and Saskatchewan rivers. The trips last 2 to 13 days, cost from C$175 to C$1,600 (US$125 to US$1,143), and are led by qualified eco-interpreters.

For additional information, contact **Tourism Saskatchewan,** 500–1900 Albert St., Regina, SK, S4P 4L9 (☎ **800/667-7191** or 306/787-2300).

FISHING   The same clear, cold northern lakes that draw canoeists hold out the chance of catching walleye, northern pike, four species of trout, and Arctic grayling. Licenses are required in both provinces.

Since Manitoba has strong catch-and-release and barbless-hook programs, the number of trophy fish is high. In 1994, 8,272 Master Angler Fish were recorded and nearly 75% released. The province is also known as the North American mecca for channel catfish, particularly along the Bloodvein River. Good fishing abounds in

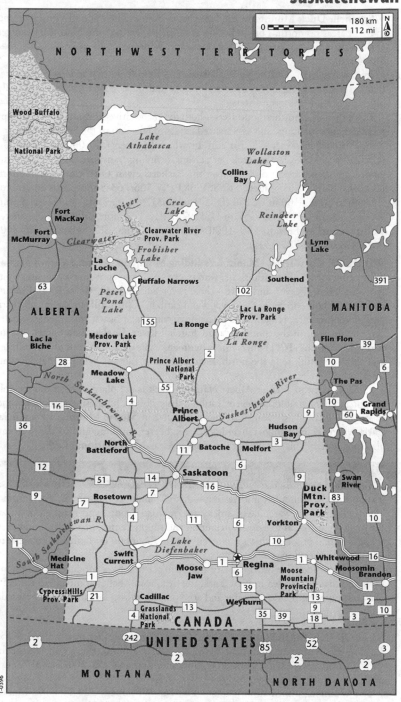

Saskatchewan

0   180 km
     112 mi

N

NORTHWEST TERRITORIES

Wood Buffalo

National Park

Lake
Athabasca

Wollaston
Lake

Collins
Bay

Cree
Lake

River

Reindeer
Lake

Fort
MacKay

Fort
McMurray

Clearwater

Clearwater River
Prov. Park

Frobisher
Lake

Lynn
Lake

La
Loche

Buffalo Narrows

Southend

391

63

Peter
Pond
Lake

102

ALBERTA

MANITOBA

155

La Ronge

Lac La Ronge
Prov. Park

Lac la
Biche

Meadow Lake
Prov. Park

Lac
La Ronge

Flin Flon

39

28

Prince Albert
National
Park

2

10

6

North Saskatchewan

Meadow
Lake

4

55

The Pas

16

Prince
Albert

Saskatchewan River

10

Grand
Rapids

36

R.

9

60

North
Battleford

11

Batoche

Melfort

Hudson
Bay

3

12

6

51

14

Saskatoon

9

Swan
River

9

7

7

16

Duck
Mtn.
Prov.
Park

83

Rosetown

4

11

6

Yorkton

10

1

South Saskatchewan R.

Lake
Diefenbaker

1

Regina

Moose
Mountain
Provincial
Park

1

Whitewood

16

Medicine
Hat

Swift
Current

Moose
Jaw

6

1

Moosomin

Brandon

1

1

Cypress Hills
Prov. Park

21

Cadillac

13

Weyburn

39

13

2

10

Grasslands
National
Park

4

35

39

18

3

CANADA

9

2

242

UNITED STATES

85

52

3

2

2

2

2

MONTANA

NORTH DAKOTA

1-0396

495

Whiteshell, Duck Mountain, the lake chains around The Pas and Flin Flon, and in fly-in areas up north. For a selection of outfitters, contact the **Manitoba Lodges and Outfitters Association,** 23 Sage Crescent, Winnipeg, MB, R2Y 0X8 (☎ 204/889-4840).

In Saskatchewan, **La Rouge, Wollaston,** and **Reindeer** are just a few of the lakes that are so densely inhabited by northern pike and walleye that you can practically pluck them from the clear waters.

More than 300 northern outfitters—both fly-in and drive-in camps—offer equipment, accommodations, and experienced guides to take you to the best fishing spots. Rates for packages vary—it can cost anywhere between C$1,000 and C$3,000 (US$715 and US$2,143) a week per person, including transportation, meals, boat, guide, and accommodations. Contact the **Saskatchewan Outfitters Association,** P.O. Box 2016, Prince Albert, SK, S6V 6R1 (☎ 306/763-5434). Boat and motor will cost about C$100 to C$250 (US$71 to US$179) a day, and guide services run about C$80 to C$150 (US$57 to US$107) a day. For more information, contact **Tourism Saskatchewan,** 500–1900 Albert St., Regina, SK, S4P 4L9 (☎ 800/667-7191 or 306/787-2300).

WILDLIFE VIEWING   Manitoba's Riding Mountain National Park is a prime destination for wildlife enthusiasts, who might be able to spot moose, coyote, wolf, lynx, black bear, beaver, and more—there's even a bison herd. **Grass River Provincial Park** is home to moose and woodland caribou. **Churchill,** in the far northern part of the province, is a fantastic place for viewing polar bears; white beluga whales can even be seen in the mouth of the Churchill River. **Kaskattama Safari Adventures** (☎ 204/667-1611) offers pricey but memorable organized trips to see the bears and the other wildlife in the north, including Cape Tatnam Wildlife Management Area.

In Saskatchewan, **Prince Albert National Park** is the place to be; you'll be able to spot and photograph moose, elk, caribou, shaggy bison, lumbering black bears, and more. It will come as no surprise that moose live in **Moose Mountain Provincial Park,** where their neighbors include deer, elk, beaver, muskrat, and coyote. You can also spot adorable black-tailed prairie dogs in **Grasslands National Park.**

2 Winnipeg

Tough, sturdy, muscular, midwestern—that's Winnipeg, the capital of Manitoba. The solid cast-iron warehouses, stockyards, railroad depots, and grain elevators all testify to its historical role as a distribution and supply center, first for furs and then for agricultural products. It's a toiling city where about 600,000 inhabitants sizzle in summer and shovel in winter.

That's one side. The other is a city and populace that have produced a symphony orchestra that triumphed in New York, the first "royal" ballet company in the British Commonwealth, and a theater and arts complex worthy of any national capital.

ESSENTIALS

VISITOR INFORMATION   Contact **Travel Manitoba,** Department SV8, 7-155 Carlton St., Winnipeg, MB, R3C 3H8 (☎ 800/665-0040, ext. SV8), or visit the **Travel Idea Centre** at The Forks in the Johnston Terminal (☎ 204/945-3777, ext. SV8).

For Winnipeg information, contact **Tourism Winnipeg,** 320-25 Forks Market Rd., Winnipeg, MB, R3C 4S8 (☎ 800/665-0204 or 204/943-1970), open weekdays from 8:30am to 4:30pm, or the **Airport InfoCentre,** Winnipeg International Airport (☎ 204/774-0031), open daily from 8am to 9:45pm.

GETTING THERE   **Winnipeg International Airport** (☎ 204/987-7832) is only about 20 minutes west-northwest from the city center (allow 30 to 40 min. in rush hours). **Air Canada** (☎ 800/776-3000) and **Canadian Airlines** (☎ 800/426-7000 in the U.S. or 800/665-1177 in Canada) serve the city.

You can get from the airport to downtown by taxi, which will cost C$10 to C$15 (US$7 to US$11), or by the city bus, which costs C$1.45 (US$1.05) and runs approximately every 15 minutes during the day, every 22 minutes in the evenings, to Portage and Garry.

If you're driving, Winnipeg is 697 kilometers (432 miles) from Minneapolis, Minnesota, and 235 kilometers (146 miles) from Grand Forks, North Dakota.

The **VIA Rail Canada** depot is at Main Street and Broadway. For information on train arrivals and departures, call ☎ 204/949-7400.

CITY LAYOUT   A native Winnipegger once said to me, "I still can't get used to the confined and narrow streets in the east." When you see Portage and Main, each 132 feet wide (that's 10 yd. off the width of a football field), and the eerie flatness that means no matter where you go, you can see where you're going, you'll understand why.

Portage and Main is the city's focal point, which is situated at the junction of the Red and Assiniboine rivers. The Red River runs north-south, as does Main Street; the Assiniboine and Portage Avenue run east-west. Going north on Main from the Portage-Main junction will bring you to the City Hall, Exchange District, the Manitoba Centennial Centre (including the Manitoba Theatre Centre), the Museum of Man and Nature, the Ukrainian Museum, and on into the North End, once a mosaic of cultures and still dotted with bulbous church domes and authentic delis. (*Warning:* At night, I'd stay away from Main Street north of the Arts Centre.)

From Portage and Main, if you go 6 blocks west along Portage, the main shopping drag, and 2 blocks south, you'll hit the Convention Centre. From here, one block south and 2 blocks west brings you to the Legislative Building, the art gallery, and south, just across the river, to Osborne Village.

GETTING AROUND   For information, contact **City of Winnipeg Transit,** 421 Osborne St. (☎ 204/986-5700). For regular buses, you need C$1.45 (US$1.05) in exact change (C85¢/US60¢ for children or seniors) to board. Call ☎ 204/986-5700 for route and schedule information, or visit the information booth in the Portage and Main concourse, open Monday to Friday from 9:30am to 5:30pm.

Taxis can be found at the downtown hotels. They charge C$2.55 (US$1.80) when the meter drops and C$1.80 (US$1.30) per mile thereafter. Try **Duffy's Taxi** (☎ 204/772-2451 or 204/775-0101), or **Unicity Taxi** (☎ 204/947-6611 or 204/942-3366).

SPECIAL EVENTS   The **Red River Exhibition,** usually held the last 10 days of June, celebrates and reflects the city's history, showcasing agricultural, horticultural, commercial, and industrial achievements. There is also a midway, a photography show, and other themed features like a lumberjack show. For more information, contact **Red River Exhibition,** 876 St. James St., Winnipeg, MB, R3G 3J7 (☎ 204/772-9464).

Folklorama, a Festival of Nations, is a 2-week cultural festival in August featuring more than 35 ethnic pavilions celebrating ethnic culture, with traditional food, dancing, music, costumes, entertainment, and crafts. For more information, contact Folklorama, 300–180 King St., Winnipeg, MB, R3B 3G8 (☎ 800/665-0234 or 204/982-6210).

The 10-day **Festival du Voyageur,** usually held in February, celebrates French Métis culture in St. Boniface (☎ 204/237-7692).

EXPLORING THE CITY
THE TOP ATTRACTIONS

At the junction of the Red and Assiniboine rivers, the **Forks Market Area** is a major city attraction created in the late 1980s when the old rail yard was redeveloped. The draw is the market—a wonderful display of fresh produce and specialty foods. There are also restaurants, specialty stores, and programs, exhibits, and events scheduled throughout the year. In summer visitors can stroll on the river walks along the Red and Assiniboine rivers; in winter there's free public skating on outdoor artificial ice or along groomed river trails. From the Forks National Historic site there's a view across to St. Boniface where all kinds of special events and interpretive programs are held. It's also a great place for a picnic. The **Manitoba Children's Museum** (☎ 204/956-5437) is here at the Forks (see below) and so too is the **Manitoba Sports Hall of Fame,** located in the Johnston Terminal. Fun Splash Dash Water Buses link the forks to The Exchange District, St. Boniface, and Osborne Village. For an update on what's going on at the Forks, call ☎ 204/957-7618.

✪ **Winnipeg Art Gallery.** 300 Memorial Blvd. ☎ **204/786-6641.** Admission C$3 (US$2.15) adults, C$2 (US$1.45) students and seniors, C$5 (US$3.55) families; children under 13 free. Oct–May Tues and Thurs–Sun 11am–5pm, Wed 11am–9pm; June–Sept Thurs–Tues 10am–5pm, Wed 10am–9pm.

A distinctive triangular building of local Tyndall stone, the Winnipeg Art Gallery houses one of the world's largest collections of contemporary Inuit art—a treasure house which includes such wry works as Leah Qumaluk Povungnituk's *Birds Stealing Kayak from Man.* Other collections focus on historic and contemporary Canadian art, as well as British and European artists. The decorative art collections feature works by Canadian silversmiths and studio potters while the photography collection contains more than 200 works by Andre Kertesz, and represents other 20th-century photographers such as Diane Arbus and Irving Penn. The penthouse restaurant overlooks the fountain and flowers in the sculpture court.

Manitoba Museum of Man & Nature. 190 Rupert Ave. ☎ **204/956-2830,** or 204/943-3139 for recorded information. Admission C$4 (US$2.85) adults, C$3 (US$2.15) seniors and children 4–17. Victoria Day to Labour Day daily 10am–6pm; Labour Day to Victoria Day Tues–Sun 10am–4pm.

Part of the Manitoba Centennial Centre, the museum is a fascinating place, with galleries that depict local history, culture, and geology through life-size exhibits such as a buffalo hunt, prehistoric creatures, pioneer life, pronghorn antelope, teepees, sod huts, and log cabins. In the Urban Gallery, you can walk down a 1920s Winnipeg street past typical homes and businesses of the era. The Boreal Forest Gallery depicts Manitoba's most northerly forested region. Climb aboard the *Nonsuch,* a full-size replica of the 17th-century ketch that returned to England in 1669 with the first cargo of furs out of Hudson Bay.

Manitoba Planetarium & Science Centre. 190 Rupert Ave. ☎ **204/943-3142** for recorded information, or 204/956-2830. Planetarium C$3.50 (US$2.50) adults, C$2.50 (US$1.80) seniors and children 4–17. Science Centre C$3.50 (US$2.50) adults, C$2.50 (US$1.80) seniors and children 4–17. Both are free for children under 4. Planetarium shows presented daily mid-May to Labour Day; Tues–Sun the rest of the year. Science Centre, Victoria Day to Labour Day daily 10am–6pm; rest of the year Tues–Sun 10am–4pm.

The planetarium, part of the Manitoba Museum of Man and Nature in the Manitoba Centennial Centre, offers shows in its 280-seat Star Theatre exploring everything from cosmic catastrophes to the reality of UFOs. The Science Centre is a hands-on science gallery containing close to 100 interactive exhibits explaining the laws of nature.

Winnipeg

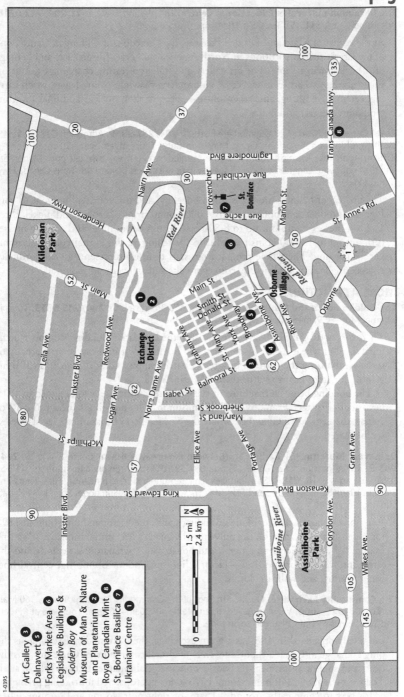

Art Gallery **3**
Dalnavert **5**
Forks Market Area **6**
Legislative Building &
 Golden Boy **4**
Museum of Man & Nature
 and Planetarium **2**
Royal Canadian Mint **8**
St. Boniface Basilica **7**
Ukranian Centre **1**

The Ukrainian Cultural & Educational Centre. 184 Alexander Ave. E. ☎ **204/942-0218.**
Admission C$2 (US$1.45). Tues–Sat 10am–4pm, Sun 2–5pm.

At the corner of Main and Disraeli Freeway, the Oseredok, or Ukrainian Centre, one
of the largest such institutions in North America, conserves the artifacts and heritage
of the Ukrainian people. The art gallery and museum feature changing exhibits on
such subjects as 18th-century icons, embroidery, weaving, painted eggs, wood carving, ceramics, clothing, and other folk arts. The gift shop stocks traditional and contemporary folk art and crafts.

Royal Canadian Mint. 520 Lagimodière Blvd. ☎ **204/257-3359.** Admission C$2 (US$1.45)
adults; children under 6 free. Open May–Aug only. Tours given every 30 min. Mon–Fri
8:30am–4pm. Take Main St. south over the Assiniboine/Red rivers, turn left onto Marion St.,
and then right onto Lagimodière. You'll see the mint rise up just beyond the Trans-Canada Hwy.
(Rte. 135).

The process of making money is mind-boggling, and this tour will prove it to you.
Dyes are produced; a roof crane lifts 4,000-pound strips of bronze and nickel; three
150-ton presses stamp out up to 8,800 coin blanks per minute; and coining presses
turn out up to 18,000 coins per hour to the telling machines that count the number for bagging. The whole process from start to finish represents an extraordinary
engineering feat streamlined by conveyor belts and an overhead monorail.

MORE ATTRACTIONS

The Golden Boy & the Legislative Building. 450 Broadway. ☎ **204/945-5813.** Tours in
summer Mon–Fri 9am–6:30pm; by reservation at other times.

There he stands, 240 feet above ground atop the Legislative Building's dome, clutch-
ing a sheaf of wheat under his left arm and holding aloft in his right an eternally lit
torch symbolizing the spirit of progress. French sculptor Charles Gardet created his
5-ton, 13^{1}/$_{2}$-foot bronze statue during World War I.

The building below, a magnificent classical Greek structure, was designed in 1919
by British architect Frank Worthington Simon. The building's focal point is, of
course, the Legislative Chamber, where the 57 members of Manitoba's legislative assembly meet.

Dalnavert Museum. 61 Carlton St. (between Broadway and Assiniboine Ave.). ☎ **204/
943-2835.** Admission C$3 (US$2.15) adults, C$2 (US$1.45) seniors and students, C$1.50
(US$1.05) ages 6–18, C$8 (US$6) families; children under 6 free. June–Aug Tues–Thurs and
Sat–Sun 10am–6pm; Sept–Dec and Mar–May Tues–Thurs and Sat–Sun noon–5pm; Jan–Feb Sat–
Sun noon–5pm.

Just 2 blocks east of the Legislative Building stands the Victorian home built in 1895
for Hugh John Macdonald, the only son of Canada's first prime minister. It's a fine
example of a late Victorian gingerbread house with a wraparound veranda and the
latest innovations of the time—electric lighting, indoor plumbing, central hot-
water heating, and walk-in closets.

The Commodity Exchange. On the 5th floor of the Commodity Exchange Tower, 360 Main
St. ☎ **204/925-5000.** Viewing gallery open Mon–Fri 9:30am–1:15pm. Tours are at 9:10am
and 12:50pm daily but call ahead to arrange.

Originally organized in 1887 as a grain exchange, the Commodity Exchange is the
only exchange in Canada that trades in agricultural commodities. Once this was the
heart and soul of Winnipeg: the world's premier grain market until World War II.
Today its has about 240 members and 77 companies registered for trading privileges.
It's best to come early around 9:15am, or right near closing at 12:45pm, when
you're more likely to see some feverish action on the floor.

Western Canada Aviation Museum. 958 Ferry Rd. ☎ **204/786-5503.** Admission C$3 (US$2.15) adults, C$2 (US$1.45) students 6–17. Mon–Sat 10am–4pm, Sun 1–4pm. Closed Dec 25–26, Jan 1, and Good Friday.

Among the historic flying treasures at the Western Canada Aviation Museum is Canada's first helicopter, designed and test-flown between 1935 and 1939. The children's interactive area is popular.

Grant's Old Mill. 2777 Portage Ave. (at the corner of Booth Dr.). ☎ **204/986-5613.** Admission by donation. June–Aug daily 10am–6pm; rest of year by appointment only.

Grant's Old Mill is a reconstruction of the water mill that was built on Sturgeon Creek in 1829, believed to be the first water mill west of the Great Lakes and the first instance of the use of hydropower in Manitoba. Grist is ground daily during the summer, and you can take away a souvenir bag of whole wheat, buckwheat, or something else.

Assiniboia Downs. 3975 Portage Ave. ☎ **204/885-3330.** Clubhouse admission C$2 (US$1.45).

Live racing begins in early May and runs to October. There's also simulcast racing from racetracks throughout North America. You can dine in the Terrace Dining Room overlooking the track. Post times are Thursday, Friday, and Saturday at 7:30pm, and Sunday and holidays at 1:30pm.

Fort Whyte Centre. 1961 McCreary Rd., Fort Whyte. ☎ **204/989-8355.** Admission C$3.75 (US$2.70) adults, C$2.70 (US$1.95) students, seniors, and children over 2. Mon–Tues and Thurs–Fri 9am–5pm, Wed 9am–9pm, Sat–Sun and holidays 10am–5pm.

About 15 minutes from downtown, some old cement quarries have been converted into several lakes at Fort Whyte Centre, and now serve as an environmental educational facility. The freshwater aquarium has many local Manitoba specimens, like the northern pike and walleye. There are self-guided nature trails, waterfowl gardens, and an interpretive center and gift shop.

A Historic District

Across the river in **St. Boniface,** a street becomes a *rue* and a hello becomes *bonjour.* Here you'll find the largest French-speaking community in western Canada, dating from 1783 when Pierre Gaultier de Varennes established Fort Rouge at the junction of the Red and Assiniboine rivers. The junction became the center of a thriving fur trade for the North West Company, which rivaled and challenged the Hudson's Bay Company. A basilica built in 1819 was dedicated to Boniface, and in 1846 four Grey Nuns arrived and began their ministry.

The original basilica was replaced in 1908 by a beautiful building that was destroyed by fire in 1968. The massive Gothic arches remain, and cradled within the shell of the old building is the new basilica, built in 1972. In front of the cathedral, the cemetery is the resting place of Louis Riel, whose grave is marked by a replica of a Red River cart. Riel, leader of the Métis uprising and president of the provincial government formed from 1869 to 1870, tried to prevent the transfer of the Red River settlement to Canada. For walking tours of St. Boniface, call the chamber of commerce at ☎ **204/235-1406.**

Parks & Gardens

Comprising 393 acres for playing, picnicking, or biking, **Assiniboine Park,** at 2355 Corydon Ave. (☎ **204/986-3050**), contains a miniature railway, a duck pond, an English garden (which opens in June), and a conservatory. During the winter there's skating on the pond and tobogganing. The park also contains a 98-acre **zoo** (see "Especially for Kids," below). Art lovers will also want to visit the **studio of Leo Mol** (☎ 204/986-6531) and see the sculpture garden containing his works. The park is open daily dawn to dusk.

Kildonan Park is quite delightful, with landscaped gardens, picnic spots, biking paths, outdoor swimming, and wading pools, as well as a restaurant and dining room overlooking a small artificial lake. Also look for the Witch's House from *Hansel and Gretel* in the park. Rainbow Stage productions are held here in July and August.

CRUISES & A STEAM-TRAIN EXCURSION

During summer, the cruise ships **MS *River Rouge*** and **MS *Paddlewheel Queen*** depart from their dock at Water and Gilroy at the foot of the Provencher Bridge on a variety of cruises, including a sunset dinner-dance cruise beginning at 7pm and a moonlight version on weekends that leaves at 10pm. Both cost C$12 (US$9). Two-hour sightseeing trips costing C$11 (US$8) depart at 2pm and provide fine views of the city from the Red and Assiniboine rivers. Occasionally the company offers longer cruises to Lake Winnipeg. For details, call ☎ 204/942-4500.

A 1900 steam-era train, the ***Prairie Dog Central,*** takes visitors on a 2-hour, 58-kilometer (36-mile) round-trip from Winnipeg north on the Oak Point line. En route you really get a feel for the prairie and what the late-19th-century immigrants might have seen when they arrived. The train operates weekends June to September. Adults pay C$13 (US$9); seniors and youths 12 to 17, C$11 (US$8); children 2 to 11, C$7 (US$5). For details, contact the **Vintage Locomotive Society** (☎ 204/832-5259).

ESPECIALLY FOR KIDS

At the Forks, there's a **Children's Museum** (☎ 204/956-1888), specially designed with participatory exhibits for 2- to 13-year-olds. At Under the Big Top they can run away to the circus and devise a show of their very own; and in the TV studio they can create their own television shows, as performers or as technicians. Admission is C$4 (US$2.85) per person; children 2 and under are free. Open Monday to Thursday from 9am to 5pm, Friday from 9am to 8:30pm, Saturday from 11am to 8pm, and Sunday from 11am to 5pm.

Assiniboine Park, at 2355 Corydon Ave. (☎ 204/986-6921), is a great place to picnic or play. Its top attraction, however, is the 98-acre **zoo** where the animals— bear, tiger, zebra, flamingo, bison, elk, and deer—are kept in as natural an environment as possible. Some exotic species on display include snow leopards, ruffed lemurs, and Irkutsk lynx. Many spectacular birds live and breed in the Tropical House. A special "Discovery Centre" for children is fun. From March to October, admission is C$3 (US$2.15) for adults, C$2.75 (US$1.95) for seniors, C$1.50 (US$1.05) for youths 13 to 17, and C$1 (US70¢) for children 2 to 12; from November to February it's C$1 (US70¢) for everyone. It's free for children under 2 year-round. The park is open daily dawn to dusk, the zoo daily from 10am to dusk. To get here, take Portage Avenue west, exit onto Route 90 South, and then turn right onto Corydon.

Darkzone, 230 Osborne St. (☎ 204/287-8710) is the hippest game at the moment for kids and adults; an advanced laser game in which as many as 30 players and three teams compete against each other in trying to deactivate the opposing players and their bases using a phaser and computerized vest. Open Monday to Thursday from 4pm to midnight, Friday from 4pm to 1am, Saturday from 10am to 1am, and Sunday from 10am to 10pm. Admission is C$5 (US$3.55), or C$14 (US$10) for three games.

Kids love the thrills at **Fun Mountain Water Slide Park,** 6 kilometers (4 miles) or so east of the mint on Highway 1 East (☎ 204/255-3910). There are 10 slides, as well as rides, including bumper boats, a giant hot tub, and a kids' playground with a wading pool. All-day admission costs C$11 (US$8) for adults and C$8.50 (US$6) for children 4 to 12; children under 4 are free. Open June to August daily from 10am to 8pm, weather permitting.

ACCOMMODATIONS

EXPENSIVE

Crowne Plaza, Winnipeg Downtown. 350 St. Mary's Ave., Winnipeg, MB, R3C 3J2. ☎ 204/942-0551. Fax 204/943-8702. 389 rms. A/C MINIBAR TV TEL. C$150 (US$107) double. Children under 18 stay free in parents' rm. Weekend packages available. AE, DC, DISC, ER, MC, V. Parking C$7.75 (US$6).

The 17-story Holiday Inn Crowne Plaza is right downtown and connected by a sky-walk to the Convention Centre. The pleasantly decorated rooms feature the usual amenities plus two telephones with fax modem capacity, coffeemakers, and irons/ironing boards. Poolside rooms are a couple of dollars more than standard rooms, while club-floor rooms include such extras as breakfast and evening hors d'oeuvres, overnight shoe-shine and in-room pants pressers, and heated tiles in the bathrooms.

Dining/Entertainment: There's the Elephant and Castle pub for all-day dining, and the Chef's Table for fine contemporary cuisine. There's also a piano bar, Tickers Lounge.

Services: 24-hour room service, laundry/valet.

Facilities: There's a skylit indoor pool plus an outdoor pool, both attractively designed with potted plants, terraces, and adjacent exercise facilities.

Delta Winnipeg. 288 Portage Ave. (at Smith St.), Winnipeg, MB, R3C 0B8. ☎ 800/268-1133 or 204/956-0410. Fax 204/947-1129. 272 rms. A/C MINIBAR TV TEL. Weekdays C$194 (US$139) double. Weekend packages available. AE, DC, ER, MC, V. Parking C$7 (US$5).

Rooms here occupy floors 15 to 29. All offer good views of the city and are well equipped, with hair dryers and coffeemakers. It's right next door to a promenade accessing the 300-plus shops in Eaton Place and Portage Place. A business lounge is on the P-level.

Dining/Entertainment: The candlelit, oak-paneled Signature's offers fine dining and piano entertainment. On the main floor is Tillie's, where sports events are shown on a big-screen TV.

Services: 24-hour room service.

Facilities: Indoor pool with an outdoor deck, whirlpool, sauna, exercise room, twin cinemas, and a free Children's Creative Centre (supervised on weekends) where kids can enjoy games, toys, and crafts activities.

The Lombard. 2 Lombard Place, Winnipeg, MB, R3B 0Y3. ☎ 800/228-3000 or 204/957-1350. Fax 204/949-1486. 350 rms. A/C MINIBAR TV TEL. C$159 (US$113) double. Weekend packages available. AE, DC, ER, MC, V. Parking C$7.50 (US$5).

Right at the corner of Portage and Main rises the 21-story white concrete Canadian Pacific Hotel, The Lombard, a few minutes' walk from the Manitoba Centennial Centre. Its rooms are furnished with white colonial-style pieces and the usual amenities, plus such extras as three phones, hair dryers, and iron/ironing boards.

Dining: The Velvet Glove features luxurious dining amid gilt-framed portraits, wood paneling, and brass torchères. You might choose an entree such as pepper-roasted wild boar with apple turnip compote or a dish featuring Canada's best—roast cedar-plank salmon and onion marmalade. Prices range from C$16 to C$25 (US$11 to US$18). Chocolate cherries, served with your coffee, are just part of the impeccable service, and if you want that C$100-plus (US$71-plus) bottle of wine, it's available. The self-serve Cafe Express offers deli sandwiches and hot specials.

Services: Concierge, 24-hour room service, laundry/valet, free local phone calls.

Facilities: Indoor pool, whirlpool, and sauna on the 21st floor; plus a fitness center.

MODERATE

Charterhouse. York and Hargrave sts., Winnipeg, MB, R3C 0N9. ☎ **800/782-0175** or 204/942-0101. Fax 204/956-0665. 86 rms. A/C TV TEL. C$125–C$135 (US$89–US$96) double. Extra person C$10 (US$7). Children under 16 stay free in parents' rm. Packages available. AE, CB, DC, DISC, MC, V. Free parking.

Right downtown, a block from the Convention Centre, the Charterhouse offers attractively decorated rooms. Top-floor rooms are designed for the business traveler, featuring ergonomically designed furniture, fax/Internet access, coffeemakers, and hair dryers. The other rooms are attractively decorated and have modern amenities including voice mail. About half have balconies. There's an outdoor swimming pool and a deck/patio.

The Rib Room is well known locally for good prime rib, ribs, steaks, and seafood, with main courses from C$13 to C$24 (US$9 to US$17). There's a coffee shop, too.

✪ **Place Louis Riel All-Suite Hotel.** 190 Smith St. (at St. Mary's), Winnipeg, MB, R3C 1J8. ☎ **204/947-6961.** Fax 204/947-3029. 277 rms. A/C TV TEL. C$100–C$110 (US$71–US$79) double. Extra person C$10 (US$7). Children under 16 stay free in parents' rm. Weekend package available. AE, DC, MC, V. Parking C$4 (US$2.85).

Right in the heart of downtown Winnipeg is a bargain that shouldn't be passed up. At the Place Louis Riel All-Suite Hotel you can stay in a studio (with a sleeping/living area partitioned from the kitchen) or a beautifully furnished one- or two-bedroom suite. All units come with a fully equipped kitchen (including a microwave and coffeemaker) and dining area. For convenience, a Laundromat, grocery store, and restaurant and lounge are located on the ground floor of the 23-floor building.

Ramada Marlborough Winnipeg. 331 Smith St. (at Portage), Winnipeg, MB, R3B 2G9. ☎ **800/667-7666** or 204/942-6411. Fax 204/942-2017. 148 rms. A/C TV TEL. C$105 (US$75) double. Children under 18 stay free in parents' rm. Special weekend (Fri–Sun) rates available. AE, DC, ER, MC, V. Free parking.

This isn't your average Ramada. Originally built in 1914, the Marlborough retains its vaulted ceilings, stained-glass windows, and Victorian Gothic exterior, but now offers all modern amenities, including a fine dining room, Victor's. There's also a coffee shop and club with live entertainment on weekends.

INEXPENSIVE

For reliable, clean, and attractively decorated rooms, the **Comfort Inn by Journey's End,** 3109 Pembina Hwy. (☎ **204/269-7390**), is hard to beat. Doubles are C$78 to C$84 (US$56 to US$60). Local phone calls are free.

Gordon Downtowner. 330 Kennedy St., Winnipeg, MB, R3B 2M6. ☎ **204/943-5581.** Fax 204/338-4348. 40 rms. A/C TV TEL. C$57 (US$41) double. Extra person C$7 (US$5). Children under 16 stay free in parents' rm. AE, DC, ER, MC, V.

Probably the best budget hotel downtown is the Gordon Downtowner, part of Portage Place. The rooms have all been renovated recently and have touches such as extra phones in the bathrooms. Amenities include a pub and a comfortable restaurant (open from 7am to 9pm).

DINING

EXPENSIVE

✪ **Le Beaujolais.** 131 Provencher Blvd. (at Tache), in St. Boniface. ☎ **204/237-6276.** Reservations recommended. Main courses C$20–C$27 (US$14–US$19). AE, ER, MC, V. Mon–Fri

11:30am–2:30pm; daily from 5pm to variable closing times, depending on the number of reservations. FRENCH.

Le Beaujolais is a comfortable place serving such traditional dishes as roast duck with cassis, veal tenderloin with Roquefort and leek sauce, and rack of lamb Niçoise (made with ratatouille). At night when candles are lit, the room, which features etched glass and glass-brick partitions, takes on a romantic air. Roasted ostrich is also a specialty. It's raised locally and served with portobello mushroom and a balsamic vinegar glaze.

Restaurant Dubrovnik. 390 Assiniboine Ave. ☎ **204/944-0594.** Reservations recommended. Main courses C$16–C$25 (US$11–US$18). AE, MC, V. Mon–Sat 11am–2pm; daily 5–11pm. CONTINENTAL.

Restaurant Dubrovnik offers a romantic setting for fine continental cuisine and Eastern European specialties. It occupies a beautiful Victorian brick town house with working fireplaces, leaded-glass windows, and an enclosed veranda. Each dining area is decorated tastefully with a few plants and colorful gusle (beautifully carved musical instruments, often inlaid with mother-of-pearl).

Start with the traditional Russian borscht, the wild-game pâté, or the Caribbean shrimp cocktail flavored with tomato, lemon, and cognac; followed by Atlantic salmon seared with a vinaigrette of basil, garlic, olive oil, and fresh dill; chicken breast with caramelized cranberries; or crisp roasted duck with a hoisin-and-plum glaze. Finish with a coffee Dubrovnik (sljivovica, kruskovac bitters, coffee, whipped cream, and chopped walnuts).

MODERATE

✪ **Amici.** 326 Broadway. ☎ **204/943-4997.** Reservations recommended. Main courses C$14–C$28 (US$10–US$20). AE, DC, ER, MC, V. Mon–Fri 11:30am–2:30pm; Mon–Sat 5–11pm. CONTINENTAL/ITALIAN.

The atmosphere at Amici is plush and comfortable and the northern Italian cuisine is tops in the city. You have your choice of 12 or more pastas, with selections like *fettucine alla boscaiola* (with wild mushrooms, veal, and lingonberries), or spaghetti alla carbonara. Or you can have such richly flavored meat and fish dishes as venison with wild mushrooms and potato gnocchi, lamb loin with spinach and mushrooms wrapped in puff pastry, medaillons of beef with a Barolo wine sauce, or sea bass in saffron broth with Mediterranean vegetables.

✪ **Bistro Dansk.** 63 Sherbrook St. ☎ **204/775-5662.** Reservations recommended. Main courses C$7.50–C$14 (US$5–US$10). AE, V. Mon–Sat 11am–3pm; Mon–Sat 5–9:30pm. DANISH.

In this warm chalet-style bistro, bright-red, gate-back chairs complement the wooden tables and raffia place mats. Main courses include seven superlative Danish specialties, such as *frikadeller* (Danish meat patties, made from ground veal and pork, served with red cabbage and potato salad), and *aeggekage* (a Danish omelet with bacon, garnished with tomato and green onions, served with home-baked Danish bread). At lunchtime, specialties include nine or so open-face sandwiches, served on homemade rye or white bread, most priced from C$3 to C$6.50 (US$2.15 to US$4.65).

Old Swiss Inn. 207 Edmonton St. ☎ **204/942-7725.** Reservations recommended. Main courses C$12–C$27 (US$9–US$19). AE, DC, ER, MC, V. Mon–Fri 11:30am–2:30pm; Mon–Sat 5–9:30pm. SWISS.

The Old Swiss Inn lives up to its name with unpretentious alpine warmth, wood paneling, pictures of mountain scenery, and Swiss specialties. At dinner, you might start with Swiss onion soup or cheese fondue and follow with veal Zurich (with white wine and mushrooms) accompanied by delicious Swiss rösti potatoes, or the house specialty, fondue bourguignonne. At lunchtime you can have Wiener schnitzel, Bratwurst mit Rösti (Swiss fried potatoes), and more.

Red Lantern. 302 Hamel Ave., St. Boniface. ☎ **204/233-4841.** Reservations recommended. Main courses C$13–C$28 (US$9–US$20). AE, ER, MC, V. Mon–Fri 11:30am–2pm; Mon–Thurs 5–9pm, Fri–Sat 5–10pm. CONTINENTAL.

A red lantern stands outside the small house occupied by this restaurant. Inside, there's a cozy dining room. The food is excellent, nicely presented, graciously served, and very reasonably priced. French background music adds to the atmosphere. Among the specialties are a breast of chicken stuffed with Brie, spinach and carrots served with thyme cream sauce, plus veal Oscar, trout meunière, steak Madagascar (with red wine, green peppercorn, and tomato demi-glace), and more.

INEXPENSIVE

D' 8 Schtove. 1842 Pembina Hwy. ☎ **204/275-2294.** Main courses C$9–C$15 (US$6–US$11). AE, DC, ER, MC, V. Mon–Sat 8am–11pm, Sun 9am–11pm. MENNONITE.

For some good, honest Mennonite cuisine, settle into this large dining room decorated with brass and wood, and order one of the borschts—*komst borscht* (made with cabbage sausages and chicken) or *somma borscht* (made primarily with potato). Follow with *jebackte rebspaa* (pork ribs baked in tomato sauce), *holupche* (cabbage rolls), beef stroganoff, slices of smoked farmer sausage in sweet-and-sour sauce, or the *wrenikje,* more commonly known as pirogies. Top it all off with rhubarb or apple strudel.

There's another location at 103–1277 Henderson Hwy. (☎ **204/334-1200**).

WINNIPEG AFTER DARK

THE PERFORMING ARTS The **Manitoba Centennial Centre,** 555 Main St. (☎ 204/956-1360), is a complex that includes the Centennial Concert Hall (home to the Royal Winnipeg Ballet, the Winnipeg Symphony, and the Manitoba Opera), the Manitoba Theatre Centre, the Warehouse Theatre, and the Playhouse Theatre.

Other spaces offering frequent concerts and performances include the **Winnipeg Art Gallery** (☎ 204/786-6641), which often features blues/jazz, chamber music, and contemporary music groups; the **Pantages Playhouse Theatre,** 180 Market Ave. (☎ 204/986-3003); and the **Convention Centre,** 375 York Ave. (☎ 204/956-1720), for popular, folk, and light orchestral musical concerts.

The world-renowned ✪ **Royal Winnipeg Ballet,** 380 Graham Ave., at Edmonton Street (☎ 204/956-0183, or 204/956-2792 for the box office), was founded in 1939 by two British immigrant ballet teachers, making it North America's second-oldest ballet company (after San Francisco's). By 1949, it was a professional troupe and in 1953 was granted a royal charter. Today its repertoire includes both contemporary and classical works, such as Ashton's *Thais, Giselle,* and *The Sleeping Beauty.* The company performs at the Centennial Concert Hall, usually for a 2-week period in October, November, December, March, and May. Tickets are C$8 to C$42 (US$6 to US$30), with a 20% discount for students and senior citizens and a 50% discount for children 12 and under.

Established in 1947, the **Winnipeg Symphony Orchestra,** 555 Main St. (☎ 204/949-3950, or 204/949-3976 for the box office), made its debut in 1978 at Carnegie Hall in New York City. The orchestra's prestige, and the genuinely superb acoustics of the Centennial Concert Hall have attracted such guest artists as Itzhak Perlman, Isaac Stern, Tracey Dahl, and Maureen Forrester. The season usually runs from September to mid-May. Tickets are C$12 to C$40 (US$9 to US$29).

The **Manitoba Opera,** Box 31027, Portage Place, 393 Portage Ave. (☎ 204/ 942-7479, or 204/957-7842 for the box office), features a season of three operas each year at the Centennial Concert Hall with performances in November, February, and April. Recent seasons have included productions of *Turandot* and *Rigoletto.* English subtitles are used. Tickets begin at C$12 (US$9).

THEATER   You can enjoy theater in the park at **Rainbow Stage,** 2021 Main St. in Kildonan Park (☎ 204/784-1281), Canada's largest and oldest continuously operating outdoor theater. The stage presents two musical classics running about 3 weeks each during July and August. Located on the banks of the Red River, Rainbow is easily accessible by bus or car. For tickets, which cost from C$10 to C$22.50 (US$7 to US$16), write Rainbow Stage, 201-320 Sherbrook St., Winnipeg, MB, R3B 2W6.

The **MTC Warehouse,** at 140 Rupert Ave. at Lily (☎ 204/942-6537), presents more cutting-edge, controversial plays in an intimate 300-seat theater. Its four-play season runs from mid-October to mid-May. Tickets range from C$25 to C$35 (US$18 to US$25).

Since its founding by Tom Hendry and John Hirsch, the **Manitoba Theatre Centre,** 174 Market Ave. (☎ 204/942-6537), has been dedicated to producing good serious theater, and this is indeed one of Canada's best regional companies. A recent season's offerings included *Hamlet* starring Keanu Reeves. The season usually features six productions and runs from October to April. Tickets are C$20 to C$50 (US$14 to US$36).

GAMBLING   On the seventh floor of the Hotel Fort Garry, visitors can play blackjack, baccarat, roulette, Caribbean poker, Super Pan 9, or pump coins into more than 200 slot machines at the **Crystal Casino,** 222 Broadway Ave. (☎ 204/957-2600). This intimate, European-style casino accommodates about 380 players. Reservations are taken. Open Monday to Saturday from 10am to 3am and Sunday from noon to 3am. The dress code is smart casual (18 years and over only).

SIDE TRIPS FROM WINNIPEG

LOWER FORT GARRY NATIONAL HISTORIC PARK   The oldest intact stone fur-trading post in North America is **Lower Fort Garry** (☎ 204/785-6050), only 32 kilometers (20 miles) north of Winnipeg on Highway 9. Built in the 1830s, Lower Fort Garry was an important Hudson's Bay Company transshipment and provisioning post. Within the walls of the compound are the governor's residence; several warehouses, including the fur loft; and the Men's House, where male employees of the company lived. Outside the compound are company buildings— a blacksmith's shop, the farm manager's home, and so on. The fort is staffed by costumed volunteers who make candles and soap, forge horseshoes, locks, and bolts, and demonstrate the ways of life of the 1850s. In a lean-to beside the fur-loft building stands an original York boat; hundreds of these once traveled the waterways from Hudson Bay to the Rockies and from the Red River to the Arctic carrying furs and trading goods.

The site is open daily from 10am to 6pm from mid-May to Labour Day. Adults pay C$5.50 (US$3.95) for admission; seniors, C$3.75 (US$2.70); children ages 6 to 16, C$2.75 (US$1.95); children under 5 are free.

STEINBACH MENNONITE HERITAGE VILLAGE   About 48 kilometers (30 miles) outside Winnipeg is the Steinbach Mennonite Heritage Village, located 2.4 kilometers (1¹/₂ miles) north of Steinbach on Highway 12 (☎ 204/326-9661). This 40-acre museum complex is worth a detour. Between 1874 and 1880, about

7,000 Mennonites migrated here from the Ukraine, establishing settlements like Kleefeld, Steinbach, Blumenort, and others. After World War I, many moved on to Mexico and Uruguay when Manitoba closed all unregistered schools between 1922 and 1926, but they were replaced by another surge of emigrants fleeing the Russian Revolution. Their community life is portrayed here in a complex of about 20 buildings. In the museum building, dioramas display daily life and community artifacts, such as woodworking and sewing tools, sausage makers, clothes, medicines, and furnishings. Elsewhere in the complex, visitors can view the windmill grinding grain, ride in an ox-drawn wagon, watch the blacksmith at work, or view any number of homes, agricultural machines, and more.

The restaurant serves Mennonite food—a full meal of borscht, thick-sliced homemade brown bread, coleslaw, pirogies, and sausage, plus rhubarb crumble, at very reasonable prices.

The village is open Monday to Saturday: May from 10am to 5pm; June, July, and August from 10am to 7pm; and September from 10am to 5pm. On Sunday the gates don't open until noon. From October to April the museum is open Monday to Friday from 10am to 4pm. Admission is C$4 (US$2.85) for adults, C$3 (US$2.15) for seniors, and C$2.50 (US$1.80) for students grades 1 through 12.

3 Manitoba's Eastern Border: Whiteshell & Atikaki Provincial Parks

Less than a 2-hour drive east of Winnipeg (144km/90 miles) lies a network of a dozen rivers and more than 200 lakes in the 2,590-square-kilometer (1,000-sq.-mile) ✪ **Whiteshell Provincial Park** (☎ 204/369-5232). Among the park's natural features are Rainbow and Whitemouth Falls; a lovely lily pond west of Caddy Lake; West Hawk Lake, Manitoba's deepest lake, which was created by a meteorite; and a goose sanctuary (best seen from mid-May to July when the goslings are about). Visitors can also view petroforms, stone arrangements fashioned by an Algonquin-speaking people to communicate with the spirits. The park is busiest in summer and spectacular in fall and winter. In fall you can witness an ancient ritual—the Indians harvesting wild rice. One person poles a canoe through the rice field while another bends the stalks into the canoe and knocks the ripe grains off with a picking stick.

During July and August the **Manitoba Naturalists Society,** headquartered at 401–63 Albert St. in Winnipeg (☎ 204/943-9029), operates wilderness programs and other workshops at their cabin on Lake Mantario. There are six self-guided trails plus several short trails that can be completed in less than 2 hours. For serious backpackers, the **Mantario Trail** is a 3- to 6-day hike over 60 kilometers (37 miles) of rugged terrain. There are also all-terrain biking trails. You can canoe the Frances Lake route, which covers 18 kilometers (11 miles) of pleasant paddling with 12 beaver-dam hauls and three portages and takes about 6 hours. There's swimming at Falcon Beach, scuba diving in West Hawk Lake, plus places to sail, windsurf, water-ski, and fish.

Horseback riding is offered at **Falcon Beach Riding Stables** (☎ 204/349-2410). In winter there's downhill skiing, cross-country skiing, snowmobiling, snowshoeing, and skating.

Within the park, **Falcon Lake** is one of Canada's most modern recreational developments, featuring tennis courts, an 18-hole par-72 golf course, hiking trails, horseback riding, fishing, canoeing and skiing. Most park resorts and lodges charge from C$70 to C$110 (US$50 to US$79) double, or C$450 to C$750 (US$321 to US$536) per week for a cabin. Camping facilities abound. For more information, contact the number above or **Travel Manitoba,** Dept. SV8, 155 Carlton St.,

Winnipeg, MB, R3C 3H8 (☎ **800/665-0040,** ext. SV8 or 204/945-3777, ext. SV8).

4 Lake Winnipeg

This 425-kilometer-long (264-mile-long) lake is the continent's seventh largest, and its shores shelter some interesting communities and attractive natural areas. At the lake's southern end, **Grand Beach Provincial Park** (☎ **204/754-2212**) has white-sand beaches backed by 30-foot-high dunes in some places. This is a good place to swim, windsurf, and fish. There are three self-guided nature trails. Campsites are available in summer only.

About 97 kilometers (60 miles) north of Winnipeg, on the western shore, the farm-ing and fishing community of **Gimli** is the hub of Icelandic culture in Manitoba. Established a century ago as the capital of New Iceland, it had its own government, school, and newspapers for many years. It still celebrates an Icelandic festival on the first long weekend in August.

Hecla Island, 185 kilometers (110 miles) northeast of Winnipeg, was once a part of the Republic of New Iceland and was, until recently, home to a small Icelandic-Canadian farming and fishing community. Today it's the site of **Hecla/Grindstone Provincial Park,** Box 70, Riverton, MB, R0C 2R0 (☎ **204/378-2945**). Open year-round, this is an excellent place to hike (with five short trails), golf, fish, camp, bird watch, canoe, swim, windsurf, play tennis (two courts), hunt, cross-country ski, snow-shoe, or go snowmobiling and tobogganing. Photographers and wildlife enthusiasts appreciate the park's wildlife-viewing tower and the **Grassy Narrow Marsh,** which shelters many species of waterfowl. There's a campground and 15 cabins available (for reservations call **Destinet** at ☎ **888/482-2267**), plus the Gull Harbour resort (listed below).

ACCOMMODATIONS IN GULL HARBOUR

Gull Harbour Resort Hotel. Box 1000, Riverton, MB, R0C 2R0. ☎ **204/475-2354.** Fax 204/279-2000. 93 rms. A/C TV TEL. C$100 (US$71) double. Extra person C$10 (US$7). Children under 18 stay free in parents' rm. Watch for specials year-round. AE, MC, V.

This is an ideal place to take the family. Though it boasts first-class resort facilities, it also reflects a concern for the environment. Beaches and woods have been left intact.

Facilities include an indoor pool, a whirlpool, and a sauna; badminton, volleyball; a game room with pool table, an 18-hole golf course, a putting green, minigolf, two tennis courts, skating rink, shuffleboard, bike rentals, and more.

5 West Along the Trans-Canada Highway to Spruce Woods Provincial Park & Brandon

About 67 kilometers (40 miles) west of Portage la Prairie, before reaching Carberry, turn south on Highway 5 to **Spruce Woods Provincial Park,** Box 900, Carberry, MB, R0K 0H0 (☎ **204/827-2543** in summer or 204/834-3223 otherwise). The park's unique and most fragile feature is Spirit Sands, large stretches of open sand that are the remains of the once wide Assiniboine Delta. Only a few hardy creatures such as the Bembix wasp and one type of wolf spider live here. The rest of the park is forest and prairie grasslands inhabited by herds of wapiti (elk).

There's camping at Kiche Manitou as well as at hike-in locations. The park is on the Assiniboine River canoe route, which starts in Brandon and ends north of

Holland. Canoes can be rented at Pine Fort IV in the park. The park's longest trail is the 40-kilometer (25-mile) Epinette Trail, but its most fascinating is the Spirit Sands/Devils Punch Bowl, accessible from Highway 5. It loops through the Dunes and leads to the Devils Punch Bowl, which was carved by underground streams. There are also bike and mountain-bike trails; swimming at the campground beach; and in winter, there's cross-country skiing, skating, tobogganing, and snowmobiling.

Brandon is Manitoba's second-largest city, with a population of 40,000. This university town features the Art Gallery of Southwestern Manitoba; the B. J. Hales Museum, with mounted specimens of birds and mammals; plus interesting tours of the Agriculture and Agri Food Research Centre. During summer, families flock to the **Thunder Mountain Water Slide,** 5 miles west of Brandon on the Trans-Canada Highway.

6 Riding Mountain National Park & Duck Mountain Provincial Park

RIDING MOUNTAIN NATIONAL PARK

About 248 kilometers (155 miles) northwest of Winnipeg, Riding Mountain National Park, Wasagaming, MB, R0J 2H0 (☎ **204/848-7275**), is set in the highlands atop a giant wooded escarpment sheltering more than 260 species of birds, plus moose, wolf, coyote, lynx, beaver, black bear, and a bison herd at Lake Audy.

The park has more than 400 kilometers (248 miles) of **hiking trails.** Twenty are easily accessible, short, and easy to moderate in difficulty; another 20 are long backcountry trails. Call the number above for more information. Many trails can be ridden on mountain bike and horseback. Bikes can be rented in Wasagaming. **Triangle Ranch,** P.O. Box 275, Onanole (☎ **204/848-2802**), offers 1-hour and day rides for C$15 and C$60 (US$24 and US$97), respectively.

Canoes and other boats can be rented at **Clear Lake Marina.** As for **fishing,** northern pike is the main game fish and specimens up to 30 pounds have been taken from Clear Lake. Rainbow and brook trout populate Lake Katherine and Deep Lake. The park also has one of the province's best **golf courses;** greens fees are C$28 (US$20). In winter there's **cross-country and downhill skiing** at Mount Agassiz on the east side of the park plus ice fishing in Clear Lake.

The **visitor center** is open daily in the summer from 9am to 9pm. For information, call or write: Superintendent, Riding Mountain National Park, Wasagaming, MB, R0J 2H0 (☎ **204/848-7275**). The park is easily accessed from Brandon, about 95 kilometers (57 miles) north along Highway 10. Entry to the park is C$3.25 (US$2.30) per adult and C$7.50 (US$5) for families; multiday passes are also available.

CAMPING & ACCOMMODATIONS

At the Shawenequanape Kipi-Che-Win (Southquill Camp), you can stay in a traditional teepee for C$50 (US$36) a night double and learn about the traditional ceremonies, arts, crafts, and culture of the Anishinabe. Each interpretive program costs C$5 (US$3.55). For information, contact Kathy Boulanger or Richard Gaywish, **Shawenequanape Camp and Cultural Tours,** 704–167 Lombard Ave, Winnipeg, MB, R3B 0V3 (☎ **204/925-2030**). Summer only.

In Wasagaming, you can stay at six park **campgrounds** or in motel and cabin accommodations for C$45 to C$130 (US$32 to US$93) double. Wasagaming also has six tennis courts, lawn-bowling greens, a children's playground, and a log-cabin movie theater in the Wasagaming Visitor Centre beside Clear Lake. There's also a dance hall, picnic areas with stoves, and a band shell down by the lake for Sunday-afternoon concerts. At the lake itself you can rent boats and swim at the main beach.

Wasagaming Campground has more than 500 sites, most of which are unserviced. Facilities include showers and toilets, kitchen shelters, and a sewage-disposal station nearby. Rates range from C$10.50 to C$13.95 (US$8 to US$10) unserviced, to C$19.50 (US$14) for full service. Other outlying campgrounds (93 sites) are at **Moon Lake, Lake Audy, Whirlpool,** and **Deep Lake.** None of these is serviced. For reservations, call ☎ **800/707-8480.** Outlying campgrounds are C$7 (US$5), site only.

Elkhorn Resort. Clear Lake, MB, R0J 2H0. ☎ **204/848-2802.** Fax 204/848-2109. 57 rms. A/C TV TEL. Lodge rm C$113–C$123 (US$81–US$88) double, C$133 (US$95) double with fireplace. Extra person C$15 (US$11). Children under 17 stay free in parents' rm. Lower off-season rates available. Chalets from C$230 (US$164) per night or C$1,200 (US$857) per week; less off-season (Mar to mid-May and mid-Oct to mid-Dec). AE, DC, ER, MC, V.

This year-round lodge is just on the edge of Wasagaming with easy access to Riding Mountain, overlooking quiet fields and forest. The rooms are large, comfortable, and nicely appointed with modern pine furnishings; some have fireplaces and private balconies. At the ranch's common room, you can join a game of bridge or cribbage in the evening. There's also an indoor pool, exercise room, game room with pool, and a 9-hole golf course. In summer, facilities include a riding stable, while in winter, pleasures include sleigh rides, cross-country skiing, outdoor skating, and tobogganing. Also on the property are several fully equipped two- and three-bedroom chalets (with fireplace, fire extinguisher, toaster, dishwasher, microwave, and balcony with barbecue) designed after Quonsets.

DUCK MOUNTAIN PROVINCIAL PARK

Northwest of Riding Mountain via Highway 10, off Route 367, Duck Mountain Provincial Park (no phone) is popular for fishing, camping, boating, hiking, horseback riding, and biking. **Baldy Mountain,** near the park's southeast entrance, is the province's highest point at 2,727 feet. **East Blue Lake** is so clear that the bottom is visible at 30 to 40 feet.

For accommodations in Duck Mountain, the place to stay is **Wellman Lake Lodge and Outfitters,** Box 249, Minitonas, MB, R0L 1G0 (☎ **204/525-4422**), which has cabins. Some are rustic, with outdoor washrooms and cold water only, but with fridges, ovens, and electricity, while others are more modern with full bath and fully equipped kitchenettes, plus a covered deck with picnic table. Two have fireplace or pellet stove. Full services for anglers and hunters are offered. There's also a beach for swimming.

7 Exploring the Far North & Churchill, the World's Polar-Bear Capital

The best way to explore the north is aboard **VIA Rail's** *Hudson Bay* on a 2-night, 1-day trip from Winnipeg to Churchill, via **The Pas,** a mecca for fishing enthusiasts, and the mining community of Thompson. No other land route has yet penetrated this remote region, which is covered with lakes, forests, and frozen tundra. The train leaves Winnipeg at about 10pm and arrives 34 hours later in Churchill. A round-trip ticket including sleeping berth costs C$1,189 (US$844) for two in high season (May 15 to October 15), C$713 (US$506) at other times. For more information, contact your travel agent or VIA Rail (☎ **800/561-3949**).

You can also fly into Churchill on **Canadian Airlines** (☎ **800/426-7000**).

If you're up this way in February, The Pas hosts the annual ✪ **Northern Trapper's Festival,** with world-championship dogsled races, ice fishing, beer fests, moose calling, and more. It's usually held the third week in February. Call ☎ **204/623-2912** for information.

Churchill is the polar-bear capital of the world. To the south and east of the city lies one of the largest known polar-bear maternity denning sites in the world. The area was placed under government protection in 1996 when the **Wapusk National Park** was established. Visit October to early November to see these awesome creatures. The area is also a vital habitat for hundreds of thousands of waterfowl and shorebirds. More than 200 species, including the rare Ross Gull, nest or pass through on their annual migration. In summer, white beluga whales frolic in the mouth of the Churchill River and seals and caribou can be sighted along the coast. You can also see the aurora borealis from here. For additional information, contact **Parks Canada,** Box 127 Churchill, MB, R0B 0E0 (☎ **204/675-8863**).

Churchill, population 1,100, is also one of the world's largest grain-exporting terminals in the world, and grain elevators dominate its skyline. You can watch the grain being unloaded from boxcars onto ships—perhaps 25 million bushels of wheat and barley clear the port in only 12 to 14 weeks of frantic nonstop operation. You can also take a boat ride to **Fort Prince of Wales** (☎ **204/675-8863**), a large, partially restored stone fort that's open in July and August. Construction started in 1730 by the Hudson's Bay Company and took 40 years. Yet after all that effort, Governor Samuel Hearne and 39 clerks and tradesmen surrendered the fort to the French without resistance in 1782, when faced with a possible attack by three French ships. From here you can observe beluga whales. Cape Merry at the mouth of the Churchill River is also an excellent vantage point for observing beluga whales and is a must for birders (it's open continuously June to August). The town's Visitor Centre is open daily from mid-May to mid-November, weekdays-only otherwise. For Churchill information, contact the **Churchill Chamber of Commerce,** Box 176, Churchill, MB, R0B 0E0 (☎ **888/389-2327**).

In town, the **Eskimo Museum,** 242 Laverendrye St., Box 10 (☎ **204/675-2030**), has a collection of fine Inuit carvings and artifacts.

Some 240 kilometers (149 miles) southeast of Churchill, the very remote **York Factory National Historic Site** was established by the Hudson's Bay Company in 1682 as a fur-trading post. It operated for nearly 2 centuries until it was abandoned in 1957. Several generations of structures have been built near or on the site. The current site referred to as York Factory III was developed after 1788. The depot building is the oldest wood structure still standing on permafrost; its unattached walls and floors allow for the buckling of the earth due to frost heaves. Across Sloop Creek are the remains of a powder magazine and a cemetery with headstones dating back to the 1700s. Guided tours are C$5 (US$3.55). The site is staffed only from June to September. Access is limited to charter planes or by canoe down the Hayes River. For more information on these sites, contact **Parks Canada,** Box 127, Churchill, MB, R0B 0E0 (☎ **204/675-8863**).

North of The Pas are two provincial parks. The first is **Clearwater Lake Provincial Park,** at the junction of highways 10 and 287; the lake lives up to its name because the bottom is visible at 35 feet. It offers great fishing, plus swimming, boating, hiking, and camping. The second is **Grass River Provincial Park** (no phone), on Highway 39, a wilderness home to woodland caribou, moose, and plenty of waterfowl. The Grass River is good for fishing and canoeing. For nearby accommodations, try **Grassy River Lodge,** Box 1680, The Pas, MB, R9A 1L4 (☎ **204/358-7171,** or 800/6379852 or 918/455-2324 in winter), which is open from mid-May to October.

Kaskattama Safari Adventures, Hudson Bay, Manitoba (☎ 204/667-1611), offers a more expensive way to view the polar bears. Their 6-day/5-night trip starts in Winnipeg, where guests stay at the Radisson before flying to Kaskattama, originally built as a fur-trading post in 1923 by the Hudson's Bay Company. Today, the storeroom and warehouse serve as the main visitor lodge and dining room. Two four-bedroom four-bath cabins, each equipped with screened porch, accommodate a maximum of 16 guests. A naturalist introduces visitors to the **Cape Tatnam Wildlife Management Area,** which is home to more than 200 species of birds, caribou, moose, black bear, Arctic wolves, fox, and the great white bears who head to land in July and can be seen foraging along the grasslands, with cubs in tow. Four days are spent at Kaska. The trip costs C$2,810 (US$1,995) per person based on double occupancy. If you like, for an additional C$282 (US$200) per person, you can take a helicopter trip to York Factory.

ACCOMMODATIONS IN CHURCHILL

Of the few choices, the following are your best bets. The 26-room **Churchill Motel,** at Kelsey and Franklin (☎ 204/675-8853), charges C$90 (US$64) for a double and has a restaurant. Additional amenities, like room service and a bar, can be found at **the Seaport Hotel,** 299 Kelsey Blvd. (☎ 204/675-8807). Their 21 rooms rent for C$95 (US$68) double. The **Tundra Inn,** 34 Franklin St. (☎ 204/675-8831), has 31 comfortable accommodations for C$95 (US$68) double.

8 Regina

Originally named "Pile O'Bones" after the heap of buffalo skeletons the first settlers found (native Canadians had amassed the bones in the belief that they would lure the vanished buffalo back again), the city has Princess Louise, daughter of Queen Victoria, to thank for its more regal name. She named the city in her mother's honor in 1882 when it became the capital of the Northwest Territories. Despite the barren prairie landscape and the infamous Regina mud, the town grew.

Today the provincial capital of Saskatchewan, with a population of 179,000, still has a certain prairie feel, although it's becoming more sophisticated, with some good hotels and some rather interesting attractions.

ESSENTIALS

VISITOR INFORMATION   Contact **Tourism Saskatchewan,** 500–1900 Albert St., Regina, SK, S4P 4L9 (☎ 800/667-7191 or 306/787-2300), open Monday to Friday from 8am to 7pm and Saturday and Sunday from 10am to 4pm.

For on-the-spot Regina information, contact **Tourism Regina,** P.O. Box 3355, Regina, SK, S4P 3H1 (☎ 306/789-5099), or visit the **Visitor Information Centre** on Highway 1 East, located just west of CKCK-TV. It's open daily from 8:30am to 4:30pm year-round, with extended hours to 7pm from mid-May to Labour Day.

GETTING THERE   **Air Canada** (☎ 800/776-3000) and **Canadian Airlines** (☎ 800/426-7000) serve Regina. The airport is located west of the city, only 15 minutes from downtown.

If you're driving, Regina is right on the Trans-Canada Highway.

VIA Rail trains pull into the station at 1880 Saskatchewan Dr., at Rose Street (☎ 800/561-8630 in Canada only).

CITY LAYOUT   The two main streets are Victoria Avenue, which runs east-west, and Albert Street, which runs north-south. South of the intersection lies the Wascana Centre. Most of the downtown hotels stretch along Victoria Avenue between Albert

Street on the west and Broad Street on the east. The RCMP barracks are located to the north and west of the downtown area. Lewvan Drive (also called the Ring Road) allows you to circle the city by car.

GETTING AROUND   Regina Transit, 333 Winnipeg St. (☎ **306/777-RIDE**), operates 9 bus routes that make it easy to get around. For schedules and maps, go to the Transit Information Centre at 2124 11th Ave., next to Eatons. Adult fare is C$1.20 (US86¢), C75¢ (US54¢) for high-school students, C65¢ (US46¢) for elementary-school students. Exact fare is required.

For car rentals, try **Dollar,** at the Regina Inn (☎ **306/525-1377**); **Hertz,** at the airport (☎ **306/791-9131**); **Tilden,** 2627 Airport Rd. (☎ **306/757-5757**); or **Avis,** 2010 Victoria Ave. (☎ **306/757-1653**).

Taxis can most easily be found at downtown hotels. They charge C$2.55 (US$1.80) when you get in and C10¢ (US7¢) per 89 meters thereafter. **Regina Cab** (☎ **306/543-3333**) is the most used.

SPECIAL EVENTS   During the first week of June, **Mosaic celebrates the city's multiethnic population. Special passports entitle visitors to enter pavilions and experience the food, crafts, customs, and culture of each group.

Regina's **Buffalo Days,** usually held the first week in August, recalls the time when this noble beast roamed the west. Throughout the city, businesses and individuals dress in Old West style, while the fair itself sparkles with a midway, grandstand shows, big-name entertainers, livestock competitions, beard-growing contests, and much, much more. For more information, contact **Buffalo Days,** P.O. Box 167, Exhibition Park, Regina, SK, S4P 2Z6 (☎ **306/781-9200**).

EXPLORING THE WASCANA CENTRE

This 2,300-acre park in the city center contains a **waterfowl park,** frequented by 60 or more species of marsh and water birds. There's a naturalist on duty from 8am to 4:30pm weekdays; call ☎ **306/522-3661** for information.

Another delightful spot is **Willow Island,** a picnic island reached by a small ferry from the overlook west of Broad Street on Wascana Drive.

Wascana Place, the headquarters building for Wascana Centre Authority (☎ **306/522-3661**), provides public information. There's a fine view from its fourth-level observation deck. It's open Monday from 8am to 4:30pm, Tuesday to Saturday from 8am to 6pm, with extended hours from May to Labour Day.

The center also contains the Legislative Building, the University of Regina, the Royal Saskatchewan Museum (which focuses on natural history), the Norman Mackenzie Art Gallery, and the Saskatchewan Centre of the Arts. Also in the park stands the **Diefenbaker Homestead** (☎ **306/522-3661**), the unassuming one-story log home of John Diefenbaker, prime minister from 1957 to 1963, which has been moved from Borden, Saskatchewan. John Diefenbaker helped his father build the three-room house, which is furnished in pioneer style and contains some original family articles. It's open daily from 10am to 7pm from Victoria Day to Labour Day.

Legislative Building. Wascana Centre. ☎ **306/787-5358.** Tours leave daily every half hour 8am–4:30pm in winter, 8am–8pm in summer.

This splendid, stately edifice built from 1908 to 1912 has 30 kinds of marble in the interior. Check out the mural *Before the White Man Came,* depicting aboriginal people in the Qu'Appelle Valley preparing to attack a herd of buffalo on the opposite shore. See also the Legislative Assembly Chamber, the 400,000-volume library, and the art galleries in the basement and on the first floor.

The Trial of Louis Riel

Louis Riel was tried and hanged in Regina in 1885. Bitter arguments have been fought between those who regard Riel as a patriot and martyr, and those who regard him as a rebel. Whatever the opinion, Riel certainly raises some extremely deep and discomforting questions. As G. F. Stanley, professor of history at the Royal Military College, Kingston, has written, "The mere mention of his name bares those latent religious and racial animosities which seem to lie so close to the surface of Canadian politics."

Even though he took up the cause of the mixed-blood population of the west, French-speaking Canadians often regarded him as a martyr and English-speaking Canadians damned him as a madman. Written by John Coulter, *The Trial of Louis Riel* is a play based on the actual court records of the historical trial. It is presented Wednesday to Friday at the Mackenzie Art Gallery during August. Nothing if not provocative, the play raises such issues as language rights, prejudice, and justice. Tickets are C$10 (US$7) for adults, C$9 (US$6) for seniors and students, and C$8 (US$6) for children 12 and under. For information or reservations, call ☎ **306/525-1185.**

Mackenzie Art Gallery. 3475 Albert St. (at Hillsdale). ☎ **306/522-4242.** Free admission. Fri–Tues 11am–6pm, Wed–Thurs 11am–10pm.

The art gallery's approximately 1,600 works concentrate on Canadian artists, particularly such Saskatchewan painters as James Henderson and Inglis Sheldon-Williams; contemporary American artists; and 15th- to 19th-century Europeans who are represented with paintings, drawings, and prints.

Royal Saskatchewan Museum. College Ave. and Albert St. ☎ **306/787-2815.** Free admission. May 1 to Labour Day daily 9am–8:30pm; Labour Day to Apr 30 daily 9am–5:30pm. Closed Christmas Day.

This museum focuses on the province's anthropological and natural history, displaying a life-size mastodon and a robotic dinosaur that comes roaring to life, plus other specimens. A video cave, rock table, and laboratory with resident paleontologist are all found in the interactive Paleo Pit. A new life-sciences gallery is scheduled to open in 2000.

MORE ATTRACTIONS

Sports fans will enjoy the **Saskatchewan Sports Hall of Fame and Museum,** at 2205 Victoria Ave. (☎ **306/780-9232**). The free museum is open May to October Monday to Friday from 8am to 5pm, Saturday and Sunday from 1 to 5pm. From November to April, it's open Monday to Friday from 8am to 5pm.

Saskatchewan Science Centre. Winnipeg St. and Wascana Dr. ☎ **306/791-7914,** or 306/522-4629 for IMAX. Admission to Powerhouse of Discovery C$5.50 (US$3.95) adults, C$3.50 (US$2.50) seniors and children 5–13, C$2 (US$1.45) children under 5. IMAX theater C$6.75 (US$4.80), adults, C$5 (US$3.55) children 5–13 and seniors, C$3.75 (US$2.70) children under 5. Combination tickets C$11 (US$8) adults, C$8 (US$6) youths and seniors, C$5 (US$3.55) children under 5. Summer Mon–Fri 9am–6pm, Sat–Sun 11am–6pm; winter Tues–Fri 9am–5pm, Sat–Sun and holidays noon–6pm.

The Saskatchewan Science Centre is home to the Powerhouse of Discovery and the Kramer IMAX Theatre. The first houses more than 80 thought-provoking, fun, hands-on exhibits that demonstrate basic scientific principles, ranging from a hot-air balloon that rises three stories in the central mezzanine to exhibits where visitors can test their strength, reaction time, and balance.

The Kramer IMAX theater shows films on a five-story screen accompanied by thrilling six-channel surround-sound. Call for show times (most are in the afternoon).

RCMP Training Academy & Museum. Off Dewdney Ave. W. ☎ **306/780-5838.** Free admission. June 1–Sept 15 daily 8am–6:45pm; Sept 16–May 31 daily 10am–4:45pm. Closed Christmas Day.

This fascinating museum traces the history of the Royal Canadian Mounted Police since 1874, when they began the Great March West to stop liquor traffic and enforce the law in the Northwest Territories. The museum uses replicas, newspaper articles, artifacts, uniforms, weaponry, and mementos to document the lives of the early Mounties and the pioneers. It traces the Mounties' role in the 1885 Riel Rebellion, the Klondike Gold Rush (when the simple requirements they laid down probably saved the lives of many foolhardy gold diggers who came pitifully ill-equipped), the Prohibition era (when they sought out stills), the First and Second World Wars, the 1935 Regina labor riot, and in the capture of the mad trapper (who was chased in Arctic temperatures for 54 days from 1931 to 1932). Kids, and adults, too, will probably love to role-play in the cockpit of the de Havilland single-engine Otter from the Air Services Division and see an audiovisual presentation of training.

A tour also goes to the chapel and, when possible, allows visitors to see cadets in training. The highlight is the Sergeant Major's Parade, which normally takes place around 12:45pm Monday to Friday. The schedule is tentative, so call before you go. In July and early August on Tuesday evenings just after 6:30pm, the Sunset Ceremony takes place, an exciting 45-minute display of horsemanship by the Mounties accompanied by pipe and bugle bands and choir.

ACCOMMODATIONS
EXPENSIVE

Hotel Saskatchewan-Radisson Plaza. 2125 Victoria Ave. (at Scarth St.), Regina, SK, S4P 0S3. ☎ **306/522-7691.** Fax 306/522-8988. 217 rms. A/C MINIBAR TV TEL. C$165 (US$118) double. Extra person C$15 (US$11). Children under 12 stay free in parents' rm. AE, CB, DC, DISC, ER, MC, V.

The hotel's ivy-covered limestone exterior has a rather solid old-world air about it, a satisfying prelude to the modern comfort within. The large, almost heart-shaped clock that hangs in the lobby is original to the 1927 Georgian-style building. The rooms have elegant high ceilings and decorative moldings; each bathroom contains a hair dryer and an additional phone.

Dining: Cortlandt Hall, with terraced seating, stately windows, and a coffered oak ceiling with brass chandeliers, specializes in grills, seafood, veal, and chicken dishes, from C$15 to C$23 (US$11 to US$16) at dinner, with a lighter selection at lunchtime.

Services: Room service until midnight.

Facilities: Fully equipped fitness center with sauna.

Ramada Plaza. 1919 Saskatchewan Dr., Regina, SK, S4P 4H2. ☎ **306/525-5255.** Fax 306/781-7188. 255 rms. A/C MINIBAR TV TEL. C$130 (US$93) double. Extra person C$15 (US$11). Children under 16 stay free in parents' rm. Weekend rates available. AE, ER, MC, V.

Conveniently located downtown in the Saskatchewan Trade and Convention Centre, the Ramada Plaza is adjacent to two large retail malls, the Cornwall Centre, and the Galleria. The modern rooms are elegantly appointed with marble vanities, sitting areas, and desks.

Dining/Entertainment: There's the casual Summerfields Cafe as well as Caper's Lounge for cocktails.

Facilities: The Waterworks Recreation Complex has a three-story indoor water slide, swimming pool, and whirlpool.

Services: Room service from 7am to 11pm.

Regina Inn. 1975 Broad St., Regina, SK, S4P 1Y2. ☎ **800/667-8162** in Canada, or 306/525-6767. Fax 306/352-1858. 235 rms. A/C TV TEL. C$140 (US$100) double. Extra person C$10 (US$7). Children under 18 stay free in parents' rm. Weekend family rates from C$65 (US$46) per night. AE, DC, ER, MC, V.

The Regina Inn occupies an entire block and offers numerous facilities within. Its rooms, most with balconies, have contemporary decor and louvered closets. Guests enjoy the sundeck and health club. The hotel offers one restaurant, lounge, and a nightspot.

MODERATE

Chelton Suites Hotel. 1907 11th Ave., Regina, SK, S4P 0J2. ☎ **800/667-9922** in Canada, or 306/569-4600. Fax 306/569-3531. 56 rms and suites. A/C TV TEL. C$119–C$160 (US$85–US$115) double (top prices for suites). Weekend rates available. AE, DC, ER, MC, V.

Conveniently located downtown, the Chelton is small enough to provide friendly personal service. The rooms, all very large, sport modern furnishings. A bedroom/sitting room will contain table, chairs, drawers, and couch, as well as a sink, fridge, microwave, coffeemaker, and private bathroom. Even the smallest rooms are bright and spacious compared to most other accommodations. Suites have a separate bedroom and living area. Facilities include a casual restaurant and lounge.

The Sands. 1818 Victoria Ave., Regina, SK, S4P 0R1. ☎ **306/569-1666.** Fax 306/525-3550. 251 rms. A/C TV TEL. C$120 (US$86) double. Children under 18 stay free in parents' rm. Weekend packages available. AE, DC, MC, V.

You notice The Sands' organic natural quality in the lobby with its earth-color stone walls and plant-filled coffee plaza. The attractive rooms have modern furnishings and all the usual amenities. Dining facilities include a restaurant and lounge. On the second floor, there's an indoor pool, sauna, sundeck, whirlpool, and exercise room. The hotel also has a children's play area.

INEXPENSIVE

Turgeon International Hostel. 2310 McIntyre St., Regina, SK, S4P 2S2. ☎ **306/791-8165.** Fax 306/721-2667. 50 beds. A/C. C$12 (US$9) members, C$17 (US$12) nonmembers. MC, V. Closed Dec 25–Jan 31. Lights out at 11:30pm.

Regina is fortunate to have one of the best youth hostels I've ever seen, if not the best. The Turgeon International Hostel is located in a handsome 1907 town house adjacent to Wascana Centre. Accommodations are in dormitories with three or four bunks; the top floor has two larger dorms, and each dorm has access to a deck. Downstairs there's a comfortable sitting room worthy of any inn, with couches in front of the oak fireplace and plenty of magazines and books. In fact, the hostel acts as a resource center for travelers. The basement contains an impeccably clean dining and cooking area with electric stoves, as well as a laundry. Picnic tables are available in the backyard. A gem!

DINING

Regina offers slim dining pickings. In addition to the steak houses listed here, try **Neo Japonica,** 2167 Hamilton St., at 14th Avenue (☎ 306/359-7669), for decent Japanese cuisine, and **Peking House,** 1850 Rose St. (☎ 306/757-3038), for Chinese.

The Diplomat. 2032 Broad St. ☎ **306/359-3366.** Reservations recommended. Main courses C$13–C$40 (US$9–US$29). AE, DC, ER, MC, V. Mon–Fri 11:30am–2pm; Mon–Sat 4pm–midnight. CANADIAN.

This old-style steak house comes complete with semicircular banquettes, and tables set with pink cloths, burgundy napkins, and tiny lanterns. Around the room hang portraits of eminent-looking prime ministers; there's a fireplace and lounge up front. The menu's main attractions are the steaks—20-ounce porterhouse, 18-ounce T-bone—along with coq au vin, veal marsala, poached salmon, and other traditional favorites.

Golf's Steak House. 1945 Victoria Ave. (at Hamilton St.). ☎ **306/525-5808.** Reservations required. Main courses C$12–C$29 (US$9–US$21). AE, DC, ER, MC, V. Mon–Fri 11:30am–2pm; Mon–Sat 4:30pm–midnight, Sun and holidays 4–11pm. CANADIAN.

In this venerable Regina institution, the atmosphere is decidedly plush (note the large fireplace, the piano and antique organ, the heavy gilt-framed paintings, and the high-backed carved-oak Charles II–style chairs). The menu offers traditional steak-house fare.

REGINA AFTER DARK

The focus of the city's cultural life is the **Saskatchewan Centre of the Arts** (☎ **306/565-4500,** or 306/525-9999 for the box office), on the southern shore of Wascana Lake. With two theaters and a large concert hall, the Centre is home to the Regina Symphony Orchestra and also features many other artists. Ticket prices vary depending on the show. The **box office** at 200 Lakeshore Dr. (☎ **306/525-9999**) is open from 10am to 6pm Monday to Saturday.

The **Globe Theatre,** Old City Hall, 1801 Scarth St. (☎ **306/525-6400**), a theater-in-the-round, presents six main-stage plays each October-to-April season. Productions run the gamut from classics (Shakespeare, Molière, Shaw, and others) to modern dramas, musicals, and comedies. Ticket prices range from C$10 to C$20 (US$7 to US$14).

Casino Regina at Broad Street and Saskatchewan Drive (☎ **306/565-3000**) is the latest year-round amusement. It has 40 gaming tables plus 500 slots. It's open daily from 9am to 4am.

A slightly older crowd (25 to 35) frequents the **Manhattan Club and Island Pub** at 2300 Dewdney St. (☎ **306/359-7771**). The upstairs dance club here is open Thursday and Saturday only.

The college crowd favors **Checker's,** at the Landmark Inn, 4150 Albert St. (☎ **306/586-5363**), a comfortable, rustic, and relaxed dance spot. In summer, the outdoor area called **Scotland Yard** is also crowded.

For more relaxed entertainment, there's the **Regina Inn lounge** (☎ **306/525-6767**) or the **Sands' Mulligan lounge** (☎ **306/569-1666**).

9 Saskatchewan Highlights Along the Trans-Canada Highway

MOOSE MOUNTAIN PROVINCIAL PARK & WEST TO REGINA

Just across the Manitoba/Saskatchewan border at Whitewood, you can turn south down Highway 9 to **Moose Mountain Provincial Park** (☎ 306/577-2131); it's also accessible from highways 16 and 13. About 106 kilometers (66 miles) southeast of Regina, this 388-square-kilometer (151-sq.-mile) park is dotted with lakes and marshes. The park harbors a variety of waterfowl and songbirds—blue-winged teal, red-necked ducks, blue heron, red-tailed hawk, ovenbird, rose-breasted grosbeak, and Baltimore oriole—and animals, including deer, elk, moose, beaver, muskrat, and coyote.

In summer, park rangers lead guided hikes. The Beaver Youell Lake and the Wuche Sakaw Trails are also easy to follow. Visitors can hike or bike along the **nature trails;** swim at the beach south of the main parking lot and at several of the lakes; cool off at the super-fun **giant water slides on Kenosee Lake,** which include an eight-story free-fall slide (open from mid-May to Labour Day); **golf** at the 18-hole course; **go horseback riding;** or play **tennis.** In winter, the park has more than 56 kilometers (35 miles) of **cross-country ski trails** and more than 120 kilometers (74 miles) of **snowmobiling trails.**

The modern, no-nonsense **Kenosee Inn** (☎ 306/577-2099) offers 30 rooms or 23 cabin accommodations (with air-conditioning, TV, and telephone) overlooking Kenosee Lake in the park. Facilities include a restaurant, a bar, an indoor pool, and a hot tub. Rates are C$85 (US$61) double for a room, C$60 (US$43) for a one-bedroom cabin, and C$75 to C$98 (US$54 to US$70) for a two-bedroom cabin, depending on its age and size. The park also has two **campgrounds.**

MOOSE JAW

Moose Jaw gained notoriety as Canada's rum-running capital; today some restored buildings still retain the underground tunnels used for the illicit trade and these can be toured (for info call ☎ 306/693-8097). The **Moose Jaw Art Museum** in Crescent Park (☎ 306/692-4471) has a fine collection of Cree and Sioux beadwork and costumes, plus art-history and science exhibits. It's open Tuesday to Sunday from noon to 5pm and Tuesday and Wednesday from 7 to 9pm. The town is also known for its **26 outdoor murals** that depict aspects of the city's heritage. For information, call Murals of Moose Jaw (☎ 306/693-4262). The **Western Development Museum History of Transportation,** at highways 1 and 2 (☎ 306/693-5989), showcases the roles that air, rail, land, and water transportation played in opening up the west. One gallery pays tribute to the Snowbirds, Canada's famous air demonstration squadron. Visitors can see a large-screen film about the squadron and experience the thrills for themselves on the flight simulator. **Wakamow Valley** (☎ 306/692-2717), which follows the course of the river through town, includes six different parks with walking and biking trails, canoeing, and skating facilities.

If you stop in Moose Jaw, the place to stay is **Temple Gardens Mineral Spa** (☎ 800/718-7727), which is right downtown. It has 44 rooms plus 25 spa suites with private mineral-water Jacuzzis. It's a full-facility resort with extra-special mineral pools where you can "take the waters." The spa offers a full range of body treatments. Rates are C$78 to C$100 (US$56 to US$71) double and from C$149 (US$106) for spa Jacuzzi suites.

For more information, contact **Tourism Moose Jaw,** 88 Saskatchewan St. E., Moose Jaw, SK, S6H 0V4 (☎ 306/693-8097).

SWIFT CURRENT, CYPRESS HILLS PROVINCIAL PARK & FORT WALSH

Swift Current, Saskatchewan's base for western oil exploration and a regional trading center for livestock and grain, is 167 kilometers (104 miles) along the Trans-Canada Highway from Moose Jaw. It's known for its **Frontier Days** in June and **Old Tyme Fiddling Contest** in September. From Swift Current it's about another 201 kilometers (125 miles) to the Alberta border.

Straddling the border is **Cypress Hills Provincial Park,** P.O. Box 850, Maple Creek, SK, S0N 1N0 (☎ 306/662-4411), and Fort Walsh National Historic Site. En route to Cypress Hills, off the Trans-Canada Highway, is **Maple Creek,** a thoroughly Western cow town with many heritage storefronts on main street. On the Saskatchewan side, the provincial park is divided into a Centre Block, off Route 21, and a West Block, off Route 271. Both blocks are joined by Gap Road, which is impassable when wet. The park's core is in the Centre Block, where there are six campgrounds; an outdoor pool; canoe, row/paddleboat, and bike rentals; a 9-hole golf course; tennis courts; a riding stable; and swimming at the beach on Loch Leven. In winter there are 24 kilometers (15 miles) of **cross-country skiing trails.** Entry to the park costs C$5 (US$3.55); camping costs C$12 to C$18 (US$9 to US$13).

The **Cypress Four Seasons** (☎ 306/662-4477) resort offers rooms plus cabin and condominium accommodations from C$65 to C$95 (US$46 to US$68) a night in high season.

Fort Walsh National Historic Site can be accessed from Route 271 or directly from the park's West Block by gravel and clay roads. Built in 1875, the fort's soldiers tried to contain the local native tribes and the many Sioux who sought refuge here after the Battle of Little Bighorn in 1876, as well as keep out American criminals seeking sanctuary. It was dismantled in 1883. Today the reconstruction consists of five buildings and a trading post staffed with folks in period costume. Open May to Thanksgiving daily from 9am to 5:30pm. Admission is C$3 (US$2.15) for adults, C$2.25 (US$1.60) for seniors, and C$1.50 (US$1.05) for children.

GRASSLANDS NATIONAL PARK

About 75 miles south of Swift Current along the U.S. border stretches Grasslands National Park, P.O. Box 150, Val Marie, SK, S0N 2T0—2 blocks of protected land separated by about 27 kilometers (17 miles).

On this mixed prairie- and grassland there's no escape from the sun and the wind. Coulees and the Frenchman River cut the west block, where the rare pronghorn antelope can be spotted. Black-tailed **prairie dogs,** which bark warnings at intruders and reassure each other with kisses and hugs, also make their home here. In the East Block, the open prairie is broken with coulees and the adobe hills of the Killdeer Badlands, so called because of their poor soil.

Although the park doesn't have facilities, there are two self-guided **nature trails,** and visitors can also climb to the summit of 113-kilometer (70-mile) Butte and no-trace camp (pack in and pack out, leaving no trace). The **information center** (☎ 306/298-2257) is in Val Marie at the junction of Highway 4 and Centre Street (closed weekends in winter).

10 Saskatoon

Saskatoon (pop. 184,000) is the progressive city on the plains. The town still retains a distinctly Western air. Downtown streets are broad and dusty and dotted in summer with many a pickup truck. Those same downtown streets just seem to disappear on the edge of town into the prairie, where grain elevators and telegraph poles become the only reference points, and the sky your only company.

Scenically, Saskatoon possesses some distinct natural advantages. The Lower Saskatchewan River cuts a swath through the city. Spanned by several graceful bridges, its banks are great for strolling, biking, and jogging. Much of the city's recent wealth has come from the surrounding mining region that yields potash, uranium, petroleum, gas, and gold; Key Lake is the largest uranium mine outside Russia.

ESSENTIALS

VISITOR INFORMATION   From around May 18 to the end of August, a booth is open at Avenue C North at 47th Street. Otherwise, contact **Tourism Saskatoon,** located at 6-305 Idylwyld Dr. N. (P.O. Box 369), Saskatoon, SK, S7K 0Z1 (☎ **306/ 242-1206**). It's open in winter, Monday to Friday from 8:30am to 5pm, and in summer, Monday to Friday from 8:30am to 7pm and Saturday and Sunday from 10am to 7pm.

GETTING THERE   **Air Canada** (☎ **800/776-3000**) and **Canadian Airlines** (☎ **800/426-7000**) fly in and out of the one-terminal airport.

If you're driving, Highway 16 leads to Saskatoon from the east or west. From Regina, Route 11 leads northwest to Saskatoon, 257 kilometers (160 miles) away.

VIA Rail trains arrive in the west end of the city on Chappel Drive. For information, call ☎ **306/384-5665;** for reservations, call ☎ **800/561-8630** in Canada.

CITY LAYOUT   The South Saskatchewan River cuts a diagonal north-south swath through the city. The main downtown area lies on the west bank; the University of Saskatchewan and the long neon-sign-crazed 8th Street dominate the east bank.

Streets are laid out in a numbered grid system—22nd Street divides north- and south-designated streets; Idylwyld Drive divides, in a similar fashion, east from west. First Street through 18th Street lie on the river's east side; 19th Street and up, on the west bank in the downtown area. Spadina Crescent runs along the river's west bank, where you'll find such landmarks as the Bessborough Hotel, the Ukrainian Museum, and the art gallery.

GETTING AROUND   You may only need to use transportation when you visit the University of Saskatchewan and the Western Development Museum. **Saskatoon Transit System,** 301 24th St. W. at Avenue C (☎ **306/975-3100** for routes and schedules), operates buses to all city areas from 6am to 12:30am Monday to Saturday and from 9:15am to 9pm on Sunday for an exact-change fare of C$1.50 (US$1.05) for adults, C$1 (US71¢) for high-school students, and C75¢ (US54¢) for grade-school students.

Car-rental companies include **Avis,** 2625 Airport Dr. (☎ **306/652-3434**); **Budget,** 234 1st Ave. S. and 2215 Ave. C N. (☎ **306/244-7925**); and **Hertz,** 16-2625 Airport Dr. (☎ **306/373-1161**).

Taxis cost C$2.10 (US$1.50) when you step inside and C10¢ (US7¢) every 90 meters. Try **Saskatoon Radio Cab** (☎ **306/242-1221**) or **United Cabs** (☎ **306/ 652-2222**), which also operates the limousine to the airport for C$7 (US$5) from downtown hotels.

SPECIAL EVENTS   Saskatoon's 8-day **Exhibition,** usually held the second week of July, provides some grand agricultural spectacles, such as the threshing competition in which steam power is pitted against gas—sometimes with unexpected results—and the tractor-pulling competition, when standard farm tractors are used to pull a steel sled weighted down with a water tank. The pay-one-price admission of C$7.50 (US$5) for adults, C$5 (US$3.55) for seniors and youths 11 to 15 (children under 11 are free), lets you in all the entertainments—a craft show, talent competitions, thoroughbred racing, midway, and Kidsville, which features clowns, games, and a petting zoo. For more information, contact Saskatoon Prairieland Exhibition Corporation, P.O. Box 6010, Saskatoon, SK, S7K 4E4 (☎ **306/931-7149**).

In mid-August, a **Folkfest** celebrates the city's many ethnic groups. The **Prairieland Pro Rodeo** is held at the Exhibition Stadium in October.

EXPLORING THE CITY

Housed in a striking modern building overlooking the South Saskatchewan River, a short walk from downtown, the **Mendel Art Gallery and Civic Conservatory,** at 950 Spadina Crescent E. (☎ 306/975-7610), has a good permanent collection of Canadian paintings, sculpture, watercolors, and graphics. It's free, and it's open Victoria Day to Thanksgiving daily from 9am to 9pm; otherwise daily from noon to 9pm (closed Christmas Day).

Nearby at 910 Spadina Crescent E. is the **Ukrainian Museum of Canada** (☎ 306/244-3800). Reminiscent of a Ukrainian home in western Canada at the turn of the century, this museum preserves the Ukrainian heritage in clothing, linens, tools, books, photographs, documents, wooden folk art, ceramics, *pysanky* (Easter eggs), and other treasures and art forms brought from the "old homeland" by Ukrainian immigrants to Canada. Admission is C$2 (US$1.45) for adults, C$1 (US70¢) for seniors, and C50¢ (US35¢) for children 6 to 12. It's open Tuesday to Saturday from 10am to 5pm and Sunday from 1 to 5pm.

At the **Saskatoon Zoo,** 1903 Forest Dr. (☎ 306/975-3382), 300 or so species of Canadian and Saskatchewan wildlife are on view—wolf, coyote, fox, bear, eagle, owl, and hawk, a variety of deer, caribou, elk, and bison. There's a children's zoo, too. During winter you can cross-country ski the 4-kilometer (2½-mile) trail. Admission is C$3.50 (US$2.50) for adults and C$2.25 (US$3.05) for seniors and children 6 to 18. It's open daily: May 1 to Labour Day from 9am to 9pm; the rest of the year from 10am to 4pm. It's in northeast Saskatoon; follow the signs on Attridge Drive from Circle Drive.

The **University of Saskatchewan** (☎ 306/244-4343) occupies a dramatic 2,550-acre site overlooking the South Saskatchewan River and is attended by some 20,000 students. The actual campus buildings are set on 360 acres while the rest of the area is largely given over to the university farm and experimental plots. The Diefenbaker Canada Centre contains the papers and memorabilia of one of Canada's best-known prime ministers and is open Monday and Friday from 9:30am to 4:30pm, Tuesday to Thursday from 9:30am to 8pm, and from 12:30 to 5pm on weekends and holidays. The observatory (open Saturday evenings after dusk) houses the Duncan telescope. The Little Stone Schoolhouse, built in 1887, served as the city's first school and community center (open May to June, weekdays from 9:30am to 4:15pm, and weekends 12:30 to 5pm; July 1 to Labour Day, weekends only, from 12:30 to 5pm). Special tours of the research farm and many of the colleges can be arranged. For information, contact the **Office of Public Relations,** University of Saskatchewan (☎ 306/966-6607). To get there, take bus no. 7 or 19 from downtown at 23rd Street and 2nd Avenue.

Western Development Museum. 2610 Lorne Ave. S. ☎ 306/931-1910. Admission C$4.50 (US$3.20) adults, C$3.50 (US$2.50) seniors, C$1.50 (US$1.05) children 5–12, C$10 (US$7) families; children under 5 free. Daily 9am–5pm. Take Idylwyld Dr. south to the Lorne Ave. exit and follow Lorne Ave. south until you see the museum on the right. Bus no. 1 from the 23rd St. Bus Mall between 2nd and 3rd aves.

The energetic years of Saskatchewan settlement are vividly portrayed by "Boomtown 1910," an authentic replica of prairie community life in that year. When you step onto the main street of Boomtown, the memories of an earlier age flood the senses. Browse through the shops, crammed with the unfamiliar goods of days gone by; savor the past through the mysterious aromas that permeate the drugstore; step aside as you hear the clip-clop of a passing horse and buggy; or wander down to Boomtown Station drawn by the low wail of an approaching steam locomotive. The museum truly comes to life during Pion-Era, when volunteers in authentic costume staff Boomtown and many pieces of vintage equipment are pressed into service once again.

Wanuskewin Heritage Park. RR #4, 5km (3 miles) north of Saskatoon on Hwy. 11. ☎ **306/ 931-6767.** Admission C$6 (US$4.30) adults, C$2.50 (US$1.80) children 5–12. Victoria Day to Labour Day daily 9am–9pm; fall and winter Wed–Sun 9am–5pm.

This park is built around the archaeological discovery of 19-plus Northern Plains Indian sites. Walking along the trails you'll see archaeological digs in progress, habitation sites, stone cairns, teepee rings, bison jumps, and other trace features of this ancient culture. At the amphitheater, native performers present dance, theater, song, and storytelling, while at the outdoor activity area visitors can learn how to build a teepee, bake bannock, tan a hide, or use a travois (a transportation device). The main exhibit halls feature computer-activated displays and artifacts, multimedia shows exploring the archaeology and culture of the Plains peoples, contemporary art, and a Living Culture exhibit that tells the stories behind the daily headlines.

SHOPPING

For Canadian merchandise, stop in at **The Trading Post,** 226 2nd Ave. S. (☎ **306/ 653-1769**), which carries Inuit soapstone carvings, native-Canadian art, Cowichan sweaters, mukluks, beadwork, and more. Some galleries showing local artists that are worth browsing include **A. K. A. Gallery,** 12–23rd St. E. (☎ **306/652-0044**); **Photographers' Gallery** (☎ **306/244-8018**), also at 12–23rd St. E.; the **Arlington Art Gallery,** 265 2nd Ave. S. (☎ **306/244-5921**); **Collector's Choice Art Gallery,** 625D 1st Ave. N. (☎ **306/665-8300**); and **Handmade House,** 710 Broadway Ave. (☎ **306/665-5542**), which specializes in crafts.

ACCOMMODATIONS

The **Sheraton Cavalier,** 612 Spadina Crescent E. (☎ **800/325-3535** or 306/ 652-6770), offers a special executive floor for businesspeople, plus a complete resort complex with adult and kiddie swimming pools and 250-foot-long water slides that attract many happy families. A double is C$99 (US$71). The **Ramada Hotel** at 90 22nd St. E. (☎ **306/244-2311**), has a very convenient location, opposite the Eatons complex and Centennial Auditorium. A double costs C$120 (US$86).

The **Saskatoon Travelodge,** 106 Circle Dr. W. at Idylwyld (☎ **800/578-7878** or 306/242-8881), has doubles for C$65 to C$85 (US$46 to US$61). There's an especially attractive pool area, plus a 250-foot-long water slide and whirlpool. For a pleasant, fairly priced room, the 80-room **Comfort Inn,** 2155 Northridge Dr. (☎ **306/934-1122**), is a good choice. Rates are C$72 (US$51) double.

Delta Bessborough. 601 Spadina Crescent E., Saskatoon, SK, S7K 3G8. ☎ **306/244-5521.** Fax 306/653-2458. 227 rms and suites. A/C TV TEL. C$160 (US$114) double; C$180 (US$129) suite. Extra person C$10 (US$7). Children under 18 stay free in parents' rm. Weekend packages available. AE, MC, V. Parking C$4 (US$2.85).

An elegant and gracious hostelry built in 1930 and finished in 1935, the Bessborough looks like a French château, with a copper roof and turrets. Inside, each room is different, although all have venerable oak entrance doors and antique or traditional furniture. Front rooms are large and most have bay windows. Riverside rooms are smaller, but have lovely views across the Saskatchewan River. There's a river-view coffee shop and the Samurai Japanese Steakhouse. Facilities include an indoor pool with whirlpool, sauna, and an exercise room.

Radisson Hotel Saskatoon. 405 20th St. E., Saskatoon, SK, S7K 6X6. ☎ **800/333-3333** or 306/665-3322. Fax 306/665-5531. 291 rms. A/C TV TEL. From C$105 (US$75) double. Extra person C$10 (US$7). Children under 16 stay free in parents' rm. Weekend packages available. AE, DC, MC, V. Parking C$4 (US$2.85).

Offering a riverside location in the heart of downtown, the Radisson is a luxury property, with attractively decorated, well-appointed rooms. About a third of the units offer river views; the corner rooms are particularly attractive. Summerfield's serves three meals daily and guests enjoy a three-story recreation complex containing a large indoor swimming pool, two indoor water slides, a sauna, and a whirlpool. Bike rentals are available and jogging and cross-country ski trails adjoin the property.

DINING

Cousin Niks. 1110 Grosvenor Ave. (between 7th and 8th sts.). ☎ **306/374-2020.** Reservations recommended. Main courses C$14–C$37 (US$10–US$26). AE, MC, V. Daily 5–11pm. GREEK/CANADIAN.

If you have only one dinner in Saskatoon, seek out the not-to-be-missed Cousin Niks. Here you'll find a delightful setting: an open courtyard garden lit from above and made even more charming by the sound of the splashing fountain. Greek rugs add color to the predominantly white background. A variety of steak and seafood dishes are offered, from baked salmon with lemon butter to rack of lamb with mint sauce. Main-course prices include *avgolemono* soup, Greek salad, and fresh seasonal fruit. On weekends there's entertainment in the lounge.

St. Tropez Bistro. 243 3rd Ave. S. ☎ **306/652-1250.** Reservations recommended. Main courses C$9–C$18 (US$6–US$13). AE, MC, V. Mon–Sat 11:30am–2pm and 5–10pm. CONTINENTAL.

One of my favorite downtown restaurants is the St. Tropez Bistro, where the background music is classical or French, and the tables are covered in Laura Ashley–style floral-design prints. For dinner, you can choose from a variety of pastas and stir-fries, or such dishes as sweet garlic veal or blackened chicken. For dessert, go for the rich chocolate fondue with fresh fruit. This is one place where you can find out what's happening culturally in Saskatoon, too.

Traegers. In Cumberland Sq., 1515 8th St. E. ☎ **306/374-7881.** Reservations recommended at lunch. Sandwiches and light fare C$4–C$9 (US$2.85–US$6). MC, V. Mon–Sat 8am–9pm, Sun 9am–8pm. LIGHT FARE/DESSERTS.

Traegers makes a very pleasant breakfast, lunch, afternoon-tea, and supper spot. The offerings include everything from Belgian waffles, croissant sandwiches, salads, quiche, schnitzel, and specialty toasts. The bakery items, though, are the most exciting—croissants, bagels, and Danish in the early morning, and richly delicious desserts like amaretto-chocolate cheesecake and Black Forest torte later in the day.

SASKATOON AFTER DARK

There's not an awful lot of nightlife in Saskatoon, but the **Saskatoon Centennial Auditorium,** 35 22nd St. E. (☎ 306/938-7800), provides a superb 2,003-seat theater, with a range of shows. The **Saskatoon Symphony** (☎ 306/665-6414) regularly performs in a September-to-April season. Tickets are C$17 to C$27 (US$12 to US$19).

Among local theater companies, the **Persephone Theatre,** 2802 Rusholme Rd. (☎ 306/384-7727), offers six shows per fall-to-spring season (dramas, comedies, and musicals); tickets are C$10 to C$23 (US$7 to US$16). **Nightcap Productions,** Box 1646, Saskatoon, SK7 3R8 (☎ 306/653-2300), produces Shakespeare on the Saskatchewan, annually from July to mid-August, in two tents overlooking the river. Two different Shakespeare plays are performed plus a special Festival Frolics during the season. Tickets are C$18.75 (US$13) for adults, C$15.50 (US$11) for seniors and students, and C$12.25 (US$9) for children 6 to 12; children under 6 are free.

For quiet drinking and conversation, you can't beat the **Samurai** lounge in the Bessborough Hotel, 601 Spadina Crescent E. (☎ **306/244-5521**). Other pleasant lounges include **Cousin Niks** (☎ **306/374-2020;** see "Dining," above). For a more pubby atmosphere, try the **Artful Dodger** on Fourth Avenue South (☎ **306/ 653-2577**).

Marquis Downs racetrack, at the corner of Ruth Street and St. Henry Avenue (☎ **306/242-6100**), is open for live and simulcast racing. The live season goes from mid-May to mid-October. The racetrack has a lounge, a cafeteria, and terrace dining overlooking the paddock and home stretch. Admission is free.

The other place to wager is the **Emerald Casino,** Prairieland Exhibition Centre (☎ **306/931-7149**), where you can play five or so table games. It opens at 5:30pm weekdays and at 2pm on weekends. Take the Ruth Street Exit off Idylwyld Freeway.

SIDE TRIPS FROM SASKATOON

FORT BATTLEFORD NATIONAL HISTORIC PARK   About 138 kilometers (86 miles), a 1¹/₂-hour drive, northwest of Saskatoon on Highway 16, this fort served as the headquarters for the Northwest Mounted Police from 1876 to 1924.

Outside the interpretative gallery, a display relates the role of the mounted police from the fur-trading era to the events that led to the rebellion of 1885. You'll see a Red River cart, the type that was used to transport police supplies into the west; excerpts from the local Saskatchewan *Herald;* a typical settler's log-cabin home, which is amazingly tiny; articles of the fur trade; and an 1876 Gatling gun.

Inside the palisade, the Visitor Reception Centre shows two videos about the 1885 Uprising and the Cree People. From there, proceed to the guardhouse (1887), containing a cell block and the sick-horse stable (1898), and the Officers' Quarters (1886), with police documents, maps, and telegraph equipment.

Perhaps the most interesting building is the Commanding Officer's Residence (1877), which, even though it looks terribly comfortable today, was certainly not so in 1885 when nearly 100 women took shelter in it during the siege of Battleford. Admission is C$4 (US$2.85) for adults, C$3 (US$2.15) for seniors, and C$2 (US$1.45) for students. Open from Victoria Day to Thanksgiving daily from 9am to 6pm. Call ☎ **306/937-2621** for further information.

BATOCHE NATIONAL HISTORIC SITE   In spring 1885 the Northwest Territories exploded in an armed uprising led by the Métis Louis Riel and Gabriel Dumont. Trouble had been brewing along the frontier for several years. The Indians were demanding food, equipment, and farming assistance that had been promised to them in treaties. The settlers were angry about railway development and protective tariffs that meant higher prices for the equipment and services they needed.

The Métis were the offspring of the original French fur traders, who had intermarried with the Cree and Saulteaux women. Initially they had worked for the Hudson's Bay and Northwest companies, but when the two companies merged, many were left without work and returned to buffalo hunting or became independent traders with the Indians in the west. When Riel was unable to obtain guarantees for the Métis in Manitoba from 1869 to 1870, even when he established a provisional government, it became clear that the Métis would have to adopt the agricultural ways of the whites to survive. In 1872 they established the settlement at Batoche along the South Saskatchewan River; but they had a hard time acquiring "legal" titles and securing scrip, a certificate that could be exchanged for a land grant or money. The

Métis complained to the government, but received no satisfactory response. So they called on Riel to lead them in what became known as the Northwest Rebellion.

Of the rebellion's five significant engagements, the Battle of Batoche was the only one that government forces decisively won. From May 9 to May 12, 1885, fewer than 300 Métis and Indians led by Riel and Dumont defended the village against the Northwest Field Force commanded by General Frederick Middleton and numbering 800. On the third day, Middleton succeeded in breaking through the Métis lines and occupying the village. Dumont fled to the United States but returned and is buried at the site; Riel surrendered, stood trial, and was executed.

At the park you can view four battlefield areas and see a film at the visitor center. It will take 4 to 6 hours to walk to all four areas, 2¹/₂ hours to complete areas 1 and 2. For more information, contact **Batoche National Historic Park,** P.O. Box 999, Rosthern, SK, S0K 3R0 (☎ **306/423-6227**). Admission is C$4 (US$2.85) for adults, C$3 (US$2.15) for seniors, and C$2 (US$1.45) for children 6 to 16. Open Victoria Day to Thanksgiving: from 10am to 6pm daily July to August and from 9am to 5pm September and October. The site is about an hour from Saskatoon via Highway 11 to 312 to 225.

11 Prince Albert National Park

This million-acre wilderness area, 240 kilometers (150 miles) north of Saskatoon and 91 kilometers (57 miles) north of the town of Prince Albert, is one of the jewels of Canada's national park system. Its terrain is astoundingly varied, since it lies at the point where the great Canadian prairie grasslands give way to the pristine evergreen forests of the north. Here you'll find clear, cold lakes, ponds, and streams created thousands of years ago as glaciers receded. It's a hilly landscape, forested with spruce, poplar, and birch.

The park offers outdoor activities from canoeing and backpacking to nature hikes, picnicking, and swimming, and great wildlife viewing. You can see and photograph moose, caribou, elk, black bear, bison, and loons. (The moose and caribou tend to wander through the forested northern part of the park, while the elk and deer graze on the southern grasslands.) Lavallee Lake is home to Canada's second-largest white-pelican colony.

In the 1930s, this park's woods and wildlife inspired famed naturalist Grey Owl, an Englishman adopted by the Ojibwa who became one of Canada's pioneering conservationists and most noted naturalists. For 7 years, he lived at in a simple, one-room cabin called Beaver Lodge on Ajawaan Lake; many hikers and canoeists make a pilgrimage to see his cabin and nearby grave site.

Entry fees are C$4 (US$2.85) per adult, C$3 (US$2.15) for seniors, and C$2 (US$1.45) per child, daily. The park is open year-round, but many campgrounds, motels, and facilities are closed after October. There are a handful of winter campsites, though, if you've come to ice fish or to cross-country ski on the more than 150 kilometers (93 miles) of trails.

The town of **Waskesiu,** which lies on the shores of the lake of the same name, is the supply center and also has accommodations.

At the **Visitor Service Centre** at park headquarters in Waskesiu, you'll find an 18-hole golf course, tennis courts, bowling greens, and a paddle wheeler that cruises Waskesiu Lake. The staff here can tell you about the weather and the condition of the trails; check in with them before undertaking any serious canoe or backcountry trip. The park's **Nature Centre** presents an audiovisual program called "Up North" daily during July and August. Together with the participatory exhibits at the center and naturalist-led programs like sunrise hikes and starlight walks, it's an excellent way to discover a hint of what awaits you in the park.

The park has 10 short **hiking trails,** plus four or so longer trails for backpackers, ranging from 10 to 41 kilometers (6.2 to 25.4 miles). Several easier ones begin in or near Waskesiu, though the best begin further north. From the northwest shore of Lake Kingsmere, you can pick up the 20-kilometer (12.4-mile) trail that leads to Grey Owl's cabin.

Canoeing routes wind through much of the park through a system of interconnected lakes and rivers. Canoes can be rented at three lakes, including Lake Waskesiu, and paddled along several routes, including the Bagwa and Bladebone routes.

There's terrific **fishing** in the park, but anglers must have a national-park fishing license. These can be purchased at the information center.

There are six **campgrounds** in the park, two with more than 100 sites and two with fewer than 30. They fill up fast on summer weekends; rates are from C$3 to C$18 (US$2.15 to US$13). The information office in Waskesiu can issue backcountry camping permits to backpackers and canoeists. Other accommodations are available in Waskesiu, including hotels, motels, and cabins, with rates starting at C$45 (US$32) double and rising to C$180 (US$129) for a suite sleeping six to eight people. Most cabins and lodges are rustic in style and often contain stone fireplaces. You could also base yourself in the town of Prince Albert and come into the park on a long day trip.

For additional information, contact **Prince Albert National Park,** P.O. Box 100, Waskesiu Lake, SK, S0J 2Y0 (☎ **306/663-4522**).

16 Alberta & the Rockies

by Bill McRae

Stretching from the Northwest Territories to the U.S. border of Montana in the south, flanked by the Rocky Mountains in the west and the Province of Saskatchewan in the east, Alberta is a big, beautiful, empty chunk of North America. At 661,188 square kilometers (255,285 sq. miles), the province has just two million inhabitants.

Culturally, Alberta is a beguiling mix of big city swagger and affluence and rural Canadian sincerity. Its cities, Calgary and Edmonton, are models of modern civic pride and hospitality; in fact, an anonymous behavioral survey recently named Edmonton Canada's friendliest city.

Early settlers came to Alberta for its wealth of furs; the Hudson's Bay Company established Edmonton House on the North Saskatchewan River in 1795. Blackfoot, one of the West's most formidable Indian nations, maintained control of the prairies until the 1870s, when the Royal Canadian Mounted Police arrived to enforce the white man's version of law and order. Open-range cattle ranching prospered on the rich grasslands, and agriculture is still the basis of the rural Alberta economy. Vast oil reserves were discovered beneath the prairies in the 1960s, introducing a tremendous 30-year boom across the province.

More than half the population lives in Edmonton and Calgary, leaving the rest of the province a tremendous amount of elbow room, breathing space, and unspoiled scenery. The Canadian Rockies rise to the west of the prairies and contain some of the finest mountain scenery on earth. Between them, Banff and Jasper national parks preserve much of this mountain beauty, but vast and equally spectacular regions of the Rockies, as well as portions of the nearby Columbia and Selkirk mountain ranges, are protected by other national and provincial parks.

All this wilderness makes outdoor activity Alberta's greatest draw. Hiking, biking, and pack trips on horseback have long pedigrees in the parks, as does superlative skiing—the winter Olympics were held in Calgary in 1988. Outfitters throughout the region offer whitewater and float trips on mighty rivers; and calmer pursuits like fishing and canoeing are also popular.

In addition, some of Canada's finest and most famous hotels are in Alberta. The incredible mountain lodges and châteaux built by early rail entrepreneurs are still in operation, offering unforgettable experiences in luxury and stunning scenery. These grand hotels established a standard of hospitality that's observed by hoteliers across the province. If you're looking for a more rural experience, head to one of Alberta's many guest ranches, where you can saddle up, poke some doggies, and end the evening at a steak barbecue.

1 Exploring Alberta & the Rockies

It's no secret that Alberta contains some of Canada's most compelling scenery and outdoor recreation. During the high season, from mid-June to August, this is a very busy place; Banff is generally acknowledged to be Canada's single most popular destination for foreign travelers.

A little preplanning is therefore essential, especially if you are traveling in the summer or have specific destinations or lodgings in mind. Accommodations are very tight throughout the province, and especially so in the Rockies. Make room reservations for Banff and Jasper as early as possible; likewise, Calgary is solidly booked for the Stampede, as is Edmonton for Klondike Days. Advance reservations are mandatory for these events.

Skiers should know that heavy snowfall closes some mountain roads in Alberta in winter. However, major passes are maintained and usually remain open to traffic. Highways 3, 1, and 16 are open year-round, though it's a good idea to call ahead to check road conditions. You can inquire locally, or call **Travel Alberta** at ☎ **800/ 661-8888** or the **Alberta Motor Association** at ☎ **403/474-8601** or check their Web site at **www.ama.ab.ca**. If you're a member of **AAA** or **CAA,** call their information line at ☎ **800/642-3810.** Always carry traction devices like tire chains in your vehicle, plus plenty of warm clothes and a sleeping bag if you're planning winter car travel.

This chapter moves along in a rough clockwise driving tour of Alberta and the Rockies: Coverage of Calgary is first, followed by day trips or short excursions into the southern part of the province. The many parks and recreation areas around Banff and Jasper national parks—including destinations in the Columbia and Selkirk mountains in nearby British Columbia—are covered next, followed by Edmonton and points north.

Don't let this structure dictate your route: There are lots of side roads and alternatives to the major destinations, and after a few days of crowds and traffic, you may be looking for a blue highway. The foothills and lakes in Kananaskis Country are a good alternative to busy Banff for campers and hikers. You can also free yourself of the crowds in the Alberta national parks by visiting the less-thronged but equally dramatic Glacier and Mount Revelstoke national parks in British Columbia.

VISITOR INFORMATION

For information about the entire province, contact **Travel Alberta,** Box 2500, Edmonton, AB, T5J 2Z4 (☎ **800/661-8888**). Be sure to ask for a copy of the accommodations and visitors guide, as well as the excellent *Traveler's Guide* and a road map. There's a separate guide for campers, which you should ask for if you are considering camping at any point during your trip.

Alberta has no provincial sales tax. There's only the national 7% goods-and-services tax (GST), plus a 5% accommodations tax.

BED & BREAKFAST NETWORKS

B&Bs are abundant in Alberta and cheaper than most hotels. The following agencies and resources make it easy to shop for B&Bs province-wide. B&B accommodations are available from **Alberta and Pacific Bed and Breakfast,** P.O. Box 15477,

M.P.O., Vancouver, BC, V6B 5B2 (☎ **604/944-1793;** fax 604/552-1659), a reservation service that maintains a network of B&B establishments throughout Alberta and BC; rates start at C$40 a day for singles, C$45 for doubles. **Alberta's Gem B&B Reservation Agency,** 11216 48th Ave., Edmonton, AB (☎ **403/434-6098**) will book bed-and-breakfast accommodations in Alberta or anywhere in North America. **Bed & Breakfast Agency of Alberta** (☎ **800/425-8160** or 403/277-8486) represents innkeepers throughout the province. Or visit the **B&B Canada** Web site, **www.bbcanada.com**, for hundreds of listings complete with photos and rates.

GUEST RANCHES

Alberta has been ranch country for well over a century, and the Old West lifestyle is deeply ingrained in Albertan culture. Indulge in a cowboy fantasy and spend a few days at one of the province's many historic guest ranches.

At Seebe, in the Kananaskis Country near the entrance to Banff National Park, are a couple of the oldest and most famous guest ranches. **Rafter Six Ranch** (☎ **403/ 673-3622**), with its beautiful log lodge, can accommodate up to 60 people. The original Brewster homestead was transformed in 1923 into the ✪ **Brewster's Kananaskis Guest Ranch** (☎ **403/673-3737**). Once a winter horse camp, the **Black Cat Guest Ranch** (☎ **403/865-3084**) near Hinton is another long-established guest ranch in beautiful surroundings.

At all of these historic ranches, horseback riding and trail rides are the main focus, but other Western activities, like rodeos, barbecues, and country dancing are usually on the docket. Gentler pursuits, like fishing, hiking, and lolling by the hot tub, are equally possible. At guest ranches, meals are usually served family-style in the central lodge, while accommodations are either in cabins or in the main lodge. A night at a guest ranch usually ranges from $C80 to C$100 (US$57 to US$72) and includes a ranch breakfast. Full bed-and-board packages are available for longer stays. There's usually an additional hourly fee for horseback riding.

Homestays at smaller working ranches are also possible. Here you can pitch in and help your ranch-family hosts with their work, or simply relax. For a stay on a real mom-and-pop farm, obtain a list of member ranches from **Alberta Country Vacation Association,** P.O. Box 396, Sangudo, AB, T0E 2A0 (☎ **403/785-3700;** Web site: www.comcept.ab.ca/cantravel/vacation.html).

HOSTELS

Alberta is rich with hostels, especially in the Rocky Mountain national parks, where they are often the only affordable lodging option. Remember: Hostels aren't just for youths anymore. All **Hostelling International** hostels in Alberta welcome guests of all ages. To find out more about Alberta hostels, check out their Web site: **www.hostellingIntl.ca/alberta**.

THE GREAT OUTDOORS

Banff and Jasper national parks have long been the center of mountain recreation for Alberta. If you're staying in Banff, Jasper, or Lake Louise, you'll find that outfitters and recreational rental operations in these centers are pretty sophisticated and professional: they make it easy and convenient to get outdoors and have an adventure. Most hotels will offer a concierge service that can arrange activities for you; for many, you need little or no advance registration. Shuttle buses to more distant activities are usually available as well.

You don't even have to break a sweat to enjoy the magnificent scenery—hire a horse and ride to the backcountry, or take an afternoon trail ride. Jasper, Banff, and Lake Louise each have gondolas to lift travelers from the valley floor to the

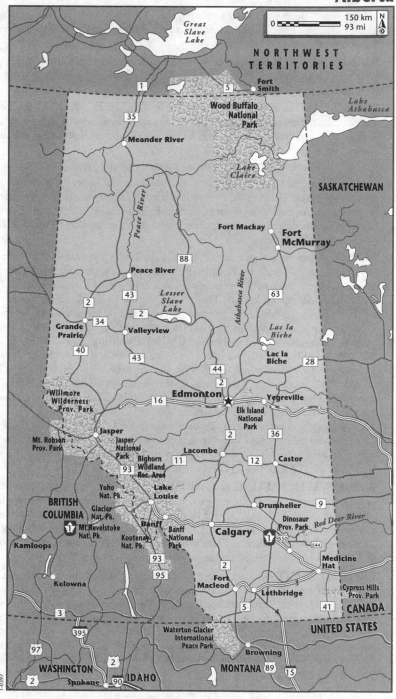

Alberta

mountaintops. Bring a picnic, or plan a ridge-top hike. If you're not ready for white water, the scenic cruises on Lake Minnewanka and Maligne Lake offer a more relaxed waterborne adventure.

BACKPACKING   Backcountry trips through high mountain meadows and remote lakes provide an unforgettable experience; Banff Park alone has 3,059 kilometers (1,900 miles) of hiking trails.

BIKING   Both parks provide free maps of local mountain-bike trails; the Bow Valley Parkway between Banff and Lake Louise and Parkway 93A in Jasper Park are both good, less trafficked roads for road biking. Bike rentals are easily available nearly everywhere in the parks.

ROCK CLIMBING, ICE CLIMBING & MOUNTAINEERING   The sheer rock faces on Mount Rundle near Banff and the Pallisades near Jasper are popular with rock climbers, and the area's many waterfalls become frozen ascents for ice climbers in the winter. Instruction in mountaineering skills, including rock climbing, is offered by **Yamnuska,** a climbing outfitter based in Canmore (☎ **403/678-4164;** e-mail: yamnuska@banffnet.net).

SKIING   There are downhill areas at Banff, Lake Louise, Jasper, and at the former Olympic site at Nakiska in the Kananaskis Country. At its best, skiing is superb here: The snowpack is copious, the scenery beautiful, après-ski festivities indulgent, and the accommodations world-class. There's a lot of value in an Alberta ski holiday— lift tickets here are generally cheaper than at comparable ski areas in North America.

Heli-skiing isn't allowed in the national parks, but is popular in the adjacent mountain ranges in British Columbia. **CMH Heli-Skiing,** 217 Bear St., Banff (☎ **800/661-0252** or 402/762-7100; fax 403/762-5879), is the leader in this increasingly popular sport, which uses helicopters to deposit skiers on virgin slopes far from the lift lines and runs of ski resorts. CMH offers 7- or 10-day trips to eight different locations; prices begin at around C$3,200 (US$2,286), all lodging, food, equipment, and transport from Calgary inclusive.

Cross-country skiers will also find a lot to like in the Canadian Rockies. A number of snowbound mountain lodges remain open throughout the winter and serve as bases for adventurous Nordic skiers. The historic ✪ **Emerald Lake Lodge** in Yoho National Park (☎ **250/343-6321**) is one of the finest.

WHITE-WATER RAFTING & CANOEING   The Rockies' many glaciers and snowfields are the source of mighty rivers. Outfitters throughout the region offer white-water rafting and canoe trips of varying lengths and difficulty—you can spend a single morning on the river, or plan a 5-day expedition. Jasper is central to a number of good white-water rivers; contact **White-Water River Adventures** (☎ **403/ 852-3370**), one of many local outfitters offering trips.

WILDLIFE VIEWING   If you're thrilled by seeing animals in the wild, you've turned to the right chapter. No matter which one you choose, the Rocky Mountain national parks are all teeming with wildlife—bighorn sheep, grizzly and black bears, deer, mountain goats, moose, coyotes, lynxes, wolves, and more. See Section 5, "Introducing the Canadian Rockies," later in this chapter, for important warnings about how to handle wildlife encounters in the parks responsibly and safely. Aside from the Rockies, there's also ✪ **Elk Island National Park** just outside Edmonton, which harbors the tiny pygmy shrew and the immense wood buffalo. The world's last remaining herd of wood buffalo lives in Wood Buffalo National Park in the far northern reaches of the province. This hard-to-reach preserve is also the only known breeding ground for the whooping crane.

2 Calgary

Historically, Calgary dates back just over a century, to the summer of 1875, when a detachment of the Northwest Mounted Police reached the confluence of the Bow and Elbow rivers. The solid log fort that they built had attracted 600 settlers by the end of the year.

Gradually the lush prairie lands around the settlement drew tremendous beef herds, many of them from overgrazed U.S. ranches in the south. Calgary grew into a cattle metropolis, a large meat-packing center by rancher standards. When World War II ended, the placid city numbered barely 100,000.

The oil boom erupted in the late 1960s, and in 1 decade the pace and complexion of the city changed utterly. The population shot up at a pace that made statisticians dizzy. In 1978 alone, $1 billion worth of construction was added to the skyline, creating office high-rises, hotel blocks, walkways, and shopping centers so fast that even locals weren't sure what was around the next corner.

The recession caused by the world's oil glut cooled Calgary's overheated growth considerably. But—at least from the visitor's angle—this enhanced the city's attractiveness. The once-ubiquitous rooftop cranes that marred its skyline have largely disappeared. However, Calgary continues to prosper. In the mid-1990s, the oil market heated up again, and Alberta's pro-business political climate tempted national companies to build their headquarters here.

In February 1988 Calgary was the site of the Winter Olympics, giving it the opportunity to roll out the welcome mat on a truly international scale. The city outdid itself in hospitality, erecting a whole network of facilities, including the Canada Olympic Park, by the Trans-Canada Highway, some 15 minutes west of downtown.

Calgary has an imposing skyline with dozens of business towers topping 40 stories. Despite this, the city doesn't seem urban. With its many parks and convivial populace, Calgary retains the atmosphere of a much smaller, friendlier town.

ESSENTIALS

VISITOR INFORMATION   The **Visitor Service Centres** at Tower Centre, 9th Avenue SW and Centre Street, and at the airport, provide you with free literature, maps, and information about the city. These are run by the **Calgary Convention and Visitors Bureau,** whose head office is at 237 8th Ave. SE, Calgary, AB, T2G 0K8. Included in their telephone services is a useful, no-charge accommodations bureau (☎ **800/661-1678** or 403/263-8510; e-mail: destination@visitor.calgary.ab.ca; Web site: www.visitor.calgary.ab.ca).

GETTING THERE   **Calgary International Airport** lies 16 kilometers (10 miles) northeast of the city. You can go through U.S. Customs right here if you're flying home via Calgary. The airport is served by **Air Canada** (☎ 800/776-3000); **Canadian Airlines** (☎ 800/426-7000); **Delta** (☎ 800/221-1212); **American Airlines** (☎ 800/433-7300); **United** (☎ 800/241-6522); **KLM** (☎ 800/374-7747); plus Time Air, Air B.C., Horizon, and several commuter lines. A shuttle service to and from Edmonton is run frequently each day by Air Canada and Canadian Airlines. Cab fare to downtown hotels from the airport comes to around C$25 (US$18). The **Airporter bus** takes you downtown from the airport for C$8.50 (US$6).

From the U.S. border in the south, Highway 2 runs to Calgary. The same excellent road continues north to Edmonton (via Red Deer). From Vancouver in the west to Regina in the east, you take the Trans-Canada Highway.

The nearest VIA Rail station is in Edmonton. You can, however, take a scenic train ride from Vancouver on the *Rocky Mountaineer* service, operated by the **Great**

Canadian Rail Tour Company (☎ 800/665-7245). The lowest priced tickets begin at C$475 (US$340) for 2 days of daylight travel, which includes overnight accommodation in Kamloops. Trains depart every 5 days.

Greyhound Buses (☎ 800/661-8747 or 403/260-0877) link Calgary with most other points in Canada, including Banff and Edmonton, as well as points in the United States. The depot is at 877 Greyhound Way SW.

CITY LAYOUT Central Calgary lies between the Bow River in the north and the Elbow River to the south. The two rivers meet at the eastern end of the city, forming St. George's Island, which houses a park and the zoo. South of the island stands Fort Calgary, birthplace of the city. The Bow River makes a bend north of downtown, and in this bend nestles Prince's Island Park and Eau Claire Market. The Canadian Pacific Railway tracks run between 9th and 10th avenues and Central Park and Stampede Park, scene of Calgary's greatest annual festival, stretch south of the tracks.

Northwest, just across the Bow River, is the University of Calgary's lovely campus. The airport is just northwest of the city.

Calgary is divided into four segments: northeast (NE), southeast (SE), northwest (NW), and southwest (SW), with avenues running east-west and streets north-south. The north and south numbers begin at Centre Avenue, the east and west numbers at Centre Street—a recipe for confusion if ever there were one.

GETTING AROUND Within the city, transportation is provided by the **Calgary Transit System** (☎ 403/276-1000). The system uses buses, plus a light-rail system called the C-Train. You can transfer from the light rail to buses on the same ticket. The ride costs C$1.50 (US$1.10) for adults and 90¢ (US65¢) for children; C-Train is free in the downtown stretch between 10th Street and City Hall (buses are not). Tickets are only good for travel in one direction.

Car-rental firms include: **Tilden,** 114 5th Ave. SE (☎ 403/263-6386); **Budget,** 140 6th Ave. SE (☎ 403/226-1550); and **Hertz,** 227 6th Ave. SW (☎ 403/221-1300). Each of these, as well as other international agencies, have bureaus at the airport.

To summon a taxi, call **Checker Cabs** (☎ 403/299-9999), **Red Top Cabs** (☎ 403/974-4444), or **Yellow Cabs** (☎ 403/974-1111).

The first thing a pedestrian will note about Calgary is how long the east-west blocks are. Allow 15 minutes to walk 5 blocks. Pedestrians will also like the "Plus-15" system, a series of enclosed walkways 15 feet above street level that connects downtown buildings. These walkways enable you to shop in living-room comfort, regardless of weather. Watch for the little "+15" signs on streets for access points.

FAST FACTS   American Express There's an office at 421 7th Ave. SW (☎ 403/261-5085).

CAA The **Alberta Motor Association,** affiliated with the Canadian Automobile Association, reciprocates with the AAA, offering members free travel information, advice, and services. The Calgary office is at 4700 17th Ave. SW (☎ 403/240-5300).

Doctors If you need nonemergency medical attention, check the phone number for the closest branch of **Medicentre,** a group of walk-in clinics open daily from 7am to midnight.

Emergency For medical, fire, or crime emergencies, dial ☎ **911.**

Hospitals If you need medical care, try **Foothills Hospital,** 1403 29th St. NW. (☎ 403/670-1110).

Calgary

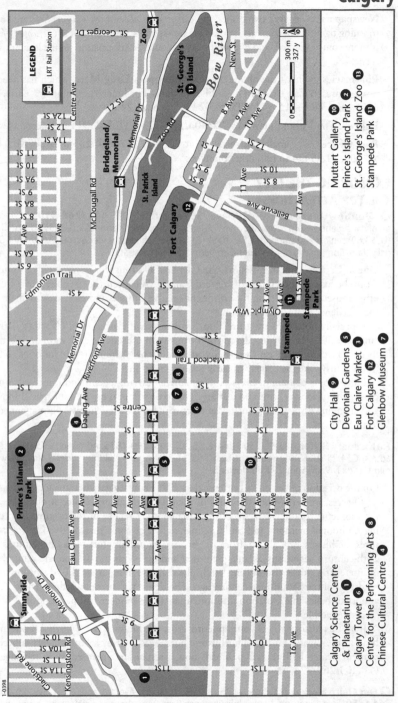

LEGEND
LRT Rail Station

Bow River

St. Georges Dr.
Zoo
St. George's Island
Bridgeland/Memorial
Memorial Dr
Centre Ave
12A St
12 St
11A St
11 St
10 St
9A St
9 St
8A St
8 St
4 Ave
2 Ave
1 Ave
McDougall Rd
6A St
9 St
Edmonton Trail
4 St
2 St
1 St
Memorial Dr
Riverfront Ave
Daqing Ave
Centre St
Prince's Island Park
Sunnyside
Memorial Dr
Gladstone Rd
Kensington Rd
11A St
11 St
10A St
10 St

St. Patrick Island
Fort Calgary
Zoo Rd
New St
8 Ave
9 Ave
10 Ave
11 St
6 St
8 St
11 Ave
Bellevue Ave
17 Ave
13 St
12 St
10 Ave
8 St

300 m
327 y

5 Ave
3 Ave
4 St
Olympic Way
13 Ave
14 Ave
15 Ave
Stampede
Stampede Park
Macleod Trail
5 St
4 St
3 St
7 Ave
1 St
Centre St
1 St
2 St
4 Ave
5 St
4 St
6 Ave
7 Ave
9 St
8 St
7 St
6 St
10 St
11 St
2 Ave
3 Ave
4 Ave
5 Ave
6 Ave
Eau Claire Ave
9 St
7 St
16 Ave
10 St
11 St

Calgary Science Centre & Planetarium ❶
Calgary Tower ❻
Centre for the Performing Arts ❽
Chinese Cultural Centre ❹

City Hall ❾
Devonian Gardens ❺
Eau Claire Market ❸
Fort Calgary ⓬
Glenbow Museum ❼

Muttart Gallery ❿
Prince's Island Park ❷
St. George's Island Zoo ⓭
Stampede Park ⓫

1-0398

535

Newspapers   Calgary's two dailies, the *Calgary Herald* and the *Calgary Sun,* are both morning papers. The local arts and events newspapers are *Avenue* and *Cityscope. Ffwd* is more youth-oriented, and is a good place to look for information on the local music scene.

Pharmacies   Check the phone book for **Shoppers Drug Mart,** which has over a dozen stores in Calgary, most open till midnight. The branch at Chinook Centre, at 6455 Macleod Trail S. (☎ **403/253-2424**), is open 24 hours.

Police   The 24-hour number is ☎ **403/266-1234.** Dial ☎ **911** in emergencies.

Post Office   The main post office is at 207 9th Ave. (☎ **403/974-2078**). Call ☎ **403/292-5434** to find other branches.

EXPLORING THE CITY
THE TOP ATTRACTIONS

✪ **Glenbow Museum.** 130 9th Ave. SE (at 1st St.). ☎ **403/268-4100.** E-mail: glenbow@glenbow.org. Web site: www.glenbow.org. Admission C$7 (US$5) adults, C$5 (US$3.60) seniors and students, C$25 (US$18) families; children under 6 free. May to mid-Oct daily 9am–5pm; mid-Oct–May Tues–Sun 9am–5pm. LRT: 1st St. E.

One of Canada's finest museums, the Glenbow is a must for anyone with an interest in the history and culture of western Canada. What sets the Glenbow apart from other museums chronicling the continent's native cultures and pioneer settlement is the excellence of its interpretation.

Especially notable is the third floor, with its vivid evocation of Canada's native cultures, and a compelling description of western Canada's exploration and settlement. The chronology isn't so strictly adhered to that there isn't time for brief asides into whimsy, like the display of early washing machines.

Other floors contain displays of West African carvings, gems and minerals, and a cross-cultural look at arms and warfare. The second floor is reserved for special shows and changing displays of paintings and artwork from the Glenbow's permanent collection.

Fort Calgary Historic Park. 750 9th Ave. SE. ☎ **403/290-1875.** Admission C$5 (US$3.60) adults, C$4.25 (US$3.05) seniors, C$2.50 (US$1.80) youths; children under 7 free. May to mid-Oct daily 9am–5pm. LRT: Bridgeland.

On the occasion of the city's centennial in 1975, Fort Calgary became a public park of 40 acres, spread around the ruins of the original Mounted Police stronghold. At the moment, volunteers are reconstructing an exact replica of the original fort, using traditional methods and building materials. The fort's Interpretive Centre captures the history of Calgary, from its genesis as a military fort to the beginnings of 20th-century hegemony as an agricultural and oil boomtown. There are a number of interesting videos and docent-led displays; always in focus are the adventures and hardships of the Mounties a century ago. The rigors of their westward march and the almost unbelievable isolation and loneliness these pioneer troopers endured now seems incredible.

If all this history whets your appetite, cross the Elbow River on 9th Avenue and head to the **Deane House.** This historic home was built by a Fort Calgary superintendent nearly 100 years ago, and is now a restaurant operated by Fort Calgary (☎ **403/269-7747**).

✪ **Eau Claire Market & Prince's Island Park.** Near 2nd Ave. SW and 3rd St. SW. ☎ **403/264-6450.** Free admission. Market building open 9am–9pm, shops and restaurants have varying hours. LRT: 3rd St. W.

The Calgary Stampede

Every year during July, Calgary puts on the biggest, wildest, woolliest Western fling on earth. To call the stampede a show would be a misnomer. The whole city participates by going mildly crazy for the occasion, donning Western gear, whooping, hollering, dancing, and generally behaving uproariously.

Many of the organized events spill out into the streets, but most of them take place in Stampede Park, a show, sports, and exhibition ground just south of downtown that was built for just that purpose. Portions of the park become amusement areas, whirling, spinning, and rotating with the latest rides. Other parts are set aside especially for the kids, who romp through Kids' World and the Petting Zoo. Still other areas have concerts, livestock shows, food and handicraft exhibitions, free lectures, and dance performances.

The top attractions, though, are the rodeo events, the largest and most prestigious of their kind in all of North America. Cowboys from all over the world take part in such competitions as riding bucking broncos and bulls, roping calves, and wrestling steers for prize money totaling C$600,000 (US$352,940). At the world-famous Chuckwagon Race you'll see old-time Western cook wagons thundering around the track in a fury of dust and pounding hooves, competing eagerly for more than C$375,000 (US$220,599) in prize money. At night the arena becomes a blaze of lights when the Stampede Grandstand—the largest outdoor extravaganza in the world—takes over with precision-kicking dancers, clowns, bands, and spectacles.

On top of that, the Stampede offers a food fair, an art show, dancing exhibitions, an international bazaar, a gambling casino, lotteries, and free entertainment on several stages.

Let me tell you right from the start that the whole city of Calgary is absolutely packed for the occasion, not just to the rafters but way out into the surrounding countryside. Reserving accommodations well ahead is essential—as many months ahead of your arrival as you can possibly foresee. (For lodging, call **Calgary's Convention and Visitors Bureau** at ☎ **800/661-1678.**) Some downtown watering holes even take reservations for space at their bar; that should give you an idea of how busy Calgary gets.

The same advice applies to reserving tickets for all of the park events. Tickets cost between C$17 (US$12) and C$43 (US$31), depending on the event, the seats, and whether it is afternoon or evening. For mail-order bookings, contact the **Calgary Exhibition and Stampede,** P.O. Box 1860, Station M, Calgary, AB, T2P 2M7 (☎ **800/661-1678;** fax 403/223-9736).

Calgary's new shopping, social, and dining center is Eau Claire Market, a car-free pedestrian zone north of downtown on the banks of the Bow River. The market itself is a huge two-story warehouse of a building, containing boutique shops; fresh fish, meat, vegetable, and fruit stalls; innumerable casual restaurants and bars; and a four-screen cinema. Also accessed from the market is the **IMAX Theatre** (☎ **403/974-4629**) with its five-story domed screen. Surrounding the market are lawns, fountains, and pathways leading to Prince's Island Park, a bucolic island in the Bow River lined with paths, shaded by cottonwood trees, and populated by hoards of Canada geese.

Eau Claire Market is extremely popular—this is where much of downtown Calgary comes to eat, drink, shop, sunbathe, jog, and hang out—it's easy to spend hours here just watching people and exploring.

○ **Calgary Zoo, Botanical Garden & Prehistoric Park.** 1300 Zoo Rd. NE. ☎ **403/232-9300.** Admission C$9.50 (US$7) adults, seniors half price Tues–Thurs, C$4.75 (US$3.40) children 2–17; discounts off season. Late May to Sept daily 9am–6pm; winter daily 9am–4pm. LRT: Zoo station.

Calgary's large and thoughtfully designed zoo lies on St. George's Island in the Bow River. The Calgary Zoo comes as close to providing natural habitats for its denizens as is technically possible—the animals live in environments rather than confines. You'll particularly want to see the troop of majestic lowland gorillas and the African warthogs. The flora and fauna of western and northern Canada is also on display, as is an amazing year-round tropical butterfly enclosure. Adjoining the zoo is the Prehistoric Park, a three-dimensional textbook of ancient dinosaur habitats populated by 22 amazingly realistic replicas. Call to inquire about special summer events, like Thursday Jazz Nights and free interpretive talks called "Nature Tales."

Calgary Tower. 9th Ave. and Centre St. SW. ☎ **403/266-7171.** Elevator ride C$5.50 (US$3.95) adults, C$2.50 (US$1.80) children. June 15–Sept 15 daily 7:30am–11pm; Sept 16–June 14 daily 8am–10pm. LRT: 1st St. E.

Reaching 626 feet (762 steps) into the sky, this Calgary landmark is topped by an observation terrace offering unparalleled views of the city and the mountains and prairies beyond. A stairway from the terrace leads to the cocktail lounge where you can enjoy drinks and a panoramic view. Photography from up here is fantastic. The high-speed elevator whisks you to the top in just 63 seconds. **The Panorama Restaurant** (☎ **403/266-7171**) is the near-mandatory revolving restaurant.

Olympic Hall of Fame and Museum. 88 Canada Olympic Park Rd. SW. ☎ **403/247-5452.** Admission C$3.75 (US$2.70) adults, C$3 (US$2.15) seniors and students, C$2.50 (US$1.80) children, C$10 (US$7) families. Summer daily 8am–9pm; off-season daily 8am–5pm. Take Hwy. 1 west.

This lasting memento of Calgary's role as host of the 1988 Winter Olympic Games stands in the Olympic Park. Three floors of exhibits contain the world's largest collection of Olympic souvenirs, such as the torch used to bring the flame from Greece, costumes and sporting equipment used by the athletes, superb action photographs, and a gallery of all medal winners since the revival of the Olympic Games in 1924. Also shown is a video presentation of the games and their history. Activities include summer luge rides, for C$13 (US$9), a new mountain-bike course, and chairlift rides up to the ski jump tower.

MORE ATTRACTIONS

Calgary Chinese Cultural Centre. 197 1st St. SW. ☎ **403/262-5071.** Building admission free. Museum C$2 (US$1.45) adults, C$1 (US70¢) seniors and students. Museum daily 11am–5pm; building hours 9:30am–9pm. Bus: 2, 3, or 17.

The new landmark and focal point of Calgary's Chinatown, this impressive structure is topped by a great central dome patterned after the Temple of Heaven in Beijing. The center houses exhibits, lecture halls, classrooms, a library, and specialized retail shops as well as a restaurant, gym, and bookstore. It covers 70,000 square feet and offers an overview of historical and contemporary Chinese cultural life, displayed underneath a gleaming gold dragon hovering 60 feet above the floor.

Devonian Gardens. 8th Ave. and 3rd St. SW, 4th floor. ☎ **403/268-3830.** Free admission. Daily 9am–9pm. LRT: 3rd St. W.

The gardens are a patch of paradise in downtown, an enclosed 2¹/₂-acre park 46 feet above street level. Laid out in natural contours with 1.6 kilometers (1 mile) of pathways and a central stage for musical performances, the gardens contain 20,000 plants (mostly imported from Florida), a reflecting pool, a sun garden, a children's playground, a sculpture court, and a water garden.

Fish Creek Provincial Park. Canyon Meadows Dr. and Macleod Trail SE. ☎ **403/297-5293.** Bus: 52, 11, or 78.

On the outskirts of town, but easily accessible, Fish Creek Park is one of the largest urban parks in the world—actually, a kind of metropolitan wildlife reserve. Spreading over 2,900 acres, it provides a sheltered habitat for a vast variety of animals and birds. You can learn about them by joining in the walks and slide presentations given by park interpreters. For information on their schedules and planned activities, visit the administration office or call the number above.

Museum of the Regiments. 4520 Crowchild Trail SW (at Flanders Ave.). ☎ **403/974-2850.** Admission by donation. Thurs–Tues 10am–4pm. Bus: 20 to Flanders Ave., then 1 block south.

The largest military museum in western Canada tells the story of four famous Canadian regiments from the turn of the century to today. A series of lifelike miniature and full-size displays re-create scenes from the Boer War in 1900 to World War II; contemporary peacekeeping operations are also depicted. You also see videos, weapons, uniforms, medals, and photographs relating the history of the regiments and hear the actual voices of the combatants describing their experiences.

Muttart Gallery. 1221 2nd St. SW, in the Memorial Library. ☎ **403/266-2764.** Free admission. Mon–Wed and Fri noon–5pm, Thurs noon–8pm, Sat 10am–5pm. LRT: 4th St. W.

The Muttart Gallery is a contemporary art gallery with special emphasis on the contribution of local talent. A good place to see Calgary's place in the modern-art scene.

ESPECIALLY FOR KIDS

Calgary Science Centre. 701 11th St. SW. ☎ **403/221-3700.** Admission (exhibits and star shows) C$9 (US$6) adults, C$7 (US$5) youths and seniors, C$6 (US$4.30) children 3–12; children under 3 free. Summer daily 10am–8pm; off-season Wed 1–9pm, Thurs–Fri 1–9:30pm, Sat 10am–9:30pm, Sun 10:30am–5pm. LRT: 10th St. W.

The Calgary Science Centre features a fascinating combination of exhibitions, a planetarium, films, laser shows, and live theater all under one roof. The hands-on, science-oriented exhibits change, but always invite visitors to push, pull, talk, listen, and play. The 360° Star Theatre opens windows to the universe.

Heritage Park Historical Village. 1900 Heritage Dr. (west of 14th St. SW). ☎ **403/ 259-1900.** Gate admission C$10 (US$7) adults, C$6 (US$4.30) children; rides extra. May–Sept daily 9am–5pm; Sept and Oct weekends and holidays 9am–5pm. Call for other times. LRT: Heritage station, then Bus 20 to Northmount.

On a peninsula jutting into Glenmore Reservoir, some 66 acres let you take a trip into the past. This Canadian pioneer turn-of-the-century township (1880–1920) has been painstakingly recreated with more than 150 buildings from frontier days. Walk down the main street and admire the "latest" fashions, drop in at the authentic soda fountain, stop at the elaborate hotel, watch the blacksmith at work, or sit on the cracker barrel of the general store. The town includes a Hudson's Bay Company fort, a native-Canadian village, mining camp, old-time ranch, steam trains, streetcars, a horse-drawn bus, and a paddle wheeler that chugs you around Glenmore Reservoir.

SHOPPING

DOWNTOWN   The city's main shopping district is found along 8th Avenue SW, between 5th and 1st streets SW. The lower part of 8th Avenue has been turned into a pedestrian zone called the **Stephen Avenue Mall,** closed to most vehicles and lined with trees, buskers, shops, and outdoor cafes. Major shopping venues lining 8th

Avenue include Eatons, the Hudson's Bay Company, and Holt Renfrew. **Banker's Hall** is an upscale, international boutique mall on 8th Avenue at 2nd Street SW.

If you're beginning to like the look of pearl snap shirts and the cut of Wranglers jeans, head to **Riley & McCormick,** 209 8th Ave. SW (☎ 403/262-1556), across from the Bay, one of Calgary's original Western apparel stores. If you're looking for cowboy boots, go to the **Alberta Boot Company,** 614 10th Ave. SW (☎ 403/263-4605), Alberta's only boot manufacturer. Buy a pair of boots off the shelf (the ABC has 10,000 pairs in stock—C$200/US$143 ought to do it), or have a pair custom made (take out a second mortgage on your house).

17TH AVENUE SW   The stretch of 17th Avenue approximately between 4th and 10th streets SW has developed a mix of specialty shops, boutiques, cafes, bars, restaurants, and delis that makes strolling and browsing a real pleasure. Many of Calgary's art galleries and interior-decorating shops are also located here. Be sure to stop in at **Provenance,** 932 17th Ave. SW (☎ 403/245-8511), which features regional Canadian arts and crafts.

KENSINGTON VILLAGE   A hip hangout for Calgary's young at heart, Kensington is just northwest of downtown across the Bow River, centered at 10th Street NW and Kensington Road. Crowded between the ubiquitous coffee shops are bicycle shops, trendy new- and used-clothing shops, bookstores, and decor boutiques.

INGLEWOOD   Calgary's principal antique-shop area is located just east of downtown, in the little neighborhood of Inglewood. Lining 9th Avenue SE near 12th Street are historic storefronts that now house dozens of shops devoted to **antiques and collectibles.**

ACCOMMODATIONS
DOWNTOWN
Very Expensive

Delta Bow Valley. 209 4th Ave. SE, Calgary, AB, T2G 0C6. ☎ **403/266-1980.** Fax 403/266-0007. 371 rms, 27 suites. A/C MINIBAR TV TEL. C$215 (US$154) double; C$235 (US$168) suite. Special weekend rate C$80 (US$57) per night, including complimentary gifts for children. Children under 18 stay free in parents' rm; children under 6 eat free from children's menu. AE, DC, ER, MC, V. Parking C$7.50 (US$5) weekdays; free on weekends.

Completely renovated in 1995, the Delta is one of Calgary's finest hotels, with excellent on-premises restaurants and a large, airy, attractive lobby. The focus of the hotel is upscale business travel, and these are some of the best facilities in the city if you're here with work to do. In their corner business suites, there are large desks completely set up for work: furnished with printer, in-room fax machine, cordless phone, and ergonomic chair; some rooms even have phones in the bathroom. And after all this there's still room for a king-size bed and a couch and chair to relax in. The standard rooms are also spacious and equipped with all the niceties you'd expect in this class of hotel.

Dining/Entertainment: Besides the classy Conservatory restaurant, there's a coffee shop and comfortable lobby bar.

Services: Rm service, laundry/dry cleaning, valet parking.

Facilities: Although primarily a business hotel, the Delta goes the distance to make families welcome. During the summer and on weekends, there's a complete children's activity center: Leave the kids here while you head out to dinner. Other pluses include a marvelous pool, hot tub, and sauna area, which leads to a rooftop deck.

✪ **Palliser Hotel.** 133 9th Ave. SW., Calgary, AB, T2P 2M3. ☎ **800/441-1414** or 403/262-1234. Fax 403/260-1260. 405 rms, 16 suites. A/C MINIBAR TV TEL. C$180–C$245

(US$129–US$175) double; from C$225 (US$161) suite. AE, DC, ER, MC, V. Valet parking C$14 (US$10) per day; self-parking C$11 (US$8).

Opened in 1914 as one of the Canadian Pacific Railroad hotels, the Palliser is Calgary's landmark historic hotel. The vast marble-floored lobby, surrounded by columns and lit by gleaming chandeliers, is the very picture of Edwardian sumptuousness. Guest rooms are large for a hotel of this vintage—the Pacific Premier rooms would be suites at most other hotels—and they preserve the Palliser's period charm while incorporating all the modern luxuries and facilities expected by today's traveler. All rooms feature cordless phones, voice mail, and business desks with easy-to-reach electrical outlets and modem jacks. Entree Gold–class rooms come with their own concierge service, express check-in, and cozy private lounge with complimentary breakfast, drinks, and hors d'oeuvres. The Palliser's C$30-million renovation continues, with new carpets, upholstery, and furniture throughout.

Dining/Entertainment: The Rimrock Room has vaulted ceilings, period Western murals, a massive stone fireplace, and hand-tooled leather panels on real teakwood beams. The lounge bar, with its towering windows, looks like a gentlemen's West End club.

Services: Concierge, 24-hour room service, secretarial services, valet parking.

Facilities: New indoor lap pool, health club, whirlpool, steam room, and sauna; staffed business center with computer and Internet access.

Expensive

Calgary Marriott Hotel. 110 9th Ave. SE. (at Centre St.), Calgary, AB, T2G 5A6. ☎ 800/228-9290 or 403/266-7331. Fax 403/262-8442. 383 rms, 10 suites. A/C TV TEL. From C$169 (US$121) double; from C$199 (US$142) suite. Ask about "Two for Breakfast" packages. AE, CB, DC, DISC, ER, MC, V. Valet parking C$13 (US$9) per day; self-parking C$10 (US$7).

The newly renovated Calgary Marriott is about as central as things get in Calgary: Linked to the Calgary Convention Centre, and convenient to the arty goings-on at the Centre for the Performing Arts and the Glenbow Museum, the Marriott is also connected via skywalk with Palliser Square, Calgary Tower, and loads of downtown shopping.

Rooms are large and nicely and subtly decorated. All rooms have windows that open, voice mail, lots of mirrors, a desk set up for the business traveler, and an ironing board and iron. Suites are especially nice; the French Parlour suites could pass for an elegant apartment. As part of Marriott's C$7.25 million makeover, all rooms have new furniture, carpets, and upholstery; the first- and second-floor lobbies have been redesigned.

Dining/Entertainment: The Wheatsheaf offers casual family dining; Traders is the hotel's fine-dining restaurant. A fireside cocktail bar, the Plaza Lounge, is the spot for cocktails and conversation.

Services: Concierge, room service, valet service, free newspapers.

Facilities: A great pool, whirlpool, sauna, and health club complex—all complimentary—which leads onto two rooftop decks. On-command video movie channels.

International Hotel. 220 4th Ave. SW, Calgary, AB, T2P 0H5. ☎ 800/637-7200 or 403/265-9600. Fax 403/265-6949. 247 suites. A/C MINIBAR TV TEL. C$170–C$225 (US$122–US$161) 1-bedrm suite; C$190–C$225 (US$136–US$161) 2-bedrm suite. Children under 16 stay free in parents' rm. AE, CB, DC, ER, MC, V. Parking C$6 (US$4.30) per day.

A soaring 35-story tower with a breathtaking view from the upper balconies, the International is an all-suite hotel. Just out the back door is Chinatown and the Eau Claire Market area; the hotel is also very convenient to adjacent business towers. These are some of the largest rooms in Calgary. The hotel was originally built as an apartment building, so the suites are up to 800 square feet and contain separate bed- and living rooms, private balcony, and large bathroom. The decor is low-key, but you get the kinds of in-room amenities that come with a four-star hotel, including an extra-large minibar. Rooms all have two TVs and telephones, and modem hook-ups. The very large two-bedroom suites are great for families. Some units have full kitchens. Recent renovations include new carpets and furniture throughout, and a face-lift to all bathrooms.

The downside? The elevators date from the days when this was an apartment building; in summer, when tour buses hit, it can be exasperating to wait for the three elevators to serve guests on all 35 floors.

Dining/Entertainment: Family-dining restaurant and lobby lounge.

Services: Room service, on-call massage treatment, newspaper delivery, courtesy car.

Facilities: There's a very attractive tiled indoor pool, a Jacuzzi, a fitness room, and sauna.

✪ Westin Hotel. 320 4th Ave. SW, Calgary, AB, T2P 2S6. ☎ **800/937-8461** or 403/266-1611. 469 rms, 56 suites. A/C MINIBAR TV TEL. C$109–C$195 (US$78–US$139) double; C$195–C$700 (US$139–US$500) suite. Weekend packages bring the price of rms under C$100 (US$72), with C$37 (US$26) worth of in-hotel coupons. AE, DC, DISC, ER, MC, V. Parking C$9 (US$6) per day.

The Westin is a massive modern luxury block in the heart of the financial district, and probably the single nicest hotel in Calgary. The entire hotel has undergone a major renovation (C$1 million was spent on the lobby alone) over the past 3 years. Gone is the anonymous business-hotel atmosphere, replaced with a subtle Western feel that's reflected in the new, very comfortable Mission-style furniture, Navajo-look upholstery, feather duvets, and in-room period photos that commemorate Calgary's bronco-busting and oil-boom past. Beautiful barn-wood breakfronts and lowboys dispel the feeling that you're in one of the city's most modern hotels. Each room has two telephones and a data port, voice-mail, as well as an iron and ironing board. For C$20 (US$14), upgrade to a Westin Guest Office Room, with fax, printer, and copier.

Dining: No fewer than seven venues, from a buffet to the exquisite Owl's Nest, one of Calgary's finest restaurants.

Services: Room service is radio-dispatched for maximum efficiency. The hotel also rolls out the welcome mat for children, with a full array of children's furniture, a streamlined check-in for families, baby-sitting service, and a special kid's menu. A family's special needs are anticipated too, from strollers, potty chairs, playpens, to room service delivery of fresh diapers!

Facilities: A panoramic 17th-floor indoor pool with sauna and whirlpool on the rooftop.

Moderate

Travelers on a budget have excellent though limited choices in downtown Calgary. Luckily, Calgary's light-rail system makes it easy to stay outside the city center, yet have easy access to the restaurants and sites of downtown.

Best Western Suites Downtown. 1330 8th St. SW, Calgary, AB, T2R 1B3. ☎ **800/528-1234** or 403/228-6900. Fax 403/228-5535. 108 rms. A/C TV TEL. C$89–C$99 (US$64–US$71) double. AE, DISC, ER, MC, V. Free parking.

This all-suites hotel is an excellent value. There's a choice of standard, one-, or two-bedroom units; some with efficiency kitchens (microwave and refrigerator). This Best Western is a few blocks from downtown, but it is near the trendy street life of 17th Avenue. The motel has its own lounge and restaurant.

✪ **Sandman Hotel.** 888 7th Ave. SW, Calgary, AB, T2P 3J3. ☎ **800/736-3626** or 403/237-8626. Fax 403/290-1238. 299 rms, 2 suites. TV TEL. C$89–C$129 (US$64–US$92) double. AE, DC, DISC, MC, V. Parking C$4 (US$2.85).

This 23-story hotel on the west end of downtown is one of Calgary's best deals. The Sandman is conveniently located on the free rapid-transit mall, just west of the main downtown core. The standard rooms are good-sized, but the real winners are the corner rooms, which are very large, with great views on two sides, and a small kitchen. All rooms were renovated throughout in 1997. The Sandman is a popular place with corporate clients, due to its central location and good value.

The Sandman has the most complete fitness facility of any hotel in Calgary. It houses a private health club, which is available free to all guests: Facilities include a large pool, three squash courts, regularly scheduled aerobic exercise groups, and weight-training facilities. A massage therapist is available by appointment. Room service is available 24 hours a day; and there are three restaurants and two bars on the premises.

Inexpensive

Lord Nelson Inn. 1020 8th Ave. SW, Calgary, AB, T2P 1J3. ☎ **800/661-6017** or 403/269-8262. Fax 403/269-4868. 55 rms, 2 suites. A/C TV TEL. C$69–C$84 (US$49–US$60) double; C$79–C$125 (US$57–US$89) suite. AE, ER, MC, V. Free parking.

One of the best deals in the city, the Lord Nelson is a modern nine-story structure with recently renovated guest rooms and suites. Although on the edge of downtown, it's just a block from the downtown's free C-Train, which will put you in the heart of things in 5 minutes. The inn has a small cozy lobby with redbrick pillars and comfortable armchairs. Adjoining are a coffee shop and the Pub, a tavern with outdoor patio. Bedrooms come with two 25-inch TVs, couch, desk, refrigerator, and balcony; the suites come with Jacuzzis.

OUTSIDE DOWNTOWN

Lodgings in the following two areas are linked to downtown via the C-Train, and each area offers a variety of moderately priced accommodations with free parking.

Moderate

MACLEOD TRAIL   Once this was a cattle track, but now it's the main expressway heading south toward the U.S. border. The northern portions of the Macleod Trail are lined with inns and motels—from upper middle range to economy. Two of the most convenient follow.

Elbow River Inn. 1919 Macleod Trail S., Calgary, AB, T2G 4S1. ☎ **800/661-1463** or 403/269-6771. Fax 403/237-5181. 78 rms. TV TEL. C$89 (US$64) double. AE, CB, DC, ER, MC, V. Free parking.

The Elbow River Inn is the Macleod Trail establishment closest to downtown, and directly opposite the Stampede grounds. The only hotel on the banks of the little Elbow River, the inn has a pleasantly furnished lobby and a dining room with a view of the water. There is also a restaurant offering hearty home-style cooking and a casino operating 6 days a week until midnight. The bedrooms are simply furnished; it's a good comfortable hostelry with near-budget rates.

Holiday Inn Macleod Trail. 4206 Macleod Trail SE, Calgary, AB, T2G 2R7. ☎ **800/661-1889** or 403/287-2700. Fax 403/243-4721. 154 rms. A/C TV TEL. C$114 (US$82) double. Weekend rates available. AE, CB, DC, DISC, ER, MC, V. Free parking.

A recently renovated property with a C-Train (light-rail station) right outside the door, the Holiday Inn is handsome and welcoming, and is located only a short stroll away from an oasis of parkland. The softly lit lobby is charming, the restaurant and lounge are elegantly furnished, and the heated indoor pool ideal for unwinding. The hotel also offers valet and secretarial services, room service, and a coin-operated laundry.

MOTEL VILLAGE   Northwest of downtown, Motel Village is a triangle of more than a dozen large motels, plus restaurants, stores, and gas stations, forming a self-contained hamlet near the University of Calgary. Enclosed by Crowchild Trail, the Trans-Canada Highway, and Highway 1A, the village is arranged so that most of the costlier establishments flank the highway; the cheaper ones lie off Crowchild Trail, offering a wide choice of accommodations in a small area with good transportation connections. If you're driving and don't want to deal with downtown traffic, just head here to find a room: except during the Stampede, you'll be able to find a room without reservations; on C-Train, use either Lions Park or Banff Park stops. A number of chain hotels are located here, including **Travelodge North,** 2304 16th Ave. NW (☎ **800/255-3050** or 403/289-0211) and the **Quality Inn Motel Village,** 2359 Banff Trail NW (☎ **800/221-2222** or 403/289-1973).

Bed & Breakfasts

If you enjoy B&Bs, ask for the yearly updated Bed and Breakfast Association of Calgary brochure from the **Calgary Convention and Visitors Bureau,** 237 8th Ave. SE (☎ **800/661-1678;** e-mail: destination@visitor.calgary.ab.ca; Web site: www.visitor.calgary.ab.ca), or call the association itself at ☎ **403/543-3900.** There are nearly 60 accredited B&Bs in Calgary, with most rates between C$40 (US$29) and C$60 (US$43) per night. The visitors bureau can also book a B&B for you.

Budget Options

The **Calgary International Hostel,** 520 7th Ave. SE, Calgary, AB, T2G 0J6 (☎ **403/269-8239;** fax 403/266-6227; e-mail: chostel@telusplanet.net), has 120 beds and charges members C$15 (US$11) and nonmembers C$19 (US$14). It's near downtown, near the bars and restaurants along Stephen Avenue and the theaters near the performing-arts center. Laundry facilities are provided, and there are two family rooms, as well as a game room and common area.

The **University of Calgary,** 2500 University Dr. NW, Calgary, AB, T2N 1N4 (☎ **403/220-3210;** fax 403/282-8443), offers accommodations to visitors from May to August, for C$28 (US$20) single, C$39 (US$28) double, and two- to four-bed suites at C$28 (US$20) per person (MasterCard and Visa accepted); parking C$2 (US$1.45) a day. The 314-acre campus of the University of Calgary is parklike and offers a vast variety of sports and cultural attractions. Facilities are excellent, including restaurants, meeting rooms, and one- to four-bedroom suites. The campus is beside the C-Train Transit line.

Camping

The **Calgary West KOA,** on the Trans-Canada Highway West (Box 10, Site 12, SS no. 1), Calgary, AB, T2M 4N3 (☎ **403/288-0411**), allows tents and pets, and has washrooms, toilets, laundry, a dumping station, hot showers, groceries, and a pool. Prices for two people are C$25 (US$18) per night; tent sites are C$17 (US$12) per night.

DINING

Eating out in Calgary is a lot of fun. The locals clearly think so, too, as restaurants are busy and full of vitality. In general, you'll find fine dining downtown, while more casual bistros and restaurants tend to be found along 17th Avenue.

DOWNTOWN

Expensive

✪ The Conservatory. 209 4th Ave. SE. ☎ **403/266-1980.** Reservations required. Main courses C$18–C$26 (US$13–US$19); table d'hôte C$33 (US$24). AE, DC, ER, MC, V. Mon–Fri 11:30am–2pm; Mon–Sat 5:30–10:30pm. FRENCH.

At this intimate restaurant in the Delta Bow Valley Hotel, the food is extremely refined—classic French technique meets the modern flavors of Alberta. The presentation is especially notable; salads come as lovely green bouquets restrained by a thin vase of sliced cucumber, vegetables are carved into fanciful shapes. Entrees, like rack of lamb with mint hollandaise and black current purée, C$25 (US$18), combine tradition with just the right touch of modern saucing savvy and showmanship. The weekly changing table d'hôte menu offers four courses; for C$18 (US$13), you can sample three glasses of wine specially chosen to complement the food.

Owl's Nest. In the Westin Hotel, 4th Ave. and 3rd St. SW. ☎ **403/226-1611.** Reservations required. Main courses C$20–C$30 (US$14–US$21). AE, DC, DISC, ER, MC, V. Daily 11:30am–2:30pm and 5:30–11pm. FRENCH/CONTINENTAL.

One of Calgary's most wide-ranging upscale menus is found in this atmospheric dining room. Entree choices range from fine hand-cut Alberta steaks and fresh lobster to continental delicacies like quail and wild mushrooms, and Dover sole with caviar. Each week, there's also a specialty menu—usually under C$30 (US$21) for four courses—often featuring an ethnic cuisine. Service is excellent and the wine list is noteworthy.

✪ River Cafe. Prince's Island Park. ☎ **403/261-7670.** Reservations recommended. Main courses C$13–C$22 (US$9–US$16). AE, MC, V. Mon–Fri 11am–11pm, Sat–Sun 10am–11pm. Closed Jan–Feb. NEW CANADIAN.

It takes a short walk through the Eau Claire Market area, and then over the footbridge to lovely Prince's Island Park in the Bow River to reach the aptly named River Cafe. On a lovely summer evening, the walk is a plus; the other attractions of the River Cafe are the lovely park-side decks (no vehicles hurtling by) and the excellent food.

Wood-fired free-range and wild-gathered foods teamed with organic whole breads and fresh baked desserts form the backbone of the menu. There's a wide range of appetizers and light dishes—many vegetarian—as well as pizzalike flat breads topped with zippy cheese, vegetables, and fruit. Specialties from the grill include Arctic char with sorrel and maple butter sauce (C$19/US$14) and duck breast with a honey and spruce reduction (C$20/US$14). Menus change seasonally, and read like a very tasty adventure novel; highly recommended.

✪ Teatro. 200 8th Ave. SE. ☎ **403/290-1012.** Reservations recommended. Main courses C$15–C$23 (US$11–US$16). AE, ER, MC, V. Mon–Fri 11:30am–midnight, Sat 5pm–midnight, Sun 5pm–10pm. ITALIAN.

Located in the handsome and historic Dominion Bank Building just across from the Centre for the Performing Arts, Teatro delivers the best New Italian cooking in Calgary. The high-ceilinged dining room is dominated by columns and huge panel windows, bespeaking class and elegance. The extensive menu is based on "Italian Market Cuisine," featuring what's seasonally best and freshest in the market, which is then cooked skillfully and simply to preserve natural flavors; some of the best dishes come from the wood-fired oven that dominates one wall. For lighter appetites, there is a large selection of antipasti, boutique pizzas, and salads; the entrees, featuring Alberta beef, veal, pasta, and seafood, are prepared with flair and innovation. Service is excellent; highly recommended.

Moderate

❂ **Buzzards Cowboy Cuisine.** 140 10th Ave. SW. ☎ **403/264-6959.** Main courses C$10–C$15 (US$7–US$11). AE, MC, V. Daily 11am–10pm. STEAK/WESTERN.

The chuck wagon of the cattle-drive days of the 1880s may seem an unlikely place to go searching for cuisine, but at Buzzards—surely one of Calgary's most unusual and interesting restaurants—the foods of the early Canadian West serve as the inspiration for up-to-the-minute fine dining. A lot of work went into the menu—the archives of the Glenbow Museum were searched for recipes and insights about the foods and ingredients of the open-range era—and that information was updated to reflect modern cooking techniques and new cultural influences. *But be warned:* Some dishes are not for the squeamish.

At Buzzards, you find the answer to what a modern-trained chef would produce if presented with the ingredients available to the chuck-wagon "Cookie." Appetizers include grilled buffalo marrow bones, julienned buffalo tongue with cranberry ketchup, and even "prairie oysters" or calf testicles, sautéed with lemon, white wine, and picked garlic. (Out here in the West, testicles are becoming a popular novelty meat, and "Testicle Festivals" are common events in small western towns.) If the above dishes don't appeal, other appetizers include Indian smoked salmon, Caesar salad, and traditional Western-style soups. Steaks—both prime beef and buffalo—lead out the entree menu: the Delmonico is crusted with malted barley and dressed with a wild-mushroom gravy, and the buffalo tenderloin is served with peppercorn and molasses sauce. The traditional "Son of a Bitch" stew is also served, as are more familiar Western dishes like meat loaf, ribs, and fried chicken; watch for Dutch oven specials. For dessert, the Saskatoon Berry Pie is near mandatory (a Saskatoon berry is a native huckleberry). The Old West dining room is charming, and there's patio seating in summer.

Divino. 817 1st St. SW. ☎ **403/263-5869.** Reservations recommended on weekends. Main courses C$10–C$15 (US$7–US$11). AE, MC, V. Mon–Sat 11:30am–10:30pm. CALIFORNIA/ITALIAN.

Divino is housed in a landmark building (the Grain Exchange) and is both a wine bar and an intimate casual bistro-style restaurant. The menu fare is both unusual and tasty—steamed mussels in ginger and garlic broth, broccoli salad with toasted almonds and ginger dressing, and a lamb pistachio burger with cambrozolo cheese, C$10 (US$7). There are also full-fledged entrees, like steak, bouillabaisse, and stuffed chicken breast, and pasta dishes. Divino is a great downtown option for tasty yet casual dining.

Grand Isle Seafood Restaurant. 128 2nd Ave. SE. ☎ **403/269-7783.** Reservations recommended on weekends. Most dishes under C$12 (US$9). AE, MC, V. Daily 10am–midnight. CANTONESE/SEAFOOD.

One of Chinatown's best restaurants, the Grand Isle's beautiful dining room overlooks the Bow River. Pick your entree from the saltwater tanks, then enjoy the view. Dim sum is served daily; there's a huge lunch buffet on weekdays, and a weekend brunch service.

Joey Tomato's. 208 Barclay Parade SW. ☎ **403/263-6336.** Reservations not accepted. Pizza and pasta C$9–C$11 (US$6–US$8). AE, MC, V. Sun–Thurs 11am–midnight, Fri–Sat 11am–1am. ITALIAN.

Located in the popular Eau Claire Market complex, Joey Tomato's is a very lively airplane hanger of a restaurant that serves great pizza and other Italian food to throngs of appreciative Calgarians. And no wonder it's often packed: The food is really good, the prices moderate (by the city's standards), and there's a lively bar scene. What more could you want in Calgary? Thin-crust pizzas come with traditional toppings, or with zippy, more cosmopolitan choices. Pasta dishes are just as unorthodox, with dishes like linguine and smoked chicken, jalapeno, cilantro, and lime cream sauce. It's a really fun, high energy place to eat, and the food is always worth trying.

The King & I. 820 11th Ave. SW. ☎ **403/264-7241.** Main courses C$7–C$20 (US$5–US$14). AE, DC, ER, MC, V. Mon–Thurs 11:30am–10:30pm, Fri 11:30am–11:30pm, Sat 4:30–11:30pm, Sun 4:30–9:30pm. THAI.

This restaurant was the first to introduce Thai cuisine to Calgary, and it still turns on the heat in carefully measured nuances. You get precisely the degree of spiciness you ask for. You also get considerable help in interpreting the menu. Chicken and seafood predominate—one of the outstanding dishes is chicken fillet sautéed with eggplant and peanuts in chili-bean sauce. For more seasoned palates there are eight regional curry courses, ranging from mild to downright devilish.

Mescalero. 1315 1st St. SW. ☎ **403/266-3339.** Reservations recommended. Most dishes around C$10 (US$7). AE, DC, MC, V. Mon–Fri 11:30am–midnight, Sat–Sun 11am–1am. SOUTHWESTERN.

One of the trendiest eateries in Calgary, Mescalero specializes in tapas—small dishes of salad, tiny sandwiches, grilled meats, zesty dips, cheese, minipizzas, and more. Assemble them into a meal as you see fit. As long as you're lucky enough to score a table, just order some wine and an ongoing series of tapas. Most dishes will provide a good-sized nibble for a table of four. More standard lunch and dinner entrees—usually Southwestern in derivation—are also available.

Stamboli Inn. 1147 Kensington Crescent. ☎ **403/283-1166.** Main courses C$10–C$15 (US$7–US$11). AE, ER, MC, V. Mon–Thurs 11:30am–2pm and 5pm–11pm, Fri 11:30am–2pm and 5pm–midnight, Sat 5pm–midnight. ITALIAN.

Located in the trendy Kensington neighborhood just northwest of downtown, Stamboli's is one of the city's favorite spots for excellent traditional Italian pasta (C$10/US$7) and pizza—the menu offers 22 different varieties. There's also a good selection of veal and chicken entrees (C$15/US$11). Stamboli's is again operated by the Stamboli family, which assures that the restaurant's traditionally high standards are observed.

Inexpensive

Budget diners have two strongholds in downtown Calgary: Chinatown and the Eau Claire Market. There are dozens of inexpensive restaurants in Chinatown, not all Chinese: check out Vietnamese and Thai options. Dim sum is widely available and inexpensive.

Eau Claire Market, just north of downtown along the river, is a food-grazer's dream. Two floors of food stalls and tiny restaurants in the market itself only begin to paint the picture. Put together a picnic with fresh bread, cheese, and wine, or grab an ethnic takeout and mosey on over to the park like everyone else in Calgary.

SEVENTEENTH AVENUE

Seventeenth Avenue, roughly between 4th Street SW and 10th Street SW, is home to many of Calgary's best casual restaurants and bistros. If you have time, take a cab or drive over and walk the busy, cafe-lined streets, and peruse the menus; the restaurants listed below are just the beginning.

Expensive

La Chaumiere. 139 17th Ave. SE. ☎ **403/228-5690.** Reservations required. Jacket and tie required for men. Main courses C$18–C$28 (US$13–US$20). AE, ER, MC, V. Mon–Fri noon–2pm; Mon–Sat 6pm–midnight. FRENCH.

Winner of half a dozen awards for culinary excellence, La Chaumiere is a discreetly luxurious temple of fine dining. Dining here is an occasion to dress up and La Chaumiere is one of the few spots in town that enforces a dress code—men must wear jackets and ties.

The impressively broad menu is based on classic French preparations, but features local Alberta meats and produce. In its new location, the Chaumiere has more room than ever, and offers plenty of patio seating in summer. If you want a special occasion restaurant in Calgary, this is it.

✪ **Savoir Fare.** 907 17th Ave. SW. ☎ **403/245-6040.** Reservations recommended. Main courses C$16–$20 (US$11–US$14). AE, DC, MC, V. Mon–Thurs 11am–11pm, Fri–Sat 11am–midnight, Sun 11am–3pm. NEW CANADIAN.

One of 17th Avenue's most coolly elegant new eateries, Savoir Fare offers a tempting selection of seasonally changing and inventive menus. Preparations tend to mix classic technique with nouveau ingredients, with very tasty results. You don't have to overindulge to enjoy yourself—there's a good selection of interesting salads and sandwiches—but entrees are hard to resist: a vegetable Napoleon or a beef tenderloin crusted with pepper and ground coffee beans are sure to please. Good wine list.

Moderate

Bistro Jo Jo. 917 17th Ave. SW. ☎ **403/245-2382.** Reservations recommended on weekends. Main courses C$12–C$16 (US$9–US$11). AE, MC, V. Mon–Fri 11:30am–2pm (except summer months) and 5:30–9:30pm, Sat 5:30–10:30pm. FRENCH.

Jo Jo's is a classic French bistro, right down to the tiled floor, mirrors, banquettes, fan-back chairs, and tiny tables. The food is Provençale French, though moderately priced for the quality and atmosphere. All your French favorites are here: duck breast, escargot, pâté, and even a warm salad of sweetbreads with lemon sauce. Desserts are worth a trip in themselves.

Cilantro. 338 17th Ave. SW. ☎ **403/229-1177.** Reservations recommended on weekends. Main courses C$9–C$20 (US$6–US$14). AE, DC, MC, V. Sun–Thurs 11am–11pm, Fri–Sat 11am–midnight. INTERNATIONAL.

Cilantro has an attractive stucco storefront, plus a pleasant garden patio with a veranda bar. The food here is eclectic (some would call it Californian). The pasta dishes are as various as beef tenderloin with wild mushrooms in a Zinfandel sauce, or ginger radiatore with julienned vegetables and chili sauce. Chicken breasts come stuffed with roasted peppers and dressed with a sauce of green onions. The wood-fired pizzas—with mostly Mediterranean ingredients—seem almost tame in comparison. However, the food is excellent, and the setting casual and friendly.

Sultan's Tent. 909 17th Ave. SW. ☎ **403/244-2333.** Reservations recommended on weekends. Main courses C$9–C$14 (US$6–US$10). AE, ER, MC, V. Mon–Sat 5:30–11pm. MOROCCAN.

Although the Sultan's Tent is located in a modern Western building, the restaurant's interior has been transformed by carpets and tapestries into a pretty good imitation of a Saharan tent. If you like great couscous or tangines, then you definitely should make this a stop in Calgary. Go all out and order the C$25 (US$18) per person Sultan's Feast, which includes all the trimmings and provides an evening's worth of eating and entertainment.

CALGARY AFTER DARK

THE TOP PERFORMING ARTS VENUES   The **Calgary Centre for Performing Arts,** 205 8th Ave. SE (☎ **403/294-7455**), gives the city the kind of cultural hub that many places twice as big still lack. The center houses the 1,800-seat Jack

Singer Concert Hall, home of the Calgary Philharmonic Orchestra; the Max Bell Theatre; Theatre Calgary; Alberta Theatre Projects; and the Martha Cohen Theatre, which puts on some avant-garde and innovative performances. Call the center or consult the newspapers for information on what is currently being performed by whom.

The magnificent **Jubilee Auditorium,** 14th Avenue and 14th Street NW (☎ **403/ 297-8000**), seats 2,700 people. An acoustic marvel, the performance hall is located high on a hill with a panoramic view. The Southern Alberta Opera Association performs three operas each year at the auditorium. Periodic productions by the young Alberta Ballet Company are also part of the auditorium's varied programs.

IMPROV & DINNER THEATER   Calgary loves dinner theater, and **Stage West,** 727 42nd Ave. SE (☎ **403/243-6642**), puts on polished performances as well as delectable buffet fare. The buffet functions from 6 to 8pm, then the show starts. Performances are Tuesday to Sunday and tickets are C$37 to C$59 (US$26 to US$42).

THE CLUB & BAR SCENE   Cover charges at most clubs range between C$5 (US$3.60) and C$10 (US$7) for live music.

There are three major centers for nightlife in central Calgary. The **Eau Claire** Market area, parklike and car-free, is also the home of the **Hard Rock Cafe,** 101 Barclay Parade SW (☎ **403/263-7625**), with its Beatles stained-glass window and 70-foot-long guitar suspended from the ceiling. The **Barleymill Neighbourhood Pub,** 201 Barclay Parade SW (☎ **403/290-1500**), is just across the square, and is a cross between a collegiate hangout and a brew pub. **The Garage,** in the Eau Claire Market (☎ **403/262-6762**), is the hip place to play billiards and listen to really loud alternative rock.

If you're looking for the dance clubs, there is a knot of five or so venues near the corner of 1st Street SW and 12th Avenue. **Crazy Horse,** 1315 1st St. SW (☎ **403/ 266-3339**), is an immensely popular, slightly precious nightclub with lines out the door; open Thursday, Friday, and Saturday only. The **Tasmanian Ballroom,** or the Taz, upstairs at 12th Avenue SW and 1st Street (no phone), is a bit grittier and even louder. Take a break from the music at **The Koop Cafe,** 211b 12th Ave. SW (☎ **403/269-4616**), a licensed coffee shop filled with dilapidated couches and graffiti-style art.

Among the trendy cafes and galleries on 17th Avenue are more nightclubs. **Republik,** 219 17th Ave. SW (☎ **403/244-1884**), is the main alternative music venue in Calgary. **Kaos Jazz and Blues Bistro,** 718 17th Ave. SW (☎ **403/ 228-9997**), is one of western Canada's top jazz clubs, frequently hosting international bands (closed Sunday). **The Ship and Anchor Pub,** 534 17th Ave. SW (☎ **403/ 245-3333**), is a youthful hangout with eclectic alternative music and two outdoor patios; expect lines out the door on summer nights. **Detour,** 318 17th Ave. SW (☎ **403/244-8537**), a lively disco, is a good place to begin exploring gay Calgary.

Put on your cowboy boots and swing your partner out to **Ranchman's,** 9615 Macleod Trail S., (☎ **403/253-1100**). Ranchman's is the best country-western dance bar in the city, and offers free dance lessons during the week at 7pm.

If you're just looking for a convivial drink, head to **Bottlescrew Bill's Old English Pub,** 1st Street and 10th Avenue SW (☎ **403/263-7900**), a friendly neighborhood pub with outdoor seating and Alberta's widest selection of beers, including many from the local Big Rock microbrewery.

GAMBLING   There are several legitimate casinos in Calgary whose proceeds go wholly to charities. None of them imposes a cover charge. **Cash Casino Place,** 4040B Blackfoot Trail SE (☎ **403/243-4812**), operates with a restaurant on the premises Monday to Saturday from noon to midnight. **The Elbow River Inn Casino,** 1919

On the Trail of Dinosaurs in the Alberta Badlands

The Red Deer River slices through the rolling prairies of Alberta east of Calgary, revealing underlying sedimentary deposits that have eroded into badlands. These expanses of desertlike hills, strange rock turrets, and banded cliffs were originally laid down about 75 million years ago, when this area was a low coastal plain in the heyday of the dinosaurs. Erosion has incised through these deposits spectacularly, revealing a vast cemetery of Cretaceous life. Paleontologists have excavated here since the 1880s, and the Alberta badlands have proved to be one of the most important dinosaur-fossil sites in the world.

Two separate areas have been preserved and developed as research and viewing areas in the badlands. Closest to Calgary, and the focus of a great day trip, is the ✪ **Royal Tyrrell Museum of Palaeontology,** P.O. Box 7500, Drumheller, AB, T0J 0Y0, (☎ **888/440-4240** or 403/823-7707; fax 403/823-7131; e-mail: rtmp@dns.magtech.ab.ca; Web site: <tyrrell.magtech.ab.ca>). Just north of Drumheller, 145 kilometers (90 miles) northeast of Calgary, this is one of the world's best paleontology museums and educational facilities. It offers far more than just impressive skeletons and life-sized models, though it has dozens of them. The entire fossil record of the earth is explained, era by era, with an impressive variety of media and educational tools. You walk through a prehistoric garden, watch numerous videos, use computers to "design" dinosaurs for specific habitats, watch plate tectonics at work, and see museum technicians preparing fossils. The museum is also a renowned research facility where teams of scientists study all forms of ancient life. The museum is open daily in summer from 9am to 9pm, in winter Tuesday to Sunday from 10am to 5pm. Admission is C$6.50 (US$4.65) for adults, C$5.50 (US$3.95) for seniors, C$3 (US$2.80) for children, and C$15 (US$11) for families.

Radiating out from Drumheller and the museum are a number of interesting side trips. Pick up a map from the museum and follow an hour's loop drive into the badlands along North Dinosaur Trail. The paved road passes two viewpoints over the badlands, and crosses a free car-ferry on the Red Deer River before returning to Drumheller along the South Dinosaur Trail. A second loop passes through

---

Macleod Trail S. (☎ **403/266-4355**), is part of a hotel by the same name (see "Accommodations," above). It offers the usual games plus a variation called Red Dog. Minimum stake is C$2 (US$1.30), the maximum C$500 (US$358). Open Monday to Saturday from 10am to 3am.

DAY TRIPS FROM CALGARY: THE OLD WEST

The Old West isn't very old in Alberta. If you're interested in the life and culture of the cowboy and rancher, then stop at one of the following sights. Both are short and very scenic detours on the way from Calgary to the Rocky Mountains.

The **Western Heritage Centre** (☎ **403/932-3514**; Web site: www.whcs.com) is 15 minutes west of Calgary in the little ranching town of Cochrane. This new museum and interpretive center is located at the Cochrane Ranche Provincial Historic Site, which preserves Alberta's first large-scale cattle ranch, established in 1881. The center commemorates traditional farm and ranch life; it also contains a rodeo hall of fame and offers insights into this most Western of sporting events. Special events—often rodeo-related—are scheduled throughout the summer; call for a schedule of

Rosedale to the south, past a ghost town, hoodoo formations, and a historic coal mine.

Dinosaur Provincial Park is in Red Deer River Valley near Brooks (about 225km/140 miles east of Calgary and 193km/120 miles southeast of Drumheller) and contains the greatest concentration of fossils from the late Cretaceous period in the world. More than 300 complete dinosaur skeletons have been found in the area, which has been named a World Heritage Site by the United Nations. Park excavations continue from early June to late August, based out of the Field Station of the Royal Tyrrell Museum. Much of the park is a natural preserve, and access is restricted to guided interpretive bus tours and hikes. Tours run daily from mid-May to Labour Day and on weekends until mid-October. Lab tours also run May to August where you can view fossil preparation. Other programs include evening hikes and campfire and amphitheater presentations in July and August. Prices for tours and hikes are C$4.50 (US$3.20) for adults and C$2.25 (US$1.60) for youths 6 to 15; children under 6 are free. Space is limited, so please be prepared to be flexible with your choices. "Rush" tickets are sold at 8:30am for that day's events. Reservations are strongly encouraged in July and August. Five self-guiding trails and two outdoor fossil displays are also available. Facilities at the park include a campground, picnic area, and a service center.

For more information, contact **Dinosaur Provincial Park,** P.O. Box 60 Patricia, AB, T0J 2K0 (☎ **403/378-4342;** fax 403/378-4247; Web site: www.gov.ab.ca/~env/nrs/dinosaur). To make tour reservations, call ☎ **403/378-4344** during the week.

If you're really keen on dinosaurs, you can **participate in one of the digs.** Day programs only are offered at the Royal Tyrrell Museum, and include a half-day kids' event, a dig watch at C$12 (US$9) for adults, or a day spent helping with the dig at C$85 (US$61) for adults. Weeklong programs only are offered at Dinosaur Provincial Park. On the Field Experience Program, you get to be part of the dig crew for 7 days for C$800 (US$572), including bed and board. For all programs, contact the Bookings Officer at the **Royal Tyrrell Museum,** P.O. Box 7500, Drumheller, AB, T0J 0Y0 (☎ **403/823-7707;** fax 403/823-7131).

upcoming events. To reach Cochrane, follow Crowchild Trail (which becomes Highway 1A) out of Calgary; or from Highway 1 to Banff, take Highway 22 north to Cochrane. Admission is C$7.50 (US$5) for adults, C$5.50 (US$3.95) for students and seniors, C$3.50 (US$2.50) for children, and C$20 (US$14) for a family pass. Open late May to early September.

An hour southwest of Calgary is another Old West destination. The **Bar U Ranch National Historic Site** (☎ **403/395-2212**) is a well-preserved and still-operating cattle ranch that celebrates both the past and the present of the area's ranching traditions. Tours of the ranch's 35 original buildings (some date from the 1880s) are available; a video of the area's ranching history is shown in the interpretive center. Special events include displays of ranching activities and techniques; this is a real ranch, so you might get to watch a branding or roundup—at the very least you'll get to see some horseplay! To reach the Bar U, follow Highway 22 south from Calgary to the little community of Longview. Admission is C$4.75 (US$3.40) for adults, C$3.75 (US$2.70) for seniors, and C$2.75 (US$2) for children. It's open mid-May to mid-October.

3 Southern Alberta Highlights

South of Calgary, running through the grain fields and prairies between Medicine Hat and Crowsnest Pass in the Canadian Rockies, Highway 3 roughly parallels the U.S.-Canadian border. This rural connector links several smaller Alberta centers and remote but interesting natural and historic sites.

MEDICINE HAT & CYPRESS HILLS PROVINCIAL PARK

Medicine Hat (291km/181 miles southeast of Calgary) is at the center of Alberta's vast natural-gas fields. To be near this inexpensive source of energy, a lot of modern industry has moved to Medicine Hat, making this an unlikely factory town surrounded by grain fields. At the turn of the century, the primary industry was fashioning brick and china from the local clay deposits. Consequently, the town's old downtown is a showcase of handsome frontier-era brick buildings; take an hour and explore the historic city center, flanked by the South Saskatchewan River.

Eighty-one kilometers (50 miles) south of Medicine Hat is **Cypress Hills Provincial Park,** 316 square kilometers (122 sq. miles) of highlands—outliers of the Rockies—that rise 1,500 feet above the flat prairie grasslands. In this preserve live many species of plants and animals, including elk and moose, that are usually found in the Rockies.

LETHBRIDGE

East of Fort Macleod (105km/65 miles north of the U.S. border, 216km/134 miles southeast of Calgary) lies Lethbridge, a delightful garden city and popular convention site (it gets more annual hours of sunshine than most places in Canada). Lethbridge started out as Fort Whoop-up, a notorious trading post that traded whiskey to the Plains Indians in return for buffalo hides and horses. The post boomed during the 1870s, until the Mounties arrived to bring order. A replica of the fort has been built in Indian Battle Park, and commemorates Whoop-up's history with interpretive programs and relics from the era.

The pride of Lethbridge is the **Nikka Yuko Japanese Garden.** Its pavilion and dainty bell tower were constructed by Japanese artisans without nails or bolts. The garden is one of the largest Japanese gardens in North America; Japanese-Canadian women in kimonos give tours and explain the philosophical concepts involved in Japanese garden design.

FORT MACLEOD

South of Calgary, a little more than 2 hours away, stands what was in 1873 the western headquarters of the Northwest Mounted Police. Named after Colonel MacLeod, the redcoat commander who brought peace to Canada's west, the reconstructed **Fort Macleod** is now a provincial park (☎ 403/553-4703). It's still patrolled by Mounties in their traditional uniforms; precision riding drills are performed four times daily.

The rebuilt fort is filled with fascinating material on the frontier period. Among its treasured documents is the rule sheet of the old Macleod Hotel, written in 1882: "All guests are requested to rise at 6am. This is imperative as the sheets are needed for tablecloths. Assaults on the cook are prohibited. Boarders who get killed will not be allowed to remain in the house." The fort grounds also contain the Centennial Building, a museum devoted to the history of the local Plains Indians.

HEAD-SMASHED-IN BUFFALO JUMP

The curiously named ✪ **Head-Smashed-In Buffalo Jump** has an interpretive center (☎ 403/553-2731) on Spring Point Road, 19 kilometers (12 miles) west of

Fort Macleod on Highway 2 (187km/116 miles southwest of Calgary, 109km/ 68 miles north of the U.S. border). This excellent museum is built into the edge of a steep cliff over which the native Canadians used to stampede herds of bison, the carcasses then providing them with meat, hides, and horns. The multimillion-dollar facility tells the story of these ancient harvests by means of films and native-Canadian guide-lecturers. Other displays illustrate and explain the traditional life of the prairie-dwelling natives in precontact times, and the ecology and natural history of the northern Great Plains. Hiking trails lead to undeveloped jump sites.

Designated a World Heritage Site, the center is open daily from 9am to 8pm in summer. Admission is C$6.50 (US$4.65) for adults, C$5.50 (US$3.95) for seniors, and C$3 (US$2.15) for children 17 and under.

4 Waterton Lakes National Park

In the southwestern corner of the province, ✪ **Waterton Lakes National Park** is linked with Glacier National Park in neighboring Montana; together these two beautiful tracts of wilderness comprise Waterton-Glacier International Peace Park. Once the hunting ground of the Blackfoot, 526-square-kilometer (203-sq.-mile) Waterton Park contains superb mountain, prairie, and lake scenery and is home to abundant wildlife.

The transition from plains to mountains in Waterton and Glacier parks is very abrupt: The formations that now rise above the prairie were once under the primal Pacific Ocean, but when the North American continent collided with the Pacific ocean floor, wedges of the ocean's basement rock broke along deep horizontal faults, cutting these rock layers free from their geologic moorings. The continued impact of the continental and ocean-floor tectonic plates gouged these free-floating rock blocks up out of the bowl they were formed in and pushed them eastward onto the top of younger rock. Under continued pressure from the elevating mass of the Rockies, the Waterton formations slid east almost 56 kilometers (35 miles) over the prairies. Almost 5 kilometers (3 miles) high, the rock block of Waterton Park— an overthrust in geological terms—is a late arrival, literally sitting on top of the plains.

During the last ice age, the park was filled with glaciers, which deepened and straightened river valleys; those peaks that remained above the ice were carved into distinctive thin, finlike ridges. The park's famous lakes also date from the ice ages; all three of the Waterton Lakes nestle in glacial basins.

The park's main entrance road leads to Waterton Townsite, with a number of hotels, restaurants, and tourist facilities. Other roads lead to more remote lakes and trailheads. Akamina Parkway leads from the townsite to Cameron Lake, glimmering beneath the crags of the Continental Divide. Red Rock Canyon Parkway follows Blackiston Creek past the park's highest peaks to a trailhead; short hikes to waterfalls and a deep canyon begin here.

The most popular activity in the park is the **International Shoreline Cruise** (☎ **403/859-2362**), which leaves from the townsite and sails Upper Waterton Lake past looming peaks to the ranger station at Goat Haunt, Montana, in Glacier Park. These tour boats leave five times daily; the cruise there and back usually takes 2 hours, including the stop in Montana. The price is C$18 (US$13) round-trip for adults, C$12 (US$9) for youths, and C$8 (US$6) for children.

For more information on the park, contact the **Park Superintendent,** Waterton Lakes National Park, Waterton Park, AB, T0K 2M0 (☎ **403/859-5109;** fax 403/ 859-2650; e-mail: angelene_mcintyre@pch.gc.ca).

ACCOMMODATIONS & DINING IN THE PARK

Prince of Wales Hotel. Waterton Lakes National Park, AB, T0K 2M0. ☎ **403/226-5551.**
(Off-season: Stn 0928, Phoenix, AZ, 85077; ☎ 602/207-6000). 89 rms. C$136–C$207 (US$97–
US$148) double. MC, V. Closed Oct–Apr.

Built in 1927 by the Great Northern Railway, this beautiful mountain lodge perched
on a bluff above Upper Waterton Lake is reminiscent of the historic resorts in Banff
Park on a smaller scale. Rooms have been totally renovated, though many are historically authentic in that they're rather small. Still, you can't beat the views or the genteel
old-world atmosphere.

The lobby and common rooms are really lovely, and the Garden Court Dining
Room is the best—and priciest—place to eat in the park. Entrees include steaks, rack
of lamb, and salmon and cost about C$25 (US$17).

5 Introducing the Canadian Rockies

Few places in the world are more dramatically beautiful than the Canadian Rockies.
Banff and Jasper national parks are famous for their mountain lakes, flower-spangled
meadows, spirelike peaks choked by glaciers, and abundant wildlife, and nearly the
entire spine of the Rockies—from the U.S. border north for 1,127 kilometers (700
miles)—is preserved as parkland or wilderness.

That's the good news. The bad news is that this Canadian wilderness, the flora and
fauna that live in it, and lovers of solitude that come here, are going to need all this
space as the Rockies become more popular. More than four million people annually
make their way through Banff National Park, and the numbers are shooting up as-
tronomically. While Draconian measures such as limiting visitors are as yet only
brought up in order to be dismissed, one thing is for certain: Advance planning for
a trip to the Canadian Rockies is absolutely necessary if you're going to stay or eat
where you want, or if you want to evade the swarms of visitors that throng the parks
during summer.

ORIENTATION

Canada's Rocky Mountain parks include Jasper and Banff, which together comprise
17,519 square kilometers (6,764 sq. miles); the provincial parklands of the Kananaskis
Country and Mount Robson; and Yoho, Kootenay, Glacier, and Mount Revelstoke
national parks to the west in British Columbia.

The parks are traversed by one of the finest highway systems in Canada, plus innumerable nature trails leading to more remote valleys and peaks. The two "capitals,"
Banff and Jasper, lie 287 kilometers (178 miles) apart, connected by Highway 93,
one of the most scenic routes you'll ever drive. Banff lies 128 kilometers (80 miles)
from Calgary via Highway 1; Jasper, 375 kilometers (225 miles) from Edmonton on
Route 16, the famous Yellowhead Highway.

Admission to Banff, Jasper, Yoho, and Kootenay parks costs C$5 (US$3.60) per
person per day, or C$10 (US$7) per group or family per day.

TOURS & EXCURSIONS

You'll get used to the name Brewster, associated with many things in these parts. In
particular, these folks operate the park system's principal tour-bus operation.

Brewster Transportation and Tours, 100 Gopher St., Banff, AB, T0L 0C0
(☎ **403/762-6767**), operates tours from Banff and Jasper, covering most of the outstanding scenic spots in both parks. Call for a full brochure, or ask the concierge at
your hotel to arrange a trip. A few sample packages:

Banff to Jasper (or vice versa): Some 9¹/₂ hours through unrivaled scenery, this trip takes in Lake Louise and a view of the ice field along the parkway. (The return trip requires an overnight stay, not included in the price.) One-way adult fare (summer) is C$79 (US$57); round-trip, C$109 (US$78).

Columbia Icefield: A 9¹/₂-hour tour from Banff. You stop at the Icefield Centre and get time off for lunch and a Snocoach ride up the glacier. Snocoach Tour is an extra C$22.50 (US$16) for adults and C$5 (US$3.60) for children, and tickets must be purchased in advance. Adults pay C$79 (US$57) (summer); children C$39.50 (US$28).

Brewster also operates an express bus between Banff and Jasper 5 days a week, costing C$49 (US$35) for adults; children are half price.

SEASONS

The parks have two peak seasons during which hotels charge top rates and restaurants are jammed. The first is summer, from mid-June to the end of August, when it doesn't get terribly hot, rarely above 80°F, though the sun's rays are powerful at this altitude. The other peak time is winter, the skiing season from December to February; this is probably the finest skiing terrain in all of Canada. March to May is decidedly off-season: Hotels offer bargain room rates and you can choose the best table in any eatery. There is plenty of rain in the warmer months, so don't forget to bring some suitable rainwear.

LODGING IN THE ROCKIES

A word about lodging in the parks. On any given day in the high season, up to 50,000 people are winding through the Canadian Rocky national parks. As growth in the parks is strictly regulated, there's not an abundance of hotel rooms waiting. The result is strong competition for a limited number of very expensive rooms. Adding to the squeeze is the fact that many hotels have 80% to 90% of their rooms reserved for coach tours during the summer. In short, if you're reading this on the day you plan to arrive in Banff, Jasper, or Lake Louise and haven't yet booked your room, start worrying. Most hotels are totally booked for the season by July 1. To avoid disappointment, **reserve your room as far in advance as you know your travel dates.**

Regarding price, it seems that lodgings can ask for and get just about any rate they want in the high season. For the most part, hotels are well kept up in the parks, but few would justify these high prices anywhere else in the world. Knowing that, there are a few choices. You can decide to splurge on one of the world-class hotels here, actually only a bit more expensive than the midrange competition. Camping is another good option, as the parks have dozens of campgrounds with varying degrees of facilities. There are also a number of hostels throughout the parks.

Outside of high season, prices drop dramatically, often as much as one-half. Most hotels will offer ski packages during the winter, as well as other attractive getaway incentives. Be sure to ask if there are any special rates, especially at the larger hotels, which have trouble filling their rooms in the off-seasons.

PARK WILDLIFE

The parklands are swarming with wildlife, with some animals meandering along and across highways and hiking trails, within easy camera range. However tempting, **don't feed the animals, and don't touch them!** There is, for starters, a fine of up to C$500 (US$350) for feeding any wildlife. There is also a distinct possibility that you may end up paying more than cash for disregarding this warning.

It isn't easy to resist the blithely fearless bighorn sheep, mountain goats, elk, soft-eyed deer, and lumbering moose you meet. (You'll have very little chance of

The Canadian Rockies

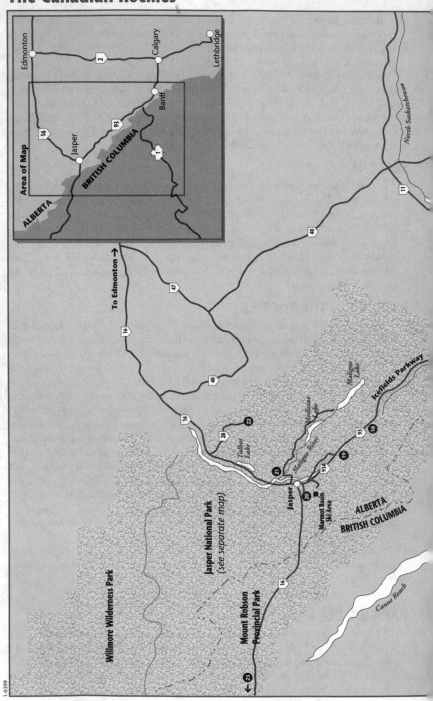

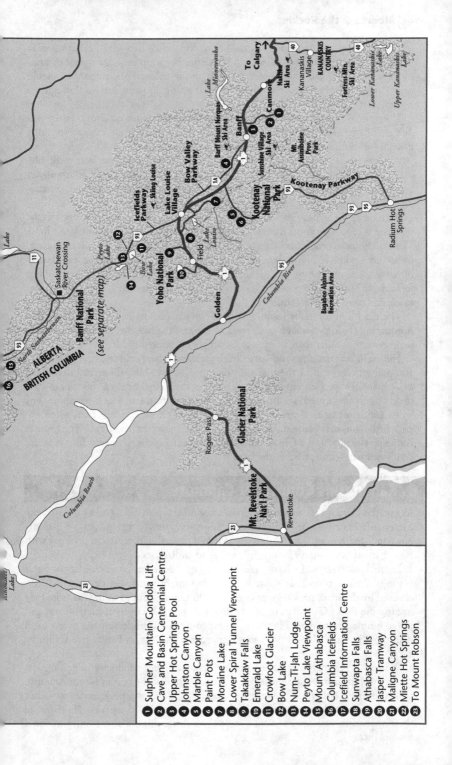

1 Sulpher Mountain Gondola Lift
2 Cave and Basin Centennial Centre
3 Upper Hot Springs Pool
4 Johnston Canyon
5 Marble Canyon
6 Paint Pots
7 Moraine Lake
8 Lower Spiral Tunnel Viewpoint
9 Takakkaw Falls
10 Emerald Lake
11 Crowfoot Glacier
12 Bow Lake
13 Num-Ti-Jah Lodge
14 Peyto Lake Viewpoint
15 Mount Athabasca
16 Columbia Icefields
17 Icefield Information Centre
18 Sunwapta Falls
19 Athabasca Falls
20 Jasper Tramway
21 Maligne Canyon
22 Miette Hot Springs
23 To Mount Robson

557

meeting the coyotes, lynx, and occasional wolves, since they give humans a wide berth.) But the stuff you feed them can kill them. Bighorns get accustomed to summer handouts of bread, candy, potato chips, and marshmallows, when they should be grazing on the high-protein vegetation that will help them survive through the winter.

Moose involve additional dangers. They have been known to take over entire picnics after being given an initial snack, chase off the picnickers, and eat up everything in sight—including cutlery, dishes, and the tablecloth.

Portions of the parks may sometimes be closed to hikers and bikers during elk calving season. A mother elk can mistake your recreation for an imminent attack on her newborn; or an unsuspecting hiker could frighten a mother from her calf, separating the two for good. Pay attention to—and obey—postings at trailheads.

Bears pose the worst problems. The parks contain two breeds: the big grizzly, standing up to 7 feet on its hind legs, and the smaller black bear, about 5 feet long. The grizzly spends most of the summer in high alpine ranges, well away from tourist haunts. As one of North America's largest carnivores, its appearance and reputation are awesome enough to make visitors beat a retreat on sight. But the less formidable black bear is a born clown with tremendous audience appeal, and takes to human company like a squirrel.

The black bear's cuddly looks and circus antics, plus its knack for begging and rummaging through garbage cans, tend to obscure the fact that these are wild animals: powerful, faster than a horse, and completely unpredictable.

Hiking in bear country (and virtually all parkland is bear country) necessitates certain precautions—ignore them at your own peril. Never hike alone, and never take a dog along. Dogs often yap at bears, then when the animal charges, they run toward their owners for protection, bringing the pursuer with them. Use a telephoto lens when taking pictures. Bears in the wild have a set tolerance range that, when encroached upon, may bring on an attack. Above all, never go near a cub. The mother is usually close by, and a female defending her young is the most ferocious creature you'll ever face—and possibly the last.

6 Kananaskis Country & Canmore

Kananaskis Country is the name given to three Alberta provincial parks on the Rocky Mountains' eastern slope. Once considered only a gateway region to more glamorous Banff, the Kananaskis has developed into a recreation destination on a par with more famous brand-name resorts in the Canadian Rockies.

Located just west of the Kananaskis and just outside the eastern boundary of Banff National Park, Canmore is a sprawl of condominium and resort development unchecked by the strict park regulations. Only 20 minutes from Banff, Canmore may not top the list of Canadian resort destinations, but the scenery is magnificent and the accommodations generally much less expensive and considerably less overbooked than those in Banff. If you can't locate affordable lodgings in Banff, give Canmore a try.

Weather is generally warmer and sunnier here, which is conducive to golfing: the championship course at Kananaskis is considered one of the best in North America. When the 1988 Olympics were held in Calgary, the national park service wouldn't allow the alpine ski events to be held at the ski areas in the parks. **Nakiska,** in the Kananaskis, became the venue instead, vaulting this ski area to international prominence.

The Kananaskis offers stunning scenery without Banff's crowds and high prices. Also, because the Kananaskis Country isn't governed by national-park restrictions, there's better road access to some out-of-the-way lakeside campgrounds and trailheads, which makes this a more convenient destination for family getaways (there are more than 3,000 campsites in the area!). This provincial parkland also allows "mixed use," including some traditional (though heavily regulated) ranching. Some of the best guest ranches in Alberta operate here. Kananaskis offers plenty of the great outdoors, including hiking, backpacking, canoeing, and fishing. For general recreation information, contact **Kananaskis Country,** Suite 100, 1011 Glenmore Trail SW, Calgary, AB, T2V 4R6 (☎ **403/297-3362;** fax 403/297-2180).

The main road through the Kananaskis Country is Highway 40, which cuts south from Highway 1 at the gateway to the Rockies and follows the Kananaskis River. Kananaskis Village, a collection of resort hotels and shops, is the center of activities in the Kananaskis, and is convenient to most recreation areas. Highway 40 eventually climbs up to 7,239-foot Highwood Pass, the highest pass in Alberta, before looping around to meet Highway 22 south of Calgary.

SKIING, GOLF & ADVENTURE SPORTS

Kananaskis offers the same mix of outdoor recreation as other parts of the Canadian Rockies, but the offerings here are highly organized. From its office in the Lodge at Kananaskis, **Mirage Adventure Tours,** P.O. Box 233, Kananaskis Village, AB, T0l 2H0, (☎ **888/312-7238** or 403/591-7773; fax 403/591-7301) represents most local outfitters and most activities available in the area: you'll find bicycle trips, horseback trail rides, rafting, hiking, sightseeing tours, and other recreational opportunities on offer. Mirage also rents cross-country skis and equipment from their shop at the lodge.

DOWNHILL SKIING   Kananaskis gained worldwide attention when it hosted the alpine ski events for the Winter Olympic Games in 1988, and skiing remains a primary attraction in the area. At world-famous **Nakiska,** skiers can follow in the tracks of winter Olympians past. A second ski area, **Fortress Mountain,** is located 19 kilometers (12 miles) south of Kananaskis Village. Although overshadowed by Nakiska's Olympic reputation, Fortress Mountain offers an escape from the resort crowd, and features overnight accommodations in an on-site dormitory. Both areas offer terrain for every age and ability, and are open from early December to mid-April. Adult lift tickets cost C$41 (US$29) at Nakiska, C$29 (US$21) at Fortress. For more information on the ski areas, call ☎ 403/591-7777 or write **Ski Nakiska,** P.O. Box 1988, Kananaskis Village, AB, T0L 2H0.

GOLF   Kananaskis also features one of Canada's premier golf resorts. **Kananaskis Country Golf Course** boasts two 18-hole par-72 championship courses set among alpine forests and streams. Contact **Golf Kananaskis,** The Kananaskis Country Golf Course, P.O. Box 1710, Kananaskis Village, AB, T0L 2H0 (☎ **403/591-7154**).

HORSEBACK TRIPS   The Kananaskis is noted for its long-established dude ranches (see "Guest Ranches," below), which offer a variety of horseback adventures ranging from short trail rides to multiple-day pack trips into the wilderness. Again, **Mirage** (see above) is a good clearinghouse for information, or contact the guest ranches themselves.

RAFTING   The Kananaskis and Bow rivers are the main draw here. In addition to half-day (C$49/US$35), full-day (C$99/US$71), and 2-day white-water trips, there are also trips that combine half-days of horseback riding or mountain biking with an afternoon of rafting. Contact **Mirage Adventure Tours,** above, for information on these packages.

ACCOMMODATIONS
KANANASKIS VILLAGE

The lodgings in Kananaskis Village were all built for the Olympics in 1988, so all are new and well maintained. There's no more than a stone's throw between them, and to a high degree, public facilities are shared among all the hotels.

Best Western Kananaskis Inn. Kananaskis Village, AB, T0L 2H0. ☎ **800/528-1234** or 403/591-7500. Fax 403/591-7500. 96 rms. TV TEL. C$125 (US$89) double; C$295 (US$211) suite. AE, DC, DISC, ER, MC, V.

This handsome wood-fronted hotel is the most affordable place to stay in Kananaskis, but don't let that diminish your expectations of high quality and service. This new hotel offers a wide variety of room types, including many loft rooms with kitchenettes, which can sleep six. There's a pool, whirlpool, and steam room.

Lodge at Kananaskis & Hotel Kananaskis. Kananaskis Village, AB, T0L 2H0. ☎ **800/441-1414** or 403/591-7711. Fax 403/591-7770. 193 rms, 58 suites in the lodge; 60 rms, 8 suites in the hotel. MINIBAR TV TEL. Peak season C$205–C$300 (US$147–US$215) double; C$252–C$365 (US$180–US$260) suite. Ski/golf package rates and discounts available. AE, ER, MC, V.

These two new resort hotels are operated by Canadian Pacific, and face each other across a pond at the center of Kananaskis Village. While they've got distinctly different lodgings, it's easiest to think of them as a unit, as they share many facilities, including a central reservation system. The lodge is the larger building, with a more rustic facade, a shopping arcade, and a number of drinking and dining choices. The rooms are large and well furnished; many have balconies, some have fireplaces. The hotel is much smaller than the lodge, and quieter. Rooms in the hotel are generally larger than those in the lodge, and they're more expensive. A full range of exercise facilities, including a swimming pool, indoor/outdoor whirlpools, aerobic studios, and a health and beauty spa, are available to guests at both lodgings.

Ribbon Creek Hostel. At Nakiska Ski Area. ☎ **403/762-3441** for reservations or 403/591-7333 for the hostel itself. Sleeps 44. C$12 (US$9) members, C$16 (US$11) nonmembers. MC, V.

This is a great place for a traveler on a budget; there are also four family rooms. The hostel is located right at the ski area, within walking distance of Kananaskis Village, and has showers, laundry facilities, and a common room with a fireplace.

CANMORE

Much of the hotel development in Canmore dates from the Calgary Olympics in 1988, and to a large degree the following hotels have very similar facilities, amenities, and prices. They even look as if they could have been designed by the same architect.

Most of Canmore's hotels are operated by the major North American chains, and rooms are large and nicely furnished; doubles range from C$130 to C$150 (US$93 to US$107) a night which is moderate in these parts. Better yet, you can usually find a room here with only a couple days' notice, unlike the booked-for-the-season reality in Banff.

Each of the following has an on-premises restaurant, an exercise room, pool, and hot tub. All are easily accessed from the freeway: **The Best Western Green Gables Inn,** 1602 2nd Ave. (☎ **800/661-2133** or 403/678-5488; fax 403/678-2670); **Greenwood Inn Hotel and Conference Centre,** 511 Bow Valley Trail (☎ **800/**

263-3625 or 403/678-3625; fax 403/678-3765); **Pocaterra Inn,** 1725 Mountain Ave. (☎ **800/661-2133** or 403/678-4334; fax 403/678-2670); **Quality Inn Chateau Canmore,** 1720 Bow Valley Trail (☎ **800/228-5151** or 403/678-6699; fax 403/678-6954).

GUEST RANCHES

✪ **Brewster's Kananaskis Guest Ranch.** Seebe (30 min. east of Banff on Hwy. 1), P.O. Box 964, Banff, AB, T0L 0C0. ☎ **800/691-5085** or 403/673-3737. Fax 403/673-2100. 33 units in cabins and chalets. C$70–C$110 (US$50–US$79) double. AE MC, V.

The Brewsters were movers and shakers in the region's early days, playing a decisive role in the formation of Banff, Jasper, and Montana's Glacier national parks, and were the first outfitters (and transport providers) in the parks. The Kananaskis Ranch was the original Brewster family homestead in the 1880s, and was transformed into a guest ranch in 1923. Located right on the Bow River near the mouth of the Kananaskis River, the original lodge buildings remain and serve as common areas. Guest rooms are fully modern, and are offered in chalets or cabins, each with full bathroom facilities. Rooms are available with full board if desired; and activities available to guests include horseback riding (varying lengths of rides) river rafting, canoeing, hiking, and more. Long-distance backcountry horseback rides are a specialty—a 3-day trip is under C$400 (US$286)—and backcountry campsites have newly constructed cabins for sleeping accommodations.

Rafter Six Guest Ranch. Seebe, AB, T0L 1X0. ☎ **403/673-3622** or 403/264-1251. Fax 403/673-3961. Accommodates 60 in log lodge and cabins. C$110 (US$79) double in lodge; cabins from C$125–C$150 (US$89–US$107) double. AE, DC, ER, MC, V.

Rafter Six is located in a meadow right on the banks of the Kananaskis River. Another old-time guest ranch with a long pedigree, the Rafter Six Ranch is a full-service resort ranch. The huge old log lodge, with restaurant, barbecue deck, and lounge, is especially inviting. Casual horseback and longer pack trips are offered, as well as raft and canoe trips. Facilities include hot tubs, an outdoor pool, a playground, and a game room. Seasonal special events are offered, like rodeos, country dances, and hay or sleigh rides.

CAMPGROUNDS

Kananaskis is a major camping destination for families in Calgary, and the choice of campgrounds is wide. There's a concentration of campgrounds at **Upper and Lower Kananaskis Lakes,** some 32 kilometers (20 miles) south of Kananaskis Village. There are a few campgrounds scattered nearer to Kananaskis Village, around Barrier Lake and Ribbon Creek. For a full-service campground with RV hookups, go to **Mount Kidd RV Park** (☎ **403/591-7700**), just south of the Kananaskis golf course.

DINING

All the hotels offer dining rooms; in fact, the two Canadian Pacific properties together offer seven different dining venues, from the upscale l'Escapades in the hotel, to tapas-style nibbling in Brady's Market in the lodge. There are also coffee shops and light entree service in the lounges. The dining rooms at both guest ranches are also open to nonguests.

7 Banff National Park

Banff is the oldest national park in Canada, founded as a modest 26-square-kilometer (10-sq.-mile) reserve by Canada's first prime minister, Sir John A. Macdonald, in

1885. The park is now 6,641 square kilometers (2,564 sq. miles) of incredibly dramatic mountain landscape, glaciers, high morainal lakes, and rushing rivers. The park's two towns, Lake Louise and Banff, are both splendid counterpoints to the surrounding wilderness, with beautiful and historic hotels, fine restaurants, and lively nightlife.

If there's a downside to all this sophisticated beauty, it's that Banff is very, very popular—it's generally considered Canada's number-one tourist destination. About four million people visit Banff yearly, with the vast majority squeezing in during June, July, and August.

Happily, the wilderness invites visitors to get away from the crowds and from the congestion of the developed sites. Banff Park is blessed with a great many outfitters who make it easy to get on a raft, bike, or horse and find a little mountain solitude. Or consider visiting the park outside of the summer season, when prices are lower, the locals friendlier, and the scenery just as stunning.

SPORTS & OUTDOOR ACTIVITIES IN THE PARK

There are lots of great recreational activities available in Banff National Park, so don't just spend your vacation shopping the boutiques on Banff Avenue. Most day trips require little advance booking—a day in advance is usually plenty—and the easiest way to find a quick adventure is just to ask your hotel's concierge to set one up for you. Multiday rafting and horseback trips do require advance booking, as places are limited and keenly sought after. There are many more outfitters in Banff than the ones listed below, but the offerings and prices that follow are typical of what is available.

SKIING   Banff Park has three ski areas. Together they have formed a partnership for booking and promotional purposes. For information on all of the following, contact **Ski Banff/Lake Louise,** Box 1085, Banff, AB, T0l 0C0, (☎ **403/762-4561;** fax 403/762-8185; e-mail: skibll@banff.net; Web site: www.skibanfflakelouise.com)

Banff Mount Norquay (formerly Mystic Ridge and Norquay) (☎ **403/ 762-4421**) are twin runs just above the town of Banff. They cater to family skiing, with plenty of day care, ski instruction, and night skiing. Rates start at C$33 (US$24) for adults for a full day.

Skiers must ski or take a gondola to the main lifts at **Sunshine Village** (☎ **403/ 762-6500**) and the Sunshine Inn, a ski-in/ski-out hotel. Sunshine is located 15 minutes west of Banff off Highway 1, and receives more snow than any ski area in the Canadian Rockies (more than 30 ft. per year!). Sunshine boasts the fastest high-speed quad chairlifts in the world. Lift tickets for Sunshine start at C$45 (US$32) for adults.

Lake Louise Ski Area (☎ **800/258-SNOW** in North America, or 403/552-3555) is the largest in Canada, with 64 kilometers (40 miles) of trails. With 11 lifts, management guarantees no long lines on major lifts, or your money back! Rates for a full day of skiing start at C$46 (US$33) for adults. Snowmaking machines keep the lifts running from November to early May.

A **special lift pass** for Banff Mount Norquay, Sunshine Village, and Lake Louise Ski Area allows skiers unlimited access to all three resorts (and free rides on shuttle buses between the ski areas). Passes for 3 days (minimum) cost C$152 (US$109) for adults and C$57 (US$41) for children.

HIKING   One of the great virtues of Banff is that many of its most dramatic and scenic areas are easily accessible by day hikes. The park has more than 80 maintained hiking trails, ranging from interpretive nature strolls to long-distance backpacking expeditions (you'll need a permit if you're planning on camping in the backcountry).

Banff Town & Banff National Park

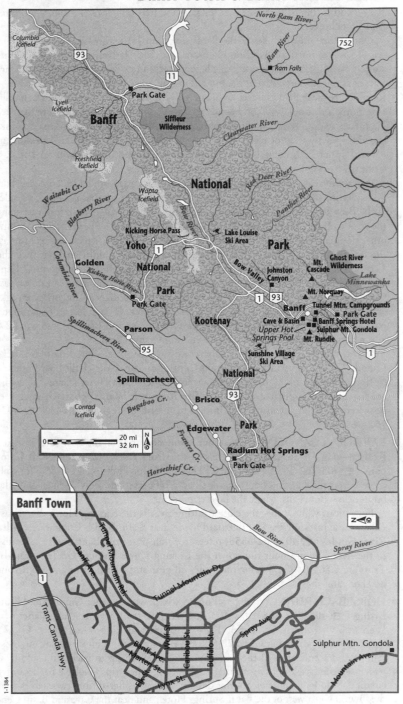

North Ram River

93

752

11

Park Gate

Ram Falls

Columbia
Icefield

Lyell
Icefield

Banff

Siffleur
Wilderness

Clearwater River

Freshfield
Icefield

National

Red Deer River

Waitabit Cr.

Wapta
Icefield

Panther River

Blaeberry River

Bow River

Kicking Horse Pass

Lake Louise
Ski Area

Park

Yoho

1

Bow Valley

Ghost River
Wilderness

Golden

National

Kicking Horse River

Johnston
Canyon

Mt.
Cascade

Lake
Minnewanka

Columbia River

Park

1

93

Mt. Norquay

Spillimacheen River

Park Gate

Banff

Tunnel Mtn. Campgrounds

Kootenay

Cave & Basin

Park Gate

Parson

Upper Hot
Springs Pool

Banff Springs Hotel
Sulphur Mt. Gondola

95

Mt. Rundle

1

Sunshine Village
Ski Area

Spillimacheen

National

Bugaboo Cr.

93

Brisco

Conrad
Icefield

Park

Edgewater

Frances Cr.

20 mi
32 km

0

N

Radium Hot Springs

Park Gate

Horsethief Cr.

Banff Town

Bow River

Spray River

N

Tunnel Mountain Rd.

1

Tunnel Mountain Dr.

Banff Ave.

Trans-Canada Hwy.

Spray Ave.

Sulphur Mt. Gondola

Banff Ave.
Marten St.
Wolf St.
Caribou St.
Buffalo St.
Lynx St.

Mountain Ave.

1-1384

For a good listing of popular hikes, pick up the free *Banff / Lake Louise Drives and Walks* brochure.

One of the best day hikes in the Banff area is up **Johnston Canyon,** 24 kilometers (15 miles) north of Banff on Highway 1A. This relatively easy hike up a limestone canyon passes seven waterfalls before reaching a series of jade-green springs known as the **Inkpots.** Part of the fun of this trail is the narrowness of the canyon—the walls are more than 100 feet high, and only 18 feet across; the path skirts the cliff face, tunnels through walls, and winds across wooden footbridges for more than 1.6 kilometers (1 mile). The waterfalls plunge down through the canyon, soaking hikers with spray; watch for black swifts diving in the mist. The hike through the canyon to Upper Falls takes 1 1/2 hours; all the way to the Inkpots will take at least 4 hours.

It's easy to strike out from Banff Townsite and find any number of satisfying short hikes. Setting off on foot can be as simple as following the footpaths along both sides of the **Bow River.** From the west end of the Bow River Bridge, trails lead east along the river to Bow Falls, past the Banff Springs Hotel, to the Upper Hot Springs. Another popular hike just beyond town is the **Fenlands Trail,** which begins just past the train station and makes a loop through marshland wildlife habitat near the Vermilion Lakes. Two longer trails leave from the Cave and Basin Centennial Centre. The **Sundance Trail** follows the Bow River for nearly 5 kilometers (3 miles) past beaver dams and wetlands, ending at the entrance to Sundance Canyon. Keen hikers can continue up the canyon another 2.4 kilometers (1 1/2 miles) to make a loop past Sundance Falls. The **Marsh Loop** leaves the Cave and Basin area to wind 2.4 kilometers (1 1/2 miles) past the Bow River and marshy lakes.

If you'd prefer a **guided hike,** there are several hikes offered daily by Parks Canada. Ask at the Banff Information Centre, or check the chalk board outside to find out what hiking options are currently offered. Some walks are free, while others (like the popular evening **Wildlife Research Walks**) charge a small fee; both require preregistration. For information and preregistration, call ☎ 403/ 762-9818.

RAFTING & CANOEING   One-hour family float trips on the Bow River just past Banff are popular diversions, and are available from **Rocky Mountain Raft Company** (☎ 403/762-3632). Trips are C$22 (US$16) for adults, C$11 (US$8) for children; rafters meet at the company's dock at Wolf Street and Bow Avenue, and take buses below Bow Falls, where the float trip begins.

For serious white water, the closest rafting river is the Kicking Horse River, past Lake Louise just over the Continental Divide near Field, British Columbia. **Hydra River Guides** (☎ 403/762-4554) offers free transport from Banff and Lake Louise to the river, and a 3-hour run down the Kicking Horse through Grade IV rapids. Trips are C$65 (US$47), which includes all gear and transport to and from your hotel or campsite.

HORSEBACK RIDING   See Banff on horseback with **Warner Guiding and Outfitting** (☎ 403/762-4551; fax 403/762-8130; e-mail: warner@telusplanet.net; Web site: www.horseback.com). Two- to 6-day trail rides—starting at C$275 (US$197) and peaking at C$1,278 (US$914)—are offered, into some of the most remote and scenic areas of the park. Some rides climb up to backcountry lodges, which serve as base camps for further exploration; other trips involve a backcountry circuit with lodging in tents. Shorter day rides are also offered from two stables near the townsite: just west of the Banff Springs Hotel, and near the Cave and Basin Centennial Site.

Operating out of Lake Louise, **Timberline Tours** (☎ 888/858-3388 or 403/522-3743) offers day trips to some of the area's more prominent beauty sites— starting at C$28 (US$20) for 90 minutes of riding. From their Bow Lake Corral, at Num-Ti-Jah Lodge, hour-long rides start at C$20 (US$14). Three- to 10-day pack trips are also offered.

FISHING   Upper Bow Fly Fishing Company, P.O. Box 2772, Banff AB, T0L 0C0 (☎ 403/760-7668; fax 403/762-8263; e-mail: ubff@banff.net) offers a number of fly-fishing expeditions on the Bow River. All levels of anglers are accommodated, and packages include part- or whole-day trips.

BICYCLING   Cycling the Rockies, Box 25 Lake Louise, AB, T0L 1E0 (☎ 888/771-9453 or 403/522-2211), makes it easy to get out on two wheels and explore the beautiful Bow Valley. Regularly scheduled guided bike trips include half-day trips around Lake Louise for C$49 (US$35), and a full-day journey between Banff and Lake Louise for C$83 (US$59). More adventuresome travelers can check out the "Peddles & Paddles" option, which combines a half day of cycling with a half day of white-water rafting on the Kicking Horse River for C$103 (US$74). Prices include cycle and helmet rental, plus snacks and meals.

If you would prefer a **self-guided tour,** simply rent a bike in Banff or Lake Louise (dozens of outfitters offer rentals) and peddle along the Bow Valley Parkway— Highway 1A—between Banff and Lake Louise, which makes an easy day trip for the average bicyclist. Hardier cyclists may want to challenge themselves with the longer Icefields Parkway between Lake Louise and Jasper. Most cyclists will need 3 days to make the trip, stopping at night in the numerous and charming hostels found along this amazing mountain road.

HELICOPTER TOURS   Alpine Helicopters (☎ 403/678-4802), operating out of Canmore, offers flights over the Canadian Rockies starting at C$110 (US$79).

GOLFING   The Banff Springs Golf Course in Banff, which rolls out along the Bow River beneath towering mountain peaks, offers 27 holes of excellent golf. Although associated with the resort hotel, the course is open to the public. Call ☎ 403/762-6801 for a tee time.

BANFF TOWNSITE

Few towns in the world boast as beautiful a setting as Banff. The mighty Bow River, murky with glacial till, courses right through town, while rearing up right on the outskirts of town are massive mountain blocks. Mount Rundle parades off to the south, a finlike mountain that somehow got tipped over on its side. Mount Cascade rises up immediately north of downtown, exposing its glaciered face at every corner. In every direction, yet more craggy peaks fill the sky.

This is a stunning, totally unlikely place for a town, and Banff has been trading on its beauty for more than a century. The Banff Springs Hotel was built in 1888 as a destination resort by the Canadian Pacific Railroad. As tourists and recreationalists began to frequent the area for its scenery, hot springs, and access to fishing, hunting, climbing, and other activities, the little town of Banff grew up to service the needs of these early travelers.

While the setting hasn't changed since the early days of the park, the town certainly has. Today, the streets of Banff are lined with exclusive boutique malls where the best names in international fashion offer their wares; trendy cafes spill out into the sidewalks, and bus after bus filled with tourists chokes the streets. Banff is particularly popular with Asian tourists; Japanese interests own many of the businesses here, and stores are often staffed by young Japanese teenagers over for the summer.

English, French, and German tourists are also very much in evidence. There's a vital and cosmopolitan feel to the town; just don't go here expecting a bucolic Alpine village. Banff in summer is a very busy place.

ESSENTIALS

VISITOR INFORMATION   The Banff Information Centre, at 224 Banff Ave., houses both the **Banff Tourism Bureau** and a national-park information center. Contact the office at P.O. Box 1298, Banff, AB, T0L 0C0 (☎ **403/762-0270;** fax 403/762-8545). Be sure to ask for the *Official Visitors Guide,* which is absolutely packed with information about local businesses and recreation.

GETTING THERE   If you're driving, the **Trans-Canada Highway** takes you right to Banff's main street; the town is 129 kilometers (80 miles) west of Calgary. There is no air or rail service to the town. **Greyhound buses** pass through Banff on their way from Calgary to Vancouver; the depot is at 100 Gopher St. (☎ **403/762-6767**). The closest **VIA Rail** train service is at Jasper, 287 kilometers (178 miles) north; Brewster offers a nontour bus between the two park centers five times weekly.

ORIENTATION   Getting your bearings is easy. The **Greyhound and Brewster Bus Depot** is located at the corner of Gopher and Lynx streets (☎ **403/762-2286**). The main street—Banff Avenue—starts at the southern end of town at the Bow River and runs north until it is swallowed by the Trans-Canada Highway. Along this broad, bright, and bustling thoroughfare, you'll find most of Banff's hotels, restaurants, stores, office buildings, and nightspots. Just beyond the river stands the park administration building amid a beautifully landscaped public garden. Here the road splits: Banff Springs Hotel and the **Sulphur Mountain Gondola** are to the left; to the right are the **Cave and Basin Hot Springs,** Banff National Park's original site. At the northwestern edge of town is the old railroad station, and a little farther northwest the road branches off to Lake Louise and Jasper. In the opposite direction, northeast, is the highway going to Calgary.

GETTING AROUND   Banff offers local bus service along two routes designed to pass through downtown and by most hotels. Service on **The Banff Bus** is pretty informal, but there's generally a bus every half hour. One route runs between the Banff Springs Hotel and down Banff Avenue to the northern end of town; the other runs between the train station and the Banff Hostel on Tunnel Mountain; the fare is C$1 (US72¢). The bus operates summer only; call ☎ **403/760-8294** for more information.

For a taxi, call **Legion Taxi** (☎ **403/762-3353**) or **Banff Taxi and Limousine** (☎ **403/762-4444**).

For a rental car, contact **Tilden Rent-A-Car,** at the corner of Caribou and Lynx streets (☎ **403/762-2688**) or **Banff Rent A Car,** 204 Lynx St. (☎ **403/762-3352**) for a less expensive but reliable used vehicle. Avis, Budget, and Hertz also have offices in Banff.

THE BANFF ARTS FESTIVAL

The **Banff Centre,** St. Julien Road (☎ **800/413-8368** or 403/762-6300), is a remarkable year-round institution devoted to art and entertainment in the widest sense. From June to August annually, the center hosts the ✪ **Banff Arts Festival,** offering a stimulating mixture of drama, opera, jazz, ballet, classical and pop music, singing, and the visual arts. Highlights include the International String Quartet Competition, with 10 world-class quartets vying for a cash prize and a national tour; the Digital Playgrounds series brings performance artists to the stage. Tickets for some of the events cost C$5 to C$27 (US$3.60 to US$19); a great many are free.

In November the center shows the **Festival of Mountain Films.** Find out what's currently on by getting the program at the Banff Tourism Bureau or by calling the center.

EXPLORING BANFF

Apart from helicopter excursions, the best way to get an overall view of Banff's mountain landscape is by the **Sulphur Mountain Gondola Lift** (☎ 403/762-2523), whose lower terminal is 6 kilometers (4 miles) southeast of Banff on Mountain Avenue. The gondolas are roomy, safe, and fully enclosed; the panoramas are stunning. At the upper terminal there's the Summit Restaurant for panoramic dining, and hiking trails along the mountain ridges. Rides cost C$12 (US$9) for adults, C$6 (US$4.30) for children 5 to 11; children under five ride free.

Lake Minnewanka Boat Tours (☎ 403/762-3473; fax 403/762-2800) offers scenic and wildlife-viewing trips in glassed-in motor cruisers on Lake Minnewanka, just 24 kilometers (15 miles) north of Banff. Trips are usually 1 1/2 hours long, and cost C$22 (US$16) for adults and C$11 (US$8) for children 11 and under. During high season, five trips depart daily; these cruises are very popular, and reservations are suggested. Buses run from the Banff bus station to the lake in conjunction with the boat departure schedules.

The **Luxton Museum** (☎ 403/762-2388) is devoted to the history of native Canada and is housed in a log fort south of the Bow River, just across the bridge. The Luxton offers realistic dioramas, a sun-dance exhibit, artifacts, weaponry, and ornaments. Adults pay C$5.50 (US$3.95); seniors and students C$4 (US$2.85), and children C$2.50 (US$1.80). The museum is open daily from 9am to 9pm.

Part art gallery, part local-history museum, the **Whyte Museum of the Canadian Rockies,** at 111 Bear St. (☎ 403/762-2291), is the only museum in North America that collects, exhibits, and interprets the history and culture of the Canadian Rockies. Two large, furnished, heritage homes on the museum grounds are open during the summer and stand as a memorial to the pioneers of the Canadian Rockies. Interpretive programs and tours run year-round. The Elizabeth Rummel Tea Room is open mid-May to mid-October and offers light lunches, desserts, and coffee. Admission is C$3 (US$2.15) for adults, C$2 (US$1.45) for seniors and students; children under 13 are free. Open daily 10am to 6pm in high season, limited hours at other times.

Housed in a lovely wood-lined building dating from the 1910s, the **Banff Park Museum,** beside the Bow River Bridge (☎ 403/762-1558), is largely a paean to taxidermy, but there's a lot to learn here about the wildlife of the park and how the various ecosystems interrelate. The real pleasure, though, is the rustic, lodge-style building, now preserved as a National Historic Site. Admission is C$2.25 (US$1.60) for adults, C$1.75 (US$1.25) for seniors, and C$1.25 (US90¢) for youths 6 to 16; children 6 and under are free. Open daily in summer from 10am to 6pm.

Although most people now associate Banff with skiing or hiking, in the early days of the park, travelers streamed in to visit the curative hot springs. In fact, it was the discovery of the hot springs now preserved as the **Cave and Basin National Historic Site** (☎ 403/762-1566) that spurred the creation of the national park in 1888. During the 1910s, these hot mineral waters, which rise in a limestone cave, were piped into a rather grand natatorium. Although the Cave and Basin springs are no longer open for swimming or soaking, the old pool area and the original hot springs cave have been preserved along with interpretive displays and films. Entrance is C$2.25 (US$1.60) for adults, C$1.75 (US$1.25) for seniors, and C$1.25 (US90¢) for youths 6 to 18; children under 6 are free. The Cave and Basin is located 1.6 kilometers (1 mile) west of Banff; turn right at the west end of the Bow River Bridge.

If you want a soak in mountain hot springs, then drive up to **Upper Hot Springs Pool** (☎ 403/762-1515), at the top of Mountain Avenue, 5 kilometers (3 miles) west of Banff. The pool and spa complex has just undergone a complete renovation. In addition to the redesigned swimming pool filled with hot, sulfurous waters, there is a restaurant, snack bar, and home spa boutique. If you're looking more for a cure than a splash, then go to the adjacent Upper Hot Springs Spa, where you get access to a steam room, massage therapists, plunge pools, and various aromatherapy treatments. Admission to the pool is C$7 (US$5) for adults, C$6 (US$4.30) for seniors, and C$3.50 (US$2.50) for children 3 to 16; family admission is C$20 (US$14). The spa is open to adults only, and costs C$30 (US$21).

The **Natural History Museum,** 112 Banff Ave. (☎ 403/762-4747), has displays of early forms of life on earth, dating from the Canadian dinosaurs of 350 million years ago, plus an "authentic" model of a Sasquatch, or "Bigfoot." Summer hours are daily from 10am to 8pm; until 10pm July and August. Free admission.

SHOPPING

The degree to which you like the town of Banff itself will depend largely upon your taste for shopping. Banff Avenue is increasingly an open-air boutique mall, with throngs of shoppers milling around, toting their latest purchases. Of course, you would expect to find excellent outdoor gear and sporting-good stores here, as well as the usual T-shirt and gift emporiums. What is more surprising are the boutiques devoted to Paris and New York designers, the upscale jewelry stores, and the high-end art galleries. What's most surprising is that it seems most visitors actually prefer to while away their time in this masterpiece of nature called Banff by shopping for English soaps or Italian shoes.

There are no secrets to shopping in Banff: arcade after arcade opens out onto Banff Avenue; you'll find everything you need. Quality and prices are both quite high.

ACCOMMODATIONS

Please note that all prices listed are for high season. Call for reduced off-season rates.

Very Expensive

Banff Park Lodge. 222 Lynx St., Banff, AB, T0L 0C0. ☎ **800/661-9266** or 403/762-4433. Fax 403/762-3553. 198 rms, 13 suites. A/C MINIBAR TV TEL. C$219 (US$157) double; C$299 (US$214) suite. AE, CB, DC, ER, MC, V. Free heated parking.

A large, handsome cedar-and-oak structure with a cosmopolitan air, the Banff Park Lodge is a quiet block-and-a-half off the main street, near the Bow River. Calm and sophisticated are the key words here: all the rooms are soundproofed, and wild, après-ski cavorting isn't the norm, or even much encouraged. The lodge seems like a happy, tranquil retreat after a day in antic Banff. The guest rooms are very spacious and exceptionally well furnished. All come with balconies and twin vanities (one inside, one outside the bathroom). The lodge, with its abundant ground-floor rooms and wide hallways, is popular with travelers with mobility concerns.

Dining: The lodge has one formal and one family-style restaurant, and a cocktail lounge.

Services: Room service, concierge, laundry/dry cleaning.

Facilities: An indoor swimming pool with whirlpool and steam room, 10 convention rooms, shopping arcade, beauty salon, heated parking.

Banff Springs Hotel. Spray Ave. (P.O. Box 960), Banff, AB, T0L 0C0. ☎ **800/441-1414** or 403/762-2211. Fax 403/762-5755. 770 rms, 105 suites. MINIBAR TV TEL. C$190–C$515 (US$136–US$368) double; C$280–C$765 (US$200–US$546) suite. AE, DC, DISC, ER, MC, V. Valet parking C$11 (US$8); self-parking C$7 (US$5).

Standing north of Bow River Falls like an amazing Scottish baronial fortress, the Banff Springs Hotel is one of the most beautiful and famous hotels in North America. Founded in 1888 as a opulent destination resort by the Canadian Pacific Railroad, this nine-story stone castle of a hotel is still the best address in Banff: especially so after the renovation of all the rooms was finished in 1997. This venerable hotel doesn't offer the largest rooms in Banff, though the amenities are all superlative. With the views, the spa, and the near-pageantry of service, this is still the most amazing resort in an area blessed with beautiful hotels.

The Springs greets you with a reception hall of such splendor that you're not in the least surprised to learn that it maintains a staff of 1,200 and holds medieval banquets for convention groups.

Dining: 15 different food outlets, from palatial to functional, and three cocktail lounges.

Services: Concierge, 24-hour room service, dry cleaning, twice-daily maid service, secretarial service, courtesy car.

Facilities: A major new addition to the hotel is Solace, a European-style health and beauty spa, complete with therapeutic mineral baths, massage treatments, aerobic and fitness training, and nutritional consultation. In addition, there are 50 stores and boutiques, an Olympic-size indoor pool, tennis courts, and business center. The 27-hole golf course is considered one of the most scenic in the world.

✪ **Buffalo Mountain Lodge.** P.O. Box 1326, Banff, AB, T0L 0C0. ☎ **800/661-1367** or 403/762-2400. Fax 403/762-4495. E-mail: bmll@telusplanet.net. Web site: www.crmr.com. 88 rms, 20 1-bedrm apts. TV TEL. C$265 (US$190) double; C$210 (US$150) 1-bedrm apt. AE, ER, MC, V.

The most handsome of the hotel and condominium developments on Tunnel Mountain, just 1.6 kilometers (1 mile) west of Banff, the Buffalo Mountain is the perfect place to stay if you would rather avoid the frenetic pace of downtown Banff and yet remain central to restaurants and activities. Its quiet location, beautiful central lodge, and choice of room types make this a good alternative to equally priced lodgings in the heart of Banff.

The lodge building itself is an enormous log cabin, right out of your fantasies. The three-story lobby is supported by massive log rafters, filled with warm Navajo-style carpets, and comfortable Western-style furniture. A huge fieldstone fireplace dominates the interior, and separates the lovely dining room and small, cozy lounge. Rooms are all located in units scattered around the forested 8-acre holding. There are three room types, ranging from cozy one-bedroom apartments with full kitchens to exceptionally handsome rooms in brand-new lodge buildings. The nicest rooms are the Premiers, which feature beautiful slate-floored bathrooms, with both a claw-foot tub and a slate-walled shower. The quality pine and twig furniture lends a rustic look to the otherwise sophisticated decor. All rooms have fireplaces (wood is free and stacked near your door), balconies or patios, and the beds have feather duvets and pillows. These are some of the most attractive rooms in Banff.

Dining: The lodge restaurant is one of the best in Banff, and in summer the excellent Cilantro Cafe opens with deck seating.

Services: Baby-sitting, dry cleaning, free coffee.

Facilities: The lodge also offers a steam room and outdoor hot tub. Premier rooms come with a VCR; all rooms have coffeemakers.

✪ **Rimrock Resort Hotel.** Mountain Ave. (5km/3 miles south of Banff; P.O. Box 1110), Banff, AB, T0L 0C0. ☎ **800/661-1587** or 403/762-3356. Fax 403/762-1842. E-mail: rimrock@banff.net. Web site: www.rimrockresort.com. 345 rms, 21 suites. A/C MINIBAR TV TEL.

C$225–C$335 (US$161–US$240) double; from C$350–C$1,200 (US$250–US$858) suite. AE, DC, DISC, JCB, MC, V. Valet parking C$10 (US$7); self-parking C$6 (US$4.30); heated garage.

If you want modern luxury and views, this should be your hotel. This enormous, stunningly beautiful hotel (completed in 1993) drops nine floors from its roadside lobby entrance down a steep mountain slope, affording tremendous views from nearly all of its rooms. Aiming for the same quality of architecture and majesty of scale as venerable older lodges, the Rimrock offers a massive glass-fronted lobby, lined with cherry wood, tiled with unpolished marble floors, and filled with soft inviting chairs, couches, and Oriental carpets. The limestone fireplace, open on two sides, is so large that staff members just step inside to ready the kindling.

The rooms are large and well appointed with handsome furniture; some have balconies. Standard room prices vary only by view; all rooms are the same size. The suites are truly large, with balconies, wet bar, and loads of cozy couches.

Dining: Two restaurants, including the four-star Ristorante Classico (see "Dining," below), and a lobby lounge.

Services: Free shuttle bus to and from downtown Banff, 24-hour room service and concierge, laundry/dry cleaning, secretarial service.

Facilities: The fitness facilities are especially notable, with an indoor pool, squash court, hot tub, workout room with regularly scheduled aerobics, and more weight training and fitness devices than many professional gyms. Rooms come with Spectravision movie channels. There's also a shopping arcade and beauty salon.

Expensive

Brewster Mountain Lodge. 208 Caribou St., Banff, AB, T0L 0C0. ☎ **800/691-5085** or 403/762-2900. Fax 403/762-2970. 63 rms. TV TEL. C$185 (US$132) double. AE, MC, V. Free heated parking.

This brand-new lodgelike hotel is right in the heart of Banff, and is operated by the Brewster family, which dominates a lot of local recreation, guest ranching, and transportation. The Brewster affiliation makes it simple to take advantage of lodging/adventure packages involving horseback riding and hiking.

This modern hotel does its best to look rustic: peeled log post and beams fill the lobby and foyer, and quality pine furniture and paneling grace the large guest rooms.

Dining: No restaurant in hotel; plenty adjacent in central Banff.

Services: Concierge.

Facilities: Whirlpool, sauna, steam room, handicapped accessible rooms.

Caribou Lodge. 521 Banff Ave., Banff, AB, T0L 0C0. ☎ **800/563-8764** or 403/762-5887. Fax 403/762-5918. 200 rms, 7 suites. TV TEL. C$170–C$190 (US$122–US$136) double; C$225–C$275 (US$161–US$197) suite. Up to 2 children under 16 stay free in parents' rm. AE, DC, DISC, ER, MC, V. Free heated parking.

Built in 1993, the Caribou, with its gabled green roof, outdoor patio, bay windows, and wooden balconies, has a Western-lodge look that blends well with the alpine landscape. The interior is equally impressive, including a vast lobby with a slate tile floor, peeled log woodwork, and a huge stone fireplace. The finely furnished bedrooms continue the Western theme with rustic pine chairs and beds with snug down comforters. The bathrooms are spacious. Some of the rooms have balconies.

The lodge is long on service and friendliness; although it's not in the absolute center of town (about 10 min. on foot), a free shuttle bus ferries guests to destinations throughout Banff.

Dining: The restaurant here, The Keg, is a favorite with locals, serving hand-cut steaks for C$14 to C$17 (US$10 to US$12).

Services: Concierge, room service, free downtown shuttle.

Facilities: The lodge has three hot tubs, a sauna, and steam room.

Ptarmigan Inn. 337 Banff Ave., Banff, AB, T0L 0C0. ☎ **800/661-8310** or 403/762-2207. Fax 403/762-3577. 164 rms, 2 suites. TV TEL. C$160–C$175 (US$114–US$125) double; C$200 (US$143) suite. Children under 16 stay free in parents' rm. AE, DC, ER, JCB, MC, V. Free heated parking.

This pine-green hotel has a few advantages over most of the other hotels along busy Banff Avenue. For one, the rooms are set well back from the street, minimizing road noise. It's also a good choice for families; some of the double rooms have sleeping areas divided by the bathroom, which makes for a little privacy for everyone. Half of the rooms have balconies; 16 rooms (the least expensive) look into the lodgelike, three-story central atrium. No-smoking rooms are located in a separate wing. Rooms have rustic-looking pine furnishings and down comforters.

Dining: A restaurant and two lounges, one with patio seating.

Services: Room service during normal restaurant hours; ski and bike rentals are available on site.

Facilities: A large hot tub and dry sauna; a massage therapist is available by appointment.

Traveller's Inn. 401 Banff Ave., Banff, AB, T0L 0C0. ☎ **800/661-0227** or 403/762-4401. Fax 403/762-5905. 89 rms. TV TEL. C$170–C$210 (US$122–US$150) double. AE, MC, V.

Located 5 minutes from downtown Banff, the Traveller's Inn recently underwent a complete renovation, and offers good value for the dollar. Rooms are quite large and pleasantly decorated, all with twin vanities and king or queen beds. Some rooms are divided into two sleeping areas by the bathroom, a great configuration for families or friends traveling together. All rooms have balconies or patio access.

Dining: A breakfast coffee shop.

Services: Ski rental is available at the hotel; ski shuttles stop at the front door.

Facilities: Sauna, whirlpool, outdoor hot tub, steam room.

Moderate

Homestead Inn. 217 Lynx St., Banff, AB, T0L 0C0. ☎ **800/661-1021** or 403/762-4471. Fax 403/762-8877. 27 rms. TV TEL. C$129 (US$92) double. Extra person C$10 (US$7). Children under 12 stay free in parents' rm. AE, MC, V.

One of the best lodging deals in Banff is the Homestead Inn, only a block from all the action on Banff Avenue. Though the amenities are modest compared to upscale alternatives, rooms are tastefully furnished and equipped with couches, armchairs, and stylish bathrooms.

King Edward Hotel. 137 Banff Ave., Banff, AB, T0L 0C0. ☎ **800/344-4232** or 403/762-2202. Fax 403/762-0876. 21 rms. TV TEL. From C$129 (US$92) double. MC, V. Free parking.

Youthful travelers—and others who don't mind the bustle—will like the moderately priced lodgings at the newly remodeled King Edward Hotel, one of Banff's originals, dating from 1904. Rooms are simply furnished but comfortable, with private baths and coffeemakers in each room. Best of all is the location, in the very heart of town and immediately next door to the epicenter of Banff nightlife. All this, and free parking, too.

Red Carpet Inn. 425 Banff Ave., Banff, AB, T0L 0C0. ☎ **800/267-3035** or 403/762-4184. Fax 403/762-4894. 52 rms. TV TEL. C$100–C$110 (US$72–US$79) double. AE, MC, V.

A handsome brown three-story brick building with a balcony along the top floors, the Red Carpet Inn is located along the long, hotel-lined street leading to downtown. Well maintained and more than adequately furnished, the Red Carpet is one of the best lodging deals in Banff. Beds and furniture are ample and new; rooms have easy chairs and a desk. There's no restaurant on the premises, but there is an excellent one right next door. The entire facility is ship-shape and very clean—just the thing if you don't want to spend a fortune in Banff.

Inexpensive

Banff International Hostel. On Tunnel Mountain Rd. (1.6km/1 mile west of Banff; P.O. Box 1358), Banff, AB, T0L 0C0. ☎ **800/363-0096** or 403/762-4122. E-mail: banff@ HostellingIntl.ca. Sleeps 154 people. C$18 (US$13) members, C$22 (US$16) nonmembers. MC, V.

With a mix of two-, four-, and six-bed rooms, this new youth hostel is by far the most pleasant budget lodging in Banff. Couple and family rooms are also available. Reserve a place at least a month in advance during the summer months. Facilities include a recreation room, kitchen area, laundry, and lounge area with a fireplace. Meals are available at the hostel's Cafe Alpenglow.

YWCA. 102 Spray Ave., Banff, AB, T0L 0C0. ☎ **403/762-3560.** Fax 403/762-2602. E-mail: lodge@ymcabanff.ab.ca. C$19 (US$14) bunk in a dorm rm (sleeping bag required); C$53–C$59 (US$38–US$42) double. MC, V.

The YWCA is a bright, modern building with good amenities just across the Bow River bridge from downtown. The Y welcomes both genders—singly, in couples, or in family groups—with accommodations in private or dorm rooms, as required. Some units have private baths. There's also an assembly room with a TV, and a guest laundry on the premises.

Bed & Breakfasts

If you prefer to stay in B&B inns, you can get a list of fairly economical establishments from the **Banff Tourism Bureau,** 224 Banff Ave. (☎ 403/762-8421). This list contains over 30 B&Bs which are screened for quality. Like other Banff lodgings, they should be booked well ahead of arrival. Some are open all year, some only from June to September or October. They accommodate from 4 to 20 guests, some have private baths, some kitchen units, and all serve the hearty breakfasts that mountain appetites require.

You'll need to make reservations through the individual B&B as there's no central booking office. Room rates range from C$30 to C$135 (US$21 to US$97)—you can expect to spend an average of about C$80 (US$57) a night.

Camping

Banff National Park offers hundreds of campsites within easy commuting distance of Banff. The closest are the three ✪ **Tunnel Mountain campgrounds,** just past the youth hostel west of town. Two of the campgrounds are for RVs only, and have both partial and full hookups; the third has showers and is usually reserved for tenters. For more information, call the park's visitor center at ☎ 403/762-1500. Campsites within the park can't be reserved in advance.

DINING

Food is generally good in Banff, although you pay handsomely for what you get. The difference in price between a simply okay meal in a theme restaurant and a nice meal in a classy dining room can be quite small. Service is often very indifferent, as most food servers have become used to waiting on the in-and-out-in-a-hurry tour-bus crowds.

An abundance of restaurants line Banff Avenue; most hotels have at least one dining room. You'll have no problem finding something good to eat in Banff, and the following recommendations are just the beginning of what's available in a very concentrated area.

Expensive

⭕ **Buffalo Mountain Lodge.** 1.6km (1 mile) west of Banff on Tunnel Mountain Rd. ☎ **403/762-2400.** Reservations recommended on weekends. Main courses C$19–C$33 (US$14–US$24). AE, DC, ER, MC, V. INTERNATIONAL NOUVELLE.

Overall, this is probably the most pleasing restaurant in Banff. The dining room occupies half the soaring, three-story lobby of a beautiful log lodge in a quiet wooded location just outside the town; and as satisfying as all this is to the eye and the spirit, the food here is even more notable. The chef brings together the best of regional ingredients—Albertan beef, lamb, pheasant, venison, trout, and BC salmon—and prepares each in a seasonally changing, international style. For example, salmon trout is baked in a potato/saffron crust (C$24/US$17), and roast free-range chicken is served with hazelnut couscous and creamed spinach (C$23/US$16). The fireplace-dominated lobby bar is a lovely place to come for an intimate cocktail.

Grizzly House. 207 Banff Ave. ☎ **403/762-4055.** Reservations required. A la carte fondue for 2 C$28–C$33 (US$20–US$24). MC, V. Daily 11:30am–midnight. FONDUE.

The Grizzly House has nothing to do with bears except a rustic log-cabin atmosphere. The specialty here is fondue—from cheese to hot chocolate, and everything in between, including seafood, rattlesnake, frog's legs, alligator, and buffalo fondue. Steaks and game dishes are the Grizzly's other specialty. The setting is cozy and the fare excellent. It gets a little rowdy in here: each of the tables (and the bathrooms) have phones, so after a couple of drinks, people start calling and talking to strangers across the room—or in the toilet stall. This isn't the place for an intimate romantic dinner; expect to have a wild, game show–style experience.

Ristorante Classico. In the Rimrock Resort, 5km (3 miles) south of Banff on Mountain Ave. ☎ **403/762-3356.** Reservations required. Main courses C$19–C$37 (US$14–US$26); 5-course table d'hôte C$48 (US$34). AE, DC, DISC, JCB, MC, V. Tues–Sun 6–10pm. NORTHERN ITALIAN.

This is the dining room with the best views in Banff, and the restaurant's four-star rating will appeal to the serious gastronome. These artfully prepared and aggressively flavored Italian dishes featuring fresh seafood, veal, fowl, and up-to-the-minute ingredients are almost as impressive as the view. Even the table settings merit a mention: Paloma Picasso designed the china—the display plates are rumored to be worth more than C$500.

The menu features a mix of updated Italian favorites, along with more inventive dishes featuring local beef, lamb, and game. Unusual combinations include venison medaillons served on barley risotto with a maple-mustard-whiskey sauce (C$32/US$23), and an arugula and baby-lettuce salad garnished with quail eggs and blood oranges (C$7/US$5).

Moderate

Balkan Restaurant. 120 Banff Ave. ☎ **403/762-3454.** Main courses C$12–C$16 (US$9–US$11). AE, MC, V. Daily 11am–11pm. GREEK.

Up a flight of stairs you'll find this airy blue-and-white dining room with windows overlooking the street below. The fare consists of reliable Hellenic favorites, well prepared and served with a flourish; Canadian dishes and burgers are also available. The Greek platter (for two) consists of a small mountain of beef souvlaki, ribs, moussaka, lamb chops, tomatoes, and salad for C$45 (US$32). If you're dining alone, you can't do better than the *logo stifado* (rabbit stew) with onions and red wine.

✪ **Coyote's Deli & Grill.** 206 Caribou St. ☎ **403/762-3963.** Reservations accepted. Main courses C$8–C$17 (US$6–US$12). AE, MC, V. Daily 7:30am–10pm. SOUTHWESTERN.

One of the few places in Banff where you can get lighter, healthier food, Coyote's is an attractive bistrolike restaurant with excellent contemporary Southwestern cuisine. There's a broad selection of vegetarian dishes, as well as fresh fish, grilled meats, and multiethnic dishes prepared with an eye to spice and full flavors. In addition, there's a deli, where you can get the makings for a picnic and head to the park. This is a very popular place, so go early or make reservations if you don't want to stand in line.

Giorgio's. 219 Banff Ave. ☎ **403/762-5114.** Reservations recommended on weekends. Pasta courses C$12–C$15 (US$9–US$11); pizza C$12–C$17 (US$9–US$12). AE, MC, V. Daily 4:30–10pm. ITALIAN.

Giorgio's is a cozy eatery dimly lit by low-hanging pink-gleaming lamps over the tables. Divided into a counter section and table portion (both comfortable), Giorgio's serves authentic old-country specialties at eminently reasonable prices. Wonderful crisp rolls—a delicacy in themselves—come with your meal. Don't miss the *gnocchi alla piemontese* (potato dumplings in meat sauce) or the Sicilian *cassata* (candied fruit ice cream).

Magpie & Stump Restaurant & Cantina. 203 Caribou St. ☎ **403/762-4067.** Reservations not accepted. Main courses C$8–C$12 (US$6–US$9). AE, MC, V. Daily noon–2am. MEXICAN.

The false-fronted Magpie & Stump doesn't really match up architecturally with the rest of smart downtown Banff, and thank goodness, neither does the food or atmosphere. The food here is traditional Mexican, done up with style and heft: Someone in the kitchen sure knows how to handle a tortilla. This isn't high cuisine, just well-prepared favorites like enchiladas, tamales, tacos, and the like. But the dishes are well priced compared to those elsewhere in town, and you won't go away hungry. The interior of the place looks like a dark and cozy English pub, except there are buffalo heads and cactus plants everywhere—plus a lot of Southwest kitsch—so you don't have to take it too seriously. This is also a good place for a lively late-night drink, as the town's young summer wait staff likes to crowd in here to unwind with an after-shift beverage—usually a beer in a jam jar.

St. James Gate Irish Pub. 205 Wolf St. ☎ **403/762-9355.** Reservations not accepted. Main courses C$10–C$17 (US$7–US$12). MC, V. Daily 11:30am–1pm. IRISH.

The St. James Gate is owned by Guinness, a company that knows a thing or two about Irish pubs. Newly created to resemble a traditional draught house, this lively pub also has a very extensive menu of bar meals to accompany its selection of draft beers and ales. Halibut-fish-and-chips is a specialty, as are traditional meat pies and sandwiches. Full meals are also available. This is a lively place, and in the Irish tradition, you never know when a table full of dislocated Finnians will break into a heartfelt ballad or two.

Inexpensive

If you're really on a budget, then you'll probably get used to the deli case at Safeways (at Martin and Elk streets), as even inexpensive food is costly here. Here are a few suggestions for fun places where you don't have to spend a fortune to fill up.

Cafe Alenglow, at the Banff International Hostel, Tunnel Mountain Road (☎ 403/762-4122), offers healthy and inexpensive food with youthful flair; they've got an outdoor patio and a liquor license. **Bruno's Cafe and Grill,** 304 Caribou St. (☎ 403/762-8115), is a coffee shop with Italian sandwiches, salads, and lunch and dinner specials. **Jump Start Coffee and Sandwich Place,** 206 Buffalo St. (☎ 403/762-0332), offers sandwiches, soup, salads, and pastries; they'll also pack a picnic for you. For great home-baked muffins and rolls, go to **Evelyn's Coffee Bar,** 201 Banff Ave. (☎ 403/762-0352); light meals are available throughout the day. For all-day and all-night pizza, head to **Aardvark Pizza,** 304a Caribou St. (☎ 403/762-5500), open from 11am to 4am.

BANFF AFTER DARK

Most of Banff's larger hotels and restaurants offer some manner of nightly entertainment. However, for a more lively selection, head to downtown's Banff Avenue. One of the best spots is **Wild Bill's,** the "legendary saloon" at 203 Banff Ave. (☎ 403/762-0333), where you can watch Asian tourists in cowboy hats learning to line dance, and **The Barbary Coast** (☎ 403/762-4616), a "California-style" bar and restaurant that features live music among the potted plants. For a little more grit, head to the **Silver City,** 110 Banff Ave. (☎ 403/762-3337), a subterranean, hammered tin–ceilinged bar where the local hard-edged youth—such as they are—go to play pool and drink gassy beer; there's nightly dancing to DJ music or live bands until 2am. The **Rose and Crown Pub,** 202 Banff Ave. (☎ 403/762-2121), brings in live entertainers all week; English-style pub grub is available late.

The new focus of young club-goers is the three-floor extravaganza at the corner of Banff Avenue and Caribou Street. **The Hard Rock Cafe,** 137 Banff Ave. (☎ 403/760-2347), takes up the main floor, while immediately below is **Outabounds** (☎ 403/762-8434), a dance club. Topping all is **King Eddy Billiards** (☎ 403/762-4629), the hip place to smoke cigars and shoot pool. **St. James Gate Irish Pub,** 205 Wolf St. (☎ 403/762-9355), is the place if you're looking for a pint and a conversation.

LAKE LOUISE

Lake Louise (56km/35 miles northwest of Banff), deep green and surrounded by forest-clad snowcapped mountains, is one of the most famed beauty spots in a park renowned for its fabulous scenery. The village that's grown up in the valley below the lake has developed in the last few years into a resort destination in its own right. Lake Louise boasts the largest ski area in Canada and easy hiking access to the remote high country along the Continental Divide.

The lake may be spectacular, but probably as many people wind up the road to Lake Louise to see its most famous resort, the Chateau Lake Louise. Built by the Canadian Pacific Railroad, the Chateau is, along with the Banff Springs Hotel, one of the most celebrated hotels in Canada. More than just a lodging, the Chateau—a storybook castle perched 1.6 kilometers (1 mile) high in the Rockies—is the center of recreation, dining, shopping, and entertainment for the Lake Louise area.

There's a reason that the water in Lake Louise is as green as an emerald: The stream water that tumbles into the lake is filled with minerals, ground by the glaciers that hang above the lake. Sunlight refracts off the glacial "flour," creating vivid colors.

Lake Louise is dramatically beautiful, and you'll want at least to stroll around the shore of the lake and gawk at the glaciers and back at the massive Chateau.

The gentle Lakeshore Trail follows the northern shore of the lake to the end of Lake Louise. If you're looking for more exercise and even better views, continue on the trail as it begins to climb. Now called the ✪ **Plain of Six Glaciers Trail,** the path passes a teahouse (5km/3 miles from the Chateau and open summers only) on its way to a tremendous viewpoint over Victoria Glacier and Lake Louise.

SEEING THE SIGHTS

The **Lake Louise Summer Sightseeing Lift** (☎ **403/522-3555**) offers a 10-minute ride up to the Whitehorn Lodge, midway up the Lake Louise Ski Area. From here the views onto Lake Louise and the mountains along the Continental Divide are magnificent. Hikers can strike out and follow one of many trails into alpine meadows, or join a free naturalist-led walk and explore the delicate ecosystem. The restaurant at the Whitehorn Lodge is much better than you usually expect at a ski area, and specially priced ride-and-dine tickets are available for those who would like to have a meal at 7,000 feet; the Canadian BBQ buffet is especially fun. The round-trip costs C$9.50 (US$7) for adults, C$8.50 (US$6) for seniors and students, and C$6.50 (US$4.65) for children 6 to 15. The lift operates from early June to mid-September.

To many visitors, ✪ **Moraine Lake** is an even more dramatic and beautiful spot than its more famous twin, Lake Louise. Here, 10 spirelike peaks over 10,000 feet each rise precipitously from the shores of a tiny gem-blue lake. It's an unforgettable sight, and definitely worth the short 13-kilometer (8-mile) drive from Lake Louise. There's a lodge on the shore of the lake with meals and refreshments, and a hiking trail follows the lake's north shore to the mountain cliffs. If the panorama looks familiar, you might have seen it on the back of a Canadian $20 bill.

ACCOMMODATIONS

✪ **Chateau Lake Louise.** Lake Louise, AB, T0L 1E0. ☎ **800/441-1414** or 403/522-3511. Fax 403/522-3834. 447 rms, 66 suites. A/C MINIBAR TV TEL. High season C$179–C$359 (US$127–US$257) double; C$270–C$1,077 (US$193–US$770) suite. Rates depend on whether you want a view of the lake or the mountains. AE, DC, DISC, ER, MC, V. Parking C$6 (US$4.30) a day.

The Chateau is one of the best-loved hotels in North America. If you want to splurge on only one hotel in the Canadian Rockies, make it this one—you won't be sorry. The Chateau Lake Louise is a massive, formal structure, blue-roofed and turreted, furnished with Edwardian sumptuousness and alpine charm. Built in stages over the course of a century by the Canadian Pacific Railroad, the entire hotel was remodeled and upgraded in 1990, and now stays open year-round. The cavernous grand lobby, with its curious figurative chandeliers, gives way to a sitting room filled with overstuffed chairs and couches; these and other common areas overlook the Chateau's gardens and the deep blue-green lake in its glacier-hung cirque. The marble-tiled bathrooms, crystal barware, and comfy down duvets in your room are indicative of the attention to detail and luxury you can expect here. The Chateau offers nine restaurants and eating facilities during the high season (including the exquisite Edelweiss room), as well as two lounge and bar areas. Chateau guests can enjoy a high tea in the afternoon and cabaret entertainment at night. Facilities include an indoor pool, whirlpool, steam room, tanning salon, and shopping arcade.

Lake Louise Inn. 210 Village Rd. (P.O. Box 209), Lake Louise, AB, T0L 1E0. ☎ **800/661-9237** or 403/522-3791. Fax 403/522-2018. 222 rms. TV TEL. High season C$128–C$264 (US$92–US$189) double. AE, DC, MC, V.

The Lake Louise Inn stands in a wooded 8-acre estate, 7 driving minutes from the fabled lake at the base of the moraine. There's forest all around and snowcapped mountains peering over the trees outside your window. The inn consists of five different buildings—a central lodge with swimming pool, whirlpool, steam room, restaurant, bar and lounge—and four lodging units. There are five different room types, beginning with standard twin rooms with double beds. The superior queen and executive rooms in Building Five (C$180/US$129) are the newest and nicest in the inn, with pine-railed balconies and a sitting area; for families, the superior lofts are capable of sleeping eight, with two bathrooms, complete kitchen (including dishwasher), living room and fireplace, and two separate bedrooms and fold-out couch—just the ticket for a family or group (C$240/US$172).

✪ **Post Hotel.** P.O. Box 69, Lake Louise, AB, T0L 1E0. ☎ **800/661-1586** or 403/522-3989. Fax 403/522-3966. 93 rms, 7 suites, 2 cabins. TV TEL. High season C$170–C$500 (US$122–US$358) double; C$440 (US$315) suite; C$300–C$340 (US$215–US$243) cabin. AE, MC, V. Closed Nov.

Discreetly elegant and beautifully furnished, this wonderful log hotel with its distinctive red roof began its life in 1942 as a humble ski lodge. Between 1988 and 1993, new European owners completely rebuilt the old lodge, transforming it into one of the most luxurious getaways in the Canadian Rockies; in fact, the Post Hotel is one of only two properties in western Canada that has been admitted into the French resort network Relais et Châteaux. The entire lodge is built of traditional log-and-beam construction, preserving the rustic flavor of the old lodge and of the mountain setting. The public rooms are lovely, from the renowned dining room (preserved intact from the original hotel) to the arched, two-story wood-paneled library (complete with rolling track ladders and river-stone fireplace) to the lobby which looks onto the peaks and glaciers behind Lake Louise and Moraine Lake.

The rooms throughout are beautifully furnished with rustic pine furniture, deep colors, and rich upholstery. Most rooms have stone fireplaces, balconies, and whirlpool tubs. Hospitality and service are top-notch.

Due to the rambling nature of the lodge, there are a bewildering 14 different kinds of rooms available. The simplest are cozy twin-bedded rooms with a balcony; "N" rooms (all rooms are known by letter) are nice for a family, as they have a separate bedroom with queen-size bed, and another queen and a twin in a loft; a fireplace; and balconies on both sides of the hotel. Newly redesigned, the "F" rooms are fantastic. Made by combining two previous rooms to make a large suite, they feature a huge tiled bathroom with both a shower and a Jacuzzi tub, a separate bedroom, a large balcony, and a sitting area with easy chairs and couch, a river-stone fireplace, and a daybed. Facilities include a notably attractive glass-encased pool, whirlpool, steam room, and meeting facilities for small groups.

DINING

Lake Louise Station. 200 Sentinel Rd. ☎ **403/522-2600.** Reservations recommended on weekends. Pizzas to C$15 (US$11); steaks and seafood C$12–C$22 (US$9–US$16). AE, MC, V. Daily 11:30am–midnight. PIZZA/STEAKS.

Located in the handsome and historic train station at Lake Louise village, this log building served as the Lake Louise train station for nearly a century, before rail service ceased in the 1980s. Now the handsome and historic building has been converted into a bar and restaurant. Dining is accommodated in the old waiting room, and the ticketing lobby is where to go for a quiet drink. Two old dining cars sit on the sidings beside the station, and are open for fine dining in the evenings. Excellent steaks and grilled meat are the specialties here.

✪ **Post Hotel Dining Rm.** In the Post Hotel, Lake Louise. ☎ **403/522-3989.** Reservations required. Main courses C$25–C$36 (US$18–US$26). AE, MC, V. Daily 7–11am, 11:30am–2pm, and 5–10pm. INTERNATIONAL/CANADIAN.

Here you'll find some of the finest dining in the Canadian Rockies. The food was famous long before the rebuilding and renovation of the old hotel, but in recent years the restaurant has maintained such a high degree of excellence that it has won the highly prized endorsement of the French Relais et Châteaux organization.

The dining room is in a long and rustic room with wood beams and windows looking out onto glaciered peaks. The dinner menu focuses on full-flavored meat and fish preparations. For an appetizer, you might try scampi, served on asparagus with both an orange and a lemon sauce; rack of lamb is served with grilled portobello mushrooms and a rosemary sauce at a cost of C$34 (US$24). Desserts are equally imaginative. Service is excellent, as is the very impressive wine list, with some good values discreetly hidden in the mostly French selection.

✪ **Walliser Stube Wine Bar.** In Chateau Lake Louise. ☎ **403/522-1817.** Reservations required. Main courses C$12.50–C$20 (US$9–US$14); fondues C$32–C$43 (US$23–US$30). AE, DISC, ER, MC, V. Daily 5–11:30pm. SWISS.

While the Chateau Lake Louise operates four major restaurants, including the formal Edelweiss Room, the most fun and relaxing place to eat is the Walliser Stube, a small dining room that serves excellent Swiss-style food and some of the best fondue ever. The back dining room is called the Library, and is indeed lined with tall and imposing wood cases and rolling library ladders. Happily, the cases are filled with wine, not books: Part of the Chateau's huge wine selection is stored here.

A meal in the Walliser Stube is an evening's worth of eating and drinking, as the best foods—a variety of fondues and raclettes—make for convivial and communal eating experiences. The cheese fondue, C$32 (US$23) for two, is fabulous; forget the stringy glutinous experience you had in the 1970s and give it another chance. Hot-meat fondues are also available, as is an excellent veal and vegetable fondue cooked in spicy wine broth, costing C$45.50 (US$32) for two. Raclettes are another communal cooking operation, where heat lamps melt chunks of cheese until bubbly, and the aromatic, molten result is spread on bread. It's all great fun in a great atmosphere—go with friends and you'll have a blast.

✪ THE ICEFIELDS PARKWAY

Between Lake Louise and Jasper winds one of the most spectacular mountain roads in the world. Called the Icefields Parkway, the road climbs through three deep river valleys, beneath soaring, glacier-notched mountains, and past dozens of hornlike peaks shrouded with permanent snowfields. Capping this 287-kilometer (178-mile) route is the **Columbia Icefields,** a massive dome of glacial ice and snow straddling the top of the continent. From this mighty cache of ice—the largest nonpolar ice cap in the world—flow the Columbia, the Athabasca, and the North Saskatchewan rivers.

Although you can drive the Icefields Parkway in 3 hours, plan to take enough time to stop at eerily green lakes, hike to a waterfall, and take an excursion up onto the Columbia Icefields. There's also a good chance that you'll see wildlife: ambling bighorn sheep, mountain goats, elks with huge shovel antlers, momma bears with cubs—all guaranteed to halt traffic and set cameras clicking.

After Lake Louise, the highway divides: Highway 1 continues west toward Golden, British Columbia, while Highway 93 (the Icefields Parkway) continues north along the Bow River. **Bow Lake,** the river's source, glimmers below enormous **Crowfoot Glacier;** when the glacier was named, a third "toe" was more in evidence, lending a resemblance to a bird's claw. Roadside viewpoints look across the lake at the glacier; **Num-Ti-Jah Lodge,** on the shores of Bow Lake, is a good place to stop for a bite to eat and some photographs.

The road mounts Bow Summit, and drops into the North Saskatchewan River drainage. Stop at the **Peyto Lake Viewpoint,** and hike up a short but steep trail to glimpse this startling blue-green body of water. The North Saskatchewan River collects its tributaries at the little community of Saskatchewan River Crossing; thousands of miles later, the Bow and the Saskatchewan rivers will join and flow east through Lake Winnipeg to Hudson Bay.

The parkway then begins to climb up in earnest toward the Sunwapta Pass. Here, in the shadows of 11,450-foot **Mount Athabasca,** the icy tendrils of the **Columbia Icefields** come into view. However impressive these glaciers may seem from the road, they are nothing compared to the massive amounts of centuries-old ice and snow hidden by mountain peaks; the Columbia Icefields cover nearly 518 square kilometers (200 sq. miles) and are more than 2,500 feet thick. From the parkway, the closest glacial fingers of the ice field are Athabasca Glacier, which fills the horizon to the west of the **Columbia Icefields Centre** (☎ 403/852-7032), a newly rebuilt lodge with restaurant and lodging, and the **Icefield Information Centre** (☎ 403/852-7030), a park service office that answers questions about the area.

From the **Brewster Snocoach Tours ticket office** (☎ 403/762-2241), specially designed buses with balloon tires take visitors out onto the face of the glacier. The 90-minute excursion includes a chance to hike the surface of Athabasca Glacier. The Snocoach Tour is C$22.50 (US$16) for adults and C$5 (US$3.60) for children 6 to 15; children under 6 are free. If you don't have the time or cash (no credit cards are accepted) for the Snocoach Tour, you can drive to the toe of the glacier and walk up onto the glacier's surface. Use extreme caution when on the glacier; tumbling into a crevasse can result in broken limbs or even death.

From the Columbia Icefields, the parkway descends steeply into the Athabasca River drainage. From the parking area for **Sunwapta Falls,** travelers can decide to crowd around the chain-link fence and peer at this turbulent falls, or to take the half-hour hike to equally impressive but less crowded Lower Sunwapta Falls. **Athabasca Falls,** further north along the parkway, is another must-see waterfall. Here, the wide and powerful Athabasca River constricts into a roaring torrent before dropping 82 feet into a narrow canyon. A mist-covered bridge crosses the chasm just beyond the falls; a series of trails lead to more viewpoints. The parkway continues along the Athabasca River, through a landscape of meadows and lakes, before entering the Jasper Townsite.

Facilities are few along the parkway. Hikers and bikers will be pleased to know that there are rustic **hostels** at Mosquito Creek, Rampart Creek, Hilda Creek, Beauty Creek, Athabasca Falls, and at Mount Edith Cavell. Reservations for all the Icefield Parkway hostels can be made by calling ☎ 403/439-3215. A **shuttle** runs between the Calgary International Hostel and hostels in Banff, Lake Louise, and along the Icefield Parkway to Jasper. You must have reservations at the destination hostel to use the service. Call ☎ 403/283-5551 for more information.

8 Jasper National Park

Jasper, now Canada's largest mountain park, was established in 1907, although it already boasted a "guest house" of sorts in the 1840s. A visiting painter described it as "composed of two rooms of about 14 and 15 feet square. One of them is used by all comers and goers, Indians, voyageurs and traders, men, women and children being huddled together indiscriminately, the other room being devoted to the exclusive occupation of Colin Fraser (postmaster) and his family, consisting of a Cree squaw and nine interesting half-breed children."

Things have changed.

Slightly less busy than Banff to the south, Jasper Park attracts a much more outdoors-oriented crowd, and hiking, biking, climbing, horseback riding, and rafting are the main activities. Sure, there's shopping and fine dining in Jasper, but it's not the focus of activity, as in Banff. Travelers seem a bit more determined and rugged-looking, as if they have just stumbled in from a long-distance hiking trail or off the face of a rock: certainly there's no shortage of outdoor recreation here.

For more information about the park, contact **Jasper National Park,** P.O. Box 10, Jasper, AB, T0E 1E0 (☎ 403/852-6176).

SPORTS & OUTDOOR ACTIVITIES IN THE PARK

A clearinghouse of local outfitters and guides is the **Jasper Adventure Centre,** 604 Connaught Dr. (☎ 800/565-7547 in western Canada, or 403/852-5595; e-mail: tours@telusplanet.net). White-water raft and canoe trips, horseback rides, guided hikes, and other activities can be ticketed out of this office.

A number of shops rent most of the equipment you'll need for an adventure. Rent a mountain bike for C$6 (US$4.30) per hour, C$18 (US$13) per day from **On-Line Sport and Tackle,** 600 Patricia St. (☎ 403/852-3630); they also rent canoes and rafts, tents, fishing gear, and skis. They can also set you up with guided rafting and fishing trips. Snowboards, cross-country ski equipment, and more bikes are available from **Freewheel Cycle,** 618 Patricia St. (☎ 403/852-3898).

SKIING   Jasper's downhill ski area is **Ski Marmot Basin,** located 19 kilometers (11.7 miles) west of Jasper on Highway 93. Marmot is generally underrated as a ski resort; it doesn't get the crowds of Banff, nor does it get the infamous Chinook winds. The resort has 52 runs and 7 lifts, and rarely any lines. Lift tickets start at C$37 (US$26). Call ☎ 403/852-3816 for more information.

HIKING   Overnight and long-distance hikers will find an abundance of backcountry trails around Jasper that reach into some of the most spectacular scenery in the Canadian Rockies. There are fewer but still good choices for day hikers.

The complex of trails around **Maligne Canyon** makes a good choice for a group, as there are a number of access points (across six different footbridges). The less keen can make the loop back and meet fellow hikers (after getting the vehicle) further down the canyon.

Trails ring parklike Beauvert and Annette lakes (the latter is wheelchair accessible), both near Jasper Park Lodge. Likewise, Pyramid and Patricia lakes just north of town have loop trails but more of a backcountry atmosphere.

The brochure *Day Hikers' Guide to Jasper National Park* costs C$1 (US75¢) at the visitor center, and details dozens of hikes throughout the park. Several outfitters lead guided hikes; contact **All Things Wild** (☎ 403/852-5193) or **Walk and Talks Jasper,** 614d Connaught Dr. (☎ 403/852-4945; e-mail: walktalk@incentre.net), for a selection of half- and whole-day hikes.

RAFTING   Jasper is the jumping-off point for float and white-water trips down several rivers. A raft trip is a good option for that inevitable drizzly day, as you're going to get wet anyway.

The mild rapids (Class II to III) of the wide Athabasca River make a good introductory trip, while wilder runs down the Maligne River (Class III) will appeal to those needing something to brag about, at a cost of C$55 (US$39). **Maligne River Adventures,** 626 Connaught Dr., Jasper (☎ 403/852-3370; fax 403/852-3405), offers trips down both rivers, as well as a 3-day wilderness trip on the Kakwa River (Class IV-plus). Note that trips down the Maligne River are currently offered only after July 1, in order to protect nesting harlequin ducks.

Wilder white-water runs (Class III to IV) are available on the Fraser River in Mount Robson Park from **Sekani Mountain Tours,** who maintain an information

Jasper Town & Jasper National Park

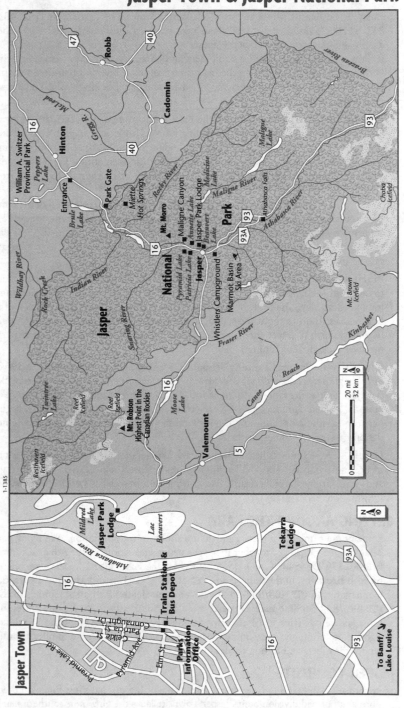

and ticket office in Jasper at the Work World Store, 618 Patricia St., (☎ **403/ 852-5211**). "Salmon spawning" floats take place on the Fraser's calmer stretches during mid-August and mid-September.

Trips generally include most equipment and transportation. Jasper is loaded with rafting outfitters; a stroll along the main streets of town reveals a half-dozen outfitters. Or just ask your hotel concierge for advice and help booking a trip. You'll have no trouble getting out onto a river.

HORSEBACK RIDING   One of the most exhilarating experiences the park can offer is trail riding. Guides take your riding prowess (or lack of it) into account and select foothill trails slow enough to keep you mounted. And the special mountain trail horses used are steady, reliable animals not given to sudden antics. For a short ride, contact **Pyramid Stables** (☎ **403/852-3562**), which offers short 1- to 3-hour trips around Pyramid and Patricia Lakes.

Long-distance trail rides take keen riders into the park's backcountry. **Skyline Trail Rides,** with an office at Jasper Park Lodge (☎ **888/582-7787** or 403/852-4215; Web site: www.discoverjasper.com/trailrides/skyline) offers a number of short day trips, and also 3- to 4-day trips to a remote albeit modernized lodge. Sleigh rides are offered in winter.

FISHING   Currie's Guiding Ltd. (☎ **403/852-5650**) conducts fishing excursions to beautiful Maligne Lake; the cost is C$149 (US$107) per person (two minimum) for an 8-hour day. Tackle, bait, and boat rentals are included in the price, as well as full lunches. Inquire about the special single and group rates. Patricia and Pyramid lakes, just north of Jasper, are more convenient to Jasper-based anglers who fancy trying their luck at trout fishing.

CLIMBING   Jasper Climbing School, 806 Connaught Dr. (☎ **403/852-3964**), offers beginner, intermediate, and advanced climbing in 1-day private courses. Basics are taught at the foot of Mount Morro, 19 kilometers (12 miles) from Jasper. The personal guided climbing fee is C$250 (US$179) a day. For C$30 (US$21), beginners can sample rappelling in a 3-hour workshop. Food, transport, and accommodations (in private homes) are extra.

GOLF   The 18-hole course at **Jasper Park Lodge,** east of Jasper Townsite, is one of the most popular and challenging courses in the Rockies, with 73 sand traps and other, more natural hazards like visiting wildlife. Call ☎403/852-6090 for information.

GETTING AROUND THE PARK

Some of the principle outfitters and guides also offer transportation to outlying park beauty spots. Organized tours of the park's major sites—notably the Athabasca snowfields (C$75/US$54 to C$80/US$57) and Maligne Lake (C$12/US$9)—are offered by both **Brewster,** in the train station (☎ **403/852-3332**), and **Maligne Tours,** 626 Connaught Dr. (☎ **403/852-3370**). **Beyond the Beaten Path,** 414 Connaught Dr. (☎ **403/852-5650;** e-mail: curries@ycs.ab.ca), offers trips to these popular destinations, as well as trips to Miette Hot Springs, (C$39/US$28) and more intimate sightseeing, photography, wildlife viewing, and picnic trips. They also offer a shuttle service for hikers and rafting parties.

JASPER TOWNSITE

Jasper isn't Banff, and to listen to most residents of Jasper, that's just fine with them. Born as a railroad division point, Jasper Townsite lacks the glitz of its southern neighbor, and also Banff's slightly precious air of an internationalized alpine fantasyland.

There's little of Banff's traffic congestion, sky-high prices, and all-out mob scenes. Jasper has a lived-in, community-oriented sense largely lacking in Banff. The streets are thronged with avid young hikers and mountain bikers, giving Jasper a recreational focus that Banff has lost to the shopping hordes. Chances are the people you meet on the streets will be a little muddy or wet, as if they've just gotten in from the river or the mountain. Chances are they have.

But development is rapidly approaching. New nightclubs, restaurants, and tourist shops are springing up along Patricia Street, and that sound in the distance is the thunder of tour buses.

ESSENTIALS

VISITOR INFORMATION   For information on the townsite, contact **Jasper Tourism and Commerce,** P.O. Box 98, Jasper, AB, T0E 1E0 (☎ **403/852-3858;** fax 403/852-4932).

GETTING THERE   Jasper is on the Yellowhead Highway System, linking it with Vancouver, Prince George, and Edmonton, and is therefore an important transportation hub. The town is 287 kilometers (178 miles) northwest of Banff.

VIA Rail connects Jasper to Vancouver and Edmonton with three trains weekly; the train station is at town center (☎ **403/852-4102**), along Connaught Street. The train tracks run due north before they start the long easterly sweep that leads to Edmonton. Also headquartered at the train station is the **Greyhound** bus station (☎ **403/852-3926**) and **Brewster Transportation** (☎ **403/852-3332**), which offers express service to Banff, as well as a large number of sightseeing excursions to scenic spots in the park.

ORIENTATION   Jasper Townsite is much smaller than Banff. The main street, Connaught Drive, runs alongside the Canadian National Railway tracks, and is the address of the majority of Jasper's hotels. Patricia Street, 1 block west, is quickly becoming the boutique street, with new shops and cafes springing up. Right in the center of town, surrounded by delightful shady gardens, is the **Parks Information Offices** (☎ **403/852-6146**). The post office is at the corner of Patricia and Elm streets. At the northern end of Connaught and Geike streets, a quarter mile from downtown, is another complex of hotels.

GETTING AROUND   **Tilden Rental Cars** is at 638 Connaught Dr. (☎ **403/ 852-3798**). Call a **taxi** at ☎ **403/852-5558** or 403/852-3600.

EXPLORING THE TOWN & ENVIRONS

The **Jasper Tramway** (☎ **403/852-3093;** Web site: www.worldweb.com/ JasperTramway/>) starts at the foot of Whistler's Mountain, 6 kilometers (4 miles) south of Jasper off Highway 93. Each car takes 30 passengers (plus baby carriages, wheelchairs, or the family dog) and hoists them 2 kilometers (1 1/4 miles) up to the summit (7,400 ft.) in a breathtaking sky ride. At the upper terminal you step out into alpine tundra, the region above the tree line where some flowers take 25 years to blossom. A wonderful picnic area carpeted with mountain grass is alive with squirrels. You'll also see the "whistlers"—actually hoary marmots—that the mountain is named for. The ride costs C$15 (US$11) for adults and C$8.50 (US$6) for children; cars depart every 10 to 15 minutes. Or consider a sunset ride followed by a three-course dinner at the terminal's restaurant for C$30 (US$21); buffet breakfast and lunch are also available.

Just northeast of Jasper, off the Jasper Park Lodge access road, the Maligne River drops from its high mountain valley to cut an astounding canyon into a steep limestone face on its way to meet the Athabasca River. The chasm of **Maligne Canyon** is up to 150 feet deep at points, and yet only 10 feet across; the river tumbles through the canyon in a series of powerful waterfalls. A sometimes-steep hiking trail follows the canyon down the mountainside, bridging the gorge six times. Interpretive signs describe the geology. A teahouse operates at the top of the canyon in summer.

An incredibly blue mountain lake buttressed by a ring of high-flying peaks, **Maligne Lake** is 45 minutes east of Jasper, and is one of the park's great beauty spots. The lake is the largest glacier-fed lake in the Rockies, and the second largest in the world. The native Canadians, who called the lake Chaba Imne, had a superstitious awe of the region. Settlers (in this case, a white woman, Mary Schäffer) didn't discover Maligne until 1908.

Today droves of tour buses go to the "hidden lake," and the area is a popular destination for hikers, anglers, trail riders, and white-water rafters. No matter what else they do, most people who visit Maligne Lake take a boat cruise to Spirit Island, at the head of the lake. The 90-minute cruise leaves from below the Maligne Lake Lodge, an attractive summer-only facility with restaurant, bar, and gift shop (no lodging, though). Cruise tickets are C$31 (US$22) for adults, C$27.50 (US$20) for seniors (65-plus), and C$15.50 (US$11) for children.

Maligne Lake waters are alive with rainbow and eastern brook trout, and the Maligne Lake Boathouse is stocked with licenses, tackle, bait, and boats. **Guided fishing trips** include equipment, lunch, and hotel transportation with half-day excursions starting at C$110 (US$79). You can rent a boat, canoe, or a sea kayak to ply the waters. Morning and afternoon **rides on horseback** up the Bald Hills depart from the Chalet at Maligne Lake. The cost is C$55 (US$39).

All the facilities at Maligne Lake, including the lake cruises and a white-water raft outfitter that offers tours down three Jasper Park rivers, are operated by **Maligne Tours.** There's an office at the lake, next to the lodge, and also in Jasper at 626 Connaught Dr. (☎ **403/852-3370;** e-mail: maligne@ycs.ab.ca; Web site: www.jaspertravel.com/malignelake), and at the Jasper Park Lodge (☎ **403/ 852-4779**). Maligne Tours also operates a shuttle bus between Jasper and the lake.

Downstream from Maligne Lake, the Maligne River flows into **Medicine Lake.** This large body of water appears regularly every spring, grows 8 kilometers (5 miles) long and 60 feet deep, then vanishes in the fall, leaving only a dry gravel bed through the winter. The reason for this annual wonder is a system of underground drainage caves. The local Indians believed that spirits were responsible for the lake's annual disappearance, hence the name.

Miette Hot Springs (☎ **403/866-3939**) lies 60 kilometers (37 miles) northeast of Jasper off Highway 16, one of the best **animal-spotting routes** in the park. Watch for elk, deer, coyotes, and moose en route. The hot mineral springs can be enjoyed in a beautiful swimming pool or two soaker pools, surrounded by forest and an imposing mountain backdrop. Campgrounds and an attractive lodge with refreshments are nearby. During summer the pool remains open from 8:30am to 10:30pm. Admission is C$5 (US$3.60) for adults, C$4.50 (US$3.20) for children and seniors, or C$14.50 (US$10) for a family.

SHOPPING

Weather can be unpredictable in Jasper. If it's raining, you can while away an afternoon in the town's shops and boutiques. The shopping arcade at the Jasper Park Lodge, called the **Beauvert Promenade,** has a number of excellent clothing and gift shops. In Jasper itself, Patricia Street contains most of the high-quality shops. A number of galleries feature Inuit and native arts and crafts: check out **Our Native Land,** 601 Patricia St. (☎ **403/852-5592**). Fashionable yet functional outdoor gear is the specialty of **Wild Mountain Willy's,** 610 Patricia St. (☎ **403/852-5304**).

ACCOMMODATIONS

In general, rooms in Jasper are slightly less expensive than those in Banff. As in Banff, there's a marked difference between high season and the rest of the year, so if you can avoid June to September, you'll find that most accommodations have reduced their prices by 50%. *Please note:* All prices listed are for high season. Call for reduced, off-season rates. You'll want to make reservations as soon as you can, as most rooms are booked well in advance. If you can't find a room, or don't want to bother with the details, contact **Reservations Jasper** (☎ 403/852-5488; fax 403/852-5489; e-mail: resjas@incentre.net). There's a fee for using the service.

Very Expensive

✪ **Chateau Jasper.** 96 Geikie St., Jasper, AB, T0E 1E0. ☎ **800/661-9323** or 403/852-5644. Fax 403/852-4860. E-mail: chjasper@agt.net. 112 rms, 7 suites. A/C TV TEL. C$275 (US$197) double; C$325–C$375 (US$232–US$268) suite. AE, CB, DC, DISC, MC, V. Free covered, heated parking.

Usually considered the Jasper Townsite's best hotel, the Chateau Jasper is a refined three-story lodging with some of the best staff and service in town. The grounds are beautifully landscaped with colorful floral patches scattered through the courtyards. All standard rooms have two double beds; about half the hotel is no-smoking (separated by floors). Rooms are nicely decorated, and come with all the amenities you expect at a four-star lodging. All suites have Jacuzzi tubs, the truly large King Suites come with both Jacuzzi and shower stall, a huge 36-inch TV, wet bar, and a nice sitting area.

Dining: The noted Beauvallon Restaurant and lounge is located just off the lobby.

Services: There's a complimentary shuttle bus to the train and bus station. Room service, dry cleaning and laundry service; baby-sitting; the Chateau Jasper is about the only downtown hotel that offers a concierge service.

Facilities: The pool and hot tub, sheltered behind glass, are connected by stairs to the large second-story sundeck. Ski lockers are provided. Spectravision movie channels; VCRs.

Jasper Park Lodge. P.O. Box 40, Jasper, AB, T0E 1E0. ☎ **800/465-7547** in Alberta, 800/441-1414 elsewhere in North America, or 403/852-3301. Fax 403/852-5107. 442 rms, suites, and cabins. C$364 (US$260) double; from C$412 (US$295) suite. AE, CB, DISC, ER, JCB, MC, V.

Jasper's most exclusive lodging, the Jasper Park Lodge was built by the Canadian Pacific Railroad, and has the same air of luxury and gentility as their other properties, but with a more woodsy feel—sort of like an upscale summer camp. The hotel's wooded, elk-inhabited grounds are located along Lac Beauvert, about 8 kilometers (5 miles) east of Jasper proper. Lodgings are all extremely comfortable, though a bit hard to characterize, as there are a wide variety of cabins, lodge rooms, chalets, and cottages; all from different eras, all set amid the forest, and all within easy walking distance of the beautiful central lodge. All rooms have the same amenities, but they vary widely in style, size, and price; it's a good idea to call and talk to the staff and find out what's available for your money, needs, and size of group. Friends or family traveling together may opt for one of the wonderful and enormous housekeeping cabins, some of which have up to eight bedrooms all with *en suite* bathrooms.

Dining: Four restaurants, including the famed four-star Edith Cavell Dining Room, with four-course dinners at C$56 (US$40); the Tent City Lounge is one of Jasper's youthful hangouts.

Services: 24-hour room service, dry cleaning/laundry, secretarial service, baby-sitting.

Facilities: Access to all the mountain sports available in Jasper, and also stables, tennis courts, outdoor swimming pool, health club, and one of the best golf courses in Canada. The lodge offers an amazing and lofty Great Room with huge fireplaces to snuggle by, and the classy Beauvert Promenade shopping arcade.

Expensive

Amethyst Lodge. 200 Connaught Dr. (P.O. Box 1200), Jasper, AB, T0E 1E0. ☎ **800/ 661-9935** or 403/852-3394. Fax 403/852-5198. 97 rms. A/C TV TEL. C$165–C$220 (US$117– US$157) double. AE, CB, DC, MC, V.

If you're sick of the faux alpine look prevalent in the Canadian Rockies, then you may be ready for the Amethyst Lodge, a comfortable and unabashed motor inn. All rooms come with two double or two queen beds; half of the rooms have balconies. The Amethyst is more central to downtown Jasper than most lodgings.

Dining: There's a large restaurant and lounge; afternoon tea is served daily in the lounge.

Services: Laundry/dry cleaning.

Facilities: Two hot tubs.

✪ **Jasper Inn.** 98 Geikie St. (P.O. Box 879), Jasper, AB, T0E 1E0. ☎ **403/852-4461.** Fax 403/ 852-5916. E-mail: jasperin@telusplanet.net. Web site: www.jasperinn.com. 143 rms, 14 suites. TV TEL. C$175–C$225 (US$125–US$161) double; from C$260–C$325 (US$186–US$232) suite. Extra person C$10 (US$7). Children under 17 stay free in parents' rm. AE, DC, ER, MC, V.

The Jasper Inn, on the northern end of town but set back off the main road, is one of the nicest lodgings in town. Rooms are available in four different buildings, and in many different size and bed configurations. If you're looking for a good value, ignore the standard and efficiency units (which are perfectly nice rooms, mind you); pay C$10 more, C$180 (US$129), and reserve a one-bedroom suite, a very spacious room with a fireplace and fully equipped kitchen. Even nicer are the rooms in the Maligne Suites unit, a separate building (all no-smoking) with extra-spacious rooms (the marble- and granite-lined bathrooms are enormous); all come with fireplaces, wet bar, Jacuzzi tubs, nice furniture, balcony, and two beds. (The top of the line is Elke Sommers's former room; ask for it by name.) Also available are two-bedroom chalet-style rooms (which can sleep up to seven). These are perfect for families, with a full kitchen, balcony, fireplace, and loads of room.

Dining: The Inn Restaurant, in a gardenlike atrium, offers tasty Canadian fare, with good prime rib, salmon, and pasta.

Services: Guest laundry.

Facilities: Sauna, steam room, hot tub, small pool, coin laundry, ski wax room, small meeting facility.

✪ **Lobstick Lodge.** 96 Geikie St. (P.O. Box 1200), Jasper, AB, T0E 1E0. ☎ **800/661-9317** or 403/852-4431. Fax 403/852-4142. 138 rms. TV TEL. C$165 (US$117) double; C$180 (US$129) kitchenette unit. Children under 15 stay free in parents' rm. AE, CB, DC, ER, MC, V.

The Lobstick Lodge was totally renovated in 1995, and now features both a lounge and elevators, good additions to one of Jasper's most popular hotels. Standard rooms here are the largest in Jasper, and all feature two double beds. Even more impressive are 43 huge kitchen units, with a complete kitchen, including full-size fridge, four-burner stove, and microwave; plus a double and twin-size bed and a fold-out couch. These are perfect for families and they go fast; so reserve them early. The upstairs meeting room has great mountain views, and guests can use it for playing cards or lounging if it's not in use.

Dining: A family restaurant and a cocktail lounge with great views.

Services: Dry cleaning/laundry.
Facilities: Indoor pool, whirlpool, two outdoor hot tubs, patio.

Marmot Lodge. 86 Connaught Dr., Jasper, AB, T0E 1E0. ☎ **800/661-6521** or 403/852-4471. Fax 403/852-3280. 107 rms. TV TEL. C$150 (US$107) double; C$180 (US$129) kitchen unit. Children under 15 stay free in parents' rm. AE, DC, MC, V.

This is one of the better deals in Jasper. At the northern end of Jasper's main street, the Marmot Lodge offers reasonable prices and very pleasant rooms. Lodging is in three different buildings, each with different types of rooms. One building has all-kitchen units with fireplaces, popular with families. The building facing the street has smaller, less expensive rooms with two singles or one queen bed, while the third building has very large "deluxe" rooms with two queen beds. All rooms have been decorated with a Native-American theme; some have tapestrylike weavings on the walls.

The Marmot has a barbecue patio, a newly renovated dining room, a fireside lounge, and a heated, picture-windowed pool with sauna and whirlpool.

Sawridge Hotel Jasper. 82 Connaught Dr., Jasper, AB, T0E 1E0. ☎ **800/661-6427** or 403/852-5111. Fax 403/852-5942. 151 rms, 3 suites. A/C TV TEL. C$175–C$229 (US$125–US$164) double; C$199–C$295 (US$142–US$211) suite. AE, ER, MC, V.

The three-story lobby of the Sawridge Hotel is large and rustic, and gives onto a very long central atrium lit with skylights, where the award-winning dining room, swimming pool, and hot tub are found. The Sawridge has one-bedroom guest rooms that face onto the atrium, or two queen-bedded rooms that overlook the town; these rooms also have balconies. The entire hotel has recently been redecorated, and the rooms are very comfortable. The hotel also has an informal garden cafe, two outdoor Jacuzzis, a lounge, and a sports bar. The Sawridge, on the northern edge of Jasper, is unique in that it's owned by the Sawridge Cree Indian Band.

Moderate

Athabasca Hotel. 510 Patricia St., Jasper, AB, T0E 1E0. ☎ **800/563-9859** or 403/852-3386. Fax 403/852-4955. 61 rms (39 with bath). TV TEL. C$99–C$129 (US$71–US$92) double with private bath; C$75–C$89 (US$54–US$64) double with shared bath. AE, DC, MC, V.

The Athabasca has a lobby like a hunting lodge, with a stone fireplace, rows of trophy heads of deer, elk, and bighorn, and a great bar with its own huge fireplace. A gray stone corner building with a homey, old-fashioned air, the hotel was built in 1929 as a destination hotel, and has a large attractive dining room and a small and trim coffee shop. Each of the bedrooms has a mountain view, although only half have private bath. The rooms are of fair size, the furnishings simple and tasteful: armchairs, writing table, and walk-in closet. The Athabasca is really quite pleasant and is one of the few good values in Jasper.

✪ Becker's Chalets. Hwy. 95 (5km/3 miles south of Jasper; P.O. Box 579), Jasper, AB, T0E 1E0. ☎ **403/852-3779.** Fax 403/852-7202. 96 chalets. TV. C$100–C$150 (US$71–US$107) 1-bedrm cabin; C$130–C$190 (US$93–US$136) 2-bedrm cabin; C$160–C$310 (US$114–US$222) 3-bedrm cabin. MC, V.

This very attractive log cabin resort offers a variety of lodging options in freestanding chalets in a glade of trees along the Athabasca River. While the resort dates from the 1940s and retains the feel and atmosphere of an old-fashioned mountain retreat, most of the chalets have been built in the last 5 years, and are thoroughly modernized. Chalets come with river-stone fireplaces, full kitchens, and color TVs. The dining room here, open for breakfast and dinner, is one of Jasper's best.

Tekarra Lodge. P.O. Box 669, Jasper AB, T0E 1E0 (1.6km/1 mile east of Jasper off Hwy. 93A). ☎ **800/661-6562** or 403/852-3058. Fax 403/852-4636. 10 lodge rms, 42 cabins. C$99

(US$71) lodge rm; C$110–C$125 (US$79–US$89) cabins for 2. Extra person C$10 (US$7). AE, DC, MC, V.

This charming log cabin resort is just east of Jasper, situated above the confluence of the Miette and Athabasca rivers. Accommodations are in the lodge, or in freestanding cabins that can sleep from two to seven people. All cabins have a kitchenette or full kitchen; 2-night minimum in summer season.

The cabins are rustic-looking and nicely furnished, but it's the location that really sets Tekarra Lodge apart. Just far enough from the bustle of Jasper, and off a quiet road in the forest, the Tekarra offers the kind of venerable charm that you dream of in a mountain cabin resort. To make the isolation more complete, none of the rooms has a private phone or television. One of Jasper's best restaurants is located in the lodge, making this a great place for a family seeking solitude and access to good food.

Inexpensive

HOSTELS   Two **Hostelling International** hostels are near Jasper and are the best alternatives for the budget traveler. Both locations have the same reservations number (reservations are strongly advised during summer) and same addresses: ☎ **403/852-3215,** P.O. Box 387, Jasper, AB, T0E 1E0; e-mail: jihostel@telusplanet.net.

The **Jasper International Hostel** is on Skytram Road, 6 kilometers (4 miles) west of Jasper. The hostel sleeps 80; rates are C$15 (US$11) for members and C$20 (US$14) for nonmembers. The closest hostel to Jasper, Jasper International is open year-round, and is especially popular in summer, when 2-week advance reservations are a good idea. There are two family rooms. The hostel rents mountain bikes, so you can get down to town and around; there's a barbecue area and indoor plumbing and hot showers. In winter, ski packages are available.

The **Maligne Canyon Hostel** is off Maligne Lake Road, 18 kilometers (11 miles) east of Jasper. The hostel sleeps 24; rates are C$9 (US$6) for members and C$14 (US$10) nonmembers. This convenient hostel is just above the astonishing Maligne Canyon and is an easy hitchhike from Jasper. Facilities include a self-catering kitchen and dining area.

PARK CAMPGROUNDS   There are 10 campgrounds in Jasper National Park. The closest to Jasper Townsite is The Whistlers, up the road toward the gondola, providing a total of some 700 campsites. You need a special permit to camp anywhere in the parks outside the regular campgrounds—a regulation necessary because of fire hazards. Contact the **parks information office** (☎ **403/852-6176**) for permits. The campgrounds range from completely unserviced sites to those providing water, power, sewer connections, laundry facilities, gas, and groceries.

Bed & Breakfasts

During high season, it seems that nearly half the dwellings in Jasper let rooms B&B fashion; contact **Jasper Home Accommodation Association,** P.O. Box 758, Jasper, AB, T0E 1E0, for a full list of such accommodations. B&Bs listed with the local visitors association have little signs in front; if you arrive early enough in the day, you can comb the streets looking for a likely suspect. Double-occupancy accommodations are in the C$40 to C$60 (US$29 to US$43) range at most homes. You'll need to pay cash for most; there is no central booking agency in Jasper, so you'll need to contact your host directly.

A Nearby Guest Ranch

Black Cat Guest Ranch. P.O. Box 6267, Hinton, AB, T7V 1X6. ☎ **800/859-6840** or 403/865-3084. Fax 403/865-1924. E-mail: bcranch@agt.net. Web site: www.agt.net/public/bcranch. 16 rms. High season C$80–C$85 (US$57–US$61) per person double. Rates include all meals. MC, V.

The Black Cat Guest Ranch is a historic wilderness retreat 56 kilometers (35 miles) northeast of Jasper. Established in 1935 by the Brewsters, the ranch is set in superb mountain scenery. The rustic two-story lodge, built in 1978—guests don't stay in the original old cabins—offers unfussy guest units, each with private bath, large windows, and an unspoiled view of the crags in Jasper Park across a pasture filled with horses and chattering birds. There's a big central fireplace room with couches, easy chairs, and game tables scattered around. Lodging prices include a big, home-cooked lunch, dinner, and breakfast, served family-style by the friendly, welcoming staff. Activities include hikes, horseback riding—C$16 (US$11) an hour for guided horseback trips—canoe rentals, murder-mystery weekends, and fishing. The ranch staff will meet your train or bus at Hinton.

DINING

Expensive

Beauvallon Dining Rm. In the Chateau Jasper, 96 Geike St. ☎ **403/852-5644.** Reservations recommended. Main courses C$15–C$39 (US$11–US$28); table d'hôte C$34 (US$24). Sunday brunch C$14.40 (US$10) adults, C$9.95 (US$7) seniors and youths. AE, DC, ER, MC, V. Daily 6:30am–2pm and 5:30–11pm. CANADIAN.

Offering one of the most ambitious menus in Jasper, the Beauvallon specializes in "classic" European preparations with Canadian meats, fish, and an extensive selection of game. The menu is seasonal, and includes dishes like Caribou Normandy: caribou loin grilled and served with calvados sauce (C$30/US$21). Another dish combines braised venison, chanterelle mushrooms, and a creamy red-wine sauce. Other dishes such as a northern Pacific seafood fricassee or a gingered breast of duck are equally complex and eclectic. Service is excellent, and the dining room—filled with high-back chairs—is cozy. The wine list is extensive, and well priced.

Becker's Gourmet Restaurant. Hwy. 93 (5km/3 miles south of Jasper). ☎ **403/852-3779.** Reservations required. Main courses C$14–C$28 (US$10–US$20). MC, V. Daily 8am–2pm and 5:30–10pm. CANADIAN.

Although the name's not very elegant, it's highly descriptive. This high-quality, inventive restaurant serves what could only be termed gourmet food, at Becker's Chalets, one of the nicest log-cabin resorts in Jasper. The dining room is very attractive, an intimate log and glass affair that overlooks the Athabasca River. The menu reads like a novel: four-nut crusted lamb chops at C$20 (US$14), chèvre Mornay sauce and dill on grilled chicken breast, and grilled venison loin with Saskatoon-berry compote.

Moose's Nook Dining Rm. In the Jasper Park Lodge, 8km (5 miles) east of Jasper. ☎ **403/852-6052.** Main courses C$17–$26 (US$12–US$19). AE, CB, DISC, ER, JCB, MC, V. Daily 6pm–10pm. CANADIAN.

This new restaurant off the Great Room of the Jasper Park Lodge features "Canadiana" specialties. With equal parts tradition and innovation, the Moose's Nook features hearty presentations of native meats, fish, and game. Pheasant breast is grilled and served with a compote of local Saskatoon berry; buffalo steak is served with a wild-mushroom, shallot, and whiskey sauce. Lighter appetites will enjoy the seafood hot pot and vegetarian cabbage rolls. Sautéed veal kidneys are offered as an appetizer, as is goose liver pâté. This hearty fare is served in a charming, wood-beamed room that could double as a hunting lodge.

Moderate

✪ **Fiddle River.** 620 Connaught Dr. ☎ **403/852-3032.** Reservations required. Main courses C$13–C$21 (US$9–US$15). AE, MC, V. Daily 5pm–midnight. SEAFOOD.

This rustic-looking upstairs retreat has panoramic windows viewing the Jasper railroad station and the mountain range beyond. The specialty here is fresh fish, though a number of pasta dishes and red-meat entrees will complicate your decision process. While there are plenty of good selections on the menu, Fiddle River offers as many daily specials: waiters pack a chalk-board tripod to your table to give you some predinner reading. Grilled salmon (one special was served with red-bell-pepper purée and dill cream sauce) comes in at C$19 (US$14), and a half-dozen oysters on the half shell is C$9 (US$6). Caribbean chicken breast, breaded in crushed banana chips and coconut, and served with mango and yogurt, is C$16 (US$11); a pepper steak with blue cheese demiglace is C$23 (US$16). There's a small but interesting wine list.

Something Else. 621 Patricia St. ☎ **403/852-3850.** Pasta and pizza C$11–C$14 (US$8–US$10); Greek dishes C$11–C$15 (US$8–US$11); other main courses C$14–C$18 (US$10–US$13). AE, DC, ER, MC, V. Daily 11am–midnight. INTERNATIONAL/PIZZA.

Something Else is accurately named: Folded together here are a good Greek restaurant and a pizza parlor, to which a high-quality Canadian-style restaurant has been added. In short, if you're with a group that can't decide where to eat, this is the place to go. Prime Alberta steaks, fiery Louisiana jambalaya and mesquite chicken, Greek saganaki and moussaka, an array of 21 pizza varieties—all the food is very well prepared and fresh, and the welcome is friendly.

Tekarra Lodge Restaurant. Hwy. 93A (1.6km/1 mile east of Jasper). ☎ **403/852-4624.** Reservations recommended on weekends. Main courses C$13–C$20 (US$9–US$14). AE, DC, MC, V. Daily 5–11pm. STEAK/INTERNATIONAL.

Located at the confluence of the Miette and Athabasca rivers, the Tekarra, a longtime favorite of the locals, has new management and a new menu. Luckily the excellent leg of lamb is still available (C$19/US$14), and it's joined by excellent steaks and other intriguing dishes like pan-seared chicken with roast grapes (C$20/US$14). The charming lodge dining room here is one of Jasper's hidden gems; the service is friendly, and the fireplace-dominated dining room is intimate and charming. In addition to the meat entrees, the Tekarra offers lighter dishes like specialty stir-fries and pasta dishes. Tekarra Lodge is a little confusing to find; ask directions before you set out.

Tokyo Tom's. 410 Connaught Dr. ☎ **403/852-3780.** Most items C$5–C$21 (US$3.60–US$15). AE, MC, V. Daily noon–11pm. JAPANESE.

Tokyo Tom's is a slice of Japan, complete with sushi bar, a karaoke lounge, intimate nooks, shoeless patrons, soft Asian mood music in the background, and service that is both fast and impeccable. The place has a studied simplicity that goes well with the traditional Japanese fare served: sukiyaki, sashimi, tempura, teriyaki.

Inexpensive

For fresh bakery goods like muffins or fresh-cut sandwiches, coffee, drinks and desserts, soup, and salad, go to **Soft Rock Cafe,** 622 Connaught Dr. (☎ 403/852-5850), a pleasant little deli in the Connaught Square Mall, in the center of town. There's also rotisserie chicken to go or eat in; and you can log on to the Web or check your e-mail at one of their computers. Another casual cafe is **Spooner's Coffee Bar,** upstairs at 601 Patricia St. (☎ 403/852-4046), with a juice bar, coffee drinks, burritos, soup, sandwiches, and other deli items.

Jasper Pizza Place. 402 Connaught Dr. ☎ **403/852-3225.** Reservations not accepted. Pizza C$7–C$12.50 (US$5–US$9). MC, V. Daily 7am–midnight. PIZZA.

One of Jasper's most popular eating spots, the highly redesigned Pizza Place agreeably combines the features of an upscale boutique pizzeria with a traditional

Canadian bar. The pizzas are baked in a wood-fired oven, and come in some very unusual—some would say unlikely—combinations. If you're not quite ready for the sour-cream and Dijon-mustard pizza, or an escargot pizza—each C$10 (US$7)—then maybe the smoked salmon, caper, and black-olive pizza will please. Standard-issue pizzas are also available, as are a selection of sandwiches and a mammoth helping of lasagna for C$9 (US$6). The bar side of things is lively, with pool tables and a lively crowd of summer resort workers on display.

Malowney's Wine Café. 606 Patricia St. ☎ **403/852-4559.** Reservations not accepted. Main courses C$6–C$12 (US$4.30–US$9). MC, V. Daily 11:30am–10pm. INTERNATIONAL.

Jasper is just *packed* with wine and liquor stores for some reason. However, Malowney's goes the extra distance and offers tasty light entrees to accompany their wines and liquors. This isn't a big place—only a handful of lucky guests score a table or a stool—but it's worth it to sit back and enjoy a toothsome light meal with a favorite beverage. Most entrees change daily and are featured on a chalkboard as you enter; lunchtime sandwiches and soups give way to pasta, grilled chicken, fish, or beef dishes at dinner. You can also come here and snack your way through some appetizers while sampling the 35 specialty martinis.

✪ **Mountain Foods Cafe.** 606 Connaught Dr. ☎ **403/852-4050.** Main courses C$6–C$10 (US$4.30–US$7). MC, V. Daily 8am–10pm. DELI.

This small deli and cafeteria is bright and friendly, and just the antidote to the stodgy food pervasive in much of the park. Most meals are light and healthful—salads, soups, and quick ethnic dishes—and specialties include burrito "wraps," sandwich "melts," and breakfast "scrambles." The deli case is filled with items available to take out. Nothing here costs much over C$6 (US$4.30). Beer and wine are served.

JASPER AFTER DARK

Nearly all of Jasper's nightlife can be found in the bars and lounges of hotels, motels, and inns. O'Shea's, at **Athabasca Hotel,** 510 Patricia St. (☎ **403/852-3386**), is usually just called the Atha'B, or simply The B, and has a changing lineup of Top-40s bands, catering to a young clientele. There's a dance floor, and movies are shown on the large-screen TV in the Trophy room. In action Monday to Saturday to 2am. Jasper's newest hot spot is **Pete's Night Club,** 610 Patricia St. (☎ **403/852-6262**), presenting live alternative and blues bands. Another youthful gathering place is **Tent City** at the Jasper Park Lodge, where you'll find billiards, loud music, and a preponderance of the JPL's 650 employees. The **D'ed Dog Bar and Grill,** 404 Connaught Dr. (☎ **403/852-3351**), is the place to find the young river and hiking guides who gather in Jasper to work every summer; Friday-night happy hour here can get pretty rowdy.

9 British Columbia's Rockies: Mount Robson Provincial Park & Yoho, Glacier, Mount Revelstoke & Kootenay National Parks

MOUNT ROBSON PROVINCIAL PARK

The highlight of this beautiful park, just west of Jasper National Park along the Yellowhead Highway, is 12,972-foot-high Mount Robson, the highest peak in the Canadian Rockies. This massive sentinel fills the sky from most vantage points in the park, making it a certainty that you'll easily run through a roll of film if the weather is good. One of the best viewpoints is from the visitor center, where the mountain looms above a wildflower meadow.

The mighty Fraser River rises in the park, and is a popular and challenging white-water adventure for experienced rafters. A number of Jasper-area outfitters offer trips down the Fraser; see the Jasper listings above.

Short 2- to 4-hour park tours are offered by **Mount Robson Adventure Holidays,** Valemount, British Columbia (☎ **250/566-4386;** fax 250/556-4351). For C$37 (US$26), visitors can choose a guided nature tour by raft, canoe, or van. Longer hiking or backpacking excursions are also available.

For more information about the park, contact P.O. Box 579, Valemount, BC, V0E 2Z0 (☎ **250/566-4325**).

YOHO NATIONAL PARK

Located just west of Lake Louise on the western slopes of the Rockies in British Columbia, Yoho National Park preserves some of the most famous rocks in Canada, as well as a historic rail line and the nation's second highest waterfall. Yoho Park is essentially the drainage of the Kicking Horse River—famed for its white-water rafting—and is traversed by the Trans-Canada Highway.

The first white exploration of this area was by scouts looking for a pass over the Rockies suitable for the Canadian Pacific's transcontinental run. Kicking Horse Pass, at 5,333 feet, was surveyed and the railroad began its service in 1884. However, the grade down the aptly named Big Hill, on the west side of the pass, was near precipitous. The steepest of any in North America, it descended the mountain at 4.5%. The first train to attempt the descent went out of control and crashed, killing three men. In 1909, after decades of accidents, the Canadian Pacific solved its problem by curling two spiral rail tunnels into the mountains facing Big Hill. Together, the two tunnels were over 6,100 feet long. At the **Lower Spiral Tunnel Viewpoint,** there are interpretive displays explaining this engineering feat, and you can still watch trains enter and emerge from the tunnels.

Thirteen kilometers (8 miles) into the park, turn north onto Yoho Valley Road to find some of the park's most scenic areas. Past another viewpoint onto the Spiral Tunnels, continue 13 kilometers (8 miles) to ✪ **Takakkawa Falls,** Canada's second highest, which cascades 1,248 feet in two drops. A short all-abilities trail leads from the road's end to a picnic area, where views of this amazing waterfall are even more eye-popping.

The Kicking Horse River descends between Mount Fields and Mount Stephen, famous in paleontological circles for Burgess Shale, fossil-rich deposits from the Cambrian era that were the subject of Stephen Jay Gould's 1988 bestseller *A Wonderful Life.* Interpretive displays about these fossil digs, which have produced organisms that seem to challenge some of the established evolutionary tenets, are found at the park's visitor center in Fields. If you're interested enough in the fossil digs to face a daylong, 19-kilometer (12-mile) round-trip hike, two groups are authorized to guide visitors to the quarries. Contact the **Yoho-Burgess Shale Research Foundation** (☎ **800/ 343-3006**) or **Canadian Wilderness** (☎ **403/678-3795**) for details. Note that collecting fossils in these areas, or in the national park in general, is prohibited.

Emerald Lake, a jewel-toned lake in a glacial cirque, is one of the Yoho Park's most popular stops. Hiking trails ring the lake, and the popular ✪ **Emerald Lake Lodge** (☎ **250/343-6321**) is open for meals and lodging year-round; this is a popular cross-country–skiing destination.

The **service center** for Yoho Park is the little town of Fields, with a half-dozen modest accommodations and a few casual restaurants. The park's visitor center is just off Highway 1 near the entrance to town. For more information, contact **Yoho National Park,** P.O. Box 99, Fields, BC, V0A 1G0 (☎ **250/343-6324**).

RAFTING THE KICKING HORSE RIVER

The Kicking Horse is one of Canada's premier white-water rivers, and a number of outfitters provide guided raft trips through its mighty canyon. While a number of Banff and Lake Louise outfitters also offer these trips, the following are based out of Golden, just west of the park. **Glacier Raft Company** (☎ 250/344-6521) offers full-day floats for C$85 (US$61) and half-day floats for C$49 to C$55 (US$35 to US$39). The price includes transportation and (for the full-day trip) a steak barbecue. **Wet 'n Wild Adventures** (☎ 800/668-9119 or 250/344-6546) offers full-day trips for C$72 (US$52) and half-day trips for C$52 (US$37), which include a lunch and a volleyball game.

GLACIER NATIONAL PARK

Located amid the highest peaks of the **Columbia Mountains,** Canada's Glacier National Park amply lives up to its name. More than 400 glaciers repose here, with 14% of the park's 2,168 square kilometers (837 sq. miles) lying under permanent snowpack. The reason that this high country is so covered with ice is the same reason that this is one of the more unsettled places to visit in the mountain West: It snows and rains a lot here.

The primary attractions in the park are the viewpoints onto craggy peaks and hiking trails leading to wildflower meadows and old-growth groves; heavy snow and rainfall lend a near rain-forest feel to forest hikes. Spring hikers and cross-country skiers should beware of avalanche conditions, an intrinsic problem in areas with high snowfall and steep slopes. Call the park information number (☎ 250/837-7500) for weather updates.

Glacier Park is crossed by the Trans-Canada Highway and the Canadian Pacific rail tracks. Each has had to build snowsheds to protect these transportation systems from the effects of heavy snows and avalanches. **Park headquarters** are just east of 4,100-foot Rogers Pass; stop here to sign up for interpretive hikes, video watching, and displays on natural and human history in the park. On a typically gray and wet day, the information center may be the driest place to enjoy the park. Two easy hiking trails leave from the center. For more information about the park, contact **Glacier National Park,** P.O. Box 350, Revelstoke, BC, V0E 2S0 (☎ 250/837-7500; e-mail: revglacier_reception@pch.gc.ca).

MOUNT REVELSTOKE NATIONAL PARK

Just west of Glacier National Park is Mount Revelstoke National Park, a glacier-clad collection of craggy peaks in the **Selkirk Range.** Comprising only 417 square kilometers (161 sq. miles), Mount Revelstoke can't produce the kind of awe that its larger neighbor can in good weather; but Revelstoke offers easier access to the high country and alpine meadows.

The most popular activity in the park is the drive up to the top of 6,000-foot Mount Revelstoke, with great views onto the Columbia River and the peaks of Glacier Park. To reach Mount Revelstoke, take the paved road north from the town of Revelstoke and follow it 23 kilometers (14 miles) to Balsam Lake. From here, free shuttle buses operated by the parks department make the final ascent up the mountain. A popular hike is the **Giant Cedars Trail,** a short boardwalk out into a grove of old-growth cedars that are over 1,000 years old.

The park is flanked on the south by Highway 1, the Trans-Canada Highway. The park has no services or campgrounds. However, all services, including a number of hotels, are available in the town of Revelstoke. For more information about the park,

contact **Mount Revelstoke National Park,** P.O. Box 350, Revelstoke, BC, V0E 2S0
(☎ 250/837-7500; e-mail: revglacier_reception@pch.gc.ca).

KOOTENAY NATIONAL PARK & RADIUM HOT SPRINGS

This national park, lying just west of Banff on the western slopes of the Canadian
Rockies, preserves the valleys of the Kootenay and Vermilion rivers. The park contains prime wildlife habitats, and a number of hiking trails. Although Kootenay's
scenery is as grand as anywhere else in the Rockies, the trails here are considerably
less thronged.

The park is linked to the other Canadian Rocky Mountain parks by Highway 93,
which departs from Highway 1 at Castle Junction to climb over the Vermilion Pass
and descend to Radium Hot Springs, the park's western entrance.

Much of the area around the pass was burned in a massive forest fire in 1968; a
number of trails lead out into the forest, and describe the process of revegetation. Be
sure to stop at **Marble Canyon,** a 200-foot-deep canyon cut through a formation of
limestone. A short hiking trail winds over and through the canyon, bridging the
chasm in several places.

Another interesting stop is the **Paint Pots.** Here, cold spring water surfaces in an
iron-rich deposit of red and yellow clay, forming intense colored pools. Early native
Canadians journeyed here to collect the ochre-colored soil for body paint; for them,
this was an area filled with "great medicine."

The highway leaves the Vermilion River valley and climbs up to a viewpoint above
the Hector Gorge, into which the river flows before meeting the Kootenay River.
From the viewpoint, also look for mountain goats, which can often be seen on the
rocky cliffs of Mount Wardle to the north (the goat is the symbol of the park).

The highway passes through one of these narrow limestone canyons after it mounts
Sinclair Pass and descends toward Radium Hot Springs. Called Sinclair Canyon, the
chasm is about 10 kilometers (6 miles) long, and in places is scarcely wide enough
to accommodate the roadbed.

Radium Hot Springs Pool (☎ 250/347-9485), a long-established hot springs
spa and resort, sits at the mouth of Sinclair Canyon. As the name suggests, the mineral waters here are slightly radioactive, but not enough to be a concern to casual soak-
ers. Stop for a swim or a soak; adults C$5 (US$3.60), seniors and children C$4.50
(US$3.20).

The town of Radium Hot Springs sits at the junction of highways 93 and 95. Not
an especially attractive place, it nonetheless offers ample motel rooms along the
0.8-kilometer (half-mile) stretch of Highway 93 just before the park gates. For more
information about the park, contact **Kootenay National Park,** P.O. Box 220,
Radium Hot Springs, BC, V0A 1M0 (☎ 250/347-9505; fax 250/347-9980; e-mail:
kootnay_reception@pch.gc.ca).

10 Edmonton

Edmonton is Alberta's capital and has the largest metropolitan population in the
province, currently around 850,000. Located on the banks of the North
Saskatchewan River, Edmonton is an outgoing and sophisticated city noted for its
easygoing friendliness—a trait that's been scientifically proven. In 1995, an independent study of Canadians' altruistic behavior found that Edmonton was the most
friendly and helpful city in the nation.

Edmonton grew in spurts, following a boom-and-bust pattern as exciting as it
was unreliable. During World War II the boom came in the form of the Alaska

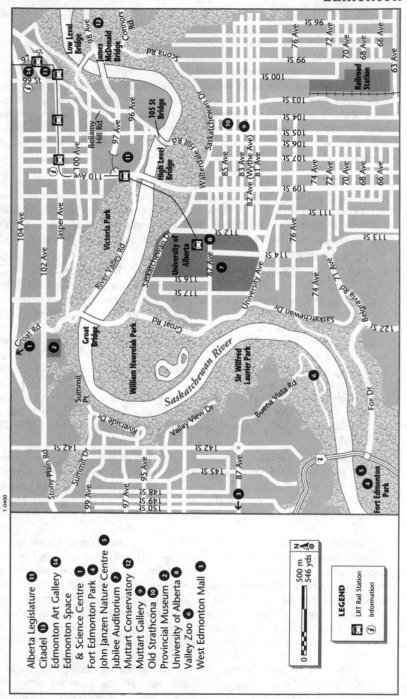

Edmonton

LEGEND

🚈 LRT Rail Station
ⓘ Information

0 | 500 m
--- | 546 yds

N

Alberta Legislature ⓫
Citadel ⓭
Edmonton Art Gallery ⓮
Edmonton Space
& Science Centre ❶
Fort Edmonton Park ❹
John Janzen Nature Centre ❺
Jubilee Auditorium ❼
Muttart Conservatory ⓬
Muttart Gallery ❾
Old Strathcona ❿
Provincial Museum ❷
University of Alberta ❽
Valley Zoo ❻
West Edmonton Mall ❸

1-0400

Highway, with Edmonton as the material base and temporary home of 50,000 American troops and construction workers.

The ultimate boom, however, gushed from the ground on a freezing afternoon in February 1947. That was when a drill at Leduc, 40 kilometers (25 miles) southwest of the city, sent a fountain of dirty-black crude oil soaring skyward. Some 10,000 other wells followed, all within a 161-kilometer (100-mile) radius of the city. In their wake came the petrochemical industry and the major refining and supply conglomerates. In 2 decades the population of the city quadrupled, its skyline mushroomed with glass-and-concrete office towers, a rapid-transit system was created, and a C$150-million civic center rose. Edmonton had become what it is today—the oil capital of Canada.

ESSENTIALS

VISITOR INFORMATION For guidance on Edmonton and its attractions, contact **Edmonton Tourism,** 9797 Jasper Ave., Edmonton, AB, T5J 1N9 (☎ 800/463-4667 or 403/496-8400). There's also a visitor information center at City Hall, and at Gateway Park, on the Calgary Trail at the southern edge of the city.

GETTING THERE Edmonton is served by most major airlines, including **Air Canada** (☎ 800/776-3000) and **Canadian Airlines** (☎ 800/426-7000), which also operates the shuttle to Calgary, a no-reservation service with over a dozen flights a day. The **Edmonton International Airport** lies 29 kilometers (18 miles) south of the city on Highway 2, about 45 driving minutes away. By cab the trip costs about C$35 (US$25); by Airporter bus, C$11 (US$8).

Edmonton straddles the **Yellowhead Highway,** western Canada's new east-west interprovincial highway. Just west of Edmonton, the Yellowhead is linked to the Alaska Highway. The city is 515 kilometers (320 miles) north of the U.S. border, 283 kilometers (176 miles) north of Calgary.

Passenger trains arrive at and depart from the **VIA Rail Station,** 104th Avenue and 100th Street (☎ 403/422-6032). **Greyhound buses** link Edmonton to all points in Canada and the United States from the depot at 10324 103rd St. (☎ 403/413-8747).

CITY LAYOUT The winding North Saskatchewan River flows right through the heart of the city, dividing it into roughly equal halves. One of the capital's greatest achievements is the way in which this river valley has been kept out of the grasp of commercial developers. Almost the entire valley has been turned into public parklands, forming 27 kilometers (17 miles) of greenery, sports, picnic, and recreation grounds.

The founding fathers decided to begin the street numbering system at the corner of 100th Street and 100th Avenue, which means that downtown addresses have five digits, and that suburban homes often have smaller addresses than businesses in the very center of town. Edmonton's main street is Jasper Avenue (actually 101st Avenue), running north of the river. The "A" designations you'll notice for certain streets and avenues downtown add to the confusion; they're essentially old service alleys between major streets, many of which now are pedestrian areas with sidewalk cafes. Get a good map and give yourself time to puzzle the city's layout; it's not entirely straightforward.

At 97th Street, on Jasper Avenue, rises the pink and massive Canada Place, the only completely planned government complex of its kind in Canada. Immediately across the street is the Edmonton Convention Centre, which stair-steps down the hillside to the river.

Beneath the downtown core stretches a network of pedestrian walkways—called Pedways—connecting hotels, restaurants, and shopping malls with the library, City Hall, and the Citadel Theatre. These Pedways not only avoid the surface traffic, they're also climate-controlled.

At the northern approach to the High Level Bridge, surrounded by parkland, stand the buildings of the Alberta Legislature, seat of the provincial government. Across the bridge, to the west, stretches the vast campus of the University of Alberta. Just to the east is Old Strathcona, a bustling neighborhood of cafes, galleries, and hip shops that's now a haven for Edmonton's student and more "alternative" population. The main arterial through Old Strathcona—which used to be its own town—is Whyte Avenue, or 82nd Avenue. Running south from here in a straight line is 104th Street, which becomes Calgary Trail and leads to the Edmonton International Airport.

West of downtown Edmonton, Jasper Avenue shifts and twists to eventually become Stony Plain Road, which passes near West Edmonton Mall, the world's largest shopping and entertainment center, before merging with Highway 16 on its way to Jasper National Park.

GETTING AROUND   Edmonton's public transport is handled by **Edmonton Transit** (☎ **403/496-1611** for information), which operates a family of services including the city buses and the LRT (Light Rail Transit). This partly underground, partly aboveground electric rail service connects downtown Edmonton with Northlands Park to the north and the University of Alberta to the south.

The LRT and the Transit buses have the same fares: C$1.60 (US$1.15) for adults and C$1 (US72¢) for seniors and children; a day pass is available for C$4.75 (US$3.40) adults, C$3.75 (US$2.70) children. You can transfer from one to the other at any station on the same ticket. On weekdays from 9am to 3pm, downtown LRT travel is free between Churchill, Central, Bay, Corona, and Grandin stations.

In addition to the following downtown locations, **Tilden,** 10131–100A St. (☎ **403/422-6097**); **Budget,** 10016–106th St. (☎ **403/448-2000**); and **Hertz,** 10815 Jasper Ave. (☎ **403/423-3431**), each have bureaus at Edmonton International Airport.

Call **Co-op Taxi** (☎ **403/425-8310** or 403/425-2525), for a ride in a driver/owner-operated cab.

FAST FACTS   American Express   There's an office at 10180 101st St., at 102nd Avenue (☎ **403/421-0608**).

CAA   The **Alberta Motor Association,** affiliated with the Canadian Automobile Association, reciprocates with the AAA, offering members free travel information, advice, and services. The Edmonton office is at 11220 109th St. (☎ **403/474-8601**).

Doctors   If you need nonemergency medical care while in Edmonton, check the phone book for the closest branch of **Medicentre,** which offers walk-in medical services 7 days a week.

Emergency   For fire, medical, or crime emergencies, dial ☎ **911.**

Hospitals   The closest hospital with emergency service to downtown Edmonton is the **Royal Alexandra Hospital,** 10240 Kingsway Ave. (☎ **403/477-4111**).

Newspapers   The *Edmonton Journal* and the *Edmonton Sun* are the local daily papers. Arts, entertainment, and nightlife listings can be found in the *See* weekly.

Pharmacies   Shoppers Drug Mart has over a dozen locations in Edmonton. Most are open till midnight. One central location is 8210 109th St. (☎ **403/433-2424**).

Post Office   The main post office is located at 103A Avenue at 99th Street.

KLONDIKE DAYS & OTHER SPECIAL EVENTS

The gold rush that sent an army of prospectors heading for the Yukon in 1898 put Edmonton "on the map," as they say. Although the actual gold fields lay 2,415 kilometers (1,500 miles) to the north, the little settlement became a giant supply store, resting place, and "recreation" ground for thousands of men stopping there en route before tackling the hazards of the Klondike Trail that led overland to Dawson City in the Yukon. Edmonton's population quickly doubled in size, and its merchants, saloonkeepers, and ladies of easy virtue waxed rich in the process.

Since 1962 Edmonton has been celebrating the event with one of the greatest and most colorful extravaganzas staged in Canada. The **Klondike Days** are held annually in late July. Street festivities last 10 days, as does the great Klondike Days Exposition at Northlands Park.

Locals and visitors dress up in period costumes, street corners blossom with impromptu stages featuring anything from country bands to cancan girls, stagecoaches rattle through the streets, and parades and floats wind from block to block.

The 16,000-seat Coliseum holds nightly spectaculars of rock, pop, variety, or Western entertainment. Northlands Park turns into Klondike Village, complete with the Chilkoot Gold Mine, Silver Slipper Saloon, and gambling casino—legal for this occasion only. The Walterdale Playhouse drops serious stage endeavors for a moment and puts on hilarious melodramas with mustachioed villains to hiss and dashing heroes to cheer.

Immense "Klondike breakfasts" are served in the open air, massed marching bands compete in the streets, and down the North Saskatchewan River float more than 100 of the weirdest-looking home-built rafts ever seen, competing in the "World Championship Sourdough River Raft Race."

The **Jazz City International Jazz Festival** is a citywide celebration of jazz that takes over most music venues in Edmonton for the last week of July and first week of August. For more information, call ☎ **403/432-7166.**

The **Edmonton Folk Music Festival** is the largest folk-music festival in North America. Held in mid-August, the festival brings in musicians from around the world, from the Celtic north to Indonesia. Recently, the festival has seen major rock musicians making appearances with acoustic "unplugged" bands. For more information, call ☎ **403/429-1899.** All concerts are held outdoors.

For 10 days in mid-August, Old Strathcona is transformed into a series of stages for a festival of alternative theater, the **Fringe Theatre Event.** Only Edinburgh's fringe festival is larger than Edmonton's—more than 60 troupes attend from around the world—making this a great event for theater lovers. For more information, call ☎ **403/448-9000.**

EXPLORING THE CITY

Royal Tours of Edmonton (☎ **403/435-6069**) offers half-day bus tours of Edmonton and its sights for C$27 to C$50 (US$19 to US$36); the bus stops at most downtown hotels. A tour is a good way to get a handle on this otherwise sprawling city.

THE TOP ATTRACTIONS

✪ **Old Strathcona.** Around 82nd Ave., between 103rd and 105th sts. Bus: 46 from downtown.

This historical district used to be a separate township, but was amalgamated with Edmonton in 1912. Due to the efforts of the Old Strathcona Foundation, the area contains some of the best-preserved landmarks in the city. It's best seen on foot, guided by the brochures given out at the **Old Strathcona Foundation office,** 8331 104th St. (☎ **403/433-5866**).

The best reason to visit Old Strathcona is to wander along the shops, stop in at street-side cafes, and people-watch. This is hipster central for Edmonton, where university students, artists, and the city's alternative community come to hang out: Old Strathcona is Edmonton's Left Bank. It's easy to spend an afternoon here, just being part of the scene. Be sure to stop in at the **Old Strathcona Farmers Market** (☎ 403/439-1844), at the corner of 83rd Avenue and 103rd Street, an open-air market with fresh produce, baked goods, and local crafts. The market is open Saturdays year-round, and also Tuesday and Thursday afternoons in summer. Another good stop for browsers is **Greenwoods Bookshop,** at 10355 Whyte Ave. (☎ 403/439-2005), Edmonton's largest and best bookstore.

✪ **Provincial Museum of Alberta.** 12845 102nd Ave. ☎ **403/453-9100.** Admission C$5.50 (US$3.95) adults, C$4.50 (US$3.20) seniors, C$2.25 (US$1.60) children, C$15 (US$11) families. High season daily 9am–8pm; winter daily 9am–5pm. Bus: 1.

Modern and expertly laid out, this 200,000-square-foot museum displays Alberta's natural and human history in three permanent galleries. The Habitat Groups show wildlife in astonishingly lifelike dioramas; these picture windows into Alberta's diverse ecosystems are sure to captivate the kids and have adults marveling at the trompe-l'oeil paint job. The Aboriginal Peoples Gallery tells the 11,000-year story of Alberta's native inhabitants. This newly redesigned gallery incorporates artifacts, film, interactive media, and native interpreters, and is one of Canada's foremost exhibits on native culture. The Natural History Gallery has fossils, minerals, and a live-bug room; and a fourth gallery features changing exhibits. The museum also presents artists and artisans and free film showings.

West Edmonton Mall. 8770 170th St. ☎ **403/444-5200.** Bus: 10.

You won't find many shopping malls mentioned in this book, but the West Edmonton Mall is something else. Although it contains 800 stores and services, including 90 eating establishments, it looks and sounds more like a large slice of Disneyland that has somehow broken loose and drifted north. The locals modestly call it the "Eighth Wonder of the World."

More theme park than mall, the West Edmonton Mall encompasses 5.2 million square feet, and houses the world's largest indoor amusement park, including a titanic indoor roller coaster, bungee-jumping platform, plus an enclosed wave-lake, complete with beach and enough artificial waves to ride a surfboard on. It has walk-through bird aviaries, a huge ice-skating palace, 19 (count 'em, 19) movie theaters, a lagoon with performing dolphins, and several absolutely fabulous adventure rides (one of them by submarine to the "ocean floor," and another simulating a white-water raft journey). In the middle of it all, an immense fountain with 19 computer-controlled jets weaves and dances in a musical performance.

Of course, you can go shopping here, and some of Edmonton's most popular restaurants are located in the mall, as well as an increasingly large share of the city's nightlife. On Saturdays at 2pm, you can even tour the rooms at the mall's excellent "theme" hotel, called Fantasyland. Admission to the mall is gratis, but some of the rides are fairly expensive. Roll your eyes all you want, but do go. You have to see the West Edmonton Mall to believe it.

✪ **Fort Edmonton Park.** On the Whitemud Dr. at Fox Dr. ☎ **403/496-8787.** Web site: www.gov.edmonton.ab.ca/fort. Admission to Fort Edmonton Park C$6.75 (US$4.85) adults, C$5 (US$3.60) seniors and youths, C$3.25 (US$2.30) children, C$20 (US$14) families; Nature Centre by donation. Fort Edmonton, mid-May to late June Mon–Fri 10am–4pm, Sat–Sun 10am–6pm; late June to early Sept daily 10am–6pm. LRT to University Station, then Bus 32.

Fort Edmonton Park is a complex of townscapes that reconstructs various eras of Edmonton's lengthy history. Perhaps the most interesting of the four sections of the park is the complete reconstruction of the old Fort Edmonton fur-trading post from the turn of the 18th century. This vast wooden structure is a warren of rooms and activities: blacksmiths, bakers, and other docents ply their trades throughout. Other sections of this very large and worthwhile park recreate Edmonton in later periods. On 1885 Street it's the Frontier Edmonton, complete with blacksmith shop, saloon, general store, and Jasper House Hotel that serves hearty pioneer meals. 1905 Street has an antique photographic studio and fire hall equipped with appropriate engines. On 1920 Street, sip an old-fashioned ice-cream soda at Bill's "confectionery." You can ride Edmonton streetcar no. 1, a stagecoach, or a steam locomotive between the various "streets."

As an open-air museum, the park is very impressive; the variety of activities and services here make this a great family destination.

Adjoining Fort Edmonton, the **John Janzen Nature Centre** (☎ 403/496-2939) offers historic exhibits, hiking trails, and lessons in nature lore. You can go bird watching, "shake hands" with a garter snake, observe a living beehive, and take courses from professionals in everything from building a log cabin to game stalking and tracking.

Muttart Conservatory. Off James MacDonald Bridge at 98th Ave. and 96A St. ☎ **403/496-8755.** Admission C$4.25 (US$3.05) adults, C$3.25 (US$2.30) seniors and youths, C$2 (US$1.45) children, C$12.50 (US$9) families. Sun–Wed 11am–9pm, Thurs–Sat 11am–6pm. Bus: 51.

The conservatory is housed in a group of four pavilions that look like I. M. Pei pyramids. They house one of the finest floral displays in North America. Each pyramid contains a different climatic zone—the tropical one has an 18-foot waterfall. The Arid Pavilion has desert air and shows flowering cacti and their relatives. The temperate zone includes a cross section of plants from this global region. The fourth pyramid features changing ornamental displays of plants and blossoms; an orchid greenhouse has newly opened. For good measure, there's also the Treehouse Café.

Edmonton Queen Riverboat. 9734 98th Ave. ☎ **403/424-2628.** Call for hours. Cruise only, C$6–C$15 (US$4.30–US$11); meal packages C$16–C$40 (US$11–US$29). Bus: 12 or 45 from downtown.

Moored just outside the convention center, this riverboat plies the North Saskatchewan River as it runs through the city's many parks. A number of different packages are offered, usually the cruise itself, or a meal package that includes lunch or dinner.

MORE ATTRACTIONS

Alberta Legislature Building. 109th St. and 97th Ave. ☎ **403/427-7362.** Web site: www.assembly.ab.ca. Free tours given daily every hour 9am–5pm, weekends and holidays noon–5pm. LRT: Grandin station.

The Alberta Legislature Building rises on the site of the early trading post from which the city grew. Surrounded by lovingly manicured lawns, formal gardens, and greenhouses, it overlooks the river valley. The seat of Alberta's government was completed in 1912; it's a stately Edwardian structure open to the public throughout the year. Free conducted tours tell you about the functions of provincial lawmaking: who does what, where, and for how long.

Edmonton Art Gallery. 2 Sir Winston Churchill Sq. ☎ **403/422-6223.** Admission C$3 (US$2.15) adults, C$1.50 (US$1.10) seniors and students; children under 12 free. Mon–Wed 10:30am–5pm, Thurs–Fri 10:30am–8pm, Sat–Sun and holidays 11am–5pm. LRT: Churchill.

Edmonton Art Gallery occupies a stately building right in the heart of downtown, immediately east of City Hall. The interior, however, is state-of-the-art modern, subtly lit, and expertly arranged. Exhibits consist partly of contemporary Canadian art, partly of international contemporary art, partly of changing works on tour from every corner of the globe. The Gallery shop sells an eclectic array of items, from art books to handmade yo-yos.

Rutherford House. 11153 Saskatchewan Dr., on the campus of the University of Alberta. ☎ **403/427-3995.** Admission C$2 (US$1.45) adults, C$1.50 (US$1.05) seniors and youths, C$5 (US$3.60) families. High season Tues–Sun 10am–5pm; winter Tues–Sun noon–5pm. LRT: University station.

The home of Alberta's first premier, Alexander Rutherford, this lovingly preserved Edwardian building gleams with polished silver and gilt-framed oils. Around 1915 this mansion was the magnet for the social elite of the province: Today, guides dressed in period costumes convey some of the spirit of the times to visitors. There's also a charming restaurant and tearoom, the **Arbour** (☎ 403/422-2697), open from 11:30am to 4pm.

Telephone Historical Centre. 10437 83rd Ave. ☎ **403/441-2077.** Admission C$2 (US$1.45) adults, C$1 (US70¢) children, C$3 (US$2.15) family. Mon–Fri 10am–4pm, Sat noon–4pm. Bus: 44.

The largest museum devoted to the history of telecommunications in North America is located in the 1912 Telephone Exchange Building. Multimedia displays tell the history of words over wire, and hints at what your modem will get up to next.

ESPECIALLY FOR KIDS

Edmonton Space & Science Centre. 11211 142nd St., Coronation Park. ☎ **403/451-3344.** E-mail: essc@planet.eon.net. Web site: www.ee.ualberta.ca/essc. Admission C$7 (US$5) adults, C$6 (US$4.30) youths, C$5.50 (US$3.95) seniors, C$5 (US$3.60) children 3–12, C$26 (US$19) families. Summer daily 10am–10pm; winter Tues–Sun 10am–10pm. Bus: 17 or 22.

This is one of the most advanced multipurpose facilities of its kind in the world. It contains, among other wonders, a giant-screen IMAX theater, the largest planetarium theater in Canada, plus many high-tech exhibit galleries (including a virtual-reality showcase and a display on robotics) and an observatory open on clear afternoons and evenings. The show programs include star shows, laser-light music concerts, and the special IMAX films that have to be seen to be believed.

Valley Zoo. In Laurier Park, 13315 Buena Vista Rd. ☎ **403/496-6911.** Admission C$4.95 (US$3.55) adults, C$3.50 (US$2.50) seniors and youths, C$2.50 (US$1.80) children under 13, C$14.95 (US$11) family. Summer daily 9:30am–8pm; winter daily 9:30am–4pm. Bus: 12.

In this charming combination of reality and fantasy, real live animals mingle with fairy-tale creations. More than 500 animals and birds are neighbors to the Three Little Pigs, Humpty Dumpty, and the inhabitants of Noah's Ark.

SHOPPING

There are more shops per capita in Edmonton than any other city in Canada. Go for it!

DOWNTOWN Most of downtown's shops are contained in a few large mall complexes; all are linked by the Pedway system, which provides pedestrians protection from summer heat and winter cold. The following malls each face onto 102nd Avenue, between 103rd and 100th streets. **Edmonton Centre** has 140 stores and shares the block with the **Hudson's Bay Company. Eaton Centre** contains over 100 stores, including the flagship Eatons. Across the street is **Manulife Place,** with 60 stores, anchored by Holt Renfrew.

OLD STRATHCONA   If you don't like mall shopping, then wandering the **galleries and boutiques** along Whyte Avenue in Old Strathcona might be more your style. About the only part of Edmonton that retains any historic structures, Old Strathcona is trend central for Edmonton's student population and the bohemian left. Shop for antiques, imported clothes, gift items, books, and crafts amid buskers and crowded street-side cafes. Be sure to stop by the **Farmers Market** at 103rd Street and 102nd Avenue.

HIGH STREET   This small district, which runs from 102nd to 109th avenues along 124th Street, has Edmonton's greatest concentration of art galleries, interior-design and housewares shops, small fashion boutiques, and bookstores. Great restaurants, too.

WEST EDMONTON MALL   The **world's largest shopping mall,** the West Ed Mall (as it's known), covers 48 square blocks near 87th Avenue and 170th Street. This is Edmonton's greatest tourist draw, with over 800 shops, plus a hotel, a waterpark and slide, performing dolphins, an amusement park, an ice-skating rink, a casino, dozens of bars and restaurants, and just about every other form of entertainment known to man. Not for the faint of heart.

ACCOMMODATIONS
VERY EXPENSIVE

✪ **Hotel Macdonald.** 10065 100th St., Edmonton, AB, T5J 0N6. ☎ **800/441-1414** or 403/424-5181. Fax 403/429-6481. Web site: www.albertahotels.ab.ca/hotelmacdonald. 198 rms. A/C MINIBAR TV TEL. High season C$219–C$257 (US$157–US$184) double. Discounts on weekends and off-season. AE, DC, DISC, ER, MC, V. Parking C$14 (US$10) a day.

The palatial Hotel Macdonald, named after Canada's first prime minister, first opened in 1915. After a long and colorful career, it was bought by the Canadian Pacific hotel chain in 1988. What ensued was a masterwork of sensitive renovation and restoration. The courtly and beautiful public rooms were left intact, and the guest rooms were completely rebuilt to modern luxury standards. While the renovation brought the rooms graciously up to date, it retained all of the original charm of the old hotel. Signature elements like the old, deep bathtubs, brass door plates, high ceilings, and handsome paneled doors were retained, while important additions like new plumbing and individual temperature controls were installed. Rooms are beautifully furnished with quality furniture, luxurious upholstery, feather duvets and pillows—and an especially thoughtful touch—a bin for recyclables. The beds are amazingly comfortable. Even the artwork, period botanical prints and fish flies, is notable.

Pacific Premier suites each have a sitting area with a couch and two chairs, and a handy dressing area off the bathroom with a vanity table. Free coffee, local phone calls, and buffet breakfast are included. Executive suites have two TVs and telephones, with a separate bedroom and a large sitting area. The eight specialty suites—which take up the entire eighth floor—are simply magnificent.

From the outside, with its limestone facade and gargoyles, the Mac, as it's known locally, looks like a feudal château—right down to the kilted service staff. High ceilings, majestic drapes, and crystal chandeliers grace the lobby, which boasts a ballroom fit for royalty. Even pets, which are welcome, get special treatment: a gift bag of treats and a map of pet-friendly parks.

Needless to say, there aren't many hotels like this in Edmonton, or in Canada for that matter. As I rode the elevator, a guest broke the silence with an effusive, voluntary, but matter-of-fact, "This is a great hotel."

Dining: The Library Bar resembles an Edwardian gentlemen's club. The Harvest Room restaurant offers views of the panoramic backdrop of the North Saskatchewan River valley, as well as an outdoor garden terrace for summer dining.

Services: Concierge, 24-hour room service, dry cleaning/laundry.

Facilities: The pool, with Roman pillars and a wading pool for children, adjoins a health club with a pro shop and juice bar, weight room, sauna, steam room, squash courts, massage therapy area, and an exercise room with personal trainers. Rooms come with Spectravision movie channels, and there's a business center available to guests.

EXPENSIVE

Crowne Plaza Chateau Lacombe. 10111 Bellamy Hill, Edmonton, AB, T5J 1N7. ☎ **800/ 661-8801** or 403/428-6611. Fax 403/425-6564. E-mail: cpcl@planet.eon.net. Web site: www.crowneplaza.net. 307 rms, 23 suites. A/C MINIBAR TV TEL. C$160–C$180 (US$114– US$129) double; C$185–C$350 (US$132–US$250) suite. Weekend packages available. AE, CB, DC, ER, MC, V. Parking C$7.50 (US$5) per day.

Centrally located downtown, the Crowne Plaza, a round 24-story tower sitting on the edge of a cliff overlooking the North Saskatchewan River, possesses some of the city's best views. The unusual design blends well with the city's dramatic skyline, yet it is instantly recognizable from afar—a perfect landmark.

The marble-lined lobby is hung with enormous chandeliers. The nicely furnished bedrooms and suites aren't huge, though the wedge-shaped design necessitates that they are broadest toward the windows, where you'll spend time looking over the city. There are two private executive floors, no-smoking floors, and wheelchair-accessible rooms.

Dining: There's a revolving restaurant, appropriately named La Ronde, at the top of the tower, plus a cocktail lounge.

Services: Concierge, room service, laundry/dry cleaning.

Facilities: Fitness center, movie channels.

Delta Edmonton Centre Suite Hotel. Eaton Centre, 10222 102nd St., Edmonton, AB, T5J 4C5. ☎ **800/661-6655** in Canada, or 403/429-3900. Fax 403/428-1566. 169 suites. A/C MINIBAR TV TEL. Standard business suite C$132–C$250 (US$94–US$179). Ask about summer family and low weekend rates. AE, DC, ER, MC, V. Parking C$8 (US$6) per day.

This all-suite establishment forms part of the upscale Eaton Centre Mall in the heart of downtown. Three-quarters of the windows look into the mall, so you can stand behind the tinted one-way glass (in your pajamas, if you like) and watch the shopping action outside.

Most units are deluxe executive suites—C$218 (US$156), or C$147 (US$105) if you're here on business—each with a large sitting area with couch, chairs, TV, and wet bar, and down a hall and behind a door, a bedroom of equal size, containing more easy chairs, another TV, a large desk, and a plate-glass wall looking into the seven-story mall atrium. Each suite has two phones. If you need lots of room, or have work to do in Edmonton, then these very spacious rooms are just the ticket. All rooms have jetted tubs. The entire hotel is nicely furnished and well decorated.

Dining: Cocoa's is the Delta's casual restaurant and lounge, just off the shopping mall.

Services: Concierge, dry cleaning/laundry, baby-sitting, valet parking.

Facilities: The hotel provides a business center with photocopy and fax machines, and a health center with exercise machines, steam bath, and whirlpool. And without having to stir out of doors, there are the 140 retail shops in the mall, plus movie theaters, an entertainment pub, and an indoor 9-hole putting green. Four other shopping malls are connected to the hotel via Pedway.

✪ **Fantasyland Hotel.** 17700 87th Ave., Edmonton, AB, T5T 4V4. ☎ **800/661-6454** or 403/444-3000. Fax 403/444-3294. 319 rms and suites. A/C TV TEL. C$155–C$260 (US$111–US$186) double. Weekend and off-season packages available. AE, ER, MC, V. Free parking.

From the outside, this solemn brown brick tower at the end of the huge West Edmonton Mall reveals little of the wildly decorated and luxurious rooms found inside. The Fantasyland is kind of a cross between a hotel and Las Vegas: The hotel contains a total of 116 "themed" rooms decorated in nine different styles (as well as 238 very large and well-furnished regular rooms).

Theme rooms aren't just a matter of subtle touches: These rooms are exceedingly clever, very comfortable, and way over the top. Take the Truck Room: Your bed is located in the back end of a real pickup (you can choose a Ford or Chevy); the pickup's bench seats fold down into a bed for a child, the lights on the vanity are real stoplights, and the lights on the roll bar are actually reading lights. Traffic signs decorate the walls. Or the Igloo Room, where a round bed is encased in a shell that looks like ice blocks; keeping company with you are statues of sled dogs; and all the walls are painted with amazingly lifelike trompe-l'oeil Arctic murals. The dogsleds even become beds for children. And so on, through the Canadian Rail Room (train berths for beds), the African Room, the Roman Room, and more. The decorations are usually ingenious, and the rooms quite luxurious. All the theme rooms come with immense four-person Jacuzzi tubs, lots of sitting room (albeit usually disguised as something else), and all the amenities that you'd expect at a four-star hotel.

It's not all fantasy here. The nontheme rooms are divided into superior rooms, with either a king or two queen beds, or executive rooms, with a king bed, four-person Jacuzzi, and masses of sitting room. The hotel has a separate business work area, with desks, modems, and printers available. There's a small workout room, and passes are offered to the mall's Waterpark. The hotel's fine-dining restaurant is quite good, and of course, the hotel provides all-weather access to the world's largest shopping mall.

If you have any doubt about the rooms, the hotel offers tours of all the different theme types on Saturdays at 2pm. After you complete the tour, you'll wish you were staying here.

Westin Edmonton. 10135 100th St., Edmonton, AB, T5J 0N7. ☎ **800/937-8461** or 403/426-3636. Fax 403/428-1454. E-mail: res@westin.ab.ca. 413 rms. A/C MINIBAR TV TEL. From C$146 (US$104) double. AE, ER, MC, V.

Located in the heart of Edmonton's downtown shopping and entertainment district, the Westin—a modern bow-shaped building—offers some of Edmonton's largest rooms. Although the lobby is a bit austere, rooms are very comfortably furnished and come equipped with nice touches like coffeemakers, two telephones, voice mail, and ironing board and iron. Rooms in the premier wing have a second TV in the bathroom! For an extra C$20 (US$14), you can request a Westin Guest Office, a room that comes with a printer, a fax, an ergonomic chair, and a proper business desk. Seventy percent of the rooms are no-smoking.

Dining: Two restaurants, including Pradera, one of Edmonton's most inventive restaurants; two lounges.

Services: Concierge, 24-hour room service, valet laundry.

Facilities: Complete exercise facilities, including indoor pool, sauna, and whirlpool.

MODERATE

Alberta Place. 10049 103rd St., Edmonton, AB, T5J 2W7. ☎ **800/661-3982** or 403/423 1565. Fax 403/426-6260. 86 suites. TV TEL. C$90 (US$65) double bed-sitter; C$104 (US$74) double 1 bdrm suite. Extra person C$8 (US$6). Children stay free in parents' rm. AE, DC, ER, MC, V. Free parking.

This downtown apartment hotel is an excellent choice for the traveler who needs a little extra space or a family that wants cooking facilities. Everything is supplied to set up housekeeping. The hotel has a swimming pool (with hot tub and sauna). The apartments, of various sizes, are very well furnished and comfortable, and each has a full kitchen, including microwave, and a large desk and working area. The hotel is located half a block from public transport, and is in easy walking distance to most business and government centers.

✪ **Edmonton House.** 10205 100th Ave., Edmonton, AB, T5J 4B5. ☎ **800/661-6562** or 403/420-4000. Fax 403/420-4008. 300 suites. TV TEL. C$99 (US$71) 1-bedrm suite. AE, DC, ER, MC, V. Free parking.

This is a great alternative to pricier downtown hotels; these are big, well-decorated rooms, and you don't have to pay stiff parking fees. With a great location right above the North Saskatchewan River, the Edmonton House all-suite hotel has one of the best views in Edmonton. The suites are large; each comes with a full kitchen and dining area, bedroom, separate sitting area with a fold-out couch and chairs, and a balcony from which to take in the view; two-bedroom suites are also available. Each room has two telephones and a computer jack; room service is available. Facilities at the hotel include a pool and sauna, exercise room, game room, and laundry facilities. On premises are both a lounge and a restaurant. Edmonton House is within easy walking distance to most downtown office areas and to public transport.

Union Bank Inn. 10053 Jasper Ave., Edmonton, AB, T5J 1S5. ☎ **403/423-3600.** Fax 403/423/4623. 14 rms. A/C TV TEL. C$125–C$145 (US$89–US$104) double. AE, ER, MC, V. Free parking.

The historic and stylish Union Bank, built in 1910, has seen many uses during its long life; however, the building—in the heart of the city—had sat vacant for years before a young businesswoman bought it and redeveloped it into an elegant restaurant and intimate boutique hotel. In order to make each of the rooms unique, the owner asked 14 of Edmonton's top interior designers each to design a room. The results are charming, each room with its own style, colors, furniture, fabrics, and layout (it has to be said that sage green was a popular color in Edmonton in 1997!).

All rooms have the same amenities, including fireplace, voice mail and modem jacks in the phones, goose-feather pillows and duvets, and a bathroom full of nice toiletries. All come with complimentary continental breakfast. Service is very friendly and professional. Rooms vary quite a bit in layout and aren't massive; if you're coming here with work to do, ask for one of the larger rooms. The main lobby restaurant/bar, Madison's, is a great place to meet friends. If you're weary of anonymous corporate hotels and would like a cozy place in central Edmonton, then this is a wonderful choice.

INEXPENSIVE

In addition to the two options below, you may want to check out the **YMCA,** 10030 102A Ave. (☎ **403/421-9622;** fax 403/428-9469), which offers 106 rooms for C$42 (US$30) double; MasterCard and Visa are accepted. It has a cafeteria, pool, weight room, gymnasium, and racquetball court, plus a TV lounge; it accommodates men, women, and couples. Only a few rooms have private bath (tub only). During summer, 1,200 dorm rooms in Lister Hall at the **University of Alberta,** 87th Avenue and 116th Street (☎ **403/492-4281;** fax 403/492-7032; e-mail: conference@ualberta.ca; Web site: www.hfs.ualberta.ca/>), are thrown open to visitors. Most rooms are standard bathroom-down-the-hall rooms with two twin beds for C$33 (US$24). Available year-round are guest suites, two-bed dorms that share a bath with only one other suite, costing C$40 (US$29). The university is right on the LRT line and not far from trendy Old Strathcona. Parking is C$3 (US$2.15) per day; MasterCard and Visa are accepted.

Days Inn. 10041 106th St., Edmonton, AB, T5J 1G3. ☎ **800/267-2191** or 403/423-1925. Fax 403/424-5302. 76 rms. A/C TV TEL. C$55–C$79 (US$39–US$57) double. Children under 12 stay free in parents' rm. Senior, AAA, and corporate discounts. AE, ER, MC, V. Free parking.

For the price, this is one of downtown Edmonton's best deals. Located just 5 minutes from the city center, this motor inn has everything you need for a pleasant stay, including guest laundry and king- or queen-size beds in comfortably furnished rooms.

Edmonton International Hostel. 10422 91st St., Edmonton, AB, T5H 1S6. ☎ **403/ 429-0140.** Fax 403/421-0131. E-mail: eihostel@hostellingintl.ca. Sleeps 50. C$13 (US$9) members, C$18 (US$13) nonmembers. MC, V.

The Edmonton hostel is air-conditioned and has mountain-bike rentals, which means you can get around town easily, even though public transportation is just around the corner. Two family rooms are available.

BED & BREAKFASTS

To book a B&B in Edmonton, ask for a list of guest houses belonging to the B&B Association of Edmonton from **Edmonton Tourism,** 9797 Jasper Ave., Edmonton, AB, T5J 1N9 (☎ **800/463-4667** or 403/496-8400). Or contact **Alberta's Gem B&B Reservation Agency,** 11216 48 Ave., Edmonton, AB, T6H 0C7 (☎ **403/ 434-6098**). Nearly all B&Bs listed charge from C$50 to C$80 (US$36 to US$57) for doubles.

DINING

Edmonton has a vigorous dining scene, with lots of hip new eateries joining traditional steak and seafood restaurants. In general, special-occasion and fine dining is found downtown, and on High Street, close to the centers of politics and business. Over in Old Strathcona, south of the river, is an area of trendy—and less expensive— cafes and bistros with up-to-the minute, cosmopolitan menus.

If you're staying downtown, one place you'll get to know well is the **Baraka Cafe,** 10088 Jasper Ave. (☎ **403/423-1819**), on downtown Edmonton's busiest corner. Baraka's has expertly made espresso drinks, two cases full of exquisite pastries and sweets, and a large selection of magazines and newspapers. With cafe tables to lounge at, this is the perfect place to caffeinate in the morning, or have a late-night dessert.

DOWNTOWN

Expensive

✪ **Hardware Grill.** 9698 Jasper Ave. ☎ **403/423-0969.** Reservations suggested. Main courses C$16–C$23 (US$11–US$16). AE, DC, MC, V. Mon–Fri 11:30am–2pm; Mon–Thurs 5–9:30pm, Fri–Sat 5–10:30pm. NEW CANADIAN.

Housed in a historic building that was once Edmonton's original hardware store, the Hardware Grill is easily one of the city's most savvy and exciting restaurants. The menu reflects new cooking styles, regional ingredients, and wonderful presentation. There are as many appetizers as entree selections, making it tempting to graze through a series of smaller dishes. Sautéed sweetbreads are served with a hearty potato hash, wild-mushroom ragout spills over grilled polenta, and smoked duck comes in crispy spring rolls. However, it's hard to resist entrees like maple-smoked pork loin with sweet corn sauce, or a lamb sirloin with herb gnocchi and mint aioli. The wine list is extensive, and witty: after the mandatory listing of chardonnays, the substantial list of other white wines is listed under "Anything but Chardonnay."

The building may be historic, but there's nothing antique about the dining room. Postmodern without being stark, the room is edged with glass partitions, with exposed pipes and ducts painted a smoky rose. The kitchen is open to the dining room, and contains a fearsome squadron of cooks. Highly recommended.

La Bohème. 6427 112th Ave. ☎ **403/474-5693.** Reservations required. Main courses C$15–C$29 (US$11–US$21). AE, MC, V. Mon–Sat 11am–3pm, Sun 11am–3:30pm; daily 5–11pm. FRENCH.

La Bohème consists of two small, lace-curtained dining rooms in a historic building northeast of downtown. The cuisine is French, of course, and so is the wine selection, with a particular accent on Rhône Valley vintages. There's a wide selection of appetizers and light dishes, including a number of intriguing salads. The entrees are hearty, classic French preparations of rack of lamb, chicken breast, and seafood. The restaurant also features daily changing vegetarian entrees. Desserts are outstanding.

Madison's at Union Bank Inn. 10053 Jasper Ave. ☎ **403/423-3600.** Reservations suggested. Main courses C$14–C$21 (US$10–US$15); table d'hôte C$25 (US$18). AE, ER, MC, V. Daily 7am–11pm. NEW CANADIAN.

One of the loveliest dining rooms and casual cocktail bars in Edmonton is Madison's, in the stylish new Union Bank Inn. Once a turn-of-the-century bank, the formal architectural details remain—columns and big moldings—but they share the light and airy space with modern art, light-wood floors, avant-garde furniture, and excellent food.

The menu is up-to-date, with grilled and roast fish and meats, pasta dishes, interesting salads (one special featured rose petals, baby lettuce, and shaved white chocolate), and several specials daily. Many dishes boast an international touch, such as prawns with cilantro and tequila lime cream served over pasta. Grilled salmon is served with cranberry-citrus salsa.

Pradera. In the Westin Edmonton, 10135 100th St. ☎ **403/426-3636.** Reservations recommended. Main courses C$15–C$25 (US$11–US$18). AE, DC, DISC, MC, V. Mon–Fri 6:30am–2pm, Sat–Sun 7am–2pm; daily 5–11pm. INTERNATIONAL.

One of downtown Edmonton's most inventive restaurants is Pradera, in the Westin Hotel, featuring creative fusion cooking. Pradera's menu free-associates across several cuisines, notably Oriental, Italian, and Canadian, to arrive at new dishes that succeed at being more than the sum of their parts. The herb-crusted rack of lamb is served with polenta and Sambuca coffee jus. Grilled mahimahi comes with a potato spring roll and papaya relish. Prime rib is served with a horseradish profiterole. Service is excellent.

Sorrentino's Bistro and Bar. 10162 100th St. ☎ **403/424-7500.** Reservations suggested. Main courses C$17–C$25 (US$12–US$18). AE, DC, MC, V. Mon–Fri 7–11am, 11:30am–2:30pm, and 5:30pm–midnight; Sat 5pm–midnight. ITALIAN.

This new and upscale branch of a local chain of Italian restaurants is a good addition to the downtown dining scene. The coolly sophisticated dining room and bar—flanked by the Havana Room, where Cuban cigars are available with port and single-malt Scotch—is a popular meeting place for the captains of the city's business and social life. The food is excellent: you can't do better than a plate from the daily appetizer table, which features grilled vegetables, bean salads, and marinated anchovies. Entrees range from risottos, to pasta and wood-fired–oven pizza, to imaginative entrees like tournedos of salmon and scallops, veal and chicken dishes, and several rotisserie specials daily.

Moderate

Bistro Praha. 10168 100A St. ☎ **403/424-4218.** Reservations recommended on weekends. Main courses C$13–C$18 (US$9–US$13). AE, DC, ER, MC, V. Mon–Fri 11am–2am, Sat noon–2am, Sun 5pm–1am. EASTERN EUROPEAN.

Bistro Praha is one of several side-by-side casual restaurants—all with summer streetside seating—that take up the single block of 100A Street (formerly a service alley). It's also the best of these restaurants, and features a charming, wood-paneled interior, a mural-covered wall, and very good Eastern European cooking. The menu offers a wide selection of light dishes, convenient for a quick meal or a midafternoon snack. The entree menu centers on schnitzels (there are three different kinds), as well as a wonderful roast goose with sauerkraut for C$15 (US$11). Desserts tend toward fancy, imposing confections like Sacher torte. Service is friendly and relaxed. This is one of downtown Edmonton's favorite casual dining houses, and the clientele is cosmopolitan, appreciative, and mainly young and stylish.

✪ Il Portico. 10012 107th St. ☎ **403/424-0707.** Reservations recommended on weekends. Main courses C$11–C$23 (US$8–US$16). AE, DC, DISC, MC, V. Mon–Fri 11:30am–2pm; Mon–Sat 5:30–11pm, Sun 5–10pm. ITALIAN.

One of the most popular Italian restaurants in Edmonton, Il Portico has a wide menu of well-prepared traditional but updated dishes. This is seriously good Italian food, with excellent selections of grilled meats, pastas, and pizza: It's one of those rare restaurants where you want to try everything. Have the Caesar salad, and remember how wonderful these salads can be if prepared properly. Service is impeccable, and the wine list one of the best in the city: Remarkably, they will open any bottle on the list (except reserve bottles) if you buy a half liter. The dining room is nicely informal but classy; there's outdoor seating in summer.

Inexpensive

At the corner of 101A Avenue and 100A Street, in the heart of downtown, are a number of street cafes with moderate to inexpensive menus. The actual restaurants seem to change frequently, but the venues remain. This is a good place to go and shop the menus for pasta, sandwiches, and burgers. There are also inexpensive food options in the Eaton Mall, at 102nd Avenue and 101st Street, and in Edmonton's compact "Chinatown" centered at 102nd Avenue and 96th Street.

Sherlock Holmes. 10012 101A Ave. ☎ **403/426-7784.** Reservations not accepted. Main courses C$6.50–C$10 (US$4.65–US$7). AE, DC, ER, MC, V. Mon–Sat 11:30am–2am. ENGLISH.

The Sherlock Holmes is a tremendously popular English-style pub with good local and regional beers on tap (as well as Guinness) and a very good bar menu. The pub is housed in a charming building with black crossbeams on whitewashed walls and a picket fence around the outdoor patio. The menu has a few traditional English dishes—like fish-and-chips, and steak-and-kidney pie for C$7 (US$5)—but there's a strong emphasis on new pub grub like chicken breast sandwiches, beef curry, burgers, and salads, from C$6 to C$10 (US$4.30 to US$7).

There are two other Sherlock Holmeses in Edmonton, one in the West Edmonton Mall and the other in Old Strathcona at 10341 82nd Ave.

HIGH STREET

High Street is a small neighborhood with galleries, classy shops, and several good restaurants, centered at 102nd Avenue and 124th Street, just west of downtown. In addition to the restaurants below, there's a lively bar and bistro called the **Iron Bridge,** 12520 102nd Ave. (☎ **403/482-5620**), with a popular summer patio.

La Spiga Restaurant. 10133 125th St. ☎ **403/482-3100.** Reservations recommended on weekends. Main courses C$13–C$23 (US$9–US$16). AE, DC, MC, V. Mon–Sat 5pm–midnight. ITALIAN.

One of Edmonton's best Italian restaurants, La Spiga is located along the gallery row in the trendy High Street neighborhood. This is nouveau Italian cooking, with an emphasis on fresh, stylish ingredients and unusual tastes and textures. The rack of lamb is marinated in fresh herbs and grappa; prawns and scallops are paired with a white-wine lemon sauce and served over angel-hair pasta.

Manor Cafe. 10109 125th St. ☎ **403/482-7577.** Reservations recommended on weekends. Main courses C$9–C$15 (US$6–US$11). AE, DC, ER, MC, V. Mon–Thurs 11am–11pm, Fri–Sat 11am–midnight, Sun 5pm–11pm. INTERNATIONAL.

Housed in a stately two-story mansion overlooking a park, the Manor Cafe offers one of the most fashionable outdoor dining patios in Edmonton, and one of its most interesting menus. Recently renamed and redesigned, this longtime favorite now offers Pacific Rim cuisine, which brings the tastes and spices of Oriental food together with international ingredients and cooking techniques. Duck breast is stuffed with apricots and served with shallot, pesto, and port sauce; hoisin lamb tenderloin is served on a bed of couscous. Smoked duck wontons are among the intriguing appetizers. The food is eclectic, but always delicious.

Sweetwater Cafe. 12427 102nd Ave. ☎ **403/488-1959.** Main courses C$5–C$12 (US$3.60–US$9). MC, V. Mon–Fri 11am–10pm, Sat 9am–10pm, Sun 10am–5pm. INTERNATIONAL/SOUTHWESTERN.

Here's a bright and lively bistro with good, inexpensive food; in summer you can sit on the charming outdoor deck in the back, thankfully far from the roar of traffic. The food here is international, leaning towards Southwestern—sandwiches are served in tortillas, and there are several types of quesadillas. Pizza and pastas are also available, and everything here—except for a handful of steak and chicken entrees—is in the C$5-to-C$7 (US$3.60-to-US$5) range.

OLD STRATHCONA

South of downtown, across the river, along Whyte Avenue (otherwise known as 82nd Avenue) in the old center of Strathcona village, is a very dynamic, youthful business district dominated by artists, students, and Edmonton's other bohemian elements. Also here, amid the busy street life, are a great many cafes, bistros, and small restaurants. This is an excellent place to come to browse your way past dozens of good places to eat. In addition to the full-service restaurants listed below, you may want to explore **Terra Natural Good Market,** 10313 82nd Ave. (☎ **403/433-6807**), a health-food store with a cafe; and ✪ **Block 1912,** 10361 82nd Ave., a friendly cafe with one refrigerated case full of great-looking salads, one full of eye-popping desserts, and an array of deli sandwiches.

Expensive

✪ **The Polos Cafe.** 8405 112th St. ☎ **403/432-1371.** Reservations suggested. Main courses C$10–C$24 (US$7–US$17). AE, DC, MC, V. Mon–Fri 11am–2:30pm; Mon–Thurs 5pm–10pm, Fri–Sat 5pm–midnight. ITALIAN/CHINESE/FUSION.

The Polo in question is Marco Polo, the first European to travel between Italy and China: as probably one of the first food-lovers to experience what we now think of as "fusion" cuisine, the 13th-century Venetian is the namesake and inspiration for this exciting restaurant. The menu brings together classic Italian and Chinese cooking in a new cuisine loftily hailed as "Orie-ital."

But it works: the food here is always interesting and delicious. Lamb rack with cumin, masala, and marsala is a typical hybrid; Italian pasta and Shanghai noodles are tossed together with a variety of Sino-Italian sauces; tea-smoked duck comes with caramelized apples in merlot. Food doesn't get much more exotic than this, and chances are you'll never see these dishes again on a menu. The dining room has art-hung mauve walls, cool pools of light, and eager diners. Definitely worth a visit.

Von's Steak & Fish House. 10309 81st Ave. ☎ **403/439-0041.** Reservations recommended on weekends. Main courses C$13–C$39 (US$9–US$28). AE, MC, V. Mon–Sat 11:30am–10pm, Sun 5–10pm. STEAK/SEAFOOD.

One of the best steak houses in Edmonton, Von's is a comfortable supper club with good Alberta beef; the prime rib here is excellent, as are the various steaks. If you've had your fill of red meat, try the pasta or fresh-fish dishes.

Moderate

Chianti. 10501 82nd Ave. ☎ **403/439-9829.** Reservations required. Main courses C$7–C$15 (US$5–US$11). AE, DC, MC, V. Daily 11am–midnight. ITALIAN.

Chianti is a rarity among Italian restaurants: The food is very good and very inexpensive. Pasta dishes begin at C$6 (US$4.30) and run to C$10 (US$7) (for fettuccine with scallops, smoked salmon, curry, and garlic), and even veal dishes (more than a dozen are offered!), and seafood specials barely top C$12 (US$9). Soups and salads start off at C$3 (US$2.15), so you can assemble a full meal here for the cost of appetizers at a pricier restaurant. Chianti is located in a handsomely remodeled post-office building; the restaurant isn't a secret, so it can be a busy and fairly crowded experience.

Da-De-O. 10548A 82nd Ave. ☎ **403/433-0930.** Main courses C$7–C$16 (US$5–US$11). MC, V. Mon–Sat 11am–2am, Sun 3pm–2am. CAJUN/SOUTHERN.

This New Orleans–style diner is authentic right down to the low-tech, juke-box-at-your-table music system. The food is top-notch, with good and goopy po'boy sandwiches from C$7 to C$9 (US$5 to US$6), fresh oysters, five kinds of jambalaya—C$10 to C$15 (US$7 to US$11)—and a big selection of blackened and *étoufée* meats and seafood. Especially good is the Sorochan Angel, seafood in Pernod cream over angel-hair pasta. There's a whole page of appetizers and salads, so you can also relax in the vinyl-covered booths, listen to Billie Holiday, and graze through some chicken wings or crab fritters with a glass of beer.

Julio's Barrio. 10450 82nd Ave. ☎ **403/431-0774.** Main courses C$9–C$14 (US$6–US$10). AE, MC, V. Mon 4–11pm, Tues–Thurs 11am–11pm, Fri–Sat 11am–midnight, Sun 2–10pm. MEXICAN.

This Mexican restaurant and watering hole is a great place to come and snack on several light dishes while quaffing drinks with friends. The food ranges from the traditional enchiladas and nachos to sizzling shrimp fajitas. The atmosphere is youthful, high energy, and minimalist-hip: no kitschy piñatas or scratchy recordings of marimba bands here.

The King & I. 10160 82nd Ave. ☎ **403/433-2222.** Main courses C$9–C$19 (US$6–US$14). AE, MC, V. Mon–Thurs 11:30am–10:30pm, Fri 11:30am–11:30pm, Sat 4:30–11:30pm. THAI.

This is the place for excellent, zesty Thai food, which can be a real treat after the heavy, beef-rich cooking of western Canada. Many dishes are vegetarian, almost a novelty in Alberta. Various curries, ranging from mild to sizzling, and rice and noodle dishes are the house specialties. For a real treat, try the lobster in curry sauce with asparagus (C$19/US$14).

✪ **Packrat Louie Kitchen & Bar.** 10335 83rd Ave. ☎ **403/433-0123.** Reservations recommended on weekends. Main courses C$8–C$19 (US$6–US$14). MC, V. Mon–Sat 11:30am–11:30pm. ITALIAN.

Bright and lively, this very popular bistro has a somewhat unlikely name, considering that this is one of Edmonton's finest purveyors of new Italian cooking. Menu choices range from specialty pizzas to fine entree salads to grilled meats, chicken, and pasta. Most dishes cast an eye toward light or healthy preparations without sacrificing complexity. A grilled chicken breast comes with an arresting mélange of puréed spinach and red bell pepper; grilled lamb chops are garnished simply with plenty of fresh tomatoes, feta cheese, and polenta.

EDMONTON AFTER DARK

Tickets to most events are available through **Ticketmaster** (☎ **403/451-8000**). For a complete listing of current happenings, check the Friday arts section of the *Edmonton Journal* or the alternative arts weekly *See.*

THE TOP PERFORMING-ARTS VENUES   A masterpiece of theatrical architecture, the **Citadel Theatre,** 9828 101A Ave. (☎ **403/426-4811**), is not a playhouse in the conventional sense, but a community project encompassing virtually every form of show craft. The complex takes up the entire city block adjacent to Sir Winston Churchill Square. It looks like a gigantic greenhouse—more than half is glass-walled, and even the awnings are glass. Apart from auditoriums, it also has a magnificent indoor garden with a waterfall, as well as a restaurant. But the best feature of the complex is that it houses, under one roof, five different theaters adapted for different productions and distinct audiences, plus workshops and classrooms. The Citadel today is one of the largest, busiest, and most prolific theaters in Canada.

The **Northern Alberta Jubilee Auditorium,** 11455 87th Ave. (☎ **403/427-2760;** fax 403/422-3750), is the setting for a great variety of concert and ballet performances. The facility was a 2678-seat multipurpose performing-arts center with another 250-seat theater on the lower level. The Jubilee is the resident home of the Edmonton Opera and the Alberta Ballet.

DINNER THEATER   The charming **Mayfield Dinner Theatre,** 16615 109th Ave. (☎ **403/483-4051**), at the Mayfield Inn, combines excellent food with light-hearted, often sumptuously equipped, stage productions. Shows go on at 8pm nightly and at brunch-time Sunday. Tickets cost C$36 to C$49 (US$26 to US$35), meals included. Spoofy comedies and musical revues are the specialty at the lively **Celebrations Dinner Theatre,** 13103 Fort Rd. (☎ **403/448-9339**), located in the Neighbourhood Inn. Shows are mounted Wednesday to Sunday evenings, and tickets cost C$34 to C$40 (US$24 to US$29), meals included.

THE CLUB & BAR SCENE   The flashy, upscale country-and-western scene is the name of the game, with new places opening up all the time. But there are plenty of options if you're not into Garth Brooks and line-dancing. Most live-music clubs charge a cover on weekends, usually C$6 to C$8 (US$4.30 to US$6).

The hottest country dance bar in town is **Cook County Saloon,** 8010 103rd St. (☎ **403/432-2665**), with a changing lineup of Western bands nightly. **Longriders Saloon,** 11733 78th St. (☎ **403/479-8700**), has live country music 6 nights a week, as does the **Wild West Saloon,** 12912 50th St. (☎ **403/476-3388**).

For something uniquely Edmonton but without the twang, check out the **Sidetrack Cafe,** 10333 112th St. (☎ **403/421-1326**), the city's most versatile music venue. You get an Australian rock group one week, a musical comedy troupe the next, a blues band the following, progressive jazz after that, and so on.

Blues on Whyte, 10329 82nd Ave. (☎ 403/439-5058), is Edmonton's best blues club. It's located in the vintage Commercial Hotel in Old Strathcona, with a popular billiard room. **The Rev,** 10032 102nd St. (☎ 403/424-2745), is the premier club for the alternative-music scene. The **Rebar,** 10551 82nd Ave. (☎ 403/433-3600) is a good, student-oriented dance club in Old Strathcona. Edmonton's gay bar of choice is **The Roost,** 10345 104th St. (☎ 403/426-3150), with a large and pleasant outdoor patio.

Straighter and more predictable is the **Hard Rock Cafe,** Bourbon Street, 1638 West Edmonton Mall (☎ 403/444-1905). Also in the mall is **Yuk Yuk's International,** Bourbon Street, 1646 West Edmonton Mall (☎ 403/481-YUKS), the Edmonton branch of a national chain of live stand-up comedy clubs. Shows are Wednesday to Saturday: weeknights at 9pm, weekends at 8:30 and 11pm. Admission is C$6.50 to C$10.75 (US$4.65 to US$8). Also at the West Ed Mall is the brand new **Planet Hollywood** (☎ 403/444-4999).

The most romantic place for a drink in the city is the **Library Bar** at the Hotel Macdonald, 10065 100th St. (☎ 403/424-5181).

GAMBLING   In Alberta, the money from casinos goes to charities. The casinos are privately owned and provide comfortable surroundings, full-service food and liquor service, and an amiable staff. The games are blackjack, roulette, baccarat, red dog, and sic bo; bets range from C$2 to C$500 (US$1.45 to US$358); and the play goes daily from 10am to 3am. Try your luck at **Casino ABS,** City Centre, 10549 102nd St. (☎ 403/424-9467), or **Casino ABS,** Southside, 7055 Argyll Rd. (☎ 403/466-9467). The **Palace Casino,** 8770 170 St. (☎ 403/444-2112), operates in the West Edmonton Mall.

DAY TRIPS FROM EDMONTON

✪ **Elk Island National Park** (☎ 403/992-5790), on the Yellowhead Highway, 32 kilometers (20 miles) east of Edmonton, is one of the most compact and prettiest in the national-parks system. It protects one of Canada's most endangered ecosystems and is the home and roaming ground to North America's largest and smallest mammals; the wood buffalo and the pygmy shrew (a tiny creature half the size of a mouse, but with the disposition of a tiger). The park has hiking trails, campgrounds, golf courses, a lake, and a sandy beach. A 1-day vehicle permit costs C$4 (US$2.85) per person per day, or C$8 (US$6) per group per day.

The ✪ **Ukrainian Cultural Heritage Village** (☎ 403/662-3640; e-mail: hssuchv@oanet.com) is an open-air museum and a park of living history 25 minutes east of Edmonton on Yellowhead Highway 16. The village has 30 restored historic buildings arranged in an authentic setting; the adjacent fields and pastures are planted and harvested according to period techniques. Visitors learn what life was like for Ukrainian pioneers in the 1892-to-1930 era through costumed interpreters who re-create the daily activities of the period. The village and interpretive center are definitely worth the drive, especially in midsummer, when you can watch horse-drawn wagons gathering hay and harvesting grain. Open from May 15 to early September daily from 10am to 6pm; early September to mid-October daily from 10am to 4pm. Summer admission is C$6.50 (US$4.65) for adults and C$3 (US$2.15) for children; children under 6 are free.

At Vegreville, 40 kilometers (25 miles) east of the Ukrainian Village, stands the **world's largest Ukrainian Easter egg,** gaily painted and towering more than 30 feet tall. This "pysanka" was constructed in 1974 to commemorate the 100th anniversary of the arrival of the Royal Canadian Mounted Police in Alberta. You can camp all around the egg and, if you get there early in July, watch the annual Ukrainian Festival with singing, music, and leg-throwing folk dances.

Located 40 minutes south of Edmonton off Highway 2, the **Reynolds Alberta Museum** (☎ 800/661-4726 or 403/352-5855; e-mail: ram@mcd.gov.ab.ca; Web site: www.gov.ab.ca/~mcd/mhs/ram/ram.htm) is a science and technology museum with specialties in transport, industry, and agricultural engineering. The collection of vintage cars and period farm equipment is especially impressive, and there are hands-on activities to keep children busy. Adjoining the museum is Canada's **Aviation Hall of Fame,** with a hangar full of vintage airplanes. Admission is C$6.50 (US$4.65) for adults, C$3 (US$2.15) for youths 7 to 17, or C$15 (US$11) for a family. The museum is open June to early September daily from 9am to 5pm; early September to May Tuesday to Sunday from 9am to 5pm.

11 Wood Buffalo National Park

Located in the far northeastern corner of Alberta is Wood Buffalo National Park, the world's second largest national park. Bigger than Switzerland, the park measures 44,807 square kilometers (17,300 sq. miles). Two-thirds lie inside Alberta, one-third in the Northwest Territories.

The park was created for the specific purpose of preserving the last remaining herd of wood bison on earth. At the turn of the century these animals were near extinction. Today some 6,000 of the creatures roam their habitat, where you can see and snap them in droves.

The park is also the only known breeding ground for the whooping crane. Some 50 of these birds live here from April until October before migrating to their winter range along the Gulf of Mexico.

One of the problems faced by would-be visitors is simply getting to the park. By vehicle, it's 1,296 kilometers (805 miles) between Edmonton and Fort Smith, the park headquarters, over mostly gravel roads. Most visitors will find it easier to fly into Fort Smith on Canadian North Airlines, and once here, hook up with an outfitter who will arrange transport to the park and activities. The tours offered by **Subarctic Wildlife Adventures,** P.O. Box 685, Fort Smith, NT, X0E 0P0 (☎ 403/872-2467; fax 403/872-2126), offer naturalist-led excursions to many of the park's best wildlife-viewing areas. The shortest excursion into the park is 3 days and explores the woods and wetlands near the park's famed salt plains, where wildlife gather to lick the naturally occurring minerals. Costs run about C$800 (US$572) per person; longer trips are also available.

For information, contact the **Park Superintendent,** P.O. Box 750, Fort Smith, NT, X0E 0P0 (☎ 403/872-2349).

17 Vancouver

by Anistatia R. Miller & Jared M. Brown

Call it Lotusland, Brollywood, or Hollywood North. Canadians have some creative nicknames for Vancouver. With its West Coast permissiveness, unique mild climate (though it does receive more rain than any other major Canadian city), thriving film industry, and seemingly endless mountains and beaches, it's a marked contrast to the snowbound and slightly staid cities dotting Canada's eastern and central provinces. Readers of *Condé Nast Traveler* have called Vancouver one of the world's top-10 destinations for the past 2 years. And *Outside* magazine recently listed Vancouver as one of the world's most livable cities.

Even with Broadway-quality theaters, nightlife to suit just about every taste, world-class museums, and miles of understreet shopping malls, Vancouver is an outdoor city, ringed by bustling harbors and snowcapped peaks. National surveys indicate that Vancouverites suffer from fewer stress-related illnesses, work the least amount of overtime, consume the most wine per capita (with the lowest incidence of alcoholism), and are statistically happier than Canadians in any other province. They also spend more money on sports equipment, running shoes, and fitness classes; own more boats per capita; and play more tennis than their neighbors.

Nearly half of British Columbia's 3,700,000 residents live in and around Vancouver. As the gateway to North America for many Pacific Rim immigrants, the city has attained a diverse cultural mosaic, representing over 70 ethnic groups. After English and Chinese, the most commonly spoken languages are Punjabi, German, Italian, French, Tagalog (Filipino), Spanish, and Japanese. And you might encounter a Chinese dragon-boat race in False Creek on one weekend, followed by a Punjabi parade down Commercial Drive the next, and then a Scottish caber-toss tourney in Vanier Park after that.

With Vancouver's perennial urban progress comes problems. Rush-hour traffic downtown has gotten worse. (The city plans to add another bridge to lighten the load on the Lions Gate Bridge.) Property-related crime has exploded, surpassing Manhattan and Miami in reported burglaries during 1997. And the drug-related crimes along East Hastings and Carrall streets have dampened the gentrification east of Gastown and north of Chinatown. In those respects, Vancouver has caught up since Expo '86 with other fast-growing North American metropolises. But quick development hasn't completely diminished the quality of life.

Out of 118 cities worldwide, Vancouver was ranked second only to Geneva in 1996 for "quality of life." But perhaps the surveyors were biased: They were from Geneva. We certainly agree with them. Where else can you ski a major mountain any time of year, sailboard, scuba dive, rock climb, golf, mountain bike, wilderness hike, and kayak all in the same day (then find a Jacuzzi, a masseuse, and an all-night pharmacy to help you recover)? And where can you find a total urban paradise? Well . . . nowhere. But we're glad Vancouver still keeps on trying.

1 Orientation

ARRIVING

BY PLANE   Daily direct flights between major U.S. cities and Vancouver are offered by **Air Canada** (☎ 800/776-3000), **United Airlines** (☎ 800/241-6522), **American Airlines** (☎ 800/433-7300), **Northwest Airlines** (☎ 800/447-4747), and **America West** (☎ 800/235-9292). **Continental Airlines** (☎ 800/231-0856) will fly you to Denver or Seattle, then put you on an Air Canada flight to complete the trip.

Vancouver International Airport is 13 kilometers (8 miles) south of downtown on Sea Island, abutting the mainland. The International Terminal features an extensive collection of native-Indian sculptures and paintings amid expanses of glass under soaring ceilings. (Turn around and look up or take the up escalator on your right just before you leave the terminal to see Bill Reid's huge bronze canoe filled with characters from local legends.) This is one of the world's most beautiful airport terminals. To pay for these improvements, you must pay an **international departure surcharge** of C$10 (US$7) when leaving the country. Domestic departures are charged C$5 (US$3.60). However, there's no surcharge on arrival.

Airport information kiosks (☎ **604/276-6101**), on levels 2 and 3 in the Main Terminal and in the International Terminal, are open daily from 6:30am to 11:30pm.

Short- and long-term **parking** (☎ **604/276-6106**) is available at the airport. Courtesy buses run to airport hotels, and a shuttle bus links the Main and International terminals to the South Terminal, where smaller and private aircraft are docked. Drivers heading into Vancouver will take the Arthur Laing Bridge, which leads directly onto Granville Street (Highway 99).

The average **taxi** fare from the airport to a downtown hotel is C$35 (US$25), plus tip. Nearly 400 taxis serve the airport. But why take a cab, when it'll cost about the same to arrive in a stretch limo from ✪ **AirLimo** (☎ **604/273-1331**), the city's only flat-rate stretch limousine service? For a flat fee of C$29 (US$21) per trip (not per person), plus tax and tip, you can stretch out, open the sunroof, turn on the stereo, roll down the windows, put on your shades, and play celebrity for half an hour. The service operates 24 hours to and from the airport, and the drivers accept all major credit cards.

Light-green **YVR Airporter buses** (☎ **604/244-9888**) operate between the airport and downtown hotels, leaving daily from the Main Terminal's Level 2 every 15 minutes from 6:30am to 10:30pm and every 30 minutes from 10:30pm to 12:15am. The ride takes about 30 minutes. The one-way fare is C$9 (US$6) for adults, C$7 (US$5) for seniors, and C$5 (US$3.60) for children; the round-trip fare is C$15 (US$11) for adults, C$14 (US$10) for seniors, and C$10 (US$7) for children.

If you don't mind transferring from one bus to another with your luggage and have spare time, you can take public transport. **BC Transit bus** no. 100 stops at both airport terminals. Once it crosses over the bridge, get off at the Marine Drive stop and transfer to either bus no. 20 or bus no. 17, both of which head into downtown Vancouver. The one-way fare is C$1.75 (US$1.25) during off-peak hours and C$2.50 (US$1.80) during rush hours.

Most major **car-rental firms** have desks and shuttle services at the airport. Make advance reservations for fast check-in and guaranteed vehicle availability, especially if you want a four-wheel-drive vehicle or compact car (see "Getting Around," below).

BY CAR U.S. Interstate 5 from Seattle and Bellingham is the most direct route to Vancouver from the United States. You pass through the Customs & Immigration checkpoint at the **Peace Arch Station** (U.S. Customs ☎ 360/332-5771; Canadian Customs ☎ 604/666-0545). Once you've cleared Customs (which may take up to 2 hours during holiday weekends), you're on Canadian Highway 99. You'll drive through White Rock, Delta, and Richmond; pass under the Fraser River through the George Massey Tunnel; and cross the Oak Street Bridge. The highway ends and becomes busy urban Oak Street. Turn left onto 70th Avenue. (A small sign suspended above the left lane at the intersection of Oak and 70th reads CITY CENTRE.) Six winding blocks later, turn right onto Granville Street. This is the business extension of Highway 99, which heads into downtown via the Granville Street Bridge.

If you arrive via the Trans-Canada Highway (Highway 1), take the Cassiar Street exit and turn left at the first light onto Hastings Street (Highway 7A), adjacent to Exhibition Park. Follow Hastings Street 6 kilometers (4 miles) into downtown. To enter North Vancouver, stay on Highway 1 and cross the Second Narrows Bridge.

BY TRAIN **VIA Rail Canada,** Pacific Central Station, 1150 Station St., Vancouver (☎ 800/835-3037), connects with the U.S. Amtrak train service at Winnipeg, Manitoba, via a connector bus from Grand Forks, South Dakota; it also connects directly to Amtrak in Toronto. From Winnipeg, you travel the spectacular Calgary-to-Vancouver route. The alpine peaks surrounding Lake Louise are just the beginning of a journey that takes you through glacial-peaked mountains, antelope-brush desert, rolling prairies, granite-walled canyons, and rich farmlands.

Amtrak (☎ 800/872-7245) also operates a run along the West Coast corridor from San Diego to Vancouver, stopping at all major U.S. West Coast cities and taking a little under 2 days for the entire journey. Fares are US$440. Substantial seasonal discounts are available. **BC Rail,** 1311 W. 1st St., North Vancouver (☎ 604/631-3500), connects Vancouver to other destinations around the province, including Whistler. The trip to Whistler is 2¹/₂ hours each way, and the fare includes breakfast or dinner. A one-way ticket is C$29 (US$21) for adults, C$26 (US$19) for seniors, C$17 (US$12) for children 2 to 12, and C$6 (US$4) for children under 2. Vancouver's **Pacific Central Station** (☎ 604/669-3050) is at 1150 Station St. You can catch a cab to downtown for about C$5 (US$3.60). Or take the SkyTrain to the Granville or Waterfront Station; the one-way bus fare is C$1.75 (US$1.25) during off-peak hours and C$2.50 (US$1.80) during rush hours.

BY BUS Both the **Greyhound Bus Lines** (☎ 604/662-3222) and **Pacific Coach Lines** (☎ 604/662-8074) debark at the Pacific Central Station. The **Quick Shuttle Bus Service** (☎ 604/940-4428) operates between Vancouver and Seattle-Tacoma International Airport. The bus stops at the Sandman Inn, 180 W. Georgia St., and at the arrivals level of Vancouver Airport's Main and International terminals. The 4-hour ride is C$38 (US$27) one-way and C$68 (US$49) round-trip.

BY SHIP/FERRY The **Canada Place** cruise-ship terminal, at the base of Burrard Street (☎ 604/666-4452), is a very visible city landmark. Topped by five distinctive Teflon sails, Canada Place pier juts out into the Burrard Inlet and is at the edge of the downtown financial district. Princess Cruises, Holland America, Royal Caribbean, Crystal Cruises, Norwegian Cruise Lines, World Explorer Majesty Cruise Line, Hanseatic, Seabourn, and Carnival Cruise Line all dock at Canada Place and the nearby Ballantine Pier to board passengers headed for Alaska via the Inside Passage. The 15-hour Inside Pasage ferry cruise aboard the MV *Queen of the North* costs only C\$102 (US\$71), and takes you from Vancouver Island's Port Hardy into an otherwise inaccessible coastline stretching north to the town of Prince Rupert and the southern tip of the Alaskan Panhandle. (If you're considering an Alaska cruise, late May and June generally offer the best weather, most daylight, and best sightseeing opportunities.)

The passenger/car ferries of **BC Ferries** (☎ 604/386-3431) dock at one of two Vancouver terminals. The **Tsawwassen terminal** is 19 kilometers (12 miles) south of Vancouver. Take Highway 17 until it joins Highway 99 just before the George Massey Tunnel, then follow the driving directions to the city given under "By Car," above. The **Horseshoe Bay terminal** is in West Vancouver. To reach downtown, take the Sea-to-Sky Highway (Highway 99) south to West Vancouver. Take the Taylor Way South exit (Exit 13) and follow the signs past the Park Royal Shopping Mall. Turn left at the intersection and cross the Lions Gate Bridge into Vancouver's West End and downtown districts.

VISITOR INFORMATION

The **Vancouver Visitor Info Centre** is at 200 Burrard St. (☎ 604/683-2000). It's open daily from May to Labour Day between 8am and 6pm; the rest of the year, it's open Monday to Saturday from 8:30am to 5:30pm. Two smaller Info Centres operate only in summer: One shares a kiosk with a local radio station, outside of Eatons department store at the corner of Georgia and Granville streets; it's open Tuesday to Friday from 10am to 5pm. The other kiosk is in Stanley Park and is open daily from 9am to 5pm.

Check out the monthly magazines *Vancouver,* 555 W. 12th Ave., Vancouver (☎ 604/877-7732), and *Vancouver Lifestyles,* 1224–1124 Lonsdale Ave., North Vancouver (☎ 604/980-7162), and the free weekly tabloid *The Georgia Straight,* 1770 Burrard St., Vancouver (☎ 604/730-7000), for up-to-date music and entertainment schedules, as well as information about what's going on in the city and environs. Another free monthly, *Coast: The Outdoor Recreation Magazine,* Glissande Publishing Co., P.O. Box 65837, Station F, Vancouver, BC, V5N 5L3 (☎ 604/876-1473), publishes schedules of mountain biking, kayaking, skiing, hiking, and climbing events. Two free monthly tabloids, *BC Parent,* 4479 W. 10th Ave., Vancouver (☎ 604/221-0366), and *West Coast Families,* 8–1551 Johnston St., Vancouver (☎ 604/689-1331), are geared for families with young children, listing many current events of interest to kids. *Terminal City,* 203–825 Granville St., Vancouver (☎ 604/669-6910), is the local alternative-music weekly. Gay and lesbian travelers will want to pick up *Xtra! West,* 501–1033 Davie St., Vancouver (☎ 604/684-9696), a biweekly tabloid available free in shops and restaurants throughout the West End.

CITY LAYOUT

Central Vancouver, downtown, and the West End are shaped roughly like a hand extended westward. Downtown Vancouver and Stanley Park are on the upraised thumb, extending away from the mitten-shaped central Vancouver peninsula. Pointing northward, this main business district is bordered on the west by English Bay, bordered on the north and east by the Burrard Inlet, and separated from central Vancouver on the south by False Creek.

Greater Vancouver

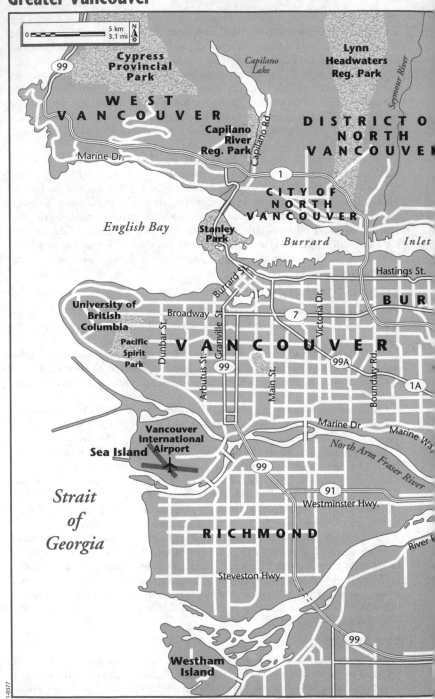

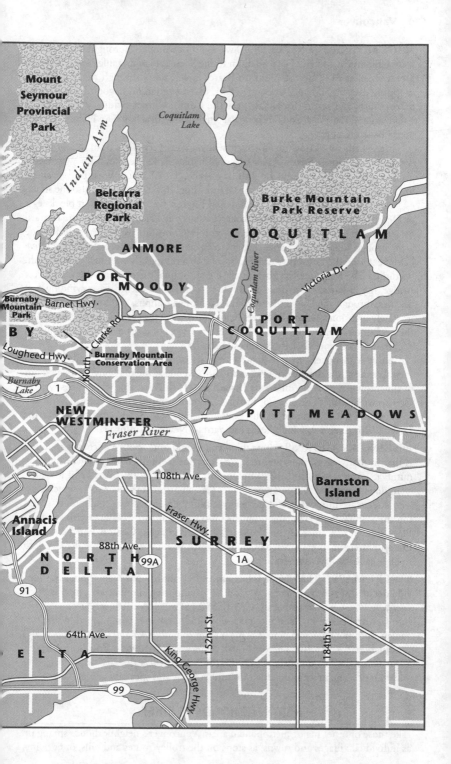

MAIN ARTERIES & STREETS   Two main downtown thoroughfares run west from Chinatown and BC Place Stadium to the West End and Stanley Park. **Robson Street** starts at BC Place Stadium on Beatty Street, flows through the West End's shopping district, and ends at Stanley Park's Lost Lagoon on Lagoon Drive. **Davie Street** starts at Pacific Boulevard near the Cambie Street Bridge, runs through Yaletown and the West End, and ends at English Bay Beach, where Denman Street meets Beach Avenue.

Three north-south downtown streets will get you everywhere both in and out of downtown. **Denman Street,** 2 blocks east of Stanley Park, stretches from West Georgia Street to Beach Avenue at English Bay Beach. This is where West End locals go to dine out or stroll and watch the sunset from English Bay Beach. It's also the shortest north-south route to Third, Second, and English Bay Beaches. Eight blocks east of Denman is **Burrard Street,** which starts at Canada Place and crosses the Burrard Street Bridge to Vanier Park, where it becomes Cornwall Avenue. As it heads due west through Kitsilano, its name changes to Point Grey Road and NW Marine Drive before entering the University of British Columbia campus. It eventually turns south, becoming SW Marine Drive, before ending at Granville Street and the Oak Street Bridge. If you have a spare hour or two, it's a wonderfully scenic drive: winding past beaches, through the University of British Columbia campus, and Shaughnessy, with its stately mansions. **Granville Street,** which starts near Canada Place to the west and the SeaBus terminal to the east, runs the entire length of central Vancouver south to Richmond, where it officially becomes Highway 99.

Central Vancouver's main east-west cross streets are successively numbered from First Avenue at the downtown bridges to 70th Avenue at the Oak Street Bridge south of downtown. Granville intersects **Broadway (10th Avenue),** which goes west to Greektown and the University of British Columbia campus and runs east all the way to Burnaby, where it becomes the Lougheed Highway. It also intersects **Marine Drive (70th Avenue),** which heads eastward to New Westminster.

FINDING AN ADDRESS   One thing you should note about Vancouver addresses is that in many cases, the suite, room, or apartment number precedes the building number. For instance, 100–1250 Robson St. is actually Suite 100 at 1250 Robson.

In downtown Vancouver, Chinatown's Carrall Street is the axis from which east-west streets are numbered and designated. Numbers increase as they progress west toward Stanley Park. The low numbers on north-south streets start on the Canada Place side and increase as they head toward False Creek. Central Vancouver uses Ontario Street as its east-west axis, and all north-south avenues from False Creek to the Fraser River have numerical names.

STREET MAPS   The Visitor Info Centres (see above) and many hotels can provide detailed downtown maps. A good all-around metropolitan area map is *Rand McNally Vancouver,* available for C$3 (US$2.15) at the Vancouver Airport Visitor Info Centre booth. The best city map we found, however, is published by the Canadian Automobile Association (CAA). It's free to both AAA and CAA members and is available at AAA offices across North America. **Worldwide Books and Maps,** 736A Granville St., downstairs (☎ **604/687-3320**), has the city's most extensive selection of Vancouver and British Columbia maps and specialty guidebooks.

NEIGHBORHOODS IN BRIEF

Like those of other major metropolitan areas, Vancouver's neighborhoods sprang up as individual villages and towns, as stops on the trolley routes and rails, or at points surrounding the many harbors. There are more than 30 neighborhoods. And the Greater Vancouver Regional District encompasses 14 incorporated cities: Vancouver, West Vancouver, North Vancouver, the district of North Vancouver, Richmond, Delta, White Rock, Port Moody, Surrey, New Westminster, Burnaby, Langley, Coquitlam, and Port Coquitlam. The following neighborhoods are of greatest interest to visitors.

Downtown   The heart of the city, downtown is a thriving urban metropolis uniquely geared to attract and entertain visitors and residents alike. Robson Street is ranked among the world's 10 best shopping streets, the Canada Place Pier with its five gleaming Teflon sails welcomes thousands of cruise-ship visitors every weekend during the Alaska cruise season, and even the financial district is lined with shops and understreet shopping malls.

The West End   It was occupied for at least 3,000 years by the Coast Salish, a Pacific Northwest native-Indian tribe. The Squamish and Musqueam tribal bands fished the harbor and lived in the old-growth western-cedar temperate rain forest that covered the peninsula. If you look up at the apartment tower next to the Sylvia Hotel on English Bay, you'll see a large tree on the roof. It was planted there to show how tall the original forest was before the West End was created by white settlers. This area was home to Vancouver's upper crust in the late 1800s and early 1900s and is now one of North America's most densely populated neighborhoods. A few Victorian houses remain nestled amid high-rises along its tree-lined streets. The West End's residents include young adults, seniors, and western Canada's largest gay and lesbian population. This area is hospitable, safe, tolerant, livable, and lively. Lined with 50 restaurants as well as coffee bars and cafes, Denman Street is the heart of the neighborhood, which is bordered on its western edge by Stanley Park.

Gastown   This area was Vancouver's first European settlement. Named after a flamboyant riverboat captain ("Gassy Jack") who opened the city's first saloon in the neighborhood, Gastown still has much of the picturesque character of a Barbary Coast port (which is why it's constantly used as a film location). There are still bars along Gastown's brick streets and wide sidewalks, but these days they're surrounded by small shops, art galleries, restaurants, outdoor cafes, and theaters instead of warehouses and shipping offices.

Chinatown   Vancouver is home to North America's third-largest Asian community (only the Chinatowns in San Francisco and New York are bigger). Even though the newest wave of immigrants are well-heeled Hong Kong families who live in nearby Richmond, Vancouver's traditional Chinatown is still a viable and historic cultural center. Worth a visit are its classic Ming Dynasty garden (the first of its kind to be built in North America), new Chinatown Museum, and many restaurants and shops. Business is primarily concentrated along Hastings, Pender, Keefer, and Georgia streets from Carrall to Gore.

Yaletown   Formerly a seedy stretch of warehouses, Yaletown has undergone a remarkable transformation. Without losing the character of its narrow streets and redbrick warehouses, the area now houses art galleries, boutiques, trendy restaurants, a microbrewery, a coffeehouse/pool hall, and loft apartments for architects, designers, and filmmakers. Much like Manhattan's TriBeCa and SoHo, this is a hip district where coffee bars and cutting-edge fashions have completely replaced the old saloons and streetwalkers.

False Creek & Granville Island   Once an industrial wasteland, False Creek has recently become a thriving residential area that encompasses Granville Island, a favorite destination for locals and visitors alike. There's a huge public market, a marina with rental boats of all sizes, a brewery, artists' studios and galleries, small shops, theaters, and restaurants concentrated into a few small blocks right on the water's edge.

Kitsilano   Kitsilano (affectionately known as "Kits") and Point Grey stretch west from Vanier Park at the mouth of False Creek to the University of British Columbia campus. Sandy beaches with names like Jericho, Kitsilano, Point Grey, Spanish Banks, and Wreck edge its coastline, while a mix of heritage houses, smaller apartment buildings, shops, and restaurants completes the makeup of this lively youthful neighborhood. **Greektown** is part of this formerly Haight Ashbury–style district, which has gentrified during the last decade.

Shaughnessy   The mansions between 16th and 41st avenues near Arbutus Street are the main attractions in the city's most elite residential district. These elegant structures proudly stand among lush gardens, golf courses, blossoming trees, and three public Elizabethan hedge mazes.

Richmond   A large island separated from the mainland by the north and south arms of the Fraser River (and directly under Vancouver Airport's landing path), Richmond boasts skyscrapers and sprawling shopping/commercial districts that hide the fact that it's home port for Canada's largest west-coast fishing fleet and contains some of the province's richest farmlands. At the island's southwestern tip, the town of Steveston was a Japanese-settled fishing village during the 19th century and is filled with wonderful seafood restaurants. Vancouver's largest Asian community resides in Richmond, so you'll find a wide range of Chinese and Japanese restaurants, markets, and shops, mainly on or near No. 3 Road.

Grandview-Woodland   This area around Commercial Drive is traditionally known as **Little Italy.** Here you can find the best espresso in town, along with myriad other Italian delicacies.

Punjabi Market   The cultural focal point for Vancouver's large East Indian population is the Punjabi Market on Main Street between 49th and 51st avenues. The local Sikh Temple and school sponsor a number of exciting, colorful parades and festivals, but you don't have to wait for a special occasion to visit; the rich silks, sparkling gold jewelry, and exotic spice shops are tempting year-round.

North Vancouver   Across the Lions Gate Bridge, the Second Narrows Bridge, or the harbor via the SeaBus, North Vancouver is a charming waterfront area with small shops and restaurants. But its real beauty lies in its natural wonders: Grouse Mountain, Capilano River Regional Park, Mount Seymour and the Seymour Demonstration Forest, Boulevard Park, Cates Park, and Deep Cove. Other points of interest are the Capilano and Lynn Canyon suspension bridges, Maplewood Farm, the Park and Tilford Gardens, and Grouse Mountain's Theatre in the Sky.

West Vancouver   Though it didn't have electricity until 1922, West Vancouver is now one of Vancouver's wealthiest and most exclusive neighborhoods, rising up the mountainside beyond the Lions Gate Bridge. It's on the route to Horseshoe Bay and Whistler but is also worth visiting on its own. West Van—as it's commonly called— has few hotels, but there are a number of lovely B&Bs, restaurants, and the Park Royal Mall (Canada's second-largest shopping mall). A seawall promenade extending from Dundareve Park to Ambleside Beach offers strollers unparalleled views; Lighthouse Park farther on is one of the cities best-kept secrets. Far above it, Cypress Park attracts hikers in summer and skiers in winter.

2 Getting Around

Bring your most comfortable shoes, because walking is the best way to discover Vancouver. The downtown district is composed of 2.6 square kilometers (1 sq. mile) of moderate hills. Gastown, Chinatown, Yaletown, False Creek, Granville Island, Sunset Beach, English Bay Beach, and Stanley Park are all within a 30-minute walk of downtown, the West End, and one another. We highly recommend strolling along the city's many beaches, thickly forested parks, and urban corridors.

BY PUBLIC TRANSPORTATION

The **Vancouver Regional Transit System (BC Transit),** 1100–1200 W. 73rd Ave. (☎ 604/521-0400), runs electrically powered buses, the SeaBus catamaran ferries, and the monorail SkyTrain. Named "North America's best public transit system" in 1995 by the American Public Transit Association, it's an ecologically conscious, highly reliable, and inexpensive way to get everywhere in Vancouver, including the ski slopes. Most buses are wheelchair accessible. Regular daily service on the main routes runs from 5am to 2am; less frequent "Owl" service operates on several downtown-suburban routes until 4:20am.

Fares are the same for the bus, SeaBus, and SkyTrain. One-way, all-zone, nonpeak fares are C$1.75 (US$1.25) in off-peak hours and C$2.50 (US$1.80) in rush hours. Free transfers are available on boarding and are good for any direction of travel as well for the SkyTrain and SeaBus; they expire in 90 minutes. DayPasses, good on all public transit, are C$6 (US$4.30) for adults and C$4 (US$2.85) for seniors, students, and children.

Some key **bus routes** are no. 8 (Robson Street), no. 51 (Granville Island), no. 246 (North Vancouver), no. 250 (West Vancouver–Horseshoe Bay), and nos. 4 and 10 (UBC-Exhibition Park via Granville Street downtown). One of the most popular summer-only routes is the hourly no. 52 "Around the Park" service that goes around the entire perimeter of Stanley Park.

The **SkyTrain** is a fully computerized rapid-transit monorail that serves 20 stations in its 35-minute ride from downtown east to the outlying towns of Surrey via Burnaby and New Westminster. Many of the stations are wheelchair accessible.

The SS *Beaver* and SS *Otter* catamaran **SeaBuses** annually serve more than 400,000 passengers on a scenic 12-minute commute between downtown's Waterfront Station and North Vancouver's Lonsdale Quay. It's wheelchair accessible, and cyclists can board with bikes during off-peak hours. On weekdays, the catamarans leave every 15 minutes from 6:15am to 6:30pm, then every 30 minutes to 1am. On weekends, the vessels run about every 30 minutes from 6:15am to 1am.

For more information about **wheelchair-accessible public transportation,** contact BC Transit (☎ **604/521-0400;** Web site: www.bctransit.com) and ask for its brochure *Rider's Guide to Accessible Transit.*

BY TAXI

Taxi fares are reasonable. In the downtown area, most trips are less than C$6 (US$4.30)—not including tip. Taxis are easy to hail on downtown streets and at major hotels. But thanks to satellite positioning systems, if you call for a cab, they can usually have a taxi meet you faster than you can go out and hail one. Call for a pickup from **Black Top & Checker Cabs** (☎ **604/731-1111**), **Yellow Cab** (☎ **604/681-1111**), or **MacLure's** (☎ **604/731-9211**). **AirLimo** (☎ **604/ 273-1331**) and **Executive Limo Service** (☎ **604/929-6000**) both offer flat-rate stretch-limo service starting at C$29 (US$21) per trip to the airport (not per person), plus tax and tip. The drivers accept all major credit cards.

BY BICYCLE

Vancouver is decidedly bicycle-friendly. There are plenty of places to rent a bike along Robson Street and Denman Street near Stanley Park. Bike lanes are designated throughout the city. Paved paths criss-cross through parks and along beaches (see "Outdoor Activities & Spectator Sports," later in this chapter), and routes are constantly being expanded. Helmets are mandatory, and riding on sidewalks is illegal except on designated bike paths.

BC Transit's Cycling BC (☎ 604/737-3034) accommodates cyclists on the SkyTrain and buses by providing "Bike & Ride" lockers at all "Park & Ride" parking lots. The department also dispense loads of information about events, bike touring, and cycle insurance. Many downtown parking lots and garages have bike racks you can use at no charge.

You can take your bike on the SeaBus any time except rush hours at no extra charge. Bicycles aren't allowed in the George Massey Tunnel, but a tunnel-shuttle operates four times daily from mid-May to September to transport you across the Fraser River. From May 1 to Victoria Day (the third weekend of May), the service operates on weekends only.

BY FERRY

Crossing False Creek to Vanier Park or Granville Island by one of the blue miniferries is cheap and fun. The **Aquabus** docks at the foot of Howe Street and takes you to Granville Island's public market, east along False Creek to Science World, and Stamps Landing. The **Granville Island Ferry** docks at Sunset Beach below the Burrard Street Bridge and the Aquatic Centre. It goes to both Vanier Park and Granville Island. Ferries to Granville Island leave every 5 minutes from 7am to 10pm. **Ferries to Vanier Park** leave every 15 minutes from 10am to 8pm. One-way fares for all routes are $1.75 for adults (US$1.25) and C75¢ (US54¢) for seniors and children.

BY CAR

Vancouver's driving laws are similar to those for much of the United States; you may turn right on red after coming to a full stop, seat belts are mandatory, children under 5 must be in a child seat, and motorcyclists must wear helmets. Daytime headlights are mandatory both in and out of the city.

Members of the American Automobile Association (AAA) can get assistance from the **British Columbia Automobile Association (BCAA),** a branch of the Canadian Automobile Association (CAA), at 999 W. Broadway, Vancouver (☎ **604/ 268-5600;** 24-hour emergency road service 604/293-2222).

RENTALS   You can rent a vehicle from the following branches of major car-rental agencies: **Avis,** 757 Hornby St. (☎ 800/879-2847 or 604/606-2847); **Budget,** 450 W. Georgia St. (☎ 800/527-0700, 800/268-8900, or 604/668-7000); **Enterprise,** 585 Smythe St. (☎ 800/736-8222 or 604/688-5500); **Hertz Canada,** 1128 Seymour St. (☎ 800/654-3131, 800/263-0600, or 604/688-2411); **National/ Tilden,** 1130 W. Georgia (☎ 800/387-4747 or 604/685-6111); and **Thrifty,** 1055 W. Georgia St. (☎ 800/367-2277 or 604/606-1666). These firms all have counters and shuttle service at the airport. To rent a recreational vehicle, contact **CC Canada Camper RV Rentals,** 1080 Millcarch St., Richmond (☎ 604/327-3003). At **Exotic Motorcycle & Car Rentals,** 1820 Burrard St. (☎ 604/644-9128; Web site: www.exoticcars.com), you can rent a Ferrari, a Viper, an NSX, a Porsche, a

Hummer, a Mercedes, a Jaguar, a Lotus, or a Corvette. There's even a wide selection of Harley-Davidsons available.

PARKING   Parking is scarce in Vancouver, especially in the West End, where nearly 95% of on-street parking is by permit only. And it's strictly enforced. As a rule, make sure that your hotel has guest parking. All major downtown hotels have guest parking; rates vary from free to C$20 (US$14), and the downtown area has garage parking available. There's public parking at Robson Square (enter at Smythe and Howe streets); the Pacific Centre (Howe and Dunsmuir streets); and The Bay (Richards near Dunsmuir Street). You'll also find parking lots at Thurlow and Georgia streets, Thurlow and Alberni streets, and Robson and Seymour streets.

BY MOPED & MOTORCYCLE

If you have a valid driver's license you can rent a moped at **Metro Scooter Rentals,** 1610 Robson St. (☎ **604/685-0009**) Prices are C$11 (US$8) per hour or C$49 (US$35) per day. If you have a valid motorcycle license, Metro also rents motorcycles for C$25 (US$18) per hour or C$75 (US$54) per day, as does **Alley Cat Rentals,** 1779 Robson St. (☎ **604/684-5117**).

FAST FACTS: Vancouver

American Express   The local branch is at 666 Burrard St. (☎ **604/669-2813**), and is open Monday to Friday from 8:30am to 5:30pm and Saturday from 10am to 4pm.

Currency Exchange   You'll obtain the best exchange rates by using your bank card at an ATM rather than exchanging cash, as there's no surcharge. For cash exchanges, banks offer a better exchange rate than most foreign exchanges. After banking hours, you'll find half a dozen currency exchanges along Robson Street. Avoid paying for purchases with American currency—hotels, restaurants, and shops set their own rates and often attach a surcharge of 5% or more.

Doctors & Dentists   Hotels usually have a doctor and a dentist on call. **Vancouver Medical Clinics,** Bentall Centre, 1055 Dunsmuir St. (☎ **604/683-8138**), is a drop-in clinic open Monday to Friday from 8am to 5pm. **Carepoint Medical Centre,** 1175 Denman St. (☎ **604/681-5338**), another drop-in medical center, is open daily from 9am to 9pm. **Dentists Denta Centre,** Bentall Centre, 1055 Dunsmuir St. (☎ **604/669-6700**), is by appointment only Monday to Thursday from 8am to 5pm.

Drugstores   **Shopper's Drug Mart,** 1125 Davie St. (☎ **604/685-6445**), is open 24 hours. Several **Safeway** supermarkets have late-night pharmacies, including one at the corner of Robson and Denman streets (☎ **604/683-0202**), which is open until midnight.

Embassies & Consulates   The **U.S. Consulate** is at 1095 W. Pender St. (☎ **604/685-4311**). The **British Consulate** is at 1111 Melville St. (☎ **604/683-4421**). The **Australian Consulate** is at 604–999 Canada Place (☎ **604/684-1177**).

Emergencies   Dial ☎ **911** for fire, police, ambulance, or poison control.

Hospitals   **St. Paul's Hospital,** 1081 Burrard St. (☎ **604/682-2344**), is the closest downtown/West End facility. Central Vancouver hospitals are **Vancouver Hospital Health and Sciences Centre,** 855 W. 12th Ave. (☎ **604/875-4111**); and **British Columbia's Children's Hospital,** 4480 Oak St. (☎ **604/875-2345**).

In North Vancouver, there's **Lions Gate Hospital,** 231 E. 15th St. (☎ **604/ 988-3131**).

Hot Lines **Crisis Centre** (☎ 604/872-3311); **Rape Crisis Centre** (☎ 604/ 255-6344); **Rape Relief** (☎ 604/872-8212); **Poison Control Centre** (☎ 604/ 682-5050); **Crime Stoppers** (☎ 604/669-8477); **SPCA animal emergency** (☎ 604/879-7343); **Vancouver Police** (☎ 604/665-3535); **Fire** (☎ 604/ 665-6000); and **Ambulance** (☎ 604/872-5151).

Liquor Laws The legal drinking age in British Columbia is 19. Spirits are sold only in government liquor stores, but you can buy beer and wine from specially licensed, privately owned stores and pubs. Last call at the city's restaurant bars and cocktail lounges is 2am.

Luggage Storage/Lockers Most downtown hotels will gladly hold your luggage before or after your stay. This service is usually free for guests. Lockers are available at the **Pacific Central Station,** 1150 Station St. (☎ **604/669-3050**). You can store your belongings for about C$1.50 (US$1.05) per day.

Newspapers The two local papers are the *Vancouver Sun* (which comes out Monday to Saturday), and the *Province* (which comes out Sunday to Friday). Other newsworthy papers are the *Financial Times of Canada* and the national *Globe and Mail.* The free weekly entertainment paper *Georgia Straight* comes out on Thursday.

Police Dial ☎ **911.** The Vancouver City Police can be reached at ☎ **604/ 665-3321.** The Royal Canadian Mounted Police can be reached at ☎ **604/ 264-3111.**

Post Office The main post office, at West Georgia and Homer streets, is open Monday to Friday from 8am to 5:30pm. You can also buy stamps at stores displaying a POSTAL SERVICES sign, such as London Drugs in the Denman Plaza Centre and City Drugs on Robson Street. These are franchised mini–post offices.

Safety Though Vancouver's violent-crime rates are relatively low, it's best not to let your guard down. Crimes of opportunity, such as the theft of items from unlocked cars, are most common, and property crime rates are higher than in New York or Miami. The areas surrounding the Pacific Central Station, Chinatown, East Hastings, and Gastown are technically skid rows that should be avoided late at night. A lot of transients mill around amid panhandlers and the homeless.

Taxes Hotel rooms are subject to a 10% tax. The provincial sales tax is 7% (it's not applied to food, restaurant meals, and children's clothing), and there's the 7% federal GST. You can receive a GST refund for purchases taken out of Canada. Refund forms are available from hotel concierges, customs offices, and duty-free shops. For specific questions, call the **BC Consumer Taxation Branch** (☎ **604/ 660-4500**).

Time Vancouver is in the Pacific time zone (as are Seattle and San Francisco). Daylight saving time applies here, too, beginning in April and ending in October.

Transit Information The **BC Transit** phone number is ☎ **604/521-0400.** BC Transit's **lost property** information number is ☎ **604/682-7887.**

Weather Call ☎ **604/664-9010** or 604/664-9032 for weather updates; on TV, weather information is available 24 hours on channel 23. Each local ski resort has its own snow-report line.

3 Accommodations

Many new hotels have opened, others have undergone extensive renovations, and good-natured competition has flourished among all the city's lodgings. No matter what your budget, there's no reason to settle for second best. Don't forget to ask about special seasonal, weekend, senior, or package discounts. If you're traveling to Vancouver on business, ask about the hotel's corporate rates. Most of the hotels below offer no-smoking rooms or floors and wheelchair-accessible rooms. Don't be timid about asking for these special accommodations if you want or need them.

Rates don't include the 10% provincial accommodations tax or the 7% goods-and-services tax (GST). Reservations are highly recommended from June to September and during holidays. If you have trouble finding a room, call Tourism Vancouver's hot line **Discover British Columbia** at ☎ **800/663-6000.** The staff can make arrangements for you by consulting their extensive listings, which are updated daily.

If you prefer to stay in a B&B, the **Beachside Bed & Breakfast Registry,** 4208 Evergreen Ave., West Vancouver (☎ **800/563-3311** or 604/922-7773), can assist you. Rates average C$95 to C$200 (US$68 to US$143) for a double and C$125 to C$300 (US$89 to US$214) for a luxury room. In addition, the listings include a few B&Bs.

See the "Downtown Vancouver" map (p.646) to locate most of the hotels in this section.

DOWNTOWN

All downtown hotels are within 5 to 10 minutes' walking distance of shops, restaurants, and attractions. But prices are also somewhat higher here than in other areas. As construction is booming, it's difficult to say (with a few exceptions) that a hotel offering magnificent harbor and mountain views will still do so 9 months later. So if you're looking for a room with a view, be sure to confirm it when you book. Granville Street offers location without the price, but there's a catch: Though it has improved, the area is still reminiscent of what New York's 42nd Street used to be like. The same applies to hotels on East Hastings Street offering rock-bottom low rates; this is Vancouver's skid row, so we don't recommend these hotels.

You can reach the downtown hotels by taking the SkyTrain to the Granville or Burrard stop, a few blocks apart. The Waterfront Station will leave you close to the Pan-Pacific and Waterfront Centre hotels. Get off at Stadium Station for the Georgian Court Hotel, Rosedale on Robson, and the YWCA. The no. 8 bus will take you to the West End hotels, and the no. 4 or 10 bus will get you to hotels near False Creek.

VERY EXPENSIVE
Four Seasons Hotel. 791 W. Georgia St., Vancouver, BC, V6C 2T4. ☎ **800/332-3442** or 604/689-9333. Fax 604/684-4555. 330 rms, 55 suites. A/C MINIBAR TV TEL. C$320–C$445 (US$229–US$318) double; C$495–C$1,020 (US$354–US$729) suite. AE, CB, DC, ER, JCB, MC, V. Parking C$18 (US$13).

This modern 28-story palace sits atop the Pacific Centre mall's 200 retail stores—a particularly appealing location for shoppers. From the street, the hotel is so well hidden that you could walk right past without noticing the enclosed driveway. Once inside, however, you're instantly immersed in understated luxury accented with wood paneling, Oriental accessories, and subdued lighting. The guest rooms aren't large, however, so for more space, try a deluxe room on one of the building's corners; a deluxe "Four Seasons" room, with a partitioned sitting area; or a spacious suite or junior suite. Wheelchair-accessible rooms are available.

Dining: Winston Churchill's country home was the inspiration for the decor and name of the hotel's superb restaurant. However, Chartwell's doesn't offer traditional British cuisine: It serves an eclectic blend of continental, West Coast, and Asian dishes.

Services: Concierge, 24-hour room service, laundry/valet service, twice-daily housekeeping, limo service. Children get cookies and milk in the evening as well as special room-service menus and robes.

Facilities: Indoor/outdoor pool, a weight/exercise room, whirlpool and saunas, sundeck, florist, cigar store.

Hotel Vancouver. 900 W. Georgia St., Vancouver, BC, V6C 2W6. ☎ **800/441-1414** or 604/684-3131. Fax 604/662-1929. 500 rms, 44 suites. A/C MINIBAR TV TEL. From C$215 (US$154) double; from C$375 (US$268) suite. AE, CB, DC, DISC, ER, MC, V. Parking C$17.50 (US$13).

With a $50-million renovation completed by Canadian-Pacific Hotels in 1996, the city's grande dame has been restored beyond her former glory. Designed on a generous scale, the Vancouver has a feeling of luxury and spaciousness. The rooms have marble baths and mahogany furnishings and offer city, harbor, and mountain views. Most have been equipped for business travelers, featuring dedicated fax and modem lines, speaker phones, coffeemakers, and desk supplies. The best rooms are on the Entrée Gold floors, with upgraded furniture and special services, like a private concierge, check-in/out, free continental breakfast and local calls, shoe-shine, and afternoon tea with hors d'oeuvres.

Dining: Serving West Coast cuisine, 900 West is one of Vancouver's hottest new fine-dining restaurants. The casual Griffins serves three meals a day. The Lobby Bar serves a light menu.

Services: Concierge, 24-hour room service, valet/laundry service.

Facilities: Indoor pool; wading pool; Jacuzzi; health club with weight room; sauna; tanning salon; day spa; shops including Vuitton, Bally, and Aquascutum.

Metropolitan Hotel Vancouver. 645 Howe St., Vancouver, BC, V6C 2Y9. ☎ **800/667-2300** or 604/687-1122. Fax 604/643-7267. 197 rms, 18 suites. A/C MINIBAR TV TEL. May–Sept C$365 (US$261) double weekdays, C$225 (US$161) double weekends; Oct–Apr C$285 (US$204) double weekdays, C$165 (US$118) double weekends. Year-round, from C$1,500 (US$1,071) suite. Children stay free in parents' rm; children under 6 eat free in the restaurant when accompanied by a paying adult. Small pets accepted. AE, DC, DISC, ER, JCB, MC, V. Underground valet parking C$18 (US$13).

In 1997, the 18-story Metropolitan underwent a $4-million renovation. It's centrally located between the financial district and the downtown shopping areas, catering to businesspeople on weekdays. All rooms offer stately dark-wood furnishings, queen-size beds, marble baths, fluffy bathrobes, and complimentary in-room coffee and morning paper; most have small balconies. We recommend the studio suites, which are much roomier and only slightly more expensive. Each business-class room and suite (C$30/US$21 extra) has a fax machine, printer, modem hookup, cordless speaker phone, power strip, and other home-office amenities. There are nine no-smoking floors.

Dining/Entertainment: Diva at the Met is one of Vancouver's hottest new restaurants, serving innovative Pacific Northwest cuisine every night to 1am; the bar features excellent martinis.

Services: Concierge, 24-hour room service, valet, limo service in hotel's Jaguar.

Facilities: Lap pool, Jacuzzi, men's steam room, squash and racquetball courts, exercise room, saunas, sundeck.

Pan-Pacific Hotel Vancouver. 300–999 Canada Place, Vancouver, BC, V6C 3B5. ☎ **800/ 937-1515** or 604/662-8111. Fax 604/662-3815. 467 rms, 39 suites. A/C MINIBAR TV TEL. May–Nov C$410–C$460 (US$293–US$329) double; C$525–C$900 (US$375–US$643) suite. Dec–Apr C$350–C$400 (US$250–US$287) double; C$480–C$700 (US$343–US$500) suite. AE, DC, ER, JCB, MC, V. Valet parking C$19.50 (US$15).

Apart from Vancouver's natural surroundings, the city's most distinctive landmark is Canada Place, with its five gleaming-white Teflon sails. The facility houses the Vancouver Trade and Convention Centre and the Alaskan cruise-ship terminal. Atop this busy pier-complex is a spectacular 23-story hotel. (If you're taking an Alaskan cruise, this is the closest accommodation.) All the guest rooms are spacious and comfortably furnished. Ask for a harborside room so that you can enjoy the view.

Dining: Whether you stay here or not, The Five Sails restaurant is worth a visit; it's one of the city's best (see "Dining," later in this chapter, for a review). The lounge has a full menu, huge picture windows, and a fountain that flows from outside into an ornate channel running through the lobby.

Services: Concierge, 24-hour room service, valet.

Facilities: Outstanding health club (extra C$15/US$11), outdoor pool and terrace overlooking the cruise ships.

✪ **Waterfront Centre Hotel.** 900 Canada Place Way, Vancouver, BC, V6C 3L5. ☎ **800/ 828-7447** or 604/691-1991. Fax 604/691-1999. 489 rms, 29 suites. A/C MINIBAR TV TEL. C$360–C$460 (US$257–US$329) double; C$375–C$1,700 (US$268–US$1,214) suite. AE, CB, DC, ER, MC, V. Parking C$15.70 (US$11).

This 23-story Canadian-Pacific Hotel takes great advantage of its location: About 70% of the rooms have spectacular harbor and mountain views through the reflective-blue glass windows. Its other plus is that there's a concourse linking the hotel to the rest of Waterfront Centre, Canada Place, and the Alaska cruise-ship terminal. Like the Pan-Pacific across the drive, the Waterfront Centre is an excellent choice if you're taking an Alaskan cruise. The rooms are large, with blond wood furnishings, original art, and spacious marble baths. Wheelchair-accessible rooms are available. Showing true concern for the environment, this hotel recycles and consciously reduces its environmental impact by using biodegradable products. And it accomplishes that without compromising on service.

Dining/Entertainment: The Heron Lounge/dining room just off the lobby offers Mediterranean cuisine from an open kitchen. Dishes are prepared with herbs from the hotel's own organic garden. It serves light meals and snacks, as well as breakfast, lunch, and dinner. The lounge has nightly piano entertainment and has seating on the outdoor terrace during summer.

Services: Concierge, 24-hour room service, valet.

Facilities: Full-service health club, heated outdoor pool.

EXPENSIVE

Georgian Court Hotel. 773 Beatty St., Vancouver, BC, V6B 2M4. ☎ **800/663-1155** or 604/ 682-5555. Fax 604/682-8830. 160 rms, 20 suites. A/C MINIBAR TV TEL. May 1–Nov 15 C$260– C$460 (US$186–US$329) double; Nov 16–Apr 30 C$195–C$460 (US$139–US$329) double. AE, DC, ER, MC, V. Parking C$7 (US$5).

This 14-story modern brick hotel, across from BC Place Stadium and near General Motors Place Stadium, is ideal for sports fans and trade-show attendees. The guest rooms are large and clean, the decor dark and masculine; some units are wheelchair accessible. The best views are from the front rooms, dominated by BC Place Stadium's white dome and distant views of False Creek and City Hall.

> ### ⊕ Family-Friendly Hotels
>
> **Four Seasons Hotel** *(see p. 627)*   The staff here gives your kids cookies and milk in the evening, as well as their own special room-service menus and robes.
>
> **Westin Bayshore** *(see p. 631)*   Its location at Coal Harbour marina makes it a great family hotel. From here, your kids can walk to Stanley Park, the Vancouver Aquarium, Nature House, and other attractions without ever crossing a street.
>
> **Quality Hotel Downtown/The Inn at False Creek** *(see p. 631)*   The family suites here are spacious and well designed. There's an enclosed balcony area in some of the upper-floor suites where your kids can play without leaving the suite. The full-kitchen facilities, casual restaurant, and off-season Adventure Passport also make this an excellent deal.
>
> **Rosellen Suites** *(see p. 632)*   The full-apartment accommodations are the ideal places to stay if you're looking for a home away from home. Their location—a block away from Stanley Park, the beaches, and Denman Street—makes it easy to do grocery shopping as well as to play.

Dining/Entertainment: The William Tell Restaurant serves classic Swiss dishes such as veal medaillons in a rich mushroom cream sauce or Wiener schnitzel Holstein prepared by 1995 Restaurateur of the Year, Erwin Doebeli. If you don't have tickets to a local game, you can always catch the action in Rigney's Bar & Grill, which was named for a former BC Lions football player. It's good, casual, cheap, and packed when there's a game on TV.

Facilities: Small exercise room with weights, Lifecycle, Stairmaster, whirlpool, sauna, indoor pool.

Rosedale on Robson Suite Hotel. 838 Hamilton (at Robson St.), Vancouver, BC, V6B 5W4. ☎ **800/661-8870** or 604/689-8033. 275 studio, 1-bedrm, and 2-bedrm suites with kitchens. A/C MINIBAR TV TEL. May–Oct C$205–C$305 (US$146–US$218) double; Nov–Apr C$135–C$225 (US$96–US$161) double. AE, DC, ER, MC, V. Parking C$8 (US$6).

You arrive at this hotel via a covered driveway and are welcomed into the grand marble lobby. You'll find Library Square, the theaters, and the stadiums all within a few blocks. The suites feature separate living rooms (except for the 12 studios), two TVs, and full kitchenettes. Dishes and cooking utensils are available on request. The rooms aren't huge, but big bay windows and scaled-down furnishings provide a feeling of spaciousness. Upper-floor suites have furnished terraces and great city views. Wheelchair-accessible rooms are available.

Dining: Rosie's Restaurant is Vancouver's only authentic New York–style deli/restaurant.

Services: Concierge, room service, computer/fax connections.

Facilities: Indoor pool, Jacuzzi, sauna, weight/exercise room, gift shop.

✪ Wedgewood Hotel. 845 Hornby St., Vancouver, BC, V6Z 1V1. ☎ **800/663-0666** or 604/689-7777. Fax 604/688-3074. 51 rms, 38 suites. A/C MINIBAR TV TEL. C$200–C$320 (US$143–US$229) double; C$420 (US$300) suite; C$520 (US$371) penthouse. AE, CB, DC, ER, JCB, MC, V. Underground valet parking C$10 (US$7).

The eclectic decor here blends French provincial, Italianate, and Edwardian styles. On weekdays, the hotel is frequented by a corporate crowd; on weekends, it becomes a romantic getaway. All the rooms have landscaped balconies overlooking Robson Square, and you'll be greeted with a box of chocolates in your room.

Dining/Entertainment: Bacchus Ristorante serves outstanding northern Italian cuisine and features live jazz nightly in the adjoining Bacchus Lounge.

Services: 24-hour room service, laundry service, nightly turndown with homemade cookies and bottled water, twice-daily housekeeping.

Facilities: Hairstylist.

MODERATE

Days Inn Downtown. 921 W. Pender St., Vancouver, BC, V6C 1M2. ☎ **800/329-7466** or 604/681-4335. Fax 604/681-7808. 80 rms, 5 suites. TV TEL. May–Oct C$145–C$175 (US$104–US$125) double; C$190 (US$136) suite. Nov–Apr C$95–C$125 (US$68–US$89) double; C$155 (US$111) suite. AE, DC, DISC, ER, JCB, MC, V. Valet parking C$8 (US$6).

The only moderately priced hotel in the downtown business center, this well-maintained seven-story property is more than 70 years old. There's no room service, no view, and only basic amenities. The guest rooms are slightly cramped but are quiet and clean. Downstairs are a restaurant and lounge.

Quality Hotel Downtown/The Inn at False Creek. 1335 Howe St. (at Davie St.), Vancouver, BC, V6Z 1R7. ☎ **800/663-8474** or 604/682-0229. Fax 604/662-7566. 157 rms, 20 suites. A/C TV TEL. May 1–Oct 12 C$150 (US$107) double; C$150–C$190 (US$107–US$136) suite. Oct 13–Apr 30 C$99 (US$71) double; C$99–C$119 (US$71–US$85) suite. AE, CB, DC, ER, MC, V. Parking C$5 (US$4).

Extensively renovated in 1997, this seven-story hotel is ideal for families. The decor blends a comfortable Southwestern style with Mexican art, pottery, and rugs. The one-bedroom suites have full kitchens. The rooms on the back side are preferable because the hotel lies beside the Granville Bridge on-ramp. The traffic noise is minimized in the front of the building, however, thanks to double-pane windows and dark-out curtains. Rooms for the hearing-impaired are equipped with strobe-light fire alarms. Some suites have separate glassed-in play areas for children, and the staff keeps a supply of board games and puzzles behind the front desk.

Dining/Entertainment: The Creekside Café serves well-prepared basic fare at reasonable prices. The Sports Lounge has a relaxed atmosphere, friendly service, and a full bar.

Services: Room service, laundry/valet service.

Facilities: Outdoor pool, complimentary fitness facilities a block away.

INEXPENSIVE

✪ **Hotel at the YWCA.** 733 Beatty St., Vancouver, BC, V6B 2M4. ☎ **800/663-1424** or 604/895-5830. Fax 604/681-2550. 155 rms (some with bath). A/C TEL. C$65–C$125 (US$46–US$89) double. Weekly, monthly, group, and off-season discounts available. MC, V. Parking C$5 (US$4).

This attractive 12-story hotel is next to the Georgian Court. It's an excellent choice for both male and female travelers or families with limited budgets. The rooms are simply furnished; some have TVs but all have minirefrigerators. While there are no restaurants in the building, there are quite a few reasonably priced ones nearby, and three communal kitchens are open to guests. (There are a number of small grocery stores nearby, and a Save-On Foods Supermarket is a 10-minute walk west on Davie Street.) There are also three TV lounges, a coin laundry, and free access to the nearby coed YWCA Fitness Centre.

THE WEST END & ENGLISH BAY
VERY EXPENSIVE

Westin Bayshore. 1601 W. Georgia St., Vancouver, BC, V6G 2V4. ☎ **800/228-3000** or 604/682-3377. Fax 604/687-3102. 484 rms, 33 suites. A/C MINIBAR TV TEL. Mid-Apr to Oct C$295 (US$211) double; C$450–C$600 (US$312–US$429) suite. Nov to mid-Apr C$224 (US$160) double; C$370–C$420 (US$264–US$300) suite. Children under 19 stay free in parents' rm. AE, CB, DC, ER, MC, V. Parking C$7 (US$5).

Perched on the water's edge in Coal Harbour at Stanley Park's eastern entrance, the Bayshore has a resort atmosphere, yet it's almost right downtown. The rooms in the original building are comfortable and well furnished; those in the newly renovated 20-story tower are larger and have balconies and bigger windows. Both towers offer unobstructed views of sailboats and luxury yachts in the harbor (many for charter through the hotel), with the park and the mountains as a backdrop. Guest Office rooms include fax/copier/printer, coffeemaker, speakerphone, and other business amenities. Two floors are wheelchair accessible.

Dining/Entertainment: Trader Vic's bar, with its South Seas decor, offers Chinese and continental cuisine with seafood specialties. The Garden restaurant is open for three meals daily as well as Sunday brunch, while the Garden lounge serves lunch by day and entertains with light jazz by night.

Services: Concierge, room service, laundry/valet service, boat charters, Westin Kids Club, bicycle and Hertz-car rental, free shuttle service downtown.

Facilities: Outdoor pool surrounded by sundeck, indoor pool, complete health club.

EXPENSIVE

Best Western Listel O'Doul's Hotel. 1300 Robson St., Vancouver, BC, V6E 1C5. ☎ **800/663-5491** or 604/684-8461. Fax 604/684-8326. 119 rms, 11 suites. A/C MINIBAR TV TEL. May–Sept C$200–C$250 (US$143–US$179) double; C$275–C$350 (US$196–US$250) suite. Oct–Apr C$135–C$165 (US$96–US$118) double; C$150–C$250 (US$107–US$179) suite. AE, DC, DISC, ER, JCB, MC, V. Parking C$10 (US$7).

Beyond the rather sparse lobby, O'Doul's has tastefully decorated and recently renovated rooms including two gallery floors with upgraded amenities, as well as works by local artists in the rooms and the halls. The upper-floor rooms facing Robson Street are worth the price because these are the only ones that have views. (The others face the alley and nearby apartment buildings.) Soundproof windows eliminate weekend traffic noise.

Dining: With tables on the sidewalk and picture windows all around, O'Doul's restaurant is a good spot for people-watching. Breakfast, lunch, and dinner basics are served all day, so whether you have a craving for eggs Benedict, penne with pesto, or a good burger, you won't be disappointed.

Services: Concierge, 24-hour room service, valet/laundry service.

Facilities: Indoor pool, exercise room.

✪ **Rosellen Suites.** 102–2030 Barclay St., Vancouver, BC, V6G 1L5. ☎ **604/689-4807.** Fax 603/684-3327. 30 apts. A/C TV TEL. High season C$175 (US$130) 1-bedrm apt; C$200–C$280 (US$143–US$200) 2-bedrm apt; C$375 (US$268) penthouse. Low season C$110 (US$79) 1-bedrm apt; C$140–C$200 (US$100–US$143) 2-bedrm apt; C$300 (US$214) penthouse. Minimum 3-night stay. Extra person C$15 (US$11). AE, DC, ER, MC, V. Free but limited parking in the rear of the building.

On a quiet residential street a few hundred yards from Stanley Park and 2 blocks from lots of restaurants, this unpretentious low-rise building was converted into an apartment-hotel in the 1960s. There's no lobby. The manager's office is open only from 9am to 5pm, but each guest receives a front-door key, a personal phone number, and voice mail. Modern and extremely comfortable, each suite features a spacious living room, separate dining area, and full kitchen. It's just like having your own corporate apartment. The autographed movie-star photos in the manager's office give you an idea of the luminaries who've stayed here. The penthouse is named after Katharine Hepburn, as this is her favorite hotel in Vancouver.

MODERATE

✪ Pacific Palisades Hotel. 1277 Robson St., Vancouver, BC, V6E 1C4. ☎ **800/663-1815** or 604/688-0461. Fax 604/688-4374. Web site: www.shangri-la.com. 233 suites. A/C MINIBAR TEL. Mid-Apr to Oct C$195–C$220 (US$139–US$157) suite; Nov to mid-Apr C$149–C$169 (US$106–US$121) suite. Year-round, from C$500 (US$357) penthouse. Full kitchen C$10 (US$7) extra. AE, CB, DC, ER, MC, V. Parking C$12 (US$9).

The Pacific Palisades is a luxury hotel in every respect, save price. It was converted from two apartment towers at the crest of Robson Street in 1991. With outstanding service, the hotel is popular with visiting film and TV production companies who demand sterling service, privacy, spacious accommodations, and more-than-great value. The suites are divided into studio, executive, and penthouse apartments; some have balconies. All rooms are spacious and have equipped kitchenettes. Extended-stay lodgings are available in a new tower next door.

Dining: The Monterey Grill is an excellent street-side restaurant featuring Pacific Northwest cuisine and outdoor seating. Monthly astrology dinners and other special events take place through the year.

Service: Concierge, 24-hour room service, valet/laundry service.

Facilities: Large fitness center with health bar, sauna, indoor pool, tanning room, and bicycle rental.

West End Guest House. 1362 Haro St., Vancouver, BC, V6E 1G2. ☎ **604/681-2889.** Fax 604/688-8812. 7 rms. TV TEL. C$145–C$205 (US$104–US$146) double. AE, DISC, MC, V. Rates include full breakfast. Free off-street parking.

On a quiet street off Barclay Heritage Square a block from Robson Street, this lavender Victorian heritage house exudes charm. There's an abundance of antiques and framed photographs in the front parlor as well as in the guest rooms. Each room comes with a teddy bear. Iced tea is served in the afternoon on a south-facing second-floor sundeck, and fresh-baked cookies or brownies appear at turndown time. An outstanding full breakfast is served in the salon, sherry is complimentary at teatime, and the pantry is stocked with tea and snacks to which you can help yourself. There are also bicycles (free for guest use) and fax service, but no smoking.

INEXPENSIVE

Sylvia Hotel. 1154 Gilford St., Vancouver, BC, V6G 2P6. ☎ **604/681-9321.** Fax 604/682-3551. 100 rms, 18 suites. TV TEL. C$75–C$150 (US$54–US$107) double; C$150 (US$107) suite. Pets accepted. AE, DC, MC, V. Parking C$5 (US$4).

Built in 1912, the Sylvia is set on English Bay overlooking the beach. It's one of Vancouver's oldest hotels (before World War II, it was the tallest building in western Canada), yet it has become deservedly trendy in recent years. The lobby sets the tone: It's small, relaxing, and dark, with red carpets, ivory drapes, and overstuffed chairs. The same atmosphere prevails in an adjoining restaurant and cocktail lounge (Vancouver's first when it opened in 1954). The restaurant serves three meals daily, specializing in meat and seafood with a continental touch. In the rooms, the furnishings are appropriately mismatched. The suites have full kitchens and are large enough for families.

CENTRAL VANCOUVER

EXPENSIVE

Granville Island Hotel. 1253 Johnston St., Vancouver, BC, V6H 3R9. ☎ **800/663-1840** or 604/683-7373. Fax 604/683-3061. 54 rms. A/C TV TEL. C$209 (US$149) double. Off-season discounts available. AE, DC, ER, MC, V. Parking C$7 (US$5).

At the east end of Granville Island surrounded by artists' studios and galleries on one side and pleasure boats on the other, this small modern hotel enjoys a unique location. It was completely renovated by new owners in 1997. The lobby is cozy and attractive with dark wood paneling and stone floors. The guest rooms feature close-up views of False Creek, skylights, marble floors, and oversize tubs; some have balconies. Downtown and English Bay are a 2-minute, C$1.75 (US$1.25) ferry ride away.

Dining: The Creek microbrewery restaurant/bar has a harborside patio and a large humidor filled with Cuban and Dominican cigars.

Facilities: Rooftop health club with fitness equipment, sauna, Jacuzzi. The staff will happily arrange boat charters in the marina.

Kenya Court Guest House. 2230 Cornwall Ave., Vancouver, BC, V6K 1B5. ☎ 604/738-7085. 4 suites. TV TEL. C$115–C$140 (US$82–US$100) suite. Rates include full breakfast. No credit cards. Street parking.

Every room in this three-story heritage apartment building at Kitsilano Beach has an unobstructed waterfront view of Vanier Park, English Bay, downtown Vancouver, and the Coast Mountains. Its location makes it an ideal launching pad for strolls around Granville Island, Vanier Park, the Maritime Museum, and other central Vancouver sights. There's also a nearby outdoor pool, tennis courts, and jogging trails. All the rooms are large and tastefully furnished. A full breakfast (including eggs and bacon) is served in a glass solarium with a spectacular view of English Bay. There's no smoking.

NORTH VANCOUVER & WEST VANCOUVER
VERY EXPENSIVE
Lonsdale Quay Hotel. 123 Carrie Cates Ct., North Vancouver, BC, V6M 3K7. ☎ 800/836-6111 or 604/986-6111. 70 rms. A/C MINIBAR TV TEL. C$250 (US$179) double. Substantial off-season discounts available. Extra person C$20 (US$14). AE, DC, DISC, ER, JCB, MC, V. Parking C$6 (US$4.30) weekdays, free on weekends. SeaBus: Lonsdale Quay.

This hotel is directly above the Lonsdale Quay Market at the SeaBus terminal. With fabulous views of the harbor, waterfront, and Vancouver skyline, it's only 20 minutes by bus from Grouse Mountain Ski Resort and Capilano Regional Park. An escalator from the market (filled with fresh produce, seafood, restaurants, and shops) leads to the front desk on the third floor. The rooms, in soft pastels, are reasonably large. Some have balconies, and most overlook the harbor. The hotel has a whirlpool, a weight/exercise room, and a restaurant and lounge.

MODERATE
✪ **Beachside Bed & Breakfast.** 4208 Evergreen Ave., West Vancouver, BC, V7V 1H1. ☎ 800/563-3311 or 604/922-7773. 3 rms. C$110–C$195 (US$79–US$139) double. Extra person C$30 (US$21). Rates include full breakfast. MC, V. Free parking. Bus: 250.

Bouquets of fresh flowers in every room are a signature touch at this beautiful Spanish-style home at the end of a quiet cul-de-sac. Its all-glass southern exposure affords a panoramic view of Vancouver. The beach is just steps from the door. You can watch the waves from the patio or outdoor Jacuzzi or spend the afternoon fishing and sailing. Hosts Gordon and Joan Gibb are knowledgeable about local history and will gladly direct you to Stanley Park, hiking, skiing, and other area highlights, as Gordon is also a registered tour guide.

INEXPENSIVE
Mountainside Manor. 5909 Nancy Greene Way, North Vancouver, BC, V7R 4W6. ☎ 604/990-9772. Fax 604/985-8484. 4 rms. TV. May–Oct C$85–C$135 (US$61–US$96) double; Nov–Apr C$75–C$120 (US$54–US$86) double. DC, MC, V. Rates include breakfast. Bus: 236.

Nestled on a peaceful tree-covered ridge adjacent to the Capilano Suspension Bridge, Grouse Mountain tram, and Baden-Powell Trail, this contemporary B&B offers a spectacular view of Vancouver and the Burrard Inlet from elegantly furnished king-size, queen-size, or twin-bedded rooms; all have coffeemakers, and one also has a Jacuzzi. There's a relaxing mountain view from the outdoor hot tub, plus an outdoor smoking area.

4 Dining

It would be impossible to give a complete listing of Vancouver's restaurants because there are more than 2,000 of them. According to a national survey, Vancouverites dine out more than residents of any other Canadian city. There's a good reason. Outstanding meals are available in all price ranges and in a wide selection of ethnic cuisines, including Chinese, Japanese, Greek, French, Italian, Spanish, Mongolian, Ethiopian, Vietnamese, and even Canadian. And main-course prices in Vancouver are arguably lower than those in most sophisticated urban areas.

The buzz words here are "Pacific Northwest" and "West Coast" cuisine. Justifiable pride in local produce, game, and seafood is combined with innovation and creativity, leading to such reduced-fat Pacific Northwest dishes as The Fish House's grilled tuna steak in green-peppercorn sauce, served with buttermilk mashed potatoes and garden-fresh asparagus. More and more restaurants are shifting to seasonal—even monthly—menus to give their chefs greater freedom. Blending fresh ingredients with a fusion of Asian and Western influences, West Coast cuisine is popular among Vancouver's chefs. While there are as many variations on this as there are fine chefs, the focus on freshness, flavor, local ingredients, and enjoyment makes this cuisine unique and unparalleled.

We've categorized our restaurant recommendations first by geographical area and then by price category. If you're staying downtown, you can walk to the West End and English Bay, Gastown, or Chinatown. Remember that there's no provincial tax on restaurant meals in British Columbia—just the 7% federal goods-and-services tax.

See the "Downtown Vancouver" map (p. 646) to locate most of the restaurants in this section.

DOWNTOWN
VERY EXPENSIVE

✪ **C.** 1600 Howe St. ☎ **604/681-1164.** Reservations recommended. Main courses C$15–C$32 (US$11–US$23). AE, DC, ER, JCB, MC, V. Daily 11:30am–11pm. SkyTrain: Burrard. SEAFOOD.

For the view alone, C is worth a visit. It sits on the water's edge facing Granville Island, so a steady stream of sailboats, kayaks, and other watercraft pass by in False Creek, and joggers, in-line skaters, cyclists, and strollers make their way along the seawall crossing in front of C's patio. The menu—developed by chef Soren Fakstop, who worked in Japan and China for years—is inventive and contemporary. The taster's box (C$19/US$14) offers grilled Monterey Bay squid, halibut sashimi, Ahi tuna tartare, and crisp soft-shelled crab. It's a great appetizer to share. The raw bar includes an impressive international selection of caviars served with blinis, red onion, and crème fraîche. Entrees show similar flair: pan-seared Wrangell Sound scallops in a five-spice crust, grilled beluga sturgeon with pressed-caviar rösti, and grilled Nova Scotia lobster with roasted-pepper flan. Lunch and brunch feature a dim-sum–style menu, giving you the freedom to sample many dishes at one sitting.

The Five Sails. In the Pan-Pacific Hotel, 999 Canada Place. ☎ **604/891-2892.** Reservations recommended. Main courses C$21–C$38 (US$15–US$27); table d'hôte C$32–C$60 (US$23–US$43). AE, DC, ER, JCB, MC, V. Sun–Fri 6–10pm, Sat 6–11pm. SkyTrain: Burrard. WEST COAST/PACIFIC RIM.

Request a table near the window when you make reservations; the view of the Coal Harbour, the Lions Gate, and the North Shore Mountains is spectacular. And so is the food. The decor is simple: white linens, candlelight, and flowers. Despite the restaurant's elegance, jackets are merely recommended and ties are optional. The dishes are an eclectic mix of Thai, Mongolian, Japanese, Vietnamese, and nouvelle influences: seared sea bass in a sweet-and-sour citrus reduction, tender grilled salmon, and steamed Atlantic mussels. The Black Angus beef fillet was as delicious as the more adventurous dishes. If you're eating late, be prepared for Stanley Park's 9pm cannon, which points toward the restaurant.

Hy's Encore. 637 Hornby St. ☎ **604/683-7671.** Reservations recommended. Main courses C$17–C$29 (US$12–US$21). AE, DC, ER, JCB, MC, V. Mon–Fri 11am–11pm, Sat–Sun 5:30–10:30pm. SkyTrain: Burrard. STEAK.

For over 35 years, Hy's has been Vancouver's premier steak house. Having weathered the lean-cuisine fads of the 1970s and 1980s, Hy's (with oak paneling, white linens, leather chairs, lamplight, and oil paintings) has come back into vogue. The list of celebrities who've dined here is impressive—from Marlene Dietrich to Rudolf Nureyev to Sonny and Cher to John Travolta to Wayne Gretzky—but not as impressive as the steaks, which are aged, marinated, and charbroiled to perfection. The selection includes filet mignon, steak au poivre, New York steak, and French-Canadian rib steak. For less carnivorous diners, there's a selection of seafood dishes as well as herb-stuffed chicken. The place is equally popular with financial-district power brokers and Japanese visitors, so book ahead.

EXPENSIVE

Il Giardino di Umberto. 1382 Hornby St. ☎ **604/669-2422.** Web site: www.umberto.com. Reservations required. Main courses C$13.95–C$32.50 (US$10–US$23). AE, DC, ER, MC, V. Mon–Fri noon–2:30pm; daily 5:30–11pm. Bus: 22 or 401. TUSCAN.

Restaurant magnate Umberto Menghi's empire in Vancouver includes Umberto's, Umberto al Porto, and Splendido. But Il Giardino has created its own niche. Decorated in burnt sienna with exposed wood beams, this restaurant has the ambiance of a seaside villa, with an enclosed garden terrace for alfresco dining and a truly Tuscan menu emphasizing pasta and game. Entrees include osso-bucco Milanese with saffron risotto, tortellini with portobellos in truffle oil, roasted reindeer loin with port-peppercorn sauce, and pheasant breast stuffed with wild mushrooms. After sampling the food you may wish to enroll in Umberto's cooking school in Tuscany.

A Kettle of Fish. 900 Pacific St. ☎ **604/682-6853.** Web site: www.andersonsrestaurants.com/kettle.html. Reservations recommended. Main courses C$14.95–C$31.95 (US$11–US$23). AE, DC, MC, V. Mon–Fri 11:30am–2pm; daily 5:30–9:30pm. Bus: 22, 401, 403, or 406. PACIFIC NORTHWEST/SEAFOOD.

Check the fresh sheet to find the best of the day's catch, then do as the sign at the entry says, "Eat Lotsa Fish." The dishes—including grilled mahimahi, Cajun-spiced BC spotted prawns, sea scallops sautéed with star fruit—are inventive and flavorful. And barbecued seafood is a house specialty. The light airy restaurant occupies the main floor of a renovated turn-of-the-century building. Try the combo dinner on your first visit; it's a great sampler.

🤸 Family-Friendly Restaurants

Romano's Macaroni Grill at the Mansion *(see p. 640)*   They draw families with an extensive children's menu and a friendly staff that'll even let your kids wander up the inviting staircase to explore the upper rooms.

Brothers Restaurant *(see p. 643)*   Here your kids get balloons along with their own menu.

Planet Hollywood *(see p. 638)*   Even though the burgers, salads, and Elvis's peanut-butter–and-banana sandwiches are expensive, the movie memorabilia from recent blockbusters, a space-age cool, and a great merchandise shop will keep your kids entertained.

Mark's Steak & Tap House *(see p. 642)*   Crayons on every paper-covered table and a friendly staff are coupled with excellent burgers and fries, pizza, pasta, and steaks.

✪ **Lola's.** 432 Richards St., at the Century House. ☎ **604/684-5652.** Reservations recommended. Main courses C$19–C$25 (US$14–US$18). AE, MC, V. Daily 11:30am–2pm and 5pm–1am. Bus: 8. INTERNATIONAL.

In a restored 1911 stone building a block southwest of Gastown, with Victorian chandeliers suspended from 20-foot vaulted ceilings painted midnight blue and trimmed with gold leaf, Lola's is gorgeous. Dark wood, deep-purple silk, and fresh flowers are reflected in the beveled-glass mirror that stretches up to the ceiling behind the marble-topped bar.

Dining here is an experience. The cocktail list is divided between martinis and champagne cocktails. Perhaps start with the tender roasted sea scallops with squash gnocchi, then follow with the grilled beef fillet with morels and roasted root vegetables in a Madeira gremolata or the bacon-wrapped sea bass with fennel. The desserts—from crème brûlée and tiramisu to chocolate saba cake—are fabulous. The terminally hip staff are surprisingly friendly.

MODERATE

Alfredo's. 1100 Melville St. ☎ **604/681-3330.** Reservations recommended. AE, DC, ER, MC, V. Main courses C$6.95–C$21.95 (US$5–US$16). Mon–Fri 11am–3pm; Mon–Sat 4:30–10pm. SkyTrain: Burrard. ITALIAN.

Nearly 5 years old and tucked away in the Plaza of Dreams, this is still one of downtown's best-kept secrets. With Rita "the Cook" presiding, Alfredo's is filled with businesspeople from the financial district at lunch (at C$9.95/US$7, the lunch specials include some fabulous pasta creations). In the evenings the mood is more romantic, especially on Friday and Saturday when there's live jazz. The menu is distinctly southern Italian, featuring antipasti, insalate, focaccia sandwiches, and everything from linguini bolognese and fettuccine primavera to "cannelloni orgasmic." The vitello marsala (veal with wild mushrooms and a hint of marsala wine) is absolutely delicious.

✪ **Joe Fortes Seafood House.** 777 Thurlow St. ☎ **604/669-1940.** Reservations recommended. Main courses C$15.95–C$23.95 (US$11–US$17). AE, DC, DISC, ER, MC, V. Sun–Thurs 11:30am–11pm; Fri–Sat 11:30am–midnight. Bus: 8. SEAFOOD.

Named after the burly Caribbean seaman who became English Bay's first lifeguard and a popular local hero, this cavernous dark-wood restaurant with an immensely popular bar is always filled with Vancouver's young and successful. The decor and atmosphere are reminiscent of a New York oyster bar, though the spacious roof garden is pure Vancouver. Pan-roasted oysters are a staple on the menu, which is supplemented by a sheet listing half a dozen varieties of oysters and twice as many daily varieties of fish. Try the gold medal–winning dark- and white-chocolate mousse cake.

Planet Hollywood. 969 Robson St. ☎ **604/688-7827.** Reservations for large parties. Main courses C$9–C$18 (US$6–US$13). AE, DC, MC, V. Daily 11am–1am. Bus: 8. AMERICAN.

If you're looking for a fabulous meal, eat elsewhere. People don't line up in front for the food, featuring expensive burgers, salads, and Elvis's peanut-butter–and-banana sandwich. This neo-kitsch theme place has all the requisite memorabilia: Sean's Connery's *Highlander* samurai sword, the robot body suit worn by Sylvester Stallone in *Judge Dredd*, Mike Myers's *Wayne's World* baseball cap, one of Mel Gibson's costumes from *Hamlet*, Alice's uniform from *The Brady Bunch*, and the drums from *The Flintstones*. The interior is space-age cool, and the merchandise shop is the best you'll find in any Vancouver restaurant.

Yaletown Brewing Company. 1110 Hamilton St. ☎ **604/681-2739.** Reservations recommended. Main courses C$9–C$15 (US$6–US$11). AE, MC, V. Sun–Wed 11:30am–midnight, Thurs–Sat 11:30am–1am. Bus: 8. WEST COAST.

In a converted warehouse with exposed-brick walls, wood floors, oak furniture, and a complete brewery in the back, the Yaletown Brewing Company attracts a wide range of customers. Models, architects, and designers from the neighborhood, sports fans and professional athletes from nearby BC Place Stadium and General Motors Place Stadium, and visitors from around the world flock here. The pizza toppings range from classic to whimsical. The hearty entrees, like goat-cheese ravioli, grilled cumin-scented salmon fillet, and baby-back ribs, are prepared with surprising delicacy and created to accompany their microbrews. Brewmaster Ian Hill oversees a range of brews, including a light lager, two light ales, a robust red bitter, a truly creamy stout, and a nut brown ale. We've sampled the wares of many microbreweries; Yaletown ranks among the best. The desserts are quite good, too.

INEXPENSIVE

The Goulash House. 1065 Granville St. ☎ **604/688-0206.** Main courses C$6.75–C$9.95 (US$5–US$7). MC, V. Mon–Fri 11:30am–8:30pm, Sat–Sun 1–8:30pm. Bus: 2, 4, 6, or 10. HUNGARIAN.

The first thing we noticed was that the interior was spotless: a rare find among Granville Street restaurants. The menu (promising goulash) and the green-and-white–checked tablecloths beckoned. We weren't disappointed. Hungarian food was never haute cuisine, but it is comfort food at its finest—from the soup to the cabbage rolls to the spaetzle (home-made noodles) and the goulash itself, we had a great meal. However, we were a little dismayed by their Reuben sandwich, served with mustard instead of Thousand Island dressing. The dessert crêpes were a remarkably light counterpoint to the heavy entrees.

Las Tapas. 760 Cambie St. ☎ **604/669-1624.** Main courses C$3.95–C$13.95 (US$3–US$10). MC, V. Mon–Fri 11:30am–2pm; Mon–Thurs 5–11pm, Fri–Sat 5pm–midnight, Sun 5–9:30pm (later if concert schedules warrant). Bus: 15 or 242. SPANISH TAPAS.

Tapas ("little dishes") allow you to order a sampling of such treats as grilled marinated lamb chops, calamari, spicy chorizo, and garlic prawns. All dishes are available in three sizes, and you'll want to try a few. For lunch, the sandwiches, including roast pork, chicken breast, and chorizo served on fresh-baked focaccia, are also tasty; skip the fish sandwich, though. The decor is distinctly Mediterranean, with whitewashed walls, exposed beams, fireplaces, and alcoves for privacy.

✪ Olympia Oyster & Fish Co. Ltd. 820 Thurlow St. ☎ **604/685-0716.** Main courses C$5.95–C$8.95 (US$4.25–US$6). AE, DC, ER, MC, V. Mon–Sat 11am–8pm, Sun noon–8pm. Bus: 8. FISH-AND-CHIPS.

In a new spot around the corner from its old location, this tiny fish store/restaurant is still a neighborhood favorite and still produces Vancouver's best fish-and-chips. There are only a few tables and a counter in the window, plus three more outside, weather permitting. The fish is always fresh and flaky and can be grilled if you prefer. The seafood platter (C$8.95/US$6) is enough for two. You can shop for smoked salmon or caviar to be shipped home or just sip a ginger beer while you wait.

THE WEST END
EXPENSIVE

Cin Cin. 1154 Robson St., 2nd floor. ☎ **604/688-7338.** Reservations recommended. Main courses C$9.95–C$27.95 (US$7–US$20). AE, DC, MC, V. Mon–Fri noon–2:30pm; daily 5–11pm. Bus: 8. On-street parking. ITALIAN.

As *Vancouver* magazine put it, Cin Cin is "known almost as well for who is eating there as for what can be eaten." Celebrities, models, politicians, and visitors in search of a meal or just a snack and a little respite from Robson Street shopping, frequent this Italian villa–style bistro. The dining room is built around the open kitchen with its huge alder-wood–fired oven, but the best spots for people-watching are the bar and heated terrace overlooking Robson. Dishes range from elegant pastas and pizzas (capellini alla Pomodoro, penne puttanesca, pizza margherita) to more substantial dishes like rosemary-marinated rack of lamb, sea bass crusted with porcinis, and smoked chicken breast. The wine list is extensive, as is the selection of wines by the glass.

The Fish House in Stanley Park. 2099 Beach Ave. (in Stanley Park). ☎ **604/681-7275.** Reservations recommended. Main courses C$13.95–C$29.95 (US$10–US$21). AE, DC, ER, JCB, MC, V. Mon–Sat 11am–10pm, Sun 11am–2:30pm. Bus: 19. PACIFIC NORTHWEST/SEAFOOD.

Reminiscent of a more genteel era, this white-clapboard clubhouse is surrounded by public tennis courts, golf and lawn-bowling greens, and ancient cedars. Three dining rooms decorated in hunter green, with dark wood and whitewashed accents, plus Lord Stanley's Oyster Bar on the Patio, complete the atmosphere. The menu includes some innovative dishes, like surprisingly tender wood-oven–roasted calamari with smoked tomato oil; seafood hot pot; and our favorite, grilled Ahi tuna steak with creamy buttermilk mashed potatoes. The oyster bar has at least half a dozen fresh varieties daily. The desserts are sumptuous and irresistible.

✪ Raincity Grill. 1193 Denman St. ☎ **604/685-7337.** Reservations recommended. Main courses C$13–C$24 (US$9–US$17). AE, DC, ER, MC, V. Mon–Fri 11:30am–2:30pm, Sat–Sun brunch 10:30am–3pm; daily 5–10:30pm. Bus: 8. WEST COAST.

With a sun-drenched patio and an extensive wine list (100 wines available by the glass), Raincity may make you feel as if you've landed a table in one of L.A.'s hottest restaurants (except that the price is roughly one-third what you'd expect to pay for this quality, and the staff is very friendly). The menu varies weekly, depending on what's exceptional at the Granville Island public market. Start out with a grilled Caesar salad with crisp capers; the grilled ratatouille; or the salmon, spinach, and chili spring rolls. Then try the rare grilled tuna steak with orange-basil marmalade and roasted red-pepper polenta, grilled lamb, or beef tenderloin. Brunches are also fabulous.

MODERATE

Café de Paris. 751 Denman St. ☎ **604/687-1418.** Reservations recommended. Main courses C$14–C$17 (US$10–US$12); 3-course table d'hôte C$13.95 (US$10) at lunch, C$24.95 (US$18) at dinner. AE, MC, V. Mon–Fri 11:30am–2pm; daily 5:30–10pm. Bus: 8. FRENCH.

An authentic Parisian bistro with dark wood, brass accents, wine racks in the dining room (wines range from C$16/US$11 to C$400/US$286), and marble-topped tables, Café de Paris is a few blocks from Coal Harbour and Stanley Park. The classic fare includes duck confit, steak tartare, and smoked rack of lamb roasted with fresh herbs. All dishes are served with Vancouver's best pommes frites.

Romano's Macaroni Grill at the Mansion. 1523 Davie St. ☎ **604/689-4334.** Reservations recommended. Main courses C$7.95–C$15.95 (US$6–US$11). AE, DC, MC, V. Daily 11:30am–10:30pm. Bus: 3 or 8. ITALIAN.

Built just after the turn of the century by sugar baron B. T. Rogers, the mansion is now the home of a casual pasta-and-pizza restaurant. The menu emphasizes southern Italian fare, and the pastas are definitely the favorite dishes. The food is simple, understandable, and consistently good. You're charged for the house wine, which you pour yourself from unlabeled bottles, based on how much you consume, as measured on the side of the bottle. Kids love the children's menu, tasty pizzas, and permissive staff, who burst into opera at the slightest provocation.

✪ **Tanpopo.** 1122 Denman St., 2nd floor. ☎ **604/681-7777.** Reservations recommended. Main courses C$7.95–C$17.95 (US$6–US$13). AE, DC, MC, V. Daily 11:30am–3pm and 5:30–10:30pm. Bus: 3 or 8. JAPANESE/SUSHI.

With a partial view of English Bay, Tanpopo has a full Japanese menu. But the lines of people waiting up to 30 minutes for a table every night are there for the all-you-can-eat sushi. The unlimited fare includes all the standards: makis, tuna and salmon sashimi, California and BC rolls, and many cooked items, such as tonkatsu, tempura, chicken kara-age, and broiled oysters. There are two secrets to getting seated: Either call ahead (if they tell you they're full, you can still show up and wait for a table) or ask to sit at the sushi bar.

INEXPENSIVE

Gyoza King. 1508 Robson St. ☎ **604/669-8278.** Main courses C$5.95–C$12.95 (US$4.25–US$9). AE, DC, JCB, MC, V. Daily noon–2:30pm; Mon–Sat 5:30pm–2am, Sun 5:30pm–midnight. Bus: 8. JAPANESE.

Gyoza King features an entire menu of gyozas—those succulent Japanese dumplings, filled with prawns, pork, vegetables, and other combinations—as well as Japanese noodles and staples like katsu-don (pork cutlet over rice) and o-den (a rich, hearty soup). This is the gathering spot for the young Japanese visitors who pour into Vancouver every year, probably because it's the closest to home cooking. There's so much to choose from under C$10 (US$7). The staff is courteous and happy to explain dishes to people not familiar with Japanese cuisine.

Just One Thai Bistro. 1103 Denman St. ☎ **604/685-8989.** Main courses C$7.75–C$13.50 (US$6–US$10). AE, MC, V. Daily 11:30am–11:30pm. Bus: 3 or 8. THAI.

The rare four-headed golden Buddha at the entrance and the collection of smaller Buddhas set into wall recesses, combined with stone floors, palm trees, and fresh flowers, give this place the serenity of a temple. The service is superb, the food the best Thai cuisine in Vancouver. While the house specialty is Thai barbecue (the beef satay is outstanding), the curries and stir-fries are equally good. If you have a cold, there's no better cure than a steaming bowl of Tom Yum Goong: a hot-and-sour soup heaping with prawns, mushrooms, and lemongrass.

Moutai Mandarin Restaurant. 1710 Davie St. ☎ **604/681-2288.** Main courses C$6.95–C$15.95 (US$5–US$11). AE, DC, MC, V. Daily 5–11pm. Bus: 3 or 8. SZECHUAN CHINESE.

The halogen lights might seem a bit bright and the ultramodern tables topped with fluorescent green metal set against a black-and-white decor might add to the brightness even with the lights dimmed, but no seems to mind. This diminutive neighborhood place serves some of the finest Szechuan cuisine in Vancouver. Don't miss the peppering wontons in a peanut, chili, ginger, and lemongrass sauce. (Order the chili wontons if you have a nut allergy.) The deluxe wonton soup lives up to its title—it's filled with prawns, wontons, green onions, and sliced pork. And the Mandarin chicken, the orange-peel beef, and the General Tzo's chicken are all delicious.

✪ **Stepho's.** 1124 Davie St. ☎ **604/683-2555.** Reservations accepted for parties of 5–8. Main courses C$4.25–C$9.95 (US$3.05–US$7). AE, MC, V. Daily 11:30am–11:30pm. Bus: 3 or 8. GREEK.

There's a reason Stepho's is packed every day—the cuisine is simple Greek fare at its finest and cheapest. Customers line up outside and wait up to half an hour to be seated. (The average wait is about 10 to 15 minutes.) Once inside, you can count on a delicious meal: generous portions of deliciously marinated lamb, chicken, pork, or beef over pilaf; *tzatziki* (yogurt dip that's a garlic-lover's dream); and heaping platters of calamari. Beware of ordering too much, as it's easy to do here. And while success is too often the downfall of a neighborhood restaurant, Stepho's recently doubled in size and was completely renovated, but didn't raise prices or compromise quality.

CENTRAL VANCOUVER
VERY EXPENSIVE

✪ **Bishop's.** 2183 W. 4th Ave. ☎ **604/738-2025.** Web site: www.settingsun.com/bishops. Reservations required. Main courses C$24–C$30 (US$17–US$21). AE, DC, MC, V. Mon–Sat 5:30–11pm, Sun 5:30–10pm. Bus: 4 or 7. PACIFIC NORTHWEST.

John Bishop doesn't behave like a guy who owns one of Vancouver's finest restaurants. He personally greets you, escorts you to your table, and introduces you to a catalog of fine wines and what he describes as "contemporary home cooking." The decor features candlelight and white linen. The service is impeccable, and the food even better. The menu changes three or four times a year. Recent dishes have included roast duck breast with sun-dried Okanagan fruit and candied ginger glacé, steamed smoked black cod with new potatoes and horseradish sabayon, and marinated sirloin of lamb with garlic mashed potatoes and a fresh mint, tomato, and balsamic vinegar reduction. If you have only one evening to dine in Vancouver, spend it here.

EXPENSIVE

Monk McQueen's. 601 Stamps Landing. ☎ **604/877-1351.** Reservations recommended. Main courses C$12–C$24 (US$9–US$17). AE, DC, ER, JCB, MC, V. Daily 11:30am–2pm and 5:30–11pm. Bus: 50. Ferry: Aquabus. SEAFOOD/CONTINENTAL.

Hop on the diminutive Aquabus over to Stamps Landing, find a table on either of two wooden decks built over False Creek, and dig into a delicious seafood dinner while the sun fades. Downstairs is Monk's Oyster Bar, where you can get a bucket of steamers and a locally brewed beer, a spicy Szechuan seafood stir-fry, or fantastic roasted prawns. McQueen's Upstairs is more formal (though still casual). Chef Robert Craig creates baked oysters, prawn-and-scallop stew, venison with pears, and grilled filet mignon with roasted garlic. The wine list, organized by price (C$21.75/US$15 to C$45/US$32), features an international mix.

✪ **Tojo's Restaurant.** 777 W. Broadway, 2nd floor. ☎ **604/872-8050.** Reservations required for sushi bar. Full dinner C$12.50–C$99.50 (US$9–US$71). AE, DC, MC, V. Mon–Sat 5–11pm. Bus: 9. JAPANESE.

The decor is unimpressive, but Hidekazu Tojo's sushi is the best in Vancouver and attracts Japanese businesspeople, Hollywood celebrities (Robin Williams, Harrison Ford), and anyone else who's willing to pay for the best. If you sit at the bar (the best seats in the house), tell him how much you want to spend and he'll prepare an incredible meal to fit your budget. The sushi menu changes with Tojo's moods, and the seasons are reflected in his abstract edible masterpieces (sea urchin on the half shell, herring roe, lobster claws, tuna, crab and asparagus). Nonsushi dishes are available from a similarly seasonal menu that in the past has included everything from tempura to teriyaki. When we walked in, he asked if we'd had sushi before. We said yes. He asked if we'd eaten in his restaurant before. We said no. "Then," he replied, "you haven't had sushi." He was right.

MODERATE

Mark's Steak & Tap House. 2468 Bayswater St., at W. Broadway. ☎ **604/734-1325.** Reservations recommended. Main courses C$6.95–C$19.95 (US$5–US$14). AE, DC, MC, V. Daily 11:30am–10:30pm. Bus: 10. STEAK.

This hip casual Kitsilano hangout, with high ceilings, exposed brick, and vintage Vancouver photos, offers a limited menu of well-executed American cuisine in the restaurant, 15 local microbrews, and a decent wine list at the bar. Appetizers include steamed mussels, fried calamari, and a delicious vegetarian baked spinach. There are seven steaks to choose from (we recommend the 10-oz. hickory-smoked New York steak). A number of inventive pasta and pizza options are also available. With a burger and fries starting at C$6.95 (US$5), crayons on every paper-covered table, and a friendly staff, Mark's is decidedly kid-friendly.

✪ **Picasso Café.** 1626 W. Broadway. ☎ **604/732-3290.** Reservations recommended. Main courses C$9.95–C$16.95 (US$7–US$12). MC, V. Mon 8:30am–2:30pm, Tues–Fri 8:30am–9pm. Bus: 10. WEST COAST/MODERN.

Are your arteries shying away from French fare and wincing at Alfredo sauce? Then visit this smoke-free place, which features surprisingly good, quite creative West Coast–influenced food, much of which lives up to the stringent HeartSmart guidelines laid down by Canada's Heart and Stroke Foundation. Framed prints by many of Vancouver's finest artists hang on the walls of this garden-style cafe. In addition, the restaurant provides culinary training for young people through the auspices of the Option Youth Society.

INEXPENSIVE

Naam Restaurant. 2724 W. 4th Ave. ☎ **604/738-7151.** Reservations not accepted. Main courses C$3.95–C$8.25 (US$2.80–US$6). MC, V. Daily 24 hours. Bus: 4 or 22. VEGETARIAN.

Naam is Vancouver's oldest vegetarian/natural food restaurant, and it's still the best. The unapologetically healthy fare ranges from open-face tofu melts, enchiladas, and burritos to tofu teriyaki, Thai noodles, and a variety of pita pizzas. Breakfast, served from 6am to 11am (Saturday to 1pm, Sunday to 2:30pm), is a testament to the variety of delicious foods available without meat; they do serve eggs and dairy products. If you're a fan of vegetarian cuisine, Naam is worth a visit.

Shao Lin Noodle Restaurant. 548 W. Broadway. ☎ **604/873-1816.** Main courses C$5.25–C$9.95 (US$3.75–US$7). No credit cards. Daily 24 hours. Bus: 10. CHINESE.

Why play with your food when you can watch the professionals do it? Traditional Chinese noodle shops are a rarity in North America, which is a shame because they're so much fun. Enclosed by glass, the noodle makers toss the pasta, stretch it over their heads, spin it around, and dramatically transform it into fine strands. Bowls of noodles are served in a vast selection of combinations with meats and vegetables. Tea is poured from a 3-foot-long teapot originally designed to allow male servants to maintain a polite distance from an 18th-century Chinese empress while serving her.

GASTOWN & CHINATOWN

EXPENSIVE

The Cannery. 2205 Commissioner St. (near Victoria Dr.). ☎ **604/254-9606.** Reservations recommended. Main courses C$16.95–C$26.95 (US$12–US$19). AE, DC, DISC, MC, V. Mon–Fri 11:30am–2:30pm; daily 5:30–10pm. Bus: 7 to Victoria Dr. From downtown, head east on Hastings St., turn left on Victoria Dr. (2 blocks past Commercial Dr.), and then right on Commissioner St. SEAFOOD.

Hidden among the Burrard Inlet wharves and built over the water, The Cannery is an upscale, unabashedly romantic restaurant filled with seafaring memorabilia. The seafood is fresh and plentiful. Start out with a bowl of creamy clam chowder or rich lobster bisque, then scan the daily fresh sheet. Those in the know order from the mesquite-grilled section. Our personal favorites are the tender sea bass served over a salad of artichokes, sun-dried tomatoes, olives, and young celery and the seafood combo platter. The Cannery's perennial gold medal–winning wine list has some good bargains, and the desserts are exquisite.

MODERATE

✪ Floata Seafood Restaurant. 400–180 Keefer St., 3rd floor. ☎ **604/602-0368.** Reservations recommended. Main courses C$9.95–C$45 (US$7–US$32); dim-sum dishes C$2.50–C$3.75 (US$1.80–US$2.70). AE, DC, ER, JCB, MC, V. Daily 8am–10pm. Bus: 19 or 22. CHINESE/DIM SUM.

The Western flagship of a renowned Hong Kong restaurant group, Floata opened in 1996 as Canada's largest Chinese restaurant. However, it's not easy to find, as it's on the third floor of a shopping plaza/parkade. (Look for the bright-red building a stone's throw from Dr. Sun Yat Sen Garden and the Chinatown museum. It's upstairs.) A safe rule of thumb with Chinese food is that the bigger and busier the restaurant, the better the dim sum is. Floata is usually packed with diners at opposite ends of the room, sitting a full block away from one another while carts loaded with shumai and hargow (steamed dumplings), dum bao (buns filled with barbecued pork), sautéed vegetables, roast duck, roast pork, spring rolls, and sausages rolled in sesame-crusted puff pastry ply the aisles (to 2:30pm; after that you can order dim sum by menu until dinner). Dinners are extravagant and priced accordingly, as dishes like shark-fin and bird's-nest soups, whole crisp sea bass in black-bean sauce, and crisp Peking duck take on entirely new dimensions in the hands of the Cordon Bleu Award–winning chef.

INEXPENSIVE

Brothers Restaurant. 1 Water St. ☎ **604/683-9124.** Reservations recommended. Main courses C$6.95–C$12.95 (US$5–US$9). AE, DC, JCB, MC, V. Mon–Thurs 11:30am–10pm, Fri–Sat 11:30am–midnight, Sun 11:30am–9pm. Bus: 1 or 50. FAMILY-STYLE.

Decorated like a Franciscan monastery complete with staff in friars' robes, Brothers has a warm ambiance that especially appeals to families and older folks. Main dishes include chowder, pastas, burgers, and serious prime rib. Children get balloons and their own menu. A bistro lounge featuring wine casks as well as sushi and oyster bars caters primarily to young adults.

Incendio. 103 Columbia St. ☎ **604/688-8694.** Main courses C$7.25–C$14.95 (US$5–US$11). AE, DC, ER, MC, V. Tues–Fri 11:30am–3pm and 5–10pm, Sat–Sun 5–11pm. Bus: 8, 14, 20, or 21. ITALIAN.

If you're looking for something casual and local that won't be full of other people reading downtown maps, this little hideaway in Gastown is sublime. There are 22 pizza combinations to choose from, all served on fresh crusts baked crisp in an old wood-fired oven. Pastas are home-made, and you're encouraged to mix and match sauces and pastas. (Try the mussels, capers, and tomatoes in lime butter.) The wine list is decent, the beer list truly inspired. (The Unibroue from Québec was recently lauded as one of the world's 10 best beers in international competition.) Sunday night features all-you-can-eat pizza for C$7.95 (US$6).

5 Seeing the Sights

Is your idea of *extreme* climbing the largest granite monolith this side of Gibraltar, skiing double-diamond trails, squeezing in 18 holes before a round of mixed doubles, or trying to cover three museums and a matinee performance and still having enough energy to go dancing? Then Vancouver has a lot to offer. This city has more natural attractions than you'll ever have time to see. Even if you stay here for a few months, you'll simply discover more things to do. Walking along the city beaches could take weeks alone. Vancouver's cultural attractions are also abundant. The museums and art galleries will astound you with rare collections you won't find anywhere else in Canada, North America, or the world. For sports fans, there's a great line-up of professional and semiprofessional teams. And for kids, there are museums and attractions that'll keep them entertained for days.

DOWNTOWN

Vancouver Art Gallery. 750 Hornby St. ☎ **604/662-4719** or 604/662-4700. Web site: www.vanartgallery.bc.ca. Admission C$7.50 (US$5) adults, C$5 (US$3.60) seniors, C$3.50 (US$2.50) students; children under 12 free. Mon–Fri 10am–6pm, Sat 10am–5pm, Sun and holidays noon–5pm. Closed Mon–Tues in Oct–May (gift shop and cafe stay open). SkyTrain: Granville. Bus: 3.

If you're curious to experience the heritage of Canadian fine art, spend an afternoon here. Formerly the provincial court house, this stately stone structure was designed in 1906 by local architect Francis Rattenbury, who also created the Roedde House in Barclay Heritage Square and the Empress and the Legislative Buildings in Victoria. It now houses an impressive collection of Canadian works by the Victoria-born artist Emily Carr and the Canadian Group of Seven—together, they comprised a "school" of 19th-century painters who documented their impressions of the Canadian prairies, mountains, and canyons in bold shapes and colors. Paintings, sculpture, graphics, photography, and video ranging from classic to contemporary created by European, North American, and Asian masters are also on display in permanent and rotating exhibits. Recent shows have included a retrospective of the late Andy Warhol's paintings. The Annex Gallery, geared to younger audiences, features rotating visually exciting and educational exhibits.

The Canadian Craft Museum. 639 Hornby St. ☎ **604/687-8266.** Admission C$4 (US$2.85) adults, C$2 (US$1.45) seniors and students; children under 12 free. Mon–Wed and Fri–Sat 10am–5pm, Thurs 10am–9pm, Sun and holidays noon–5pm. Closed Tues Sept–May. SkyTrain: Granville. Bus: 3.

Across Georgia Street from the Hotel Vancouver, this museum occupies a voluminous gallery/work space complex. The gallery presents a vast collection of Canadian and international crafts in glass, wood, metal, clay, and fiber, appealing to anyone who devours interior design and architectural magazines. Recent shows have included an impressive display of carved Chinese signature seals and calligraphy, native-Indian artist Bill Reid's gold and silver jewelry, and furnishings created by Canada's best industrial designers. You can also purchase unique, creatively designed ceramics, sculptures, and crafts in the gift store.

✪ **BC Sports Hall of Fame & Museum.** BC Place Stadium, Gate A, Beatty and Robson sts. (777 Pacific Blvd. S.). ☎ **604/687-5520.** Admission C$6 (US$4.30) adults, C$4 (US$2.90) seniors and students; children under 5 free. Daily 10am–5pm. SkyTrain: Stadium. Bus: 15.

A great destination for sports-minded, active children who never seem to run out of energy, the museum's Participation Gallery features interactive running, climbing, throwing, riding, rowing, and racing competitions where kids can pit themselves against video-simulated competitors. There's even a climbing wall, throwing cages, and stationary bikes. For parents, the Hall of Champions and Builders Hall document the achievements of British Columbia's greatest athletes, such as runners Terry Fox and Rick Hansen, referees, and coaches in video and photographic displays.

WEST END

✪ **Vancouver Aquarium.** Stanley Park. ☎ **604/682-1118.** Admission C$12 (US$9) adults, C$10.50 (US$8) seniors and students, C$8 (US$6) children 4–12; children under 4 free; rates are lower off-season. June 23–Sept 4 daily 9:30am–8pm; Sept 5–June 22 daily 10am–5:30pm. Bus: 19; "Around the Park" bus.

North America's third-largest aquarium, the Vancouver Aquarium is home to more than 56,000 marine species, making it a must-see for adults and children alike. One viewing gallery is dedicated to local coastal marine life, such as a giant octopus, orcas, beluga whales, sea otters, harbor seals, and Stellar sea lions. We silently watched a 6-foot baby beluga whale (the first ever born in captivity) and her mother effortlessly glide in the still blue waters of the underground gallery a week after she was born. We spent nearly an hour observing a male orca as he delicately played with an oak leaf that had landed in his pool, while his mate and her Dall porpoise pal enjoyed a quick round of hide-and-seek in the adjoining pool. Regal angelfish glide through a re-created coral reef, and black-tip reef sharks menacingly scour the waters. Human-size freshwater fish await you in an Amazonian rain forest. An hourly rainstorm thunders over your head while you meet crocodiles, poison-dart tree frogs, piranha, and two-toed sloths.

CENTRAL VANCOUVER

Pacific Space Centre. 1100 Chestnut St., in Vanier Park. ☎ **604/738-STAR.** Web site: www.pacific-space-centre.bc.ca/. Admission to special shows C$6.50–C$7.75 (US$4.65–US$6) adults, C$5–C$7.75 (US$3.55–US$6) seniors and students; Tues seniors admitted free to all regular shows. Tues–Sun 10am–5pm and 7–11pm. Occasional unannounced closures; call ahead. Bus: 22.

Greatly expanded in 1997, this space center and observatory has something for every amateur astronomy buff. Both adults and kids can travel to Mars in BC's first full-motion simulator, see an engine from the *Apollo 17* manned satellite, and try your hand at designing a spacecraft or manipulating lunar robots. You can learn more about Canada's contributions to the joint North American space program in the Groundstation Canada theater, surf the Internet from the Centre's terminals, or view the skies from the Geosphere's satellite-image display system. The center also offers a number of daily shows, like the history of Chinese astronomy, and nightly laser-light shows. And on selected nights, you can shoot the moon through a half-meter telescope for C$10 (US$7) per camera; call ☎ **604/736-2655** for details.

✪ **Science World British Columbia.** 1455 Québec St. ☎ **604/268-6363.** Web site: www.scienceworld.bc.ca. Admission C$10.50 (US$8) adults, C$7 (US$5) seniors, students, and

Downtown Vancouver

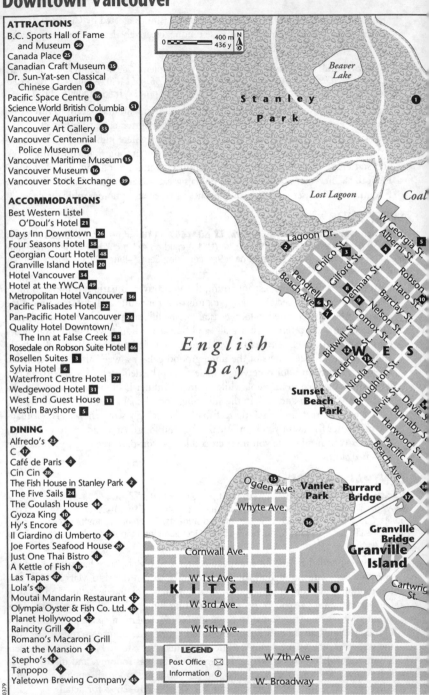

ATTRACTIONS
B.C. Sports Hall of Fame
  and Museum 50
Canada Place 25
Canadian Craft Museum 35
Dr. Sun-Yat-sen Classical
  Chinese Garden 41
Pacific Space Centre 16
Science World British Columbia 51
Vancouver Aquarium 1
Vancouver Art Gallery 33
Vancouver Centennial
  Police Museum 42
Vancouver Maritime Museum 15
Vancouver Museum 16
Vancouver Stock Exchange 39

ACCOMMODATIONS
Best Western Listel
  O'Doul's Hotel 21
Days Inn Downtown 26
Four Seasons Hotel 38
Georgian Court Hotel 48
Granville Island Hotel 20
Hotel Vancouver 34
Hotel at the YWCA 49
Metropolitan Hotel Vancouver 36
Pacific Palisades Hotel 22
Pan-Pacific Hotel Vancouver 24
Quality Hotel Downtown/
  The Inn at False Creek 43
Rosedale on Robson Suite Hotel 46
Rosellen Suites 3
Sylvia Hotel 6
Waterfront Centre Hotel 27
Wedgewood Hotel 31
West End Guest House 11
Westin Bayshore 5

DINING
Alfredo's 23
C 17
Café de Paris 4
Cin Cin 28
The Fish House in Stanley Park 2
The Five Sails 24
The Goulash House 44
Gyoza King 10
Hy's Encore 47
Il Giardino di Umberto 19
Joe Fortes Seafood House 29
Just One Thai Bistro 8
A Kettle of Fish 18
Las Tapas 47
Lola's 40
Moutai Mandarin Restaurant 12
Olympia Oyster & Fish Co. Ltd. 30
Planet Hollywood 42
Raincity Grill 7
Romano's Macaroni Grill
  at the Mansion 13
Stepho's 14
Tanpopo 9
Yaletown Brewing Company 45

1-0379

646

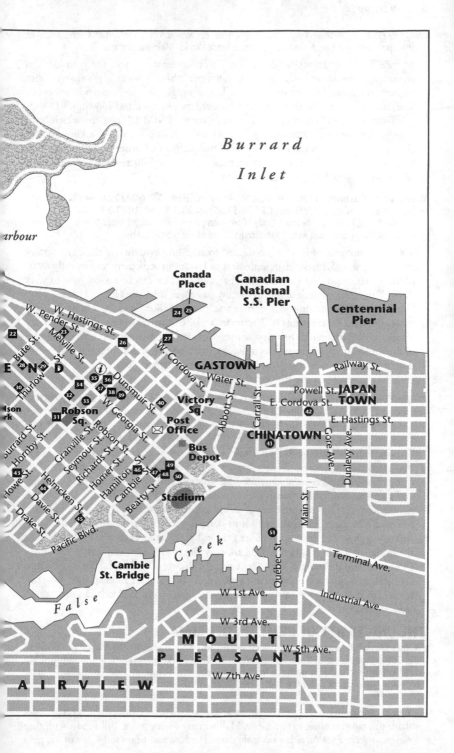

Burrard

Inlet

arbour

Canada Place

Canadian National S.S. Pier

Centennial Pier

W. Hastings St.

W. Pender St.

Melville St.

Bute St.

22

E N D

28

Thurlow St.

30

ison rk

31

34

35 36

Dunsmuir St.

37

38 39

32 33

Robson Sq.

W. Georgia St.

40

Victory Sq.

Post Office

Bus Depot

GASTOWN

Water St.

Railway St.

Powell St. JAPAN

E. Cordova St. TOWN

42

E. Hastings St.

CHINATOWN

41

W. Cordova St.

Abbott St.

Carrall St.

Gore Ave.

Dunlevy Ave.

26

27

24 25

urrard St.

Hornby St.

Granville St.

Seymour St.

Robson St.

Richards St.

Homer St.

Hamilton St.

Cambie St.

Beatty St.

43

owe St.

44

Helmcken St.

Davie St.

45

Drake St.

Pacific Blvd.

46

47 49

48 50

Stadium

51

Main St.

Québec St.

Terminal Ave.

Industrial Ave.

Cambie St. Bridge

Creek

W 1st Ave.

W 3rd Ave.

M O U N T

P L E A S A N T

W 5th Ave.

False

A I R V I E W

W 7th Ave.

children; children under 4 free. Combination tickets available for OMNIMAX film. Mon–Fri 10am–5pm, Sat–Sun 10am–6pm. SkyTrain: Science World–Main St. Station.

Science World is a hands-on scientific discovery center where you and your kids can create a cyclone, blow square bubbles, watch a zucchini explode as it's charged with 80,000 volts, stand in the interior of a beaver lodge, play wrist-deep in magnetic liquids, create music with a giant synthesizer, and watch mind-blowing 3-D slide and laser shows and other optical effects. In the OMNIMAX Theatre, which has a huge projecting screen and surround-sound, you can feel as if you're taking a death-defying flight through the Grand Canyon and performing other spine-tingling acts. Science World also hosts many spectacular traveling exhibits. Backyard Monsters, with giant robotic bugs, is a recent favorite.

Vancouver Museum. 1100 Chestnut St., in Vanier Park. ☎ **604/736-4431.** Web site: www.vanmuseum.bc.ca. Admission C$5 (US$3.55) adults, C$2.50 (US$1.80) children, seniors, and students, C$10 (US$7) families. Daily 10am–5pm; Sept–June closed Mon. Bus: 22, then walk 3 blocks south on Cornwall Ave. Boat: Granville Island Ferry or Aquabus.

This museum opened in 1894, dedicated to amassing evidence of the city's history from its days as a native-Indian settlement to European settlement and its early 20th-century maturation into a modern urban center. The exhibits allow you to walk through the steerage deck of a 19th-century passenger ship, peek into a Hudson's Bay Company frontier trading post, or have a seat in an 1880s Canadian-Pacific Railway passenger car. Re-creations of Victorian and Edwardian rooms show how early Vancouverites decorated their new homes. Rotating exhibits include a recent display of the museum's collection of neon signage that's been rescued from the city's abandoned buildings: representatives of Vancouver's former glory as the west coast's glitziest metropolis in the 1940s and 1950s.

✪ **Vancouver Maritime Museum.** 1905 Ogden Ave., in Vanier Park. ☎ **604/257-8300.** Admission C$6 (US$4.30) adults, C$3 (US$2.15) seniors and students, C$14 (US$10) families; children under 6 free. Daily 10am–5pm; Sept to mid-May closed Tues. Bus: 22, then walk 4 blocks north on Cypress. Boat: False Creek Ferries dock at Heritage Harbour.

This museum houses the RCMP Arctic patrol vessel *St. Roch,* the first vessel to have navigated the Northwest Passage from west to east and the first to have made it through in both directions. Intricate ship models, antique wood and brass fittings, and prints and other documents fill the other galleries. Pirates Cove is a new permanent gallery that's a treasure chest of pirate lore, artifacts, a "jolly roger," and pieces of eight. The most successful exhibit to date, it also houses a miniature pirate ship where your kids can dress up in pirate gear and play. The aft cabin of a schooner and the bridge of a modern tugboat lead the way to the Children's Maritime Discovery Centre, where there are computers, a wall of drawers filled with ship models and artifacts, and observation telescopes aimed at the ships in English Bay. You can maneuver an underwater robot in a large water tank, and your kids can dress up in naval costumes.

THE UNIVERSITY OF BRITISH COLUMBIA

✪ **Museum of Anthropology.** University of British Columbia, 6393 NW Marine Dr. ☎ **604/822-5087.** Admission C$6 (US$4.30) adults, C$3.50 (US$2.50) seniors and students, C$15 (US$11) families; children under 6 free. Free Tues evenings. June–Sept Tues 10am–10pm, Wed–Sun 10am–5pm; Oct–May Tues 11am–9pm, Wed–Sun 11am–5pm. Closed Dec 25–26. Bus: 4 or 10.

You enter through a huge carved bent-cedar box. Articles from potlatch ceremonies flank the ramp leading to the Great Hall's many totem poles. Bill Reid's sculpture *Raven and the First Men,* his pettable carved cedarwood bear, and some of his gold

Hollywood North

The **BC Film Commission** runs a hot line (☎ 604/660-3569) and posts a list of the film and TV production companies currently shooting in town. The list is available at the SeaBus terminal, 601 W. Cordova St., 2nd floor; it's open Monday to Friday from 8:30am to 4:30pm.

On one afternoon's stroll, we found five production sets between Stanley Park and Thurlow Street, from Sunset Beach to Robson Street. In recent years, films such as *Legends of the Fall, Little Women, Man of the House, Roxanne, Cousins, The Fly 2, Look Who's Talking, Who's Harry Crumb?, Narrow Margin, Timecop, The Never-Ending Story,* Jackie Chan's *Rumble in the Bronx, Intersection,* and *Jumanji* were filmed here. Most of Sylvester Stallone's *Rambo: First Blood* was filmed in Lynn Canyon Park. Many TV shows have also had Vancouver as a backdrop: Examples are *The X-Files, Millennium, MacGyver, Sabrina: Teenage Witch, The Sentinel, The Outer Limits, 21 Jumpstreet, Poltergeist: The Legacy,* and *Highlander.*

Stargazing in Vancouver can be easier (and more successful) than touring the homes of the stars in Beverly Hills. The first American filmmaker to shoot in British Columbia? Thomas Edison in the early 1900s.

and silver creations are also displayed. In the Visible Storage Galleries, you can open the glass-topped drawers to view small treasures from around the world and look at larger pieces in the tall glass cases along the gallery walls. The Koerner Ceramics Gallery contains a collection of European ceramics unique to North America. The gift shop has an extensive selection of books, prints, carvings, and jewelry. After touring the museum, take a walk through the grounds in back. Two cedar longhouses positioned on the traditional north-south axis, 10 totem poles, and a few contemporary native-Canadian carvings overlook Point Grey.

GASTOWN & CHINATOWN

✪ **Vancouver Centennial Police Museum.** 240 E. Cordova St. ☎ **604/665-3346.** Admission C$2 (US$1.45) adults, C$1 (US70¢) seniors and children. May–Aug Mon–Sat 11:30am–4:30pm; Sept–Apr Mon–Fri 11:30am–4:30pm. Bus: 4 or 7.

Originally the home of the Vancouver Coroner's Court and the place where actor Errol Flynn was autopsied after his accidental death, this museum will definitely appeal to those fascinated by the criminal underworld. The museum's morgue, simulated autopsy room, and re-creations of Vancouver's most infamous (and unsolved) murder and crime scenes are on display. There are also displays of police equipment and a coroner's forensic exhibit. It's an intriguing way to pass the time on a dark and stormy day.

NORTH VANCOUVER & WEST VANCOUVER

Grouse Mountain Resort. 6400 Nancy Greene Way, North Vancouver. ☎ **604/984-0661.** Admission C$15.95 (US$11) adults, C$14.95 (US$10) seniors, C$9.95 (US$7) students, C$5.95 (US$4.25) children 6–12; children under 6 free. Skyride free with advance Grouse Nest restaurant reservation. Daily 10am–10pm. SeaBus to Lonsdale Quay, then transfer to bus no. 236.

On a clear day, Grouse Mountain offers an impressive view of the Vancouver skyline. (When it's cloudy, the 10-minute trip up is a sensory-deprivation experience.) The cable car on the Skyride tram lifts you to the 3,700-foot summit. Only a 20-minute drive from Vancouver by car (about an hour by public transit), the resort offers hiking in summer and day and night skiing, cross-country skiing, snowboarding, snowshoeing, and sleigh riding in winter (see "Outdoor Activities & Spectator Sports," later in this chapter). There are interpretive nature trails, "Born to Fly" (a spectacular high-definition video montage of southern British Columbia through the eyes of an eagle), a snack bar, the Spirit Gallery and Inpost shops, and daily summertime logger-sports events. For the kids, there's the Adventure Playground. The Grouse Nest Restaurant serves continental and West Coast cuisine.

Capilano Canyon Suspension Bridge & Park. 3735 Capilano Rd., North Vancouver. ☎ **604/985-7474.** Web site: www.capbridge.com. Admission C$8.95 (US$6) adults, C$7.50 (US$5) seniors, C$6 (US$4.30) students, C$3 (US$2.15) children 6–12; children under 6 free. Winter discounts. May–Sept daily 8:30am–dusk; Oct–Apr daily 9am–5pm. Closed Dec 25. Bus: 246.

It's about a 15-minute drive to the city's oldest sightseeing attraction, the 450-foot-long Capilano Suspension Bridge (a cedar and steel-cable footbridge), which gently sways 230 feet above the Capilano River. You nervously cross above kayakers who are shooting the rapids. The 1911 trading post at the bridge houses the souvenir shop, and the elegant Bridge House Restaurant is open year-round. The Canyon Café and Loggers' Grill are casual dining spots but are open only from May to September. Carvers demonstrate their traditional skills at the Totem Park Carving Centre and the Longhouse. The Living Forest and Rock of Ages exhibits explain the region's delicate environmental balance as well as introduce you to the diverse flora and fauna that live in this area. Tour greeters and guides provide complimentary history and nature tours from May to September.

ESPECIALLY FOR KIDS

Pick up copies of the free monthly *BC Parent,* 4479 W. 10th Ave., Vancouver (☎ **604/221-0366**), and *West Coast Families,* 8–1551 Johnston St., Vancouver (☎ **604/689-1331**), whose centerfold "Fun in the City," as well as an event calendar, lists everything currently going on, including IMAX and OMNIMAX shows and free children's programs.

Most of the following attractions are covered in detail earlier in this section.

Animal lovers will have a ball at **Stanley Park's petting zoo,** where peacocks, rabbits, calves, donkeys, and Shetland ponies eagerly await kids' attention. The **Vancouver Aquarium,** with its playful sea otters, harbor seals, orcas, and beluga whales, is always a popular spot. The nearby water park at Lumberman's Arch lets kids do a little splashing of their own during summer.

Budding scientists can get their hands into everything in **Science World**'s displays. They can go to Mars or see the moon in **Pacific Space Centre**'s flight simulator and observatory telescope. They can also maneuver the **Maritime Museum**'s underwater robot or board the RCMP icebreaker *St. Roch.*

Future athletes can run amok at the **BC Sports Hall of Fame's Participation Gallery,** where they can jump, climb, race, throw fastballs, and attempt to beat world records. At Granville Island's **Water Park and Adventure Playground,** 1496 Cartwright St. (☎ **604/665-3425**), they can *really* let loose with movable water guns and sprinklers. They can also get wet on the water slides or in the wading pool throughout summer from 10am to 6pm. Admission is free. There are changing facilities right next door at Isadora's Restaurant.

At the **Capilano Canyon Suspension Bridge,** kids can brave the bridge, walking high above lush forests and roaring rivers. **Mount Seymour Provincial Park** (see "Outdoor Activities & Spectator Sports," later in this chapter) offers **Children's Ski Programs** (☎ **604/986-2261**) for kids 4 to 16.

Kids who love to shop will find heaven at Granville Island's **Kids Only Market,** 1496 Cartwright St., open daily from 10am to 6pm (closed Monday except in summer). Playrooms and 21 shops filled with toys, books, records, clothes, and food are all kid-oriented. They'll also love taking the Aquabus or Granville Island ferry to get to the market.

6 Parks, Gardens, Nature Preserves & Beaches

PARKS & GARDENS

Stanley Park (☎ 604/257-8400) is named after the Lord Stanley whose name is synonymous with professional hockey playoffs—the Stanley Cup. The park is a 1,000-acre forest of western red cedars, lagoons, walking paths, lawns, and gardens surrounded by water, except for part of its eastern edge, which connects it to the West End. It boasts abundant wildlife (beaver, coyote, bald eagles, raccoon, trumpeter swans, brant, duck, and skunk), pristine natural settings, and amazing marine views. This is where the locals go to run, skate, bike, walk, or just sit. As North America's largest urban park, it's 20% larger than New York's Central Park. It's also considerably safer.

In Chinatown, a tranquil oasis is concealed behind high white-washed walls: Gnarled limestone scholar rocks jut skyward amid pine, bamboo, winter-blooming plum, and dark reflective pools filled with turtles and koi (decorative carp), with tiled paths meandering through it all. The **Dr. Sun Yat-Sen Classical Garden,** 578 Carrall St. (☎ 604/689-7133), was built in the Suzhou province of northern China around 1492 and relocated to Vancouver before Expo '86. It was packed in more than 900 crates, and 52 artisans took nearly 10 years to reassemble it. It's the only one of its kind in the Western Hemisphere and is serenely beautiful year-round.

Central Vancouver's **Queen Elizabeth Park,** Cambie Street (at West 33rd Avenue), sits atop a 500-foot-high extinct volcano and is the highest southern vantage point south of downtown. Its well-manicured gardens are a profusion of colorful flora. There are areas for lawn bowling, tennis, pitch-and-putt golf, and picnicking. Next to a huge sunken garden—an amazing reclamation of an abandoned rock quarry—stands the **Bloedel Conservatory** (☎ 604/872-5513). A 140-foot-high domed structure with a commanding 360° city view, the conservatory houses a tropical rain forest with more than 100 plant species as well as free-flying tropical birds. Conservatory admission is C$3 (US$2.15) for adults and C$1.50 (US$1.05) for seniors and children.

The University of British Columbia campus incorporates a number of parks and gardens. The **UBC Botanical Garden,** 6250 Stadium Rd., Gate 8 (☎ 604/ 822-4208), which has 70 acres of formal alpine, herb, and exotic plantings, was established nearly a century ago. Nearby is the **Nitobe Memorial Garden,** 6565 NW Marine Dr., Gate 4 (☎ 604/822-9666), a traditional Japanese garden. A double-entry ticket is C$5.75 (US$4.10) for adults.

Opened in 1989, **Pacific Spirit Park**'s 1,885 acres of temperate rain forest, marshes, and beaches completely surround the UBC campus and include nearly 35 kilometers (22 miles) of maintained trails suited for hiking, riding, mountain biking, and beach combing. Open from 8am to dusk, this university endowment land is free of admission and open to the public.

Capilano River Regional Park, 4500 Capilano Rd., North Vancouver (☎ 604/ 666-1790), surrounds the Capilano Canyon Suspension Bridge & Park (see above). Hikers can trek along the Capilano trails for 7 kilometers (4½ miles) down to the

Lions Gate Bridge or 1.6 kilometers (1 mile) upstream to a launching point for kayakers and canoers wishing to run the rapids under the suspension bridge.

Lynn Canyon Park, Park Road, offers a great free attraction: the **Lynn Canyon Suspension Bridge.** Built in 1912, it rivals the footbridge over Capilano Canyon (see above). Measuring 225 feet from end to end, it's half as long but 10 feet higher than the Capilano Suspension Bridge. Best of all, it's free. A 10-minute walk upstream, 30-Foot Pool is a popular spot for swimming and sunning.

Eight kilometers (5 miles) west of Lions Gate Bridge is **Lighthouse Park,** Marine Drive West, West Vancouver (☎ 604/922-1211), a 185-acre rugged terrain forest that you can traverse on its 13 kilometers (8 miles) of trails. One of the paths leads to the 60-foot-tall Point Atkinson Lighthouse, on a rocky bluff overlooking the Straits of Georgia with a panoramic view of Vancouver. It's an easy trip on bus no. 250.

Driving up-up-up the mountain from **Lighthouse Park** will eventually get you to the top at **Cypress Park.** Stop halfway up at the scenic viewpoint for sweeping views of Vancouver, the harbor, and the islands, with Washington State's Mount Baker looming above the eastern horizon. The park is 12 kilometers (7½ miles) north of Cypress Bowl Road and the Highway 99 junction in West Vancouver: part of the North Shore mountain chain overlooking Vancouver. At the park you'll find an intricate network of trails for hiking: trails that turn into ski trails—both downhill and cross-country—during winter.

Rising 4,767 feet above Indian Arm behind North Vancouver, ✪ **Mount Seymour Provincial Park,** 1700 Mt. Seymour Rd., North Vancouver (☎ 604/986-2261 or 604/872-6616), offers another view of the area's Coast Mountain range. The road to this park roams through stands of Douglas fir, red cedar, and hemlock. At a higher altitude than Grouse Mountain, Mount Seymour has a spectacular view of Washington State's Mount Baker on clear days. It has challenging hiking trails that go straight to the summit, where you can see Indian Arm, Vancouver's bustling commercial port, the city skyline, the Straight of Georgia, and Vancouver Island. The trails are open all summer for hiking; in winter, the paths are maintained for skiing, snowboarding, and snowshoeing. A cafeteria and gift shop are open year-round. Mount Seymour is open daily from 7am to 10pm (see "Outdoor Activities & Spectator Sports," later in this chapter).

NATURE PRESERVES

Thousands of migratory birds following the Pacific Flyway rest and feed in the 850-acre **George C. Reifel Migratory Bird Sanctuary,** 5191 Robertson Rd., Westham Island (☎ 604/946-6980), which was created by a former bootlegger and bird lover. More than 263 species have been spotted, like Temminck's stints, spotted red-shanks, bald eagles, Siberian and trumpeter swans, peregrine falcons, blue herons, owls, and coots. An observation tower, over 3 kilometers (2 miles) of paths, free bird seed, and picnic tables make this an ideal destination from October to April. The sanctuary is wheelchair accessible and open daily from 9am to 4pm. Admission is C$3.25 (US$2.30) for adults and C$1 (US70¢) for seniors and children.

The **Capilano Salmon Hatchery** (☎ 604/666-1790) is on the river's east bank, one-half kilometer (a quarter mile) below the Cleveland Dam. About two million coho and chinook salmon are hatched here annually in glass-fronted tanks connected to the river, through which you can observe the departing fry (baby fishes) and returning mature coho and chinook salmon. It's free and open daily from 8am to 7pm (to 4pm in winter). Take the SeaBus to Lonsdale Quay and transfer to bus no. 236; the trip takes less than 45 minutes.

BEACHES

English Bay Beach, at the end of Davie Street off Denman Street and Beach Avenue, is an ideal spot to watch Vancouver's spectacular sunsets. On Stanley Park's western end, **Second Beach** is a quick stroll north from English Bay Beach. A playground and a freshwater lap pool make this a convenient family spot. Secluded **Third Beach,** off Stanley Park Drive, is also easily accessible via the seawall. Between English Bay Beach and the Burrard Street Bridge is **Sunset Beach.** At the edge of Sunset Beach is the **Aquatic Centre,** with an indoor public pool and other facilities.

Affectionately called Kits Beach, **Kitsilano Beach,** along Arbutus Drive near Ogden Street, draws a younger crowd. **Jericho Beach** (Alma Street off Point Grey Road) is another local after-work social spot. **Wreck Beach** is Vancouver's immensely popular nude beach; you get there by taking Trail 6 on the UBC campus near Gate 6 down through the woods to the water's edge. **Ambleside Park,** at the northern foot of Lions Gate Bridge, is a popular north-shore spot.

7 Special Events & Festivals

The first event every year is the annual New Year's Day **Polar Bear Swim** (☎ 604/732-2302); thousands of hardy citizens take their first dip of the year in English Bay's frigid waters. In late January or early February, the **Chinese New Year** (☎ 604/687-6021) is celebrated with 2 weeks of festivities, including firecrackers, dancing-dragon parades in Chinatown, and a special weekend kickoff at the Plaza of Nations.

The **International Wine Festival** (☎ 604/827-6622), in late March and early April, is a major event that takes place at the Vancouver Convention Centre. You're handed a glass at the door and can try the latest vintages from around the world, sampling cheeses and pâtés along the way. Even the event's rarest wines are usually available in the on-site wine shop.

During the second or third week of April, the **Vancouver Sun Run** (☎ 604/689-9540) takes place at BC Place Stadium. It's a charity race that attracts 17,000 runners, joggers, and walkers. And runners from all over the world gather during the first weekend in May for the **Vancouver International Marathon** (☎ 604/872-2928).

Kids love the **International Children's Festival** (☎ 604/687-7697), held the last week in May or the first week in June in Vanier Park on False Creek. Activities, plays, music, and crafts, all for children, are featured.

On June 6 and 7, 1998, Vancouver will host the **Sumo Basho** (☎ 604/682-2222), the world championships of Sumo wrestling. This 2,000-year-old event has never been staged in Canada.

In mid-June, the **Vancouver Storytelling Festival** (☎ 604/876-2272) keeps people of all ages spellbound as some of the world's greatest raconteurs spin their tales. Around the same time the **National Aboriginal Day Community Celebration** (☎ 604/873-3761) offers the public an opportunity to learn about native-Canadian Indian cultures.

During the **Canadian International Dragon Boat Festival** (☎ 604/688-2382), held the third week of June, you can watch the races from False Creek's north shore, where 150 local and international teams compete. Four stages of music, dance, and Chinese acrobatics are also staged at the Plaza of Nations as part of the event.

From late June to early July, more than 800 international jazz and blues performers come here to take part in the **du Maurier International Jazz Festival** (☎ 604/682-0706), at venues ranging from the Orpheum Theatre and the Yaletown Hotel to the Plaza of Nations.

On July 1, **Canada Day** (☎ 604/641-1987), Canada Place Pier hosts an all-day celebration that begins with the swearing-in of new citizens. Music and dance acts perform outdoors, and a fireworks display over the harbor tops off the entertainment. There's also a salmon barbecue and fair in Steveston.

The second or third weekend of July brings the **Vancouver Folk Music Festival** (☎ 604/879-2931). International folk music is played outdoors on Jericho Beach Park. At about the same time, **SeaFest** (☎ 604/684-3378) takes place on and around Kits Beach with a parade, salmon barbecues, concerts, and fireworks. The highlight is the arrival of the competitors of the Nanaimo-to-Vancouver bathtub race (yes, bathtubs with outboard motors). They abandon their boats at the shore and dash up Kits Beach hoping to be first to ring the brass bell that marks the finish of their comically grueling race.

At the end of July there's the **Powell Street Festival** (☎ 604/682-4355), an annual festival of Japanese culture with music, dance, and food. There's also the **Obon Festival** (☎ 604/253-7033), the Japanese full-moon festival that takes place in Oppenheimer Park with kimonoed classical dancers and heart-quaking koto drummers. The **Ecomarine Kayak Marathon** (☎ 604/689-7575) takes place the last week in July, with competitors racing sea kayaks in Georgia Strait's open waters. The Jericho Sailing Centre, at Jericho Beach, hosts the race and can provide details.

Three international fireworks companies compete for a coveted title and put up their best displays with accompanying music over English Bay Beach in the ✪ **Benson & Hedges Symphony of Fire** (☎ 604/738-0883), held from the end of July to the first week in August. Don't miss the big finale on the fourth evening.

From mid-August to Labour Day, Vancouver puts on the **Pacific National Exhibition** (☎ 604/253-2311). The 10th-largest fair in North America has everything from big-name entertainment to a demolition derby, livestock demonstrations, and logger-sports competitions. On Labour Day weekend, the **Molson Indy Vancouver** (☎ 604/684-4639, or 604/280-4639 for tickets) roars through Yaletown and False Creek, attracting more than 500,000 spectators to this 3-day event.

From early to mid-October, the highly acclaimed **Vancouver International Film Festival** (☎ 604/685-0260) features 250 new works, revivals, and retrospectives from more than 40 countries. Attendance is over 120,000, not including the stars and celebrities who appear annually.

In addition to adorning the city in a festival of lights, Vancouver stages a **Christmas Carol Ship Parade** (☎ 604/682-2007) on English Bay every December. You can book seats on any of the dozens of charter boats that join in the procession around the bay and harbor.

8 Outdoor Activities & Spectator Sports

OUTDOOR ACTIVITIES

The city's hottest outdoor sports are skiing, mountain biking, sailing, and in-line skating, which you can do year-round. Pick up a copy of the free monthly *Coast: The Outdoor Recreation Magazine* (☎ 604/876-1473), which lets you in on the latest snow conditions, bike trails, climbing spots, competitions, races, and the like.

Below are specialized rental outfitters listed according to activity. For a one-stop outlet, try **Recreational Rentals,** 2560 Arbutus St. (☎ 604/733-7368).

BIKING Helmets are required both on- and off-road. Cyclists have separate lanes on developed park and beach paths. Some West End hotels offer guests bike storage or rentals. Vancouver's hot ○ **bicycle runs** are Stanley Park and the Seawall Promenade; English Bay to Sunset Beaches; Granville Island to Vanier Park; Kitsilano Beach; Jericho Beach; Pacific Spirit Park; and the 7-Eleven Bicycle Path.

Local mountain bikers love hitting **Hollyburn Mountain** in Cypress Provincial Park in West Vancouver. **Grouse Mountain**'s backside trails are some of the best around. Mount Seymour's very steep **Good Samaritan Trail** connects up to the Baden-Powell Trail and the Bridle Path near Mount Seymour Road. **Cycling Vancouver** (☎ 604/737-3034) has a group ride and special-events **hot line** (☎ 604/731-3165).

Rentals run around C$3.90 to C$6 (US$2.80 to US$4.30) per hour or C$16 to C$24 (US$11 to US$17) per day. Bikes, helmets, locks, and child trailers are all available on an hourly or daily basis at **Spokes Bicycle Rentals & Espresso Bar,** 1798 W. Georgia St. (☎ 604/688-5141). **Alleycat Rentals,** 1779 Robson St., in the alley (☎ 604/684-5117), is a popular shop among locals.

BOATING   You can find bareboat rentals of 15- to 17-foot power boats for a few hours or several weeks at **Stanley Park Boat Rentals Ltd.,** Coal Harbour Marina (☎ 604/682-6257). **Delta Charters,** 3500 Cessna Dr., Richmond (☎ 800/661-7762 or 604/273-4211), has weekly and monthly rates for 32- to 58-foot powered bareboat craft.

CANOEING & KAYAKING   Both placid, urban False Creek and the wilder 29-kilometer (18.2-mile) North Vancouver fjord—Indian Arm—have launching points you can reach by car or bus. Granville Island's **Ecomarine Ocean Kayak Centre,** 1668 Duranleau St. (☎ 604/689-7575), has 2-hour, daily, and weekly kayak rentals. They have another office at the **Jericho Sailing Centre,** 1300 Discovery St., at Jericho Beach (☎ 604/689-7575). **Deep Cove Canoe & Kayak Rentals,** at the foot of Gallant Street, Deep Cove (☎ 604/929-2268), near Indian Arm, offers hourly and daily canoe rentals, single and double kayak rentals, and customized tours.

DIVING   Scuba diving in the chilly Georgia Straight is popular. Wreck diving here is rated as some of the world's best. (More than 2,000 ships have gone to "the Graveyard of the Pacific" in the last 2 centuries.) Cates Park in Deep Cove, Whytecliff Park near Horseshoe Bay, and Lighthouse Park (see "Parks, Gardens, Nature Preserves & Beaches," earlier in this chapter) are nearby dive spots. **Rowand's Reef Scuba Shop Ltd.** (☎ 604/669-3483), based on Granville Island, offers instruction, equipment rental, and charters. The **Diving Locker,** 2745 W. 4th Ave. (☎ 604/736-2681), rents equipment and offers courses.

FISHING   Five species of salmon, rainbow and Dolly Varden trout, steelhead, and even sturgeon abound in local waters. To fish, you need a nonresident license. There are separate ones for saltwater and for freshwater. Tackle shops sell licenses and have information on current restrictions. **Hanson's Fishing Outfitters,** 102–580 Hornby St. (☎ 604/684-8988) downtown; **Bonnie Lee Fishing Charters Ltd.,** on the dock at the entrance to Granville Island (mailing address: 744 W. King Edward Ave., Vancouver, BC, V5Z 2C8; ☎ 604/290-7447); and **Granville Island Boat Rentals** (☎ 604/682-6287), 1696 Duranleau St., on Granville Island, are all outstanding Vancouver outfitters.

Corcovado Yacht Charters Ltd., 1676 Duranleau St. (☎ 604/669-7907), also on Granville Island, has competitive rates. **Reel Adventures,** 1334 Larkspur Dr., North Vancouver (☎ 604/945-6755), specializes in wilderness sportfishing.

The *Vancouver Sun* newspaper prints a **fishing report** in the sports section detailing which fish are in season and where the best spots are.

GOLF This is a year-round Vancouver sport, except when it's raining too hard, of course. With five public 18-hole courses and pitch-and-putt courses in the city and dozens more nearby, Vancouver ensures that no golfer is far from his or her love. The **University Golf Club,** 5185 University Blvd. (☎ **604/224-1818**), is a great 6,560-yard, par-71 public course; or call **A-1 Last Minute Golf Hotline** at ☎ **800/684-6344** or 604/878-1833 for substantial discounts and short-notice tee times on more than 30 Vancouver area courses; there's no membership fee.

HIKING **Stanley Park** has some gorgeous back trails through the towering cedars that are favorites with flatland hikers and runners, like the trail to **Beaver Lake.**

On the right, just a few yards from the entrance to Grouse Mountain Resort, is an entry to the world-famous 42-kilometer (26-mile) **Baden-Powell Trail.** The trail, with thick forest, rocky bluffs, and snow-fed streams racing through ravines, stretches from Cates Park to Horseshoe Bay. Even if you only want to hike the Grouse Mountain leg, start early and be ready for some steep ascents. (You can buy a one-way ticket on the Skyride so that you don't have to hike both ways.)

Lynn Canyon, Lynn Headwaters, Capilano Regional Park, Mount Seymour Provincial Park, and Cypress Provincial Park have good trails of all difficulty levels. Pay attention to the posted trail warnings: Some paths do cross black-bear habitats. Always remember to sign in with the park service at the start of your trail. Golden Ears and the Lions in Golden Ears Provincial Park are for serious hikers only.

ICE-SKATING Robson Square has free skating on a covered ice rink from November to early April. Rentals are available in the adjacent concourse. The **West End Community Centre,** 870 Denman St. (☎ 604/257-8333), rents skates at its enclosed rink from October to March. The **Ice Sports Centre,** Burnaby (☎ 604/291-0626), is the Vancouver Canucks' official practice facility. It has eight rinks, is open year-round, and offers lessons and rentals.

IN-LINE SKATING You'll find locals rolling along beach paths, streets, park paths, and promenades. If you didn't bring a pair of blades, go to **Alleycat Rentals** (see "Biking," above), the preferred local outfitter; rentals run C$4.50 (US$3.20) per hour (2-hour minimum) or C$15 (US$11) per day or overnight.

JOGGING Runners should head for Stanley Park's Seawall Promenade, Lost Lagoon, and Beaver Lake. The scenery is spectacular, and there are no motor vehicles.

SAILING Charter a sailboat on Granville Island at **Cooper Boating Centre,** 1620 Duranleau St. (☎ 604/687-4110), which has cruises, bareboat rentals, and sail-instruction packages on 20- to 43-foot boats; or at **Seafari Sailing,** 1521 Foreshore Walk, (☎ 604/683-6837), which also offers a range of courses and charters.

SKIING & SNOWBOARDING While it seldom snows in the city's downtown and central areas, there are three ski resorts in the north-shore mountains. Vancouverites frequently ski in the morning before work or take advantage of after-dinner night skiing.

Grouse Mountain, 6400 Nancy Greene Way, North Vancouver (☎ 604/984-0661, or 604/986-6262 for a snow report), is 3 kilometers (2 miles) from Lions Gate Bridge. The resort has a 300-foot half pipe for snowboarders, night skiing, special events, instruction, trails ranging from beginner to expert, and a spectacular view. Lift tickets good for the entire day plus night skiing are C$19 (US$14) weekdays and C$25 (US$18) weekends for adults.

Mount Seymour Provincial Park, 1700 Mt. Seymour Rd., North Vancouver (☎ 604/986-2261, or 604/879-3999 for a snow report), has the area's highest base elevation. It's accessed by four chairs and a tow. Lift tickets are C$18 (US$13) all day on weekdays, C$12 (US$9) for evening-only on weekdays, and C$26 (US$19) all day on weekends.

Cypress Bowl, 1610 Mt. Seymour Rd. (☎ **604/926-5612,** or 604/926-6007 for a snow report), has the area's highest vertical drop (1,750 ft.), challenging ski and snowboard runs, and 16 kilometers (10 miles) of track-set cross-country skiing trails, including 5 kilometers (3 miles) set aside for night skiing and a shuttle service that picks you up and drops you off at **Cypress Mountain Sports** (☎ **604/878-9229**) in the Park Royal Shopping Centre in West Vancouver (C$9/US$6 per round-trip).

SWIMMING Vancouver's midsummer saltwater temperature rarely exceeds 65°F. However, Stanley Park's Second Beach has a large freshwater pool. See "Parks, Gardens, Nature Preserves & Beaches," earlier in this chapter, for a rundown of city beaches.

TENNIS Vancouver's 180 city-maintained, outdoor public hard courts have 1-hour limits; operate on a first-come, first-served basis; and are free (except for the Beach Avenue courts, which charge a nominal fee). Stanley Park has 21 courts, Queen Elizabeth Park 18, and Kitsilano Beach Park 10. The **UBC Tennis Training Centre,** on Thunderbird Boulevard (☎ **604/822-2505**), has 10 outdoor and 4 indoor courts that you can reserve for C$10 (US$7) per hour. **Bayshore Bicycle and Rollerblade Rentals,** 745 Denman St. (☎ **604/688-2453**), and 1601 W. Georgia St. (☎ **604/689-5071**), rents tennis racquets for C$10 (US$7) per day.

WILDLIFE WATCHING During winter, thousands of bald eagles line the banks of Indian Arm fjord to feed on spawning salmon. The Capilano Salmon Hatchery (see "Parks, Gardens, Nature Preserves & Beaches," earlier in this chapter) is overflowing with leaping salmon.

Orcas (killer whales) also watch the salmon migration, as salmon are their favorite food. In 1997, orcas were even spotted in Burrard Inlet and off Spanish Banks. Companies offering whale-watching trips are **Corcovado Yacht Charters Ltd.** (see "Fishing," above), and **Ecomarine Coastal Kayaking School** (☎ **604/689-7520**) (see "Canoeing & Kayaking," above).

Even **Stanley Park** is home to a heron rookery. (You can see these primitive birds nesting outside the Vancouver Aquarium.) But ravens, dozens of species of waterfowl, raccoon, skunk, beaver, even coyote are also full-time residents. And over 260 bird species have been spotted at the **George C. Reifel Migratory Bird Sanctuary** (see "Parks, Gardens, Nature Preserves & Beaches," earlier in this chapter).

WINDSURFING Windsurfing isn't allowed at the mouth of False Creek near Granville Island, but you can bring a board to Jericho and English Bay beaches or rent one there. You can find equipment sales, rental (including wet suits), and instruction at **Windsure Windsurfing School,** 1300 Discovery St., at Jericho Beach (☎ **604/224-0615**), or **Boards Unlimited,** 3743 W. 10th Ave. (☎ **604/228-0256**).

SPECTATOR SPORTS

You can get information about all major events and buy tickets at the **Vancouver Visitor Info Centre,** 200 Burrard St. (☎ **604/683-2000**).

BASEBALL The **Vancouver Canadians** draw up to 6,500 spectators per game to their home at the Nat Bailey Stadium, 33rd Avenue at Ontario Street, near Little Mountain Park (☎ **604/872-5232**).

BASKETBALL Vancouver was just awarded the NBA's 29th franchise and began play in the 1995–96 season. The **Vancouver Grizzlies** play at General Motors Place Stadium, 800 Griffith Way (☎ **604/899-7469;** event hot line 604/899-7444).

FOOTBALL   The Canadian Football League **BC Lions** (☎ 604/583-7747) play at BC Place Stadium, 777 Pacific Blvd. S., at Beatty and Robson streets.

HORSE RACING   Hastings Park Racecourse, Exhibition Park (☎ 604/254-1631), has thoroughbred racing from mid-April to October.

ICE HOCKEY   The NHL's **Vancouver Canucks** play at General Motors Place Stadium, 800 Griffith Way (☎ 604/899-4600).

SOCCER   APSL's **Vancouver 86ers** (☎ 604/273-0086) play at **Swangard Stadium** (☎ 604/435-7121) in Burnaby.

9 Shopping

The late Italian designer Gianni Versace once said that Robson Street is "one of 10 streets in the world where you have to have a store." It's hard to spend time in Vancouver without going on a shopping spree: Robson Street is unarguably the street to stroll for trendy fashions; Granville Island has crafts and kids' stuff; Kerrisdale offers reasonably priced clothing; Gastown is filled with native-Canadian Indian art; Yaletown has hip designer wear and furniture; and downtown Vancouver is laced with designers' boutiques, including Valentino, Fendi, Cartier, Dolce y Gabbana, Ferragamo, Chanel, Armani, Polo/Ralph Lauren, and Versace.

Vancouver's real finds, however, are the pieces made by the numerous local fashion designers and craftspeople. Don't miss the bold native Indian–influenced appliquéd leather vests and coats at **Dorothy Grant**'s boutique or **Zonda Nellis**'s sumptuously soft handwoven and hand-painted creations.

You don't have to purchase an antique to acquire a high-quality original native-Indian work of art. As experts at the **Museum of Anthropology** will tell you, these cultures aren't dead. If a work is crafted by a talented Pacific Northwest tribal artisan, it's a real piece of tribal art.

The province's **wines**—especially rich, honey-thick ice wines, such as Jackson-Triggs gold-medal 1994 Johannesburg Riesling Ice wine and bold reds such as the Quails' Gate 1994 Limited Release Pinot Noir—are worth buying by the case. Five years of restructuring, reblending, and careful tending by French and German master vintners have won these vineyards world recognition. John Simes of Mission Hill won the 1994 Avery's Trophy for his 1992 Grand Barrel Reserve Chardonnay at the London International Wine and Spirits Competition.

In Vancouver, you'll find **salmon** everywhere. Many shops pack whole fresh salmons with ice for U.S. visitors to bring back with them. Shops also carry delectable smoked salmon in travel-safe, vacuum-packed containers. Some offer decorative cedarwood gift boxes; most offer overnight air transport. Try treats made of salmon, including salmon jerky and Indian candy, available at public markets like the Lonsdale Quay Market and Granville Island Public Market.

SHOPPING A TO Z

ANTIQUES   The **Vancouver Antique Centre,** 422 Richards St. (☎ 604/669-7444), contains 15 shops specializing in everything from china, glass, Orientalia, and jewelry to militaria, sports, toys, and watches. **Uno Langmann Ltd.,** 2117 Granville St. (☎ 604/736-8825), specializes in European and North American paintings, furniture, silver, and objects from the 18th to early 20th centuries.

ARTS & CRAFTS   Even if you're not in the market, go gallery-hopping to see works by native-Indian artists Bill Reid (perhaps the best-known native artist) and Richard Davidson and photographer David Neel.

Images for a Canadian Heritage, 164 Water St. (☎ 604/685-7046), and the Inuit Gallery of Vancouver, 345 Water St. (☎ 604/688-7323), are government-licensed galleries featuring traditional and contemporary works. Hill's Indian Crafts, 165 Water St. (☎ 604/685-4249), is where you'll find Cowichan sweaters, moccasins, ceremonial masks, wood sculptures, totem poles worth up to C$35,000 (US$25,000), serigraphic prints, soapstone sculptures, and jewelry.

BOOKS   At World Wide Books & Maps, 736A Granville St., across from Eatons (☎ 604/687-3320), you'll find specialty travel guides, travelogues, topographical maps, globes, marine charts, and such. Duthie Books, 650 W. Georgia St. (☎ 604/684-4496), with locations around Vancouver, and Blackberry Books, 2855 W. Broadway (☎ 604/739-8116), are Vancouver's homegrown booksellers and have extensive selections of Canadiana. Little Sister's Book & Art Emporium, 1238 Davie St. (☎ 604/669-1753), has a large selection of lesbian and gay books, videos, and magazines, as well as a huge adult-novelties department.

DEPARTMENT STORES   Since the 1670s, Hudson's Bay Company has sold quality Canadian goods. The Bay, 674 Granville St. (☎ 604/681-6211), is still the place to buy a Hudson's Bay woolen point blanket (the colorful stripes originally represented how many beaver pelts each blanket was worth) as well as Polo, DKNY, Anne Klein II, and Liz Claiborne. The store's modern trading post is filled with British Columbia souvenirs. Eatons, Pacific Centre Mall, 701 Granville St. (☎ 604/685-7112), is filled with fashions from the classic to the outrageous, housewares, gourmet foods, and books. The seventh-floor bargain annex sells discount children's and men's clothing.

FASHION   International designers with boutiques here include Chanel, 103–755 Burrard St. (☎ 604/682-0522); Salvatore Ferragamo, 918 Robson St. (☎ 604/669-4495); Gianni Versace's Istante, 773 Hornby St. (☎ 604/669-8398); Polo/Ralph Lauren, The Landing, 375 Water St. (☎ 604/682-7656); and Plaza Escada, Sinclair Centre, 757 W. Hastings St. (☎ 604/688-8558).

❂ Dorothy Grant, Sinclair Centre, 250–757 W. Hastings St. (☎ 604/681-0201), boasts an exciting Feastwear collection with exquisitely detailed native Haida motifs appliquéd on coats, leather vests, jackets, caps, and accessories. Zonda Nellis Design Ltd., 2203 S. Granville St. (☎ 604/736-5668), features imaginative handwoven separates, pleated silks, sweaters, vests, and soft knits as well as a new line of hand-painted silks and velvets that coordinate with her signature weaves. Carol Claffey, 3302 Granville St. (☎ 604/731-6828), is a new local designer, and her casual, office, and evening wear are feminine, flattering, and comfortable. Iago-go, 1496 Cartwright St. (☎ 604/689-2400), will delight your kids with one-of-a-kind colorful clothes by local designers. This Granville Island shop, in the Kids-Only Market, has colorfully printed handcrafted children's fashions.

FOOD   At Au Chocolat, 1702 Davie St. (☎ 604/682-3536), grab a table inside or on the patio and indulge. It carries the most delectable handmade Belgian chocolate truffles and other treats and will even ship your purchases. Chocolate Arts, 2037 W. 4th St. (☎ 604/739-0475), also makes handmade chocolates and truffles, produced with the finest Belgian chocolate.

The Lobsterman, 1807 Mast Tower Rd., on Granville Island (☎ 604/687-4531), can pack for air travel any of the live seafood in the store's tanks—from lobsters and Dungeness crab to oysters, mussels, clams, geoduck, and scallops. Salmon Village, 779 Thurlow St. (☎ 604/685-3378), has a great selection of prepackaged gift boxes and individual items like smoked salmon, salmon jerky, Indian candy, and caviar that can be wrapped and shipped home.

GIFTS & SOUVENIRS **Canadian Impressions at the Station,** 601 Cordova St. (☎ 604/681-3507), carries lumberjack shirts, Cowichan sweaters, T-shirts, baseball caps, salmon jerky, maple syrup, and shortbread cookies. Aside from an extensive run of T-shirts and trinkets, at the **Capilano River Trading Company,** 1060 Robson St. (☎ 604/682-2676), you'll find Tilley hats, Australian outback oilskin jackets, polar fleece vests, shearling coats, down booties, and other outdoor weekend clothing.

JEWELRY **Henry Birks & Sons Ltd.,** Vancouver Centre, 710 Granville St. (☎ 604/669-3333), has been designing and creating beautiful jewelry and watches for more than a century. **Karl Stittgen + Goldsmiths,** 2203 Granville St. (☎ 604/737-0029), creates gold pins, pendants, rings, and other accessories that highlight their commitment to fine craftsmanship.

MARKETS The 50,000-square-foot **Granville Island Public Market,** 1669 Johnston St., Granville Island (☎ 604/666-5784), has food counters selling Chinese, vegetarian, and Mexican fare or just about anything else you could want. There's usually live entertainment, and there's always a lot to see daily from 9am to 6pm (open at noon on Sunday and closed Monday in winter except public holidays).

Lonsdale Quay Market, 123 Carrie Cates Ct., at the SeaBus terminal, North Vancouver (☎ 604/985-6261), is filled with fashions, gift shops, Kids' Alley (dedicated to children's shops and containing a play area), food counters, coffee bars, and bookstores. It's open Monday to Thursday and Saturday from 9:30am to 6:30pm, Friday from 9:30am to 9pm.

SHOPPING CENTERS **Pacific Centre Mall,** 700 W. Georgia St. (☎ 604/688-7236), is a 3-block complex containing 200 shops and services including Godiva, Benetton, Crabtree & Evelyn, and Eddie Bauer. Underground concourses make it a pleasant rainy-day experience. Across the Lions Gate Bridge, **Park Royal Shopping Centre,** 2002 Park Royal S., West Vancouver (☎ 604/925-9576), consists of two facing malls on either side of Marine Drive. The Gap, Disney, Marks & Spencer, Eatons, The Bay, Coast Mountain Sports, Cypress Mountain Sports, and a public market are just a few of the more than 200 stores in the complex.

TEA **T Oasis in Nobo,** 2460 Heather St. (☎ 604/874-8320), doesn't serve a traditional afternoon tea, but something equally warm, comforting, and herbal. Teas and requisite paraphernalia from around the world are available.

TOYS The **Kids Only Market,** 1496 Cartwright St., Granville Island (☎ 604/689-8447), is a 24-shop complex that sells toys, craft kits, games, computer software, and books for kids.

WINES **Marquis Wine Cellars,** 1034 Davie St. (☎ 604/684-0445), carries a full range of BC wines and an exceptional array of international vintages.

10 Vancouver After Dark

You can find current events and nightclub listings in the monthly *Vancouver* magazine; *The Georgia Straight,* a weekly tabloid; or *Xtra! West,* the gay and lesbian biweekly tabloid.

The **Vancouver Cultural Alliance Arts Hotline,** 938 Howe St., in the Orpheum Theatre (☎ 604/684-2787; Web site: www.culturenet.ca/vca), has 24-hour information on all major cultural events and instructions on where and how to get tickets.

THE PERFORMING ARTS

You can buy tickets for major performances at the Visitor Info Centre (see "Visitor Information," earlier in this chapter). Tickets for clubs, local theater, and special attractions are available at the **Community Box Offices,** 1234 W. Hastings St. (☎ 604/280-2801), open Monday to Saturday from 9am to 5:30pm. Or call **Ticketmaster,** 1304 Hornby St. (☎ 604/280-4444).

VENUES   There are four venues where major touring shows appear: the **Orpheum Theatre,** 801 Granville St. (☎ 604/299-9000); the **Queen Elizabeth Complex,** 600 Hamilton St. (☎ 604/299-9000); the **Vancouver Playhouse,** at the corner of Hamilton and Dunsmuir streets (☎ 604/299-9000); and the **Ford Centre for the Performing Arts,** Homer Street off Robson Street (☎ 604/280-2222).

In a converted turn-of-the-century church, the **Vancouver East Cultural Centre,** 1895 Venables St. (☎ 604/254-9578), presents avant-garde theater productions, performances by international musical groups, various festivals and cultural events, children's programs, and art exhibits.

THEATER   Theater isn't confined to the theaters here; in summer, it heads outdoors with events like the Shakespearean series **Bard on the Beach,** at Vanier Park (☎ 604/737-0625), and **Theatre Under the Stars,** in Stanley Park (☎ 604/687-0174). Major Broadway productions also book into Vancouver, so you can see *Les Misérables, Miss Saigon, Sunset Boulevard, Phantom of the Opera, Kiss of the Spider Woman, Showboat,* or the like.

Originally Vancouver's Firehouse No. 1, the **Firehall Arts Centre,** 280 E. Cordova St. (☎ 604/689-0926), is the home of three cutting-edge companies—the Firehall Theatre Co., the Touchstone Theatre, and Axis Mime. The center also presents dance events, arts festivals, and concerts.

Two Granville Island theaters are note worthy. The **Arts Club Theatre,** 1585 Johnston St. (☎ 604/687-1644), has two stages. The 425-seat Granville Island Mainstage presents major dramas, comedies, and musicals with postperformance entertainment in the Backstage Lounge. The Arts Club Revue Stage is a cabaret-style showcase for improvisation nights, small productions, and musical revues such as *Ain't Misbehavin'.* The **Waterfront Theatre,** 1412 Cartwright St. (☎ 604/685-6217), is the home of the Carousel Theatre and School; it also hosts both touring and local dance, music, mime, and theater companies.

OPERA   The repertoire of the **Vancouver Opera** (☎ 604/682-2871), whose season runs from October to June, ranges from Puccini, Strauss, Verdi, Gounod, Bizet, and Rossini classics to 20th-century works by Benjamin Britten and Kurt Janacek as well as esoteric modern productions. The English supertitles projected above the stage of the Queen Elizabeth Theatre help you follow the operatic dialogue.

CLASSICAL MUSIC   The **Vancouver Symphony Orchestra** (☎ 604/684-9100 from 9am to 5pm or 604/876-3434 from 9am to 9pm) presents a number of classical, pop, and children's programs at their Orpheum Theatre home. Their traveling summer concert series takes them from White Rock and Cloverdale on the U.S. border to the Whistler area.

DANCE   If you love dance, catch the September **Dancing on the Edge Festival,** presenting 60 to 80 pieces over 10 days. You'll see works by local companies, including the **Anna Wyman Dance Theatre** (☎ 604/926-6535) and the **Karen Jamieson Dance Company** (☎ 604/872-5658).

The 12-year-old **Ballet British Columbia** (☎ 604/732-5003) regularly performs at the Queen Elizabeth Theatre. The innovative company presents works by choreographers such as John Alleyne and John Cranko. They also host soloists such as Mikhail Baryshnikov and companies such as American Ballet Theatre and the National Ballet of Canada.

COMEDY & MUSIC CLUBS

COMEDY Paul Wildman and J. O. Mass host a leading lineup of Canadian and American stand-ups at **Yuk Yuk's Komedy Kabaret,** Plaza of Nations, 750 Pacific Blvd. (☎ **604/687-5233**). Amateurs take the stage on Wednesday. It's a 200-seat theater, so it's hard to get a bad seat. Cover is C$3 to C$10 (US$2.15 to US$7), and show times are 9 and 11pm.

JAZZ, BLUES & FOLK The **Coastal Jazz and Blues Society** (☎ **604/ 682-0706**) has information on all current jazz and blues music events.

The elegant **Bacchus Piano Lounge,** in the Wedgewood Hotel, 845 Hornby St. (☎ **604/689-7777**), features live jazz music Monday to Saturday nights. The fireplace makes it cozy on rainy evenings. People show up in everything from suits to jeans in this richly appointed room. There's an excellent full restaurant menu, a light-snack menu, plus a great wine and drink list. Evening entertainment begins around 7pm.

Long John Baldry, Junior Wells, Koko Taylor, John Hammond, Jim Byrne, and many other blues masters have played at the **Yale Hotel,** 1300 Granville St. (☎ **604/ 681-9253**), a late-19th-century hotel. If you're a serious blues fan, this is the place to go. The room is nicely arranged for dancing and for sitting back and just enjoying the show. There's also a billiard corner set away from the stage. Cover is C$5 to C$7 (US$3.60 to US$5).

ROCK Rock clubs bloom and fade here as rapidly as they do in many metropolitan areas. At the **Mighty Niagara,** 435 Pender St. (☎ **604/688-7574**), look for the vintage neon NIAGARA FALLS sign out front. Here you'll find ska, thrash, heavy metal, and other genres, except Wednesdays, when Gin & Sin night turns the club into a lounge with jazz, a cigarette girl, and a dress code.

Richards on Richards, 1036 Richards St. (☎ **604/687-6794**), with two floors, four bars, a laser-light system, and valet parking, plays recorded music and hosts acts from blues sensation Junior Wells to the acid jazz sounds of Groove Collective.

Live bands play 1950s, 1960s, and 1970s classic rock at the **Roxy,** 932 Granville St. (☎ **604/684-7699**), which has showmen bartenders. Theme parties, old movies, and Wednesday Student Nights add to the entertainment. Cover is C$3 to C$6 (US$2.15 to US$4.30). The **Starfish Room,** 1055 Homer St., near Helmcken Street (☎ **604/682-4171**), is a large club with a huge dance floor that hosts international recording acts, as well as local artists. Monday and Tuesday are DJ nights. Cover is C$2 to C$6 (US$1.45 to US$4.30).

LOUNGES The week begins on Sunday at the Havana-style **Babalu,** 654 Nelson St., at Granville Street (☎ **604/605-4343**), with Vancouver radio personality Jason Manning's Martini Madness party. Mondays it's crooner Brian Evans. The rest of the week is a mix of Motown, salsa, and acid jazz. Babalu has a full menu, a well-stocked humidor, and a pool table. The **Chameleon Urban Lounge,** 801 W. Georgia St., entrance on Howe Street (☎ **604/669-0806**), is a plush basement space with live jazz most evenings and a full martini menu. **The Purple Onion,** 15 Water St., in Gastown (☎ **604/602-9442**), offers dancing, dining, cigars, and cocktails. The emphasis is on jazz and funk, with a side of salsa.

DANCE CLUBS

Big Bamboo, 1236 W. Broadway (☎ **604/733-2220**), is a warehouse space playing Gen-X industrial dance music. Wednesday is reggae night. Sport your best cyberwear to dance here. Cover is C$3 (US$2.15). **The Rage,** Plaza of Nations, 750 Pacific Blvd. S. (☎ **604/685-5585**), spins techno, disco, world-beat, and other dance music, complete with lights, smoke machines, and crowds of 21- to 30-year-olds. Occasional headline acts appear here, too.

The **Blue Note,** 455 W. Broadway (☎ **604/872-8866**), is a New York–style supper club. The generally relaxed audience includes a lot of couples. Cover is C$2 (US$1.45) on weekends, and there's a C$6 (US$4.30) drink minimum all week.

Learn to lambada and have a few Spanish and Mexican tapas for rejuvenation at **Mesaluna Latin American Dine & Dance,** 1926 West St. (☎ **604/739-1025**), a live-music supper club that also features a full menu and tequila drinks. It's open Thursday to Saturday with a variety of international bands.

BARS

Vancouver's bar scene is closely linked with its restaurant life. Because of the city's liquor laws, most hot spots for drinks also have full menus, and most restaurants have full bars, such as one of our favorites, the **Yaletown Brewing Company** (see "Dining," earlier in this chapter). Drinks generally cost between C$3 and C$6 (US$2.15 and US$4.30) in bars and lounges; closing times are around 2am (midnight on Sunday). Following are some of Vancouver's few bars:

Checkers, 1755 Davie St. (☎ **604/682-1831**), is a friendly West End bar where you can listen to classic rock inside or head for their small terrace for a people-watching view of English Bay. The **Rusty Gull,** 175 E. 1st St., North Vancouver (☎ **604/988-5585**), attracts gourmet beer drinkers who love the 13 local brews on tap at this live-entertainment watering hole. **Stamp's Landing,** 610 Stamp's Landing (☎ **604/879-0821**), is where the False Creek Marina yachting crowd hangs out.

GAY & LESBIAN BARS

The **Gay & Lesbian Centre,** 110 Bute St. (☎ **604/684-6869**), and the **Vancouver Lesbian Centre,** 876 Commercial Dr. (☎ **604/254-8458**), have information on the current hot spots. Vancouver's gay and lesbian scene is comfortable and open without the cloistered feeling you'll find in some other North American cities. A lot of the clubs feature theme nights and dance parties.

The **Heritage House Hotel,** 455 Abbott St., in Gastown (☎ **604/685-7777**), has three gay bars: **Charlie's Lounge** on the main floor is casual and elegant; **Chuck's Pub,** with a pool table and big-screen TVs, attracts both men and women; and the downstairs **Lotus Cabaret** lesbian bar is open Tuesday to Saturday, and only women are admitted on Wednesday and Friday.

The **Dufferin Pub,** 900 Seymour St. (☎ **604/683-4251**), opens every day at noon. Fourteen nude go-go boys set the party atmosphere, as divas of drag like Mz. Adrien and Myria Le Noir command the room. Various DJs and karaoke provide the background for this Vancouver institution.

CASINOS

Try your luck at blackjack, roulette, seven-card stud, Texas hold'em, sic-bo, red dog (diamond dog), and Caribbean stud poker. The casinos here aren't open 24 hours, don't feature floor shows, and don't have slot machines (though they may be added in the near future). One downtown option is the **Royal Diamond Casino,** 750 Pacific Blvd. S., at the Plaza of Nations (☎ 604/685-2340), which is informal and friendly. It's open daily from 6pm to 2am. Another is the **Great Canadian Casino–Renaissance Hotel Downtown,** 1133 W. Hastings St. (☎ 604/303-1000), a few blocks from Canada Place, open from noon to 2am.

Victoria & the Best of British Columbia

by Anistatia R. Miller & Jared M. Brown

British Columbia runs the length of Canada's west coast, from the Washington border to the Alaskan panhandle. Roughly 590,733 square kilometers (366,255 sq. miles), it's more than twice the size of California, though the population (3.7 million) is roughly a quarter the size of Los Angeles's. The majority of the residents live in the greater Vancouver and Victoria areas in the southwest, along a coastline dotted with beachfront communities, modern cities, and belts of rich farmland. But just a few hours' drive to the north on any of BC's three mostly two-lane highways, the communities are tiny, the sparse population is scattered, and the land is alternately towering forest, fields of stumps left by timber harvests, and high alpine wilderness. Between these extremes are the areas covered in this chapter.

British Columbia's outstanding feature is its variety of scenery, climates, and cultures. The wide-open ranch lands of the High Country and Kamloops contain the last vestiges of North America's legendary Wild West, with cowboys riding herd, prospectors staking claims, cattle drives crossing the high plains, and Indians struggling to reclaim ancestral lands. The rough-hewn mountains of the Cariboo and Chilcotin regions are topped with glaciers that run off into hidden lakes. Alpine meadows, buried under snow all winter, burst forth with a profusion of blossoms every summer. The rugged fjords and misty islands along the coast from the Queen Charlotte Islands to Howe Sound are home to much of the world's population of orcas, most of the world's remaining old-growth temperate rain forests, and some of North America's earliest human settlements. The arid Okanagan Valley is filled with fruit trees and surrounded by vineyards and wineries on the hillsides, and it boasts sagebrush and sand deserts. And hundreds of lakes, sheltered beaches, and majestic mountains stretch across the province, separating each region from the others yet interlacing them all.

1 Exploring British Columbia

There's more to British Columbia than Vancouver's urban bustle. In fact, the other Vancouver—Vancouver Island—is 90 minutes from Vancouver by ferry. On Vancouver Island is the province's capital, **Victoria.** It's a lovely seaport city that's proud of its Scottish and British roots, its lavish Victorian gardens, and its picturesque port.

Southern British Columbia

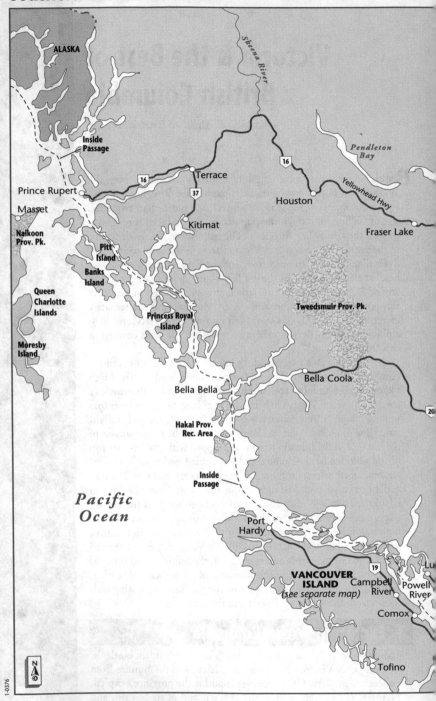

ALASKA

Skeena River

Inside Passage

Pendleton Bay

16

Terrace

16

Prince Rupert

37

Houston

Yellowhead Hwy

Masset

Kitimat

Fraser Lake

Naikoon Prov. Pk.

Pitt Island

Banks Island

Queen Charlotte Islands

Princess Royal Island

Tweedsmuir Prov. Pk.

Moresby Island

Bella Coola

20

Bella Bella

Hakai Prov. Rec. Area

Pacific Ocean

Inside Passage

Port Hardy

VANCOUVER ISLAND
(see separate map)

19

Lu

Campbell River

Powell River

Comox

Tofino

N

1-0376

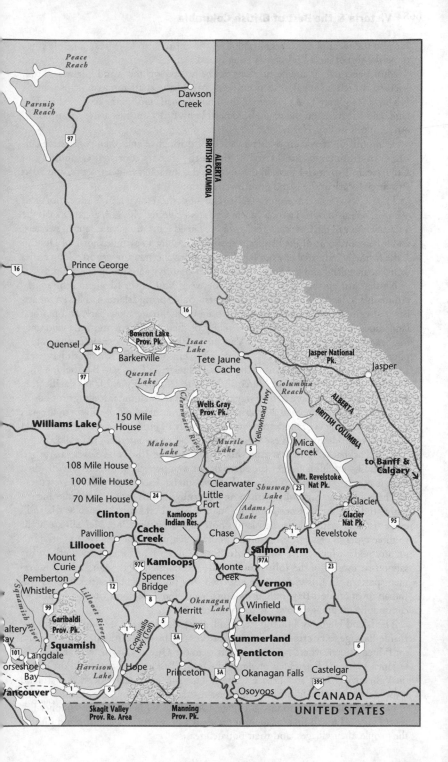

It's also the ideal place to begin exploring the entire island—which is nearly three times the size of New York state's Long Island.

Most Vancouver Island destinations can be reached via the Island Highway. From Victoria, which is Mile 0, to Nanaimo, it's part of the coast-to-coast Trans-Canada Highway (Highway 1). At Nanaimo, the Trans-Canada crosses the ferry to the mainland, and the route up the island becomes Highway 19 until its arrives at its northern terminus in Port Hardy.

Along this route you encounter a variety of distinctive and often contrasting cultures, environments, and lifestyles—from the heavily touristed tranquillity of **Goldstream Provincial Park** in the south to the untamed wilderness of **Cape Scott Provincial Park** at the island's northwestern tip.

The "City of Totem Poles"—**Duncan**—in the Cowichan Valley, north of Victoria, reveals another facet of Vancouver Island culture. This lush green valley is the ancestral home of the Cowichan tribe, who are famed for crafting hand-knitted sweaters, and it contains some of the island's best wineries. Only a few miles north of Duncan is the formerly industrial city of **Nanaimo,** the arrival center for visitors taking ferries from the mainland and the site of a major 19th-century coal-mining operation.

Nestled just off the island's east coast between Vancouver Island and the southern mainland lie the Gulf Islands. The largest, **Salt Spring Island,** is a haven for artists and craftspeople who are attracted to its mild climate, slow pace, and pastoral landscapes. In sharp contrast to the serenity of the east-coast islands, the wild, raging beauty of the Pacific Ocean on Vancouver Island's west coast entices photographers, hikers, kayakers, naturalists, and divers to explore **Pacific Rim National Park, Long Beach,** and the neighboring towns of **Ucluelet, Tofino,** and **Bamfield.** Thousands of visitors arrive between March and May to see as many as 20,000 **Pacific gray whales** pass close to shore as they migrate north to their summer feeding grounds in the Arctic Circle. More than 200 **shipwrecks** have occurred off the shores in the past 2 centuries, luring even more travelers to this eerily beautiful underwater world. And the park's world-famous **West Coast Trail** beckons an international collection of intrepid backpackers and "extreme" hikers to brave the 10-day hike over the rugged rescue trail—established after the survivors of a shipwreck in the early 1900s died from exposure on the beach because there was no land access route for the rescuers.

The bohemian charm of **Denman and Hornby islands** complements the ancient native-Indian culture of neighboring **Quadra Island** off central Vancouver Island's east coast. The waters along the island's northeast coast near **Port McNeill** are home to three types of orca pods: stationary pods, which live in the area consistently; migratory pods, which move annually from the Queen Charlotte Strait south to the salmon-rich waters of the **Johnstone Strait;** and transient pods with no fixed movement pattern. In this vicinity are also two tiny unique communities: the native-Indian town of **Alert Bay,** on Cormorant Island, and **Telegraph Cove,** a boardwalk community on pilings above the rocky shore.

The Island Highway's final port of call, **Port Hardy** is the starting point for the **Inside Passage ferry cruise** up the northern coast. The ferry carries passengers bound for Prince Rupert, where it meets the ferries to the **Queen Charlotte Islands.**

Since 1966, BC Ferries has operated the Inside Passage ferry between Port Hardy on Vancouver Island and Prince Rupert. This rugged, thickly forested mainland coastline is the highlight of the Vancouver-to-Alaska cruises and the ancestral home of native-Indian tribes who intrigued late-19th-century American photographer Edward Curtis so much that he spent more than a decade photographing and filming the people, their villages, and their potlatch feasts.

The ferry system also connects Prince Rupert to the remote **Queen Charlotte Islands,** the ancestral home of the Haida tribe and the location of the UNESCO World Heritage Site, **Haida Gwaii.** The remains of untouched Haida villages, abandoned more than 400 years ago, stand amid a thick rain forest of old-growth Sitka spruce. Cedar totem poles, sculptures, funerary boxes, and longhouses are all that remains of the culture that flourished there for nearly 10,000 years—and inspired Victoria-born artist Emily Carr's now-famous paintings and drawings, which you can see at the Vancouver Art Gallery.

On the mainland, the Yellowhead Highway (Highway 16) follows the lush Skeena River Valley from Prince Rupert on the coast of the Inside Passage to the province's interior. The Skeena Valley is home to a diverse community of fishers, loggers, and aluminum and paper mill workers in **Terrace.** The valley is also occupied by the Gitksan, Haisla, and Tshimshian (Nisga'a) tribes, whose ancestors lived in the area more than 8,000 years ago. The site of Canada's most recent volcanic activity, the **Nisga'a Memorial Lava Beds Provincial Park,** near Terrace, stands as a silent memorial to the villages that were buried in the lava flow that consumed the 60-square-kilometer (23-sq.-mile) area in 1750.

Heading south from Prince George and the Yellowhead Highway, you'll discover that the Canadian Wild West hasn't changed too much in the past century. This is Cariboo Country, the scene of the 1860s Cariboo Gold Rush. The town of **Lillooet,** "Mile 0" of the Old Cariboo Highway, was the starting point of a 250-mile journey taken by prospectors and settlers who sought their fortunes in the northern Cariboo goldfields.

The gold-rich town of **Barkerville** sprang up after a British prospector named Billy Barker struck it rich on Williams Creek. But gold isn't the only thing that attracts thousands of visitors to this area year-round. Cross-country skiers and snowmobilers explore the creek-side paths during the winter. And canoeists head a few miles north of Barkerville to a 72-mile circular paddling and portage route called **Bowron Lakes.**

It's only a 96.6-kilometer (60-mile) drive from Lillooet (and a 120.7km/75-mile drive from Vancouver) to North America's most popular ski resort—the glacial peaks of **Whistler and Blackcomb mountains.**

Whistler is also a popular summertime getaway, where you can ski or snowboard the Horstman Glacier at the top of Blackcomb Mountain, paddle the raging glacier-fed Green River or the placid River of Dreams, mountain-bike down the slopes of Whistler Mountain, or fish in the icy waters of **Birkenhead Lake Provincial Park.**

Due east, on the opposite side of Cariboo Country, the High Country's arid and hilly lowlands attract fishermen and boaters to the shores of the lower Thompson River and **Shuswap Lakes.** But rising up from this dry terrain as you head north to the town of **Clearwater** is a majestic 3,211,000-acre forested mountain wilderness formed by glaciers and volcanoes, **Wells Gray Provincial Park.**

Due south of the High Country on Highway 97, the arid **Okanagan Valley** and its long chain of crystal-blue lakes lure sports enthusiasts and wine lovers to its **fruit orchards, vineyards, golf courses, waterskiing,** and **ski resorts** in and around the towns of **Kelowna, Penticton,** and **Vernon.**

VISITOR INFORMATION

Contact **Tourism British Columbia,** 865 Hornby St., 8th Floor, Vancouver, BC, V6Z 2G3 (☎ 604/663-6000), and the **Tourism Association of Vancouver Island,** 302-45 Bastion Sq., Victoria, BC, V8W 1J1 (☎ 250/382-3551), for information about travel throughout the province. Contact the individual regional tourism associations and Visitor Info Centres listed in this chapter for more detailed local information.

DRIVING TIPS

Members of the American Automobile Association (AAA) can get assistance from the **BC Automobile Association** (BCAA) by calling ☎ **800/222-4357** or 604/ 293-2222. Seat belts and daytime headlights must be used while driving in the province.

THE GREAT OUTDOORS

It's hard to believe the province's variety of sports and other outdoor activities. Even the most cosmopolitan British Columbians spend their leisure time mountain biking, windsurfing, skiing, or hiking in the surrounding mountains, rivers, and meadows. The province's varied and largely uninhabited terrain seems to lure visitors to get close to nature.

To find out what's happening in the great British Columbian outdoors, pick up a copy of the free bimonthly tabloid *Coast: The Outdoor Recreation Magazine* (☎ **604/876-1473**). It contains up-to-date info on mountain-bike races, kayaking competitions, eco-challenges (an international pentathlon-style competition encompassing kayaking, horseback riding, hiking, mountain biking, and skiing). It's available at outfitters, recreational-equipment outlets, and community centers throughout the province.

BIKING   There are countless marked mountain-bike trails and cycling paths throughout British Columbia. In **Victoria,** the 8-mile Scenic Marine Drive has an adjacent paved path following Dallas Road and Beach Drive, then returning to downtown via Oak Bay Avenue (see "Victoria," below). On **Newcastle Island Provincial Park,** off the Nanaimo coast, the Shoreline Trail circles the lovely island, which was once a holiday resort (see "Side Trips from Victoria," below). There are plenty of marked trails to explore on **Salt Spring Island** in the Gulf Islands group between Vancouver Island and the mainland. The thick forests on both **Hornby Island** and neighboring **Denman Island** are best suited to rugged mountain-bike exploration (see "Central Vancouver Island," below).

The best **Okanagan Valley** off-road bike trail is the incredible **Kettle Valley Railway** route. The **Myra Canyon** railway route near Kelowna crosses over 18 trestle bridges and passes through two tunnels carved through the mountains (see "The Okanagan Valley," later in this chapter).

In the **Shuswap Lakes** region of the High Country, off-road trails run through the hilly terrain surrounding the lakes and rivers that attract hordes of houseboaters and anglers. It's also the location of the world's largest salmon run (see "Wells Gray Provincial Park & Shuswap Lakes," below).

The ski runs on the lower elevations of both **Whistler and Blackcomb mountains** are transformed into mountain-bike trails during summer. Bikes are permitted on the gondola ski lift, allowing you to reach the peaks where the winding, marked trails begin. From here, experts, intermediates, and novices barrel down through the colorful alpine slopes. Bike challenges take place regularly on both mountains from June to September (see "Whistler," below).

In town, the **Valley Trail** offers 20 kilometers (12 miles) of paved paths that pass through residential areas and around alpine lakes. Located next to the Chateau Whistler Golf Course, the **Lost Lake Trails** feature numerous unpaved alternate routes that fan out from the main lakeside trail (see "Whistler," below).

Touring cyclists take Highway 99 north to the neighboring towns of Pemberton and Mount Currie, a hilly but scenic 33.3 kilometers (20 miles) away.

BOATING & SAILING While you're in **Victoria,** take a leisurely cruise south to Sooke Harbour or up the Strait of Georgia in a rental boat or a skippered vessel. There are many outfitters at the **Brentwood Bay** and **Oak Bay marinas** (see "Victoria," below).

On **Salt Spring Island,** you can take the wheel of a 30-foot sailing craft or enjoy a skippered cruise on a power catamaran around the Gulf Islands. The remote **Queen Charlotte Islands** offer a world of marine beauty that can best be discovered by taking a guided cruise on a skippered schooner. The crews are familiar with the history and lore of the mysterious waters surrounding the home of the Haida Native-Indian tribe (see "The Inside Passage").

Back on the mainland, more than a dozen **Okanagan Valley** lakes lure boaters, houseboaters, and water-sports enthusiasts. Whether you're into waterskiing, fishing, jet skiing, house- or pleasure boating, local marinas offer full-service rentals (see "The Okanagan Valley," below).

CAMPING British Columbia's national parks, provincial parks, marine parks, and private campgrounds are generally filled during summer weekends. Most areas are first-come, first-served, so stake your claim early in the afternoon (for weekends, arrive by Thursday). However, you can now book a campsite up to 3 months in advance by calling **Discover Camping** (☎ **800/689-9025** in North America, or 604/ 689-9025) from March 1 to September 15. It's open Monday to Friday from 7am to 9pm and Saturday and Sunday from 9am to 5pm. There's a nonrefundable service fee of C$6 (US$4.30), and reservations can be confirmed only with MasterCard or Visa.

The provincial park campgrounds charge C$9 to C$12 (US$6 to US$8) per site. There's a 2-week maximum for individual campsite stays. Facilities vary from rustic (walk-in or water-access) to basic (pit toilets and little else) to luxurious (hot showers, flush toilets, and sani-stations). All provincial drive-in campgrounds offer precutwood piles, grill-equipped fire pits, bear-proof garbage cans, pumped well water, and well-maintained security, and are filled with congenial campers. The rustic wilderness campgrounds provide minimal services—a covered shelter, or simply a cleared patch of ground, and little else. You'll find our favorite campgrounds listed throughout this chapter.

CANOEING & KAYAKING Visitors will quickly discover why sea kayakers rate **Vancouver Island's west coast** as the world's second-best place to paddle (after New Zealand's coastline). Novice and intermediate paddlers launch from the passenger ferry MV *Lady Rose* into the sheltered waters of **Clayoquot Sound** and **Barkley Sound.** Surf kayakers are drawn to the tidal swells that crash along the shores of **Long Beach,** which is part of Pacific Rim National Park. And the **Broken Island Group's** Meares and Flores islands offer paddlers an excellent site for overnight expeditions amid the primeval beauty of Sitka-spruce rain forests and a warm, comforting hot spring (see "The West Coast of Vancouver Island," below).

On Vancouver Island's east coast, the **Johnstone Strait** lures paddlers to the world's largest orca (killer whale) population, and to ancient native-Indian villages (see "Northern Vancouver Island," below).

In **Whistler,** paddlers are treated to an exhilarating stretch of glacial waters that runs behind the village itself. Some savvy kayakers and canoeists call it the "River of Dreams" (see "Whistler," later in this chapter). In the province's Cariboo Country, a circle of lakes attracts paddlers from around the world. Located north of Barkerville, **Bowron Lakes** offers a placid yet challenging chain of lakes for canoeists and kayakers who portage and camp their way through a relatively pristine alpine mountain setting. The entire route takes approximately 7 days (see "Cariboo Country," below).

Shipwrecks & Sea Creatures:
British Columbia's World-Class Dive Sites

An amazing array of colorful marine life flourishes amid the 2,000 shipwrecks that have become artificial reefs off the coast of British Columbia. Divers from around the world visit the area year-round to encounter the Pacific Northwest's unique underwater fauna and flora, and to swim among the ghostly remains of 19th-century whaling ships and 20th-century schooners.

The Pacific Rim National Park's **Broken Islands Group** is home to branching bryozoans (microscopic sea creatures) that create coral-like reefs where brittle stars, juvenile crabs, and ring-top snails live in protected clusters. The underwater drop-offs shelter large populations of feather stars, numerous varieties of rockfish, and wolf eels that grow as long as 7 feet and occasionally poke their heads out of their underwater caves.

The waters off the park's **West Coast Trail** are known throughout the world as "the graveyard of the Pacific." Hundreds of 19th- and 20th-century shipwrecks silently attest to the hazards of sailing without an experienced guide in these unforgiving waters. The Cousteau Society rates this dive area as one of the world's best, second only to the Red Sea. There are even underwater interpretive trails that narrate the area's unique history. Contact the **Ocean Centre,** 800 Cloverdale Ave., Victoria, BC, V8X 2S8 (☎ 250/475-2202); **Seaker Adventure Tours,** 950 Wharf St., Victoria, BC, V8W 1T3 (☎ 250/480-0244); or the **Victoria Dive Tourism Association,** 2853 Graham St., Victoria, BC, V8T 3Z3 (☎ 250/725-3318), to book a 2- to 6-day diving cruise. Prices usually include on-board food and accommodations.

A rare species of primitive six-gill shark resides in the deep reefs around **Denman and Hornby islands** off Vancouver Island's east coast. Don't worry—the 12-foot-long denizens of the deep are very slow-moving because of the unusually warm water

CLIMBING & SPELUNKING   Off Valleyview Road, east of Penticton in the Okanagan Valley, **Skaha Bluffs** has more than 400 bolted routes set in place. For information about organized climbing trips throughout the province, contact the **Federation of Mountain Clubs of BC,** 1367 W. Broadway, Vancouver, BC, V6H 4A9 (☎ 604/737-3053).

FISHING   Numerous fishing packages depart from the **Victoria** docks, where charters run to the southern island's best catch-and-release spots for salmon, halibut, cutthroat, and lingcod. Thirteen kilometers (8 miles) north of Victoria, **Elk & Beaver Lakes Provincial Park's** Beaver Lake is stocked with steelhead, rainbow trout, kokanee, Dolly Varden char, and smallmouth bass (see "Victoria," below). And a 31.1-kilometer-long (19-mile-long) fishing path follows the **Cowichan River** near Duncan. This is a good bet any time of year for fly fishermen interested in trout and steelhead (see "Side Trips from Victoria," below).

Year-round sportfishing for salmon, steelhead, trout, Dolly Varden char, halibut, cod, and snapper lures anglers to the waters near **Port Alberni** and **Barkley Sound.** Nearby **Long Beach** is great for bottom fishing (see "The West Coast of Vancouver Island").

Located on Vancouver Island's east coast, **Campbell River** is the home of **Painter's Lodge.** A favorite Hollywood getaway for over 50 years, it has entertained

temperature. In fact, they seem to enjoy the company of human divers who come to mingle with them near the Flora Islet during the summer. But more than marine life attracts divers to these waters. Built in 1900, the iron steamer *Alpha* ran aground off **Chrome Island** just south of Denman Island in the 1920s, and is just one of the many shipwrecks divers encounter.

Off the shores of **Campbell River,** dive sites with enticing names like Row and Be Damned, Whisky Point, Copper Cliffs, and Steep Island attract more than strawberry anemones and sponges to the clear tidal waters. **Beaver Aquatic,** 760 Island Hwy., Campbell River, BC, V9W 2C3 (☎ **250/287-7652**), rents scuba equipment for about C$55 (US$39) per day and can provide site information and diving advice.

Pink hydrocorals, rose soft corals, plumose anemones, and basket stars inhabit the lush underwater kelp forests of the northern **Johnstone Strait.** Sixteen-and-a-half kilometers (10 miles) north of Port Hardy on Hurst Island, **God's Pocket Resort,** Box 130, Port Hardy, BC, V0N 2P0 (☎ **250/949-9221**), offers both divers and anglers all-inclusive holiday packages.

The shipwrecks off the Cape Scott coast attract experienced divers. **All Kinds Trips & Charters,** Box 1620, Port Hardy, BC, V0N 2P0 (☎ **250/949-7952**), escorts divers, kayakers, and canoeists to Cape Scott Wilderness Provincial Park aboard a motorized cruiser.

Cape Saint James on Moresby Island in the Queen Charlotte Islands is an important summer rookery for northern sea lions. Divers often encounter playful young pups and curious adults as they roam the protected waters. Underwater visibility is excellent during summer, and swimming with the creatures is an unforgettable experience.

Bob Hope, John Wayne (a frequent guest), and Goldie Hawn (see "Central Vancouver Island," below).

The **Queen Charlotte Islands** were only recently opened to sportfishermen, and the fish stories about 70-pound tyee salmon and 125-pound halibut emanating from these misty shores are true. **Langara Island and Naden Harbour on Graham Island** are perfect salmon-fishing spots where anglers commonly release catches under 30 pounds as they aim for the big fish (see "The Inside Passage," below).

The long fjords and many islands near the **Skeena River Valley** provide shelter for the salmon, cod, halibut, and snapper that feed and spawn in the slow-moving river waters and nearby inland channels. Fishing lodges dot the coastline, which is home to bald eagles, grizzlies, black bears, seals, sea lions, and orcas. Resort operators encourage fisherman to release catches under 17 pounds! The question here isn't whether you'll reach your catch limit, but whether you'll have a trophy catch (see "The Skeena River Valley," below).

The desertlike **Okanagan Valley** summers are far too hot for fish and fisherman, but for the region's **Okanagan, Kalamalka, and Skaha lakes,** spring and fall are bountiful seasons. The best summer fishing centers around the small hillside lakes surrounding the valley. These spots brim with trout, steelhead, Dolly Varden char, and smallmouth bass (see "The Okanagan Valley," later in this chapter).

Sportfishing is the best reason to visit the **Cariboo Country lakes,** about 250 of which are accessible by road. Some lakes are nestled at altitudes as high as 6,000 feet and can be reached by booking a guided floatplane trip (see "Cariboo Country," below).

In the **Shuswap Lakes** area, weed beds nurture the shrimp, sedge, and insects that rainbow trout thrive on. Many of these lakes are considered trout factories. The area is close to civilization, but it's not hard to get away by helicopter or floatplane to isolated Bonaparte Plateau fishing resorts for even more excitement (see "Wells Gray Provincial Park & Shuswap Lakes," below).

Whistler's **Green River** and nearby **Birkenhead Lake Provincial Park** have runs of steelhead, rainbow trout, Dolly Varden char, cutthroat, and salmon that attract sport anglers from around the world (see "Whistler," below).

GOLFING   Considering **Victoria's** Scottish-British heritage and its lush, rolling landscape, it's no wonder that golf is a popular pastime. The three local courses offer terrain—minus thistles—similar to Scotland's, too (see "Victoria," below).

There are also a number of outstanding layouts in central **Vancouver Island,** including an 18-hole course designed by golf legend Les Furber. The **Morningstar** championship course is in Parksville. The **Storey Creek Golf Club** in Campbell River also has a challenging course design and great scenic views (see "Central Vancouver Island," below).

There are 9- and 18-hole golf courses in the **Okanagan Valley,** including the **Gallagher's Canyon Golf & Country Club** in Kelowna, **Predator Ridge** in Vernon, and the **Harvest Club** in East Kelowna (see "The Okanagan Valley," later in this chapter). Visitors to **Whistler** can tee off at the **Chateau Whistler Golf Course,** located at the base of Blackcomb Mountain, or the **Nicklaus North** golf course on the shore of Green Lake (see "Whistler" below).

The **Salmon Arm Golf Course, Shuswap Lakes Estates Golf & Country Club,** and **Quaaout Lodge's** golf course offer beautiful terrain, great values on greens fees, and more than your fair share of bunkers, traps, and ascents (see "Wells Gray Provincial Park & Shuswap Lakes"). But we must admit that we were more than a little surprised at the 9-hole **Sheep Pasture Golf Course,** in Lillooet, when a sheep strolled by (see "Cariboo Country," below).

HIKING   Among the best nature walks on Vancouver Island, the lush temperate rain forest of **Goldstream Provincial Park** offers hikes through centuries-old stands of Douglas fir (see "Side Trips from Victoria," below). Accessible by ferry from Nanaimo, **Newcastle Island Provincial Marine Park** has trails that meander through the wooded interior and along the sandy shoreline (see "Side Trips from Victoria," below).

On Vancouver Island's west coast, the world-famous **West Coast Trail** is considered by many seasoned hikers to be the challenge of a lifetime. The boardwalked **Clayoquot Witness Trail** near Tofino provides a contemplative stroll through a Sitka-spruce temperate rain forest, as does the **Big Cedar Trail** on Meares Island. The trails that follow **Long Beach** allow hikers a close-up glimpse of the marine life that inhabits the tidal pools in the park's many quiet coves (see "The West Coast of Vancouver Island," below).

At Whistler, **Lost Lake Trails'** 30 kilometers (18 miles) of marked trails around creeks, beaver dams, blueberry patches, and lush cedars are ideal for biking, Nordic skiing, or just quiet strolling and picnicking. The **Valley Trail System** provides hikers with a well-marked, paved trail that connects residential subdivisions of Whistler and is ideal for itinerant shoppers determined to cover both villages in 1 day. The

Ancient Cedars area of Cougar Mountain above Whistler's Emerald Estates is an awe-inspiring grove of towering old-growth cedars and Douglas firs.

Garibaldi Provincial Park's **Singing Pass Trail** is a 4-hour, moderately difficult hike that winds from the top of Whistler Mountain down to the village via the Fitzsimmons Valley. North of Whistler, **Nairn Falls Provincial Park** features a gentle 1.6-kilometer-long (mile-long) trail that leads to a stupendous view of the icy-cold Green River as it plunges 196 feet over a rocky cliff into a narrow gorge. There's also an incredible view of Mount Currie peaking over the treetops.

In the High Country, **Shuswap Lakes Provincial Park** was the site of a gold-mining operation during the 1930s and 1940s. Today, the old-growth ponderosa pines and second-growth red cedar and Douglas fir form a towering canopy over an extensive network of trails. And nearby **Copper Island** has a pleasant circular trail leading to elevated views of the surrounding countryside.

HORSEBACK RIDING   Besides booking a trip to one of the **Cariboo Country guest ranches** (see "Cariboo Country," below) or the outfitters and guest ranches near **Wells Gray Provincial Park** (see "Wells Gray Provincial Park & Shuswap Lakes," below), equestrian visitors can take an afternoon ride along a wooded trail near Victoria's Buck Mountain. A guided ride through the 800-acre area around the slopes of **Salt Spring Island's** Mount Maxwell with a knowledgeable guide promises an afternoon of wondrous scenery. In Whistler, there are riding trails along the Green River and across the Pemberton Valley, and even up on Blackcomb Mountain itself (see "Whistler," below).

RAFTING   Whistler's **Green River** offers novices small rapids and views of snowcapped mountains for their first rafting runs (see "Whistler," below). Intermediate and expert rafters can take on the **Elaho and Squamish rivers,** which offer Class 4 runs.

SKIING & SNOWBOARDING   Cross-country and powder skiing are the **Okanagan Valley's** main winter attractions. **Big White Ski Resort** gets an annual average of 18 feet of powder and has more than 20 kilometers (12 miles) of cross-country trails. **Apex Resort** maintains 56 downhill runs and extensive cross-country trails. And **Silver Star Mountain Ski Resort & Cross-Country Centre** offers cross-country skiers 93.3 kilometers (56 miles) of trails (including 6.6km/4 miles lit for night skiing), plus 50 kilometers (30 miles) of trails in the adjacent Silver Star Provincial Park. The ski-in-ski-out resort resembles a 19th-century mining town. For off-piste fanatics, some of Canada's most extreme verticals are here among the resort's 72 downhill runs. Nearby **Crystal Mountain** caters to intermediate and novice downhill skiers and snowboarders (see "The Okanagan Valley," below).

There are 63 downhill runs and two snowboarding half pipes at the High Country's **Sun Peaks Resort.** Up in the mountains of **Wells Gray Provincial Park,** outfitters offer expert guidance through the miles of cross-country skiing trails surrounding Trophy Mountain (see "Wells Gray Provincial Park & Shuswap Lakes," below).

And then there's **Whistler Mountain.** With a 5,006-foot vertical and 100 marked runs, this is the cream of the province's ski resorts. And **Blackcomb Mountain,** which shares its base with Whistler, has a 5,280-foot vertical and 100 marked runs. Dual-mountain passes are available. **Helicopter skiing** makes another 100-plus runs accessible on nearby glaciers. **Lost Lakes Trails** are converted into miles of groomed cross-country trails, as are the **Valley Trail System, Singing Pass,** and **Ancient Cedars** (see "Whistler," later in this chapter).

WILDLIFE WATCHING   Whether you're in search of the 20,000 **Pacific gray whales** that migrate to **Vancouver Island's** west coast (see "The West Coast of Vancouver Island," below), resident **orcas** (killer whales) in the east coast's Johnstone Strait (see "Northern Vancouver Island," below), or thousands of ✪ **bald eagles** in Goldstream Provincial Park (see "Side Trips from Victoria," below), there are land-based observation points and numerous knowledgeable outfitters who can guide you to the best nature and bird-spotting areas the island has to offer.

On the mainland near **Prince Rupert** and **Terrace,** you'll find two rare species of bear: the *kermodei,* a subspecies of black bear, and **grizzly bears.** Two protected provincial park reserves have been set aside to safeguard the fragile ecosystems these bears inhabit, though authorized outfitters are allowed to bring visitors in (see "The Skeena River Valley," below).

If you take the ferry cruise up the **Inside Passage,** you have a great opportunity to spot **orcas, Dall porpoises, salmon, bald eagles,** and **sea lions.** While on the Queen Charlotte Islands, you can observe **peregrine falcons, Sitka deer, horned puffins, Cassin's auklets, Steller's sea lions,** and the world's largest **black bears** (see "The Inside Passage," below).

2 Victoria

British Columbia's provincial capital is a historic seaport city. It bears the name of the monarch who ruled the British territory of Canada when Victoria was established as a frontier outpost. It's been described as being "more British than the British." And the city has reason to boast of its proud Scottish and British roots, which began when Hudson's Bay Company executive James Douglas chose the Inner Harbour as an outpost site in 1843. (The company feared the loss of its posts south of the 49th Parallel in the U.S.-Canadian boundary settlement, and Victoria's safe, three-tiered harbor had an ideal south-facing location.) In the century that followed, whaling ships and trade vessels docked in Victoria's harbors, bringing new immigrants and exporting Vancouver Island's coal, lumber, and furs to the world.

Even today, getting to Victoria and Vancouver Island from the mainland is half the fun. Though you can fly into Victoria or hop a helicopter, the best way to arrive is by ferry. (At least that's how John Wayne, Richard and Pat Nixon, numerous other celebrities, and millions of modern-day visitors have made the crossing.)

Victoria is symbolically linked to the rest of Canada by the Trans-Canada Highway (Highway 1), which begins at the base of the city's Beacon Hill Park and makes the long trek to Prince Edward Island. At Canada's southwest corner, Victoria is "Mile 0" on the coast-to-coast roadway. The highway heads north before crossing the same route many ferry travelers take, leaving the Nanaimo docks and arriving at Horseshoe Bay on the mainland.

ESSENTIALS

VISITOR INFORMATION   Across from the Empress is the **Tourism Victoria Visitor Info Centre,** 812 Wharf St., Victoria, BC, V8W 1T3 (☎ **250/382-2160**). If you didn't reserve a room before you arrived, you can visit this office or call the **reservations hot line** for last-minute bookings (☎ **800/663-3883**). The center is open September to March daily from 9am to 5pm (summer to 8pm or 9pm).

GETTING THERE   You can reach Victoria from the mainland by ferry from Vancouver or Washington, by plane or helicopter, or by train or bus.

By Ferry   **BC Ferries** (☎ **250/386-3431**) has three Victoria-bound routes. The most direct route from Vancouver is the **Tsawwassen–Swartz Bay ferry,** which operates daily on the hour from 7am to 9pm. The actual crossing takes 95 minutes, but schedule an extra 3 hours for travel to and from the ferry terminals, including waiting time at the docks.

The **Horseshoe Bay–Nanaimo ferry** has eight daily sailings, leaving Horseshoe Bay near West Vancouver and arriving 95 minutes later in Nanaimo. From there, passengers bound for Victoria board the E&N Railiner (see "By Train," below) or drive south on the Island Highway (Highway 1).

The **Mid-Island Express** operates between Tsawwassen and Nanaimo. The 2-hour crossing runs six times daily from 5:30am to 11pm.

These large ferries offer on-board facilities such as restaurants, snack bars, gift shops, business-center desks with modem connections, and comfortable indoor lounges. The one-way fare is C$8 (US$6) for adults, C$4 (US$2.85) for children ages 5 to 11, and C$30 (US$21) per car; children under 5 are free.

Three ferry services offer daily, year-round connections between Port Angeles, Bellingham, and Seattle, Washington, and Victoria. **Black Ball Transport** (☎ 250/386-2202 in Victoria or 360/457-4491 in Port Angeles) operates between Port Angeles and Victoria. One-way fares start at C$9.45 (US$7) for adults and children 12 and up or C$4.75 (US$3.40) for children 5 to 11; children under 5 are free.

Clipper Navigation, 1000A Wharf St., Victoria (☎ 800/288-2535 in North America or 250/382-8100 in Victoria), operates the *Princess Marguerite III,* a 1,070-passenger, 200-vehicle ferry. The *Princess Marguerite III* leaves Seattle's Pier 48 at 1pm and arrives at Victoria's Ogden Point at 5:30pm. On board are restaurants, snack bars, a cocktail lounge, gift shop, and duty-free shop. One-way fares start at C$40.60 (US$29) for adults, C$35 (US$25) for seniors, and C$20.30 (US$15) for children ages 1 to 11. Day rooms are an extra C$40.60 (US$29) per room. Vehicle fares run from C$28 to C$35 (US$20 to US$25). Group and overnight packages are available.

From June to October, Victoria San Juan Cruises' **MV *Victoria Star*** (☎ 800/443-4552 in North America, or 360/738-8099) departs from the Fairhaven Terminal in Bellingham at 9:30am and arrives in Victoria at 2pm, making a stop in the San Juan Islands at Friday Harbor. One-way fares start at C$58.80 (US$42). Food is available on board for an extra charge. The return trip leaves the Victoria docks at 4:30pm and a salmon dinner is included in the fare.

By Train Travelers on the Horseshoe Bay–Nanaimo ferry can board a train that winds down the Cowichan River valley through Goldstream Provincial Park into Victoria. The VIA Rail's **E&N Railiner** leaves Courtenay at 1:15pm daily and arrives in Nanaimo at about 3:07pm and in Victoria at 5:45pm. The Victoria **E&N Station,** 450 Pandora Ave. (☎ 800/561-8630 in Canada), is located near the Johnson Street Bridge. The one-way fare is C$19.25 (US$14) for adults, C$17.10 (US$12) for seniors and students, and C$9.50 (US$7) for children 3 to 11. Seven-day advance-purchase discounts are available; all prices include unlimited stopover privileges.

By Bus   Pacific Coach Lines (☎ 800/661-1725 in Canada, or 250/385-4411) operates bus service between Vancouver and Victoria. The 5-hour trip from the Vancouver bus terminal (Pacific Central Station, 1150 Terminal Ave.) to the Victoria Depot (710 Douglas St.) includes passage on the Tsawwassen–Swartz Bay ferry. One-way fares are C$16.50 (US$12) per person. Service runs daily from 6am to 9pm (winter to 8pm); times vary depending on space availability.

By Plane Air Canada (☎ 800/776-3000 in the U.S. or 800/361-6340 in Canada), **Canadian Airlines** (☎ 800/426-7000 in the U.S. or 800/363-7530 in Canada), and **Horizon Air** (☎ 800/547-9308) have direct flights from Seattle and Vancouver to **Victoria International Airport,** 26.6 kilometers (16 miles) north of the city. **Air BC**

(☎ 604/688-5515), **Harbour Air** (☎ 604/688-1277), and **Kenmore Air** (☎ 800/ 543-9595) operate provincial commuter flights and floatplanes to the city. **Helijet Airways** (☎ 800/665-4354 in Canada, or 250/382-6222) offers direct helicopter transport from Vancouver to Victoria. Its service from Boeing Field in Seattle, Washington, to downtown Victoria operates three times daily and costs C$238 (US$170) round-trip.

All the major car-rental firms have desks at the airport (see "Getting Around," below). From the airport, the Patricia Bay Highway (Highway 17) heads directly into downtown Victoria. A cab ride from the airport to downtown Victoria costs approximately C$40 (US$29) plus tip. Both **Empress Cabs** and **Blue Bird Cabs** (see "Getting Around," below) make airport runs.

The airport bus service, operated by **PBM Transport** (☎ 250/475-2010), makes the trip into town in about half an hour. Buses leave every 30 minutes from 5:25am to 11:55pm daily; the one-way fare is C$12 (US$9).

CITY LAYOUT   Victoria rests on Vancouver Island's southeastern tip, surrounded by suburban residential districts. Victoria's **downtown/Olde Towne** area embraces the Inner Harbour, an offshoot of Victoria Harbour, which, in turn, leads out to the Upper Harbour. The **Ross Bay** and **Oak Bay** residential districts overlook the open waters of the Haro Strait with Washington's Olympic Mountains in the distance. Dallas Road and Beach Drive pass through these lovely coastal communities.

The city's central landmark is the **Empress** on Government Street directly across from the Inner Harbour wharf. If you turn your back to the hotel, the northern edge of the **James Bay** residential area, the Seattle–Port Angeles ferry terminal, and the provincial **Legislative Buildings** on Belleville Street will be on your left. The **Tourism Victoria Visitor Info Centre** on Wharf Street and the beginning of the **downtown shopping district** on Government Street will be on your right.

GETTING AROUND   Although Victoria is a very walkable city, you can also use the efficient public transit system, take cabs, or rent a car, bike, or motor scooter to get around.

By Bike   Biking is the easiest way to get around Victoria. There are designated bike lanes as well as park and beach paths. Helmets are mandatory. It's illegal to cycle on sidewalks, except on designated paths. You can rent bikes and scooters for C$5 to C$8 (US$3.55 to US$6) per hour or C$15 (US$11) per day from **Budget,** 757 Douglas St. (☎ 250/953-5300). **Cycle Victoria Rentals,** 327 Belleville St. (☎ 250/ 385-2453), rents scooters, bikes, in-line skates, tandems, and strollers for about the same prices.

By Bus   The **Victoria Regional Transit System** (BC Transit), 520 Gorge Rd. (☎ 250/382-6161; Web site: www.bctransit.com), operates 40 bus routes throughout greater Victoria, including the neighboring towns of Sooke and Sidney. Regular daily service operates from 6am to 12:15am. Schedules are available at the Visitor Info Centre.

Fares are charged on a per-zone basis. One-way, single-zone fares are C$1.50 (US$1.05) for adults and C$1 (US70¢) seniors and children ages 5 to 13. Transfers can be used to board more than one bus route for any one-way destination that does not include stopovers. A **DayPass** gives you unlimited travel throughout the day; fares are C$6 (US$4.30) for adults and C$4 (US$2.85) for seniors and children 5 to 13. You can buy a DayPass at the Visitor Info Centre and at convenience stores and ticket outlets displaying a FARE DEALER sign.

By Cab You can usually take a cab between two downtown destinations for less than C$6 (US$4.30) per trip. It's best to call ahead. Drivers don't always stop on city streets for flag-downs, especially when it's raining. Call **Empress Cabs** (☎ 250/383-8888) or **Blue Bird Cabs** (☎ 250/382-8294).

By Car Make sure your hotel has parking. Street parking is at a premium. Metered on-street parking is hard to come by, and the regulations are strictly enforced. Unmetered parking on side streets is risky. You will more than likely get towed or spend hours circling the neighborhood in search of a spot at night. There are **parking lots** on View Street between Douglas and Blanshard streets; on Johnson Street off Blanshard Street; on Yates Street north of Bastion Square; and at The Bay department store on Fisgard and Blanshard streets.

Right turns are allowed at red lights. Seat belts are mandatory, as are daytime headlights.

You can rent a car from **Avis,** 1001 Douglas St. (☎ 250/386-8468); **Budget,** 757 Douglas St. (☎ 250/953-5300); **Hertz Canada,** 102–907 Fort St. (☎ 250/388-4411); and **Tilden International,** 767 Douglas St. (☎ 250/386-1213). These major firms also have desks at the airport.

FAST FACTS   American Express The office at 1203 Douglas St., Victoria, BC, V8W 2E6 (☎ 250/385-8731), is open Monday to Friday from 8:30am to 5:30pm and Saturday from 10am to 4pm. The branch accepts mail (letters only) for visiting cardholders.

Area Code The area code for Victoria and all of Vancouver Island is **250.**

Dentists & Doctors Most major hotels have a dentist and doctor on call. **Cresta Dental Centre,** 28-3170 Tillicum Rd. (at Burnside Street), Tillicum Mall (☎ 250/384-7711), and the **James Bay Treatment Center,** 100–230 Menzies St. (☎ 250/388-9934), are additional resources.

Hospitals Local hospitals include the **Royal Jubilee Hospital,** 1800 Fort St. (☎ 250/370-8000; emergency 250/370-8212); and **Victoria General Hospital,** 35 Helmcken Rd. (☎ 250/727-4212; emergency 250/727-4181).

Police Dial ☎ **911** in an emergency. The Victoria City Police can be reached at ☎ 250/384-4111. The Royal Canadian Mounted Police can be reached at ☎ 250/380-6161.

Safety Crime rates are relatively low in Victoria, but transient panhandlers are stationed throughout the downtown and Olde Towne areas. As in any city, stay alert to prevent crimes of opportunity.

SPECIAL EVENTS Watch local Victorians and British Columbians throw stones (the 40-lb. curling kind) on the ice at the **Mixed Curling Bonspiel** (☎ 250/474-8604). It takes place during the third week in January at the Juan de Fuca Recreation Centre, 1767 Island Hwy.

So many flowers bloom during the temperate month of February in Victoria and the surrounding area that the city holds an annual **Flower Count** (☎ 250/477-2412). The third week in February is a great time to see the city as it comes alive in vibrant color.

During the second week in April, the city hosts the **Terrif Vic Dixieland Jazz Party** (☎ 250/953-2011). Bands from New Orleans, England, and Latin America perform swing, Dixieland, honky-tonk, fusion, and improv before dedicated audiences at venues all over Victoria.

During the last 2 weeks in June, the Market Square courtyard and other locations stage swing, bebop, fusion, and improv performances as part of **Jazz Fest International** (☎ 250/388-4423). During the same 2 weeks, folk performers take part in **Folkfest** (☎ 250/388-4728) in Centennial Square.

From the second week of July to the third week of August, the annual **Victoria Shakespeare Festival** (☎ 250/360-0234) takes place around the Inner Harbour.

The annual **First Peoples Festival** (☎ 250/953-3557 or 250/384-3211) highlights the culture and heritage of the Pacific Northwest native-Indian tribes, featuring dances, performances, carving demonstrations, and displays at the Royal British Columbia Museum during the second week in August.

During the second week in November, **the Great Canadian Beer Festival** (☎ 250/952-0360), at the Victoria Conference Centre, 720 Douglas St., features samples from the province's best microbreweries.

Victoria rings in the New Year with **First Night** (☎ 250/380-1211). A number of downtown venues join to throw a performing-arts, alcohol-free celebration for thousands of local and visiting revelers.

EXPLORING THE CITY
THE TOP ATTRACTIONS

✪ **Butchart Gardens.** 800 Benevenuto Ave., Brentwood Bay (21.6km/13 miles north of Victoria). ☎ **250/652-4422,** or 250/652-8222 for dining reservations. Admission C$15.50 (US$11) adults, C$7.75 (US$6) children 13–17, C$2 (US$1.45) children 5–12. Winter discounts. Daily from 9am. Call for seasonal closing times. AE, MC, V. Bus: 75.

These internationally acclaimed gardens were born after Robert Butchart exhausted the limestone quarry near his Tod Inlet home. His wife, Jenny, gradually landscaped the deserted eyesore into a resplendent Sunken Garden, opening it for public display in 1904. A Rose Garden, Italian Garden, and Japanese Garden were added. And as the fame of the 50 acres of gardens grew, the Butcharts also transformed their house into an attraction. Butchart's grandson now owns and operates the splendid gardens, which have more than a million plants on display throughout the year. The gardens are illuminated from June 15 to September 15 for evening strollers. Musical entertainment is provided free. You can even watch firework displays on Saturday nights during July and August. Lunch, dinner, and afternoon tea are offered in the Dining Room Restaurant in the historic residence; casual family fare is served in the Blue Poppy Restaurant. There's also the Seed and Gift Store, where you can buy some of the seeds of the plants you've seen, gardening books, cards, calendars, and other items.

Fort Rodd Hill & Fisgard Lighthouse NHS. 603 Fort Rodd Hill Rd. ☎ **250/478-5849.** Admission C$3 (US$2.15) adults, C$2.25 (US$1.60) seniors, C$1.50 (US$1.05) children 6–16; children under 6 free. Family discounts. Daily 10am–5:30pm. Bus: 25.

Perched on an outcrop of volcanic rock, the Fisgard Lighthouse has guided ships toward Victoria's sheltered harbor for more than 135 years. Built in 1873, this is the oldest beacon on Canada's west coast. Its heritage is displayed on two floors of exhibits that narrate the stories of the lighthouse, its keepers, and the terrible shipwrecks that gave this coastline its ominous moniker, the "graveyard of the Pacific." Adjoining Fort Rodd Hill lets visitors relive the excitement of this 1890s coast artillery fort, which still sports camouflaged searchlights, underground magazines, and its original guns. Audiovisual exhibits bring the fort to life with the voices and faces of the men who served at this key outpost. Displays of artifacts, room re-creations, and videos of historic film footage add to the experience.

Victoria

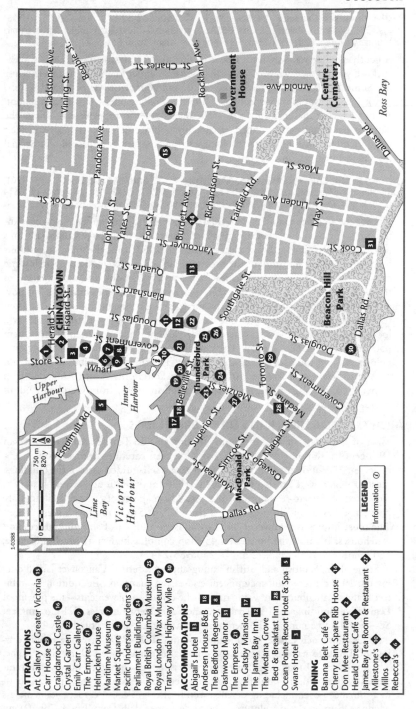

ATTRACTIONS
Art Gallery of Greater Victoria 15
Carr House 29
Craigdarroch Castle 16
Crystal Garden 22
Emily Carr Gallery 9
The Empress 21
Helmcken House 26
Maritime Museum 7
Market Square 4
Pacific Undersea Gardens 20
Parliament Buildings 24
Royal British Columbia Museum 25
Royal London Wax Museum 19
Trans-Canada Highway Mile 0 30

ACCOMMODATIONS
Abigail's Hotel 13
Andersen House B&B 18
The Bedford Regency 8
Dashwood Manor 31
The Empress 21
The Gatsby Mansion 17
The James Bay Inn 12
The Medana Grove
Bed & Breakfast Inn 28
Ocean Pointe Resort Hotel & Spa 5
Swans Hotel 3

DINING
Banana Belt Café 23
Cherry Bank Spare Rib House 14
Don Mee Restaurant 2
Herald Street Café 1
James Bay Tea Room & Restaurant 27
Milestone's 10
Millos 11
Rebecca's 6

Pacific Undersea Gardens. 490 Belleville St. ☎ **250/382-5717.** Admission C$7 (US$5) adults, C$6 (US$4.30) seniors, C$3.50 (US$2.50) children 5–11; children under 5 free. Family discounts. May–Sept daily 9am–5pm; Sept–Apr daily 10am–5pm. Bus: 5, 27, 28, or 30.

A gently sloping stairway leads down to this unique marine observatory's glass-enclosed viewing area, where visitors can observe the Inner Harbour's marine life close up. Some 5,000 creatures feed, play, hunt, and court in these protected waters. Sharks, wolf eels, poisonous stonefish, flowery sea anemones, starfish, and salmon are just a few of the organisms that make their homes in these waters. One of the harbor's star attractions is a huge, remarkably photogenic octopus. Seals and their pups are cared for in holding pens alongside the observatory as part of a provincial marine-mammal rescue program.

✪ **Royal British Columbia Museum.** 675 Belleville St. ☎ **800/661-5411** or 250/387-3701. Admission C$7 (US$5) adults, C$3.20 (US$2.30) seniors, C$2.15 (US$1.55) children 6–18, C$14 (US$10) family. Daily 9am–5pm. Closed Christmas and New Year's Day. Bus: 5, 28, or 30.

Outside the entrance to this modern trilevel concrete-and-glass museum, you encounter a glass-enclosed display of towering totem poles and other large sculptural works produced by Pacific Northwest native-Indian artisans. Inside the museum, exhibits highlight the natural history of the province, including presentations of prehistoric fossils, a temperate rain forest, a seacoast, a live tidal pool, and a re-creation of the ocean floor. The top-floor exhibits are dedicated to demonstrating how archaeologists study ancient cultures and their artifacts, using examples gathered from the numerous local native-Indian tribes. Be sure to stop by Thunderbird Park, located behind the museum, where a cedar longhouse and contemporary totem poles are on permanent display. There might even be a guest carver working on a pole or mask in the park during the summer. The traveling exhibition "Leonardo da Vinci: Scientist, Inventor, Artist," will make its only North American stop (other than the Museum of Science in Boston in 1997) from October 1998 to February 1999.

ARCHITECTURAL HIGHLIGHTS & HISTORIC HOMES

Most of the retail establishments in Victoria's Olde Towne area are housed in 19th-century shipping warehouses that have been carefully restored as part of a heritage-reclamation program. Visitors can take a **self-guided tour** of the buildings, most of which were erected between the 1870s and 1880s and whose history is recounted on easy-to-read outdoor plaques. The majority of restored buildings are between Douglas and Johnson streets from Wharf Street to Government Street. The most impressive, however, used to house a number of shipping offices and warehouses. It's now the home of a 45-shop complex known as **Market Square,** 560 Johnson St./255 Market Sq. (☎ **250/386-2441**).

Some of the Scottish and British immigrants who settled Vancouver Island during the 19th century built magnificent estates and mansions. In addition to architect Francis Rattenbury's crowning turn-of-the-century achievements—the provincial **Legislative Buildings,** 501 Belleville St., and the opulent **Empress,** 721 Government St.—you'll find a number of other magnificent historic architectural sites.

✪ **Craigdarroch Castle,** 1050 Joan Crescent (☎ **250/592-5323**), was built during the 1880s to serve as Scottish coal-mining magnate Robert Dunsmuir's home. The four-story, 39-room Highland-style castle is topped with stone turrets and chimneys. It's filled with the opulent Victorian splendor one would expect to read about in a romance novel, including detailed woodworking, Persian carpets, stained-glass windows, paintings, and sculptures. The castle is open daily from 9am to 7pm (10am to 4:30pm September 1 to June 14). Admission is C$7.50 (US$5) for adults, C$5

(US$3.55) for students, and C$2 (US$1.40) for children 6 to 12; children under 6 are free.

To get a taste of how upper-middle-class Victorians lived, visit the **Carr House,** 207 Government St. (☎ **250/387-4697**), where the painter Emily Carr was born; and the **Helmcken House,** 675 Belleville St. (☎ **250/387-4697**), which was the residence of a pioneer doctor who settled in the area in the 1850s. The doctor's house still contains the original imported British furnishings and his medicine chest. **Craigflower Farmhouse,** 110 Island Hwy., in the View Royal district (☎ **250/387-3067**), was built in 1856 by a Scottish settler who brought many of his furnishings from the old country.

The Carr House, Helmcken House, and Craigflower Farmhouse are open during summer, Thursday to Monday from 11am to 5pm. Admission is C$3.25 (US$2.30) for adults, C$2.25 (US$1.60) for seniors and students, and C$1.25 (US90¢) for children 6 to 12; children under 6 are free. A three-site discount pass is available.

MUSEUMS & GALLERIES

Maritime Museum. 28 Bastion Sq. ☎ **250/385-4222.** Admission C$5 (US$3.55) adults, C$4 (US$2.85) seniors, C$3 (US$2.15) students, C$2 (US$1.45) children 6–12; children under 6 free. Family discounts available. Daily 9am–4:30pm. Closed Christmas Day. Bus: 5.

Housed in the former provincial courthouse, this museum is dedicated to Victoria's rich maritime heritage. The 1889 building contains more than 5,000 artifacts, including two European shipping vessels and an impressive collection of ship models, photographs, and journals.

Royal London Wax Museum. 470 Belleville St. ☎ **250/388-4461.** Admission C$7 (US$5) adults, C$3 (US$2.15) children. Daily 9am–7:30pm. Bus: 5, 27, 28, or 30.

Adjacent to the Pacific Undersea Gardens (see "The Top Attractions," above), this museum houses 300 costumed wax figures that were handcrafted at the world-famous Madame Tussaud's Wax Museum in London, England. It also features a few eerie emissaries from the famed Chamber of Horrors collection.

PARKS & GARDENS

In addition to Butchart Gardens (see above), there are several city parks that attract strollers and picnickers in summer. The 154-acre **Beacon Hill Park** stretches from Southgate Street to Dallas Road between Douglas and Cook streets. In 1882, the Hudson's Bay Company gave this property to the city. Stands of indigenous Garry oaks (found only on Vancouver Island, Hornby Island, and Salt Spring Island) and manicured lawns are interspersed with floral gardens and ponds. Hike up Beacon Hill to get a clear view of the Strait of Georgia, Haro Strait, and Washington's Olympic Mountains. The children's farm (see below), aviary, tennis courts, lawn-bowling green, putting green, cricket pitch, wading pool, playground, and picnic area make this a wonderful place to spend a few hours with the entire family. The Trans-Canada Highway's Mile 0 marker stands at the edge of the park on Dallas Road.

There's an indoor garden that originally opened as an Olympic-sized saltwater pool in 1925 and was converted into a big-band dance hall during the World War II. The **Crystal Garden,** 731 Douglas St. (☎ **250/381-1277**), is filled with rare and exotic tropical flora and fauna. The ground-floor souvenir plaza doesn't hint at what you'll find upstairs in this re-created jungle setting with coral flamingoes, macaws, pygmy marmosets, butterflies, and other wildlife. The garden is open daily from 10am to 5:30pm (extended hours in summer). Admission is C$7 (US$5) for adults, C$6 (US$4.30) for seniors, and C$4 (US$2.85) for children. Family and group discounts are available.

ESPECIALLY FOR KIDS

Kids can ride a pony and pet goats, rabbits, and other barnyard animals at the **Beacon Hill Children's Farm,** Circle Drive, Beacon Hill Park (☎ 250/381-2532). The farm is open mid-March to September daily from 9am to 5pm. Admission is by donation. Most visitors are asked to give C$1 (US70¢) toward the park's continued upkeep.

The awesome array of tropical plants and animals in the enclosed **Crystal Garden** (see "Parks & Gardens," above) makes this a delightful rainy-day destination. At the **Pacific Undersea Gardens'** underwater observatory (see "The Top Attractions," above), your kids can meet a wolf eel eye-to-eye, view a giant octopus up close, and watch harbor seals cavort underwater with their pups.

Youngsters also enjoy the **Royal British Columbia Museum** (see "The Top Attractions," above), which presents the intriguing life and culture of the Pacific Northwest native-Indian tribes who've inhabited the province for over 10,000 years, as well as the majestic beauty of the province's temperate rain forests and coastlines.

Kids love the **Royal London Wax Museum** (see "Museums & Galleries," above), where they can encounter Madame Tussaud's world-famous wax figures, including some spine-tingling denizens of the Chamber of Horrors.

TOURS & EXCURSIONS

Gray Line of Victoria, 700 Douglas St. (☎ 250/388-5248), conducts tours of Victoria and the Butchart Gardens. The 1 1/2-hour "Grand City Tour" costs C$13.75 (US$10) for adults and C$6.95 (US$4.95) for children. Summer departures occur every 30 minutes from 9:30am to 7pm; from December to mid-March there are two daily departures, at 11:30am and 1:30pm.

The same company operates a **wheeled-trolley service,** which runs every 40 minutes from 9:30am to 5:30pm on a circuit of 35 hotels, attractions, shops, and restaurants. A 24-hour day pass allows you to stop and reboard at the destinations of your choice throughout the day and costs C$7 (US$5) for adults and C$4 (US$2.85) for children.

Heritage Tours and Daimler Limousine Service, 713 Bexhill Rd. (☎ 250/474-4332), guides you through the city, Butchart Gardens, and Craigdarroch Castle in a six-passenger British Daimler limousine. Rates start at C$62 (US$44) per hour per vehicle (not per person).

The bicycle-rickshaw tours operated by **Kabuki Kabs,** 15–950 Government St. (☎ 250/385-4243), usually "park" in front of the Empress. Prices are individually negotiated with each driver; the average cost is C$30 to C$40 (US$21 to US$29) per hour.

Tallyho Horse Drawn Tours, 2044 Milton St. (☎ 250/383-5067), has conducted tours of Victoria in horse-drawn carriages since 1903. Tours start at the corner of Belleville and Menzies streets; fares are C$12 (US$9) for adults, C$7 (US$5) for students, C$5 (US$3.55) for children 17 and under. Family discounts are available. Tours operate daily every 20 minutes from 9:30am to 7pm (10am to 5:30pm in late March, April, May, and September).

To get a bird's-eye view of Victoria, take a 30-minute seaplane tour with **Harbour Air Seaplanes,** 1234 Wharf St. (☎ 250/361-6786). Rates are C$72 (US$51) per person; flights depart at 10am, noon, and 4pm.

For a pleasant and informative stroll in summer, join a guided walking tour through the downtown and Olde Towne neighborhoods. **Lantern Tours in the Old Burying Ground,** Box 40115, Victoria, BC, V8W 3R8 (☎ 250/598-8870), begin at the cemetery gate at 9pm daily in July and August. **Murder, Ghost & Mayhem Walking Tours,** 78 San Jose Ave. (☎ **250/385-2035**), specializes in Olde Towne walks that introduce you to the city's darker heritage. And **Victoria's Haunted Walk & Other Tours,** 103–2647 Graham St. (☎ **250/361-2619**), introduces you to some of the city's nefarious ghosts and spirits.

SHOPPING

Victoria has dozens of specialty shops that offer a fine selection of high-quality classic woolens, ethnic clothing, jewelry, unique craft items, and a wide selection of marine and camping gear. Stores in the downtown area are generally open Monday to Saturday from 10am to 6pm. Some downtown stores are open on Sunday from noon to 5pm during summer.

A shopping spree can easily become a stroll through Victoria's history (see "Architectural Highlights & Historic Homes," above). An excellent example of this trend toward the revitalization of existing property can be seen at **Market Square,** 560 Johnson St./255 Market Sq. (☎ 250/386-2441), a restored complex of 19th-century warehouses and shipping offices. Forty-five small shops and restaurants surround a central courtyard where live performances take place throughout summer.

ARTS & CRAFTS   Cowichan Trading Ltd., 1328 Government St. (☎ 250/ 383-0321), has been dealing in Pacific Northwest native-Indian crafts and clothing at this location for more than 50 years. It features a good selection of hand-knitted sweaters and affordable crafts. **Alcheringa Gallery,** 665 Fort St. (☎ 250/383-8224), handles the artwork of dozens of regional master artists, including native-Indian carver Richard Hunt, a member of the Kwakiutl tribe, and printmaker Robert Davidson, a Haida tribal artisan.

BOOKS   Munro's Book Store, 1108 Government St. (☎ 250/382-2464), housed in a Victorian heritage building, is a great source for books about the region as well as fiction by local authors such as Anne Cameron, author of *The Daughters of Copper Woman.* **The Field Naturalist,** 1126 Blanshard St. (☎ 250/388-4174), stocks a great selection of naturalist titles and field guides, as well as binoculars, telescopes, spotting charts, and other nature-watching equipment.

CLOTHING   You can find men's, women's, and children's classic woolen fashions at great prices. **Avoca Handweavers,** 1009 Government St. (☎ 250/383-0433), specializes in Irish woolen apparel, blankets, and crafts. **The Edinburgh Tartan Shop,** 921 Government St. (☎ 250/388-9312), has a wide selection of tartan plaid garments and thick Aran-style cable-knit wool sweaters.

For something out of the ordinary, **Carnaby Street,** 538 Yates St. (☎ 250/ 382-3747), features ethnic clothing such as Mexican cotton wedding dresses and Moroccan caftans, as well as imported textiles, jewelry, and carpets.

DEPARTMENT STORES   Two major Canadian department stores have branches in Victoria. **The Bay (Hudson's Bay Company),** 1701 Douglas St. (☎ 250/ 382-7141), and **Eatons,** Victoria Eaton Centre, Government and Fort streets (☎ 250/382-7141), offer everything from apparel and dinnerware to camping gear and maple-sugar candies.

If you crave a taste of Olde England, such as chocolate-covered tea biscuits or lemon curd, head to **Marks & Spencer,** Victoria Eaton Centre (☎ 250/386-6727). This Canadian branch of the time-honored British department store carries a wide assortment of traditional British and Scottish treats such as frozen bangers (sausages), butter tarts, and "spotted dick" (a traditional steamed pudding), as well as mint sauce, tea biscuits, and candies.

JEWELRY   At **The Rockhound Shop,** 777 Cloverdale Ave. (☎ 250/475-2080), you'll find rough and polished gemstones that are indigenous to the island, such as jade, quartz, and argillite. The shop also carries a lovely selection of stone jewelry, gift items, crystal-mineral display pieces, rock polishers, and lapidary tools.

OUTDOOR GEAR   Suit up at the century-old **Jeune Bros. Great Outdoors Store,** 570 Johnson St. (☎ 250/386-8778), or at our favorite outdoor outfitter, **Ocean River Sports,** 1437 Store St. (☎ 250/381-4233). Both shops carry clothes and equipment designed for hikers, kayakers, campers, skiers, sailors, and canoeists.

SPORTS & OUTDOOR ACTIVITIES

BIKING   Cycling is one of the best ways to get around Victoria. You can rent a bike for a few hours or a few days right in the downtown area (see "Getting Around," above). The 8-mile **Scenic Marine Drive** bike path begins on Dallas Road and Douglas Street at the base of Beacon Hill Park. The paved path follows the walkway along the beaches, winding up through the residential district on Beach Drive. It eventually turns left and heads south toward downtown Victoria on Oak Bay Avenue. The **Inner Harbour pedestrian path** also has a bike lane for cyclists who want to take a leisurely ride around the entire city seawall.

BOATING   Bareboat rentals and chartered vessels can be booked for a few hours or a couple of weeks at **Brentwood Inn Resort Boat Rentals,** 7176 Brentwood Dr., Brentwood Bay (☎ 250/652-3151). And **Cuda Marine,** 2849 Santana Dr. (☎ 250/812-6003), charters diving and fishing trips as well as 2- and 3-hour tours aboard their 25-foot power boats, which launch off the docks at Courtney and Wharf streets. There are also a number of independent charter companies docked at the **Oak Bay Marina Group,** 1327 Beach Dr. (☎ 250/598-3369). For example, the **Horizon Yacht Centre,** at the Oak Bay Marina Group (☎ 250/595-2628), offers sailboat charters, lessons, and navigational tips geared toward familiarizing you with the surrounding waters. Skippered charters in the area run about C$600 (US$429) per day. Bareboat rentals average around C$125 (US$89) for a couple of hours. If you're taking the wheel yourself, don't forget to check the **marine forecast (☎ 250/ 656-7515)** before casting off.

CANOEING & KAYAKING   ✪ **Ocean River Sports** (see "Shopping," above), can equip you with everything from single-kayak, double-kayak, and canoe rentals to lifejackets, tents, and dry-storage camping gear. Kayak rentals range from C$7 (US$5) per hour to $35 (US$25) per day. Weekly rates are also available. The company also offers group tours of Vancouver Island's west coast and the Johnstone Strait, as well as kayaking lessons and clinics.

FISHING   Anglers in search of trout and bass often get lucky at **Elk & Beaver Lakes Provincial Park** (☎ 250/479-2213), 13.3 kilometers (8 miles) north of Victoria on Elk Lake Drive off Patricia Bay Highway (Highway 17). You can also reach the park on the no. 70 and 75 bus routes. Ocean anglers should contact the local boat charters (see "Boating," above) or the **East Sooke Fish Corp.,** 6638 E. Sooke Rd., Sooke (☎ 250/642-7078), which combines fishing charters with whale watching and birding. While trolling for chinook or coho salmon, passengers can observe orcas, seals, bald eagles, and porpoises in their natural habitat off the southern tip of Vancouver Island. To fish here, you need a nonresident license, and there are separate ones for saltwater and for freshwater catches. Tackle shops sell licenses, have information on current restrictions, and often carry copies of the current publications *BC Tidal Waters Sport Fishing Guide* and *BC Sport Fishing Regulations*

Synopsis for Non-Tidal Waters. Independent anglers should also pick up a copy of the *BC Fishing Directory and Atlas.* **Robinson's Sporting Goods Ltd.,** 1307 Broad St. (☎ 250/385-3429), is a reliable source for information, recommendations, lures, licenses, and other gear.

GOLFING   The **Cedar Hill Municipal Golf Course,** 1400 Derby Rd. (☎ 250/595-3103), is an 18-hole public golf course 3.3. kilometers (2 miles) from downtown Victoria. The **Cordova Bay Golf Course,** 5333 Cordova Bay Rd. (☎ 250/658-4075), is northeast of the downtown area. Designed by Bill Robinson, this 18-hole course features 66 sand traps and some tight fairways. The **Olympic View Golf Club,** 643 Latoria Rd. (☎ 250/474-3673; Web site: www.sunnygolf.com/ov/ov.html), is one of the top 35 golf courses in Canada. Amid 12 lakes and a pair of waterfalls, this 18-hole, 6,414-yard course is open daily, year-round. Facilities include shuttle service from downtown hotels, cart rentals, pro shop, dining room, coffee shop, and lounge. Tee times are generally easy to reserve a day in advance; greens fees range from C$22 to C$48 (US$16 to US$34).

WATER SPORTS   The **Crystal Pool & Fitness Centre,** 2275 Quadra St. (☎ 250/380-7946, or 250/380-4636 for schedule), is Victoria's main aquatic facility. The 50-meter lap pool, children's pool, diving pool, sauna, whirlpool, steam, weight, and aerobics rooms are open daily from 6am to midnight. **Beaver Lake** in Elk & Beaver Lakes Provincial Park (see "Fishing," above) has lifeguards on duty as well as picnicking facilities along the shore. **All Fun Recreation Park,** 650 Hordon Rd. (☎ 250/474-4546 or 250/474-3184), operates a 1.2-kilometer-long (three-quarter-mile-long) water-slide complex that's ideal for cooling off on hot summer days. And **Ocean Wind Water Sports Rentals,** 5411 Hamsterly Rd. (☎ 250/658-8171), rents nearly every form of popular water-sport gear, including parasails.

　　Windsurfers skim along the Inner Harbour and Elk Lake when the breezes are right. In a long weekend, **Active Sports,** 1620 Blanshard St. (☎ 250/381-SAIL), can teach anyone who's ready to learn how to maneuver a parasail.

WHALE WATCHING & BIRDING   The waters surrounding the southern tip of Vancouver island are home to orcas, harbor seals, sea lions, bald eagles, and porpoises. **Seacoast Expeditions,** Ocean Pointe Resort Hotel & Spa, 45 Songhees Rd. (☎ 250/383-2254; Web site: www.islandnet.com/~seacoast), offers 2-hour whale-watching trips on Zodiac boats from April to October. Guaranteed sightings make this trip worthwhile. Both adults and kids will learn a lot from the naturalist guides who explain the behavior and nature of the orcas, gray whales, sea lions, porpoises, cormorants, eagles, and harbor seals. Fares are C$75 (US$54) for adults, C$50 (US$36) for children 10 to 16, and C$30 (US$21) for children under 10 (however, it's not recommended for kids under 5). **Pride of Victoria Cruises,** Oak Bay Beach Hotel, 1175 Beach Dr. (☎ 250/592-3474), offers 3¹/₂-hour whale-watching charters daily from March to October (only on Saturday the rest of the year) on a fully equipped 45-foot catamaran that can handle up to eight passengers and has washroom facilities and bar service. A picnic-style lunch is served on the cruise. Fares are C$79 (US$56) per person; lunch is C$5 (US$3.55) per person in summer and free the rest of the year.

ACCOMMODATIONS

Reservations are a must at Victoria hotels from June to September and during holiday periods. If you haven't booked a room before your arrival, contact **Tourism Victoria's** reservation hot line (☎ 800/663-3883 or 250/382-1131) or visit the Visitor Info Centre (see above) for last-minute accommodations.

VERY EXPENSIVE

The Empress. 721 Government St., Victoria, BC, V8W 1W5. ☎ **800/441-1414** or 250/ 384-8111. Fax 250/381-4334. 474 rms, 37 suites. MINIBAR TV TEL. Canadian-Pacific rms: Mid-May to mid-Oct C$295–C$360 (US$211–US$257) double; mid-Oct to mid-May C$170–C$260 (US$121–US$186) double. Year-round C$325–C$1,400 (US$232–US$1,000) suite. AE, CB, DC, DISC, ER, MC, V. Underground valet parking C$14.50 (US$10). Bus: 5.

Opened in 1908 by the Canadian-Pacific railway, this ivy-covered landmark hotel has a commanding view of the Parliament Buildings and the Inner Harbour from its central location on Government Street. The hotel staff has hosted its share of celebrities, from author Rudyard Kipling and the King of Siam to Queen Elizabeth II and President Richard M. Nixon. In fact, everyone who stays here feels like a VIP. Guest rooms are filled with restored Victorian antique furnishings. The deluxe rooms have harbor views, and the eight honeymoon suites, which feature four-poster canopy beds, are accessible via a private stairway. Wheelchair-accessible rooms are available.

Dining: The Bengal Lounge serves curry buffets and an à la carte menu; the Empress Dining Room serves Pacific Northwest cuisine in an elegant and formal setting; and the more affordable Kipling's serves regional cuisine in a casual setting. The famous afternoon tea (C$29.95/US$21 per person) is served under the stained-glass dome of the Palm Court and in the Lobby Lounge.

Services: Concierge, room service, dry cleaning, laundry, massage, secretarial service, valet.

Facilities: Indoor 40-foot lap pool, children's wading pool, health club, sauna, whirlpool, shopping arcade, meeting/banquet space for up to 1,500 people in the conference center, and car-rental desk.

✪ **Ocean Pointe Resort Hotel & Spa.** 45 Songhees Rd., Victoria, BC, V9A 6T3. ☎ **800/ 667-4677** or 250/360-2999. Fax 250/360-1041. Web site: www.oprhotel.com. 250 rms, 34 suites. A/C MINIBAR TV TEL. Jan 1–May 31 C$169–C$229 (US$121–US$164) double; June 1–Oct 13 C$209–C$279 (US$149–US$199) double; Oct 14–Dec 31 C$164–C$214 (US$117–US$153) double. Year-round C$399–C$595 (US$285–US$425) suite. AE, DC, ER, MC, V. Underground valet parking C$9 (US$6). Bus: 24 to Colville.

Located on the Inner Harbour's north shore, this luxurious modern waterfront hotel boasts a commanding view of Victoria, set against a backdrop of the snowcapped Olympic Mountains. The hotel's Inner Harbour rooms offer the best views, but guest rooms that face the Outer Harbour feature floor-to-ceiling bay windows. All rooms are tastefully decorated in soft beige and pale earth tones to accent the natural wood furnishings. Wheelchair-accessible units are available.

Dining/Entertainment: The Victorian Restaurant offers elegant West Coast cuisine; the Boardwalk Restaurant is more casual. Rick's Lounge & Piano Bar is a warm, friendly room with a harbor view.

Services: Concierge, 24-hour room service, laundry, valet, shuttle service.

Facilities: In the lower concourse, the hotel's complete European spa and health club feature facial and body treatments, aesthetics treatments, workout equipment, and a pool. Other concourse facilities include a wine shop that specializes in British Columbian wines, and the whale-watching outfitters Seacoast Expeditions (see "Sports & Outdoor Activities," above).

Sooke Harbour House. 1528 Whiffen Spit Rd., RR #4, Sooke, BC, V0S 1N0. ☎ **250/ 642-3421.** Fax 250/628-6988. E-mail: shh@islandnet.com. 13 rms. TEL. C$260–C$360 (US$186–US$257) double. Rates include breakfast and lunch. Dinner C$56 (US$40) extra. Off-season discounts. AE, MC, V. Free parking. Take the Island Hwy. (Hwy. 1) to the Sooke/ Colwood turnoff (Junction Hwy. 14). Follow Hwy. 14 to Sooke. About 1.6km (1 mile) past the town's only traffic light, turn left onto Whiffen Spit Rd.

This famous inn boasts wonderful waterfront views from every room, privacy, seclusion, refined European-style service, and a renowned restaurant. Each guest room is uniquely decorated and has a fireplace and a hot tub or whirlpool tub. For example, the Victor Newman Longhouse Room reflects the influence of the Pacific Northwest native-Indians in its motifs and use of natural wood. The Herb Garden Room is appointed in pale shades of mint and parsley and opens onto a private patio. The hosts leave a bouquet of flowers or a decanter of port in every room.

Dining: See "Dining," below.

Services: Massage therapist by appointment, in-room breakfast, and optional in-room dinner.

EXPENSIVE

Abigail's Hotel. 906 McClure St., Victoria, BC, V8V 3E7. ☎ **250/388-5363.** Fax 250/388-7787. 16 rms. C$139–C$299 (US$96–US$214) double. Rates include full breakfast. Midweek discounts. MC, V. Free parking. Bus: 1.

This four-story gabled Tudor building is the quintessential small European-style luxury inn. All of the guest rooms seem to be tailor-made for honeymooners or lovers, with touches like crystal chandeliers, stained-glass windows, fresh flowers, and goose-down comforters. Most rooms also have private Jacuzzis or deep soaking tubs, and a few are equipped with fireplaces, four-poster canopy beds, or both. Breakfast is served in the sunroom at 8am. There's an afternoon social hour in the library, where the hosts serve mulled wine and snacks. There are a piano and a games table in the library, and a beautiful floral garden outside. Be sure to check in before 10pm; you can't get in after that unless you already have your room key.

Oak Bay Beach Hotel. 1175 Beach Dr., Victoria, BC, V8S 2N2. ☎ **800/668-7758** or 250/598-4556. Fax 250/598-4556. 43 rms, 7 suites. TV TEL. C$174–C$325 (US$124–US$232) double; C$325–C$399 (US$124–US$285) suite. Off-season discounts. Golf, Romantic, and Train packages available. AE, DC, ER, MC, V. Free parking. Bus: 2.

Surrounded by an extensive garden, this Tudor-style inn is perched at the edge of the Haro Strait, overlooking the San Juan Islands. It attracts an older crowd, but the hotel is casual and comfortable. The lobby is a huge living room that features a century-old baby grand piano, Edwardian and Victorian antiques, and a big fireplace. Every guest room is uniquely decorated with antique British furnishings and priced according to size and view. The residential side is the cheapest, with waterside views slightly higher. The second-floor fireplace suites are the best choice, with bay windows, private balconies overlooking the serene waterfront, and—of course—fireplaces. The junior suites and one-bedroom suites are also good values.

Dining/Entertainment: The Snug is a British pub that's been a local favorite for over a century; Bentley's on the Bay offers outdoor seating and a four-course set menu that emphasizes West Coast cuisine.

Services: Room service, laundry, newspaper, valet, complimentary shuttle service, morning coffee, hot chocolate and cookies in the evening.

Facilities: The hotel's private yacht can be booked for dinner cruises, sightseeing, and fishing charters.

MODERATE

✪ **Andersen House B&B.** 301 Kingston St., Victoria, BC, V8V 1V5. ☎ **250/388-4565.** Fax 250/388-4563. Web site: www.islandnet.com/~andersen. 5 rms. TV TEL. C$135–C$235 (US$96–US$168) double. Off-season discounts. Rates include breakfast. MC, V. No smoking. No children under 8. Free, limited parking. Bus: 30.

It's a short walk from the busy downtown area to the Andersen House, which was built for a sea captain in 1891. It's an ornate Queen Anne–style wooden structure with 12-foot-high ceilings and stained-glass windows. The decor throughout is an eclectic mix of antiques, modern paintings, hand-knotted Persian rugs and carpets, and Japanese *raku*-style ceramics. Each guest room has a private entrance, CD/cassette player, selection of CDs, VCR, and a king- or queen-size bed. The bathrooms have pedestal sinks, tiled showers, slipper tubs, and marble accents. Three rooms overlook a lovely British-style floral garden. The Captain's Apartment is ideal for a family, featuring a king-size bed in one room and twin beds in another. The 700-square-foot room also contains a soaking tub, shower, and wet bar. But our favorite room is 2 blocks from the house, on Janet and Max Andersen's gorgeous 1927 teakwood 50-foot motor yacht, the *Mamita*, docked in the harbor. Breakfast for all guests is served in the house.

The Boathouse. 746 Sea Dr. (in the Brentwood Bay district), RR #1, Victoria, BC, V0S 1A0. ☎ **604/652-9370.** 1 unit. TEL. C$120 (US$86) double. Rate includes continental breakfast. MC, V. Free parking.

It's a short stroll (or row) to Butchart Gardens from this tiny, secluded red cottage, perched on pilings over the waters of the Saanich Inlet, which was converted from a boathouse. In fact, the only passersby you're likely to encounter during your stay are seal, bald eagles, otter, heron, and raccoon. The cottage is situated at the end of a very long flight of stairs behind the owner's home. Inside, there's a sofa bed, dining table, kitchen area with small refrigerator and toaster oven, electric heater, and a reading alcove that overlooks the floating dock. Full toilet and shower facilities are located in a separate bathhouse a short stroll back uphill. All the makings for a delicious continental breakfast are provided in the evening, and guests also have use of a private dinghy.

The Gatsby Mansion. 309 Belleville St., Victoria, BC, V8V 1X2. ☎ **250/388-9191.** Fax 250/920-5651. 20 rms. TV TEL. C$135–C$275 (US$96–US$196) double. Rates include full breakfast. AE, MC, V. Free parking. Bus: 5 to Belleville and Government.

Harking back to the elegant atmosphere of a 1920s seaside resort, crystal chandeliers hang from the recently restored frescoed ceilings of this charming B&B. You won't be disappointed by the rooms, which feature down duvets, fluffy linens, and an array of Victorian antiques. Some have views of the Inner Harbour, while others feature private parlors. This establishment is across the street from the Seattle–Port Angeles ferry terminal.

The formal dining room is open for breakfast, lunch, and dinner. Main courses at dinner range from C$13.95 (US$10) for pasta dishes to C$22.95 (US$16) for a charbroiled T-bone steak. The adjoining martini lounge features 2-ounce martinis for C$5.95 (US$4.25).

✪ Swans Hotel. 506 Pandora Ave., Victoria, BC, V8W 1N6. ☎ **800/668-7926** or 250/361-3310. Fax 250/361-3491. 29 suites. TV TEL. C$135–C$165 (US$96–US$118) suite. Off-season discounts. AE, MC, V. Parking C$8 (US$6). Bus: 23 or 24.

Located in a restored 1913 heritage warehouse, this small, friendly boutique hotel offers families something truly special: space, and lots of it. Unlike the diminutive lobby, the upstairs suites are spacious. Many feature bilevel layouts with open lofts. All accommodations have full kitchens, separate dining areas, and living rooms. The two-bedroom suites are particularly suited for families. The furnishings and decor are clean and basic, featuring white and natural woods. But the original artwork on the walls and the vases of fresh flowers on the tables add to this establishment's pleasant atmosphere.

The Fowl Fish Café Ale & Oyster House serves lunch and dinner daily. Swans also offers guests a cooked breakfast menu, with free-range eggs and fresh baked goods. The adjoining and often-crowded Swans Brewpub is a casual hangout popular with locals (see "Victoria After Dark," below) that serves traditional pub fare, burgers, salads, and ales brewed on the premises.

INEXPENSIVE

✪ The Bedford Regency. 1140 Government St., Victoria, BC, V8W 1Y2. ☎ **800/665-6500** or 250/384-6835. Fax 250/386-8930. 40 rms. TV TEL. C$89–C$215 (US$64–US$154) double. Off-season discounts. Rates include full breakfast and afternoon tea. AE, MC, V. Parking C$15.65 (US$11). Bus: 5.

This small downtown hotel was built in 1930. Today, it's a real find. The colorful flowerpots perched on the outside window ledges and the spacious vintage lobby are a preview of the charm you'll find in the guest rooms. As in many older hotels, the rooms vary considerably in size, shape, and decor. Most have brass fixtures, well-stocked bookshelves, goose-down comforters, dark-stained wood furnishings, double-headed showers, and luxurious amenities. Some rooms even feature wood-burning fireplaces and Jacuzzis. Complimentary coffee, free local calls, and concierge service are offered. Children are welcome, but all rooms are equipped with one queen-size bed, so the hotel management recommends booking a second room for them.

The Red Currant restaurant serves three meals daily in the summer (breakfast and lunch only during the winter) and a reasonably priced, classic British afternoon tea year-round. The Garrick's Head Pub is a friendly spot for a drink or a casual meal.

Dashwood Manor. 1 Cook St., Victoria, BC, V8V 3W6. ☎ **800/667-5517** or 250/385-5517. 15 suites. TV. C$95–C$265 (US$68–US$189) suite. Rates include in-rm breakfast. AE, DC, ER, MC, V. Free parking. Bus: 5.

This cozy Tudor manor overlooking the Strait of Juan de Fuca was built in 1912. The beach and Beacon Hill Park are directly across the street, and downtown is a 20-minute stroll away. Inside, the manor is Edwardian. Deep-stained oak paneling and burgundy carpeting lead up to the suites. Each unique suite has a queen-size bed and a well-stocked kitchen (breakfast foods and coffee service are self-catered and included in the price). You might also find an "extra" like a fireplace, Jacuzzi, private balcony, or a crystal chandelier amid the blend of antique and contemporary furnishings. Complimentary sherry, port, and wine are set out during the evening hours in the lobby. Don't expect a raucous crowd: Most of the guests are couples, and romance is hard to avoid.

The James Bay Inn. 270 Government St., Victoria, BC, V8V 2V2. ☎ **250/384-7151.** Fax 250/ 381-2115. 50 rms (41 with bath). TV TEL. C$95–C$105 (US$68–US$75) double. Off-season weekly discounts. MC, V. Free, limited parking. Bus: 5 or 30.

This Edwardian manor, which faces Beacon Hill Park, was built in 1907 and was the last home of the famed Victoria-born painter Emily Carr. The lobby and rooms are decorated in subtle Spanish-Mediterranean style, with dark-wood furnishings. The inn's tranquillity makes it popular with vacationing retirees.

The restaurant serves three meals daily, and the adjacent neighborhood pub is popular with the locals. Guests of the inn receive a 15% discount in both establishments.

The Medana Grove Bed & Breakfast Inn. 162 Medana St., Victoria, BC, V8V 2H5. ☎ **800/ 269-1188** or 250/389-0437. Fax 250/389-0425. 2 rms. TV. May 15–Oct 15 C$85–C$110 (US$61–US$79) double; Oct 15–Mar 15 C$65–C$85 (US$46–US$61) double; Mar 15–May 15 C$75–C$95 (US$54–US$68). Off-season discounts. Rates include full breakfast. MC, V. Street parking. Bus: 5 to Simcoe.

This charming little 1908 James Bay home is a short walk from downtown, the Inner Harbour pedestrian path, and Beacon Hill Park. Tucked away on a block-long, tree-lined street, the inn has a comfortable, cheery living room with a welcoming fireplace, TV, and a small library. The dining room is filled with turn-of-the-century antiques; a full gourmet breakfast is served there every morning. No smoking or pets.

DINING

EXPENSIVE

Sooke Harbour House. 1528 Whiffen Spit Rd., Sooke. ☎ 250/642-3421. Reservations required. Main courses C$16–C$28 (US$11–US$20). AE, ER, MC, V. Daily seatings at 6:30 and 7:30pm; closes at 9:30pm. Take the Island Hwy. to the Sooke/Colwood turnoff (Junction Hwy. 14). Continue on Hwy. 14 to Sooke. About 1.6km (1 mile) past the town's only traffic light, turn left onto Whiffen Spit Rd. PACIFIC NORTHWEST.

Situated in a rambling white house on a bluff overlooking Sooke's Whiffen Spit, this restaurant and hotel (see "Accommodations," above) offers spectacular waterfront views and a quiet, relaxed atmosphere. Hosts Frederica and Sinclair Phillips will immediately make you feel at home as you dine on imaginatively prepared Pacific Northwest cuisine, featuring local seafood and organically grown herbs and vegetables that are picked fresh from the Phillipses' garden. Halibut baked in an herb, sunflower-seed, and Parmesan crust is accompanied by a roasted-carrot, coriander, and parsley purée, and roasted veal is served with a wild-mushroom, port-wine, and lovage sauce.

MODERATE

Cherry Bank Spare Rib House. 825 Burdett Ave. ☎ 250/385-5380. Reservations accepted. 3-course rib special C$11.75 (US$8); main courses C$11.75–C$16.75 (US$8–US$12). AE, DC, MC, V. Daily 11:30am–2pm and 5–9pm. Bus: 5. RIBS.

Located in an 1897 landmark hotel, the Cherry Bank has been Victoria's top rib house for more than 40 years. You won't find another place in town that serves up fresh, healthy portions at such a reasonable price. The friendly staff serves up large, tangy racks of ribs accompanied by salad, potatoes, vegetables, and garlic bread to a family-oriented clientele. The menu also offers huge portions of scampi, fresh fish, seafood, chicken, and steaks.

Herald Street Café. 546 Herald St. ☎ 250/381-1441. Reservations required. Main courses C$10.95–C$19.95 (US$8–US$14). AE, ER, MC, V. Wed–Sat 11:30am–3pm, Sun 10am–3pm; Sun–Wed 5:30–10:30pm, Thurs–Sat 5:30pm–midnight. Bus: 5. PASTA/WEST COAST.

Young, hip locals flock to the excellent Sunday brunch at this casual bistro. Located in a 19th-century heritage building, the dining room is filled with potted palms and floral arrangements. Paintings and drawings by local artists decorate the exposed-brick walls. And the chef's own creations—fresh pastas, venison, or steamed mussels served with prawns, ginger, and roasted cashews—grace patrons' tables. The award-winning wine list highlights the province's best vintages and has won the restaurant almost as much recognition as its inventive menu.

✪ James Bay Tea Rm & Restaurant. 332 Menzies St. ☎ 250/382-8282. Reservations recommended. Main courses C$12–C$15 (US$8–US$11); tea C$6.55 (US$4.70). MC, V. Mon–Sat 7am–9pm, Sun 8am–9pm. Tea service offered all day. AE, MC, V. Bus: 5 or 30. ENGLISH.

For decades, this country-style British home filled with quaint clutter and royal memorabilia has served Victoria's best afternoon tea. Sandwiches, tarts, and scones with cream and jam accompany pots of piping-hot tea. Located 1 block from the Parliament Buildings, the James Bay Tea Room also features traditional British favorites at breakfast, lunch, and dinner. You'll find kipper and eggs, steak-and-kidney pie, Cornish pasties, mixed grill (lamb chop, liver, sausage, bacon, onions, and tomato), and roast prime rib of beef with Yorkshire pudding. There's often a line for afternoon tea, but it's a very civil line.

Rebecca's. 1127 Wharf St. ☎ **250/380-6999.** Reservations accepted. Main courses C$12.95–C$18.95 (US$9–US$14). AE, MC, V. Daily 11:30am–10pm. Bus: 5, then walk 2 blocks west. PACIFIC NORTHWEST.

A team of eight chefs creates the pastas and baked goods featured at this spacious wharf-front restaurant. The seasonal menus include specials such as a whole Dungeness crab topped with a Chardonnay and roasted-garlic cream sauce; or grilled halibut steak served with toasted almonds in strawberry-balsamic vinaigrette. The cappuccino bar is situated right by the large front windows, making it a perfect spot for people-watching. The outdoor cafe is open for summer dining.

INEXPENSIVE

Banana Belt Café. 281 Menzies St. ☎ **250/385-9616.** Reservations not accepted. Breakfast and lunch C$4.25–C$9.25 (US$3.05–US$7). No credit cards. Tues–Sun 8am–3pm. Bus: 5. WEST COAST.

It doesn't matter if you crave a quesadilla stuffed with cheese and avocados, a fresh-juice-and-yogurt shake, a good old-fashioned burger, or eggs and bacon. Just bring a healthy appetite to this tiny cafe, a favorite local hangout where breakfast is a serious matter. Don't let items like "the Sensitive New Age Guy Omelette" (filled with Monterey Jack, Brie, and avocados) fool you. This is not a "weeds-and-seeds" dive—it's a good, simple establishment with a great sense of humor.

♦ Don Mee Restaurant. 538 Fisgard St. ☎ **250/383-1032.** Main courses C$4.95–C$10.35 (US$3.55–US$7); 4-course dinner for 2 C$16.95 (US$12). AE, DC, MC, V. Mon–Fri 11am–2:30pm, Sat–Sun and holidays 10:30am–2:30pm; daily 5pm–10:30pm. Bus: 5. CANTONESE/SZECHUAN.

Since the 1920s, Don Mee's has been serving up delightful Hong Kong–style dim sum, hearty San Francisco–style chop suey and chow mein, piquant Szechuan seafood dishes, and delectable Cantonese sizzling platters. You can't miss this second-story restaurant. A huge Chinese lantern made of neon looms above the small doorway. A 4-foot-tall gold-leafed laughing Buddha greets you at the foot of the stairs that lead up to the huge dining room. The dinner specials for two, three, or four people are particularly good deals if you want to sample lots of everything on the menu.

Milestone's. 812 Wharf St. ☎ **250/381-2244.** Main courses C$5.95–C$12.95 (US$4.25–US$9). AE, DC, MC, V. Mon–Thurs 11am–10pm, Fri 11am–11pm, Sat 10am–11pm, Sun 10am–10pm. Bus: 5. WEST COAST.

This waterfront bistro has Victoria's best view of the Inner Harbour: It's downstairs from the Visitor Info Centre, right on the wharf. The success of this chain restaurant can be attributed to its casual, upscale atmosphere, waterside outdoor patio, and hearty menu, which includes bountiful grilled-chicken Caesar salad, grilled seafood, barbecued ribs, broiled steaks, and overstuffed sandwiches. The bar serves nightly drink specials and innovative martinis.

Millos. 716 Burdett Ave. ☎ **250/382-4422** or 604/382-5544. Reservations recommended. Main courses C$8.95–C$24.95 (US$6–US$18). AE, DC, ER, MC, V. Mon–Sat 11:30am–4:30pm; daily 4:30–11pm. Bus: 5. GREEK.

Millos is not hard to find: Just look for the blue-and-white windmill behind the Empress. Flaming saganaki (a sharp cheese sautéed in olive oil and flambéed with

Greek brandy), grilled halibut souvlaki, baby-back ribs, and succulent grilled salmon are just a few of the menu items at this lively five-level restaurant. Kids get their own menu. Folk dancers and belly dancers highlight the evening's entertainment lineup on Friday and Saturday nights. (The wait staff is remarkably warm and entertaining every night of the week.)

VICTORIA AFTER DARK

It may appear to be a sleepy city after sunset, but Victoria does have its share of nighttime diversions, ranging from the performing arts and the local pub scene to cigar-and-martini lounges. The **Community Arts Council of Greater Victoria,** 511–620 View St. (☎ 250/381-2787), operates an information hot line, with updated events listings and schedules for performances at various venues. Tickets to special events can be purchased at the **Tourism Victoria Visitor Info Centre** (see "Visitor Information," above). And *Monday Magazine* (☎ 250/727-5272), a weekly tabloid that's published on Thursdays, is your best bet for information about local bands, club dates, and lounge life.

THE PERFORMING ARTS   The theater is alive and well in Victoria. Staging the works of Canadian playwrights as well as masters such as Harold Pinter, Stephen Sondheim, and William Shakespeare, the **Belfry Theatre,** 1291 Gladstone Ave. (☎ 250/385-6815), is a nationally acclaimed company that performs five productions per season (October to April) in a small, intimate playhouse. **Theatre Inconnu,** Box 8796, Victoria, BC, V8W 3S3 (☎ 250/360-0234), presents "Shakespeare in the Giant Tent" on the Inner Harbour from mid-July to mid-August. Tickets are C$5 to C$13 (US$3.55 to US$9.30).

The **Victoria Operatic Society,** 798 Fairview Rd. (☎ 250/381-1021), produces Broadway musicals such as *Evita, The Mikado,* and *Into the Woods* throughout the year at the **McPherson Playhouse,** 3 Centennial Sq. (☎ 250/386-6121). Ticket prices range from C$12.50 to C$19.50 (US$9 to US$14).

The **Victoria Symphony Orchestra,** 846 Broughton St. (☎ 250/385-9771), performs weekly from August to May, kicking off each season with "Symphony Splash," a free concert on a downtown barge. "Summer Pops" is a favorite Friday event that takes place at the **Royal Theatre,** 805 Broughton St. (☎ 250/361-0820, or 250/386-6121 for box office). During the rest of the year, the orchestra performs at a various area venues. Tickets for most concerts are C$12 (US$9) for adults. Senior, student, and group discounts are available.

LIVE-MUSIC CLUBS   Most Victoria nightclubs are open Monday to Saturday until 2am, and on Sunday until midnight. **Harpo's,** 15 Bastion Sq. (☎ 250/385-2626), is an intimate waterfront venue featuring high-profile recording artists as well as popular reggae and rock bands. Admission varies from C$3 to C$15 (US$2.15 to US$11). Drinks are C$3 (US$2.15) and up.

Hermann's Dixieland Inn, 753 View St., near Blanshard Street (☎ 250/388-9166), is Victoria's best jazz venue. It's a low-lit supper club specializing in Dixieland jazz, and sometimes features fusion jazz and blues acts. There's usually no cover charge; drinks are C$3 (US$2.15) and up.

Lounge culture has arrived in Victoria. **Euphoria,** 1208 Wharf St. (☎ 250/381-2331), is a "swank" cocktail lounge that pipes in world-beat, salsa, lounge, and some Top-40 tunes, shakes up some mean martinis, and stocks fine Cuban and Honduran cigars in a temperature-controlled humidor. There's a C$3 (US$2.15) cover most nights; drinks are C$3 (US$2.15) and up. And, of course, a "lounge wear" dress code (jackets for men, cocktail outfits for women; no jeans, please) is enforced.

The **Drawing Room,** 751 View St. (☎ **250/920-7797**), is perched on top of a downtown office building. Open Tuesday to Saturday nights, this "high-life" lounge has an excellent, well-stocked humidor of Cuban cigars and an extensive martini menu. The swank, upscale lounge attracts the city's young and beautiful set. Cover is C$3 (US$2.15); drinks are C$2.50 (US$1.80) and up.

PUBS   Traditional British-style pubs and microbreweries are the center of social life in Victoria, as they are in the rest of the province. **Garrick's Head Pub,** 64 Bastion Sq., in the Bedford Hotel (☎ **250/384-6835**), serves classic pub food like shepherd's pie, ploughman's lunch, and beer-and-ale pie without the glitz and high prices of the *faux* pubs nearby. A meal and a pint of ale costs less than C$7.95 (US$6).

✪ **Swans Brewpub,** 506 Pandora Ave., in Swans Hotel (☎ **250/361-3310**), is the city's hottest nightspot for the young professional crowd. This brass-and-fern establishment has a glassed-in patio and offers good pub food along with traditional ales brewed on the premises by Buckerfields Brewery. (Free tours are conducted at 2pm on weekdays.)

GAY & LESBIAN CLUBS   The scene here is small, intimate, and friendly. Nightlife centers around **Rumors,** 1325 Government St. (☎ **250/385-0566**), which serves as a hangout, dance hall, and social center. Rumors is open daily from 9pm until 2am. There's no cover charge, and there are nightly drink specials.

CASINOS   Victoria has two casinos. They don't offer floor shows or entertainment, but you'll find blackjack, roulette, sic-bo, red dog (diamond dog), and Caribbean stud-poker games at both **Casino Victoria,** 716 Courtney St. (☎ **250/380-3998**), and the **Great Canadian Casino,** 3366 Douglas St. (☎ **250/384-2614**). Both are open daily from 6pm to 2am.

3 Side Trips from Victoria: Goldstream Provincial Park & Duncan

The **E&N Railiner** winds through this forested wonderland on its route from Victoria to Nanaimo, and the natural beauty of **Goldstream Provincial Park** attracts hikers, campers, and birders who stop for a few hours or days to observe the wildlife in the beautiful temperate rain forest.

The Island Highway continues north from Goldstream Provincial Park, heading into the Cowichan Valley and the city of **Duncan** (pop. 5,100) about 50 kilometers (30 miles) farther. This is the ancestral home of the Cowichan tribe, famed for crating hand-knitted sweaters. Five of the island's best wineries are in the valley. The city of Duncan also serves as a jumping-off spot for fly-fishing trips on the Cowichan River or a self-guided walking tour of the city's 41 totem poles.

ESSENTIALS

VISITOR INFORMATION   Contact **Goldstream Provincial Park,** Sooke Lake Road, Malahat (☎ **250/387-4363,** or 250/478-7411 for group camping; mailing address: 2930 Trans-Canada Highway, RR #6, Victoria, BC, V9E 1K3). The park's **Freeman King Visitor Centre** (☎ **250/478-9414**) offers guided walks, talks, displays, and programs throughout the year. It's open daily from 10am to 6pm. The **Duncan–Cowichan Visitor Info Centre,** 381 Trans-Canada Highway, Duncan, BC, V9L 3R5 (☎ **250/746-4636**) is open daily from 10am to 6pm.

GETTING THERE   The **Island Highway** (Highway 1 and Highway 19) runs through the center of Goldstream Provincial Park. It's a 20-minute drive north from Victoria.

Duncan is 61.6 kilometers (37 miles) north of Victoria. Take the Island Highway (Highway 1), which passes through the center of town. The VIA Rail's **E&N Railiner** (see "Getting There" in section 2) leaves Courtenay at 1:15pm daily and stops in Nanaimo and Duncan before arriving in Victoria at 5:45pm. **Island Coach Lines** (☎ **250/385-4411**) operates regular daily service between Victoria and Duncan; fares start at C$15 (US$11) one-way.

GETTING AROUND   You'll need a car to visit Goldstream Provincial Park and Duncan.

SPECIAL EVENTS   Three species of salmon (chum, chinook, and steelhead) make the **annual salmon runs** up Goldstream River during October, November, December, and February. You can easily observe this natural wonder along the riverbanks. Contact the park's **Freeman King Visitor Centre** (☎ **250/478-9414**) for details.

During the second week in November, the **Native Heritage Annual Art Show & Sale** presents the works of local Cowichan tribal artists and craftspeople at the Native Heritage Centre, 200 Cowichan Way (☎ **250/746-8119**).

EXPLORING GOLDSTREAM PROVINCIAL PARK

This tranquil arboreal setting overflowed with prospectors during the 1860s gold-rush days. Park trails take you past abandoned mine shafts and tunnels as well as 600-year-old stands of towering Douglas fir, lodgepole pine, red cedar, indigenous yew, and arbutus trees. The **Gold Mine Trail** leads to Niagara Creek and the abandoned gold mine that was operated by Lt. Peter Leech, a Royal Engineer who discovered gold in the creek in 1858. **The Goldstream Trail** leads you to the salmon-spawning areas. (You might also catch sight of mink and river otters racing along this path.)

ACCOMMODATIONS

Goldstream Provincial Park maintains 141 **tent sites** and 9 **RV/trailer sites.** There are no electric or water hookups, but the camping facilities include hot showers, flush toilets, well-pumped water, fire wood, and grill-equipped fire pits. The campsites cost C$9.50 (US$7) per site, per night.

✪ **The Aerie.** 600 Ebedora Lane (mailing address: Box 108), Malahat, BC, V0R 2L0. ☎ **250/743-7115.** Fax 250/743-4766. 24 suites. A/C TV TEL. Apr 25–June 30 and Sept 5–Oct 14 C$180–C$240 (US$129–US$171) double, C$275–C$375 (US$196–US$268) suite; July 1–Sept 4 C$195–C$260 (US$139–US$186) double, C$295–C$425 (US$211–US$304) suite; Oct 15–Apr 24 C$150–C$200 (US$107–US$143) double, C$250–C$300 (US$179–US$214) suite. Rates include full breakfast. Combination accommodation and dinner packages available. AE, MC, V. Free parking. Take Hwy. 1 to the Spectacle Lake turnoff; take the first right and follow the winding driveway up.

Nestled atop the Malahat summit at the park's northern end is a little bit of heaven. In this elegant Mediterranean-style villa, each pastel-hued hideaway suite has a large handcrafted bed, a sumptuous bathroom, a Jacuzzi, a wet bar and refrigerator, and a fireplace in front of a white leather sofa. Most of the suites have decks positioned to ensure complete privacy and a breathtaking view. And although it's the kind of exclusive, opulent getaway you'd expect to see featured on "Lifestyles of the Rich and Famous" (in fact, it appeared three times on that TV show), there's no pretension here, just remarkable service and hospitality.

Dining: The hotel's restaurant, overlooking Spectacle Lake, is a singularly pleasant experience (see "Dining," below).

Facilities: Five acres of private walking trails, helipad, heated indoor pool, outdoor hot tub, tennis courts, full spa (massage, facials, wraps, aesthetics), outdoor wedding chapel.

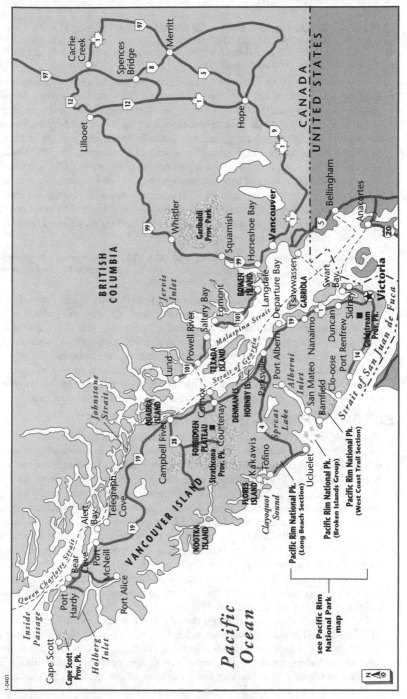

Vancouver Island

Pacific Ocean

Inside Passage
Queen Charlotte Strait

Cape Scott
Cape Scott Prov. Pk.
Holberg Inlet

Port Alice
Port Hardy
Bear Cove
Port McNeill
Alert Bay
Telegraph Cove

Johnstone Strait

19

Campbell River

QUADRA ISLAND

28
FORBIDDEN PLATEAU
Strathcona Prov. Pk.

Comox
Courtenay

VANCOUVER ISLAND

NOOTKA ISLAND

FLORES ISLAND

Clayoquot Sound

Kakawis
Tofino

Ucluelet

Pacific Rim National Pk.
(Long Beach Section)

Pacific Rim National Pk.
(Broken Islands Group)

Pacific Rim National Pk.
(West Coast Trail Section)

see Pacific Rim National Park map

4
Sproat Lake
Port Alberni
Alberni Inlet

San Mateo
Bamfield
Clo-oose
Port Renfrew
14

DENMAN IS.
HORNBY IS.
Parksville

Strait of Georgia

TEXADA ISLAND

Lund
101
Powell River
Saltery Bay

Malaspina Strait

Egmont
101
Langdale

BOWEN ISLAND
Departure Bay
GABRIOLA
19
Nanaimo
Duncan

Tsawwassen
Swart Bay
Sidney

Victoria
★
Goldstream Prov. Pk.

Strait of San Juan de Fuca

1

Jervis Inlet

BRITISH COLUMBIA

Whistler
Garibaldi Prov. Park
99
Squamish
99
Horseshoe Bay

Vancouver
1

CANADA
UNITED STATES

5
Bellingham
20
Anacortes

97
Cache Creek
1

Spences Bridge
8
Merritt
97

12
Lillooet
12
1
5

Hope
9
1

N

1-0401

DINING

○ **The Aerie.** 600 Ebedora Lane, Malahat. ☎ **250/743-7115.** Fax 250/743-4766. Reservations required. Main courses C$27.50–C$32 (US$20–US$23); 7-course set menu C$55 (US$39). AE, MC, V. Daily 5–10pm. Free parking. Take Hwy. 1 to the Spectacle Lake turnoff; take the first right and follow the winding driveway up. FRENCH.

This luxurious restaurant features a 24-carat gold-leaf ceiling, an open-hearth stone fireplace, and breathtaking, lofty views of Spectacle Lake and the Olympic Mountains. Serving three meals daily to the hotel's guests, this establishment is open to the public for dinner only. Local venison-and-pistachio pâté with a dried-fruit compote, juniper-and-port glaze, and herb sunflower croutons is just one overture in master chef Chris Jones's dining symphony, which is served by an impeccable staff. The entrees are also composed from fresh local ingredients. A grilled halibut fillet is delicately seasoned with fried-caper and balsamic vinaigrette. An oven-roasted lamb chop and loin are glazed with currants and cracked pepper and served with rhubarb and lemon thyme chutney, and roasted eggplant blinis. A Belgian chocolate and hazelnut-nougat pyramid is topped with Frangelico ganache and fruit coulis. An excellent brandy and Kona coffee completes a memorable experience.

Six Mile House. 494 Island Hwy., Victoria. ☎ **250/478-3121.** Reservations for large parties requested. Main courses C$4.50–C$7.50 (US$3.20–US$5). ER, MC, V. Daily 11:30am–2pm and 6–9pm. Pub Mon–Sat 11am–1am, Sun 11am–11pm. PUB.

This 1855 heritage building was originally the site of Parson's Bridge Hotel. It was a favorite drinking haunt for naval personnel stationed at Esquimalt Harbour. A fire consumed the original structure in 1898, and a Tudor-style pub with a mahogany ceiling, stained-glass windows, Persian carpets, and brass railings took its place. The Six Mile has a loyal local crowd who come for the atmosphere and classic British pub dinner specials, which include prime rib, lamb stew, and beef-and-ale pie—all seasoned with herbs fresh from the pub's garden. The Fireside Room boasts an oak bar and other classically British touches, and there's beautiful scenery from the outdoor patio.

EXPLORING DUNCAN: THE CITY OF TOTEM POLES

The Cowichan Valley native-Indian tribes are famous for their bulky, durable sweaters knitted with bold motifs from hand-spun raw wool. But there's more to learn about this ancient living culture. Visiting the ○ **Native Heritage Centre,** 200 Cowichan Way (☎ 250/746-8119), is a visually enlightening experience. You can walk through displays of ancient artifacts and multimedia presentations, speak with master and apprentice carvers as they work on totem poles and ceremonial masks, watch textile and beading artisans create intricately designed fabrics and garments, have a native-Indian meal in the Riverwalk Café or the Big House, or join in the many summer events, including the "Mid-Day Salmon Barbecue Show." Shoppers will find a wide assortment of Cowichan sweaters and jewelry in the two gift shops, as well as books, serigraphic prints, handcrafted ceremonial masks, totem poles, and other craft items. The center is open daily from 9:30am to 5pm; admission is C$7 (US$5) for adults and C$6.15 (US$4.40) seniors and children.

The Cowichan River runs through the city. A few miles from the city center, a 31.6-kilometer (19-mile) **fishing path** winds from the Robertson Road clubhouse to Cowichan Lake, where you'll find brown trout, cutthroat, rainbow trout, and steelhead salmon. Some sections of the riverbank are designated strictly for fly-fishing. To get there, drive west from Duncan along Highway 18 toward Cowichan Lake. To fish here, you need a nonresident freshwater license. Pick up a license, lures, and gear at **Robinson's Sporting Goods Ltd.,** 1307 Broad St., Victoria (☎ 250/385-3429).

TAKING THE WINERY TOURS

The vintners of the Cowichan Valley have gained a solid reputation for producing fine wines. Five of the establishments have opened their doors for winery tours and tastings. Located less than half an hour's drive from Duncan, the hour-long winery tours are a great introduction to novice aficionados and include a tasting of the vintner's art as well as a chance to purchase bottles or cases of your favorites.

Cherry Point Vineyards, 840 Cherry Point Rd., Cowichan (☎ 250/743-1272), conducts tours daily from 11:30am to 6pm. **Venturi-Schulze Vineyards,** 4235 Trans-Canada Highway, Cowichan Station (☎ 250/743-5630), provides tours by appointment only and is a must for veteran oenophiles. And **Blue Grouse Vineyards,** 4365 Blue Grouse Rd., Mill Bay (☎ 250/743-3834), conducts tours on Wednesday and Friday to Sunday from 11am to 5pm.

FERRYING TO NEWCASTLE ISLAND

Just off the Nanaimo coastline, **Newcastle Island** is an ideal destination for hikers, cyclists, and campers. Trails around the island lead you through quiet woodlands onto beaches, around caves, and up to high overlooks.

To get there, take the **ferry** (☎ 250/753-5141, or 250/387-4363 off-season). It leaves daily from the wharf behind Mafeo–Sutton Park's Civic Arena (just north of downtown) from May to October; departures occur almost hourly from 10am to 7:30pm. The 15-minute crossing costs C$4.25 (US$3.05) round-trip; bikes costs an extra C$1.50 (US$1.05).

Newcastle Island Provincial Marine Park, 2930 Trans-Canada Hwy. (☎ 250/ 387-4363), was at one time a bustling island community. Two Salish native-Indian villages were established here before coal was discovered on the island, in 1849, by British settlers. The Canadian-Pacific Steamship Company purchased the island in 1931, creating a resort with a dance pavilion, teahouse, picnic areas, changing houses, soccer field, wading pool, and a floating hotel.

The island became a provincial marine park in 1961, and now attracts hikers, bikers, and campers to its many trails. The popular **Mallard Lake Trail** leads through the wooded interior toward a freshwater lake, while the **Shoreline Trail** runs across steep sandstone cliffs, onto sand and gravel beaches, past caves and caverns, and up to a great eagle-spotting perch, Giovando Lookout.

The park also maintains 18 **campsites** for tenters on the island's southern tip. Toilets, wood, fire pits, and water are strategically placed at three points on the campgrounds. Rates are C$9.50 (US$7) per site.

ACCOMMODATIONS

Village Green Inn. 141 Trans-Canada Hwy., Duncan, BC, V9L 3P8. ☎ 800/665-3989 in Canada, or 250/746-5126. Fax 250/746-5126. 80 rms and suites. TEL. C$64 (US$46) double; C$79 (US$56) suite. Kitchen C$10 (US$7) additional. Senior discounts. AE, MC, V.

Situated right on the Island Highway (Trans-Canada Highway) near the Native Heritage Centre (see "Exploring Duncan," above), this inn offers large rooms and one-bedroom suites. All accommodations offer tastefully decorated surroundings in muted tones that highlight the dark-wood furnishings; all offer ample amounts of peace and quiet. Some accommodations are equipped with kitchenettes and air-conditioning. Free local calls and in-room coffee are offered. An indoor pool, a sauna, tennis courts, a cold-beer and wine store, and a licensed family-style restaurant and bar and grill are on the premises.

NEARBY DINING

✪ The Crow & Gate. 2313 Yellow Point Rd. **☎ 250/722-3731.** Reservations recommended. Main courses C$7.95–C$12.95 (US$6–US$9). AE, MC, V. Mon–Thurs 11am–11pm, Fri–Sat 11am–midnight. Take the Island Hwy. (Hwy. 19) north past Cassidy. Turn right on Cedar Rd., which leads onto Yellow Point Rd. Drive 1.6km (1 mile). PUB.

This classic Tudor-style pub was built in 1972 on a 10-acre working farm. It's a friendly haven of English style and hospitality. The handcrafted beams, tables, and chairs are complemented by a large brick fireplace and leaded-glass windows. The menu offers the best British cuisine, including roast beef and Yorkshire pudding, shepherd's pie, and roasted Cornish game hens. But the pub's owners also pay homage to the province's Scottish and Australian heritage with special events like Robert Burns Night, which features *haggis* (sheep's stomach stuffed with oats and herbs) that's ceremonially sliced open with a sword.

BUNGEE JUMPING

Take the plunge off a 140-foot trestle at **The Bungy Zone** (**☎ 250/753-5867** or 250/716-7874; mailing address: Box 399, Station A, Nanaimo, BC, V9R 5L3), off the Island Highway about 15 minutes south of Nanaimo. North America's only legal bridge jump sends you over the Nanaimo River from a specially constructed steel trestle bridge. The first jump costs C$95 (US$68), the second leap C$75 (US$54). It's open daily from 10am to 4:30pm year-round. Reservations are recommended from June to August. For a C$2 to C$4 (US$1.40 to US$2.85) admission charge, you can observe jumpers. There's free shuttle service from Victoria and Nanaimo. Or drive 68.3 kilometers (41 miles) north from Victoria on the Island Highway (highways 1 and 19) or 13.3 kilometers (8 miles) south from Nanaimo, then follow the exit signs.

4 The West Coast of Vancouver Island: Pacific Rim National Park, Tofino, Ucluelet & Bamfield

In sharp contrast to the tranquillity found on Vancouver Island's east coast, the wild, weather-ravaged beauty of the Pacific Ocean on the island's west coast has changed little since native-Indian tribes settled its shores thousands of years ago. Today, Vancouver Island's west coast is a favorite haunt for photographers, hikers, kayakers, and divers. And it's the home of the **Pacific Rim National Park** group, established in 1971 as Canada's first marine park.

The town of **Ucluelet** ("You-*clue*-let," meaning "safe harbor") is British Columbia's third-largest fishing port, but has a winter population of only 1,900. Thousands of visitors arrive between March and May to see as many as **20,000 Pacific gray whales** pass close to the shore as they migrate north to their summer feeding grounds in the Arctic Circle. The town is only a 15-minute drive from **Long Beach** (part of the Pacific Rim National Park group), which is a haven for an abundance of marine life.

Scuba divers are lured by the numerous **shipwrecks** beneath the waves in and around the town of **Tofino** (pop. 1,300). Sea-going kayakers and canoeists also come here to board sail-charter excursions headed toward Pacific Rim National Park's **Broken Islands Group** and **Meares Island,** where the serene waters of the sound are an ideal area for intermediate paddlers.

The park's world-famous **West Coast Trail** is considered the adventure of a lifetime by intrepid backpackers and "extreme" hikers from around the world, who flock to the tiny town of **Bamfield** (pop. 383) and Port Renfrew to begin their odyssey. Thousands have braved the 10-day hike over this rugged rescue trail, which was established after the survivors of a shipwreck in the early 1900s died from exposure on the beach because there was no land access for the rescuers. The trail includes basket rides over deep canyons, moss-covered many-hundred-step stairways in and out of gorges, beach treks that must be completed at low tide, and rain-forest conditions.

Even if you're not an outdoor adventurer, the sandy beaches of Tofino, Ucluelet, and Long Beach beckon you to beachcomb along the tide pools and experience the area's amazing beauty.

ESSENTIALS

VISITOR INFORMATION The **Tofino Visitor Info Centre,** 380 Campbell St., Tofino (☎ **250/725-3414;** mailing address: Box 476, Tofino, BC, V0R 2Z0), is open March to September, Monday to Friday from 11am to 5pm. The **Ucluelet Visitor Info Centre,** Junction Highway 4, Ucluelet (☎ **250/726-4641;** mailing address: Box 428, Ucluelet, BC, V0R 3A0), is open only from July to September, during the same hours.

The **Long Beach Visitor Information Centre,** about a mile from the Highway 4 junction to Tofino, is open daily from mid-March to September from 10am to 6pm. You can get trail maps and trail-condition updates here; the adjoining Wickaninnish Restaurant has ecological and historical information about the area.

For **West Coast Trail** permits and information, contact **Discover BC** (☎ **800/ 663-6000**) between March 1 and September 1.

GETTING THERE Visitors to the west coast can drive, take a coach bus or ferry, or fly into this remote region.

By Bus Island Coach Lines (☎ **250/724-1266**) operates regular daily bus service between Victoria and Port Alberni. The 3¹/₂-hour trip costs C$26.40 (US$19) each way. The 2-hour shuttle that links Port Alberni with Tofino and Ucluelet costs C$15 (US$11) each way.

The daily **West Coast Trail Express** (☎ **250/380-0580**) provides Victoria-Bamfield service from May to September. Because it partially travels along an unpaved logging road, the ride is usually about 4 hours long.

The **Pacheenaht Band Bus Service** (☎ **250/647-5521**) operates on-call, summer-only service between Bamfield and Port Renfrew for a minimum of four people. The one-way fare is C$40 (US$29) per person.

By Car & Ferry From Nanaimo, take the Island Highway (Highway 19) north for 51.6 kilometers (31 miles). Just before the town of Parksville is a turnoff for Route 4, which leads to the midisland town of Port Alberni (about 38.3km/23 miles west). From this central location you can reach the coastal towns of Tofino (135km/81 miles west of Port Alberni), Ucluelet (103.3km/62 miles west), and Bamfield (103.3/ 62 miles southwest).

You'll have to drive almost 2 hours on an unpaved logging road that's open only during summer to get to Bamfield, at the West Coast Trail's northern trailhead. However, the ferry from Port Alberni (see "By Ferry," below), makes this town accessible year-round.

By Ferry A 4¹/₂-hour ride aboard the **Alberni Marine Transportation** (☎ **250/ 723-8313**) passenger ferry, MV *Lady Rose,* takes you from Port Alberni through the Alberni Inlet fjord to the boardwalk fishing village of Bamfield or to Ucluelet. It makes brief stops along the way to deliver mail and packages to solitary cabin dwellers along the coast, and to let off or pick up kayakers bound for the Broken Islands Group. The *Lady Rose,* which was built in Scotland in 1937, departs three times a week to each destination from Alberni Harbour Quay's Angle Street. The one-way fare to Bamfield is C$16 (US$11); one-way to Ucluelet is C$20 (US$14); the round-trip fare is C$36 (US$26) to Bamfield and C$40 (US$29) to Ucluelet.

By Plane   North Vancouver Air (☎ 800/228-6608) operates twin-engine, turbo-prop plane service daily between Vancouver or Victoria and Tofino from May to September; it runs five times a week from October to April. **Northwest Seaplanes** (☎ 800/690-0086) and **Sound Flight** (☎ 800/825-0722) offer floatplane service between Seattle and Tofino during the summer.

SPECIAL EVENT   In the second week of March, the **Pacific Rim Whale Festival** (☎ 250/726-4641) is held in both Tofino and Ucluelet. Live crab races, the Gumboot Golf Tournament, guided whale-watching hikes, and a native-Indian festival are a few of the events celebrating the annual Pacific-gray-whale migration.

EXPLORING THE PACIFIC RIM NATIONAL PARK GROUP

During the 1800s, a huge whale population resided in this area. Massive herds of humpbacks, Pacific gray whales, Baird's beaked whales, and gigantic blue whales roamed the island's west coast. From 1905 until the late 1920s, whaling fleets harvested whales from these rich waters for their valuable oils until the populations were nearly extinct. It wasn't until 1972 that the Canadian government banned whaling in these waters. Miraculously, the Pacific-gray-whale population has returned in recent years to its historic level: about 20,000 migrate here annually.

Generally, the island's west-coast lifestyle is oriented toward outdoor activities, and there are outfitters, facilities, and itineraries suited to every interest and experience level. But whale watching is the main attraction. Charters and land-based viewing points are filled with whale watchers during the spring, and the towns of Tofino and Ucluelet celebrate the yearly return by hosting the Pacific Rim Whale Festival (see "Special Event," above).

The 7-mile stretch of rocky headlands, sand, and surf along **Long Beach Headlands Trail** is the most accessible section of the park system, which incorporates Long Beach, the West Coast Trail, and the Broken Islands Group. No matter where you go in this area, you're bound to meet whale watchers in the spring, surfers and anglers in the summer, hearty hikers during the colder months, and kayakers year-round.

In and around **Long Beach,** numerous marked trails 0.83 to 3.3 kilometers (¹/₂ mile to 2 miles) long take you through the thick temperate rain forest that edges the shore. The **Gold Mine Trail** (3.3km/2 miles long) near Florencia Bay still has a few artifacts from the days when a gold-mining operation flourished amid the trees. And the partially boardwalked **South Beach Trail** (less than a mile long) leads through the moss-draped rain forest onto small quiet coves such as Lismer Beach and South Beach, where you can see abundant life in the rocky tidal pools.

The ✪ **Broken Islands Group,** located in Barkley Sound, is the park's canoeing, diving, and kayaking paradise. The reefs teem with beautiful marine life, and there are ancient shipwrecks to explore (see the box "Shipwrecks & Sea Creatures," above). Before you set out, pick up a copy of Marine Chart 3670 at **Worldwide Books and Maps,** 736A Granville St. (downstairs), Vancouver (☎ 604/687-3320), or at **Jeune Bros. Great Outdoors Store,** 570 Johnson St., Vancouver (☎ 604/386-8778). You can take the MV *Lady Rose* (see "Getting There," above) to the main launch site on Gibraltar Island. Once you're in the water, paddle to the nearby sheltered lagoons, where resident bald eagles soar overhead and salmon swim below.

Hot Springs Cove is Vancouver Island's only natural hot spring. Located 66.6 kilometers (40 miles) north of Tofino, the cove is accessible only by water. Sail,

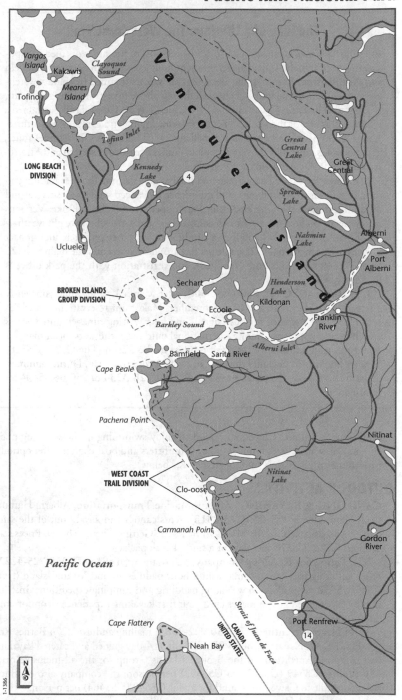

Pacific Rim National Park

The Hike of a Lifetime: The West Coast Trail

After the SS *Valencia* ran aground in 1906 and most of the survivors died of exposure on the beach, the Canadian government built a rescue trail between Bamfield and Port Renfrew. For years, the lifesaving trail was maintained by solitary watchmen who groomed the trail and checked the telephone line strung along the path.

Upgraded by Parks Canada in the 1970s, the ✪ **West Coast Trail** has gained a reputation as one of the world's greatest extreme hiking and camping adventures. About 9,000 people hike the entire challenging 70-kilometer (43¹/₂-mile) route, and thousands more hike the very accessible **7-mile oceanfront stretch** at the northern trailhead near Bamfield each year.

Planning (get a topographic map and tidal table), stamina (besides hiking, you should train for rock climbing), and experience (advanced wilderness survival and minimum-impact camping knowledge) are imperative for the full hike. Veterans recommend you go with at least two companion hikers, pack lightweight weatherproof gear, and bring about 50 feet of climbing rope per person. To reduce impact on the environment, only 52 people per day are allowed to enter the main trail (26 from Port Renfrew, 26 from Bamfield), and registration with the park office is mandatory.

Call **Discover BC** (☎ **800/663-6000**) after March 1 to schedule your entry reservation for the coming May to September. Make your reservations as early as possible and be prepared for busy signals and long waiting times. Limited access and increased popularity among international outdoor enthusiasts mean that you might not gain admission if you call too late in the season. The C$25 (US$18) advance booking fee includes the price of a waterproof trail map. During summer, you can also contact the **parks service** at ☎ **250/728-3234** or 250/647-5434 for information.

---

canoe, or kayak up to Clayoquot Sound to enjoy swimming in the steaming pools and bracing waterfalls. A number of kayak outfitters and boat charters offer optional trips to the springs (see "Outdoor Activities," below).

OUTDOOR ACTIVITIES

CANOEING & KAYAKING   Alberni Marine Transportation, Alberni Harbour Quay, Port Alberni (☎ 250/723-8313), rents canoes and kayaks out of the same office that sells tickets for the MV *Lady Rose* (see "Getting There," above). Prices start at about C$28 (US$20) per day for a single kayak package.

The **Tofino Sea-Kayaking Company,** 320 Main St., Tofino (☎ 250/725-4222), offers kayaking packages ranging from 4-hour paddles around Meares Island (from C$45/US$32 per person) to weeklong paddling and camping expeditions. Instruction by experienced guides makes even your first kayaking experience a comfortable, safe, and enjoyable one.

Wild Heart Adventures (☎ 250/722-3683; mailing address: 2774 Barnes Rd., Site H2, RR #2, Nanaimo, BC, V9R 5K2) offers 4-day guided and catered kayaking and camping expeditions to the Broken Islands Group for the all-inclusive price of C$449 to C$549 (US$321 to US$392) per person; the company also conducts a 6-day paddle to Clayoquot Sound for about C$649 (US$464) per person.

Victoria-based **Ocean River Sports** (see "Shopping" in section 2) organizes weeklong group trips with experienced guides, instruction, and equipment through this area ranging in price from C$450 to C$800 (US$312 to US$571) per person.

DIVING See the box "Shipwrecks & Sea Creatures," near the beginning of this chapter.

FISHING Sportfishing for salmon, steelhead, rainbow trout, Dolly Varden char, halibut, cod, and snapper is excellent near Port Alberni and the Broken Islands Group. The nearby provincial fish hatchery releases more than 10 million fish into these waters annually. Long Beach is also great for bottom fishing. To fish here, you need a nonresident license: one for saltwater and one for freshwater catches. Tackle shops sell licenses, have information on current restrictions, and often carry copies of the current publications *BC Tidal Waters Sport Fishing Guide* and *BC Sport Fishing Regulations Synopsis for Non-Tidal Waters.* Independent anglers should also pick up a copy of the *BC Fishing Directory and Atlas.* **Alberni Pacific Charters,** 5440 Argyle St., Port Alberni (☎ 250/724-3112), organizes fishing charters throughout the area, including Barkley Sound. Prices start at about C$50 (US$36) per hour.

HIKING If you're canoeing or kayaking around Clayoquot Sound or Barkley Sound and the Broken Islands Group, there are two other trails to discover. The boardwalked **Clayoquot Witness Trail,** north of Tofino, winds through a towering old-growth temperate rain forest of Sitka spruce and western red cedar. The **Big Cedar Trail** (☎ 250/725-3233) on Meares Island is a 2-mile boardwalked path that was built in 1993 to protect this old-growth temperate rain forest. Maintained by the Tla-o-qui-aht native-Indian band, the trail has a long staircase leading up to the Hanging Garden Tree, the province's fourth-largest western red cedar.

WHALE WATCHING & BIRDING A number of local outfitters conduct tours through this region, which is inhabited by gray whales, bald eagles, porpoises, orcas, seals, and sea lions. **Chinook Charters,** 450 Campbell St., Tofino (☎ 800/665-3646 or 250/725-3431), offers whale-watching trips in Clayoquot Sound on 25-foot Zodiac boats. The company also conducts trips to Hot Springs Cove on its 32-foot Chinook Key. **Jamie's Whaling Station,** 606 Campbell St., Tofino (☎ 250/725-3919), uses a glass-bottomed 65-foot power cruiser as well as a fleet of Zodiacs for tours to watch the gray whales from March to October. A combined Hot Springs Cove and whale-watching trip aboard a 32-foot cruiser can be booked year-round. Fares for expeditions conducted by both establishments start at C$75 (US$54) per person for a 3-hour tour; customized trips can run as high as C$200 (US$143) per person for a full-day trip.

Remote Passages, Meares Landing, 71 Wharf St., Tofino (☎ 800/666-9833 or 250/725-3330), organizes hour-long whale-watching tours in Clayoquot Sound on Zodiac boats daily at 9am, noon, and 3pm from March to November. Fares are C$35 (US$25) for adults and C$20 (US$14) for children under 12. The company also conducts a 7-hour combination whale-watching and hot-springs trip. Fares are C$55 (US$39) for adults and C$40 (US$29) for children under 12. Reservations are recommended.

SHOPPING

While you're in **Tofino,** take a peek at the **Eagle Aerie Gallery,** 350 Campbell St. (☎ 604/725-3235), which is constructed in the style of a native-Indian longhouse. The gallery features the artwork of Roy Henry Vicker, a hereditary chief and son of a Tsimshian native-Indian fisherman, including serigraphs, sculptures in glass and wood, carved panels, and totem poles. The **House of Himwitsa,** 300 Main St. (☎ 250/725-2017), is also native-Indian—owned and operated. The quality and craftsmanship of the shop's artwork, masks, baskets, totems, gold and silver jewelry, and apparel are excellent. In **Ucluelet,** the **Treasure Chest,** Davison Plaza, 1636

Peninsula Rd. (☎ 250/726-7337), has a fine selection of handcrafted silver and gold jewelry as well as souvenirs created by local native craftspeople. It's open daily year-round.

ACCOMMODATIONS

The 94 year-round campsites on the bluff at **Green Point** are maintained by Pacific Rim National Park. The grounds are full every day in July and August, and the average wait for a site is 1 to 2 days. Leave your name at the ranger station when you arrive to be placed on the list. For C$14 to C$15 (US$10 to US$11) per site in summer (C$6/US$4.30 per night Thanksgiving to Easter), you're rewarded with a magnificent ocean view, pit toilets, fire pits, pumped well water, and free firewood. There are no showers or hookups.

Bella Pacifica Resort & Campground, 3.3 kilometers (2 miles) south of Tofino on the Pacific Rim Highway (☎ 250/725-3400; mailing address: Box 413, Tofino, BC, V0R 2Z0), is privately owned. It has 160 campsites from which you can walk to Mackenzie Beach or take the resort's private nature trails to Templar Beach. Flush toilets, hot showers, water, laundry, ice, fire pits, firewood, and full and partial hookups are available. Rates are C$18.70 to C$26.20 (US$13 to US$19) per site.

IN BAMFIELD

Bamfield Lodge. 275 Boardwalk (mailing address: Box 23), Bamfield, BC, V0R 1B0. ☎ 250/728-3419. Fax 250/728-3417. Web site: www.alberni.net/bamfieldlodge/. 2 rms, 2 cottages; one 2-bedrm house. C$75 (US$54) double; C$100 (US$71) cottage; C$250 (US$179) house. Off-season discounts. No refunds Aug–Sept. V. Take Hwy. 4 to Port Alberni. There are no access roads. The owners pick up guests by boat and transport them to the location.

A pair of rustic cottages, a lodge, and a two-bedroom house are the waterfront accommodations at this marine education center and retreat. The rustic, wood-paneled accommodations are simply decorated in earth-tone fabrics. The twin-bed and double-bed cabins and the guest house have fully equipped kitchens. No pets. Moorage is available if you boat to the lodge. The staff can also arrange hiking, kayaking, fishing, diving, whale watching, and intertidal field trips.

Bring your own food (freezer space is available) or partake of the lodge's gourmet meals. The restaurant is open to the public at dinnertime. Main dishes are priced from C$7 to C$18 (US$5 to US$13). Sip an espresso in the resort's cappuccino bar while watching the birds, whales, and boats pass by.

✪ **Woods End Landing Cottages.** 168 Wild Duck Rd., Bamfield, BC, V0R 1B0. ☎ 250/728-3383. Fax 250/728-3383. Web site: www.futuresite.com/woodsend. 6 cottages. C$95–C$185 (US$68–US$132) per cottage for up to 4 people. Off-season discounts. MC, V. Take Hwy. 4 to Port Alberni. There are no access rds. The owners pick up guests by boat and transport them to the location.

The picturesque timbered cottages on this secluded waterfront wilderness property offer fully equipped kitchens, propane barbecues, and private porches that look out on the 2-acre perennial gardens. The decor features Canadiana antiques and collectibles as well as double-size hand-hewn log beds, duvets, large farmhouse tables, exposed timber beams, and skylights. Gas barbecues are just outside your door. Hiking, fishing, whale watching, diving, eagle and sea-lion watching, Keeha Beach, part of the West Coast Trail, and the Cape Beale Lighthouse are within walking distance. A private dock, moorage, freezer space, a canoe, and fishing tackle are available for guests' use. No smoking. No pets.

IN TOFINO

Mackenzie Beach Resort. 1101 Pacific Rim Hwy. (mailing address: Box 12), Tofino, BC, V0R 2Z0. ☎ **250/725-3439.** 14 cottages, 25 campsites. TV. C$119–C$170 (US$85–US$121) double. Extra person C$20 (US$14). C$28–C$32 (US$20–US$23) campsite; extra C$2 (US$1.40) electric hookup, C$1 (US70¢) water hookup, C$1 (US70¢) sewer hookup. MC, V. Located 1.6km (1 mile) south of Tofino on Mackenzie Beach. Take the Pacific Rim Hwy. north from the Hwy. 4 junction and exit at Mackenzie Beach.

This popular and often crowded (but very civilized) bay-side resort is open year-round, offering one- and two-bedroom cottages with fully equipped kitchens and barbecues. Some units have fireplaces. The resort also has 25 tent and RV campsites with full hookups, barbecues, and hot showers. An indoor heated pool and spa are open to overnight guests, as well as others, who can spend the day fishing in the bay or playing golf at a nearby course. No pets.

✪ **The Wickaninnish Inn.** Osprey Lane at Chesterman Beach (mailing address: Box 250), Tofino, BC, V0R 2Z0. ☎ **800/333-4604** in North America, or 250/725-3300. Fax 250/725-3110. E-mail: wick@island.net. 43 rms, 3 suites. Mar 1–June 25 C$170–C$210 (US$121–US$150) double; June 26–Sept 30 C$240–C$280 (US$171–US$200) double; Oct 1–Nov 1 C$180–C$220 (US$129–US$157) double; Nov 2–Feb 28 C$140–C$180 (US$100–US$129) double. Special packages available year-round. AE, MC, V. Free parking. Drive 5km (3 miles) south of Tofino toward Chesterman Beach to Osprey Lane.

No matter which room or suite you book in this beautiful new cedar, stone, and glass lodge, you'll wake to a magnificent view of the untamed Pacific. The inn is on a rocky promontory, surrounded by an old-growth spruce-and-cedar rain forest and the sprawling sands of Chesterman Beach. You do have to make some choices: select king- or queen-size beds. Rustic driftwood, richly printed textiles, and local artwork highlight the room decor. Each spacious guest room features a fireplace, down duvet, soaker tub (26 rooms have tubs with an ocean view), and balcony. Winter storm-watching packages have become so popular that the inn is as busy in winter as it is in summer.

Dining: The Pointe Restaurant & On-the-Rocks Bar (see "Dining," below) serves three meals daily and features an oceanfront view.

Facilities: The staff can arrange whale-watching, golfing, fishing, and diving packages. No-Stress Express packages include air transport and accommodations.

IN UCLUELET

✪ **Canadian Princess Fishing Resort.** Peninsula Rd. at the Boat Basin (mailing address: Box 939), Ucluelet, BC, V0R 3A0. ☎ **800/663-7090** or 250/726-7771. 51 rms on shore, 30 rms aboard ship. C$55–C$89 (US$39–US$92) double on ship; C$95–C$109 (US$68–US$78) double on shore. AE, ER, MC, V. Closed Oct–Apr.

Permanently moored in Ucluelet harbor, this restored steamship was built in 1932 and called the *William J. Stewart*. It served as a hydrographic vessel and was assigned Royal Canadian Naval duties during World War II. The 228-foot vessel was retired in 1975 and became a floating resort 4 years later. Renamed the *Canadian Princess*, it's decked out in authentic nautical decor. Berth staterooms have washbasins and shared baths. Spacious rooms are available in the adjacent lodges on shore; all have private baths and televisions. The open-beam cedar chalet-style rooms feature pastel walls and upholstery as well as wood furnishings. A few rooms have fireplaces. The brass-and-dark-wood dining room and lounge offer a beautiful waterfront view (see "Dining," below). The staff can arrange whale-watching and fishing trips. No pets.

DINING

Offerings here range from hearty pub food to elegant Pacific Northwest cuisine featuring fresh seafood and local produce. Campers can stock up on provisions at the **Block & Cleaver Deli,** 1790 Peninsula Rd., Ucluelet (☎ **250/726-7314**), which carries fresh meats and poultry as well as deli meats and cheeses; and the **Ucluelet Consumers Co-operative,** 1580 Peninsula Rd., Ucluelet (☎ **250/726-4231**), which carries groceries and essential camping and fishing supplies. If you're headed to Bamfield, you can pick up groceries in Port Alberni at **Safeway,** 3756 10th Ave. (☎ **250/723-6212**).

IN TOFINO

The Loft. 346 Campbell St., Tofino. ☎ **250/725-4241.** Main courses C$4.95–C$11 (US$3.55–US$8). AE, DC, DISC, MC. Daily 7am–10pm. CANADIAN.

If you're looking for big portions of wholesome, tasty food at breakfast, lunch, or dinner, this is the place. We can vouch for the tasty eggs Benedict and the hearty sandwiches.

The Pointe Restaurant. The Wickaninnish Inn. Osprey Lane at Chesterman Beach, Tofino. ☎ **250/725-3110.** Reservations recommended. Main courses C$18–C$30 (US$13–US$21). MC, V. Daily, breakfast 8am–11:30am; lunch and brunch 11:30am–2:30pm; snacks 2pm–5pm; dinner 5pm–9:30pm. PACIFIC NORTHWEST.

Perched on the water's edge at Chesterman Beach is the Pointe, where a 280° view of the roaring Pacific is the backdrop to a dining experience that can only be described as pure Pacific Northwest. Chef Rodney Butters (who's cooked for top hotels such as the Pacific Palisades in Vancouver and the Chateau Whistler in Whistler) applies his talents to an array of local ingredients, including Dungeness crab, spotted prawns, halibut, salmon, quail, lamb, and rabbit. His signature version of bouillabaisse, called Wickaninnish Potlatch, is a chunky, fragrant blend of soft and firm fish, shellfish, and vegetables simmered in a thick seafood broth. Offerings include delectable appetizers like goat-cheese tarts and shaved fennel salad, and entrees such as grilled lamb chops served with new potatoes, fresh artichokes, and sea asparagus. Butters's signature dessert—a double chocolate, mashed-potato brioche—is superb when accompanied by a glass of raspberry wine.

IN UCLUELET

Canadian Princess Fishing Resort. Peninsula Rd. at the Boat Basin, Ucluelet. ☎ **800/663-7090** or 250/726-7771. Main courses C$8.95–C$19.95 (US$6–US$14). AE, ER, MC, V. Daily 4:30am–10:30am, 11:30am–2:30pm, 5–10pm. SEAFOOD.

Permanently moored in Ucluelet harbor, this beautiful vessel houses not only a hotel (See "Accommodations," above) but also an elegant restaurant that serves healthy portions of tasty seafood specialties like steamed Dungeness crab caught right off the dock, and blackened halibut steak served with garden-fresh vegetables and rice. The menu also includes nonseafood items like juicy prime rib, chicken cordon bleu, pasta dishes, and vegetarian stir fry.

✪ **Wickaninnish Centre & Restaurant.** Long Beach, Pacific Rim National Park. ☎ **250/726-7706.** Main courses C$11.50–C$24 (US$8–US$17). MC, V. Daily 11am–9:30pm. Closed mid-Oct to mid-Mar. Drive 1.6 kilometers (1 mile) from the Hwy. 4 junction northward on the only road to Tofino. SEAFOOD.

Sixteen and one-half kilometers (10 miles) north of Ucluelet you'll find this beautiful weathered-wood beachfront lodge with an eclectic rustic decor, which adjoins the Pacific Rim National Park Interpretive Centre. The Wickaninnish serves the best seafood, pasta dishes, meats, and desserts in the area. Grilled salmon fillets are served with rosemary butter, seasonal vegetables, and rice. The West Coast Bouillabaisse for two brims with a variety of fish and shellfish in a tomato saffron broth. The sirloin of venison is roasted with a Dijon mustard and garlic crust. The desserts are also inventive. For example, the mocha pecan torte is topped with a Jack Daniels whiskey–laced caramel sauce.

5 Central Vancouver Island: The East Coast & the Offshore Islands

THE EAST COAST: CAMPBELL RIVER

Vancouver Island's east coast is a fishing, diving, and golf haven where the look and feel of the waterfront resorts reflects their elegant 1920s roots. **Campbell River** is the home of movie star John Wayne's favorite fishing camp, the Painter's Lodge Holiday & Fishing Resort (see "Accommodations," below). Masterfully designed 18-hole golf courses in Campbell River, Courtenay, and Parksville have breathtaking views of the mainland coast (see "Sports & Outdoor Activities," below). And **dive sites** with names like Row and Be Damned, Whisky Point, Copper Cliffs, and Steep Island attract divers from around the world to discover the marine life that inhabits the shipwrecks that stud this rugged coastline (see the box "Shipwrecks & Sea Creatures," near the beginning of this chapter).

ESSENTIALS

VISITOR INFORMATION   Area information centers are open daily year-round from 9am to 6pm. The first one you'll reach as you drive up the Island Highway (Highway 19) is the **Parksville Visitor Info Centre,** 1275 East Island Hwy. (mailing address: Box 99), Parksville, BC, V9P 2G3 (☎ 250/248-3613). The **Campbell River Visitor Info Centre** is at 1235 Shopper's Row (mailing address: Box 44), Campbell River, BC, V9W 5B6 (☎ 250/287-4636).

GETTING THERE   There are four convenient ways to reach this portion of Vancouver Island. Most visitors drive up the Island Highway, but you can also take a coach bus, train, or ferry.

By Bus   Island Coach Lines (☎ 250/287-7151) operates daily bus service from Victoria to Port Hardy, making stops in Nanaimo, Courtenay, and Campbell River. The 3-hour trip costs C$35 (US$25) for adults and C$14.50 (US$10) for children under 12; senior discounts are available.

By Car   On the Island Highway (Highway 19), Parksville is 38.3 kilometers (23 miles) north of Nanaimo; Qualicum Beach is 10 kilometers (6 miles) north of Parksville; Courtenay is 61.6 kilometers (37 miles) north of Qualicum Beach; and Campbell River is 51.6 kilometers (31 miles) north of Courtenay.

By Ferry   BC Ferries (☎ 250/386-3431) operates a 75-minute crossing from Powell River on the mainland to Campbell River. The one-way fare is C$6 (US$4.30) per passenger and C$21.50 (US$15) per vehicle.

By Train   The **E&N Railiner** operates daily between Courtenay and Victoria (see "Getting There" in section 2 of this chapter).

SPORTS & OUTDOOR ACTIVITIES

DIVING   See the box "Shipwrecks & Sea Creatures," near the beginning of this chapter.

FISHING   There's more to lure freshwater and saltwater anglers to this area than indigenous cutthroat and rainbow trout and the fabulous local fishing resorts. The coho salmon in these waters weigh up to 20 pounds, and even these are dwarfed by the tyee salmon. Some catches have tipped the scales at more than 75 pounds, but average around 30 pounds. Between mid-July and mid-September, fishermen vie for membership in the **Tyee Club.** The requirements include fishing from an unpowered, guided rowboat in a small, designated area called a tyee pool. Only certain types of poles and line weights can be used to catch a record-weight tyee salmon. To fish here, you need nonresident saltwater and freshwater licenses which you can purchase at **Painter's Lodge Holiday & Fishing Resort,** 1625 MacDonald Rd. (mailing address: Box 560), Campbell River, BC, V9W 5C1 (☎ **250/286-1102**). The staff can also provide you with additional information on guided boats and all fishing rules. This resort is also the perfect place to view the action from their beautiful waterfront lounge or on the deck.

For a C$1 (US70¢) admission fee, you can fish off **Discovery Pier,** in Campbell River right at Campbell Harbour. Cutthroat and rainbow trout inhabit the nearby rivers.

GOLFING   Golfers find this part of Vancouver Island a little bit of paradise because of its outstanding courses. When he designed the **Morningstar,** 525 Lowry Rd., Parksville (☎ **250/248-8161**), Les Furber used large lakes in open areas to integrate several seaside links and rolling fairways that run in and out of the woods. This 18-hole championship par-72 course has a 74 rating. Because it was carved out of a dense forest, you may see wildlife grazing on the fairway and roughs at **Storey Creek Golf Club,** Campbell River (☎ **250/923-3673**). Gentle creeks and ponds also wind through this course. Greens fees range from C$74 to C$125 (US$53 to US$89), and tee times are easy to arrange a day in advance.

ACCOMMODATIONS & DINING

Hotels and B&Bs in this area offer fine and casual dining, fully equipped kitchens for guests, or all three. There are a few good basic restaurants on Comox Avenue in Comox, Fifth Street in Courtenay, the Island Highway in Parksville, and Cliff Avenue in Cumberland. And you'll find a number of stores selling groceries and supplies in Campbell River if you need to stock up.

Best Western Austrian Chalet Village. 462 S. Island Hwy., Campbell River, BC, V9W 1A5. ☎ **800/667-7207** in Canada, or 250/923-4231. Fax 250/923-2840. 55 rms. TV TEL. C$94–C$129 (US$67–US$92) double. Extra person C$10 (US$7). Kitchen units C$10 (US$7) extra. Off-season discounts. AE, MC, V.

Overlooking Discovery Passage, this newly renovated oceanfront hotel is conveniently located right on the Island Highway. You'll have a choice of regular or housekeeping rooms (with fully equipped kitchenettes and refrigerators). Some units are in loft chalets.

Dining/Entertainment: On the premises are a licensed restaurant that serves three meals daily, as well as a casual pub.

Facilities: Indoor pool, sauna, whirlpool, table tennis, and a mini putting green. The staff can arrange whale-watching, fishing, or golfing trips.

✪ **Painter's Lodge Holiday & Fishing Resort.** 1625 MacDonald Rd. (mailing address: Box 560), Campbell River, BC, V9W 5C1. ☎ **800/663-7090** in Canada, or 250/286-1102. Fax 250/598-1361. 90 rms, 4 cottages. TV. C$99–C$150 (US$71–US$107) double; C$150–C$325 (US$107–US$232) cottage. Off-season discounts. AE, MC, V. Closed Nov–Mar.

This has been a favorite fishing hideaway for film stars like John Wayne, Bob Hope, and Goldie Hawn and Kurt Russell. We can see why, for the wooded coastal location is awe-inspiring. The excellent restaurant menu features hearty servings of expertly prepared seafood and meat dishes. And the staff provides sterling service. Built in 1924 on a point overlooking the Discovery Passage, this lodge retains a rustic grandeur, with spacious lodge rooms and suites decorated in natural wood and pastels. Secluded self-contained cottages nestled near the lodge are also available.

Dining/Entertainment: The Legends Dining Room, Tyee Pub, and Fireside Lounge serve breakfast, lunch, dinner, cocktails, and nightcaps.

Facilities: Guided fishing trips, tennis courts, fitness center, and airport shuttle.

THE OFFSHORE ISLANDS: HORNBY, DENMAN & QUADRA

"Flower children" were attracted to rural Hornby (pop. 1,300) and Denman (pop. 1,200) during the 1960s and 1970s. They started organic farms and thriving art communities on the tiny islands off the coast of Vancouver Island. Both islands have maintained their bohemian charm. In contrast, nearby Quadra (pop. 3,200) retains much of its native-Indian heritage. The Cape Mudge band of the Kwakiutl tribe made Quadra Island its home thousands of years before white settlers set foot on this remote island.

ESSENTIALS

VISITOR INFORMATION   On Denman Island, the **Denman General Store,** 1069 Northwest Rd., Denman Island, BC, V0R 1T0 (☎ 250/335-2293), serves as **Denman/Hornby Visitor Services.** It offers a free island guide as well as a brochure listing the small arts and crafts galleries that are open to the public. For information about Quadra Island, talk to the staff at the **Kwakiutl Museum** (see "Exploring the Islands," below).

GETTING THERE   The islands are accessible only by water. Visitors regularly cross by ferry, canoe, or kayak.

By ferry   Local **BC Ferries** (☎ 250/386-3431) operate year-round between these islands and Vancouver Island. The dozen daily ferry trips to each island take 10 minutes each way and cost C$3.25 to C$7.25 (US$2.30 to US$5) per person; vehicles cost extra. The ferry from Buckley Bay to Denman Island operates from 7am to 11pm; the ferry from Denman Island to Hornby Island operates from 8am to 6:35pm; and the ferry from Campbell River to Quadra Island operates from 6:40am to 10:30pm.

GETTING AROUND   Public transportation on Hornby Island directly reflects this gentle culture: The **Hornby Blue Bus** (☎ 250/335-0715) is a funky 1960s International Harvester. Passengers negotiate with the driver to determine the fare from the ferry.

The islands are great for two-wheel exploration. Visitors can bring bikes on the ferry or go to the **Hornby Island Off-Road Bike Shop,** next to the Co-Op market (☎ 250/335-0444), or **Cycledeli Bike Shop,** 3646 Denman Rd., Denman Island (☎ 250/335-1797). Both rent mountain bikes for C$10 (US$7) per hour or C$25 (US$18) per day.

SPECIAL EVENT   During the first 2 weeks in August, the **Hornby Festival** (☎ 250/335-2734) is held at the Community Hall on Hornby Island. Events include live music and theatrical and dance performances.

EXPLORING THE ISLANDS

Hornby and Denman islands are pleasant destinations for strolling or cycling along the sandy beaches, like the ones at **Hornby Island's Tribune Bay** and **Whaling Station Bay.** Hornby is also a great destination for birding. The Heliwell Bluffs in **Heliwell Bay Provincial Park** are home to thousands of birds that nest in the high cliffs along the coast.

   Denman Island also has its share of sandy beaches, including **Bayle Point,** which also has a spectacular view of the Chrome Island Lighthouse. The majestic stands of old-growth Douglas fir in **Fillongley Provincial Park** are an inspiration to many of the local artisans. There's also plenty to see at the island's many **open studios.** Potters, jewelers, painters, and sculptors open their doors so visitors can view their work during the summer months.

   On Quadra Island, Cape Mudge Village operates the **Kwakiutl Museum,** WeiWai Road (☎ **250/285-3733**). It has a beautiful collection of artifacts, ceremonial masks, and tribal costumes that were used in the elaborate potlatch ceremonies conducted to celebrate births, deaths, tribal unity, the installment of a new chief, marriages, and other important occasions. Potlatches became more and more ostentatious as the centuries went by, on the islands and the mainland. Bands and villages spent months, even years, planning feasts and performances, carving totem poles, and amassing literally tons of gifts for their guests. The Canadian government outlawed the practice in 1922 as part of the short-lived enforced-assimilation policy, and lifted the ban in 1951. The museum is open Monday to Saturday from 10am to 4:30pm. During the summer, it's also open on Sunday from noon to 4:30pm. Across from the museum is a park where a series of petroglyphs (ancient drawings painted on stone) document a few of the island's ancient legends.

TOURS & EXCURSIONS

Adventurers can combine camping with sailing or kayaking lessons at ✪ **T'ai Li Lodge,** Cortes Bay, Read Island (☎ **250/935-6749**). The staff will pick up visitors and their gear from Quadra Island or Cortes Island and transport them to the beautiful wilderness hideaway. To arrive under your own power, you can sail or kayak to the docks by following Marine Chart 3538. This is a challenging but rewarding destination to reach. Rooms in the lodge are rustic, and the services are basic. Guests share shower, sink, and toilet facilities. Meals are included in the price of C$85 (US$61) per lodge room. Campsites are C$10 (US$7) per night. There's a solar-heated shower and pit toilet for campers' use. The views are breathtaking and wildlife abounds.

ACCOMMODATIONS & DINING

On Denman Island

Late risers can get breakfast until 11am at **Jan's Cafe Next Door,** Central Road, Denman Island (☎ **604/335-1487**). The lunch menu features burgers, sandwiches, and absolutely scrumptious desserts and pastries. Most courses are under C$7 (US$5); no credit cards are accepted. It's open daily from 7:30am to 3pm (to 5pm on weekends).

Denman Island Guest House. 3808 Denman Rd., Denman Island, BC, V0R 1T0. ☎ **250/ 335-2688.** 5 rms (none with bath). C$50 (US$36) double. Rates include breakfast. MC, V.

   This turn-of-the-century farmhouse has a laid-back island atmosphere and rustic guest rooms with a shared bath. For visitors exploring the island, this is a good location to rest up and have a huge, country-style breakfast before heading out on the overland and marine trails.

With garden views, the hotel restaurant is more than passable. The menu changes with the availability of local seafood and produce. Dinner is served Wednesday to Sunday from 4:30 to 9:30pm, and main courses run C$12 to C$17 (US$9 to US$12).

Hawthorn House Bed & Breakfast. 3375 Kirk Rd., Denman Island, BC, V0R 1T0. ☎ **250/ 335-0905.** 3 rms. C$65–C$70 (US$46–US$50) double. Rates include full breakfast. No credit cards. From the ferry, take Denman Rd. to Northwest Rd., turn left, continue to Kirk Rd., then turn left.

Children are welcome at this restored 1904 heritage house, which is tastefully decorated with Canadiana. The sitting room features a beautiful stone fireplace. The one single and two double rooms have private baths. The property's ocean and mountain views are complemented by a secluded garden. Dinner can be prepared for guests on request. Also on the premises are a hot tub, bikes for rent, and a friendly dog. Smoking is permitted outside only. No pets.

On Hornby Island

Hornby Island Resort & Thatch Pub. 4305 Shingle Spit Rd., Hornby Island, BC, V0R 1Z0. ☎ **250/335-0136.** 4 cottages, 10 campsites. C$60–C$75 (US$43–US$54) double; C$12–C$18 (US$9–US$13) campsite; C$1 (US70¢) electric hookup. MC, V. No pets.

Make reservations months in advance for the cottages and campsites of this popular waterfront resort located next to the ferry terminal. The rustic cottage rooms are basically furnished; the campsites are well maintained and adequately spaced. Campground facilities include hot showers and laundry. There's a playground on the beach, boat rental and moorage service, and a tennis court on the grounds.

The resort has a licensed restaurant and pub with a waterfront view, and casual indoor and outdoor dining year-round as well as barbecues on the deck during the summer. The Thatch Pub is a popular local nightspot with live music Thursday to Saturday.

On Quadra Island

April Point Lodge & Fishing Resort. April Point Rd., Quadra Island (mailing address: Box 1, Campbell River, BC, V9W 4Z9). ☎ **250/285-2222.** 30 rms, 6 guest houses. C$99–C$195 (US$71–US$139) double; C$195–C$395 (US$139–US$282) guest house. Extra person C$25 (US$18). AE, MC, V.

The secluded April Point Lodge, world-famous for its freshwater fishing charters, has magnificent views of the Johnstone Strait in a tranquil private setting. The one- to six-bedroom guest houses at the water's edge have hot tubs, fireplaces, and kitchens. They're comfortable and tastefully furnished. Lodge suites are also spacious and nicely appointed.

Dining/Entertainment: A licensed restaurant, sushi bar, and cocktail lounge are on the premises.

Services: Helicopter access and seaplane service to Vancouver, BC, and Seattle, Washington, are available.

○ **Tsa-Kwa-Luten Lodge.** Lighthouse Rd. (mailing address: Box 460, Quathiaski Cove, Quadra Island, BC, V0P 1N0). ☎ **250/285-2042.** 30 suites, 5 cabins. TEL. C$80–C$115 (US$57– US$82) suite; C$115–C$125 (US$82–US$89) cabin (double or triple). AP available. MC, V. Closed Oct 16–Apr 14.

Overlooking the Discovery Passage, this island resort offers both lodge suites and waterfront cabins. Some suites have lofts, Jacuzzis, or fireplaces; all have twin-, queen-, or king-size beds. The two- and four-bedroom waterfront cabins have fully equipped kitchens. Some have fireplaces and hot tubs. All rooms are beautifully decorated with native-Canadian–inspired furnishings and accessories. The main lodge resembles a Pacific Northwest tribal longhouse.

Dining/Entertainment: The restaurant features fresh seafood and native cuisine such as alder-wood-smoked salmon, marinated venison, and bannock bread. There's also a cocktail lounge.

Facilities: Fitness center, sauna, and gift shop. Guided fishing trips and heli-fishing charters, and boat, mountain-bike, and moped rentals are arranged by the staff.

6 Northern Vancouver Island: Port McNeill, Alert Bay, Telegraph Cove & Port Hardy

It's a winding 198-kilometer (124-mile) drive through thickly forested mountains along the Island Highway (Highway 19) from Campbell River to **Port McNeill** in northern Vancouver Island. But the majestic scenery, the crystal-clear lakes, and the unique wilderness along the way make it worthwhile. This area is home to a number of orca pods, which migrate annually from the Queen Charlotte Strait south to the adjoining salmon-rich waters of the **Johnstone Strait.** (Orcas, or killer whales, are actually the largest members of the oceanic dolphin family and live in groups from a few to 50 individuals, known as pods or herds.) There's plenty to see in the small nearby community of **Alert Bay** (pop. 1,350) and in **Telegraph Cove,** a boardwalk community of only 12 residents.

The Island Highway's terminus, **Port Hardy,** is 51.6 kilometers (31 miles) north of Port McNeill. Though it's a remote community of only 5,500, Port Hardy is the starting point for three unique experiences: the **Inside Passage ferry cruise** (see "The Inside Passage," below) to Prince Rupert, **the Discovery Coast ferry cruise** (see "The Inside Passage"), and **Cape Scott Wilderness Provincial Park's** untamed rain forest and coastline.

ESSENTIALS

VISITOR INFORMATION The **Port McNeill Visitor Info Centre,** 1626 Beach Dr. (mailing address: Box 129), Port McNeill, BC, V0N 2R0 (☎ 250/956-3131), is open May 15 to September 15 from 10am to 6pm. The **Alert Bay Visitor Info Centre,** 116 Fir St. (mailing address: Box 28), Alert Bay, BC, V0N 1A0 (☎ 250/ 974-5213), is near the ferry terminal. It's open daily during summer from 9am to 6pm and Monday to Friday from 9am to 5pm the rest of the year. The **Port Hardy Visitor Info Centre,** 7250 Market St. (mailing address: Box 249), Port Hardy, BC, V0N 2P0 (☎ 250/949-7622), is open June 1 to Labour Day Monday to Friday from 8am to 9pm and Saturday, Sunday, and holidays from 9am to 9pm; Labour Day to October 20, Monday to Friday from 9am to 5pm and Saturday, Sunday, and holidays from 9am to 9pm; October 21 to May 31, Monday to Friday from 8:30am to 4:30pm (May 1 to 31, Saturday, Sunday, and holidays from 9am to 5pm). Although there's no official visitor center in **Telegraph Cove,** you can contact **Information for Tourists,** Telegraph Cove, BC, V0N 3J0 (☎ 250/ 928-3185).

GETTING THERE There are three ways to get to Vancouver Island's northern-most towns and islands: by car, coach bus, and ferry.

By Bus **Island Coach Lines** (☎ 250/385-4411) operates service between Nanaimo and Port McNeill. The daily 9am departure arrives at 3:15pm. The fare is C$32.30 (US$23). The return trip leaves Port McNeill at 9:15am and arrives in Nanaimo at 2:55pm. The company also offers service between Nanaimo and Port Hardy.

By Car   Telegraph Cove is 198.3 kilometers (119 miles) north of Campbell River along the Island Highway (Highway 19). Port McNeill is another 8.8 kilometers (5 miles) north.

By Ferry   BC Ferries (☎ 250/386-3431) operates between Port McNeill and Alert Bay 10 times daily from 8:40am to 9:50pm. The crossing takes about 45 minutes.

SPECIAL EVENTS   Even at Vancouver Island's northernmost point, you'll find daring swimmers diving into the icy waters on New Year's Day at the annual **Polar Bear Swim** (☎ 250/949-7622) on Seagate Dock in Port Hardy.

During the second week of June, the Nimpkish Reserve hosts **June Sports & Indian Celebrations** (☎ 250/974-5556) on the soccer field in Alert Bay. Traditional tests of strength and agility are demonstrated by the island's tribal members.

On Canada Day (July 1), Alert Bay hosts an annual **Soap Box Derby** (☎ 250/974-5430) on Cedar Street. It attracts some great junior drivers and vehicles from the surrounding areas.

EXPLORING THE AREA: SPOTTING ORCAS & MORE

Port McNeill has ferry service to Malcolm Island and Alert Bay. This side trip offers visitors an opportunity to explore this amazing wilderness and meet the people who have coexisted with its remarkable marine inhabitants for centuries.

Eight kilometers (5 miles) south of Port McNeill, **Telegraph Cove's** 12 residents live in one of the few remaining elevated-boardwalk villages on Vancouver Island, overlooking Johnstone Strait and Robson Bight. This postcard-perfect fishing village's buildings are perched on stilts over the water, making it an entertaining destination for a stroll, especially since whales have been spotted close to shore many times.

Alert Bay on Cormorant Island has a rich native-Indian heritage that can be seen in the architecture and artifacts that are proudly preserved on the tiny island. It has been a Kwakiutl tribal village for thousands of years. The integration of Scottish immigrants into the area during the 19th and 20th centuries is clearly depicted in the design of the **Anglican Church** on Front Street in Alert Bay (☎ 250/974-5213). The cedar building was erected in 1881. The stained-glass window designs reflect a fusion of native Kwakiutl and Scottish design motifs. It's open Monday to Saturday from 8am to 5pm in summer.

Walk 1.6 kilometers (1 mile) from the ferry terminal along Front Street to the island's two most interesting attractions. A 173-foot **totem pole** stands next to the Big House (the tribal community center), which is not open to the public. Visitors are welcome, however, to enter the outside grounds to get a closer look. Erected in 1973, this cedar totem pole features 22 hand-carved figures of bears, orcas, and ravens, plus a sun at the top.

A few yards down the road from the Big House and totem pole is the **U'Mista Cultural Centre,** Front Street, Alert Bay (☎ 250/974-5403), which displays a collection of carved-wood ceremonial masks, cedar baskets, copper jewelry, and other potlatch artifacts that were confiscated by the Canadian government when the potlatch was banned in 1922. The items were only recently returned to the island's native-Indian community. Revolving exhibitions explain the Kwakiutl tribe's culture and history. Admission is C$5 (US$3.55) for adults, C$4 (US$2.85) for seniors, and C$1 (US70¢) for children under 12. The museum is open daily from 9am to 5pm (on weekends and summer holidays it opens at noon). During the winter, the museum closes on legal holidays.

The best way to closely observe the many **orca pods** (families of killer whales) that inhabit the Johnstone Strait is to kayak out to where you can also observe sea lions as they cavort along the shore. You can paddle to overnight campgrounds at any of the marine parks and explore abandoned Kwakiutl villages. This area is ideal for novice kayakers; the placid, sheltered waters provide a safe, inspiring entry to this growing sport (see "Tours & Excursions," below).

There's one very special observation point in this area. Sixteen and one-half kilometers (10 miles) south of Telegraph Cove and accessible by boat charter, the **Robson Bight Ecological Reserve** provides some of the most fascinating whale watching in the province. Orcas, some the size of small school buses, regularly beach themselves in the shallow waters of the Bight's world-famous pebbly "rubbing beaches" to remove the barnacles from their tummies.

Port Hardy is the final stop on the Island Highway. It's the point of departure for the Inside Passage and Discovery Coast ferry cruises, which transport residents and visitors to the remote villages on the mainland coast, the northern town of Prince Rupert, and the misty Queen Charlotte Islands. It's also the launching point for a land-based journey to Cape Scott.

TOURS & EXCURSIONS

Stubbs Island Charters Ltd. (☎ **250/928-3185** or 250/982-3117; mailing address: Box 7, Telegraph Cove, BC, V0N 3J0) operates from Telegraph Cove from June to mid-October, conducting tours to Robson Bight and the Johnstone Strait on 60-foot cruisers outfitted with hydrophones so passengers can hear as well as see the orcas.

Seasmoke Tours (☎ **250/974-5225;** mailing address: Box 483, Alert Bay, BC, V0N 1A0) offers sailing trips from June to October. Trips through the Johnstone Strait aboard a 44-foot yacht include a seafood lunch and Devonshire tea. This boat is also outfitted with a hydrophone. Half-day tours with both outfitters cost between C$75 and C$115 (US$54 and US$82) per person.

Discovery Kayaks, 2755 Departure Rd., Nanaimo (☎ **250/758-2488**), offers guided kayaking trips to the Johnstone Strait orca feeding grounds. **Northern Lights Expeditions,** based in Seattle, Washington (☎ **206/483-6396**), conducts 6- to 8-day expeditions to Robson Bight. The guides can identify many individual whales who return to these waters every year. All-inclusive tour packages start at C$750 (US$536) per person.

ACCOMMODATIONS & DINING

IN ALERT BAY

Groceries and supplies are available at the **Blueline Supermarket** (☎ **250/974-5521;** mailing address: Box 349, Alert Bay, BC, V0N 1A0). The store is open Monday to Friday from 9am to 9pm, Saturday from 9am to 6pm, and Sunday from 10am to 5pm.

Oceanview Camping & Trailer Park, Alder Road, Alert Bay, BC, V0N 1A0 (☎ **250/974-5213**), has a great view of the Johnstone Strait. A number of nature trails fan out from the 20 campsites. Rates are C$10 to C$15 (US$7 to US$11) per vehicle. Full hookups, flush toilets, free hot showers, a free boat launch, boat charters, and boat tours make this a great deal.

Ocean View Cabins. 390 Poplar St., Alert Bay, BC, V0N 1A0. ☎ **250/974-5457.** Fax 250/974-2275. 12 cottages (2 with shower only). TV. C$45–C$50 (US$32–US$36) double. Extra person C$5 (US$3.55). MC, V.

Overlooking Mitchell Bay only a mile from the ferry terminal, this quiet waterfront resort is the island's best value. Reserve a few months in advance. This property offers simply furnished, comfortable cabins with queen-size beds, kitchens, and full baths (in all but two cabins).

IN PORT HARDY

Groceries are available at supermarkets such as the **Overwaitea,** Thunderbird Mall, 8950 Granville St., Port Hardy (☎ 250/949-6455), and there are a few restaurants along Market Street in Port Hardy.

The shaded **Wildwood Campsite,** Forestry Road (mailing address: Box 801), Port Hardy, BC, V0N 2P0 (☎ 250/949-6753), is on the road to the Port Hardy ferry terminal. The 60 campsites are a great value, offering fire pits, hot showers, toilets, picnic tables, beach access, and moorage for C$5 to C$15 (US$3.55 to US$11) per vehicle. There's a store on the premises.

✪ **Duval Point Lodge.** Goletas Channel (mailing address: Box 818), Port Hardy, BC, V0N 2P0. ☎ **250/949-6667.** 8 rms. C$180 (US$129) per person per night. Rate includes transportation from Port Hardy. V. Closed Oct–May.

Located on the Goletas Channel, this floating fishing lodge is almost all-inclusive. It's accessible only by boat or floatplane; pickup and drop-off service from and to Port Hardy is included in the price. The resort's 4- to 5-day packages include a boat, gas, fishing gear, and comfortable rooms equipped with fireplaces and kitchens. Guests must bring their own food and purchase a fishing license, but if dawn-to-dusk fishing in a 16-foot welded aluminum boat outfitted with fish finders and top-of-the-line equipment sounds like your idea of vacation heaven, then every moment is worth the price.

Kay's Bed & Breakfast. 7605 Carnarvon Rd. (mailing address: Box 257), Port Hardy, BC, V0N 2P0. ☎ **250/949-6776.** 4 rms (2 with shared bath). C$45–C$65 (US$32–US$46) double. Rates include continental breakfast. No credit cards.

This conveniently located B&B offers free pickup service from the Port Hardy ferry terminal and has a lovely ocean view. Each room is self-contained, furnished with a comfortable queen-size bed and a fully equipped kitchen. Breakfast features fresh baked goods, jams, and coffee.

IN PORT MCNEILL & TELEGRAPH COVE

Groceries are available at supermarkets such as **IGA Plus,** 1705 Campbell Way (☎ 250/956-4404). There are a number of restaurants along Beach Drive in Port McNeill. **Sportsman's Steak & Pizza** on Beach Drive in Port McNeill (☎ 250/956-4113) offers a hearty menu of basics like roast chicken, steaks, burgers, and pizzas for C$4.95 to C$19.95 (US$3.55 to US$14). It's open daily from 11am to 9:30pm.

The 121 wooded campsites at **Telegraph Cove Resorts** (☎ 250/928-3131; mailing address: Comp 1, Box 1, Telegraph Cove, BC, V0N 3J0) are a short walk from the cove and the boardwalk town. Open from May to October, the resort provides hot showers, laundry, toilets, fire pits, fishing licenses, charters, a marina, whale-watching trips, and drinking water. Sites are C$17.25 to C$21.25 (US$12 to US$15). Hookups are C$3 (US$2.15). There's a small convenience store on the grounds.

Hidden Cove Lodge. Lewis Point (mailing address: Box 258), Port McNeill, BC, V0N 2R0. ☎ **250/956-3916.** 6 rms. C$115–C$125 (US$82–US$89) double. Extra person C$25–C$30 (US$18–US$21). Rates include continental breakfast. MC, V. Closed Dec–Apr. Take the Island Hwy. (Hwy. 19) to Telegraph Cove/Beaver Cove; turn right and follow the signs. The lodge is 6.6 km (4 miles) from Telegraph Cove.

This beautiful 2-story lodge is nestled in a secluded cove overlooking the Johnstone Strait. Rooms are cozy and rustic, and the hosts can arrange whale watching, bird and nature watching, guided fishing, heli-fishing, and hiking tours. No smoking.

7 The Inside Passage: Prince Rupert & the Queen Charlotte Islands

The ferry cruise along British Columbia's **Inside Passage** combines the best scenic elements of Norway's rocky fjords, New Zealand's majestic South Island, Chile's Patagonian range, and Nova Scotia's wild coastline. Less than half a century ago, there were only two ways to explore this rugged coastline. One was to book the 4-day passage on an Alaska-bound cruise ship or freighter. The other was to spend 2 or 3 days driving the Cariboo and Yellowhead highways to Prince Rupert, missing views of the thickly forested, craggy coastline and its resident orcas, sea lions, seals, and sea otters.

Since 1966, BC Ferries has operated the **Inside Passage ferry** between **Port Hardy** on Vancouver Island and **Prince Rupert** on the mainland, with stops at the small Discovery Coast communities of Bella Coola, Ocean Falls, Shearwater, McLoughlin Bay, and Klemtu. These stopovers became so popular that in 1994, the company added the **Discovery Coast ferry** to its schedule.

The ferry system also connects Prince Rupert to the remote **Queen Charlotte Islands,** the ancestral home of the Haida tribe. The misty archipelago known as **Haida Gwaii** has been designated as a UNESCO World Heritage Site and is managed by the Gwaii Haanas Reserve. Amid the lush old-growth Sitka spruce in this temperate rain forest are the remains of untouched Haida villages that were abandoned over 400 years ago. The most famous of these sites is **Ninstints** on Anthony Island, where cedar totem poles and longhouses stand in mute testament to a culture that flourished there for nearly 10,000 years. An epidemic spread by European explorers in the 1890s wiped out 90% of the Kunghit Haida tribe. The village was abandoned in 1900.

ESSENTIALS

VISITOR INFORMATION Contact the **North by Northwest Tourism Association,** 11–3167 Tatlow Rd. (☎ **250/847-5227;** mailing address: Box 1030, Smithers, BC, V0J 2N0). The **Prince Rupert Visitor Info Centre,** 100 1st Ave. E. (at the corner of McBride St.), Prince Rupert, BC, V8J 3S1 (☎ **800/667-1994** in Canada, or 250/624-5637; mailing address: Box 669), is open daily year-round from 9am to 5pm. The **Queen Charlotte Islands Visitor Info Centre,** 3220 Wharf St., Queen Charlotte, BC, V0T 1S0 (☎ **250/559-8316;** mailing address: Box 819), is open daily from May 1 to September 4 from 9am to 5pm. On Graham Island, the **Masset Visitor Info Centre,** 1455 Old Beach Rd., Masset, BC, V0T 1M0 (☎ **250/ 626-3982;** mailing address: Box 68), is open daily in July and August from 9am to 5pm.

GETTING THERE The saying "getting there is half the fun" sums up all the routes to Prince Rupert, and from there to the Queen Charlotte.

By Car The 1,518-kilometer (943-mile) drive from Vancouver to Prince Rupert begins on the Sea-to-Sky Highway (Highway 99), which intersects the Cariboo Highway (Highway 97) after passing through Whistler, Pemberton, and Lillooet. The town of Prince George is 811.6 kilometers (487 miles) north of Vancouver. At this central junction, head east for 745 kilometers (447 miles) on the Yellowhead Highway (Highway 16). This isolated stretch of thickly forested wilderness passes over the towering Coast Mountain Range before descending into the glacier-fed Skeena River Valley (see "The Skeena River Valley," below).

By Ferry   BC Ferries' (☎ 250/386-3431) flagship cruisers MV *Queen of the North* and MV *Queen of Prince Rupert* have made this route a popular and affordable summertime destination. The daytime crossing from Port Hardy to Prince Rupert takes about 15 hours. Humpback whales, orcas, Dall porpoises, salmon, bald eagles, and sea lions line the route past the relatively uninhabited coastline and through countless forested islands like **Princess Royal Island** in the Douglas Channel (see "The Skeena River Valley," below).

The 410-foot *Queen of the North* ferry crosses every other day from June to mid-October, leaving Port Hardy at 7:30am and arriving in Prince Rupert at 10:30pm. The *Queen of Prince Rupert* makes the same run, stopping at Bella Coola, Ocean Falls, Shearwater, McLoughlin Bay, and Klemtu. Both ferries briefly encounter open ocean before passing behind Calvert Island and entering Fitz Hugh Sound. From there, the vessels cruise through the protected waters of Finlayson Channel and Grenville Channel to Prince Rupert, the last Canadian town on the coast.

The ferries carry up to 750 passengers and 157 vehicles. You can wander around the ferry and lounge on inside and outside deck seating or rest in a private dayroom or overnight cabin. On board you'll find buffet-style dining, a cafeteria, snack bar, playroom, business center, and gift shop.

Reservations are required. The one-way passenger fare is C$102 (US$73) for adults, C$68 (US$49) for seniors, and C$51 (US$36) for children ages 5 to 11; children under 5 are free when accompanied by a paying passenger. For an extra charge of C$22 to C$117 (US$16 to US$84), you can reserve a dayroom or overnight cabin. Cars cost an additional C$210 (US$150) each way; mountain bikes cost an additional C$6.50 (US$4.65) each way. Land accommodations should also be booked in advance at both ports of call. The ferry has weekly sailings during the rest of the year, but summer is the best time to make the trip. The weather is remarkably pleasant, with warm, sunny days only occasionally broken by dramatic ocean mists and mild storms.

From Prince Rupert, you can continue north to Skagway, Alaska, on the **Alaska Marine Highway System ferry** (☎ 907/465-3941; fax 907/277-4829), which docks at the same terminal. Or you can travel to the Queen Charlotte Islands on the **Prince Rupert–Skidegate ferry,** which leaves Prince Rupert late in the morning and arrives about 6¹/₂ hours later at Skidegate in the Queen Charlotte Islands. The one-way fare in the high season is C$23 (US$16) for adults, C$15.50 (US$11) for seniors, and C$11.50 (US$8) for children. Car transport is an additional C$83 (US$59). A dayroom or overnight cabin is an additional C$22 to C$117 (US$16 to US$84).

By Plane   Air BC (☎ 604/688-5515), **Canadian Regional Airlines** (☎ 800/426-7000 in the U.S. or 800/363-7530 in Canada), and **Harbour Air** (☎ 604/688-1277 or 250/637-5350) serve Prince Rupert and the Queen Charlotte Islands.

By Train   The **VIA Rail** (☎ 888/842-7245 or 800/561-3949) passenger train departs from Prince George on Monday, Thursday, and Saturday at 7:45am and arrives in Prince Rupert at 8:30pm. One-way fares start at C$85.60 (US$61) per person. However, the round-trip fare is C$102 (US$73) per person with a 7-day advance purchase. The train follows the same route as the Yellowhead Highway. **BC Rail's** *Cariboo Prospector* route (☎ 604/984-5246) from North Vancouver to Prince George connects with this service. It departs three times a week from North Vancouver at 7am, stops at Whistler, Lillooet, 100 Mile House, Williams Lake, and Quesnel, and arrives in Prince George at 8:30pm. The one-way fare is C$190 (US$136).

GETTING AROUND   In the Queen Charlotte Islands, the island-to-island **Skidegate–Alliford Bay ferry** operates 12 daily sailings between the main islands. The fare is C$3 (US$2.15) each way; C$8.50 (US$6) per vehicle.

   Budget (☎ **250/559-4675**), **Rustic Car Rentals** (☎ **250/559-4641**), **Tilden** (☎ **250/626-3318**), and **Thrifty** (☎ **250/559-8050**) have car-rental offices on the islands.

SPECIAL EVENTS   During the second week in June, Prince Rupert hosts **Seafest** (☎ **250/624-9118**), which features a fishing derby, parades, games, food booths, the annual blessing of the fleet, and bathtub races.

EXPLORING PRINCE RUPERT

Prince Rupert gets more than 18 hours of sunlight a day during the summer. And despite its location, this coastal city of 18,000 residents enjoys a mild climate most of the year. Mountain biking, cross-country skiing, fishing, kayaking, hiking, and camping are just a few of the region's popular activities. Northern British Columbia's rich native-Indian heritage has been preserved in its museums and archaeological sites.

   The **Museum of Northern British Columbia,** 100 1st Ave. (☎ 250/624-3207), recently underwent a major renovation. It displays artifacts created by the Tsimshian/Nisga'a and Haida tribes, who've inhabited this area for over 10,000 years. There are also artifacts and photographs from Prince Rupert's 19th-century European settlement. In summer, the museum's Archaeological Harbour Tours allow you to see the area's many active dig sites at ancestral villages that date back more than 5,000 years. The historic **Cow Bay** district on the waterfront reminds visitors that both fishing and logging attracted European settlers to this remote outpost in the 1800s. The many art galleries, gift shops, and craft stores along the water invite perusal.

   And 20 kilometers (12 miles) south of Prince Rupert, the province's oldest working salmon-cannery village, built in 1889, is located at Prince Edward and has a picturesque boardwalk. Every summer, fishing fleets dropped off their catches at the cannery, which employed hundreds of native-Indian and Asian seasonal workers. Managed by the **North Pacific Cannery Village Museum** (☎ 250/628-3538; mailing address: Box 1104, Prince Edward, BC, V0V 1G0), the working museum allows visits to the manager's house, cannery store, workers' mess, canning buildings, and seasonal workers' cabins, which are open year-round.

SPORTS & OUTDOOR ACTIVITIES

BIKING   **Vertical Ski & Cycle,** 212 3rd Ave. W. (☎ 250/627-1766), rents mountain bikes during the summer for about C$15 (US$11) per day. The staff can direct cyclists to the best trails and advise on weather and trail conditions.

HIKING   **Kalen Sports,** 344 2nd Ave. W. (☎ 250/624-3633), and **Far West Sports,** 221 3rd Ave. W. (☎ 250/624-2568), are the two best sources for information about hiking trails and directions. The area experiences annual as well as seasonal changes in trail conditions, and some hiking and backcountry ski areas are too challenging for beginners. Both of these outfitters can supply clothing or camping, climbing, and skiing equipment, but it's advisable to call ahead with special requests.

KAYAKING & CANOEING   The waters surrounding Prince Rupert are tricky, and rough tidal swells and strong currents are common. **Sea Sports,** 295 1st Ave. E. (☎ 250/624-5336), rents kayaks and gear only to experienced paddlers. Rates start at C$35 (US$25) per day; weekly rates and canoes are available.

SKIING Vertical Ski & Cycle, 212 3rd Ave. W. (☎ 250/627-1766), rents cross-country skis and gear for about C$29 (US$21) per day. The staff can direct skiers to the best trails and advise on weather and trail conditions.

ACCOMMODATIONS

A mile from the ferry terminal, **Park Avenue Campground,** 1750 Park Ave. (☎ 250/624-5861; fax 250/627-8009; mailing address: Box 612, Prince Rupert, BC, V8J 4J5), has 97 full-hookup and tenting sites. Facilities include laundry, hot showers, flush toilets, a playground, mail drop, and pay phones. Make reservations in advance during the summer months because this campground is the best in the area. It's also an ideal location if you're catching the morning ferry to Port Hardy or to Skagway, Alaska. Rates are C$9 to C$16 (US$6 to US$11) per campsite.

✪ **Rainforest Bed & Breakfast.** 706 Ritchie St., Prince Rupert, BC, V8J 3N5. ☎ **250/ 624-9742.** 3 rms (1 with bath). C$60–C$70 (US$43–US$50) double. Rates include full breakfast. MC, V. From the ferry terminal, drive 3 min. (0.8km/0.5 mile) on Hwy. 16, which is also called Park Ave. on the coast side of town. Turn right on Ritchie St.

Located in a quiet, residential section of Prince Rupert, this cozy, homey B&B offers guests a shared kitchenette for making lunch or dinner, and a TV room. Breakfast, served in the dining room, includes fresh-squeezed juices and delicious homemade cinnamon rolls.

Totem Lodge Motel. 1335 Park Ave., Prince Rupert, BC, V8J 1K3. ☎ **800/550-0178** in North America, or 250/624-6761. Fax 250/624-3831. 31 rms. TV TEL. C$65–C$75 (US$46– US$54) double. Kitchen units C$5 (US$3.55) extra. AE, ER, MC, V. Hwy. 16 becomes McBride St. when it first enters town. It then becomes 3rd Ave. and finally Park Ave. From the ferry terminals, drive 1.6km (1 mile) into town on Park Ave.

This motel offers tidy, quiet, simply furnished rooms with kitchens, combination baths, and cable and satellite TV. It's the closest lodging to the Alaska and BC ferry terminal. Facilities include car storage and coin laundry. No pets.

DINING

For 60 years, **Smile's Seafood Café,** 113 Cow Bay Rd. (☎ 250/624-3072), has served seafood in every shape and form, from oyster burgers and seafood salads to heaping platters of fried fish. Located in the historic Cow Bay district, this small establishment is always busy during the summer, but it's always worth the wait. Main courses range from C$4 to C$22 (US$2.85 to US$16). During summer, it's open daily from 10am to 10pm; the rest of the year, daily from 11am to 9pm.

Right next door is **Breakers Pub** (☎ 250/624-5990), a popular local pub with a harbor view and tasty fare like fish-and-chips, barbecued ribs, and stir-fries. It's open Monday to Saturday from noon to 2am and Sunday from noon to midnight).

EXPLORING THE QUEEN CHARLOTTE ISLANDS

The misty and mysterious Queen Charlotte Islands inspired 19th-century painter Emily Carr to document her impressions of the towering carved-cedar totem poles and longhouses at the abandoned village of **Ninstints on Anthony Island.** The islands still lure artists, writers, and photographers wishing to experience their haunting beauty.

On **South Moresby Island,** you'll discover an array of rare fauna and flora, including horned puffins, Cassin's auklets, waterfowl raptors, gray whales, harbor seals, Steller's sea lions, and the world's largest black bears—all framed by moss-covered Sitka spruces, western hemlocks, and red cedars.

Graham Island's **Naikoon Provincial Park** is a 180,000-acre wildlife reserve where whales can be spotted from the beaches, peregrine falcons fly overhead, and Sitka deer silently observe you as you walk along trails through the dense temperate rain forest. And just outside the town of Masset, the **Delkatla Wildlife Sanctuary** is a birder's paradise. It's the first landfall for the 113 migrating species of bird life that use the Pacific Flyway.

Gwaii Haanas: The Land Where Time Stood Still

Ninstints on Anthony Island is an ancient native-Indian village revered as sacred ground by the modern-day Haida tribe. The island and surrounding area are a designated UNESCO World Heritage Site called **Gwaii Haanas** (also known as South Moresby National Park Marine Reserve). Centuries-old totem poles and longhouses proudly stand in testimony to the culture's 10,000-year heritage. According to local legends, the Haida people were created on this island by the "Raven who captured the Sun" after he brought the life-giving light to the dark, ice-encrusted earth.

Gwaii Haanas is accessible only by sea kayak and sailboat. For permission to enter the area, contact the **Haida Gwaii Watchmen** (☎ 250/559-8225; mailing address: Box 609, Skidegate, Haida Gwaii, BC, V0T 1S0), who act as site guardians and area hosts. Their office is at Second Beach, just north of Skidegate Landing on Highway 16.

Tours & Excursions

Outfitters offer all-inclusive kayaking packages to this area that suit all ages and experience levels. **Super Natural Adventures,** 626 W. Pender St., Vancouver (☎ 604/683-5101), offers a "Butterfly Tour" to Gwaii Haanas. The single-person kayak adventure includes an experienced guide, paddling and camping equipment, and provisions. Equipment is provided if you want to take over the cooking duties from your host. The same company arranges charter-boat and floatplane transport to Sandspit.

Tofino Expeditions Ltd., 202–1504 Duranleau St., Vancouver (☎ 604/687-4455), conducts 6- to 8-day group kayaking trips for about C$850 (US$607) per person. Tours depart from Port Hardy. Upon your arrival in Sandspit, a floatplane transports you to the launch site. No prior kayaking experience or equipment is necessary. The single-person kayak, paddling, camping, and first-aid equipment, transport, and meals are included. The company offers 6-day-long kayaking/camping trips to Ninstints for C$1,350 (US$964) per person.

The **Royal British Columbia Museum** (☎ 250/387-5745) in Victoria (see "Victoria," earlier in this chapter) offers educational expeditions to the Haida Gwaii archaeological sites on South Moresby Island from June to October. The skippered 6-day sailing trips are accompanied by full crew and an anthropologist who explains the area's remarkable history. Package tours include meals, transport, and accommodations at around C$2,300 (US$1,643) per person.

Queen Charlotte Adventures (☎ 250/559-8990) offers package tours to Ninstints on a 53-foot schooner. Prices include accommodations and meals on board as well as a knowledgeable skipper and crew. A 6-day all-inclusive package starts at C$2,000 (US$1,429) per person.

✪ **Langara Lodge, Ltd.,** 436 W. 2nd Ave., Vancouver, BC, V5Y 1E2 (☎ 604/873-4228; fax 604/873-5500), offers the most complete all-inclusive package to the islands, and is one of the most beautiful lodges in western Canada. Geared toward anglers and ecotourists who want to be pampered, the lodge picks up guests in a private aircraft at Vancouver Airport's Southern Terminal and delivers them to Sandspit.

From there it's a quick hop by floatplane to Langara Island, just north of Graham Island. The rooms at this log-lodge complex overlooking the harbor are large and luxurious. The bathrooms even have gold-plated fixtures. The lounge has vaulted ceilings and a massive river-rock fireplace. There's also a game room with a pool table and dartboard, outdoor decks, and a dining room that serves expertly prepared Pacific Northwest dishes complemented by an impressive wine list. Fishing packages include round-trip air transport from Vancouver, accommodations, meals, boats, tackle, weather gear, survival suits, and freezing, canning, and taxidermy services. Guided fishing costs extra, as do whale-watching, ecotouring, and heli-touring charters. Rates start at C$3,125 (US$2,232) per person for a 4-day trip.

ACCOMMODATIONS & DINING

After a long day of exploration, stop in at **Daddy Cool's Neighbourhood Pub,** Collison Avenue at Main Street, Masset (☎ 250/626-3210), for a pint and a fish tale or two. The **Café Gallery,** Collison Avenue at Orr Street, Masset (☎ **250/ 626-3672**), serves hearty portions of fresh seafood, steaks, pasta dishes, sandwiches, and salads. Main courses range from C$12 to C$16 (US$9 to US$11). It's open Monday to Saturday from 9:30am to 9pm.

Dorothy & Mike's Guest House. 3127 2nd Ave. (mailing address: Box 595), Queen Charlotte City, BC, V0T 1S0. ☎ **250/559-8688.** Fax 250/559-8439. 5 suites (3 with bath). C$50–C$60 (US$36–US$43) suite. Rates include breakfast. No credit cards. Closed Oct–Mar. Drive 3.3km (2 miles) away from the Skidegate ferry terminal on 2nd Ave.

The atmosphere here has an island flavor: A large deck overlooks the Skidegate Inlet, and a serene garden surrounds the house. The warm, cozy guest suites are filled with local art and antiques, with full kitchen facilities. It's within walking distance of the ocean, restaurants, and shopping.

✪ **Spruce Point Lodging.** 609 6th Ave., Queen Charlotte City, Graham Island, BC, V0T 1S0. ☎ **250/559-8234.** 7 rms. TV TEL. C$65 (US$46) double or triple. Kitchen unit C$10 (US$7) extra. Rates include breakfast. MC, V. Drive 0.8km (0.5 mile) away from the Skidegate ferry terminal on 6th Ave.

This rustic inn, overlooking the Hecate Strait, features rooms with private entrances as well as excellent views. But there are other reasons why this is a great spot to stay with your friendly hosts. Each of the double-, twin-, and queen-bedded rooms has a refrigerator and a choice of either a private shower or a bath. Some rooms even have full kitchen facilities, and all have complimentary tea and coffee service. The shared balcony is used as a guest lounge. Your hosts can also arrange kayaking packages to the surrounding islands.

8 The Skeena River Valley: Terrace & Nisga'a Memorial Lava Beds Provincial Park

The Yellowhead Highway (Highway 16) follows the lush Skeena River Valley from Prince Rupert on the coast of the Inside Passage to the province's interior. It's the gateway to the land-based return route from the Inside Passage ferry cruise. The long, winding valley is home to a diverse community of fishers, loggers, and aluminum and paper mill workers in **Terrace** and is the ancestral home of the Gitksan, Haisla, and Tshimshian (Nisga'a) tribes, who've lived in the area for over 8,000 years.

Another point of interest is the **Nisga'a Memorial Lava Beds Provincial Park** near Terrace. Vegetation has only recently begun to reappear on the lava plain created by a volcanic eruption and subsequent lava flow, in 1750, that consumed this area and nearly all of its inhabitants.

ESSENTIALS

VISITOR INFORMATION   The **North by Northwest Tourism Association,** 11-3167 Tatlow Rd. (mailing address: Box 1030), Smithers, BC, V0J 2N0 (☎ **250/ 847-5227**), can provide extensive and detailed information on the area. The **Terrace Visitor Info Centre,** 4511 Keith Ave., Terrace, BC, V8G 1K1 (☎ **250/635-2063**), is open June 1 to September 30, daily from 10am to 6pm; October 1 to May 31, Monday to Friday from 10am to 6pm.

GETTING THERE   The Skeena River Valley is accessible by car or train.

By Car   Terrace is 151.6 kilometers (91 miles) east of Prince Rupert on the Yellowhead Highway (Highway 16). To reach it from Vancouver, follow the directions to Quesnel (see "Cariboo Country," below), and continue 123.3 kilometers (74 miles) north of Quesnel on Highway 97 to Prince George. From there, take the Yellowhead Highway 643 kilometers (386 miles) west to Terrace.

By Train   The **VIA Rail** (☎ **888/842-7245** or 800/561-3949) passenger train departs from Prince George on Monday, Thursday, and Saturday at 7:45am and arrives in Prince Rupert at 8:30pm, making a stop in Terrace. The train follows the same route as the Yellowhead Highway. **BC Rail's** *Cariboo Prospector* route (☎ **604/ 984-5246**) from North Vancouver to Prince George connects with this service. It departs three times a week from North Vancouver at 7am; stops at Whistler, Lillooet, 100 Mile House, Williams Lake, and Quesnel; and arrives in Prince George at 8:30pm. The one-way fare is C$190 (US$136).

EXPLORING TERRACE & NISGA'A MEMORIAL LAVA BEDS

Many native-Indian legends focus on the Skeena River Valley surrounding the city of **Terrace** (pop. 13,400), as do stories about the incredibly rare wildlife in this region. Forty kilometers (25 miles) northwest of town, the **Khutzeymateen** (meaning "confined space of salmon and bears") is the province's first official grizzly-bear sanctuary. Established in 1994, the 622-square-kilometer (240-sq.-mile) reserve protects the **50 grizzlies** that live in a fragile estuary habitat. You need special permission to enter the park, and you must be part of an authorized group or accompanied by a park ranger to observe these amazing creatures.

North America's rarest subspecies of black bear, the **kermodei,** also makes its home in the valley and on Princess Royal Island in the Douglas Channel. The kermodei is unique, a nonalbino black bear born with white fur, ranging from dark chestnut blond to blue-gray glacier white. One of every 10 black bears born here is a kermodei. Its teddy-bear face, small eyes, and round ears are endearing, but the kermodei is even larger than the impressive Queen Charlotte Islands black bear.

Tsimshian (Nisga'a) legends describe the kermodei's supernatural powers, which were bestowed on it by the Raven who brought the Sun's warmth and light to the earth and its people. The Raven created the kermodei (which means "spirit bear") to remind the people of the dark days and of his promise that those days would never return so long as the kermodei remained in the valley. This amazing animal was on the verge of extinction until a decade ago, when naturalists managed to prevent the logging industry from decimating its remaining territory.

The valley is also known for a tragic event that befell the Wolf Clan of the Tsimshian. The incident occurred in September 1750, while the salmon were spawning. The young men were torturing the fish with burning pitch despite the elders' warnings that the spirit would be angered by their cruelty. Suddenly, a "spirit drum" thundered and the volcano that overlooked the villages exploded. The subsequent lava flow consumed 38.3 square kilometers (23 sq. miles) of valley floor, dammed up the T'seax River's northward flow to the Nass River, and subsequently created Lava Lake. Two thousand Nisga'a villagers were buried alive.

The route to this near-lunar landscape, the **Nisga'a Memorial Lava Beds Provincial Park,** begins in Terrace at the intersection of the Yellowhead Highway (Highway 16) and Kalum Lake Road (Nisga'a Highway). Follow the narrow gravel highway north along the Kalum River past Kalum Lake. Along the way, there's a **pioneer graveyard** and the **Deep Creek Fish Hatchery** (☎ 250/635-3471; mailing address: Box 21, Terrace, BC, V8G 4A2), which releases chinook salmon from August to September and coho salmon from October to November. Just past the tiny settlement of Rosswood is **Lava Lake,** then the town of **New Aiyansh** (the valley's largest Nisga'a village), and finally the park. The entire trip is 80 kilometers (48 miles), but allow at least 2 hours.

SHOPPING IN TERRACE

There are two shops in Terrace that you shouldn't miss. The **Northern Light Studio,** 4820 Halliwell Ave. (☎ 250/638-1403), has a Japanese-style garden and a walkway built completely out of British Columbia jade. The art studio features jewelry, fine arts, native crafts, totem poles, and an herb garden.

The **House of Sim-oi-ghets,** off Highway 16 (☎ 250/635-6177), is a cedar longhouse decorated with traditional Nisga'a motifs in red, black, and white. The store features jewelry, wood carvings, moccasins, bead and leather work, and books. Owned by the Kitsumkalum tribal band, the complex also includes a convenience store and a riverside campground.

ACCOMMODATIONS & DINING

✪ **Miles Inn on the T'seax.** Nass Valley (mailing address: Box 230, New Aiyansh, BC, V0J 1A0). ☎ and fax **250/633-2636.** E-mail: milesinn@kermode.net. Web site: www.kermode.net/milesinn. 4 rms (2 with bath). C$75 (US$54) double. Rates include breakfast. No credit cards.

Overlooking the Nisga'a Memorial Lava Beds Provincial Park, this beautiful lodge is nestled in the Nass River valley. Two guest rooms feature queen-size beds and private baths. The other two share a bath. A large hot tub is available for relaxing tired muscles after a day of hiking the lava beds and crater, rock climbing, canoeing or kayaking the Nass river, salmon or trout fishing in the T'seax River, or simply lounging around the lodge. Guests select the breakfast menu before going to bed. A home-cooked dinner is also available for an extra charge. No smoking.

Terrace Inn. 4551 Greig Ave., Terrace, BC, V8G 1M7. ☎ **250/635-0083.** Fax 250/635-0092. 68 rms. A/C TV TEL. C$80–C$99 (US$57–US$71) double. Family, group, and weekend discounts. AE, MC, V. Airport limo and free parking.

Overlooking the surrounding mountains, these comfortable, well-appointed rooms with queen- and king-size beds feature a number of little touches not normally found this far into the backcountry: complimentary coffee, a clock radio, and a hair dryer. On the premises, you'll also find a licensed restaurant, piano bar and lounge, and a casual pub with live entertainment.

9 Cariboo Country

South of Prince George along the Yellowhead Highway (Highway 16) and beyond into British Columbia's interior, the Canadian Wild West hasn't changed much in the past century. This is Cariboo Country, a vast landscape that changes from alpine meadows and thick forests of Douglas fir and lodgepole pine to rolling prairies and arid, granite-walled canyons before it encounters the gigantic glacial peaks of Whistler Mountain (see "Whistler," below). The Cariboo's history is synonymous with the word *gold.*

The Sea-to-Sky Highway (Highway 99) from Vancouver through Whistler and the Cayoosh Valley eventually descends into the town of **Lillooet,** which was Mile 0 of the Old Cariboo Highway during the gold-rush days of the 1860s. Prospectors and settlers made their way north up what's now called the **Cariboo Gold Trail** (highways 99 and 97).

Highway 97 follows the gold-rush trail through **70 Mile House, 100 Mile House, 108 Mile House,** and **150 Mile House.** The towns were named after the mile-marking roadhouses patronized by prospectors and settlers headed north to the goldfields.

The gold-rich town of **Barkerville** sprang up in the 1860s after a British prospector named Billy Barker struck it rich on Williams Creek. Completely restored by the parks service, the town brings the rough gold-rush days to life. The streets are only 18 feet wide (thanks to a drunken surveyor). And the town burned to the ground in 1868, when a miner knocked over an oil lamp while in hot pursuit of a dance-hall girl. It was rebuilt almost overnight, but abandoned after World War II. Nowadays, you can try your hand at panning for the shiny gold flakes and nuggets that still lie deep in Williams Creek.

Gold isn't the only thing that attracts thousands of visitors to this area year-round. Cross-country skiers and snowmobilers take to the creek-side paths during the winter. And canoeists head a few miles north of Barkerville to a 120-kilometer (72-mile) circular paddling route called **Bowron Lakes.**

LILLOOET
ESSENTIALS

VISITOR INFORMATION Contact the **Cariboo Tourist Association,** Box 4900, Williams Lake, BC, V2G 2V8 (☎ **800/663-5885** or 250/392-2226). The **Lillooet Visitor Info Centre** is at 790 Main St. (mailing address: Box 441), Lillooet, BC, V0K 1V0 (☎ **250/256-4308**). Situated inside the Lillooet Pioneer Museum, the center is open May 24 to October 31 daily from 10am to 6pm.

GETTING THERE Whether you travel by train or by car, the trip from Whistler to Cariboo Country is a visually exhilarating experience.

By Car The entire drive up Highway 99 from Whistler to Lillooet takes 1 1/2 to 2 hours. From Whistler, drive north on Highway 99 through Pemberton and Mount Currie. About 6.6 kilometers (4 miles) later, you begin your ascent up a number of switchbacks into the spectacular Cayoosh Valley. For 100 kilometers (60 miles), this portion of Highway 99 winds through rolling alpine meadows. The icy waters of the valley's creeks race along the roadside. The scenery suddenly changes to stark granite walls and cavernous canyons that plunge hundreds of feet below the roadway. Suddenly, you find yourself in a mountainous antelope-brush desert. Lillooet is nestled in this valley, where the muddy Thompson River is fed by the crystal-clear waters of the Cayoosh Valley creeks.

By Train BC Rail's (☎ **604/984-5246**) *Cariboo Prospector* departs from the North Vancouver train station three times a week at 7am. Passing through Howe Sound, Whistler, and the Pemberton Valley, it arrives in Lillooet at 12:35pm. The one-way fares start at C$63 (US$45) per person.

SPECIAL EVENT A parade, exhibits, live performances, and food highlight the agenda at **Only in Lillooet Days** (☎ 250/256-7972) during the second week in June.

SEEING THE TOWN

The **Lillooet Pioneer Museum,** 790 Main St., Lillooet (☎ **250/256-4308**), is housed in a former Anglican church. Built in the 1960s, it's a replica of the original structure, which was carried in pieces by miners who were headed up the Cariboo Gold Trail in 1860. The museum houses an eclectic collection of memorabilia, including native-Indian tools and artifacts, farming tools, mining implements, furnishings, and camel saddles. (Believe it or not, miner John Callbreath brought 23 camels from San Francisco in 1862 to work on road construction! Their tender feet and foul odor put an end to his plan.) The printing presses that produced "Ma" Murray's politically controversial newspaper stand silent in the lower level. The museum is open daily from 9am to 5pm; admission is by donation.

This was Mile 0 of the 1860s **Cariboo Gold Rush Trail.** In 1858, a trail was established from the Fraser Valley goldfields in the south to the town of Lillooet. At the big bend on Main Street, a cairn marks "Mile 0" of the original Cariboo Wagon Road, cut in 1861 as an access route to the newly discovered gold-rich creeks of Barkerville. The towns along this road (now Highway 97) are named after the roadhouses along the way: 70 Mile House, 100 Mile House, 108 Mile House, and 150 Mile House.

There are still signs of **"gold fever"** in and around Lillooet. Visitors try their luck, panning a few shovelfuls along the river's edge. The **Chinese Rock Piles** just outside of town were formed by early Chinese prospectors who patiently gathered minute grains of gold from the remains of spent claims abandoned by miners looking for fist-sized nuggets.

The nearby **gold-rush ghost towns** of Bradian and Brexton in the Bridge River valley are accessible by car. The tiny settlements of **Bralorne** and **Gold Bridge** were established when the Pioneer-Bralorne mine was built in the 1930s. The mine produced over C$145 million in gold and employed 5,000 miners before it closed in 1970. You can reach these inhabited towns on the unpaved Hurley River Road above Lillooet.

ACCOMMODATIONS & DINING

The 26 campsites at **Marble Canyon Provincial Park,** Highway 99 between Lillooet and Highway 97 (☎ **250/851-3000;** mailing address: 1210 McGill Rd., Kamloops, BC, V2C 6N6), are popular summer-weekend retreats for Vancouverites. Open from April to November, the campgrounds offer excellent canoeing, fishing, kayaking, and swimming opportunities, but minimum facilities (pit toilets, fire pits, and pumped well water). The ideal location, well-positioned campsites, and surrounding views balance out the rustic atmosphere. Campsites are $9.50 (US$7) per night.

Tyax Mountain Lake Resort. Tyaughton Lake Rd., Gold Bridge, BC, V0K 1P0. ☎ **250/238-2221.** Fax 250/238-2528. 35 rms, 7 campsites. TEL. C$96–C$115 (US$69–US$84) double; C$20 (US$14) per 2-person site. Drive 2 hours (86km/40.8 miles) from Lillooet up the unpaved Tyaughton Lake Rd. Follow signs to the resort.

Set high above the town of Lillooet, Tyaughton Lake is the perfect alpine setting for a romantic vacation. On its shores stands this huge log lodge, which offers guests luxurious accommodations and a host of activities ranging from heli-fishing and heli-skiing trips to barbecues on the lake. Guest rooms are comfortably furnished with queen-size beds.

The resort has a restaurant that serves Pacific Northwest cuisine, and a cocktail lounge. There is also a sauna, fitness center, outdoor whirlpool, and tennis court on the premises. Fly-out fishing charters, floatplane sightseeing, canoe rentals, horseback riding, cross-country ski trails, heli-skiing, heli-fishing, and mountain-bike rentals are available.

SPORTS & OUTDOOR ACTIVITIES

FISHING   Anglers hit the surrounding mountain lakes, rivers, and creeks for ko-kanee, rainbow trout, and lake trout at places like Tyaughton Lake, Hat Creek, Crown Lake, and Turquoise Lake. To fish here, you need a nonresident freshwater license. Pick up a license before you arrive at **Whistler Backcountry Adventures,** 4314 Main St., Whistler (☎ 604/932-3474). The staff can also give you advice on lures, regulations, and necessary gear.

GOLFING   The **Sheep Pasture Golf Course,** just outside of Lillooet (☎ 250/256-4484; mailing address: Box 217, Lillooet, V0K 1V0), is a 9-hole course with a pro shop, clubhouse, driving range, and sheep. That's right, loads of sheep. The course is located on a working sheep ranch that was established in 1858. The views and the warm desert climate make this course a welcome diversion. Tee times are not required, pull carts are available for rent, and the sheep keep the greens neatly trimmed. Greens fees start at C$20 (US$14) per person.

SKIING   Miles of cross-country ski trails weave around near Gold Bridge and Bralorne above Lillooet, especially the trail that encircles Tyaughton Lake. You need to bring your own cross-country skis or rent a full equipment package at **Cypress Mountain Sports** (☎ 604/878-9229), in the Park Royal Shopping Centre, West Vancouver, before you head up. Prices, including boots, skis, and poles, start at C$19 (US$14) per day.

BARKERVILLE & BOWRON LAKES

The **Cariboo Gold Rush Trail** winds up Highway 99 north from Lillooet to the tiny settlement of **Pavilion,** where the province's first privately owned post office is still in operation in the town's general store (where, incidentally, they make great milkshakes). The trail heads east, meets Highway 97, and continues north to the goldfields of **Barkerville, Richfield,** and **Likely.**

Before the Klondike prospectors trudged to the frozen goldfields of the Yukon and Alaska in 1897 and 1898, fortune hunters hiked up from the Fraser River valley to the Cariboo's gold-rich creeks (Antler, Keithley, Lightning, and Lowhee creeks) during the 1860s. Many of these claims continued to produce well into the 1930s, and there are still prospectors and active gold claims in the area.

In the woodlands of the Cariboo mountains, the **Bowron Lakes** (a chain of six major and a number of smaller interconnecting lakes) attract canoeists and kayakers who paddle and portage around the entire 72-mile circuit.

ESSENTIALS

VISITOR INFORMATION   The **South Cariboo Visitor Info Centre,** 422 Cariboo Hwy. 97 S. (Box 2312), 100 Mile House, BC, V0K 2E0 (☎ 250/395-5353), is open September 1 to May 31, Monday to Friday from 10am to 4pm; June 1 to August 31, daily from 8am to 7pm.

GETTING THERE   Barkerville and Bowron Lakes are more than 83.3 kilometers (50 miles) from the last sizable town, Quesnel.

By Car   Highway 99 runs north and east from Lillooet for 59 kilometers (37 miles) until it meets Highway 97. Turn left and continue on Highway 97, heading north to Quesnel, which is about 400 kilometers (250 miles) from Lillooet. Follow the signs in town to Highway 26 east. The 86.6-kilometer (52-mile) drive to Barkerville takes you deep into the moss-covered forests of the Cariboo mountains, where moose, black bears, and deer are often seen on the road. The highway ends at the entrance to Barkerville. Bowron Lakes is another 30 kilometers (18 miles) northeast of Barkerville on the Bowron Lakes Road.

By Plane & Car   Air BC (☎ 604/688-5515) flies into Quesnel from Vancouver. Fares start at C$159 (US$114) round-trip for a long weekend. You'll need to rent a car once you arrive. **National Tilden** (☎ 800/387-4747) has a rental desk right at the airport to assist you.

By Train   BC Rail's (☎ 604/984-5246) *Cariboo Prospector* departs North Vancouver three times per week at 7am. After passing through Howe Sound, Whistler, Pemberton, and Lillooet, it arrives in Quesnel at 6:41pm. One-way fares to Quesnel start at C$154 (US$110) per person.

The company offers a 3-day, 2-night getaway package, the **"Barkerville Gold Rush Tour,"** which takes passengers up to the historic gold town on the *Cariboo Prospector* and returns them to Vancouver by air from Quesnel. The round-trip, all-inclusive package is C$535 (US$382) per person. Custom all-rail packages are available.

SPECIAL EVENT   The Quesnel Rodeo, a horseshoe tournament, river-raft races, and more than 100 other events attract thousands to Quesnel during the second week of July for **Bill Barker Days** (☎ 800/992-4922 in Canada, or 250/992-8716).

EXPLORING BARKERVILLE: AN OLD WEST GHOST TOWN

The 1860 Cariboo Gold Rush was the reason thousands of miners made their way north from the played-out Fraser River gold deposits to Williams Creek, east of Quesnel. The town of **Barkerville** was founded on its shore after a British immigrant, Billy Barker, discovered one of the region's richest placer (not embedded in rock) gold deposits 50 feet below the water line in the summer of 1862. The town sprang up practically overnight. It was reputedly the largest city west of Chicago and north of San Francisco that year. The adjoining settlements of Camerontown and Richfield absorbed the overflow.

A bar of soap was a buck, and so was a dance with a hurdy-gurdy girl. Billy married a woman who spent every dollar he made, but a few years later he struck it rich a second time in Horsefly, 66.6 kilometers (40 miles) east of 150 Mile House. Unfortunately, he also remarried, and is buried in a pauper's grave in Victoria. Miners pulled C$50 million in gold (at C$16 per oz.) out of Williams Creek. A mining company is still dredging gold out of the creek just outside the provincial park grounds.

The big nuggets ran out around 1930, and Barkerville's population moved on, leaving behind an intact ghost town that was designated a historic park in the 1950s. The original Anglican church (built in 1869) and 125 other buildings have been lovingly reconstructed or restored. The church holds daily services. And aside from the **visitor center** (☎ 250/994-3302) at the park's entrance, very little has changed. The Richland courthouse (a 30-min. hike from Barkerville) stages trials from the town's past.

From May to September, the "townspeople" dress in period costumes and bring the town back to life. Visitors can pan for gold outside the general store, learn about the big strikes and the miners' lives from the local miners, take a stagecoach ride, or attend a criminal trial. The Theatre Royal actors also perform dramatic productions in the town hall. You can have a root beer at the town saloon or a meal in the Chinatown section (early photos in the Chinese restaurant show how accurate the restoration is).

During the winter, the town becomes a haven for cross-country skiers, who take to the trail from Barkerville and Richfield down to Likely and Quesnel Forks. And Barkerville hosts a special Victorian Christmas celebration.

Two-day admission to the town is C$5.50 (US$3.95) for adults, C$3.25 (US$2.30) for seniors and students, and C$1 (US70¢) for children 6 to 12. Barkerville is open daily from dawn to dusk year-round.

EXPLORING BOWRON LAKES: A CANOEIST'S PARADISE

Thirty kilometers (18 miles) northeast of Barkerville over an unpaved road, there's access to a circle of lakes that attract canoeists and kayakers from around the world. The 304,000-acre ✪ **Bowron Lakes Provincial Park** is a majestic paddler's paradise set against a backdrop of glacial peaks.

The 7-day circular route is 120 kilometers (72 miles) of unbroken wilderness. It begins at Kibbee Creek and Kibbee Lake, flows into Indianpoint Lake, Isaac Lake, and the Isaac River, and continues to McCleary, Lanezi, Sandy, and Una lakes before entering the final stretch: Babcock Lake, Skoi Lake, the Spectacle Lakes, Swan Lake, and finally Bowron Lake. The long, narrow lakes afford visitors a close look at both shores. More than occasionally, you'll catch sight of the moose, caribou, mountain goats, beaver, black bears, and grizzly bears that inhabit the area. Be prepared to portage for a total of 8.3 kilometers (5 miles) between some of the creeks that connect the lakes. The longest single portage is 2.9 kilometers (1³/₄ miles). You must pack everything in and out of the wilderness camps that are plotted at frequent intervals. Reservations, required prior to arrival, can be made through **DJ Park Contractors,** 358 Vaughn St., Quesnel, BC, V2I 2T2 (☎ **250/992-3111**). You must report to the park's Registration Centre before embarking. All visitors begin by portaging to Kibbee Creek before entering the official launch point at Indianpoint Lake.

You don't have to make the entire journey to enjoy this incredible setting. Open from May to October, the campground at the park's entrance is a relaxing spot to camp, fish, boat, or simply relax and observe the abundant flora and fauna.

For information or to make reservations, contact **Bowron Lakes Provincial Park,** 181 1st Ave., Williams Lake, BC, V2G 1Y8 (☎ **250/398-4414**), or contact **Bowron Lake Lodge & Resorts** at Bowron Lake (☎ **250/992-2733;** mailing address: 672 Walken St., Quesnel, BC, V2J 2J7). This reliable outfitter not only arranges canoe, mountain-bike, and boat rentals, it's also an excellent place to dine and stay in the park (see below).

ACCOMMODATIONS & DINING

There are three campgrounds in **Barkerville Provincial Park,** Highway 26, Barkerville (☎ **250/398-1414;** mailing address: 181 1st Ave. N., Williams Lake, BC, V2G 1Y8), all open year-round. **Lowhee Campground** is the best and closest to the park entrance. The well-spaced sites accommodate both tents and RVs. Hot showers, flush toilets, pumped well water, and a sani-station are available on the well-maintained grounds. The other two campgrounds are not as attractive and don't offer as many amenities: One is next to the town cemetery and the other is hidden behind a working mine operation that starts up daily at dawn. The 168 campsites

City Slickers & Saddle Sores: Guest Ranches

Cariboo Gold Rush Trail guest ranches offer visitors luxurious accommodations and a variety of outdoor activities year-round, and the restored, working ranches also provide glimpses into the region's rich cowboy heritage.

The **Big Bar Guest Ranch,** Big Bar Road (mailing address: Box 27), Clinton, BC, V0N 1K0 (☎ and fax **250/459-2333**), is just north of Clinton off Highway 97. The centerpiece of the property is the **Harrison House,** a hand-hewn log home built by pioneers in the 1800s. Besides taking horseback-riding and pack trips year-round, you can canoe, fish, hike, pan for gold, and cross-country ski on the beautiful grounds. The 12 guest rooms in the lodge have private baths; the four self-contained log cabins have kitchens, baths, and wood-burning fireplaces. There are six campsites on the grounds. The licensed family-style dining room serves hearty Western barbecue dishes. There's also a fireside lounge, a billiard room, and an outdoor hot tub. Rooms and cabins cost C$60 to C$99 (US$43 to US$71) for a double. Campsites are C$30 (US$21) per night. American Express, Discover, MasterCard, and Visa are accepted.

There's even a year-round spa resort in the Cariboo. The **Hills Health & Guest Ranch,** Highway 97, 108 Mile House (☎ **250/791-5225;** fax 250/791-6384; mailing address: 108 Ranch, Comp. 26, BC, V0K 2Z0), offers guests a full complement of beauty and health treatments as well as outdoor activities such as horseback riding, hayrides, guided hiking trips, and cross-country skiing on more than 166.6 kilometers (100 miles) of private trails. There are golf courses nearby. The 46 guest rooms are large, with ranch-style natural pine decor. The resort has recently added two new lodges, the Ranch House and Manor House, as well as self-contained chalet accommodations that feature kitchens and full baths and sleep up to six people. The health spa offers indoor exercise classes, health programs and wellness workshops, an aerobics studio, hydrotherapy pools, massage, herbal wraps, facials, reflexology, and body packs. The restaurant serves guests and the public a unique blend of cowboy favorites and spa cuisine, such as Italian fish stew made with fresh cod fillets or roasted Cornish hens scented with cloves and orange peel. It's open daily from 8am to 9pm, and reservations are recommended. Main courses cost C$9 to C$27 (US$6 to US$19). Or choose a meal and horseback-ride package for an unforgettable picnic experience. There are 10 campsites on this amazing property as well. Room rates range from C$79 to C$139 (US$56 to US$99). All-inclusive packages are available. Campsites are C$15 (US$11) per night. American Express, Discover, MasterCard, and Visa are accepted.

cost C$9.50 to C$12 (US$7 to US$9) per campsite from June to September; they're free the rest of the year. No credit cards are accepted.

During summer, groceries and camping supplies are available at the **Grubstake,** up the hill from the Lowhee campground on the Old Cariboo Highway. It's open daily from 8am to 9pm and offers a better selection of frozen meats and canned goods than can be found in the nearby town of Wells.

✪ **Bowron Lake Lodge & Resorts.** Bowron Lake (mailing address: 672 Walken St., Quesnel, BC, V2J 2J7). ☎ **250/992-2733.** 24 rms, 50 campsites. $C65–C$75 (US$46–US$87) double, kitchen C$10 (US$7) extra; C$16–C$20 (US$11–US$14) campsite. MC, V. Closed Nov–Apr.

This rustic, lakeside lodge resort provides all the creature comforts you could ask for in a wilderness setting. Guests can choose from comfortable lodge rooms with double beds, full private baths, and optional fully equipped kitchens; self-contained cabins; or tree-shaded campsites by the lake.

Mountain-bike rentals, canoe rentals, and motorboat rentals are available. The lodge has 5 kilometers (3 miles) of private hiking trails, 2,000 feet of private sandy beach, a private airstrip, and a licensed restaurant and cocktail lounge.

The Wells Hotel. Pooley St. (mailing address: Box 39), Wells, BC, V0N 2R0. ☎ **800/ 860-2299** in Canada, or 250/994-3427. Fax 250/994-3494. 17 rms. C$59–C$120 (US$42–US$86) double. Rates include breakfast. AE, MC, V.

Established in 1933, this restored country inn is filled with lovely antique furnishings and offers amenities that you can truly appreciate after hiking, canoeing, skiing, or gold panning in Barkerville or Bowron Lakes: fine dining, a frothy cappuccino, and a soothing hot tub. All guest rooms are tastefully decorated in earth-tone textiles and locally executed artwork. Some rooms have fireplaces. There are a licensed cafe and a cappuccino bar on the premises.

10 Whistler: North America's Most Popular Ski Resort

It's only a 90-minute drive up the Sea-to-Sky Highway (Highway 99) from downtown Vancouver and a 97-kilometer (60-mile) drive from Lillooet and the Cayoosh Valley to North America's most popular ski resort—Whistler. For 5 years running, the twin glacial peaks of ✪ **Whistler and Blackcomb mountains** have been rated the best year-round ski destination by both *Ski* and *Snow Country* magazines.

It all started in 1914, when Alex and Marybeth Philip bought 10 acres of land on Alta Lake for C$70 an acre. They spent the summer building a resort, the Rainbow Lodge. It gradually gained a reputation as the best ski resort west of Jasper, attracting European, Canadian, and American enthusiasts of the new sports crazes: downhill and cross-country skiing. As the sport's popularity grew after the World War II, so did the number of lifts and trails on the nearby peaks and valleys.

Whistler's reputation soared during the 1980s with the opening of the Upper Village's Blackcomb Mountain, which boasts a mile-high vertical drop—North America's highest. Its population has ballooned in the past few years to 7,300 permanent residents. But the best part about skiing on Whistler or Blackcomb Mountain is that you can walk, ski, or snowshoe from your hotel, condo, or chalet onto a ski lift or into the village's two main shopping and dining areas. The mountains (and villages) are less than 5 minutes apart on foot and can be reached quickly by walking trail or paved road. There's ample free parking for daytime visitors near the base of both mountains.

And if that's not enough, the price of lift tickets puts every other top North American ski resort to shame. A dual-mountain, 3-day pass is C$138 (US$99). That's C$23 (US$16) a day per mountain!

Whistler isn't limited to the ski season. The number of visitors is the same year-round. It's not unusual for Vancouverites to brave the Friday-night traffic on Highway 99 throughout the year to reach their favorite weekend-getaway spot. At the crack of dawn, you'll find people lined up for lift tickets, toting snowboards, skis, snowshoes, mountain bikes, day packs, and parawings. Or standing in the next line, waiting for horses.

The towns north of Whistler, **Pemberton** and **Mount Currie,** are refreshment stops for touring cyclists and hikers, and the gateway to the icy alpine waters of **Birkenhead Lake Provincial Park** (see "Fishing," below) and the majestic **Cayoosh**

Valley, which winds through the glacier-topped mountains to the Cariboo town of Lillooet (see "Cariboo Country," above).

ESSENTIALS

VISITOR INFORMATION   The **Whistler Visitor Info Centre** is at 2097 Lake Placid Rd. (in the Whistler Conference Centre), Whistler, BC, V0N 1B0 (☎ **604/ 932-5528**). It is open year-round daily from 10am to 6pm. An **information kiosk** on Village Gate Boulevard at the entry to Whistler Village is open from mid-May until early September during the same hours. The **Whistler Resort Association** is at 4010 Whistler Way, Whistler, BC, V0N 1B0 (☎ **604/932-3928**).

GETTING THERE   The drive up the scenic Sea-to-Sky Highway (Highway 99) from downtown Vancouver to Whistler takes about 90 minutes. The 121-kilometer (75-mile) route winds along the craggy, tree-lined coast of Howe Sound through Brittania Beach, Shannon Falls, Brackendale, Squamish, and Garibaldi Provincial Park. Many of the areas along the route have been backdrops for movies and television shows—it's that beautiful. You can also take a bus or a train to Whistler.

By Bus   Perimeter Transportation Ltd., 8695 Barnard St., Vancouver (☎ **604/ 266-5386** in Vancouver or 604/905-0041 in Whistler), operates bus service from Vancouver International Airport to the Whistler Bus Loop at 11am and 6:30pm daily. The trip takes about 3¹/₂ hours; one-way fares are C$45 (US$32) for adults and C$23 (US$16) for children. Reservations are required year-round.

   Maverick Coach Lines, Pacific Central Station, 1150 Station St., Vancouver (☎ **604/662-8051** in Vancouver or 604/932-5031 in Whistler), operates bus service from the Vancouver Bus Depot to the Whistler Bus Loop at 8am, 11am, 1, 3, 5, and 7pm daily. The trip takes about 3 hours; one-way fares are C$17 (US$12) for adults and C$8.50 (US$6) for children 5 to 12; children under 5 ride free.

By Train (☎ **604/984-5246**) operates the *Cariboo Prospector* through-out the year. It leaves the North Vancouver train terminal daily at 7am and chugs up the Howe Sound coastline through the Cheakamus River valley and Garibaldi Provincial Park until it reaches the Whistler train station on Lake Placid Road. The same train leaves Whistler at 6:10pm and returns to the North Vancouver train terminal at 8:45pm.

   The 2¹/₂-hour trip includes breakfast or dinner. A one-way ticket is C$29 (US$21) for adults, C$26 (US$19) for seniors, C$17 (US$12) for children 2 to 12, and C$6 (US$4.30) for children under 2.

GETTING AROUND   The walk between the Whistler Mountain (Whistler Village) and Blackcomb Mountain (Upper Village) resorts takes about 5 minutes.

By Bus   There's also a year-round **public transit service** (☎ **604/932-4020**) that operates on frequent daily schedules from Tamarisk and the BC Rail Station to Nester's Village, Alpine Meadows, and Emerald Estates. One-way fares are C$1.50 (US$1.05) for adults and C$1.25 (US90¢) for seniors and students; children under 5 are free.

By Cab   The village's taxis operate around the clock. Taxi tours, golf-course transfers, and airport transport are also offered by **Airport Limousine Service** (☎ **604/273-1331**), **Whistler Taxi** (☎ **604/938-3333**), and **Sea to Sky Taxi** (☎ **604/932-3333**).

By Car Rental cars are available from **Budget** at the Holiday Inn Sunspree, 4295 Blackcomb Way (☎ **604/932-1236**), and **Thrifty,** in the Listel Whistler Hotel, 4121 Village Green (☎ **604/938-0302**).

SPECIAL EVENTS Dozens of downhill-ski competitions are held between December and May. They include the **Owens-Corning World Freestyle Competition** (January), **Power Bar Peak to Valley Race** (February), **Kokanee Fantastic Downhill Race** (March), **World Ski & Snowboard Festival** (April), and **Whistler Snowboard World Cup** (December).

During the third week in July, the villages host **Whistler's Roots Weekend** (☎ **604/932-2394**). Down in the villages and up on the mountains, you'll hear the sounds of Celtic, zydeco, bluegrass, Delta blues, Latin, folk, and world-beat music at free and ticketed events.

The **Whistler Classical Music Festival** (☎ **604/932-2394**) is held during the second weekend in August. The highlight event is the "Whistler Mountain-Top Concert," featuring the Vancouver Symphony Orchestra at Whistler Mountain's natural amphitheater.

The **Alpine Wine Festival** (☎ **604/932-3434**) takes place on the mountaintop during the first weekend in September. Featuring wine tastings and events that highlight North America's finest vintages, the festival has become a summer classic.

And the second weekend in September ushers in the **Whistler Jazz & Blues Festival** (☎ **604/932-2394**), featuring live performances in the village squares and the surrounding clubs.

EXPLORING WHISTLER: A STEP BACK IN TIME

If you want to learn more about Whistler's heritage, flora, and fauna, visit the **Whistler Museum & Archives Society,** 4329 Main St., off Northlands Boulevard (☎ **604/932-2019**). Established in 1986, the museum has exhibits that reveal the life and culture of the native-Indian tribes that have lived in the lush Whistler and Pemberton valleys for thousands of years. There are also portrayals of the village's early settlement by Scottish and British immigrants during the late 1800s and early 1900s. That's when the railway, logging companies, and the first ski resort changed the face of the region. During the summer, the museum is open Sunday to Thursday from 10am to 4pm and Friday and Saturday from 10am to 6pm. Admission is C$1 (US70¢) for adults; children under 18 are free.

For centuries, the arid canyons, alpine meadows, and crystal-clear lakes of the area between Whistler and Kelly Lake were inaccessible to all but the most experienced hikers. However, **BC Rail's** (☎ **604/984-5246**) *Whistler Explorer* offers visitors a leisurely way to see the remote landscape. Departing from the Whistler train station on Lake Placid Road at 8:30am, the *Explorer* rambles through Pemberton Valley and past Seton Lake and Anderson Lake before arriving at Kelly Lake, which is adjacent to the historic Cariboo Gold Rush Trail.

After a 1-hour stretching-and-strolling break, passengers reboard the *Explorer,* returning to Whistler at 6:10pm. The round-trip fare is C$109 (US$78) for adults, seniors, and children over 12, and C$75 (US$54) for children 2 to 12.

ESPECIALLY FOR KIDS

Whistler's a great family destination. Whistler Village and the Upper Village sponsor daily activities near the base of the mountains that are tailor-made for active kids of all ages. There are mountain-bike races, an in-line skating park, trapeze, trampoline, and wall-climbing lessons, summer skiing, snowboarding, and snowshoeing. There's even a first-run multiplex movie theater.

Based at Blackcomb Mountain, the **Dave Murray Summer Ski Camp** (mailing address: Box 98), Whistler, BC, V0N 1B0 (☎ **604/932-3141** or 604/687-1032), is North America's longest-running summer ski camp. Junior programs cost about C$850 (US$607) per week. The packages include food, lodging, and lift passes as well as tennis, trampoline, trapeze, and mountain-biking options. The comprehensive instruction and adult supervision at this activity-oriented camp are excellent.

SHOPPING

The **Whistler Marketplace,** in the center of Whistler Village, and the area surrounding the **Blackcomb Mountain lift** brim with clothing, jewelry, craft, specialty, gift, and equipment shops that are open daily from 10am to 6pm. **Horstman Trading Company** (☎ **604/938-7725**), beside the Chateau Whistler at the base of Blackcomb, carries men's and women's casual wear to suit seasonal activities, from swimwear and footwear to polar-fleece vests and nylon jacket shells. **Escape Route** at Whistler Marketplace and Crystal Lodge (☎ **604/938-3228**), has a great line of outdoor clothing and equipment. The **Durango Boutique,** 4227 Village Stroll (☎ **604/932-6987**), carries fashionable, casual, and Western clothing. **For Nature's Sake,** in the Timberline Shops Mall (☎ **604/938-9453**), carries hiking canes, bear bells, books, gifts, and more. And **Whistler Backcountry Adventures,** 4314 Main St. (☎ **604/932-3474**), sells fishing licenses and carries a great selection of fishing rods, tackle, sports gear, and outdoor clothing.

HITTING THE SLOPES

Whistler Mountain (☎ **604/932-3434,** or 604/687-6761 for snow report; e-mail: whistler@whistler.net; Web site: www.whistler.com) has a 5,006-foot vertical and 100 marked runs that are serviced by a high-speed gondola and eight chairlifts, plus four other lifts and tows. Helicopter service from the top of the mountain makes another 100-plus runs on nearby glaciers accessible. There are a cafeteria and gift shop on the peak as well as a fully licensed restaurant.

Blackcomb Mountain, 4545 Blackcomb Way, Whistler, BC, V0N 1B4 (☎ **604/932-3141,** or 604/687-7504 for snow report), has a 5,280-foot (1.6km/1-mile) vertical and 100 marked runs that are serviced by nine chairlifts, plus three other lifts and tows. The huge cafeteria and gift shop aren't far from the peak, and the fully licensed restaurant is worth the gondola trip even if you're not skiing. The view is spectacular, the food decent.

During the **summer season,** Whistler Mountain is open daily from late June to September 28 (weekends-only in October). The gondolas are open from 9am to 5pm daily. Lift tickets are C$19 (US$14) for adults, C$16 (US$11) for seniors and children 13 to 18; children under 12 ski free. Summer-season passes are C$99 (US$71) for adults and C$79 (US$56) for seniors and children 13 to 18. For more information on summer activities (such as the Music on the Mountain events) and weather conditions, contact **Guest Relations** at ☎ **604/932-3434.**

Blackcomb Mountain is open from May through July. Horstman Glacier is open for snowboarding, skiing, and snowshoeing from 9am to 3pm from May to mid-June, and noon to 3pm from mid-June to August 4. Lift tickets are C$30 (US$21) for adults and C$23 (US$16) for seniors and children 13 to 18; children under 12 ride free. Summer-season passes are C$169 (US$121). Saturday nights are a special treat during the summer, when Blackcomb Mountain conducts **weekly guided stargazing and moonrise tours.** For information on other summer activities and weather conditions, contact **Guest Experience** at ☎ **604/938-7747.**

During winter, lift tickets are C$49 (US$35) per day for either mountain or C$51 (US$36) per day for a dual-mountain pass. A 3-day dual-mountain pass is C$138 (US$99), and 4- and 6-day dual-mountain passes are available for C$180 to C$220 (US$129 to US$157).

There are well-marked, fully groomed cross-country trails throughout the area. For example, the 30 kilometers (18 miles) of easy to very-difficult marked trails at **Lost Lake** actually start a block away from the Blackcomb Mountain parking lot. They're groomed for track skiing and for ski-skating. Passes are C$8 (US$6); a 1-hour cross-country lesson runs about C$35 (US$25). The **Valley Trail System** in the village becomes a well-marked cross-country ski trail during the winter (see "Hiking," below). **Garibaldi Provincial Park** (☎ 604/898-3678) maintains marked, groomed trails at **Singing Pass** and **Cheakamus Lake.** On Highway 99 north of Mount Currie, **Joffre Lakes Provincial Park** is a tranquil, forested area with a few trails that wind deep into the forest and circle the glacial lakes.

OTHER OUTDOOR ACTIVITIES

BIKING   Some of the best mountain-bike trails in the village are on Whistler and Blackcomb mountains. It's not unusual to see bikers loading into the gondolas at both lifts during the summer (see "Hitting the Slopes," above). Some of the backcountry trails at Lost Lake (see "Hiking," below) are also marked for mountain biking. Lift tickets at both mountains range from C$19 to C$30 (US$14 to US$21) per day, and discounted season mountain-bike passes are available. You can rent a mountain bike from **Blackcomb Ski & Sports,** Blackcomb Mountain Day Lodge, Upper Village (☎ 604/938-7788); **Trax & Trails,** Chateau Whistler Hotel, 4599 Chateau Blvd., Upper Village (☎ 604/938-2017); **The Whistler Bike Company,** Delta Whistler Resort, 4050 Whistler Way, Whistler Village (☎ 604/938-9511); and **McCoo's Too,** Whistler Village Centre, Whistler Village (☎ 604/938-9954). Prices range from C$7 (US$5) for an hour to C$30 (US$21) per day.

CANOEING & KAYAKING   The 3-hour River of Golden Dreams Kayak & Canoe Tour offered by **Whistler Sailing & Water Sports Centre Ltd.** (☎ 604/932-7245; mailing address: Box 1130, Whistler, BC, V0N 1B0) is a great way for novices, intermediates, and experts to get acquainted with an exhilarating stretch of racing glacial water that runs between Green Lake and Alta Lake behind the village of Whistler. Packages range from C$29 (US$21) per single kayak to C$45 (US$32) per canoe, double kayak, or pair of single kayaks. Prices include all gear and return transportation to the village center.

FISHING   Spring runs of steelhead, rainbow trout, and Dolly Varden char, summer runs of cutthroat and salmon, and fall runs of coho salmon attract anglers from around the world to the many glacier-fed lakes and rivers in the area and to **Birkenhead Lake Provincial Park,** 66.6 kilometers (40 miles) north of Pemberton. Bring your favorite fly rod and don't forget to buy a fishing license at **Whistler Backcountry Adventures,** 36–4314 Main St., Whistler (☎ 604/932-3474). **Whistler River Adventures** (see "Jet Boating," below), **Sea to Sky Reel Adventures** (☎ 604/894-6928 or 604/905-7058; mailing address: Box 776, Pemberton, BC, V0N 2L0), and **Off the Beaten Track Wilderness Expeditions** (☎ 604/938-9282; mailing address: Box 1085, Whistler, BC, V0N 1B0) offer half-day and full-day catch-and-release fishing trips in the surrounding glacier rivers. Rates range from C$99 to C$250 (US$71 to US$179) per person, which includes all fishing gear, transport to and from the Whistler Village Bus Loop, and a snack or lunch.

GOLFING Robert Trent Jones's **Chateau Whistler Golf Club,** at the base of Blackcomb Mountain (☎ **604/938-2092,** or 604/938-2095 for pro shop), is an 18-hole, par-72 course with a gradual 300-foot ascent on the first few holes, which overlook cascading creeks and granite rock faces. Midcourse, there's a panoramic view of the Coast Mountains. Greens fees range from C$74 to C$114 (US$53 to US$81), which includes power cart rental. **Nicklaus North at Whistler** (☎ **604/938-9898**) is a 5-minute drive north of the village on the shores of Green Lake. The par-71 course's mountain views are spectacular. Greens fees range from C$75 to C$108 (US$54 to US$77).

A-1 Last Minute Golf Hotline (☎ **800/684-6344** or 604/878-1833) can arrange a next-day tee time at Whistler golf courses. Savings can be as much as 40% on next-day, last-minute tee times. No membership is necessary. Call between 3pm and 9pm for the next day or before noon for the same day.

The **Harvest Club,** 2725 KLO Rd., Kelowna, BC, V1W 4S1 (☎ **250/ 862-3101**), has an 18-hole, par-72 course, with a pro shop and two restaurants. The greens fee is C$70 (US$49).

HIKING There are numerous easy hiking trails in and around Whistler. Besides taking a lift up to Whistler and Blackcomb Mountain's high mountain trails during the summer (see "Hitting the Slopes," above), you have a number of other choices.

Lost Lake Trail starts at the northern end of the Day Skier Parking Lot at Blackcomb Mountain. The lake is less than a mile from the entry. The 30 kilometers (18 miles) of marked trails that wind around creeks, beaver dams, blueberry patches, and lush cedar groves are ideal for biking, Nordic skiing, or just strolling and picnicking.

The **Valley Trail System** is a well-marked, paved trail that connects parts of Whistler. The trail starts on the west side of Highway 99 adjacent to the Whistler Golf Course and winds through quiet, residential areas as well as golf courses and parks.

Garibaldi Provincial Park's **Singing Pass Trail** is a 4-hour hike of moderate difficulty. The fun way to experience this trail is to take the Whistler Mountain gondola to the top and walk down the well-marked path that ends in the village on an access road. Winding down from above the tree line, the trail takes you through stunted alpine forest into Fitzsimmons Valley.

Nairn Falls Provincial Park is 33.3 kilometers (20 miles) north of Whistler on Highway 99. This provincial park features a 1.6-kilometer-long (mile-long) trail that leads you to a stupendous view of the icy-cold Green River as it plunges 196 feet over a rocky cliff into a narrow gorge on its way downstream. There's also an incredible view of Mount Currie peeking over the treetops.

The **Ancient Cedars** area of Cougar Mountain is an awe-inspiring grove of towering cedars and Douglas firs. (Some of the trees are over 1,000 years old and measure 9 feet in diameter.) This 4-kilometer (2.5-mile) hike can be made even more exciting by taking a Land Rover 4x4 up the backcountry route. **Off the Beaten Track Wilderness Expeditions** (see "Fishing," above) offers this unique off-road experience and provides a knowledgeable guide and snacks. Three- and 6-hour tours depart from the Whistler Village Bus Loop. Prices range from C$59 to C$89 (US$42 to US$63) per person.

HORSEBACK RIDING **Whistler River Adventures** (see "Jet Boating," below) offers 90-minute and 3-hour trail rides along the Green River, through the forest, and across the Pemberton Valley from its 10-acre riverside facility in nearby Pemberton. Shuttle service takes riders out to the site from the Whistler Mountain Village Gondola Base. Prices range from C$45 to C$90 (US$32 to US$64) per person.

JET BOATING   Whistler River Adventures, Whistler Mountain Village Gondola Base (☎ **604/932-3532;** fax 604/932-3559; e-mail: raftnjet@whistler.net; mailing address: Box 202, Whistler, BC, V0N 1B0), takes guests up the Green River just below Nairn Falls, where moose, deer, and bear sightings are common in the sheer-granite canyon. The Lillooet River tour goes past ancient petroglyphs, fishing sites, and the tiny native-Indian village of Skookumchuk.

Whistler Jet Boating Company Ltd. (☎ **800/303-BOAT** or 604/894-5200) runs sightseers down the icy rapids of the Green River or speed-cruising through the Lillooet River valley throughout the summer. Tours by both companies range from hour-long trips for C$55 (US$39) to 4-hour cruises for C$109 (US$78). Discounts for children 3 to 12 are available.

RAFTING   Whistler River Adventures (see "Jet Boating," above) offers 2-hour and full-day round-trip rafting runs down the Green River that include equipment and ground transport for C$47 to C$119 (US$34 to US$85). Novices are taken to the Green River, where small rapids and snowcapped mountain views highlight a half-day trip. Experts are transported to the Birkenhead River for half-day runs and the Elaho or Squamish rivers for full-day, Class 4 excitement on runs with names like Aitons Alley and Steamroller. From May to August, trips depart at 9:30am, 12:30pm, and 4pm. The company also conducts 3-hour round-trip jet-boat tours of the river for C$63 (US$45) per person, which includes ground transport and wet suit.

For first-timers, **Wedge Rafting,** Carleton Lodge, Whistler Village (☎ **604/ 932-3288;** e-mail: wedge@whistlernet.com; mailing address: Box 453, Whistler, BC, V0N 1B0), offers a Green River Tour. The entire trip takes about 3 hours. The shuttle picks rafters up in Whistler and takes them to the wilderness launch area for briefing and equipping. It's an exciting hour or more on the icy, bubbling rapids of the Green River. After the run, rafters can relax at the outfitter's log lodge for a snack and soda before being shuttled back into town. Tours cost C$48 (US$34) and depart at 9am, noon, and 3:30pm daily.

TENNIS   Whistler Racquet & Golf Resort, 4500 Northland Blvd. (☎ **604/ 932-1991;** e-mail whisracq@whistler.net), features three covered courts, seven outdoor courts, and a practice cage, all open to drop-in visitors. Adult and junior tennis camps are offered during the summer. Camp prices range from C$36 (US$26) per day to C$353 (US$252) per week. **Mountain Spa & Tennis Club,** Delta Whistler Resort, Whistler Village (☎ **604/938-2044**), and the **Chateau Whistler Resort,** Chateau Whistler Hotel, Upper Village (☎ **604/938-8000**), also offer courts to drop-in players. There are **free public courts** (☎ **604/938-PARK**) at Myrtle Public School, Alpha Lake Park, Meadow Park, Millar's Pond, Brio, Blackcomb Benchlands, White Gold, and Emerald Park.

ACCOMMODATIONS

Whistler Village and the Upper Village offer you a choice of more than 1,000 self-contained accommodations. The one- to four-bedroom, fully furnished and equipped condos, town houses, and chalets are available year-round. Prices range from C$60 to C$1,400 (US$43 to US$1,000) per night. **Whistler Chalets and Accommodations Ltd.,** 4360 Lorimer Rd., Whistler, V0N 1B0 (☎ **800/663-7711** in Canada, or 604/932-6699; Web site: www.whistlerchalets.com), and **Rainbow Retreats Accommodations Ltd.,** 2129 Lake Placid Rd., Whistler, BC, V0N 1B0 (☎ **604/ 932-2343;** Web site: www.whistler.net/rainbow) have many properties to suit every budget and group size. Make reservations for the winter season before September.

The park service maintains two campgrounds in **Garibaldi Provincial Park.** Ten kilometers (6 miles) north of Squamish is the campground that Vancouverites have rated as their favorite weekend getaway: **Alice Lake** off Highway 99 (☎ 604/898-3678). Its 88 campsites are considered the most family-friendly in the province. Free hot showers, flush toilets, and a sani-station are just the beginning of a long list of available facilities. Hiking trails, picnic areas, sandy beaches, swimming areas, and fishing spots are all on the grounds. Sites are C$15.50 (US$11) per night.

Twenty-six kilometers (16 miles) north of Whistler, the campground at **Nairn Falls** on Highway 99 (☎ 604/898-3678) is more adult-oriented, with pit toilets, pumped well water, fire pits, and firewood, but no showers. Its proximity to the roaring Green River and the town of Pemberton makes it appealing to many hikers, and the sound of the river is sweeter than any lullaby. Prices for the 88 campsites are C$9.50 (US$7) per night.

✪ **Canadian Pacific Chateau Whistler Resort.** 4599 Chateau Blvd., Whistler, BC, V0N 1B4. ☎ 800/441-1414 in the U.S., 800/606-8244 in Canada, or 604/938-8000. Fax 604/938-2055. 516 rms, 47 suites. MINIBAR TV TEL. Summer C$299–C$335 (US$214–US$239) double; C$425–C$1,000 (US$304–US$714) suite. Winter C$385–C$435 (US$275–US$311) double; C$570–C$1,200 (US$407–US$857) suite. AE, ER, MC, V. Underground valet parking C$15 (US$11).

This Upper Village hotel provides sterling service and excellent accommodations, and is ideally situated right next to the Blackcomb Mountain ski lift. The rooms and suites feature double-, queen-, and king-size beds, down duvets, bathrobes, comfortable sitting areas, wonderful views, and spacious marble-tiled bathrooms. The decor highlights the country-style textile prints and artwork in each room. The split-level, 1^1/$_2$-bath executive suites with dining areas and fireplaces offer mesmerizing views from supertall windows. The lobby resembles a gigantic stone-and-wood hunting chalet that's filled with country-style Canadian antiques. Wheelchair-accessible rooms are available.

Dining/Entertainment: The after-ski Mallard Bar has a great view of the Blackcomb lifts. With comfy armchairs and sofas, a warm, relaxed ambiance, cocktails, coffee, and light meals, it's the quintessential civilized après-ski spot. The village's best buffet-style brunch (C$16.95/US$12 per person, C$8.50/US$6 for children 6 to 12) is served daily in the Wildflower Restaurant from 7am 11pm.

Services: Concierge, room service, coffee service.

Facilities: Ski and bike storage, full-service spa, massage therapy, heated indoor/outdoor pool, sauna, whirlpool, steam room, and weight room. Terrace barbecue, pool deck, rooftop garden terrace with gazebo and outdoor fire pits, tennis courts, and an 18-hole, par-72 golf course on the grounds.

Cedar Springs Bed & Breakfast Lodge. 8106 Cedar Springs Rd., Whistler, BC, V0N 1B8. ☎ 604/938-8007. Fax 604/938-8023. 9 rms (5 with bath), 1 suite. C$60–C$119 (US$43–US$85) double; C$169 (US$121) suite. Rates include full breakfast. MC, V. Take Hwy. 99 north toward Pemberton 4km (2.4 miles) past Whistler Village. Turn left onto Alpine Way. Drive 1 block to Rainbow Dr. and turn left. Drive 1 block to Camino St. The lodge is 1 block down at the corner of Camino and Cedar Springs Rd.

Rooms at this charming modern lodge have a choice of king-, queen-, or twin-size beds. The honeymoon suite has a fireplace, balcony, and private bath. The guest sitting room has a TV, VCR, and video library. The gourmet breakfast is served in the dining room by the fireside. Owners Joerne and Jacqueline Rohde can also provide box lunches and special-occasion dinners at this warm, cozy hideaway.

✪ **Durlacher Hof Pension Inn.** 7055 Nesters Rd. (Box 1125), Whistler, BC, V0N 1B0. ☎ 604/932-1924. Fax 604/938-1980. 8 rms. C$110–C$195 (US$79–US$139) double.

Extra person C$30 (US$21). Rates include full breakfast and afternoon tea. Summer discounts. MC, V. Free parking. Take Hwy. 99 north 0.8km (0.5 mile) north of Whistler Village to Nester's Village. Turn left and the inn is immediately on the right.

Owners Peter and Erika Durlacher have a lovely Austrian mountain chalet that fits perfectly with its surroundings. Guests will feel completely spoiled by the fine European service, decor, and cuisine. Each room has a goose-down duvet on the extra-long twin- or queen-size bed and an incredible mountain view from a private balcony. The licensed cocktail lounge has a welcoming fireplace. On selected nights, dinners are offered for an additional charge, and they're often prepared by a celebrated guest chef. There are a sauna and whirlpool on the premises.

DINING

A number of Vancouver-based restaurants have branched out to Whistler. A quick meal for gourmets on the go can be found at **Chef Bernard's,** 4573 Chateau Blvd., Whistler Village (☎ **604/932-7051**). It serves full breakfasts, soups, salads, and sandwiches, as well as hot entrees—like quiche, chicken with penne, cannelloni, and an incredible fried meat-loaf sandwich topped with mushroom-and-red-wine sauce, cambozola cheese, and a side of roasted garlic mashed potatoes—for C$4.95 to C$8.25 (US$3.55 to US$6). It's open daily from 7am to 5pm.

Citta Bistro, in Whistler Village Square (☎ **604/932-4177**), is the locals' favorite dining- and nightspot. It serves thin-crust pizzas like the Californian Herb, topped with spiced chicken breast, sun-dried tomatoes, fresh pesto, and mozzarella; gourmet burgers like the Citta Extraordinaire, topped with bacon, cheddar, garlic mushrooms, and Dijon-pepper mayonnaise; and finger foods like bruschetta, spring rolls, and nachos. Besides having great food and good prices (main courses range from C$6.95 to C$10.95/US$4.95 to US$8), it has umbrella-covered tables on the terrace, the best people-watching corner in town.

✪ **Araxi Ristorante.** 4222 Village Sq., Whistler. ☎ **604/932-4540.** Main courses C$10.95–C$26.95 (US$8–US$19). AE, MC, V. Daily 11am–10:30pm. ITALIAN.

In the heart of the village square, this lovely Italian restaurant might remind you of the elegant alfresco establishments of Rome or Venice. Diners relax at the cocktail bar inside while waiting for a prime table outside on the patio or in the romantic main dining room. For starters, try the grilled portobello mushroom served on a bed of arugula and topped with a port-and-red-wine reduction and shaved Romano cheese. Then choose one of the captivating pasta dishes such as oven-cured tomato fettuccine served with fresh mussels and a fennel-scented cream sauce. Or try a plate of delicately sautéed medaillons of venison topped with a sun-dried cherry and port-wine sauce accompanied by garlic mashed yams, braised cabbage, and pea greens. The tiramisu—a luscious concoction of lady fingers soaked in espresso and layered with a coffee-liqueur-laced mascarpone cream—is only one of the restaurant's signature desserts.

Monk's Grill. 4555 Blackcomb Way (at the Blackcomb ski lifts), Whistler. ☎ **604/932-9677.** Main courses C$9.25–C$18.95 (US$7–US$14). Daily 11am–2am. Brunch Sat–Sun 11am–2pm. AE, DC, MC, V. CANADIAN.

Besides having a spectacular view of the busy Blackcomb Mountain slopes, Monk's has a menu that offers everything from ocean-fresh salmon and oysters, "25¢ a piece" steamed prawns, slow-roasted Alberta prime rib, and grilled steaks, to pasta dishes and salads. There's seating in the formal dining area, in the casual Mountainside Lounge, on the outdoor patios, and in the bar where there are pool tables and a wide array of draft ales and lagers, including a few outstanding local brews.

WHISTLER AFTER DARK

Citta's (see "Dining," above) is the local gathering place. Start your evening sipping a cocktail or having a quick meal before heading around the corner to the **Savage Beagle,** 4222 Village Sq., Whistler Village (☎ **604/938-3337**), a theme-based night-club that features DJs and live bands. (The latest Sunday-night special features salsa and Latin-beat sounds spun by Tio Roly.) **Barefoot Bistro,** 4122 Village Green (☎ **604/932-6613**), draws a lively local crowd and occasionally offers live entertainment by the likes of Melissa Etheridge, Edgar Winter, and the Tragically Hip. Tuesday is comedy night, and the sizable drinks start at C$3 (US$2.15).

11 Wells Gray Provincial Park & Shuswap Lakes

The High Country's landscape is arid and hilly in the lowlands along the Trans-Canada Highway (Highway 1), which follows the shores of the lower Thompson River and Shuswap Lakes. The acres of undulating sheets of black mesh draped along the hillsides are actually shading field after field of cultivated ginseng.

The **Shuswap Lakes** are popular with houseboaters. It's easy to navigate the region's 1,000 kilometers (600 miles) of waterways, landing at campsites and beaches along the way that are accessible only by boat. The Adams River sockeye-salmon run is an annual event, but the dominant runs that occur every 4 years are worth the wait (the next one is due in 1998). Rent a houseboat in the nearby town of **Salmon Arm** (pop. 15,034), then spend a relaxing vacation at one of the area's marine parks.

Rising up from this dry terrain, heading north along Highway 5, the road enters the cool, green forests of the High Country. And high above the town of **Clearwater** (pop. 5,500) is the pristine wilderness of **Wells Gray Provincial Park.** The cascading waters of **Helmcken Falls** and **Dawson Falls** are not the only natural wonders you'll find in the 3,211,000-acre wilderness. Drive up the winding dirt road to the **Green Point Observatory** for a perfect overview of the park from the three-story wooden observation tower.

ESSENTIALS

VISITOR INFORMATION   Contact the **High Country Tourism Association,** 2–1490 Pearson Place, Kamloops, BC, V1S 1J9 (☎ **250/372-7770**); it's open Monday to Friday from 8am to 4:30pm. The **Clearwater Visitor Info Centre,** 425 E. Yellowhead Hwy. 5 (mailing address: Box 1988, RR #1), Clearwater, BC, V0E 1N0 (☎ **250/674-2646**), at the intersection of Highway 5 and Wells Gray Park Road, is open October 16 to April 14, Monday to Saturday from 9am to 5pm; April 15 to June 30 and September 1 to October 15, daily from 9am to 6pm; July 1 to September 1, daily from 8am to 8pm. The **Salmon Arm Visitor Info Centre,** 751 Marine Park Dr. NE (mailing address: Box 999), Salmon Arm, BC, V1E 4P2 (☎ **250/832-2230**) is open September 2 to May 30, Monday to Friday from 9am to 5pm, and June 1 to September 1, daily from 9am to 5pm. The staff can help with travel plans throughout the Shuswap Lakes region.

GETTING THERE   You need a car to explore the best areas of the High Country, especially Wells Gray Provincial Park.

By Car   To get to **Wells Gray Provincial Park** from Quesnel, take Highway 97 south to 100 Mile House. Follow the signs to Highway 24 east. Partially paved and well-maintained, Highway 24 runs through the small towns of Lone Butte and Bridge Lake before arriving in Little Fort, 83.3 kilometers (50 miles) farther. At Little Fort, take the Yellowhead Highway (Highway 5) north 31.6 kilometers (19 miles) to Clearwater.

To get to the **Shuswap Lakes** from Vancouver, take the Trans-Canada Highway (Highway 1) through Cache Creek and Kamloops to Chase (about 420km/252 miles) or Salmon Arm (473.3km/284 miles), in the heart of the Shuswap Lakes region.

From the Okanagan Valley, take Highway 97 north, pick up the Trans-Canada Highway just outside Kamloops, then head east 58.3 kilometers (35 miles) to Chase.

By Plane & Car You can fly into Kamloops, a 50-minute flight from Vancouver, and rent a car at the airport. **Air BC** (☎ 604/688-5515) and **Canadian Regional Airlines** (☎ 800/426-7000 in the U.S. or 800/363-7530 in Canada) operate daily flights. The major car-rental firms have desks at the airport.

SPECIAL EVENTS The **Reino Keski-Salmo Loppet** (☎ 250/832-7740) attracts cross-country skiers from across North America to the Larch Hills Cross-Country Ski Hill in Salmon Arm during the second week in January.

The **Wells Gray Loppet** (☎ 250/674-3657) in Wells Gray Provincial Park during the first week of February is a doubly enjoyable event for cross-country skiers. The hilly 41.6-kilometer (26-mile) course attracts more contestants in all age groups and levels each year, and the scenery is spectacular.

The annual **Salmon Arm Bluegrass Festival** (☎ 250/832-3258), in Salmon Arm's R. J. Haney Heritage Park during the first weekend in July, features performers from Canada, the United States, and Europe.

Departing from a different Cariboo ranch each year, the annual ✪ **Charity Cattle Drive,** Box 1332, Kamloops, BC, V2C 6L7 (☎ 250/372-7075; e-mail: cattledr@mail.netshop.net), has grown immensely popular over the past 7 years. More than 1,000 people participate in the 8-day ride during the second week in July. Cattle, cowboys, and visitors from around the world ride through the High Country's rolling prairies for 5 days, finishing with a grand arrival and a big party in Kamloops. Horses, gear, and even seats on the chuck wagons are available for rent.

One of nature's most amazing phenomena, the **Adams River Salmon Run,** takes place annually in late October. Every 4 years, an estimated 1.5 to 2 million sockeye salmon struggle upstream to spawn in the Adams River near Squilax. These "dominant" runs have recently occurred in 1990 and 1994. The 1998 and 2002 runs are projected to be even larger. Trails provide riverside viewing. A "Salute to Salmon" program is scheduled, with displays and trained staff in attendance to interpret this spectacle. Take the Trans-Canada Highway (Highway 1) to Squilax (about 10km/ 6 miles east of Chase). Follow the signs north to Roderick Haig-Brown Provincial Park.

EXPLORING WELLS GRAY PROVINCIAL PARK

Established in 1939, **Wells Gray Provincial Park** (☎ 604/371-6400) is British Columbia's second-largest park, encompassing more than 1.3 million acres of virgin wilderness: mountains, rivers, volcanic formations and outcroppings, lakes, glaciers, forests, and alpine meadows. Wildlife abounds, including mule deer, moose, caribou, grizzly and black bears, beaver, coyote, rufous hummingbirds (we saw 26 in a single morning), timber wolves, mink, wolverine, marmot, and golden eagles.

Twice as tall as Niagara Falls, the park's **Helmcken Falls** is an awesome sight that can be reached by paved road. So can the broad cascade known as **Dawson Falls.** Boating, canoeing, kayaking, and fishing are popular pastimes on **Clearwater** and **Azure Lakes, Mahood Lake,** and **Murtle Lake.** The wilderness campgrounds along the lakes make perfect destinations for overnight canoe or fishing trips.

We've spent days exploring the area around Ray Farm Homestead, and hiked up the trail to Rays Mineral Spring and along the thickly forested **Murtle River Trail.** It leads to **Majerus Falls, Horsehoe Falls,** and **Pyramid Mountain,** a volcanic upgrowth that was shaped when it erupted beneath miles of glacial ice that covered the park millions of years ago.

TOURS & EXCURSIONS

Besides excellent accommodations, **Trophy Mountain Buffalo Ranch** and **Wells Gray Park Backcountry Chalets** (see "Accommodations," below) offer half-day to weeklong horseback-riding, cross-country skiing, and hiking trips. Prices start at C$35 (US$25) per person for a couple of hours at both companies.

Wells Gray Guest Ranch, Wells Gray Road (mailing address: RR #1, Box 1766), Clearwater (☎ **250/674-2774** or 250/674-2792), offers guided trips and packages that include hiking, canoeing, white-water rafting, fishing, mountain biking, and motorboating (on Clearwater and Azure lakes) during summer; and dogsledding, cross-country skiing, downhill skiing, snowshoeing, snowmobiling, and ice fishing during the winter. Excursions range from half-day to weeklong trips.

Crazy Moon Enterprises, Helmcken Falls Lodge, Wells Gray Road, Clearwater (☎ **250/674-3657**), offers half- and full-day guided hikes and canoeing trips through the park and environs.

Interior Whitewater Expeditions (☎ **250/674-3727**) conducts a variety of rafting and kayaking packages, ranging from half-day to 5-day trips, on some of the wildest, most beautiful stretches of the North Thompson River.

ACCOMMODATIONS

Most campers head to Wells Gray Provincial Park's **Spahats, Clearwater,** and **Dawson Falls campgrounds** (☎ **250/851-3000**). Only 88 available sites are in the park, so check the sign outside the Clearwater Visitor Info Centre to make sure the grounds aren't full before driving all the way up to the park. Sites are C$9.50 (US$7) per night. Facilities include fire pits, firewood, pumped well water, pit toilets, and boat launches at the lakes.

✪ **Nakiska Ranch.** Trout Creek Rd. (off Wells Gray Park Rd.), Clearwater, BC, V0E 1N0. ☎ and fax **604/674-3655.** 4 rms, 2 cabins. Summer C$85 (US$61) double; C$85–C$165 (US$61–US$118) cabin. Winter C$69 (US$49) double; C$85–C$135 (US$61–US$96) cabin. Rates include full breakfast. MC, V. Drive up Wells Gray Park Rd. for 41.6km (25 miles). The road actually takes about 40 min. to drive. Turn right at the ranch sign onto Trout Creek Rd.

Gorgeous log cabins, acres of mowed meadows, and Wells Gray's majestic forests and mountains surround the main log house on this working ranch. The RUSTIC CABINS sign at the entrance describes only the exteriors of these pristine hideaways. The immaculate interiors of both the lodge and the individual cabins are straight out of the pages of *House Beautiful,* featuring open kitchens, hardwood floors and walls, lots of windows, and Scandinavian-style wood furnishings. The two-story cabins can sleep up to six comfortably. Breakfast is served in the lodge house, but you must bring your own groceries for lunches and dinners. The lodge guests can ask for access to the large house kitchen. (It's a 30-minute drive to the nearest restaurant or store.) The park entrance is a 10-minute drive from the ranch.

✪ **Trophy Mountain Buffalo Ranch Bed & Breakfast & Campground.** RR #1 (mailing address: P.O. Box 1768), Clearwater, BC, V0E 1N0. ☎ **250/674-3095.** Fax 250/674-3131. 4 rms (2 with private bath), 20 campsites, 4 camping cabins. C$45–C$60 (US$32–US$43) double; C$13.50–C$16.50 (US$10–$12) campsite; C$11 (US$8) cabin. Rm rates include breakfast. MC, V. Drive up Wells Gray Park Rd. for 33.3km (20 miles). The road actually takes about 30 min. to drive. Turn left at the ranch sign.

You can't miss the small buffalo herd casually grazing in a fenced pasture as you drive up the Wells Gray Park Road. Beyond this pastoral setting stand a log lodge, campsites, and four cabins nestled in the woodlands. The four lodge rooms are cozy and clean, featuring warm comforters and soft pillows. A hearty breakfast welcomes you in the dining room. The camping cabins, tent sites, and separate RV sites are also extremely well kept. Dishwashing sinks are set up on the deck of the shower house, where hot water flows liberally. There's plenty of free firewood; fire-pit grills are available for a nominal fee. Hiking and horseback-riding trails surround the ranch. In fact, horses are available for rent, and guided trail rides run through the forest to the cliffs overlooking the Clearwater River valley and to the base of a secluded 115-foot waterfall. Prices start at C$43 (US$31) for a 2¹/₂-hour trip. If you get a sudden urge to venture deep into the woods near Trophy Mountain, your hosts can give you directions and outfit you with rental gear, from canoes and tents to cookware.

Wells Gray Park Backcountry Chalets. Box 188G, Clearwater, BC, V0E 1N0. ☎ **888/ SKI-TREK** or 250/587-6444. Fax 604/587-6446. 3 chalets. Chalet only, summer C$25 (US$18) per person; winter C$33 (US$24) per person. MC, V. Drive up Wells Gray Park Rd. for 36.6km (22 miles). The road actually takes about 35 min. to drive. Turn left at the ranch sign.

Ian Eakins and Tay Briggs run a family-owned outdoor guiding company that maintains three year-round chalets nestled deep in the park. The chalets sleep up to 12 people and are fully equipped with kitchens, furniture, bedding, books, a sauna, and propane-generated lighting and heat. It's the best of both worlds: You can experience untrammeled wilderness and great rural hospitality. Two of the nicest people you could hope to have as guides and hosts, Ian and Tay are very knowledgeable about the wildlife and history of the park. They offer guided or self-catered hiking and cross-country ski packages that include stays in these backcountry hideaways as well as guided 3-day and 6-day canoe trips on Clearwater and Azure lakes in Wells Gray Provincial Park that are custom-built for families. Fully catered and guided trips are available in 3- to 8-day packages. Summer hikes are C$100 (US$71) per person per day; winter cross-country ski trips are C$110 (US$79) per person per day.

DINING

There aren't many restaurants in Clearwater. Campers usually stock up on provisions at the **Safety Mart,** Brookfield Mall, Old North Thompson Highway, Clearwater. It's open daily from 9am to 6pm. The **Chuckwagon Restaurant & Saloon,** Old North Thompson Highway (☎ 250/674-3636), serves decent diner-style basics like roast turkey, burgers, and lasagna at reasonable prices. The **Helmcken Falls Lodge,** Wells Gray Park Road, Clearwater (☎ 250/674-3657), and the **Wells Gray Guest Ranch,** Wells Gray Park Road, Clearwater (☎ 250/674-2774), offer buffet-style dinners at 7pm sharp daily for C$21 (US$15) per person.

AFTER DARK

Clearwater's nightlife consists of two saloons. The **Wells Gray Guest Ranch Saloon,** Wells Gray Park Road, Clearwater (☎ 250/674-2774), is open daily from 4pm to midnight. It's a great place to share stories of world travels with the many Swiss and German hikers who frequent this area. The **Chuckwagon Saloon,** Old North Thompson Highway (☎ 250/674-3636), attracts a local crowd, including ranchers, fishermen, and farmers. There's a huge covered porch where you can enjoy the cool evening air and a pint of ale.

EXPLORING THE SHUSWAP LAKES

One of the world's greatest natural wonders, the **Adams River Sockeye Salmon Run,** takes place in this area annually. Millions of crimson fish fight their way upstream from the Pacific Ocean to spawn in the placid Shuswap waters at the Roderick Haig-Brown Provincial Park. Once every 4 years the run reaches an unbelievable level. The next major peak is expected in 1998. (See "Special Events," above).

Fishing and boating are the area's biggest lures. With 1,000 kilometers (600 miles) of shoreline filled with sandy beaches, private coves, and narrow channels, visitors come to while away the summer days aboard houseboats or fishing charters, enjoying the tranquil beauty of the lakes.

SPORTS & OUTDOOR ACTIVITIES

BIKING   In the **Shuswap Lakes** region of the High Country, off-road trails lead you through the hilly terrain surrounding the beautiful lakes and rivers, which also attract houseboaters and anglers. Nearby **Full Boar Mountain Bike Tours,** Kamloops (☎ 250/376-5532), rents mountain bikes and offers half-day to multiday guided trips through the area. Prices start at C$35 (US$25) for a 1-day rental; guided trips start at C$75 (US$54) per person for a half-day trip.

FISHING   To fish here, you need a nonresident freshwater license. Pick up copies of *BC Tidal Waters Sport Fishing Guide* and *BC Sport Fishing Regulations Synopsis for Non-Tidal Waters.* Independent anglers should also pick up a copy of the *BC Fishing Directory and Atlas.* For licenses, equipment, and advice, try **Wilderness Outfitters,** 1304 Battle St., Kamloops (☎ 604/327-2127). An authorized Orvis shop, it stocks a great selection of rods, reels, flies, and tying supplies. It's open Monday to Saturday from 9am to 5:30pm.

GOLFING   The **Salmon Arm Golf Club,** 3641 Hwy. 97B SE, Salmon Arm (☎ 250/832-4727; e-mail: sagolf@jetstream.net) is an 18-hole, par-72, 6,738-yard course. **Shuswap Lakes Estate Golf & Country Club,** 2404 Centen-nial Rd., Sorrento (☎ 800/661-3955 in Canada, or 250/675-2315), offers an 18-hole, par-71, 6,438-yard course. Greens fees at both start at C$65 (US$46) per person. **Quaaout Lodge,** Little Shuswap Lake Road (mailing address: Box 1215), Chase (☎ 250/679-3090), offers an 18-hole course as well as deluxe resort accommodations and dining at its lodge. Golf packages start at C$65 (US$46) per person.

HIKING   On the northern shore of Shuswap Lake near the town of Squilax, **Shuswap Lake Provincial Park** (☎ 250/851-3000) was the site of a gold-mining operation during the 1930s and 1940s. The original mineral-bearing creek no longer flows through this rich delta, but the area offers wonderful strolling, with abundant old-growth ponderosa pines and second-growth red cedar and Douglas fir.

About a mile offshore, **Copper Island** has a pleasant circular trail that leads to a high point where boaters looking for a dry-land hiking experience can survey the lake and surrounding countryside, and catch a glimpse of the many mule deer that inhabit the island.

SKIING   **Sun Peaks Resort,** Tod Mountain Road, Heffley Creek (☎ 250/578-7232, or 250/578-7232 for snow report), is a great powder-skiing and open-run area with a vertical rise of 2,854 feet. The 63 runs are serviced by one high-speed quad chair with bubble cover, one fixed-grip quad chair, one triple chair, one double chair, one T-bar, and one beginner platter. Snowboarders have a choice of two half pipes, one with a superlarge boarder-cross. At the bottom of this 3,000-foot run are handrails, cars, a fun box, hips, quarter pipes, burly tabletops, transfers, and fat gaps that were designed by Ecosign Mountain Planners and some of Canada's top amateur riders. Cross-country and snowmobile trails are also available. Lift tickets are C$41 (US$29) for adults, C$36 (US$26) for children over 12, and C$23 (US$16) for children under 12.

ACCOMMODATIONS & DINING

The 280 campsites at **Shuswap Lake Provincial Park** (☎ 250/851-3000), 31.6 kilometers (19 miles) northeast of Highway 1 at Squilax, cost C$15.50 (US$11) per night. Facilities include free hot showers, flush toilets, a playground, and a nature house. The 35 sites at **Silver Beach Provincial Park** (☎ 250/851-3000) are accessible by an unpaved road from the town of Anglemount, by ferry from Sicamous, or by boating to the north end of Seymour Arm. Facilities include pit toilets and fire pits; sites are C$7 (US$5) per night. And there are 51 campsites at **Herald Provincial Park** (☎ 250/851-3000), 15 kilometers (9 miles) northeast of Highway 1 at Tappen. Facilities include free hot showers, pit toilets, a sani-station, and a boat launch. Sites are C$15.50 (US$11) per night.

Quaaout Lodge. Little Shuswap Lake Rd. (mailing address: Box 1215), Chase, BC, V0E 1M0. ☎ 800/663-4303 or 250/679-3090. Fax 604/679-3039. 72 rms. TV TEL. C$103–C$135 (US$74–US$96) double. AE, MC, V. On the Trans-Canada Hwy. (Hwy. 1), drive through the town of Chase. About 16km (10 miles) east, turn left at the Squilax Bridge underpass. Take the overpass and the lodge is on the first road on the left.

This gorgeous resort draws heavily on native-Indian tradition in its design and decor. Set on the sandy shores of Little Shuswap Lake, it is owned and operated by the Shuswap band of the Secwepemc tribe, who built it in 1992. Six of the well-appointed rooms have fireplaces and Jacuzzis.

Dining: The hotel's excellent licensed restaurant offers a menu featuring many traditional dishes, including alder-smoked salmon, grilled duck breast with wild rice, venison, and a fluffy fried bread called bannock.

Facilities: Indoor pool, Jacuzzi, fully equipped gym, 18-hole golf course (See "Golfing," above), and saunas. Hiking and biking trails, fishing, cross-country skiing, canoeing, and a playground (adventurous kids can opt to spend a night in a large teepee provided by the lodge). Rental canoes and mountain bikes are available at the lodge.

HOUSEBOATING

The best way to see the lakes is to rent a houseboat for a few days. After all, Shuswap is the "Houseboating Capital of Canada." For C$125 to C$531 (US$89 to US$379) per day you can rent a fully equipped houseboat that sleeps up to 10 people. **Three Buoys Houseboat Vacations,** 710 Riverside (mailing address: Box 709), Sicamous, BC, V0E 2V0 (☎ 250/836-2403), **Twin Anchors Houseboat Vacations,** 101 Martin St. (mailing address: Box 318), Sicamous, BC, V0E 2V0 (☎ 250/836-2450), and **Bluewater Houseboats,** 110 Weddup (mailing address: Box 248), Sicamous, BC, V0E 2V0 (☎ 250/836-2255), are just a few of the area outfitters.

12 The Okanagan Valley

Just south of the High Country on Highway 97, the arid **Okanagan Valley** with its long chain of lakes is the ideal destination for freshwater-sports enthusiasts, golfers, skiers, and wine lovers. The climate is hot and dry during the summer high season (when, one local told us, the valley's population increases five-fold from its winter average of about 28,000).

Ranches and small towns have flourished here for more than a century; the region's **fruit orchards and vineyards** will make you feel as if you've been transported to the Spanish countryside. Summer visitors get the pick of the fruit crop at insider prices from the many fruit stands that line Highway 97. Be sure to stop for a pint of cherries, a basket of apples, homemade jams, and other goodies.

An Okanagan region chardonnay won gold medals in 1994 at international competitions held in London and Paris. And more than 2 dozen other wineries produce vintages that are following right on its heels. Despite this coveted honor, the valley has received little international publicity. Most visitors are Canadian, and the valley is not yet a major tour-bus destination. Get here before they do.

Many Canadian retirees have chosen **Penticton** as their home because it has relatively mild winters and dry, desertlike summers. It's also a favorite destination for younger visitors, drawn by boating, waterskiing, sportfishing, and windsurfing on 100-kilometer-long (62-mile-long) Lake Okanagan.

Remember to bring your camera when you head out on the lake. If you spot its legendary underwater resident, **Ogopogo,** take a picture. The shy monster (depicted in ancient petroglyphs found in the valley as a snakelike beast with a horselike head) is said to be a distant cousin of Scotland's Loch Ness monster. Ogopogo's actually the monster's English-language name, a palindrome derived from a 19th-century English music-hall tune, the "Ogopogo Song." Local tourism authorities have offered a C$1 million reward to anyone who can confirm Ogopogo's existence.

The town of **Kelowna** in the central valley is the hub of the BC wine-making industry and the valley's largest city. And the town of **Vernon** is a favorite destination for cross-country and powder skiers, who flock to the northern valley's top resort—**Silver Star Mountain.**

ESSENTIALS

VISITOR INFORMATION   Contact the **Okanagan Similkameen Tourism Association,** 1332 Water St., Kelowna, BC, V1Y 9P4 (☎ 250/860-5999). The Okanagan Valley's visitor information centers are open daily year-round from 9am to 6pm. The **Penticton Visitor Info Centre** is at 185 Lakeshore Dr., Penticton, BC, V2A 1B7 (☎ 800/663-5052 or 250/493-4055). The **Kelowna Visitor Info Centre** is at 544 Harvey Ave., Kelowna, BC, V1Y 6C9 (☎ 250/861-1515). And the **Vernon Visitor Info Centre** is at 6326 Highway 97 North (mailing address: Box 520), Vernon, BC, V1T 6M4 (☎ 250/542-1514).

GETTING THERE   From Vancouver, the Okanagan Valley is less than an hour away by commuter jet, and it's a 6-hour drive.

By Car   The 387-kilometer (242-mile) drive from Vancouver to Penticton via the Trans-Canada Highway (Highway 1) and Highway 3 rambles through rich delta farmlands and the forested mountains of Manning Provincial Park and the Similkameen River region before descending into the Okanagan Valley's antelope-brush and sagebrush desert.

For a more direct route to the valley towns of Kelowna and Vernon, take the Trans-Canada Highway to the Coquihalla Toll Highway, which eliminates more than an hour's driving time. The 203-kilometer (126-mile) route runs from Hope through Merritt over the Coquihalla Pass into Kamloops. The highway toll is C$10 (US$7) per car.

By Plane   Canadian Airlines (☎ 800/426-7000 in the U.S. or 800/363-7530 in Canada) has frequent daily commuter flights from Calgary and Vancouver to Penticton and Kelowna.

SPECIAL EVENTS   Colorful balloons meet to fly the valley's air thermals during the first and second weeks in February at Vernon's **Annual Winter Carnival & Hot Air Balloon Festival** (☎ 250/545-2236). Indoor and outdoor events like arts and crafts exhibits, food stands, and live musical entertainment take place at locations throughout the city.

Taste the valley's bountiful harvest of fine vintages and local produce at the **Okanagan Spring Food & Wine Festival** (☎ 250/861-6654) during the first week in May at wineries and restaurants throughout Penticton.

For a taste of the Canadian Old West, join the festivities and live performances at the **Annual Cowboy Festival** (☎ 250/542-7868) at the O'Keefe Historic Ranch near Vernon.

Be the first to taste the valley's best chardonnay, pinot noir, merlot, and ice wines at the **Okanagan Wine Festival** (☎ 250/861-6654), during the first and second weeks in October at wineries and restaurants throughout Penticton.

TASTING THE FRUITS OF THE VINEYARDS

British Columbia has a long history of producing wines, ranging from mediocre to really, truly bad. A missionary, Father Pandosy, planted apple trees and vineyards in 1859 and produced sacramental wines for the valley's mission. Other monastery wineries cropped up, but none of them worried about the quality of their bottlings. After all, the Canadian government has a long history of subsidizing domestic industries to promote entrepreneurial growth, including the book-publishing industry and cleric wineries.

In the 1980s the government threatened to pull its support of the industry unless it could produce an internationally competitive product. The vintners listened. Root stock was imported from France and Germany. European-trained master vintners were hired to oversee the development of the vines and the wine-making process. The climate and soil conditions turned out to be some of the best in the world for wine making, and today, British Columbian wines are winning international gold medals. Competitively priced, in the C$7 to C$50 (US$5 to US$36) per bottle range, they represent some great bargains in well-balanced chardonnays, pinot blancs, and gewürztraminers, full-bodied merlots, pinot noirs, and cabernets, and dessert ice wines that surpass the best muscat d'or.

Because American visitors are allowed to bring 33.8 ounces (1 liter) of wine per person back home without paying additional duty, you can bring a bottle (about 750ml) of your favorite selection home with you if you've visited Canada for more than 24 hours. (The duty on additional bottles can be as high as US24¢ per ounce!)

The valley's more than 2 dozen vineyards and wineries conduct free tours and wine tastings throughout the year. Here are a few of our favorite stops:

The town of **Okanagan Falls** is 20 kilometers (12 miles) south of Penticton along Highway 97. Adjacent to a wilderness area and bird sanctuary overlooking Vaseaux Lake, **Blue Mountain Vineyards & Cellars,** Allendale Road (☎ 250/497-8244; mailing address: RR #1, Site 3, Comp 4, Okanagan Falls, BC, V0H 1R0), offers tours by appointment and operates a wine shop and tasting room.

Wild Goose Vineyards and Winery, Sun Valley Way (☎ 250/497-8919; mailing address: RR #1, Site 3, Comp 11, Okanagan Falls, BC, V0H 1R0), conducts daily tours and operates a wine shop and tasting room from April to October from 10am to 5pm. From November to March, tours are conducted by appointment only.

Even if you're not a serious wine aficionado, there's one estate that's worth visiting just for the views and the heritage buildings. Overlooking Skaha Lake, **LeComte Estate Winery,** Green Lake Road (☎ 250/497-8267; mailing address: Box 480, Okanagan Falls, BC, V0H 1R0), conducts tours daily from April to October from 10am to 5pm. The wine shop and tasting room are housed in a restored early-1900s settlers' house.

In and around **Kelowna** are some of the biggest names in British Columbia's wine-making industry. **Calona Wines,** 1125 Richter St., Kelowna, BC, V1Y 2K6 (☎ 250/762-3332), conducts tours through western Canada's oldest and largest (since 1932) winery. Many antique wine-making machines are on display alongside the state-of-the-art equipment the winery now uses. Tours are given hourly from 10am to 4pm daily from May to September. The wine shop is open from 9am to 6pm daily from May to August, and from 10am to 5pm September to April.

Summerhill Estate Winery, 4870 Chute Lake Rd., Kelowna, BC, V1W 4M3 (☎ 800/667-3538 in Canada, or 250/764-8000), conducts tours daily from 10am to 6pm year-round. The wine shop and tasting room are also open year-round.

The neighboring town of Westbank is home to two award-winning wineries. Established in 1981 and winner of the 1994 Avery Trophy for its 1992 Grand Reserve Chardonnay and a gold medal for its 1994 Pinot Noir, **Mission Hill Wines,** 1730 Mission Hill Rd., Westbank, BC, V4T 2E4 (☎ 250/768-7611), conducts tours and operates its wine shop from May to October from 10am to 6pm, and November to April from 10am and 4pm.

Another experience worth savoring even if you're not an oenophile is the Quail's Gate estate. If ice wines are your favorite dessert potable, visit **Quail's Gate Vineyards Estate Winery,** 3303 Boucherie Rd., Kelowna, BC, V1Z 2H3 (☎ 250/769-4451). Tours are conducted daily at 11am, 1pm, and 3pm. The wine shop and tasting room are housed in the restored log home of the Allison family, pioneers who arrived in the valley during the 1870s. The shop is filled with historic regional artifacts and is open from 10am to 6pm daily from June to September; from 10am to 5pm the rest of the year.

Located 43.3 kilometers (26 miles) north of Penticton, **Hainle Vineyards Estate Winery,** 5355 Trepanier Bench Rd. (☎ 250/767-2525; mailing address: RR #2, Site 27A, Comp 6, Peachland, BC, V0H 1X0), was the first Okanagan winery to produce ice wine. Tours through the winery and wine shop operate May to October from 10am to 5pm Tuesday to Sunday. From November to April, the winery and shop are open for tours and tastings only Thursday to Sunday from 1 to 5pm.

Sumac Ridge Estate Winery, 17403 Hwy. 97 (☎ 250/494-0451; mailing address: Box 307, Summerland, BC, V0H 1Z0), conducts tours daily May to October from 9am to 6pm; November to April on weekends only from 11am to 5pm. Besides operating a wine shop and tasting room, the winery features a dining room that's open in summer and autumn.

SPORTS & OUTDOOR ACTIVITIES

BIKING The best **Okanagan Valley** off-road bike trail is the old **Kettle Valley Railway** route. The tracks and ties have been removed, making way for some incredibly scenic biking. The **Myra Canyon** railway route near Kelowna crosses over 18 trestle bridges and passes through two tunnels that were carved out of the mountains. Guided biking tours are organized by **Vintage Cycling Tours,** 4847 Parkridge Ave., Kelowna (☎ 604/764-7223), and **Silver Star Mountain Resort** (see "Skiing & Snowboarding," in section 1 of this chapter).

BOATING & WATER SPORTS The Okanagan Valley's numerous local marinas offer full-service boat rentals. **Okanagan Boat Charters,** 291 Front St., Penticton (☎ 250/492-5099), rents houseboats with fully equipped kitchens that can accommodate up to 10 people. A 3-day weekend rental costs about C$750 (US$536); a 4-day week runs about C$700 (US$500); and weekly rental of a 27-foot sailboat costs C$545 (US$389).

The **Marina on Okanagan Lake,** 291 Front St., Penticton (☎ **250/492-2628**), rents ski-boats, Tigersharks (similar to Jet-Skis or Sea-Doos), fishing boats, and tackle.

GOLFING The greens fees throughout the Okanagan Valley range from C$72 to C$112 (US$51 to US$80) and are a good value not only because of the beautiful locations but also for the quality of service you'll find at each club. Les Furber's **Gallagher's Canyon Golf and Country Club,** 4320 McCulloch Rd., Kelowna (☎ **250/861-4240**), has an 18-hole course that features a hole overlooking the precipice of a gaping canyon and another that's perched on the brink of a ravine. It also has a 9-hole course, a midlength course, and a new double-ended learning center.

Resting high on a wooded ridge between two lakes, Les Furber's **Predator Ridge,** 360 Commonage Rd., Vernon (☎ **250/542-3436**), has hosted the BC Open Championship in recent years. The par-5 fourth hole can only be played over a huge midfairway lake; it's a challenge even for seasoned pros.

A-1 Last Minute Golf Hotline (☎ **800/684-6344** or 604/878-1833) can arrange a next-day tee time at local golf courses. Savings can be as much as 40% on next-day, last-minute tee times. No membership is necessary. Call between 3pm and 9pm for the next day, or before noon for the same day.

SKIING Cross-country and powder skiing are the Okanagan Valley's main winter attractions. Intermediate and expert downhill skiers frequent the **Apex Resort,** Green Mountain Road, Penticton (☎ **800/387-2739,** 250/492-2880, 250/292-8111, or 250/492-2929, ext. 2000 for snow report), where 56 runs are serviced by one quad chair, one triple chair, one T-bar, and one beginner tow/platter. The 51.6 kilometers (31 miles) of cross-country ski trails are well marked and well groomed, offering both flat stretches and hilly ascents. Facilities include an ice rink, snow golf, sleigh rides, casino nights, and racing competitions.

Only a 15-minute drive from Westbank, **Crystal Mountain Resorts Ltd.** (☎ **250/768-5189,** or 250/768-3753 for snow report; mailing address: Box 26044, Westbank, BC, V4T 2J9), has a range of ski programs for all types of skiers, specializing in clinics for children, women, and seniors. Celebrating its 30th anniversary during the 1997–98 ski season, this friendly family-oriented resort lets you ski free on your birthday as one of its regular promotions. The resort's 20 runs are 80% intermediate-to-novice grade, and are serviced by one double chair and two T-bars. The runs are equipped for day and night skiing. There's also a half pipe for snowboarders. Lift tickets start at C$28 (US$20) for adults, C$24 (US$17) for youths, and C$19 (US$14) for juniors. Half-day and nighttime discounts are available.

If you yearn for hip-deep dry powder, then head to **Big White Ski Resort,** Parkinson Way, Kelowna (☎ **250/765-3101,** or 250/765-SNOW for snow report, or 250/765-8888 for lodge reservations). The resort spreads over a broad mountain, featuring long, wide runs. Skiers here cruise open bowls and tree-lined glades. There's an annual average of 18 feet of fluffy powder, so it's no wonder the resort's 57 runs are so popular. There are three high-speed quad chairs, one fixed-grip quad, one triple quad, one double chair, one T-bar, one beginner tow, and one platter lift. The resort also offers more than 21 miles of groomed cross-country ski trails, a recreational racing program, and night skiing 5 nights a week.

ACCOMMODATIONS

The **BC Provincial Parks Service/Okanagan District** (☎ **250/494-6500**) maintains a number of provincial campgrounds in this area. They're open from April to October, and fees range from C$9.50 to C$14.50 (US$7 to US$10) per night. There are 41 campsites at **Haynes Point Provincial Park** in Osoyoos, which has flush toilets, a boat launch, and visitor programs. This campground is popular with naturalists interested in hiking the "pocket desert." **Vaseaux Lake Provincial Park,** near Okanagan Falls, offers 12 campsites and great wildlife-viewing opportunities; deer, antelope, and even a number of California bighorn sheep live in the surrounding hills. And **Okanagan Lake Provincial Park** has 168 campsites nestled amid 10,000 imported trees. Facilities include free hot showers, flush toilets, a sani-station, and a boat launch.

IN PENTICTON

The (Clarion) Penticton Lakeside Resort. 21 West Lakeshore Dr., Penticton, BC, V2A 7M5. ☎ 800/663-9400 or 250/493-8221. 194 rms, 10 suites. A/C TV TEL. C$155 (US$111) double; C$159–C$195 (US$114–US$139) suite. AE, DC, MC, V. Follow the signs to Main St. when you arrive in town. Lakeshore Dr. is at the north end of Main St.

On the water's edge, the Penticton Lakeside Resort has its own stretch of sandy Lake Okanagan beachfront where guests can sunbathe or stroll along the adjacent pier. This year-round resort is also close to great golf courses and the Apex Mountain ski area. The deluxe suites feature Jacuzzis. And the lakeside rooms are highly recommended for their view.

Dining: The menus at the fully licensed Okanagan Surf N' Turf Company Restaurant and the Barking Parrot Bar & Patio feature locally grown ingredients.

Facilities: Indoor pool, sauna, whirlpool, fitness center with complete Nautilus circuit, tennis courts, hair salon, gift shop, volleyball, and running trails.

IN KELOWNA

The Grand Okanagan Lakefront Resort & Conference Centre. 1310 Water St., Kelowna, BC, V1Y 9P3. ☎ 800/465-4651 or 250/763-4500. Fax 250/763-4565. 205 rms, suites, and condos with full kitchens. A/C TV TEL. C$190–C$230 (US$136–US$164) double; C$325–C$370 (US$232–US$264) suite/condo. Extra person C$15 (US$11). Off-season discounts. AE, MC, V. Free parking. On Hwy. 97, cross the Lake Okanagan Bridge. At the first set of lights, turn left onto Abbott St. At the second set of lights turn onto Water St.

This elegant lakeshore resort is on 25 acres of beach and parkland. The atmosphere is reminiscent of Miami Beach in the 1920s. The atrium lobby of the modern hotel has a fountain with a sculpted dolphin as its centerpiece. The rooms, suites, and condos are decorated in salmon, sea blue, and shell white and exude a relaxed yet elegant atmosphere. It's an ideal location for visitors who want to feel pampered in the resort's very sophisticated surroundings during their stay.

Dining/Entertainment: The Dolphins Restaurant and Vines cocktail lounge overlook the resort's private marina, where guests can moor their small boats and relax over a tasty meal served on the patio.

Facilities: Heated outdoor pool, salon, shops, and fitness center. Motorized swans and kid-sized boats offer fun for children in a protected waterway.

Hotel Eldorado. 500 Cook Rd. (at Lakeshore Rd.), Kelowna, BC, V1W 3G9. ☎ 250/763-7500. Fax 250/861-4779. 20 rms. TV TEL. C$89–C$165 (US$64–US$118) double. AE, DC, MC, V. Free parking. From Hwy. 97, cross the Lake Okanagan Bridge. Turn right at the second set of traffic lights onto Pandosy Rd. Drive 1.6km (1 mile) past the hospital and the shopping center. Turn right on Cook Rd. and drive 1 block to Lakeshore Rd.

One of Kelowna's oldest hotels, the Eldorado was floated down the lake from its original location to its present site on the water's edge north of downtown. It's been fully restored and is decorated with a unique mix of antiques. The third-floor rooms with a lake view are the largest and quietest. Some rooms also feature lakeside balconies. No pets.

Dining/Entertainment: There are a fully licensed boardwalk cafe, cocktail lounge, and formal dining room on the premises.

Facilities: The staff can arrange boat moorage, boat rental, or waterskiing lessons.

Lake Okanagan Resort. 2751 Westside Rd., Kelowna, BC, V1Y 8B2. ☎ **800/663-3273** or 250/769-3511. Fax 250/769-6665. 100 1-bedrm suites, 40 3-bedrm suites. A/C TV TEL. C$130–C$185 (US$93–US$132) suite. Off-season discounts and packages available. AE, MC, V. Drive 18.3km (11 miles) up Westside Rd., which overlooks the lake.

The long, winding coastline road that leads to this secluded hideaway is a sports-car driver's dream come true. And there are many more activities to keep guests interested once they arrive at this beautiful, woodsy resort, with its country-club atmosphere. Located on 300 acres of Okanagan Lake's hilly western shore, the resort offers one-bedroom units with kitchenettes, as well as suites and rooms. Because the resort is built on a hillside, every room has a terrific view of the lake.

Dining/Entertainment: A patio cafe, two elegant restaurants, and a poolside bar.

Facilities: Three heated outdoor pools, indoor and outdoor Jacuzzis, cabana, fitness center, par-3 golf course, seven tennis courts (including three nighttime courts), horseback riding, mountain-bike and hiking trails, sandy private beach, marina, nature program, and summer kids' camp.

DINING
IN KELOWNA

MV *Fintry Queen*. On the dock off Bernard Ave., Kelowna. ☎ **250/763-2780.** Reservations recommended. Dinner cruise C$27.50 (US$20); lunch cruise C$17.50 (US$13); cruise only C$9 (US$6). MC, V. Lunch cruises Mon–Sat noon–2pm, Sun 1–3pm. Dinner cruises Mon–Fri 7:30–9:30pm, Sat 9pm–midnight, Sun 5:30–8:30pm. Closed Oct–Apr. CANADIAN.

Built in 1948, this paddle wheeler was once a working ferry that transported residents and visitors across the lake. A bridge now spans the water, so the MV *Fintry Queen* was converted into a restaurant. It offers à la carte lunch buffet cruises as well as dinner-dance cruises that feature a full hot and cold buffet filled with fresh seafood, roasted meats, and salads.

IN & AROUND PENTICTON

The Historic 1912 Restaurant. Lakehill Rd., Kaleden. ☎ **250/497-6868.** Reservations recommended. Main courses C$14.95–C$21.95 (US$11–US$16). MC, V. Tues–Sun 5:30–10pm. Drive 5 min. south of Penticton on Hwy. 97. Take the second left after the Okanagan Game Farm onto Lakehill Rd. CONTINENTAL.

This is a quintessential romantic hideaway. At the end of a long, winding road, the lakeside restaurant is in a stone building that served as a general store when it was built in 1912. The decor is Victorian and romantic, featuring dark-wood paneling, white linens, and soft lights. The menu offers seafood specialties like lemon vodka prawns, pasta dishes, steaks, cheese fondues, and Kahlúa-laced chocolate dessert fondue.

Theo's Greek Restaurant. 687 Main St., Penticton. ☎ **250/492-4019.** Reservations accepted. Main courses C$9.95–C$15.95 (US$7–US$11). AE, DC, ER, MC, V. Mon–Sat 11am–11pm, Sun 5–11pm. GREEK.

Theo's is a slice of Athens. The casual taverna-style dining room has whitewashed walls, a stone floor, and plenty of lush greenery. The traditional menu features delectable calamari, succulent marinated lamb, and standard favorites like dolmades and moussaka. Even the requisite BC salmon is baked with an oregano-and-garlic crust.

Three Mile House. 1507 Naramata Rd., Penticton. ☎ **250/492-5152.** Reservations recommended. Main courses C$12.95–C$23.95 (US$9–US$17). AE, MC, V. Tues–Sun 6–11pm. FRENCH.

Hosts George and June McLeod have created a haven for lovers of fine country-style French dishes such as pâté de maison and grilled tenderloins of filet mignon. And they've added a few local touches, creating combinations such as oysters Florentine, Okanagan fruit soup, halibut steak au poivre, wild-boar cutlets in red-wine sauce, and roast pheasant. Save room for the signature Belgian chocolate mousse.

19

The Yukon & the Northwest Territories: The Great Northern Wilderness

by Bill McRae

The Far North of Canada is one of the last great wilderness areas in North America. The Yukon, Northwest Territories, and the far north of British Columbia are home to the native Inuit and northern Indian tribes like the Dene, vast herds of wildlife, and thousands of square miles of tundra and stunted subarctic forest. For centuries, names like the Klondike, Hudson's Bay, and the Northwest Passage have had the power to conjure up powerful images. For an area so little visited and so distant, the North has long played an integral role in the history and imagination of the western world.

Yet the North isn't eternal, and it's changing before our eyes. The changes are creating a whole pattern of paradoxes. The Arctic is a hotbed of mineral, oil, gas, and diamond exploration. Jobs and schools have brought Inuit and Indian natives from the hunting camps to town, where they live in prefabs instead of igloos and drive trucks and snowmobiles out to their traplines. But the money they spend in supermarkets is earned by ancestral hunting skills and their lifestyle remains based on the pursuit of migrating game animals and marine creatures.

The **native Canadians** (Indians) and the **Inuit** make up the majority of the North's population, particularly when you add the **Métis** offspring of white and native-Canadian couples. All the natives were originally nomadic, covering enormous distances in pursuit of migrating game animals. Today nearly all First Nation people, as native Canadians are often called, have permanent homes in settlements, but many of them spend part of the year in remote tent camps hunting, fishing, and trapping. And although nobody lives in igloos anymore, these snow houses are still built as temporary shelters when the occasion arises.

Survival is the key word for the native Canadians. They learned to survive in conditions unimaginably harsh for southern societies, by means of skills that become more wondrous the better you know them. The early white explorers soon learned that in order to stay alive, they had to copy those skills as best they could. Those who refused to "go native" rarely made it back.

The first white man known to have penetrated the region was **Martin Frobisher.** His account of meeting the Inuit, written 400 years ago, is the earliest on record. About the same time, European whalers, hunting whales for their oil, were occasionally forced ashore by storms or shipwrecks and depended on Inuit hospitality for survival. This almost legendary hospitality, extended to any stranger who came to them, remains an outstanding characteristic of the Inuit.

Whites began to move into the Canadian Arctic in greater number during the great "fur rush" of the late 18th century. In the wake of the fur hunters and traders came Roman Catholic and Anglican missionaries, who built churches and opened schools.

For most of its recorded history, the Far North was governed from afar, first by Great Britain, then by the Hudson's Bay Company, and from 1867 by the new Canadian government in Ottawa. At that time the Territories included all of the Yukon, Saskatchewan, Alberta, and huge parts of other provinces.

Then, in 1896, **gold** was discovered on Bonanza Creek in the Klondike. Tens of thousands of people descended onto the Yukon in a matter of months, giving birth to Dawson City, Whitehorse, and a dozen other tent communities that went bust along with the gold veins. The Yukon gold rush was the greatest in history; more than C$500,000 in gold was washed out of the gravel banks along the Klondike before industrial mining moved in. With its new wealth and population, the Yukon split off from the rest of the Northwest Territories in 1898.

The rest of the Northwest Territories didn't receive its own elected government until 1967, when the center of government was moved from Ottawa to Yellowknife, and a representative assembly was elected. However, with 3.4 million square kilometers (1.3 million sq. miles), the territory has proved to be an unwieldy piece of real estate to govern, and the process of self-determination continues. In 1999, the eastern section of the Northwest Territories will become a separate and autonomous territory, known as **Nunavut** (meaning "our land"). The rump Northwest Territories, which roughly speaking consists of the drainage of the Mackenzie River, including Yellowknife, and the Arctic coast west of Coppermine, has not decided on a new name for itself, though the odds are good that it'll be called the Western Arctic.

1 Exploring the North

The Arctic isn't like other places. That observation may seem elementary, but even a well-prepared first-time visitor will experience many things here to startle—and perhaps offend—the senses.

No matter where you start from, the Arctic is a long ways away. By far the easiest way to get there is by plane. Whitehorse, Yellowknife, and Iqaluit each have airports with daily service from major Canadian cities. Each of these towns is a center for a network of smaller airlines with regularly scheduled flights to yet smaller communities; here you'll also find charter services to take you to incredibly out-of-the-way destinations.

CLIMATE & SEASONS

During summer, the farther north you travel, the more daylight you get. Yellowknife and Whitehorse, in the south, bask under 20 hours of sunshine a day, followed by 4 hours of milky twilight bright enough to read a newspaper by. But in northern Inuvik or Cambridge Bay, the sun shines 24 hours around the clock. In winter, however, the northern sun doesn't rise above the horizon at all on certain days.

The North is divided into two climatic zones: subarctic and Arctic, and the division does not follow the Arctic Circle. And while there are permanent ice caps in the far northern islands, summer in the rest of the land gets considerably hotter than you might think. The average high temperatures in July and August are in the 70s and 80s, and the mercury has been known to climb into the 90s. However, even in summer you should bring a warm sweater or ski jacket—and don't forget a pair of really sturdy shoes or boots.

In winter, weather conditions are truly Arctic. The mercury may dip as low as –60 for short periods. You'll need heavily insulated clothing and footwear to travel during this time of the year. Spring is an increasingly popular time to visit, with clear sunny skies, highs in the 20s, and days already longer than seems reasonable.

DRIVING THE NORTH

Setting out to drive the back roads of the Far North has a strange fascination for many people, most of whom own RVs. The most famous route through the North is the **Alaska Highway,** which linked the wartime continental U.S. with Alaska via northern BC and the Yukon. Today the route is mostly paved and isn't the adventure it once was. Off-road enthusiasts may prefer the **Mackenzie Highway,** which links Edmonton to Yellowknife. Even this road is mostly paved nowadays, which leaves the **Dempster Highway,** between Dawson City and Inuvik, as one of the few real back roads left in the North.

Much of the North is served by good roads, though driving up here demands different preparations that you might be used to. It's a good idea to travel with a full 5-gallon gas can, even though along most routes gas stations appear frequently. However, there's no guarantee that these stations will be open in the evenings, or on Sunday, or at the precise moment you need to fill up. By all means, fill up every time you see a gas station in remote areas.

In summer, dust can be a serious nuisance, particularly on gravel roads. When it becomes a problem, close all windows and turn on your heater fan. This builds up air pressure inside your vehicle and helps to keep the dust out. Keep cameras in plastic bags for protection.

It's a good idea to attach a bug or gravel screen and plastic headlight guards to your vehicle. And it's absolutely essential that your windshield wipers are operative and your washer reservoir full. In the Yukon, the law requires that all automobiles drive with their headlights on; it's a good idea while traveling on any gravel road.

April and May are the spring slush months when mud and water may render some road sections hazardous. The winter months, from December to March, require a lot of special driving preparations; winter isn't a good time to plan a road trip to the North.

SHOPPING FOR NATIVE ARTS & CRAFTS

The handiwork of the Dene and Inuit people is absolutely unique. Some of it has utility value—you won't get finer, more painstakingly stitched cold-weather clothing anywhere in the world.

Baffin Island communities are famous world-wide for their **stone, bone,** and **ivory carvings.** Inuit artists also produce noted weavings, prints, and etchings with native themes; clothing articles made of sealskin are also common. The Dene produce caribou-skin moccasins and clothing, often with beaded decoration.

Most arts-and-crafts articles are handled through community cooperatives, thus avoiding the cut of the middleman. This is an important business in the Territories, with sales averaging around C$10 million (US$7.2 million) a year. Official documentation will guarantee that a piece is a genuine native-Canadian object. Don't hesitate to ask retailers where a particular object comes from, what it's made of, and who made it. They'll be glad to tell you, and frequently will point out where the artist lives and works. In the eastern Arctic particularly, artists will often approach tourists in the streets or in bars and restaurants, seeking to sell their goods. While these articles

The Yukon & the Northwest Territories

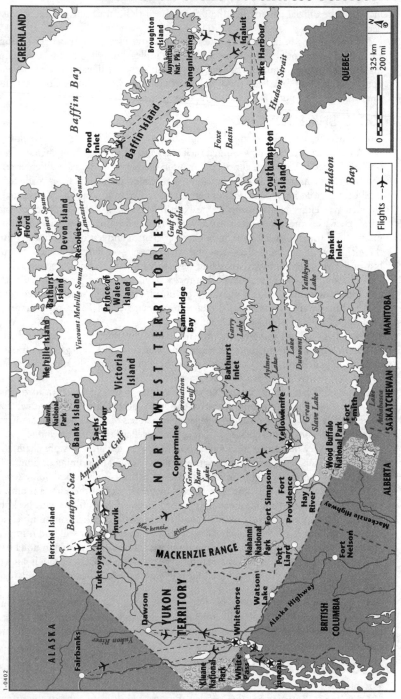

may lack the official paperwork, the price is often right; use your judgment when deciding to buy.

Before investing in native art, make sure you know what the **import restrictions** are in your home country. In many countries, it is illegal to bring in articles containing parts of marine mammals (this includes walrus or narwhal ivory, as well as whale bones or polar-bear fur). Sealskin products are commonly prohibited. Consult a customs office to find out what restrictions are in place.

FOOD, DRINK & LODGING

Northerners traditionally lived off the land by hunting and fishing (many still do), and Arctic specialties have now worked their way onto many fine dining menus. **Caribou** and **musk ox** appear on almost all menus in the North, and offer a different taste and texture for meat-eaters. Good caribou, sometimes dressed in sauces made from local berries (wild blue- or Saskatoonberries) tastes like mild venison, and is usually cheaper than either beef or lamb in the North. Musk ox is rather stronger tasting, with a chewy texture, and is often served with wild mushrooms. **Arctic char** is a mild, pink-fleshed fish, rather like salmon but coarser grained and less oily. You won't find the mainstays of the Inuit diet—seal and whale meat—on most restaurant menus, but in outlying communities you won't have to look hard to find someone able to feed you some *muktuk* or seal meat. **Bannocks,** a type of baking-powder biscuit, and **Eskimo doughnuts,** a cousin of Indian fry bread, are popular snacks to feed tourists. You may want to keep your distance from what's called **Eskimo ice cream,** a concoction made of whipped whale fat.

Vegetarians are not going to find much to eat in the North. The traditional Arctic diet doesn't include much in the way of fruits or vegetables, and green stuff that's been air-freighted in is pretty sad-looking by the time it reaches the table. *Bring your own dietary supplements if you have a restricted diet.*

No matter what you eat in the North, it is going to be expensive. In towns like Yellowknife, Inuvik, and Iqaluit, a normal entree at a decent hotel restaurant will cost at least C\$25 (US\$18); at outlying villages, where hotels offer full board, a sandwich with fries will run C\$20 (US\$14). Chances are excellent that, for the money, your food will be very pedestrian in quality. In most towns, the grocery-store chain The Northern shelters a few fast-food outlets, usually the only other dining option.

Alcohol is banned or highly restricted in most native communities. Some towns are completely dry: no one, not even visitors in the privacy of their hotel rooms, is allowed to possess or consume alcohol. In some locales, RCMP officers will check the baggage of incoming travelers and will confiscate alcohol. In other communities, alcohol is legal but regulated to such a degree that the casual visitor will find it impossible to get hold of a drink. In other communities, alcohol is available in hotel bars or restaurants, but not available in stores (or even by room service). Alcohol is a major social problem in the North, so by all means respect the local laws that regulate alcohol consumption.

Lodging is the most expensive day-to-day outlay in the North. Almost every community, no matter how small, will have a hotel, but prices are very high. You can save some money with B&Bs or homestays, which also have the advantage of introducing you to the locals.

VISITOR INFORMATION

For information, write **Tourism Yukon,** P.O. Box 2703, Whitehorse, YT, Y1A 2C6, (☎ 867/667-5340; fax 867/667-3546). Be sure to ask for a copy of the official vacation guide *Canada's Yukon.* You can also check out Tourism Yukon's Web site at **www.touryukon.com**; its e-mail address is yktour@yknet.yk.ca.

For the Northwest Territories, contact **NWT Arctic Tourism,** P.O. Box 1320, Yellowknife, NT, X1A 2L9 (☎ **800/661-0788** or 867/873-7200; fax 867/873-0294; Web site: www.nwttravel.nt.ca). Ask for the free map of the province (it is almost impossible to find a map of the Territories elsewhere) and *The Explorers' Guide,* with full listings of accommodations and outfitters.

For Nunavut and Baffin Island, contact **Nunavut Tourism,** P.O. Box 1450, Iqaluit, NT, X0A 0H0 (☎ **800/491-7910** or 867/979-6551; e-mail: nunatour@nunanet.com; Web site: www.nunanet.com/~nunatour). Ask for the *Arctic Traveller,* which has full listings of destinations, accommodations, and outfitters.

THE GREAT OUTDOORS

OUTFITTERS Outdoor enthusiasts in many parts of the world can simply arrive at a destination and then put together a recreational trip when they get there. That is not the case in the North. If you want to get out onto the land, or the water, or the glacier, you will definitely need to have the assistance of an outfitter or local tour provider. There are no roads to speak of in the North, so you'll need help simply to get wherever you're trying to go; this usually involves a boat or airplane trip. Sports-equipment rental is all but unheard of in the North; and it's very foolish to head out into the wilds (which start at the edge of the village) without the advice and guidance of someone who knows the terrain, weather, and other general conditions. For all these reasons—and for the entree you'll get into the community—you should hire an outfitter. While it may seem like an unnecessary expense, you will end up saving money, time, and frustration.

SUMMER TRAVEL Hiking and naturalist trips are popular in late July, August, and in early September. The ice is off the ocean, allowing access by boat to otherwise remote areas. Auyuittuq National Park, with its famed long-distance hiking and rock climbing, is a popular destination for the experienced recreationalist. Float trips on the Soper River in Katannilik Park, are popular for those seeking adventures that are a bit softer. Naturalist-led hikes out onto the tundra make popular day trips. The South Nahanni River, in Nahanni National Park, is popular for weeklong raft or canoe trips below massive 316-foot Virginia Falls.

WINTER & SPRING TRAVEL While it may seem natural to plan a trip to the Arctic in the summer, in fact the Far North is a year-round destination. Dogsledding trips out into the frozen wilderness are popular late-winter trips for adventurous souls. In May and June from Pond Inlet, dogsled or snow-machine trips visit the edge of the ice floe, where wildlife viewing is superb. And, in the dead of winter, there's the 24-hour darkness and the **northern lights,** which lure people north to have a look.

MOSQUITOES, DEERFLIES & OTHER CRITTERS During the summer especially, two of the most commonly heard sounds in the North are the rhythmic buzzing of winged biting insects and the cursing of their human victims. **Insect repellent** is a necessity, as is having a place you can get away from the mosquitoes for a while. Some hikers wear expedition hats or head nets to ward off the worst attacks. Mosquitoes can go through light fabric, which is why it is better to wear sturdy clothes even on the hottest days. Wasps, hornets, and other stinging insects are common in the north. If you're allergic, be ready with your serum.

CANOEING & DOGSLEDDING If you want to see the land as early explorers and natives did, try exploring the North via these two traditional transportation methods. The following outfitters usually offer recreation in more than one part of the North; or different recreational pursuits depending on the season.

Canoe Expeditions   The early French-Canadian trappers, or *voyageurs,* explored the North—particularly the Yukon—by canoe, and outfitters now offer multiday expeditions down the region's wide and powerful rivers. A good place to go for advice and a wide range of guided tours on Northwest Territory rivers is **Canada's Canoe Adventures,** P.O. Box 398, 446 Main St. W., Merrickville, ON, K0G 1N0 (☎ 613/269-2910; fax 613/269-2908). Over 60 different destinations are offered; all trips are with accredited outfitters. For more information, see their Web site at **www.crca.ca** or contact them via e-mail at staff@crca.ca. **Kanoe People,** P.O. Box 5152, Whitehorse, YT, Y1A 4S3 (☎ 867/668-4899; fax 867/668-4891; e-mail: kanoe@yknet.yk.ca), offers a number of guided canoe trips down several of the Yukon's most historic rivers, past mining ghost towns and native-Canadian villages. Trips are offered on the Teslin, Yukon, and Big Salmon rivers, and range in length from 4 days at C$1,050 (US$750) to 11 days at C$1,620 (US$1,158). Bring your own sleeping bag; everything else, including transportation from Whitehorse, is included.

In southern Baffin Island, the Soper River, which flows past innumerable waterfalls in Katannilik Park, is the most famous canoeing river. **NorthWinds,** P.O. Box 849, Iqaluit, NT, X0A 0H0 (☎ 867/979-0551; fax 867/979-0573), offers 6-day trips down this beautiful river—gentle enough for family groups—starting at C$1,100 (US$787).

Dogsledding   An even more indigenous mode of transport in the north is travel by dogsled. While few people actually run dogs as their sole means of getting around any longer, the sport of dogsledding is hugely popular, and dogsledding trips to otherwise-snowbound backcountry destinations make a great early spring adventure. On Baffin Island, **NorthWinds** (see above) offers a variety of dogsled trips, ranging from day trips to 7-day expeditions, costing C$2,300 (US$1,144), out to see the northern lights; you'll also get a chance to learn how to run the dogs!

In the Yukon, **Michie Creek Mushing,** RR #1, Site 20, Camp 104, Whitehorse, YT, Y1A 4Z6 (☎ 867/667-6854; fax 867/668-2933), offers 1- to 6-day guided backcountry trips out into the wilderness, where you, your hosts, and the sled team stay in old trapper's cabins. Six-day trips are available for C$1,650 (US$1,180); day packages start at C$130 (US$93) per person. For more information, check out their Web site at **users.yknet.yk.ca/bbdo/michie**.

WILDLIFE VIEWING   It's easy to confuse **caribou** with reindeer because the two species look very much alike. Actually, caribou are wild and still travel in huge migrating herds stretching to the horizon, sometimes numbering 100,000 or more. They form the major food and clothing supply for many of the native people whose lives are cycled around the movements of caribou herds.

The mighty **musk ox** is indigenous to the Arctic. About 12,000 of them live on the northern islands—immense and prehistoric looking, the bulls weigh up to 1,300 pounds. They appear even larger because they carry a mountain of shaggy hair. Underneath the coarse outer coat, musk oxen have a silky-soft layer of underwool, called *qiviut* in Inuit. One pound of qiviut can be spun into a 40-strand thread 25 miles long! As light as it is soft, a sweater made from the stuff will keep its wearer warm in subzero weather. And it doesn't shrink when wet. Qivuit is extremely expensive: Once spun, it sells for C$70 (US$50) an ounce.

The monarch of the Arctic, the **polar bear** roams the Arctic coast and the shores of Hudson Bay; you'll have to travel quite a way over mighty tough country to see one in its habitat. Weighing up to 1,450 pounds, they're the largest predators on the

North American continent. Grizzly bears are found in the boreal forests and river basins. Both animals are very dangerous; if encountered, give them a wide berth.

The North is full of other animals much easier to observe than the bears. In the wooded regions you'll come across wolves and wolverines (harmless to humans, despite the legends about them), mink, lynx, otter, ptarmigan, and beaver. The sleek and beautiful white or brown Arctic foxes live in ice regions as well as beneath the tree line and near settlements.

From mid-July to the end of August, seals, walruses, narwhals, and bowhead and beluga whales are in their breeding grounds off the coast of Baffin Island and in Hudson Bay. And in the endless skies above there are eagles, hawks, huge owls, razor-billed auks, and ivory gulls.

2 The Alaska Highway

Constructed as a military freight road during World War II to link Alaska to the Lower 48, the Alaska Highway (also known as the Alcan Highway) is now a popular tourist route to the Last Frontier. Now as much a phenomenon as a road, the Alaska Highway has become something of a pilgrimage route. The vast majority of people who make the trip are recent retirees, who take their newly purchased RVs and head up north; it's a rite of passage.

Strictly speaking, the Alaska Highway starts at the Mile 1 marker in **Dawson Creek,** on the eastern edge of British Columbia, and travels north and west for 2,452 kilometers (1,520 miles) to **Fairbanks, Alaska,** passing through the Yukon along the way. Even a decade ago, much of the talk of the Alaska Highway had to do with conditions of the road itself: where the really torn-up sections were, making it through soupy roads during freak rain and snowstorms, and how to make it between far-flung gas pumps. However, for the road's 50th anniversary in 1992, the final stretches of the road were paved.

While the days of tire-eating gravel roads and extra gas cans are largely past, there are several considerations before casually setting out to drive this road. First, this is a very *long* road. Popular wisdom states that if you drive straight out, it's a 3-day drive between Fairbanks and Dawson Creek. If you are in that big of a hurry to get to Fairbanks, then consider flying: Much of the road is very winding, slow-moving RV traffic is heavy, and a considerable amount of the road is under reconstruction every summer. If you try to keep yourself to a 3-day schedule, you are going to have a miserable time.

DRIVING THE ALASKA HIGHWAY

The route begins (or ends) at Dawson Creek in British Columbia, and before long crosses the Peace River and passes through **Fort St. John.** There are ample tourist facilities throughout this stretch of the highway. The highway continues north, parallel to the Rockies. The forests thin, with pointy spruce trees replacing pine and fir trees. Wildlife viewing is good; moose are often seen from the road.

From Fort St. John to **Fort Nelson,** there are gas stations and cafes every 65 to 81 kilometers (40 to 50 miles), though lodging options are pretty dubious. At Fort Nelson, the Alaska Highway turns west and heads into the Canadian Rockies; from here too, graveled Highway 7 continues north to Fort Liard and Fort Simpson, the gateway to **Nahanni National Park.** Fort Nelson is thick with motel rooms and gas stations; hours from any other major service center, this is a good place to spend the night.

The road through the Rockies is mostly narrow and winding; you can pretty much depend on finding a construction crew working on reconstruction along this stretch. The Rockies are relatively modest mountains in this area, not as rugged or scenic as they are further south in Jasper Park. Once over the Continental Divide, the Alaska Highway follows tributaries of the Liard River through Stone Mountain and Muncho Lake provincial parks. Rustic lodges and cabin resorts are scattered along the road for accommodations; this is also a good place to find a campsite.

At the town of **Liard River,** be sure to stop and stretch your legs or go for a soak at Liard Hot Springs. The provincial parks department maintains two nice soaking pools in the deep forest; the boardwalk out into the mineral water marsh is pleasant even if you don't have time for a dip.

As you get closer to **Watson Lake** in the Yukon, you'll notice that mom-and-pop gas stations along the road will advertise that they have cheaper gas than Watson Lake. Believe them, and fill up: Watson Lake is an unappealing town whose extortionately priced gasoline is probably its only memorable feature. If you don't plan your trip well, you may end up spending the night here.

The long road between Watson Lake and **Whitehorse** travels through rolling hills and forest to Teslin and Atlin lakes, where the landscape becomes more mountainous and the gray clouds of the Gulf of Alaska's weather systems hang menacingly in the western horizon. Whitehorse is the largest town along the route of the Alaska Highway, and unless you're in a great hurry, plan to spend at least a day here. You'll want to wash the dust off the car at the very least, and eat a decent meal before another day of driving on the way to Alaska.

Hope for good weather as you leave Whitehorse, since the trip past **Kluane National Park** is one the most beautiful parts of the entire Alaska Highway route. The two highest peaks of Canada straddle the horizon, while glaciers push down mountain valleys. The road edges by lovely Kluane Lake before passing Beaver Creek and crossing over into Alaska. From the border crossing to Fairbanks is another 481 kilometers (298 miles).

A number of guidebooks deal exhaustively with driving the Alaska Highway; particularly good is the mile-by-mile classic, the annual *Alaska Milepost.*

WHAT TO EXPECT

Summer is the only window of opportunity to upgrade or repair the road, so construction crews really go to it; depend on lengthy delays and some very rugged detours. During the summer of 1995, total delays of 2 to 4 hours were common in each daylong segment of the trip. Visitor centers along the way get a fax of daily construction schedules and conditions. Stop and ask if you don't want to be surprised by the delays you'll almost certainly encounter; or call ☎ 867/667-5893 for **24-hour highway information.**

While availability of **gasoline** isn't the problem that it once was, there are a couple of things to remember. Gas prices are high, about a third higher than in Edmonton or Calgary. While there's gasoline at most of the little communities that appear on the provincial road map, most close up early in the evening, and some outfits are less than friendly. There are 24-hour gas stations and plenty of motel rooms at Dawson City, Fort St. John, Fort Nelson, Watson Lake, and Whitehorse.

Try to be patient when driving the Alaska Highway. During the high season, the entire route, from Edmonton to Fairbanks, is one long caravan of RVs. Many people have their car in tow, a boat on the roof, and several bicycles chained to the spare tire. Thus encumbered, they lumber up the highway at top speeds of 72 kilometers per hour (45 m.p.h.); loath (or unable) to pass one another, convoys of RVs stretch on forever, the slowest of the party setting the pace for all. If you're not part of the RV crowd, driving the Alaska Highway will demand a lot of patience.

3 Whitehorse

Once part of the Northwest Territories, the Yukon is now a separate territory bordering on British Columbia in the south and Alaska in the west (when locals refer to the United States, they nearly always mean Alaska). Compared with the Northwest Territories, it's a mere midget in size, but with 200,000 square miles, it's immense by most other standards.

The entire territory has a population of only 33,400—two-thirds of them living in Whitehorse. The capital of the Yukon is a late arrival on the scene. It was established only in the spring of 1900, fully 2 years after the stampeders had swarmed into Dawson City. But Whitehorse, located on the banks of the Yukon River, is the logical hub of the Territory and became the capital in 1953 after Dawson fizzled out along with the gold.

ESSENTIALS

GETTING THERE   The airport, placed on a rise above the city, is served by **Canadian Airlines** (☎ 800/426-7000) from Vancouver; flights range from C$980 to C$1,750 (US$700 to US$1,250) round-trip. **Air North** (☎ 867/668-2228) flies from Juneau to Whitehorse for C$231 to C$431 (US$165 to US$308) round-trip; their Klondike Explorer Pass allows travelers to travel to many Yukon and Alaska destinations for C$550 (US$393). Cab fare to downtown is around C$8 (US$6). Whitehorse is 458 kilometers (284 miles) southeast of Beaver Creek (the Alaskan border).

VISITOR INFORMATION   Your first stop should be the **Whitehorse Visitor Reception Centre,** 302 Steele St. (☎ 867/667-7545), where you'll get a smiling reception plus armloads of information about hotels, restaurants, shopping, and excursions. The center is open daily from 8am to 8pm. Information about the Yukon in general is found at the **Yukon Visitor Reception Centre** (☎ 867/667-2915), on the Alaska Highway near the Whitehorse airport.

CITY LAYOUT   The city's layout is straightforward: Streets run vertically, avenues—First to Eighth—bisect them horizontally, and roads run around the periphery. Whitehorse centers on Main Street, which has 4 blocks of stores and a busy pace.

GETTING AROUND   Public transit is handled by **Whitehorse Transit** (☎ 867/668-2831). Car rental is available from **Tilden** (☎ 867/668-6872), **Avis** (☎ 867/667-2847), **Budget** (☎ 867/667-6200), and **Norcan** (☎ 867/668-2137). If you need a taxi, try **Yellow Cabs** (☎ 867/668-4811) or **Co-op Cabs** (☎ 867/668-2358).

SPECIAL EVENTS   February is a happening month in Whitehorse. One of the top dogsled races in North America, the **Yukon Quest** begins in Whitehorse and runs to Fairbanks. The town is filled with hundreds of yapping dogs and avid mushers, eager to vie for the C$100,000 (US$71,428) top prize. Making even more noise is the **Frostbite Music Festival,** which attracts musicians and entertainers from across Canada. Immediately afterward is the **Yukon Sourdough Rendezvous,** a midwinter festival that commemorates the days of the gold rush with various old-fashioned competitions, like dog pulls, fiddling and costume contests, and a "mad trapper" competition.

EXPLORING WHITEHORSE

✪ **Yukon Transportation Museum.** Adjacent to the Yukon Visitor Centre, Mile 915 on the Alaska Hwy. ☎ **867/668-4792.** Admission C$3.50 (US$2.50) adults, C$2.75 (US$2) seniors and students, C$2 (US$1.45) children. Mid-May to Sept daily 10am–7pm.

In a remote area like the Yukon, the history of white settlement is essentially the story of its transportation systems. In this fascinating museum, the development of travel, from dogsled to railway to bush plane and through the building of the Alaska Highway, is presented. You'll come away with a new appreciation of what it was to travel to the Yukon in the past. The exhibits and vintage photos on travel by dogsled are especially interesting. There's a replica of the historic aircraft *Queen of the Yukon*, the sister aircraft of *The Spirit of St. Louis*, plus a film on the building of the White Pass Railroad from Skagway to Whitehorse.

SS *Klondike*. Anchored at the Robert Campbell Bridge. ☎ **867/667-4511.** Admission C$3.50 (US$2.50) adults, C$2.50 (US$1.80) seniors, C$2 (US$1.45) students, C$8 (US$6) families. Tours on the half hour daily 9am–5:30pm.

The largest of the 250 riverboats that chugged up and down the Yukon River between 1866 and 1955, the *Klondike* is now permanently dry-docked beside the river. The boat has been restored to its 1940s glory.

✪ **MacBride Museum.** First Ave. at Wood St. ☎ **867/667-2709.** Admission C$4 (US$2.90) adults, C$3.50 (US$2.50) seniors, C$2.50 (US$1.80) students. Daily 10am–6pm.

The MacBride Museum covers half a city block, with four galleries, open-air exhibits, and a gift shop. Within the museum compound you'll also find Sam McGee's Cabin (read Service's poem on the cremation of same) and the old Whitehorse Telegraph Office. The log-cabin museum is crammed with relics from the gold-rush era, and has a large display of Yukon wildlife and minerals. It's interesting material, lovingly arranged by a nonprofit society.

Yukon Art Centre. Yukon Place at Yukon College, off Range Rd. N. ☎ **867/667-8575.** Free admission. Mon–Fri 11am–5pm, Sun 1–4pm.

The gallery at the Yukon Art Centre has changing exhibits that feature regional artists, photographers, and themes. The exhibits are free and are open daily. The art center also houses a tearoom and a theater that functions as Whitehorse's performing-arts center.

Yukon Beringia Interpretive Centre. Adjacent to Yukon Transportation Museum, Alaska Hwy. milepost 915. ☎ **867/667-8855.** E-mail: yktour@yktour.yk.ca. Web site: www.touryukon.com. C$6 (US$4.30) adults, C$5 (US$3.60) seniors, C$4 (US$2.90) students. Late May to mid-Sept daily 8am–9pm.

During the last ice age, a land bridge joined Asia to Alaska and the Yukon. These lands, and the exposed Bering Sea floor, formed a subcontinent now known as Beringia. Bordered on all sides by glaciers, this region was home to woolly mammoths and other Pleistocene-era animals, as well as cave-dwelling humans. This new museum highlights the archaeological and paleontological past of this part of North America, with exhibits on the prehistoric ecosystem, skeletons and other remains of ancient life, multimedia displays, and films.

Old Log Church. Elliott St. at Third Ave. ☎ **867/668-2555.** Admission C$2.50 (US$1.80) adults, $2 (US$1.45) seniors, C$1 (US70¢) children, C$6 (US$4.30) family. Mon–Sat 9am–6pm, Sun noon–4pm.

When Whitehorse got its first resident priest in 1900, he lived and held services in a tent. By the next spring the Old Log Church and rectory were built, and are now the only buildings of that date in town still in use. The Old Log Church was once the Roman Catholic cathedral for the diocese—the only wooden cathedral in the world—and contains artifacts on the history of all churches in the Yukon. Mass is every Sunday morning at 10:30am. (On the next block over are two "log skyscrapers"—that is, old two- and three-story log cabins, still used as apartments and offices. One of the buildings is the local office for the Yukon member of parliament.)

Takhini Hot Springs. On the Klondike Hwy., 27km (17 miles) north of Whitehorse. ☎ 867/ **633-2706.** Admission C$4 (US$2.85) adults, C$3.50 (US$2.50) seniors and students, C$3 (US$2.15) children. Daily 7am–10pm.

A swimming pool fed by natural hot springs and surrounded by rolling hills and hiking trails, the developed Takhini Hot Springs might be just what you need after days on the Alaska Highway. After swimming you can refresh yourself at the coffee shop. Horseback riding is also available.

Whitehorse Rapids Dam. At the end of Nisutlin Dr., in suburban Riverdale. Free admission. Daily 8am–10pm.

The native chinook salmon that pass by Whitehorse are completing one of the longest fish migrations in the world, and to bypass the Whitehorse Rapids Dam, they climb the world's longest wooden fish ladder. Interpretive displays and an upper viewing deck show you the entire process by which the dam has ceased to be an obstruction to the salmon migration.

TOURS & EXCURSIONS

HISTORICAL WALKING TOURS   The Yukon Historical and Museums Association, Donnenworth House, 3126 Third Ave., behind the Chamber of Commerce Visitors Centre (☎ 867/667-4704), offers Whitehorse Heritage Buildings Walking Tours on the hour from 9am to 4pm, Monday to Saturday. The 45-minute tour costs C$2 (US$1.45) and passes many of the gold-rush-era structures and historic sites, and offers a good introduction to the town.

WILDLIFE TOURS   The Yukon Wildlife Preserve covers hundreds of acres of forests and meadows. Roaming freely throughout are bison, moose, musk ox, elk, snowy owls, and the rare peregrine falcon. Tours of the preserve depart daily at 10:30am and 6:30pm. The cost is C$15 (US$11) for adults and C$7.50 (US$5) for children. Book through **Gray Line,** 208G Steele St. (☎ 867/668-3225).

RIVER CRUISES   The MV *Schwatka* is a river craft that cruises the Yukon River through the famous Miles Canyon. This stretch—once the most hazardous section of water in the Territory—is now dammed and tamed, though it still offers fascinating wilderness scenery. The cruise takes 2 hours, accompanied by narration telling the story of the old "wild river" times. Adults pay C$18 (US$13), children half price. For reservations, call ☎ 867/668-4716; the boat leaves 5 kilometers (3 miles) south of Whitehorse; follow signs for Miles Canyon.

A more authentic river experience is offered by the *Emerald May,* a steel pontoon raft that closely duplicates (but this one is completely safe and motorized) the style of boat used by the original 98ers, the gold-rush prospectors who stormed through the Yukon on their way to the Klondike in 1898. Instead of shooting dangerous rapids, today's trips focus on wildlife viewing and historic sites. Excursions are offered by **Taste of 98 Tours** (☎ 867/633-4767) and leave daily from the log cabin on First Avenue, across from the MacBride Museum; tickets are C$17 (US$12).

SHOPPING

The **Yukon Gallery,** 2093 Second Ave. (☎ 867/667-2391), is Whitehorse's best commercial visual-arts gallery, featuring a large show space devoted to Yukon and regional artists. There's an extensive display of paintings and prints, as well as some ceramics and Northern crafts, like moose-hair tufting.

Northern Images, 311 Jarvis St. (☎ 867/668-5739), is the best gallery in the Yukon for native-Canadian art, in particular Inuit carvings and native masks.

Yukon Native Products, 4230 Fourth Ave. (☎ 867/668-5955), is an unusual garment factory combining traditional native-Canadian skills with the latest computer technology. You can watch the stylish double-shell Yukon parka being designed by computer and assembled by humans. Alongside the parkas are examples of mukluks, slippers, and beadwork found in the North.

Mac's Fireweed Books, 203 Main St. (☎ 867/668-2434), is the best bookstore in town.

SPORTS & OUTDOOR ACTIVITIES

CANOEING   Many of these rivers were explored by French-Canadian voyageurs in canoes, and the wide, swift-flowing rivers of the Yukon still make for great canoe trips. In addition to their multiday expeditions (see "The Great Outdoors," above), **Kanoe People** (☎ 867/668-4899) offers evening trips on the Yukon River for C$45 (US$32); they also rent canoes and sea kayaks. **Prospect Yukon** (☎ 867/667-4837; fax 867/668-5728) offers 6-hour trips on the Yukon River for C$49 (US$35) per person; they also offer longer trips down other major Northern rivers. For day rentals, which cost C$25 (US$18), and a selection of easy day canoe trips, contact **Up North** (☎ 867/667-7905), located right on the Yukon River across from the MacBride Museum. You can also rent a canoe for a day and shoot the once-harrowing 25-mile Miles Canyon—C$45 (US$32) pays for two shuttles and the canoe rental.

DOGSLEDDING   If you're in the Yukon during the late winter or spring, go for a day-long dogsledding trip, or plan a long-distance cross-country trip with dogsled support. **Michie Creek Mushing** offers both day and custom trips with their 16-dog team; day trips start at C$125 (US$90). For information, see "The Great Outdoors," above.

HIKING   The **Yukon Conservation Society,** 302 Hawkins St. (☎ 867/668-5678), offers free guided nature walks in the Whitehorse area. Hikes are offered Monday to Friday, and on most days several different destinations are offered (most walks are only a couple of hours long). Self-transport is necessary; bring comfortable shoes and insect repellent.

If you're looking for a nice hike on your own, cross the Second Avenue Bridge, and follow the riverside path past the Whitehorse Dam and up to **Miles Canyon.** Here, the Yukon River cuts a narrow passage through the underlying basalt. Although not deep, the canyon greatly constricts the river, forming rapids that were an object of dread to the greenhorn 98ers in their homemade boats. Three kilometers (2 miles) up the canyon, a footbridge crosses the canyon, leading to both the Miles Canyon Road (arrange a pickup here) and a series of footpaths on the opposite side of the canyon.

HORSEBACK RIDING   White Horse Riding Stable (☎ 867/663-3086) is located 8 kilometers (5 miles) south of Whitehorse, just before the Miles Canyon turnoff.

ACCOMMODATIONS

Whitehorse has more than 20 hotels, motels, and chalets in and around the downtown area, including a couple just opposite the airport. This is far more than you'd expect in a place its size, and the accommodation standards come up to big-city levels in every respect.

EXPENSIVE

Edgewater Hotel. 101 Main St., Whitehorse, YT, Y1A 2A7. ☎ **867/667-2572.** Fax 867/668-3014. 30 rms. TV TEL. C$110–C$132 (US$79–US$95) double. AE, ER, MC, V.

At the end of Main Street, overlooking the Yukon River, this small vintage hotel has a distinct old-fashioned charm of its own, plus an excellent dining room, the Cellar. The lobby and bedrooms are cozy, and there's a well-appointed lounge. The rooms are newly renovated, kept in soft pastel colors, and equipped with extra-long beds and individual heat/air-conditioning units.

Dining: Two dining rooms, including the excellent Cellar Restaurant.

Services: Room service, newspaper delivery.

Facilities: Kitchenettes with coffeemakers and refrigerators, VCRs.

✪ **Westmark Whitehorse.** 201 Wood St. (P.O. Box 4250), Whitehorse, YT, Y1A 3T3. ☎ **800/544-0970** or 867/668-4700. Fax 867/668-2789. 180 rms. TV TEL. C$148 (US$106) double. Children under 12 stay free in parent's rm. AE, DC, ER, MC, V.

Centrally located in downtown Whitehorse, this representative of a national chain has one of the busiest lobbies in town, nicely fitted with armchairs and settees. There's a small arcade alongside, housing a gift shop, barber, and hairdresser, plus a travel agency. The guest rooms, including rooms for nonsmokers and travelers with disabilities, are spacious, well furnished, and well decorated.

Dining/Entertainment: The Westmark has a combination dining room, coffee shop, and cocktail lounge. The hotel is also host to one of Whitehorse's popular musical revues, the Frantic Follies.

Facilities: The most complete conference facilities in the Territory, guest laundry.

MODERATE

✪ **Best Western Gold Rush Inn.** 411 Main St., Whitehorse, YT, Y1A 2A7. ☎ **800/661-0539** in western Canada, 800/764-7604 in Alaska, or 867/668-4500. Fax 867/668-4432. 80 rms (24 with kitchenette). TV TEL. C$115 (US$82) double. AE, DC, ER, JCB, MC, V.

Modern but with a Wild West motif, the Gold Rush Inn is one of the most comfortable and centrally located lodgings in Yellowknife, within easy walking distance of attractions and shopping. All rooms, recently remodeled, have refrigerators and hair dryers; some come with kitchenettes. There are meeting facilities and a Jacuzzi. The restaurant here is good, and the convivial tavern is the scene of one of Yellowknife's evening theaters.

Bonanza Inn. 4109 Fourth Ave., Whitehorse, YT, Y1A 1H6. ☎ **867/668-4545.** Fax 867/668-6538. 53 rms. TV TEL. C$80 (US$57) double. Children under 12 stay free in parents' rm. AE, DC, ER, MC, V.

The Bonanza has a great location, at the heart of Whitehorse dining and entertainment. The rooms are good-sized and comfortably furnished with fully modern facilities; there's also a restaurant and lounge on the premises. Altogether, this is one of the better deals in Whitehorse.

Hawkins House. 303 Hawkins St., Whitehorse, YT, Y1A 1X5. ☎ **867/668-7638.** Fax 867/668-7632. 4 rms. TV TEL. C$95–$150 (US$68–$107) double. MC, V.

All guest rooms have private baths and balconies in this modern but stylishly retro Victorian home. Rooms are decorated according to theme, but tastefully so: The Fireweed Room has rustic pine furniture à la Klondike, while the Fleur de Lys Room recalls belle-epoque France. Rooms are furnished with worktables and computer jacks, and there are free laundry facilities. Breakfast is not included in the rate, but is available for C$7 (US$5).

Regina Hotel. 102 Wood St., Whitehorse, YT, Y1A 2E3. ☎ **867/667-7801.** Fax 867/668-6075. 53 rms. TV TEL. C$70–C$80 (US$50–US$57) double. Extra person C$10 (US$7). AE, ER, MC, V.

One of the oldest establishments in the Yukon, completely rebuilt in 1970, the Regina stands beside the Yukon River and breathes territorial tradition. Don't judge by the rather plain exterior; the rooms are large and fully modern and represent a good deal in an otherwise expensive town. The lobby is crowded with Old Yukon memorabilia, from hand-cranked telephones to moose antlers. You can't beat the location either: The Regina is located right on the Yukon River, across the street from the MacBride Museum, and only 1 block from Main Street.

Yukon Inn. 4220 Fourth Ave., Whitehorse, YT, Y1A 1K1. ☎ **800/661-0454** or 867/667-2527. Fax 867/668-7643. E-mail: yukoninn@polarcom.com. 92 rms. TV TEL. C$95–C$110 (US$69–US$79) double. AE, DC, DISC, MC, V.

The Yukon Inn is located on the edge of Whitehorse, near the malls, bars, and restaurants that make up the newer commercial strip north of downtown. This is a large and busy complex, with a lively bar and restaurant at one end; there's also a hair salon and gift shop in the lobby.

The rooms are good-sized and unfussy, and come equipped with standard amenities. The Yukon Inn is a favorite of local Yukoners; the hotel has even set aside a special meeting- and workroom for its First Nation guests.

CAMPGROUNDS & RV PARKS

There are a great number of campgrounds in and around Whitehorse; they represent the best alternative for travelers watching their money.

Tenters will like the **Robert Service Campground,** South Access Road (☎ 867/668-3721), close to downtown and free of RVs. There are 48 unserviced tent sites, plus fire pits, washrooms, showers, and a picnic area. The rate is C$11 (US$8) per tent. There are a number of lakeside territorial parks with campgrounds just north of Whitehorse on the Dawson City road. At Lake Laberge Park, you can camp "on the marge of Lake Lebarge" with the creatively-spelled verses of Robert Service filling your thoughts.

Most convenient for RVers is **Downtown Sourdough Park,** on Second Avenue north of Ogilvie (☎ 867/668-7938), with 146 campsites, most of them full-service, with showers, laundry, and a gift shop. Sites range from C$14 to C$18 (US$10 to US$13).

DINING

Food generally is more expensive in Whitehorse than in the provinces, and this goes for wine as well. Be happy you didn't come during the gold rush, when eggs sold for C$25 each—in 1899 money!

EXPENSIVE

Cellar Dining Room. In the Edgewater Hotel, 101 Main St. ☎ **867/667-2572.** Reservations recommended. Main courses C$19–C$40 (US$14–US$29). AE, MC, V. Mon–Fri 11:30am–1:30pm; daily 5–10pm. CANADIAN.

This plush lower-level establishment has a big local reputation. You'll enjoy whatever you order, but expect to pay top dollar. Pasta dishes start at C$19 (US$14); you can't go wrong selecting either the king crab, lobster and prawns, or the excellent prime rib (C$27/US$19). Dress casually, but not too casually. For good food—including steaks and prime rib—at a cheaper price point, eat at the Gallery, just upstairs from The Cellar.

Panda's. 212 Main St. ☎ **867/667-2632.** Reservations recommended. Main courses C$18–C$45 (US$13–US$32). AE, DC, MC, V. Mon–Fri 11:30am–2pm; Mon–Sat 5:30–10pm. July and Aug only, Sun 5:30–10pm. INTERNATIONAL.

Panda's is possibly the finest and certainly the most romantic restaurant in the Territory. The decor is a mixture of restrained elegance enlivened by traditional Klondike touches, the service smoothly discreet. This is one of the few establishments in town to offer daily specials apart from the regular menu. Dishes are classic European, like beef Wellington (C$30/US$21), pheasant breast with juniper berries, and veal Chanterelle (C$29/US$21), with a seafood curry dish thrown in for spice.

MODERATE

If you're looking for a moderately priced and copious lunch, try one of two good Asian buffets, both served weekdays from 11:30am to 2pm for C$9 (US$6). **The China Garden,** 309 Jarvis St. (☎ **867/668-2899**), and **Tung Lock Seafood Restaurant,** 404 Wood St. (☎ **867/668-3298**), also serve full dinners from their extensive menus.

✪ **Angelo's Restaurant on Top.** 202 Strickland St. ☎ **867/668-6266.** Reservations recommended. Pasta C$14–C$19 (US$10–US$14); pizzas (medium) C$15–C$20 (US$11–US$14); main courses C$19–C$39 (US$14–US$28). AE, MC, V. INTERNATIONAL.

This is one of Whitehorse's most popular restaurants, with good reason. The menu is extensive, ranging from pizzas to pasta (there are nearly 20 different choices, including some vegetarian options) and on to lamb, seafood, and steaks. If the restaurant has a specialty, it's the Greek souvlaki, which comes in six different meat choices. What's more, the preparations are tasty, and the staff does a good job of table service—when they're not called on to enforce crowd control (word is out on the tour-bus circuit).

✪ **No Pop Sandwich Shop.** 312 Steele St. ☎ **867/668-3227.** Reservations recommended. Sandwiches C$4–C$7 (US$2.90–US$5); dinner main courses C$10–C$15 (US$7–US$11). MC, V. Mon–Thurs 9am–9pm, Fri 9am–10pm, Sat 10am–9pm, Sun 10am–3pm. COFFEE SHOP/SANDWICHES.

Whitehorse's hip and "alternative" eating spot is No Pop. Part bakery, part espresso shop, and part evening bistro, this friendly restaurant is just about the only postmod 1990s restaurant in town. The baked goods are especially notable (try a raisin cinnamon roll), and the midday sandwiches meaty and happily retro. At night, the extensive sandwich menu is available, as well as a number of daily changing special entrees, usually featuring fresh fish. On Sunday, this is the place for brunch, with omelets and crêpes leading the menu. True to its name, no soft drinks are served (though there's coffee, juices, beer, wine, and a full bar), nor are there male employees in evidence. For a place with such a casual fare and attitude, it's somewhat odd that reservations are necessary for most meals.

INEXPENSIVE

Pasta Palace. 209 Main St. ☎ **867/667-6888.** Main courses C$8–$11 (US$6–$8). MC, V. Daily 11:30am–10pm. ITALIAN/TAPAS.

This is one of the few inexpensive restaurants in Whitehorse where you don't feel you're eating on a budget. The best thing about the menu is the extensive selection of tapas and appetizers, available throughout the day. The selection includes bruschettas, salads, and satays, all between C$5 and C$6 (US$3.60 and US$4.30). Full entrees are also good bargains, with full-flavored pasta dishes starting at C$8 (US$6), and steaks, chops, and a selection of kabobs topping out at C$11 (US$8). Everything is à la carte, but you can still have a full meal and get change back from C$12 (US$9). The dining room isn't fancy, but the service is prompt and friendly.

WHITEHORSE AFTER DARK

The top-of-the-bill attraction in Whitehorse is the ✪ **Frantic Follies,** a singing, dancing, clowning, and declaiming gold-rush revue that has become famous throughout the North. The show is a very entertaining mélange of skits, music-hall drollery, whooping, high-kicking, garter-flashing cancan dancers, sentimental ballads, and deadpan corn, interspersed with rolling recitations of Robert Service's poetry. Shows take place nightly at the **Westmark Whitehorse Hotel,** 201 Wood St.; for reservations call ☎ **867/668-2042.** Tickets cost C$18 (US$13) for adults and C$9 (US$6) for children.

Another musical comedy, called the *1940's Canteen Show,* is a paean to the era when the U.S. Army laid down the Alaska Highway through the Yukon, precipitating a boom for Whitehorse. The revue promises to bring out the lighter side of the war years, complete with skits and period songs and dancing. The show runs nightly May to September; tickets are C$16.50 (US$12) for adults and C$8 (US$6) for children. The show is held at the Capitol Hotel, 103 Main St. (☎ **867/667-3652**).

4 Kluane National Park

Tucked into the southwestern corner of the Yukon, a 2-hour drive from Whitehorse, these 22,015 square kilometers (8,500 sq. miles) of glaciers, marshes, mountains, and sand dunes are unsettled and virtually untouched. Bordering on Alaska in the west, Kluane National Park contains **Mount Logan** and **Mount St. Elias,** respectively the second- and third-highest peaks in North America.

The park also contains an astonishing variety of **wildlife.** Large numbers of moose, wolves, red foxes, wolverines, lynx, otters, and beavers abound, plus black bears in the forested areas and lots of grizzlies in the major river valleys.

Designated as a **UNESCO World Heritage Site,** Kluane Park lies 158 kilometers (98 miles) west of Whitehorse—take the Alaska Highway to Haines Junction. There, just outside the park's boundaries, you'll find the **Visitor Reception Centre,** which is open year-round (☎ **867/634-2345**). The center has information on hiking trails and canoe routes and shows an award-winning audiovisual presentation on the park. Admission to the park is free.

OUTDOOR ADVENTURES

Because this park is largely undeveloped and is preserved as a wilderness, casual exploration of Kluane is limited to a few day-hiking trails and to aerial sightseeing trips on small aircraft and helicopters. **Kluane Park Adventure Centre** (☎ **867/ 634-2313**), along the main road in Haines Junction, is a good clearinghouse of fishing, hiking, aerial sightseeing, and river-rafting outfitters. As many adventure trips require a minimum number of participants, this service can often put together a last-minute trip more easily than individual outfitters.

The shortest hike up to a glacier follows the **Slims East Trail,** leaving from south of the Sheep Mountain Information Centre. To reach Kaskawulsh Glacier and return will take at least 3 days, but this is an unforgettable hike into very remote and dramatic country. If you're interested in exploring the backcountry, you'll need to be in good shape and have experience with mountaineering techniques.

Day hikers have a few options, mostly near Haines Junction and south along Haines Road. Stop at lovely **Kathleen Lake,** where there's an easy interpreted hike or else a longer trail along the lake's south bank. Stop at the visitor center for more information on hikes in Kluane.

KLUANE AREA OUTFITTERS

The vast expanse of ice and rock in the wilderness heart of Kluane is well beyond the striking range of the average outdoor enthusiast. The area's white-water rafting is world-class, but likewise not for the uninitiated. The Tatshenshini and Alsek rivers are famous for cold and wild white water that flows through magnificent mountain and glacier scenery. Some raft trips pass through iceberg-filled lakes just below huge glaciers!

To explore this part of Kluane, contact an outfitter. **Ecosummer Expeditions,** Box 5095, Whitehorse, YT, Y1A 4Z2 (☎ 867/633-8453; e-mail: joycefill@hypertech.yk.ca), takes guided backpacking, mountaineering, and white-water rafting parties to Kluane National Park. Individual trips can feature either trekking or rafting, while others combine the two in one trip. Trekking expeditions include an 8-day naturalist tour and a 12-day expedition across the park; both are C$1,695 (US$1,212). Rafting trips include trips down the Alsek and Tatshenshini; 4- to 11-day trips run C$895 to C$2,495 (US$640 to US$1,784). Ecosummer also offers Sila Sojourns, backcountry trips—some for women only—that combine adventure travel and components of artistic creativity, such as writing, sketching, or photography workshops.

Also offering white-water trips is **Tatshenshini Expediting,** 1602 Alder St., Whitehorse, YT, Y1A 3W8 (☎ 867/633-2742; fax 867/633-6184; e-mail: tatexp@polarcom.com; Web site: www.yukon.wis.net/tourism/tatshenshini.html). Trips range from a 1-day run down the Tatshenshini, costing C$100 (US$72), to a 10-day trip down the Tatshenshini from Dalton Post and down the Alsek River to the Pacific, costing C$2,500 (US$1,781). Four- and 6-day trips down the Alsek are also available.

AERIAL SIGHTSEEING

Purists may object, but the only way the average person is going to have a chance to see the backcountry of Kluane Park is by airplane or helicopter. The most popular glacier-viewing trip is flown by **Trans North Helicopters** (☎ 867/841-5809). Three trips are offered, ranging from C$35 to C$210 (US$25 to US$150) per person. Short trips provide a panorama of Kluane Lake and the foothills of the park; longer trips explore the glaciers. **Sifton Air** (☎ 867/634-2916) also has three airplane flights over the park; two fly over either Kaskawulsh or Lowell glaciers for C$90 (US$65) per person (which one you fly over may depend on the weather); the longer trip, costing C$125 (US$89), loops over both.

5 Chilkoot Trail & White Pass

South of Whitehorse, massive ranges of glacier-chewed peaks rise up to ring the Gulf of Alaska; stormy waters reach far inland as fjords and enormous glaciers spill into the sea (the famed Glacier Bay is here). This spectacularly scenic region is also the site of the Chilkoot Trail, which in 1898 saw 100,000 gold-rush stampeders struggle up its steep slopes. Another high mountain pass was transcribed in 1900 by the White

Pass and Yukon Railroad on its way to the goldfields; excursion trains now run on these rails, considered a marvel of engineering.

To see these sites, most people embark on long-distance hiking trails, rail excursions, or cruise boats. Happily, two highways edge through this spectacular landscape; using the **Alaska Marine Highway ferries** (☎ **800/642-0066**), this trip can be made as a loop trip from either Whitehorse or Haines Junction. As the ferries keep an irregular schedule, you'll need to call to find out what the sailing times are on the day you plan to make the trip.

THE CHILKOOT TRAIL

In 1896, word of the great gold strikes on the Klondike reached the outside world, and nearly 100,000 people set out for the Yukon to seek their fortunes. There was no organized transportation into the Yukon, and the stampeders resorted to the most expedient methods. The Chilkoot Trail, long an Indian trail through one of the few glacier-free passes in the Gulf of Alaska, became the primary overland route to the Yukon River, Whitehorse, and the goldfields near Dawson City.

The ascent of the Chilkoot became the stuff of legend, and pictures of men and women clambering up the steep snowfields to Chilkoot Summit are one of the enduring images of the stampeder spirit. The North Western Mounted Police demanded that anyone entering the Yukon carry with them a ton of provisions (literally); there were no supplies in the newly born gold camps on the Klondike, and malnutrition and lack of proper shelter were major problems. People were forced to make up to 30 trips up the trail in order to transport all of their goods into Canada. Once past the RCMP station at Chilkoot Summit, the stampeders then had to build some sort of boat or barge to ferry their belongings across Bennett Lake and down the Yukon River.

HIKING THE CHILKOOT TRAIL   Today, the Chilkoot Trail is a national historic park jointly administered by the Canadian and U.S. parks departments. The original trail is open year-round to hikers who wish to experience the route of the stampeders. The route also passes through marvelous glacier-carved valleys, passing through coastal rain forest, boreal forest, and alpine tundra.

However, the Chilkoot Trail is as challenging a trail today as it was 100 years ago. Although the trail is a total of 53 kilometers (33 miles) in length, the vertical elevation gain is nearly 3,700 feet (1100m); much of the trail is very rocky. Weather, even in high summer, can be extremely changeable, making this always-formidable trail sometimes a dangerous one.

Most people will make the trip from **Dyea,** 15 kilometers (9 miles) north of Skagway in Alaska over the Chilkoot Summit (the U.S.-Canadian border) to **Bennett** in northwest British Columbia, in 4 days. The third day is the hardest, with a steep ascent to the pass and a 12-kilometer (7¹/₂-mile) distance between campsites. Once at Bennett, there's no road or boat access; from the end of the trail, you'll need either to make another 6-kilometer (4-mile) hike out along the railroad tracks to Highway 2 near Fraser, British Columbia (the least expensive option), or you can ride the White Pass and Yukon Railway (see below) from Bennett for C$20 (US$14) a person out to Fraser, or for C$60 (US$43) down to Skagway.

The Chilkoot Trail is not a casual hike; you'll need to plan and provision for your trip carefully. Nor is it a wilderness hike; between 75 to 100 people start the trail daily. Remember that the trail is preserved as a historic park; leave artifacts of the gold-rush days—the trail is strewn with boots, stoves, and other effluvia of the stampeders—as you found them.

For information on the Chilkoot Trail, contact the **Klondike Gold Rush National Historic Park,** P.O. Box 517, Skagway, AK 99840 (☎ 907/983-2921); or **Canadian Parks Service,** P.O. Box 5540, Whitehorse, YT, Y1A 5H4 (☎ 867/668-2116).

WHITE PASS & YUKON ROUTE

In 1898, engineers began the task of excavating a route up to White Pass. Considered a marvel of engineering, the track edged around sheer cliffs on long trestles and tunneled through banks of granite. The train effectively ended traffic on the Chilkoot Trail, just to the north.

The White Pass and Yukon Route now operates between Skagway, Alaska, and Bennett, British Columbia. Several different excursions are available on the historic line. Trains travel twice daily from Skagway to the summit of White Pass, a 3-hour return journey for C$78 (US$56) per adult. Roughly twice a month, a train makes a round-trip from Skagway to Lake Bennett, the end of the Chilkoot Trail; tickets for this 8-hour excursion cost C$150 (US$107) (hikers on the Chilkoot Trail can catch this train on its downhill run). Connections between Fraser and Whitehorse via motor coach are available daily. Prices for children are half of the adult fare.

The White Pass and Yukon excursion trains operate from mid-May to the last weekend of September. Advance reservations are suggested; for more information, contact the **White Pass and Yukon Route,** P.O. Box 435, Skagway, AK 99840 (☎ 800/343-7373 or 907/983-2217; e-mail: ngauge73@aol.com; Web site: www.whitepassrailroad.com).

6 Dawson City

Dawson is as much of a paradox as a community today. Once the biggest Canadian city west of Winnipeg, with a population of 30,000, it withered to practically a ghost town after the stampeders stopped stampeding. In 1953 the seat of territorial government was shifted to Whitehorse, which might have spelled the end of Dawson—but didn't. For now, every summer, the influx of tourists more than matches the stream of gold rushers in its heyday. The reason for this is the remarkable preservation and restoration work done by Parks Canada. Dawson today is the nearest thing to an authentic gold-rush town the world has to offer.

However, Dawson City is more than just a gold-rush theme park; it's a real town with 1,800 year-round residents, many still working as miners (and many as sourdough wanna-bes). The town still likes to party, stay up late, and tell tall tales to strangers, much as it did 100 years ago.

ESSENTIALS

VISITOR INFORMATION   The **Visitor Reception Centre,** Front and King streets (☎ 867/993-5566; fax 867/993-7298), provides information on all historic sights and attractions; the national park service also maintains an information desk here. A walking tour of Dawson City, led by a highly knowledgeable guide, departs from the center once a day; the tour costs C$5 (US$3.60).

GETTING THERE   From Whitehorse you can catch an **Air North** plane for the 1-hour hop (☎ 867/668-2228); with 7-day advance purchase, tickets are roughly C$215 (US$154).

If you're driving from Alaska, **take the Taylor Highway (Top of the World)** from Chicken to Dawson. The **Klondike Highway** runs from Skagway, Alaska, to Whitehorse, and from there north to Dawson City via Carmacks and Stewart Crossing. The

537 kilometers (333 miles) from Whitehorse to Dawson City is a very long and tiring drive even though the road is fine.

SPECIAL EVENTS The next few years promise to be one big party in the Yukon, as the 100th anniversary of the discovery of gold in the Klondike and the gold rush rolls around. **Discovery Days,** held in mid-August, commemorates the finding of the Klondike gold a century ago with dancing, music, parades, and canoe races.

The winter's big party, held in mid-March, is the **Percy De Wolfe Memorial Race and Mail Run,** a 210-mile dogsled race from Dawson City to Eagle, Alaska.

EXPLORING DAWSON CITY & ENVIRONS

All of Dawson City and much of the surrounding area is preserved as a National Historic Site, and it's easy to spend a day wandering the boardwalks, looking at the old buildings, shopping the boutiques, and exploring vintage watering holes. About half the buildings in the present-day town are historic; the rest are artful contemporary reconstructions. Between the town and the mighty Yukon River are a series of dikes, which channel the once-devastating floodwaters. A path follows the dikes, and makes for a nice stroll. The SS *Keno,* a Yukon riverboat, is berthed along the dike. Built in Whitehorse in 1922, the boat was one of the last riverboats to travel on the Yukon—there were once more than 200 of them.

A MUSEUM

✪ **Dawson City Museum.** Fifth Ave. ☎ **867/993-5291.** E-mail: dcmuseum@yknet.yk.ca. Admission C$4 (US$2.90) adults, C$2.25 (US$1.60) students and seniors; small children free. May 20 to Labour Day daily 10am–6pm.

Located in the grand old Territorial Administration building, this excellent museum should be your first stop on a tour of Dawson City. Well-curated displays explain the geology and paleontology of the Dawson area (this region was on the main migratory path between Asia and North America during the last ice age), as well as the history of the native Han peoples. The focus of the museum, of course, is the gold rush, and the museum explains various mining techniques, and one of the galleries is dedicated to demonstrating the day-to-day life of turn-of-the-century Dawson City.

Various tours and programs are offered on the hour, including two video programs. Costumed docents are on hand to answer questions and recount episodes of history. On the grounds are early rail steam engines that served in the mines.

KLONDIKE NATIONAL HISTORIC SITES

There are currently eight buildings and sites preserved by the national parks service in and around Dawson City. The Parks Service has recently instituted a fee, usually C$5 (US$3.60) for adults per site, for most of its sites and services. However, you can get a yearlong pass to all the Park Service's Dawson City sites for C$15 (US$10).

Robert Service Cabin. Eighth Ave. Admission C$6 (US$4.30) adults, C$2.50 (US$1.80) children. Daily 9am–noon and 1–5pm; recitals daily at 10am and 3pm.

The poet lived in this two-room log cabin from 1909 to 1912. Backed up against the steep cliffs that edge Dawson City, Service's modest cabin today plays host to a string of pilgrims who come to hear an actor recite some of the most famous verses in the authentic milieu. In this cabin, Service composed his third and final volume of *Songs of a Rolling Stone,* plus a middling awful novel entitled *The Trail of Ninety-Eight.* Oddly enough, the bard of the gold rush neither took part in nor even saw the actual stampede. Born in England, he didn't arrive in Dawson until 1907—as a bank

The Klondike Gold Rush

The Klondike gold rush began with a wild war whoop from the throats of three men—two native Canadians and one white—that broke the silence of Bonanza Creek on the morning of August 17, 1896: "Gold!" they screamed, "gold, gold, gold!" That cry rang through the Yukon, crossed to Alaska, and rippled down into the United States. Soon the whole world echoed with it, and people as far away as China and Australia began selling their household goods and homes to scrape together the fare to a place few of them had ever heard of before.

Some 100,000 men and women from every corner of the globe set out on the Klondike Stampede, descending on a territory populated by a few hundred souls. Tens of thousands came by the Chilkoot Pass from Alaska—the shortest route, but also the toughest. Canadian law required each stampeder to carry 2,000 pounds of provisions up over the 3,000-foot (1000m) summit. Sometimes it took 30 or more trips up a 45° slope to get all the baggage over, and the entire trail—with only one pack—takes about 3¹/₂ days to hike. Many collapsed on the way, but the rest slogged on—on to the Klondike and the untold riches to be found there.

The riches were real enough. The Klondike fields proved to be the richest ever found anywhere. Klondike stampeders were netting C$300 to C$400 in a single pan (and gold was then valued at around C$15 an ounce)! What's more, unlike some gold that lies embedded in veins of hard rock, the Klondike gold came in dust or nugget forms buried in creek beds. This placer gold, as it's called, didn't have to be milled—it was already in an almost pure state!

The trouble was that most of the clerks who dropped their pens and butchers who shed their aprons to join the rush came too late. By the time they had completed the backbreaking trip, all the profitable claims along the Klondike creeks were staked out and defended by grim men with guns in their fists.

Almost overnight, Dawson boomed into a roaring, bustling, gambling, whoring metropolis of 30,000 people, thousands of them living in tents. And here gathered those who made fortunes from the rush without ever handling a pan: the supply merchants, the saloonkeepers, dance-hall girls, and cardsharps. There were also some oddly peripheral characters: A bank teller named Robert Service who listened to the tall tales of prospectors and set them to verse (he never panned gold himself). And a stocky 21-year-old former sailor from San Francisco who adopted a big mongrel dog in Dawson, then went home and wrote a book about him that sold half a million copies. The book was *The Call of the Wild,* and the sailor, Jack London.

By 1903 more than C$500 million in gold had been shipped south from the Klondike and the rush petered out. A handful of millionaires bought mansions in Seattle, tens of thousands went home with empty pockets, thousands more lay dead in unmarked graves along the Yukon River. Dawson—"City" no longer—became a dreaming backwater haunted by 30,000 ghosts.

teller—when the rush was well and truly over. He got most of his plots by listening to old prospectors in the saloons, but the atmosphere he soaked in at the same time was genuine enough—and his imagination did the rest.

Jack London's Cabin. Eighth Ave. ☎ **867/993-5575.** Free admission. Daily 10am–5pm; recitations daily at 1pm.

Jack London lived in the Yukon less than a year—he left in June 1898 after a bout with scurvy—but his writings immortalized the North, particularly the animal stories like *White Fang* and "The Son of Wolf."

Bonanza Creek. West on Bonanza Creek Rd., 5km (3 miles) south of Dawson City.

The original Yukon gold strike and some of the richest pay dirt in the world was found on **Bonanza Creek,** an otherwise insignificant tributary flowing north into the Klondike River. A century's worth of mining has left the streambed piled into an orderly chaos of gravel heaps, the result of massive dredges. The national park service has preserved and interpreted a number of old prospecting sites; however, most of the land along Bonanza Creek is owned privately, so don't trespass, and by no means should you casually gold-pan.

The **Discovery Claim,** 16 kilometers (10 miles) up Bonanza Creek Road, is the spot, now marked by a National Historic Sites cairn, where George Carmack, Skookum Jim, and Tagish Charlie found the gold that unleashed the Klondike Stampede in 1896. They staked out the first four claims (the fourth partner, Bob Henderson, wasn't present). Within a week, Bonanza and Eldorado creeks had been staked out from end to end, but none of the later claims matched the wealth of the first. Fifteen kilometers (9 miles) up Bonanza Creek is **Dredge no. 4,** one of the largest gold dredges ever used in North America. Dredges, which augured up the permafrost, washed out the fine gravel, and sifted out the residual gold, were used after placer miners had panned out the easily accessible gold along the creek. Dredge no. 4 began operations in 1913. It could dig and sift 18,000 cubic yards in 24 hours, thus doing the work of an army of prospectors. Tours are offered of the dredge. You can do some panning yourself at Claim 33, 11 kilometers (7 miles) up Bonanza Road—at C$5 (US$3.60) per pan.

The next drainage up from Bonanza Creek is **Bear Creek,** which became the headquarters for the dredge gold mining that dominated the Klondike area from 1905 to 1965, after the bloom went off placer mining. Parks Canada has developed a 65-building interpretive site that explores the history of industrial mining, including a dredge, hydraulic monitor, and a gold mill, where the gold nuggets were cleaned, melted down, and cast into bullion. The turnoff for Bear Creek is 16 kilometers (10 miles) south of Dawson City, off the Klondike Highway.

TOURS & EXCURSIONS

The national park service offers a **daily walking tour** of Dawson City; sign up at the information center; the cost is C$5 (US$3.60). **Gold City Tours** (☎ 867/ 993-5175) offers a minibus tour of Dawson City and the Bonanza goldfields, as well as a late-evening trip up to Midnight Dome for a midnight-sun panorama of the area. The office is on Front Street, just across from the riverboat *Keno*.

The *Yukon Queen* is a stately twin-deck craft carrying 49 passengers over the 108-mile stretch of river from Dawson City to Eagle, Alaska. Tickets include meals; the daylong journey runs daily from mid-May to mid-September. Passengers can choose either one-way or round-trips. Adults pay C$181 (US$129) round-trip, C$108 (US$77) one-way. Book at **Gray Line Yukon** on Front Avenue near the visitor center (☎ 867/993-5599); tickets go quickly, so try to reserve well in advance.

ACCOMMODATIONS

There are about a dozen hotels, motels, and B&B establishments in Dawson City. Most of them are well appointed, but none are particularly cheap. Only the Eldorado and Downtown hotels and a couple of the B&Bs remain open year-round.

EXPENSIVE

Downtown Hotel. Corner of Second and Queen sts., Dawson City, YT, Y0B 1G0. ☎ **867/ 993-5346.** Fax 867/993-5076. 60 rms. TV TEL. C$124 (US$89) double. AE, DC, DISC, ER, MC, V.

One of Dawson City's originals, the Downtown has been completely refurbished and updated with all modern facilities, yet preserves a real Western-style atmosphere.

Dining/Entertainment: The Jack London Grill and Sourdough Saloon look right out of the gold-rush era; they're definitely worth a visit.

Services: Airport pickup.

Facilities: Jacuzzi, winter plug-ins for head-bolt heaters.

Eldorado Hotel. Third Ave. and Princess St., Dawson City, YT, Y0B 1G0. ☎ **867/993-5451.** Fax 867/993-5256. 52 rms. TV TEL. C$121 (US$86) double. AE, DC, DISC, MC, V.

Another vintage hotel made over and modernized, the Eldorado offers rooms in its original building or in an adjacent modern motel unit. Some rooms feature kitchenettes.

Dining/Entertainment: Licensed dining room and separate lounge.

Services: Complimentary airport pickup.

Facilities: Guest laundry, winter plug-ins.

MODERATE

Dawson City B&B. 451 Craig St., Dawson City, YT, Y0B 1G0. ☎ **867/993-5649.** Fax 867/ 993-5648. 7 rms (some with shared bath). C$79–C$99 (US$56–US$71) double. Senior discounts. DC, MC, V.

This large, nicely decorated home is on the outskirts of Dawson City. Your hosts will also provide use of bicycles and fishing rods.

Dawson City Bunkhouse. Front and Princess sts., Dawson City, YT, Y0B 1G0. ☎ **867/ 993-6164.** Fax 867/993-6051. 27 rms, 5 suites. TV TEL. C$50–C$95 double; C$95 (US$68) suite. MC, V.

One of the few good lodging values in Dawson City, this handsome hotel looks Old West, but is brand new. Rooms are small, but are bright and clean; beds all come with Hudson's Bay Company wool blankets. The cheapest rooms have their own toilets, but showers are down the landing. Only the queen (sleeps three) and king (sleeps four) suites have private bathrooms.

Westmark Inn. Fifth and Harper sts., Dawson City, YT, Y0B 1G0. ☎ **800/544-0970** or 867/ 993-5542. 136 rms. TV TEL. C$90–C$119 (US$64–US$85) double. AE, MC, V.

The Westmark only looks old; on the inside, it reveals itself to be a modern hotel. Facilities include a Laundromat, a cafe with courtyard deck, a gift shop, and a traditional cocktail lounge.

INEXPENSIVE

Dawson City River Hostel. Located across the river via the free ferry from Dawson City (P.O. Box 32), Dawson City, YT, Y0B 1G0. ☎ **867/993-6823.** 30 cabin bunks, plus campsites. C$13–C$15 (US$9–US$11) bunk, C$10 (US$7) campsite. No credit cards. Closed Oct to mid-May.

Check this out for a no-frills, dirt-cheap stay popular with young adventurers. Cabin rooms house up to five people; four rooms are reserved for couples. You won't find electricity here, but there is a hot-water shower house. If you don't mind using an outhouse, this could be for you.

DINING

Food is generally good in Dawson City, and considering the isolation and transport costs, not too expensive. The hotels all have good dining rooms and are open for three meals a day. Many restaurants close in winter, or keep shorter hours.

A cheerful place for a lunchtime burger, at C$4 to C$6 (US$2.85 to US$4.30), or an evening steak or grilled salmon fillet, **Nancy's** (☎ **867/993-5633**), First Avenue and Princess Street, has a large outdoor deck.

Klondike Kate's Restaurant. At the corner of Third Ave. and King St. ☎ **867/993-6527.** Main courses C$5–C$22 (US$3.60–US$16). MC, V. Daily 7am–11pm. CANADIAN.

This friendly and informal cafe is located near the theaters and casino, and serves tasty uncomplicated meals from a small but dependable menu. The atmosphere is Old Dawson, and weather permitting, there's dining on the veranda.

✪ **Marina's.** Fifth Ave. (between Princess and Harper sts.). ☎ **867/993-6800.** Main courses C$13–C$24 (US$9–US$17). MC, V. Daily 11am–10pm. PIZZA/STEAKS/PASTA.

Housed in an attractive, historic-looking building, Marina's offers Dawson City's best dining, with a wide menu offering everything from salads to fine seafood. The pasta and steaks here are truly good, and the pizza's not bad either. The bow-tied wait staff give prompt and professional service.

River West Food & Health. Front and York sts. ☎ **867/993-6339.** Sandwiches and other items C$5–C$8 (US$3.60–US$6). No credit cards. Daily 9am–6pm. SANDWICHES/HEALTH FOOD.

This health-food shop and cafe is a good place to get a decent cup of coffee and order sandwiches either to eat in or take out for picnics. There are soup and salad specials daily.

DAWSON CITY AFTER DARK

Dawson City is still full of honky-tonks and saloons, and most have some form of nightly live music. On warm summer evenings all the doors are thrown open and you can sample the music by strolling through town on the boardwalks; the music is far better than you'd expect for a town of fewer than 2,000 people. A couple of favorites: Both the lounge bar and pub at the **Midnight Sun,** at Third Avenue and Queen Street, have live bands nightly; the bar at the **Westminster Hotel,** between Queen and Princess on Third, often features traditional Yukon fiddlers.

Diamond Tooth Gertie's. Fourth and Queen sts. ☎ **867/993-5575.** Admission C$4.75 (US$3.40).

Canada's only legal gambling casino north of the 60th parallel has an authentic gold-rush decor, from the shirt-sleeved honky-tonk pianist to the wooden floorboards. The games are blackjack, roulette, 21, red dog, and poker, as well as slot machines; the minimum stakes are low and the ambiance is friendly rather than tense. There's a maximum set limit of C$100 (US$72) per hand. The establishment also puts on three floor shows nightly: a combination of cancan dancing, throaty siren songs, and ragtime piano. Gertie's is open May to September daily from 7pm to 2am.

Palace Grand Theatre. King St. ☎ **867/993-6217.** Tickets C$15–C$17 (US$11–US$12).

Built at the height of the stampede by "Arizona Charlie" Meadows, the original Palace Theatre and dance hall had its slam-bang gala premiere in July 1899. Now totally rebuilt according to the original plans, the Palace Grand serves as showcase for the *Gaslight Follies,* a spoofy musical comedy revue that's silly and fun in about equal measure. Performances take place May to September from Wednesday to Monday at 8pm.

7 The Top of the World Highway

This scenic road links Dawson City to Tetlin Junction in Alaska. After the free Yukon River ferry crossing at Dawson City, this 175-mile gravel road rapidly climbs up above the tree line, where it follows meandering ridge tops—hence the name. The views are wondrous: Bare green mountains undulate for hundreds of miles into the distance; looking down, you can see clouds floating in deep valley clefts.

After 106 kilometers (66 miles), the road crosses the U.S.-Canadian border; the border crossing is open in summer only, from 8am to 8pm Pacific time (note that the time in Alaska is an hour earlier). There are no rest rooms, services, or currency exchange at the border. The quality of the road deteriorates on the Alaska side.

The free ferry at Dawson City can get very backed up in high season; delays up to 3 hours are possible. Commercial and local traffic have priority and don't have to wait in line. The Top of the World Highway is not maintained during the winter; it's generally free of snow from April to mid-October.

8 North on the Dempster Highway

Forty kilometers (25 miles) east of Dawson City, the famed ✪ **Dempster Highway** heads north 735 kilometers (456 miles) to Inuvik, Northwest Territories, on the Mackenzie River near the Arctic Ocean. The most northerly public road in Canada, the Dempster is another of those highways that exudes a strange appeal to RV travelers; locals in Inuvik refer to these tourists as "end-of-the-roaders." It's a beautiful drive, especially early in the fall when frost brings out the color in tiny tundra plants and migrating wildlife is more easily seen. The Dempster passes through a wide variety of landscapes, from tundra plains to rugged volcanic mountains; in fact, between Highway 2 and Inuvik the Dempster crosses the Continental Divide three times. **North Fork Pass** in the Ogilvie Mountains, with the knife-edged gray peaks of Tombstone Mountain incising the horizon to the west, is especially stirring. The Dempster crosses the Arctic Circle—one of only two roads in Canada to do so—at Mile 252.

The Dempster wasn't completed until 1978, and special construction techniques were developed to accommodate Arctic conditions. Normal road grading is impossible; if the tundra surface of permafrost is disturbed, the underlying ice begins to melt; over a period of years a marshy sinkhole develops, eventually drowning the road. Much of the Dempster is highly elevated above the tundra, in order that the warm roadbed (during periods of 24-hour sunlight, the exposed soil can absorb a lot of heat) doesn't begin to melt the permafrost.

The Dempster is a gravel road and is open year-round. It's in good shape in most sections, though very dusty; allow 12 hours to make the drive between Inuvik and Dawson City. There are services at three points only: Eagle Plains, Fort McPherson, and Arctic Red River. Don't depend on gas or food outside of standard daytime business hours. At the Peel and the Mackenzie rivers are free ferry crossings during summer; during winter, vehicles simply cross on the ice. For 2 weeks, during the spring thaw and the fall freeze up, through traffic on the Dempster ceases. For information on ferries and road conditions, call ☎ **800/661-0750.** Our coverage of Inuvik begins on page 789.

9 Yellowknife

The capital of the Northwest Territories and the most northerly city in Canada lies on the north shore of Great Slave Lake. The site was originally occupied by the Dogrib tribe. The first white settlers didn't arrive until 1934, following the discovery of **gold** on the lakeshores.

This first gold boom petered out in the 1940s, and Yellowknife dwindled nearly to a ghost town in its wake. But in 1945 came a second gold rush that put the place permanently on the map. The local landmarks are the two operating gold mines that flank Yellowknife: Miramar Con and Giant Yellowknife.

Most of the old gold-boom vestiges are gone—the bordellos, gambling dens, log-cabin banks, and never-closing bars are merely memories now. But the original **Old Town** is there, a crazy tangle of wooden shacks hugging the lakeshore rocks, surrounded by bush-pilot operations that fly sturdy little planes—on floats in summer, on skis in winter.

Yellowknife is a vibrant, youthful place. The white population of Yellowknife is mostly made up of people in their late 20s and 30s. Yellowknife attracts young people just out of college looking for high-paying public-sector jobs, wilderness recreation, and the adventure of living in the Arctic. However, after a few years, most people head back south to warmer climes; not many stay around to grow old. Yellowknife is also the center for a number of outlying native communities, which roots the city in a more long-standing traditional culture.

People are very friendly and outgoing and seem genuinely glad to see you. The party scene here is just about what you'd expect in a town surrounded by native villages and filled with miners and young bureaucrats. There's a more dynamic nightlife here than the size of the population could possibly justify.

ESSENTIALS

VISITOR INFORMATION   For information about the territory in general or Yellowknife in particular, contact one of the following: The **Northern Frontier Regional Visitors Centre,** No. 4, 4807 49th St., Yellowknife, NT, X1A 3T5 (☎ **867/873-4262;** fax 867/873-3654; e-mail: nfva@internorth.com); or **NWT Arctic Tourism,** P.O. Box 1320, Yellowknife, NT, X1A 2L9 (☎ **800/661-0788** or 867/873-7200; fax 867/873-0294; Web site: www.nwttravel.nt.ca).

Another useful phone number for motorists is the **ferry information line** (☎ **800/ 661-0751**), which lets you know the status of the various car ferries along the Dempster and Mackenzie highways. At break-up and freeze-up time, there's usually a month's time when the ferries can't operate and the ice isn't yet thick enough to drive on.

GETTING THERE   NWT Air, a division of Air Canada (☎ **800/776-3000** in the U.S. or 800/332-1080 in Alberta), and **Canada North,** a division of Canadian Airlines (☎ **800/426-7000**), fly into Yellowknife from Edmonton; flights range from C$700 to C$1,085 (US$500 to US$775). Canada North also provides daily flights to and from Ottawa and Toronto; round-trip tickets range from C$1,680 to C$2,380 (US$1,200 to US$1,700). Yellowknife Airport is 5 kilometers (3 miles) northeast of the town.

If you're driving from Edmonton, take Highway 16 to Grimshaw. From there the **Mackenzie Highway** leads to the Northwest Territories border, 475 kilometers (295 miles) north, and on to Yellowknife via Fort Providence. The total distance from

Edmonton is 1,524 kilometers (945 miles). Most of the road is now paved, though construction continues throughout the summer.

CITY LAYOUT The city's expanding urban center, **New Town**—a busy hub of modern hotels, shopping centers, office blocks, and government buildings—spreads above the town's historic birthplace, called **Old Town.** Together the two towns count about 17,200 inhabitants, by far the largest community in the Territories.

Most of New Town lies between rock-lined Frame Lake and Yellowknife Bay on Great Slave Lake. The main street in this part of town is **Franklin Avenue,** also called 50th Avenue. Oddly, early town planners decided to start the young town's numbering system at the junction of 50th Avenue and 50th Street; even though the downtown area is only 10 blocks square, the street addresses give the illusion of a much larger city.

The junction of 48th Street and Franklin (50th) Avenue is pretty much the center of town. A block south is the post office and a number of enclosed shopping arcades (very practical up here, where winter temperatures would otherwise discourage shopping). Turn north and travel half a mile to Old Town and **Latham Island,** which stick out into Yellowknife Bay. This is still a bustling center for boats, floatplanes, B&Bs, and food and drink.

South of Frame Lake is the modern residential area, and just west is the airport. If you follow 48th Street out of town without turning onto the Mackenzie Highway, the street turns into the **Ingraham Trail,** a bush road heading out toward a series of lakes with fishing and boating access, hiking trails, and a couple of campgrounds. This is the main recreational playground for Yellowknifers, who love to canoe or kayak from lake to lake, or all the way back to town.

GETTING AROUND Monday to Saturday, the **City Bus** (☎ 867/873-4892) makes a loop through Yellowknife once an hour. The fare is C$2 (US$1.45).

For car rentals, **Avis** (☎ 867/920-2491) and **Budget** (☎ 867/873-3366) both have offices at the airport. **Rent-A-Relic,** 356 Old Airport Rd. (☎ 867/873-3400; e-mail: xferrier@ssimicro.com), offers older models at substantial savings—and they'll deliver a vehicle to your hotel or campsite. **Tilden,** at 5118 50th St. (☎ 867/ 873-2911), has a range of rental vehicles from full-size cars to half-ton four-speed vans. At all these operations, the number of cars available during the summer season is rather limited and the demand very high. You may have to settle for what's to be had rather than what you want. Try to book ahead as far as possible. To rent an RV, contact **Frontier RV Rentals,** P.O. Box 1088, Yellowknife, NT, X1A 2N7 (☎ 867/ 873-5413).

Taxis are pretty cheap in Yellowknife; call **City Cabs** (☎ 867/873-4444) or **Gold Cabs** (☎ 867/873-8888) for a lift. A ride to the airport costs about C$10 (US$7).

SPECIAL EVENTS The **Caribou Carnival,** held from March 17 to March 25 annually, is a burst of spring fever after a very long, very frigid winter (one of the fever symptoms consists of the delusion that winter is over). For a solid week Yellowknife is thronged with parades, local talent shows, and skit revues with imported celebrities. Some fascinating and specifically Arctic contests include igloo building, Inuit wrestling, tea boiling, and the competition highlight: the Canadian Championship Dog Derby, a 3-day, 240-kilometer (150-mile) dogsled race, with more than 200 huskies and their mushers competing for the C$30,000 (US$21,375) prize.

Summer comes but once a year and doesn't last long in Yellowknife, so the locals make the most of it with a profusion of festivals. **Mining Week** commemorates the city's gold-mine heritage, and offers such unique features as underground mine rescue competitions. Held during the second week of June, Mining Week is the only time that the area's mines are open for tours. The **Festival of the Midnight Sun** is an arts festival held in mid-July. There's a one-act play competition, various arts workshops (including lessons in native beading and carving), and fine art on display all over town. **Folk on the Rocks,** an outdoor music festival, takes over the shores of Long Lake in late July.

EXPLORING YELLOWKNIFE

Visitors to Yellowknife should stop by the **Northern Frontier Regional Visitor Centre** (☎ 867/873-3131) on 48th Street on the west edge of town. There are a number of exhibits that explain the major points of local history and native culture; you'll want to put the kids on the "bush-flight" elevator, which simulates a flight over Great Slave Lake while slowly rising to the second floor. Also pick up a free parking pass, which enables visitors to escape the parking meters.

The ✪ **Prince of Wales Northern Heritage Centre,** on the shore of Frame Lake (☎ 867/873-7551), is a museum in a class all its own. You'll learn the history, background, and characteristics of the Dene and Inuit peoples (the Métis and pioneer whites) through dioramas, artifacts, and talking, reciting, and singing slide presentations. It depicts the human struggle with an environment so incredibly harsh that survival alone seems an accomplishment. Admission is free and it's open daily from June to August from 10:30am to 5:30pm; September to May it's open Tuesday to Friday from 10:30am to 5:30pm.

The **Bush Pilot's Memorial** is a stone pillar rising above Old Town that pays tribute to the little band of airmen who opened up the Far North. The surrounding cluster of shacks and cottages is the original Yellowknife, built on the shores of a narrow peninsula jutting into Great Slave Lake. It's not exactly a pretty place, but definitely intriguing. Sprinkled along the inlets are half a dozen bush-pilot operations, minuscule airlines flying charter planes as well as scheduled routes to outlying areas. The little floatplanes shunt around like taxis, and you can watch one landing or takeoff every hour of the day. About 100 yards off the tip of the Old Town peninsula lies Latham Island, which you can reach by a causeway. The island has a small native-Canadian community, a few luxury homes, and a number of B&Bs.

TOURS & EXCURSIONS

Raven Tours (☎ 867/873-4776; fax 867/873-4856; e-mail: raventours@ yellowknife.com), which operates out of the visitor center, and the **Yellowknife Tour Company** (☎ 867/669-9402), which operates across from the Wildcat Café in Old Town, both offer a standard 3-hour city tour, as well as a number of more specialized trips (boat, waterfall, and wildlife tours, and more). The standard tour costs C$20 (US$14); call to find out what other tours are offered during your visit. Raven also offers aerial sightseeing trips, wildlife-viewing tours, as well as fishing trips on Great Slave Lake. Yellowknife Tour Company can also set you up with a rental bike or canoe.

Bluefish Services (☎ 867/873-4818) is a boat-tour operator that offers a number of excursions onto Great Slave Lake. The 2-hour interpretive boat tour of the Yellowknife area costs C$25 (US$18) and takes in the Old Town and the mining areas, as well as the native villages of N'Dilo and Detah. Bluefish also offers a longer boat trip out to one of the many islands in the lake, where your guide/chef cooks up fresh fish for dinner at a cost of C$65 (US$46). It's a great evening out (remember that during the summer, the sun doesn't go down till midnight!) Bluefish also offers guided fishing trips on the lake.

Natural-history tours of the Yellowknife area, with an emphasis on subarctic ecology, bird watching, and geology, are offered by **Cygnus Ecotours** (☎ 867/873-4782). Some tours focus on the ecosystem near town, while other trips journey out along the Ingraham Trail to more distant lakes; hikes to Cameron Falls are also available.

Cruise Canada's Arctic in the **MS *Norweta,*** a modern diesel-engine craft equipped with radar and owned by NWT Marine Group, 5414 52nd St., Yellowknife, NT, X1A 3K1 (☎ 867/873-2180). For part of the summer, the *Norweta* is in Yellowknife and offers a number of day excursions and dinner cruises. Call ahead to make reservations and to make sure the boat is available. Twice a summer, the *Norweta* conducts 5-day cruises of the scenic East Arm of Great Slave Lake, at a cost of C$1,700 to C$2,000 (US$1,210 to US$1,424). The *Norweta* also makes one trip up and back on the mighty Mackenzie River to Inuvik, costing C$4,000 (US$2,848).

SHOPPING

Yellowknife is a principal retail outlet for Northern artwork and craft items, as well as the specialized clothing the climate demands. Some of it is so handsome that sheer vanity will make you wear it in more southerly temperatures.

Northern Images, in the Yellowknife Mall, 50th Avenue (☎ 867/873-5944), is a link in the cooperative chain of stores by that name that stretches across the entire Canadian North. The premises are as attractive as they are interesting—exhibitions as much as markets. They feature authentic native-Canadian articles: apparel and carvings, graphic prints, silver jewelry, ornamental moose-hair tuftings, and porcupine quill work.

Although fairly new, the log cabin–style **The Trappers Cabin,** 4 Lessard Dr., Latham Island (☎ 867/873-3020), is the nearest thing to an old-time frontier store Yellowknife can offer. You drop in there not just to buy goods, but to have coffee and snacks, book cruises and excursions, listen to gossip, and collect information. Hours are daily from 9am to 10pm.

SPORTS & OUTDOOR ACTIVITIES

The town is ringed by hiking trails, some gentle, some pretty rugged. Most convenient for a short hike or a jog is the trail that rings **Frame Lake,** accessible from the Northern Heritage Centre and other points.

The other major focus of recreation in the Yellowknife area is the **Ingraham Trail,** a paved and then gravel road that starts just west of town and winds east over 73 kilometers (45 miles) to Tibbet Lake. En route lie a string of lakes, mostly linked by the Cameron River, making this prime canoe and kayak country. Ingraham Trail also crosses by several territorial parks, two waterfalls, the Giant Mine, and waterfowl habitat, plus lots of picnic sites, camping spots, boat rentals, and fishing spots.

One of the largest lakes along the trail is Prelude Lake, 32 kilometers (20 miles) east of town; it's a wonderful setting for scenic boating and trout, pike, and Arctic-grayling fishing. The **Prelude Lake Lodge** (☎ 867/920-4654) rents motorboats and rowboats.

CANOEING & KAYAKING   When you fly into Yellowknife, you'll notice that about half the land surface is comprised of lakes, so it's no wonder that kayaking is really catching on hereabouts. **Above and Below Sports,** 4100 Franklin Ave. (☎ 867/669-9222), offers rentals and instruction, as well as guided tours of Great Slave and Prelude lakes.

The visitor center offers maps of seven different canoe paths through the maze of lakes, islands, and streams along the Ingraham Trail; with a few short portages, it's possible to float all the way from Prelude Lake to Yellowknife, about a 5-day journey. Canoes are available for rent from either the **Sportsman,** in downtown Yellowknife at 50th Street and 52nd Avenue (☎ **867/873-2911**), or more conveniently, from **Eagle Point Rentals** (☎ **867/873-1683**), located at the Yellowknife River Bridge, 8 kilometers (5 miles) north of town on the Ingraham Trail. A daylong rental is around C$45 (US$32).

FISHING TRIPS   Traditionally, fishing has been the main reason to visit the Yellowknife and the Great Slave Lake area. Lake trout, Arctic grayling, northern pike, and whitefish grow to storied size in these Northern lakes; the pristine water conditions and general lack of anglers mean that fishing isn't just good, it's great. Some outfitters, like **Bluefish Services** (☎ **867/873-4818**) listed above, offer fishing trips on Great Slave Lake directly from town, but most serious anglers fly in floatplanes to fishing lodges, either on Great Slave or on more remote lakes, for a wilderness fishing trip.

One of the best of the lodge outfitters on Great Slave Lake is Jerry Bricker's **Frontier Fishing Lodge** (☎ **867/465-6843,** or 867/370-3501 in summer only). A 3-day all-inclusive guided fishing trip will cost around C$1,700 (US$1,215). Nearly 2 dozen fishing-lodge outfitters operate in the Yellowknife area; contact the visitor center or consult the *Explorers' Guide* for a complete listing.

HIKING   The most popular hike along Ingraham Trail is to **Cameron River Falls.** The well-signed trailhead is located 48 kilometers (30 miles) east of Yellowknife. Although not a long hike—allow 1¹/₂ hours for the round-trip—the trail to the falls is hilly. An easier trail is the **Prelude Lake Nature Trail,** which winds along Prelude Lake through wildlife habitat. The 90-minute hike begins and ends at the lakeside campground. Closer to Yellowknife, the **Prospectors Trail** at Fred Henne Park is an interpreted trail through gold-bearing rock outcroppings; signs tell the story of Yellowknife's rich geology.

ACCOMMODATIONS

Yellowknife now has more than 500 hotel and motel rooms in a wide range of prices. Hotel standards are good; in parts, excellent. The **visitor center** (☎ 867/873-3131) also operates as a room-reservation service, which is especially handy for locating rooms at local B&Bs.

EXPENSIVE

✪ **Explorer Hotel.** 48th St. and 48th Ave., Yellowknife, NT, X1A 2R3. ☎ **800/661-0892** or 867/873-3531. Fax 867/873-2789. 126 rms, 2 suites. A/C TV TEL. C$172 (US$122) double; from C$225 (US$161) suite. AE, ER, MC, V.

The Explorer Hotel is a commanding eight-story snow-white structure that overlooks both the city and a profusion of rock-lined lakes. The Explorer has long been Yellowknife's premier hotel—Queen Elizabeth herself has stayed here. The lobby is large and comfortable, with indoor greenery and deep armchairs and sofas.

The guest rooms are spacious and uncluttered, all equipped with a color TV, a writing desk, and table. A no-smoking floor is available.

Dining: The Factors Club dining room is one of the Territories finest restaurants.
Services: Room service, dry cleaning, laundry service.
Facilities: Conference rooms, gift shop.

MODERATE

Captain Ron's. 8 Lessard Dr., Yellowknife, NT, X1A 2G5. ☎ **867/873-3746.** 4 rms (with shared bath). C$90 (US$64) double. Rates include breakfast. MC, V.

Located on Latham Island on the shores of the Great Slave Lake, Captain Ron's is reached by causeway. It's a cozy and picturesque place with four guest rooms and a reading lounge with fireplace and TV. You can arrange fishing trips with Captain Ron (he really exists and used to skipper a cruise vessel).

Discovery Inn. 4701 Franklin Ave., Yellowknife, NT, X1A 2N6. ☎ **867/873-4151.** Fax 867/920-7948. 41 rms. A/C TV TEL. C$120 (US$86) double. AE, MC, V.

A small two-story modern brick building with friendly awnings and a huge neon sign, the Discovery Inn has a central downtown location. There's a lively bar with pool table, video games, and nightly entertainment, plus a family restaurant. Six of the rooms have kitchenettes.

Igloo Inn. 4115 Franklin Ave. (P.O. Box 596), Yellowknife, NT, X1A 2N4. ☎ **867/873-8511.** Fax 867/873-5547. 44 rms. TV TEL. C$99 (US$71) double. Rates include continental breakfast. AE, MC, V.

An attractive two-story wood structure, the Igloo sits at the bottom of the hill road leading to Old Town. Complimentary coffee is served all day in its breakfast room. Thirty-three of the units have pleasantly spacious kitchenettes stocked with electric ranges and all the necessary utensils. Altogether, it's a great value for your money.

✪ Yellowknife Inn. 5010 49th St., Yellowknife, NT, X1A 2N4. ☎ **867/873-2601.** Fax 867/873-2602. 130 rms. TV TEL. C$130 (US$93) double. Rates include breakfast. AE, DC, ER, MC, V.

The Yellowknife Inn is right in the center of Yellowknife, and has recently been completely refurbished and updated. The new lobby is joined to a large shopping and dining complex, making this the place to stay if you're arriving in winter. The rooms are fair-sized, some with minibars, and offer guest amenities that have won an International Hospitality award. The walls are decorated with Inuit art. Guests receive a pass to local fitness facilities and complimentary shuttle rides to and from the airport. The fourth floor is reserved for nonsmokers.

INEXPENSIVE

Eva and Eric Henderson. 114 Knutsen Ave., Yellowknife, NT, X1A 2Y4. ☎ **867/873-5779.** Fax 867/873-6160. 3 rms (with shared bath). TEL. C$70 (US$50) double. Rates include breakfast. No goods-and-services tax (GST) added to room rates. No credit cards.

Located handy to the airport, Eva and Eric Henderson have three rooms available for nonsmokers. There's a shared lounge with color TV, a shared bathroom, kitchen for guests, a library, and Northern foods for breakfast (if requested). The Hendersons are some of the nicest and most welcoming people around; you'll enjoy staying here.

CAMPGROUNDS

The most convenient campground to Yellowknife is **Fred Henne Park** (☎ **867/920-2472**), just east of the airport right on Long Lake. Both RVs and tents are welcome; there are showers and kitchen shelters, but no hookups. Campsites are C$12 (US$9). At **Prelude Lake Territorial Park** (☎ **867/920-4674**), 29 kilometers (18 miles) east of Yellowknife, there are rustic campsites without camping fees; although there are no facilities beyond running water, boat rental and food service is available at the nearby **Prelude Lake Lodge** (☎ **867/920-4654**).

DINING
EXPENSIVE

Factors Club Dining Room. In the Explorer Hotel, 4825 49th Ave. ☎ **867/873-3531.** Reservations recommended. Main courses C$17–C$33 (US$12–US$24). AE, ER, MC, V. Daily 5:30–10pm. NORTHERN/INTERNATIONAL.

Factors offers some of the best Northern cooking in the Northwest Territories. The menu offers a number of game dishes peculiar to the region (caribou and musk ox) but prepared with French sauces and finesse. Other dishes, like Jamaican chicken and game hen with coconut curry sauce, prove quite a shock to those innocent visitors who expected log-cabin cuisine in the Territories. The logs are there all right, but they're on the ceiling and in the immense enclosed fireplace with a copper chimney that forms the centerpiece. The service is as smooth and silent as you'd find in top-ranking metropolitan restaurants.

The Office. 4915 50th St. ☎ 867/873-3750. Reservations recommended. Main courses C$9–C$26 (US$6–US$19). AE, MC, V. Mon–Sat 11:30am–10pm. CANADIAN/NORTHERN.

This sophisticated retreat sports elegant decor and paintings by local artists. House specialties include Northern fare, like the frozen thinly sliced Arctic char and caribou steak. Otherwise the menu is top-grade Anglo: roast lamb, beef with Yorkshire pudding, roast duckling, great steaks, and a large selection of seafood. The eggs Benedict served here is famous among the lunchtime crowd. And The Office puts on possibly the best salad bar in the north.

MODERATE

L'Attitudes Restaurant & Bistro. Center Square Mall, 5010 49th St. ☎ **867/920-7880.** Pizza C$10–C$12 (US$7–US$9); pasta C$12–C$15 (US$9–US$11); main courses C$12–C$26 (US$9–US$19). MC, V. Daily 7:30am–8pm. INTERNATIONAL/NORTHERN.

L'Attitudes is one of Yellowknife's newest and most attractive restaurants and reflects its youth with lighter, more eclectic offerings. The menu ranges from boutique pizzas to pasta, barbecued ribs, and chicken, and on to intriguing Northern specialties like a rack of caribou with rosemary mint sauce (C$25/US$18). If you're more interested in grazing through several dishes, there's a snack menu, with salads and nibbles available all day; you can also caffeinate on espresso drinks. There are more vegetarian selections here than anywhere else in Yellowknife.

Sam's Monkey Tree. Range Lake Road Mall. ☎ 867/920-4914. Most items C$8–C$14.95 (US$6–US$11). MC, V. Mon–Thurs 4–11pm, Fri 4pm–midnight, Sat–Sun 11am–10pm. INTERNATIONAL/CHINESE.

Sam's is actually two different establishments operating under one name, but serving quite distinct menus. The first is a pub restaurant with a country-inn flavor, a dartboard, and outdoor patio. The second is a good Chinese eatery with take-out service and Szechuan and Cantonese fare. Between them the two manage to please most palates, including vegetarians'.

✪ Wildcat Café. Wiley Rd., Old Town. ☎ 867/873-8850. Reservations not accepted. Main courses C$7–C$17 (US$5–US$12). MC, V. Mon–Sat 7am–9:30pm, Sun 10am–9pm. Closed in winter. NORTHERN.

The Wildcat Café is a tourist site as much as an eatery. A squat log cabin with a deliberately grizzled frontier look, the Wildcat is actually refurbished in the image of the 1930s original. The atmospheric interior is reminiscent of Yellowknife in its pioneer days, and the cafe has been photographed, filmed, painted, and caricatured often enough to give it star quality. The menu changes daily, but focuses on local products like caribou and lake fish, in addition to steaks. Seating is along long benches, and you'll probably end up sharing your table with other diners.

INEXPENSIVE

The coffee shop at the **Northern Heritage Centre,** on Frame Lake (☎ 867/873-7551), has a good selection of inexpensive luncheon items; this is a good place to go for soup, salad, or sandwiches, whether or not you plan on visiting the museum. For good and inexpensive family dining, go to the **Country Corner,** 4601 Franklin Ave. (☎ **867/873-9412**), a log cafe just north of downtown. Come here for breakfast when the line snakes out the door at the Wildcat.

Brand-name fast-food is present in Yellowknife, and for people on a tight budget, this is probably the way to avoid the otherwise rather high cost of dining here. All of the downtown shopping arcades have inexpensive food outlets as well.

YELLOWKNIFE AFTER DARK

By and large, people in Yellowknife aren't scared of a drink, and nightlife revolves around bars and pubs. Increasingly, there's a music scene in Yellowknife; a number of local bands have developed national followings.

The Float Base, at the corner of 50th Avenue and 51st Street (☎ **867/873-3034**), is a jolly neighborhood basement pub with polished cedar tables and upholstered swivel chairs. Floatplane bits and photos are used for decoration.

Yellowknife's first brew pub, the ✪ **Bush Pilot,** 3502 Wiley Rd. (☎ **867/ 920-2739**), is where Arctic Ales are served up on a bar made from the wing of a plane. On Sunday the establishment becomes a teahouse: Darjeeling and cream cakes share the billing with clairvoyants and tarot-card readers. This fun pub has a great location on the water in Old Town.

Officially called Bad Sam's, the **Gold Range Tavern,** in the Gold Range Hotel, 5010 50th St. (☎ **867/873-4441**), is better known by its local nickname—"Strange Range." There is nothing really strange about it; the Gold Range is exactly what you'd expect to find in a Northern frontier town.

The Range is an occasionally rip-roaring tavern that attracts the whole gamut of native and visiting characters in search of some after-dinner whoopee. The nightly entertainment is supposedly country-and-western music, but that doesn't really describe it. Anybody is liable to join in with an offering—such as an elderly French-Canadian fur trapper who comes to town on a snowmobile and accompanies himself on a plywood guitar. There is also dancing and a pool table, the second-highest per-capita beer consumption in Canada, and, periodically, a brawl, very quickly subdued by the most efficient bouncers in the Territory. You don't come here for a quiet evening, but you can't say you've seen Yellowknife if you haven't seen the Strange Range.

10 Nahanni National Park

A breathtaking, unspoiled wilderness of 4,766 square kilometers (1,840 sq. miles) in the southwest corner of the Territories, Nahanni National Park is accessible only by foot, motorboat, canoe, or charter aircraft. The park preserves 295 kilometers (183 miles) of the **South Nahanni River.** One of the wildest rivers in North America, the South Nahanni claws its path through the rugged Mackenzie Mountains, at one point charging over incredible **Virginia Falls,** twice as high as Niagara (at 105m/316 ft.) and carrying more water. Below the falls, the river surges through one of the continent's deepest gorges, with canyon walls up to 1,333 meters (4,000 ft.) high.

White-water rafting from Virginia Falls through the canyon is the most popular, but not the only, white-water trip in the park. The trip from the falls (you'll need to fly in, as this is a roadless park) to the usual take-out point takes at least 6 days or more, depending on the amount of time spent hiking or relaxing en route. The best white water in the park is actually far above the falls, beginning at Moose Ponds and continuing to Rabbitkettle Lake, near an impressive hot-springs formation.

A number of outfitters are licensed to run the South Nahanni River. For a full listing and for further information about the park, contact the Superintendent, **Nahanni National Park,** Postal Bag 300, Fort Simpson, NT, X0E 0N0 (☎ **867/695-3151**). As an example, **Nahanni River Adventures,** P.O. Box 4869, Whitehorse, YT, Y1A 4N6 (☎ **867/668-3180;** fax 867/668-3056; e-mail: nahanni@yknet.yk.ca; Web site: users.yknet.ca/bbdo/nahanni), operates a 6- to 10-day trip from the falls through the canyon with either canoes or inflatable raft for C$2,200 (US$1,573).

A number of charter airlines also offer daylong aerial sightseeing trips into the park. **Deh Cho Air** (☎ 867/770-4103) operates out of Fort Liard, and **Simpson Air** (☎ 867/695-2505) operates out of Fort Simpson. Each offers half-day charters to Virginia Falls for C$150 (US$107) (minimum numbers required).

11 The Arctic North

Canada's Arctic North is one of the world's most remote and uninhabited areas, but one that holds many rewards for the traveler willing to get off the beaten path. Arctic landscapes can be breathtaking: the 72-kilometer-wide (45-mile-wide) wildlife-filled delta of the **Mackenzie River** or the awesome fjords and glaciers of **Baffin Island.** In many areas, traditional Indian or Inuit villages retain age-old hunting and fishing ways, but welcome respectful visitors to their communities. The **artwork** of the North is famous worldwide; in almost every community, artists engage in weaving, print-making, or stone, ivory, and bone carving. Locally produced artwork is available from community co-ops, galleries, or from the artists themselves.

Traveling the wilds of the Canadian Arctic is a great adventure, but frankly it isn't for everyone. Most likely the Arctic isn't like anywhere you've ever traveled before, and while that may be exciting, there are some realities of Arctic travel that you need to be aware of before you start making plans.

PRICES   The Arctic is a very expensive place to travel. Airfare is very high (many tourists travel here on frequent-flier miles, one of the few ways to get around the steep ticket prices). While almost every little community in the Arctic has a serviceable hotel/restaurant, room prices are shockingly high; a rustic, hostel-style room with full board costs as much as a decent room in Paris. Food costs are equally high (remember that all of your food was air-freighted in) and quality is poor. Also, don't plan on having a drink anywhere except Inuvik or Iqaluit—also expensive, at C$5 (US$3.60) a bottle for beer.

FLYING IN THE BUSH   Except for the Dempster Highway to Inuvik, there is no road access to any point in the Arctic. *All public transportation is by airplane.* To reach the most interesting points in the North, you'll need to fly on floatplanes, tiny commuter planes, and aircraft that years ago passed out of use in the rest of the world. Of course, all aircraft in the Arctic are regularly inspected and are regulated for safety, but if you have phobias about flying, then you might find the combination of rattly aircraft and changeable flying conditions unpleasant.

CULTURE SHOCK   The Arctic is the homeland of the Inuit. Travelers are made welcome in nearly all native villages, but it must be stressed that these communities are not set up as holiday camps for southern visitors. Most people are not English speakers; except for the local hotel, there may not be public areas open for non-natives. You are definitely a guest here; while people are friendly and will greet you, you will probably feel very much an outsider.

The Inuit are hunters: On long summer nights, you'll go to sleep to the sound of hunters shooting seals along the ice floes. Chances are good that you'll see people butchering seals or whales along the beaches. You may be lucky enough to visit an Inuit village during a traditional feast. All the meat, including haunches of caribou, entire seals, and slabs of whale, will be consumed raw. Nor is the Arctic a pristine place. Garbage and carcasses litter the shoreline and town pathways. Don't come to the North expecting to find a sanitized, feel-good atmosphere.

If these realities are a problem for you, then you should reconsider a trip to the Arctic. If not, then traveling to a traditional Inuit village under a 24-hour summer sun to partake of native hospitality is a great adventure; this is surely one of the last truly traditional cultures and unexploited areas left in North America.

INUVIK: END OF THE ROAD

Inuvik, 771 kilometers (478 miles) from Dawson City, is the town at the end of the long Dempster Highway—the most northerly road in Canada—and the most-visited center in the western Arctic. Because of its year-round road access (the Dempster Highway reached here in 1978) and frequent flights from Yellowknife, Inuvik is becoming a major tourist destination in itself, and is the departure point for many tours out to more far-flung destinations. However, don't come to Inuvik looking for history: the town was built by the Canadian government in the 1950s and improved on by the oil boom in the 1970s. While there's not much charm to the town beyond its many-colored housing blocks, it does have all the comforts and facilities of a midsized town: nice hotels, hospitals, good restaurants, schools, banks (and cash machines), shops, a Laundromat, and one traffic light. All this 2° north of the Arctic Circle!

Inuvik is home to a population of 3,400, comprised of near equal parts of **Inuvialuit,** the Inuit people of the western Arctic; of **Gwich'in,** a Dene tribe from south of the Mackenzie River delta; and of more recent white settlers, many of whom work at public-sector jobs.

ESSENTIALS

Inuvik is on the Mackenzie River, one of the largest rivers in the world. Here, about 129 kilometers (80 miles) from its debouchment into the Arctic Ocean, the Mackenzie flows into its vast delta, 88 kilometers (55 miles) long and 65 kilometers (40 miles) wide. This incredible waterway, where the river fans out into a maze containing thousands of lakes, dozens of channels, and mile after mile of marsh, is a rich preserve of wildlife, especially waterfowl and aquatic mammals. Inuvik is also right at the northern edge of the taiga, near the beginning of the tundra, making this region a transition zone for a number of the larger Northern animals.

GETTING THERE   The drive from Dawson City along the Dempster usually takes 12 hours, and most people make the drive in 1 day (remember, in the summer, there's no end of daylight). It's best to drive the road after July 1, when the spring mud has dried up. There is summer bus service between Inuvik and Dawson City: **Arctic Tour Co. (☎ 867/777-4100)** offers buses Tuesday and Thursday for a round-trip fare of C$350 (US$250). One flight a day links Inuvik to Yellowknife on both **NWT Air (☎ 800/776-3000** in the U.S. or 800/332-1080 in Alberta) and **Canada North (☎ 800/426-7000);** with 7-day advanced purchase, the fare is around C$630 (US$450).

VISITOR INFORMATION   For more information about Inuvik and the surrounding area, contact the **Western Arctic Tourism Association,** P.O. Box 2600, Inuvik, NT, X0E 0T0 (☎ **800/661-0788** or 867/777-4321; fax 867/777-2434; Web site: www.inuvik.net).

WEATHER   Weather can change rapidly in Inuvik. In summer, a frigid morning, with the winds and rains barreling off the Arctic Ocean, can change to a very warm and muggy afternoon in seemingly minutes. (Yes, it does get hot up here.) During the summer, there is nearly a month when the sun doesn't set at all, and 6 months when there is only a short dusk at night. Correspondingly, there are about 3 weeks in winter when the sun doesn't rise.

SPECIAL EVENTS   July is festival season in Inuvik. The **Great Northern Arts Festival,** which begins the third week of July and runs into August, is a celebration of the visual and performing arts, with most regional artists displaying works for sale; artists also give workshops on traditional craft techniques. The festival also includes Musicfest, a weekend of traditional fiddling, drumming, and jigging. The last week of July, Inuvik hosts the **Northern Games,** a celebration of traditional native sports and competitions, including drumming, dancing, high-kicking, craft displays, and the unique "Good Woman" contest, in which Inuit women show their amazing skill at seal and muskrat skinning, bannock baking, sewing, and other abilities that traditionally made a "good woman."

WHAT TO SEE IN INUVIK

The most famous landmark in Inuvik is **Our Lady of Victory Church,** a large round structure with a glistening dome, usually referred to as the Igloo Church. Visitors should definitely stop at the **Western Arctic Visitors Centre** (☎ **867/777-4518**) on the south end of town. Exhibits provide a good overview of the human and natural history of the area, and of recreation and sightseeing options.

Several art and gift shops offer local Inuit and Indian carvings and crafts; probably the best is **Northern Images,** 115 Mackenzie Rd. (☎ **867/777-2786**). Don't miss **Boreal Bookstore,** 181 Mackenzie Rd. (☎ **867/777-3748**), for a great selection of books on all things Northern.

EXPLORING OUTSIDE INUVIK

Unless you're a die-hard "end-of-the-roader," you'll want to hitch up with a local tour company and get out onto the Arctic Ocean or Mackenzie Delta. The best of the local tour operators is **Arctic Nature Tours,** P.O. Box 1530, Inuvik, NT, X0E 0T0 (☎ **867/777-3300;** e-mail: archcnt@internorth.com). This family-operated business also owns a charter airline, so there's no problem lining up planes and pilots for expeditions. Trips to all the following destinations are offered. **Arctic Tour Company,** P.O. Box 2021, Inuvik, NT X0E 0T0 (☎ **800/661-0721** in western Canada, or 867/777-4100), also offers tours to many of the same destinations, plus an imposing list of other, more specialized tours. However, as minimum numbers are necessary for all tours, don't count on specific trips to run while you're visiting.

TUKTOYAKTUK   On the shores of the Beaufort Sea, 161 kilometers (100 miles) south of the permanent polar ice cap in the Arctic Ocean, and popularly known as "Tuk," this little native town is reached by a short flight from Inuvik (in winter, the frozen Mackenzie River becomes an "ice road" linking the two towns by vehicle). Most tour operators in Inuvik offer 2-hour tours of Tuk for around C$125 (US$89) (including the flight), focusing on the curious "pingos" (volcanolike formations made of buckled ice that occur only here and in one location in Siberia) and the Inuvialuit culture. Stops are made at the workshops of stone carvers and other artisans, and you'll get the chance to stick your toe in the Arctic Ocean. Although there are a couple of hotels in Tuk, there's really no reason to spend more than a couple of hours up here; even as Arctic towns go, Tuk is pretty desolate.

MACKENZIE DELTA TRIPS When the Mackenzie River meets the Arctic Ocean, it forms an enormous basin filled with a multitude of lakes, river channels, and marshlands. River trips on the mazelike delta are fascinating: One popular trip visits a fishing camp for tea, bannock, and conversations with local fishers who prepare Arctic char by age-old methods; the cost is C$45 (US$32). Other river tours include dinner or a midnight-sun champagne cruise. (You can also arrange to fly to Tuk, and return by boat to Inuvik up the Mackenzie River.)

HERSCHEL ISLAND This island, located 241 kilometers (150 miles) northwest of Inuvik, sits just off the northern shores of the Yukon in the Beaufort Sea. Long a base for native hunters and fishers, in the late 1800s Herschel Island became a camp for American and then Hudson's Bay Company whalers. Today, Herschel Island is a territorial park, preserving both the historic whaling camp and abundant tundra plant- and wildlife (including Arctic fox, caribou, grizzly bear, and many shorebirds).

Tours of the island are generally offered from mid-June to mid-September, when the Arctic ice floes move away from the island sufficiently to allow floatplanes to land in **Pauline Cove,** near the old whaling settlement. This is a great trip to an otherwise completely isolated environment. A day trip to the island, costing C$240 (US$172), includes a brief tour of the whaling station and a chance to explore the tundra landscape and Arctic shoreline. On the flight to the island, there's a good chance of seeing musk ox, nesting Arctic swans, caribou, and grizzly bear. Longer expeditions to the island can be arranged.

BANKS ISLAND Located in the Arctic Ocean, Banks Island is home to the **world's largest herds of musk oxen,** and to remote Aulavik National Park. The daylong flight-seeing trips out to Banks Island and its small Inuvialuit community of Sachs Harbour aren't cheap—the basic trip costs C$400 (US$286)—but the absolute remoteness of the destination and the chance to see vast herds of shaggy musk oxen make this a worthwhile trip.

ACCOMMODATIONS

Rooms are expensive in Inuvik. It's not cheap to operate a hotel up here, and realistically, you're not likely to drive on to the next town looking for better prices. However, all the following accommodations are fully modern and quite pleasant.

There are also two bed-and-breakfasts open year-round that welcome families and accept MasterCard and Visa for payment. The **Hillside B&B,** 68 Reliance St. (☎ 867/777-2662), offers two guest rooms with shared bath. Rates with continental breakfast are C$75 to C$85 (US$54 to US$61). **Robertson's B&B,** 41 Mackenzie Rd. (☎ 867/777-3111; fax 867/777-3688; e-mail: robertbb@permafrost.com), has three guest rooms with shared bath. Rates, including full breakfast, are C$70 to C$80 (US$50 to US$57).

Right in Inuvik is **Happy Valley Campground,** operated by the territorial parks department, with showers and electrical hookups. Between Inuvik and the airport is **Chuk Campground,** with no hookups. The camping fee for both is C$12 (US$9).

✪ **Finto Motor Inn.** P.O. Box 1925, Inuvik, NWT, X0E 0T0. ☎ **800/661-0843** or 867/777-2647. Fax 867/777-3442. 42 rms. A/C TV TEL. C$110 (US$79) double. AE, ER, MC, V.

The newest and quietest place to stay in Inuvik is the Finto Motor Inn, a large, wood-sided building on the southern edge of town. Rooms are good-sized and nicely furnished, all with computer jacks; some have kitchenettes. This is where most government people stay when they come up for business, as it's the most modern and comfortable hotel in Inuvik. The lobby and common areas are warm and welcoming and the restaurant here is the best in town. In summer a dinner theater operates from the hotel.

Mackenzie Hotel. P.O. Box 1618, Inuvik, NWT, X0E 0T0. ☎ **867/777-2861.** Fax 867/777-3317. E-mail: mack@permafrost.com. Web site: www.inuvik.net/mack. 32 rms. TEL TV. C$120 (US$86) double. AE, DC, MC, V.

The Mackenzie is the oldest of Inuvik's hotels (which only makes it 30 years old) and is centrally located in the town center. Rooms are large and nicely furnished, and come with a couch, a couple chairs, a desk, and a full-sized closet. The staff is very friendly and welcoming. There's a coffee shop, laundry, free passes to a local health club, a fine dining room, and a popular bar and dance hall on the main floor. On the weekends, ask for a room away from the bar entrance and parking area.

DINING

The fine dining establishments detailed below offer high quality and high prices. Unfortunately, there aren't many other choices in Inuvik. A good break from the high prices and game meat is the **Cafe Gallery,** 105 Mackenzie Rd. (☎ 867/777-2888), a small cafe in the front of an art gallery, where you can get an espresso and fresh-baked muffin or slice of pie—home-baked cheesecake is a specialty. They also make sandwiches to order for lunch. There's also the unlikely combination of Chinese food and pizza at the **Peking Garden,** in the Finto Motor Inn, 288 Mackenzie Rd. (☎ 867/777-2262).

Green Briar Dining Room. In the Mackenzie Hotel, downtown Inuvik. ☎ 867/777-2861. Main courses C$13–C$20 (US$9–US$14). AE, ER, MC, V. Tues–Sat 6–9pm. NORTHERN CANA-DIAN.

The Mackenzie's fine dining room has reopened after a makeover, and the menu has reemerged with a wide selection of Northern and mainstream dishes, and at prices that make this place attractive in several senses of the word. Caribou makes a number of appearances: It's pot-roasted in red wine (C$15/US$11) and served as scaloppini with rye whiskey demiglace (C$17/US$12). Musk ox and local fish are also standbys. There's a whole page of meat dishes in more international guises, including a pork tenderloin with curry sauce (C$14/US$10). Desserts and a number of salads round out the menu.

Peppermill Restaurant. In the Finto Motor Inn, 288 Mackenzie Rd. ☎ 867/777-2999. Main courses C$18–C$28 (US$13–US$20). AE, MC, V. Mon–Sat 7am–10pm, Sun 8am–10pm. NORTHERN CANADIAN.

Generally considered the best restaurant in Inuvik, the Peppermill offers gourmet renditions of local game and fishes, in addition to traditional steaks and other meats. Arctic lake trout is fried and served with pink peppercorn sauce (C$23/US$16), while caribou medaillons are grilled and served with a wild-cranberry/blueberry sauce (C$24/US$17). Other local delicacies include Arctic char and musk ox. You can try a serving of three Northern dishes on the popular Arctic platter, which costs C$30 (US$21). While there's not much for a vegetarian here (the Caesar salad not withstanding), the steaks and rack of lamb will comfort nongame eaters. The dining room is pleasantly decorated, surmounted by an enormous pepper mill. The Sunday brunch is a major social event in Inuvik.

BAFFIN ISLAND

One of the most remote and uninhabited areas in North America, rugged and beautiful Baffin Island is an excellent destination for the traveler willing to spend some time and money for an adventure vacation; it's also a great place if your mission is to find high-quality Inuit arts and crafts.

It's easy to spend a day or two exploring the galleries and museums of Iqaluit, but if you've come this far, you definitely should continue on to yet more remote and traditional communities. Iqaluit is the population and governmental center of Baffin, but far more scenic and culturally significant destinations are just a short plane ride away. The coast of Baffin Island is heavily incised with fjords, which are flanked by towering, glacier-hung mountains. Life in the villages remains based on traditional hunting and fishing, though some of the smallest Baffin communities have developed worldwide reputations as producers of museum-quality carvings, prints, and weavings.

Though Baffin is the fifth-largest island in the world, it has a population of only 11,000. However, it will be the largest population and cultural center in the new territory of Nunavut, which will split off from the rest of the Northwest Territories in 1999. Iqaluit will become the new capital city. As 85% of the population in the Nunavut region are Inuit, the new territorial government will almost certainly concentrate more heavily on native interests, and will work to preserve the viability of the traditional Northern lifestyle. While tourism will play a role in the economic development of small Inuit communities, don't expect a Club Med anytime soon; culturally sensitive tourism will be the focus of the new government's policies.

ESSENTIALS

VISITOR INFORMATION For information about Baffin Island communities, direct inquiries to **Nunavut Tourism,** P.O. Box 1450, Iqaluit, NT, X0A 0H0 (☎ **800/491-7910** or 867/979-6551; fax 867/979-1261; e-mail: nunatour@nunanet.com; Web site: nunanet.com/-nunator). Any serious traveler should get hold of *The Baffin Handbook,* an excellent government-sponsored guide that's available from local bookstores.

GETTING THERE Iqaluit, 2,266 kilometers (1,405 miles) from Yellowknife, is the major transport hub on Baffin, and is linked to the rest of Canada by flights from Montréal, Ottawa, Winnipeg, and Yellowknife on **First Air, Air North,** and **NWT Air.** Flights are very expensive; full-coach tickets from Yellowknife are nearly C$1,600 (US$1,143). To make airfare more affordable, consider using frequent-flier miles.

As there are no roads linking communities here, travel between small villages is also by plane. First Air is the major local carrier, centering out of Iqaluit; a bevy of smaller providers fill in the gaps. If you're planning on traveling much around Baffin Island, chances are good that your local travel agent won't know much about the intricacies of travel up here. Don't hesitate to contact a local travel agent for ticketing and reservations; try **Canada North Travel** in Iqaluit (☎ **800/263-4500** or 867/979-6492; fax 800/461-4629).

IQALUIT: GATEWAY TO BAFFIN ISLAND

Located on the southern end of the island, Iqaluit is the major town on Baffin, and like most Inuit settlements, is quite young; it grew up alongside a U.S. Air Force airstrip built here in 1942. The rambling village overlooking Frobisher Bay now boasts a population of more than 2,500, and is a hodgepodge of weather-proofed government and civic buildings (the futuristic grade school looks like an ice-cube tray lying on its side) and wind-beaten public housing.

When the district of Nunavut becomes its own territory in 1999, Iqaluit will become the territorial capital. There's already a lot of activity here, with children roaring down the steep, rocky hills on mountain bikes; planes roaring; and husky pups yelping for attention. As in all Arctic towns, at any given time in summer, the entire population seems to be strolling somewhere. Even though no roads link Iqaluit to anywhere else, everyone seems to have at least one vehicle to drive endlessly around the town's labyrinth of dusty paths. There are no street addresses in Iqaluit, because there are few roads organized enough to bother calling streets.

Special Events

A festival of spring, called **Toonik Tyme,** is held the last week of April, featuring igloo building, ice sculpture, dogsled racing, and reputedly the toughest snowmobile race in the world. Cultural activities include Inuit dancing and singing, an arts fair, and traditional competitions like harpoon throwing and whip cracking. After a long winter, the locals are apt to be just a little silly and engage in more lighthearted events like "honey bucket" races, and a 9-hole golf tournament on the sea ice.

What to See in Town

Begin your explorations of Iqaluit at the **Unikkaarvik Visitor/Information Centre** (☎ 867/473-8737), overlooking the bay, with a friendly staff to answer questions, and a series of displays on local native culture, natural history, and local art. There's even an igloo to explore.

Immediately next door is the **Nunuuta Sunakkutaangit Museum** (☎ 867/979-5537), housed in an old Hudson's Bay Company building. The collection of Arctic arts and crafts here is excellent; this is a good place to observe the stylized beauty of native carvings.

If you aren't planning to go any farther afield in Baffin, you may wish to catch a taxi out to **Sylvia Grinnel Park** and take a hike on the tundra. The park is only 5 kilometers (3 miles) from Iqaluit, but is on the other side of the ridge from town; it's a relatively quiet and protected place to see wildflowers and walk along an Arctic river. Another good hiking trail runs from Iqaluit to the "suburb" of Apex, following the beach and headland above Frobisher Bay. The trail begins near the Iqaluit cemetery; watch for the "inuksuks," or manlike stone cairns, that mark the trail.

Iqaluit is the primary center for **Baffin Island art.** Local galleries carry works from communities around the island; ask for a map of arts and crafts locations from the visitor center if you're interested in buying; prices here can be at least half of what they are down south.

Accommodations

Accommodations by the Sea. P.O. Box 341, Iqaluit, NT, X0A 0H0. ☎ **867/979-6074** or 867/979-0219. 10 rms. TV. C$95–C$110 (US$68–US$79) double. No credit cards.

The lodgings that comprise this two-unit establishment are private homes a couple of miles east of Iqaluit proper in the village of Apex. If you want quiet and the comforts of home, then this is a great lodging choice. The original building is a modern wood residence; three guest rooms have access to a kitchen, laundry, and large eight-sided living area with great views over Frobisher Bay. A newer, town-house–style condo offers six bedrooms with access to a kitchen and public rooms. Although meal service is available by request, à la B&B, most people set up housekeeping on their own or share meals with other guests. If you're traveling with a small group, then either of these units makes a great place to stay. There's free pickup and drop-off at the Iqaluit airport.

✪ **Discovery Lodge Hotel.** P.O. Box 387, Iqaluit, NT, X0A 0H0. ☎ **867/979-4433.** Fax 867/979-6591. 52 rms, 1 suite. TV TEL. C$140–C$185 (US$100–US$132) double; C$235 (US$167) suite. AE, DC, ER, MC, V.

Located about halfway between town and the airport, the Discovery Lodge is a newer hotel with nicely furnished, good-sized rooms, and an inviting public sitting area. All rooms come with two beds (some are specially designed, wedge-shaped beds meant to save space). No-smoking rooms (a rarity in the North) are in their own wing. The Discovery Lodge in general has better maintenance than most Arctic hotels; for many travelers who have been to the North before, the fact that there's no public bar in the hotel will be a plus. The on-premises restaurant is good (you can have a drink with a meal); there are also laundry facilities.

The Navigator Inn. P.O. Box 158, Iqaluit, NT, X0A 0H0. ☎ **867/979-6201.** Fax 867/979-4296. 35 rms. TV TEL. C$187 (US$134) double. AE, ER, MC, V.

The Navigator has some of the newest rooms in Iqaluit, as it has recently expanded in anticipation of the town's imminent status as a capital. The restaurant is a favorite with locals, the coffee shop is handy for lighter meals, and there's a lounge for a reasonably quiet drink.

۞ Pearson's Arctic Home Stay. P.O. Box 449, Iqaluit, NT, X0A 0H0. ☎ **867/979-6408.** Can sleep up to 8. C$100 (US$72) per night per person. No credit cards.

At Iqaluit's premier B&B, you get to stay with the town's former mayor, in a lovely home filled with Inuit carving and artifacts.

Regency Frobisher Inn. P.O. Box 610, Iqaluit, NT, X0A 0H0. ☎ **867/979-2222.** Fax 867/979-0427. 49 rms. TV TEL. C$160 (US$114) double. AE, ER, MC, V.

Located high above the town, the "Frobe," as it's known by regulars, is in the same complex of buildings that houses the regional government offices, a small shopping arcade, and the municipal swimming pool. If you want to be central, this is it. Rooms are well heated, pleasantly furnished and decorated, and come with a desk, dresser, and two chairs. The views on the bay side are quite panoramic. There's a very lively bar in the facility, as well as an excellent restaurant.

Dining

The three major hotels above each have popular dining rooms; they're the best (and just about the only) places to eat in town. Menus and prices in each are remarkably similar: Menus feature Northern specialties like Arctic char, caribou, and musk ox, along with steaks, trout, pork, and lamb. Prices for dinners will run between C$20 and C$35 (US$14 and US$25).

In general, the dining room at the ۞ **Frobisher Inn** is the nicest place to eat, and has the only view in town. The menu is extensive, with an emphasis on French preparations, though this is one of the only places in the North where you can actually order whale meat. The locals like **The Navigator** because it has the largest portions. **The Discovery Inn** has the most formal dining room in terms of atmosphere, and a small, well-chosen menu. For cheaper eats, there's a snack bar with fried chicken and pizza a block north of the visitor center.

A Baffin Island Outfitter

۞ **NorthWinds,** P.O. Box 849, Iqaluit, NT, X0A 0H0 (☎ **867/979-0551;** fax 867/979-0573), is Baffin Island's leading adventure-tour operator and provides year-round adventures. A specialty of NorthWinds is its dogsledding expeditions. The 7-day Arctic Odyssey tour involves 5 days on the sea ice amid the amazing fjords of the Baffin coast; all members of the party get a chance to drive the dogs; the cost is C$2,300 (US$1,638). NorthWinds also offers a 12-day tour to Lake Harbour at C$3,500 (US$2,492). In spring, NorthWinds offers a wildlife viewing tour at the floe edge off Bylot Island to view narwhals, polar bears, seals, and birds, at a cost of C$3,750 (US$2,670). In summer, NorthWinds leads hiking expeditions—10 and 14 days, costing C$2,300 and C$2,950 (US$ 1,638 and US$2,100)—into Auyuittuq National Park and 8-day walking and rafting trips through Katannilik Park (C$1,950/US$1,388).

PANGNIRTUNG & AUYUITTUQ NATIONAL PARK

Called "Pang" by Territorians, Pangnirtung is at the heart of one of the most scenic areas in the Northwest Territories. Located on a deep, mountain-flanked fjord, Pang is the jumping off point for 21,497-square-kilometer (8,300-sq.-mile) Auyuittuq National Park, often referred to as "the Switzerland of the Arctic." Pang is served by daily flights from Iqaluit on First Air.

Pang itself is a lovely little village of 1,200 people, with a postcard view up the narrow fjord to the glaciered peaks of Auyuittuq. The local population is very friendly and outgoing, which isn't the case in some other Inuit villages. The **Angmarlik Visitor/Interpretive Centre** (☎ 867/473-8737) is definitely worth a stop, with its well-presented displays on local Inuit history and culture. Immediately across the street are print and weaving shops, where local artisans can be visited.

The most popular day trip from Pang is to **Kekerten Historic Park,** an island in Cumberland Sound that served as the base of American and Scottish whaling around the turn of the century. To reach Kekerten, you'll need to sign on with an outfitter, who will boat you the 29 kilometers (18 miles) to scenic Cumberland Bay and back; lunch is usually included in the price, and whales and other sea mammals are frequently seen during the trip. Visitors can also hike from Pang up to a 2,200-foot viewpoint above town, or up to a series of waterfalls on the Duval River.

Most people go to Pang to reach **Auyuittuq National Park,** 31 kilometers (19 miles) further up Pangnirtung Fjord. *Auyuittuq* means "the land that never melts" and refers to 5,698-square-kilometer (2,200-sq.-mile) Penny Ice Cap, which covers the high plateaus of the park, and the glaciers that edge down into the lower valleys and cling to the towering granite peaks. Landscapes here are extremely dramatic: Cliffs rise from the milky-green sea, terminating in hornlike, glacier-draped peaks 7,000 feet (2,333m) high; in fact, the world's longest uninterrupted cliff face (over 0.8km/0.5 mile of sheer rock) is in the park. Auyuittuq is largely the province of long-distance hikers and rock climbers; the park's principal trail leads from the end of Pangnirtung Fjord up a glacial-carved valley to a high pass, and then down a second valley to another mountain-lined fjord. It takes 5 days to hike the entire trail, but many people choose to hike in for a couple days and explore from base camps beside glacial lakes. Access to both ends of the main trail is by boat (from Pangnirtung from the south, and from Broughton Island from the north); outfitters are available to ferry visitors in and out from both ends of the park for C$75 to C$100 (US$54 to US$71) per person.

While the logistics might seem daunting, a trip to Auyuittuq isn't very hard to arrange; if you're looking for an adventurous walking holiday in magnificent scenery, this might be it. The best time to visit is July to mid-August, when the days are long and afternoons bring short-sleeve weather. For more information, contact the Auyuittuq Park Superintendent, P.O. Box 353, Pangnirtung, NT, X0A 0R0.

ACCOMMODATIONS & DINING The only year-round place to stay and eat in Pang is **Auyuittuq Lodge** (☎ 867/473-8955; fax 867/473-8611), which is more a hostel than a hotel. There are 25 clean and cheerful rooms, all with two twin beds and bathroom down the hall. Meals are served family-style in the pleasant guest lounge and at set times only. Simple lodging is C$100 (US$72) a night per person;

for three meals, it's an additional C$65 (US$46) a day (MasterCard and Visa are accepted). Nonguests are welcome for meals; reservations are requested. In summer there is a free campground on the edge of Pang.

OUTFITTERS   The best of the local outfitters is **Joavee Alivaktuk,** a very personable Pang native with 20 years of experience as a professional guide. Joavee provides boat service to Auyuittuq for C$75 (US$54) and also operates day trips to Kekerten Historic Park for C$140 (US$100), Arctic char–fishing trips, and whale-watching trips into Cumberland Sound. Contact **Alivaktuk Outfitting Services** at P.O. Box 3, Pangnirtung, NT, X0A 0R0 (☎ and fax **867/473-8721**).

POND INLET

In many ways, the best reason to make the trip to Pond Inlet on Baffin's northern shore is simply to see the landscape. On a clear day, the flight from Iqaluit up to Pond is simply astounding: hundreds of miles of knife-edged mountains, massive ice caps (remnants of the ice fields that once covered all of North America), glacier-choked valleys, and deep fjords flooded by the sea. It's an epic landscape; in all of the country, perhaps only the Canadian Rockies can match the eastern coast of Baffin Island for sheer scenic drama.

Pond Inlet sits on **Eclipse Sound,** near the top of Baffin Island in the heart of this rugged beauty. Opposite the town is **Bylot Island,** a wildlife refuge and part of the soon-to-be established North Baffin National Park. Its craggy peaks rear 6,500 feet (2,167m) straight up from the sea; from its central ice caps, two massive glaciers pour down into the sound directly across from town.

Considering the amazing scenery in the area, Pond Inlet is relatively untouristed. The peak tourist season is in May and June, when local outfitters offer trips out to the edge of the ice floes, the point where the ice of the protected bays meets the open water of the Arctic Ocean. In spring this is where you find much of the Arctic's wildlife: seals, walruses, bird life, polar bears, narwhals, and other species converge here to feed, often on each other. A wildlife-viewing trip out to the floe edge (by snowmobile or dogsled) requires at least 3 days, with 5-day trips advised for maximum viewing opportunities. Other recreation opportunities open up in August, when the ice clears out of Eclipse Sound. Bird-watching boat trips out to Bylot Island are offered (the rare ivory gull nests here), as well as narwhal-watching trips in the fjords. Hill walking to glaciered peaks, sea kayaking in fjords, and superlative Arctic char fishing are also popular summer activities. It's best to allow several days in Pond Inlet if you're coming for summer trips; weather is very changeable this far north.

ACCOMMODATIONS & DINING   The local co-op also operates the **Sauniq Hotel** (☎ **867/899-8928;** fax 867/899-8770), with 12 rooms, all with private bathrooms and in-room TVs. Rooms are C$180 (US$129) a night, which includes full board. First Air flies into Pond Inlet 5 days a week from Iqaluit.

OUTFITTERS   Two outfitters operate out of Pond Inlet. The local **Toonoonik Sahoonik Co-op** offers a variety of trips throughout the year; contact them at General Delivery, Pond Inlet, NT, X0A 0S0 (☎ **867/899-8847;** fax 867/899-8770). **Polar Sea Outfitting,** P.O. Box 60, Pond Inlet, NT, X0A 0C0 (☎ **867/899-8870;** fax 867/899-8817), is operated by Scottish-born John Henderson, and offers naturalist-guided floe-edge trips, and guided hiking and boat trips in summer; Polar Sea is the best contact for sea kayaking or narwhal-watching trips on Milne Ilet.

LAKE HARBOUR: STONE CARVERS & KATANNILIK TERRITORIAL PARK

The center for Baffin Island's famed **stone-carving industry,** Lake Harbour is located along a rocky harbor, directly south of Iqaluit on the southern shore of Baffin Island. While many people make the trip to this dynamic and picturesque community to visit the workshops of world-renowned carvers, Katannilik Territorial Park is a preserve of Arctic wildlife and lush tundra vegetation and offers access to Soper River. The Soper, a Canadian Heritage River, is famed for its many waterfalls in side valleys, and for its long-distance float and canoe trips.

Many people visit **Katannilik Park** for a less demanding version of rugged Auyuittuq National Park further north. Wildlife viewing is good, and hiking trails wind through the park. Canoeing or kayaking the Soper River is a popular 3-day trip that's full of adventure but still suitable for a family. For more information on the park, contact the Katannilik Park Manager, Lake Harbour, NT, X0A 0N0 (☎ 867/939-2416; fax 867/939-2406). For information on canoe rentals and guided trips through Katannilik Park, contact NorthWinds (see above).

To watch local artists at work, visit the carving studio across from the tourist office. For a selection of local carvings, go to the co-op store.

ACCOMMODATIONS & DINING　Lodging is available in Lake Harbour at the **Kimik Co-op Hotel** (☎ 867/939-2093; fax 867/939-2005), with eight rooms. Lodging is C$125 (US$89) a night, with full board available for an additional C$60 (US$43).

OTHER ARCTIC DESTINATIONS

BATHURST INLET　One of the most notable Arctic lodges, **Bathurst Inlet Lodge** was founded in 1969 for naturalists and those interested in the natural history and ecology of the Arctic. The lodge is located at the mouth of the Burnside River, in a rugged landscape of tundra and rocky cliffs, housed in the historic buildings of a former Oblate mission and the old Hudson's Bay Company trading post.

The lodge offers a varying schedule of guided walks, boat trips, camping trips, and lectures, all focusing on the plant and animal life of the inlet. A naturalist is on staff to lead excursions and to answer questions. Other programs focus on the area's archaeology and the culture of the Inuit.

The lodge takes guests for minimum 1-week stays. The weekly rate of C$2,200 (US$1,573) includes round-trip airfare from Yellowknife, a full week's bed and board, and most guided excursions. For more information, contact **Bathurst Inlet Lodge,** P.O. Box 820, Yellowknife, NT, X1A 2N6 (☎ 867/873-2595; fax 867/920-4263; e-mail: bathurst@internorth.com; Web site: www.virtualnorth.com/bathurst).

ELLESMERE ISLAND NATIONAL PARK RESERVE　A good part of the intrigue of Ellesmere Island is its absolute remoteness. A preserve of rugged glacier-choked mountains, ice fields, mountain lakes and fjords, and Arctic wildlife, Ellesmere Island National Park is the most northerly point in Canada. During the short summer, experienced hikers and mountaineers make their way to this wilderness area to explore some of the most isolated and inaccessible land in the world.

Getting to Ellesmere is neither easy nor cheap. From Resolute Bay (served by regularly scheduled flights on Air North and First Air), park visitors must charter a private airplane for the 960-kilometer (600-mile) flight further north. There are no facilities or improvements in the park itself, so park visitors must be prepared for extremes of weather and physical endurance. The most common activity is hiking from Lake Hazen at the center of the park to Tanquary Fjord in the southwest corner. This 129-kilometer (80-mile) trek crosses rugged tundra moorland, as well as several glaciers, and demands fords of major rivers. Needless to say, Ellesmere Island Park is not for the uninitiated.

For more information and an up-to-date listing of outfitters who run trips into the park, write to **Parks Canada,** P.O. Box 353, Pangnirtung, NT, X0A 0R0 (☎ 867/473-8828; fax 867/473-8612).

Index